P9-BZD-844

A Prophet with Honor

Also by William Martin

These Were God's People, 1966
Christians in Conflict, 1972
My Prostate and Me, 1994
With God on Our Side, 2005

A Prophet with Honor

The Billy Graham Story

William Martin

ZONDERVAN®

ZONDERVAN

A Prophet with Honor

Requests for information should be addressed to:
Zondervan, *3900 Sparks Dr. SE, Grand Rapids, Michigan 49546*

ISBN 978-0-310-35392-8 (international trade paper edition)

ISBN 978-0-310-35333-1 (audio)

ISBN 978-0-310-35332-4 (ebook)

Library of Congress Cataloging-in-Publication Data

Names: Martin, William C. (William Curtis), 1937- author.
Title: A prophet with honor : the Billy Graham story / William Martin.
Description: Updated edition. | Grand Rapids, Michigan : Zondervan, [2018] | Originally published in 1991. | Includes bibliographical references and index.
Identifiers: LCCN 2017046017 | ISBN 9780310353300 (hardcover)
Subjects: LCSH: Graham, Billy, 1918- | Evangelists – United States – Biography.
Classification: LCC BV3785.G69 M278 2018 | DDC 269/.2092 [B] – dc23 LC record available at https://lccn.loc.gov/2017046017

Cover design: Matthew P. Van Kirk
Cover image: © Bettmann / Corbis
Back cover images: Russ Busby
Interior design: Michelle Espinoza

First printing January 2018 / Printed in the United States of America

To Patricia

Contents

Preface to This Edition

Life is unpredictable. As explained in the preface to the original edition of this book, an unexpected invitation from Billy Graham in 1985 led to five years of near total immersion in the life of the famed evangelist and the people who held up his arms during more than five decades of public ministry. And then, with the completion of the research and publication of the book, immersion dwindled to a sprinkling. I continued to receive *Decision* and monthly letters and press releases and exchanged the occasional letter or telephone call with Billy Graham. I wrote articles for magazines and newspapers and talked to dozens (perhaps hundreds) of reporters whenever Billy Graham was scheduled to hold a crusade in their cities or suffered an illness and as he passed the torch, in stages, to his son Franklin. But personal contact with people who had filled my life was largely absent—and missed. Then, to my delight, Zondervan—now, like my original publisher William Morrow, under the HarperCollins tent—asked me to bring the 1991 edition up to date. For the most part, I happily relied on many of the same people who had been so helpful to me in preparing the first edition. Particularly helpful were John Akers, David Bruce, Russ Busby, Roger Flessing, Rick Marshall, Tex Reardon, Larry Ross, Maury Scobee, Norman Sanders, Tedd Smith, Stephanie Wills, and various staff members at the Billy Graham Evangelistic Association and the DeMoss Group, which handles much of the public relations activities of BGEA and Samaritan's Purse. I also cherished the opportunity to have a good visit with each of the Graham progeny: GiGi, Anne, Franklin, Ruth (formerly Bunny) and Ned. Their valuable contributions to the new chapters will be quite clear to readers. I also deeply appreciate the wise professional counsel and encouragement I received from Zondervan, particularly from Stan Gundry and Jim Ruark, who shepherded this edition to completion.

As with the first edition, I have tried to tell the story of Billy Graham as accurately as I am able. I do not doubt that additional information about Mr. Graham will surface from time to time after the publication of this book. I suspect, with good reason, that some of the Graham offspring will publish memoirs that will add to our understanding of their father and mother. If I am granted sufficient additional years, I may participate in some widening and deepening of the story. But whatever the future, I feel enormous gratitude for the opportunity I have been given and satisfaction that the work already published has been well received. I trust that this expanded version will also make a contribution to understanding the life and work of a truly remarkable man and the movement he led for much of the twentieth century.

William Martin
March 2018

Preface and Acknowledgments

I can scarcely remember a time when revivals and revivalists did not fascinate me. As a small boy in Devine, Texas, in the late 1940s, I relished having the visiting evangelist over to our house for dinner during the annual "gospel meeting." When the Baptists held a revival down the street, I often dropped in for a sermon or two, and numerous times I stood at the edge of a Pentecostal tent wondering what might be going on inside the minds and bodies of folk being whipped into a holy-rolling frenzy by the sweating, shouting, shirt-sleeved man striding back and forth on the flimsy little stage.

I didn't hold any revivals myself until I was fourteen, but they were authentic for their time and place—held in the open air, illuminated by yellow bulbs, with the crowd seated on wooden-slatted church pews and singing from tattered softback songbooks. Not all of my outings were a success. One dismal, week-long revival seldom brought more than a dozen people out to sit in the oppressive August heat, and it was hard to be confident I had the full attention even of that faithful remnant, since the bare, unfrosted floodlight directly over my head not only drew hundreds of night bugs but, with the intense glow of its high wattage, fairly baked my crew-cut scalp and forced my auditors to look off to one side to avoid permanent damage to their stricken eyes.

Still, I was a pretty good speaker, and my sermons were of sufficient quality to have merited previous publication—one of my favorites featured a stinging attack on the Bolsheviks—and when kindly church ladies said, "I'd sure love to hear you preach twenty years from now," I never doubted they would have the chance. As it happens, I don't preach much anymore—haven't for over twenty years—but I am still intrigued by those who do and are really good at it. Thus, when the opportunity came to chronicle and assess the life and ministry of the world's best-known and, arguably, most successful preacher, I saw it immediately as the remarkable pleasure and privilege it has turned out to be. Some explanation of how this happened and what followed seems in order.

Throughout the 1970s, after joining the sociology department at Rice University in Houston, I wrote a series of magazine articles about popular religion, my primary academic specialty. Several of these appeared in *Texas Monthly*. In 1978 William Broyles, Jr., then editor of that excellent magazine, asked me to consider writing a profile of Billy Graham, whose Texas connections were numerous and strong. I already knew a fair amount about Graham and had even spent several days interviewing members of his staff and meeting briefly with him during a crusade in Jackson, Mississippi, so the assignment was a relatively easy one. The article, which appeared in the March 1978 issue of *Texas Monthly*, was generally favorable toward the evangelist, but it was by no means a puff piece, and because I had liked and been treated graciously by every member of Graham's staff whom I met, I had some apprehensions about how it would be received. When the time comes to write, I have no conscious hesitation about trying to say exactly what I believe and feel about people and organizations I have studied, but I do not enjoy hurting people's feelings, and because I consider it of paramount importance to be fair in what I write, I like to be perceived as fair. On occasion, I have written things that ruptured or forever precluded the possibility of friendship. I will doubtless do so again. I can live with that, but it brings me scant satisfaction. I do not write as a means of venting repressed anger. When Graham and his chief lieutenant, T. W. Wilson, both wrote notes expressing appreciation for the article, and particularly for its fairness, I was pleased. Still, I knew enough about the evangelist's legendary graciousness toward the press not to imagine that the article had actually made any lasting impression on him. And I expected that my study of Billy Graham had ended.

Three years later Graham held a crusade in the football stadium at Rice University. I urged my students to attend and attended several services myself but made no attempt to make contact with Graham or any of the staff members I had met several years earlier. I was quite surprised, therefore, to receive a letter from him several weeks after the crusade stating that one of the biggest disappointments of his stay in Houston was not getting to see me and expressing a hope that we might be able to sit down together for lunch sometime. I responded, letting him know that I felt sure I could work him into my schedule, but, quite frankly, I assumed that his staff had prepared a list of people he might meet while in Houston, and that he was dispatching brief courtesy notes to those he had missed lest someone be unnecessarily offended.

Thus, despite these expressions of appreciation for my acumen and literary style, I was somewhat astonished when in November 1985 I received a letter from Mr. Graham in which he asked if I would be interested in writing "a book concerning my life, ministry, and any niche in history our work may have." Several scholars and journalists had approached him about such a book, he said, but he had decided not to offer his cooperation to anyone else until checking with me about my interest and availability. As it happened, I was due for a sabbatical the following academic year and had not yet fully decided on a primary project. To be sure, I was interested, but I was also uncertain as to what Graham would expect of me and whether I would feel comfortable under conditions he might set. I let him know that I continued to think well of him but would feel obliged to tell the story as accurately as I could, whatever that might entail. A few weeks later, we met for several hours in a New York hotel room. I thought it possible he might ask me to produce an in-house, "authorized" account of his ministry, one guaranteed to view him favorably. I would have regretted turning down the chance to look at him and his organization carefully, but I was prepared to do so if those were the conditions. I also wondered, though I considered it less likely, if he might expect me to pledge some portion of whatever income I derived from the book to the Billy Graham Evangelistic Association. To my pleasant but perplexed surprise, we talked about our children and our wives, about what directions his ministry had taken lately and where he thought it might go in the future, and about why it would be simpler just to order sandwiches from room service than to go into a restaurant where people would almost certainly interrupt our conversation. Finally, when I knew we had to start talking about the ostensible reason for our visit, he asked, "Well, do you want to do the book?" I told him of course I did but would need to find out what the conditions might be. He said, "There are no conditions. It's your book. I don't even have to read it. I want you to be critical. There are some things that need criticizing." He asked if I had an agent. I told him I did, and he correctly suggested that I should find a publisher. "We don't want any part of the income from the book," he said, "but you'll have a lot of expenses. How do you think that ought to be handled?" He indicated that friends of his organization could provide expense money if that were necessary, but he clearly had reservations, even about an arms-length arrangement. I told him I thought it would be best if I took care of my own expenses. He readily agreed. "That's great," he said. "If we gave you money, I think you would know there were no strings attached, but others might not believe it, and I don't want anyone to think this is a 'kept' book." He then gave me the names, addresses, and telephone numbers of people who held the keys to various treasure-houses of information, assured me he would tell them I'd be in touch, and invited me to attend his upcoming crusade in Washington, D.C. Shortly afterward, he gave me a letter to present to publishers confirming his willingness to cooperate with me and assuring them that neither he nor any person associated with him reserved any right of approval or editorial control over anything I might write.

Mr. Graham proved true to his word. Over the next five years—two or three longer than either of us had imagined at the outset—I enjoyed cooperation of the sort that scholars and journalists dream about but seldom experience. Long interviews with Graham himself had to be scheduled during down times between crusades and major conferences, but he was always generous with his time on those occasions, spending most of several days with me at his home or office in Montreat, North Carolina, over three years, and making himself available for long telephone conversations on other occasions. In addition, he sent word up and down the line of his organization that his friends and colleagues should feel free to speak openly with me, which more than a hundred did. At the several crusades I attended (Washington, D.C.; Paris; Denver, Colorado; and Columbia, South Carolina), at the mammoth International Conference for Itinerant Evangelists, held in Amsterdam in 1986 (See Chapter 32), and at a Team and Staff Conference at the Homestead in 1987, I was given the opportunity to visit with scores of key personnel and access to any aspect of the operation I had sense enough to inquire about. On rare occasion Graham chose not to respond to a question, usually indicating that he had pledged not to discuss the topic (for example, private conversations with presidents or other world leaders), that he preferred not to discuss the topic while other parties to an incident were still alive, or that he did not wish to cause undue pain to some person. In most cases, he was willing to answer the same or a similar question a year or two later. The few instances in which I felt he was less than fully forthcoming are noted in the text. This same generally open atmosphere prevailed at Billy Graham Evangelistic Association (BGEA) offices in Minneapolis, London, and Montreat, where I received warm and extremely helpful assistance virtually every time I requested it. Also of inestimable value was the assistance I received from Dr. Lois Ferm, who serves as BGEA's liaison with the Billy Graham Center Archives at Wheaton College. Certain materials in the archives, particularly oral histories, were donated with the understanding that they would be sealed until a certain date. Others were available only with express permission from Dr. Ferm. The wish of donors was always correctly observed, of course, but in no case was I ever denied permission to examine any archival file over which BGEA held sole control. Dr. Ferm expressed her conviction that early acquisitions by the archives had been placed under unnecessary restrictions; later additions have seldom been subject to such stringent regulations. As the person who conducted virtually all the oral-history interviews, Dr. Ferm assured me that those still closed to inspection held no dark secrets. Given my experience with several dozen such interviews whose time limitations ran out during the course of my research, I have no reason to doubt her word. Finally, various personnel at Walter Bennett Communications, BGEA's media representative and public relations agency, as well as people holding similar positions within BGEA itself, have repeatedly furnished me with books, magazines, videotapes, transcripts, photocopies, and incidental bits of information that have proved invaluable in my research.

As agreed in my early discussions with Billy Graham, I attempted to pay virtually all of the considerable expenses involved in preparing this book. On two occasions, when BGEA's large-scale dealings with its travel agent made it sensible and economical for the organization to furnish me with tickets for last-minute flights to major conferences, I accepted the tickets and soon afterward made contributions to the association in excess of what I believe the actual costs to have been. On numerous occasions I was able to take advantage of special hotel rates negotiated by BGEA on behalf of its members. And though I always offered to pick up the check, some members of the Graham "team" paid for various meals during my visits to crusades or BGEA offices. In similar fashion, I have tried to make contributions to BGEA or Samaritan's Purse (an Evangelical social service organization headed by Graham's eldest son, Franklin) in excess of any financial expense directly incurred by BGEA on my behalf.

To imagine, however, that writing a few checks cancels any debt I might owe to Billy Graham and his organization would be legalistic and naive. I would not try, or even begin to know how, to pay for the favors, assistance, goodwill, and gracious treatment I have received from numerous individuals, only some of whom are named below. They knew, of course, that I would write about Mr. Graham and his organization and that treating me kindly and well would enhance the likelihood that I would speak of them favorably. But I want to believe and do believe that they treated me kindly and well because they tend to be, as a group, remarkably kind and well-meaning people. As I have written this book, I have constantly examined what I have said in an effort to make sure that I was neither shading the truth in Graham's or his associates' favor out of gratitude for their helpfulness, nor taking an inappropriately negative slant as a way of emphasizing that I had not been taken in by slick manipulation. Admittedly, I enjoyed writing about their strengths more than about their weaknesses. But since Billy Graham and his associates, like all humankind, have weaknesses, I determined not to gloss these over. I have tried to be scrupulously fair, not only because I do not wish the taint of unfairness to mar the most notable scholarly enterprise in which I have engaged to date but also because I regard fairness as a cardinal virtue. I do not imagine, of course, that my judgment is flawless. I am certain it is not. But the account and the assessments I have rendered here have been given with great care.

My debts, as I have indicated, are many and substantial. I owe early and long appreciation to Dr. Kenneth Chafin, former pastor of Houston's South Main Baptist Church and former dean of the Billy Graham School of Evangelism. At our first meeting in 1974, when I was interviewing him about a different subject, Dr. Chafin half-seriously suggested that I consider writing a biography of Billy Graham. A year later, he invited me to spend several days at a crusade in Jackson, Mississippi. That visit led to the *Texas Monthly* article, which led to the invitation to write this book. I haven't talked to Ken Chafin much since he moved to Louisville, Kentucky, but I haven't forgotten him.

T. W. Wilson, Graham's personal assistant and traveling companion, repeatedly went to extra lengths to help coordinate my visits with Graham, to provide entree to interviewees and access to materials, and to supply me with various other kinds of information. It was easy to understand why Billy Graham has come to rely upon him so heavily and to relish his company.

Cliff Barrows, even while recovering from a life-threatening illness, spent several days reviewing films of Graham's early ministry and sharing observations and insights gleaned during an adult lifetime spent at Billy Graham's side as his music director and vice-chairman of BGEA.

George Wilson and John Corts, former and present chief of operations of BGEA, gave me broad access to the association's facilities and staff, and graciously met any need I expressed.

Sterling Huston, director of North American Crusades, saw to it that I got every piece of information I requested about Graham's crusade operations and enabled me to get a worm's-eye view of crusades in progress.

Maurice Rowlandson, director of BGEA's London office, shared his extensive knowledge of Graham's ministry in Great Britain, arranged interviews with key church leaders in England, and, with his wife, Marilyn, offered gracious personal hospitality and other kind assistance on several occasions.

Dr. Alexander S. Haraszti was a meticulously inventoried storehouse of detailed information about Graham's visits to the Soviet bloc countries. Dr. John Akers and Edward E. Plowman supplemented his accounts with their own observations and insights. Both these men also offered candid and astute reflections on other aspects of Graham's organization and ministry.

Bob Williams gave hours of his time, even when swamped with responsibility, to help me gain a better understanding of the International Conference for Itinerant Evangelists and the saturation evangelism effort known as Mission World.

Russ Busby, BGEA's photographer, recorded hundreds of scenes that enabled me to picture exactly how an event looked, recommended several photos for use in this book, and furnished a stack of verbal snapshots that no camera could capture.

I am indebted, of course, to every person I interviewed. I hope each of them, including those not mentioned in the footnotes, will accept as sufficient my blanket expression of gratitude. Some, however, stand out for their willingness to engage in repeated conversations, for their assistance in providing access to other people, and for myriad other thoughtful deeds. I think especially of Dr. Akbar Abdul-Haqq, Gerald Beavan, Ralph Bell, Bill Brown, Dr. David Bruce, Blair Carlson, Elwyn Cutler, J. D. Douglas, Fred Durston, Allan Emery, Jr., Colleen Townsend Evans, Dr. Robert Evans, Roger Flessing, Leighton Ford, Ernest Gibson, Melvin Graham, Roy Gustafson, Henry Holley, Mike Hooser, Dr. Arthur P. Johnston, Howard Jones, Johnny Lenning, Dr. Robert L. Maddox, Dr. Victor Nelson, Roger Palms, Dr. Tom Phillips, Texas E. Reardon, Charles Riggs, Tedd Smith, Walter Smyth, Charles Templeton, Dr. Calvin Thielman, Bill Weldon, Dr. John Wesley White, Ralph Williams, and Grady Wilson.

My research efforts were wonderfully extended by a competent corps of co-workers. None was more valuable than my prize daughter, Dale Martin Thomas, who worked at my side for two summers and made further valuable contributions by writing her senior thesis at Yale on the conflict between Billy Graham and the Fundamentalists, and whose research for that project is reflected in Chapter 13. She also enlisted her friend and classmate, Jim Ford, who provided me with information about Graham's visits to Yale in 1957 and 1982. Alongside her in importance is Jane Washburn Robinson, whose enterprising, painstakingly thorough, and expertly organized and documented research provided the basis for the chapters on the relationship between Graham and Richard Nixon. Though she was able to assist me for only one summer, and most of that via computer modem, Christiane Pratsch also proved to be as able a second set of hands, eyes, and mind as one could hope for. And during the final push to get all the footnotes correct, Shay Gregory displayed remarkable diligence, ingenuity and cheerfulness as she hunted down every straggler who lacked a proper name or identifying mark.

The bulk of my archival research was done at the Billy Graham Center at Wheaton College. The extensive and well-ordered collection at the center's archives is a priceless resource for students not only of Billy Graham's ministry but also of other facets of Evangelical Christianity. Archives Director Robert Shuster and his associates, Lannae Graham, Frances Brocker, Paul Ericksen, and Jan Nasgowitz could not have been more helpful or gracious during the several weeks I spent in their midst. I received similar assistance from the center's library director, Feme Weimer, and her co-worker, Judy Franzke. As already noted, my work at the archives was greatly facilitated by the good offices of Dr. Lois Ferm, who was at pains to see to it that I had access to every piece of material that was legally possible for me to see. She was also helpful in suggesting places to look. In addition, my candid conversations with her and her husband, Dr. Robert Ferm, associated with Billy Graham for over forty years, provided many valuable insights.

One of the most valuable sources of assistance was the staff of Walter Bennett Communications, which has long handled public relations and media operations for the Graham ministry. Fred and Ted Dienert gave me open access to backstage operations of the television productions. Larry Ross repeatedly shared his time and insights into Billy Graham's phenomenal success in gaining the confidence of the world's media. And Noel Wilkerson Lee, again and again and again, found and sent videotapes, transcripts, press releases, and whatever other materials I requested, all in good time and good humor.

Sarah Clemmer of the *Charlotte Observer* also smoothed my way to effective research in that newspaper's extensive files on Graham.

As with virtually any historical project, I have depended upon the work of those who have plowed the ground before me. Earlier biographies, particularly those by John Pollock, William McLoughlin, Marshall Frady, and Patricia Daniels Cornwell, have been helpful for their insights and for guiding me to materials I might otherwise have found less easily or missed altogether. In addition, I have benefited from the work of numerous journalists who have written books and thousands of articles about Billy Graham. I have given credit for every known debt in the footnotes, but I take this opportunity to pay additional thanks to them all.

From the beginning, secretaries have played crucial roles. Billy Graham and his colleagues are blessed—I have no more hesitation to use the word than they—with a phalanx of extraordinarily able and unfailingly helpful assistants. Stephanie Wills served as lifeline to Billy Graham himself, relaying queries accurately, dispatching all sorts of materials immediately, and giving information and advice that was invariably on target and often delivered with a wry sense of humor. Cathy Wood, secretary to Sterling Huston, not only provided me with abundant assistance at and regarding crusades and other aspects of the ministry but repeatedly did so in the midst of hectic workdays that lasted at least fifteen hours. During the several weeks I spent in Amsterdam in 1986, Susan Cherian, Bob Williams's secretary, offered similar help with equal good cheer. Belma Reimers was especially helpful in arranging my meetings with Cliff Barrows and Johnny Lenning. Ruth Graham's secretary, Maury Scobee, helped me several times with appointments and travel arrangements and proved to be a delightful friend as well. I had only limited personal contact with Mary Becker in BGEA's Minneapolis office, but I was regularly grateful to her for faithfully sending me a full set of newly updated statistics every few weeks during the entire five years. And George Wilson's longtime assistant, Esther LaDow, managed to find copies of almost any obscure publication or document I felt I needed. In addition, and absolutely without exception, numerous other secretaries at various levels within BGEA, in both the Montreat and Minneapolis offices, rendered friendly and competent assistance whenever they had opportunity. I am deeply grateful.

On the home front, my several computers, whose value has been incalculable, made it unnecessary for me to rely heavily on the official skills of university secretaries in the actual research and preparation of the manuscript. Still, the friendship, forbearance, load-lifting good humor, and able assistance on other fronts consistently furnished by Kathy Koch, Crystalyn Williams, Nancy Dahlberg, and Rita Loucks during years of single-minded pursuit of a goal and absentminded loss (usually temporary) of essential items have been a source of comfort.

I can scarcely imagine how I could have written this book had I not been able to spend eighteen months in practical isolation in comfortable dwellings graciously made available to me by thoughtful and generous people. Loise H. Wessendorff's picturesque and peaceful retreat center, Wellspring, not only provided much-needed solitude during the early stages of the writing but rekindled a deep affection for the Texas Hill Country. The roar of the ocean at Lamar and Penny Vieau's Seabean helped drown my inner moanings during the wintriest period of the entire project. The delightful nineteenth-century farmhouse at Pecan Mill, from whose windows I could watch champion cutting horses grazing in the fields, gave me a marvelous place to work and, just as important, enabled me to renew my ties with my cousins, Mike, Jerry, and Bill McLennan. And the magnificent view of the mountains from the window of the study in Steven and Sandra Rudy's charming cottage in Crested Butte, Colorado, made it easy to get through the final revisions and copyediting. I expect to write my next book at a place called Canaan, not far from Wellspring. All these will be welcome there.

My several visits to Wheaton were made immeasurably more pleasant by Bill, Donna, Bruce, and Vicky Bond, who welcomed a stranger into their home and made him feel a part of their family. And my sojourn in Paris, a delightful assignment in itself, was enhanced by the hospitality and companionship of Spencer and Marlene Hays and Herve Odermatt.

For more than twenty years, I have enjoyed an unusual degree of support and encouragement from my colleagues on the faculty and in the administration of Rice University. With scarcely a murmur of discontent, my dear friends in the Department of Sociology—Chandler Davidson, Chad Gordon, Stephen Klineberg, Elizabeth Long, and Angela Valenzuela—my two deans, Joseph Cooper and James Pomerantz, and George Rupp, president of Rice University, agreed to my taking a two-and-a-half-year leave to work on this book. I do not take such an environment for granted.

The folks at William Morrow showed great confidence in this book, making it possible for me both to take time away from my teaching and to afford the research I needed to perform. I commend them for their generosity, thank them for their patience, and hope their judgment will be vindicated. I am also grateful to their counterparts at other publishing houses, particularly at Macmillan/Free Press and Houghton Mifflin/Ticknor and Fields, who helped convince them that a book about Billy Graham would have wide appeal.

Many people at a publishing house are involved in the production of a book, but none more intimately than the editor. My editor, Maria Guarnaschelli, is a remarkable woman. When we first met, I was overwhelmed by her enthusiasm for the book. In the intervening years, I have been repeatedly overwhelmed by her capacity to demonstrate a range and intensity of emotion that exceed my own to a noticeable degree. Maria not only possesses superb technical skills as an editor; she also has two other gifts that make her a valuable collaborator: the ability to teach and the ability to learn, gifts that enabled me to find and to write the book I wanted to write. Two freelance editors also gave good assistance. After reading the first version of the manuscript, Joy Parker furnished thirty pages of thoughtful analysis and encouragement that proved extremely helpful, and Ellen Joseph helped pare that first version to a more manageable size. And finally, copy editor Michael Goodman patiently checked facts, spotted typographical errors and inconsistencies, and brought the manuscript into line with William Morrow's stylistic conventions.

Gerry McCauley has been my literary agent for twenty years. We have been friends throughout that period, but never have I valued the friendship so highly as during these past five years. From his wise and effective assistance in helping arrange for the original contract, through regular telephone calls to calm my fears and assure me that all books were difficult and that many authors actually finish them, to reading and commenting on various drafts of the manuscript itself, he demonstrated a care and concern that went far beyond a mere professional relationship. And now, perhaps, we can talk about baseball without being distracted.

My wife, Patricia, has been her dependably wonderful self throughout this long process. When it became clear that the only way to get the book written was to retreat from the city, she bore my long absences with un complaining grace, brightened my weekends with her warm and cheerful presence, gave and resisted giving criticism in just the proper proportion, and appeared never to doubt that I could and would eventually finish. My sons, Rex and Jeff, their wives, Mary and Suzanne, and my son-in-law, Rupert Thomas, were less directly involved, but they supported me with their encouragement and love, as did my longtime friends David Berg, John Boles, Sidney and Mary Lee Burrus, Allen Matusow, and Richard and Michael Parten.

I understand that I am a fortunate man.

William Martin

Part 1

Genesis

1

Mr. Graham Goes to Washington

Billy Graham arrived at precisely the right moment. Some who jammed the interview room at the National Press Club looked as if they might be first-assignment reporters for their church's weekly newsletter, but most had the countenance and equipment of men and women accustomed to confronting the familiar figures who provide grist for the evening news and the morning editions in the nation's capital. Still, even those well-seasoned veterans seemed to acknowledge the sheer physical presence radiated by the world's most famous preacher, a man who is by almost any measure the most successful evangelist in Christian history.

As Graham and his small retinue took their places at a table, it was hard not to be surprised that despite his six-foot-three-inch height, his shoulders are rather narrow, his chest thin, and his legs, outlined when he crosses them in a loose-jointed way, almost skinny; only the large expressive hands seem suited to a titan. But crowning this spindly frame is that most distinctive of heads, with the profile for which God created granite, the perpetual glowing tan, the flowing hair, the towering forehead, the square jaw, the eagle's brow and eyes, and the warm smile that has melted hearts, tamed opposition, and subdued skeptics on six continents.

After a press-club welcome and warm praise from the cochairs of the 1986 Greater Washington Crusade, Billy Graham took center stage. With a manner that suggested he still marveled that a simple country preacher found favor with famous and powerful people, he recalled how legendary House Speaker Sam Rayburn arranged for him to use the Capitol steps for the closing service of his 1952 crusade, mentioned that Ben Bradlee asked what the *Washington Post* could do to help the present effort ("I told him that all we want is the first headline every day for eight days"), revealed that he had discussed the crusade at private dinners with President and Mrs. Reagan, Vice-President and Mrs. Bush, and Secretary of State George Shultz and at meetings with Defense Secretary Caspar Weinberger and other cabinet members. He told of an international conference his organization would host that summer at a cost of more than 20 million dollars and revealed an ambitious plan to use satellite technology to preach the gospel simultaneously to virtually the entire world. Then, after lamenting the return of the Elmer Gantry image among television preachers, Billy spoke of his anguish over continuing racism, his concern for the hungry and homeless, and his determination to do what he could to foster bilateral nuclear disarmament and world peace.

When he opened the floor for questioning, noting ahead of time that he would "sort of beat around the bush" on purely political issues, Graham displayed a well-honed skill at fielding and finessing what turned out to be a quite routine set of inquiries. Forty minutes later, as the reporters packed up their gear, Graham's lifetime friend and primary gatekeeper T. W. Wilson, drew public relations specialist Larry Ross into a corridor for a quick assessment. They agreed the conference had been a bit of a letdown. Graham had prepared for a tough session and got nothing to hit but softballs. None of it would win much airtime or newspaper space. They also registered disappointment over a *Washington Post* article that appeared that morning. "That guy spent two hours with Billy, but it didn't reflect it." They had higher hopes for a *New York Times* story because the reporter was a Christian. "Give the *Times*, *USA Today*, and the other big papers all the time they need," Wilson said. "Try to spare Billy from the others. We need to move out of here as soon as possible and get over to CNN."

Two days before the crusade would begin, Graham met with his "team" for a serve-yourself continental breakfast in a conference room at the Key Bridge Marriott Hotel in Alexandria. All but he and two or three of his closest aides stayed at the Marriott; to protect himself from a potentially endless parade of supplicants, Graham nearly always maintains separate quarters, taking most meals in his room. Typically, he stays in a comfortable suite in a good hotel, but lest the press find out and create an unfavorable impression, he seldom accepts the ultraluxurious suites pressed on him by admiring hoteliers. The precrusade team breakfast is one of the few occasions when most staff members will see him, except on the crusade platform. In public Graham wears well-tailored suits that give him the look of a statesman or an investment banker. Here, among his friends, some of whom have worked with him for forty years, he sported his favorite informal outfit: moccasin-style gum-soled shoes, nondescript gray trousers, and an off-the-rack bright blue blazer. His hair, as usual, needed trimming and would have benefited either from a new application of Grecian Formula 16 (a concession to television rather than vanity) or simple recognition that longevity is one of his greatest assets, of which a mane of gray would be a fitting symbol. Most of the men on his staff appeared to have chosen their clothes for utility rather than style.

Several sported toupees; only one had bothered to try for a match with the texture and color of his own hair. They make up one of the most efficient and effective event-producing organizations in America; they remind one of the Lions Club in Dothan, Alabama. The women, mostly wives and secretaries, cut a similar figure: neat but unflashy, competent but ever friendly, well able to take care of themselves but accustomed by ethos and experience to attend to the needs of others. As a group, these pleasant, unassuming, thoroughly dedicated men and women represent the elite of Evangelical Christianity and the middle of the middle class.

Graham opened the meeting with a few words about the importance of the crusade, then relinquished the chair to Sterling Huston, director of North American Crusades for the Billy Graham Evangelistic Association (BGEA). A trim, diplomatic man who favors precise speech and is ever at pains to shine the best possible light on the evangelist and the association, Huston urged the team to regard its interaction with the Marriott staff as a kind of ministry, taking care to display a consistently courteous and friendly attitude and inviting them to the crusade services. On a practical note, he reminded them that the hotel restaurant's cold breakfast buffet would provide as much as they wanted to eat, with plenty of cereal and fresh fruit at about half the cost of the hot buffet.

There followed a series of brisk reports, most packed with statistics, in which various team members summed up the preparation and current status of the aspects of the crusade under their direction. Washington crusade director Elwyn Cutler, one of several BGEA staffers who move to cities a year or two in advance to oversee the development of committees and other crusade preparations, declared how amazing it had been "just to stand back and see how the Lord worked, in ways beyond human understanding, to bring to the front the leadership He wanted for this crusade." To illustrate his point, various team members told how sixteen major committees, all carefully integrated and headed by black and white cochairs, had organized 8,000 volunteers into an elaborate network of prayer, Bible study, and work groups. Workers had issued over 500,000 personal invitations and distributed 400,000 packets of promotional material to homes in the Greater Washington area. Thousands of small prayer groups had met regularly for months, and thousands more who belonged to national "prayer chains" had implored God to smile on this effort. Nearly 4,000 people had been taught how to counsel those who would "come forward" at the crusade services, and another thousand would lead "nurture groups" for new converts after the crusade ended. The Billy Graham School of Evangelism, an intensive training program held in conjunction with every Graham crusade, would enroll 1,750 pastors from 79 denominations and all 50 states in a five-day program designed to help them become more effective evangelists in their home communities. In similar fashion, other team members reported on special efforts to minister to blacks, young people, college students, military personnel, political leaders, and prisoners, and on the Love-in-Action program that collects food for disbursement to the crusade city's hungry and homeless.

As a capstone to this triumphalist litany, United States Senate chaplain Richard Halverson spoke almost worshipfully of Graham's visits on Capitol Hill. "When Billy Graham comes to the Capitol," he said, "suddenly, the Senate and Congress are unimportant. To me, it's a miracle. Wherever Billy is, there is the gospel of Christ. Everybody knows what he stands for, so he says it without a word. Just yesterday, after he opened the Senate with prayer, it was almost impossible to get away. Pages wanted to get his autograph. Senators kept coming off the floor to talk with him. It was just absolutely exciting. Here is a man who personifies the gospel of Christ, the love of God in Christ. Wherever he goes, all over the world, it's not like they are receiving just him; it's like they are receiving Christ. I wish that were true of more of us."

Such a potent witness apparently has its downside. Graham observed that "the Devil is also at work," citing as proof the afflictions that had befallen three of the men who had stood at his side in virtually every crusade since the 1940s. His longtime song leader, Cliff Barrows, crusade pianist Tedd Smith, and Associate Evangelist Grady Wilson, a high school friend who had been present when Graham preached his first sermon in 1936, were all ailing. "I'm sure this is an attack of Satan," Graham said. "We've had a number of things happen that have no other explanation to me, and we need to build a wall of prayer." At his direction, the people at each table began to pray, softly lifting petitions for the matters that burdened their hearts. As the room filled with the earnest sounds of heaven-directed entreaties, Billy Graham prayed especially for "those who think they are not interested in religion but are, for those who laugh at cocktail hours but are not happy." Others prayed for the hotel staff, for team members out visiting prisons, and for those trying to solve parking problems around the downtown convention center. When enough time had passed to ensure that most key needs had been covered, Chaplain Halverson brought the meeting to a close by asking everyone in the room to touch Billy Graham or someone who was touching him. Then, as they linked in an unbroken chain of support, Halverson offered a fervent prayer commending the evangelist to the Almighty as "Mr. Gospel, the incarnation of the teachings of Jesus Christ."

An old black prophet shuffling along inside a word-jammed sandwich board tried to convince the thousands who streamed past him into the convention center that Billy Graham was an aide-de-camp to the Antichrist, but they did not buy it. To them, as to Chaplain Halverson, he was the living symbol of Evangelical Christianity, the man who had preached Christ to hundreds of millions of people throughout the world and now brought his message to the capital of what many still regarded as the Redeemer Nation, the "nation with the soul of a church."

Inside, some grabbed Cokes or hot dogs at concession stands. Others lingered at tables set up in the center's cavernous lobbies, browsing over devotional guides, souvenir picture books, how-to manuals on personal evangelism, and rapidly shrinking stacks of volumes by and about Graham and sundry relatives and associates. For the most part, the assembling multitude was solidly middle- and working-class: clean, neat, and conforming to standards of dress and decorum they felt best reflected their self-image as the good, decent people who affirm and embody the core values of American society. A well-schooled usher corps funneled folks into the stands or to special areas for the deaf or for those who spoke one of the eight foreign languages into which the service was being translated.

In the cramped quarters of a TV-production truck parked at a loading dock off the main hall, a small crew checked monitors and controls as they prepared to transform a live service into a television program that would be seen by millions a few weeks later. Meanwhile, in one of the center's many conference rooms, Elwyn Cutler gave instructions and seating assignments to the ministers and other professional churchmen whose contribution to the crusade would be honored by a spot on the platform, a tangible symbol of importance to massage their egos, impress their parishioners, and consequently boost attendance. In another room, comfortably furnished with sofas and chairs and stocked with an abundance of soft drinks and snacks, Billy Graham spent the last few minutes before the service visiting with former District of Columbia mayor Walter Washington, Mayor Marion S. Barry, Jr., and Vice-President George Bush.

When the appointed moment approached, T. W. Wilson unobtrusively indicated it was time for this inner circle to join Elwyn Cutler's larger group in its procession to the platform. Inside the arena the choir fell silent and attention shifted to the stage, where the organ, piano, and synthesizer sounded the first notes of "Jesu, Joy of Man's Desiring." Moments later, as Graham and his party mounted the rear steps and came into view, 25,000 people rose in sustained ovation.

Because it was the opening service, introductions ran somewhat longer than usual, but they provided a good view of the thin line between Church and State and of Billy Graham's position as an icon not just of American Christianity but of America itself. Mayor Washington, noting that he had raised the first dollar to build the magnificent convention center, announced that Billy Graham came to Washington, like Queen Esther in the Bible, "for such a time as this." Mayor Barry, observing that it was he who brought the ninety-eight-million-dollar facility to completion, praised Graham's stand against apartheid in South Africa and racism in America, then assumed the evangelist's support of the mayor's own programs regarding drugs, unemployment, the rehabilitation of prisoners, and sex education for young people. To close, Barry wrapped his own career in the mantle of God's providence, noting that his rise from a sharecropper's shack in Mississippi to the leadership of this great city and a spot on the platform with Billy Graham proved that "the Lord moves in mysterious ways, his wonders to perform." George Bush provided the final cachet. "We welcome to America's city," he said, "America's pastor, Dr. Billy Graham." He affirmed his own belief in the separation of Church and State but insisted the nation would be strong only so long as its faith is strong, and he thanked Graham for his role in reawakening the faith of citizens in "this one nation, *under God*, the last, best hope of man on earth."

Other preliminaries included a stirring religiopatriotic song and a low-key collection. Then, just before Graham spoke, "America's beloved singer of sacred songs," George Beverly Shea, a gentle bear of a man who became the first member of Graham's team in 1944, stepped to the microphone, anchored himself to the pulpit with both hands, and sang, "In times like these we need the Bible.... This rock is Jesus ... Yes, He's the one." At seventy-seven, Shea sounded twenty years younger, his deep rich voice rolling out over the auditorium and settling on the audience like a down comforter.

With no further fanfare—at most services, Graham receives no introduction whatever—America's Pastor began to speak. He commended local officials for giving "the greatest cooperation we have ever received in any crusade we have ever held," announced that on Tuesday night he would talk about "The Richest and Sexiest Man Who Ever Lived," and urged everyone to make a special attempt to fill RFK Stadium for the final service the following Sunday. Then, apparently because he feels a preacher ought to tell a few jokes to show he is a regular fellow, he related a couple of the small handful of stories he has been repeating for decades. Neither was a four-star anecdote, but the crowd laughed generously, as crowds often do when famous noncomedians tell jokes.

The sermon, when he finally got to it, was a classic piece of Graham homiletics. Its theme was Christ and its five subheadings were the Creative Christ, the Compassionate Christ, the Crucified Christ, the Conquering Christ, and the Coming Christ. As in virtually all his sermons, he recited a laundry list of problems: poverty, drugs, broken hearts, emptiness, guilt, loneliness, spiritual blindness, and fear. He knew these were problems and that secular remedies were bound to fail because one of the greatest biochemists in the world and rocket scientist Wernher von Braun and Harvard president Derek Bok had told him so. He had other evidence as well: "a Roman Catholic priest studying for a Ph.D. in Chicago ... Simon LeBon of the rock group Duran Duran ... a girl in Japan ... the managing partner of one of Washington's most prestigious law firms ... a new movie out ... a recent Gallup poll ... a magazine cover story ... a taxicab driver on *Donahue* ... a letter that came to me last month.... "And most important of all, "the Bible says...."

To no one's surprise, Graham proclaimed, with monumental conviction and certainty, that the sole and sufficient answer to these problems is Jesus Christ. In the early years of his ministry, he spoke with such volume and driving rapidity that journalists dubbed him "God's Machine Gun." He can still generate considerable intensity when the topic and occasion demand it, but his style has become almost conversational, and the conversation has a tendency to ramble despite his increasing use of full manuscripts. Nonetheless, many of the familiar gestures—the clenched fist, the pointing finger, the ambidextrous slashes, the two-pistol punctuation, the hands drawn down to the Bible like twin lightning bolts—are still there and still riveting in their effect.

The sermon moved inexorably to its goal: the "invitation"—to accept Christ for the first time, to receive assurance that one's prior acceptance and salvation are still under warranty, or to acknowledge a backslid condition and to rededicate oneself to walking a straighter and narrower path. "Life is uncertain," he said. "God does not give us the date of our death." And then, the words that bring virtually every sermon of his to an end: "I'm going to ask you to get up out of your seat and come and stand here in front of the platform, and say by your coming, 'Tonight, I want Christ in my heart.'" As he suddenly fell silent, his head bowed in prayer, chin resting on right fist, elbow cradled in left hand, the convention center swelled with the simple melody and words of the quintessential invitation hymn:

Just as I am, without one plea,
But that Thy blood was shed for me,
And that Thou bidd'st me come to Thee,
O Lamb of God, I come, I come.

And from every section of the auditorium, they came, they came. Serious of mien but devoid of tears or other overt signs of emotion, more than a thousand souls answered Billy Graham's call to be washed in the blood of the Lamb.

The response pleased the crew in the television truck:

"Pan around and pull, [Camera] Three. Let them walk through. We want movement. Stand by, One.... Give me the shot with the aisles. A little further right. That's nice."

"Would you look at that! They're still coming."

The program would not air for several weeks, but Graham stepped back into the pulpit to say, "To you watching on television, at home, in a hotel room, in a college dormitory, wherever you are, call that telephone number you see on the screen." Then, to the "inquirers" who had streamed into a large open space immediately in front of the platform, he said:

> You have not come to Billy Graham. I have no special powers. I'm just another human being like you. I'm just the messenger. The message comes from God. You have asked for his forgiveness. I want to tell you on the authority of Scripture that he will give you that forgiveness. Not because you deserve it, but because Christ died for you. And he rose again, and he's alive, and he's willing to come into your heart now by the Holy Spirit and give you a new power, a new strength, a new joy, and a new peace.

He then led them through the "sinner's prayer":

> O God,... I am a sinner.... I'm sorry for my sins.... I'm willing to turn from my sins.... I receive Christ as my savior.... I confess him as Lord.... From this moment on.... I want to follow him ... and serve him ... in the fellowship of his church.... In Christ's name, Amen.

This ostensibly life-changing transaction so simply accomplished, he urged them to read the Bible every day, to pray regularly, and to witness for Christ by inviting others to become Christians and by manifesting a loving and helpful spirit, particularly across racial lines. Finally, he encouraged them to affiliate with a church and worship regularly, not just stay home and watch TV preachers: "Many are far better than I'll ever be, but Christians need to worship *together*." With that, Graham left the platform and his associates took control, making sure all inquirers were matched with counselors who would help them clarify and confirm their decisions. As the last remaining strays found shepherds, the area began to hum with quiet conversation and prayer. Counselors helped their charges fill out decision cards and gave them a booklet entitled *The Living Christ*, a copy of the Gospel according to John, a brief Bible correspondence course, and suggestions for further study. The cards would reveal that few inquirers were confirmed pagans. Most already had some connection to a church or had come to the crusade as the guest of a church member.

Within minutes, runners rushed the decision cards to rooms where a Co-Labor Corps of over two hundred volunteers waited to feed them into an elaborate follow-up procedure designed to link them to cooperating pastors and channel them into local congregations. The head of this operation, Dr. Robert L. Maddox, who had served as Jimmy Carter's liaison to the religious community before becoming executive director of Americans United for Separation of Church and State, admitted that the crusade could not be expected to reshape Greater Washington. "Billy will go home next week and the city will swallow him up and the effects will be gone. But as a matter of fact, in the lives of individuals, it may be absolutely pivotal. I have seen that happen. It won't rock Washington, D.C., for the Lord, but it might make some congressman struggling with key legislation think a little bit differently. Last night, I watched two or three guys that I know who grew up out here in Virginia and were as segregationist as they could be. They were working right alongside black people without any regard to color at all. When this is over, white churches will still do their thing and black churches will do theirs, and there is not going to be any great crossing of that line. But there will be greater understanding. It could have some impact."

Back on the sidewalk outside the convention center, the old prophet had retired for the night, but a squad of grim-faced young men in slacks and white shirts and severe long-haired women in ankle-length homemade dresses passed out cheaply printed pamphlets that condemned Graham for his apostate theology, coming down especially hard on his faulty understanding of the purpose and proper mode of baptism. Most people declined their publications and tried to ignore them, but one Graham supporter vociferously responded to their challenge. While they argued, a policeman who had asked a departing counselor for an inquirer's packet and had, after a brief conversation, "trusted Christ," held up his hand to stop traffic for one of the last groups to leave the building. He was singing a gospel song.

2

A Great Cloud of Witnesses

The path Billy Graham trod to triumph in the nation's capital in 1986 stretched backward across 350 years through gigantic stadiums and two-pole tents, brush arbors and open fields, ornate auditoriums and simple meeting-houses, to the waters of Massachusetts Bay, where the leader of four hundred brave and devout souls prepared them for their "errand into the wilderness" not by reading a manifesto but by preaching a sermon. From the day John Winthrop proclaimed to the passengers of the *Arbella* that God Almighty had dispatched them to New England to establish "a city upon a hill" for all mankind to behold and emulate, Americans have been moved and molded by men and women who assayed to speak for God. Over the centuries, the vectors and vagaries of history have eroded their influence and power, so that no contemporary clergyman enjoys the submissive respect routinely accorded to ministers in the early years of the New England Way, but no one who has paid attention in recent years can doubt that the Word and those who preach it still find a vast audience perpetually open to the prophetic exhortation, "Seek good, and not evil, that you may live."

When Winthrop and the first wave of English Puritans in the Great Migration set sail from Southampton in search of a land where pure and undefiled religion might flourish, they were seen off by John Cotton, a brilliant young Cambridge-trained cleric who warned them that "as soon as God's Ordinances cease, your Security ceaseth likewise; but if God plants his Ordinances among you, fear not, he will maintain them." Within five years those settlers formed the core of a thriving social experiment like none the world had ever seen, and John Cotton, whose devotion to Puritan ideals had moved him to join them, was their most prominent spiritual teacher.

Cotton's sermons were solid food, and those who heard him were expected both to chew and to digest it. Most of his sermons dealt with the topic that dominated the Puritan psyche: eternal salvation. The Reformed (Calvinist) theology espoused by the Puritans held that before the beginning of time, an absolutely sovereign and righteous God had predestined the eternal fate of every person who would ever live. The elect would bask in the sunlight of his glory and rejoice in the company of angels; the damned, in cosmic contrast, would writhe forever in the raging torments of hell. Since the differences in destination were so great and the reservation open-ended, most could not avoid trying to discern whether they might possibly be numbered among the elect. Thus, Cotton's parishioners did not ask "What must I *do* to be saved?" but "How can I *know* I am saved?" The desperate desire for blessed assurance produced a strenuous regimen of Bible study, prayer, meditation, and intense inward searching for sparks of saving grace among the ashes of sinful Adamic nature. It also promoted careful attention to sermons designed to fan these sparks into a reassuring flame.

The first decade of the New England Way was a glorious success. Prosperity, an impressive level of political autonomy, and widespread concern with godly living brought a steady flow of new settlers and led John Cotton to write that both Church and Commonwealth were progressing so well that he could not help but think of the biblical image of "the New Heaven and the New Earth." But that golden age, like all before and since, soon passed. The satisfactions produced by prosperity led many to pursue even greater prosperity, not always to the benefit of pure motive and behavior. Freedom from oppression by Anglican bishops attracted some, particularly Baptists and Quakers, who wished to be free of Puritan domination as well. And the glowing accounts of political autonomy seemed a bit hollow to those denied access to the levers of self-government because they could not convince themselves or others that God had saved them.

All these developments affected the church. Piety declined, dissent increased, and when a dwindling migration cut off the flow of new saints from England during the 1640s, membership rolls began to shrink, despite a rapidly growing population. By 1660 less than half of New England's inhabitants were church members, and ministers began to lower the standards of membership to avoid further losses. When Solomon Stoddard came to the frontier parish of Northampton in 1669, the church had fourteen adult members and attendance was meager. He decided it was time for change. John Cotton had preached to people already on the road to regeneration; Stoddard stirred their interest in the journey. Though a graduate of Harvard, he aimed for the heart more often than the head, pioneering a homiletic strategy that would become the staple of evangelistic preaching. Preaching without notes and using plain speech, familiar examples, graphic imagery, and fervent emotion, he terrified his listeners with vivid descriptions of hellfire and its horrors. Then, when fear had done its work, he held out the hope of new life in Christ, life filled with joy rather than despair, with light rather than darkness, life crowned at the end with eternal bliss. What he described was the "New Birth." His predecessors had viewed regeneration as a lifelong process; Stoddard pressed for a more immediate and dramatic response, a relatively brief episode a person could identify as the time he or she had been "born again." He still believed that God alone selected those on whom his regenerating Spirit would fall, but he did what he could to make sure hearts were open when the Spirit was in the neighborhood. In a real sense, Solomon Stoddard was the father of evangelism in America, and his critics, put off by his transparent enjoyment of fame and ecclesiastical power, found their barbs deflected by the same shield that would protect his successors in later generations: "He gets results."

Stoddard was succeeded at Northampton by his grandson, Jonathan Edwards, who presided over the first manifestations in New England of what historians have called the Great Awakening, a revival that began in rural New Jersey and rapidly swept through the Colonies. During 1734 and 1735 Edward's earnest preaching resulted in the conversion of several people, including a young woman known to be "one of the greatest company-keepers in the whole town." Her example led to other conversions, and soon the whole town was astir, marveling at what the Spirit was doing in their midst. Worship became a vital experience, with attentive hearers frequently breaking into tears, some with joy and love, others with sorrow and distress over the state of their own souls or those of their neighbors.

In the course of six months, Edwards recorded approximately three hundred conversions, and people came from all over New England to hear him preach. Toward the end of 1735, there began to be signs of a withdrawal of the Spirit, and by 1737 the revival was "very much at a stop." Its effects, however, did not quickly pass away, and some time later Edwards was able to report, "I know of no one young person in the town who has returned to former ways of looseness and extravagance in any respect.... God has evidently made us a new people." Similar showers of blessings fell on more than thirty towns in the region, creating a sense of contagion and community, as well as readiness for the torrent soon to follow.

Local pastors stirred these early revivals. In 1740 this pattern suddenly and permanently changed with the coming of "the Grand Itinerant," George Whitefield, a twenty-six-year-old free-lance evangelist who quickly became a celebrity from Georgia to New England. The fiery young Oxford-trained Anglican had created a sensation in England by preaching in open fields in an attempt to reach working people who would not come to the churches. In 1739 he toured the southern and middle Colonies, in part to raise money for an orphanage he had established near Savannah. Wherever he went, great crowds gathered to hear him, even without formal publicity. Months before he invaded New England, Boston newspapers reported his activities and printed testimonies to his piety and character, so that when he arrived in September 1740, he preached several times daily to crowds so large and tumultuous—on one occasion, five people leapt to their death from the balcony—that he was forced to move into open fields to accommodate gatherings of more than

5,000 anxious souls. As a climax to his Boston meetings, he enthralled more than 20,000 people on the Common in the largest assembly ever gathered on American soil to that point. In the course of 45 days, Whitefield preached more than 175 sermons, and most New Englanders heard him at least once. Not everyone liked his preaching, but no one forgot it. Equipped with a silver tongue, galvanized tonsils, and lungs of the finest-grain cowhide, he spoke in a loud and clear voice, articulated perfectly, and used such crowd-pleasing techniques as telling Bible stories by taking all the roles himself, a skill enhanced by childhood experience on the stage. Despite evidence of memorization and practice, Whitefield conveyed an impression of spontaneity and immediacy. He spoke without manuscript or notes and contended that any man who had not lost "the old Spirit of Preaching" would do the same. And however much he prepared, he had a powerful gift for extemporaneous communication and great skill at seizing an immediate stimulus, such as a thunderclap or a rainbow or an incident in the congregation, and turning it to dramatic advantage. In contrast to the ponderous scriptural exposition, elaborate theological reflection, and grave ethical instruction favored by local pastors concerned to transmit "the whole counsel of God," Whitefield based his sermons on catchy biblical snippets that served less as a text to be explained than as a teaser to be exploited, usually as a springboard to a sermon on the New Birth, the chief matter of all his preaching. It was not enough to feed a flock for a lifetime, but for the moment it made a delicious plateful.

As he basked in his success and gained confidence in his standing with the people, Whitefield sounded a note that would become characteristic of itinerant evangelists. Local pastors had never seen such results, he observed, because they spoke of "an unknown, unfelt Christ." They were "unconverted dead men who did not experimentally know Christ" and who preached "almost universally by note," which practice was itself "a symptom of the decay of religion." "The reason why congregations have been dead," he concluded, "is because they have dead men preaching to them.... How can dead men beget living children?" The "unconverted" ministers of New England unleashed a bitter and sustained attack against Whitefield and his methods, but "the Word ran like lightning," and according to one chronicler of the revival, not since the earthquake of 1727 had the multitudes shown such concern for their souls.

Lesser lights than Whitefield carried the revival to every corner of New England, and many settled ministers adopted revivalistic techniques as well. Young people flooded into the churches, religious societies sprang up to supplement regular church services with special gatherings for prayer and discussion of devotional literature, and Bostonian Thomas Prince founded *The Christian History*, America's first religious magazine, to report glad tidings of revival in the Colonies. The effects seem to have been greatest where roots ran shallow—in newer towns and more unstable urban areas, for example—but the awakening was much as numerous observers described it: "great and general." Jonathan Edwards declared that the world could not be far away from "the dawn of that glorious day" when the millennium would begin and New England would take its place as the center of "a kind of heaven upon earth."

Despite its momentum, revival gave way to revolution as the leading item on the American agenda during the latter half of the eighteenth century. When George Whitefield returned to New England in 1744, he found many churches closed to him and was unable to rekindle the fires he had started just four years earlier. But the changes he and his colleagues had wrought in that brief, glorious period endured. Though the size of the Christian community did not change dramatically as a result of the revival, life within it did. In revivalistic churches, power passed from the clergy to the laity. Instead of formal training and theological acumen, the test of leadership became the ability to appeal to the heart, to rouse men and women to seek and find the New Birth. Preachers attained authority and power in direct democratic fashion from the people who heard them preach and chose to accept or reject what they heard. American religion and culture would never be the same again.

During the decades following the Revolution, many thoughtful observers concluded that American religion had seen its brightest day. In New England, neither the liberal rationalists nor the more orthodox Congregationalists wanted a revival. The spiritual descendants of Jonathan Edwards professed to want one, but could not produce it. In the South, Presbyterians, Baptists, and Methodists continued to chip away at the flinty frontier heart, with discouraging results. On the southern and western frontiers, life was hard and rough and almost wholly lacking in the spiritual and cultural influences present in the East. Sparse population, scattered settlements, and limited transportation left settlers in a state of isolation unlike that experienced by farm people anywhere else in the world. Occasional spurts of revival lifted spirits here and there, but the mood within the churches was gloomy to the point of desperation. Chief Justice John Marshall, of the U.S. Supreme Court, wrote that the church in Virginia was "too far gone ever to be redeemed," and Voltaire and Tom Paine gloated over the prospect that "Christianity will be forgotten in thirty years."

Surprisingly, some began to interpret this season of barrenness as God's chastening, a cleansing preparation for a coming mighty work. In response, frontier preachers began to speak expectantly of revival, and small groups of struggling Christians joined together in intense sessions of prayer and fasting, calling upon the Lord to send refreshing showers of spiritual blessing. When the new century arrived, no harvest seemed in sight, but the ground was ready, so that when the heavenly rains fell, America experienced its second Great Awakening, or more simply, the Great Revival. The first phase of this revival, the southern and western camp meetings, turned the American South into one of the most distinctively and self-consciously religious regions in Christendom. The second, symbolized by the urban revivals of Charles Grandison Finney, came remarkably close to achieving the Evangelical dream of making America a Christian nation.

The primary catalyst for the frontier awakening was a Presbyterian minister named James McGready. Though described by his contemporaries as ugly and uncouth, McGready preached with compelling power. Like increasing numbers of revivalist Presbyterians, he gave the doctrine of election a polite nod, then proceeded to ignore it, stressing the need and ability of all alike to offer themselves in conscious obedience to God's saving grace. In sermons evoking the odor of flaming sulfur and summoning the strains of heavenly harps, he called on people to experience a New Birth so dramatic and glorious that they would forever be able to identify and relate the exact time and circumstances of its occurrence. His preaching often stimulated uncommon emotional displays, including copious crying, screaming, and an exercise in which persons "slain in the spirit" fell to the ground, where they lay still as corpses or writhed in apparent agony while groaning, praying, and crying out for mercy. Such irregularities, coupled with his pointed attacks on immorality and materialism, made McGready a controversial figure in many quarters, but it won him the adulation of scores of young men who entered the ministry with a conscious intent to emulate him.

In the summer of 1800, McGready sent out broadsides announcing a continuous outdoor service to be held at the Gasper River Church, one of several he served in Logan County, Kentucky. By encouraging people to camp out on the grounds for the duration of the services, McGready not only organized what was probably the first planned camp meeting held in America but inaugurated one of the most successful revival techniques ever developed. The harvest at Gasper River was great and other successful camp meetings followed, but none would match the historic gathering at Cane Ridge, Kentucky, in August 1801.

Organized, advertised, and overseen by Barton W. Stone, a Presbyterian converted by McGready, the Cane Ridge camp meeting was perhaps the most electrifying, exhilarating, sensuous, unforgettable communal event in the history of American religion. Over a week-long span, crowds variously estimated at between 10,000 and 25,000 people (the latter is probably an exaggerated figure, given the population of the region at the time) gathered in a forest clearing for a nonstop assault on their senses and their souls. At the central log meetinghouse and across a gently sloping hillside crowded with tents and wagons and horses and people, dozens of preachers held forth for hours at a time from platforms, wagon beds, and tree stumps, threatening whatever crowds they could gather with "liquid boiling waves" and the fiery darkness of "the deepest caverns in the flaming abyss," and promising redemption to those who would repent of their sin-soaked habits, experience the New Birth, and embark on a life of pure and undefiled religion. As this message pierced vulnerable hearts and occasionally broke through the proud armor of sightseers and scoffers, the wounded engaged in remarkable demonstrations of "acrobatic Christianity." At times, the "slain in the spirit" numbered into the hundreds and had to be dragged aside and laid in neat rows to prevent their being trodden under foot by ecstatic multitudes. Some lay motionless so long that doctors bled them to revive them, with the result that "the ground was crowded with bleeding bodies like a battlefield." Others experienced violent spasms in which they jerked their heads rapidly from side to side or whipped their bodies forward and backward with such force that kerchiefs and hairpins flew from the heads of the women. Still others danced or ran or rolled or erupted in fits of laughing and barking and ecstatic moaning. Each sign of the Spirit's work prompted outbursts of joy or longing from those already saved and those afraid they might not be until the din reached such a level that "the noise was like the roar of Niagara."

No revivals in American history have matched the results of the second Great Awakening in the South. Though it broke no new theological ground, the Great Revival deepened the furrows and set the boundaries within which southern Evangelical religion would subsequently flourish. At its heart was total acceptance of the Bible as the literal, true, and completely dependable Word of God. Since the frontier attracted few Deists or New England–style "supernatural rationalists," southern preachers faced little skepticism on this issue. The question was not whether the Bible was trustworthy, but what it said. Disagreement existed over details, but its central message was crystal clear: All humans are sinners and will spend eternity in hell unless their sins are forgiven; forgiveness is possible because Jesus Christ died on the cross. Evangelicals differed on the source and nature of human sin, the precise process by which Christ's merit was transferred into human accounts, and the ability of individual humans to draw on those accounts, but predestination was clearly losing ground. Though Presbyterians and many Baptists continued to subscribe to some form of election, the manner and content of their preaching presupposed that humans could and should respond to God's gracious offer of salvation through Christ. Neither they nor the Methodists, who did not subscribe to the doctrine of election, imagined for a moment that salvation was possible apart from God's grace, but for men and women who had traveled beyond the rivers of the East to claim a part of America for their own, any religion that did not offer an equal chance to stake out a homestead in the promised land of paradise held little appeal. The revivals also made an uneducated ministry acceptable, as the proper test of a minister came to be his ability as a soul winner, not whether he had been to seminary. So thoroughly did this belief take root in Evangelical Christian thinking that from the beginning of the nineteenth century to the present an extraordinarily small proportion of popular evangelists in America have possessed standard educational credentials.

On an everyday level, the revival's more immediately important theological product was a vigorous emphasis on "sanctification," often called "perfectionism." The belief that Christians should live sinless lives was promoted most strongly by the Methodists but soon became a central preoccupation of all Evangelical Christians. In its individualistic concern for personal piety and opposition to common frontier vices such as alcohol, gambling, fornication, profanity, and dishonesty, it could exempt devout believers from feeling responsible for political decisions, economic policies, or such egregious social ills as slavery. It could also produce a narrow and unlovely legalism and a nearsighted hypocrisy. Still, the pervasive (sometimes obsessive) concern for purity helped civilize the frontier, encouraging the pioneers to live more sober and decent lives.

The Great Revival had peaked in the South by 1805, but Baptist farmer-preachers, Methodist circuit riders, and a fresh crop of itinerant evangelists inspired by the camp meetings kept it going at a less feverish pitch for several more decades. In New England Yale University became the focus and fomenter of revivalist thought and action. The primary catalyst for Yale's activity was Jonathan Edwards's grandson, Timothy Dwight, who became its president in 1795. Dwight held to a conservative ideal of society, with the church as its bedrock institution, and he sought to enlist Yale in the service of that ideal. When he ascended to the presidency, almost none of the college's 110 students were professing Christians. Dwight stormed this bastille of unbelief with a four-year series of weekly sermons that when finished, he began anew. In 1801, after seven lean years of unflagging effort, Yale experienced a dramatic revival that brought the conversion of fully half its students, many of whom eventually entered the ministry.

A major key to the resurgence of revivalism at Yale and, indeed, to the subsequent astonishing growth of Evangelical religion throughout America, was a Scottish philosophical import known as commonsense realism. To advocates of this view, developed in the universities at Edinburgh and Aberdeen and championed at Yale for a time, the observations and intuitions of common sense are dependable, the world is much as it appears to be, and attention to the moral laws imprinted on one's conscience will lead to appropriate behavior. Obviously, such an optimistic view of human nature fit marvelously with democratic values. If every person could discern dependable truth, it was safe to take power from the hands of kings and bishops and put it into the hands of ordinary people who could use their innate common sense to figure out what to do with it. After a brief period of popularity, commonsense realism faded from the European intellectual scene by the end of the eighteenth century, but in America it became almost a national philosophy during the first half of the nineteenth century, quite apart from whether its adherents had ever heard of Edinburgh or Aberdeen. Nowhere did it have greater impact than within Evangelical Christianity, where its principles still hold dominion, though most of its practitioners are unaware of its influence on their lives.

Applied to religion, commonsense philosophy decreed that the Bible was not a volume filled with dark mysteries and knotty conundrums but a straightforward book easily accessible to straightforward people without assistance from learned philosophes and theologues. In the words of a phrase still repeated in Bible classes throughout Evangelical America, "It means what it says and says what it means." Since no tenet of Calvinism, still the dominant form of Protestant orthodoxy in America, offended common sense more than the doctrine of original sin, which held that all people not only share the guilt incurred by Adam's fall but have inherited a totally depraved nature, commonsense theologians concluded that Calvin must have been wrong. Sin, they insisted, is in the sinning, not the nature. Whatever guilt humans bear derives from sins *they* have committed, not from sins committed by Adam. Further, since a loving and reasonable God would not hold anyone guilty for sins not committed, he would not predetermine who should be saved and who damned but would offer salvation to everyone and give it to those who accepted the offer. Thus, election and predestination cannot be what the Bible teaches, or revival preaching would make no sense, and anyone could see the positive effects of revival preaching. What the Bible teaches, therefore, is that all persons are able to repent, accept God's grace, experience regeneration, and receive salvation. Commonsense theology gave revivalism what it needed: a clear mandate to confront sinners with what they must do to be saved and persuade them to do it. It was ideally suited for the Jacksonian popular democracy about to sweep the young nation and would provide a powerful warrant for evangelists to justify their methods by the results they achieved.

The key figure of the northern revival was a young maverick named Charles Grandison Finney. A former teacher and lawyer converted to Christ at age twenty-nine, Finney launched his preaching career with a series of strikingly successful revivals in upstate New York. Wherever he preached, his straightforward insistence that people were responsible for their own sinfulness and possessed the freedom and ability to lay hold of salvation roused dozens, sometimes hundreds, from their lethargy. But more than theology was at work. Using to the fullest his clear, theatrical voice, his hypnotic gaze, and dramatic skills polished in the courtroom, he presented his case less like a traditional preacher than like an attorney addressing a jury. He also served as prosecutor and judge, denouncing accused as heinous offenders whose guilt could not be doubted. In strong, vituperative, even coarse language, he blistered them for their hard-hearted sinfulness, telling them they deserved to spend eternity in a hell prepared for them by a wrathful God. The effect was shattering, "like cannonballs through a basket of eggs."

Within three years, Finney's phenomenal success attracted national attention and a flood of invitations to preach. He also attracted widespread criticism for his theology, his harsh preaching, and his increasing reliance on "new measures." Even his supporters acknowledged that his pulpit style was "somewhat dictatorial," and he began to take pains to limit the grosser displays of emotion, even noting that "weepers seldom receive any lasting good." He did, however, employ new measures. In one of the first known accounts of the now-familiar invitation, he challenged people to stand or come to the front of the assembly, indicating their readiness to accept Christ. Finney believed conversion could be instantaneous and did not hesitate to use social pressure, such as praying for reluctant sinners by name, to bring it about.

As Finney's reputation grew, he moved inevitably from the towns and villages of New York to the major population centers of the eastern seaboard. In the fall of 1829, he came to New York City to help write a new and vital chapter in Evangelical history. During the first half of the nineteenth century, optimistic Americans were joining together to establish an incredible array of voluntary associations aimed at accomplishing the reforms and improvements they felt would generate a perfect society. Though some were secular in origin, most of these vessels rode a booming tide of millennial expectations set in motion during the first Great Awakening. Evangelistic Christians were consumed with the conviction that their efforts could ring in the millennium, a literal thousand years of peace and prosperity that would culminate in the glorious second advent of Christ. This potent belief produced a campaign of social reform so massive and multifaceted that it came to be known as the Benevolent Empire and the Evangelical United Front. No problem seemed too great to tackle, and few were deemed so minor as to require no attention. Reform-minded Christians threw themselves into fervent campaigns to eradicate war, drunkenness, slavery, subjugation of women, poverty, prostitution, Sabbath breaking, dueling, profanity, card playing, use of fermented wine in the Communion, and poor eating habits.

In the vanguard of this phalanx of millennial harbingers marched a cadre of wealthy New York entrepreneurs and bankers calling themselves the Association of Gentlemen. Frustrated by the lack of a dynamic preacher to represent their position in the city's Presbyterian pulpits, the association, led by Arthur and Lewis Tappan, persuaded Finney to join their cause. When Finney entered their circle, he became part of a progressive Evangelical network whose members would interact and depend on one another's counsel and collaboration to a degree that was remarkable, given the state of travel and communication at the time. This pattern, in which a small number of key actors assume leading roles in a linked chain of major ventures—a kind of pious power elite—would also come to characterize Evangelical Christianity.

In 1834, in an effort to rescue a floundering publication established to promote his revivals, Finney delivered a series of lectures on the techniques of revival and allowed the journal to reprint them, first as a series of articles and then as a book. The result was an Evangelical classic. The *Lectures on Revivals of Religion*, a detailed manual of new measures, sold 12,000 copies on the day it hit bookstores in America, became a sensation in Great Britain (one publisher alone printed 80,000 copies), and was still in print 150 years later. In the *Lectures*, Finney expressly denied there was anything supernatural about revival. "It is not a miracle, or dependent on a miracle, in any sense," he insisted. "It is a purely philosophical result of *the right use of the constituted means*—as much so as any other effect produced by the application of means." Jonathan Edwards felt revivals had to be "prayed down"; Charles Finney believed they could be "worked up" and developed a clear-cut system for doing so.

To Finney, the primary object of effective preaching is to cause one's hearers to make a decision for Christ, and to that end, any device within the bounds of common decency is not only acceptable but recommended. A successful revivalist, according to Finney, would give attention not just to content and organization but to style as well, and seminary training would not help much on this score. It is, he declared, "a SOLEMN FACT that the great mass of young ministers who are educated accomplish very little. When young men come out from the seminaries, are they fit to go into a revival?... Seldom." The most effective sort of preacher, he reckoned, would resemble the self-educated Charles Finney. He would speak without notes in a conversational and colloquial manner—much as an attorney might speak to a jury. He would use "the language of common life" because "that is the way Jesus Christ preached. And it is the only way to preach." When possible, his illustrations would come from everyday life. A good preacher would also pay attention to the faces of his auditors, and if he sensed they had not understood a point, he would repeat it until they did. And finally, an effective preacher would not hesitate to use theatrics if they helped him communicate his message. The calculation implicit in Finney's lectures and reflections struck some as undignified and out of keeping with the spirit of the gospel. Finney's response was characteristic: "When the blessing evidently follows the introduction of the measure itself, the proof is unanswerable but the measure is wise." And the measure of wisdom, he said, "is to be decided, 'other things being equal,' by the *number* of cases in which [the evangelist] is successful in converting sinners."

The *Lectures* also made the link between revival and reform unmistakably explicit. In keeping with his conviction that "the great business of the church is to reform the world—to put away every kind of sin," and that true

Christians must be "useful in the highest degree possible," Finney asserted that new converts should set about immediately to improve their society and, in the process, to bring in the millennium. In a famous burst of optimism, he estimated that, if the church would only do her duty, "the millennium may come in this country in three years.... If the whole church as a body had gone to work ten years ago, the millennium would have fully come in the United States before this day." To his credit, he did not shrink from addressing the volatile issue of slavery. Revivals are hindered, he said, when ministers take the wrong stand on questions involving human rights. "The church cannot turn away from this question," he insisted. "[T]he silence of Christians upon the subject is virtually saying *that they do not* consider slavery a sin." As various historians have noted, Finney's converts became active participants in most of the progressive social movements of their era. Wherever he preached Christians turned their hands to reform.

At about this same time, an ardent admirer of Finney's established an undergraduate college in the rural community of Oberlin, Ohio, where students who paid for their education by manual labor could receive a wholesome Christian education free from the amusements and temptations of the Babylonish cities of the East. The Tappans quickly offered their support, with the stipulation that Charles Finney become its first professor of theology. Finney hesitated to take the assignment, but Arthur Tappan pushed him to accept. Under Finney's influence, Oberlin became the western center of social radicalism. Students and faculty alike enjoyed complete freedom of speech on all reform issues, and the school was involved in both the feminist and the antislavery movements. It was, in fact, the first co-educational college in the world and produced the first American woman to be ordained in the ministry. Black students were also fully integrated from the beginning, and the college soon gained notoriety as a major station on the Underground Railway that spirited fugitive slaves to freedom.

By the midnineteenth century, America had become, more fully than ever before or again, a Christian republic, and the dominant expression of that Christianity was Protestant, Evangelical, and revivalistic. Church membership vaulted to the highest levels in American experience, and virtually all the new growth occurred in Evangelical ranks. Individuals and churches exposed to revival preaching and thought were energized with new hopes, new drives, a sense of community with others of like belief, and a conviction that they were engaged in a grand effort to save the republic and with it the world. Driven by millennial hopes and pulled by perfectionist goals, they further democratized their churches and pioneered in the development of voluntary associations whose focused attention to single issues made them highly efficient instruments of reform and, in the process, provided models that were soon reflected in business and political organizations and would still be a prominent feature of Evangelicalism nearly 150 years later.

For all its success, however, the Evangelical United Front began losing some of its unity. Growing denominations withdrew from ecumenical voluntary societies to erect their own benevolent and missionary structures, with a resulting decline in interdenominational cooperation. Baptists, Methodists, and Presbyterians split over slavery. Revivalism itself, familiar to all and approved by most, was still criticized. Although Finney established itinerant evangelism as a respectable profession, men of less ability and integrity reduced it to a trade, and not always a respectable one. Numerous evangelists took advantage of the ecstatic feelings they stirred in the bosoms of their female auditors, and others drew fire for bombastic theatricality and unvarnished greed.

During 1857 and 1858 the nation experienced a throwback to the Great Awakening in New England and a precursor of the charismatic revival that began in the 1960s. The revival broke out among laymen in New York in 1857, when economic indicators pointed to a major financial upheaval. When the stock market crashed in October, setting off an epidemic of bankruptcies, similar meetings began, and within six months more than 10,000 men were meeting daily for prayer in gatherings throughout the city. At a time when urbanization and technology were disrupting whole communities and creating new lines of division between social groups, this truly nonsectarian revival, though it crested rather quickly, provided a basis for new community and had lasting consequences. At a tangible level, it introduced the widespread use of tents as gathering places for revival and reinvigorated the YMCA, which would serve as a key operation base for later evangelists. It also eased some tensions between religion and business. If God could generate such revival in the hearts of men and women engaged in capitalistic commerce, was this not clear and sufficient proof that he smiled on their endeavors? Finally, by providing participants with a sense of solidarity with fellow worshipers throughout the nation, the mass media—in the form of newspapers and the telegraph—laid an early foundation stone of what would come to be called the electronic church.

The decades that followed the revival of 1857–1858 were of course among the most tumultuous in the history of the republic. The Civil War and Reconstruction left scars that have never disappeared from the body and soul of the nation. Despite this national trauma, however, the war threatened the survival of religion less than did other factors. Many Christians, particularly Northerners, were able to interpret the suffering as punishment for grievous sin; others, particularly Southerners, viewed it as part of the unjust pain often visited upon the righteous. Ultimately more upsetting were the combined forces of industrialization, urbanization, and immigration, which replaced the relative homogeneity and social cohesion of an earlier time with multiple subcultures divided by class, ethnicity, and language.

As these social forces shook the ground beneath them and changed the society around them, Evangelicals began to suffer an even more devastating set of crises within their hearts and minds. Charles Darwin's account of the *Origin of Species* (1859) and *The Descent of Man* (1871) cast doubt not only upon the veracity of the opening chapters of Genesis but upon the entire doctrine of human nature and destiny. An even more serious threat came in the form of historical criticism of the Bible. Imported from German universities into American seminaries and pulpits, this approach questioned the traditional authorship and dating of the books of the Bible, dismissed the miracle stories as naive magical nonsense, and asserted that so-called prophecies were either written after the events they allegedly predicted or had been inappropriately twisted to fit situations that bore no relation to the original intent of the passages. It also raised serious questions about whether the New Testament picture of Jesus was reliable in any meaningful sense. Many Protestants, including some from the revivalist tradition, adjusted to these challenges. They set forth theories of "theistic evolution" and interpreted the days of the Genesis creation story as ages that were as long as God needed to get the job done. Most Evangelicals, however, chose to ignore or deny them. The Bible could still be accepted at face value, they insisted; it still said what it meant and meant what it said. The vehicle they used to deliver this reassuring message to the new urban frontier was the same one that had worked so well on other frontiers: revival. And the man who epitomized revival for this era was Dwight Lyman Moody.

A native of Northfield, Massachusetts, Moody struck out for Chicago, where he found quick success as a sales representative for a shoe company. Converted shortly before he left Massachusetts in 1856, Moody became active in a Congregational church and participated happily in the laymen's prayer revival that came to Chicago a year later. The desire of businessmen involved in this revival to provide young employees who worked for them with a wholesome social and spiritual atmosphere led them to found Chicago's first YMCA. Moody had lived at the Y in Boston for a time and threw himself enthusiastically behind this effort. Ever the salesman and promoter, he rented several pews at his church and began packing them with strangers cajoled in from the streets. When church members criticized this unorthodox approach, in part because many of his recruits were not of the middle classes, he organized his own Sunday school in a rented hall and attracted hundreds of poor children with candy, picnics, and pony rides. As the children and their parents were converted and needed a church to attend, Moody established the independent Illinois Street Church and served as its spiritual leader; since he was never ordained, he could not serve as pastor. In 1860 Moody quit his secular job to become the Chicago YMCA's first full-time employee. Nothing illustrated his native pragmatic shrewdness better than his skill at fund-raising. To raise money for the first fully equipped YMCA in America, he persuaded Cyrus McCormick to contribute $10,000 and to allow that fact to be made public, explaining to the inventor and manufacturer that "the public will think, if you take hold of it, it must succeed." The support of men like McCormick, of course, legitimated not only the YMCA but other projects headed by D. L. Moody.

In 1867 Moody traveled to England to meet with YMCA founder George Williams. While there he became acquainted with "dispensationalist premillennialism," a new scheme of biblical interpretation that would have an incalculable impact on Evangelical theology. Premillennialism holds that Christ will return prior (pre-) to establishing a glorious thousand-year reign on earth. Dispensationalism's distinctive contribution to premillennial thought was its positing of a series (usually seven) of distinct eras (dispensations) in God's dealing with humanity, and its keen interest in reading the signs of the times in the light of biblical prophecy, to see just how close the Second Coming might be. The triggering action for the millennial age, the last dispensation, will be "the rapture," at which point faithful Christians will be "caught up together to meet the Lord in the air," leaving the rest of humanity to face an unprecedented congeries of calamities known as the tribulation. The main protagonist of the seven-year tribulation will be the Antichrist, who will seek total control by requiring every person to wear a mark or number (probably 666, "the mark of the beast" [Revelation 13:16–18]). The tribulation will end with the Second Coming of Christ and the battle of Armageddon, to be followed by the millennium and ultimately the Last Judgment and eternity of bliss for the redeemed and agonizing punishment for the wicked.

Moody fully accepted the premillennial teaching that the world was rushing headlong toward moral and social disaster from which only the second coming and millennial reign of Christ offered hope for the redeemed. The task, then, was to help as many people as possible prepare for that blessed event. In perhaps the most frequently quoted of Moody's observations, he said, "I look on this world as a wrecked vessel. God has given me a life-boat, and said to me, 'Moody, save all you can.'"

By 1870 Moody was an Evangelical celebrity in both the United States and England, receiving numerous invitations to speak at conferences and churches and ready to embark on a full-time career as an itinerant evangelist. During an extended tour of the British Isles, he and his musical assistant, Ira D. Sankey, drew great crowds and honed the techniques of their new profession. When he returned to America in 1875, he found himself with more opportunities than he could accept and went from victory to victory in Brooklyn, Philadelphia, New York, and Chicago during the next two years.

There was nothing mysterious about Moody's success. His theology, style, and technique were perfectly suited to his age. Lacking time and inclination for subtle theological disputation, he summed up essential doctrine in the simple assertion that humans are fallen and that Christ came to seek and save them. He believed all were sinners, but sinners in the hands of a loving God who offered peace and comfort and refuge from the storm. Since Americans obviously have free will, so must all people. If they wish to accept salvation, it is a simple, straightforward choice, like voting for the right political party: "a fair, square, practical thing, isn't it?" He acknowledged that conversion might involve cataclysmic upheaval but knew from his own experience that it might also be marked by nothing more dramatic than an improvement in daily habits, greater feelings of happiness, loss of the fear of death, and heightened interest in religious activities.

As a preacher, Moody suffered from several disabilities; foremost of these was his meager education. His grammar was so poor that a deacon told him he would probably do more harm than good by attempting to tell others about Christ. With help from his wife and exposure to people of wider experience, he improved, but his letters reveal that he never mastered the rules of grammar and spelling, and his English supporters once canceled a scheduled appearance at Eton, fearing that his unpolished manner of speaking would embarrass them. In many ways, however, his style fit the taste of the times. He spoke rapidly, like a door-to-door salesman, described biblical people and events in the vernacular, and told syrupy stories of the sort that abounded in the popular literature of the period. When he was not exhorting his audiences with slogans that would have delighted an advertising man—"Ruined by Sin, Redeemed by Christ, and Regenerated by the Holy Spirit"—he was wooing them with tears and treacle. If he spoke of hell, it was with compassion in his eyes, not fire in his nostrils and brimstone on his breath.

Perhaps aware of Charles Finney's dictum that "the commonsense people *will* be entertained" and that a successful preacher must take this into account, Moody and Sankey offered revival crowds an evening of wholesome family enjoyment, highlighted by Sankey's enormously popular renditions of such comforting gospel songs and spiritual ballads as "Rescue the Perishing" and "Safe in the Arms of Jesus." After Moody, all successful revivalists would make extensive use of music in their campaigns. Probably even more crucial to Moody's success than his message and style was his talent as an organizer and manager. Historian William McLoughlin has aptly observed that "Charles Finney made revivalism a profession, but Dwight L. Moody made it a big business." He studied the techniques of other evangelists and, by the time of his great meetings in the 1870s, had developed a detailed program for organizing and executing revivals, or, as he preferred to call them, "preaching missions." He accepted invitations only when the major Evangelical churches in a city would agree to support the meetings on a nonsectarian basis. Prior to each campaign, he met with local clergymen to respond to any concerns they might have about his coming to their city, stressing always that the success of the endeavor depended on their wholehearted support. When the meetings ended, he met with them again to thank them for the key role they had played. To promote a nondenominational atmosphere, he appointed a prominent layman to serve as general administrator for the campaign, and he chose neutral sites for the meetings, hiring public halls or erecting temporary buildings large enough to accommodate crowds that would neither attend nor fit into a conventional church building. Moody received honoraria for his revivals, and he lived quite comfortably, but much of his money went to various institutions and projects he believed in, and he was not personally wealthy. He left a modest estate and a reputation for financial integrity that later evangelists have seldom equaled.

Moody's early revivals were the greatest triumphs of his career. When subsequent efforts failed to match them, he turned increasingly to perpetuating his contribution through the establishment of two college preparatory schools, the Northfield School for girls and the Mt. Hermon School for boys, both located in his hometown of Northfield, where he moved his family after leaving Chicago. As he grew increasingly pessimistic about the direction of American society, he retained his belief that the conversion of individuals was the only plausible response but realized the battle could not be won without more trained warriors. Evangelical schools and seminaries might produce competent Christian soldiers, but the numbers were too small and the process too long. To meet the immediate challenge, he created the Chicago Evangelization Society, aimed at rapidly transforming eager laymen into consecrated minutemen who would "stand in the gap" for God, both at home and abroad. Later renamed the Moody Bible Institute and characterized as the West Point of Christian Service, this school served as a model for dozens of similar institutions and still exercises great influence in Evangelical circles.

Other evangelists followed in Moody's train, some with notable success, but the country's enthusiasm for revivals seemed clearly on the wane. Churches began to question whether revivals actually produced much long-term growth, Evangelicals more attuned to the social gospel grew uncomfortable with the one-sided emphasis on personal morality, and many pious souls were put off by the flamboyance and secular nature of evangelistic services. In addition, some evangelists fell under suspicion because of excessive emphasis on collections and alleged inconsistencies between public and private behavior. Those ready to pronounce itinerant evangelism terminally ill, however, soon learned that the sound they heard in the distance was not a dirge sung by mourners of the late revival tradition but the tooting and blaring of "the Calliope of Zion," the Reverend Billy Sunday.

Billy Sunday grew up in Iowa, played baseball in the National League, and found Jesus in Chicago by listening to a street preacher holding forth outside a saloon where he and several other ballplayers had gone to drink. No one could question the sincerity of his conversion. He gave up alcohol immediately and refused to play ball on Sundays, using the time to give talks at local YMCAs instead. Sunday was not a great player, but he was a good one. He once batted .291 (though his average for eight seasons was only .248), and he stole 84 bases in 117 games during the 1890 season. (This record stood until Ty Cobb surpassed it in 1915 with 96 thefts in 156 games, setting a mark that endured for another 47 years, when Maury Wills stole 104 bases in 165 games.) When he left baseball in 1891 to work full-time for the Chicago YMCA, it was not because his career was fading; he had just been offered a new contract for the then-handsome sum of $500 a month, nearly six times what the Y would pay him.

Sunday's position with the YMCA put him in contact with Moody's friends, and he soon went to work as advance man and manager for J. Wilbur Chapman, whom Moody regarded as the greatest evangelist of the day. When Chapman abruptly retired from the field to become pastor of a church in Philadelphia, Sunday struck out on his own, armed with a handful of his mentor's sermons and a handful of confidence. Over the next five years, he held over sixty revivals in towns and small cities of the Midwest. As he gained experience and built a reputation, he and his wife, Nell (better known as Ma Sunday in later years), worked out a system that surpassed even Moody's in its detail and efficiency, and he honed a style of preaching that was perhaps the most distinctive and flamboyant ever to erupt from an American pulpit.

For the first several years, Sunday held most of his revivals in tents, but after 1901 his reputation and success were such that he was able to demand construction of large wooden tabernacles designed to hold 10 percent of the population of smaller cities or, in the case of major cities, at least 20,000 people. Since loudspeakers did not exist, anything larger would have been pointless. Moody and others had used specially constructed tabernacles on occasion, but they were so identified with Sunday's ministry that some older evangelists still speak of revivals they held in "old Billy Sunday-type tabernacles." One common feature of these structures, the spreading of sawdust on the floor or ground, not only deadened the noise of shuffling feet and chairs but introduced a memorable term into the language of American popular religion: "hitting the sawdust trail."

In his early talks, Sunday spoke in a restrained, even dignified manner, avoiding slang or other rhetorical devices that might obscure his message. Out on the revival circuit, he decided that a preacher should "put his cookies on the lower shelf." So, he said, "I took out the old gospel gun and loaded her up with rock salt, ipecac, barbed wire, carpet tacks, and rough-on-rats. I lowered the hindsight and blazed away, and the gang's been ducking and the devil's been hunting his hole ever since!" As he became flashier and more colloquial, people began to wait eagerly to hear him scream his anger at some "bull-necked, infamous, black-hearted, white-livered, hog-jowled, god-forsaken, hell-bound gang" that had stirred his ire; or to ridicule "those ossified, petrified, mildewed, dyed-in-the-wool, stamped-in-the-cork, blown-in-the-bottle, horizontal, perpendicular Presbyterians"; or to condemn Pilate as "just one of those rat-hole, pin-headed, pliable, stand-pat, free-lunch, pie-counter politicians," and to denounce Pilate's wife as "a miserable, plastic, two-faced, two-by-four, lick-spittle, toot-my-own-horn sort of woman." Such outbursts eventually became so renowned that newspapers printed the latest "Sunday-isms." Sunday supplemented invective with jokes, mimicry, mockery, dialects, homey illustrations, and a keen sense of timing, all sharpened to perfection as he repeated the same sermons dozens (or hundreds) of times. And, lest the ear say to the eye, "I have no need of you," he used his athleticism to full advantage, pacing (an estimated one-and-a-half miles per sermon), running, whirling, pounding on the floor, leaping onto a chair or swinging it around his head, and after shedding his coat and tie and rolling up his sleeves, sliding baseball fashion across the platform-level press table, causing startled reporters to recoil in astonishment and the audience to roar with laughter.

Sunday preached the same simple gospel proclaimed by Moody: "With Christ you are saved, without him you are lost.... You are going to live forever in heaven or you are going to live forever in hell. It's up to you and you must decide now." He characterized the atonement as a business deal: Christ had paid the price for salvation, and God had canceled the debt; not to accept the offer meant "not giving God a square deal." What he preached, Sunday said, "is the fact that a man can be converted without any fuss." For some men, admittedly, conversion might involve a considerable transformation. But "multitudes of men live good, honest, upright, moral lives. They will not have much to change to become a Christian." All they required, in fact, was to hit the sawdust trail, shake Billy Sunday's hand for approximately one second, and live according to middle-class mores. "So it sums up," he summed up, "that all God wants is for a man to be decent. Gee whizz!" Indeed, what could be simpler?

After the early years, Billy left most of the actual operations of his revivals to Ma Sunday and his associates, but he took understandable pride in his organization's businesslike efficiency. Noting that "this is a day of specialists," he hired assistants to stimulate interest, generate financial support, handle publicity, get the tabernacle built, recruit tens of thousands of volunteers, organize hundreds of cottage prayer meetings, work with special-interest groups, organize delegations and assign specific nights they would be expected to attend the services (thus assuring a good crowd every night), help him with sermon preparation and Bible study, and compile statistics. Nothing was intentionally left to chance.

During his heyday Sunday gleaned an annual income of approximately $80,000, which he showed off by dressing sharply and sporting such expensive accoutrements as diamond rings and stickpins. Predictably, critics carped at both the high cost of his campaigns and the good living they provided him, but his supporters accepted his claim that no man alive could produce a comparable harvest at the same price. Given the ease with which salvation could be obtained, Sunday had little difficulty coaxing people to accept it, but anecdotal responses from individual pastors and more systematic studies by both friends and critics of his revivals revealed that between 50 percent and in some cities, as many as 80 percent of trail hitters were either church members who simply checked "reconsecration" on their decision cards or the children of members who would probably have joined the church eventually without any boost from Sunday. As for "first timers," once the out-of-towners and fictitious names and false addresses were eliminated, a discouragingly small percentage ever affiliated with a church.

The simple decency that Sunday wanted Christians to manifest amounted to little more than adhering to dominant political and economic orthodoxies and upholding the moral standards of the Anglo-Saxon Protestant middle class. He further asserted that "there can be no religion that does not express itself in patriotism." To express his own patriotism during World War I, he appeared with Will Rogers at "Wake Up America" rallies, vehemently damned the Germans (even teaching children to hiss the German flag), encouraged young men to volunteer for the army, recommended the jailing of those who criticized President Woodrow Wilson and his policies, and, at the President's request, helped sell an estimated 100 million dollars in Liberty bonds. His economic views consisted of an unreflective espousal of laissez-faire free enterprise. He occasionally acknowledged the distortions unchecked capitalism produced but opposed any government interference, insisting that anyone who made a reasonable effort could succeed in America. He characterized the Social Gospel espoused by the new Federal Council of Churches (founded in 1908 and later renamed the National Council of Churches) as "godless social service nonsense," un-American in motivation and result. Like Horatio Alger, he counseled poor people to view their poverty as an opportunity to demonstrate grit and move up the ladder, perhaps by taking his advice to "go out west and study and be a horticulturist."

For the most part, Sunday's moral and social agenda amounted to little more than a kind of muscular perfectionism, with an emphasis on personal vices. Wherever he went, he cooperated with Prohibitionist forces, and his booze sermon was often the high point of his revivals. Renouncing these manly vices, however, would not make a man a Milquetoast. After all, Billy Sunday had given them up, and who could name a manlier man than he? By being pure and tough, Sunday asserted, the good people of America could regain control of their lives and their country itself. They could close down the saloons, defeat the kaiser and his pagan hordes, drive skeptics and evolutionists whimpering into a corner, and beat back the challenges to traditional

Protestant hegemony posed by the foreigners who were trying to take over American cities. He saw his own role in this process as being "a giant for God" who could, by his preaching and example, make it "easier for people to do right and harder for them to do wrong." Despite the scorn he drew from some religious and political critics, Sunday was unquestionably a national hero. Laudatory books about him became best-sellers, public-opinion polls regularly placed him high on the lists of greatest living Americans, national and state legislative bodies invited him to pray or address their assemblies, and presidents received him at the White House.

As Sunday rode the crest of his popularity, Evangelical Christianity seemed to have regained its stride. It possessed a well-thought-out and consistent view of the inspiration of the Scriptures, worked out during the 1880s at Princeton Theological Seminary, which had become the movement's intellectual center. Between 1910 and 1915, a widely distributed set of twelve volumes entitled *The Fundamentals: A Testimony of the Truth*, set forth the movement's basic doctrines and proved crucial in getting the name *Fundamentalist* established as the most common appellation for the conservative Protestant wing of the church.

The war and the Bolshevik Revolution of 1917 provided Fundamentalism with what was to become one of its major elements: religious nationalism. Sunday and other Fundamentalist leaders declared that Satan himself was directing the German war effort and implied it was part of the same process that began with the development of biblical criticism in German universities. Modernism, they asserted, had turned Germany into a godless nation and would do the same thing to America. When the rise of communism and the rash of strikes, bombings, and advocacy of radical causes immediately following the war helped produce the Red Scare, Fundamentalists were among the most scared. In 1919 Sunday offered his audiences his solution for dealing with radicals: "If I had my way with these ornery wild-eyed socialists and IWW's, I would stand them up before a firing squad." As for Reds, he said he would "fill the jails so full ... that their feet would stick out the windows."

Sunday's career reached its apex with his New York City revival in 1917, a campaign that reaped a harvest of over 98,000 trail hitters in ten weeks. Then, with marked suddenness, he lost his grip on the national consciousness. He remained active on the revival field until his death in 1935, but the great cities of the North and East stopped inviting him, and he played out the string in smaller southern cities and towns. Billy Sunday left little tangible legacy—no important writings, no college or training school, no distinctive approach others have preserved. Still, the simple fact that he held over three hundred revivals, spoke without a loudspeaker to audiences whose aggregate number exceeded one hundred million, and registered more than a million trail hitters (whatever their motivation) won for him a permanent place in the first rank of American evangelists.

Sunday's decline coincided with a decline of revivalism in general, and some observers believed he was surely the last great warrior of his tribe. But the line had not come to an end. A scant year before Sunday died, November 6, 1935, a gangly teenager strolled self-consciously into an itinerant evangelist's "Billy Sunday-type tabernacle" in Charlotte, North Carolina. As a child, he had heard Sunday preach, but stepping into the famed evangelist's shoes could not have been further from his mind. And when he hit the sawdust trail later that evening, neither he nor anyone who watched him stride nervously down the aisle could have suspected that the boy who would become the most famous preacher of all time had just declared his intention to spend his life preaching the gospel of Jesus Christ.

Part 2

America's Sensational Young Evangelist (1918–1949)

3

Billy Frank

The first pains struck as the hall clock announced the beginning of November 7, 1918. Throughout the long night and the longer crystal-bright day, Morrow Graham labored to bring forth her first child. Finally, as the light began to fade from the late-autumn sky, William Franklin Graham, Jr., issued his first call on the world's attention. A year earlier, Billy Sunday had marked the zenith of his career with a triumphant ten-week campaign in New York City. No one imagined this tiny creature, wiggling his toes as his father examined him proudly by the light of the evening fire, would one day surpass any achievement by Sunday or Moody or Finney or Whitefield. No more than the usual number of dark red apples fell from the huge tree in the front yard, and no aged Simeon appeared at the two-story farmhouse to declare he was ready to depart this life, having seen at last the child the Lord had promised. Still, less from any premonition of greatness than from a deep-seated desire to seek and do God's will, Frank and Morrow Graham hoped and earnestly prayed that their firstborn son, Billy Frank, might one day feel himself singled out for special assignment by the Lord of the Universe.

The Grahams' Scotch-Irish forebears had immigrated to the Carolinas before the American Revolution. Both their fathers had fought for the Confederacy during the Civil War. Ben Coffey, Morrow's father, lost a leg and one of his piercing blue eyes on Seminary Ridge during the first day of fighting at Gettysburg in 1861, and Crook Graham carried a Yankee bullet in his leg till the day he died in 1910. Coffey, not yet twenty when he went off to war, passed the next fifty-five years in tranquil anonymity, scratching a living from a small vegetable farm in the Steele Creek community near Charlotte, North Carolina. He and his wife Lucinda reared their third daughter, Morrow, to be a classic Southern Christian Lady, attentive to Scripture, faithful in public worship at the Steele Creek Presbyterian Church and in her personal devotions at home, and schooled for a year at Charlotte's Elizabeth College in music, manners, and public speaking of the sort befitting a proper lady. She was small, and her clear blue eyes and long blond hair gave her a delicate look, but her strong chin and forthright smile conveyed an impression of will and character, a signal that was not misleading. William Crook Graham, in noisy contrast to Ben Coffey, was an uproarious rascal, a sometime Klansman and full-time whiskey-drinking hell-raiser with a great black beard, a penetrating gaze, and a blustery rambunctiousness that kept him in or near trouble all his life. Moderate in nothing but work, Crook produced a brood of eleven children, the eighth of whom, Frank, seemed almost his polar opposite. The last words his God-fearing, long-suffering mother spoke to him before she died, when he was about ten, were "Frank, be a good boy," and he had tried to honor her memory. Though he grew to be large and strong like his father, with dark wavy hair and steel-blue eyes, he was polite, restrained, unpretentious, and devoid of vices other than card playing and an occasional cigar. He had seen the demon in the bottle, and he wanted no commerce with it. He gave himself so fully to work that he found it difficult to relax and impossible to play; his children doubt he ever played a game or went fishing, and they tell of occasional trips to the shore when he would roll up his trousers, splash about for a few moments in his bare feet, then abruptly retire to his accustomed spot on the sidelines of worldly pleasure. He enjoyed telling jokes and spinning yarns, but those who knew him insist they never heard him utter a word of profanity or repeat an off-color story. When Crook died in 1910, twenty-year-old Frank just naturally took charge of the run-down four-hundred-acre farm his father had staked out four miles from Charlotte. Aided by his younger brother, Clyde, with whom he eventually split the property, he quickly worked it into a prosperous enterprise. In the process, he established himself as one of the most eligible and attractive young bachelors in Mecklenburg County.

When Morrow Coffey spotted Frank at a lakeside amusement park one summer evening, spiffily splendid in his favorite ensemble of navy-blue jacket, white trousers, and Panama hat, she welcomed his attentions and happily accepted his offer of a ride in his snappy new buggy. If he moved with speed and confidence that evening, he soon adopted a more measured step. Frank wanted a wife, but not until he was certain he could support her comfortably and he was already responsible for Clyde, an older sister, a niece, and a cousin, all of whom lived with him at the family farm, so he courted Morrow steadily and exclusively for six years before they finally wed. After a five-day honeymoon at the plush Biltmore House near Asheville, he moved her out to the farm flanking the one-lane sand-clay thoroughfare known grandly as Park Road. Billy Frank was born two years later, followed soon by Catherine, then Melvin, and, after an eight-year gap, Jean. To make room for his growing brood, Frank purchased a house across the road for his siblings and other relatives.

Old Crook Graham had not put much value on education, and Frank's scant three years of formal schooling gave him but the barest acquaintance with reading and writing, so Morrow kept the production records and took care of the billing. Working with and aided by a growing contingent of tenant farmers, the Grahams built one of the largest dairy farms in the area, with seventy-five cows and four hundred regular customers, and Frank installed his family in a handsome new colonial-design brick home with indoor plumbing. With its red barns trimmed in white, its towering silos, and its corn and hay crops growing tall right up to the well-tended fences, the Graham farm resembled a calendar picture of rural America. To keep farm work from grinding down his delicate wife, Frank brought in city water and electricity, projects most neighbors thought unrealistic because of the distance from the edge of town. Even so, Morrow carried her share of the load, rising early to fix a five-o'clock breakfast for the milkers, cooking all day on a wood stove for extra field hands during harvest season, and putting up hundreds of jars of fruits and vegetables each year.

Billy Frank sometimes tested his mother's patience and nerves by his constant "running and zooming" through the house. Even though he was sick more than the other children, Morrow remembered that "there was never any quietness about Billy. He was always tumbling over something. He was a handful. I was relieved when he started school." Apparently hyperactive before the term was invented, he careened through early childhood at full throttle, gleefully overturning egg baskets, knocking plates from the kitchen table, sending a bureau chest crashing down a full flight of stairs, and pelting a passing auto with rocks, all less from any obvious sense of meanness than from a simple desire to see what effect his actions would produce. At one point the Grahams took him to a doctor, complaining that "he never wears down." They were told, "It's just the way he's built." Fortunately, little of the boy's boundless energy fueled anger or rebellion. Mother and siblings alike remember him as an essentially happy child, given to no more than ordinary mischief and blessed with a remarkable ability to please and charm. His first string of spoken words—"Here comes Daddy, sugar baby"—echoed the tones in which his mother introduced him to the world and presaged the gentle, optimistic sweetness that would smooth his way through life. Morrow also taught him the value of a thoughtful gesture. As he waited for the bus to take him to the second day of first grade at the little Sharon school, she suggested he take a handful of flowers to his teacher, who would "just love you for it." The fear that new schoolmates would tease him and that his teacher might think him a peculiar child mortified Billy Frank, but he did as Mother suggested and, as Mother had predicted, the teacher found favor with both the gift and the giver. The boy found such satisfaction in the episode that until he was fifteen or sixteen, he seldom passed a week without romping into the woods back of the big barn to gather a bouquet of wildflowers or some other treasure to bring home to his mother. As one might guess, Mother just loved him for it.

The Graham home, however, was not all sugar babies and wildflowers. Frank and Morrow held their children to a stern discipline. A simple directive brought obedience in most matters, but neither parent saw anything amiss in the frequent use of corporal punishment, and Billy Frank felt the sting of Morrow's hickory switches and the bite of Frank's belt hundreds of times during his first dozen years. Looking back, Morrow once suggested they could have gotten by with a lighter touch and admitted she had sometimes turned her head while Frank applied his belt to a young transgressor's backside: "I knew what he was doing was biblically correct," she conceded, "and the children didn't die," but "I think I would use a lot more psychology today." Not all forms of psychology were entirely absent; on the day Mecklenburg County went "wet," Frank used a bit of homegrown aversion therapy on Billy and Catherine, forcing them to drink beer until they vomited.

This seriousness of purpose and wariness of the world had its roots and reinforcement, not surprisingly, in church. As part of his effort to be a good boy, Frank "got religion" when he was eighteen. It had not been easy. He had been feeling that "things were not right in his heart," so when three old confederate veterans held a revival at a Methodist chapel known as the Plank Meetinghouse, he decided to seek whatever peace of soul they might be offering. On the first night, when the preacher gave the "altar call," Frank went down to the "mourner's bench" and prayed for salvation or deliverance or assurance or whatever it was folk were supposed to find there, but as an old friend put it, "He just couldn't see the light or 'pray through.'" For the next nine nights, he returned to the meeting in an increasingly desperate quest for some sign of God's favor. Failing to experience anything he could identify as positive, he began to worry that he had unwittingly committed the unpardonable sin and that God had hidden his face from him forever. He lost his taste for food, and the same friend recalled, "He wouldn't have picked up a five-dollar bill if he had seen it in the road." On the tenth night, as he headed his buggy toward the chapel, the bright moonlight glinting off his rig and team seemed to illuminate his soul and assure him that Jesus Christ had paid the debt for *his* sin—not just the sin of the world, but *the sin of Frank Graham of Charlotte, North Carolina*—on the cross of Calvary. At that moment, as he related it, he put his faith in Christ alone, and the burden of his heart rolled away. When he pulled up to the chapel, a friend who saw his beaming face recognized immediately that he had been born again, and Brother Coburn, one of the old preachers, proclaimed his own confidence that "this young man is going to preach Christ." That spur-of-the-moment prophecy haunted Frank for decades, but he was not a public man and he decided that until the Lord gave him a more definite sign, he would keep on plowing corn and milking cows. No such sign ever came and, indeed, that one brief episode of internal tension and release seems to have been the sole occasion when Frank Graham's religion exhibited any signs of what William James called the "tender mind." He attended church and lived circumspectly, and that seemed to him to be sufficient.

Morrow neither suffered the doubts nor felt the exhilarations her husband had experienced. "I couldn't tell you the day or hour when I was converted," she would later say, "but I knew I was born again." When the Grahams married, they dedicated their union to God, reading the Bible and praying together on their wedding night, and keeping the "family altar" each night in their home. The primary impetus for that practice seems to have come from Morrow, who thought it would be a positive influence for her new relatives. Even if they chose not to participate, which was usually the case, she recalled, "They knew it was going on." From the start, at Morrow's suggestion, the Grahams attended the Associate Reformed Presbyterian Church, a small sect whose rock-ribbed Calvinism featured complete acceptance of the literal truth of the Bible and full adherence to the seventeenth-century Westminster Confession of Faith. Morrow drummed Bible verses into Billy Frank's head as she scrubbed his back in the washtub; fittingly, the first one she taught him was that great golden text of evangelism, John 3:16: "For God so loved the world, that he gave his only begotten Son, that whosoever believeth in him should not perish, but have everlasting life." She also kept a Scripture calendar on the breakfast-room wall, and each morning she tore off a verse the children were expected to memorize before they left for school or, during the summer, before they went out to play. "She wasn't real, real strict about it," Melvin recalled, "but she constantly kept it before us, so that if you didn't do it, you'd get to feeling a little bit guilty." Prayer accompanied every meal, of course, and each evening after dinner, the family gathered in the family room for further devotions. Morrow would read Scripture and other inspirational material, and Frank would pray. "He could really pray a good prayer," Melvin says admiringly. "His hands would tremble and his voice would shake a little, but people used to love to hear him pray." The children, as soon as they were old enough, would recite or read verses and offer simple prayers. By age ten, each child memorized the Shorter Catechism, a marvel of pedagogy that compresses the heart of Calvinist theology into 107 concise questions ("Are there more gods than one?") and authoritative answers ("There is but one only, the living and true God") and proclaims that "man's chief end is to glorify God, and enjoy him forever."

Though by no means entirely cheerless and gray, religion as practiced in the Graham household tended to find its form in rules to keep, its motive power in terrors to fear. On weekends Morrow cooked all of Sunday's food on Saturday so that no work other than milking and feeding the cows needed be performed on the Lord's day. The children observed a sabbatical ban on games and newspaper comics, and Melvin still recalls the amazement he felt when his father signaled the first break with this austere legalism by taking the family to an ice-cream parlor on the way home from church one Sunday evening. The major terrors were hell and a leather belt, but even religious diversion had ominous overtones. When Billy Sunday came to Charlotte in

1923, Frank took his five-year-old boy to hear him, but the only thing Billy remembers is that "my father said, 'Be quiet, or he'll call your name from the platform.' I sat there frightened to death." If the strictness of his upbringing produced a certain gravity in Billy Frank, it did not break his spirit or drain his energy. Early on, he learned to channel aggression into practical jokes and to allay anger by his ever-present and overwhelming affability. A school-bus driver whom he tormented by cutting off the vehicle's external gas valve, making the bus sputter to a stop a few moments after the Graham children dismounted, admitted that "you couldn't get mad at the skinny so-and-so." A classmate concurred. "He just liked everybody so enthusiastically that everybody had to like him," she recalled. "It was just this lovable feeling that he himself seemed to have for everybody. You couldn't resist him."

Because they lived in the country, the Graham children had few playmates. When he was about ten or eleven, Billy Frank solved this problem by developing an unexpected addiction to reading. "Read!" marvels Melvin, "he could outread anybody I ever saw!" He read Tarzan, then clamored into the woods to reenact the stories, usually casting Catherine and Melvin as obedient simians. He rode the purple sage with Zane Grey and explored distant lands with Marco Polo. And with the aid of an abridged edition of Gibbon's classic Morrow found in a secondhand book shop, he traced *The History of the Decline and Fall of the Roman Empire* before he turned fourteen. Morrow also obtained, and Billy Frank seemed to enjoy, biographies of preachers and stories of brave missionaries in faraway lands. The hundreds of hours spent with books—in the hayloft, in his large, cluttered upstairs bedroom, or most often, lying on his back in the middle of the living room floor with his legs propped up on a chair and chewing his fingernails to the quick—did little to improve a generally lackluster performance in school ("He didn't pick up his lessons too quick," brother Melvin noted), but exposure to worlds beyond the Piedmont stirred a lifelong fascination with the unfamiliar and a longing to explore new territory. His appetite for learning also produced an abiding ability to listen intently when others were talking. When guests came to visit, he typically staked out the largest available chair and sat wide-eyed and wordless, gnawing his nails and soaking up every sentence.

As he grew, Billy Frank became a full-fledged member of the dairy's workforce, rising at two-thirty or three o'clock to milk the cows, then returning from school to haul and pitch hay before it was time to milk again, and working in the fields during the hot, humid summers. Melvin relished these tasks and tagged along at his father's side from early boyhood, eager to take his turn long before he was able. This pleased Frank Graham, who felt a real man would work with his hands, work hard, and like it. Billy Frank did as he was told, but only because he was told. To finish the job and get back to the house as quickly as possible, he became the fastest milker on the farm, but he never came to view manual labor as inherently virtuous. He did, however, learn and reap the benefits of diligence. The Grahams weren't exactly wealthy, but they always had enough and the income was steady, so that even a bank failure that cost them their savings in 1933 put no real dent in a fairly comfortable lifestyle. In a 1964 autobiographical series for *McCall's*, Graham wrote of "the hard red clay where my father eked out a bare existence." But the reality was a good deal rosier. His schoolmates remember him as the most affluent member of their circle, and a former tenant recalls that Frank Graham confided to him in the middle of the Great Depression that the dairy was bringing in a clear profit of $500 a month, a sum roughly equivalent to an annual income of $50,000 in the 1990s. Frank also managed to augment his farm income by shrewd trades of cars and real estate. Melvin recalled that "Daddy might buy a car for a thousand dollars, drive it for a year, and sell it for fifteen hundred dollars. I was amazed. My daddy was my idol."

When adolescence attacked, Billy Frank eagerly embraced its two leading attractions: baseball and girls. For several years, he spent most of his spare daylight hours on the ball field and dreamed the big-league dream—"That was just his life, to play ball"—but desire could not offset the lack of several crucial skills, most notably the ability to hit. He played first base on his high school team for a season, filled in for four innings with a semipro team, and shook Babe Ruth's hand when the Bambino came through town on a barnstorming tour, but these were the high points of his diamond career. He had greater success with the girls. Catherine recalls that "he was in love with a different girl every day. He really did like the girls. And they liked him." In appearance, he was as unfinished as a young giraffe. His pipe-cleaner limbs and narrow torso seemed almost too spindly to support the large head, but his broad smile and the blue laser eyes that flashed out from their dark surrounds gave him a unique appearance that if not yet handsome, was certainly arresting. In any case, access to his father's car counted for more than a Charles Atlas frame and facilitated long pleasurable evenings in the company of young ladies. He acknowledges having enjoyed spending time with girls but insists that other liberties remained in the realm of fantasy: "I never went any further. I never touched another woman till I was married, in any way beyond kissing." He credits this triumph of virtue over hormones to parental influence, noting that Frank and Morrow Graham expected their children "to be clean, and never doubted that we would be. They trusted us and made us want to live up to their confidence."

Effective as it was at filling young minds with Scripture and keeping their bodies pure, the legalistic piety practiced by the Grahams lacked the comforting assurance and energizing power of full-bore Evangelical religion. That changed, decorously but decisively, in 1933. The first shift came when Morrow's sister, Lil Barker, urged her "to get down deep into the Word and see what God really has to say to you," and persuaded her to attend an independent Bible class taught by a Mrs. Whitted. This class introduced her to the writings of such Evangelical giants as Arno Gaebelein and Donald Grey Barnhouse, whose books she acquired from mail-order houses in New York. It also introduced her to dispensationalist teachings, which she found fascinating. Encouraged by Lil and her husband, Simon, a fervent dispensationalist, Morrow eventually began attending evening Bible classes at the Plymouth Brethren Church, a sect once led by John Nelson Darby, the father of dispensationalist teaching. Frank's difficulty with reading made Bible classes an unpromising avenue of spiritual growth, but the loss of his savings in the bank failure and a near-fatal farm accident, in which a chunk of wood thrown off by a mechanical saw smashed his face, underscored the essential fragility of life and moved him to take a more active interest in matters spiritual.

The following spring, in a desperate attempt to break free of the miasmic lassitude produced by the depression, with its merciless mortgage foreclosures, ruinous bank failures, and debilitating disappearance of businesses and jobs, a group of thirty or so members of the Charlotte Christian Men's Club, a men's group formed in the aftermath of Billy Sunday's 1924 revival, met in a grove of trees in Frank Graham's pasture for a daylong session of prayer and fasting. At the same time, Morrow hosted an all-day prayer meeting in her home. Standing, sitting or kneeling on blankets, and leaning against their cars, the men importuned God for some insight, some direction, some inspiration that would enable them to endure the doldrums in which they were adrift. In particular, they girded themselves for an evangelistic effort they hoped would generate some wave of vitality in what they regarded as Charlotte's moribund spiritual life. The percentage of churchgoing folk in Charlotte was reportedly the highest in the nation, but these men felt the churches had become self-satisfied and smug, with little real concern for lost souls. As the intensity and confidence of their prayers began to mount, they called on God to use them "to shake up the whole state of North Carolina for Christ." Before long they had expanded their horizons to include the entire world. No transcript of this session exists, but one shining arrow fired toward heaven in a moment of high aspiration has been recovered, perhaps polished a bit, and set aside like a museum piece. At some point, Vernon Patterson, the group's leader, launched what must have seemed an improbable entreaty when he earnestly prayed that "out of Charlotte the Lord would raise up someone to preach the Gospel to the ends of the earth." Surely, none of the modest group gathered there among the pines considered for a moment that the evangelist envisioned in that long-shot request was pitching hay into feed troughs a few hundred yards away, and no one would have been more surprised than he. When a friend who had come home with him after school asked why all the cars were there, Billy Frank told him, "Oh, I guess they are just some fanatics who talked Dad into letting them use the place."

The revival for which the men were preparing stretched from late August to the Sunday after Thanksgiving and featured the vivid, fire-breathing preaching of a colorful old war-horse named Mordecai Ham. True to revivalist tradition, Brother Ham had a reputation for attacking the lethargy of the local clergy, which doubtless influenced the Charlotte ministerial association's decision not to support his meeting. He also generated controversy and opposition (as well as approval) by anti-Semitic rantings and racist slurs so notable that newspaper editors sometimes urged him to leave their cities. In the Charlotte campaign, however, he seemed to have concentrated mostly on those durable touchstones of revival preaching: sin and salvation.

Perhaps because their minister was cool toward the revival, the Grahams did not attend for the first week or so, but Billy Frank eventually accepted an invitation from his father's chief tenant, Albert McMakin, to drive a truckful of young people to the services. About the same time, Frank and Morrow also began attending, and the revival became the family's major evening activity for the next two months. When he joined the 4,000 eager souls inside the sprawling sawdust-floored, tin-roofed, raw-pine tabernacle, Billy Frank quickly succumbed to the aroma of the evangelist's sulfuric fulminations. "This man would stand up there and point his finger at you and name all the sins you had committed," he recalled, years later. "It made you think your mother had been talking to him." To avoid Ham's penetrating gaze, Billy Frank joined the choir, despite a consensus view that he "couldn't sing a lick." There he sat down by Grady Wilson, who shared his nonmusical motivation. Grady and his older brother, T.W., were sons of a plumber who knew Frank Graham from the Christian Men's Club and had been present at the prayer meeting on the Graham farm. T.W., often shortened just to T, was tall and handsome, with large, surprised eyes and an insouciant nose that a decade later, often caused people to mistake him for the popular young radio comedian, Bob Hope. Grady was shorter and stockier, with an open, happy face, an irrepressible enthusiasm, and a rustically humorous slant on life that enabled him to spot the comic wherever it existed and invent it where it did not. Billy Frank knew of the two boys but since they attended different high schools, they had never been around each other much until the revival. The friendship that grew out of experiences they shared on those cool fall evenings would endure for the rest of their lives.

As proprietor of a bulging mental storehouse of Scripture and vice-president of his church's youth group, Billy Frank probably never imagined he was not a true Christian, but Ham's preaching magnified his consciousness of sin, convincing him he had not fully surrendered his life to Christ. Finally, when the evangelist made his appeal and while the congregation sang an invitation hymn whose closing words were "Almost persuaded ... Almost—but lost!" Billy Frank Graham and Grady Wilson "went forward" to register a decision that would forever alter their lives. *Decision* is the proper word, as Graham has related to many an audience: "I didn't have any tears, I didn't have any emotion, I didn't hear any thunder, there was no lightning. I saw a lady standing next to me and she had tears in her eyes, and I thought there was something wrong with me because I didn't feel all worked up. But right there, I made my decision for Christ. It was as simple as that, and as conclusive." The conclusiveness seems more solid in retrospect. At home later that evening, Billy Frank announced to his approving parents, "I'm a changed boy," but upstairs in his bedroom, he privately wondered if he would feel any different the next day. Finally, he dropped to his knees by the side of his bed and said, "Oh God, I don't understand all of this. I don't know what's happening to me. But as best I can figure it, I have given myself to you." Since he had no truly impressive sins to repudiate, he made mental notes on the modest improvements available to him: greater seriousness about his schoolwork, increased consideration for others, more attention to Bible study and prayer, and, most importantly, a resolve to manifest that distinctive mark of the Evangelical Christian, bearing witness to the Good News. Family members have found it a bit difficult to depict the occasion as a momentous turning from darkness unto light. Catherine said, "He was much nicer to me after that" and remembered that he stopped attending movies for several years. At the Junior-Senior Banquet, he abandoned his date rather than hang around where others would be dancing. Melvin also saw a shift in his brother's priorities but allowed that "it didn't change all at once, now. It took a little while."

Billy Frank's new dedication neither dimmed his delight in the company of young ladies nor stemmed his growing enthusiasm for racing his father's Plymouth along back roads or driving it "right up on the sidewalk" in downtown Charlotte. In fact, when the family began attending the Tenth Avenue Presbyterian Church in Charlotte, a group of devoted young people who called themselves the Life Service Band turned down his application for membership on the grounds that he was "just too worldly." At school his grades improved a bit, but he had to retake a final exam before he could graduate. "He wasn't any dumb bunny," close friend Wint Covington remembered, "but he certainly wasn't the smartest one." Neither did he completely conquer a tendency toward vainglory. Covington, whose father also made a good living, recalled that "we both had wristwatches, and none of the others did. During the depression, something like that would kind of lift you above the crowd. When we'd go into Charlotte for a movie, we wore jeans, but we'd roll up our sleeves to show our watches, to indicate we weren't down and out."

An objective observer might have concluded that Billy Frank's conversion was shallow, but, "deep down inside me," he has often insisted, "I knew something was different. I began to want to tell others what had happened to me. I began to want to read the Bible and to pray. I got hold of a little hymn book and began to memorize those hymns. I would say them because I couldn't sing." As a sign of the new maturity he sought, he dropped the second of his names. The double name, he felt, had a juvenile ring to it, "like

Sonny, Buddy, or Junior." Still, he gave little thought to a career in preaching, even when the Wilson boys and several other young men influenced by Mordecai Ham announced their intention to enter the ministry, but he was impressed by his friends' efforts and has often recalled the first time he heard Grady preach. "Grady borrowed my watch to time his sermon. He preached on 'Four Great Things God Wants You to Do,' and he went on for about an hour and a half. He was nervous"—Grady contended his anxiety stemmed from seeing his girlfriend and Billy hold hands throughout the sermon—"and all the time he was preaching, he was winding my watch, so when he finally got through, he had wound the stem off my watch and ruined it. But I was so impressed. I thought to myself, 'I'd give anything in the world if I could stand up in front of people like Grady did and preach. That'll never happen to me, I know.'" His occasional attempts to testify during sidewalk services organized by his church's youth group were timid, fumbling efforts, more embarrassing than edifying. Still, he was fascinated by preachers, particularly the itinerants who passed through Charlotte and stayed with the Grahams or their friend, Vernon Patterson. He listened raptly to their expositions, fixed on their thrilling stories, and imitated their pulpit styles in front of a mirror, but the thought of actually joining their ranks lay distant on the horizon, like a cloud no bigger than a man's hand.

4
The Boy Preacher

Despite Billy's modest academic record, he expected to attend college when the time came. He favored the University of North Carolina, less because of its academic reputation than because two of his cousins had gone there, and because its president was a distant relative. Morrow Graham's exposure to Fundamentalist culture, however, convinced her that the road to hell passed straight through the campuses of state universities, and she longed for him to attend one of the fundamentalist schools advertised in the *Moody Monthly*. Wheaton College in Illinois was her first choice, but it was so expensive and so far away that she began to consider other options. Her husband, who regarded college as an extravagance, wanted his son to stay home and help with the farm. An apparent solution presented itself when one of the South's best-known evangelists, Bob Jones, came to Charlotte for a short series of meetings during Billy's senior year in high school. Large and imposing, self-assured past the point of arrogance, unflinching in his willingness to say exactly what he believed, and equipped with a gift for ear-catching rhetoric, Jones had founded Bob Jones College (BJC), a small Bible school in Cleveland, Tennessee. The unaccredited school had no standing in professional educational circles, but it was gaining a reputation as a place where Fundamentalist young people could insulate themselves from the chilling winds of doubt that blew across secular campuses. Billy Sunday himself had given it his blessing, and Ma Sunday served on its board of trustees. Jones's blunt, uncompromising style fascinated Frank Graham, and he decided his son could use some exposure to the hardheaded discipline that characterized the young school, particularly since the cost of attending was pegged at approximately one dollar a day. If Billy wanted to attend Bob Jones College, Frank would agree to send him. Billy resisted a bit, but when T. W. Wilson, who had "got saved" during Jones's meeting and had gone to BJC for the 1936 spring semester, came home with glowing reports, he grew accustomed to the idea. The convincing argument came from Jimmie Johnson, a twenty-three-year-old evangelist who was Billy's current idol. Johnson, who had stayed in the Graham home for a time during the summer of 1935, had his own portable tabernacle and enjoyed a rapidly growing reputation as a soul winner.

"He was a handsome fellow and really did know his Bible," Melvin Graham recalled. "Billy Frank thought if he could just preach like Jimmie Johnson, there wouldn't be anything higher." Johnson was also an ardent BJC alumnus, and that was all Billy needed. Bob Jones would be his college.

After Billy graduated from high school in 1936, Albert McMakin, who had left the Graham farm for a career in sales, cajoled him and the Wilson brothers into spending the summer in his crew of Fuller Brush salesmen, peddling their wares in the small towns and rural areas of the Carolinas. Some doubted Billy would succeed as a salesman. He didn't really need the money and had never shown much enthusiasm for hard work. When McMakin picked him up at the start of the summer, Uncle Clyde made no effort to hide his skepticism. "You really taking him?" he asked. "Two weeks. I'll give him two weeks to wire home for money." Clyde's gibe had its effect; when Billy lost all the money he made during the first week, he refused to seek help from home. The doubt had been unfair. Cows had not been Billy's calling, but he proved well suited to salesmanship. He worked hard, he learned how to make customers pay attention while he rummaged for their free gift at the bottom of his bag, he prayed before he began his calls and between houses, and he believed in the product. "Sincerity," he would later observe, "is the biggest part of selling anything, including the Christian plan of salvation." He learned how to talk his way into front doors and out of hostile or embarrassing situations. And as successful salesmen will, he got caught up in the selling process itself. "Selling those brushes became a cause to me. I was dedicated to it, and the money became secondary. I felt that every family ought to have Fuller brushes as a matter of principle." Even though he confesses to having spent a fair amount of time enjoying the sun and sand at Myrtle Beach, he netted between fifty and seventy-five dollars a week, and when the summer ended, his sales topped those of any other Fuller salesman in North or South Carolina.

Life on the road had its surprises. In one episode the boys found particularly shocking, they recognized a drunken man as an acquaintance from Charlotte, a man they had believed to be an upright Christian. Apart from adultery, few behaviors seemed more egregious to southern Fundamentalists than the use—not to mention abuse—of alcohol. Grady recalled that the sight of the stumbling, disheveled sinner stunned Billy, causing him to determine to put his confidence "in Christ, not man," since "man is weak and made of clay." To counteract such disillusioning wickedness, the boys spent their evenings in Bible study and prayer, and they hooked up with Jimmie Johnson every chance they got. One Saturday night in Monroe, North Carolina, where Johnson was holding a revival, mosquitoes and bedbugs drove Billy and T.W. out of their fifty-cents-a-head tourist court. Knowing the evangelist wouldn't mind, they took shelter in his tabernacle. Grady and Albert McMakin lasted the night at the tourist court but joined them early the next morning. When Johnson showed up, he was glad to see the boys and talked Billy and Grady into going with him to the city jail for a service. Neither boy had ever been inside a jail, and the sights and sounds and smells still hanging over Saturday night's ingathering of miscreants assaulted their senses with striking impressions of fallen mankind, but they watched in silent admiration as their hero delivered a short homily. Then, at least in part as a practical joke not uncommon among preachers, Johnson introduced Billy as a new convert who wanted to tell what Jesus had done for him. As Jimmie had known it would, the request caught Billy off guard, but he had heard plenty of testimonies and knew approximately what to do, so he sucked in his breath and offered the remarkably inappropriate greeting, "I'm glad to see so many of you out this afternoon." As he continued, he warmed to his task, to the point of overstating the darkness of his own preconversion condition: "I was a sinner and a no-good! I didn't care anything about God, the Bible, or people!" Then he launched into the time-honored proclamation he had heard Mordecai Ham and a procession of other revivalists make, and had practiced before the mirror himself: "Jesus changed my life! He gave me peace and joy! He can give you peace and joy! He will forgive your sins as He forgave mine if you will only let him into your heart! Jesus died so he could take your sins on His shoulders." Then, his heart still pounding with excitement, he picked up his sample case and hurried from the jail. He had offered no invitation and no prisoners had made "decisions," but the basic affirmation of that first impromptu sermon — that Jesus died so that sinners might be forgiven, have their lives transformed, and find peace with God — would remain the central tenet of his preaching for more than fifty years.

At the end of the summer, Frank Graham drove Billy and the Wilson brothers down to Tennessee to enroll in Bob Jones College. As soon as they spied out the land, Billy and Grady began figuring ways to conquer it. In his first foray into politics, he plotted with Grady to "take over the freshman class!" His plan was simple: "I'll nominate you for president, then you nominate me for vice-president." His rousing nominating speech propelled Grady into office as planned, but when the new president took the chair, he no longer had the opportunity to nominate his friend, and Billy got no office. From this botched beginning, the rest of the semester went downhill. Dr. Bob, who saw himself, and wanted others to see him, as the South's premier evangelist and Fundamentalism's most influential leader, resolutely sought to mold students in his own likeness. On the positive side, he was unquestionably talented and committed to high academic and spiritual standards, as he understood them, and students at his college kept a packed schedule of classes punctuated by daily chapel services, evening vespers, and regular devotions in dormitories. Less admirably, he was obsessively self-important, rigidly dogmatic, and vehemently intolerant of anything that resembled an opinion different from his own. The educational goal he set for his students was mastery of carefully screened material and suppression of independent or original thinking. Jones also felt a special need to corral the "lust of the flesh" in his young charges. To this end, he forbade students to have any kind of physical contact, including hand holding, with members of the opposite sex. Dates amounted to fifteen minutes of conversation, once a week, in a chaperoned parlor. The administration also monitored mail to make sure that nothing lascivious, doctrinally unsound, or uncomplimentary to the institution passed between it and the threatening world outside. Students who chafed under such measures learned to heed the warning of signs posted in dormitories: "Griping Not Tolerated." The slightest infraction of this or any other rule, stated or unstated, could draw a heavy dose of demerits, and a student who amassed 150 demerits faced automatic expulsion.

Billy tried to fit in, but he and a new friend, Wendell Phillips, grew a bit careless about some of the regulations, amassing a perilous stack of demerits—Phillips estimated that "we both had about 149." To make matters worse, Billy's classwork was a shambles. He had never learned to study in high school, and he simply could not keep up the frenetic pace the school imposed. In his disillusioned and depressed state, allergies and the flu found him an easy target. He began to lose weight and spent long spells in the school's infirmary. When he went home for Christmas, a Charlotte doctor suggested he might fare better in a warmer climate. Fortuitously, an evangelist visiting in the Graham home recommended the Florida Bible Institute (FBI), a new school in Temple Terrace, just outside Tampa. Morrow had seen an advertisement for the school in the *Moody Monthly* and persuaded Frank to take the family to visit one of her sisters, who had just bought a small hotel in Orlando. During that four-day visit, which included a reconnaissance of the Bible college, Billy fell in love with Florida, whose warm climate and lakes and palm trees and flowers seemed paradisiacal in contrast to the wintry cheerlessness at Bob Jones.

When the holiday ended and he returned to BJC, Billy told Wendell Phillips of Florida's wonders. Phillips was looking for an excuse to leave, and a last-straw confrontation with Dr. Bob sealed both their decisions. Jones found out that the boys were speaking positively about another college and summoned them to his office for a maledictory address. The old tyrant charged both of them with disloyalty, one of the most serious sins in his catalogue. Phillips acknowledged that he was leaving and, while Jones fulminated, "just looked him straight in the eye and grinned. That was *bad*." Billy, however, retreated "like a wounded dog with his tail between his legs. He wouldn't even look at Dr. Bob. He just sat there and bit his nails. He was quite a nail biter." The college's founder had already written off Phillips as worthless, but he somehow sensed Billy's potential. "Billy," he prophesied, "if you leave and throw your life away at a little country Bible school, the chances are you'll never be heard of. At best, all you could amount to would be a poor country Baptist preacher somewhere out in the sticks." Then, unexpectedly, Jones softened his tone. "You have a voice that pulls," he said. "Some voices repel. You have a voice that appeals. God can use that voice of yours. He can use it mightily."

Billy's deep reluctance to challenge authority made it hard for him to act on his inclinations, but Wendell Phillips set out for Florida immediately. Within a few days, he was writing letters in which he described Florida Bible Institute as a Shangri-la where students free from stifling regulations could pluck luscious temple oranges from trees right outside their dormitory windows and could swim and play golf all year round. In the days that followed, Wendell received several phone calls from Billy, who had gotten sick again and sought some final bit of evidence that he ought to join his friend in paradise. Then came a call from Morrow, who had only one question: "Wendell, do they teach the Bible there? That's what I want to know." Phillips assured her that "they teach nothing but the Bible. There is hardly any other subject. It is not a liberal arts school. You couldn't go on to be a schoolteacher, or anything else, except something with the church." That was good enough for Morrow, and a few days later, the Grahams loaded up the gray Plymouth one more time and headed for Tampa. The decisive break between Billy Graham and the Fundamentalism symbolized by Bob Jones would not come for twenty more years, but the first fissures had already appeared.

Florida Bible Institute suited Billy perfectly and offered delights he had never known. Its main facility was a former country club and luxury hotel that had gone broke during the depression—an early brochure included a picture of a roulette wheel left by the original owners, a testimony to the transformation that had occurred. The school's founder-president, W. T. Watson, himself a Bible-school product, had acquired the property on very favorable terms and ingeniously turned it into a hybrid college, conference center, and Fundamentalist resort hotel, with most of the ninety or so students defraying the cost of their schooling by serving as staff. Billy wasted no time getting involved with the program. Within hours of his arrival, an administrator gave him keys to a car and asked him to take a group of guests on a tour of Tampa. Higher education had not rusted his skills as a salesman: "I spent the afternoon explaining the virtues of Tampa, which I didn't know anything about, and they seemed happy." Their happiness, no doubt, reflected his own. His father sent him six dollars a week to cover his expenses, and he logged enough hours as a bellhop, waiter, caddy, and high-speed dishwasher to keep him in spending money, but he never ran out of time to play. He swam and canoed in the swampy, snake-infested Hillsborough River, which bordered the campus. He played tennis with about the same proficiency he had shown in baseball. And he spent as much time as he could on the school's eighteen-hole golf course, whacking the ball with an awkward cross-handed grip and wielding a putter as if it were a croquet mallet or sometimes just loping joyously across the fairways, a lanky Ichabod with a scout knife dangling from the belt of his chartreuse slacks. He admitted that for most of the first year, "I was really just a glorified tourist who was taking a few Bible courses," and a more studious classmate acknowledged that "he was not a digger. He got a lot by osmosis."

Academically, the institute represented little, if any, improvement over Bob Jones College, but Watson supplemented the work of the regular faculty, most of whom were pastoring local congregations as well, by inviting a stream of big-name Fundamentalist leaders to serve as short-term visiting instructors. Billy reveled in their presence. As he had once fastened onto the minor-league revivalists who passed through Charlotte on their way up, he now took every opportunity to learn from such old-timers as William Evans (a friend of D. L. Moody's and the first graduate of Moody Bible Institute), E. A. Marshall (who taught the first missions course at Moody) radio preachers Gerald Winrod and R. R. Brown, evangelists Gipsy Smith and Vance Havner ("the Will Rogers of the Pulpit"), A. B. Winchester (whose trademark was the catchphrase "My Bible says"), Billy Sunday's old chorister, Homer Rodeheaver, and Fundamentalist patriarch William Bell Riley. As these venerable veterans warmed themselves over the embers of adulation offered by older people who still remembered them and tried to build a new fire in the young men they hoped might take their place, Billy studied their strengths and weaknesses, determined to find some way he could perform comparable service to the Lord and to the church. ("Billy always wanted to do something big," Dr. Watson remembered; "he didn't know exactly what yet, but he couldn't wait just to do something big, whatever it was.") He attended their lectures and took notes on their sermons. He sat in rapt fascination while they held forth in informal sessions in the hotel's lounges. He served their tables, he polished their shoes, he caddied for them, he carried their bags, he had his picture taken with them, and he wrote home to tell his mother how much he longed to be like this one or that one—"It's hard to find any particular one that you could say affected him," Watson noted; "I think they all had a part; he's a combination man, Billy is"—and eventually to reveal that "I think the Lord is calling me to the ministry, and if he does it will be in the field of evangelism."

The young aspirant observed that an evangelist could regard a comfortable lifestyle as his proper due; a big-name preacher whose bags he had carried gave him a dollar tip, five times what he could earn in an hour of dishwashing, and told him, "Young man, apply yourself to your work and study diligently, and some day you can tip also, for there is more where this came from." He also learned that an evangelist could come to think of himself more highly than he ought. When Gipsy Smith refused his request for an autograph, on the grounds that too many other students would want one, Billy silently pledged that should anyone ever care to have his autograph, he would never refuse it. From Dr. Watson he learned more strongly than ever to rely on prayer to see an institution through crisis and help it accomplish its goals. In one memorable episode of the sort that becomes part of the mythology of such institutions, Watson summoned the students together after breakfast one morning and explained that the institute might have to close its doors if the Lord did not provide $10,000 immediately. As they were expected to do, Billy and his classmates dutifully fell to praying, beseeching God nonstop right through lunch and into the early afternoon. Then, as if by a miracle, Watson's secretary handed the president a telegram from a northern businessman who reported that as he had been driving through Mount Vernon, Ohio, that very morning, he had suddenly "felt a burden" for Florida Bible Institute and was sending a check for $10,000. This experience moved Billy far more than the old evangelist's generous tip, but the lesson was the same: "There is more where this came from."

Billy's most significant "father in the faith" during his Florida days was the Reverend John Minder. Academic dean of the college and pastor of the Tampa Gospel Tabernacle, "Minder couldn't preach for sour apples," but he was "an all-round wonderful man" who had what the Apostle Paul labeled "the gift of helps." Minder himself liked to say, "I polish the apple for the other fellow to eat." When he saw young men and women with promise, he did what he could to encourage them. Billy's boundless energy and unquenchable ebullience, his willingness to work hard, his popularity, and, most of all, his obvious sincerity and dedication to God impressed the dean, who adopted him as a special project. During the Easter vacation that spring of 1937, Minder invited Billy to join him and his family at a conference center he owned up near the state's northern border, west of Jacksonville. On Easter afternoon, they drove over to Palatka to visit Cecil Underwood, a bivocational Baptist preacher who supported himself by painting and sanding floors while pastoring a church in the little community of Bostwick. When Underwood invited Minder to preach that evening, the dean grinned and said, "Billy's preaching tonight." Billy gasped and protested that he had never preached before, but Minder had heard him give his testimony at a student-conducted meeting and ignored his protests. He told him, "You go ahead and preach. When you run out, I'll take over. I never run out." As a matter of fact, Billy was not wholly unprepared. He had known such a day was bound to come and had secretly cribbed, embellished, and practiced four sermons from a book published by the Moody Press. That Sunday evening, to no more than twenty-five or thirty deep-country Baptists whose dogs scratched around outside the little clapboard church while their masters belted out lively gospel songs and asked forgiveness for what they had done and left undone, Billy Graham preached his first real sermon. To be precise, he preached his first four real sermons. He had calculated that any one of them would run over half an hour, but anxiety had so accelerated his delivery and short-circuited his recall that he finished all four in less than eight minutes. He has said of this initial outing, "Nobody ever failed more ignominiously." Dean Minder, a beneficent spirit, recalled it as "a very nice message." This first sermon was a simple historical milestone, a formal beginning of no great immediate consequence either to Billy or his auditors, and he still felt no clear call to preach, though he obviously planned to be ready if it came. But if God was not yet ready to call him, John Minder was. A few weeks later, he invited Billy to join him at the Tampa Gospel Tabernacle as youth director, a post he held until he graduated three years later. A clipping from a Tampa newspaper's church page gave an early progress report: "Three months ago when Mr. Graham took charge of this department the young people were a somewhat discouraged group. But now after much prayer and hard work it has become one of the most promising organizations of the Tabernacle. The present enrollment is 52." Contrary to Wendell Phillips's description, FBI did not lack for rules and regulations. Smoking and drinking were absolutely forbidden, and dating, while freely allowed, was still a noncontact sport and subject to strict curfews. But these were the same rules Billy and most of the other students had obeyed all their lives, so they posed no obstacle to any pleasure they considered legitimate. An incident early in Billy's career at the school illustrates the importance the community placed on being "clean." When two highly regarded individuals were discovered to be in at least the planning stages of adultery, a band of scandalized students tracked them to their trysting place and exposed their liaison to public inspection. To these sheltered, pietistic young people, for whom forbidden sexual activity essentially exhausted the category of immorality, the effect was electrifying. Because, like virtually everyone else in his circle of acquaintances (including, no doubt, the hapless culprits in this poignant episode), he subscribed unquestioningly to an ideal of sexual chastity, Billy was stunned to realize that anyone—*anyone!*—could succumb to the lures of this world, with devastating consequences. The only safe course, he resolved, would be to insulate himself against even the most tentative appearances of fleshly temptations.

This renewed pledge of purity did not involve a commitment to celibacy. On the contrary, as if to make up for time lost at Bob Jones, Billy quickly started prospecting among the school's forty or so female students as soon as he hit the campus. His colorful clothes and friendly manner made him an immediate hit with the girls, but he soon narrowed the field to a bright, vivacious, dark-haired beauty named Emily Cavanaugh. He fell quickly and hard, and that summer, at age eighteen, he asked her to marry him. Emily found Billy admirable, fascinating, lovable; yet, she hesitated. Naturally, this troubled him. In January 1938, when she had still not given him an answer, he wrote to his parents, who had met her and agreed she was a true prize: "Emily thinks a great deal of me, and I believe she loves me, but she is not sure. She won't give me a definite answer yet as to whether she loves me enough to settle it for life,... but it's all in the hands of the Lord and I don't worry about it. God is directing my life and He will do the very best for those who leave the choice to Him." Emily confirmed his confident faith a few weeks later when she accepted his proposal, but she continued to seem unsure of her decision. One afternoon late in the spring, she broke their engagement and returned his high school ring.

Billy was staggered, unable to understand how Emily could fail to reciprocate his love. He sought comfort at Dean Minder's house, where he wept disconsolately for the rest of the evening. A few days later, he wrote a dramatic letter to Wendell Phillips, who had moved to Pennsylvania to take a pastorate. "All the stars have fallen out of my sky," he lamented. "There is nothing to live for. We have broken up." Not long afterward, Emily began to date Charles Massey, an older student who seemed headed for a successful career in the ministry. In a search for solace after this rebuff, Billy turned to prayer and the Scriptures. He later attributed his decision to enter the ministry as stemming, at least in part, from a desire to share with others the comfort and assurance he had found during that period. His sister Catherine characterized the episode as "definitely traumatic" and conceded it probably pushed Billy toward greater seriousness. Melvin was a bit more blunt: "She wanted to marry a man that was going to amount to something, and didn't think he was going to make it. I never will forget that. We figured she was right. It so broke him up. I think that was a big turning point. He just got down and asked the Lord to really give him something he could hold on to."

Billy's sense that he had lost Emily because of insufficient promise may have heightened his determination to do "something big," but his theology and his deep need for absolute certainty kept him from announcing just how he planned to make his mark. He was clearly aiming toward the ministry, but he believed that men do not choose to be evangelists or pastors; God chooses them, and when He chooses, they will know it. Like Puritans awaiting the seal of saving grace, they can be ready, but they cannot, must not, force God's hand. The search for certainty spoiled Billy's sleep for much of that spring of 1938. Night after insomnia-wracked night he stalked the streets of Temple Terrace or roamed the lush, humid countryside for three and four hours at a time, praying aloud as he walked. He protested to God and to himself that he lacked the eloquence to be an evangelist. At the same time, the hours he had spent in the company of Fundamentalist firebrands had filled him with visions of what might be, and "in the most unusual way," he recalled, "I used to have the strangest glimpses of the crowds that I now preach to." Finally, inevitably, he reached the only conclusion he was prepared to accept. Around midnight one evening, as he returned to the campus from one of his brooding walks, he knelt alongside the eighteenth green of the golf course and said, "All right, Lord, if you want me, you've got me. I'll be what you want me to be and I'll go where you want me to go." And that was it. It may not have been loud, but he had his call. Now, he had to preach.

Having set his hand to the plow, Billy Graham never looked back. Dean Minder let him fill in at the tabernacle from time to time and encouraged his minister friends to give the young man a chance, but Billy created most of his own opportunities. On weekends he and a soloist or a gospel quartet would drive John Minder's wood-paneled station wagon into Tampa or out to the dog track at Sulphur Springs and hold seven or eight outdoor services a day. Street preachers were scarcely more welcome in those days than now, and Billy had to endure the embarrassed avoidance and derisive heckling Salvationist sorties can generate. Once, when he started damning sin at the doorway of a saloon on one of Tampa's rawest streets, the angry bartender knocked him down and shoved him face-first into the mud. Such rebuffs only convinced him he was suffering for Christ's sake and redoubled his determination to miss no opportunity to declare the wonders of God's grace. On Sunday afternoons, he preached repentance to sinners who had spent the night in the "Stockade," the jail at Sulphur Springs. To fill his Sunday evenings, he got himself appointed chaplain to the Tampa Trailer Park, a thousand-space facility advertised as "the tin-can tourist capital of the world." During the peak of the winter vacation season, he often drew several hundred vacationers to services in its central pavilion, where they heard him preach the polished version of the sermon he had already delivered several times over the weekend. In addition to these regular rounds, he preached in a Spanish mission—his first experience with using a translator—and in converted meat markets and onion sheds and tents and anywhere else he could get someone to listen. When the opportunity came to speak on the *Back Home Hour*, a radio program produced by the institute, he readily accepted, launching his first-ever appearance in the electronic pulpit with the trembling entreaty, "Folks, pray for me, for I have never done this before." As one of his contemporaries noted, "his gospel gun was always loaded."

As Billy gained experience and skill, country churches that relied on young men from the institute as "supply preachers" began to invite him to speak. The honoraria were always modest, but he made enough to buy an old car, which enabled him to accept almost any invitation he received. From the outset, for reasons that defy facile explanation, Billy's preaching demonstrated a phenomenal characteristic that it never lost: When he gave the invitation at the conclusion of his sermons, people responded, usually in numbers far exceeding what anyone would have predicted. The first time he offered a full-fledged invitation, to a gathering of no more than a hundred in a storefront church in the Gulf Coast town of Venice, thirty-two people came forward—more than many preachers would harvest in a year. The church's Sunday-school superintendent observed, "There's a young man who is going to be known around the world." That summer of 1938, Billy held his first revival, at the East Palatka Baptist Church. The campaign was sponsored by the youth group from the nearby Peniel Baptist Church, where Cecil Underwood now served as pastor. Billy stayed with the Underwoods, downing a quarter pound of butter every day as part of his perpetual effort to gain weight, and helped the pastor paint and sand floors, but at night he became a preaching machine. The community's weekly newspaper described the revival as "the greatest meeting in the history of the church" and noted that "young Graham does not mince words when he tells church members that they are headed for the same hell as the bootlegger and racketeer unless that they get right and live right."

The East Palatka meeting, which Billy claimed gave him "the first little inkling I had that maybe the Lord could use me in evangelism," also marked his formal switch from the Presbyterian to the Southern Baptist denomination. Baptists take their name from the importance they assign to the ordinance of baptism. Unlike some Fundamentalists, they do not regard it as essential to salvation, but they believe a saved person should be baptized, by immersion, soon after "accepting Jesus as their personal savior" (being born again) and they require it for church membership. Baptism is ostensibly offered only to adults, but the lower limit of this category extends to almost any child able to state with some conviction that he or she understands and affirms the essence of the gospel. It emphatically does not include infants sprinkled shortly after birth. When Brother Underwood and the deacons learned that their young soul winner was a Presbyterian who had never been immersed according to the biblical pattern, they persuaded him to join a clutch of his converts in being baptized in nearby Silver Lake. Billy would never completely shake his Presbyterian beliefs, but exposure to the parade of stalwarts who passed through the institute undercut any strong sense of brand loyalty he might have had. If folk believed the essentials—that they were sinners, that God loved them, and that Christ had died that they might have eternal life—that was good enough for him. Besides, a young man determined to be an evangelist would receive far more encouragement and support from Baptists than from Presbyterians. In any case, he found the transition to Baptist ways an easy one and, several months later, received ordination as an evangelist from the St. John's Baptist Association of Northern Florida.

Like Billy, most of the several dozen young men at Florida Bible Institute intended to preach. Most undoubtedly loved God and felt genuine concern for lost souls. Some probably had comparable natural talent as preachers. What distinguished Billy from the rest was that he poured every possible ounce of his talent and commitment into his preaching. Using a technique common to young preachers, he raided books of printed sermons, gleaning illustrations, borrowing outlines, and, quite often, memorizing the entire text of sermons first preached in Chicago or Philadelphia or London, and now about to be reproduced in Sulphur Springs and East Palatka. Nearly every afternoon when classes ended, he took a book of sermons, went into an old shed next to his dormitory, and excoriated oil cans and lawnmowers for their hard-hearted faithlessness, or he paddled a canoe to a lonely spot on the Hillsborough River where he named the sins of snakes and alligators and called on stumps to repent or perish. He practiced not just the words but the precise gestures he would use to drive them home. One afternoon, Dr. Watson heard him holding forth in his dormitory room. When he peeked through the slightly opened door, he saw his four-year-old son Bobby perched on top of Billy's dresser serving as the audience while the intense young preacher rehearsed his performance, aligning each gesture and expression with the words he was speaking. "Poor little Bobby had to take everything Billy could give him," Watson recalled with amusement. "I looked through that cracked door and Billy was putting that finger right there, just letting him have it." Another time, a student passing by the school auditorium heard someone preaching as if to a multitude. When she peeked inside, she found Billy at the podium addressing empty seats and working to dramatize the story of creation by raising his hands high over his head and flinging his fingers outward, as if he were God casting the planets and stars into space. His exuberant gestures and high-speed delivery won him the nickname, the Preaching Windmill, and nearly everyone who heard him mentioned the uncommon amount of noise he could generate in the pulpit. Even Morrow Graham, whose memory of her son's career was unfailingly rosy, acknowledged that his preaching during the Florida days was "awfully loud," though she quickly added, in the soft Carolina tones that smooth out even the gentlest criticism, "Billy's fervor has always been of such intensity that he couldn't restrain himself."

Unlike many Fundamentalist preachers, Billy wrote out his sermons in great detail, giving them such catchy titles as "Who's Who in Hell" and "Mobilization Under the Blood-Spangled Banner." A portion of a sermon manuscript from 1940, his last year at FBI, suggests he had already found the formula that typified his later preaching. He began by announcing that "crime has increased 500% in the last thirty years and costs the gov't $50,000,000,000 in the last ten years or three times the cost of the World War." He observed that three times as many young women were selling liquor as were going to college and asserted that "75,000,000 people see moving pictures every day and half of these are children, and 75% of the pictures are immoral." He spoke of pestilence, earthquakes, astronomical phenomena, and a worldwide increase in natural disasters. Then he surveyed political developments in Europe, where Nazi Germany was moving against its neighbors. These events might confound the secular world, he said, but they did not surprise Fundamentalist Christians: "Amist it all and the ones that were not shocked was those that had studied their Bibles.... Twenty-five hundred years ago God saw the political situation of the world as we are seeing it fulfilled today in the present setup." Since those ancient prophecies were now being fulfilled, the second coming of Christ and the end of the present dispensation were obviously just around the corner, so anyone not in a right relationship with God should correct that situation immediately. This sermon also reflects an imprecision of language and carelessness with facts that would often appear in his later preaching. In addition to "Amist," Billy spoke of "epidemics of desise," "the 14th [and 15th and 17th] centry," "hurricuns," and problems befalling "Londen" and "Porto Rico." These errors offend the eye more than the ear, but he was capable of startling mispronunciations, and he often failed to recognize that some of the "facts" he cited were quite improbable. Depending on what one included as a governmental cost of crime, a fifty-billion-dollar outlay over ten years might be plausible, even during the depression. It is less likely that every child in America between the ages of three and eighteen attended 365 movies in 1940, which is what his statistics would require, or that the same two-minute whirlwind that descended on Miami in 1927 and had "blown to bits that great concrete and steel city" had then "passed on to Japan and India doing fearful damage." Such flaws would never disappear from his preaching; neither, however, would they obscure his central message or pose much of a problem for his congregations.

Billy was willing to practice his sermons in an empty auditorium, but when the time came to face a live audience, he wanted those seats full. From the beginning, he showed keen appreciation for the role self-promotion could play in an evangelist's career. To advertise his appearance at a little mission church, he paid a sign painter $2.10—more than two thirds of the love offering he received—to make a banner that encouraged people to "Hear Billy Graham." He distributed handmade fliers that asked, "Have you heard the young man with a burning message?" As his reputation and self-confidence grew, he billed himself as "Dynamic Youthful Evangelist Billy Graham," "A Great Gospel Preacher at 21," and, even more grandly, "Billy Graham, One of America's Outstanding Young Evangelists—Dynamic Messages You Will Never Forget." He also learned to advertise the fact that the services included plenty of consecrated entertainment ("Good Songs Each Night—-Trios, Quartets, Duets, Solos, Orchestra" and "The Melody Three—The Foremost Ladies Trio in America") and abundant opportunity to socialize ("Your Friends Will Be There—Why Not You?") Sometimes, his exaggerated assessment of his stature and his quest for crowds had hubristically comic results. Back in Charlotte one summer, Grady Wilson received a handbill advertising Billy's revival at the First Baptist Church of Capitola, Florida.

On it Billy had scrawled "Big Baptist church in the capitol of Florida. Pray for me." When Grady decided not only to pray but to travel from Charlotte to attend the revival, he discovered that Capitola, far from being a nickname for Tallahassee, was little more than a logging camp, and that the revival had been canceled when its student pastor, one of Billy's classmates, had gone home unexpectedly. Grady never let Billy forget this bit of puffery, but he acknowledged his admiration for his friend's optimism: "The printer said Billy had ordered a thousand fliers for that little two-hundred-person community. He was ready to go after it."

If Billy had pursued his dream of attending the University of North Carolina, these activities would have marked him as an exceedingly peculiar young man, a butt of jokes, a last resort as a date. At the institute, where the highest accolade was to earn the tag "soul winner," he stood out like Saul among the Benjaminites. His peers elected him president of the eleven-member senior class and named him the outstanding evangelist in their ranks. At commencement in June 1940, valedictorian Vera Resue observed that in times of crisis, "God has chosen a human instrument to shine forth His light in darkness. Men like Luther, John Wesley, D. L. Moody and others were ordinary men, but men who heard the voice of God. The time is ripe for another Luther, Wesley, Moody. There is room for another name in this list." Billy may have wished to pencil his name into the space Miss Resue left blank in the published version of her speech, but he realized that God's next hero might need more formidable credentials than a Christian Worker's Training Course Diploma from an unaccredited Fundamentalist school. During his three-and-a-half years at the institute he acquired a nearly unshakable faith in the Bible as the inspired and literal word of God, and he learned a great deal about preaching, but Bible colleges did not pretend to offer a broad curriculum, and he knew there were yawning gaps in his education. As much as he wanted to spend every waking hour in active evangelism, he wisely decided to accept a remarkable offer he had received a few months earlier. During the winter, a party of tourists associated with Wheaton College had spent a few days at the institute's hotel. They heard Billy preach at the Tampa Gospel Tabernacle and were impressed but felt he needed some broadening and deepening. Elner Edman, the brother of Wheaton's president, V. Raymond Edman, told him he should go to Wheaton. Billy said, "That's what my mother wanted, but it's too expensive." A day or two later, Edman and another man, whose brother was the chairman of Wheaton's board of trustees, asked Billy to caddy for them. On the golf course, they offered to pay for his first year at Wheaton and to use their influence to try to get him a scholarship for succeeding years. To Billy, it was an answer to prayer. Some of his friends advised against accepting their offer. He already possessed an undisputed talent for winning souls. Why risk tainting it or watering it down with more education? But he never seriously hesitated.

After another summer of revivals, including a Pennsylvania campaign not far from where his grandfathers had fought to save the Confederacy, he shifted the center of his world to the placid Chicago exurb of Wheaton, Illinois, now (after the loss of Princeton to the Modernists) the intellectual and political center of the Fundamentalist world.

5

Ruth

Theologically, Wheaton was a Lamb's-blood relative of Bob Jones College and Florida Bible Institute, and the motto carved on the cornerstone of Blanchard Hall—For Christ and His Kingdom—clearly expressed the dominant ethos, but Wheaton embodied the broadest spirit of American Fundamentalism in the 1930s. As an accredited and academically respectable liberal arts college, it attracted the offspring of many of America's most affluent and influential Fundamentalist families. Because Wheaton gave him almost no credit for his courses in Florida, Billy, now almost twenty-two, had to enroll as a freshman. If his bright clothes, Li'l Abner brogans, and North Carolina accent caused people to think him a naive country boy, his age and status as an ordained minister with real preaching experience gave him a jump on other neophytes, and he soon emerged as a well-known campus figure. He had not yet drawn many invitations to preach, and Frank Graham had stopped sending him money, so he found a job working for another student who hauled luggage and furniture in a battered old yellow pickup. The CEO of the Wheaton College Student Trucking Service was preparing for mission work in China and introduced his new assistant to Ruth Bell, a second-year student who, as the daughter of a Presbyterian medical missionary, had grown up in Tsingkiang, China. Ruth claims not to remember their first meeting with any real clarity. Billy fell in love with her immediately and informed his mother of that fact before he ever got up the courage to ask for a date.

In many respects, Ruth's and Billy's childhoods could hardly have differed more. He had pored over books about faraway lands; she lived about as far away from Charlotte as it was possible to get. He had heard sermons on the wickedness of card playing and swearing; her regular path to school took her alongside putrid streams where dogs ate the tiny carcasses of infants slain by their parents because they were female or deformed. She knew of children kidnapped by bandits and sold into slavery or prostitution, and of missionaries who had been murdered or who had killed themselves in despair over the wretchedness of their circumstances. Billy arose at 2:30 A.M. to milk cows; Ruth often still lay awake at that hour, unable to sleep because of the noise from gunfire and bombs, or from fear of rats and scorpions that even the strictest measures could not eliminate. In Mecklenburg County, the religiously peculiar were those who insisted on singing hymns without an organ or who kept the Sabbath as if they were Jews; Billy's father had once warned him to be wary of Lutherans because they held "very strange beliefs." In North Kiangsu province, nine thousand miles away, the heretics were the Christians, foreign devils with their peculiar belief in only one God, and that one a wrathful being who permitted the death of his only son.

Despite these differences, striking points of contact existed between the two young people. Ruth's father, Dr. L. Nelson Bell, not only loved baseball but had signed a contract with a Baltimore Orioles farm team shortly before he got caught up in the Student Volunteer Movement for Foreign Missions (inspired by D. L. Moody) and dedicated himself to medical missions. As head of the Tsingkiang General Hospital, founded in 1887 by Pearl Buck's father, Dr. Bell proved to be a talented surgeon and, like Frank Graham, a resourceful provider. Also like the Grahams, the Bells steeped their brood in Presbyterian piety, rearing them on daily doses of private and family devotions and expecting them to commit large sections of Scripture to memory. Ruth's religion, however, took a serious turn far earlier than did Billy's. By the time she was twelve, she was pointing toward a career as an old-maid missionary to Tibet and praying regularly for a martyr's death. As another measure of her devotion, she loved to conduct animal funerals, complete with hymns and eulogies, before interring the dearly departed in her own pet cemetery. Of these leanings, Dr. Bell observed in a note to her teacher, "We feel Ruth has a slight tendency to revel in the sad side of things, letting her religion (which is exceedingly real and precious to her) take a slightly morbid turn." As she matured, the darker side of her piety gave way to a spunky willingness to tackle the world head-on rather than look for avenues of escape, but she continued to cling to the vision of a solitary mission to nomadic Tibetan tribes, at least in part, because it seemed like the hardest challenge she could possibly undertake.

During 1935 and 1936, the Bells spent a furlough year in Montreat, North Carolina, a picturesque mountainside village that served as a conference center and retirement community for Southern Presbyterians. Both Ruth and her sister Rosa finished high school that year. Rosa entered Wheaton in the fall of 1936, and Ruth followed a year later. Though obviously of modest means—her dress wardrobe consisted of one good black dress, a blue tweed suit she had picked up at a street bazaar in Chicago, and some dime-store pearls—Ruth's vivacious beauty, a young lifetime of unusual experiences that fascinated Christian youth who considered the mission field the highest of human callings, and her well-known piety (she rose regularly at 5:00 A.M., for prayer and Bible reading) made her the prize catch of her class.

Though Ruth felt no thunderbolt when she met Billy Graham during the fall semester of 1940, he impressed her a few days later by the fervor of his prayer at an informal church meeting. "I had never heard anyone pray like [that] before," she said. "I sensed that here was a man that knew God in a very unusual way." When he eventually summoned the courage to ask her to accompany him to a performance of Handel's *Messiah*, she readily accepted. After the concert and a slow, snowy walk to a professor's house for tea, he wrote home again, announcing that he planned to marry this new girl who reminded him so much of his mother. The Grahams took note but made no wedding plans. As younger sister Jean recalls, "He had fallen in love so many times, we didn't pay much attention to him." Ruth, always more private, chose to let God alone know that "if you let me serve you with that man, I'd consider it the greatest privilege in my life." Their courtship was a strange one. Well aware that a young woman might not return his affection in full measure, Billy seemed to doubt he deserved or could win Ruth's love. Their next date came six weeks later, after she invited him, by mail, to a party at her boardinghouse. A week later, he asked her out again and clumsily sputtered that he had been reluctant to pursue his interest in her because he did not feel a definite call to the mission field, a revelation that seemed a bit premature for a third date. He followed this by asking her out, then ignoring her, then asking if he was embarrassing her by taking her out too frequently. He also told her that he had asked the Lord to give her to him if that was his will, but to keep him from loving her if that would be best for both of them. She was clearly intrigued and wrote to her parents about this "humble, thoughtful, unpretentious, courteous" young man with an uncommon determination to discern and do God's will, but she found his courtship rituals a bit peculiar and began to date other students. This produced the desired result, and Billy delivered an ultimatum: "Either you date just me, or you can date everybody *but* me!" That also worked, and they began to go out on a regular basis, usually to some kind of preaching service. He impressed her with his "fearless, uncompromising presentation of the Gospel," but she later confessed she thought his preaching was too loud and too fast, and it took her some time to get used to the fact that, almost invariably, it produced an impressive harvest at the invitation.

As Billy grew surer of their relationship, he began to assume the authoritarian, patriarchal manner he had learned at home. He told Ruth what to eat and sat across from her until she complied. He insisted she get more exercise and personally put her through a rigorous program of calisthenics. She confided to her parents that Bill (she never called him Billy) "isn't awfully easy to love because of his sternness and unwavering stand on certain issues," but his assurance that he did what he did because he loved her invariably melted her resistance. They talked of the future in terms of their respective "calls." She still clung to her dream of evangelizing Tibet. He respected this noble aspiration but, since he felt no Himalayan call himself, tried to convince her that the highest role a woman could fill was that of wife and mother. Both agreed to read the Bible and pray for God's leading. No burning light of revelation came, so Billy decided to proceed without it. At the end of the spring semester, just before they parted for the summer of 1941, he asked Ruth to marry him. She did not respond immediately, but a few weeks later, while he was filling in for John Minder in Tampa, she wrote that she believed their relationship was "of the Lord" and would be pleased to become his wife. On July 7, she acknowledged to her parents, "To be with Bill in [evangelistic] work won't be easy. There will be little financial backing, lots of obstacles and criticism, and no earthly glory what-soever," but added, "I knew I wouldn't have peace till I yielded my will to the Lord and decided to marry Bill." At this point, they had yet to kiss.

That summer, Billy met the Bells, who had finally been forced out of China by the Japanese, and Ruth came to Charlotte to visit the Grahams. Both visits went well. At the end of the summer, Billy went to Montreat, North Carolina, where the Bells had settled permanently, and presented Ruth with an engagement ring. Then, just as she prepared to return to school, Ruth grew so ill that her parents feared she might have malaria and decided to put both her and Rosa, who was suffering from tuberculosis, into a Presbyterian sanatorium in New Mexico. The rest restored Ruth's health—Rosa also recovered, though much more slowly—but the equanimity she experienced during the separation resurrected old doubts. Eventually, she wrote Billy that she had grown unsure of her love for him and thought it best to break their engagement. He was crushed but decided not to react hastily. When she returned to school in January 1942, he offered to take back the ring, but she hesitated, explaining that the real problem was that she still felt called to be a missionary. Sensing an opening, he used an approach whose efficacy he would not forget: He convinced her that not to do what he wanted would be to thwart God's obvious will. "Do you or do you not think the Lord brought us together?" he asked. She admitted she thought that was indeed the case. He pointed out that the Bible says the husband is head of the wife and declared, with an authoritativeness probably grounded on shifting sand, "Then I'll do the leading and you do the following." Ruth Bell eventually surrendered her missionary vocation, but only the blindest of observers would conclude that she also surrendered her will or her independence.

Billy and Ruth set their wedding date for August 1943, still more than eighteen months away. In the meantime, they finished school. Ruth majored in art, with a minor in Bible. In the eyes of most of their friends, then and thereafter, she was the better student, he the charismatic communicator, but Billy took his studies more seriously than ever, developing the healthy conviction that he always needed to know more. Under the influence of an outstanding professor teaching at Wheaton between stints at the University of Pennsylvania, Billy decided to major in anthropology. Instead of leading him toward cultural relativity, with its assumption of the absence of a dependable yardstick of truth and value, the Wheaton version of anthropology provided instead a reassuring affirmation that people in every culture are essentially alike and therefore equally open to a straightforward explanation of their problem (sin and separation from the one true God) and its solution (acceptance of the saving grace made possible through Christ).

In addition to his studies, Billy continued to preach at every opportunity, and the opportunities multiplied as his skills and reputation grew. Under the auspices of the Wheaton Christian Student Union, which he served as president during his senior year, he spoke at numerous small churches across the upper Midwest, establishing himself as a dynamic and popular speaker: "A Young Southern Evangelist with a Burning Message You Will Never Forget!" As an indication of his stature, when President Edman resigned his post as the regular preacher at Wheaton's United Gospel Tabernacle, known as the Tab to the students and faculty who made most of its membership, he asked Billy to replace him. During these years, Billy also enjoyed the encouragement of old friends Jimmie Johnson, who decided he needed some more education, and Grady Wilson, who ran afoul of Dr. Bob and, after a period on the evangelistic field, transferred to Wheaton with the encouragement and financial support of R. G. LeTourneau, an Evangelical industrialist who admired his preaching but felt he needed more schooling. LeTourneau, known in Evangelical circles as "America's Number One Christian Layman," had spoken at John Minder's Tabernacle during Billy's tenure as assistant pastor. Impressed with Billy, he was pleased to help Grady follow the same path. The reunion of these young men, who had learned to preach from the same books and had practiced their sermons on each other, had its comic aspects. Once, when Jimmie Johnson filled a local pulpit a week after Billy spoke there, he preached the identical sermon—Scripture, text, outline, illustrations, and all.

Early in 1943 a local businessman named Robert Van Kampen, head of a large printing and publishing company, spoke in the Wheaton chapel. Afterward, he fell into conversation with Billy, who told him he planned to be a preacher. Van Kampen invited him to speak at a small and struggling Baptist church he attended in nearby Western Springs. The church's physical plant consisted of nothing but a roofed basement, the first installment of what its several dozen members hoped might eventually become a full-fledged edifice. Billy's first sermon, delivered at his usual speed and volume level, bounced off the stucco walls and wooden theater seats like a fusillade from a Gatling gun, but it impressed his listeners and led to an offer to become pastor of the church upon graduation at a salary of forty-five dollars a week. Other churches had shown an interest in Billy, but with the prospect of having to support a wife looming large, he accepted the offer without consulting Ruth, an oversight that led to a spirited discussion of the distinction between authority and thoughtfulness. At least part of her irritation stemmed from her fear that a pastorate would deter Billy from evangelism. She need not have worried. He apparently never intended to stay in Western Springs for long. The war had stirred his patriotic fires, and he decided to enlist. When his professors persuaded him he could do more good as a minister, he applied for commission as an army chaplain, stating a preference for a battlefront assignment. Twice, the army rejected his application on the grounds that he lacked pastoral experience and was underweight.

After their wedding in Montreat on Friday the thirteenth of August, Ruth caught a chill on the trip back to Western Springs from their seven-day honeymoon at a tourist home in Blowing Rock, North Carolina. Instead of calling to cancel a routine preaching engagement in Ohio so that he could stay at the bedside of his brand-new bride, a reason his hosts would surely have accepted graciously, Billy checked her into a local hospital and kept the appointment, sending her a telegram and a box of candy for consolation. She felt hurt at this apparent lack of concern for her condition and feelings but soon learned that nothing came before preaching on her husband's list of priorities and that this would not be the last time he would leave a hospital bed (including his own) or miss key moments of sorrow or celebration because of a promise to preach.

Despite the brevity of the only eighteen months he would ever spend as a pastor, Billy displayed talents and received opportunities at Western Springs that proved crucial in his rise to national prominence. He had come to think of himself as a Baptist—indeed, he had stirred Ruth's ire by suggesting that if Dr. Bell were a true Christian, he would also become a Baptist—but he was unwilling to draw lines that would limit his reach and persuaded the deacons to change the name of the Western Springs Baptist Church to the more inclusive Village Church. He launched a businessmen's dinner series at which prominent Evangelical speakers addressed as many as five hundred men. He also helped the church begin a mission program, retire a long-standing mortgage, and make plans to add an above-ground sanctuary. He was not, however, particularly skilled at such staples of pastoral work as personal visitation and managing conflict within the congregation. "Billy's not a pastor," a close friend from this period observed. "This kind of thing was very difficult for him—not to do, but to like. He'd rather preach, and be in association with other men who were preaching." One man who recognized this most clearly was Torrey Johnson, the enterprising and extraordinarily persuasive young pastor of Chicago's thriving Midwest Bible Church. Johnson knew Graham through Wheaton and the National Association of Evangelicals. He had heard him preach on several occasions and was impressed with his prowess; in fact, he had countered Billy's desire to get additional theological training with a classic soul-winner's admonition: "Get in there and preach. That's the theological school you need." Johnson produced a popular Sunday-evening radio program, *Songs in the Night*, aired over the fifty-thousand-watt clear-channel station WCFL from Chicago. When the crush of his pastoral duties and another radio program proved too great a burden, he approached Billy about taking his place on *Songs in the Night*. Billy immediately recognized the possibilities and convinced the church to take up the challenge, even though the program's weekly budget of nearly $150 would exceed the congregation's pledged income.

Billy's instincts proved correct. With a confidence bordering on gall, he persuaded bass-baritone George Beverly Shea, already well-known among Evangelicals in the Chicago area for a program on the Moody Bible Institute station (WMBI), to become the show's primary musical performer. Beginning in January 1944, from ten-thirty to quarter past eleven every Sunday evening, the program originated live from the basement sanctuary of "the friendly church in the pleasant community of Western Springs." Between Bev Shea's unadorned yet rich renderings of hymns and gospel songs and the peppier trillings of a girls' quartet known as The King's Karrolers, Billy, sitting at a table outlined in colored lights to provide a dramatic aura for the live audience, offered brief meditations. Many of these pointed out the relevance of the Christian message to various contemporary problems and situations: the loneliness of families separated by war, the need for courage and confidence in the face of danger and fear, the perils of succumbing to the lures of alcohol and licentiousness, the relevance of biblical prophecy for understanding world events. Back in Charlotte, too far from Chicago for the Philco in the Grahams' den to pick up the program unless the weather cooperated, Frank and Morrow sat in their car long past their regular bedtime, turned on the Plymouth's stronger radio, and strained through the static to hear that familiar and increasingly distinctive voice. "Imagine!" they sometimes said. "That's our Billy Frank."

The program caught on quickly, and contributions from listeners relieved the church of any financial burden. Requests for sheet music of Bev Shea's songs led Robert Van Kampen to launch the Van Kampen Press, which eventually grew into a major Evangelical publishing house whose substantial profits supported a variety of Evangelical missions. The program also boosted Billy's reputation, generating more invitations to speak at churches throughout the region, a result that irritated parishioners who felt a pastor needed to be at home, tending the sheep. Ever his defender, Bob Van Kampen helped keep the criticism from getting out of hand. Once, after accompanying Billy on a two-week tour through the Midwest, he reported to the deacon's meeting that "there is only one thing that I can say, and that is that God has laid upon Billy a special gift of evangelism and someday he could be another Billy Sunday or D. L. Moody." Recalling this occasion decades later, Van Kampen observed, "That's in the minutes of the church. I wasn't being prophetic. It was obvious." For his part, Billy was beginning to understand that a free-lance ministry of the sort that seemed to fit his talent and ambition might flourish best when free of the inevitable parochial concerns of a conventional congregation. While his parishioners chafed, he began to move in directions that would change the course of his career and, indeed, of Evangelical Christianity.

Meanwhile, Evangelical Christianity was moving in new directions of its own. During the height of Billy Sunday's popularity, Fundamentalism had appeared to be in reasonably good shape. It had a coherent view of Scripture to defend against Modernist critics, it was riding a crest of patriotism, and it had shared in what was ostensibly a stunning moral victory by helping to bring about Prohibition, which went into effect in 1920. Yet, within ten years, this formidable movement was devastated by defeat and dissension. At the Scopes trial in 1925, famed defense attorney Clarence Darrow failed to have his client acquitted for the crime of teaching evolution in the Dayton, Tennessee, high school, but he and the world press still managed to make Fundamentalists look like monkeys. On the heels of that embarrassment, Princeton Theological Seminary and several major denominations—most notably the Presbyterian Church in the U.S.A. and the Northern Baptists—repelled the Fundamentalist challenge to modern biblical criticism and, in effect, drove most Fundamentalists from their midst. As a final symbolic blow, Prohibition was repealed in 1933. Fundamentalism, it appeared, had been defeated and relegated to a minor position in American culture. Its tendency toward intellectual rigidity, its propensity for attracting and lending support to anti-Semitic, anti-Catholic, and other nativist and right-wing political elements, and its often uncritical equation of Christianity and Americanism had all helped its decline, a decline many observers felt would continue inexorably until the last Fundamentalist had withered and died with a sour whimper.

Fundamentalism did indeed pass through a wilderness, but it did not enter the grave. It not only failed to disappear during the 1930s but underwent a transformation that left it in a reasonably strong position by the end of the decade. That transformation involved shifting, realigning, and reorganizing its base. Instead of trying to fight off liberals within mainstream denominations, Fundamentalists began to form themselves into large independent congregations, usually centered around a notable preacher, and to join alliances such as the World Christian Fundamentalist Association. An even more significant development was the substantial increase in the number of Bible colleges and institutes favoring impeccably orthodox teaching and practical instruction in Christian service over the liberal arts they felt had undermined commitment to truth more narrowly conceived. The model, of course, was Moody Bible Institute, which had trained more than 69,000 students by 1930. The Bible Institute of Los Angeles (BIOLA) enjoyed a similar status on the West Coast. By 1940 more than a hundred such institutions had sprung up all over America. Fundamentalists also made extraordinarily wide use of publications and radio; by 1943, BIOLA graduate Charles Fuller's programs were carried by over a thousand stations, and generous donations from loyal listeners enabled him to found Fuller Theological Seminary, which would become one of the most respected and influential of Evangelical schools.

Not only had dozens of Fundamentalist editors and radio ministers kept Evangelical doctrines before the people but they had made it clear that unnumbered legions still built on the firm foundation, still walked on the ancient pathways, and would teach their children to do the same. In 1941 two new organizations were formed, representing the extreme and moderate branches of the movement. The American Council of Christian Churches, founded by the cantankerous archconservative, Carl McIntire, banned from its membership churches or denominations that had truck with Modernists or belonged to the liberal Federal Council of Churches. Reacting against this extreme separatist position, a more temperate coalition established the National Association of Evangelicals. A third organization, formed during this period to save young people from modernists, communists, and worldliness, called itself Youth for Christ International. Youth for Christ produced many new and dynamic leaders, but none of its young stars would outshine Billy Graham.

6

"Geared to the Times, Anchored to the Rock"

The social, economic, and psychic dislocations created by the twenties, the Great Depression, and global war generated enormous concern over the welfare of the young. Conservative Christians shared with many Americans the struggle to keep food on the table and the fear that their adolescent sons might soon be facing enemy guns in Europe or in the Pacific, but what troubled them more deeply was the possibility that their beloved children would abandon faith in God, would live and die outside the community of the redeemed, and thus spend eternity in a hell of fire and brimstone, where thirst is never slaked and the worm dieth not. To ward off this specter, Evangelical and Fundamentalist leaders all over the country began holding Saturday-night rallies designed to offer young people, especially young soldiers and sailors stationed far from the safe harbor of their homes, a blend of wholesome entertainment, patriotic fervor, and revivalist exhortation.

Because significant efforts were beginning almost simultaneously, the chronology of this movement is a bit imprecise, but certain key leaders stand out. Clearly, one of the first and most important was Jack Wyrtzen, a New York City bandleader-turned-minister whose *Word of Life* radio broadcast and rallies began in 1940 and by 1944 were packing Carnegie Hall and Madison Square Garden. In Toronto a handsome, spellbinding young preacher named Charles Templeton enjoyed comparable success, as did alert and enterprising leaders in Indianapolis, Detroit, St. Louis, Philadelphia, and other cities throughout the United States and Canada. Though less a commanding public figure than these men, one of the most enterprising participants in the rapidly spreading movement was George Wilson, a layman who owned a Christian bookstore and served as business manager for William Bell Riley's Northwestern Schools in Minneapolis.

Torrey Johnson had attended rallies in Indianapolis, St. Louis, and Minneapolis and determined to start a similar program in Chicago, where Bev Shea had been urging him to do something for the hundreds of thousands of soldiers stationed in the Chicago area and spending their weekends aimlessly wandering its downtown streets. Johnson leased the three-thousand-seat Orchestra Hall, next door to the USO, and invited Billy Graham to speak at the inaugural rally of the Chicagoland Youth for Christ. On May 27, 1944, ten days before D day, the young pastor got his first real taste of mass evangelism. Backstage before the service, as he paced back and forth, biting his nails and fearing in equal measure that no one would show up to hear him or that he would fail in front of a large crowd, he suffered what he remembers as "the worst fit of stage fright of my life." His anxiety did not abate when he stepped onstage before a huge crowd of almost three thousand, by far the largest audience he had ever faced. But when he began to preach, fear departed and fire roared. He electrified the gathering with his exuberance and command of Scripture, and when he gave the invitation, forty-two people responded.

Torrey Johnson had made no provision to funnel these young trail hitters into churches or to put servicemen in contact with military chaplains, but he satisfied his conviction that such rallies could stir the hearts of the young and serve as a catalyst for revival. The Orchestra Hall meetings continued all summer (until the Chicago Symphony reclaimed the building for its fall season) and proved popular not only with servicemen but also with sheltered young people who relished the excuse and opportunity to be downtown on Saturday night. In October, following a rally that drew a capacity crowd of nearly thirty thousand to Chicago Stadium, the series moved into the Moody Church, where crowds grew so large that Johnson often scheduled two identical programs back-to-back. Similar meetings were occurring in at least two hundred other cities, and Torrey Johnson, now being called the "Bobby-Sox Evangelist" and "the Second Moody," spent much of his time on the telephone trying to help ministers across the country get still more programs under way.

Just as these meetings were giving Billy a glimpse of what the future might hold, the army finally accepted him for the chaplaincy and gave him a commission as a second lieutenant. As he prepared to leave for the government's chaplaincy training program at Harvard Divinity School, he contracted a severe case of the mumps, "with all the complications." During six extremely painful bedridden weeks, his temperature reached 105 degrees, he suffered bouts of delirium, and at times it seemed doubtful he would survive. Even after the crisis passed, doctors told him he might never have children. When listeners to *Songs in the Night* learned of his condition, one compassionate woman sent him a hundred dollars, with the request that he and his wife spend it on a restful convalescence. A few days later, he and Ruth drove to Miami to spend a few days in the Florida sun. Torrey Johnson happened to be in Miami at the time and offered to take Billy fishing. On the boat, where no telephone calls could interrupt his sales pitch, Johnson laid out a plan. If he could get Chuck Templeton and George Wilson and other young leaders to cooperate, he wanted to coordinate existing youth programs and establish new ones under the aegis of a single organization, to be known as Youth for Christ International. With compelling conviction and persuasiveness, Johnson convinced Billy that if they could sweep young people into a great tide of revival, they could place Evangelical Christianity at the heart of a movement to revitalize American culture. "If I can swing it, will you come join us?" he asked. "We'll pay you seventy-five dollars a week."

Billy found the offer appealing. At this point he knew little about Evangelical history and certainly had no vision of recreating the hegemony Charles Finney and his friends had enjoyed a century earlier. Neither was he involved in the strategies of the new National Association of Evangelicals in more than a casual way. His main motive, by now his abiding obsession, was "to win as many to Christ as I could," and this seemed to be the best chance he was likely to get. It also promised to feed his pleasure at standing in the circle of Christian leaders. More mundanely, he relished the chance to see the country, and he and Ruth sorely needed an increase in salary. Ruth also liked the idea; for some time, she had been chipping away, reminding him that God had called him to evangelism, not the pastorate. Since the church expected him to leave for the army, the cutting of that tie would not be difficult. Billy found it awkward to resign his chaplaincy commission after pushing so hard to obtain it, but when he learned that the weight loss and weakness caused by his illness would limit him to a stateside desk job, he requested and received permission to be released from his commitment. Soon afterward, early in 1945, he accepted Johnson's invitation, with the stipulation that his duties include "not one bit of paper work."

Chicago's importance as a cultural and economic center, its location in the heartland of midwestern Evangelical Christianity, and Torrey Johnson's dynamism combined to move the Chicagoland Youth for Christ into the front rank of the most notable youth movement in America at the time. In July 1945 more than six hundred youth leaders from all over North America met at the famed Fundamentalist conference center at Winona Lake, Indiana, and formed Youth for Christ International. They accepted the doctrinal statement fashioned by the National Association of Evangelicals in 1942 and held themselves out as a viable alternative to theological liberalism. Torrey Johnson was elected president, George Wilson was named secretary, and at Chuck Templeton's nomination, Billy Graham became the organization's first official field representative, a role he had already been filling unofficially for several months. Significantly, none of the participants paid much attention to denominational labels. "We never inquired as to a man's background," Johnson noted. "It didn't even occur to us. We just loved Jesus Christ supremely."

As field representative, Graham traveled almost constantly, speaking at rallies of high school and college students, addressing civic clubs and Gideons and Christian businessmen's groups, and showing ministers and youth leaders how to establish Youth for Christ (YFC) chapters in their cities. More than once he had to dissociate YFC from free-lance evangelists who had built up extravagant expectations, then absconded in the wake of financial or moral misadventures. Seeing the terrible disillusionment trusting church folks had suffered stirred deep revulsion within him and added an increasingly dogged determination to adhere to high standards of morality and ethics. During 1945, with the help of a credit card provided by one of the organization's wealthy backers and automobiles furnished by car dealers and other supporters, Graham visited forty-seven states, logging at least 135,000 miles and receiving United Airlines's designation as its top civilian passenger. Perhaps sensing the start of a lifelong pattern, and pregnant with their first child, Ruth Graham packed their meager possessions and moved in with her parents, who had settled in Montreat after the war forced them out of China. Her mother taught her skills of homemaking that had not come naturally to her. More important, her parents provided her with companionship to ease the loneliness she felt during her husband's long absences, and family to share important moments—when their first child, Virginia (always called "GiGi"), was born on September 21, 1945, Billy was away on a preaching trip. Though she found great comfort in the bosom of her family, Ruth displayed an unusual capacity for solitariness, and she soon developed a stock response she would still be repeating decades later: "I'd rather have a little of Bill than a lot of any other man."

The rounds of meeting with eager church leaders during the day, preaching to thousands of excited young people in the evenings, then piling back onto a noisy DC-3 for a bumpy all-night ride to the next city where the whole process began anew the next morning, was exhilarating but exhausting. Graham and Johnson needed help and persuaded Chuck Templeton to leave Toronto to work full-time for YFC. Graham then lured T. W. Wilson from a Georgia pastorate by providing him with a plane ticket to Los Angeles, arranged for him to address a crowd of 6,000—by far the largest he had ever faced—and pointed out, "T, you could be doing this all the time." These were heady days for the young movement. As Chuck Templeton observed, "We were just these dynamic, handsome young guys, you know, full of incredible energy, full of vitality, and we were totally committed ... every one of us. We really thought we were involved in a dramatic new resurgence of revivalism over the country." To underline their announcement that Christianity did not have to be drab and dismal but could provide "Old-fashioned Truth for Up-to-date Youth" and be "Geared to the Times, but Anchored to the Rock," YFC leaders wore colorful suits and sport coats, neon "glo-sox," garish hand-painted ties, and gaudy bow ties, some of which lit up. The rallies themselves were a sort of Evangelical vaudeville, with usherettes, youth choirs and quartets and trios and soloists, "smooth melodies from a consecrated saxophone," Bible quizzes, patriotic and spiritual testimonies by famous and semifamous preachers, athletes, entertainers, military heroes, business and civic leaders, and such specialty acts as magicians, ventriloquists, and a horse named MacArthur who would "kneel at the cross," tap his foot twelve times when asked the number of Christ's apostles and three times when asked how many persons constituted the Trinity, a performance that led emcees to observe that "MacArthur knows more than the Modernists." The sermon, of course, was the climax toward which all the preliminaries pointed. As Billy Graham observed, "We used every modern means to catch the attention of the unconverted—and then we punched them right between the eyes with the gospel."

George Wilson once produced a show that included a sonata for one hundred pianos, but no program ever packed more excess wallop than Torrey Johnson's Soldier Field rally on Memorial Day, 1945. Johnson's friends had warned him he could never hope to fill Chicago's largest facility, but his faith was such that he mortgaged his home to guarantee the twenty-two-thousand-dollar rental fee. Spurred by the twin specters of humiliation and homelessness, he spared no effort to prove the doubters wrong. For weeks beforehand, five evangelistic teams held one-night rallies in 150 cities and towns in the Chicago area to drum up a crowd, and Evangelical publications carried stories promising a grand spiritual extravaganza. The publicity worked, and on the appointed day 70,000 young people packed the cavernous stadium to the light poles. Few could have felt Torrey Johnson had not delivered what he had promised. A 300-piece band accompanied a 5,000-voice choir and soloist Pruth McFarlin, "America's greatest negro tenor." Bev Shea sang, and an ensemble of eight grand pianos, eight marimbas, and one vibraharp entertained the crowd with "a heartwarming medley of old-fashioned hymns and classics." In keeping with the organization's admiration for a kind of muscular Christianity, a natural theme for virile young men in a wartime atmosphere, world-champion miler Gil Dodds ran an exhibition race, and a young man from the University of Virginia told how Christ had helped him become national intercollegiate boxing champion in the 155-pound class. A missionary pageant followed, featuring hundreds of young people dressed in costumes "representing the bleeding nations of the world and disclosing their spiritual need." As part of its unabashed patriotic emphasis, especially appropriate on this Memorial Day as the first troops were returning from Europe after the German surrender, the program gave proof through the night that our flag was still there. In addition to an abundant display of flags and the singing of "The Star-Spangled Banner," four hundered white-clad nurses formed a marching cross that entered the field as the band played "The Battle Hymn of the Republic." Then, while every serviceman stood to receive the applause of the grateful and admiring throng, Rose Arzoomanian sang "God Bless Our Boys," and four hundered high school students placed a memorial wreath on a platform crowned by a large blue star. After taps was sounded, Lieutenant Bob Evans, a Wheaton graduate and chaplain who had been wounded several times and had pledged to return to Europe to preach the gospel in the very places where he had fallen, appealed to the crowd to sign applications for war bonds while a lone drummer played a dramatic solo from the middle of the field. Finally, after a stirring challenge from featured speaker Percy Crawford, another pioneer in the youth-rally movement, all the lights in the stadium went out. As the choir sang "The Gospel Light house," a strong beacon circled the stands, falling on the crowd to remind them of their own obligation to be "the light of the world." Then, while George Wilson pronounced the benediction in total darkness, a huge black-light sign, high on the platform and hidden till this moment, eerily proclaimed the heart of the Evangelical message: "JESUS SAVES."

Torrey Johnson had a habit of making assignments by telling his young assistants, "I believe God wants you to go to. . . ." At least in retrospect, two such directives must have seemed especially providential to Billy Graham. On one of his earliest trips for YFC, he spoke at a Minneapolis rally, where he formed an immediate and durable bond with George Wilson. Then, during the summer of 1945, while trying to spend more time at home with Ruth during her pregnancy, he spoke at the Ben Lippen Conference Center in neighboring Asheville. Shortly before the meeting was to begin, he discovered that his regular song leader had unexpectedly returned to Chicago. Someone suggested he enlist Cliff and Billie Barrows, two young musicians who were spending their honeymoon in the area. Both Cliff and Billie had attended Bob Jones College, and Cliff had heard Graham speak, but they had never met. Barrows, an appealing young California athlete with a radiant wholesomeness that could light up a tabernacle, had served as a chorister for Jack Shuler, a young evangelist at least as popular as Graham. Billy was less than enthusiastic about using an unknown musical team but had little choice. That night Billie Barrows played the piano, Cliff sang a solo, the two of them sang a duet, and Billy Graham preached on "Retreat, Hold the Line, and Advance." Graham must have shared Cliff's assessment that "we had a wonderful evening together"; within a year, they formed one of the closest and most enduring partnerships in evangelistic history.

In the spring of 1946, YFC earned its "International" designation. While some of its young dynamos whirled off to Japan, China, Korea, India, Africa, and Australia, Graham, Templeton, Johnson, and singer Stratton Shufelt made a forty-six-day tour of the British Isles and the Continent, accompanied by Wesley Hartzell, a reporter for William Randolph Hearst's *Chicago Herald-American*. Hartzell, a committed Christian, had been a delegate at YFC's founding meeting at Winona Lake, but he was assigned to this trip on an editor's inspired hunch that "Graham might turn out to be a top newsmaker." Hearst had already shown considerable interest in YFC, apparently because he liked its patriotic emphasis and felt its high moral standards might help combat juvenile delinquency. Not incidentally, he also figured that any movement attracting nearly a million people to rallies every Saturday night might help him sell some newspapers. According to Johnson, who never had any direct contact with Hearst, the reclusive publisher sent his Chicago editor a telegram shortly after the Soldier Field rally. It contained only two words: "PUFF YFC." A short time later, all twenty-two Hearst papers carried a full-page story on the YFC movement. Further coverage followed, and other papers picked up the story. In February 1946, *Time* devoted four columns to the movement, quoting President Truman as saying, "This is what I hoped would happen in America." *Time* also noted that some Americans viewed "the pious trumpetings of the Hearst press on YFC's behalf" as ominous, apparently fearing the movement might become an instrument of Hearst's conservative social and political views. As the old titan watched the organization grow, he apparently realized that Graham and Templeton were its two brightest stars and decided to assign someone to chronicle their ascent. Hartzell's reports of the British trip appeared not only in the Hearst papers but on the International News Service wire as well, providing potential exposure to virtually every significant newspaper in America.

Johnson, Graham, and Templeton understood the value of such publicity and did what they could to live up to their billing. Before they left, they held large send-off rallies in Charlotte, Toronto, Detroit, and Chicago, then booked the first-ever commercial flight from Chicago to London. To make sure they received a share of the free publicity this inaugural flight generated, they arranged for a large party to see them off at the airport, and they knelt in prayer as long as photographers requested. The experience of playing to crowds that consistently bolstered their sense of being conquerors for Christ led to a telling brush with hubris on this trip. During a weather-induced stopover at an American air force base in Newfoundland, Torrey Johnson led the base's social director to believe that the group was "sort of like the USO" and wangled an invitation to present a program to the airmen. Accustomed to speaking to servicemen and excited by the prospect of addressing a captive audience, the young preachers failed to reckon with the fact that their stateside audiences were hardly a random selection of the population, and that the wholesome fare that wowed sheltered Evangelical youngsters might not have the same appeal for a cross section of enlisted men starved for a little excitement. Chuck Templeton served as master of ceremonies and introduced the troupe. The men quickly registered their disappointment at the absence of women in the group, and after Strat Shufelt's helplessly wholesome version of "Shortnin' Bread," Torrey Johnson's hokey appeal to regional pride ("How many are here from Chicago? How many from Philadelphia? How many from Charlotte?"), and Templeton's own rendition of "The Old Rugged Cross," the mood in the Quonset-hut auditorium turned ugly, with boos and whistles and curses. Templeton thought they should bail out and cut their losses before the situation got even worse and refused to go back onstage. Graham was also uneasy about the turn things had taken but felt he should not pass up the chance to preach. After a brief prayer, Templeton recalled, "Billy went out there and preached in typical, absolutely unvarying fashion from what he usually did. He told a couple of jokes and then just waded on into a regular sermon." When he finished, the base commander was waiting in the wings, white with rage. While he herded Johnson into his office to vent his anger, Templeton and Graham rushed outside and began to pray in agony, begging God to forgive them for flying under false colors. "It was essential Billy," Templeton observed. "He was fearless when he went out to face that crowd, and completely true to his beliefs. Then, when he realized we were in the wrong, he just opened his heart to God's reproval. We were pretty cocky. We needed to be reproved. It was probably a good thing."

This first international trip, one of six Graham would make during the next three years, was a true case of innocents abroad. Shufelt was the only member of the group ever to have been to Europe, and none of them had much sense of history, customs, or even of the distances between major cities. In a nation still climbing out of the rubble of war, still frequently dark from voluntary and involuntary blackouts, still devoid of all but the most basic consumer goods, the sight of these exuberant, backslapping young Americans in pastel suits, racetrack sport coats, and rainbow ties scandalized some but captivated others. Tom Rees, a London lay evangelist who had organized Britain's Youth for Christ meetings before he ever heard of Torrey Johnson, described the young evangelists as "like a breath from heaven in a suffocated time, men who brought brightness in the midst of all our darkness." And in Manchester, when the group interpreted the astonished gapes of a welcoming party as disapproval and changed into more conservative clothes for dinner, their hosts insisted, "Please go up and change your clothes again. We want you just like you were." Before the trip was over, they had given away most of their loudest neckties to sober-sided English clergymen, sometimes because they mistook astonishment for admiration.

Their enthusiastic preaching style stimulated a similar response. Anglican cleric Tom Livermore recalled the first time he heard Graham speak, his bright red bow tie poking out over the top of a clerical robe. "He spoke for fifty-seven minutes, which was an All-England record at the time. The English people wanted to take breaths for him. Stenos estimated he was speaking 240 words per minute, but they couldn't keep up with him. People were just overcome. He bashed the Bible into them. He bashed the message into the minds of the people. This didn't make his work any easier." If Billy's machine-gun delivery put off some of its audience, it did not completely miss the mark. Overall, Livermore said, "It was terrific. Forty people came forward." Though they arrived with almost no specific agenda and few contacts to help them implement one, they managed to organize rallies that drew an aggregate attendance estimated at more than 100,000. Response on the Continent was mixed. The young preachers met resistance to their simplistic attitude toward Scripture and their non-Calvinist confidence in the ability of humans to lay hold of salvation. And when theology posed little problem, they were still so ... American. Nevertheless, they managed to found YFC organizations in numerous major cities, often with the help of American servicemen. Key assistance in gaining the cooperation of American military personnel and local officials throughout occupied Europe came from Paul Maddox, Chief of Chaplains for the European Command and a man who would eventually come to work for Graham in America.

Graham returned to England in the fall of 1946 for a six-month tour. This time he invited Cliff and Billie Barrows to serve as his musical team. Barrows had joined YFC and was enjoying notable success not only as a singer and gospel trombonist but also as an evangelist. He intended to continue preaching but readily accepted the opportunity to assist Graham. Despite their drive, both men possessed amiable, conflict-avoiding spirits and a genuine appreciation for the other's abilities. It was during that first trip that according to Barrows, "God really knit our hearts together in a special way."

The winter was bitterly cold, the worst in decades, and economic conditions had improved little since the first visit. To save money, the group frequently boarded in homes rather than in hotels, and Graham and George Wilson often slept in the same bed fully dressed and wearing shawls over their heads to keep warm. On occasion they spoke in stone churches so cold and dank that fog obscured part of the congregation from their view. These hardships, however, neither dampened their spirits nor cooled their ardor. Over a six-month period, Graham spoke at 360 meetings, with extended campaigns in Manchester, Birmingham, Belfast, and London. The Manchester effort early in 1947 marked his first true citywide campaign, but the Birmingham meetings stood out because of opposition from the local clergy, who not only refused to cooperate but persuaded the city council to withdraw permission for him to use the civic auditorium. Instead of following the venerable revivalist tradition of seeking popular support by skinning the local clergy for their hide-bound, moss-backed resistance to God's will, Graham chose a more winsome and successful course: He spoke to his critics directly and simply melted their resistance. Armed with a list of clergymen most opposed to his efforts, he called on each one, "not to argue, only to explain, and if you don't mind, to pray." In almost every case, he won them over with his warmth and sincerity, humbly acknowledging his own shortcomings as a preacher and easily convincing them that his only interest was in helping them further the cause of Christ in their country. One vocal critic of "America's surplus saints" described his own capitulation: "Billy called on me. He wasn't bitter, just wondering. I ended up wanting to hug the twenty-seven-year-old boy. I called my church officers and we disrupted all our plans for the nine days of his visit. Before it was over, Birmingham had seen a touch of God's blessing. This fine, lithe, burning torch of a man made me love him and his Lord." The city council reversed its decision, and by the end of the meetings, the twenty-five-hundred-seat auditorium was packed each night for what newspapers called "the greatest spiritual revival the city had experienced in a generation."

From a spiritual standpoint, the key development was Graham's encounter with Stephen Olford, an eloquent and powerful young Welsh evangelist whose missionary father had been converted by R. A. Torrey. The two men met briefly during the spring visit, and Graham had been impressed by a powerful sermon Olford had given on the work of the Holy Spirit in a person's life. This time the men spent two days together, except for evening services, in the cold, drab bedroom of a miner's home in the little Welsh town of Pontypridd, not far from Olford's home in Newport, South Wales. In that bleak setting, Olford led Billy step by step through the process that had produced a profound spiritual renewal in him a few months earlier. "The first day we spent on the Word; not memorizing texts—he was quite good at that—but on what it really means to expose oneself to the Word in one's 'quiet time.' Billy admitted that he'd never had a quiet time in the sense in which I'd described it. That seemed to make a tremendous impression. He was so teachable, so beautifully humble and reflective. He just drank in everything I could give him."

The effects of the first day's conversation did not show immediately. Graham preached that evening and Olford thought, "Quite frankly, it was very ordinary. Neither his homiletics nor his theology nor his particular approach to Welsh people made much of an impact. The Welsh are masters of preaching, and the Welsh people expect hard, long sermons with a couple of hours of solid exposition. Billy was giving brief little messages. They listened, but it wasn't their kind of preaching." The crowd was small and response to the invitation meager. The next day in the bedroom, Olford concentrated on the work of the Holy Spirit. "I gave him my testimony of how God completely turned my life inside out—an experience of the Holy Spirit in his fullness and anointing. As I talked, and I can see him now, those marvelous eyes glistened with tears, and he said, 'Stephen, I see it. That's what I want. That's what I need in my life.'" Olford suggested they "pray this through," and both men fell on their knees. "I can still hear Billy pouring out his heart in a prayer of total dedication to the Lord. Finally, he said, 'My heart is so flooded with the Holy Spirit,' and we went from praying to praising. We were laughing and praising God, and he was walking back and forth across the room, crying out, 'I have it. I'm filled. This is the turning point in my life.' And he was a new man."

Whether this experience was ultimately more critical than Billy's decision at Mordecai Ham's tabernacle or his surrender on the golf course at

Temple Terrace is impossible to measure, but it clearly had an impact, and his Welsh audience seemed to sense it. That evening, Olford recalled, "for reasons known to God alone, the place which was only moderately filled the night before was packed to the doors. As Billy rose to speak, he was a man absolutely anointed." Perhaps conscious that it was a significant moment, or perhaps short of sermons, Graham preached an old favorite, based on the biblical story of the Feast of Belshazzar, and the normally unemotional Welsh jammed the aisles as soon as he began his invitation. "Practically the entire audience responded," Olford remembers. "My own heart was so moved by Billy's authority and strength that I could hardly drive home. My parents were still alive then, and when I came in the door, my father looked at my face and said, 'What on earth has happened?' I sat down at the kitchen table and said, 'Dad, something has happened to Billy Graham. The world is going to hear from this man. He is going to make his mark in history.' His response was absolutely wonderful. He said, 'It won't be the first time America has taken a lead in evangelism.'" Others shared Olford's sense that Graham's preaching had taken on a new dimension, that he was not simply delivering sermons but speaking of a God whom he knew in a close, personal way. Chuck Templeton also noticed that Billy's preaching "seemed to be taking on, more and more, a largeness and authority in the pulpit, to be going for a certain magnificence of effect. It became fascinating, really impressive, to watch him."

By mid-1947, Youth for Christ and the similar Southern Baptist Youth Revival movement it spawned constituted a phenomenon sufficiently significant to attract the attention of secular and theologically liberal critics. With memories of the Hitler Youth fresh in their minds, some feared that these patriotic, Fundamentalist rallies, which by now were attracting perhaps a million young people each week, could easily become authoritarian, proto-fascist gatherings, manipulated by political opportunists whose hand-painted ties barely covered hearts of darkness. To these, the young who streamed into auditoriums and stadia in over a thousand cities were simply "dumb sheep," differing little from those who had flocked to hear the fanatical bleating of Father Charles Coughlin and Huey Long, anti-Semites Gerald Winrod and Gerald L. K. Smith, and various spellbinding Communist orators. William Randolph Hearst's appraisal of YFC as a "good and growing thing" that "will never be good enough or big enough until it involves all of our young people in this country" served only to confirm their troubled suspicions. Insofar as YFC had a political orientation, it was indeed largely conservative, but apart from a decided anticommunism and a strong patriotic strain, politics was neither its manifest nor hidden agenda. It was, as it purported to be, a religious movement, a resurgence of the Fundamentalism that had been licking its wounds for two decades, awaiting just such an opportunity to challenge the liberal Protestantism that had held undisputed sway since the mid-1920s.

Billy Graham had at least some self-conscious inkling of what was happening. He declared that his travels had convinced him that Modernism was on the ropes and that Evangelicals had a real chance to deliver a knockout blow, not only in America but around the world. To a nation that had emerged victorious from war on two far-flung fronts and welcomed whatever help it could get in its efforts to redrop its anchors and reattach its roots, his bold and confident assertion that a virile, athletic, victorious, freedom-creating Christ was the answer held enormous appeal. Though he remained largely unknown outside Evangelical circles, song sheets from his rallies scarcely exaggerated when they described him as "America's foremost youth leader ... whose ministry God is blessing more than any other young man in his generation." As a YFC headliner, Graham was widely sought for rallies throughout the country, but the addition of dozens of full-time staffers and evangelists enabled him to obtain some respite from the grueling round of travel. He used this opportunity to move into a more general kind of evangelism, remaining under the aegis and on the payroll of YFC but holding longer campaigns aimed not just at youth but at the general public. Still, a 1947 publicity brochure for his first American citywide campaign, in Grand Rapids, Michigan, contained a strong pitch to youth, calling him "A Young Athlete with a Twentieth-Century Gospel Message" and promising "terrific programs paced to a teenage tempo ... fastmoving ... enjoyable ... captivating."

The key campaign of the 1947 fall season took place in Charlotte. The invitation, from the same Christian Men's Club that had invited Mordecai Ham a dozen years earlier, arrived while he was in London. The committeemen failed to take the six-hour time difference into account and telephoned him in the middle of the night, but he accepted without hesitation. As the day approached, however, anxiety seized him and he began to fear that the honor achieved abroad would be without profit in his own country. Almost obsessively determined not to fail at home, he drove his advance men to a thorough job of preparation and spent heavily on a professional saturation-advertising campaign that included airplane-drawn sky banners and leaflet bombings, regular press releases to thirty-one local newspapers, and five thousand telephone calls a day, in addition to the standard run of brochures, billboards, bumper stickers, bus cards, radio spots, window placards, and personal appearances at civic clubs and school assemblies. He also plumped up the services with a gaggle of gospel variety acts that included a Salvation Army band, a brass quartet from Bob Jones College, a child piano prodigy, and the "world's foremost marimba player." On opening night Gil Dodds ran an exhibition race against a miler from the University of North Carolina. As the rubber-soled tennis shoes of the two harriers flapped around the wooden floor of the armory, Grady Wilson, not easily embarrassed by incongruity, thought to himself, "This is awfully silly. This is really a little absurd." But the crowd seemed impressed when Dodds mounted the platform and said,

"I wonder how many of you here tonight are doing your best in the race for Jesus Christ," and when Graham gave the invitation, an unusually high number of young people responded. The eighteen-service campaign drew 42,000 people and marked the first time the original Graham team—Billy, Cliff, Grady Wilson ("We didn't really ask Grady to come with us," Graham recalled; "he just joined us and we paid him a little salary"), and Bev Shea—-worked together in a campaign. Because he wanted to keep Shea with him, Billy persuaded the Charlotte committee to raise the singer's pay twice during the meetings.

The Charlotte campaign marked one of the first recorded instances of Graham's warnings against communism, a theme that would occupy a major place in his preaching over the next decade. The local boy who had toured a ravaged Europe himself and who regularly received firsthand reports from YFC colleagues in other lands warned the home folks that "Communism is creeping inexorably into these destitute lands; into war-torn China, into restless South America.... You should see Europe. It's terrible. There are Communists everywhere. Here, too, for that matter." The only hope, he thundered, is worldwide revival. "Unless the Christian religion rescues these nations from the clutches of the unbelieving, America will stand alone and isolated in the world." He also struck another note that he would sound again and again in this age that thrilled (or shuddered) at the words and deeds of such titans as Hitler, Stalin, Churchill, Roosevelt, de Gaulle, MacArthur, Patton, and Eisenhower: the deep-seated need for an exemplar, a hero. "American youth must have a hero," he proclaimed. "It may be a football player, a general in the army, or some other glamorous person." This perception doubtless underlay the packing of evangelistic services with appearances by Christian celebrities, but their task was, like his own, to point beyond themselves to the Star of Stars, the Hero of Heroes: "Jesus Christ is the Hero of my soul and the coach of my life."

One further momentous and largely unsought accomplishment remained for 1947. When the YFC evangelists spoke at George Wilson's rallies at the First Baptist Church in Minneapolis, the church's old and ailing pastor and Fundamentalist patriarch, William Bell Riley, always made it a point to attend the services, observing from a wheelchair or, when weather permitted, from a convertible pulled into a doorway. Well past eighty, Riley was actively seeking someone to take the reins of his Northwestern Schools, which consisted of a Bible school, a seminary, and a brand-new liberal arts college, touted in Evangelical publications as having a "course and bearing [that will] save our young people from the poisonous sting of pagan philosophies which have become the devil's substitutes, and which have been palmed off under the high-sounding and yet empty phrase of: 'EXACT SCIENCE.' The college is coeducational, fundamental, and millennial." Riley talked to both Graham and Torrey Johnson about becoming president of the schools. When Johnson made it clear he was staying with Youth for Christ, the old man turned all his attention to Graham, whose career he had followed since their first meeting at Florida Bible Institute. He broached the subject on several occasions, but Billy balked, objecting that he had little talent or inclination for administration and could not hold evangelistic campaigns and run the schools at the same time, a point Torrey Johnson had made. Riley countered by pointing out that the crusades would feed students and money into the schools and that when his glory days on the revival circuit passed, as they surely would, he would need a permanent home base. Graham professed to be flattered but continued to insist he did not feel led of God to accept the opportunity. "I have been waiting for Heaven's signal," he wrote. "I have not received it." Privately, he also harbored doubts about the wisdom of assuming a mantle stiffened by Riley's intransigent Fundamentalism—in many ways, the very kind of pugnacious dogmatism the National Association of Evangelicals was seeking to avoid—and stained with anti-Semitic and anti-Catholic bile foreign to Billy's irenic spirit.

Accustomed to getting his way and quite willing to invoke the authority of heaven in support of his position, Riley summoned Graham to his sickbed during the summer of 1947, pointed a bony finger directly at him, and, as portentous lightning and thunder streaked and crashed outside the window, declared imperiously, "Beloved, as Samuel appointed David King of Israel, so I appoint you head of these schools. I'll meet you at the judgment-seat of Christ with them." Unable to resist the combination of biblical precedent, deathbed dramatics, and celestial fireworks, Graham relented, but only to the point of agreeing to serve as interim president if Riley died before July 1, 1948, which would cover the next academic year. When the old man died on December 6, 1947, Billy Graham became, at twenty-nine, the youngest college president in America. After six months as interim and six more as acting president, Graham accepted full-time status, but he drew no salary and spent little time on campus. Fearing the job would divert him from evangelism, and opposing it from the outset, Ruth showed no interest in being the first lady to a husband unlikely to spend more time in Minneapolis than he was spending in Montreat. When a school administrator called to ask when she would be moving into the president's mansion, she gave a clipped and accurate answer: "Never." A few months later, shortly after the birth of a second daughter, Anne, she borrowed $4,000 to buy a small house across the street from her parents in Montreat.

As a largely absentee president, Graham established a pattern of leadership he would follow throughout his career: He raised money, enlisted boosters, stayed in touch by telephone, left the day-to-day administrative work to a coterie of trusted associates, and occasionally complicated their jobs by making decisions and commitments based more on well-meaning impulse than on informed understanding of relevant facts and issues. In one of his first moves, he persuaded T. W. Wilson to become Northwestern's vice-president and de facto chief administrator. Wilson was understandably hesitant. One of YFC's most successful evangelists, he wanted to pursue his career. Moreover, he realized he was no more qualified than Graham to run a college. "I told him," Wilson recalled, "that I would be a miserable flop, but he called me every night for about ten nights, wanting to know if I had made up my mind yet." Then, as later, Graham tended to identify making up one's mind with accepting his wishes; T.W. finally caved in under the pressure and moved to Minneapolis. George Wilson was already on hand as business manager, and Graham quickly put his confidence in Gerald Beavan, a professor of psychology, theology, and Hebrew whom he appointed registrar. When he discovered that Beavan also had experience in advertising and journalism, he enlisted him to prepare publicity for his preaching campaigns and to make sure that news of his successes reached the relevant media.

Graham had little feel for the way academic institutions operate. He began his first letter to the faculty with the salutation "Dear Gang." He awarded raises without consulting department chairmen, deans, or financial committees. He hired a man trained in English to teach math. "He hired him because he liked him," T.W. explained. "Some of the students knew more about math than he did. We had to make some adjustments there." He appeared at board meetings to discuss issues or projects that would normally require weeks or months of research and discussion by faculty and administrative committees and expected the board to reach a decision in time for him to catch a plane. When he felt he had given the matter all the time he could spare, he would look at his watch and tell his faithful vice-president, "T, you better do the rest. Good-bye." Several of Graham's associates from this period have tactfully observed that "Billy was called to be an evangelist, not an educator," but his tenure at Northwestern was by no means a failure. His growing prominence in Evangelical circles attracted students to all three schools, causing a jump from eight hundred to approximately twelve hundred students. On the map of American higher education, the schools were little more than an obscure dot, but in the parochial universe of Fundamentalist Christianity, they were rising stars. And their leader's lack of appropriate academic credentials was soon papered over with the first four of what would become a stack of honorary doctorates. Ironically, one of the first schools to honor the Reverend Dr. Graham was Bob Jones College. YFC had funneled hundreds of students to the college, and Dr. Bob was duly grateful. In a reciprocal gesture of reconciliation, Graham invited Jones to speak at Northwestern's 1948 commencement, the first to be held during his presidency.

In late summer of 1948, Graham attended (as an official observer, not a delegate) the founding assembly of the World Council of Churches (WCC). He was uncomfortable with the liberal theology dominating the WCC and the ecumenical movement it represented, but he remembered that two of the movement's most important spiritual ancestors had been D. L. Moody and one of Moody's close friends, John R. Mott, and he felt Evangelicals had been partly to blame for the direction it had taken, since they had pulled out to maintain their separatist purity instead of remaining involved and trying to check the movement's drift to the left. The vision of a unified Christian community so captured his expansive nature that he later characterized his attendance at these meetings as "one of the most thrilling experiences of my life up to that moment."

In the fall of that year, Graham and Barrows took a leave of absence from YFC to devote full time to their own campaigns. For Graham, the move to a wider and independent ministry had come to seem inevitable. He had emerged from the pack as the most successful YFC evangelist, his meetings garnering more space in Evangelical publications than any other young preacher, including Chuck Templeton and Jack Shuler, his only real competitors. For Cliff Barrows, however, becoming the second member of the Graham/Barrows Campaign team meant the subordination of his own ministry to Graham's. Such a subordination was not easy. When he and Billie were not traveling with Graham in Europe, they were enjoying considerable success with their own revivals, mostly on the West Coast. Cliff was a gifted preacher, and he and Billie combined talent, enthusiasm, transparent sincerity, and a remarkable lack of egotism into a highly winsome package. They clearly had the option to remain in a leading role with YFC or to establish their own independent evangelistic ministry, or to get off the road and serve as a pastor or minister of music. Yet Cliff not only recognized that he would probably never quite equal Graham's success as an evangelist; he also saw that their most notable abilities were complementary rather than competitive and that they could accomplish far more together than either could alone or, for that matter, in tandem with anyone else they knew. One evening in Philadelphia, Cliff and Billie came to Graham's hotel room to give him their decision. "Bill," Cliff said, using that address to distinguish his friend from his wife, "God has given us peace in our hearts. As long as you want us to, from now till the Lord returns, or whenever, I'll be content to be your song leader, carry your bag, go anywhere, do anything you want me to do." It was a notable surrender of self, all the more so because it was volunteered rather than demanded. Forty years later, in a nearly empty cafeteria near his home in Greenville, South Carolina, Barrows reflected on the sacrifice of ego he had made and said in a quiet tone, utterly free of dissimulation, "I still have that same peace of mind and heart. I think Bill knows that."

Graham remained on YFC's board of directors and still actively promoted and encouraged its activities, but he was now largely on his own, receiving his primary support from love offerings collected in crusade services. At this point he still took no salary from the Northwestern Schools, which he continued to direct by telephone and proxy. His fame was confined mainly to the

Evangelical world, and when he hit the front pages of the nation's newspapers and magazines a year later, he appeared to be an overnight sensation, an inexplicable meteor. In fact, much of the success he would shortly enjoy could be traced directly to his four years with Youth for Christ. In that brief but critical period, he obtained preaching opportunities and experience few free-lance evangelists could have matched, and they had their effect. In keeping with YFC's pledge to be "Geared to the Times," Billy made it a standard aspect of his preaching to proclaim the "good news" against a contrasting background of bad news from contemporary events and circumstances, leading numerous observers to say that he preached as if he had "a Bible in one hand and a newspaper in the other." He spoke of "how sleek Russian bombers are poised to drop death upon American cities; how Communism and Catholicism are taking over in Europe; how Mohammedanism is sweeping across Africa and into Southern Europe." And in good dispensationalist fashion, he interpreted these dreadful portents, particularly when coupled with the imminent establishment of the state of Israel, as indisputable signs that the second coming of Christ lay but a short time in the future.

As important as becoming a more competent practitioner of his craft, Graham also established strong bonds with the small handful of men who would remain at his side for the rest of their lives, and he built a network of contacts with ministers and leading laymen who trusted him and would welcome the opportunity to work with him in his own citywide crusades. He learned that Charles Finney had been justified in commending "the right use of the constituted means," and that revivals and successful evangelistic efforts are more likely to be "prayed down" when they have also been "worked up" by meticulous organization and copious publicity. Finally, in his role as college president, he was continuing to become aware of his strengths and, not insignificantly, his weaknesses as a leader. At age thirty, a precedented point at which to begin a wider ministry, Billy Graham was ready for higher ground.

7

The Canvas Cathedral

On countless occasions over the past forty years, usually at a press conference preceding a major crusade, Billy Graham has declared that he sensed religious revival was breaking out and about to sweep over the land. In 1948 he happened to be right. During the 1940s church membership in America rose by nearly 40 percent, with most of the growth coming after the end of the war, when the nation tried to reconstruct normalcy on the most dependable foundation it knew. Church building reached an all-time high, seminaries were packed, and secular colleges added programs in religious studies. Religious books outsold all other categories of nonfiction, and Bible sales doubled between 1947 and 1952—the new Revised Standard Version of the Bible sold two million copies in 1950 alone. While Graham and his colleagues in Youth for Christ and the Southern Baptist Youth Revival movement were packing civic auditoriums and stadia William Branham, Jack Coe, A. A. Allen, and Oral Roberts were filling stupendous nine-pole circus tents with Pentecostal believers desperate to see afflictions healed, devils cast out, and the dead raised.

For evangelists it was like being a stockbroker in a runaway bull market. As in other fields, however, the boom attracted some whose motives and methods were less than sanctified, who fell prey to the temptations described in Scripture as "the lust of the flesh, and the lust of the eyes, and the pride of life" (I John 2:16), but better known by their street names: sex, money, and power. Despite good intentions and behavior, Graham and his associates occasionally found themselves the objects of suspicion and condescension from ministers and laypeople alike. They learned that Elmer Gantry, whom Sinclair Lewis had assembled from skeletons and scraps found in the closets of real-life evangelists, was a deeply entrenched cultural stereotype. As they contemplated the checkered history and contemporary shortcomings of itinerant evangelism (the term itself had a kind of siding salesman's rhinestone ring to it) and talked with veteran campaigners, they realized that much of the skepticism was warranted. To prepare his own defenses, Graham called Bev Shea, Grady Wilson, and Cliff Barrows to his hotel room during a campaign in Modesto, California, in November of 1948. "God has brought us to this point," he said. "Maybe he is preparing us for something that we don't know. Let's try to recall all the things that have been a stumbling block and a hindrance to evangelists in years past, and let's come back together in an hour and talk about it and pray about it and ask God to guard us from them."

The assignment was easy. They had all seen enough evangelists rise and fall or leave town in a cloud of disillusionment to be able to pinpoint the key problems readily. When they regrouped in Graham's room later in the afternoon, each had made essentially the same list, which came to be known in the oral tradition as the Modesto Manifesto. The first problem was money. The most rectitudinous of men could find it difficult not to pull out a few extra flourishes when the love offering was collected. When he traveled for YFC, Graham turned offerings over to local or national bodies and was paid a straight salary, but no parent body existed to fund his independent revivals, so the group saw no viable alternative to the love-offering system, even though it made them uncomfortable. They did, however, pledge not to emphasize the offering and to try to keep themselves as free as possible of suspicion regarding the way they handled the money by asking members of the sponsoring committee to oversee the payment of all bills and disbursement of funds to the revival team. On one occasion, Bev Shea sent the sponsoring committee a check for thirty dollars, just in case the hotel had levied a charge for extra laundry service for his infant son.

The second potential problem was immorality. As energetic young men in full bloom, often traveling without their families, charged with the raw excitement of standing before large and admiring crowds, and living in anonymous hotels and tourist courts, all of them knew well the power and possibilities of sexual temptation, and all of them had seen promising ministerial careers shipwrecked by the potent combination of lust and opportunity. They asked God "to guard us, to keep us true, to really help us be sensitive in this area, to keep us even from the appearance of evil," and they began to follow simple but effective rules to protect themselves. They avoided situations that would put them alone with a woman—lunch, a counseling session, even a ride to an auditorium or an airport. On the road, they roomed in close proximity to each other as an added margin of social control. And always, they prayed for supernatural assistance in keeping them "clean."

Two other problems, less imperious in their proddings than money or sex but capable of generating cynicism toward evangelists, were inflated publicity and criticism of local pastors. Because it helped win invitations to bigger churches and cities and thus fed their egos and fattened their pocketbooks, evangelists had grown accustomed to exaggerating their crowds and their results, both in advance publicity and in reports to Evangelical publications. Critics accused them of counting arms and legs instead of heads, and the phrase *evangelistically speaking* signified that anyone interested in accuracy should discount an itinerant's reports of his own accomplishments. D. L.

Moody refused to keep statistics lest he be drawn into exaggeration or boasting. Billy Graham and his team were too wed to the modern ethos to adopt that approach, but they did begin to use a consistent procedure. Instead of generating their own figures, they usually accepted crowd estimates given by police or the fire department or arena managers, even when they felt the official estimate was too low, and they readily admitted that many who came down the aisles during the invitation were counselors assigned to help inquirers, not inquirers themselves. As for the criticism of pastors, they had heard Mordecai Ham and his ilk attack the local clergy to gain attention and make themselves look good, then leave town while the hapless pastors tried to regain the confidence of their parishioners. Graham was determined to avoid this destructive course. He would gladly meet with pastors who criticized him but would not publicly criticize men who planted the seed and tilled the fields that he swooped in to harvest.

The next several months passed uneventfully with a return visit to England and respectable but modest outings in Miami and Baltimore. Then came an effort in Altoona, Pennsylvania, that Graham and his colleagues remember as the nadir of their public careers. Grady Wilson, given to plain speech, called it "the sorriest crusade we ever had," adding that "Billy was about ready to give up the ministry after Altoona." Less bluntly, Cliff Barrows conceded that "several contributing factors combined to keep it from standing out as one of the most blessed of events." The problems began as soon as Graham hit town and learned that the several invitations he had received to hold a campaign had not been repeated requests from a single body, as he had hoped, but separate inquiries from rival ministerial associations that were at each other's throats and not about to cooperate in a joint venture. Once the meeting started, a large mentally deranged woman repeatedly interrupted the services by threatening to kill Cliff Barrows if she ever saw him on the street, screaming that Indians were about to attack Billy Graham, and rushing the platform with such determination to cause trouble that it took Grady Wilson and two ushers to restrain her. Overall, Barrows recalled that "we didn't do much in Altoona but pray and wonder what had happened and wish the meeting would get over with so we could get out of town."

Grady's comment about Billy's leaving the ministry was intentionally hyperbolic, but the bloom of the YFC triumphs did seem to fade a bit, and Graham's confidence that God was preparing him for a glorious ministry began to falter. Simple ambition played its part here; Billy had always liked standing out from the crowd, and he must have enjoyed the intoxicating rush that few experiences can provide so fully as drinking in the attention and adoration of a rapt multitude. But there was more, and not to appreciate that would be to misunderstand Billy Graham, who has carried with him since his midteens an obsessive determination to discern and perform the will of God. A small but telling incident shortly after the Altoona meeting offered a glimpse of this compulsion. During a gathering at a Michigan Fundamentalist conference center whose very name, Maranatha ("Come, Lord"), signified its eschatological orientation, Graham and two other featured speakers, including Roy Gustafson, an old friend from Florida Bible Institute, went out into a field one evening after the services to see the aurora borealis. As they contemplated the beauty and mystery of the northern lights, they fell easily to talking of the celestial manifestations that might accompany the Second Coming. None of them doubted that the rapture and the millennium would soon bring the present "dispensation" to an end, and all three assumed they would be in the company of those whisked into the clouds, so the prospect held no terror whatever for them. But Graham raised a lone qualification to his basically joyful anticipation: "I want the Lord to come," he said, "but I sure would like to do something great for him before he comes." He knew salvation was by grace, but he aspired to enter God's presence at the Judgment with a suitable token of gratitude. Typically, the men ended their reflections in prayer. Gustafson, who went first, knelt on his handkerchief to protect his trousers from dampness and grass stains. When Billy's turn came, his friends heard not his customary clear resonance but a muffled groaning. When Gustafson cocked open an eye to discover the cause of the unusual sounds, he saw that Billy, still wearing his suit and tie and far away from any crowd that might acclaim his piety and humility, had thrown himself face forward onto the ground in abject prostration and was beseeching God for an opportunity to serve him more fully. A second incident at the same conference made it clear that Graham did not view greater service as an avenue for greater gain. When conference leaders gave him a twenty-three-hundred dollar love offering for his efforts, he handed the entire amount to Roy Gustafson, who was about to leave on a Central American mission.

Graham's fear that he might fall short in his efforts to serve God had another source that was far more troubling than the mediocrities of Miami and Baltimore and the depressing failure of Altoona. If he had a peer among his YFC colleagues, it was unquestionably Chuck Templeton. Darkly handsome, intelligent, and intellectually curious despite his lack of a high school education, and more worldly wise than most of his colleagues by dint of a troubled homelife that had forced him to fend for himself since his early teens, Templeton was generally acknowledged to be the most versatile of the YFC evangelists, able to preach a soul-winning message or lead a devotional service or emcee a stadium rally with great and equal effectiveness. "He was not an expositor of the Word," Torrey Johnson recalled. "He did not know his Bible as thoroughly as some others, [but] he loved it and preached it. The only danger with him was that he was so eloquent, you were taken up with his eloquence more than with the substance." Templeton himself, while deeply fond of Billy Graham, had no doubt his own preaching was superior to Graham's in both technique and content, though he acknowledged that no one could match Billy's success when it came to inviting people to accept Christ. "He got more results than anybody," Templeton remembered. "We would travel together and preach on consecutive nights. He would get forty-one; I would get thirty-two. In the next town, I would get seventeen, he would get twenty-three, or I would get two hundred and he would get three hundred. Very clearly, he was going to be a well-known figure." Still, in the early years of YFC, most observers would probably have put their money on Templeton; in 1946, when the National Association of Evangelicals published a pictorial spread of Evangelicals "best used of God" in the organization's five-year history, it named both Johnson and Templeton but omitted Billy Graham. And a YFC veteran looking back on these exciting days remembered that "this boy Charlie Templeton could just preach fantastically. That was before he went to seminary."

The ominous overtone of that brief assessment pointed to the heart of the crisis both Graham and Templeton faced. After three years on the rally and revival circuit, Templeton had come to believe that the success he and the other young lions of the YFC enjoyed was illusory, that they were offering their audiences meringue instead of meat, and garnering their "decisions" by force of personal attractiveness rather than by convincing presentation of a substantial message grounded on a solid rock of understanding. Increasingly troubled, he decided to resign from YFC and his flourishing independent church in Toronto to pursue a formal education. Even without a high school diploma, he managed to gain admission to Princeton Theological Seminary and prepared to enroll in the fall of 1948. Knowing that Graham shared at least some of his feelings about the need for further disciplined study, he went to Montreat to enlist him as a partner in the venture. He said, "Bill, we are getting by on animal magnetism and youthful enthusiasm and natural talent, but that's not going to work when we're forty or fifty. You've got to come with me." The idea intrigued Graham, but he protested that increased evangelistic opportunities, his duties at Northwestern, and the incongruity of a college president's returning to school would make enrollment in an American seminary unfeasible. Lest his friend think these were polite dodges, however, he made a counterproposal. "I never will forget," Templeton recalled. "He got up out of his chair and walked across the floor with his hand out. And he said, 'Chuck, go to Oxford and I'll go with you." Templeton regarded Graham's proposal to devote at least two years to graduate work at Oxford as genuine but chose to stay his own course. "It had been an enormous problem to get into Princeton," he explained, "and I couldn't change my mind at this stage, but if I had shaken his hand I have no doubt in the world that the whole history of evangelism would have changed. Billy would have been ruined by going to Oxford, or he would have left at midterm. It undoubtedly would have diminished him in some way. I'm not saying this in a disdainful way, but

Billy was not interested in the scholarly side of things. He was not interested in reaching for conceptual or intellectual horizons."

Graham undoubtedly valued the immediate satisfactions of packed auditoriums and crowded aisles and growing schools more than the less tangible pleasures of the life of the mind, but he did begin to read serious academic theology, some of it suggested by John Mackay, then president of the Princeton seminary. Over the following academic year, when his travels brought him to New York, he and Templeton met several times in a room in the Taft Hotel, just off Times Square, for long bouts of prayer and discussion in which he struggled to defend received belief against the attacks Templeton mounted with his newly acquired weapons from the seminarian's armamentarium: historical and literary criticism of the Bible, theology viewed as a creative enterprise rather than scrupulous adherence to a blueprint, epistemological allegiance to the methods and findings of natural science, and the relativizing lessons of anthropology, sociology, and psychology. At one point Graham uttered what Templeton called "a declaratory sentence in the evolution of Billy Graham." Flustered by his inability to counter Templeton's arguments, he said, "Chuck, look, I haven't a good enough mind to settle these questions. The finest minds in the world have looked and come down on both sides of these questions. I don't have the time, the inclination, or the set of mind to pursue them. I have found that if I say, 'The Bible says' and 'God says,' I get results. I have decided I am not going to wrestle with these questions any longer." Exasperated by this unblinking abdication of the struggle that was wrenching his own soul, Templeton issued a sharp rebuke: "Bill, you cannot refuse to think. To do that is to die intellectually. You cannot disobey Christ's great commandment to love God 'with all thy heart and all thy soul and all thy *mind!*' Not to think is to deny God's creativity. Not to think is to sin against your Creator. You can't stop thinking. That's intellectual suicide."

Templeton's charge stung, and Graham continued to wrestle with both conscience and intellect. His dilemma was real and threatening. If Scripture were not truly God's inspired revelation, God's literal *Word*, directly transmitted to the human agents who committed it to writing and trustworthy in every respect, how could he continue to preach it with the same assurance and power? How could he remain as president of a school founded on unquestioned faith in the absolute dependability of Scripture? Indeed, if any portion of the Bible were seen to be unreliable, how could one trust any other portion, including the central affirmations of the Christian faith? On the other hand, if the Bible were all he believed and desperately wanted it to be, why couldn't he answer Chuck Templeton's questions? And why did the faculty and students at the world's best universities seem, when confronted with the evidence, to move inexorably away from the positions he held? For an honest young Fundamentalist, there could scarcely be a greater threat. Perhaps for the first time in his life, Billy Graham understood more fully than ever before the Apostle Paul's observation that "if Christ is not risen" (which is to say, if what believers affirm about Jesus is not true) then "we are of all men most miserable."

The resolution came at a student conference at Forest Home, a retreat center in the San Bernadino Mountains near Los Angeles. Both Graham and Templeton were featured speakers, and their conversations, joined by others asking similar questions, rekindled Billy's doubts. In fresh turmoil, he went for a walk in the serene pine forest. About fifty yards off a main trail, he sat for a long time on a large rock, his Bible spread open on a tree stump. As he struggled once more with his doubts and his commitment, he finally made the pragmatic decision to abandon doubt and cling to commitment. With the same spirit of surrender he had shown on the eighteenth green at Temple Terrace, he said, "Oh, God, I cannot prove certain things. I cannot answer some of the questions Chuck is raising and some of the other people are raising, but I accept this Book by faith as the Word of God." Chuck Templeton could not or would not make such a surrender, but he understood Graham's reaction. "I could not live without facing my doubts," he said. "Billy could not see but that doubt was sin. It flew in the face of being a southern country boy, raised in a religious family, married to a missionary's daughter. To doubt God was to do wrong." After completing his studies at Princeton and serving for a time as a successful evangelist for the National Council of Churches—Princeton's dean called him "the most gifted and talented young man in America today for preaching mission work"—Templeton recognized he was no longer a believer in any kind of orthodox sense and that it was intellectually dishonest to pretend otherwise. Shortly afterward he left the ministry and returned to Toronto, where he pursued a multifaceted career as a newspaper columnist and editor, radio and TV commentator, novelist, and screenwriter. In sharp contrast, Graham's conscious resolution that he would never again entertain any doubts whatsoever about the authority of Scripture galvanized his faith and, as he later observed, "gave power and authority to my preaching that has never left me. The gospel in my hands became a hammer and a flame I felt as though I had a rapier in my hands and through the power of the Bible was slashing deeply into men's consciousness, leading them to surrender to God." Today, at Forest Home, a bronze tablet identifies the Stone of Witness where Billy Graham accepted, once and for all, the absolute authority of the Scriptures.

Fortified with his newly refinished faith, Graham plunged headlong into the campaign that would make him a national figure. For several years, a group of laymen operating under the banner of Christ for Greater Los Angeles sponsored revivals featuring a well-known preacher who could be counted on to draw a respectable crowd of fellow Fundamentalists and perhaps a smattering of the unsaved. Jack Shuler had been the evangelist for two of their meetings, and Chuck Templeton had shared the preaching with another

YFC evangelist two years earlier. For the 1949 edition, they invited Billy Graham. The sponsoring committee enjoyed good support from approximately a quarter of Los Angeles—area churches, so a respectable outing seemed assured, but Graham wanted more than that, and he set about to get it. For the first time, a Billy Graham campaign began to assume what would eventually become its mature form. Nine months before the meetings began, the organizers engaged veteran revivalists J. Edwin Orr and Armin Gesswein to conduct preparatory meetings throughout the Los Angeles area. As a result of their efforts, nearly eight hundred small groups were meeting regularly to pray for the campaign long before it began in September. Then, two weeks before opening night, Grady Wilson flew in from South Carolina to organize still more prayer meetings, some lasting all day or all night, and around-the-clock prayer chains involving hundreds of people. The supernatural benefits of prayer are inherently impossible to measure, no matter what one believes about the practice, but the mobilizing of thousands into prayer groups undoubtedly stimulated their enthusiasm for the campaign and must have boosted Graham's confidence. As further support, Cliff Barrows recruited a large choir, and Dawson Trotman, founder and leader of The Navigators, a live-wire group of young people who emphasized personal evangelism, trained counselors to help inquirers clarify their decisions and direct them into Bible-believing churches.

Graham may have surrendered his doubt and pride at Forest Home, but he did not relinquish his faith in publicity. On the contrary, he pressured a wary committee into spending $25,000 for posters, billboards, radio announcements, and newspaper ads urging Los Angelenos to "Visit the Canvas Cathedral with the Steeple of Light," to hear "America's Sensational Young Evangelist," and enjoy old-fashioned revival services featuring a "Dazzling Array of Gospel Talent." The Canvas Cathedral, a Ringling Brothers circus tent pitched at the corner of Washington and Hill streets and sporting a garish midway-style picture of Graham on a long cloth marquee, was itself a grand attention getter. Billy's fascination with celebrities and his keen appreciation for the role they could play in lending both legitimation and panache to a cause blossomed in this city of radio and movie stars. Through Henrietta Mears, a wealthy and flamboyant woman who grew up in W. B. Riley's church in Minneapolis, founded Forest Home, and taught a Sunday school class of several hundred members at the First Presbyterian Church in Hollywood, Graham gained access to the Hollywood Christian Group, an organization of mostly minor actors and other media personalities he hoped would lend their names and influence to the campaign. One of the best known but least devout, Stuart Hamblen, agreed to plug the meetings on his popular western-flavored radio show. Graham also cultivated high-level official support and won public endorsemerit from the city's mayor. Filling a 6,000-seat tent remained a daunting task, but a good meeting seemed assured.

Two years of campaigning had helped the Graham team evolve a style that toned down the gaudier aspects of the YFC rallies while retaining enough enthusiastic flash to attract and hold attention. Cliff Barrows played his trombone and led the singing with a cheerleader's vivacity, but the hymns were familiar, designed to reassure the timid that despite the circuslike trappings, the services themselves were much like those in the churches in which most had been reared. Barrows kept applause to a minimum, and if guest performers ever crossed the line of propriety and good taste, Bev Shea's dignified renditions always restored a sense of seriousness before Graham entered the pulpit. Billy (Cliff was now introducing him as "Dr. Graham") still spoke with great intensity and fervor, but he never slipped into the wild hysteria or demagogic rantings that drew unfavorable attention to some of the stars of the Pentecostal healing revival, and he told reporters that "I want to do away with everything that is criticized in mass evangelism. We believe it is a spiritual service. We don't believe it is a concert or a show."

Whether traceable to his Forest Home experience or simply to the realization that never before had he possessed such an opportunity, Graham preached with a force and authority that impressed even his colleagues. Standing behind a pulpit with a plywood facade cut to suggest a giant open Bible, he began most of his sermons by reading a lengthy passage of Scripture and launching immediately into a ringing litany of what would happen if folks did not heed the clear lessons contained in that portion of God's Word. Throughout virtually the entire performance, he stayed in motion, using a lapel microphone that gave him freedom to stalk back and forth across a long platform while Cliff Barrows played the cord in and out to keep him from getting tangled in it. Some observers calculated that he walked at least a mile per sermon, and some found his pacing a distraction, but it kept attention riveted on him, and it made listeners in all sections of the tent feel he was speaking directly to them at least part of the time, particularly when he stopped suddenly, leaned forward with both hands on his knees, and announced with glowering ferocity the judgment of God upon them, their city, and their nation. Little of this was accidental. Graham acknowledged that he not only rehearsed his sermons but sometimes listened to a wire recording of previous presentations to make sure he had every nuance down pat, and he was clearly aware of the importance of nuance. "I've learned to look straight at them," he explained. "Say I'm preaching to an audience of three or four thousand. I can look straight at them, and I can tell when a man way back in the auditorium blinks his eyes. When he does that, I know it's time for a change of pace, or I'll lose some of the people. That's what I've trained my voice for. It's a change of pace that's the secret. I speak in loud tones—oh, not boisterous, but good and loud—and then I soften the voice. It's that difference in delivery that holds them." The more turbulent aspects of his style would eventually disappear along with his hand-painted ties and bright argyle socks and the voluminous double-breasted suits that hung on his bony frame like a scarecrow's garment, but films from this campaign show the trademark gestures that already connected speech and sinew in easily recognizable patterns. He shaped his hands into pistols and fired his accusations into the transfixed crowd. His arms became machetes as he hacked his way through the jungle of contemporary sin. His clenched fist descended with such power and fury that none could doubt he had made the wrath of God his own. And over and over, again and again, as he held the limp-backed book high overhead or drew his hands down like lightning to where it lay open on the pulpit, he declared that his words should be heeded not because they were his but because "the *Bible* says . . . !"

The content of Graham's sermons also foreshadowed his later preaching. At the opening service, he ran through the catalogue of problems—adultery, divorce, crime, alcohol abuse, suicide, materialism, love of money, and general moral "deteriation"—that marked Los Angeles as a "city of wickedness and sin" and warned that the only choices before it were "revival or judgment." These, of course, were evangelistic evergreens, safely transplantable in any urban soil. During this campaign, however, Billy alarmed his audiences with a brand-new threat: atomic-powered communism. A year earlier he had ventured an opinion that the Soviet Union had the bomb and was prepared to use it on America or any other country that dared defy it. Now, reality replaced speculation. Just two days before the campaign began, President Truman announced that the Russians had successfully tested an atomic bomb and for two years had been building a nuclear arsenal that would drastically alter the imbalance of power America had enjoyed since the end of World War II. Graham seized upon this stunning revelation and hammered it home throughout the campaign. Reminding his audiences that he had visited a devastated Europe six times since the war, he declared that "across Europe at this very hour there is stark, naked fear among the people. . . . An arms race, unprecedented in the history of the world, is driving us madly toward destruction!" The line had been drawn, he thundered, between communism and Western culture, and no accommodation was possible. "Western culture and its fruits had its foundation in the Bible, the Word of God, and in the revivals of the Seventeenth and Eighteenth Centuries. Communism, on the other hand, has decided against God, against Christ, against the Bible, and against all religion. Communism is not only an economic interpretation of life—Communism is a religion that is inspired, directed, and motivated by the Devil himself who has declared war against Almighty God." The fire of that war, he warned, would fall directly upon them, because "the Fifth Columnists, called Communists, are more rampant in Los Angeles than any other city in America. . . . In this moment I can see the judgment hand of God over Los Angeles. I can see judgment about to fall."

The only hope, the prophet said, was repentance and revival. "It is the providence of God," he declared, "that he has chosen this hour for a campaign—giving this city one more chance to repent of sin and turn to a believing knowledge of the Lord Jesus Christ.... This may be God's last great call!" And who would issue that call? "Let me tell you something," Graham said. "When God gets ready to shake America, He may not take the Ph.D. and the D.D. God may choose a country boy. God may choose the man that no one knows, a little nobody, to shake America for Jesus Christ in this day, and I pray that He would!"

Graham's preaching drew fair crowds and produced acceptable conversion rates, but at the end of the three scheduled weeks, little other than expense distinguished the revival from those of previous years. The weather was unseasonably cold, attendance was flagging—workers spaced the seats to make the crowds appear larger than they actually were—and Billy was out of sermons. It was customary to extend a successful revival, but several committee members thought it time to bring this one to a close. After some discussion, one man suggested they "put out a fleece" and let God decide. If the cold weather continued, they would end the campaign; if a warm front blew in by the time the services ended that same evening, they would take that as a sign God wanted the meetings to continue. Weather miracles are hard to count on or certify, and no record exists to indicate whether or not the gentleman had already checked the forecast for that day, but a few hours later, while Graham preached, committee members on the platform noticed a flutter in the audience as people began to fan themselves with programs and song sheets. Soon, Billy himself noticed the heat and asked ushers to raise the flaps on the west side of the tent to let in fresh air. The committee had its miracle, and when the sermon ended, the man who had challenged God to show his hand happily announced that the services would continue on a week-to-week basis.

Almost immediately, that decision proved to be a good one. Stuart Hamblen had made good on his promise to plug the meetings on his radio program and had attended several services, apparently enjoying his role as a prominent patron. The son of a Methodist minister and one of the original members of the Stars Christian Fellowship Group, Hamblen was also well-known as a backslider who drank, gambled, sang with dance bands and owned a stable of racehorses, all significant transgressions in Evangelical eyes. Graham regarded Hamblen as "a key man in the area with tremendous influence" and appreciated his encouragement but eventually concluded that the singer's public show of piety was an unacceptable pose and made a pointed public effort to bring him to repentance, declaring from the pulpit that "there is someone in this tent who is leading a double life. There is a person here tonight who is a phoney." The barely veiled accusation offended Hamblen, but it also hit the mark. When he realized that an extended campaign meant further attacks, his resistance crumbled. After a terrifyingly violent mountain storm ended a drunken hunting trip, taken in part to get away from his wife Suzy's insistent nagging that he "get saved," Hamblen showed up at Graham's apartment in the middle of the night. When Grady sleepily opened the door, Hamblen lurched in, fell on his knees, grabbed Billy around the legs, and boozily begged for help in straightening out his life. Billy, not at his best when awakened unexpectedly said, "Stand up, Stuart. You're drunk. You don't know what you're doing." Hamblen acknowledged his condition but insisted Graham help him, so they sat down at the kitchen table and Billy began to read the Bible to him and explain what he needed to do. Finally, at the climax of an extended and tearful prayer session, Hamblen declared, "Lord, you're hearing a new voice," and asked God to forgive his sins. At that moment, he later recounted, "I heard the heavenly switchboard click." Improbable as it seemed to skeptical acquaintances, Hamblen's conversion took. He told his radio audience of his experience, urged them not to smoke or drink the products advertised on his program (a move that cost him his job), promised to sell all but one of his racehorses ("I will keep El Lobo [who had won a fifty-thousand-dollar race at Santa Anita], but only for sentimental reasons. I will never race him again"), and invited his listeners to come to the big tent, where he would sing and give his testimony. A few days later, his overjoyed parents flew in from Texas to praise Billy Graham for his role in bringing their prodigal son home. When good friend John Wayne commented on the remarkable transformation, Hamblen told the Duke, "It is no secret what God can do." Wayne suggested he write a song about it, and the result, beginning with those same words, became a country-music standard.

The publicity boomlet detonated by Hamblen's conversion more than justified the decision to continue the revival, but it paled beside what followed. Apart from ads, newspaper coverage of the campaign had been limited to a brief account of the opening service and stories in the Saturday religion section. Then, one evening, quite without warning, a cluster of reporters and photographers met Graham when he arrived at the tent. Puzzled, even somewhat frightened, Billy asked a reporter what had happened. "You have just been kissed by William Randolph Hearst. Look here." He showed him a scrap of paper torn from a wire-service machine. "Here's what's happened. The boss has said, 'Puff Graham.'"

Accounts of Graham's career have typically portrayed the Hearst endorsement as a complete surprise, unsought and unexpected. The reality was less dramatic. All the Hearst papers had boosted YFC—Hearst had sent his "Puff YFC" telegram in 1946—but none had done more for the organization than the *Los Angeles Examiner*, the largest West Coast newspaper at the time. Its publisher, R. A. Carrington, though not particularly religious himself, admired the organization, gave its activities good coverage in the newspaper, did much of its printing free of charge, and arranged for the paper to sponsor various YFC projects. Most notably, Carrington had given YFC leader Roy McKeown a weekly column in the Sunday *Examiner* to report on YFC activities for a five-state region. A committee member for the revival, McKeown contacted Carrington to ask if the paper might give Graham and the meetings special attention. Carrington met with Graham, then telephoned "the chief" (Hearst), and the rest was publicity. Billy's YFC days had convinced him Hearst's endorsement could be valuable, but he feared the notorious old titan's strong opinions and unconventional lifestyle, particularly his widely publicized liaison with actress Marion Davies, might contaminate any stream of publicity. Filled with anxiety and indecision, Graham pulled Edwin Orr aside to ask for advice. Orr's response was simple: "Billy, if this is of God, he will make the press work for you for nothing." Graham accepted this counsel and became a truly national figure almost overnight. The next morning, the *Examiner* and the city's other Hearst paper, the *Herald*, gave him banner headlines, and twelve other papers in the Hearst chain also gave the campaign extensive coverage. Within days the Associated Press, the United Press, and the International News Service picked up the story, and *Time*, *Newsweek*, and *Life* followed soon afterward with major feature stories. Strangely, Graham never met his benefactor—"I never wrote him, I never thanked him, I never had any correspondence or telegrams or anything else. I suppose I could have met him, but I never thought he would see a person like me at that time"—and still professes not to know exactly why Hearst decided to back his ministry. An ardent anti-Communist, Hearst may have been attracted by Graham's stern warnings against the Red Menace. Another possibility is that he regarded Graham as a positive moral influence, a successor to Billy Sunday, whose career he had also boosted. The tycoon's son, William Randolph Hearst, Jr., may have provided the most likely explanation when he observed that quite simply his father was interested in whatever attracted the greatest number of people. He saw that Graham had an uncommonly accurate bead on the anxieties of a large segment of the American public and was more than happy to use him to sell papers.

As the revival stretched from three to eight weeks, Graham had to call on friends for sermon ideas and outlines. A missionary just back from Korea offered him his entire stock of sermons. At one point, he resorted to reading Jonathan Edwards's classic, "Sinners in the Hands of an Angry God," word for word except for a few minor emendations. Out of illustrations, he fell back on more copious use of Scripture, a technique he felt improved his sermons. Whether it was his preaching or the publicity or, as all participants felt, the prodding of God's Spirit, the crowds grew so large that a tent expanded to seat 9,000 (with the seats scrunched together) was sometimes full hours before the service started, forcing thousands of latecomers to listen from the periphery and creating such a traffic problem that police eventually closed off a street rather than try to keep it clear.

The conversion of Olympic miler and war hero Louis Zamperini and gangland wiretapper Jim Vaus stimulated further publicity. Zamperini, who created a minor sensation at the 1936 Berlin Olympics when he pulled down a Nazi flag from Hitler's Reichstag, had spent forty-six days bobbing about on a raft in the Pacific, followed by a harrowing stay in a Japanese POW camp. When the war ended, he never managed to put his life back together and had begun to drink heavily. Dragged to the revival by his wife, Zamperini saw Graham more "as an athlete than as a man of God" and reached out in desperation for the new life he offered. Vaus's conversion rivaled Hamblen's for its publicity value. Fundamentalist religion was hardly alien to Jim Vaus. Before being expelled, he had studied for the ministry at the Bible Institute of Los Angeles, where his father was a professor, and he spent a year at Wheaton, where he got into trouble for wiretapping a girls' dormitory. Deciding he had misread his call, Vaus turned to crime, which led to a term in state prison for armed robbery. After release, he served in the military and, despite a court-martial sentence for misappropriation of government property, earned an honorable discharge, but soon turned again to crime and became an assistant to the notorious West Coast crime czar, Mickey Cohen. Vaus knew Stuart Hamblen, and when he read of the singer's return to God, he decided to attend Graham's revival. He insisted he went largely because he had nothing better to do. Once inside, however, he found himself enfolded in the familiar environment in which he had been reared, and he struggled only briefly before stepping forward to accept Billy Graham's invitation.

Predictably, the reclamation of an authentic gangster drew the media's attention, but the real publicity bonanza came when Vaus arranged a late-night meeting between Graham and Mickey Cohen at the mobster's home. Cohen had dismissed his servants and was in the house alone. Neither man's experience had furnished him with a clear sense of protocol for dealing with the other, but both were anxious to please. To prove he was not wicked as the preacher might have heard, Cohen talked of the charitable causes he supported and, after searching the bookshelves and tabletops in several rooms, triumphantly produced a Bible he had received in appreciation for his fund-raising efforts on behalf of the new state of Israel. Graham was careful not to offend the gangster, but he gingerly presented an outline of the gospel Jim Vaus had embraced. Cohen gave no sign he was "almost persuaded," but to demonstrate his goodwill, he took the evangelist back to his bedroom, showed him his huge closets full of expensive suits, and gave him a necktie as a souvenir of the visit. As they parted, he told Graham a bit ruefully, "I've given Jim everything he ever wanted, but now he leaves me and he's going with you." Then, according to Vaus, he turned to his former henchman and said, "Jim, if the whole world turns against you for the decision you made, remember that there's one little Jew who thinks the world of you for that decision and for the guts you've had to stand up for it." The visit was supposed to have been secret, but the next day's headlines trumpeted the nocturnal meeting between the gangster and the preacher. Graham was chagrined that the story had leaked, but Cohen did not complain—an insatiable publicity seeker, he may well have leaked the story himself—and the revival received another round of front-page coverage.

As the campaign entered its "Sixth Great Sin-Smashing Week," such notables as Gene Autry and Jane Russell began to attend, and Cecil B. De Mille, the father of cinematic biblical epics, offered Graham a screen test. The wife of the head of Paramount Studios hosted a ladies luncheon for him at the Wilshire Country Club. Louella Parsons interviewed him at a posh Sunset Strip restaurant and wrote a gushing column about the appeal of "this really naive, humble man." The AP called the revival "one of the greatest the city ever has witnessed," *Life* pronounced it "the biggest revival in Los Angeles since the death of Aimee Semple McPherson," and *Time* declared that "no one since Billy Sunday" had wielded "the revival sickle" with such success as "this thirty-one-year-old, blond, trumpet-lunged North Carolinian." Back in North Carolina, Morrow Graham wanted desperately to accept Billy's invitation to join him at the scene of his triumph, but "Mr. [Frank] Graham never enjoyed trips—he just didn't like to travel—and I wouldn't go without him." By the time the revival ended on November 20, a day on which a large contingent of prostitutes and skid-row derelicts showed up to ask someone to pray for them, aggregate attendance for the eight weeks approached 350,000, with inquirers numbering approximately 3,000. Nearly seven hundred churches, almost three times more than at the beginning, were lending at least some measure of support. Charles Fuller and another famed radio preacher, "Fighting Bob" Shuler (Jack Shuler's father), had thrown their full weight behind Graham, and a number of preachers who had been cool toward the campaign at the beginning came around "to ask forgiveness for a few things they had said about evangelism, Youth for Christ, and some of the 'hot-rodders' in wide ties.'" Suddenly, whatever Billy Graham said on any subject was likely to find its way into the newspapers, a phenomenon that justifiably stirred his anxiety. Shortly after the revival began to boom, Graham called Armin Gesswein in Chicago to say, "You better get back out here real fast, because something has broken out that is way beyond me." In the months that followed, he had little time to reflect on just what it was that had happened or his capacity to handle it. On the train back to Minneapolis, conductors and passengers treated him like a hero, reporters crowded on board to press their inquiries, and a band of Northwestern colleagues welcomed him home in the middle of the night. The next day, while reporting on the campaign to a Northwestern audience, he faltered, then sat down without finishing, overcome by the magnitude of the turn his life had taken.

Part 3

"From Vict'ry Unto Vict'ry" (1950–1960)

8

Evangelism Incorporated

Billy Graham opened the second half of the century with a little-heralded campaign in Boston. The leaders of the Evangelistic Association of New England, who had watched Billy Sunday's 1917 crusade spawn over fifty new churches, hoped Graham might kindle similar fire in a region whose religious life was now shaped by a Roman Catholic majority and a cultural elite comprised largely of Unitarians, Congregationalists, and Episcopalians. Actual expectations, however, were modest. After a delegation scouted Graham's 1949 Baltimore campaign, the association decided to sponsor only one service, on New Year's Eve. They felt Graham's style was too intense to appeal to New Englanders, and his reputation insufficient to justify a greater commitment. Allan Emery, Jr., whose father had brought Billy Sunday to Boston, served as general chairman for the service and helped persuade his pastor, Harold John Ockenga, to invite the young evangelist for a ten-day continuation effort at the venerable Park Street Church, New England's most prestigious Evangelical congregation. Ockenga, a scholarly man and probably the single most influential figure in Evangelical circles at the time, had refused a YFC request to have Graham hold a rally in 1947, primarily because he knew nothing about him and was not inclined to throw his prestige behind an untested product, particularly a southern Bible school preacher with a known penchant for loud suits and hand-painted ties. In the interim, however, he had learned more about Graham and figured that at worst, he could do no real harm in ten days.

Helped by publicity from the recent Los Angeles revival, the sparsely advertised New Year's Eve service at Mechanics Hall drew more than 6,000 people, a surprise that led Ockenga to reserve the auditorium and announce a service for the next afternoon. That impromptu and (apart from announcements in churches the next morning) unpublicized gathering packed the building again. The scheduled evening service a few hours later filled the Park Street sanctuary and two auxiliary rooms and left more than 2,000 would-be worshipers frustrated because they could not get in. This unexpected response unnerved Graham. Though he believed God had been at work in Los Angeles, he also knew that months of preparation, thousands of dollars spent on promotion, and a windfall of publicity had contributed to that campaign's success. But in Boston, with little preparation or publicity, the response was similar. This both exhilarated and terrified him. As soon as the service ended, he called Emery and Ockenga into a room and asked them to pray "that the Lord will keep reminding me of the fact that this is all of grace and to Him is all the glory, because I realize if I take the smallest credit for anything that has happened so far, that my lips will turn to clay." Emery was astonished: "Instead of praying for the various problems we might foresee, such as finances, follow-up, converts, or anything else, here, after this unexpected triumph, Billy's concern was that the Lord keep his hand on him. He also wanted us to [help] him continue moment to moment to give God the glory. This is something we had never seen before. I will never forget it, because as I look back and as I continue to see his ministry, I see that same ingredient, that same principle at work in his life: 'To Him is all the glory.' He has wanted to stand behind, to hide, as it were, so there wouldn't be any temptation for him to take credit for what he sincerely believes and knows to be the work of God himself." If what followed fell short of the Great Awakening stirred by Jonathan Edwards and George Whitefield, it did cause dry bones to rattle in normally sedate New England. The announced run of nine days stretched to eighteen, and under pressure from crowds that consistently exceeded the capacity of every venue, the revival itself became itinerant, moving, as booking schedules permitted, from Park Street Church to Mechanics Hall, to the opera house, to Symphony Hall, back to Mechanics Hall, and finally to Boston Garden for a climactic service that attracted more than 25,000, of whom 10,000 were turned away. The crowds themselves drew attention, not only for their size, but also for their practice of singing hymns as they walked along the streets or rode home on subways and buses after the meetings. One lifelong New Englander remembered that "there was just a spirit of unanimity, joy, and happiness that I've never seen since."

That Graham created a sensation in Los Angeles probably impressed few Bostonians, but the press could not afford to ignore stories in *Time* and *Life* and on the major wire services. Still, a precampaign press conference at the Hotel Bellevue drew few of the city's top reporters. Graham opened the session in disarming fashion by good-naturedly chiding his sponsors for referring to him as "Doctor," noting that the title was honorary, not earned, but the questioning was rather perfunctory until a reporter asked Graham how much money he expected to garner from the effort. The evangelist explained that the Northwestern Schools paid him $8,500 a year (he had finally started accepting a salary), that he would receive no income from the crusade, and that a committee from the Park Street Church would release a full, audited financial statement when the meetings ended. The reporter kept pressing Graham to admit he expected to get rich from his campaigns. Seldom has an evangelist been armed with a better reply to this ubiquitous question. Just before the press conference began, a bellman handed Graham a telegram, which he read and stuck in his pocket without comment or discernible reaction. "I can still see him," Allan Emery recalled. "He took out that crumpled telegram and said, 'Sir, if I were interested in making money, I would take advantage of something like this.'" The telegram, according to Emery, offered Graham a substantial sum—"something like $250,000"—to star in two Hollywood films. As the reporters passed it around, judging both it and Billy Graham to be authentic, their attitude visibly changed. "From then on," Emery said, "we got nothing but the top reporters, and we got front-page coverage on every single one of the five dailies."

Whatever the precipitant, the coverage was remarkable. Graham was the hottest thing around in the dead of a typical New England winter, and newspapers outdid themselves to see who could depict him and his crusade in the most vivid terms. Describing him as a "swashbuckling southerner" whose "chic gray suit with draped lapels and bright blue and orange tie" made him look "as if he belonged in the star's dressing room of a musical comedy rather than in a pulpit," they gave every service extensive space, in editorials and cartoons as well as news stories, and frequently printed his words in bold type, a journalistic equivalent to a red-letter New Testament. In return he rewarded them with some of the most colorful preaching of his career—so colorful, in fact, that although he began to disown some of his statements within a year or two, he had not completely lived them down four decades later.

Railing against communism as "a fanatic religion supernaturally empowered by the devil to counteract Christianity," he predicted the "imminent deification of Joseph Stalin" in the Soviet Union, with "his birthday celebrated as we do Christ's." While being careful not to set precise dates, he predicted Christ would return within ten to fifteen years and offered a memorable image of the tumult the rapture would cause: "Wait till those gravestones start popping like popcorn in a popper. Oh boy! Won't it be wonderful when those gravestones start popping?" Graham could look forward to the rapture with such joyful anticipation because he had no doubt he would be caught up with Jesus in the clouds to flourish during the millennium, and would have no reason to shudder when, at the Last Judgment, God gives the awesome command, "Start up the projector!" Because he had accepted God's gracious gift of salvation, he felt certain he would spend eternity in heaven, which he regarded as a place "as real as Los Angeles, London, Algiers, or Boston." He informed his Boston audience that heaven is "sixteen-hundred miles long, sixteen-hundred miles wide, and sixteen-hundred miles high ... as much as if you put Great Britain, Ireland, France, Spain, Italy, Austria, Germany, and half of Russia in one place. That is how big the New Jerusalem is going to be. Boy, I can't wait until I get up there and look around." His view of how the redeemed would spend eternity was equally concrete: "We are going to sit around the fireplace and have parties and the angels will wait on us and we'll drive down the golden streets in a yellow Cadillac convertible." Food for these parties would be plucked from "trees bearing a different kind of fruit every month," and Graham himself might provide entertainment and organize the recreation since he "hoped to be able to sing, play the trombone and violin, and play football and baseball as well as the best." He also depicted hell in vivid terms, asserting that its denizens would meet regularly to hold prayer meetings, begging for mercy and remembering the times they had passed up the chance to respond to the invitation at an evangelistic meeting.

Graham also amazed his Boston audiences with his use of a technique George Whitefield had used to good effect in these same environs two hundred years earlier, that of dramatizing biblical stories by slangily updating the lines and acting out all the parts. Appearing in the title role of "The Feast of Belshazzar," a favorite sermon he had honed and polished on the YFC circuit, he preened and strutted and boasted that "I'm going to put on a party that will be the biggest shindig in Babylon." Slipping deftly into the role of narrator, he observed that Belshazzar "was one of those smart fellows who think they can do as they please and forget all about God. But, brother, that's where he was wrong. That's where everyone is wrong who thinks he can get away with any kind of living. It makes no difference if you are the king of Babylon or the President, or anybody important. You are no exception to the law of God. He don't care how big your name is or whether you came over on the *Mayflower*." Then, introducing Daniel, who interpreted "the handwriting on the wall" that foreshadowed Belshazzar's imminent assassination, Graham explained that "Daniel was a pal of the boss—the King of the Medes and Persians. Some jealous guys were out to get him, so they trained their spyglass on him one morning when he was praying and had his Venetian blinds up. They tattled to the King. The King was on the spot, so he said to his lawyers, 'Find me a couple of loopholes so I can spring my pal, Dan.' They just couldn't find a loophole and the King had to send Dan to the lions." Matching actions to words, he described what happened next: "Old Daniel walks in. He's not afraid. He looks the first big cat in the eye and kicks him and says, 'Move over there, Leo. I want me a nice fat lion with a soft belly for a pillow, so I can get a good night's rest.... "In another sermon he recreated the plight of the Prodigal Son, tossing imaginary slop to invisible hogs with such flair that "hundreds of persons who had never fed a hog nor seen one fed felt sure that Billy Graham must have learned firsthand how that was done." Then he pranced around like an uppity pig to make the point that "even if you gave a pig a bath, gave it a Toni, and sprinkled it with Chanel No. 5, it would still, like an unregenerate sinner, revert to the mud puddle as soon as you let it loose."

Graham's theatrics captivated some observers. After hearing him deliver several such sermons, one reporter wrote admiringly of the evangelist's dramatic range: "He prowls like a panther across the rostrum.... [H]e becomes a haughty and sneering Roman, his head flies back arrogantly and his voice is harsh and gruff. He becomes a penitent sinner; his head bows, his eyes roll up in supplication, his voice cracks and quavers. He becomes an avenging angel; his arms rise high above his head and his long fingers snap out like talons. His voice deepens and rolls sonorously—the voice of doom. So perfect are the portrayals that his audience sits tense and fascinated as his sermons take on a vividness, a reality hard to describe." Others admitted the tension but had little difficulty describing the reality. Ruth Graham, for one, thought it an unseemly display and did not hesitate to let him know it. "As an actor," she volunteered, "I'm afraid he is pretty much a ham. When he starts that kind of acting sermon, I usually start to squirm. If I'm anywhere in sight, he is sure to see me and know what's the matter." Her counsel to him was simple and direct: "Bill, Jesus didn't act out the Gospel. He just preached it. I think that's all He has called you to do!"

Reporters loved Ruth's candor on this and other matters, such as her husband's penchant for bright clothes—"We have a domestic compromise," she revealed. "I buy my hats. He buys his ties"—and gave her ample opportunity to fashion responses she would use again and again over the years as their counterparts all over the world asked her what it was like to be the wife of a famous evangelist. She conceded that "the kids get so they don't know what their daddy looks like" but contended that having her parents live just across the street made her job easier and allowed her to slip away to spend a few days with her husband during most of his meetings. People often asked, she acknowledged, how she and the wives of Graham's associates could stand to have their husbands away from home for so long. Her answer was a blend of piety and pragmatic realism: "We know how important their work is. Then, too, we are spared the monotony of ordinary married life.... When we do have a chance to talk together, there are so many things we want to say. Every conversation is important. It's more than news about the office or what happened at the grocery store, so I always get a lift in talking with Bill." She and Billie Barrows, both quite lovely women still in their twenties, also pointed out that good conversation was not the only pleasure provided by reunions with their husbands. "Every time we get together," they agreed, "It's like another honeymoon," though Ruth revealed that the hectic pace of crusades so tired Billy that he typically slept through most of his first few days at home following a campaign. "It's like being married to Rip Van Winkle," she said, but she reiterated her now-standard declaration that "I'd rather have Bill part-time than anybody else full-time."

Graham professed to feel resistance to his efforts: "There are thousands in Boston who wish his revival would hurry and get over.... They don't want a revival. They don't want people to be saved. They hate the gospel." But if such animosity existed, it was either suppressed or voiced only in private; among the five daily newspapers, not one published a negative article about either Graham or his campaign. The *Globe* ventured that he was "perhaps the lowest-paid evangelist of modern times," and a *Herald-Traveler* editor wrote that "Graham is not mercenary. He takes the stigma of money off evangelism.... He should have the support of every Christian church in America." As the campaign continued, the papers treated him not only as an evangelist but as the public figure he was rapidly becoming, complete with appropriate myths. In a special souvenir edition, the *Boston Post* reported he had played professional baseball in North Carolina and was aiming for diamond greatness before entering the ministry. Reporters pressed for his opinion on such topics as the death penalty and received the cautious responses that would come to characterize his public style: "I don't say [the defendant in a controversial mercy-killing case] deserves death, but if we let this pass, who is to say who is to die and who is to live?" Occasionally, he ventured further, then stepped back quickly to avoid giving offense. Asked his views on foreign aid, he asserted that revival would do more than the Marshall Plan to combat evil and warned that "we are going to spend ourselves into a depression. We can't keep on taking care of the whole world." Then, when he noticed that every reporter present was writing down what he had said, he became flustered and added with a sheepish grin, "But don't anybody tell Mr. Truman I said so." As a measure of his growing stature, he was invited to offer prayer at a session of the Massachusetts House of Representatives, where a rising young legislator, Thomas "Tip" O'Neill, introduced him to the assembly.

Graham had not expected all this success and attention, and when the overflow turnout at the Boston Garden indicated the revival still had plenty of fire left in it, he was, like the Apostle Peter on the Mount of Transfiguration, reluctant to come down. Prior commitments and increasing difficulty in hiring suitable auditoriums led him to leave the field temporarily, but not before announcing he would return as soon as possible in the spring. On the train west, he seriously considered turning back but did not. Among the hundreds, perhaps thousands, of opportunities chosen or waived during his long career, Graham always looked back on the decision to end the Boston campaign as one of two or three times when he "possibly disobeyed the voice of God" by allowing the demands of his schedule to overpower the inclination of his heart.

The next major campaign, a three-week stint in Columbia, South Carolina, marked a further stage in the growth and maturation of Graham's revival machine. At his suggestion, the sponsoring Layman's Evangelistic Club hired Willis Haymaker, who had done advance work for Gipsy Smith and Bob Jones senior and junior to organize prayer groups, encourage cooperation across denominational lines, and arrange for scores of small gatherings at which Billy and his associates could appear before and during the crusade. Haymaker also installed Billy Sunday's delegation system, in which cooperating churches reserve large blocks of tickets for specific nights, a technique that assured good attendance at every service. The veteran advance man proved so effective that Graham persuaded him to join the team as his chief crusade organizer, a position he held until his retirement in 1979. It was Haymaker who suggested using *crusade*, instead of the more modest *campaign*, a change first implemented at the Columbia meeting. Graham also added Tedd Smith, a young classical pianist just out of the Royal Conservatory of Music at Toronto. The basic "platform team" formed at this 1951 crusade—Graham, Barrows, Shea, Grady Wilson, and Smith—was still intact thirty-six years later when the evangelist returned for his second Columbia crusade in the spring of 1987. More significant than the size and enthusiasm of its crowds—more than 40,000 attended the closing service at the University of South Carolina stadium—the Columbia crusade enabled Graham to forge stronger bonds with the political and cultural establishment. Governor Strom Thurmond underscored his personal endorsement of the crusade with a notable disdain for the ostensible barrier between Church and State. He brought prominent guests to services and insisted that Billy and Grady stay in the governor's mansion. He invited the evangelist to address the state's general assembly, arranged for him to speak at school assemblies, and declared the closing day of the crusade South Carolina Revival Rally Day. Then, when the crusade ended, he provided Graham and his team with a police escort for a quickly arranged two-week preaching tour of the state that included a triumphant return to Bob Jones University, where Bob Jones, Jr., introduced him to a packed house and those who could not get in heard his sermon about Belshazzar broadcast live over the campus radio station, WMUU (an acronym for World's Most Unusual University).

The most celebrated of Governor Thurmond's "pew packers" was Henry R. Luce, publisher of *Time* and *Life*. Both magazines had already run stories about Graham, but Luce himself had not paid much attention until financier and statesman Bernard Baruch, who had a home in South Carolina, showed him a Columbia newspaper's account of the young evangelist's speech to the general assembly. Luce, himself the son of missionaries, was interested in the possibility of religious revival and was also impressed by Graham's emphasis on Russia's possession of the atomic bomb. Since he and his wife, Clare, were vacationing in Charleston, he went to Columbia to attend the crusade and spent long hours with Billy at the executive mansion, also as Governor Thurmond's guest. The following week *Time* carried a substantial article that if not entirely complimentary—it pointed out that the 7,000 decisions registered in Graham's crusade seemed meager compared to the 25,000 souls harvested in Columbia by Billy Sunday in 1923 and noted that 80 percent of the inquirers were already church members—still enhanced Graham's position as a man worth watching.

Immediately after the South Carolina tour, Graham made good on his promise to return to New England. After a brief stand in the Boston Garden, he launched a sixteen-city tour, accompanied this time by a press corps shepherded by Gerald Beavan, who had taken leave from Northwestern to help with media relations and publicity. On the first trip, Grady Wilson had pecked out press releases in his hotel room, and Robert Van Kampen, who had come from Illinois to help out, had done his best to answer the mail and filter requests for interviews. As executive secretary and public relations director, Beavan now took on both of these men's roles, controlling access to Graham and serving as an almost constant companion. When Graham fell ill in Hartford for several days (Jack Wyrtzen drove up from New York to fill in for him), Beavan stayed at his bedside and read to him from Bishop Fulton Sheen's *Peace of Soul* and Rabbi Joshua Loth Liebman's *Peace of Mind*. From that experience, Graham began to consider writing a book on the same theme. Published in 1953, it bore the title *Peace with God*.

If Strom Thurmond's political patronage boosted Graham's career, his next brush with secular power nearly undid him. Billy had an uncommon determination to stand out from the herd. In part, this impulse involved nothing more complicated than a desire to be admired, a need sufficiently well distributed as to require little explication. Without question, Billy Graham wanted to be somebody—somebody important, somebody famous, somebody who stood in the circle of other somebodies. In part he fastened himself to the Fundamentalist luminaries who visited Florida Bible Institute, curried the favor of rich Evangelicals like R. G. LeTourneau and British weapons manufacturer Alfred Owen, delighted in winning the souls of pop stars and athletes and gangsters, and reveled in the attention paid him by William Randolph Hearst and Henry Luce because they gratified that portion of his ego that conversion and baptism and agonizing prayers of surrender would never fully regenerate or subdue. But to dismiss his fascination with celebrity, influence, and power as nothing more than garden-variety social climbing is to misunderstand Billy Graham quite seriously, for even more consuming than his desire to find favor with his fellows was his passion to be approved by the Ultimate Somebody: Almighty God. Nothing impelled Graham more powerfully than the hope he expressed while contemplating the northern lights at Maranatha: "to do something great for the Lord." From the earliest stages of his ministry, he understood intuitively that his message would reach more people, appear more legitimate, and have a greater impact if he were viewed as an important man whose friendship and opinion and counsel mattered to people of property, power, and prestige. He also understood that his lower-order ambitions could easily overwhelm and corrupt his higher desires. Awareness of this vulnerability would haunt him throughout his career as he wrestled to conquer his humanity.

By 1950 Graham had experienced notable popular acclaim, won respect in Evangelical circles, and shown that like Finney and Moody and Sunday, he would have no trouble financing his ministry. The key realm he had yet to penetrate was politics, and since much of his preaching featured political themes, he sought to ingratiate himself with political figures with an eagerness that seemed almost desperate. Strom Thurmond's blessing was his first breakthrough, but it was not his first effort. Early in 1949, in what seems to have been a clear case of overreaching, he wrote President Truman to request a brief visit with him. When the President's secretary reported that Mr. Truman's schedule was too packed to permit an appointment, Graham wrote that he understood but asked the secretary to let the President know that "over 1,100 students at these Northwestern Schools are praying daily that God will give him wisdom and guidance" and that "we believe our President to be a man of God. We believe him to be God's choice for this great office." While in Boston he told a reporter that his whole ambition was "to get President Truman's ear for thirty minutes, to get a little help" in spreading the gospel, and he worked hard to satisfy that ambition. He sent a telegram urging the President to declare a national day of repentance and prayer as a step toward lasting peace. After Communist forces invaded South Korea a few weeks later, he sent another wire with the following bit of encouragement and foreign-policy advice: "MILLIONS OF CHRISTIANS PRAYING GOD GIVE YOU WISDOM IN THIS CRISIS. STRONGLY URGE SHOWDOWN WITH COMMUNISM NOW MORE CHRISTIANS IN SOUTHERN KOREA PER CAPITA THAN IN ANY PART OF THE WORLD WE CONNOT LET THEM DOWN. EVANGELIST BILLY GRAHAM."

Perhaps feeling that his telegrams had endeared him to Truman, he renewed his request for a personal visit. The President resisted, but with the assistance of Massachusetts congressman John McCormack, Graham finally obtained an appointment for July 14, 1950. When he managed to get the invitation widened to include Barrows, Beavan, and Grady Wilson, the four of them got so excited, Grady recalls, that "we were jumping up and down in our hotel room." As they puzzled over how to make a good impression on Truman, Grady remembered that newspapers often pictured Truman wearing a Hawaiian sport shirt and white buck shoes at his Key West retreat and suggested they meet the chief executive in bucks of their own. Graham, who already had a pair of the shoes, loved the idea and dispatched Grady to a Florsheim store to purchase three more pairs for his friends. Thus shod, and attired in matching ice cream suits and colorful hand-painted ties that made them look like hospital orderlies at the racetrack, they readied themselves for a visit with the most powerful leader in the non-Communist world. The meeting was scheduled for noon, and Truman's appointments secretary recommended they arrive a few minutes early. That suggestion was hardly needed. Often nervous and always punctual, Billy had broken his watch and, according to Barrows, pestered his friends for the time "on an average of twice a minute." When the four awestruck men finally entered the Oval Office, Truman received them warmly, listening courteously to Graham's call for a national day of prayer and sharing a few observations about the possibility that some kind of police action might be needed to resist communism in Korea. As their scheduled thirty minutes drew to a close, Graham asked the President if they might "have a word of prayer." The chief executive, not famous for piety, said, "I don't suppose it could do any harm." Billy put his arm around Truman and began to pray, Cliff chimed in with "Do it, Lord" and several fervent "Amens," and Grady peeked to find the President taking in the scene with what appeared to be bemused detachment.

As the group left the President's office, a clutch of reporters descended on them, and Graham, unaware he was violating protocol, freely related what Truman had said and acknowledged they had prayed together. He balked when photographers asked him to re-create the pose they had struck, explaining he thought it improper to simulate prayer, but not wanting to disappoint them, he said, "On second thought, my team and I were going to go out on the White House lawn and just give God thanks for this privilege of visiting with the President of the United States. I suppose you could take a picture of that." The next morning, newspapers all over America ran a photograph of the young innocents, dazzling in their white raiment and poised on one knee like a southern gospel quartet. With typical generosity, Billy described the President as "very gracious, very humble, very sweet," but the stories and photographs irritated Truman mightily. Washington columnist Drew Pearson reported that the evangelist was persona non grata at the White House, but Graham seemed oblivious to his gaffe. When he sent a thank-you note a few days later, he requested an autographed picture, reiterated his call for a day of repentance and prayer, and let the President know that his was a voice worth hearing. "It is my privilege," he observed, "to speak to from five to twenty thousand people a night in each and every section in America. I believe I talk to more people face-to-face than any living man. I know something of the mood, thinking, and trends in American thought." Having established his credentials, he repeated his hard-line position on foreign policy, urging Truman to order "total mobilization to meet the Communist threat, at the same time urging the British commonwealth of nations to do the same. The American people are not concerned with how much it costs the taxpayer if they can be assured of military security." Graham got the photograph he requested but little else. A few months later, the President curtly declined a request to send a telegram in support of a Rose Bowl rally at which Billy was the headliner, and not until long after he left office did Truman come to regard his erstwhile prayer partner as much more than a publicity-grubbing God huckster. Graham has retold the story of this abortive visit so frequently, often to justify his refusal to reveal the substance of his conversations with other world leaders, that the embarrassment it caused him obviously ran deep. The best analysis, however, came from Grady Wilson who, chuckling and shaking his head as he recalled the incident, offered the uncomplicated but irrefutable observation: "We were so naive."

Naivete notwithstanding, Billy Graham had made astonishing strides in less than twelve months, emerging from relative obscurity to become the best-known evangelist of his generation. He scored resounding triumphs in settings as strikingly different as Los Angeles, New England, and Bible-belted South Carolina. And he assembled a team of colleagues who, when it came to evangelistic campaigns, not only knew exactly what they wanted to do and how to do it but were rapidly gaining the confidence to insist it be done their way. Both the Boston and Columbia crusades had been hampered and ultimately cut short in full flower by the lack of suitable auditoriums. For the Portland, Oregon, crusade, which began in July 1950, Graham persuaded the sponsoring committee, led by an old friend from Youth for Christ, to construct a 12,000 seat wood-and-aluminum tabernacle the size of a football field, but even this proved inadequate. The opening service drew a standing-room-only crowd of well over 20,000, the first week's attendance exceeded 100,000, and an estimated 250,000 tried to get in during the second week. At times the enthusiasm for the young preacher resembled that associated with movie stars. When approximately 30,000 women gathered for a "Ladies Only" meeting one hot August morning, they tore down traffic barriers, climbed on automobiles, and generally behaved so boisterously that team members had to call police to keep the dear sisters from wrecking the tabernacle. By the time the crusade ended its six-week run, the aggregate attendance exceeded a half million, even by conservative estimates.

Successful as it was, the Portland crusade's status as a landmark in Graham's ministry owes less to what occurred inside the tabernacle than to external developments that happened to fall into place during that period. The first involved Graham's entry into major-league religious broadcasting. As he contemplated his remarkable success and increasing fame, he naturally considered various means of expanding and extending his ministry. The most obvious route seemed to be through radio or, possibly, the fledgling medium of television. A few months before the second New England tour, when spring was still too raw to attract many visitors to the New Jersey shore, Dr. Theodore Eisner, pastor of an interdenominational Evangelical church in Philadelphia and president of the National Religious Broadcasters (NRB), followed what he regarded as an "impression" from God and drove down to Ocean City to spend the night in a cabin he and his son-in-law had rented. The next morning, when he entered a diner in nearby Somers Point, he heard cries of "Doc! Doc!" coming from a booth in the back where Billy Graham and Cliff Barrows, who were attending a conference in the area, were having breakfast. "We were just talking about you," Billy said. "We want to do something on radio or television, and we don't know how to do it. We need help."

As president of NRB, founded by the National Association of Evangelicals to protect and promote Evangelical programs, Eisner understood religious broadcasting well and was able to help them sharpen their focus. He also promised to tell his son-in-law, Fred Dienert, an advertising and public relations man, of their interest in developing a program.

Dienert and his partner, Walter Bennett, specialized in religious accounts and leapt at the chance to work with Graham, but they soon discovered that Eisner had not handed them a neatly wrapped gift. Throughout his ministry, Graham's pattern would be to pursue a new idea or opportunity with great enthusiasm, perhaps committing substantial money and personnel to its exploration and execution. Then, as he reflected on the time and expense and effort it would require and contemplated visions of failure and embarrassment, he would either retreat, convinced the idea could not possibly succeed, or agree to continue only after assuring himself and others that he would bail out at the first sign of trouble. By the time Dienert and Bennett approached him a few days after the conversation with Eisner, he had already cooled on the whole idea. When they went to Montreat soon afterward with word that the ABC network would offer him a prime Sunday-afternoon slot, Graham remained adamant. Though they assured him the program could originate from any city where his travels took him, he reckoned the demands of a weekly program to be excessive and the cost—$92,000 for thirteen weeks—astronomical.

The two agents, certain Graham would change his mind, waited for his call, but none came. At first they told themselves he was contacting wealthy friends, trying to raise money for the venture. Finally, with no invitation or advance notice, they flew to Portland to press him for a decision. Graham never liked to transact business during a crusade, and for several days, he refused even to see them. Finally, as they prepared to return to the East Coast, he called them to his hotel room. Dienert recalled that "the room was very unpretentious—a little room with one table and one chair and a single bed. Billy had on a baseball cap and a pair of green pajamas and was walking back and forth, back and forth. He told us some friends had indicated they would do something to help, but nothing definite. Frankly, I think he might have been a little discouraged. We explained to him that if he could raise just $25,000, that would pay for at least three weeks, and contributions from listeners should take care of it after that. Then he said, 'Guys, let's pray.' I have never been in a prayer meeting like that in my life, and I never expect to be in another one like it. You could feel the power of God in that room. Walter got down on one side of the bed, and I got down on the other. Billy knelt at the one chair and started to pray. I can't tell you all that was in the prayer, but I know this: The pipeline was open. I knew he was talking to the Lord, and I knew the Lord was listening. He said, 'Lord, I've got this little house in Montreat. I'll be glad to put a mortgage on it. I'll do whatever you want me to do. You know my heart. We don't have the money, but I would like to do it.' It was a great prayer, a really terrific prayer! Then Billy said, 'Lord, I want to put out a fleece. I want $25,000 by midnight.' Well, I've heard a lot of prayers, but I never heard anybody proposition God like that: $25,000 tonight or we don't go! On the way out of the room, I said, 'Billy, how about giving the little people a chance?' And he said, 'I'll do it tonight.' Well, he was drawing 20,000 a night in Portland, so we figured if he got just a dollar apiece, that would be $20,000 and, frankly, if you ask God for $25,000 and he gives you $20,000, that's pretty close."

At the service that evening, Graham's unwillingness to push the issue seemed almost perverse. He made no mention of a radio program at the time of the offering. When he finally did speak of it, he rested content with noting that "a couple of men are here to see us about going on radio. The time is available; we can let the tobacco people have it, or we can take it for God. If you want to have a part in this, I'll be in the little room by the choir area after the service tonight." Dienert sank in his seat, certain "the whole thing was shot." To make matters worse, a guest preacher sharing the service that evening not only spoke too long but, when Graham gave the invitation, got up again and confessed his own shortcomings at length. By the time he finished, the entire crowd had stood for twenty-five minutes. Dienert thought to himself, "By Golly, can't somebody make it easier? Who, after standing this long, is going to line up and give Billy another gift?"

What followed became one of the favorite stories in the Graham hagiography. People did indeed line up, dropping checks, bills, pledges, even a few coins into a shoe box held to receive their offerings. When the money was counted, Billy had $23,500 in cash and pledges for the program. Dienert and Bennett were ecstatic until Graham reminded them, "I didn't ask for $23,500. I asked for $25,000." To accept this as a sign from God, he cautioned, might be to fall into a Satanic trap. For the same reason, he refused Bennett's offer to have the agency make up the difference. As the two befuddled and crestfallen admen sought consolation in the company of Barrows and several other friends at Louie's-on-the-Alley, a little seafood restaurant favored by the team, Graham and Grady Wilson returned to the Multnomah Hotel, where the desk clerk greeted them with two envelopes and several telephone messages. The two letters were from wealthy Texas businessmen Bill Mead and Howard Butt, Jr., both of whom were avid believers in evangelism—Butt, a supermarket magnate known as God's Groceryman, had himself been a leading figure in the Southern Baptist Youth Revival movement of the 1940s. Accounts of the number and distribution of checks and pledges vary, but all agree that contributions from Mead and Butt were crucial and that these last-minute gifts brought the total to *exactly* $25,000. To Graham, not unreasonably, it seemed a clear sign God was calling him to a radio ministry.

The shoe box full of money posed a problem. Graham learned that if he deposited it in his own name, even temporarily, he would be liable for personal income taxes, and contributors could not claim their gifts as deductions. Probably because they feared a network radio program could easily become a financial albatross, Northwestern's board felt any such venture should be independent of the schools. Graham called George Wilson for advice, and Wilson offered a simple solution: "You need a little nonprofit organization, with you and your wife and myself on the board, and you can control it." Graham replied, "Well, get some papers together and come on out here." Anticipating such a need, Wilson had collected sample incorporation documents from several nonprofit organizations: "So I dictated the articles and bylaws, and took it to a lawyer and had him put in a few commas and *whereases*. One thing I didn't want changed was Article 1: 'To spread the gospel by any and all means.' Knowing Billy, I knew he wasn't going to stick just to crusades. So that covered it, and still does: 'any and all means.'" Armed with the articles of incorporation, Wilson flew to Portland where he joined Cliff Barrows, Grady Wilson, and Billy and Ruth Graham as the charter members of the Billy Graham Evangelistic Association (BGEA), a name reportedly chosen over Graham's strenuous objections. On his return to Minneapolis, George Wilson leased a one-room office near the Northwestern Schools, hired a secretary, and began thirty-six years of day-to-day control of the organization.

Graham's film ministry began in Portland as well. A year earlier in Los Angeles, a young filmmaker, Dick Ross, had talked to him about extending his reach through motion pictures. As their first major venture, Ross produced a color documentary called *The Portland Story*, later renamed *Mid-Century Crusade* and widely used to publicize Graham's ministry and to show potential sponsors how a crusade worked and could benefit churches in their city. Within a year, Billy Graham Evangelistic Films, later renamed World Wide Pictures, with headquarters and studios in Burbank, California, began turning out a steady stream of documentary and fictional films, the latter mostly retellings of broken lives mended by attendance at a Billy Graham crusade. Ross also helped produce Graham's new radio program, the *Hour of Decision*, a name Ruth suggested. The first broadcast, originating from the Atlanta crusade in the Ponce de Leon baseball stadium on November 5, 1950, opened with Tedd Smith's adaptation of "The Battle Hymn of the Republic," introductory remarks by Cliff Barrows ("each week at this time ... for *you* ... for the *nation* ... *this* is the *Hour of Decision!*"), and songs from the choir and congregation. Jerry Beavan described the 10,000-seat steel and canvas tabernacle centered on second base and noted that "where short days ago baseball pitches rocketed across home plate, now the Gospel message is driven home to the multiplied thousands who have been in attendance for every service." Then Grady Wilson read Scripture, and George Beverly Shea intoned "I Will Sing the Wondrous Story." These preliminaries over, Cliff Barrows announced dramatically, "And now, as always, a man with God's message for these crisis days, Billy Graham."

True to his billing, Graham began his sermon on an arresting note: "An Associated Press dispatch from Hong Kong in the Atlanta *Constitution* this morning states . . ." Three days earlier, Chinese troops had entered the Korean conflict, a development Billy managed to inflate into a precursor of imminent world war, possibly involving a hydrogen bomb. Declaring those "crisis days" to be "the most tragic and fateful hour in world history," he proclaimed that none but the Prince of Peace could bring true and lasting tranquillity to individuals and nations and called on listeners, wherever they might be, "to say an eternal yes to Christ." Then, after a short prayer, he closed with the signature benediction: "And now, until next week, good-bye and may the Lord bless you, *real good*." The team was elated with the smoothness of the production, but perhaps no one found greater satisfaction than Frank Graham, who had driven down from Charlotte to share in his son's hour of triumph. Frank's pleasure went beyond fatherly pride; at last, it seemed, he felt relieved of the burden old Brother Coburn had placed on him at the Plank Meetinghouse by predicting he would become a preacher. When an Atlanta reporter asked Mr. Graham when Billy had been called to preach, he told him, "About ten years before he was born."

No mention of money occurred on that first program, but Barrows did ask people to let them know if they felt the broadcasts "meet a need across the land." Soon he began to remind listeners, in the briefest manner possible, that the program's continued existence depended on freewill offerings: "Send your letters to Billy Graham, Minneapolis, Minnesota. That's all the address you need." No greater urging was needed. The *Hour of Decision* caught fire immediately and within five weeks attracted the largest audience the Nielsen rating service had ever recorded for a religious broadcast. In his cautiousness, Graham had ordered the Bennett agency to contract for only 150 stations, the smallest segment of the network ABC would sell, and had made it clear he would cancel immediately if contributions from listeners did not cover the costs. Within a few months, the program aired on all 350 network stations, soon spread to nearly 1,000 stations in the United States, and reached many other parts of the world on at least 30 shortwave stations. Graham's entry into electronic evangelism stretched him and his ministry in other ways. During the YFC days, a talented preacher could build a reputation with two or three good sermons, and even the longer crusades required no more than a relatively modest stock of material. A weekly program, however, heard by an estimated twenty million people, forced Graham to expand his reading and seek assistance in satisfying the relentless need for fresh material. With Dick Ross's help, Cliff Barrows quickly assumed primary responsibility for production, overseeing both the more nerve-racking live broadcasts of crusade services and the composite programs in which he blended taped segments from various crusades with a studio sermon from Graham. In mid-1951, Graham launched a television version of the *Hour of Decision*. Some programs featured filmed segments from live crusades, where Graham was at his best, but most were studio productions that showed him in a study or living room setting. They often included obviously rehearsed interviews and did not allow him to preach with the kind of intensity and effectiveness he could manifest before a large crowd, though he did eventually become more at ease with the conversational format. The program ran for nearly three years on the fledgling ABC television network, but neither Graham nor his associates have ever regarded it as a particularly memorable or effective effort. Years later, he told an interviewer, "They are interesting films, but I can't find anyone who ever saw one! Prime time on Sunday nights on network TV, and no one remembers."

The media ministry required dramatic changes in the scope of Graham's organization and outreach. The most significant immediate result was the flood of mail that cascaded into the Minneapolis headquarters. From a small packet a postman could carry in one hand, the response grew to more than 178,000 letters during 1951, and twice that the next year. Back in Florida, W. T. Watson had stressed the importance of a mailing list. Billy now told his associates, "Let's collect all the names we can. I'd rather have the name and address of somebody who supports us than a dollar bill." Thereafter, in crusades and on the radio, the team put more emphasis on gathering names than on asking for contributions. Badgering people into giving money could offend them; contacting them several times a year with requests for prayer and low-key reminders of financial need would surely prove more effective in the long run. George Wilson, initially skeptical about the value of a mailing list, became one of the leading direct-mail experts in the country. Throughout his ministry, Graham would use a variety of assistants and ghostwriters to help with sermons and publications, but with rare exceptions, he would personally write every letter going out to the list over his signature. "That's been my own thing," he explained, "because I felt that God had given me a rapport with our listeners, and people, and I felt I knew what to say."

Mainly to take care of the mail, BGEA purchased a modest office building and expanded the staff from George Wilson and a secretary to approximately eighty employees by 1954, and by half again that many a year later. The letters brought more than enough money to ease Graham's anxiety over paying for the *Hour of Decision* and enabled him to be a bit bolder in seizing other opportunities for ministry. They also brought so many requests for personal and spiritual advice that in 1952, at Walter Bennett's suggestion, he began his syndicated newspaper column, "My Answer." Then, as requests mounted for sermons, books, sheet music, and recordings aired on the programs, Graham and Wilson formed a retail company called Grason, a tax-paying entity whose profits were fed back into BGEA.

The ministry's growth and the accompanying increase in income both called for and made possible a more businesslike arrangement for handling the team's compensation. Despite aggregate attendance of 500,000 and successful inauguration of the *Hour of Decision*, the Atlanta crusade produced a major embarrassment for Graham. Though he had not sought it, the crusade committee had taken up a substantial love offering for him and his team at the closing service. The next day, the Atlanta *Constitution* ran two pictures side by side. One showed a group of happy ushers, holding up four large sacks of money; the other showed Billy Graham waving and smiling broadly as he got into a car in front of the Biltmore Hotel, just prior to leaving Atlanta. The pictures appeared in newspapers throughout the country, implying once again that itinerant evangelists, Billy Graham included, were still trying to prove that one could serve both God and mammon. Deeply stung, Graham determined to put all trace of the Elmer Gantry image behind him and asked Jesse Bader, secretary for evangelism at the National Council of Churches, for advice. Bader advised him to have BGEA put him and his team on fixed salaries unrelated to the number of crusades they might hold in a given year. Graham agreed and pegged his own salary at $15,000, comparable to that received by prominent urban pastors at the time but less than he could have made from love offerings—his income from the Atlanta crusade alone came to $9,268.60. He would later accept money for his newspaper column and royalties from some of his books, but never, after the system took effect in January 1952, would he or his team accept another honorarium for their work in a crusade.

In addition to the thousands of dollars pouring into Minneapolis each week, mostly in small amounts, Graham's widely publicized pronouncements on the Satanic evils of communism, the God-blessed superiority of the free-enterprise system, and the need to return to the old-fashioned values and virtues of individualist America attracted the favor of several folk able to offer more substantial support. During his 1951 Fort Worth crusade, the crusty Texas oilman, Sid Richardson, less well-known for piety than profanity, took a special liking to him and introduced him to other rich and powerful people, including his personal attorney, John Connally. Another early backer was millionaire industrialist and investor Russell Maguire, an ardent anti-Communist who made a fortune in oil and the manufacture of electrical equipment and Thompson submachine guns, and who contributed a substantial amount of it to various organizations described as fascist by the U.S. attorney general. Not long before he met Graham, Maguire had stirred a controversy by backing the distribution of *Iron Curtain over America*, a book the Methodist publication *Zion's Herald* described as the "most extensive piece of racist propaganda in the history of the anti-Semitic movement in America." He had also been forced out of a Wall Street brokerage position for "flagrant violations" of the law. Maguire invited Graham to his Palm Beach estate and offered to underwrite the salaries and expenses for him and ten other evangelists selected by him just to keep preaching what he was already preaching. Graham graciously declined this offer, explaining that unfortunately, he did not know ten evangelists with whom he would be willing to be associated in such a venture. When Maguire then offered to free him from all fund-raising activities by underwriting anything he wanted to do, Billy still demurred. W. T. Watson, who helped arranged the meeting and was present at the conversation, marveled at Graham's reaction. "Most folks would have thought the millennium had come," he said, "but Billy didn't bat an eye. He said, 'Mr. Maguire, I can't accept it. My work is a spiritual work. We're getting about fifteen thousand to twenty thousand letters a week. Not all of those letters have a little money in them, but every one of them will say, 'We're praying for you.' If they know there's a rich man underwriting my work, they'll stop praying and my ministry will take a nosedive. I can't accept it." He did, however, accept $75,000 to help with his new film ministry. Given the backing of such men as Richardson and Maguire, it was probably not sheer coincidence that the first two fictional features produced by Graham's studio were *Mr. Texas*, the story of a hard-drinking Texas cowboy who found Christ at the end of his rope, and *Oiltown U.S.A.*, which tells of a millionaire Houston oilman's conversion and was promoted as "the story of the free-enterprise system of America . . . of the development and use of God-given natural resources by men who have built a great new empire." The televised version of the *Hour of Decision* also benefited from a healthy infusion of funds from wealthy Texas supporters. Perhaps influenced by this rewarding association with Texas, Graham began wearing a large western hat, providing newspaper photographers with a favorite image until he decided it was drawing too much attention and put it into retirement, along with a pair of green suede shoes and a shiny green suit that had prompted one reporter to describe him as a "Gabriel in Gabardine."

Other 1951 events confirmed Graham's place as an increasingly popular public figure. In Memphis, at the invitation of the Chicago & Southern Airline, he held an airborne service aboard a four-engine Super Constellation plane that had been outfitted with a portable pump organ and a small gray pulpit from which he preached on "Christianity vs. Communism" and prayed that "the great C & S Airline may be blessed as never before." Noting that it was the first time he had ever preached above Memphis or any other city, and probably the first time God's Word had been proclaimed on a commercial airline, he declared optimistically, "I think this trip will set a precedent." In Seattle, Governor Arthur Langlie served as cochairman of his crusade. Back in Los Angeles, 25,000 people, including Cecil B. De Mille and other moguls of the motion-picture industry, attended the gala premiere of *Mr. Texas*. The projector broke in the middle of the screening, the film was achingly amateurish—at the film's climax, the penitent cowboy says, "All my life, I've been riding the wrong trail.... I'm turning back. I'm going God's way. I think it's going to be a wonderful ride"—and reviews were terrible, but five hundred people answered the invitation at the picture's conclusion, a response Graham regarded as "God's seal of approval on our weak and faltering beginning in making dramatic motion pictures." Overseen from Washington, D.C., by Walter Smyth, who had previously headed Youth for Christ in Philadelphia, the film ministry's first efforts did have a definite catch-as-catch-can quality to them. Dave Barr, another Youth for Christ veteran who was the first man Smyth hired to help in the new venture, recalled the early days with amusement. "Redd Harper [a singing cowboy who starred in *Mr. Texas*] and I would go around and show it in churches and auditoriums. We'd have a can of film, a guitar, two suitcases, and a bunch of copies of the Gospel of John. Walter would call us every day to tell us where to go next. My job was to introduce Redd. He would sing a little and give his testimony, then we'd take an offering, show the film, and give the invitation. Many times we were so disorganized that we'd just throw the offering in a cardboard box in the back of the car and take it to the bank the next day. There was no blueprint to follow, but thousands of people came to see that film. It was the first Christian western. When *Oiltown* came along, we tried to profit by what we'd learned, and pretty soon we were in bigger auditoriums, with more publicity and counselor training. And it just grew from there."

Despite the increased emphasis on media, crusades remained the heart of Graham's ministry, and they reached almost full maturity by 1951 with the installation of an extensive counseling and follow-up program overseen by Dawson Trotman, who agreed to spend six months a year helping Graham increase the likelihood that those who made decisions in his crusades would be incorporated into active churches. By early 1952 the evangelistic ministry so consumed Graham's time and energy and imagination that he began to doubt he could carry on much longer. In what witnesses described as a "low, resigned, and reflective" voice, he told a group of Pittsburgh churchmen: "I've always thought my life would be a short one. I don't think my ministry will be long. I think God allowed me to come for a moment and it will be over soon." On another occasion, he volunteered that he thought his name was high on "Communist purge lists" and that he expected to die the death of a martyr. With encouragement from Ruth, he resigned his post at Northwestern, but this was hardly preparation for shutting down his ministry. Free at last of a responsibility he had never sought, Graham was poised to attempt to win for Evangelical Christianity a status it had not enjoyed since the days of Charles Grandison Finney.

9
Principalities and Powers

In a span of seven years, Billy Graham had rocketed out of a basement in northern Illinois to become the best-known, if not yet the most influential, leader of a resurgent Evangelical movement. Not since the 1830s had revivalistic Christianity enjoyed the popularity it experienced during the postwar years, and not since Charles Finney had an Evangelical preacher been so in tune with the mood of a nation and so ready to become the symbol of one of its most vital religious traditions as was Billy Graham in 1952. In the years immediately following the war, the nation had thrown itself into an effort to reestablish a semblance of normalcy and stability. In some respects, it succeeded tremendously, but the euphoria stimulated by victory and postwar prosperity soon gave way to new attacks of anxiety. Because it won the war and rebuilt an economy that had lain in ruins a decade earlier, America was thrust into the unsought but well-earned role as leader of the free world. By pumping billions of dollars into foreign aid between 1947 and 1952, it helped its battered allies and enemies avoid total collapse but also inherited some of the resentment aimed at those countries by their colonies and by developing nations unhappy with Western domination. The greatest threat, however, came from the Soviet-led Communist bloc. The temporary sense of atomic invulnerability vanished in a mushroom cloud when Russia crashed the nuclear club in 1949. Communism seemed to be spreading all over the world, and the United States felt it had no choice but to try to contain it. That entailed frustrating efforts to influence the United Nations, where the Soviet Union repeatedly and effectively vetoed most attempts to check its tentacular reach and increased deployment of resources and personnel to lands where Americans were not always welcome and where those in power were not always paragons of democratic government. When Graham and his team met with President Truman in the summer of 1950, the Commander in Chief had mentioned the possibility of sending troops to Korea. A few weeks later, just five years after America concluded what it hoped would be its last war, its young men were once again bound for a distant land, a land most Americans knew or cared little about, in an attempt to rescue it from Communist invasion. A nation so recently proud and confident had been cast anew into turmoil. In this anxious state, it was vulnerable to two ancient and proven appeals: the placing of blame on a scapegoat and the assurance that old, familiar truths were still valid. Billy Graham intuitively understood how to seize that moment. He hammered away at communism, accusing it of trying to undermine the very foundations of Western civilization and damning any effort at appeasement or compromise. At the same time, he trumpeted assurance that the world had not slipped from God's pocket, that those who were vigilant and put their trust in the verities that had brought them this far could manage an uncertain future with confidence because God was on their side.

Graham's largest campaigns in 1952 were in Houston, Texas, and Jackson, Mississippi, but the most important was a five-week crusade in the nation's capital. Morrow Graham feared her son was taking on too much, too soon, and warned, "Billy, you are now going to your Waterloo." Her assessment proved overly pessimistic. BGEA claimed a total attendance of 307,000. *Time* placed the figure at 500,000 and implied, by failing to point out that many people attended the crusade more than once, that Graham had preached to one third of Greater Washington's 1.5-million population. But even the more modest figure represents a good response for the dead of winter, and attendance would surely have been greater had it not been for the National Guard armory's 5,310-person capacity. The high point of the crusade was a climactic rally that drew 40,000 people to the steps of the Capitol despite a steady rain. When Graham first broached the idea of preaching and originating an *Hour of Decision* broadcast from the Capitol, he was told it would be impossible to arrange, but a call to Sid Richardson, one of House Speaker Sam Rayburn's key supporters, led to an act of Congress permitting Graham to hold the first-ever formal religious service on the Capitol steps. "In those days," Graham later observed, "you didn't need anything but Sam Rayburn's word for almost anything in Washington. And so we used the Capitol steps."

That Billy Graham was able to stimulate acts of Congress signaled his growing influence in the political realm. The invitation to hold the crusade had been initiated by a bipartisan group of senators and representatives, several of whom attended regularly and worked as volunteers at the services, and he managed to forge important and enduring links to power during his sojourn in the capital. Unhappily for him, he was not able to repair the damage done by his 1950 White House prayer meeting. That abortive episode might have convinced a man of less ambition and confidence that he had tried to play out of his league. But Graham's determination to gain approval for himself and the movement he fronted did not permit retreat. He had acted in naive ignorance, but he meant the President no harm or embarrassment; surely, so innocent a mistake would not be held against him for long. He sometimes poked fun at Truman—"Harry is doing the best he can," he would say. "The trouble is that he just can't do any better"—but the President was used to harsher criticism than that. Besides, Truman's stock was not at its highest, and surely he could understand that association with a popular young preacher carried a symbolic blessing, even if the preacher was not his staunchest defender.

Harry Truman did not subscribe to this line of reasoning. After leaving the presidency, he once observed that Graham had "gone off the beam. He's . . . well, I hadn't ought to say this, but he's one of those counterfeits I was telling you about. He claims he's a friend of all the Presidents, but he was never a friend of mine when I was President. I just don't go for people like that. All he's interested in is getting his name in the paper." Apparently, Truman eventually softened his assessment of the evangelist, but he had not done so by January 1952, and Graham had made little effort to mend the rift, if he even knew it existed. The communication between the evangelist and the White House regarding this crusade provides an illuminating contrast between a man whose desire for affirmation was a mainspring of his personality and a man barely able to summon conventional courtesy toward those whom he wished to avoid. A few weeks prior to the crusade, Truman informed his aides that "when, as, and if a request comes for Billy Graham to be received at the White House, the President requests that it be turned down. . . . "Unaware of Truman's directive, Graham sent him a detailed preview of the campaign, noted that Oklahoma senator Robert Kerr would serve as crusade chairman, and added, "I would count it a high privilege and distinct honor if you could bring a few words of greeting [on opening day] and, if possible, stay for the entire service. We would be particularly thrilled to have Mrs. Truman and Miss Margaret join you on that occasion." Graham then cannily suggested that such a favor could benefit the President and his party. Truman had talked of appointing an ambassador to the Vatican. Republicans saw this as a cynical political maneuver designed to nail down the Catholic vote in an election year, and many Protestants, whatever their party affiliation, opposed such an appointment on religious grounds. Aware that the President was in a tight spot, Graham said, "Due to some of the unfavorable publicity connected with the Vatican issue, I sincerely believe it would be of some advantage to you to join with us on that opening Sunday. You may be interested to know that I have refused to make any comment on the Vatican appointment because I didn't want to be put into the position of opposing you." A few days later, a White House memo reported that "at Key West, the President said very decisively that he did not wish to endorse Billy Graham's Washington revival, and particularly, he said, he did not want to receive him at the White House. You remember what a show of himself Billy Graham made the last time he was here. The President does not want it repeated." When the inevitable request came, Harry Truman's "very decisive" declination was sanitized by his secretary into a polite "I'm very sorry I must send you a disappointing reply."

"Graham was disappointed, to be sure. The President's approval would be a marvelous coup, irrefutable evidence that he and his ministry had national significance. At the same time, he felt Mr. Truman was making a tactical error. Just four days before the opening service, he wrote to the President's secretary, informing him that "this campaign is being watched with probably more interest than probably any religious event since the founding of the World Council of Churches in Amsterdam, and I do feel it would be advantageous for the President to give some word or to make a personal appearance at some time during these meetings." The President was not persuaded, but Graham would not give up. Like Jacob wrestling with the angel, he seemed determined not to let go until he had wrung a blessing from his adversary. When Truman made good on his promise not to attend the opening service, Graham set a new goal. If Sam Rayburn and Congress could set aside normal regulations to permit him to preach on the Capitol steps, surely the President could set aside an hour or two to attend that service. Jerry Beavan sent Truman a resolution by 225 ministers who urged him to be present at that rally. Graham followed immediately with a letter noting that ABC would broadcast the service coast-to-coast and that "the clergy of the Washington area, together with literally thousands of their colleagues, would rejoice to know that their chief executive was in attendance on this occasion." He then called the White House to issue a personal plea that Truman attend the service. An aide who took the call reported that Graham stressed that he "believes the President will go down in history as one of the most courageous men of all times," reiterated his refusal to speak out on the Vatican issue, and observed that his ministry had received "some favorable publicity from various publications." This time, Truman's secretary informed Graham that "a previous engagement" would preclude the President's attendance at the service, but that he "is nonetheless grateful for the kind thought which prompted your invitation and sends you his best wishes." Finally, Graham stopped pestering the White House. He recognized he had been rebuffed—a *Time* magazine story described Truman's nonappearance as a "snubbing"—but he resisted prophetic rebuke, limiting himself to a mild "I guess he was just too busy or something." Privately, he may have taken pleasure in reports that the rally drew a bigger crowd than had Truman's inauguration.

Harry Truman may have regarded Graham as a rube to be avoided, but other politicians saw him either as a kindred spirit or as someone whose friendship could convey a blessing. Approximately one third of all senators and one fourth of House members asked for a special allocation of seats for crusade services, and scores of congressmen attended the Capitol rally. With the help of such friends, Graham secured permission to hold prayer sessions at the Pentagon each noon throughout the crusade. Virginia senator A. Willis Robertson, father of religious broadcaster and 1988 Republican presidential candidate M. G. "Pat" Robertson, boosted Graham by authoring a unanimous Senate resolution to be read at a crusade prayer service, urging Americans to pray that "God may guide and protect our nation and preserve the peace of the world." Graham's sojourn in Washington also led to acquaintance with two men who would become his close and controversial friends, Richard Nixon and Lyndon Johnson, the latter another favorite of Sid Richardson's. Of greater immediate moment, however, the attention he received apparently convinced Graham that he and his supporters wielded considerable political clout. Late in 1951 he had expressed the opinion, foreshadowing later predictions by the religious right, that "the Christian people of America will not sit idly by in 1952. [They] are going to vote as a bloc for the man with the strongest moral and spiritual platform, regardless of his views on other matters. I believe we can hold the balance of power." This bloc, he suggested, would be a coordinated effort in which church members would follow "the instructions of their religious leaders." During the Washington crusade, he announced his desire to interview every potential candidate from both parties, revealing he had already met with Senator Estes Kefauver and General Douglas MacArthur ("He is one of the most inspirational men I have ever met.... He is deeply religious"), and expected to visit General Eisenhower during a March visit to Supreme Headquarters Allied Powers Europe (SHAPE) near Paris. "The only one who has turned me down," he noted pointedly, "is President Truman. I will not ask for another appointment." Though careful to note that he would refrain from a public endorsement, he told reporters that he might well share his personal choice with a number of religious leaders "who probably will use my views as a guide." He was also willing to commend his views to candidates. "If I could run for President of the United States today," he volunteered, "on a platform of calling the people back to God, back to Christ, back to the Bible, I'd be elected. There is a hunger for God today." At first Graham brushed off any suggestion of personal desire for political office, but statements such as this stirred some imaginations, and a few months later, he told reporters that "numerous congressmen" and a former member of Roosevelt's cabinet had approached him to run for the United States Senate from North Carolina, or perhaps even to consider the presidency in 1956. Apparently, he did not consider such suggestions far-fetched. America had not yet reached a crisis that demanded he sacrifice his ministry to enter politics, he said, but if that should happen, he stood ready to help: "If the country ever comes close to communism, I will offer myself in any capacity to lead the Christian people of this country in the preservation of their God-given democratic institutions." In the meantime, he estimated he could swing at least sixteen million votes to the cause or candidate of his choice.

Despite Graham's profession of neutrality during the early stages of the presidential campaign, it appears he already suspected who his choice would be. Several months earlier, in a letter to Sid Richardson, he expressed a highly positive evaluation of Dwight Eisenhower (named, it was said, for Dwight

Moody) and a hope that the general would seek the presidency. Richardson shared the letter with Ike, who wrote to Graham in November 1951, thanking him for "the overgenerous personal allusions your letter made to me" and commending him for his "fight for the old-fashioned virtues of integrity, decency, and straightforwardness in public life." Richardson then proposed to Graham that he "write General Eisenhower some good reasons why you think he ought to run for the presidency." Graham protested: "Mr. Sid, I can't get involved in politics." The canny old operator pushed this objection aside. "There's no politics," he said. "Don't you think any American ought to run if millions of people want him to?" When Graham agreed, Richardson grumped, "Say that in a letter," and Graham did as he was bidden. Eisenhower's earlier note to Graham was apparently a formal courtesy, and his compliments were generated by Sid Richardson's appraisal of the evangelist rather than any firsthand knowledge. But this missive caught his attention, and he asked Richardson, "Who was that young preacher you had write me? It was the darndest letter I ever got. I'd like to meet him sometime." Given this encouragement, Graham promptly requested an interview and Eisenhower agreed, though he insisted that his position as SHAPE commander ruled out any early declaration of intentions. In later years Graham has minimized his role in Eisenhower's decision to seek the presidency, claiming his was just one voice among many. According to Jerry Beavan, who met with Eisenhower and his staff at Fontainebleau to iron out details of Graham's visit, Richardson and several of his Texas cronies specifically assigned Billy the task of persuading the general to enter the campaign, and the Fontainebleau meeting proved pivotal in that decision.

Graham continued to feign impartiality, even to the point of declining invitations by both major parties to lead the opening prayer at their national conventions, but it was not hard to discern where his sentiments lay. He repeatedly criticized the Truman administration for the way America had entered the Korean conflict and for lack of resolve in pursuing victory. "How many of you voted to go into the Korean War?" he often asked, noting that "I never did." The decision had been made by "one man sitting in Washington," and just as all inherit the burden of Adam's original sin in the Garden of Eden, "when Mr. Truman went to war in Korea, you and I went to war in Korea whether we liked it or not." He told a Houston audience in May 1952, "The Korean War is being fought because the nation's leaders blundered on foreign policy in the Far East. I do not think the men in Washington have any grasp of the Oriental mind; Alger Hiss shaped our foreign policy and some of the men who formulate it [now] have never been to the East." The administration then compounded its *original error, he charged, by refusing to follow General MacArthur's advice* to take whatever measures were necessary to win, choosing instead to drag out the war in a "cowardly" and "half-hearted" fashion at a cost of nearly two thousand American lives each week.

Throughout the spring and summer, Graham echoed the sentiments and sometimes the exact phrases of the Republican campaign, observing that it was "time for a change," time to elect new leaders who would "clean up the mess in Washington," time to get "a new foreign policy to end this bloodletting in Korea." Asserting that "we all seem to agree there's a mess in Washington," he proclaimed that "the nation desperately needs a strong spiritual leader" who has "the fortitude and moral courage to clean out the 'grafters and hangers-on'," "a Moses or a Daniel [or a general] to lead them in this hour." After Eisenhower gained the Republican nomination, Graham visited him at the Brown Palace Hotel in Denver and presented him with a red Bible, which the general apparently kept with him and read frequently throughout the campaign. At this same meeting Eisenhower confided his concern that the public did not perceive him to be a religious man. To make a show of religion during a campaign, he feared, would appear insincere, but he told Graham he intended to join a church immediately following the election, win or lose. Whether the general's approach was guileless or craftily calculating, it won Graham's admiration, and the story found its way into the newspapers. Without question, Eisenhower recognized the potential value of Graham's goodwill. In the early stages of the campaign, he wrote to Washington governor Arthur Langlie, cochair of Graham's 1951 Seattle crusade, acknowledging Graham's power to reach millions of voters and expressing his pleasure in the evangelist's commendation of his "crusade for honesty in government" during several *Hour of Decision* radio broadcasts. Clearly, Eisenhower hoped for more, even though he recognized Graham and other religious leaders would have to be circumspect in their support. "Since all pastors must necessarily take a nonpartisan approach," he conceded, "it would be difficult to form any formal organization of religious leaders to work on our behalf. However, this might be done in an informal way, and I am passing a copy of this letter ... on to [campaign adviser] Arthur Summerfield. If you have further thoughts along this line, I would be most grateful for them." Perhaps because they doubted his influence or feared some kind of backlash, Eisenhower's staff was ambivalent toward Graham. They acknowledged that the general "likes and admires" the evangelist, but attempted to limit the number and length of his visits.

Keeping Graham's favor proved wise. Not only did he continue to make Republican-flavored comments, but a few days before the November election, he revealed to the press that although he was still not taking sides, a personal survey of nearly 200 churchmen and religious editors from 30 states and 22 denominations indicated that 77 percent favored Eisenhower for president, while only 13 percent indicated an intention to vote for Democratic candidate Adlai Stevenson. Predictably, such gestures won Eisenhower's appreciation and affection and, after his thumping victory in the election, led to

Graham's being asked to serve as a religious consultant for the inauguration ceremonies.

The Washington crusade and his developing relationship with Eisenhower enhanced Graham's symbolic importance as an official spokesman for Protestant Christianity. During the fall of 1952, he began to receive letters from chaplains and servicemen asking him to visit troops in Korea during the Christmas season. Cardinal Spellman visited the troops under the auspices of the Defense Department, but Graham was unable at first to obtain government sponsorship for his trip and was obliged to pay his own expenses, an inequity Harold Ockenga and other Evangelicals vehemently criticized. Jerry Beavan and friends in Congress, however, helped reduce Pentagon resistance to a morale-boosting visit, and accompanied by Grady Wilson and Bob Pierce, president of the Evangelical relief organization, World Vision, Graham soon set out on his first visit to the Far East, grandly announcing his plan to duck from bunker to bunker along the front "to assure the boys that prayers are being said for them at Christmastime." In Tokyo, where he lunched with the emperor's brother, visited wounded soldiers, and addressed nearly 750 missionaries ("I was told," he reported, "that this was the largest gathering of missionaries on a mission field in history"), he was called in for an unexpected visit with General Mark Clark, Supreme Allied Commander in the Far East. On the day following that visit, Graham and his party received word that the Pentagon had decided not only to sponsor their trip but had ordered first-class treatment throughout their stay in Korea. With clear delight, Billy exulted, "We all became VIPs!" and, on returning home, disingenuously told his supporters of a privileged train trip in a general's private command car, of having "a full escort with about ten jeeps to meet us" and an "entire staff lined up for review," of "being briefed by every commanding general in every area," and of being repeatedly offered "the seat assigned by protocol to [generals]."

The tour, however, was hardly an exercise in vainglory. At almost every stop, Graham and his colleagues visited orphanages set up by American GIs (and, in many cases, supported by World Vision) to care for children who had lost their families in the war. He was equally diligent in visiting numerous hospitals and MASH (mobile army surgical hospital) units where wounded soldiers were being treated. He saw, for the first time, sights that exceeded his imagination: "men with their eyes shot out—their arms mutilated—-gaping wounds in their sides and back—their skin charred by horrible burns," a "big, tough Marine" so shredded by enemy bullets that "there was not enough body left to be made whole again." When one man, permanently paralyzed and lying facedown in a canvas and aluminum rigging, said, "Mr. Graham, I would like to see your face," Billy lay on his back, fighting tears as he softly talked and prayed with him. Seeing his countrymen suffer strengthened his conviction that Washington should seek a swift and decisive end to such carnage, but it did not make him a war monger. "I wish every American could stand [in the hospitals] with me," he said. "They would have a new sense of the horror of war." And he recognized that Americans were not the only ones to suffer. After seeing a Communist POW who had been "burned by a liquid fire," he said, "Watching him I could not help but think of the terrible suffering that goes on in the Communist armies as well. I offered a prayer for them, too, for our God is not only the God of the Americans, but also of the Communists. I am convinced that we as Christians should pray daily for our Communist enemies." Graham reckoned he had "wept more in Korea than in the past several years put together. These experiences changed my life. I could never be quite the same again.... I felt sadder, older. I felt as though I had gone in a boy and come out a man."

Billy was scarcely less moved by his encounters with Korean Christians, who were already showing the dedication that would produce explosive Christian growth over the next forty years. In Pusan, shielded from subfreezing winds by a fleece-lined parka and heavy boots, and from possible Communist attack by a phalanx of military police brandishing rifles and machine guns, he spoke for four nights from an open-air platform to several thousand Koreans and GIs who sat on tiny straw mats or stood in the mud to hear him. In Seoul he attended prayer meetings that began at five o'clock in the morning. And in Taegu and other cities, he was shamed by Korean pastors who gripped his hand in gratitude for his coming, great tears coursing down their cheeks. "I felt so humble as I stood with these men," he said. "I was not worthy to loosen their shoe latchets. These men had suffered persecution for Christ—their families had been killed because of their testimony for Christ—their homes were gone, they had nothing of worldly possessions—and here they were, coming to listen to me preach the Gospel and thanking me for it. They were preaching to me, but they did not know it." He was particularly moved by two pastors he invited to speak on an *Hour of Decision* broadcast he was sending back to America. Neither had ever spoken on the radio and Graham noticed one turning his head to brush back a tear just before his turn to speak. "Here," he marveled, "were men who had faced death a hundred times, and who had suffered untold agonies for Christ—afraid before a microphone. My heart was deeply touched."

As promised, Graham spent several days, including Christmas, at the battlefront itself. Flying in small planes and helicopters through thick fog, and so close to enemy artillery that exploding shells jarred the aircraft several times, he landed at tiny airstrips, donned a helmet and flak jacket as soon as he hit the ground, and preached to hundreds of grimy, unshaven, and fully armed GIs, some of whom had just returned from combat. On one hillside he preached from a makeshift platform decorated with an enormous painting of Jesus watching over a marine who had dropped his head on his arms to get a moment of rest during a break from battle; the picture had been painted in a frontline trench and trundled forty miles undercover of darkness in time for the service. After preaching, he spent as much time as possible visiting with the men, signing their Bibles—"usually I avoid signing my name in Bibles," he said, "but here it was a privilege. Some of these Bibles were pierced and torn by bullets or shrapnel. All of them looked used and well read"—and going into trenches and bunkers to talk with those on active duty. Without exception, Graham found the men unusually receptive to his message, which he delivered without adornment.

The brevity of his trip did not deter Graham from feeling he had obtained a good grasp of the situation in Korea. Typically, and for the most part, he was highly positive. After a visit with South Korean president Syngman Rhee, arranged with the assistance of General James Van Fleet, he judged that the president "seems to have a firm grip on the country." Virtually every general he met impressed him as a gracious man of out standing character, and he declared he had "never seen a private organization operate as efficiently as does the army.... The food is excellent, and medical care is unsurpassed anywhere." The soldiers he talked to were "the finest of American youth." Every one was "a rugged he-man ... a courageous, red-blooded American," yet with such an interest in spiritual matters that he "never saw a pinup picture at the front." Within a few days of his arrival, he blithely offered the rather damning and simplistic observation that if President Truman had taken time to visit Korea, he would have ended the war. Then, apparently to compensate for Truman's oversight, he announced he had his own plan to end the conflict and hoped to share it with president-elect Eisenhower as soon as he returned to the United States. His plan was a national day of prayer for God's help in finding the precise solution to the war. Eisenhower apparently decided to rely on secular military expertise; the war continued for sixteen more months.

Graham wielded greater influence in the spiritual realm. Eisenhower became the first President ever to lead a prayer as part of his own inauguration, and shortly afterward he was baptized and became a communicant in the Presbyterian Church. Graham insists that both these actions were at the President's own initiative, but he quickly stepped forward to applaud them and to assure his followers that the nation was in good hands once again. "It has been my privilege during the past year to talk with Mr. Eisenhower on two occasions," he told his radio audience. "I have been deeply impressed by his sincerity, humility, and tremendous grasp of world affairs. I also sense a dependence upon God. He told me on both occasions that the hope of building a better America lay in a spiritual revival." He added, "Another thing that encourages me about Mr. Eisenhower is that he is taking advice from some genuine, born-again Christians."

In 1953 Graham conducted crusades in half a dozen American cities, the most successful a four-week effort in Dallas, at whose climactic closing service he filled the 75,000-seat Cotton Bowl in the largest evangelistic meeting ever held in America to that point. (In what would become a regular practice, he sent Eisenhower a report on the crusade, noting that the record-breaking crowd had lit matches and asked God's blessing on the President. He then asked, in what would become a typical gambit, if it might be possible "to have a short chat with you about a matter of great importance.") This crusade was also notable in that it marked the occasion of Graham's formally placing his membership with the First Baptist Church in Dallas. His reason for maintaining membership in a church so far from his home in Montreat was disarmingly simple: "If I belonged to a Baptist church in the neighborhood, they would continually be asking me to work in church affairs. When I'm at home I attend my wife's Presbyterian church and naturally they don't ask me to do anything." He did not mention that the Dallas church was also the largest Southern Baptist congregation in the world. That year Graham also published *Peace with God*, an extended statement of the theology and social thought contained in his sermons. A *Christian Century* reviewer declared that "as writing, it is just the dullest in a long, long time. The great evangelists wouldn't have been caught dead preaching this pedestrian stuff. It never gets off the ground and so help me I can't see how any amount of triple-fortissimo sincerity ever gives it flight." He also predicted that ministers who had welcomed Graham's crusades would withdraw their support after seeing what he really believed. In an ironic coincidence, the same reviewer praised a book written by Charles Templeton, describing Graham's old friend as "alone in the Billy Sunday line in the verve and vitality of his preaching. The great ones were original and repeatable and quotable and aphoristic. Among the headliners today only Templeton is that ... he is by himself in the grand tradition." Despite such criticism, *Peace with God*, "written not for the theologians and philosophers but for the man in the streets," and subsequently translated into thirty-eight languages, has sold more than two million copies and remains a useful compendium of the essential content of Billy Graham's theology and preaching. He sent one of the first copies to President Eisenhower.

As he would throughout his life, Graham struggled with his fame and success. He realized he was achieving near-iconic status in the minds of a great many people. Near the conclusion of his Greensboro crusade, he told his audience, "I know you are going to be attached to this place. When this tabernacle is torn down a month from now, thousands of you will cry, and you'll come in here and pick blades of grass to keep in your Bibles as souvenirs. I know you will. I have seen it happen." Allowing his associates and others to refer to him as "Dr. Graham" on the grounds that the honorific title was useful in "appealing to a higher type of social strata" reflected his striving for human approbation, just as his soon-expressed preference for "Mr. Graham" or simply "Billy" reflected his concern that such striving was inappropriate. His currying favor with presidents and other notables made it clear that at some level not far beneath the surface, he relished the publicity and prestige he attained, but he passed over handsome opportunities to capitalize on them as fully as he might have. He rejected an opportunity to play Billy Sunday in a feature film, and when NBC offered him a million dollars a year to host a regular television program, he turned it down with scarcely a second thought, observing that he would not be willing to trade with the richest man on earth if it meant detracting from his work as an evangelist.

While Billy built his career as an itinerant evangelist, Ruth worked with comparable intensity to construct a stable homelife for their growing family. A third daughter, named Ruth but known from birth as Bunny ("because she looked like a rabbit"), had arrived late in 1950, and in 1952 the Grahams finally got a son, William Franklin III—"I'd have loved another girl," Billy said, "but every man needs a son." With the aid of the Bells, who lived across the street and served as full-time grandparents, Ruth gave the children a great deal of nurturing attention, but Billy's long absences from Montreat could not but take a toll. Once, when Ruth brought Anne to a crusade and let her surprise her father while he was talking on the telephone, he stared at the toddler with a blank look, not recognizing his own daughter. In a turnabout a few years later, young Franklin greeted his father's homecoming from a crusade with a puzzled "Who he?" The rest of the world, however, knew who he was, and that inevitably impinged on the family's privacy. "We were on the sight-seeing tour," Ruth recalled. "If the cars just kept going, we thought they were probably from the Episcopal center. If they just slowed down, we thought they were probably Presbyterians. The ones that actually stopped, got out of the bus, came down and looked in the bedroom windows and wandered all over—we knew they were from Ridgecrest," a Baptist conference center on the other side of Black Mountain. "It got to be a joke. Bill said I was prejudiced against the Baptists, but that's the way they were. They were so friendly—*too* friendly." Displaying a bit of their father's enterprise, the children capitalized on the attention. GiGi and Anne once stretched a rope across the road and demanded a dollar from those who stopped to look at their home. Bunny used a more subtle form of extortion. When Ruth commented that she always seemed to have more money than her allowance would warrant, Bunny innocently told her, "Just watch the next time a bus stops." Ruth recalls, not without some pleasure, that "we watched, and she had her little red pocketbook on her arm and she wandered up to the gate where the bus was parked with her wistful little face and the pocketbook on her arm, and the inevitable happened. I put a stop to that."

Ruth practiced a somewhat more lax form of discipline than Billy Frank and his siblings had endured. Despite Billy's occasional comments on the benefits of corporal punishment and the children's memory of frequent spankings, some acquaintances from this period remember that the Graham youngsters were less than models of decorum in their behavior at church and other public gatherings. Few, however, would criticize the children's spiritual development. Motherhood and other domestic demands had not altered Ruth's lifelong devotional bent. She usually kept an open Bible out on a counter and sometimes carried one in her hand to read while she vacuumed the floor. She saw to it that the children observed a daily "family altar," similar in form and content to those on which she and Billy had been reared, though she always kept it short, lest the children come to resent it. She also took special pains to make her husband's absences seem normal, following the advice of an old black man who had told her, "Make the least of all that goes, and the most of all that comes." Leave taking was always kept unemotional, as if it were no more significant than a trip to the hardware store, and if the children commented on their father's absence, they were told he had "gone somewhere to tell the people about Jesus." GiGi remembered that "Mother never said 'Daddy's going away for a month.' Instead, she would say, 'Daddy will be home in a month. We'll do such and such before he comes back.'" She also noted, particularly when she was younger, that "I thought everyone's daddy was gone. And my granddaddy was such a father figure for us that it never hit me that it was all that unusual." Whether perceived as unusual or not, the children did notice their father's absence. Once, Ruth saw one of the girls sitting on the lawn, staring wistfully at an airplane in the distance and calling out, "Bye, Daddy! Bye, Daddy!" A plane meant Daddy was going somewhere. "How much we missed him," Ruth said, "only each one knows." She read Billy's letters aloud, guided the children as they prayed for their father and his work, and, on Sunday afternoons, gathered them together to listen to his voice on the *Hour of Decision* broadcast. Afterward, he usually called to talk with each of them. It was not easy, but both Billy and Ruth were determined not to let his career exact the kind of painful price the children of evangelists too often paid. "I like to think," Graham reflected, "that we learned something about satisfying a growing child's need for a father, even though he was so often away from home."

10

Trust and Obey

In keeping with his modest aspiration to know nothing "save Jesus Christ and him crucified," Billy Graham's theology was anything but abstruse. The heart of his preaching was and would ever remain a short list of straight forward affirmations. A sovereign God has revealed his will to humans in the Bible, his inspired, accurate, and fully dependable Word. Humans are sinful and corrupt, but if they accept God's offer of grace, made possible by the redeeming work of the crucified, risen, and living Christ, their sinful nature can be supernaturally transformed—"born again"—and after death they will live forever in heaven. Without question, the simplicity of this scheme helps account for the widespread and enduring popularity of Evangelical Christianity. It is easily understood and, despite its negative view of human nature, essentially optimistic; though it may not be easy, humans can readily do what they need to do, God will do the rest, and the rewards are infinite. To many, many people, that is indeed "good news."

Later in his career Graham would devote entire books to such subjects as the Holy Spirit, angels, and the problem of suffering, but during these early years, in his sermons, newspaper columns, and *Peace with God* he simply delivered this *kerygma* (the Greek word for "proclamation," often used to describe the bare-bones gospel message) with little attempt at elaboration or defense. His task, as he had understood it since the day he knelt by the rock at Forest Home, was not to ask hard questions of Scripture but to follow the advice of the old revival hymn, "Trust and Obey." If a skeptic asked how he could be sure of the existence of God, he answered guilelessly, "I spoke to him this morning," or told the story of a boy whose kite had disappeared in the clouds but who knew it was there because "I can feel the tug." Such answers did little to help inquirers who were truly struggling with theism, but they were sufficient for the many in his audience who needed only a one-liner or an anecdote to make them feel they had wrestled with the world's doubt and won handily. As Creator and Sustainer of the universe, God is able both to raise up individuals and nations, and to bring them down if they betray the purpose for which he has exalted them. He also intervenes, as it pleases him, in the minutest aspects of everyday life. Graham did not doubt that God acts directly in human affairs, or that diligent, disciplined prayer would be rewarded with discernible blessings, but he was realistic enough to admit that the correlation between request and benefaction is imperfect. During the Washington crusade, when asked if he believed God had stopped the rain to allow the rally on the steps of the Capitol to proceed, he replied, "I believe God does intervene. I also believe that God did intervene today, as he has in days gone by when we have prayed concerning the matter of the weather." Then, with a slight smile, he added, "But in all fairness, I have to remember that we prayed once out in Portland, Oregon, and it poured down." Overall, Graham's view of God during the early years of his prominence emphasized justice and wrath more than grace and mercy. "[God] is not a jolly fellow like Santa Claus," he warned. "He is a Great Bookkeeper. And he is keeping the book on you! I am a Western Union boy! I have a death message! I must tell you plainly—you are going to Hell! You listen! Don't you trifle with God! Don't you think you can barter! You are a sinner! You have come short of God's requirements! Your punishment is sure!"

Graham also believed in an equally real Satan who stands in cosmic opposition to God, battling for control of the universe and the allegiance of every human soul. His own obsession with avoiding temptation was based in large measure on enormous respect for Satan's powers and prowess. "The devil," he wrote, "is a creature of vastly superior intelligence, a mighty and gifted spirit of infinite resourcefulness.... His reasoning is brilliant, his plans ingenious, his logic well-nigh irrefutable. God's mighty adversary is no bungling creature with horns and tail—he is a prince of lofty stature, of unlimited craft and cunning, able to take advantage of every opportunity that presents itself, able to turn every situation to his own advantage. He is unrelenting and cruel." Fortunately, since God possesses three qualities the Prince of Darkness lacks—omnipotence, omniscience, and omnipresence—-the Almighty will ultimately defeat the Enemy, as Scripture teaches, but his power and craft are so great that only those safely inside God's mighty fortress, the Church, will be able to resist him and escape eternal damnation.

The cornerstone of Graham's theology, of course, was his unshakable belief that the Bible is God's actual Word. His literalism required him to reject evolution of the human species and to believe that Adam and Eve were actual historical beings, "created full-grown with every mental and physical faculty developed," but it was Adam's nature, not his origin, that played the key role in his theology and preaching. Adam, in the orthodox Evangelical view, was created sinless but equipped with free will. Because he used that freedom to disobey God and eat of the tree of the knowledge of good and evil, he fell into a state of sinful, guilt-ridden rebellion against God, a state passed along to all of his descendants. Left to their own devices, humans will live a miserable, unsatisfying life and spend eternity separated from God and the only relationship upon which true peace and happiness can be based.

Billy Frank *(back row, second from left)* stands out among his Sharon High School classmates, 1936.

Billy Frank (about 1935).

The Canvas Cathedral, at the corner of Washington and Hill streets in Los Angeles, 1949.

America's Sensational Young Evangelist addresses a crowd of forty thousand in the University of South Carolina stadium, Columbia, South Carolina, 1950.

Graham warns a gathering of New York church leaders that no place is "more ripe for judgment, or closer to catastrophe than this city," 1951.

© Bettmann/CORBIS

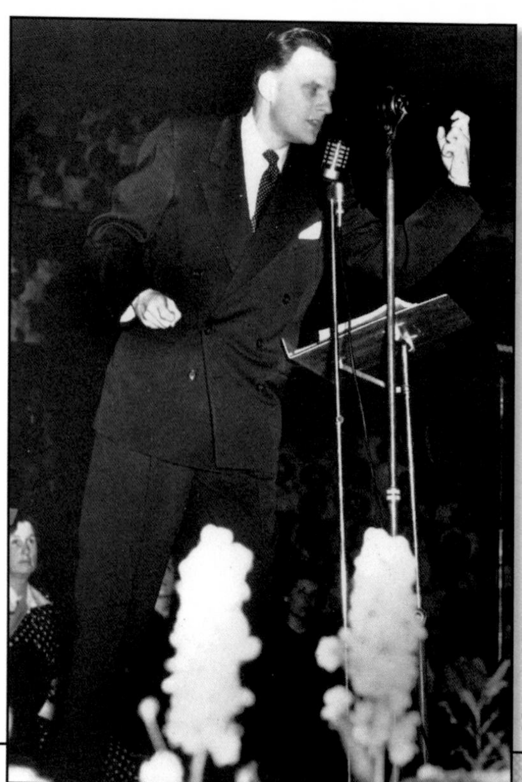

Graham's dynamic speaking style electrifies an English audience in London's Albert Hall, 1952.

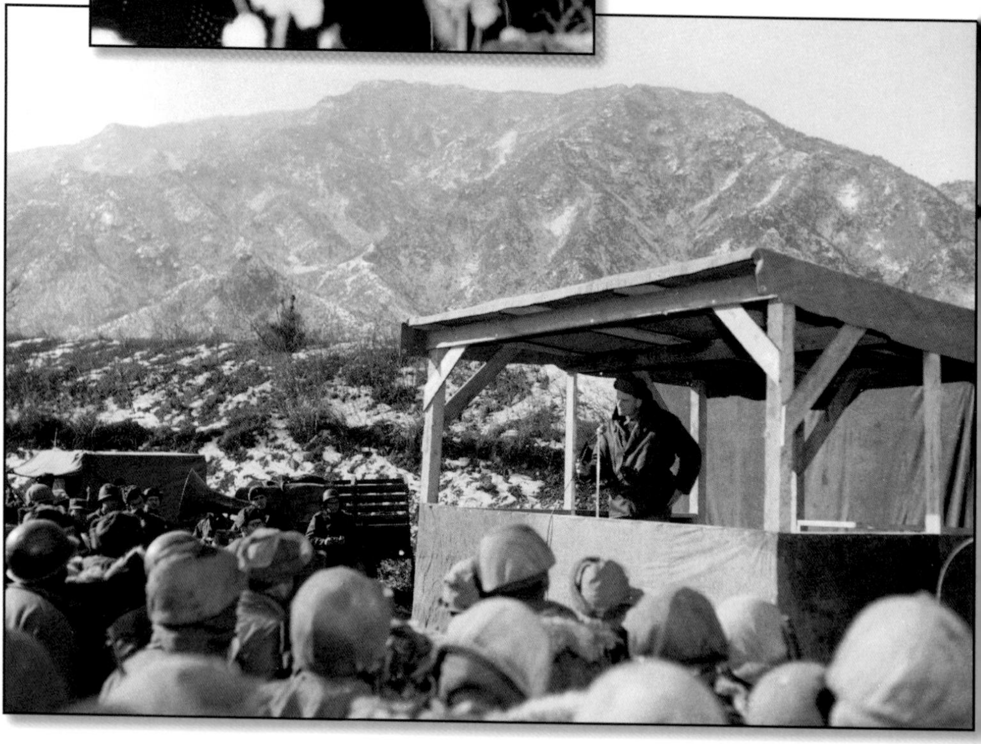

Graham addresses an audience of U.S. soldiers at Christmastime in Korea, 1952.

An open-air service in London's Trafalgar Square, 1954, draws an estimated twelve thousand people, the largest crowd to gather there since V-E day.

On the closing day of the 1954 London crusade, at Wembley Stadium, Graham addresses the largest crowd ever assembled in Great Britain for a religious event.

Graham greets Dwight Eisenhower, 1962, the first president with whom he developed a close friendship.

Graham astounded skeptical observers by packing Madison Square Garden for sixteen weeks over the summer of 1957.

Religious News Service Photo

Speaking from the steps of Federal Hall National Memorial on Wall Street in 1957, Graham tells a noontime crowd that money and the things it can buy will not bring lasting satisfaction.

Ruth and Billy with their children. *From left:* Franklin, Ned (with Ruth), Anne, GiGi, and Ruth, 1963.

Ruth

Even in their depravity, however, they possess sufficient reason to understand what they must do to escape from their wretched state, and sufficient free will to enable them to do it. And what they need is justification. A just God, Graham proclaimed, had no choice but to demand that all sin, from Adam onward, be punished by a sentence of death. Since "all have sinned and come short of the glory of God," the only hope for fallen humanity was for someone to volunteer to die, physically and spiritually, as a substitute offering to God. In a succinct statement of his doctrine of atonement, Graham wrote, "God demands death, either for the sinner or a substitute. Christ was the substitute!" Because he did not deserve to die, since he had not sinned, his merit could be transferred into the accounts of those who would accept it. Here then was the heart of Graham's theology and preaching: "God so loved the world, that he gave his only begotten Son, that whosoever believeth in him should not perish, but have everlasting life" (John 3:16).

Graham frequently asserted that only born-again Christians could ever know true happiness and genuine peace of mind, but he never promised that conversion would cure all ills; on the contrary, he warned that the disciplined life of a true Christian could be difficult and that taking a stand for Christ might create entirely new and quite serious problems. Still, he believed that "only the Christian knows how to live," and his thumbnail sketch of the Christian life looked remarkably like an idealized self-portrait: "The Christian should stand out like a sparkling diamond against a rough background. He should be more wholesome than anyone else. He should be poised, cultured, courteous, gracious, but firm in the things that he does and does not do. He should laugh and be radiant, but he should refuse to allow the world to pull him down to its level." The hallmarks of Christian life are the disciplined practice of specific spiritual exercises and personal purity, particularly with regard to sex. In a 1952 sermon, "The Life That Wins," he told his radio audience that "your quiet time (your prayer time and the time you spend in the Word) is absolutely essential to a happy Christian life. You cannot possibly be a powerful Christian without such a daily walk with Christ." He was able to imbue these words with convincing force because he made it clear, somewhat more frequently than absolute humility required, that he followed such a regimen himself. In sermons and articles and interviews and printed excerpts from his diaries, he often spoke of long stretches of prayer, of praying immediately upon arising, of an entire afternoon spent pouring out his heart to the Lord, of walking out under the starry sky to pray, of a delightful prayer time with a close circle of friends, and of dropping to his knees again and again as he wrestled with some decision or difficulty. Such descriptions, which clearly portrayed him as a spiritual exemplar, could easily have been viewed as immodest and self-serving. They seem also to have been accurate.

A person properly fortified by prayer and Bible study would, Graham believed, live a disciplined moral life. In keeping with Evangelical practice, he tended to identify morality with avoiding specific behaviors, primarily sins of the tongue and the flesh. He spoke against the profanity he heard among politicians, university professors, and other men in high places, but warned that many common expressions used by professing Christians are simply disguised ways of taking the name of the Lord in vain. He also condemned lying, including the shadings of truth that often occur in business, politics, and everyday social intercourse. As for sins of the flesh, Graham appeared to share the common Fundamentalist conviction that alcohol is scarcely less pernicious and damnable than heroin or cocaine and was willing to put at least a bit of his weight behind occasional last-wheeze efforts at legal prohibition. In 1950 he spoke so forcefully to the Georgia state senate about the need for an all-out revival against sin that two hours later, that body passed a bill to make the state totally dry; the state's House of Representatives, however, managed to arrange that bill's death by neglect. In Jackson two years later, Graham commended Mississippi for being one of the few dry states in the nation and said, "I hope it will remain so." And in his first two feature films, alcohol served as a key symbol of the lost condition of the male protagonists. Clearly, Graham felt the bottle held a powerful demon. Still, far more dangerous than lying, swearing, or drinking was sex, the primary temptation Satan uses to lure people down that broad path to hell. Graham readily admitted to being a sexual person and spoke glowingly of the joys to be found in a God-blessed marital bed, but he followed Evangelical practice by using *immorality* as a code word for sexual transgressions and devoted what was clearly a disproportionate, if not in ordinate, amount of attention to sex-related topics. In an early collection of his best "My Answer" columns, for example, over a hundred selections deal with some aspect of sex—adultery, fornication, petting, pornography, smutty stories, illegitimacy, abortion, rape, impure thoughts, immodest apparel, and "living in sin," among others. Graham's basic position on these topics was predictably condemnatory, or at least full of caution. Speaking to teenagers about sexual temptation, he stated flatly, "You'll never make it to the top until you lick this thing, and you'll never lick it without Christ!" He pointed out that adultery is one of the few sins for which God demanded the death penalty in the Old Testament and consistently warned against any behavior that would increase the likelihood of falling into this grievous sin. To a man who defended his ostensibly platonic friendship with a woman other than his wife, he warned, "You are living a double existence and you are playing with fire. What can so easily start as an 'innocent friendship' has within it the seed of untold sorrow for all concerned and of the eternal loss of your soul." At the same time, he refrained from a bluenosed, unforgiving priggishness that would demand some modern equivalent to a scarlet letter. He reminded sinners that as bad as it is, adultery can be forgiven as easily as lying, cheating, or stealing, and told them they must not fear that God would not welcome them back into his loving arms. He told women who suspected their husbands of infidelity that "before I did anything at all, I would make certain that my suspicions were justified." If the test proved positive, they should confront the offender directly: "I've known men to grow up overnight when wives reminded them that from now on it is an 'either/or' deal." Moreover, he said to one woman who had failed to take this step, "I must frankly say that your meek silence is in part to blame for your husband's philandering. He either thinks you don't love him, you don't care, or that you are not smart enough to know what is going on right under your nose." To those who wondered if they should confess their past infidelities, he counseled against either a public confession before the church or a private confession to one's mate: "I don't think this is always advisable or necessary. I have known of homes that were wrecked by such confessions." Interestingly, on the question of abortion, which was not hotly debated at the time, Graham ventured that if it were necessary to save the mother's life, abortion might be acceptable, though he felt it should not be employed simply "for selfish reasons."

Graham's prescriptions for a happy Christian home included a similar blend of biblical precept and commonsense. The husband, he said, should provide for the support of his family and serve as "the master of the house, the one who organizes it, holds it together, and controls it." The wife is "his chief assistant in this work" and has every right to expect her husband to be demonstrative, courteous, polite, loving, and gentle toward her, but she is nevertheless to remain in subjection to him and adapt herself continually to "his interests, his experiences, his progress.... When he comes home in the evening, run out and meet him and give him a kiss. Give him love at any cost. Cultivate modesty and the delicacy of youth. Be attractive. Read as much as you can to keep up on world events and developments." Given his own marriage to a strong and capable woman, Graham had to admit that "in one sense, the husband and wife are co-equal in the home; but when it comes to the governmental arrangement of the family, the Bible, from Genesis to Revelation, teaches that man is to be the head of the home.... He is the king of the household, and you, his wife, are the queen." A proper queen, he said, would prepare the king's favorite dishes, have the meals on time, make their home as attractive and comfortable as possible, and feel "it is her duty, responsibility, and privilege to remain at home with the children." She is not, however, a plaything or chattel without basic rights. She should satisfy her husband's sexual desires, but the decision to bear children should be hers: "Surely a woman is entitled to choose when she will undertake the burden she alone must carry in bearing a child. No woman should be called upon to pass through [childbirth] involuntarily, nor should she be obliged to live in constant dread of doing so." To a husband who asserted his right to impregnate his wife against her will, Graham flatly answered, "In my opinion, you are totally in the wrong. You and your wife should lovingly and prayerfully agree on this point."

Graham believed children in a Christian home should be subordinate to both parents and did not hesitate to recommend spankings, pointing out that "the pain of corporal punishment administered in love is insignificant compared with the evil and pain resulting from the habits of disobedience." Accordingly, he decried modern psychology's tendency toward permissiveness. "Psychologists are saying, 'Don't spank your children; you'll warp their personality.' I stand here before you tonight in a warped personality because I got plenty of spankings. There are plenty of calluses on my backbone that were put there by a razor strap. If you haven't had that kind of discipline in your home, you'd better start it, because God demands it. Our children tonight are roaming the streets because there is no home discipline or restraint." Despite these strong words, Graham acknowledged that punishment is inherently negative and that children differ in their reaction to punishment: "It may not be necessary for you to resort to the rod. I am saying, do not be afraid to use it when there is no other way." As for religious training, he cautioned against forcing children to perform unpleasant or meaningless exercises. It is better, he counseled, to let them see their parents pray, to set aside special times for family worship, and to make such experiences as pleasant as possible. Graham felt confident that couples who followed these directions would be able to establish happy homes, a vital need not only for individuals but for the nation as well, since, "almost every historian will agree that the disintegration of the Roman Empire was due largely to the broken home." He informed an *Hour of Decision* audience that only one in fifty-seven marriages ended in divorce when the families were regular in their church attendance; in homes where daily Bible reading and prayer occurred, the ratio dropped to only one in five hundred. "This amazing survey," he proclaimed, "gives us two significant facts: that divorces in America are mostly among nonreligious people, and a Christian home is the best possible insurance against a broken home."

Nothing in Graham's theology or recipes for Christian living was unique, or even rare, but he proclaimed his convictions with an urgency and style that caught and held attention, and he undergirded them with a character and personality that made them compelling to those disposed to listen. As he gained experience, first-person dramatizations of the exploits of biblical heroes disappeared along with his argyle socks and flashy ties. Occasionally, he displayed a purplish school-declamation kind of eloquence, as when he declared that "the secret of America is not found in her whirling wheels or streamlined industry, nor in the towering skyscrapers of our teeming cities where clever men of commerce meet, [nor] in the rich, lush prairies laden with golden grain, nor in her broad green meadows where fat cattle graze ... [but] in the faith that abides in the hearts and homes of our fair land." He also sometimes illustrated his sermons with Moody-like stories of the praying mother who left the front door wide open for years, winter and summer alike, so that a wayward daughter would always know she was welcome at home;

of the father who turned away from the saloon when he noticed his young son walking behind him, "stepping in Daddy's tracks"; of the fatally ill girl who lamented that her mother had taught her how to dance and smoke and drink, but not how to die. But he was never truly comfortable with either poetry or pathos, and though he acknowledged it was possible to move audiences by eloquence, deathbed tales, and heart-tugging illustrations, he felt the result was too often insubstantial. "It may look genuine," he said, "but the people are weeping over the story told and not over the conviction of sin by the Holy Spirit." In consequence these rhetorical techniques came to play less and less a role in his mature style, a style that reflected elements from most of his major forerunners but that borrowed most heavily from the earliest and latest forms of mass communication in America, the jeremiad and the network newscast.

In the manner of YFC speakers, as well as of many a southern preacher, Graham usually began by relating a few warm-up jokes, often mangling the punch line, to relax the audience and let them know that despite the hard things he had to say, he was really a good fellow not much different from themselves. As soon as he got through these relaxation exercises, he shifted gears and set about to create a high level of tension in his listeners. He observed that revival is more likely to occur in a time when people feel unable to cope with the problems they face, and he used a variety of techniques to make his audiences believe their lives were filled with such problems. In some sermons he proceeded carefully from point to next logical point. In others his subject and text served merely to launch him into a barely related discourse on teenage sex, drugs, loneliness, communism, or atomic war. But whatever the mode of organization, he typically began by ticking off a list of individual or social problems he had observed or heard about on the news or seen mentioned in an article by J. Edgar Hoover or personally discussed with Henry Luce and President Eisenhower or read about in *Reader's Digest* or gleaned from the works of British historian Arnold Toynbee and Danish philosopher Soren Kierkegaard and Dr. P. A. Sorokin of Harvard and the famous psychiatrist, Erik Erikson, and the great Russian novelist Ivan Turgenev. He pointed out that like the rich young ruler in the parable, many seem to have everything but inside are lonely, restless, empty, despondent, and depressed. They seek pleasure in nightclubs and casinos, but their faces wear no smiles when they leave. And even those whose personal lives seemed rich and fulfilling must live in a world filled with terror and threat. As a direct result of sinful humanity's rebellion against God, our streets have become jungles of terror, mugging, rape, and death. Confusion reigns on campuses as never before. Political leaders live in constant danger of the assassin's bullet. Racial tension seems certain to unleash titanic forces of hatred and violence. Communism threatens to eradicate freedom from the face of the earth. Small nations are getting the bomb, so that global war seems inevitable. High-speed objects, apparently guided by an unknown intelligence, are coming into our atmosphere for reasons no one understands. Clearly, all signs point to the end of the present world order.

These assertions flashed like a fusillade from an automatic weapon, fired in unrelenting staccato bursts that could not be ignored but allowed no time to run for cover. Indeed, Graham's basic mode of preaching in these early years was assault. To keep entire arenas alert and at bay, he stalked and walked and sometimes almost ran from one end of the platform to the other, his body now tense and coiled, now exploding in a violent flurry. His arms slashed and crushed and shattered, his hands chopped and stabbed and hammered, his fingers pointed and sliced and pierced. And his words kept coming, a stream of arresting, often violent and frightening, images. He never faltered, never groped for a word, never showed the slightest doubt that what he said was absolutely true. Then, when he had his listeners mentally crouching in terror, aware that all the attractively labeled escape routes—alcohol, sexual indulgence, riches, psychiatry, education, social-welfare programs, increased military might, the United Nations—led ultimately to dead ends, he held out the only compass that pointed reliably to the straight and narrow path that leads to personal happiness and lasting peace. "The *Bible* says," Billy said, that the only Way worth following, the only Truth worth knowing, the only Life worth living is that offered to those who acknowledge their helplessness, throw themselves on God's grace and mercy, and turn their lives over to Jesus Christ, who is able to answer their deepest need. "Christ died for your sins," he proclaimed. "They hung him on a cross, and his blood was flowing, and they taunted him, 'Come down, come down. You saved others; save yourself.' And he said, 'No, I love them. I'm dying for people in 1952 in Washington, D.C. I'm dying for those people in generations yet unborn. I'm going to bear their penalty and their punishment, and take it upon myself.'" That offer, Graham stressed, as he moved to close the sale, was the most spectacular any person could receive, but it would not forever be available. Even if Christ did not soon return, each individual's life is of brief and uncertain span. Think, he reminded them, of the movie stars and sports heroes and political leaders who had recently died, some at the peak of their careers. How could anyone be sure he or she would be alive twenty-five or fifteen or ten or two years from now? What about a week? A day? How easy it would be to die in an automobile accident on the way home from the service, and then face God at the Judgment, aware of having passed up this one last opportunity to escape an eternity of separation from his blessed countenance. Life is uncertain. Tomorrow's sun may never rise. Eternity may be but a heartbeat away.

Graham did not wring such themes for every ounce of anxiety and fear they might hold, but seldom did he let an invitation pass without giving them at least a twist or two. It was not high pressure, but it was pressure nonetheless, and he felt no qualms in using it to move them to make the decision toward which all his preaching pointed. "I'm going to ask you to get up out of your seats," he would announce, "and come and stand in front of the platform, and say, 'Tonight, I want Christ in my heart.'" And then, suddenly and unlike most revivalists, who continued to badger and plead and cajole throughout the invitation hymn, he stopped talking, closed his eyes, rested his chin on his right fist, cradled his right elbow in his left hand, and waited—for the Holy Spirit to move, for men and women and boys and girls to decide that *this* would be the day of their salvation.

For all his vitality and carefully honed technique, Graham was far from flawless as a preacher. He often insisted he was no scholar or intellectual, and his sermons were studded with garish justification of his modesty. He seemed to specialize in sweeping generalization and oversimplification, as when he declared that "almost all ministers of the gospel and students of the Bible agree that [the postwar rise of Russia] is masterminded by Satan himself" or blithely proclaimed in a sermon on "The Sins of the Tongue" that "the problems of the world could be solved overnight if the world could get victory over the tongue." In similar fashion he asserted that the major reasons for the immorality of youth in midcentury America were the troubled marriages of Lana Turner and Rita Hayworth, Ingrid Bergman's notorious affair with Roberto Rossellini, and too-frank discussions of marital problems. On other occasions he offered dubious or glaringly erroneous renderings of the thought of authorities he cited, as when he overlooked Thomas Jefferson's well-known Deism and credited him with having "believed that [man's] salvation, his only real freedom, is found in a personal knowledge of Jesus Christ, because he gives freedom from fear of death, from sin," or when he lumped Nietzsche, Freud, and Schleiermacher together under the heading of "behavioristic philosophies."

Such naive statements gave more learned and sophisticated critics ample excuse to dismiss Graham as an undereducated zealot, but they detracted hardly at all from the quality that gave his preaching its strength and power: the unmistakable authority of his proclamation. The source of his authority, of course, was the Bible and his absolute confidence in its truth. It was for him a saber whose strength and sharpness he used to slash deeply into the consciousness of his hearers. He understood intuitively that countless multitudes—not everyone, to be sure, but far more than enough to fill the largest arena in any city—want to be told what to believe by someone who believes it himself. He advised ministers to hide whatever doubts they might have and to preach what they do believe with full conviction. "People want to be told authoritatively that this is so," he said, "not be given pro and con arguments.... The world longs for finality and authority. It is weary of theological floundering and uncertainty. Belief exhilarates people; doubt depresses them." His own belief was final and unshakable, if not fully explicable, and because he had no doubts, he was able to convey in his voice, his gestures, and his absolute forthrightness a personal authority that bolstered and exemplified the authority of Scripture. He did not defend his belief; he proclaimed it in clear and perfectly intelligible language, so that no one could doubt or misunderstand what he wanted them to do.

Though Graham often spoke of social problems of national and global magnitude, he offered few suggestions for dealing with them other than accepting Christ as one's personal savior. In part, this was because he considered himself an evangelist, not a theologian or social reformer. More crucial was his conviction, widely shared among Evangelicals, that the only way to change society is to change individual men and women, who would then act as a leavening agent to make society more Christian, which he seemed to assume would naturally cause it to resemble the decent, hardworking, middle-class, patriotic, capitalist society to which he belonged and in which he felt most comfortable. He and his fellow Evangelicals did not expect to bring about widespread and basic social change by promoting legislation or disobeying laws that seemed clearly unjust.

In 1947, Carl F. H. Henry, one of the most prominent and perhaps the most gifted of young Evangelical theologians, wrote a pivotal book, *The Uneasy Conscience of Modern Fundamentalism*, in which he lamented his own movement's lack of sensitivity to social problems. Modernists had an insufficient view of the gospel, he believed, but they often demonstrated a concern for society that put Fundamentalists to shame. If Evangelicals were to have the impact they ought to have, they must develop a more progressive social message. Harold John Ockenga agreed. Evangelicals, he insisted, "must concern [themselves] not just with personal salvation and doctrinal truth "but also with the problems of race, of war, of class struggle, of liquor control, of juvenile delinquency, of immorality, and of national imperialism.... [O]rthodox Christians, cannot abdicate their responsibility in the social scene." Also in 1947, radio preacher Charles Fuller, with strong encouragement from Henry, Ockenga, and other leading Evangelicals, founded Fuller Theological Seminary, one of whose goals was to encourage a more socially enlightened ministry. Graham was aware of these currents of modest change and was particularly impressed by Carl Henry's book, but his overriding passion for winning souls outweighed his social concerns, and his solutions to major social problems were typically those of Evangelical individualism and pietistic moralism—get individuals to attend church, read their Bibles, and pray, and social problems will vanish—and he showed only limited appreciation for corporate efforts to effect social change. He occasionally conceded that organized labor had helped reduce exploitation and ameliorate insufferable conditions in the workplace. He noted with pride that Wesley's revivals had stimulated improvements in working conditions in England and often noted that Keir Hardy, the founder of the British Labor party, had been one of D. L. Moody's converts. He was careful to point out that employers should regard their workers not just as "man power" but as human beings, should provide them with a safe and pleasant work environment and treat them with fairness, generosity, and respect, and that responsible workers should give an honest day's work for an honest day's pay and "not stoop to take unfair advantage" of their employers. To encourage such a whistle-while-you-work atmosphere, his associates visited industrial sites in every crusade city, setting up prayer groups they hoped would improve relations between employers and employees, and he urged employers and workers to save a seat for Jesus at the bargaining table. "I guarantee," he said, "that if labor and management alike would bow their knees to almighty God and ask him for a solution, they would solve their problems overnight. If Christ reigned in these labor discussions, . . . we would enter an industrial Utopia." Still, his reference to the Garden of Eden as a Paradise in which there were "no union dues, no labor leaders, no snakes, no disease," clearly reflected his preference for a world free of unions and the conflict they produced. Neither Graham's supporters nor his critics expected or demanded much more of him on most problems facing society during the 1950s, but he could not easily avoid more comprehensive attention to two issues threatening to rend the fabric of unity woven by the war and the following period of recovery. Those issues were communism and racism. The first, he could not resist; the second, he could not avoid.

To Graham, communism was such an unqualified evil that he regarded attacks on it as but the slightest departure from his ostensible political neutrality. At a precrusade press conference, he told newspeople that "not once will you hear from this platform an attack, by implication or otherwise, against any religious or political group. The only one I mention from the platform occasionally is Communism, which is anti-God, anti-Christ, and anti-American." On the *Hour of Decision* he declared that the struggle between Communism and Christianity was "a battle to the death—either Communism must die, or Christianity must die because it is actually a battle between Christ and Anti-Christ," and he told an Asheville reporter, "I think it gets its power from the devil." In keeping with that conviction, the first printed sermon he distributed to *Hour of Decision* listeners was "Christianity Versus Communism." In it he characterized Communists as devotees of a religion "created and directed by Satan himself. . . . The Devil is their god; Marx, their prophet; Lenin, their saint; and Malenkov, their high priest." These "disciples of Lucifer," he charged, "seek in devious and various ways to convert a peaceful world to their doctrine of death and destruction."

Graham, like many Americans, expressed admiration for those claiming to find subversives in government and elsewhere in American society. When Senator Joseph McCarthy, frustrated by witnesses who refused to answer his badgering questions, called for changes in the Fifth Amendment, Graham recommended that if that was what it took, "Then let's do it." Even after McCarthy's and similar committees came under heavy fire for their abusive and demagogic tactics, Graham persisted in his admiration for their efforts. In a 1953 sermon, a year before the Senate censured McCarthy, he said, "While nobody likes a watchdog, and for that reason many investigation committees are unpopular, I thank God for men who, in the face of public denouncement and ridicule, go loyally on in their work of exposing the pinks, the lavenders, and the reds who have sought refuge beneath the wings of the American eagle and from that vantage point, try in every subtle, undercover way to bring comfort, aid, and help to the greatest enemy we have ever known—Communism." As McCarthy became more intemperate, and as his opponents began to demonstrate that he was a liar and a charlatan, Graham began to back away from him and his ilk. He admitted that while there might be some leftist, Marxist thinking in American churches, as McCarthy and others charged, he did not know of any such cases personally and was opposed to having people "put under suspicion without solid documentary facts and proof." And in 1954, when reporters pressed him for a statement, he said, "I have never met McCarthy, corresponded with him, exchanged telegrams or telephone him. I have no comments to make on the Senator." When they asked whether, simply as a Christian leader, he did not have some opinion on McCarthyism, he replied, "I am not answering that." A few weeks later, he informed President Eisenhower that "most people are laughing off the McCarthy hearings" and were not giving them the kind of seriousness they had earlier received. Later that year, however, when the Senate voted to censure McCarthy, Graham observed that like Nero during the burning of Rome, the Senate was fiddling over "trifles" and "bringing disgrace to the dignity of American statesmanship" by making such a fuss. Other patriotic Americans besides Billy Graham (including Robert F. Kennedy, who worked for McCarthy for six months before becoming disillusioned) had been taken in by the junior senator from Wisconsin, and despite his apparent willingness to modify the Constitution if it would help ferret out enemies of freedom, Graham's tolerant spirit made him uncomfortable with McCarthy's excesses once he understood their implications. Still, his conviction that America was locked in a death struggle with Satan's own ideology kept him from ever declaring flatly that Joseph McCarthy had also been an enemy of freedom.

Graham by no means believed that all of America's problems were caused by Communists themselves. Equally at fault were American leaders who had underestimated the Communist threat, had listened to bad advice, and had followed a course of appeasement that encouraged Communist aggression of the very sort that led to the war in Korea. "We've lost prestige in the Far East, shown weakness, betrayed friends," he lamented. "Our morally weakened allies are now calling for the admission of Red China into the United Nations and crying for the scalp of Generalissimo Chiang Kai-shek on Formosa." Such a faltering approach, he warned, was doomed to fail. "There can be no bargaining, there can be no parleying or compromising with evil."

America must stand firm, "no matter what it costs." Firmness did not necessarily entail support of the United Nations. In a 1953 sermon, "America's Decision," he observed that "we have been caught in the web of the United Nations," then quoted a *Life* editorial that had said of the UN's intervention in Korea, "They set the policies, we shed the blood and pay the bills." Though Graham would come to have a higher opinion of the UN in later years, he criticized it during the Korean conflict for its failure "to stand up to Russia" and ventured that a root cause of its some times spineless behavior was its lack of a clear theistic foundation: "At the first meeting of the United Nations in San Francisco, there was no prayer made to God for guidance and blessing. We were afraid that the Godless, atheistic Communists would not like it, so we bowed in deference to Russia." Such statements earned Graham recognition as a staunch anti-Communist. The *Chicago Daily News* characterized him as "Communism's Public Enemy Number One," and the Soviet Army newspaper, *Red Star*, denounced him as a quack, a charlatan, and a howling hysteric whose comments on world affairs impressed only "simpletons inexperienced in politics." With equal vehemence, East German papers depicted him as a hypocritical demagogue fronting for a war-mongering White House and soulless Wall Street capitalists. Clearly, however much impact they assigned to his efforts, the Communists regarded Graham as something more than just another itinerant missionary.

For all the seriousness of the Communist threat, attacking it was a relatively risk-free enterprise. Evangelists since Billy Sunday had pounded on communism with impunity; not many Communists wandered into their tabernacles, and few Fundamentalists held up a hand to argue that their Communist friends had been misunderstood. All Graham had to do was avoid looking foolish. Racism posed a much trickier problem. Many Christians, as well as many observers who were not Christians, felt Graham ought to use all his influence to denounce segregation and prejudice. At the same time, others among his supporters, particularly in the South, continued to defend racist policies and practices and did not want him to meddle with what they regarded as a God-ordained system. To complicate matters even further, increased reliance by blacks on various forms of public protest ran counter to Graham's own deep abhorrence for conflict and impropriety. The complexities of that problem would dog him for decades.

As a son of the South, Graham inherited a view of blacks as a qualitatively different and inferior people. "It was sort of an unspoken assumption that we were in a different class," he recalled. "Whether it was master/servant, I don't know. It was with some people, I'm sure. I don't think I ever analyzed it when I was a boy." Like many southerners, however, he was not exposed to a particularly virulent form of racism. His father used the word *nigger*, later softening it to *nigra* and then to *negro*, but he also hired Reese Brown, a black man who had been to school and served as a sergeant in World War I, to be foreman of the dairy farm. Billy admired Brown, worked alongside him, learned from him, played with his children, and shared meals at his table, experiences that made it difficult to sustain any notion of blacks as subhuman creatures. He often claimed that after his conversion he found it difficult to reconcile racial discrimination with worship of a God who is "no respecter of persons," but these misgivings remained latent for a number of years. Bob Jones College and Florida Bible Institute were whites-only schools, and issues of racial justice did not arise. Wheaton College had been founded by abolitionists, and its student body included a sprinkling of black students, some of whom Billy befriended. His anthropology studies taught him that *race* is a quite imprecise term and concept often used by laypeople to explain such obviously nongenetic traits as language, religion, and social values. He also learned that most of the world's peoples, including those responsible for some of humanity's greatest achievements, are of mixed heritage. But these experiences and insights demanded no radical response. Most Evangelicals, even in the North, did not think it their duty to oppose segregation; it was enough to treat the blacks they knew personally with courtesy and fairness, and Billy found that quite easy to do. Dr. Bell, whom he admired tremendously, saw no contradiction between being a Christian and endorsing traditional southern racial attitudes, and he strongly urged his son-in-law to stay away from social-reform efforts that might deflect him from his primary task of winning souls.

During the early years of his independent ministry, Graham followed the example set by Billy Sunday and others by holding segregated meetings wherever that was the local custom. In Los Angeles and New England, blacks were welcomed and free to sit wherever they liked, but the few who supported his crusade in Columbia, South Carolina, were obliged to sit in a clearly designated "colored section." When he returned to New England for his reprise tour, reporters grilled him about his acquiescence to this racist practice. He had no persuasive defense for not taking a stronger stand, but he affirmed his belief that the gospel is for all people, regardless of color, and that spiritual revival, which he professed to see on every hand, was the only dependable way to break down racial barriers. He managed to avoid a major controversy, but awareness that a skeptical public would be watching everything he did pricked his increasingly uneasy conscience. In Portland that summer, he objected to the automatic assumption that just because he was a Southern Baptist, he also favored racial inequality. "All men are created equal under God," he said flatly. "Any denial of that is a contradiction of holy law." Brave words and good copy, but two months later, he accepted just such a denial and contradiction by preaching to segregated audiences throughout his Atlanta crusade. Though Georgia was experiencing considerable racial tension at the time, Graham railed against the evils of alcohol, drugs, crime, divorce, and suicide, but said nothing about the evils of racism. It troubled him that few blacks attended his services and that the black ministerial association indignantly refused, and the leading black newspaper vigorously criticized, his offer to hold a special service for blacks only. Unfortunately, he was not sufficiently troubled either to speak out boldly against racism or to demand that his next several southern crusades—in Fort Worth, Shreveport, Memphis, Greensboro, and Raleigh—be integrated. It bothered him that blacks stayed away, but he resisted any action that might engender conflict or offend his white hosts. During his brief Hollywood Bowl crusade in 1951, he tried to play both sides of the issue, announcing that he personally favored improved race relations but that organized reform efforts were likely to do more harm than good, especially since it seemed to him that Communists and Communist sympathizers were at the root of most such efforts. Once again, he could imagine no route to racial harmony that did not run past the cross. "You can't clean up a city," he said, "until you clean up the hearts and minds of individuals, and the only successful method of accomplishing this is to lead them to an acceptance of Christian faith."

Graham's insistence on individual rather than social change doubtless gave comfort to advocates of racial gradualism and massive resistance alike since it placed the onus of conflict on those who wanted to change the system, but it was not a hypocritical dodge. He genuinely believed he was right, and he began ever so gingerly, to suggest it was time for individual Christians to start accepting the implications of a gospel whose central assertion is that Christ died for *all* people, whatever their color. On the *Hour of Decision* he declared that for America to remain strong, its people would have to affirm and demonstrate confidence in one another, "race with race, creed with creed, color with color." Before his 1952 Washington crusade he announced there would be no discrimination in seating arrangements, and when liberal Washington clergymen criticized his lack of a coherent social message, he replied that at conversion "you become obedient to spiritual laws. You begin to love persons of all races, regardless of the color of their skin. It's just love, love, love—love for all people of the world." In Houston a few weeks later, he acceded to the local committee's desire for segregated seating but set aside a shady portion of Rice University stadium for blacks instead of assigning them to the less desirable sunny section, as was customary. In addition, he held a special service, this time at their request, for nearly five hundred black leaders, whom he warned not to make their problems worse by turning them over to "a gang of international bandits." Then, at the 1952 Southern Baptist Convention, he startled some of his brethren by asserting that it was the Christian duty of every Baptist college to welcome academically qualified Negro students. "The moral stature of the Baptist people," he warned, "can rise no higher than the policies of the Baptist educators."

Graham clearly felt an obligation to speak against segregation, but he also believed his first duty was to appeal to as many people as possible. Sometimes he found these two convictions difficult to reconcile. That summer in

Jackson, Mississippi, in the heart of the black belt, he accepted segregated seating but defied Governor Hugh White's request that he hold entirely separate services for blacks. During that crusade a white minister who had been president of a black college made him understand that his growing prominence meant he could not avoid such public stands. "Human justice is on their side," the man said, "but more than that, religion is, too. You're taking leadership in the field of evangelism, and this is something you're going to have to face." Near the close of the crusade, Graham took another step by not only proclaiming that God's love knows no racial barriers but by identifying Jackson's two greatest social problems as illegal liquor (Mississippi was still dry) and segregation. With respect to the latter, he said, "There is no scriptural basis for segregation. It may be there are places where such is desirable to both races, but certainly not in the church." He acknowledged that he accepted it in his southern crusades, where local custom demanded, but said it made him uncomfortable to do so. "The ground at the foot of the cross is level," he said, and "it touches my heart when I see whites stand shoulder to shoulder with blacks at the cross." These statements stirred a chorus of amens and hallelujahs from the black section and applause from the editors of the *Christian Century*, who predicted his forthrightness would hurt him in the South. Both responses were correct, and when segregationists criticized him, he immediately backtracked. He told the local newspaper, "I feel that I have been misinterpreted on racial segregation. We follow the existing social customs in whatever part of the country in which we minister. As far as I have been able to find in my study of the Bible, it has nothing to say about segregation or non-segregation. I came to Jackson to preach only the Bible and not to enter into local issues." Just one day earlier, preaching the Bible required that segregation be condemned and characterized the practice as on a par with bootlegger's moonshine, only one rung lower than immorality on the ladder of major sins. When it appeared that such a message might shrink the size of his potential audience, Graham decided it was no longer "unscriptural" but simply a "local issue" that had mischievously popped up where it did not belong. Not long afterward, he covered this fast-rising waffle with still another topping. In a letter to one of the leaders of a crusade planned for Detroit, he included a copy of the news story about his bold statements (but not the story of his "clarification") with the comment, "I am certain this will be of interest to our colored brethren. I cannot be hypocritical on this matter. I do not preach one thing in the North and change my message in the South. This is a moral issue, and we take our stand. To take one's stand in Mississippi is not too popular, but we had very little repercussions from this statement. Our Negro friends have attended in large numbers."

Graham's behavior had not quite matched his alleged boldness, but the statement expressed truth as he wanted it to be, and that ideal pulled him along toward consistency. In March 1953, more than a year before the

Supreme Court, in *Brown* v. *Board of Education of Topeka, Kansas*, ruled that segregated schools were unconstitutional, and more than a decade before the Civil Rights Act of 1964, Graham told the sponsoring committee of his Chattanooga crusade that he could not countenance the usual practice of segregated seating. When the committee balked, he went to the crusade tabernacle and personally removed the ropes marking the section reserved for blacks. In fact, few blacks dared to move into the white sections, and many people may not have realized what Graham had done—the incident passed without comment in the local papers—but he could not know what might happen, and the gesture was significant. In Dallas a few months later, he backslid a bit by accepting the sponsoring committee's designation of separate seating areas for blacks and whites, but ushers made no attempt to hinder the small number of blacks who chose to sit in areas reserved for whites. When a black Detroit newspaper reported the segregated arrangements in Dallas, the pastor of a Baptist church in that city informed Graham that his church would not participate in the upcoming crusade and blasted him for bowing to racist practices. Crusade director Willis Haymaker responded that Dallas law mandated segregated seating and that however much they might dislike certain laws, they felt bound to obey them. Billy Graham, he asserted, was deeply committed to improving race relations, but he intended to do it by preaching the gospel, not by breaking the law. Some black churchmen in Detroit continued to doubt Graham's commitment, but others participated actively on various committees and were quite visible on the platform and in the choir and usher corps. Reassured and buoyed by the harmony of the meetings, Graham proclaimed that "the church must practice the Christianity it professes. The state, the sports world, and even the business field are way ahead of the church in getting together racially. And church people should be the first to step forward and practice what Christ taught—that there is no difference in the sight of God." Racial discrimination, he warned, hurt American foreign policy and frustrated the work of Christian missionaries. Still, without explaining why secular institutions were moving more quickly toward racial harmony than was the church, or why the plight of blacks seemed particularly discouraging in that section of the country most heavily populated with born-again Christians, he reaffirmed his basic conviction that "a great spiritual revival is needed to relieve the racial and political tensions of today." The *Christian Century*, though skeptical of Graham's individualistic approach to social issues, commended him for his statements in Detroit and acknowledged his growing insistence on integrated crusades.

While in Detroit, Graham explicitly rejected as unbiblical the racist contention that dark skin and the inferior social position of blacks derived from a curse Noah placed on Canaan, the son of Ham (Genesis 9:22–27), and were therefore part of a divinely sanctioned and unchangeable order. A few weeks later, in his syndicated column, he addressed the same issue from both a biblical and an anthropological perspective. To the question Does the Bible teach the superiority of any one race? he replied: "Definitely not. The Bible teaches that God hath made of one blood all the nations of the world.... Anthropologists have come to two very important biological observations. First, there are no pure races. Second, there are no superior or inferior races. We know from history that all people upon contact have crossed their genetically based physical traits. We know from human anatomy that in fundamental structure all people are identical. As far as biological man is concerned, what he is is related to his cultural environment, rather than to any inherited ability or aptitude." Then, in oblique but unmistakable fashion, he lumped racists with Nazis. "There is no 'German Race,'" he observed, "only a German nationality. There is no 'Aryan race,' only an Aryan language. There is no Master Race, only a political bombast!" In *Peace with God*, he again indicted the church for allowing secular institutions to outshine its commitment to racial justice. "The church should have been the pacesetter," he lamented. "The church should voluntarily be doing what the federal courts are doing by pressure and compulsion." And they should be doing it because the Holy Spirit had transformed their hearts and their perceptions. When true Christians look at other people, they see "no color, nor class, nor condition, but simply human beings with the same longings, needs and aspirations as our own." Billy Graham was now fully on the record against segregation and for racial equality. After the Supreme Court decision on May 17, 1954, he no longer permitted any form of enforced segregation in his meetings, even in the Deep South, though he sometimes seemed less concerned with the intrinsic injustice of racial discrimination than with the effect on his ministry's image. Before his Nashville crusade in the fall of 1954, for example, he wrote to the crusade chairman, urging him to "keep in mind that my ministry is now worldwide, and I have to be extremely careful in everything I do. Therefore, I would suggest that Negroes be allowed to sit anywhere they like in the open-air stadium and that nothing be said one way or the other about it. It might be well if once a week you had a Negro pastor lead in prayer.... There will likely be only a small group of Negroes come anyway, but if they were roped off or segregated into the back, it might cause trouble." Graham obviously felt no strong need to incorporate blacks into the crusade as he had in Detroit, and they apparently got the message. Few attended the services, and those who did, though not required to, sat where black folk usually sat in that stadium. Consistent with his pacific and conciliatory nature, Billy would always prefer decorum to bold example, and he would never be comfortable with violent protest or even with nonviolent socially disruptive measures aimed at changing the standing order. Neither, however, would he ever retreat from the higher ground he had seized.

11
Harringay

None of Graham's predecessors was able to maintain peak levels of performance and response for more than a decade. In contrast, he would hold large and successful meetings for more than forty years. Still, no crusade looms larger in the collective memory and mythos of the Graham organization than a twelve-week effort at London's Harringay Arena in 1954. This campaign so defied expectations, so triumphed over skepticism and opposition, and so captured the attention and imagination of the English-speaking world, particularly the British Empire, that participants found it easy to believe they were living in the days foreseen in the rousing revival standard: "From vict'ry unto vict'ry / His armies shall he lead / Till ev'ry foe is vanquished / And Christ is Lord indeed."

The impetus for the Billy Graham Greater London Crusade, as it was officially known, came from Britain's Evangelical Alliance, whose members came to know him during his Youth for Christ campaigns. Even within that body, the Salvation Army and Plymouth Brethren were more favorable toward him than were Baptist or Anglican Evangelicals. The official invitation came in 1952, after Graham held a large rally at Royal Albert Hall and met with nearly seven hundred clergymen at Westminster to confront their fears and reservations about a full-scale crusade. Even so, the British Council of Churches, representing the great majority of British Christians, chose not to join in the invitation, and the archbishop of Canterbury left no doubt about his reservations concerning such a campaign.

Resistance took several forms. "His theology," one liberal critic wrote "is fifty years behind contemporary scholarship. He gives no sign of having read any of it from the last three decades. He is completely out of step with the majority of ministers and pastors." Strict Calvinists objected to his use of the invitation, contending that salvation is by God, not something humans can simply choose to accept or reject. And to hard-line Fundamentalists, Graham's willingness to associate with those considered theologically unsound, which in their minds included not only most Anglicans but many members of the Evangelical Alliance, marked him as one to be shunned rather than encouraged. Also at work, of course, was a lingering streak of anti-Americanism and resistance to what many perceived as "hot gospel," high-pressure salesmanship. This lack of broad-based support gave Graham pause, but he hoped the extensive network of friendships formed during his YFC tours would rally the support he needed. He did not expect to change the life of Britain, he admitted, but he did hope "to start a spark that may some day ignite something."

Determined not to let the crusade fail for lack of preparation, Graham ordered full-scale deployment of the two weapons he trusted most: prayer and publicity. Well before the crusade started, more than 18,000 people in Great Britain were praying for its success, as were thousands of Americans, including Supreme Court chief justice Earl Warren, who led "a contingent of high government officials" at a Washington send-off prayer rally for Graham. Though Billy regarded prayer as the key instrument of assault on the spiritual vacuum he professed to find in England, he provided impressive backup support from a Beavan-engineered promotional campaign so dazzling that both the Publicity Club and the Advertising Club of London named it the top advertising effort of the year, the first time an American had won either award and the first time a single campaign had won both awards. The blitz, whose £50,000 price tag astonished the crusade committee, included nearly 10,000 press announcements, almost 30,000 posters bearing the evangelist's picture and the simple directive, "Hear Billy Graham," and hundreds of thousands of handbills. In addition, Graham discussed the campaign thoroughly with President Eisenhower and informed crusade director Willis Haymaker that the President "not only heartily endorses it" and would be praying for its success "but is using his great influence behind the scenes to help." Secretary of State John Foster Dulles, who agreed that "Britain must have a spiritual renaissance to survive," would also be "using his considerable prestige to help by writing letters to all of his friends and contacts in England." Perhaps at Dulles's recommendation, American ambassador to Great Britain, Winthrop Aldrich, promised his assistance as well.

With prayer, publicity, and political patronage lined up in support, Graham set sail for London in February 1954. Three days before the *United States* reached Southampton, he learned that a crucial fourth ingredient, the press, had waded in against the tide to urge that he turn back from England's shores. Early press response to the precrusade publicity barrage had been largely negative, filled with derisive barbs aimed at Graham's style and substance. In a typical story, the London *Evening News* called him an "American hot gospel specialist" who served as "actor-manager of the show," and declared that "like a Biblical Baedeker, he takes his listeners strolling down Pavements of Gold, introduces them to rippling-muscled Christ, who resembles Charles Atlas with a halo, then drops them abruptly into the Lake of Fire for a sample scalding." Such appraisals stung, but they were hardly unique and not nearly so problematic as the newest charge being leveled. Now, the press claimed,

Billy Graham not only had the gall to decide that England's religious life needed reviving but had attacked a major aspect of its political life as well.

The new charge stemmed from an organizational snafu. Because of the difficulty and expense of arranging for large auditoriums for long campaigns, and particularly because London lacked what Graham considered a satisfactory arena, he had accepted R. G. LeTourneau's proposal to design and build an immense portable aluminum tabernacle (300 feet in diameter, with a seating capacity of 12,000 to 14,000), constructed of a series of concentric rings that could be hoisted, rather like an inverted collapsible camper's cup, to form an all-weather dome. The initial cost would be high, but it would ultimately be a great money saver, and the publicity value of such a futuristic structure—plopped, for example, along the banks of the Thames like a gleaming spaceship—would be enormous. To raise money for the venture, Jerry Beavan designed an expensive oversize brochure to be sent to a small number of wealthy American backers. In describing the tabernacle's proposed use in the London crusade, he described England as a nation that lost its historic faith during and immediately following World War II until "the churches still standing were gradually emptied." The text left no doubt where to place the blame: "And when the war ended a sense of frustration and disillusionment gripped England and what Hitler's bombs could not do, Socialism with its accompanying evils shortly accomplished." When Beavan showed proofs of the brochure to a member of Parliament with ties to the Conservative party in June 1953, the MP found misspellings of several British names and a misquotation of Shakespeare. He also noted that the reference to socialism, particularly if written with a capital *S*, would offend members and supporters of the Labor party, which had played a key role in rebuilding Britain after the war and regarded *socialism* as an honorable term. As it happened, the brochure was never distributed. Buckminster Fuller's new invention, the geodesic dome, might well have served Graham's needs; R. G. LeTourneau's concentric rings turned out to be less than an architectural breakthrough. During the summer of 1953, Hugh Gough, Anglican bishop of Barking and chair of the Greater London Crusade, flew to Texas to allay his doubts about the fantastic structure. As he stood in the broiling sun at LeTourneau's Longview plant, sweat drenching his dust-stained purple dickey while he watched workmen struggle to attach the third ring to the two already in place, the entire contraption collapsed in a groaning, clanging heap. The bishop drily observed, "I say, I don't think it is going to work." He was right, and when he returned to London, the crusade committee made arrangements to hire Harringay Arena, a drab barnlike structure used mostly for boxing matches and located next door to a dog track in a run-down and unattractive section of North London. They feared Christian people might resist coming to the arena because of its association with gambling, but they had no better option.

With the tabernacle project aborted, Beavan scrapped the brochure and gave it no more thought. Back in Minneapolis, however, George Wilson saw an uncorrected copy and used some of its text, including the reference to socialism, in a 1954 calendar sent to BGEA supporters to keep them aware of the year's major activities. As soon as someone aware of the brochure's history saw the first copies off the press, the offending word was changed to *secularism*, but at least one of the uncorrected versions found its way to England. The MP's apprehensions had been correct. In a stinging attack in the London *Daily Herald*, columnist Hannen Swaffer quoted the calendar and asked just which "evils" Graham was laying at the feet of socialism: "The abolition of the Poor Law? The National Health Service ...? Town planning? Family allowances? Improved educational facilities?" Charging that the calendar's assertion was a "foul lie," he demanded that Graham "apologize ... or stay away!" Labor MP Geoffrey de Freitas sounded the same note and announced plans to challenge Graham's admission to England on the grounds that he was "interfering in British politics under the guise of religion." The Central Council of the Socialist Christian League also characterized the statements as an attack on "the British Labor government which was in power from 1945 to 1951."

When the *United States* docked briefly at Le Havre, France, a crew of reporters came on board to question him about his alleged attitude toward socialism. Off Southampton, a tug pulled alongside the liner, and several dozen reporters and photographers boarded to launch another assault. Graham's response was immediate and abject. First by cablegram and then by telephone, he assured the editor of the *Daily Herald* that it had all been "a horrible mistake," that the calendar had been prepared by a New York advertising firm, and that the key word should have read *secularism* instead of *socialism*. Further, he insisted that he had "never attacked Socialism," that he wished to apologize to all who may have been offended, and that his visit had no political implications whatever. Back in Minneapolis, George Wilson took full blame for not having caught the mistake, but none was more willing to fall on his pen than Jerry Beavan, who insisted that Graham had neither written nor approved the calendar's text. He further observed that even the original use of the word *socialism* contained no veiled reference to the Labor party, because when spelled with a lowercase *s*, the word "means in America theater-going, social life, materialism, and so on."

Such explanations, dismissed by a Labor MP as "fatuous," and acknowledged by some of Graham's staunchest supporters to be less than fully convincing, were at best disingenuous. Just three months earlier, Graham had described Karl Marx as "a subtle, clever, degenerate materialist" who, "having filled his intellectual craw with all the filth of Europe's gutters, and garbling perverted German philosophies and half truths," had "spewed this filthy, corrupt, ungodly, unholy doctrine of world socialism over the gullible people of a degenerate Europe." On various occasions, the evangelist had called for "a revolt against the tranquil attitude to[ward] communism, socialism, and dictatorship," predicted that England would turn to Marxist socialism within five years, indicated he might go there to help halt this trend, and described Socialist leader Aneurin Bevan, the major architect of the highly regarded National Health Service, as "a dangerous man" involved in "Communist advance." Even more pointedly, he had observed in 1949 that "the present government, Labor, is killing all initiative and free enterprise. The system has not solved one of Britain's economic ills. Instead, it has created a thousand economic problems." These views, neither uncommon nor unpopular in Eisenhower-era America, were sufficiently well reported to have gained the attention and approval of Kenneth De Courcey, the outspoken editor of London's extremely conservative *Intelligence Digest*, which hailed Graham as "the most important single figure in the religious world today," described him as "without doubt not very partial to Socialism," and predicted that a major Evangelical awakening "would detach hundreds of thousands, if not millions, from the Socialist concept." As a further show of his support, De Courcey arranged to reprint some of Graham's sermons and inaugurated a new paper, the London *Free Press*, which was advertised as possessing "a strong editorial slant fully supporting the Billy Graham message." In light of such evidence, Graham's insistence that he bore no animus toward socialism seemed quite unconvincing. And yet he not only weathered the storm but soon turned most of his attackers into docile admirers. Within a few days, he visited the House of Commons as the guest of several Labor MPs, including Geoffrey de Freitas, who declared he had accepted Graham's apology for the offensive calendar and was "impressed by [his] sincere Christianity."

Ironically, the calendar flap made Billy and his crusade front-page news. When he arrived at Waterloo Station, he was met by a crowd judged to be the largest to gather for any celebrity since Mary Pickford and Douglas Fairbanks visited London in 1924. An eyewitness reported that "women screamed and fainted, babies and children were passed over the heads of the crowd, newspaper stands were overturned, and burly railway policemen were swept aside, and a harassed station official complained, if these are Christians, it's time we let out the lions!" None of this calmed Graham's deep-seated fear that he was facing certain and humiliating failure. On the evening of the opening service, March 1, as he and Ruth prepared to leave their modest quarters over a shoe shop near Oxford Circus, he received word that Senators Stuart Symington and Styles Bridges, who had promised to say a few words at the service, had backed out, ostensibly because of a conflicting dinner engagement. Ambassador Aldrich had already distanced himself from Graham as a result of the calendar flap, and Billy wondered if Symington and Bridges had been persuaded to abandon him as well. To make matters worse, a steady mixture of sleet and freezing rain might well discourage people from leaving home. When Jerry Beavan called to report on the status of last-minute preparations, he noted that several hundred journalists were present, but the crowd was still quite small. Given his state of mind, Graham found it easy to envision newspapers and television screens filled with pictures of an empty arena. Ruth, who was writing in her diary when the call came, penned the following observation: "Jerry just called.... Some of the [team] are getting discouraged. Bill looked sort of stunned when he told me, and I thought I heard him praying in the other room just now." In fact, Beavan had not been concerned, but a team member who took his call had misunderstood his message, and Billy characteristically feared the worst. As he and Ruth rode to the arena in a chauffeured car furnished by the Ford Motor Company of England, they held hands and Billy stared into the drizzly darkness, mute with dread of humiliating failure. When they arrived at the warehouselike arena, he saw no one outside and steeled himself to face what he imagined would be a gang of mocking reporters, ready to slice him apart as he tried to communicate with scattered clumps of wet, dispirited Fundamentalists. Then he saw Willis Haymaker rushing toward them, obviously filled with excitement. "The building is packed," he exclaimed, "and thousands are on the other side trying to get in. They've come in the last twenty minutes from everywhere. Listen to them sing!" Tears filled Billy's eyes as he thanked God he had not been forsaken. When he entered the room that would serve as his office, he found Senators Symington and Bridges standing there smiling. They had broken loose from a cocktail party and would arrive late at their appointment—dinner with Foreign Secretary Anthony Eden. When at last it was time to mount the platform, Billy saw the jammed auditorium for himself. Filled with exhilaration, he could hardly wait to preach. He spoke too fast and his was voice too loud, but the invitation reaped a harvest of 178 souls, a standard proportion (1.5 percent) for Graham crusades, but eye-popping to the reticent British, and the most remarkable religious revival in modern British history was under way. On the second evening, snow and rain kept the crowd a bit below capacity, but on no more than two or three nights of the remaining twelve weeks did a single spot in the 12,000-seat arena go unfilled. On weekends extra services were scheduled to accommodate overflow crowds. Each night coachloads of pilgrims traveled hundreds of miles to attend the services, and entire tube trains rang with a chorus that would become a standard in Graham crusades. "To God be the glory, Great things He hath done."

Harringay marked the introduction of a new technique that would become a vital and standard part of subsequent crusades. Stephen Olford, who led Billy into a "deeper walk" with the Holy Spirit during those memorable sessions at Pontypridd, had left itinerant evangelism to become pastor of London's Duke Street Baptist Church. From his own experience he knew that most people who attended evangelistic services were already affiliated with a church, and he puzzled over ways to increase the proportion of the unchurched at such meetings and to make sure they did not simply drift back into the night after the services. His solution was biblical, elegantly simple, and remarkably effective. The Duke Street Church would furnish free transportation and arrange for reserved seating for any member who wished to attend the crusade. Bus and crusade tickets were free, but they came in batches of no less than two, and all church members who received a ticket for themselves were obliged to bring at least one unconverted person with them, preferably a friend, relative, or associate. "It was," Olford recalled with considerable satisfaction, "entirely my vision, entirely my procedure." He called it Operation Andrew, after the apostle whose primary recorded contribution to Jesus' ministry was inviting his brother, Peter, to meet the Messiah (John 1:40–42). The scheme, Olford recalled, proved to be a smashing success: "We drove multitudes of people to Harringay. "*Multitudes!* And we trebled our membership at Duke Street. Actually trebled! I knew what it took, and we proved it could work." Veteran team members dispute Olford's claim to sole credit for Operation Andrew but freely acknowledge it was a British invention and quickly made it a regular part of crusade operations.

As the crusade gathered momentum, the problem was not how to fill Harringay but how to reach other multitudes for whom regular attendance was simply not feasible. At the suggestion of an ABC engineer who came along to help with *Hour of Decision* broadcasts, and in keeping with Evangelical openness toward any innovation that promised to lengthen the reach or enhance the effectiveness of efforts to fulfill the Great Commission, to preach the gospel to all nations, the team experimented with landline relays that transmitted the service over telephone lines to loudspeakers set up in churches or rented halls. After a single installation at the Troccet Cinema in South London showed the technique would work, other lines were hired, and by May the crusade was going out to 430 churches and rented halls in 175 different cities and towns in England, Ireland, Scotland, and Wales. In these services, team members or local church leaders led the singing and prayers and took an offering to pay the cost of the relay and hall rental. Then, when the time for the sermon came, the landline transmission began. In Liverpool the congregation looked at a six-foot-high portrait of Graham while they listened to his voice over the loudspeaker; in most locations they simply sat and listened. In virtually all cases, the clarity of the transmission—often noticeably better than the sound in Harringay—made it easy to concentrate on the sermon, and observers noticed that the level of attention and response at the invitation was at least as good and often better than at the live services. At the same time, because those who conducted the services were usually local churchmen and attendance seldom exceeded a few hundred, critics could hardly claim that response to the invitation was a product of an emotionally charged mass meeting manipulated by charismatic professionals.

Popular acclaim helped Graham gain entry to more elite circles as well. Near the end of the crusade, he addressed almost two hundred British political and social elites who gathered at the posh Claridges hotel for a white-tie dinner ostensibly hosted by Lord Luke of Pavenham, a dedicated Evangelical Anglican, but actually paid for by Sid Richardson. At Cambridge and Oxford he drew capacity crowds, and then he addressed large gatherings at the University of London, Imperial College in Kensington, and at the London School of Economics (LSE). Graham approached the LSE appearance with trepidation. Though invited by the school's Christian Union, he was well aware of its openly secular orientation and an outspoken leftist element. A few moments after he was introduced by a professor who noted he was the first minister ever to speak from that platform, a student crashed through an upper window and stood scratching himself like an ape, an obvious gibe at Fundamentalism's rejection of evolution. Graham instantly made the connection and, when he finished laughing, quipped, "He reminds me of my ancestors." The students roared appreciatively, and then he added, "Of course, all my ancestors came from Britain." This brought the house down, and from then on he had them. Whether or not any of them changed their mind about his message, they listened in complete silence to his brief gospel presentation.

Similar triumphs attended the rest of the crusade. Nearly every day, Graham addressed a new group or met with religious or political leaders. The pace exhausted him. He lost weight, and the circles around his eyes darkened even more, but the thrill and satisfaction of doing "some great thing for God" kept him moving from glory to glory. An open-air service in Trafalgar Square drew an estimated 12,000 people, the largest crowd to gather there since V-E day. More than 40,000 children assembled one Saturday morning at the dog track next to Harringay to hear Roy Rogers and Dale Evans (and Trigger, "the Gospel Horse") entertain and give their testimony. A Good Friday rally in Hyde Park attracted another 40,000, and two services on the closing day, one at White City Stadium and the other at mammoth Wembley Stadium, drew, despite driving rain, overflow audiences totaling at least 185,000, the largest crowds ever assembled for a religious event in British history, and larger than any crowd at the 1948 Summer Olympics at Wembley. The lord mayor of London attended the Wembley service, in official capacity, as did the archbishop of Canterbury, Geoffrey Fisher, who sat on the platform and pronounced the benediction. The archbishop's coolness toward the crusade had been obvious since the outset, and this was the first service he bothered to attend. Even then, some felt his implicit endorsement was not all it might have been. Bishop A. W. Goodwin-Hudson, one of Graham's champions in the Anglican hierarchy, recalled that the archbishop took out a piece of paper, fidgeted with it, and then read his benediction. "He must have done it a million times before. He did not declare himself. It was perfunctory. It could have been better." The archbishop, however, may have been overwhelmed, not diffident. When the service ended, he turned to Grady Wilson and said with a bit of wistful wonder in his voice, "I don't think we'll ever see a sight like this again until we get to heaven." The southern plumber's son, never one to stand on ceremony and perhaps unaware that the customary form of direct address was "Your Grace," threw a beefy arm around the prelate, gave him a good squeeze, and said, "That's right, Brother Archbishop! That's right!"

His Grace was not the only clergyman to manifest a change of heart. Less than two weeks after the crusade started, the Church of England asked for a special series of training classes to equip its members to participate in the counseling and follow-up aspects of the crusade. The Reverend Frank Martin, writing in the *Sunday Graphic*, proclaimed after his first exposure to the evangelist's preaching that "this Billy Graham line just won't do!... Just pelting us with texts will never convert British sinners. The whole thing is (and I say it in all charity) too spiritually bouncy and immature." Eleven weeks later, at the close of the crusade, Martin wrote, "Thank you, Billy. You've done us a power of good. Come again soon." Donald Soper, president of the Methodist Conference and known for his ardent defense of various social-welfare causes, refused to budge from his charge that "there is not a single reputable theologian in the churches who agrees with what is promulgated at Harringay," but his equally respected colleague, Leslie Weatherhead, then president-designate of the Methodist Conference, asked, "And what does fundamentalist theology matter compared with gathering in the people we have all missed and getting them to the point of decision? Theology comes much later." Once again, as had been the case throughout the history of evangelistic preaching, criticisms of substance and method had to move to the side to make room for the converts who were crowding the aisles.

Graham's ability to win the support of his clerical critics turned in no small measure on his consistent manifestation of humility in the face of criticism. Colleen Townsend Evans, who had abandoned her movie career for Christian service and had come to London to assist with the crusade, recalled being in a small group as a team member read an article in which a London clergyman had "absolutely blasted" the evangelist. "He listened very thoughtfully and carefully, and finally, when he had heard the whole tirade, he lifted his head and looked at all of us and said very thoughtfully, 'Well, I guess if I had been in that man's place, I might have thought the same thing about me." Whether present on that occasion or not, the often-critical *Christian Century* found evidence of the same spirit. Billy Graham, the magazine observed, "is revealing himself as extraordinarily teachable and humble, considering that he is surrounded with the fevered adulation of crowds so much of the time. He will learn a great deal in London and will, if he keeps up the growth which has characterized his last three years, put what he learns to good use for Christ and the church."

The secular press also experienced a conversion of sorts. With the exception of Hannen Swaffer, whose disdain continued unabated, Graham's open friendliness, transparent sincerity, and disarming humility transformed acid into warm milk. *Daily Express* columnist William Hickey admitted he was inclined to be rude to Graham at an interview, but he wrote, "[T]hat is where the personality of the man comes into the picture—he is not a man you can be rude to, for the simple reason that a voice inside you tells you that this is a man of integrity." While admitting he might be wrong, Hickey said, "I think he is a good man. I am not so sure that he isn't a saintly man. I just don't know. But make no mistake about this.... Billy Graham is a remarkable man.... He is an American. He hasn't the inhibitions we suffer from. Perhaps he is what Britain needs.... It is a bitter pill to swallow." As if this were not sufficient, at the end of the interview, when Hickey shook Graham's hand ("He has the firm, self-conscious grip of the American executive"), wished the evangelist Godspeed and left his presence, he was stunned to realize that "my eyes were scalding with tears." William Conner, writing in the *Daily Mirror* under the pen name Cassandra, did a similar turnabout. After suffering two acerbic attacks, Graham wrote a short note asking Conner for the opportunity to meet him. "While your articles about me were not entirely sympathetic," he graciously observed, "they were two of the most cleverly written that I have ever read." In a nice bit of irony, Cassandra suggested they meet at a pub called Baptist's Head. After their meeting, at which Conner had a beer and Graham a soft drink, the columnist described Graham as having "a kind of ferocious cordiality that scares ordinary sinners stone cold" and confessed to an urge "to set about some devilment as soon as he switched on his looming, bulging goodness of heart." But it would not work. "I never thought that friendliness had such a sharp, cutting edge," he marveled. "I never thought that simplicity could cudgel a sinner so damned hard. We live and we learn.... The bloke means everything he says."

The massive crowds and widespread acclaim were so dramatic that they helped Graham gain one of the most treasured moments of the campaign: a meeting with Prime Minister Winston Churchill. Graham had, of course, invited Churchill to the crusade and had sought to arrange a personal meeting with the great man through one of his private secretaries, but Churchill declined both requests. The Wembley rally, however, piqued his curiosity and he agreed to receive the evangelist for a courtesy visit of five minutes, probably calculating that he and his party could not be hurt by a nod of recognition to the man who had so captured the nation's attention. Precisely at noon on the second day after the Wembley service, Billy Frank Graham of Charlotte, North Carolina, was ushered into the Cabinet Room at 10 Downing Street to meet the most formidable figure of the midtwentieth century. Ironically, Churchill may have been more anxious than Graham; before Billy arrived, he paced back and forth, wondering aloud what one talked about with an American evangelist. When Billy entered the room, whose dim light suggested dusk rather than midday, he found the prime minister standing at the center of a long conference table, fingering one of his famous cigars, still unlit. He was surprised to discover that his host was such a short man but still felt awed in his presence. Churchill seemed depressed. Several times he said, "I am an old man, without any hope for the world." Then he asked Graham, "What hope do you have for the world, young man?" Whether by design or accident, the prime minister had hit upon the perfect topic to discuss with an American evangelist. Billy reached into his pocket, withdrew his little New Testament, and earnestly burbled, "Mr. Prime Minister, I am filled with hope!" Gesturing with his Testament, he said, "Life is very exciting, even if there's a war, because I know what is going to happen in the future." He then proceeded to give Churchill a recitation of the significance of the life, death, and resurrection of Christ and professed his strong belief that Christ would come again to bring human history to a glorious conclusion. Churchill said little, but he listened closely as the visit stretched to forty minutes. He told Graham that perhaps the only hope for humanity was, indeed, a return to God, and he asked that the details of their conversation remain private. His aides later indicated that he had been impressed with the earnest young American. Certainly, Graham had been impressed with him. "I felt," he said, "like I had shaken hands with Mr. History."

Sinners, critics, and skeptics were not the only ones who changed. At the suggestion of advisers, Billy reduced both the speed and volume of his delivery, further reined in his tendency to pace about the stage and dramatize his stories, and even disowned some of his most egregious literalisms. Of his 1950 description of heaven as a sixteen-hundred-mile cube, for example, he said, "It is a statement I do not make any longer, something I no longer hold. But there seems to be no way I can live it down." It was sufficient, he thought, to know that "to live with God is called heaven." As for hell, he told reporters that "I do believe in hell. I believe there is a hell on earth for those who break the moral laws of God, and I believe there is a hell to come; but whether there is fire there I do not know." In keeping with this progressive move toward decorum and respectability, Cliff Barrows retired his trombone, and when reporters suggested that people responded to the invitation because of the almost hypnotic effect of the music, he stopped using an invitation hymn for a time, with no effect on the response. Graham also moderated some of his political views. Not long after arriving in London, he conceded that "you can say what you like about socialism, but it's done a lot of good here." More substantially, he repeatedly touted the labor-union movement as one of the proudest legacies of Wesley's and Moody's revivals, and he urged the churches to show as much concern for unions as for other economic groups. At the same time, those who viewed him as a crass American entrepreneur who used professional revival techniques to extract money from the gullible could not but fall silent when they learned that BGEA was picking up over half the £150,000 cost of the crusade, and that Graham had permitted the sponsoring committee to stop taking collections at services long before the crusade ended, even though this increased the burden on his organization.

The critical test of an evangelistic crusade, of course, is not the amount or quality of press coverage, nor the number of famous people met and favorably impressed, but the lasting impact on individuals and institutions. Some results were easy to quantify. When relay services and meetings held by associate evangelists were added to those at which Graham preached, the total attendance for the twelve-week crusade topped two million. Of that number, 36,431 filled out decision cards and received counseling. According to BGEA figures, 90 percent of those reported some kind of church connection, but 75 percent regarded themselves as making a first-time decision, suggesting the connection was quite nominal. Approximately half of all inquirers described themselves as essentially "unchurched." Enthusiastic British Evangelicals almost uniformly credited the crusade with producing the greatest wave of religious interest since the onset of World War I, and some boldly compared it to Wesley's efforts, which had led to the founding of the Methodist Church. Those who regarded its results more modestly took pleasure in seeing religion, particularly Evangelical religion, become front-page news and a topic of general conversation. Even the venerable London *Sunday Times* noted that the churches had been astonished to discover that the spirit of materialism they believed had caused people to lose interest in spiritual matters had been exposed as no more than a veneer covering a widespread and genuine religious longing.

Eventually, of course, church leaders and journalists and sociologists began to look at the results more closely and critically. As would prove to be the case throughout Graham's ministry, the spectacles through which the investigators examined the data tended to affect their methods and their findings. Seven months after the crusade ended, a London *Evening Standard* poll of the city's 20 largest Anglican parishes found that over two thirds of the 336 inquirers referred to them were already members or regular attenders of the churches that received their cards; of the remaining 110 people, only 35 were still attending church. If these proportions held good for other congregations, the net gain in new members for all of Great Britain's churches would be 4,000 people, a mere 11 percent of all inquirers. Evangelicals responded by noting that limiting the survey to Anglican churches could skew the results, since the most vigorous supporters of the crusade had been non-Anglican Evangelical bodies. The *British Weekly*, a nondenominational Christian paper that had backed the crusade, eventually conceded that "the main impact was among already sympathetic church members. The effect outside the Church, speaking generally, appears to have been very little indeed in terms of figures." The archbishop of Canterbury expressed a similar sense of mild disillusionment. Immediately after the crusade, he wrote a quite positive assessment of Graham's work for the *Canterbury Diocesan Notes*; three years later, he reluctantly concluded that "there is very little to show" for the Harringay crusade. Graham's supporters typically defended the crusade with anecdotes rather than with statistics, telling of churches directly across the street from each other, one of which had supported the crusade wholeheartedly, while the other remained disdainful and aloof, with the result that the standoffish church got no new members, and the active church soon had to add new services to accommodate a swarm of converts. The lesson seemed clear: Churches got from a crusade what they put into it. But not every case supported this analysis. Some active churches gained few or no new members, but many pastors reported that even with little tangible growth, they saw increased vitality in their congregations and indicated they would welcome another Billy Graham crusade. Perhaps the most significant tangible impact of the Harringay crusade was its role in persuading an unusually large number of young men to enter the ministry, and to do so with explicitly Evangelical beliefs and motives. Before the crusade, only 7 percent of Anglican seminarians and ordinands identified themselves as Evangelicals; the rest tended to be theological liberals, with little or no interest in evangelism. In 1956, twenty-three of thirty-three men ordained in the various Anglican dioceses of London were Evangelicals. A year later the proportion was twenty-two of thirty-two. Other dioceses and other denominations reported similar figures. From that time until the present, according to knowledgeable Anglican churchmen, Evangelical theological schools have consistently enrolled far more students than their liberal counterparts, and numerous key British church leaders, Anglicans and non-Anglicans alike, trace either their conversion or their decision to enter the ministry to the Harringay crusade.

No individual experienced a greater impact from the crusade than Billy Graham himself. However one might assess the effects of his preaching on others, Harringay gave his own career an incalculable boost. By touching London, he touched the entire British Empire, whose tentacles reached around the globe. By leaving his mark on this great world capital, he transformed himself into a world figure. Both the American ambassador and the British home secretary credited him with doing more for Anglo-American relations than any man or diplomatic effort had been able to achieve since the end of the war. In reporting that bit of intelligence to President Eisenhower, he offered an observation that might well have expressed his feelings about all the accolades and generous assessments tossed his way in Harringay's aftermath: "This may be an exaggeration, but if these meetings have helped, I am deeply grateful."

12

Fields White Unto Harvest

In the years following the triumph at Harringay, Graham did his best to fulfill Jesus' directive to "preach the gospel to the whole creation" (Mark 16:15), or at least enough of it to satisfy his 1954 aspiration to be a true world evangelist. Though he held only eight full-scale crusades in the United States between Harringay and the end of the decade, he kept busy spreading his message from Berlin to New Delhi to Tokyo. As a result of his worldwide successes, he advanced from being the popular young favorite of Evangelical Christianity's key leaders to occupying a position of unchallenged prominence in their front rank.

Immediately following Harringay, Billy and a small band of associates set out on a whirlwind tour of European cities. Bob Evans had planned a series of modest rallies, but the news from Harringay stimulated such interest that most of these were transferred to the largest stadium in each city. The overflow crowds clearly justified the change. In Stockholm 65,000 thronged Skansen arena for the largest religious meeting ever held in Sweden. In Copenhagen 15,000 stood outdoors in a pouring rain to hear Billy speak in the city square. In Amsterdam he preached to 40,000. But it was in Germany that he experienced both the heaviest criticism and greatest success. Repeatedly, he came under fire for what his critics saw as a uniquely American blend of commercialism and sensationalism. They characterized him as "a Hollywood version of John the Baptist" and "a salesman in God's company" who "advertises the Bible as if it were toothpaste or chewing gum" and is overly concerned with the size of the commission. Critics also scored him for a theology they judged to be superficial and naively literalistic, citing such statements as "from birth to grave, God has a TV camera focused on you, and every bad word is being taped." His proclamation that people could be born again simply by professing their belief in Christ ran counter to the time-honored process of catechism and confirmation practiced in the Reformed (Lutheran and Calvinist) traditions and to some seemed tantamount to heresy. To step forward at Billy Graham's invitation as a sign they were accepting Christ as their savior seemed to call into question the validity of the entire confirmation process, and thus of the theology the ministers held dear. Both the individualism and pluralism implicit in revivalist preaching—decisions are personal and differences in belief and practice are downplayed—contrasted sharply with the more hierarchical and communal ethos of the European parish, creating another source of discomfort.

The sharpest attacks, however, came from the East German press, which charged him with being a spy, a tool of Texas oilmen, a front man for weapons manufacturers (a reference to Alfred Owen), an envoy of American imperialism and capitalism, and a demagogue who used the same techniques employed by Hitler. One paper published a cartoon that showed him flying over Berlin with a Bible in one hand and an atom bomb in the other while Secretary Dulles cheered in the background. Several papers cited his address to American military personnel at Frankfurt, in which he had praised West Germany's postwar recovery and observed that to deter Soviet aggression, the country should be equipped with the most modern and effective weapons available, a statement that also stirred a furor in London, which viewed any encouragement of German rearmament with deep suspicion. In what would become a familiar tactic, Graham denied he had any political agenda, insisting that the opinion he had expressed was not his own but simply an observation he had heard others make. In light of later controversial statements, it seems likely he was expressing a political opinion he felt would please his immediate audience without adequate consideration of its probable reception in other quarters. But whatever the accuracy of the charges leveled against him, they did little to dampen enthusiasm for his mission.

The emotional and statistical high point of the German tour occurred in Berlin. The rally was scheduled for the great Olympic stadium where Hitler and Goebbels had goaded a nation into war, and Graham had learned that large numbers of East Germans would be present—the Berlin Wall had not yet been erected. The symbolic aspects of proclaiming the crucified Christ in what had been a shrine of the twisted cross of Nazism did not escape Billy. A few hours before the rally, he lay writhing in agony in his hotel room, suffering from a kidney stone but refusing to take strong painkillers because they would make him too dopey to preach. Wrestling anew with the forces of ambition and humility that warred within him, he speculated to a friend that perhaps God had sent this affliction to remind him that he should not allow the recent triumph at Harringay or the huge crowds he was attracting in Europe to cause him to believe he could depend on his own strength or rhetorical power, since that would be to repeat the tragic hubris Hitler had displayed in the same stadium where he would speak that very afternoon. His friend could understand that fear better than most. John Bolten had been a confidant of Hitler's during the early years of his rise to power. When Hitler began to unleash his maniacal hatred of Jews, a group of industrialists persuaded Bolten to convey their objections to this policy, and Hitler reacted with such rage that Bolten fled to America, settling in Boston and gradually building a new fortune to replace the one he had left behind in his homeland. He had rededicated his life to Christ during Graham's 1950 Boston campaign and had become one of the evangelist's key supporters. Now, back in his native country to help smooth Graham's way, he pondered the irony of riding in a motorcade, along the same route Hitler had taken to the same stadium less than two decades earlier, in the company of "a young Timothy with a very different message" but nonetheless a charismatic orator whose ability to sway masses of people was propelling him to heights of power.

Inside the stadium, 80,000 people—at least 20,000 from East Germany—sang Protestant hymns where Nazi war anthems had once been raised, and the banner that hung in the swastika's place proclaimed Jesus' assertion, "I am the Way, the Truth, and the Life." The tremendous turnout and the strong response to the invitation—stadium officials would not permit people to come forward out of the stands, but thousands filled out cards asking for an opportunity to discuss the Christian faith—was a victory for Graham and his message. Having failed at keeping people away from the rally, the Communist press tried to discredit Graham by reporting that he had taken his team to East German nightclubs, where he had ordered liquor by the case and then been thrown into jail for trying to sneak out without paying the bill, but the story received no more credibility than it deserved.

In 1955 Graham returned to both the United Kingdom and the Continent. His tour of the UK included a six-week stand in Glasgow's Kelvin Hall as well as a week-long stint in Wembley Stadium in London, and was, by any normal standard of measurement, a success. A Good Friday service, for example, was broadcast from Kelvin Hall by both BBC radio and television—the first time any preacher used the combined networks for a religious program—and reached a larger audience than any program in the history of British television, save for the Queen's coronation. Yet some of the bloom had faded from the Evangelical rose since Graham told *U.S. News & World Report* shortly after Harringay that Great Britain was at "the beginning of what could be the greatest spiritual awakening of all times." Despite record crowds, the public impact of this second tour simply did not compare with the first. Several factors contributed to the lessened enthusiasm, including disillusion among Church of England clergy about the long-term results of Graham's approach, as well as the simple fact that Billy Graham was now old news. Nevertheless, Graham did see thousands respond to the invitation and no doubt took personal pleasure from his association with the highest social stratum in Anglo-American society, the royal family. Queen Elizabeth and several members of the family had viewed the Good Friday broadcast from Kelvin Hall, and it was rumored that Princess Margaret had attended at least one service at Wembley. Whether true or not, she and the Queen Mother did entertain Billy and Ruth at Clarence House, and on the Sunday following the crusade, Graham preached to the queen and other members of the family in the royal chapel at Windsor Great Park. This was the first time an American preacher had been accorded this honor.

After the Wembley crusade, Graham made another whistle-stop tour of twelve European cities, where he experienced what was becoming the standard response: opposition or foot-dragging resistance from established clergy claiming his message and methods were unsound and too unsophisticated to appeal to Europeans, and stadium-packing crowds who seemed not to have realized they were above this sort of thing. The longest of these ventures was a four-day effort in Paris, the first time Protestants had mounted a major evangelistic effort in modern France's history. Reminiscent of the flap over the "socialism" calendar in England, Graham stirred a small controversy by declaring at a press conference that "France is like a watch without its mainspring. It has run down. The French just sin and sin, and get weaker." Americans accustomed to being damned by preachers may have taken such an assessment in stride, especially when coming from one of their own; self-assured Frenchmen were less willing to be so harshly judged. When called to account for his unflattering assessment, Graham resorted to an increasingly familiar ploy: He claimed these were not necessarily his own feelings, but that he had been quoting the remarks of a Far Eastern diplomat, that he regretted very much that anyone had misconstrued his statement, and that he wished the papers had quoted the many wonderful things he had said about France at the same press conference. In any case the damage was minor. Crowds were surprisingly good for a country that was largely either Roman Catholic or openly secular, and the prestigious newspaper, *Le Monde*, counseled Parisians not to mock the "American style of such a religious manifestation" but to "bow before [Graham's] spiritual dynamism. His technique may offend European intellectuals, but the fact remains he is successful. French Protestants who, despite some reservations, did not hesitate to ask him to come to our country, made no mistake."

Later that same year, Graham returned to England to conduct a brief mission at Cambridge University. The customary resistance to his message in such settings was increased by the fact that he came at the invitation of the Cambridge Intercollegiate Christian Union (CICCU, pronounced "kick you"), an aggressively Evangelical organization noted for its buttonholing tactics and lack of cooperation with other Christian groups. Most of the college chaplains and theology professors expressed open skepticism or outright opposition to the Fundamentalism they believed he represented, and an exchange in the London *Times* made the visit and the nature of Fundamentalism itself a matter of some national debate, particularly in religious circles. Graham, ever insecure about his lack of advanced theological education, dreaded the meetings and feared that a poor showing might do serious harm to his ministry and affect "which way the tide will turn in Britain." Had he been able to do so without a complete loss of face, he would have canceled the meetings or persuaded some better-qualified man to replace him. "I am scared stiff about preaching at Cambridge," he told Stephen Olford, who counseled him "not to get involved in a philosophical approach or to try to do something that was out of his depth, lest he be discredited for inaccuracies," and to remember that he was preaching not to students but to sinners, and should keep things simple.

Graham found Olford's advice hard to accept. In the first two or three meetings he tried to be at least somewhat intellectual but found his sermons falling flat. Finally, midway through the series, he abandoned the effort and addressed them as if they had gathered at Harringay or Kelvin Hall, not the hallowed university church. Neither approach got high marks from the Cambridge dons who bothered to attend the services, but he did generate an enthusiasm among students that some compared to D. L. Moody's historic visit in 1882. At one address a divinity professor who introduced him pointedly noted that he "could not agree with his doctrinal views." Graham countered this chill-inducing remark with a warm smile and observed that he did not pay great attention to theological differences. "We are all Christians," he said, "and we love one another." With that as a basic foundation, soul winning is more important than hairsplitting. "A minister is not a minister," he asserted, "unless he is winning men for Christ. If theological students don't think they can do that, they should quit studying for the ministry." The students, many of whom were preparing to be ministers, applauded him for a full three minutes.

With repeated successes in Great Britain and on the Continent under his belt, Graham decided to challenge the Far East. During the 1955 Wembley crusade, he met with Jack Dain, an Anglican who spent many years as a missionary to India and was intimately familiar with the religious situation in that country, and asked him to help set up a month-long tour. Dain quickly sketched a map of India on a breakfast napkin, scribbling in the cities they should visit and the route they should follow. With his typical trust in the expertise of his advisers, Graham accepted Dain's recommendations completely and asked him to take charge of the campaign. Dain had seen what Graham had wrought in London and Scotland, and the prospect of similar triumphs in his adopted homeland excited him mightily, but his faith was not boundless. "The Christian Church is such a small minority in India," he noted. "We had never considered, ever, anything like a citywide evangelistic crusade. Those of us who knew Billy knew what God was doing with him, but I think I've got to be honest and say that we had our doubts as to whether this could happen in India." But when Dain spread the word that Graham was willing to come, invitations from his many contacts in India poured in, so that the tour, while technically at the invitation of Indian Christians, was able to follow the exact route he had sketched on the napkin.

Graham faced the trip with his usual mixture of trepidation and boldness, fearing he could fail miserably yet believing the tour might mark a turning point in the history of Indian Christianity. He carried with him the good wishes of Church and State alike. Harold John Ockenga, still the dominant figure of Evangelical Christianity, reminded him of God's words to young Joshua when he assumed the leadership of Israel: "As I was with Moses, so will I be with thee." President Eisenhower sent him an encouraging telegram shortly before he departed, and John Foster Dulles, whose enthusiasm for Graham apparently matched Eisenhower's, invited him to his home for an hour-long briefing on world affairs. Dulles, a minister's son who had often sounded the need for a "righteous and dynamic faith" to counteract the quasi-religious zeal of dedicated Communists, commended him for not watering down his message in foreign lands but also gave him a bit of political advice, perhaps hoping Graham would not make statements that ran counter to U.S. foreign policy. The secretary referred to the evangelist's recent recommendations that American farm surpluses be sent immediately to needy peoples, pointing out that such a policy would have negative effects on the agricultural economy of such nations as Australia and Argentina. He also brought him up to date on the relationship between the United States and India, which were experiencing some tension over Prime Minister Jawaharlal Nehru's attempt to carve out for his young democracy a then-unheard-of position as a nonaligned nation. The Eisenhower administration did not believe such a position was tenable, and many suspected Nehru of using this approach as a rather transparent front for a tilt toward Russia—a recent visit by Soviet leaders Khrushchev and Bulganin had drawn large and enthusiastic crowds. Dulles thought it crucial to bring India into the U.S. camp to prevent other nations from adopting a similar nonaligned stance and seemed to think Graham might be an effective advocate for U.S. interests. According to Graham, the secretary told him that one of India's greatest needs was for someone like him to proclaim the Christian message of discipline and authority to its masses, particularly at this time, when the favorable memory of the Russian leaders was still fresh. Graham apparently saw no conflict between the roles of soul saver and semiofficial representative of American foreign policy. Whatever was bad for communism and good for capitalism must obviously be a plus for Christianity.

Thus prepared, Graham set sail for India. When he arrived, the country obviously astonished and enchanted him, its exotic nature gratifying his lifelong desire to visit strange lands and stimulating the curiosity about other cultures that his anthropological studies at Wheaton had encouraged. At times he was simply overwhelmed by the magnitude of the Indian population and its problems. He tried to keep a vow, made back at Florida Bible Institute, to sign autographs for anyone who asked him, but crowds he could never have imagined as he roamed the streets of Temple Terrace made it impossible. The poverty he saw on every hand tugged at his compassion. "Beggars were all around in Bombay," he wrote to Ruth, who had stayed behind in Montreat, "some men with their legs gone, others with their arms that had been eaten by disease, and blind men everywhere, all asking for money. It was one of the most heartbreaking scenes that I had seen since I left Korea. I wanted to give every one of them the message of Christ and give them all money." Ignoring the warnings of missionary friends, he did give some of them money, distributing "as many rupees as I possibly could to as many people as I saw in need" until he found himself engulfed by a teeming whirlpool of beggars screaming and fighting for more, forcing him to concede that his advisers were right—he could not, by him self, alleviate poverty in India.

At first, the campaign itself seemed in danger of being overwhelmed by the tumultuous country, as Graham arrived in the midst of wild riots and turmoil caused by the government's redivision of Indian states. An American reporter, whose dispatches from the tour would become a laudatory book later in the year, dismissed the upheaval with the observation that "authorities agreed that the riots were inspired by Communists, who brought in goon squads," and noted that a young man who was asked why he was throwing stones had answered, "I don't know. Somebody told me to." Whatever the degree of Communist involvement, the riots clearly had nothing to do with Graham, and he felt remarkably unthreatened by them. "All people will respond to a smile and affection," he later observed. "In Bombay, rioters were throwing rocks at each other, but as I passed, I smiled and they smiled back." He could not, it seemed, conceive of the possibility that a riot might be an expression of justifiable discontent and anger rather than the work of evil conspirators, nor could he move beyond his conviction that all problems, and their solutions, are ultimately individualistic. However deep-seated it may or may not have been, the turmoil was sufficient to compel cancellation of a large stadium rally slated for Bombay. Several small indoor services and a large meeting with ministers went on as scheduled, and Graham received wide public exposure through a press conference at which he spent most of his time explaining the basics of Evangelical Christian belief rather than answering the questions about American political issues he had expected to receive.

As Graham and his small band of associates moved southward, the tour finally assumed its hoped-for contours, including crowds far larger than anyone had publicly predicted. In many respects, the rallies and crusades during this portion of the tour resembled those in America and Europe, a circumstance aided by the fact that most were scheduled in the Indian Bible Belt, where the majority of the nation's Christians were concentrated and could be counted on to generate a good turnout for the meetings. In each city the sponsoring committee followed standard operating procedures and launched a publicity barrage that included advertising sheets nailed to trees and loudspeaker trucks that rumbled through cities and villages inviting people to hear the dynamic young Christian from America. Wherever he went, Billy preached the same things he had preached from the swamps of Florida to the venerable halls of Cambridge University: Belshazzar's Feast, John 3:16, and the Second Coming. In Madras attendance over three days exceeded 100,000 with 4,000 to 5,000 inquirers, a response that swamped the counseling corps and moved Billy to marvel that "all you could hear was just the tramp, tramp, tramp of bare feet and sandaled feet as they were coming forward quietly and reverently. This was God. Yes, the same God that was with us at Wembley and Harringay and Kelvin Hall has been with us here in India." His basic crusade, Graham learned, in a lesson that would be crucial to his career, could be packaged and delivered with amazingly little alteration to a land whose history and culture could hardly differ more strikingly from those of North Carolina, particularly if he restricted himself primarily to areas already familiar with the Christian message.

But despite this apparent success, even Graham admitted that the enormous crowds resulted in part from the novelty of his being an American, and it seems clear that some non-Christian observers were baffled by what they heard and saw. One Indian reporter marveled at the strangeness of his message. Graham, he wrote, "propounds the theory that the reproductive act, for instance, is in itself sinful, 'the whole business being a legacy from Adam and Eve.' He insisted that his son, age three, was a liar, and asserted that he himself had wallowed in 'evil' pleasures until, at the age of seventeen, a 'voice' had asked him to spread the divine message." The reporter acknowledged, however, that these peculiarities notwithstanding, "Dr. Graham can be dreadfully effective."

The high point of the crusade as a whole, however, came at Kottayam, a city of only 50,000 located in the heart of India's largest Christian population. Aware that no existing setting would accommodate the anticipated throngs, local church leaders commissioned the construction of a massive temporary amphitheater around the athletic field of a school belonging to the Church of South India. Using small hand tools and baskets, a corps of young girls labored for hours carving terraces into a hillside to provide seating areas for worshipers, segregated by sex as was customary, with women sitting at levels lower than those occupied by men.

Graham's host in Kottayam was Bishop Jacob, spiritual leader of the Church of South India and vice-president of the World Council of Churches. Upon the evangelist's arrival, the bishop told him, with a straight face but perhaps with an inner smile, that just a week earlier, snake charmers had captured twenty-six cobras in the front yard. He assured him, however, that "very rarely do the cobra come in the house," and that even though people were bitten every day, "many of them survive." Given this bit of intelligence, Graham may not have slept well that night under any circumstances, but when a strange communal buzz awakened him at 4:00 A.M., he looked out a window in his room to see an amazing sight: Five thousand worshipers had already assembled and were conducting a massive prayer service, entreating God to bless the American evangelist's visit to their country. This was only the beginning. Throughout the following day, Billy and his team watched in wonder as little knots of pilgrims, all dressed in white and many with large Bibles under their arms, drifted in from every direction and found places, sitting on palm leaves to protect themselves from the ground's slight chill. More than half had traveled at least ten miles; some had walked fifty or sixty miles. All day, they continued to arrive, filling the amphitheater until the crowd had grown to an astounding 75,000 by the time Graham spoke that evening, their garments gleaming in the glare of the powerful arc lights, a dazzling company of Christians larger than any the region had ever seen. Though most were Christians and almost worshipful in their attitude toward him, Graham admitted to some anxiety. "When I leave the platform at night," he wrote to Ruth, "the Bishop always takes me through the milling crowd. It's in a sense a terrifying experience with the crowd pressing in close with their dark faces peering at you, trying to get us in view; and you could imagine that anything could happen if they became excited."

Those who shared those moments still speak of the miracle of Kottayam, but the most powerful sense of supernatural forces at work was unleashed at Palamcottah, deep in southern India. Graham had read and seen enough of Hindu religion to be aware of its ability to incorporate new beliefs and deities into its fantastically elaborate mythology. Indeed, he was quite aware that Hindus, who could co-opt both Christ and Buddha into their system, were far more likely to attend his meetings than were Muslims, who regarded the Christian doctrine of Jesus' divinity as blasphemy. He also knew of their reverence toward holy men of varied stripe, and had become somewhat accustomed to having villagers gather at the windows of his street-level rooms in primitive hotels to peer wordlessly through tattered curtains at the tall white figure who prayed and read his strange limber book till far into the night. Still, he was not prepared for the response at Palamcottah, where the crowd's response to his personal power reached new heights.

The evening service did not begin in promising fashion. The huge crowd, estimated at over a hundred thousand people, had trouble settling down, and a cranky loudspeaker system made it difficult for many people to hear. Some began to shout and scream until the missionaries feared a riot might erupt. Frustrated by the lack of attention, Graham resorted to the one weapon he hoped would work: prayer. "I bowed my head," he wrote, "and prayed a prayer I have not prayed in a long time. It was almost a prayer of commanding, a prayer of authority. I remember I opened my hand as though to come down upon the crowd, and I said, 'Oh God, stop the noise; quiet the people now.' " For whatever reason, the power possessed by charismatic leaders manifested itself dramatically. "Immediately a deathlike hush came on the crowd, and it became the quietest, most reverent meeting we have had in India yet. It was like the breath of God had suddenly fallen. You couldn't hear a sound." Graham preached to the suddenly silent crowd for about an hour, feeling a "tremendous power and liberty." Then, he recalled, "Pentecost fell. People began to run forward and fall upon their knees. Some of them began to scream to God for mercy; others were saying, 'Jesus, save me, Jesus, save me,' until about 3,000 to 4,000 people had come, and we had to stop the invitation because there was no room for anyone else. They were falling on their knees like flies. It was almost as if they were being slain by the Lord." Inquirers outnumbered trained counselors by at least ten to one, so that long after the formal service ended, the meeting ground twinkled with the light of lanterns whose flames struggled with the darkness, providing just enough light to allow counselors to read from the Bible to the little groups of seekers huddled around them across the hillside. In his room that evening, Graham wrote, "Certainly tonight's demonstration of the Spirit is the deepest and greatest that I have ever sensed.... It is almost like something you read about in the ministry of Charles Finney."

Word of the evangelist's presence and power spread quickly through the countryside around Palamcottah. The next morning, when he arrived at the cathedral to address a meeting of women, he found the sanctuary jammed with 5,000 people. At least an equal number stood outside, clamoring to squeeze inside, and the streets were lined with still others trying to get at least a glimpse of the man who had created such excitement. "As we got to the Cathedral," he recalled, "the press of the crowd was so great that our car could not get through. The people were pressing and fighting. I almost thought the car would overturn, they were pushing it, grabbing. Many of them were trying to touch us.... Jack Dain is fearful that many of the Hindus are beginning to accept me as a god. Many of them fall down and practically worshipped me as I come by. Many of them try to get in my shadow." The looming specter of a jealous deity who does not share his glory filled Graham with a frantic compulsion to disavow whatever illicit thrill the moment may have provided. If seeing his name in lights made him uneasy, seeing himself treated as a god absolutely terrified him. "I told them time after time, very much as Peter, that I am not a god but a man; but the word is spreading all over the southern part of India as to what God is doing, and people are coming for miles to see and hear the revival."

Despite denying he had a political agenda, Graham made his customary attempt to forge links with his host country's most powerful and prestigious leaders. He liked to say that "the ground is level at the foot of the cross," but the VIP section of the sprawling canvas-covered and neon-lit *shamiana* (a kind of flat-topped sideless tabernacle) featured armchairs for ambassadors and embassy staff members, while others sat or squatted on the ground. Prominent local government officials had been gracious toward the evangelist in most cities, and in Bombay the head of Nehru's Congress party had met him at the airport, informed him that he often quoted him in his speeches, and announced his intention to attend all his meetings in that city. But the real prize was an appointment with Prime Minister Jawaharlal Nehru, who had maintained a polite distance, perhaps waiting to see how Graham would comport himself.

As always, Billy had behaved in public in an almost painfully gracious manner, making every effort not to offend any segment of the population and taking scrupulous care not to utter any public criticism of Hinduism. While privately abhorring much that he saw—in his journal he described the spectacle of priests laying offerings before phallic sculptures in a Benares temple, a scene he said made him aware of "the powers of darkness and heathenism more in Benares than in any city in which I've ever been"—Graham remained a model guest throughout his tour. Nehru may have appreciated Graham's gentlemanliness, but his close identification with America and the Republican administration made the prime minister wary. He had accompanied Khrushchev and Bulganin on their tour of the country and had closed schools and government offices in an effort to swell attendance at their appearances. The word in unofficial channels was that it troubled him a bit to see Graham visiting many of the same cities without government sponsorship, yet attracting larger crowds than he and the Soviet leaders had drawn. The prime minister agreed to see the evangelist not from any strong personal curiosity but because Dulles and Richard Nixon, working through Ambassador John Sherman Cooper, had urged him to. Striving to maintain a delicate balancing act of remaining poised between the two superpowers, Nehru evidently felt receiving Graham was a requirement—a testimony to the political clout Billy had acquired—but he made no particular effort to make him feel welcome.

Graham knew it would be hard to make a strong impression on Nehru, and his confidence was not increased by the behavior of Dag Hammarskjöld, secretary general of the United Nations, whose appointment with the prime minister immediately preceded his own. As Hammarskjöld crossed the room on his way out, he looked at Graham but did not speak, either not sure that he recognized him or not interested in meeting him. When Graham entered Nehru's office, his host greeted him cordially but then fell silent, leaving the conversational shuttlecock in the evangelist's court. At Dulles's suggestion, Billy spoke of how much Americans admired and respected India and its great leader. Nehru did not respond. Graham volunteered that his tour had given him a much better appreciation for India's problems. Still no response.

Graham later acknowledged his uneasiness, perhaps unconsciously fingering the reason for Nehru's reticence: "When I got through what I considered a rather pleasant speech, he didn't say anything. He just sat there with a letter opener in his hand, twiddling it." Then, when he began a recital of the high points of his tour, the prime minister stared at the ceiling. "I had never had an interview quite like it," Graham recalled, so he fell back on the one topic with which he felt entirely comfortable, regardless of the reaction it stirred. "I decided I'd tell him what Christ had done for me, and I told him in no uncertain terms ... how He had changed me and given me peace and joy, and how He had forgiven my sins. Then immediately, he began to be interested. He began to ask some questions." Graham pointed out that he had no interest in preserving Christianity as an outpost remnant of British imperialism; indeed, he had repeatedly told his audiences that Jesus was an Asian like themselves, with skin a bit lighter than theirs but darker than his own, and had urged them to make their churches indigenous and self-supporting. Nehru warmed to that line of conversation and said he had no objection to Christian missionaries in India as long as they refrained from political activity. He conceded that Graham's presence in India seemed to have a salutary effect and offered to help in any way he could during his sojourn in New Delhi. Once again, Graham's simple, sincere testimony, cut loose from State Department cant, melted a potential opponent's icy reserve and won for himself, if not a friendship, at least an attitude of tolerant respect.

Graham reported that even though Nehru had said nothing when he ventured that peace would come only "when people turn by faith to Christ," he sensed the prime minister was "pro-Christian." But Billy frequently divined in people, particularly those in positions of power, sentiments that may not have been present. He seemed to assume, in the absence of compelling counterevidence, that deep down most people saw the world much as he did. His belief in the universality of the deepest human needs and characteristics bespoke a large and admirable spirit but made it difficult for Graham to accept the brute fact that human cultures and the people they comprise can differ radically over quite basic issues. Throughout most of his public ministry, he had hammered away at the Satanic nature of communism, and yet when he met real Communists, he found it hard to believe they understood what they were ostensibly espousing. When he saw Indian Communists marching in the streets, waving Communist flags, shouting Communist slogans, and singing Communist songs, he walked along beside them and directed his photographer to take pictures. "We marched along for about three or four hundred yards with one group," he reported. "I would wave at them and smile, and they would smile back, because of course most of them, even though they were in red shirts, waving the hammer and sickle, did not know what it was all about. I am convinced that the average Communist in India doesn't know what it's all about."

The positive side of Graham's attitude was that he believed, and some times demonstrated that openhearted friendliness could overpower ideology. On hearing of the hospitality and warmth the Indians extended to Khrushchev and Bulganin, and experiencing a similar response himself, he observed that "if Eisenhower came to India, he would get the most overwhelming reception of his life, and it would do America a whale of a lot of good. They don't care two hoots for all the money we give them, but they are thrilled to death when we come in person to visit them." Graham's intuitive grasp of the fact that a symbolic gesture may do more to win a people's allegiance than more substantive measures was accurate, but it led him to make a foreign-policy recommendation that must have had diplomats in both capitals groaning. At the airport in Bangalore, he had seen a beautiful plane the Russians had given to Nehru to commemorate their leaders' visit. "We give fifty million dollars in economic aid to India," he wrote, "and it appears on the third page. Mr. Nehru is given an airplane costing probably a million dollars and it's front-page news and people talk about it everywhere. There is a showmanship in the way the Russians give that puts all of our giving in the shade. I thought: wouldn't it be a wonderful thing if we gave to India perhaps a beautiful new air-conditioned train; or we might give to Mr. Nehru a white air-conditioned Cadillac. This would cause the people of India to talk more than all of our economic aid put together."

Before leaving the country, Graham took steps to preserve and extend the achievements of the campaign by making outreach to India an official element of BGEA activities. To do this he conferred the mantle of leadership he had been weaving upon Dr. Akbar Abdul-Haqq, a Methodist scholar who had been his interpreter in New Delhi. A formal and formidable man, Abdul-Haqq had been lukewarm about Graham's visit, but the experience of holding a large throng in absolute thrall, even if the words belonged to another man, had their effect. After only one sermon, he confided to Graham that "I believe God has called me tonight to be an evangelist." Graham persuaded Abdul-Haqq to come to America to learn the trade of evangelism by pointing out that part of his own success in drawing great crowds stemmed from the novelty of his being an American, but that would fade. "I'm not the man to be used for spiritual awakening here," he told Abdul-Haqq. "It has to be an Asian. I think you are the man." Eight months later, after a visit to Graham's crusade in Louisville, Kentucky, Akbar Abdul-Haqq held the first of a still-continuing string of crusades in North India.

Apart from the initiation of this ongoing effort, the impact of Graham's Indian campaign is difficult to assess. Without question, it stood out as a brief, shining moment in the life of the Indian church in the regions he visited. It demonstrated that it was possible to conduct large-scale evangelistic crusades in India, a hypothesis that had not been rigorously tested. It also lent encouragement to scattered bands of believers who, like the prophet Elijah, may have imagined that they alone had not bowed the knee to Baal (or Siva or Krishna or Vishnu). They could now see some strength in the cause they espoused and could continue in the face of ridicule or persecution from relatives and fellow villagers.

Unfortunately, much of whatever goodwill Graham generated by his attempts to be a gracious guest was erased by an apparent failure to recognize that India, though far away from the United States, was not completely insulated from Western media. A few months after the tour, Chattanooga *Free Press* reporter George Burnham, an Evangelical journalist who chronicled Graham's British and European tours and traveled with the team to the Far East, published a book that included such condescending observations of his own as "a majority of the economic problems now suffered in India could be wiped out overnight if they would eat their cows instead of worshiping them." It also contained unflattering comments Graham had recorded in his diary or in letters to Ruth and had unwisely allowed Burnham to quote. The book drew heavy fire from the Indian government and the religious community, both of which felt the evangelist had dissembled by displaying apparent openness to Indian culture while in fact regarding it as decidedly inferior to that of the West. Deeply chagrined that he had offended his hosts, Graham wrote an abject apology for the Madras *Sunday Standard*, noting somewhat lamely that although he had written an introduction to the book, he had not taken the time to read it and therefore had not been aware of Burnham's ethnocentric bias. Ultimately, since several of the offending quotations were from his own hand, all he could do was pledge to himself not to repeat his mistake in the future. "I have learned a lesson," he ruefully admitted to Jack Dain, "and it will never happen again." It is difficult to know exactly what other lessons Graham learned on this tour, how his first exposure to a culture so deeply different from his own affected his view of life and the world. His abhorrence of Hindu rituals involving sexuality and his shock over the crushing poverty he saw must have strengthened his beliefs in sexual reserve and the American economic system, just as his exposure to the deep spirituality of the Indian people may have contributed to a gradual widening of his vision and a loosening of the bonds of Fundamentalist separatist dogma. But in large measure, it appears Graham came away relatively unscathed by whatever reflections he entertained. Near the end of the trip, in a tone one observer perceptively likened to that a boy might use in capsuling a good summer-camp experience, he observed that "everything has been absolutely perfect. I have not been sick one single day. I do not have any cold, sore throat, or stomachache.... I have not lost my temper once and try to wait patiently on everybody." In the same vein, he reported on returning home that "I don't think that in any place I've ever been they've had finer platforms for me to speak from, better amplification systems, and finer arrangements."

While Billy stumped the world preparing people for an eternal home, Ruth stayed back on Black Mountain building an earthly one. As their children grew and their privacy diminished, she set about to construct an environment that suited both her uncompromising aesthetic tastes and her preference for solitude. In 1954 the Grahams had the chance to buy a heavily wooded 150-acre cove between two hogback ridges rising up behind Montreat. This was at a time when more people wanted to move into town than out to the country and two mountain families offered the land for sale at $12.50 an acre. The narrow, steep, and winding clay road was barely passable, and Billy wondered at the wisdom of trying to build a home on the side of a mountain, but he left the decision to her. To his mild alarm, she made it. While he was on a trip to the West Coast, she borrowed the money from the bank and bought the land. She fixed up a pole cabin one of the mountain families had abandoned, and the family used it for a time as a weekend retreat from tourists. Then, while Billy was in Europe and the Far East during 1955 and 1956, she scoured the North Carolina mountains, bouncing her red jeep up and down back roads and into remote hollows, popping into gas stations and little grocery stores with bread signs stenciled into the screen door to ask if anybody knew of a log cabin she could buy. Some of the citizens found it hard to believe the feisty creature in blue jeans and army jacket was the wife of their state's most famous citizen, or that she was serious about wanting to buy old houses, but her scavenging turned up five cabins and several truckloads of lumber, well-weathered bricks, cords of crooked fence rails, and a yard sale's worth of rough-hewn rustic *authentica*.

Ruth hired an architect to draw plans for the house but served as counter-architect and project manager herself. Her task was not easy. Local workmen found it hard to understand why a woman whose husband had a good job would want a house made out of old logs instead of clean brick or brand-new lumber covered with asbestos siding, and then want to fill it with country junk instead of going to Sears, Roebuck and buying furniture that matched and wasn't all scratched up as if somebody else had used it. Billy himself had some preference for the new and modern—"When Bill gets to heaven and finds it's not like a Holiday Inn or Marriott," Ruth joked, "he'll be back"—but he let his wife build it to suit herself, stipulating only that it have comfortable chairs and plenty of good lighting. Several of the craftsmen never caught her vision. One carpenter finally quit when she insisted he hang weather-beaten cabin doors in the front hall closets. "I weren't mad at none of you men," he told his co-workers, "but everything I done up there I had to do wrong. A man can't take no pride in this kind of work." But others eventually came to share at least a bit of her affection for "mountain primitive," and one finally conceded, "You know, this house kind of grows on you, and before you know it, you catch yourself a-liking it."

Little Piney Cove is not hard to like. The view across the mountains, framed in great sweeping windows that fill the high-ceilinged, rough-beamed living room, dining room, and large functional kitchen is beyond price. The rooms themselves are large, warm, and rich with wood and books and mementos and the redolence of four fireplaces, the largest of which, in the living room, is of walk-in dimensions and crowned with a mantle (fashioned from an old diving board) carved with the words *Eine feste Burg ist unser Gott* ("A Mighty Fortress Is Our God"). To the question of how many rooms it has, Ruth laughs and gives a stock answer: "The architect told me, 'Ruth, if you are smart, you will never count the rooms in this house.' So I never have. You have to decide what's a room and what's not a room. Ned [their youngest son, born in 1958] always slept in what was supposed to be the linen closet."

Isolated as it was, Little Piney Cove did not permit complete withdrawal from the world. Graham's foreign tours had enabled him to avoid direct involvement with mounting racial tensions in the United States during 1955 and the early part of 1956, but as he faced repeated questioning about the American situation and watched with a mixture of dismay and fascination at the nonviolent protests led by fellow Baptist preacher Martin Luther King, Jr., he began to ponder what he might do to help. Others had been pondering the same question. Alabama congressman Frank W. Boykin, a friend and supporter, wrote to President Eisenhower, recommending that he enlist the evangelist to help the South make the transition to integration—"to quiet it down and to go easy and, in a godlike way instead of trying to cram it down the throats of our people all in one day, which some of our enemies are trying to do." Eisenhower, whose chances of reelection could be hurt by racial turmoil, seized immediately on Boykin's suggestion and dictated a long letter to Graham. The President referred to a previous conversation in which they had discussed "the opportunity open to ministers of promoting both tolerance and progress in our race relations problem" and listed several gradualist measures he thought might help reduce tensions. "Could we not begin to elect a few qualified Negroes to school boards?" he asked. "Could not universities begin to make entrance into their graduate schools strictly on the basis of merit—the examinations to be conducted by some Board, which might even be unaware of the race or color of the applicant?" Might it not be possible to develop flexible seating plans for public buses so that blacks would not be left waiting at bus stops while seats reserved for whites went vacant? "It would appear to me," the President ventured, "that things like this could properly be mentioned in a pulpit."

Graham's response, dispatched by return mail and followed with a visit to the White House two days later, not only reflected his willingness to use his influence to help ameliorate an important social problem but showed his oft-repeated claim of political neutrality to be less than fully accurate. He assured Eisenhower he would convene a meeting of the leaders of the major southern denominations and would urge them to call on their people to show moderation, charity, and compassion as they moved toward compliance with the Supreme Court's decision. He also noted that he had talked with Governors Luther Hodges of North Carolina and Frank Clement of Tennessee and had urged them "to consider the racial problem from a spiritual point of view." Then, moving from the role of minister to partisan tactician, he said, "Immediately after the election, you can take whatever steps you feel are wise and right. In the meantime, it might be well to let the Democratic party bear the brunt of the debate. Your deeds are speaking for you. You have so wonderfully kept above the controversies that necessarily rage from time to time. I hope particularly before November you are able to stay out of this bitter racial situation that is developing."

As promised, Graham met with a wide range of black and white southern religious leaders, both in groups and privately, laying before them "what I considered to be a sensible program for better race relations." He had little doubt that like the President and himself, God approved of a gradual approach to integration. "I believe the Lord is helping us, and if the Supreme Court will go slowly and the extremists on both sides will quiet down, we can have a peaceful social readjustment over the next ten-year period." Like many another moderate, however, he soon found that standing in the middle affords more people an opportunity to shoot. On the Right, staunch resisters of desegregation denounced him as a meddler and traitor to his people. On the Left, liberal Christians wondered why he demanded that some sins be renounced immediately and totally but thought it permissible to repent of racism a step or two at a time. Reinhold Niebuhr, perhaps the most acute and influential religious thinker in America at the time, scolded Graham in *Christian Century* for a moderate approach that failed to take black suffering seriously and that looked pale and timorous when compared to Charles Finney's vigorous support of abolition.

To have become the sort of bold prophet Niebuhr and others wanted him to be was ideologically and temperamentally impossible for Billy Graham. He sincerely believed that laws cannot change hearts, and he found it extremely painful to make people angry enough to renounce him. But if he could not directly confront, he could attempt to persuade, and he did so quite publicly. That fall, in *Life* magazine, he issued a plea for an end to racial intolerance. He assured a national audience that most southern ministers believed segregation should be ended on buses, in railroad and bus stations, in hotels, and in restaurants, but that it was "far too early to implement school integration in some sections of the Deep South." Still, he did not lay all the blame at the feet of extremists and outsiders. "We have sown flagrant human injustice," he confessed, "and we have reaped a harvest of racial strife." But southerners, he noted, were not the world's only racists. Jains discriminate against people of low caste in India, the British look down on Jamaican blacks, Arabs and Jews dislike each other, white Americans behave unjustly toward Mexicans and Indians as well as blacks, and blacks themselves often manifest prejudice toward whites. He reiterated his conviction that none of these attitudes could be justified from Scripture—"Let's not make the mistake of pleading the Bible to defend it"—and noted that after an earlier period of bowing to local custom, he now refused to hold a crusade unless blacks were permitted to sit wherever they pleased, even though his conversations with blacks revealed that they usually felt comfortable sitting by themselves. Parents, he said, should actively teach their children to love people of other races lest they pass on the sin of prejudice, and all Christians should "take a stand in your church for neighbor love.... Take courage, speak up, and help the church move forward in bettering race relations." All things considered, it was hardly a pathbreaking statement, but it was a statement, and it called on Christians to take responsibility for building a better world.

13

New Evangelicals, Old Fundamentalists

As the scope of his ministry expanded, Graham's supporting nucleus swelled proportionately. When the Minneapolis staff grew to more than 125, prompting a move to larger quarters, BGEA purchased a plain but roomy Standard Oil building that provided twice as much space at less cost than the previous annual rent. Negotiations for the building reveal a telling aspect of Graham's leadership style, a style that enabled him to husband his energies and concentrate on matters more directly related to ministry. After resigning from the Northwestern Schools, he spent little time in Minneapolis, content to leave the day-to-day operation to George Wilson. He liked the arrangement and saw no reason to alter it, even for something as important as choosing the ministry's basic administrative facility. When Wilson called repeatedly to laud the advantages of the building, he was both astonished and gratified to hear his boss say, "Man, if you need a building, go ahead and buy it. Don't bother me with details."

Graham was, however, willing to take a stronger hand in augmenting his personal circle. Throughout his ministry, when he needed someone to fill a particular role, instead of launching a formal or informal search for a person with appropriate credentials, he has selected someone he liked and trusted, whatever the shape or content of his portfolio. He has done whatever it took to persuade that person to join him, then endued him with confidence to accomplish the task for which he had been chosen. As he moved more and more in circles of strangers, new friends, and high-powered casual acquaintances, he felt the need for the reassurance that only old friends can provide. And as he had done while in YFC and at Northwestern, he called on one of his oldest and most trusted friends, T. W. Wilson.

After leaving Northwestern along with Graham, T. W. had gone back into an evangelistic ministry and was achieving considerable success with his own team. He had felt like a misfit at Northwestern and admitted he suspected it was Billy Graham, not God, who had called him to that particular position. When Graham invited him to join his crusade team in 1956, he resisted. Wilson was flourishing financially, a pleasant experience for a man reared in poverty, and admitted that "for me to be willing to take a big cut in salary was my big problem." Instead of offering to match his current income, Graham used a bit of spiritual jujitsu on Wilson. "T," he said, "why don't you come [with me] and just take a salary. I know what kind of offerings you get, but I believe your ministry would be more constructive, more helpful, more edifying, and freer from criticism." Wilson struggled with the decision but finally gave in. "In a sense, it was a selfish thing," he acknowledged, "and yet, I wanted to do what was honorable and right. I took a salary of just about one third of what I had been accustomed to, but I was happy about it, and it made me feel more like a gentleman." Over the next thirty years, no one, including Ruth, would spend more time at Billy's side than T. W. Wilson.

A second major addition came with the recruitment of Leighton Ford, an impressive young Canadian whose life Graham had already touched in important ways. Ford, an able preacher and youth leader while in high school, met Graham at a YFC conference at Winona Lake. Their paths crossed again in January 1949, when Billy spoke at a Canadian Youth Fellowship meeting at Ford's invitation. When only one young woman came forward at the close of Graham's sermon, Leighton was crushed, apparently feeling he was somehow responsible for not having produced a more receptive audience. After the service, as he stood by the side of the platform, tears of disappointment streaming down his face, he felt the presence of the tall young evangelist he so admired standing beside him. Graham recognized, of course, that Leighton was in no way responsible for the meager response, but he took his young friend's concern seriously. "Billy put his arms around me," Ford recalled, "and said, 'Leighton, God has given you a burden, and He always blesses somebody with a burden." Graham perceived that Leighton Ford had exceptional promise as a preacher and Christian leader, and he determined to see it realized.

Shortly afterward, he contacted President Edman of Wheaton and got him to accept Ford as a student. Then, not content with the role of college recruiter, he decided to become a matchmaker. In his subsequent letters to Leighton and even in a carbon copy of a letter he sent to Edman, he managed to mention that his younger sister, Jean, would also be enrolling at Wheaton in the fall. If Ford understood this simply to be incidental news, his mother did not. Throughout the spring and summer, whenever he dated a girl, she would remind him that he should not get serious, because "you haven't met Billy Graham's sister yet." On the home front, Graham was telling Jean about Leighton. Perhaps sensing that once Billy decided what people ought to do with their lives, the chances of getting him to relent were minimal, the two young people accepted their fate and were married in December 1953; the bride's older brother performed the ceremony. During the summer of 1952, Ford worked for BGEA as a representative of the film ministry, arranging screenings for *Mr. Texas* in churches and rented halls throughout the

Midwest. In 1955 he was a student at Columbia (Presbyterian) Theological Seminary in Georgia and spent the summer in Scotland holding one-night meetings aimed at keeping Graham's Kelvin Hall inquirers plugged into local churches. He proved so effective that Graham persuaded him to return to Toronto in the fall to help with a three-week crusade in his home city. Soon afterward, he became a full-time associate evangelist with the team, a position he would hold for thirty years.

That Graham was able to summon men to his side attested to his status as a key leader and the most prominent public figure in a movement that had assumed definite shape and called itself the New Evangelicalism. The term, coined by Harold John Ockenga, signified a form of conservative Christianity that consciously marked itself off from old-line Fundamentalism in several crucial respects. Its adherents clung loyally to such basic tenets of Fundamentalism as the inspired and fully reliable nature of Scripture, the Virgin Birth, the sinfulness of humanity, the substitutionary atonement, the Resurrection, and the Second Coming, but tended to be rather tolerant of minor theological differences among themselves. Upward mobility, education, travel, and the associations they afforded helped them understand that good and sincere people could look at the world quite differently and that these differences need not always be threatening. They tended to feel more comfortable in Evangelical congregations, denominations, and parachurch organizations but did not insist these were the only bodies in which one could serve God. If an Evangelical believer chose to remain affiliated with a mainline denomination, as had Nelson Bell and Harold Ockenga, that was acceptable, perhaps even desirable, since they might counteract tendencies toward liberalism in those bodies. Most were skeptical of the tongue speaking and healing that occurred in Pentecostal denominations, but they hesitated to define the work of the Holy Spirit too narrowly, and they regarded the Pentecostals who belonged to the National Association of Evangelicals as brothers and sisters in Christ. Similarly, though they deemed Modernist theology to be both erroneous and threatening to true Christianity, their opposition lacked the hysterical brittleness manifested by Carl McIntire and men of his ilk. To the New Evangelicals, it was far more important to proclaim the gospel than to defend it.

Despite their conviction that theological disputation should take second place to evangelism, the New Evangelicals were by no means anti-intellectual. On the contrary, Ockenga and Bell and Carl F. H. Henry, as well as other leaders of the movement, had high regard for serious intellectual work and devoutly believed that Evangelical convictions could and should be set forth and defended according to the same rigorous canons of scholarship observed in liberal and secular universities and seminaries. For true Christianity to commend itself to modern men and women, it had to be intellectually respectable. It could announce that "the Bible says," but it had to show why that announcement deserved special notice. It might ultimately reject evolution, but it would address the same evidence secular scientists considered and not simply declare that evolution could not be true because it differed from the Genesis account of creation.

As part of their willingness to take a hard look at positions long held, many New Evangelicals began to reexamine some of their distinctive and cherished beliefs, including that hallmark of Fundamentalist doctrine, dispensationalism. Few surrendered their conviction that Christ would one day return to bring human history to a divinely ordained consummation, probably including a glorious millennial reign. Some key leaders, however, rejected the dispensationalist notion that history is following a blueprint so detailed and immutable that human attempts to affect its course are futile, a belief that underlay Fundamentalism's notorious lack of concern for social reform. Speaking directly to this issue, Ockenga asserted that the New (and true) Evangelical "intends that Christianity will be the mainspring in many of the reforms of the societal order. It is wrong to abdicate responsibility for society under the impetus of a theology which overemphasizes the eschatological." By the mid-1950s, they had not only rejected the narrowness of the Fundamentalist vision but had begun to believe they might have an outside chance to regain a kind of cultural hegemony Evangelicals had not known, outside the South at least, since the Civil War. Modernist faith in the inherent goodness of humanity and the inevitability of progress had taken a terrible pounding in the previous two decades, making the biblical view of a tragically flawed humanity seem quite plausible and the offer of radical transformation quite attractive. In apparent response to this circum stance, America was experiencing unmistakable religious revival, evinced in part by the growing popularity of Billy Graham. Many New Evangelicals dared hope that with God's help and Billy Graham's connections, they might revitalize Evangelical Christianity, and through it, America and the world.

Graham and President Eisenhower had regular, if not particularly frequent, contact. The evangelist visited at Gettysburg, where the former general gave him a private tour of the battlefield where Morrow Graham's father had been wounded. Before his foreign trips, Graham tried to drop by the White House to let Eisenhower know where he would be going and to learn if he needed to watch for any special diplomatic opportunities or pitfalls. When he returned he typically sent a long report on what he had observed or requested the opportunity to discuss "an urgent matter" or to deliver "extremely vital information" to the Commander-in-Chief. After major crusades he routinely dropped the President a line, letting him know the size of the crowds and assuring him that most of the people he had met in the crusade city admired and prayed regularly for him. Graham made no attempt to mask either his delight at their relationship or his political leanings. Once, after Eisenhower gave him a ride in the presidential limousine, he called the brief excursion "an unforgettable experience that I shall cherish the rest of my life." In the same letter, he noted that he had recently heard Republican congressman Walter Judd speak in Asheville. "I told him afterward," he noted, "that if he could give that same address on all the television networks, we wouldn't have to worry about Congress remaining GOP-controlled this fall." Like any politician interested in reelection, the President kept up his end of the exchanges, but the tone and content of his letters suggest that genuine affection nourished the friendship at least as much as perfunctory, pragmatic politics. By the summer of 1955, Graham, who signed his letters with such effusive tributes as "still thinking you are the greatest President in American history, I am cordially yours," was comparing Ike to Lincoln and urging him to seek reelection in 1956. "You have," he pledged, "my unqualified support."

Contact with the White House led naturally to further exposure to Nixon, whose fervent anticommunism and Evangelical associations (though a Quaker, Nixon had been converted by evangelist Paul Rader, and his parents were active in California Evangelical circles) attracted Graham to him. Their similarity in age also made it easy to develop what would become a long and fateful friendship. While many found it difficult to admire or even to trust the Vice-President, Graham quickly became an enthusiastic booster and solicitous counselor. In the summer of 1955 he observed that "[Nixon's] sincerity, strong convictions, and humility are evident and catching. Your speech is also sparked with a sense of humor that is all-important." These winsome qualities, he thought, bode well for the Republican ticket in the 1956 election, and he revealed that he was suggesting to friends in "high ecclesiastical circles" that Nixon be invited to address various religious assemblies during the following year. He also hoped he might benefit firsthand from the Vice-President's charm and wit. "Anytime that you have a few days this winter," he volunteered, in an uncommon show of scheduling flexibility and willingness to travel, "we can take a swim or play a game of golf in Florida or, better still, in Hawaii."

By October, when Nixon was standing in for Eisenhower, who had suffered a heart attack, Graham had already begun to envision him as a candidate for president, if not in 1956, then certainly in 1960. Given that likelihood, he felt the Vice-President needed to pay close attention to his public image. "Governor Dewey said to me a few weeks ago," he confided, "that you were the most able man in the Republican party. He has great confidence in you but seems to be a little fearful that you may be taken over unwittingly by some of the extreme right-wingers. He feels that in order to be elected President of the United States, a man is going to have to take a middle-of-the-road position. I think he is right!" He then cautioned Nixon against drawing too heavily on his anti-Communist credentials. "In my opinion, there is so much goodwill bubbling out of Moscow that the issue of Communism is no longer as potent as it was politically in the U.S." The Reds were still a menace, he conceded, but it might not be wise to harp on it too loudly. That said, he promised, "You will have my constant prayers and I will put in a word here and there and use my influence to show people that you are a man of moral integrity and Christian principles." In his reply a short time later, Nixon indicated he had taken the evangelist's counsel to heart. "I think your political advice was right on the beam," he said, "and, as you probably have noted, I have been trying to follow the course of action you recommended during the past few weeks."

The frequency and informality of these exchanges grew as the election approached. The evangelist called the Vice-President "Dick" and remained "Cordially yours, Billy." Nixon reciprocated the familiarity, and the two men cemented their friendship with further notes and golf games and gifts. Once, after Nixon sent a set of three "Mr. Vice-President" golf balls, Billy gushed in gratitude that prompted a non sequitur "How thoughtful of you. No wonder you are one of the youngest Vice-Presidents in history." Graham did not restrict his praises and favors to private communication. He told *U.S. News & World Report* that Nixon was "very respected around the world as a man of the people" and arranged to have the Vice-President, whom he characterized as "a splendid churchman," speak at major Methodist, Baptist, and Presbyterian conferences in North Carolina during the summer, even supplying him with an unsolicited speech he thought Nixon might want to use. He also offered to invite several key religious leaders, including a Methodist and an Episcopal bishop, the president of the Southern Baptist Convention, and the moderator of the Presbyterian Church in the United States (South), to have lunch with the Vice-President at the Graham home in Montreat. Graham felt exposure to these and other religious leaders would help Nixon immensely. "Very frankly," he said, "you are in need of a boost in Protestant religious circles. I am asked about you almost everywhere I go in religious circles. I think it is time that you move among some of these men and let them know you. There is nothing like personal contact. They will become completely sold on your sincerity and ability, just as I have been." He assured Nixon, however, that the trip would not be a weekend of sackcloth and ashes. In addition to promising him "three air-conditioned rooms with a king-sized double bed," Billy offered to be his host at "the exclusive Biltmore Club in Asheville, where General Eichelberger and I have lockers side by side."

After the Republican convention in San Francisco in August, Graham wrote Eisenhower that he was "absolutely convinced" that the contrast between the decorum at the GOP gathering and the raucous disorder at the Democratic convention in Chicago "won millions of thoughtful Americans. As you, Mrs. Eisenhower and the Nixons were bowing in prayer, all of us seemed to sense that here were dedicated people to a cause that cannot lose. I shall do all in my power during the coming campaign to gain friends and supporters for your cause. As always, you have my complete devotion and personal affection." On the same day, he told Nixon, "There is no doubt about it that the Democrats are going to use every trick in the bag, but in my opinion, you do not have to stoop to the gutter with them to win." Once again, Graham made no official public endorsement, but such pointed comments as his lament that divorce no longer seemed to disqualify a person from being a presidential candidate—Adlai Stevenson, the Democratic nominee was divorced—left little doubt where he stood. After the election Graham wrote not only to congratulate Nixon on the victory and commend him for "adhering to highest moral and spiritual principles" but also to note, in easy-to-decipher code, that "this campaign has lifted your prestige higher than ever. I think some of the possibilities we talked about concerning the future are definitely in the making." Then, in a reference that made it clear that at least some of his political views were grounded in his understanding of the Bible, he added, "Some of the things that are now happening in the Middle East are highly significant from the Bible point of view. I hope the U.S. does not make a serious mistake at this crucial hour of history." In a subsequent letter, he raised a similar point, observing that "it is amazing how these scriptures are being fulfilled before our very eyes. Sometimes, perhaps we will have opportunity to go over these again privately, because it may help you in determining future courses of action, in case added responsibilities are yours."

Graham was not alone in his efforts to inject Evangelical Christianity into the veins of the body politic. In Washington a seldom-publicized organization, International Christian Leadership (ICL), set up a "Christian embassy" under the low-key but effective direction of Abraham Vereide, known in Evangelical circles as Mr. Christian of Washington. Vereide's primary strategy was to organize breakfast prayer groups for government leaders and workers and, more dramatically, to conduct "spiritual installations" for government officials entering new positions or feeling the need for a spiritual booster shot. In 1953 Vereide also organized the first annual Presidential Prayer Breakfast. These breakfasts brought leading Evangelicals together with some of the nation's most powerful figures. At the 1954 edition, which doubled as the opening meeting of ICL's annual conference, Eisenhower, several cabinet members, and a flock of influential senators and congressmen attended; featured speakers included hotel magnate Conrad Hilton, Richard Nixon, and Chief Justice Earl Warren. Billy Graham did not speak, but he was prominently present, and at the close of the session, George Beverly Shea led the six hundred guests in singing President Eisenhower's favorite hymn, "What a Friend We Have in Jesus."

While Graham and Vereide and others worked the corridors of political power, Harold Ockenga, Carl Henry, and a small cadre of men more oriented to scholarship tended a new young sapling in the groves of academe. When

Charles Fuller first spoke to Ockenga about using his radio ministry to generate income to found an undergraduate school of evangelism and missions, Ockenga (who held a Ph.D. from the University of Pittsburgh) countered with a vision of a first-rate graduate seminary to fill the gap created when Princeton moved into the liberal camp and to equip Evangelicals for the formidable task of articulating and defending conservative Christianity in the face of liberal theology and secular materialism. The idea captured Fuller's imagination, and in 1947 Fuller Theological Seminary welcomed an inaugural class of thirty-nine members—an impressive number in itself, and all the more so because it included students from Harvard, Dartmouth, Berkeley, and USC—to its Pasadena campus, a lovely facility acquired by Fuller at a good price from a millionaire's estate. Its founding fathers expansively predicted it would soon achieve a status comparable to that of another Pasadena institution, making it "a Cal Tech of the Evangelical World." A decade would pass before Billy Graham established a formal tie with Fuller Seminary as a member of its board of trustees, but his admiration for its founder and faculty translated easily into unabashed enthusiasm for the new school and its mission. He liked being plugged into a serious academic institution, and the men at Fuller relished the visibility their ties with him provided their little school.

Despite his confidence in the faculty and students at Fuller, Graham worried that their impact would be too long in coming and began to dream of a way to present the beliefs and concerns of the New Evangelicalism to America's pastors, who could, in turn, communicate them to their parishioners. In the service of that dream, in 1956 he established what would quickly become the most widely read serious religious journal in the nation, *Christianity Today*. Early in 1951, Fuller professor Wilbur Smith, whom he greatly respected, wrote to him of the need for "a periodical so important that it would be absolutely indispensable for every serious-minded Christian minister in America." Such a publication would, in Smith's vision, contain exposition of Scripture, explication of biblical prophecy and its application to current affairs, reviews of important books, and religious news. It would also, he insisted, pay "no attention to trash." At that hectic point in his career, when he was trying to hold crusades, run the Northwestern Schools by telephone, keep BGEA afloat, and prepare a weekly radio broadcast, Graham had been in no position to act on Smith's suggestion, and it is not clear he gave it much consideration. As he became more solidly established, however, and began to be criticized by liberal churchmen, particularly in the *Christian Century*, which the secular media seemed to regard as a kind of semiofficial voice of Protestant Christianity, he began to reflect on the need for a comparable publication to represent an Evangelical perspective. Late in 1953, as he told it, he got out of bed in the middle of the night, went to his desk, and started writing down ideas for an Evangelical publication, similar in format to *Christian Century*, that "would give theological respectability to Evangelicals." He made a list of the various departments the magazine should have, decided to call it *Christianity Today*, and even drew up a tentative budget. The next morning, he shared his ideas with Ruth, who suggested they "make it a matter of prayer." When prayer produced no negative indicators, Graham took the matter to Dr. Bell, who had founded the *Presbyterian Journal*; his father-in-law was enthusiastically receptive. Billy's crusade experience had convinced him that many ministers in mainline denominations held Evangelical convictions but were timid about expressing them lest more liberal colleagues hold them up to scorn. Also, the fragmentation so characteristic of Fundamentalists and Evangelicals often left them isolated and unconnected to those sharing their beliefs and values. "Evangelicals needed a rallying point," Graham recognized; "perhaps a dynamic magazine could help."

A full schedule of crusades, including Harringay, moved the project to Graham's back burner during 1954, but with BGEA's underwriting the cost of his travel and correspondence, Nelson Bell diligently contacted hundreds of Evangelical leaders to gauge the interest in such a magazine and to identify potential editors, writers, and financial supporters. With few exceptions, he found generous encouragement. By 1955, Graham was ready to move, and it was clear he had been thinking about the character of the publication. In a letter to Fuller professor Harold Lindsell, he elaborated on his plans. The magazine would, he wrote, "plant the Evangelical flag in the middle of the road, taking a conservative theological position but a definite liberal approach to social problems." It would be critical of both the National and World Council of Churches when that was appropriate but would also commend them for their good work rather than align itself in unvarying opposition, in the manner of Carl McIntire's journal, the *Christian Beacon*. It would, of course, promulgate a high view of biblical authority, but "its view of inspiration would be somewhat along the line of [*The Christian View of Science and Scripture*] by Bernard Ramm," an Evangelical scholar's book that challenged the belief that the Bible could be taken as authoritative on scientific matters and left open the possibility that a divinely guided form of evolution might have played a role in the origin of species and the development of humankind. Graham's positive assessment of Ramm's controversial book was significant in that despite his unshakable confidence in the trustworthiness of Scripture, he was wary of making stronger claims for the Bible than the Bible makes for itself and was opting for an approach sure to draw fire from many Fundamentalists. Graham felt it was crucially important to "present a positive and constructive program" rather than to use "the stick of denunciation and criticism.... We would attempt to lead and love rather than vilify, criticize, and beat. Fundamentalism has failed miserably with the *big stick* approach; now it is time to take the *big love* approach."

As part of its mission to influence national policy, the magazine would emanate from Washington, D.C. Graham had seriously considered moving BGEA's offices to Washington—he thought it would be impressive to tell his radio listeners to write to "Billy Graham, Washington, D.C. That's all the address you need." It was even more important, he believed, for the capital to serve as the new journal's home base. "I felt a magazine coming from Washington would carry with it an unusual authority. We also wanted our editor to mingle with congressmen, senators, and government leaders so he could speak with firsthand knowledge on the issues of the day." Certainly, the editors must have felt they were at the center; from their tenth-floor offices at the corner of Pennsylvania Avenue and Fifteenth Street, they looked down on the White House lawn and the Treasury building.

Graham felt confident that tens of thousands of pastors would welcome such a publication, but he realized it would take years to build a substantial subscription list, and Evangelicals did not have years to spare. In one of the boldest aspects of the entire enterprise, he resolved to send the magazine free of charge for two full years to every minister and ministerial student in the United States, Canada, Great Britain, Australia, and New Zealand, as well as to English-speaking missionaries on foreign fields—a total of nearly 200,000 unpaid subscribers, the largest list of Protestant ministers ever assembled for any purpose. He was prepared to throw his weight behind the new venture and expected to be part of "a silent non-published group of men who actually control the paper," but he did not think it should be a BGEA house organ, and his association would not be able to foot the entire bill. He persuaded old friends Howard Butt and John Bolten to pledge sizable sums, and he wrung substantial amounts from such newer supporters as shoe magnate Maxey Jarman and advertising executive Carl Fleming, but the angel whose wings would cast the largest shadow over the publication was J. Howard Pew, the president of Sun Oil Company and an active Presbyterian layman whom Billy had met through Nelson Bell. Despite his admiration for and self-proclaimed expertise in the theology of John Calvin, who advocated a theocratic state, Pew was an ardent conservative who virtually identified Christianity with his own version of pure laissez-faire economic individualism and who insisted the church should keep itself strictly free of entanglement in controversial social issues. He was also a fervent anti-Communist and had recently severed longstanding and close ties with the National Council of Churches because he felt its policies would "inevitably lead us into Communism." He believed the ministry of liberal denominations contained "a few Communists, a larger percentage of Socialists, and a still larger percentage of what I might term fellow travelers." Pew was far more of an ideologue than Billy Graham—he believed the United States should break off diplomatic relations with all Communist countries and drive them from the United Nations—but he approved of Graham's anticommunism and of a magazine that would attempt to raise the level of scholarship in the ministry, on the apparent assumption that when people truly understood the Bible and classical Reformation theology, they would come to agree with him. Even Pew's critics conceded the sincerity of his convictions, but the near fanaticism with which he held them was bound to create problems for an enterprise committed to standing in the middle of the road. Still, *CT*, as the magazine soon came to be known in Evangelical circles, would probably never have seen the light of day had it not been for Pew's confidence in Billy Graham and his willingness to plow large sums of money into virtually anything the evangelist recommended. When Graham assured him in April 1955 that "I am determined to see this vision that I believe is from God carried out and properly controlled," Pew agreed to stand in the gap for whatever amount might be needed to get the magazine started and to keep it in operation for its first several years. He pledged $150,000 for each of the first two years and continued to provide major support of the magazine for several additional years.

CT's first board of trustees illustrated once again that a small number of men, most with close ties to Billy Graham, were at the center of the major developments in Evangelical Christianity during the 1950s. In addition to Graham and Howard Pew, the founding board included Nelson Bell, Jerry Beavan, John Bolten, Walter Bennett, Maxey Jarman, Howard Butt, and National Association of Evangelicals president Paul Rees. The first president was Harold Ockenga. Graham tried to persuade Wilbur Smith to leave Fuller to serve as the magazine's first editor. When Smith declined after a period of longing indecision, the job went to Carl Henry. Interestingly, though he admired Henry's administrative ability and intellect, Graham had reservations about his suitability for the post. His primary fear was that Henry, a man not inclined to undervalue his own positions, might show insufficient tolerance toward both Fundamentalists and liberals. He asked Lindsell, "Would Carl be ready to take a certain amount of criticism from typical Fundamentalist leaders? Would he be ready to come out in the middle, recognizing that even among American Baptists and U.S.A. Presbyterians there are good elements, God-fearing people, and devout ministers?" Along the same line, Graham feared that Henry's writings had made him "too well known as a Fundamentalist," so that his name on the mast head might generate a negative response among liberals, no matter how irenic the magazine's tone. To offset that problem, Billy even raised the possibility of having Henry edit the magazine under an assumed name for a year or two until readers grew accustomed to its approach. Graham also wondered whether Henry would be able to produce the type of journalism the magazine needed. "The journalism that I envision for this magazine," he told a friend, "must be intellectual but popular.... To put my thought at this point rather bluntly, Carl's writing has a tendency to be rather heavy. I have read most of his writings, and though

I am a minister of average intelligence, it has been very difficult for me to follow."

Graham was not the only one with reservations. Henry himself wondered if he was right for the job. On the one hand, he felt the middle of the road might be a dangerous place to stand. Though he agreed that a charitable spirit would be necessary, he insisted on theological integrity. "Liberalism and Evangelicalism," he said, "do not have equal rights and dignity in the true church." On the other hand, despite his staunch anticommunism and Republican confidence in the superiority of capitalism to other economic systems, he believed that "capitalism is not beyond Christian criticism" and thought it a mistake to assume that "American capitalism [is] the ideal economic form of the Kingdom of God." If Howard Pew's underwriting of the magazine meant such sentiments must be stifled, then perhaps Graham should seek another editor. This insistence on independence worried Graham, and he asked if Henry would consider soft-pedaling his differences with liberals for two years, stressing instead the beliefs and practices Evangelicals held in common with the so-called mainline denominations. Henry would not. "The truth," he snapped, "is still the indispensable human factor in Christian apologetics; truth without love will be usually ignored, but love without the truth is not even real love." If they wanted to come back to him after two years of shading their true colors, he might be interested, but he could not agree to hide his light under a bushel, even on a temporary basis. Because Henry was not only the best man available but objectively a quite good choice, Graham and the board finally offered him the editorship, which he accepted. Nelson Bell gave up his surgical practice to become the magazine's full-time executive editor, and Marcellus Kik, a Reformed Church minister who had helped Bell lay the groundwork for the magazine, became associate editor.

Not everything went smoothly. Pew's experience with the National Council of Churches and other ventures he had supported had made him wary of relinquishing control. He decided, and got Ockenga to agree, that the editors should submit all articles to the board for approval before publication. Henry bridled immediately, telling Bell that were such a measure implemented, he would have no choice but to resign. In a notable, if reluctant, show of courage, both Bell and Graham sided with Henry, even though they realized doing so might undermine the entire venture. Bell informed the board that "none of us is willing to have *Christianity Today* bought by any interests. . . . If this position entails a loss of certain financial support, we will seek it elsewhere." Graham then called Pew, whose support he desperately wanted to retain, to tell him his efforts to assert control over *CT* would destroy the magazine. A board has the right to fire an editor, he argued, but "if it hires him, it should trust and support him." Pew never admitted his impulse was wrong, but he did drop his demands.

The fortnightly journal made its first appearance in mid-October 1956. Paul Harvey mentioned it on his national radio program, *Newsweek* made it the lead article in its religion section, and AP religion writer George Cornell gave it generous coverage. The *Christian Century* did not acknowledge its existence for four months. The inaugural forty-page issue demonstrated its founders' aspirations to bridge the gap between serious theological discussion and practical preaching. Dutch theologian G. C. Berkouwer discussed the "Changing Climate of European Theology." This was followed by Billy Graham's ringing affirmation of the role of "Biblical Authority in Evangelism," Carl Henry's reflections on "The Fragility of Freedom in the West," a mélange of other articles, editorials, news, and book reviews, a bit of strained humor under the heading, "Eutychus and His Kin" (named for a man who fell asleep while listening to the Apostle Paul preach), and nearly ten pages of advertising—an encouraging sign for a new publication. The masthead listed forty-nine contributing editors and seventy-three correspondents, a virtual roll call of Evangelical elites. A few days after the first issue went out, Graham sent Henry a six-page critique in which he judged it "not strikingly good, considering the terrific roster of editors and correspondents." He reported that several people had indicated his own article contained "a bit too much spinning dust and purple prose" and several misleading and ineffective illustrations. As for Henry's contribution, Graham said his informants had thought it was "too verbose" and gave the impression of "obscurity reaching for profundity." Noting that these and most other criticisms had been voiced by others—"Personally, I was delighted with the magazine ... for the first issue, I thought it was great"—and urging "beloved Carl" not to become discouraged, Graham said, "I felt that you would like to know the hard, cold facts, because it will help us in the future."

Like most new magazines, *CT* got off to a shaky start. No one on the too-small staff had any previous experience in advertising or circulation, and it showed. Eager for revenue, they ran an early series of ads for Vita Safe and Supra Vite, nostrums designed to bring "fun and excitement" back into marriages whose female members were complaining about their husband's "age." Medically dubious and therefore particularly embarrassing to Dr. Bell, these ads were dropped as soon as the term of the contract expired. Both staff and board were naive about circulation. Graham, for example, felt confident he could generate 25,000 subscriptions by an appeal to his mailing list; he received 3,622 positive responses. With counsel from *U.S. News & World Report* editor David Lawrence, who admired the evangelist and gave his crusades extensive coverage, the staff trimmed expectations to match probability, exchanged lists with other conservative publications, and made good use of its institutional friends, as when it arranged to have Fuller Seminary's mailing operation address thousands of envelopes to send to prospective subscribers. All these measures helped. By the time the ninth issue appeared in February

1957, the paid subscription list stood at 35,000, equal to that of the *Christian Century*, and *Christianity Today* assumed an apparently permanent position as the nation's most widely read serious religious publication.

Financial and personnel problems notwithstanding, most of those associated with the new magazine delighted in its early success. Graham's decision to send it to all the nation's Protestant ministers had instantly given it an audience no other serious religious journal could match, and that audience was beginning to respond positively. Positive response meant a great deal to Billy Graham and his friends at *CT*. They looked backed yearningly to a time a hundred years earlier when *Evangelical* and *Christian* and *American* had been virtual synonyms. They also looked back (and around) at a time when *Evangelical* and *Fundamentalist* had come to mean "obscurantist" and "marginal." Now, some dared hope they might look forward to a time, perhaps not far away, when Evangelicals would once again move to and stand at the center of the culture, defining and shaping its ethos. They understood that their little magazine was only part of the effort and that it was far from perfect, but they clearly saw it as a key weapon in their struggle to regain respectability. *Look* magazine declared that "among the so-called think magazines, *Christianity Today* is most stimulating." The World Council of Churches invited Carl Henry to attend a conference at Oberlin College, Catholic scholar Gustave Weigel asked him to address a group of three hundred priests at the Jesuit seminary in Woodstock, Maryland, and the secular press began to refer to him as "the thinking man's Billy Graham," a sobriquet that caused some embarrassment within the Evangelical network but signaled awareness that Graham and *CT* were closely related elements of the same movement. An excellent news department drew such attention to the magazine that it soon became one of the nation's most frequently quoted religious publications. Perhaps most important of all to the folk at *CT*, their magazine was giving the *Christian Century*, the loudest voice of liberal ecumenical Protestantism, more than a run for its money.

When the New Evangelical founders and shapers of *Christianity Today* declared their intention to fashion a new umbrella under which Christians of many denominations could unite, they found themselves arrayed against a formidable foe: the old Fundamentalists. Their differences, often hardly comprehensible to those who stood outside both camps but nevertheless real and significant, had been papered over to some extent by their mutual admiration for Billy Graham. It was therefore fitting, or at least historically symmetrical, that when they finally separated into distinct and often warring camps, Billy Graham stood at the center of the fray.

Evangelicals differed little from Fundamentalists on matters of doctrine. What distinguished them was their strategy regarding what to do with that doctrine. They saw their task as twofold: First, they felt it imperative to proclaim the gospel to as wide an audience as ability, opportunity, resources, and technology allowed; second, they sought to regain a hearing and respectability for orthodox belief within mainline denominations. Fundamentalists paid lip service to evangelism, but proclaiming their faith was never as important to them as protecting it and themselves from error. Their strategy of protection involved meticulous attention to the jots and tittles of Christian teaching and obsessive concern with contamination by those who were not pure. They believed in the Great Commission—"Go ye into all the world, and preach the gospel to every creature" (Mark 16:15)—but felt it should be interpreted in light of the Apostle Paul's equally binding directive, "*Be ye not unequally yoked together with unbelievers*: for what fellowship hath righteousness with unrighteousness? And what communion hath light with darkness?... Wherefore *come out from among them, and be ye separate*" (II Corinthians 6:14–17) [Emphasis added]. Any attempt to preach the gospel, they insisted, would be undermined and ultimately turned into a victory for Satan if it involved fellowship with those whose minds had been clouded by Modernism, whose hearts had been cooled by compromise. Some thought it sufficient merely to separate themselves from unbelievers and liberals and ecumenists; a more extreme group thought purity also required separation from those who chose not to separate.

Billy Graham found it difficult to repudiate people who appeared to be sincere, professed to believe in at least some of the same things he believed, and treated him with courtesy and kindness. He doubtless intended to keep himself and his crusades free from Modernist contamination, but success weakened his resolve. As non-Evangelicals watched the streams of people who responded to his invitation, they wanted to channel at least a trickle of them into their own churches. As they saw it was possible to cooperate with his crusades without having him attack their beliefs from the pulpit, they began to join in the invitations, and when he agreed to come to their cities, to volunteer for committees. At first Graham was uneasy with non-Evangelical support but soon convinced himself that as long as no one tried to tell him what he could or could not preach, there could be no real harm in accepting the assistance and encouragement of people whose beliefs differed from his own at some points. After all, a key part of New Evangelical strategy was to gain a hearing for Evangelical doctrine in mainline denominations; might not his crusades be the perfect instrument of that strategy? Increasingly, and particularly after extensive cooperation with liberal state churches in England, Scotland, and on the continent, Graham came to accept, then to welcome, then virtually to require, the cooperation of all but the most flagrantly Modernist Protestant groups, such as Unitarians, or such bodies as Mormons and Jehovah's Witnesses, whose teachings excluded them from both Evangelical and mainline circles and who seldom showed any interest in taking part in his crusades.

The strictest of the separatists opposed Billy Graham from the beginning. Carl McIntire, who had never cooperated long with any person or organization he could not control, disliked the evangelist because of his close ties with the National Association of Evangelicals (NAE), which McIntire regarded as little better than the National Council of Churches. He also resented Graham's friendship with Harold Ockenga, his chief rival within conservative circles. Others shared McIntire's distrust of the New Evangelicals but were so proud of Graham's accomplishments that they supported him as long as their convictions would allow. Bob Jones had been forced to renounce his prediction that Billy Graham would never amount to anything, and their relationship had been cordial while Graham was with YFC and at Northwestern. But when Jones withdrew from the NAE over what he regarded as excessive ecumenism, he soon fixed his gimlet eye on Graham, accusing him of peddling a "discount type of religion" and "sacrificing the cause of evangelism on the altar of temporary convenience." Genuine doctrinal convictions doubtless played a role in Dr. Bob's criticisms of Billy Graham, but the old tyrant's legendary ego may well have been the decisive factor in creating an irreparable breach between the two men. For years Jones had repeatedly boasted that he had preached to more people than any person in history except Billy Sunday, that he was the highest-paid evangelist in America, and that "his boys"—students trained at Bob Jones College—had a corner on effective evangelism. Then, rather suddenly and wearing neither his mantle nor his blessing, Billy Graham had eclipsed him. "And the more well-known Billy got," one observer said, "the more Dr. Bob turned against him."

Some of the most thoroughgoing and sustained criticism of Graham's ministry came from a third prominent Fundamentalist, John R. Rice, a man who stood by his side long after others had written him off as an apostle of the Antichrist. In 1934, the same year Billy Graham hit the sawdust trail in Mordecai Ham's tent, Rice founded the *Sword of the Lord*, a militant journal whose masthead identified it as "An Independent Christian Weekly, Standing for the Verbal Inspiration of the Bible, the Deity of Christ, His Blood Atonement, Salvation by Faith, New Testament Soul Winning and the Premillennial Return of Christ. Opposes Modernism, Worldliness and Formalism." By mid-century it was the most popular and influential journal in the Fundamentalist orbit. Rice was fully as willing as McIntire and Jones to draw a circle and shut others out, but even as the *Sword* slashed at the ties that bind true Christians to dupes and pretenders, he supported Billy Graham and gave his campaigns extensive coverage, fiercely proud that conservative Christianity once again had a world-famous evangelist in its ranks.

Graham appreciated Rice's goodwill and encouragement but did not make his admirer's job an easy one. When the National Council of Churches published the new Revised Standard Version (RSV) of the Bible in 1952, Carl McIntire led a vitriolic Fundamentalist attack against it, charging that it was part of an ecumenical, possibly Communist, plot to undermine sound doctrine. Fundamentalists ferreted out numerous alleged inaccuracies in the RSV, but none so egregious as its translation of Isaiah 7:14, cited in Matthew 1:23 as a prophecy foretelling the birth of Jesus. In the King James Version, the verse read, "a *virgin* shall conceive and bear a son." The RSV correctly translated the Hebrew phrase to read, "a *young woman* shall conceive." Even though the new translation retained *virgin* in Matthew's quotation and clearly depicted Mary as a virgin in the gospel accounts, many Fundamentalists viewed the translation as a Modernist assault on one of the cardinal affirmations of their faith. Acceptance or rejection of the RSV soon became a litmus test in Fundamentalist circles. Most professors at Fuller Seminary held positive views toward the new book, a fact that reportedly cost Charles Fuller thousands of supporters. In this climate Graham might easily have chosen to stand apart from the fray, since he had more to lose than to gain, but he did not. Instead, asserting that he favored making the Bible easier to read and understand, he issued a statement endorsing the new version and encouraging his supporters to give it a try.

As a further sign he was veering to the left, Graham began to accept invitations to speak at liberal seminaries. At Colgate Rochester Divinity School, he attempted to bridge the differences between his own theology and that of the eminent neoorthodox theologian and social critic, Reinhold Niebuhr. When he spoke of "the central need for a personal experience of Jesus Christ," he added, as if they were synonymous conceptions, "or what Niebuhr would call an encounter with the living God." A Fundamentalist reporting on this event objected that "no one in his right mind would believe for a moment that what the neo-orthodox Niebuhr means by 'an encounter with the living God' and what Jesus Christ defined as being 'born again' are one and the same." At New York's Union Theological Seminary, Graham had the temerity to say kind words about "known liberals," including his old friend Chuck Templeton, who was then serving as an evangelist for the National Council of Churches. His hobnobbing with Anglicans in Great Britain and with Church of Scotland pastors in Glasgow added fuel to the fire. To make matters worse, he had invited some prominent American ministers, including New York pastor John Sutherland Bonnell, whose stated views on heaven and hell, the Virgin Birth, the Resurrection, and the inerrancy of Scripture struck fundamentalists as suspiciously liberal, to sit on the platform with him during some of the services at Kelvin Hall. When Scottish reporters tried to pin down Graham's location on the contemporary spectrum, he declared, in a statement that mightily offended his conservative critics, "I am neither a fundamentalist nor a modernist." To make matters worse, he told another reporter, "The ecumenical movement has broadened my viewpoint and I recognize now that God has his people in all churches."

Such statements drew a storm of protest from Carl McIntire and a host of minor-league detractors, but John R. Rice remained loyal for as long as he could. In the late spring of 1955, he came to Graham's defense in two long articles, "Questions Answered About Billy Graham" and "Billy Graham at Union Seminary." He admitted that some of the things Billy had done troubled him but insisted that "no one could possibly say that Billy Graham is a modernist or tending toward modernism." Rice conceded that Graham sometimes drifted into treacherous waters and "unwisely had fellowship with modernists on some occasions" but affirmed that "I believe he is God's anointed man, being used tremendously in great revivals, and that every Christian in the world ought to rejoice in these revivals."

Rice's defense helped maintain a fragile accord for a while. Carl McIntire continued to fire his loose cannon at anything that moved even slightly to the left, but Bob Jones, probably at Rice's behest, refrained from criticizing the evangelist by name in his weekly column in the *Sword*, and men like Jack Wyrtzen fretted more in private than in public, continuing to hope that Graham's flirtation with Modernists would pass and that he would return to the Fundamentalist fold a chastened and wiser man. But about the same time he took the first steps to found *CT*, Graham dashed those hopes and severed whatever threads of unity remained between the New Evangelicals and old Fundamentalists by accepting an invitation from the Protestant Council of the City of New York, an affiliate of the liberal National Council of Churches, to hold a crusade in Madison Square Garden during the late spring of 1957.

Graham had turned down invitations to come to New York in 1951 and 1954, both times because he felt the group offering the invitation was too heavily weighted with Fundamentalists and therefore did not represent the broad spectrum of the city's Protestant churches. The Protestant Council represented 1,700 churches, 94 percent of all Protestant bodies in the metropolitan area. In fact, the council's leadership was less than enthusiastic about a Billy Graham crusade, but the idea received strong support from some wealthy and influential constituents, including Chase Manhattan Bank chairman George Champion, a southern Evangelical layman who chaired the council's Department of Evangelism, and Mrs. Cleveland Dodge, a wealthy laywoman whose family had backed Finney, Moody, and Sunday, as well as some of the city's leading clergymen, including Norman Vincent Peale.

In April Rice argued that Modernist opposition to the crusade proved the evangelist was preaching the truth, but over the next seven months, except for two mildly negative articles by nonregular contributors, neither Graham's name nor face appeared in the pages of the magazine that had featured him and his ministry on virtually a weekly basis. When Rice finally broke his silence in November, it was clear Graham had lost the last major Fundamentalist in his camp. The title of Rice's editorial, "Which Way, Billy Graham?" suggested ambiguity, but he had made up his mind where Graham's ministry was headed. Apparently, Graham had also made up his mind to worry no longer about pleasing the Fundamentalists. In an interview published in the June issue of *Christian Life* he said that "the fighting, feuding and controversies among God's people ... is a very poor example" and charged that a key reason true revival had not come to America was the "name-calling and mudslinging" so prevalent among Evangelicals. As for his coming to New York under the aegis of the Protestant Council, he asked, "What difference does it make who sponsors a meeting?" Paul had preached at Mars' hill at the invitation of Greek philosophers, and George Whitefield had said that if invited, he would gladly preach to the pope.

Always eager to spot any sign of weakness, Fundamentalist wolves pounced on Graham's exposed neck. Yes, they conceded, Paul had permitted Athenian philosophers to "sponsor" him, but he did not give the names of his converts to the priests of pagan temples. Graham's appeal to peace and harmony, they hooted, was just the sort of thing to expect from a man who had gone soft on doctrine. Graham resisted lashing back but made little attempt to change his course. However much he wanted the support of Fundamentalists, for both strategic and emotional reasons, he realized he could do without them. Their numbers were relatively small, and their obstreperous exclusiveness would always keep them out of the cultural mainstream where he was determined to swim. He was ready to make the break. When John R. Rice asked him to indicate in writing that he still held to the *Sword's* statement of faith, Graham not only declined but asked to be dropped from the magazine's board. The break was final. In his editorial, which took the form of an open letter to Graham, Rice sadly conceded that the constellation of true believers had lost one of its brightest stars. "I understand that you are generally sound in doctrine," he wrote, "but I know now that the *Sword of the Lord* does not speak for you when it defends fundamentalists, [because] you do not claim to be a fundamentalist."

In an April 1957 article entitled "Billy Graham's New York Crusade," Rice announced he would trace the "breaking down of convictions" in the "new Evangelicalism" and the unfortunate changes in Billy Graham's policies and evangelistic program. Over the next several months, almost every issue of the *Sword of the Lord* contained a long article or editorial detailing the danger Graham and his Modernist New York crusade posed to Bible-based Christianity. In a notable shift in tactics, Rice began to criticize not only Graham's misguided behavior but also his motives. Billy had rejected the invitation of faithful Fundamentalists, he charged, because he wanted "the prestige, the financial backing, and worldly influence" of the liberal council. In an unusually explicit defense offered at a meeting of the National Association of Evangelicals, Graham called his critics "extremists," and said flatly, "I would like to make myself clear. I intend to go anywhere, sponsored by anybody, to preach the Gospel of Christ if there are no strings attached to my message. I am sponsored by civic clubs, universities, ministerial associations, and councils of churches all over the world. I intend to continue." As a consequence of this tolerance for impurity, Rice solemnly intoned, "Dr. Graham is one of the spokesmen, and perhaps the principal spark plug of a great drift away from strict Bible fundamentalism and strict defense of the faith."

The Fundamentalists' rage increased as plans for the New York crusade moved forward. As the committees took shape, it became clear that Graham did indeed plan to hold an ecumenical crusade. One critic charged that of the 140 people on the General Crusade Committee, at least 120 were "reputed to be modernists, liberals, infidels, or something other than fundamental." When Carl McIntire heard Graham refer to such men as National Council of Churches leader Jesse Bader and noted preacher Ralph Sockman as "godly men," it was "almost too hard to swallow!... They are *not* godly men." Graham further manifested his ostensible lack of concern for sound doctrine not only by such statements as "the one badge of Christian discipleship is not orthodoxy, but love," but also by his apparent willingness to send decision cards to Catholic and Jewish clergy. Given the choice, the follow-up committee would always send an inquirer's card to a Protestant congregation, but if an inquirer specifically asked to be referred to a Catholic church or Jewish synagogue, that request would be honored. "After all," he explained, "I have no quarrel with the Catholic Church. Christians are not limited to any church. The only question is: Are you committed to Christ?" This justification did not seem to apply to Jews, but Graham was quoted by several newspapers as having explicitly said that "we'll send them to their own churches—Roman Catholic, Protestant, or Jewish.... The rest will be up to God."

Not all of Graham's Fundamentalist critics saw him as a willing tool of Satan, sent forth to do the work of the Antichrist. Some concluded that he wanted to be faithful to God's commands, but his desire for acceptance and his lamentable tendency to see the best in others short-circuited his ability to recognize error and excise it from the body of Christ. One prominent Fundamentalist observed that "those who know Billy best say that it is his amiable personality that makes him believe that he can become a sort of pontiff—or bridge builder—between Bible-believing Christians and those attractive personalities who are the proponents of the non-redemptive gospel. [At a recent breakfast], he pleaded with us to recognize that many of the liberals were good men, loved the Lord, and perhaps could be won over to the conservative position—Billy spreads himself too thin; he tries not to offend anybody in any way—[B]y not making war on some things he has gone to the other extreme, and made peace, not with the doctrines of apostasy, but with those who preach the doctrines of apostasy. This, I believe, is deadly and will one day defeat the whole cause for which this man of God is laboring."

This furor upset Graham, not only because it threatened the crusade but also because it pained him to lose the confidence and affection of men who had worked at his side. He decided, however, not to respond to their criticisms directly. Years earlier, when his sudden rise to national prominence had made him an inviting target for both religious and secular detractors, he had told his radio audience that "the devil starts many deliberate lies about God's servants, and thousands of Christians grasp them, believe them, and pass them on in ugly gossip.... I make it a policy never to answer critics, but to go on in the center of God's will, preaching the everlasting Gospel of Christ. Satan would like nothing better than to have us stop our ministry and start answering critics, tracking down wretched lies and malicious stories." Fundamentalists whose orthodoxy "knows nothing of the spirit of God or the love for their own brethren" and the dissension they stir, he charged, are "a stench in the nostrils of God" and thwart revival in the church. "By God's grace," he pledged, "I shall continue to preach the Gospel of Jesus Christ and not stoop to mudslinging, name-calling, and petty little fights over nonessentials." That approach had served him well on three continents, and he decided to stick with it. Stephen Olford, who had come from England to help with the crusade, remembered reading some of the letters the evangelist received from his Fundamentalist critics—"They were vitriolic, sarcastic, devastating." But Billy decided to turn the other cheek. "Stephen," he said, "I've prayed this through. All I'm going to do is write them little love notes—'I'll weigh what you say, but I love you.'"

Graham's refusal to respond directly did not mean he was unwilling to have others fight in his stead. Nelson Bell wrote a long and widely circulated letter to Bob Jones offering point-by-point response to the charges Jones had made against his son-in-law. Carl Henry also wrote a series of articles in *CT,* charging Fundamentalism with "a harsh temperament, a spirit of lovelessness and strife contributed by much of its leadership in the recent past," and declaring that "in this contemporary expression [it] stands discredited as a perversion of the biblical spirit." He called on readers to repudiate this disposition and adopt the more open attitude represented by the New Evangelicalism. And Robert O. Ferm, who had joined BGEA as a researcher and all-purpose intellectual, wrote an entire book, *Cooperative Evangelism*, in which he contended that all the great evangelists—Wesley, Whitefield, Finney, Moody, Sunday, and others, including Bob Jones and John R. Rice themselves in earlier years—had willingly cooperated with a wide range of churchmen in order to fulfill the Great Commission to preach the gospel to all humankind. "No major evangelist in history," Ferm asserted, "has ever too closely analyzed the orthodoxy of his sponsors."

The New York crusade did not cause the division between the old Fundamentalists and the New Evangelicals; that had been signaled by the nearly simultaneous founding of the National Association of Evangelicals and McIntire's American Council of Christian Churches fifteen years earlier. But it did provide an event around which the two groups were forced to define themselves. Many outsiders would be unaware of what was happening within the ranks of this segment of conservative Christianity, and many would never fully recognize or understand their differences, but during the struggle that came to a head in 1957, the mask of Evangelical unity was lifted, and the terms *Fundamentalism* and *Evangelicalism* came to refer to two different movements.

14

God in the Garden

New York, the town Billy Sunday couldn't shut down, was a town Billy Graham feared he might not wake up. "We face the city with fear and trembling," he said. "I'm prepared to go to New York to be crucified by my critics, if necessary. When I leave New York, every engagement we have in the world might be canceled. It may mean that I'll be crucified—but I'm going." In part, this ominous assessment was hyperbole, of a piece with his more common anticipation that a given crusade might ignite a revival that would sweep across the land to inaugurate a new and greater awakening than America (or England or Europe or India) ever experienced. Billy Graham seldom, if ever, spoke of his crusades or other endeavors simply as members of a series, no one of which was likely to differ much from the others, but in this case both his hopes and fears were well grounded. New York *was* unique. Whether he succeeded or failed, everyone would know—and remember. If he drew mediocre crowds and could persuade only token numbers of them to come down the aisle at the invitation, the mocking publicity sure to follow might indeed consign him to the same fate Billy Sunday faced after leaving New York: playing out the rest of his ministry in the second-line cities of the South and Midwest. If he succeeded, if he came to this citadel of secularism and kept the Garden full and the aisles packed with inquirers, no one could ever again dismiss him as a short-term wonder. It was critically important that he succeed.

For nearly two years, Willis Haymaker, Charlie Riggs, Jerry Beavan, Leighton Ford, and other team members worked to develop a failure-proof crusade machine. Seldom, if ever, has a crusade been able to boast of more competent and influential leadership. The crusade committee, chaired by Roger Hull, vice-president of Mutual of New York, included in its number Chase Manhattan's George Champion, Norman Vincent Peale, longtime Graham backers Russell Maguire and J. Howard Pew, corporate executives Walter Hoving, Eddie Rickenbacker, and Jeremiah Milbank, *Reader's Digest* senior editor Stanley High, and media moguls Henry Luce, William Randolph Hearst, Jr., *Herald Tribune* editor Ogden Reid, and ABC president Robert Kintner. With this kind of clout at the top, and with solid encouragement from members of the Dodge, Phelps, Vanderbilt, Gould, and Whitney families, all of whom had supported Graham's storied predecessors—the Phelpses, like the Dodges, had joined the Tappan brothers in bringing Charles Finney to New York, and all five families backed Moody and Sunday—-finance chairman Howard Isham, vice-president and treasurer of U.S. Steel, found it relatively easy to raise a large portion of the projected $600,000 budget.

Once again, the team organized a massive worldwide prayer effort. By the time the crusade began, more than 10,000 prayer groups in at least seventy-five countries were meeting daily to beg God's blessing on Billy Graham and the New York crusade. Illiterate African tribesmen sent a document signed with their thumbprints, promising to pray for the evangelist as he bore witness to the civilizing power of the gospel. In India clumps of Christians in five cities met regularly to pray through the night. In Formosa intercessors formed more than thirty groups, including one comprising Madame Chiang Kai-shek and several of her close friends. In Japan a band of convicts converted while awaiting execution prayed that Americans lost in sin might find the secret of abundant life in Madison Square Garden. The primary effort, of course, was in New York itself, where at least 150,000 people signed prayer-pledge cards. A daily radio program, *Noontime Is Prayer Time*, encouraged countless others to pray, and 75,000 plastic disks slipped over telephone dials in homes and offices reminded people to "Pray for the Billy Graham New York Crusade." Other aspects of crusade preparation proceeded with the same bureaucratic thoroughness. The tragic and untimely death of Dawson Trotman, who drowned during the summer of 1956, was a blow to the counselor-training program, but Charlie Riggs, an unassuming Navigator veteran who had worked on Graham crusades since Harringay, stepped into the breach and proved no less effective at screening prospective counselors, gently recommending that they use deodorants and keep a roll of breath mints handy, reminding them to avoid discussing minor theological points that might offend or confuse an inquirer, and patiently teaching them how to help inquirers articulate their decisions and fill out inquirer cards properly. So well did Riggs perform that thirty years later he was still serving as overall director of counselor training for Graham's crusades. To complement Riggs's efforts, a retired air force colonel came in to overhaul the processing of decision cards and follow-up mail, and National Council of Churches executive Jesse Bader, who in 1951 advised Graham to pay himself a straight salary, headed up the postcrusade visitation program. And as always, Jerry Beavan mounted a media campaign that kept Graham's name and face in the public's eye and ear. Billy professed that "every time I see my name up in lights, it makes me sick at heart, for God said He will share His glory with no man. Pat me on the back and you will ruin my ministry." Despite this alleged aversion to publicity, he permitted his organization to spend fifty times more than Billy Sunday laid out for the same purpose forty years earlier. In view of this extraordinary level of preparation, the *Christian Century* made the cynical but perceptive observation that "the Billy Graham campaign will spin along to its own kind of triumph because canny experienced engineers of human decision have laid the tracks, contracted for the passengers, and will now direct the traffic which arrives on schedule.... Anticipation has been adroitly created and built up by old hands at the business, and an audience gladly captive to its own sensations is straining for the grand entrance." The "Graham procedure," complained the *Century*, "does its mechanical best to 'succeed' whether or not the Holy Spirit is in attendance."

Not all of Graham's efforts were mechanical. To help create an awareness that he could communicate with young people, and also to associate himself with a venerable academic and evangelistic tradition that harked back to Jonathan Edwards and Timothy Dwight, Graham made a four-day visit to Yale in February. No sweeping revival occurred, but the thirty-eight-year-old product of a backwater Bible institute and a midwestern Christian college left his mark. He spoke to overflow crowds in venerable Woolsey Hall and spent many additional hours talking with small groups and counseling individual students. The *Yale Daily News* described him as "looking like a combination Norse god and prep school headmaster," characterized his preaching as "embarrassingly overdramatic and clearly underintellectual," chided him for his "banal insights," and commented on "the irrelevance of his message to the special problem of the Yale undergraduate." Still, even his detractors acknowledged his genuineness and a *Daily News* editor admitted that "the ultimate effect of [Graham's] appearance here was incontrovertibly tonic." According to the newspaper, at least half the audience at each address stood when he offered the invitation, and "for at least one week in more years than you can count, this University has become a hotbed of violent and concerned religious controversy." Back in Manhattan, as opening night drew closer, Lane Adams, a former nightclub singer who came to BGEA through Leighton Ford, whom he met while studying at Columbia Theological Seminary, sought to win support in another distinctive community by organizing an outreach program aimed at actors and other entertainers along the Great White Way. Commenting on Graham's leadership style, Adams recalled that Graham gave him but the barest instructions as to the nature of his task. "Billy has the talent of a master artist," he observed. "He brought me in, showed me the canvas, which already had a beautiful frame around it, grabbed a palette and paintbrush, daubed a few things on it, and said, 'Now you get the picture of what I want you to do. You figure out the rest of it.' Since I had never done it before, all I could do was fumble along, and it worked out pretty well."

In spite of all the efforts to generate success, anxiety kept Billy gnawing at his fingernails. Fundamentalist charges that he had "sold out to the Modernists" continued to trouble him, despite his determination to proceed without their support. At the same time, not all of the liberal churchmen to whom he had allegedly sold out showered him with pieces of silver. Union Theological Seminary's Reinhold Niebuhr repeatedly attacked him in the pages of *Christian Century* and *Christianity and Crisis*. Niebuhr warned that simplistic revivalism would accentuate the antireligious prejudices of enlightened people, that Graham's sermons produced an artificial crisis that prompted shallow and essentially meaningless conversions, and that individualistic pietism would divert attention and resources from pressing social problems such as racial prejudice. In an article for *Life*, he acknowledged that Graham was "obviously sincere" but questioned the promise of "a new life, not through painful religious experience, but merely by signing a decision card." It simply would not do, wrote the theologian whose own keen insights into the ambiguity and inevitable sinfulness of all human beings (whether once- or twice-born) were perhaps unmatched in this century, to pretend that by walking down the aisle, repeating a "sinner's prayer," and checking a box on a quadruplicate form, one could suddenly be freed of past sins and given a new nature that was miraculously oriented in a totally new direction. He marveled that Graham could declare without blinking that "every human problem can be solved and every hunger satisfied and every potential can be fulfilled when a man encounters Jesus Christ and comes in vital relation to God in him." A message of that sort, Niebuhr said, "is not very convincing to anyone—Christian or not—who is aware of the continual possibilities of good and evil in every advance of civilization, every discipline of culture, and every religious convention." The success of evangelism, he asserted, has always rested on oversimplification of difficult issues, but Graham, whom Niebuhr regarded as "better than any evangelist of his kind in American history," had imbued evangelism with "even less complicated answers than it had ever before provided." In Niebuhr's eyes, theologically and socially responsible Protestant churches compromised their dignity and integrity by endorsing such a simple message in the hope, probably vain, that they might add a few members to their church rolls.

Graham responded with disarming humility, telling the *Saturday Evening Post*, "When Dr. Niebuhr makes his criticisms about me, I study them, for I have respect for them. I think he has helped me to apply Christianity to the social problems we face and has helped me to comprehend what those problems are." He added, however, that "I disagree with Dr. Niebuhr in one respect. I don't think you can change the world with all its lusts and hatred and greed, until you change men's hearts. Men must love God before they can truly love their neighbors. The theologians don't seem to understand that fact." The evangelist acknowledged Niebuhr's superior intellect—"I have read nearly everything Mr. Niebuhr has written," he told one reporter, "and I feel inadequate before his brilliant mind and learning. Occasionally I get a glimmer of what he is talking about"—but he was not tempted to adopt his adversary's tolerance of ambiguity. "If I tried to preach as he writes," he explained, "people would be so bewildered they would walk out." Neither did he shrink from confronting Niebuhr directly. Perhaps remembering his conquest of his critics in London, Graham tried to arrange a personal conversation, but Niebuhr refused to meet with him, even after George Champion prevailed on the chairman of Union Seminary's board of trustees to urge the theologian to grant Graham the courtesy of at least a perfunctory encounter. Graham was disappointed, but not surprised. "I knew he wouldn't see me," he told Champion, "because he's a Socialist." Catholics also took critical aim at Graham's crusade, but with a blend of warmth and wariness that reflected a fascinating ambivalence toward him. Graham shared in a general Evangelical antipathy toward Catholicism, but Catholics benefited from his uncommon spirit of openness and conciliation toward those with whom he disagreed. Team members might speak of Catholics who had been "won to Christ," clearly implying they had moved from a lost to a saved state, but Billy himself had never engaged in the Catholic bashing to which many Fundamentalists were prone, and Catholics seemed to appreciate this. Still, some priests feared he might rustle sheep from their flocks. Jesuit scholar Gustave Weigel, while commending the evangelist for eschewing hucksterish excesses and demagogic attacks on Catholics, lamented the thinness of intellectual content in his sermons: "He lacks the scholarship of the Catholic Church.... He can no doubt tell us what the Bible says, but can he really tell us what the Bible means?" His simple invitation to trust and obey "can be exhilarating; it can be transforming; but it is an uncritical, nonintellectual way of answering the questions of man's ultimate concern." Weigel acknowledged, however, that the fundamentals Graham emphasized were clearly essential to vital Christianity, and he declared that he hoped and prayed "that God will lead him to the one true Church." Other Catholics were less generous. Specifically linking its directive to Graham's crusade, the archdiocese ordered parish priests to preach a series of nine sermons on basic Catholic doctrines, emphasizing that Christianity involved not simply seeking peace with God or joining the church of one's choice but adherence to the doctrinal truths contained in the historic creeds and interpreted by the magisterium of the church. Even more pointedly, the Reverend John E. Kelly, representing the National Catholic Welfare Council, expressly forbade Catholics to attend the crusade services at the Garden, to listen to Graham on radio or television, or to read his books or sermons, charging that Graham was "a danger to the faith" who promulgated false and heretical doctrines in such an enticing manner that total abstinence was the only safe course. Even so, Kelly admitted that Graham was "a man of prayer, humble, dedicated," and one for whom all Catholics should pray. Moreover, he asserted, "Catholic projects for evangelizing the unchurched would be much more effective if they were administered with even half the efficiency of the Graham team."

These deprecations had their effect. Graham later told one reporter that about a month before the crusade began, his heart had grown cold: "I didn't have the passion and love I should have had for the souls in New York. I don't know why. Maybe some of the criticism centered around the campaign got into my heart unawares and brought on the coldness." The loss of the soul winner's ardor was only temporary. Stephen Olford, on hand to assist with counseling and follow-up, remembered a visit to Graham's suite on the top floor of the New Yorker Hotel a few days before the crusade opened. "We walked on to the balcony, looking out over the city, and were standing there discussing the crusade, speculating about who would come and how the Lord would work. While we were talking, suddenly I was aware of this big, tall, broad-shouldered man heaving and breaking down with convulsive weeping. It was almost embarrassing. Billy was crying over the city, like our Lord weeping over Jerusalem."

Graham realized, of course, that an observer standing on the same parapet months later might perceive little change. In the first of one hundred front-page columns he wrote for the *Herald Tribune*, he raised the possibility that the crusade "might have tremendous impact on the entire world ... and could change the course of history by putting a new moral fiber into our society." He conceded, however, that "when these meetings are over, it may be possible that outwardly New York will seem unchanged. Times Square will still be crowded with tens of thousands seeking peace and happiness that seem so elusive. Probably outwardly, most of the same problems will still exist. But this we know by past experience: Many people will have their decisions for Christ and will be transformed by the power of God. These few, we pray, may begin a spiritual chain reaction in the pulsing life of this great metropolis which will inevitably make its impact upon the future.... We sincerely believe that thousands of individuals will be very wonderfully changed inwardly in their relationship with God, a change which certainly will make itself felt in better human relationships."

The crusade opened on May 15 to a crowd of 18,000 that if not quite a full house, was duly noted as the largest-ever opening-night attendance at an American crusade. With occasional exceptions, newspapers gave Graham generous coverage. In a singular nod to Evangelical Christianity, the *New York Times* devoted two full pages to the first service, including a verbatim transcript of his sermon. The front page of the tabloid *Journal-American* blared, "BILLY GRAHAM PLANS FOR BIG NY CRUSADE," in garish red headlines. A *World-Telegram and Sun* reporter gushed that Graham "is part Dick Nixon and part Jack Kennedy, with overtones of the young executive behind a Madison Avenue desk." The *Telegraph* assigned him to sales rather than to management but was equally complimentary: "He is like an excellent salesman: he describes the goods in plain terms, lets you see them and decide on them. He avoids the old, ranting ways and the pulpit thumping. He is a skilled and wise and practiced salesman of a commodity he truly believes should be in every home. The shrill ways of the medicine pitch, the arch and subtle ways of the stock and bond pitch, the snarled pitch of the Broadway showman never are heard or seen. He is plausibility to the final degree." Other papers, particularly the *Herald Tribune*, also provided saturation coverage, even to the point of announcing what his sermon topics would be in upcoming services, and *Life* magazine put him on its cover.

The inaugural crowd was no fluke. On evenings when the arena would not contain the crowd, Graham conducted impromptu services on Forty-ninth Street for the overflow. The crusade was originally scheduled to run six weeks, but Graham had taken an option on the Garden for a full five months. Within two weeks, when he saw the sustained level of attendance, he decided to extend at least three weeks into July. On June 12 attendance passed the half-million mark, and the campaign seemed to be gaining rather than losing momentum. More than in any previous campaign, television played a major role in focusing widespread attention on Graham. Besides numerous appearances on local stations, Walter Cronkite interviewed him on CBS, John Cameron Swayze visited with him on ABC, and he talked with Steve Allen, Dave Garroway, and Tex McCrary and Jinx Falkenberg on NBC. He also appeared as a guest on *Meet the Press*. In addition, the team produced a program that aired each night on WPIX-TV at 11:30 P.M., providing news and human-interest stories from the crusade and inviting viewers to call counselors for help with spiritual or other problems. This marked Graham's first attempt at a telephone ministry, and it proved so successful that by the third week of services, additional phone lines had to be installed to handle calls that came in until one-thirty or two o'clock in the morning.

The real media breakthrough, however, occurred when Graham decided to air his Saturday-evening services live, over the ABC television net work. As soon as it became clear that Billy could fill the Garden regularly, Charles Crutchfield, an old friend who owned a television station in Charlotte, urged him to put the crusade on TV. A few days later, apparently at Crutchfield's suggestion, Leonard Goldenson, instrumental in getting the televised version of the *Hour of Decision* on ABC, visited Billy at his hotel and proposed that ABC air the crusade once a week. "I thought it would be tremendous," Graham recalled, "because nobody else was on nationwide television at that time. But I was scared about the money because ABC had to sell us the time. So I called Mr. Howard Pew and asked him if he would back us if we went in the hole." Pew balked at first but finally pledged $100,000, enough to underwrite the first two programs, with the expectation that viewer contributions would cover expenses for further programs. As a measure of their confidence, Walter Bennett and Fred Dienert contracted with ABC for four weeks.

The first broadcast, on June 1, posted an 8.1 Trendex rating (against Jackie Gleason's 12.5 and Perry Como's 20.0), which translated into approximately 6.4 million viewers, enough to fill the Garden to capacity every day for an entire year, and more than enough to convince Billy Graham that he had finally found the most effective way to use this powerful new medium. The cameras bothered him, his gestures proved too sweeping for the small screen, and technical problems marred the initial telecast. One TV critic wrote that "this is not a good TV program. It is too much sermon, not enough color, not enough music, and misses the climax. [Graham] uses his hands as if they were a windmill, so that the person in the living room loses the Gospel message and becomes just a watcher of the hands." *Variety* was more charitable: "As a one-man evangelism show, it was a revelation and a close insight into why audiences respond to this religious phenomenon. As a showman, Graham's hour performance had all the click elements that translated, say, into the pop music area, make a Lawrence Welk tick.... Few performers, whether on TV, stage or film, have the dynamic qualities of Graham or are as sure of themselves, or can 'treat' a script with such positive aggressiveness. There's no unctuous quality, no sanctimonious persuasion. The voice is strong, never borders on hysteria...." The same reporter also had a positive reaction to Graham's gestures. "He's a man of perpetual motion," he conceded, but "the constant gesturing is never accidental, for the vast sweep of both his hands and arms propels and holds the visual attention. This, in addition to the voice that never falters, never gropes for a word or a phrase and is as assured as his beliefs, holds his audiences with almost mesmeric power."

More important than reviews was the impact on viewers. Almost immediately, letters began to pour in at a then-incredible rate of 50,000–75,000 per week, containing enough money to make it unnecessary to collect Howard Pew's pledge. In fact, contributions so exceeded expenses that the Council of Churches and several charitable organizations expressed considerable unhappiness with BGEA's decision to keep the money (approximately $2,500,000, according to Graham's recollection) to fund future TV ventures. The proportion of viewers volunteering to make some kind of decision for Christ was approximately equal to that registered in the Garden and far outstripped any response generated by the original televised version of the *Hour of Decision*. The first telecast alone garnered 25,000 inquirers, more than had come forward in the Garden during the first nine weeks of the crusade, and a Gallup poll revealed that 85 percent of American adults could correctly identify Billy Graham; moreover, nearly three quarters of that number regarded him favorably. In an innocent masterpiece of understatement, *Christian Life* cautiously observed, "Undoubtedly, this fact will affect Graham's ministry."

Perhaps no one explained the success of the live broadcasts more perceptively than a journalist who wrote: "When the average, moral, reputable American sees Dr. Graham in a studio telling him he needs to be 'born again,' his first impulse will be to discredit him as a religious fanatic. But if the viewer sees thousands of respectable, normal people listening and consenting to all this he hears, and then sees hundreds voluntarily get up and walk to the front in response to a low-pressure request, he'll begin to consider the message and situation with some sincere, honest interest. It's much easier to say a single speaker is wrong than to discredit the conviction and decision of thousands." Graham accepted that assessment. For the next thirty years, while other religious broadcasters experimented with a variety of formats, his television programs continued to be little more than slightly edited reproductions of services at which Billy Graham stands in front of large audiences and preaches what he freely acknowledges is essentially the same sermon.

With network television exposure serving as a kind of ultimate legitimation, the crusade boomed along from triumph to triumph. In addition to the nightly gatherings in the Garden, Graham held several massive outdoor rallies. A noontime meeting on the steps of the Federal Hall National Memorial on Wall Street drew a crowd variously estimated at between 7,500 and 30,000. Whatever the size of the crowd, and pictures show it was indeed quite large, its members listened respectfully as Bev Shea sang his own composition, "I'd Rather Have Jesus Than Silver or Gold," and as Graham warned that money and the things it could buy would not provide lasting satisfaction. On July 20, at what had been planned as the closing service until Graham announced another three-week extension, 100,000 people jammed Yankee Stadium in 105-degree heat, and at least 10,000 others were turned away, smashing the stadium's previous attendance record of 88,150, set when Joe Louis fought Max Baer in September 1935. Richard Nixon addressed the crowd and brought greetings from the President. When noise from airplanes departing and landing at La Guardia Airport threatened to detract from Graham's sermon, a call by a team representative to the airport manager resulted in a quick change in the flight pattern.

Somewhat disconcertingly, Graham's triumphs in Madison Square Garden and the financial district and Yankee Stadium had no counterpart north of 125th Street. Racial tension continued to mount in the South, and Martin Luther King's boycotts, sit-ins, and other forms of nonviolent resistance were turning up the pressure. Graham still felt confrontation was a perilous tactic but was beginning to acknowledge that something more than preaching might be required to secure basic civil rights for minorities. In an interview with the *New York Times* a few weeks before the crusade, he stressed that the most effective action would be "setting an example of love," then added, "as I think Martin Luther King ... has done in setting an example of Christian love." Given the time and his constituency, this on-the-record endorsement of the controversial civil rights leader was a notable step for the cautious evangelist. However, if he expected it to generate enthusiasm in black churches for the Garden crusade, he was disappointed. Officially, black support of the crusade was heartening; fifty black churches pledged their support, and several black pastors took active roles on crusade committees. Still, the crowds in the Garden were mostly white, and that bothered Graham and his team, who hoped to set an example of interracial fellowship and cooperation. In his *Life* article the previous fall he had set forth his clear belief that racial prejudice was a sin, and he followed that with similar statements in interviews and press conferences prior to the crusade, observing on one occasion that those who say they love Jesus but hate those whose skin is a different color not only break the commandment to love their neighbor, but by claiming to love God, also take his name in vain. Furthermore, since to hate someone is to wish him dead, such people, he asserted, are guilty of the sin of murder. Some blacks took note of his words; just as the crusade began, a group of black North Carolina ministers invited him to lead a crusade against segregation in his own home state. Still, despite such affirmations and growing awareness of his stand, blacks were not coming out to hear him. Rather than rest content to have it both ways—speaking out against discrimination while letting racist supporters see that his was still a ministry aimed primarily at white people—Graham took concrete steps to follow his own recommendation of "setting an example of love."

His first move was to integrate his own organization by inviting Howard O. Jones, a young black pastor from Cleveland, to join his team. Jones organized black youth rallies and spearheaded a service in Harlem at which Graham spoke to a packed house of several thousand blacks. He also helped facilitate a rally at a black church in Brooklyn, where Graham admitted, apparently for the first time in public, that antisegregation legislation would be required to end discrimination, though he added that it would come to naught unless it were supplemented by a strong manifestation of Christian love. These efforts helped increase black attendance at the crusade; *U.S. News & World Report* estimated that by the end of the crusade, blacks composed almost 20 percent of the typical audience. But more essential at this point than any specific task or result was Jones's mere presence on the team, and that presence did not go unnoticed. Ostensible Christians, outraged by Graham's integrationist action, bombarded the New York and Minneapolis offices with angry telephone calls and vile letters. The notorious southern racist John Kasper branded Graham a "negro lover" and attacked him for spreading the Christian religion among black people, for whom it was obviously never intended. On the positive side, *Ebony* magazine did a feature story on Graham in which he said, "There are a lot of segregationists who are going to be sadly disillusioned when they get to heaven—if they get there," and pointed out that the absence of a color line in heaven, which he believed the Bible taught, seemed to require that Christians observe no color line on earth.

Graham was just warming up. Despite his reservations about confrontational tactics, he took an unexpectedly bold step by inviting Martin Luther King to visit with his team and to participate in a crusade service. Behind the scenes, King met with Graham and team members to brief them on the racial situation in America and to sensitize them to key issues, including changes in terminology they needed to know about if they were to relate to blacks effectively. At a private dinner for King in a hotel suite, Graham asked how he and his followers had avoided violence during the Montgomery bus boycott. King gave the perfect answer: "Prayer and the Holy Spirit." Graham needed nothing more to convince him that King was a man to be trusted and encouraged. On July 18, before a capacity crowd at the Garden, he invited the black leader to join him on the platform and to lead the congregation in prayer. In his introduction he said, "A great social revolution is going on in the United States today. Dr. King is one of its leaders, and we appreciate his taking time out of his busy schedule to come and share this service with us tonight." The words did not explicitly condone either the revolution or King's part in it, and King's prayer called for nothing more revolutionary than "a brotherhood that transcends color," but the implication was unmistakable: Billy Graham was letting both whites and blacks know that he was willing to be identified with the revolution and its foremost leader, and Martin Luther King was telling blacks that Billy Graham was their ally. According to both Graham and Jones, King also told the evangelist that "your crusades do more with white people than I could do. We help each other. Keep on." That public, mutual quasi-endorsement, Howard Jones remembered, "brought the house down on Billy." A fresh batch of irate responses repeated accusations that Graham was "a straight-out integrationist," "nigger lover," and troublemaker; declared he had "lost the South" by abandoning evangelism to jump into politics; and even offered the unlikely explanation that his association with King had finally revealed him for what he was: a Communist. Bob Jones, Sr., a staunch foe of integration, pronounced Graham's ministry dead in the South. "Dr. Graham has declared emphatically," he said, "that he would not hold a meeting anywhere, North or South, where the colored people and the white people would be segregated in the auditorium, and I do not think any time in the foreseeable future the good Christian colored people and the good Christian white people would want to set aside an old established social and religious custom...." In fact, Graham had no southern crusade scheduled for the next twelve months, but his views were sufficiently well known and his influence so great that he could not escape involvement in the agony of that troubled region.

By midsummer, Graham was exhausted. He lost so much weight—thirty pounds by crusade's end—that, after seeing one of the telecasts, Richard Nixon's mother called from California to tell him he looked sick and needed to get some rest. He took her advice and began to spend most of the day in bed, working on sermons and husbanding his energy for the daytime appointments he could not avoid and for the enervating combat with Satan each evening in the Garden. Once, he was so distracted that when an attractive woman spoke to him in an elevator, he returned her greeting with a kind of noncommittal friendliness. Not until she got off the elevator did he realize that he had failed to recognize his own wife.

After a final three-week extension, the crusade finally came to an end on Labor Day, September 2. Jerry Beavan had studied the possibilities for a dramatic finish to the campaign. In a letter to Graham not long after the Yankee Stadium rally, he admitted that "we could quite conceivably let the crusade close without another big meeting ... but the London crusade is most remembered around the world for those two great meetings on that one final day, rather than for all the other terrific meetings along the way. We can never use mere crowds as the sole criterion for the meeting, but the crowds certainly are a yardstick that the public uses." A second gathering in Yankee Stadium could not possibly draw a bigger crowd, and if even one seat were empty, "it would be racked up as a failure." One promising option might be to schedule three consecutive services in different locations, one at the Polo Grounds, one at Ebbets Field, and one at Roosevelt Field in New Jersey. Speakers and the press corps would travel to each one and people could be urged to "avoid the congestion; attend the meeting nearest your home." Such an extravaganza, Beavan suggested, could be advertised as "the evangelistic meeting of all time." If Graham thought the logistics of a triple service were too complicated, Beavan suggested that perhaps a single holiday rally in Times Square might work. With a keen sense of the dramatic, Graham chose the latter option. On the evening of Labor Day, from a platform set in the midst of neon lights that hawked some of the most tawdry and temporary of the world's pleasures, he faced a crowd that jammed Times Square and stretched upward along Broadway for block after block to form a shoulder-to-shoulder ribbon of souls apparently numbering well above the one hundred thousand who had filled Yankee Stadium. His voice crackling through the urban canyon, Billy made one final call for spiritual revival. "Let us tell the whole world tonight," he boomed, "that we Americans believe in God.... that our trust is not in our stockpile of atomic and hydrogen bombs but in Almighty God.... that we are morally and spiritually strong as well as militarily and economically.... Let us tonight make this a time of rededication—not only to God but to the principles and freedoms that our forefathers gave us. On this Labor Day weekend, here at the Crossroads of America, let us tell the world that we are united and ready to march under the banner of Almighty God, taking as our slogan that which is stamped on our coins: 'In God we trust.'"

Postcrusade assessments contained the familiar recitations of "firsts" and "mosts." With an average attendance of nearly 18,000 per service, the campaign had been the longest-running and most heavily attended event in the history of Madison Square Garden. Counting the crowds at outdoor rallies, total attendance topped 2,000,000 with over 55,000 recorded decisions for Christ. More than 1,500,000 letters had cascaded into Minneapolis in direct response to the weekly telecasts, and at least 30,000 of those told of additional decisions made in the privacy of homes. Lane Adams's outreach to entertainers resulted in the conversion or rededication of 500 people and led to the founding of the Christian Arts Fellowship, with opera singer Jerome Hines serving as director. This program also helped keep the platform and "celebrity gallery" stocked with well-known figures—Stuart Hamblen, Dale Evans, Walter Winchell, Ed Sullivan, Dorothy Kilgallen (who wrote a multipart profile of Graham for the *Journal-American*), Pearl Bailey, John Wayne, Edward G. Robinson, Greer Garson, Gene Tierney, ice-skating star Sonja Henie, boxing great Jack Dempsey, Dodger pitcher Carl Erskine, Giant shortstop Alvin Dark, sportscaster Red Barber, and born-again Peruvian headhunter Chief Tarari, among others—who provided the meetings with publicity and legitimation. Society hostess Perle Mesta gushed, "Isn't it fantastic! I think he is just wonderful! Certainly we need this. It's all that's going to save the world." He, in turn, thought well of them and was pleased to return the compliments. After meeting Gloria Swanson on the *Dave Garroway Today Show*, he observed that "America would be a wonderful place if more of our film stars were like Gloria Swanson."

However much they hoped the stars might be attending the crusade from sincere interest in the Christian gospel, Graham and his team understood that his own considerable celebrity, which they promoted relentlessly, was part of the attraction. To achieve and maintain celebrity, one does well to appear at places where other celebrities (and the people who take their pictures) gather. Sometimes the mixed agendas proved awkward. Gangster Mickey Cohen, fighting to stay out of prison, made an appearance at the crusade and hosted Graham for lunch in his suite at the Waldorf-Astoria. In later years Cohen claimed that Graham's people tried to bribe him into becoming a "trophy" convert. Graham and his team flatly deny the allegation, and it seems far more likely Cohen was trying to cast himself in a sympathetic light. But some celebrities, such as black singer and actress Ethel Waters, attended the crusade in a genuine search for meaning. Waters, whose personal life was in serious crisis, found the crusade services a joyful and reassuring return to the simple Christianity in which she had been reared. She soon began singing in the choir and performing solo numbers, including a signature piece, "His Eye Is on the Sparrow." The crusade marked a profound turnaround for her, and she played a lead role in *The Heart Is a Rebel*, a World Wide Pictures feature film centered on the New York campaign. Throughout the rest of her life, she appeared as a regular guest performer in Graham's crusades and remained close to the team, particularly to Grady Wilson, until her death in 1977.

Analysis of decisions registered at the crusade produced results similar to those of other Graham campaigns. In an ambitious study performed by

Robert Ferm, approximately one in five inquirers could not be contacted, some because they had given false addresses. Of the remainder, nearly one in three claimed no church affiliation prior to the crusade, but more than 90 percent of these reported that they had become members of a church or were studying to do so. A similar proportion of those who were already church members prior to the crusade claimed to be aware of a significant difference in their lives since their decision. The Protestant Council of New York estimated that 6,000–10,000 new members were added to the metropolitan area's 1,700 churches, a welcome but not astonishing gain. A few churches saw a substantial influx of new people. Nearly half of the 373 people referred to Norman Vincent Peale's Marble Collegiate Church—the largest number referred to any single congregation—were previously unknown to the ministers; all were tracked down, and nearly 100 joined the church. The Calvary Baptist Church baptized 30 people as a direct result of the crusade, and other churches reported attendance increases of from 10 percent to 40 percent. At the low end of the spectrum, however, a Christian and Missionary Alliance tabernacle near Times Square received ninety cards. Three came from current members; of the remaining eighty-seven, not a single one showed the slightest interest in further contact with the church. More commonly, a high proportion of the people referred to ministers for follow-up were already members of their congregation or denomination, but pastors reported they had become more effective members, forming the nucleus for new prayer and study groups and participating more vigorously in other aspects of the church's program. Hoping to improve this yield, Graham returned to the city a few weeks after the crusade ended in an attempt to enlist 1,500 ministers and churches in a massive follow-up campaign in which church members would call on 200,000 homes. That effort, however, fell far short of its goal and reaped no notable harvest. Graham and his team would wrestle with the problem of adequate follow-up for the rest of his career, but given the unavoidable reliance on clergy whose attitude toward them would vary from total commitment to barely concealed cynicism, they would never find a fully satisfactory solution.

Few would admit they were disappointed, but even fewer would claim the crusade's tangible results had exceeded their expectations. On his last night in the Garden, Graham said, "I believe that history will say that 1957 was the year of spiritual awakening," but it was clear he had not turned New York upside down. "New York probably looks the same," he admitted. "The crowds still throng Times Square. There are still people going to nightclubs. There's still lots of crime in the city. Yes, but there is one difference. One tremendous difference! That difference is in the lives of thousands of men and women who will never be the same." The claim, though difficult to document in a statistically satisfying way, was rendered quite plausible by the thousands of letters that poured into BGEA's Minneapolis headquarters claiming just such a profound change as a direct result of responding to the invitation Graham offered. In the years to follow, this would become the orthodox interpretation of crusade results. It would not satisfy critics. It would disappoint many supporters, who had worked and hoped for more. But it would be enough to keep the gospel locomotive rolling on down the line.

15

Reaping the Whirlwind

As expected, the New York crusade made the breach with the Fundamentalists permanent. Early in 1958, John R. Rice, the Bob Joneses (an equally fractious Bob junior had joined his father's battle with Billy) and a number of lesser evangelists signed a pledge never to accept meetings sponsored by nonorthodox groups. Graham not only ignored this show of purity but offended his critics even more deeply by courting and receiving new levels of approval for his May 1958 crusade in the Cow Palace in San Francisco. The crusade received the endorsement of both the Oakland and San Francisco Council of Churches, the Episcopal Diocese of California, and the Presbytery of San Francisco, and enjoyed the participation of numerous other non-Evangelical churches as well. Some extreme liberals took the usual potshots, with the usual lack of effect. Several dozen Fundamentalist pastors, mostly Baptists, opposed and attacked the crusade, but their efforts attracted such meager support that in the words of one observer, they "became quiescent." Clearly, Graham's decision to occupy the middle ground had been a successful one. *Christianity Today* said of the San Francisco crusade, "The great central segment of Protestantism was committed to a mass evangelistic effort as never before.... There was a polarization of extremes; many of those opposed at the beginning were more so at the ending. Yet in the center, there seems to have taken place a wonderful warming and softening of hearts.... A real secret of Billy Graham's power was manifest—his ability to bring believers into touch with each other by omitting the things which divide them."

For a brief period, Graham attempted to repair, or at least to justify, the breach with the Fundamentalists. In a twelve-page open letter released during the San Francisco crusade, he urged his critics to realize that "many men are mistakenly called 'liberal' or 'modernist' by uninformed Evangelicals. I have found in my contacts that hundreds of men are warm, Godly men who hold to the essentials of the Christian faith but who for various reasons do not want to be identified with modern-day Evangelicalism, its organizations and institutions.... We should be extremely careful that we do not become as the Pharisees of old, thinking we have a 'corner' on the gospel." The spiritual defects of extreme liberalism, he warned, are no more odious than those that cause the "bitterness, jealousy, rancor, division, strife, hardness, a seeking after revenge, and vindictiveness that characterizes a few fundamentalists." Apart from this one effort, Graham restrained himself and responded to the long vitriolic letters he received from McIntire and Jones with no more than brief notes. "I soon learned there was no way I could answer them," he recalled. "But I'd always write back and say, 'Thank you for your letter. I've noted its contents and God bless you,' or something to that effect." He could not recall ever meeting Carl McIntire, but he did make one attempt to effect a reconciliation with Dr. Bob. While meeting informally in Birmingham, Alabama, with a group of twenty or so men who had fallen out of favor with Jones, Graham learned that Jones, who had been to nearby Dothan to inspect a statue of himself that he had recently commissioned, was staying in the same hotel. Graham asked his old adversary if he could call on him in his room: "I wanted to tell him that I still loved him and would answer any question he had about my ministry. It wasn't an organized meeting; some of us just came in to visit. I remember Dr. Bob was in bed, and he was as nervous as a cat." One participant recalled that Graham greeted Jones warmly and told him he was "looking great." Instead of returning the compliment, Jones harrumphed, "You're on your way down, Billy." Graham said, "If that's the way God wants it, then it's settled." The reason, Jones said, was because "your converts don't last." Graham turned the other cheek: "I don't have any converts. I have never led anybody to Christ. Missionaries can say they have done that; I can't. There are so many factors—prayer, Bible classes, pastors, hard work by lots of people. I come along and point to the door. I can't claim any as mine." Graham's self-effacing responses fell on stony ground. "We're taking over evangelism in America, Billy," Jones announced, "Jack Shuler is going to be the man now. I know, because I trained him." Eventually, the men in the room shook hands and prayed together, but the hoped-for reconciliation did not occur. When Jones died a few years later, Bob Junior took the trouble to send T. W. Wilson a telegram informing him that neither he nor, by clear implication, any of Graham's colleagues would be welcome at the funeral. "Dr. Bob had a terrific philosophy," Graham observed years later, "but he didn't live up to it. He said, if a hound dog barks for Jesus, then I'll be for him,' but when I came along and was the hound dog, he wasn't for me.... I suspect it was a little like Saul and David. Saul had slain his thousands and David his ten thousands. But I don't want to be judgmental. I believe Dr. Bob loved the Lord." He paused for a moment, then said, "It shows me how to act as an older man."

The loss of Fundamentalist support disappointed Graham, but he and his New Evangelical colleagues had clearly won the war, and he had emerged as the most prominent figure in a revitalized national social movement. Harold Ockenga, who could legitimately claim to be the father of this movement, explicitly identified Graham as "the spokesman of the convictions and ideals of the New Evangelicalism." Some Evangelicals remained wary, fearful that worldly success in the form of larger numbers and popular recognition might corrupt their purity. The *Moody Monthly*, for example, which had regularly extolled Graham's triumphs, omitted all mention of the San Francisco crusade and maintained a cautious attitude toward the evangelist for another four or five years. This reticence, however, was more than offset by Charles Fuller's naming Graham to the board of Fuller Seminary in 1958, thus forging a visible bond between the leading evangelists of two generations. In retaliation, Bob Jones took Fuller's *Old Fashioned Revival Hour* program off WMUU.

If some Evangelicals worried that success might spoil their young champion, others delighted in his triumphs and basked in the respectability he had won for their movement. When newspaper and television reporters asked his opinions, he articulated Evangelical beliefs and values in a manner that made them plausible, perhaps even convincing, to mainstream America. When talk-show hosts interviewed him, Evangelicals appreciated that one of their own was accorded the same respect enjoyed by movie stars and sports heroes and famous authors and prominent politicians. When the Gallup poll repeatedly listed him among the "most admired men" in the nation, as it had every year since 1955, they felt their own judgments about him had been confirmed by the populace as a whole. And when Ralph Edwards retold his story on *This Is Your Life*, with Richard Nixon as a participant, they felt their own lives—which were, after all, not radically different from his—had been declared legitimate and worthy of honor.

Graham took his celebrity seriously. Not only did he persist in his determination to keep his life free of recognizable stain, but he also showed remarkable grace and apparently indefatigable patience toward those who encountered him in more private circumstances. To protect himself against being nibbled into fragments by well-wishers and autograph seekers and desperate souls who sought his ministrations, he seldom ate in well-known restaurants or took the long walks that had been a lifelong habit. During crusades he spent most of his unscheduled time in his hotel room, at the homes of friends, or on the golf course, which offered him a chance to relax, socialize, and get some exercise without constant interruptions. Beavan and other associates served as gatekeepers, winnowing those who sought an audience to a manageable few and politely attempting to discourage strangers from accosting him unannounced. Graham wanted and needed these hedges against constant intrusion, but whenever an admirer or supplicant breached the thin protective barrier, his long habit of wanting to please overpowered any impulse toward resentment. Lane Adams recalled an airplane flight during which "the copilot, the engineer, all the stewardesses, and at least half the passengers at some time got up and came forward into the section where we were and said, 'I don't want to bother you, Mr. Graham, but I just have to shake your hand.' Billy was exhausted and was sitting by the window, hoping to get a little rest, but he always stood up and shook their hand. He bumped his head on the overhead compartment nearly every time, but each time he acted just thrilled to meet them and to listen to their inane comments. Finally, the captain came back and said, 'We'd like to show you what the cockpit of a DC-7 looks like.' He said, 'I'd love that.' Later, I said, 'Be honest with me. How many cockpits of DC-7's have you seen?' He said, 'I've lost count. But I didn't want to disappoint him.' He had probably been in planes the pilot had never seen, but that's just the way Billy is."

Celebrity impinged on the Grahams' family life as well. Their mountainside manse was hard to find, and thoughtful neighbors learned not to give directions to curious pilgrims, but some inevitably made their way up the narrow, steep road to the house, where they knocked to ask for directions, pretending to be lost, or just wandered around in the front yard, hoping to get a glimpse of the famous evangelist or some member of his family. Ruth tended to ignore them. If Billy happened to be home, she seldom informed him they had visitors; if he spotted them, he often went outside to greet them and chat for a few minutes. Eventually, however, he agreed to the installation of a security fence with electronic gates and acquired two German shepherd guard dogs, Belshazzar and Samson, whose alleged viciousness seems never to have been put to a definitive test. Ruth understood that she could do little to protect her husband from his own gregariousness, but she steadfastly refused to expose her children to public gaze. They were not available to make comments—charming, revealing, or merely childlike—to inquiring reporters. They were not trotted out on crusade platforms to give their personal testimony or to tell adoring crowds what a wonderful man their father was. And they were subjected to a rather stern and consistent discipline at home. GiGi observed that "because she had full-time help, Mother didn't get upset about dirty clothes or little things like that. But she was strict, and she did spank us. I got spanked nearly every day. Franklin, too. Anne didn't seem to need it. She had those great big blue eyes that filled up with tears, and Mother's heart would melt. Also, I was usually the instigator of the trouble anyway. Mother was fair. She was particularly strict on moral issues, and respect for adults was a moral issue for her. My son calls me 'Dude.' My mother would not have allowed that. But she had a great sense of humor, and we had a lot of fun. I have no memories of a screaming mother." Ruth would be pleased at that memory, since she sometimes worried that she was becoming shrewish. In one diary entry, she reflected, "The children misbehave. I reprimand them more sharply—more probably, peevishly. The very tone of the voice irritates them. (I know because if it were used on me it would irritate me.) They answer back, probably in the same tone. I turn on them savagely. (I hate to think how often. And how savage a loving mother can be at times.) And I snap, 'Don't you speak to your mother like that. It isn't respectful.' Nothing about me—actions, tone of voice, etc.—commanded respect. It doesn't mean I am to tolerate sass or back talk. But then I must be very careful not to inspire it either."

When Billy was home, which was less than half the time, much of Ruth's disciplinary regimen went out the window. "Mother would have us in a routine," GiGi recalled. "She monitored our TV watching, made us do our homework, and put us to bed at a set time. Then, when Daddy was home, he'd say, 'Oh, let them stay up and watch this TV show with me,' or he'd give us extra spending money for candy and gum. Mother always handled it with grace. She never said, 'Well, here comes Bill. Everything I'm trying to do is going to be all messed up.' She just said, 'Whatever your Daddy says is fine with me.' We just slipped in and out of two different routines. As a mother, I look at it with wonder now, but it wasn't an issue. It was just two routines." It was also a different routine for Ruth. "They were always very affectionate," GiGi noted. "Whenever he was at home, they were always hugging or holding hands, or he'd have her sitting in his lap. They mutually adored one another, and it was very evident. They still do."

GiGi offered a possible explanation of her father's more relaxed approach. "Once, he disciplined me for something I did. I don't even remember what it was about, but we had some disagreement in the kitchen. I ran up the stairs, and when I thought I was out of range, I stomped my feet. Then I ran into my room and locked my door. He came up the stairs, two at a time it sounded like, and he was angry. When I finally opened the door, he pulled me across the room, sat me on the bed, and gave me a real tongue-lashing. I said, 'Some dad you are! You go away and leave us all the time!' Immediately, his eyes filled with tears. It just broke my heart. That whole scene was always a part of my memory bank after that. I realized he was making a sacrifice too. But it does seem like he didn't discipline us much after that."

Over time, Ruth also became more flexible, reducing the number of her demands on the children to those she felt were essential. She claimed to have obtained some of her most effective child-rearing techniques from a dog-training manual whose directives included keeping commandments simple and at a minimum, seeing to it that all commands were obeyed, rewarding obedience with praise, and being consistent. Even then, GiGi found it difficult to stay in line. According to Ruth, her eldest daughter "tried harder to be good than anyone—but couldn't." Once, after a day in which she had been a particular trial, she asked at bedtime, "Mommy, have I been good enough today to go to heaven?" Ruth wrote in her diary, "Now how much should I impress on her Salvation by Grace when really for a child of her disposition one could be tempted to think salvation by works would be more effective on her behavior?" Whatever her faults, GiGi did display a talent for practical theology. Ruth once caught her slapping docile Anne on the cheek, insisting that she had a duty to turn the other for equal assault. On another occasion, to resolve an argument among the three girls over ownership of pictures cut from the *TV Guide*, Anne and Bunny prayed and decided they should burn all the pictures rather than let them become a source of conflict. GiGi countered by announcing that Jesus would not mind if they kept the better pictures. In 1958, when a fifth child, Ned (a contraction of Nelson Edman, after Nelson Bell and former Wheaton president V. Raymond Edman), was born, GiGi, just shy of her thirteenth birthday, was shipped off to Hampden-Dubose boarding school in Florida. T.W. and Grady Wilson had both sent their children to the school, and GiGi's best friend was going, which made the decision seem attractive, but GiGi admitted she never adjusted well and "cried for four years," adding that "when Anne went away and cried for a few days, they let her come back home, but I had to stay all four years. I didn't like it, I was scared, and I missed my family, but the Lord led them, and I can't thank him enough now. I married young, and it was great preparation time for me. The Lord knew."

Whatever Billy Graham's private feelings about fame, and even his most loyal and admiring friends acknowledge he does not find it entirely onerous, he instinctively understood its value to his ministry. He also understood that his ties to the Eisenhower-Nixon administration were his optimum public credential, and he worked assiduously to maintain them. In public he continued to insist that "I don't think politics is part of my work. My work is winning persons for Christ. I follow [politics] as closely as I do religion, but I never take sides." In private he continued to act like a Republican strategist. In December 1957 he told Nixon, "I think your political stock is extremely high, although I fear there are many factors working against any Republican being elected in 1960. Senator Kennedy is getting a fantastic buildup in certain elements of the press. He would indeed be a formidable foe. Contrary to popular opinion, when the chips are down, I think the religious issue would be very strong and might conceivably work in your behalf." A few months later, he observed that "there is a growing possibility of a split deep within Democratic ranks on the race issue. Therefore, I think there is every reason for at least mild optimism."

Graham's critics not only scoffed at his claims to neutrality but explicitly charged him with cozying up to the White House as a way of boosting his own image and stature. Billy wrestled inwardly with both critiques, probably recognizing the elements of truth in each and attempting to convince himself as well as others that they were not valid. In a letter asking Nixon to address a Presbyterian meeting, he noted that he turned down most requests to intercede with the President or Vice-President lest he be accused of exploiting their friendship but justified this exception on the grounds that "it would give you an excellent platform to say some of the things you would like to say along moral and spiritual lines." In similar fashion, just as he had importuned

Truman to show up at a service during the 1952 Washington crusade, he had asked Eisenhower on several occasions to make an appearance at Madison Square Garden, venturing that "I am convinced that if you visited Madison Square Garden some evening in August, it would become one of the most historic events of your administration and would leave an indelible impression on the minds and hearts of millions, not only in this country but abroad." To his disappointment, the President passed up the chance to make history.

Inevitably, standing close to the center of power involved Graham in the struggles that occupy power's attention. In September, just as the New York crusade was drawing to a close, schools were about to open and dozens of southern cities and towns were in turmoil as citizens tried to deal with a series of federal court orders designed to end school desegregation. In Graham's hometown of Charlotte, fifteen-year-old Dorothy Counts, a black minister's daughter, was driven away by a barrage of sticks and rocks when she tried to enter previously all-white Harding High School. Her plight moved Billy to write her a stiffly awkward letter of encouragement. "Dear Miss Counts," he wrote, "Democracy demands that you hold fast and carry on. The world of tomorrow is looking for leaders and you have been chosen. Those cowardly whites against you will never prosper because they are un-American and unfit to lead. Be of good faith. God is not dead. He will see you through. This is your one great chance to prove to Russia that democracy still prevails. Billy Graham, D.D." It was not Charlotte, however, that drew Graham's primary attention. In what some regarded as a self-conscious strategic test of resistance to federal demands, the focus of the civil rights crisis shifted from the Deep South to Little Rock, Arkansas, where Governor Orval Faubus (who had attended a crusade service in the Garden earlier in the summer) provoked a showdown in the confrontation created by the federal government's determination to enforce the Supreme Court's school-desegregation order and the stubborn refusal of southern states to obey it. The mayor, the school board, and a substantial proportion of Little Rock's ministers declared themselves in favor of obeying a federal judge's explicit directive to delay integration of the city's schools no longer, but on the pretext that he feared an outbreak of violence if blacks sought to enter the all-white Central High School, Faubus deployed 270 members of the Arkansas National Guard to stop them. On the first day of school, no blacks appeared, but a white crowd raucously shouted its defiance of the court order. On the second day, when nine black students tried to enter, the troops turned them away, to the delight of a jeering crowd. President Eisenhower counseled restraint on all sides and informed Faubus that the federal government would not pay the Guard's expenses and salary, since it was acting on behalf of the state of Arkansas, not the United States. In an obvious grandstanding effort, Faubus sent the President a wire accusing the FBI of tapping the phone lines to the executive mansion (a charge FBI director J. Edgar Hoover emphatically denied) and urging Ike to stop "unwarranted interference by Federal agents." Eisenhower countered with his own wire, putting Faubus on notice that he intended to "uphold the Federal Constitution by every legal means." The President's press secretary, James Hagerty, told reporters that Eisenhower was firmly against the use of federal troops but left a bit of maneuvering room by acknowledging that the Commander in Chief had not anticipated a situation in which state troops would be used to bar children from attending school. To that, Faubus boasted, ambiguously but ominously, that Arkansas could defend itself, adding that at least half the southern states had vowed to help. In an attempt to break the impasse, Faubus flew to Newport, Rhode Island, where Eisenhower was vacationing, for a highly publicized meeting. The governor asked for a one-year cooling-off period; the President gave him until the following Monday to pull the troops out and allow the black students, who had already missed two weeks of classes, to enter Central High. Faubus withdrew the Guard as ordered and dispatched fifty Arkansas state troopers to help protect any black students who tried to enter the school. Hate groups flooded Little Rock with racist literature, the segregationist White Citizens' Council announced it planned to hold anti-integration rallies, and pulpits rang with calls for calm and patience. When the nine students approached the school on Monday morning, September 23, a violent mob forced them to withdraw. Black and white newsmen, often lumped with Communists and the NAACP as outside agitators determined to stir up trouble, were attacked and twenty-four demonstrators were arrested.

Pressed for a comment, Billy Graham recommended that the white citizens of Little Rock submit to the court order: "It is the duty of every Christian, when it does not violate his relationship to God, to obey the law. I would urge them to do so in this case." These words differed little from his earlier justification for having accepted segregated seating in his southern crusades and hardly constituted a ringing denunciation of discrimination. Graham also followed his practice of absolving most southerners of blame for the worst of the problems. The turmoil in Little Rock, he theorized, had been instigated by outsiders and was "giving the Communists one of their greatest [propaganda] weapons in years." (In fact, Communist newspapers were paying close attention. *Pravda* clucked that Little Rock was showing the true face of "free America," and a headline in the Italian Communist paper *Unita*, trumpeted, "SHAME OF ARKANSAS ENVELOPS AMERICA."). Newspapers were not alone in their interest in Graham's views on the Little Rock situation. With George Champion as intermediary, former Health, Education, and Welfare secretary Oveta Culp Hobby suggested that Graham consider a special nationwide broadcast on the need for peaceful integration. Billy also discussed the problem during a half-hour visit with Richard Nixon but would not reveal the substance of their conversation. Undoubtedly, Graham would have preferred to be out of the eye of this particular storm. If he said nothing or made excuses for southern racists, he risked losing the support of black Evangelicals and drawing the fire of white Christians committed to racial justice. If he spoke or acted in opposition to those resisting integration, he risked alienating a wide segment of his audience and support. But when the President, who had used him as a sounding board on racial questions for some time, called to tell him he was thinking of sending troops into Little Rock, Graham told him, "Mr. President, I think that is the only thing you can do. It is out of hand, and the time has come to stop it." About an hour later, Nixon called to get a second reading on Graham's inclination. Graham gave him the same answer he had given Eisenhower. That afternoon, a thousand troops of the 101st Airborne Division, together with additional members of the National Guard, rolled into Little Rock.

Graham revealed that he had been in touch with several Little Rock ministers and offered to visit the city if it appeared he could make some useful contribution. Some clergymen urged him to come to Little Rock, but Fundamentalists, who tended to be unsympathetic to both his racial views and his alleged doctrinal laxity, opposed any such visit on the grounds that it would just stir up more trouble. He chose to stay away, noting that he had "no intention of going there without an invitation." This response may have been a model of thoughtful courtesy, and it surely reflected Graham's distaste for conflict, but it hardly exemplified the stance of the biblical prophets, whose passion for justice sometimes took them into settings where their presence was not entirely welcome. Graham's quite genuine but restrained support of the movement toward integration inevitably left many dissatisfied. Racists saw him as the critic and opponent that indeed he was. Those pushing hardest against the barriers to equality labeled him an equivocator and compromiser, always ready to step back from risking his popularity on a bold and courageous stand. And southern governors and other politicians, whatever their deepest feelings about integration, found it difficult to accept his siding with the federal government in the most notable challenge to the autonomy of the southern states since the Civil War. The disaffection of such a large segment of his constituency troubled him deeply, but he seems not to have doubted that the President had made the right decision, and for the right reasons. In a letter to Eisenhower a few weeks later, he gushed, "Just a note to say that you are about the most remarkable man in history. I think your going to church [Thanksgiving] morning sent a sigh of relief throughout the entire world. It also indicated to millions that your faith was in God."

During the following two years, Graham's growing reputation as an integrationist created both conflict and opportunity to set a positive example. He met each in the cautious, measured fashion that irritated his critics but kept him out of trouble. In the fall of 1958, he planned a rally on the lawn of the South Carolina statehouse in Columbia, where he had held his first major southern crusade. Governor George Bell Timmerman, a hard-shell segregationist, opposed the rally on the grounds that allowing Graham to speak on state property would be tantamount to an official endorsement of racial mixing, the very sort of thing that had caused all the trouble in Little Rock. "While most Columbians were enjoying their sleep," Timmerman solemnly reported, "I took this problem to my God in prayer and concluded that I should speak out in protest." Despite this claim of divine warrant, some churchmen, including the pastor of the city's largest Southern Baptist congregation, felt Graham should come to show the rest of the country that not all southerners shared the governor's racist views. Rather than challenge Timmerman's stand on segregation, however, Graham asserted that the purpose of his proposed visit to Columbia was to proclaim the gospel, not to promote integration. "I am certain," he ventured, that "no citizen would object to people being won to Christ on the Capitol grounds." This did not mollify the governor, who observed that having an evangelist speak on the statehouse lawn would violate the historic principle of the separation of Church and State—a principle South Carolinians had apparently not thought violated when in 1950 Governor Strom Thurmond, who had arranged for Graham to address the state legislature and public-school gatherings, proclaimed a "South Carolina Revival Rally Day" and dispatched a police escort to accompany him on a whirlwind preaching tour of the state. To Graham's great relief, the impasse was broken and further conflict avoided when the commanding officer of Fort Jackson offered to host the rally on the army base. Billy told the press, "I certainly would not want to be a party to breaking any state laws" but refused further comment on the controversy surrounding the rally or the racial situation itself. Sixty thousand people attended the rally, described as "the first nonsegregated mass meeting in South Carolina's history" and "the largest religious gathering ever held in the southeast." Graham struck a gentle blow for integration when he introduced W. O. Vaught, Jr., a Baptist pastor who played a major role in restoring peace to Little Rock during the previous year's racial turmoil, and commended him for having "stayed by his stuff." But he also gave a prominent seat on the platform to former governor James Byrnes, an ardent foe of integration. During his sermon he commended Columbians for what he perceived to be a "warm friendship between the races," an assessment that though perhaps accurate in some respects, ignored the clear fact that the conflict his visit had generated revealed some rather telling imperfections in that friendship. As usual, this moderate approach drew fire from both sides. John Sutherland Bonnell comforted him by writing, "The stand you took was very courageous and I believe truly Christian. Even the *Christian Century* had to take off its hat to you! I know that such a stand cost you a great deal in the matter of relations with some of the brethren in the South, but God will be able to use you even more effectively as the result." Less sympathetic critics fastened on Governor Byrnes's presence on the platform and contended that Graham should have stuck to his plan of meeting on the capitol steps, even though it might have provoked a riot.

About the same time, racists bombed the newly integrated high school in Clinton, Tennessee. Newspaper columnist Drew Pearson took the lead in raising money to rebuild the school and challenged Graham to join him. Graham not only accepted but agreed to serve on the executive committee of the Americans Against Bombs of Bigotry. He also pointedly observed that bombings of schools and churches were "symptomatic of the type of thing that brought Hitler to power. It could eventually lead to a union between forces of crime and hate groups which would lead to anarchy.... Every Christian should take his stand against these outrages." In mid-December, he went to Clinton to speak at a fund-raising rally. Addressing an integrated audience of approximately 5,000 in the badly damaged school's still-standing gymnasium, Graham called for "tolerance, forgiveness, cool heads and warm hearts," noting that "hot heads and cool hearts never solved anything," and declaring that "we must not even hate the depraved minds who commit acts of hatred and violence, but we must have the grace to forgive them." He further urged that southern Christians allow neither integration nor segregation "to become our Gospel. Our Gospel must be Jesus Christ and the Cross." When he offered the invitation at the close of his address, which Pearson described as "a fine and inspiring sermon," no one moved for a full two minutes. Then, the dam broke and scores of people streamed forward, including, according to one account, "a white racist who had vowed to wreck the meeting."

Graham had avoided Little Rock at the height of its troubles, but he came to the city for two large rallies in September 1959. While some still found him overly cautious in his efforts to boost integration, none doubted where his sentiments lay, as evidenced by the criticisms leveled against him by the Ku Klux Klan and the White Citizen's Council, which distributed thousands of leaflets attacking him for his antisegregation views and criticizing him for inviting Martin Luther King to participate in the New York crusade. More positively, Governor Faubus called on citizens not to oppose Graham, whom he commended as "a great gospel speaker," and indicated his intention to attend at least one of the rally services. In his own show of conciliation, Graham went to the city jail to visit several men who had set off dynamite in the school-board office, the mayor's office, and the fire chief's car. He reported that "these men received me very cordially. We had quite a talk and I said a prayer with each of them privately. They were very humble and, I would say, repentant." In his sermons and public statements, Graham lamented the conflict Little Rock had experienced and hinted that much of the blame for the troubles should be laid at the feet of those trying to force integration. Such intimations predictably displeased those who painted Little Rock's preriot tranquillity in a less rosy light, but Billy's moderate approach surely succeeded in softening some racist hearts. In a letter to Graham a week after he left Little Rock, integrationist pastor W. O. Vaught told the evangelist that "there has been universal agreement in all the churches and out across the city that your visit here was one of the finest things that ever happened in the history of Little Rock. So very many people have changed their attitude, so many people have washed their hearts of hatred and bitterness, and many made decisions who had never expected to make such decisions." Several years later, Vaught reaffirmed his original assessment when he wrote, "The influence of this good man was a real factor in the solution of our racial problems here in Little Rock."

As Graham's reputation and influence continued to grow, he began to seek other ways of using them to enhance his ministry and Evangelicalism in general. *Christianity Today* had won a secure place in religious publishing, but it still addressed itself primarily to ministers. He sensed a need for a more popular magazine aimed at the lay Christian, a magazine that would be "thought-provoking, devotional and evangelistic, with a breezy, easy-to-read style." It would also be, in a way *Christianity Today* could never be, an official organ of his ministry, reporting on his crusades and other activities, as well as those of his associate evangelists, and gently reminding subscribers of the ministry's continuing financial needs. Some of his colleagues and supporters, aware of the financial and personnel problems that typically attend the launching of a new magazine, tried to dissuade him, but he was determined. During the 1958 San Francisco crusade, he developed a friendship with Sherwood Wirt, a Congregational minister who was so impressed by Graham that he jettisoned the liberal theology he had been preaching and began to proclaim a more Evangelical message. At Graham's urging, Wirt wrote glowing accounts of the crusade for several Evangelical publications, including *Christianity Today*, and later expanded them into a book, *Crusade at the Golden Gate*. As a younger man, he had worked as a newspaper editor in Alaska and had earned a doctorate from the University of Edinburgh, a combination of practical experience and academic credential that Graham found irresistible. Two years later, in November 1960, with former pastor Wirt at the helm, the first issue of *Decision* magazine reached a remarkable 253,000 charter subscribers generated by radio, television, crusade, and direct-mail appeals. Circulation increased with every issue until five years later, *Decision* went into 5,000,000 homes, making it by far the most widely received religious publication in the country.

At times it must have seemed, even to Graham, that virtually any enterprise he conceived would automatically come to successful, perhaps glorious, fruition, but that was not quite the case. During the preparation for the New York crusade, the evangelist became convinced that the northeastern portion of the nation desperately needed a Christian university, "a university that would be what Harvard and Yale and Dartmouth started out to be, with a Christian philosophy of education," a university to which soon-to-be lesser schools like Wheaton and Houghton could turn when they needed professors for their own institutions. The positive response by young people at Madison Square Garden intensified that conviction. With encouragement from *Reader's Digest* owner DeWitt Wallace, former New York governor Thomas E. Dewey, Vice-President Nixon, and the active participation of southern department-store magnate Henderson Belk (who pledged major support), radio commentator Paul Harvey (who agreed to serve as chairman of the finance committee), veteran Wheaton professor and administrator Enock Dyrness, and the usual cast of Evangelical entrepreneurs—J. Howard Pew, Roger Hull, Carl Henry, Harold Ockenga, and Nelson Bell—Graham convened several meetings to explore the feasibility of establishing such an institution, preferably in New Jersey, as close to New York City as possible. A brochure entitled *A Time for Decision in Higher Education: Billy Graham Presents Crusade University* depicted a fifteen-building campus (complete with a football stadium) on five hundred to one thousand acres, projected a seventy-member faculty that would receive salaries above the national median, and described in general terms a liberal arts curriculum that would match its commitment to the highest possible academic standards with equal faithfulness to the Bible, "with emphasis on its absolute validity." Keeping a customary eye for maximum public impact, the target date for opening the first phase of the institution, the undergraduate college, was set for the fall of 1963 "so as to capitalize on the World's Fair to be held in New York in 1964." Impressive as it was, the brochure probably contained the seeds of its failure in an open letter from Graham in which, despite his endorsement of the project, he said, "I am not an educator and have no intention of entering that field." Graham's decision not to play even a ceremonial role, however, seems to have doomed the project before it got off the ground, and the complete history of Crusade University is contained in a thin manila folder in the Billy Graham Archives at Wheaton College, the institution it was expected to supersede.

Graham repeatedly justified both his break with the Fundamentalists and his decision not to take a more prophetic stance on race and other social issues by pointing out that God had not called him to theological disputation or headline-grabbing social action. His call, he insisted, was to "do the work of an evangelist," and he ended the decade as he had begun it, with an intense flurry of preaching. During 1959 and 1960, he held rallies and crusades in 40 cities on four continents, speaking in person to more than 5 million people and adding 227,000 more inquirers to his carefully kept box score. The most memorable of these campaigns were a 1959 tour of Australia and New Zealand, which still ranks as one of the most successful of his entire ministry, and a less triumphant but still notable 1960 safari for souls in nine nations of Africa.

16

Unto the Uttermost Parts of the Earth

By 1959 Billy Graham was an internationally renowned figure, sought after by Protestant churchmen and civic leaders throughout the world. Still, the nations beneath the Southern Cross seemed a formidable challenge. Less than a third of Australians attended church with any regularity, and the stereotype of a hard-drinking, rough-and-ready, egalitarian, and largely secular people—happy pagans, they were sometimes called—seemed to fit a substantial segment of the population. Certainly, the Australians had shown little enthusiasm for itinerant evangelists. They treated Billy Sunday and Aimee Semple McPherson with virtual contempt, and in 1956 rowdy Melbournites disrupted an Oral Roberts meeting with a stink bomb, then cut down his tent and tried to set fire to his equipment, causing him to cut short his campaign and return to Tulsa in humiliating defeat. Graham was aware of this history but took some comfort from the fact that he was not coming as an unwelcome interloper. On the contrary, the impetus for the invitation, issued at the height of the New York crusade in 1957, grew out of an initiative led by the archbishop of Sydney, primate of the Anglican Church in Australia, who was joined by most Anglican leaders and prominent churchmen from other Protestant bodies. When the archbishop died in 1958, he was replaced by Hugh Gough, bishop of Barking, a vigorous supporter of Graham's Harringay crusade who hoped for an Australian rerun of that great triumph. The chief justice of the state of Victoria headed the group offering a parallel invitation to Melbourne, suggesting a crusade would enjoy significant civil legitimation as well.

When Jerry Beavan visited both cities a few months later, he found even broader support than anticipated. Still, Graham left nothing to chance. In 1958–1959 Beavan moved to Sydney and Walter Smyth, yet another Youth for Christ leader who had joined the team, opened a crusade office in Melbourne. Both men set about to solidify organizational and financial support from the churches, to arrange for crusade sites, bus reservations, landline relays to more than four hundred communities, and contracts for radio and television, and to launch the inevitable barrage of publicity. To build excitement, they scheduled screenings of several of Graham's films, including *Souls in Conflict* and *Miracles in Manhattan* which told the fictionalized stories of several converts in the Harringay and New York crusades. Attendance consistently outran expectations, and police occasionally had to be called to provide adequate crowd control. On the more explicitly spiritual side, Graham benefited from preparatory work by a team of teachers led by Edwin Orr, who toured churches much as he had done before the Los Angeles crusade, trying to gather the kindling and stack the wood that Billy's torch might ignite a roaring blaze. Graham originally planned to spend six or seven weeks in Australia, mostly in Sydney, with short visits to Melbourne and Brisbane. Sensing a real hunger for revival, however, Beavan persuaded him to plan major crusades for both Melbourne and Sydney, with shorter campaigns in the capitals of other Australian states and in three New Zealand cities. Associate evangelists Grady Wilson, Leighton Ford, and Englishman Joe Blinco, who joined the team after Harringay, would be the primary speakers in the smaller crusades, with Graham appearing for two or three climactic meetings at the end. This first use of "associate crusades" proved so successful that they became a permanent aspect of Graham's ministry.

Despite all this preparation, the mission nearly had to be canceled. Shortly before they were to leave for Australia, Graham and Grady Wilson went out for one of their frequent rounds of golf. "I noticed that several times, Billy would swing at the ball and just miss it completely," Grady recalled. "He said, 'It looks to me like the ground has ridges in it.' I said, 'You've got to come up with a better one than that.' I didn't take him seriously, but he insisted he was serious, and he even got down on the green and felt it." Suddenly, a stabbing pain assaulted his left eye and he lost all peripheral vision in that eye. An ophthalmologist in Louisville sent him to the Mayo Clinic in Minnesota, where his condition was diagnosed as angiospastic edema of the macula, an abnormal swelling of the blood vessels brought on by muscle spasms in back of the retina and directly traceable to overwork and exhaustion. He might have suffered a bleeding ulcer or a heart attack; instead, he seemed in danger of losing his sight in at least one eye. His doctors gave him appropriate drugs, but insisted he take a long rest immediately and return to work only at a much reduced pace. According to Grady, "They said it would be a whole lot better for him if I would just take a two-by-four and knock him in the head. They were about half-serious about it, too." Fortunately, such an extreme measure was unnecessary. Through the generosity of a Canadian millionaire who had been converted in the Toronto crusade, Billy was able to take his prescribed rest at a lovely estate in Hawaii, and he used the opportunity to prepare himself mentally and spiritually for the crusade. BGEA paid to have Wheaton's longtime president, V. Raymond Edman, join the Grahams and the Wilsons in Hawaii for several weeks, "just to teach us the scriptures." Grady remembered that, "for a couple of hours each morning, each of us would read from a different version of the Bible, then Dr. Edman would call on us to talk about it. That's the way he taught us the scriptures. That really refreshed Billy's heart for the Australia crusade. I can see now that God just set him aside for that month of time to sort of get his spiritual batteries recharged and all, to get him ready for the crusade."

Graham's inability to cultivate the media and local church and civic leaders in customary fashion did not seem to hinder the crusade. As Jerry Beavan had discerned, Australian churches, many stimulated by Edwin Orr's diligent efforts, were ready for revival, and Billy Graham's straightforward simplicity was well suited to their temperament. In Melbourne, so many people had to be turned away from the 10,000-seat indoor arena during the first week that the crusade moved to an outdoor music bowl, where crowds of up to 70,000 blanketed a grassy hillside. Long-scheduled events forced still another move, this time to the agricultural showgrounds located several miles from the center of the city and next to a malodorous slaughterhouse. At least in part because of a spell of heavy rains, attendance fell off but still ranged between 10,000 and 28,000. At the final service on March 15, over 143,000 people jammed the stands and manicured turf of the magnificent Melbourne Cricket Grounds, obliterating (by 27,000) previous highs recorded during soccer finals and the 1956 Olympics, and achieving a personal best for Graham as well. Normally, noisy trains rattled past the grounds—no serious problem for a cricket or soccer match, but potentially disruptive for a worship service. On this day, however, at the personal order of the chief officer of the state railway commission, the trains slowed to an inobtrusive crawl as they passed. The railroad commissioner was not the only civil official to take note of the gathering; the queen sent her personal representative, the governor of Victoria read the twenty-third Psalm, and Graham read a letter of greeting and congratulation from his old friend Dwight Eisenhower. The response in Sydney and in the three largest cities of New Zealand (Auckland, Wellington, and Christchurch) was, if anything, even more remarkable than in Melbourne. An estimated 20 percent of New Zealanders attended the associate crusades and relay services. In Sydney volunteers attempted to deliver an invitation at every home in the city, a technique that paid off handsomely. Total attendance for four weeks of meetings fell just short of 1 million, with 150,000 appearing for the closing rally at the Sydney Showgrounds and adjoining cricket club. To a degree that exceeded even Harringay, Billy Graham became a national figure. Observers doubted any visitor to Australia ever received as much space in the press; certainly, no religious event had been treated so favorably.

Other media also raised public awareness of the crusade. Television had come to Australia only two years earlier, and Billy Graham was its first national attraction. The major network, Australian Broadcasting, aired numerous features and bulletins about Graham before and during the crusade. When Melbourne station GTV got a large positive response to a taped replay of a sermon, it broadcast others and found itself with a star on its lens. To encourage the crusade and no doubt to build its audience, the station let the team use its studios as headquarters for the telephone-counseling operation, and announcers encouraged viewers to call the number appearing on their screens. The first night, telephone calls mounted into the hundreds over the course of the evening; on the second night, an estimated 10,000 calls (many of them repeat tries by the same people) were attempted during the first hour, overloading Melbourne's automatic telephone network to such an extent that few people making any kind of call were able to obtain anything but a constant busy signal for several hours. On subsequent evenings callers simply gave their numbers, which were then relayed to freshly recruited counselors who called them back as soon as possible, thus alleviating frustration on the part of seekers and keeping public resentment to a minimum. GTV also obliged Graham by letting him conduct a studio service one Saturday evening when trotting races crowded the crusade out of the agricultural showgrounds; the live program was viewed by an estimated 200,000 people. Stations in Sydney and New Zealand were not as directly involved, but they also continued to give Graham extensive attention so that he dominated television in both countries for nearly three months. "It was," one Graham admirer said, "the closest to national adulation of an overseas figure, other than the Queen, that Australia has ever seen."

When the time came for summing up, the results were impressive. An Anglican bishop declared the crusade to be "the biggest thing that ever happened in the church history of Australia," and the data seemed to support him. Total attendance for all services exceeded three million, and countless others heard the evangelist on television. Known inquirers numbered almost 150,000, three quarters of whom claimed to be making first-time decisions. Reflecting defensiveness about stereotypes of Evangelicals as unsophisticated people, crusade supporters proudly noted that the ranks of inquirers included the wife of a state governor, many students from top universities, scores of lawyers, dozens of doctors, more than a thousand nurses, and over eight hundred high-ranking business executives.

As always, distribution of the harvest was uneven. No church prospered more than Sydney's St. Stephen's Presbyterian, which took in 310 new members during the first year after the crusade, compared to an annual average intake of less than 50. Two years later, at least half of these remained active and enthusiastic; about one fourth appeared to have fallen away. Reports from other quarters painted a familiar picture. When the pastor and members actively participated in crusade programs, some increase in membership was likely; renewed vitality was almost inevitable. When participation was half-hearted or negligible, congregations experienced little or no growth and tended to regard results such as those at St. Stephen's as freakish anomalies. Nearly all clergymen, however, registered appreciation for Graham's efforts, and many expressed gratitude at a new spirit of unity they had found in cooperating with clergy and laity from other denominations.

Increases in church membership were not the only gains attributed to Graham's efforts. Charitable organizations reported a substantial growth in the number of volunteer workers. The Bible Society sold over $125,000 worth of Bibles, and managers of several bookstores reported that their entire stock of Scripture had been cleaned out. The magistrate of Sydney reported that some types of crime—specifically, those associated with alcohol, such as assault, indecent behavior, and drunk and disorderly conduct—dropped by at least 50 percent during the crusade. The record on this score was not perfect, however. At a landline service in a church hall in Katoomba, sixty miles west of Sydney, a man listening to Graham preach about love went berserk, stabbing one woman to death and critically wounding two others. As at Harringay, perhaps the most important long-term result was the increase in the number of men inspired by Graham to enter the ministry. In general, Anglican churches experienced less revitalization immediately following the crusade than did other Protestant bodies, but Jack Dain, who later transferred from India to become a coadjutant bishop in Sydney, noted that sixty-five clergymen in that diocese alone traced their decision to enter the ministry to the 1959 campaign, and that fully half of the students in the diocesan seminary during the decade of the 1960s were there because of Graham's influence. In 1986 Dain asserted that "[Today,] the Anglican Church in Sydney is totally Evangelical." For all this, however, the 1959 meetings seemed also to prove that the days when an evangelist could truly make a dramatic and lasting impact on a secular culture were long past. As Edwin Orr, who became one of Evangelical Christianity's foremost historians of revivalism, ruefully observed in 1986, "They were the greatest crusades Australia has ever seen, but Australia is still far from revived."

From Australia Graham flew to England, where he visited with the queen and Prince Philip on Philip's thirty-eighth birthday. They talked, Graham reported, about "the upsurge of spiritual feeling which is taking place here," and drank "tea out of big cups—really good." The queen poured. "It was just like having tea with any nice English family," he revealed. "It was all rather wonderful." Unfortunately, the perfection of that visit was spoiled by walks through three London parks where he saw people openly "smooching"—and worse. "I could hardly believe my eyes," he said. "Once upon a time, people went to the parks to see the birds and feed the ducks. It looked as though your parks had been turned into bedrooms, with people lying all over the place in all sorts of conditions." In fact, Billy was not the only one to notice an increase of open sexual activity in the park; in the three months prior to his comments, London police had made 538 arrests for forbidden sexual behavior, but the deterrent effect of the crackdown seemed minimal. When a reporter asked Graham why he had said nothing to couples he saw doing in public "what is usually done in bedrooms," he replied, "There were hundreds doing it." Overemphasis on sex, he warned, yet again, would bring Western nations down. A few months earlier he had offered the remarkable opinion that "if the female bosom were completely covered, that would solve many problems in every realm of life." Now he lamented that "the new generation coming along is far better acquainted with Jayne Mansfield's statistics" than with the Ten Commandments. From Las Vegas, where she was appearing at the Tropicana Hotel, Miss Mansfield replied, "I can't help it if I'm on their minds. It's a free country and I'm flattered that the youth of America is thinking about me." She noted that her figure had been given to her by God and by nature and was therefore no cause for shame. And besides that, she revealed, she received more fan mail from twelve-year-old boys than from members of the army and navy, a response she felt conclusively proved it was not her figure but "their liking for me as a person" that accounted for her popularity. Mercifully, Graham did not enter into a continuing debate with Miss Mansfield. He made it clear, however, that he did not intend to tar all of England with the same brush he had used to depict the denizens of its public parks. Without citing specific evidence, he declared, "I think the British people have a higher standard of morals than the entire western world."

Unsettling exposure to sex outside the home perhaps helped account for Graham's unexpectedly warm response to moral and spiritual conditions he found a few days later during a visit to Russia. Though he had been invited by the Moscow Baptist Church, the trip was officially billed as simply a tourist trip. When he attended the packed 3,500-seat church on Sunday morning, he and his associates sat inconspicuously in the balcony. Though church officials reserved a pew for him and provided an interpreter, he was not introduced to the assembly, and he took no part in the service. Some day, he reported, his fellow Baptists hoped to see a great stadium filled with people yearning to hear the gospel, but he anticipated no such occasion in the near future." "The official said we have to move step by step and I feel this visit is an important step." He was not at all surprised to hear that atheism was declining and religion on the rise throughout the Soviet Union, since, quite predictably, he "could read on the faces of the people a great spiritual hunger and some sort of insecurity that only God can solve." This "deepening hunger for God that penetrates even behind the Iron Curtain," he noted, "gives cause for hope and optimism." He was also impressed by what he took to be a high standard of personal morality among the Soviet people. "In the Moscow parks," he reported, just a few days after his upsetting stroll in London, "I saw thousands of young people but I did not see a single couple locked in an embrace. I hate Communism, but I love the Russian people and the moral purity I found among the Muscovites." This encomium to Soviet morality drew scornful fire from some quarters where he had been viewed as a champion. In New York, the director of the anti-Communist Research Institute of America snorted, "If by morality the Reverend Billy Graham means that the Russians wear longer bathing suits than we do, he's quite right. If his evidence has persuaded him that in the Soviet Union the entire culture places a lesser emphasis upon sex than is the case in the United States and the countries of Western Europe, that is also entirely true. These, however, are purposeless manifestations of morality when contrasted with the fact that those who first enslaved and then butchered the Hungarians, who were simply seeking freedom, were also Russians." Asked why he had not criticized the darker aspects of Soviet life, such as slave camps, Graham resorted to an easy disclaimer: "I didn't criticize Russian slave camps because I didn't see them. I am aware they exist." He preferred to emphasize what he had seen. He took particular delight in the sight of the crosses on top of the onion-domed churches inside the walls of the Kremlin itself, venturing that "to have this religious spirit in the heart of the Kremlin is symbolic of some future date." And outside the Kremlin walls, in Red Square, he paused to pray that if it be God's will, he might be present on that historic date. Back home a few weeks later, he recommended that President Eisenhower do his part for Russian revival by inviting Soviet premier Nikita Khrushchev to church during his upcoming visit to Washington, noting that, as a houseguest, "if he should refuse to go, it will put Khrushchev on the spot."

Early in 1960, Graham embarked on an eight-week, sixteen-city tour of eleven African countries, adding a fifth continent to his career itinerary. This tour, chronicled in *Safari for Souls*, a Graham-sanctioned book by a South Carolina newspaper reporter and captured on film in a World Wide Pictures documentary, was notable in that it aroused in Graham a keen awareness of the need and potential for an Evangelical witness in Africa. At the same time, he seems to have sensed that he was not ideally suited to be the point man for any such attempt. Over the next thirty years, he would return to most of the sites where he conducted large crusades during the early years of his ministry, but with the exception of a 1973 crusade in South Africa, which he had refused to visit until guaranteed that all racial groups would be admitted and seated on a nondiscriminatory basis, he never attempted another large-scale African tour. He accounted for this as largely a matter of circumstance: Other opportunities seemed more promising, other groups exerted greater pressure, Africa lacked adequate television coverage. Quite likely, however, at least part of the reason he limited his efforts in Africa is that despite sizable and enthusiastic crowds in some areas, he and his team faced vehement opposition in other locales and at times seemed so out of place culturally that they could as easily have come from Pluto as from North Carolina.

The tour began in Liberia, whose Christian heritage dated back to 1822, when freed slaves from the United States, with the aid of American colonization societies, founded it to serve as a home for other freedmen in the hope of helping to solve the problem of American slavery. Graham's black associate, Howard Jones, who spent several months of each year in Liberia and had a thriving radio ministry over that country's powerful Christian station, ELWA, helped organize the meetings. Graham could not have asked for more enthusiastic official cooperation. He came with a state invitation tendered by President William V. S. Tubman, who was also a Methodist minister. Baptist pastor William R. Tolbert, who doubled as the nation's vice-president, served as crusade chairman. As a further sign of state approval, Billy was made a Grand Commander of the Humane Order of African Redemption, Liberia's second-highest civil honor.

Despite support at the highest levels, the total attendance for five days of meetings in Liberia was less than 13,000. Graham preached to similarly unimpressive crowds in Ghana, where the Accra *Evening News* blasted him for his refusal to comment on plans by the French to conduct atomic bomb tests in the Sahara. Graham was warmly received when he called on President Kwame Nkrumah, whose own quasi-messianic aspirations had led him to erect a statue of himself emblazoned with the words "Seek ye first the political kingdom and all other things shall be added unto it," a blatant lifting of Jesus' classic directive in the Sermon on the Mount, "Seek ye first the kingdom of God, and his righteousness; and all these things shall be added unto you" (Matt. 6:33). In a reciprocal gesture of courtesy, the World Wide Pictures documentary *Africa on the Bridge* offered a brief criticism of Nkrumah's this-worldly (and decidedly leftist) orientation but was generally positive toward his achievements, noting especially the improved status of women in that country.

From Ghana, Graham proceeded to Nigeria. He drew well in Lagos—128,600 in seven days—and enjoyed hospitable treatment there and in Ibadan and Euegu. But in Kaduna, Kano, and Jos, all in the Islam-dominated northern part of the country, he not only attracted modest crowds but stirred strident criticism and resistance from Muslims, who, by his estimate, were winning ten converts from tribal religions for every one converted to Christianity. Here and elsewhere, Muslims appreciated Graham's emphatic insistence that he was an ordinary man with no supernatural powers, a stance that contrasted with the claims of tribal shamans and fit with Islamic teachings about the nondivine status of all of God's spokesmen, including Muhammad himself. They disagreed, however, with his claims for the deity of Christ and resented the straightforward criticism of Islam in his sermons. They were also disappointed when he declined a challenge to debate one of their scholars on theological doctrine or even to meet privately with Muslim leaders. On a more secular level, the strong endorsement he received from Christian political leaders led some Muslims to fear that he was trying to help boost a Christian government into power, a charge for which there was little evidence, though he did subsequently urge President Eisenhower to visit Nigeria to build better relations between the two nations and perhaps even to use the occasion of Nigeria's becoming independent of England later that year to identify himself and the United States with the interests of African nationalism.

Muslims in Sudan managed to rescind Graham's invitation to preach in that country, apparently because they feared he might disrupt proper observance of Ramadan, the sacred month during which Muslims severely restrict normal activities. The most explicit and memorable Muslim challenge, however, came in Kenya, where Maulana Sheikh Mubarak Ahmad, chief of the Ahmadiyya Muslim Mission in East Africa, hurled a challenge reminiscent of that proposed by the prophet Elijah in his famous contest on Mount Carmel with the priests of Baal (I Kings 18:20–40). In a letter to Graham, the Muslim leader proposed that thirty individuals—ten Europeans, ten Asians, and ten Africans, all certified by the director of medical services of Kenya to be incurable by scientific medicine—be assigned by lot into two groups and that he and Graham, together with a small band of associates, beseech God to heal the group assigned to them "to determine as to who is blessed with the Lord's grace and mercy and upon whom His door remains closed." If Graham declined, Ahmad argued, "[I]t will be proved to the world that Islam is the only religion which is capable of establishing man's relationship with God." A group of American Pentecostals cabled him to "accept the challenge; the God of Elijah still lives," but Graham neither picked up the gauntlet nor offered any comment to the press.

Throughout much of Africa, Graham had to confront a force more deeply rooted and, for that reason, less familiar and harder to combat than Islam: the indigenous tribal beliefs and practices of animism, augury, juju, shamanism, and idolatry. In Liberia, at a tribal dancing exhibition, a little man clad in a "country-devil" costume—a huge black mask attached to a kind of grass poncho that completely covered his body—repeatedly tapped Graham on the chest, muttering, "I'm the devil; I'm the devil; give me a dollar; give me two dollars." Billy lifted his arm and pointed to the man, exclaiming, "I've come to cast out the devil." Then, less dramatically, he knelt and grasped the man's hand in an attempt to make contact with the universal human component hidden beneath the fantastic costume. At Ki-sumu, Kenya, three men in full witch-doctor regalia walked forward and took positions directly in front of the platform, standing stiffly and staring straight at Graham as if working a curse. Instead of calling for security personnel to remove them, Graham addressed them directly, announcing to them that "God loves you, and Jesus died on the cross for you." They did not respond, then or at the invitation, and Graham suffered no ill effects from their imprecations—no surprise, since they had been hired by a news photographer to dress up and help him obtain a colorful photo.

Not every encounter left the evangelist so untouched. During a preaching stint in Kaduna, Nigeria, a Southern Baptist missionary invited Graham and his team to visit a leprosarium near that city. The missionary told Graham that Christians at the leprosarium knew who he was and had built a brush arbor of limbs and straw in the hope that he might pay them a visit and hold a brief service. To a man with such a strong preference for cleanliness and propriety, the sight of a village filled with people whose toes and fingers and noses and ears had been eaten away by leprosy must have been a horrifying sight, but Billy preached a passionate sermon, assuring his audience that God loved them no matter what their physical condition and that Christ had died to make it possible for them to have a new and perfect spiritual body in heaven. When he gave the invitation, dozens raised deformed and scarred hands to signify their desire to accept the salvation he proclaimed. As the team prepared to leave, a small woman with nothing more than stubs for hands approached him to say, with the missionary acting as interpreter, "Mr. Graham, before today we had never seen you. But since your London crusade in 1954, we Christians have been praying for you. Here in our little leprosarium we have been keeping up with your ministry." Lifting an envelope toward him with her two nubbed arms, she said, "This is just a little love gift for you and your team for your worldwide ministry." Deeply moved, Billy grasped her nubs in his hands and thanked her. As she walked away, the missionary translated a note she had included: "Wherever you go from now on, we want you to know we have invested in some small way in your ministry and given, in a sense, our widow's mite. We send our love and prayers with you around the world." Inside the envelope were two Nigerian pound notes worth approximately $5.60 in American money at the time. Graham turned away to look across the vast brushland. After a few moments, he turned to Grady and Cliff, tears trickling down his face. "Boys," he said, "that's the secret of our ministry."

To accommodate the low level of education in many quarters, as well as to try to overcome language barriers, Graham deliberately "put the cookies on a lower shelf," using concrete sensory language and speaking in short repetitive sentences to facilitate translation, but he still worried that he was being misunderstood. On several occasions, the response to his invitation was so large and general that in an effort to winnow out those who were simply going along with the crowd or seeking to please the American visitor, he took pains to stress that becoming a Christian meant a complete repudiation of idols and other aspects of tribal religion. Even so, his efforts to bridge the chasm between cultures, though always transparently sincere, seemed at times more poignant than potent or prophetic. In one little village where some of the women squalled and fled when he appeared in the midst of their huts, he preached a simple sermon and returned to his car, optimistically observing that "just this little visit and somebody could be converted." Another time, in Tanganyika (now Tanzania), he visited a Sekei village where a drunken dance was in progress. His white shirt, blond hair, and open grin offering anemic contrast to the half-naked painted and festooned bodies writhing about in inebriated ecstasy, he did the only thing he knew to do in such a situation: He took out his New Testament and tried to tell one of the men how he might be saved from the chaos swirling about him. He might as well have been trying to sell the *Watchtower* in the middle of the Super Bowl. The hapless tribesman, more baffled than angry at the incongruous apparition squatting beside him, kept saying, "I too drunk. I do not understand." Finally conceding that his message was falling on rocky ground, Graham consoled himself in the knowledge that he had tried and politely stood back to watch as his camera crew documented the great gulf between depraved juju worshipers and the sober God-fearing folk who would see their film.

Africans and others seeking to discredit Graham could easily seize upon his open and clearly stated opposition to communism, Islam, and tribal religion. They had less success in painting him as a white supremacist. Wherever he went, he emphasized, as he had in India, that Jesus was not a white man. "People stumble," he observed on returning to America, "because Christ is often presented as a European" and thus associated with colonialism and imperialism. "All over Africa, faces lit up as we told how Christ belongs to all races.... that he was born near Africa, that he was taken to Africa for refuge, and that an African helped carry his cross." In Kenya and elsewhere, white and black Christians underwent counselor-training sessions together and sat intermingled at the services. In Northern and Southern Rhodesia, (known today as the independent nations Zambia and Zimbabwe, respectively) Graham insisted that blacks be admitted to services, making them the first integrated public meetings ever conducted in either country, and that his sermons be translated into the native tongues, not given only in English as some of the Europeans on the sponsoring committees desired, hoping to discourage African attendance. He repeatedly reminded the mostly white crowds that the ground beneath the cross of Christ is level and that all who stand there are equals. "God doesn't look to see the color of your skin or how much money you have," he insisted. "An impartial God looks on the heart. He does not look on the outside." It pleased him that many newspapers, including South African publications, duly reported that "smartly dressed White women stood shoulder to shoulder with African servants." Further, the filmed account of the tour, shown to American audiences during the controversial sit-ins that were forcing drastic changes in southern society, showed black workers in Rhodesian copper mines and observed that "while

African laborers appear content with wages and working conditions, there are increasing evidences of unrest, and many Africans include in their vision of tomorrow a dream of equal opportunity and an equal wage."

Despite their officially integrated status, Graham's crowds in Rhodesia were overwhelmingly white, and most Rhodesians would never learn of his oblique criticisms of their society. Morever, black African nationalists objected to his repeated insistence that only by sitting down together in a spirit of Christian love could any nation hope to solve its racial problems. In Kitwe, Northern Rhodesia, they swept through housing projects urging blacks not to attend his meetings, then followed up by heckling and tossing stones at the few who did show up. In nearby Chingola, where Grady Wilson was preaching, a more determined effort led to a clash between boycotters and police, breaking up the service and sending several people to the hospital for treatment of their wounds. His opposition to racial discrimination took sharper form in his explicit and well-publicized refusal to preach in South Africa after being told blacks would not be permitted to attend his meetings. To underline his position, he chose to follow a circuitous and time-consuming flight schedule rather than a much easier route that would have included a stop in South Africa, specifically because he feared that country's racial practices might embarrass Howard Jones. When sixty-four South African ministers chartered a plane to attend his crusade in Bulawayo, Southern Rhodesia, he told reporters he was tempted to reconsider his boycott of South Africa but pressed for what he regarded as inevitable changes in racial attitudes and policies. "I don't see how the South African approach can possibly work," he said. "Race barriers will ultimately have to end. I cannot presume to suggest a solution in the Rhodesias or for the Union [of South Africa] problem, because we have our own problem in the States. Before I can preach about colour in Africa we must apply Christ in the United States." He continued to insist, however, that the key to any change in policy would have to be a change of heart of the sort that only true conversion to Christ was likely to bring. On his return to the United States later in the spring, he declined to comment on the lunch-counter sit-ins in progress in the South on the grounds that he knew too little about them, but he said of the South African situation that "to keep the races in total separation is a policy that won't work and is immoral and unchristian," adding pointedly that "I would say the same of our past treatment of the Indians, as we look back on it." The reference to Indians was a sign of still-widening social conscience, not an attempt to finesse the current racial unrest among blacks; Graham explicitly warned that American failure to solve its own racial problems was a key factor in the appeal of communism to many Africans. "They doubt the United States will be a true friend," he explained. "Somehow, Americans of both races are going to have to find an amicable solution or we may lose the friendship of this richest continent on earth." The alternative to a peaceful solution, he feared, was too dreadful to contemplate. "Seventy percent of the world's population is colored," he pointed out. "They will exterminate the white race if we don't end discrimination." Once again he asserted the only way either America or South Africa could summon the insight and moral courage to institute these changes was through sweeping religious revival. Only religion, he said, can create "an atmosphere [in which] all racial differences can be settled."

The soul safari wound up with visits to Addis Ababa, Ethiopia, where he was received by the patriarch of the Ethiopian Orthodox Church and Emperor Haile Selassie, a longtime friend of Evangelical missions. After Ethiopia Graham drew 10,000 people to a rally held under a giant crimson tent in Cairo, apparently the first such Christian meeting in Egyptian history. Arrangements for both visits had been smoothed by assistance from Vice-President Nixon's office. Later, Graham revealed that he had been invited to hold a full-scale crusade in the Egyptian capital but decided against it, explaining that "such a crusade in the United Arab Republic would cause thousands and thousands of Christians to be publicly identified with a white Western American evangelist. I would not want anyone to suffer needlessly for their loyalty to Christ and most certainly never to be injured or abused by their appearance at one of our rallies."

True to the vow he made to Jack Dain following his Indian tour, Graham largely avoided condescending assessments of African culture when he returned to the United States. He spoke of communism as erroneous and dangerous, and he lamented the "fanatic devotion" he found among Africa's Muslims, but he clearly regarded both ideologies as formidable forces. The film *Africa on the Bridge* referred to tribal idols that "can neither see nor speak" and included scenes of tribesmen having their faces scarred in religious ceremonies, but the narrator said without obvious condescension that beliefs that are "to us, foolishness, [are] to millions of Africans the final word about God and the world about them." When portraying other aspects of African life, the documentary took a decidedly nonjudgmental tack. Bare-breasted women were shown suckling their young or simply walking along the roadside, with no clucking judgments about their lack of modesty. (In an amusing juxtaposition that must have caused consternation when it was shown in Evangelical congregations that frowned on any public exposure of the body, including swimming in mixed groups, the film contained a sequence in which the world's most famous evangelist and his faithful side kicks were shown lounging on the deck of a river launch clad in nothing but swimsuits.) Perhaps reflecting Graham's own love of animals—recalling his boyhood fantasies of playing Tarzan in the woods behind the dairy barn, he relished telling of how he and Cliff Barrows had whooped with delight as the little plane in which they were riding flew over great herds of elephants, zebras, antelopes, and buffalo in Kenya—the film also included extended scenes of African wildlife, including one in which lions stalked and killed a waterbuck, and another in which members of the team delighted in the antics of a band of baboons. Similarly, scenes of tribal dances, which might have been lambasted as depraved pagan rituals, were presented as joyous occasions that proved "the African has great talent for sheer showmanship." Implicit throughout, of course, was a recognition that Africa was in large measure still a backward continent, but this assumption took on a descriptive rather than evaluative tone. The primary message was that the continent had great potential, that it was poised promisingly, if somewhat precariously, on the bridge to full modernity, and that all it needed to lead it across was the enabling power of Christ.

As a reprise to the African tour, Graham visited both Jordan and Israel, neither of which was overjoyed. Jordan, in fact, had banned him from entry, charging him with propaganda and fund-raising activities on Israel's behalf. The evangelist acknowledged having friends in Israel but denied he had raised money or assisted that country in any notable way. "As a Christian," he said, "I'm both pro-Jew and pro-Arab." After an amusing exchange of disclaimers—a BGEA spokesman said the Jordanian embassy in Washington recommended the ban, an embassy spokesman said he had never heard of Billy Graham and knew of no ban, and Graham said that as far as he knew, he had made no request to visit Jordan but hoped he would be able to—a Muslim businessman in Charlotte contacted an influential relative in Jordan and managed to get the ban lifted. If resistance truly existed, it posed no obvious problem. King Hussein welcomed him for a brief visit, and, in a singular gesture of ecumenical good will, a Muslim radio station recorded his sermon on John 3:16, replaying it several times while he was in the country.

Israeli authorities gave Graham a warmer official welcome but refused to let the sponsoring Christian Council rent large halls for public meetings. As a further restriction, in an off-the-record agreement that *Time* magazine got hold of, Prime Minister David Ben-Gurion enjoined the evangelist from mentioning Jesus while speaking to Jewish audiences. Graham graciously indicated he would accept both limitations. At a press conference in the King David Hotel, he noted that one of his reasons for coming to Israel was to preach the gospel, then added, "but I want to make it clear that I am going to address only Christian audiences. I have no intention of proselytizing. In fact, I must be grateful to you for proselytizing me. For Jesus Christ was a Jew, all the apostles were Jews, and the whole early church was Jewish." At the same gathering, he expressed his delight at being able to see "the new nation where the Star of David now flies again after twenty-four centuries." These generous gestures softened most of whatever resistance remained, so that some Israelis protested the restrictions on Graham, and when he preached an unapologetically evangelistic message to an audience that was ostensibly

Christian but which some observers guessed to be 70 percent Jewish, no complaint was raised. To avoid any unpleasantness, Graham offered no invitation but suggested that any who wished to receive Christ should contact representatives of the Christian Council. While in the country, Graham visited with Israeli president Ben-Zvi and established friendships of long standing with Israeli political giants Abba Eban and Golda Meir. A few years later, Ms. Meir presented him with one of his most treasured possessions, a Bible inscribed "To a great teacher in all the important matters to humanity and a true friend of Israel." He also visited with the head of the Ministry of Religion, Rabbi Toledano. When Graham inevitably affirmed his own belief that Jesus is the promised Messiah, the white-bearded rabbi softly observed, "When the Messianic times come, then we will know the truth."

The African tour capped slightly more than a decade of activity during which Billy Graham emerged from virtual anonymity outside Evangelical circles to become one of the best-known and most widely admired men in the world—the Luce Clipping Service reported that it processed more than 5,000 articles about him each month, more than Franklin D. Roosevelt generated during his heyday. He was clearly the primary spokesman for Evangelicalism and, in the eyes of many, for Protestant Christianity as a whole. According to some, his fame and the accompanying attention paid to religious revival played a significant role in increasing the amount of coverage given to religion in daily newspapers and stimulated *Time* and *Newsweek* to initiate a regular section devoted to religion. As he had risen from preaching to drunks and brawlers in saloons and stockades to addressing tens of thousands in Olympic stadia and storied arenas, and to sharing his faith quietly with kings and queens, presidents and prime ministers, captains of industry and masters of mass media, he had led his people out of a cultural wilderness, had helped make them feel that America was once again "one nation under God," and that they were among its finest citizens. From this pinnacle of accomplishment and renown Graham could see "all the kingdoms of the world and the glory of them." He had faced and fought bravely with powerful temptations, so that even his harshest critics acknowledged his genuineness. He lived well, but not nearly so well as he might have, and no hint of scandal tarnished his public or private image. He was clearly fascinated by fame, but his omnipresent fear of the very celebrity he sought kept the excesses of that particularly treacherous lust in harness, if not completely subdued. Fame and recognition had brought influence and power. He had made modest efforts to use them, with results that both encouraged and disquieted him, but the greatest opportunities, and with them the deepest pitfalls, still lay ahead.

Part 4

The Kingdoms of the World and Their Glory (1960–1974)

17

Election and Free Will

When Graham returned to America after his African tour, he gave a full report to President Eisenhower, Vice-President Nixon, and Secretary of State Christian Herter, who assembled a handful of top aides for an informal briefing that lasted several hours, an indication that the White House regarded him not simply as a goodwill ambassador but as a man whose contacts and observations might make him a valuable diplomatic resource. Eisenhower seemed to appreciate the contact and information, and Graham urged him to visit Nigeria at his earliest opportunity to help prevent that pivotal nation from falling into Communist hands. This visit to the White House renewed Graham's sense of standing near the center of power and doubtless reinforced his desire to remain there — a prospect that was less than certain. The President would soon be stepping down. It seemed obvious Richard Nixon would be the Republican nominee, though it was no secret Eisenhower was less than enthusiastic about him, and the growing possibility that the attractive young senator from Massachusetts, John F. Kennedy, might get the Democratic nomination made it far from certain Nixon could win the election without a real struggle. Because he felt close to the Vice-President and because he enjoyed a personal relationship he had little chance of duplicating with Kennedy, Graham began to explore ways in which he might help his friend hold on to power.

Billy always found fewer faults in his friends than others managed to see. If they liked him, he liked them, and was inclined to think the best of them and to regard patent shortcomings as little more than a failure to let the sterling character he was sure they possessed manifest itself with sufficient force. Nearly a decade of friendship with Nixon — nurtured by occasional games of golf, ritual exchanges of gifts and greetings, Graham's behind-the-scenes support of the Republican ticket in 1956, and Nixon's reciprocal appearance at the 1957 Yankee Stadium rally — had left Billy with remarkably few reservations about the Vice-President, and in private conversations, he tried to allay Eisenhower's anxieties at the prospect of a Nixon presidency. Still, he sometimes wished his friend would make it easier for him to offer his wholehearted support. In 1959 he told Nixon, "If I have one suggestion for you, it is this:

there are many, many reasons why I would strongly urge you to attend church regularly and faithfully from now on. I am convinced that you are going to have the backing of the overwhelming majority of the religiously minded people in America. It would be most unfortunate if some of your political enemies could point to any inconsistency." He also noted that he had mentioned Nixon several times on his *Hour of Decision* broadcasts and "practically came out in full support of you a few weeks ago by saying that you were the best-qualified and best-trained man in America for the presidency."

In May 1960, as Kennedy's prospects improved, Graham told a group of reporters that "this is a time of world tension. [It] is a time for a man of world stature. I don't think it is a time to experiment with novices." He added that while he intended to stay out of politics, he had deep personal convictions on the matter. When asked if his convictions stemmed from his friendship with Nixon, he replied with a smile, "Might be. But I'm not taking sides." According to one columnist's report, "The fifty correspondents roared with laughter." Two days later Graham contacted the Nixon staff to say that "after deep and long consideration," he was coming out publicly on the Vice-President's behalf. He also indicated, a Nixon aide reported, "that he was going to be on *Meet the Press* sometime early in June and that if [we] felt that was the time for him to do it, he would use that as the forum." Between them, Graham and Nixon apparently decided that something less than a flat-out endorsement would better serve the interests of both men, at least for the time being.

As the campaigns heated up, Graham warmed to the task of giving advice, often on matters with a less than obvious connection to eternal salvation. After Eisenhower denied, then subsequently admitted, that the U-2 aircraft downed by the Russians was indeed a U.S. spy plane, Graham told Nixon, "In my opinion, the current U-2 incident is political dynamite. My advice, for what it's worth, would be to keep as quiet as possible. It is difficult to tell which way sentiment is going to turn. I think the mood of the people at the moment is to resent this incident being used for political advantage by either party." He went on to offer his observations about possible Communist attempts to influence the coming election, revealing continued respectful fear of the enemy's diabolical cleverness. "It's been my contention since the beginning," he volunteered, "that Mr. Khrushchev is interjecting himself into the American political campaign." Without suggesting how the Soviet leader might accomplish his aim, he said, "I believe he is hopeful that he can force one of the parties to nominate a man that he can 'get along' with. After the nomination of such a man, the left-wingers and fellow travelers in this country will go all out to elect him.... I am more convinced than ever that you will be the next President of the United States."

Although Graham had suggested earlier that if Kennedy were elected, the religious issue could work in Nixon's favor, he now saw another side to the situation. "If Senator Kennedy is nominated," he predicted, "he will capture the Catholic vote—almost one hundred percent. No matter what concessions you make to the Catholic Church or how you play up to them—even if you had a Catholic running mate, you would not even crack five or ten percent of the Catholic vote." Adding that "Johnson, Smathers, Rayburn and others agree with me at this point!" he concluded, "Since the Protestant voters outnumber the Catholics three to one, you must concentrate on solidifying the Protestant vote. In my opinion, if you make a mistake of having a Catholic running mate, you will divide the Protestants and make no inroads whatsoever in the Catholic vote. Therefore I hope you will discard this idea at all costs. It is imperative for you to have as your running mate someone in the Protestant church, someone the Protestant church can rally behind enthusiastically. I can think of only one man in the Republican party who has the support of both liberals and conservatives in the Protestant church, and that is Dr. Walter Judd," a former Evangelical missionary whom Graham greatly admired and who he undoubtedly hoped could bolster the efforts of New Evangelicals to influence national policy. "They don't all agree with him," he conceded, "but they deeply respect him. Having been a missionary and being one of the ablest speakers in America, it is my opinion he would be almost a must. With Dr. Judd, I believe the two of you could present a picture to America that would put much of the south and border states in the Republican column and bring about a dedicated Protestant vote to counteract the Catholic vote." Aware that this kind of specific political advice ran directly counter to his professions of non-partisanship, Graham added, "I would appreciate your considering this letter in utter confidence. You would do me a favor by destroying it after reading it."

Kennedy allegedly sought to short-circuit anti-Catholic bias by asking Graham and other prominent clergymen to sign a pledge not to bring religion into the campaign. Graham refused to sign, and in announcing that refusal, Grady Wilson tossed in the unlikely and never-verified allegation that Roman Catholics in Latin America had recently conducted a special mass during which they had prayed that the plane bringing Billy Graham to Brazil that summer would crash and kill the evangelist. Wilson's statement, made on a local radio program, drew sharp objection from Kennedy's press secretary, Pierre Salinger, who denied any effort to get anyone to sign a pledge, but Grady stuck by what he had said. Graham, however, wrote to Lyndon Johnson, asking him to assure Senator Kennedy that he did not intend to raise the religious issue "publicly" and hoped "to stay out of the political campaign as much as possible." A week later, Johnson sent a note thanking Graham and noting that Kennedy had been "obviously impressed by your attitude."

In midsummer, both parties chose their candidates. Ignoring Graham's advice, Nixon opted for Henry Cabot Lodge; in a cannier but ambivalent move, Kennedy sought to appeal to the South and Southwest by selecting Lyndon Johnson. Graham's expressed intention to stay out of the campaign was short-lived. Two weeks after his letter to Johnson, he returned from a meeting of the Baptist World Alliance in Rio de Janeiro filled with fresh concern that Nixon was floundering. "This conference of religious leaders all agree," he wrote, "that your people are not nearly so well organized as the Kennedy people. I heard this from man after man representing different parts of the nation." He noted that Kennedy was getting his name in the papers more often than Nixon and that despite a recent Gallup poll showing that Nixon's chances were improving, he felt Kennedy was still ahead. He then added presciently, "Your debates with him on television will be decisive in the minds of millions!"

Graham predicted trouble on both the racial and religious fronts. He had traveled to and from the Baptist conference with Martin Luther King, Jr., and learned that King had met with Kennedy at Joseph Kennedy's apartment in New York and had been "tremendously impressed" by the senator. In other accounts of the meeting, King was said to have found Kennedy pleasant but lacking a "depthed understanding" of the racial situation, but Graham felt the black leader was "just about sold" on the senator. "I think I at least neutralized him," he noted, but ventured that "if you could invite him for a brief conference, it might swing him. He would be a powerful influence." Dr. King, like Dr. Graham, was determined not to endorse either party's candidates, asserting that his cause transcended partisan politics, but Graham's perception that Kennedy was capable of loosening the Republican grip on the black vote was accurate. Nixon decided against contact with King, probably feeling blacks would not desert the party of Lincoln (60 percent of the black vote in 1956 went to Eisenhower) and that association with the controversial leader would alienate white voters, particularly in the South. Ultimately, however, after both John and Robert Kennedy made telephone calls that offered encouragement to Coretta King and helped free her husband from a Georgia prison a few days before the election—facts disseminated to black churches on the Sunday before the election—Kennedy garnered a stunning 70 percent of the black vote, even though King maintained to the end his refusal to give an explicit endorsement. Graham must have been surprised at what appeared to be a tactical mistake on Nixon's part, since his close scrutiny of the campaign had led him to believe that "God has been giving you supernatural wisdom in handling difficult situations." On the other hand, he and Norman Vincent Peale had been commissioned by a gathering of ministers to urge the Vice-President to say more about religion in his addresses, and he told Nixon, "These men reported that throughout Protestantism there is running a question as to your religious convictions. They report that many people are concerned at this point. I informed them of your reticence to use religion for political purposes. They felt people had a right to know. Therefore, I would urge you to weave this into your addresses." He noted that Peale would soon be coming out flat-footed in favor of Nixon, a move he estimated might prove extremely costly to the popular minister.

Overall, Graham was optimistic. He thought the proportion of Protestant clergy now supporting Nixon (an estimated 76 percent) would probably increase, and expressed satisfaction that the Catholic bloc vote would not be quite as solid as he once supposed. He also reported that he had written to his mailing list, which included two million American families, urging them to organize their Sunday school classes to get out the vote. He suspected the majority of these people were registered as Democrats or Independents, but because of his well-known friendship with the Vice-President, he felt a concerted effort to stimulate the vote might produce a significant swing in Nixon's direction and was encouraging other religious organizations likely to be favorable to Nixon to follow his lead. He urged Nixon not to give up on southern and border states. In spite of lingering southern animosity toward Eisenhower for forcing compliance with federal court-desegregation orders, Graham felt the more conservative platform of the Republican party, combined with the religious issue, "could well put some of these states in your column."

Graham also had some tactical advice for Eisenhower. In a confidential letter sent after the convention, he urged the President to stump the southern states on Nixon's behalf. "With the religious issue growing," he observed, "I believe you could tip the scales in a number of key states from Kentucky to Texas. I believe Nixon has a fighting chance only if you go all out." In a characteristic flight of hyperbole, he said, "I know this would mean two months of hard work, but I believe the rewards to the nation would be as great as when you led the armies at Normandy." He further suggested that the President, whom he once again compared to Lincoln, not limit his efforts to the hustings. "It is also my opinion," he volunteered, "that you must win the battle in the coming special session of Congress. It seems to me that you could send so many dramatic messages to Congress that you could keep Kennedy and Johnson off-balance and capture the headlines during that period."

Perhaps unfortunately for Nixon's campaign, Graham was holding crusades in Europe during most of August and September, but he assured the Vice-President that the election would not be far from his thoughts. He would be on the transatlantic phone constantly, he said, and "would be delighted to be of any service I possibly can." In a remarkable change from the days in which he begged for the approval of his ministry by politicians, Graham suggested that Nixon's cause might be helped by a trip to Montreat as soon as possible after the European tour ended. Such a visit, he wrote, "would certainly be a dramatic and publicized event that I believe might tip the scales in North Carolina and dramatize the religious issue throughout the nation, without mentioning it publicly. This is just a suggestion, and we would be delighted to cooperate in it if you think it has any merit."

The highlight of Graham's two-month European tour was a seven-day crusade in West Berlin. In what the East Berlin government unsurprisingly regarded as a direct affront, the crusade's closing rally was held in a huge tent set up in front of the old Reichstag building, just three hundred yards from the Brandenburg Gate. The Berlin Wall would not be erected for another year, but the Communist government dispatched 150 police officers to the Brandenburg Gate and sent scores of others to patrol other crossing points in an effort to discourage East Germans from attending the services. However much they might deride the content of his messages, they respected his ability to draw huge crowds, and they knew that his ever-present anti-Communist rhetoric could only be detrimental to their efforts to maintain ideological uniformity. An East German daily charged that "whenever the American imperialists begin their provocative act, wherever the policy of the Washington and Bonn warmongers is shaky, Billy Graham and his 'staff officers' are sent." East Berlin mayor Waldemar Schmidt warned that if the tent remained in place, West Berlin would "suffer the consequences," without specifying just what that might entail. West Berlin mayor Willy Brandt curtly indicated he had no intention of calling for the tent to be moved, but Graham minimized tensions by refraining from any mention of politics in his sermon to the 25,000 people, many of whom were East Germans who had made it through the police blockade.

Though he remained quiet on the eastern front, Graham made good on his promise to stay abreast of the election campaign at home. Most of his colleagues in the New Evangelical camp would probably vote for Nixon no matter whom the Democrats put forward, but Kennedy's religion led them to view the 1960 election as particularly portentous. In a sermon preached at Park Street in June and subsequently published, Harold John Ockenga articulated concerns he felt all Protestant Christians ought to share. While acknowledging that a Catholic had every right to run for the presidency, he observed that a keystone of American democracy is the separation of Church and State, and that the Roman Catholic Church had not been a notable champion of that particular principle. He noted that "a prominent candidate in this coming election" had insisted that "whatever his religion was in private it could not take precedence over his oath as President of the United States," but he pointed out that several Roman Catholic publications had sharply criticized the unnamed candidate for such statements. A strong individual might ignore such criticism, Ockenga admitted, "but the pressures would always be there for him to succumb, especially when there is the possibility of excommunication for disobedience and such excommunication could mean the loss of his soul." If the American Catholic hierarchy were to acknowledge that America is a pluralistic society and bring pressure on the Vatican to renounce policies aimed at exerting control over the temporal realm, then Americans might have little to fear from a Catholic president. But unless and until that happened, Protestants would do well not "to aid and abet [the movement toward Roman Catholic domination of America] by electing a President who has more power to advance such a goal than any other person."

In a speech entitled "Protestant Distinctives and the American Crisis" and reprinted as a tract, Graham's father-in-law painted a similar picture. Catholics observed American rules and conventions regarding religious freedom, Dr. Bell contended, only because they had to. He characterized the Roman Catholic Church as "a political system that like an octopus covers the entire world and threatens those basic freedoms and those constitutional rights for which our forefathers died in generations past" and warned that "once a nation becomes 51% Catholic, the pressure increases, and as the percentage rises in favor of that Church, tolerance recedes and oppression intervenes." He pointed to suppression of Protestant beliefs and practice in Italy and in various Latin American countries, adding ominously, "Rome never changes."

Ockenga and Bell were hardly voices crying in a wilderness. In the Fundamentalist camp, John R. Rice, Bob Jones, Sr., and Carl McIntire predictably sounded even more strident notes, and the executive director of the National Association of Evangelicals wrote a moderate but clearly pessimistic booklet entitled *A Roman Catholic President: How Free from Church Control?* The NAE also sent a "Plan of Action" letter to Evangelical pastors, suggesting they emphasize the dangers of Roman Catholicism as well as the evergreen threats of Communist infiltration and general spiritual and moral decay. "Public opinion is changing," the letter warned, "in favor of the Church of Rome. It is time for us to stand up and be counted as Protestants. We dare not sit idly by—voiceless and voteless—and lose the heritage for which others have died." *Christianity Today* conjured similar visions of dark days ahead if a Catholic occupied the White House, and a BGEA flyer advertising the inaugural issue of *Decision* magazine reminded Evangelicals of their responsibility to participate in government. "We Christians," it asserted, "must work and pray as never before in this election or the future course of America could be dangerously altered and the free preaching of the gospel could be endangered." On the campus of Evangelical colleges, students expressing a preference for Kennedy were open to accusations of spiritual laxity. At Wheaton College prejudice made the short leap to overt discrimination, as students favoring Nixon were permitted free use of the college service to tout their candidate, while the few Kennedy backers were charged regular rates to mail their literature.

Not all such forebodings came from Evangelicals and Fundamentalists. A group of Protestant clergymen led by Norman Vincent Peale and calling themselves the National Conference of Citizens for Religious Freedom asserted that Kennedy could not withstand the Roman hierarchy's determined efforts "to breach the wall of separation of church and state." G. Bromley

Oxnam, chairman of the Methodist Church's Council of Bishops and president of both the Federal and World Council of Churches, and Presbyterian Eugene Carson Blake, president of the National Council, both acknowledged they were "uneasy" that a Roman Catholic president could strengthen Catholic influence in government and society and felt it might be difficult for him to square his political duties with obligations to his church when it came to such matters as parochial schools, birth control, and the separation of Church and State. They did, however, profess an admiration for Kennedy and said they would consider voting for him.

If pressed on the matter, Billy Graham could contend that he was not personally responsible for any of these statements, even those produced by his own organization but he shared at least some of these apprehensions. In his letter urging Eisenhower to take a more active role in supporting Nixon, he expressed concern that if Lyndon Johnson were to become vice-president, Roman Catholic Mike Mansfield would be in line to become Senate majority leader. With Massachusetts congressman John McCormack as floor leader in the House, Catholics would hold two extremely powerful positions. "The Roman Catholic Church," Graham warned, "will take advantage of this." A few days later, reporters quoted him as saying that "a man's religion cannot be separated from his person: therefore, where religion involves political decision, it becomes a legitimate issue." When asked if the religious issue would be important in this election, he replied, "Yes, I have been informed by political experts that it will be deeper than in 1928 [when Roman Catholic Al Smith ran against Herbert Hoover] because people are better informed." He added that "some Protestants are hesitant about voting for a Catholic because the Catholic Church is not only a religious, but a secular institution which sends and receives ambassadors from secular states." Seeing his own words in print, however, caused second thoughts, and he quickly sent statements to both *Time* and *Newsweek* denying he had John Kennedy in mind when he made these observations about religion and politics.

Despite this waffling, Graham's interest in the religious issue stemmed less from fear of Kennedy's Catholicism than from awareness that raising the specter of religious bigotry could help Kennedy's campaign. He also recognized that some objections to Kennedy were just what they were portrayed to be—bigotry—and that troubled him. He told Nixon early in September that he was "detaching myself from some of the cheap religious bigotry and diabolical whisperings that are going on. I am not so much opposed to Kennedy as I am FOR YOU." He also strongly urged Nixon not to participate in any such attacks. "At all costs," he urged, "you must continue to stay a million miles from the religious issue at this time."

As Graham feared, Kennedy adroitly turned his Catholicism to his own advantage. In a bold move, his religious adviser, James Wine, a Presbyterian elder and former official of the National Council of Churches, arranged a

September meeting with a large group of ministers in Houston, a hotbed of anti-Catholic sentiments. A master at handling hostile questions in extempore fashion, Kennedy faced his antagonists head-on and gave them unambiguous, reassuring answers about his relative allegiance to the Constitution and the Roman magisterium. Repeatedly and without hesitation, he made it clear that if in his role as president he faced a conflict between his obligation to America and his obligation to the Vatican, either he would give precedence to his obligation to America, or he would vacate his office. The Houston meeting was a pivotal event in the campaign, and Graham knew it. He told Nixon that Kennedy's tactic seemed to be working, and that a high-ranking Democratic leader had told him Kennedy might be elected solely on the religious issue. Graham recommended that Nixon put his enemies on the defensive by having Eisenhower, Senator Jacob Javits, and Thomas Dewey point out that the Democrats had led both Protestants and Catholics into a political trap by highlighting religious prejudice. In view of a fusillade of criticism the press and some liberal religious leaders had launched against Norman Vincent Peale after he both endorsed Nixon and questioned whether Kennedy could govern free of Vatican control, Graham felt it imperative that he not make any public statement on the religious issue. "Not only would [the press and liberal religious leaders] crucify me," he explained, "but they would eventually turn it against you, so I must be extremely careful. I have been avoiding the American press the last few weeks like the plague. But when I arrive home next week, I will make statements that will by implication be interpreted as favorable to you without getting directly involved. As the campaign moves on, I may be forced to take a more open stand if I feel it will help your cause, but we shall wait for the developments."

Graham's public reticence masked intense private concern over the election. With the exception of a three-day crusade aimed at Hispanics in New York City, his fall schedule was light, and he spent at least part of his free time concocting political strategy. In an October 17 letter marked "confidential and urgent," he offered several concrete suggestions for Nixon's consideration. First, he counseled, the Vice-President should take a strong position critical of Cuba's turn toward communism, an issue on which Kennedy was scoring the administration. In what seems an astonishing willingness to manipulate foreign policy for partisan political advantage, Graham recommended that Nixon urge the President to take some dramatic action, perhaps even to break diplomatic relations with Cuba. His other recommendations involved rhetoric more than policy but reflected relish at being part of the competition. When Kennedy talked of the loss of Cuba and the Congo to communism, he counseled that Nixon should mention the countries that went Communist under Democratic administrations. "I believe there are at least twenty countries. This would be tremendously impressive and would shut the mouth of your opponent on this point." Candidates and office holders get an abundance of unsolicited advice, but Nixon and his staff apparently took Graham's counsel seriously. In a memo regarding Graham's suggestion that he take a harder line on Cuba, Nixon told his aides, "I think [this] makes a hell of a lot of sense.... Please note the paragraph where he is talking about the Cuban situation. I would like you, Len [Hall], to go over and have a chat with the President about that situation. I don't know whether anything can be done about it, but it does show what the reactions are."

Graham continued to be vexed that Kennedy had turned his Catholicism and a perception of religious prejudice to political advantage. To offset this, he felt Nixon simply had to persuade some leading Republican to show that Democrats were deliberately using the religious issue to "(1) solidify the Catholic vote, (2) split the Protestants, (3) make a martyr out of Kennedy, and (4) obscure the more basic issues in the campaign." Graham regarded this plan as a deliberate and cynical strategy: "Protestants and Catholics alike have been caught in a deliberate political trap set for them." Graham urged Nixon to speak out on the need for spiritual revitalization and greater dependence on God and prayer. "I wonder if you couldn't say in your next debate that whoever is elected, he is going to have to depend upon God for wisdom, striking a note of humility and saying frankly that you don't have all the answers but that whoever is elected should look to God for strength, guidance, and leadership, as Washington and Lincoln did. Many of my advisers believe that a few statements along that line would convince tens of thousands of the uncommitted." He also recommended that "you must somehow show that if Kennedy wins, this is going to be a personal repudiation of Eisenhower. [A Kennedy victory] will be one of the greatest propaganda weapons that Khrushchev ever had." In closing, Graham revealed his belief that the same combination of prayer and pragmatic technique used in his crusades was appropriate to the political realm as well. "You will be interested to know," he said, "that thousands of prayer meetings have been organized across America to pray about this election. I am certain that during the next few days you are going to sense supernatural wisdom in answer to prayer. I have a sneaking suspicion that by midnight on November 8, we are all going to be rejoicing. In the meantime, a great deal of hard work and praying needs to be done."

Billy was ready to do some of that work himself. As his concerns mounted, he sought Henry Luce's advice. Luce suggested that the evangelist write an article for *Life* setting forth his own candid evaluation of Nixon. Graham had doubts about such an assignment but agreed to do it, in part, he admitted, because he "felt under such obligation to him for all of his references [in Luce publications]." He wrote that the Vice-President did not "have the slightest inkling that I am writing this article and probably would have advised against it," but asserted that he had a right and responsibility to speak out just as Reinhold Niebuhr and [Union Theological Seminary president and professor] John Bennett had spoken out on behalf of John Kennedy. Noting that this election was "the most crucial our nation has ever confronted" because Americans were in effect choosing "the President of the world," he observed that it would be inappropriate to choose a candidate simply because he was "more handsome or charming" or to follow "the dubious path of tradition and say, 'I'll vote for my party, right or wrong.'" Moreover, he had more faith in the American people than to believe a presidential election could actually be bought by a candidate who happened to be richer, better organized, and more ruthless. If pressed, Graham could claim that these were neutral observations that could apply to any election, but since none of the descriptions other than ruthlessness could possibly fit Nixon, all but the densest readers would construe them as a barely concealed attack on Kennedy.

Turning to an explicit consideration of his own favorite, Graham acknowledged that some regarded Nixon as cold, calculating, politically expedient, and intellectually lightweight but volunteered that "I have found him totally different. Richard Nixon to me is the epitome of warmth, affability, and sincerity. He has qualities that are found in few people.... He has sincere concern for the underprivileged people of the world." In fact, he ventured, Nixon's outstanding quality was sincerity: "His mind doesn't seem to reach for political gimmicks. He inspires confidence and commands respect. He has no characteristics of a demagogue. [He has a] deep personal faith in God.... Although he doesn't flaunt his faith publicly, I know him to be a deeply religious man."

Luce liked the article and scheduled it to run the week before the election. Graham then got cold feet and called several politically astute friends to let them know what he had done. Republican Senator Frank Carlson expressed reservations but basically approved. *U.S. News & World Report* publisher David Lawrence and radio commentator Paul Harvey absolutely opposed it, even though both supported Nixon. Graham also tried to reach Nixon during that period, but for never-explained reasons, the Vice-President's staff did not put him through and according to Graham, "seemed terribly indecisive" about the proposed article. "They were not sure whether it would hurt or help [Nixon]. This indecisiveness was a contributing factor to my own dilemma." Ruth Graham also felt it was a mistake that would jeopardize Graham's own ministry and destroy any possible chance Nixon had of appealing to Roman Catholics. The anxious couple prayed that if Luce did run the article, God would use it for good, but that if it happened not to meet with divine approval, the Almighty might deploy some small miracle to keep it from appearing. News traveled fast, and the next morning Senator George Smathers, North Carolina governor Luther Hodges, and Frank Clement all called to express concern. Later in the morning, Henry Luce called to say that he had informed Kennedy of the article and the senator had strongly urged that Reinhold Niebuhr be asked to write a balancing article. To give him time to consider that request, Luce had pulled the article temporarily but planned to run it the following week. Taking this as the divine portent he had been seeking, Graham told Luce of his misgivings and asked him not to run the article. In its place he submitted a nonpartisan article on why Christians should vote, and Luce agreed to run it. After that, Graham said, "I had peace, for I found the Lord had intervened in some strange and mysterious way. I may never know why until I stand before him at the judgment."

After Luce let him off the hook, Graham was quoted as saying he was not going to give a straight endorsement of Nixon. "I have come to the conclusion," he said, "that my main responsibility is in the spiritual realm and that I shouldn't become involved in partisan politics." But two days later, he was back in the fray, albeit behind the scenes. With less than a week before the election, as it became clear that Kennedy stood a good chance of winning, Graham's advice to Nixon assumed a desperate tone. "There is a great deal of evidence," he alleged, "to indicate that the Democrats have deliberately printed hate material and spread it in Catholic areas to incite the Catholics against you." To counter that effort, he suggested that some leading Republican, probably Eisenhower or Rockefeller, should film a rebuttal and the campaign should buy as much time as possible in the key electoral states and show the film over and over until the election. Forget money, he urged: "You should purchase cream time at any cost." Temporal tactics alone, however, would not suffice. Noting that he had received numerous letters from supporters reporting dismay over Nixon's failure to emphasize spiritual matters, Graham counseled the Vice-President to emphasize his own convictions about the importance of spiritual guidance. "State frankly," Graham proposed, "that you are a firm believer, putting the election in God's hands and saying, 'Thy will be done.'" He then recommended a course that had worked well for him: "Indicate also that you have little personal ambition in this matter, but that you have represented a cause in which you sincerely believe." He noted that voters were not the only pertinent observers. "God may be searching your heart," he cautioned, "to see where you stand before Him. I am convinced that without His help you cannot win this election." To enhance the likelihood that the much-needed divine assistance would be forthcoming, Graham flew to South Carolina the next day to give the invocation at a Nixon rally and to be photographed at the candidate's side as they stood under a banner that defiantly challenged complacent Democrats to recognize that Dixie Is No Longer in the Bag.

With or without God's help, Nixon lost one of the closest elections in American history. When the last returns finally trickled in on the morning after the election and it became clear that John Kennedy would be the next president, Graham sent Nixon a consoling telegram: "BELIEVE YOUR GREAT CAMPAIGN HAS WON MORAL VICTORY. AM CERTAIN GOD WILL USE YOU GREATLY IN THE FUTURE." Even so, he gave up grudgingly. Ten days after the election, he said, "I understand there is to be a recount of votes in Illinois. Nixon may win there. And they may recount the votes in New Mexico. Those Mississippi electors could still be important. Technically, you know, the President isn't chosen until December 19th." Despite such grasping at straws, Graham must have felt in his heart of hearts that his days of first-name intimacy with the White House were over, at least until 1964, when Nixon might try again. Still, he prudently refrained from any action or statements that would alienate Kennedy, and the president-elect responded in kind. Kennedy would never extend to Graham the right hand of fellowship both Eisenhower and Nixon had proffered, but he understood that it would serve no purpose to harden Graham's resistance to him. Within two weeks Florida Democratic senator George Smathers, whose campaign manager was an old friend of Graham's, arranged for Graham to have lunch with Kennedy at Key Biscayne. Though pleased to be sought out, Graham hesitated lest he seem to be fickle or unduly opportunistic. When he ultimately accepted the invitation, he called Nixon's offices to let the Vice-President know that the meeting in no way detracted from his wholehearted support.

The luncheon took place in January, a few days before the inauguration. Both men got what they sought. Graham kept open at least a narrow channel to the White House and had the satisfaction of feeling he might ultimately exert some spiritual influence over the new President. He has often recalled how the dashing young politician suddenly pulled the white Lincoln convertible to the side of the road on the way back from their golf game at Palm Beach, and looking directly at Graham, blurted out, "Billy, do you believe that Jesus Christ is going to come back again?" Without hesitation, Graham answered, "I do." Kennedy pondered the matter a moment, then said, "My church teaches it in its creeds, but I don't hear much about it." He also inquired, Graham recalled, about the triumph of the kingdom of God and numerous other topics—"He must have asked a hundred separate questions"—but that exchange appears to have been the extent of theological discussion between the two men. Still, it gave Graham two things every preacher needs: hope of success and a good sermon illustration. In return, Graham gave Kennedy an even greater gift. At a press conference that evening, without prior warning to his guest, Kennedy said that Dr. Billy Graham was present and would answer questions about the religious issue that had drawn so much attention during the campaign. Graham recalled that "I was scared to death, but I stood up and tried to walk the middle line as much as I could." Few men have proved more adroit at walking the middle line, and Billy's balance and agility did not fail him on this occasion. A *New York Times* article titled "Dr. Graham Hails Kennedy Victory" reported that "the Reverend Dr. Billy Graham declared tonight that the election of John F. Kennedy, a Roman Catholic, had promoted a better understanding between the Protestant and Catholic churches in the United States. Dr. Graham, the evangelist, said Mr. Kennedy's victory had proved there was not as much religious prejudice as many had feared, and probably had reduced forever the importance of the religious issue in American elections." The article went on to note that Dr. Graham "commended Mr. Nixon and his running mate, Henry Cabot Lodge, for not bringing up the religious issue. He also praised Mr. Kennedy for 'facing' the issue forth-rightly, thereby easing 'many fears' held by some voters about a Catholic in the White House." Graham said he would not be able to attend the inauguration—though his crusade schedule would have permitted it—but he would watch and pray for the new President. Kennedy's embrace was similarly restrained. Press Secretary Pierre Salinger approved sending Graham photographs of the two men taken at the press conference but directed aides to make it clear "in writing" that "these pictures are for Mr. Graham's personal use" and not for reproduction in his magazines or other publications.

Richard Nixon accepted Graham's decision in the *Life* episode with rueful grace, calling the unused article "probably the best and most effective statement in my behalf in the entire campaign" but allowing that the decision not to use it had been proper. Still, he was pleased Billy had felt able to say such kind things about him. "I have deeply appreciated the spiritual inspiration and guidance that you have given me," he wrote, shortly before leaving the capital for California, "but in addition to that, your political advice has been as wise as any I have received from any man I know. I have often told friends that when you went into the ministry, politics lost one of its potentially greatest practitioners!" In an interesting glimpse at the fruitful technique of pretending to greater intimacy than may actually exist, Nixon added a postscript: "Pat joins me in sending our very best wishes to Ruth and to you." The draft of the letter contained a parenthetical note: "Ck for sure that his wife's name is 'Ruth.'"

Nixon may have forgiven, but he had not forgotten. A few months later, ostensibly as part of his research for the book *Six Crises*, he asked Graham to provide an account of the factors that led to his decision not to publish the article for *Life*. Graham recounted his version, stressing that he had been wholeheartedly for Nixon and had harbored numerous reservations about Kennedy, but that he had not wanted to solidify the Catholic vote or be branded a bigot. Then, in a gentle dig at Nixon, he said, "The more I listened to Mr. Kennedy, the less fear I had that all would be lost if he were elected. In fact, he began to say some of the things that I had hoped you would say," mentioning specifically Kennedy's call for sacrifice and dedication on the part of Americans. When Nixon did not respond immediately, Graham grew anxious and wrote another letter to see if his remarks had somehow offended his friend. After an additional period of awkward silence, Nixon again let Billy off the hook, but he could not entirely conceal his disappointment. "In retrospect," he said, "the *Life* article should have been published and would have been a definite plus."

Graham and Nixon remained in occasional contact. After the former vice-president's infamous "you-won't-have-Nixon-to-kick-around-anymore" press conference, following his unsuccessful bid for the California governorship in 1962, Graham sent a warm pastoral letter urging his friend not to become bitter or to withdraw into a shell and exclude those who care for him. "A man's true character," he said, "is seen in the midst of disappointment and defeat." The petulant behavior at the press conference had given "the impression that you were a poor loser and bitter." To correct that impression, he recommended that Nixon hold a combination press conference and party for reporters at which he should apologize for his behavior at the previous gathering. A show of humility, Graham suggested, would silence his critics and bring a wave of sympathy. "You could turn the entire feeling and comment to a tremendous advantage." The concerned pastor apparently also thought his counselee needed some internal rehabilitation. "It would be the greatest tragedy I can think of," he said, "for you to turn to drink or any of these other escapisms. Millions of Americans admire you as no other man of our time." Rather than let disappointment drag him down, Graham urged Nixon to "start reading the Bible, learning the value, power, and secrets of prayer, and attending church with new faithfulness." He closed on a note that helped explain the uncommon loyalty he demonstrated to Nixon in later years. "Dick, I have thousands of friends, but very few close, intimate friends. There are few men whom I have loved as I love you. My friendship for you was never because you were Vice-president or an international figure. It was far deeper than that, and I hope we can continue our friendship on a warmer basis than ever before."

18

The Kennedy Years

His main bridge to the White House temporarily washed out, his fight with Fundamentalism all but over, and his position on integration no longer requiring daily defense, Billy Graham spent most of the Kennedy years doing what he did best: holding crusades and broadening his base of support. A decade of marathon campaigns had taken such a toll on his physical stamina that he occasionally told reporters he doubted he would live much longer. To give both body and spirit a rest, he began to trim the length of his crusades, moving gradually toward the eight-day (usually Sunday to Sunday) format used in most of his meetings since the mid-1960s. He spent the first four months of 1961 in Florida holding a three-week crusade in Miami and a series of one- and two-day meetings in a dozen other cities. He also spent a fair amount of time on the beach and the golf course, basking in the warm sunshine he had come to love during his days at the Bible institute. He followed the Florida campaign with a less-than-brilliant three-week crusade in Manchester, England, and wound up the season with good outings in Minneapolis and Philadelphia.

In 1962 Graham added another continent to his list by making two month-long forays into South America. Shortly before the first of these, he met with President Kennedy, who was also about to visit South America. In a conversation Graham recounted with obvious pleasure, the President told the preacher, "I'll be your John the Baptist," graciously implying that he would prepare the way for one who would follow with a greater message. According to Graham aides, Kennedy felt Graham's visit to South America would strengthen goodwill between the United States and its neighbors unless he became the target of anti-Protestant hostility. He apparently asked what kind of treatment Graham expected from Catholics, an indication he recognized that his coreligionists could be highly resistant to Protestant incursions on what they regarded as their rightful turf, particularly when the intruders were Americans. These apprehensions were not unfounded. In Colombia the mayor of Barranquilla, apparently acting under pressure from Catholic clergy, denied Graham permission to speak at that city's largest baseball stadium, forcing a move to the grounds of an American Presbyterian school. In Maracaibo, protesters tore down crusade placards, replacing them with leaflets warning citizens not to attend the meetings. And while Graham spoke at a government building, they pounded on the doors, fired guns into the air, and brandished signs that read, Yankee No, Down with Kennedy, and Castro Si, forcing the evangelist and his team to beat a hasty retreat through a back door. (Team photographer Russ Busby recalled with amusement his own unwillingness to follow Graham's suggestion that he "stick around and try to get some pictures. This could be real interesting.") This incident, which occurred on the fourth anniversary of a Communist defeat in Venezuela, seems to have been more political than religious in nature, fixing on Graham because he was a prominent American rather than because he was a Protestant, and he subsequently preached unmolested to a crowd of 4,000 at a baseball park. The reception in Cali, Colombia, was friendlier, and in the Venezuelan capital of Caracas, a city with only 5,000 Protestants, 32,000 people crowded into a bullfight arena to hear him.

Response to Graham's visit to Paraguay was both intense and unambiguously Catholic in origin. The archbishop, whom one Graham aide described as "a well-known flagrant homosexual who had corrupted the lives of hundreds of young men," led the opposition, directing local priests to warn their parishioners not to attend Graham's meetings. In addition, church leaders organized a protest parade through the streets of Asuncion on the afternoon before the opening service of the crusade in the city. With the unmistakable implication that more than coincidence had been at work, a team member who witnessed the parade recalled a great storm that suddenly blew up while the parade was in progress. "The wind blew trees down, and flipped DC-3s over at the airport," he remembered. "It blew the Virgin they were carrying around off her pedestal and broke her arm. The rain was incredible. It was a complete disaster. Then, about an hour before the crusade, the weather changed. The stars came out and we had a lovely, cool evening. It was just a fantastic thing." Even so, crowds were modest, though not embarrassingly small, in both Asuncion and Montevideo, Uruguay.

Graham preached to large crowds in Chile, Argentina, and Brazil, and encountered little organized opposition. Overall, the trip was less than a smashing success. BGEA crusade statistics, which typically list every city in which Graham has held a major public meeting, write off nine weeks of preaching in South America under two brief entries, both consisting of "Tour—South America." Similarly, authorized histories of Graham's ministry devote only two or three sentences to the campaign without naming a single country visited. Still, the tour gave Protestant Christianity valuable exposure in newspapers and on television, and veteran Latin American missionary Kenneth Strachan called it a watershed event in South American

Evangelicalism, claiming it provided an important impetus for a broad movement of aggressive evangelistic efforts that led to a well-documented surge of Protestantism in many sectors of South America.

As Graham faced his other major challenge of 1962, he must have wondered if the cooperative spirit he had worked so hard to forge was being eroded. Despite his many contacts in the area, he had not held a crusade, or even an outstanding rally, in Chicago since his YFC days in the 1940s. An effort to wangle an invitation in 1958 had come to naught after Mayor Richard Daley, allegedly under pressure from Catholic leaders, openly opposed a Graham crusade, and the Protestant Church Federation of Greater Chicago expressed strong reservations about the high-powered bureaucratic approach Graham's team imposed on churches in a crusade city. Despite this rebuff, Graham's Evangelical supporters in the Chicago area continued to aim for a full-scale crusade, often working through enthusiastic laymen who brought pressure on their more reticent pastors. Two years later, at a breakfast meeting with nearly seven hundred Chicago-area ministers, many of whom had been negative about a crusade, the evangelist patiently addressed their concerns and doubts. When he finished, the chair of the meeting, an old friend of Graham's who had supported him since the YFC days, asked the men to indicate by standing if they wished to invite Billy to hold a crusade in Chicago. All seven hundred stood. After the meeting, Graham acknowledged that the procedure had "looked to some as if it were a bit high-pressure," but the chairman insisted there was no way such a procedure could be viewed as an attempt to pressure the clergymen, pointing out, apparently as proof, that Graham himself had proposed the rising vote.

While the ostensibly unanimous vote of the clergymen did not quell all doubts, it clearly shifted the balance of power to those favoring a crusade, and in the summer of 1962, Graham preached for three weeks to a packed house at the new McCormick Place arena. Then, at the closing service in Soldier Field, he addressed 116,000 souls, his largest American audience yet. That service was notable in other respects as well. Chicago was suffering from a sweltering heat wave that caused a plague of vapor lock to descend on the long lines of approaching cars, creating a cacophonous tangle outside the stadium. Inside, the sun's rays seemed to concentrate on the unshaded platform, and the television lights made the pulpit area even hotter, so that Graham risked a heatstroke just by preaching a sermon of normal length. At one point, sweat-soaked and sagging, his head throbbing with pain, he apparently came close to blacking out; though he never stopped talking, one observer later recalled that he suspected an uncut film would reveal several moments of incoherence. Waving his aides away, however, Graham cut the sermon short and managed to offer the invitation. The response was substantial, and the service drew to a close with no further problems, but Graham went immediately to his hotel to sleep off his affliction and weariness.

The evening, however, was not over. After years of practice, Graham had learned to time his sermon so that his television crew could wind up with a film that required only minimal editing to produce an hour-long program. Because of his problems with the heat, however, the service had ended seven minutes early. Since the crew would depart the next day, something had to be done immediately. Aware that Graham was exhausted and asleep, some felt it would be best to have him tape a short concluding message the next morning, but Cliff Barrows had a more dramatic idea. He rousted Graham out of bed and trundled him back to Soldier Field. When viewers saw the program weeks later, the usual closing shots of inquirers streaming toward the platform were suddenly replaced by a slow, sweeping panoramic shot of a littered and empty stadium, deserted except for Billy Graham, who sat alone on the platform, obviously weary, his eyes circled in darkness. "I have come back here to Soldier Field to talk to you," he said. "I talked on Agrippa almost being persuaded to follow Christ. Some of you during this meeting have almost been persuaded to give your life to Jesus Christ, but you haven't done it.... And as this stadium is empty now, your heart is empty." For most of seven minutes, he told them that no matter what they had done, no matter where they were, no matter how many times they had previously rejected Christ, it was not too late. And then he said, in what had become one of Evangelical Christianity's most famous phrases, "I'm going to ask you right now...." Within a few days, the mail and telephone response generated by that dramatic scene outstripped that for any previous appeal in Graham's ministry.

Two aspects of the Chicago crusade drew little public attention but proved to be of considerable long-term significance for the Graham organization. After the 1957 New York crusade, during which he organized the recruitment of show-business people, Lane Adams found that the hands-on experience gained while working with prospective and new converts translated easily into a more effective ministry in a local pastorate. He felt every pastor ought also to be an evangelist but realized that most seminaries did not provide the skills he had learned while working with the Graham team. At Adams's instigation, seven students from Columbia Presbyterian Theological Seminary, which he had attended, received internships (paid for by an affluent student at the seminary) to work with the team during a month-long crusade in Philadelphia in the fall of 1961. About the same time, a wealthy California layman, Lowell Berry, was thinking along similar lines. Berry, whose theological leanings had been somewhat liberal before his participation in Graham's highly successful 1958 San Francisco crusade, had been convinced of both the plausibility of a more Evangelical theology and the effectiveness of high-powered evangelism of the sort Graham practiced. George Wilson recalled that Berry approached BGEA representatives several times, indicating his interest in underwriting a program to enable seminary students and young ministers to obtain intensive instruction in evangelistic theory and methods during Graham crusades. Wilson was not particularly open to the idea, responding that such a program would require a great deal of money. Berry's simple response—"Well, I have a great deal of money"—cast a different light on the matter, and at the Chicago crusade, twenty-seven seminarians from seven schools received seminar training and practical field experience in evangelism. The Chicago experience proved so successful that Berry continued his support. Robert Ferm developed a more structured program for an El Paso crusade later in the year, and the Billy Graham School of Evangelism was under way. A year later, a hundred men, including young clergy as well as seminarians, attended a School of Evangelism attached to a Graham crusade in Los Angeles, spending their days in classes taught by members of the team and invited guests, and their evenings watching the master evangelist at work. In subsequent years, the program catered less to seminarians than to pastors, but each major crusade eventually came to include evangelistic training for several hundred ministers. Long after Berry's death, most of the expense, including travel and lodging for less affluent ministers, was picked up by the Berry Foundation.

A second little-noticed development of the Chicago crusade involved a shift in T. W. Wilson's role. After Graham persuaded him to come to work for BGEA in 1956, Wilson served as an associate evangelist, using team-developed techniques and personnel to hold crusades on his own, quite independent of Graham's schedule, or conducting "satellite crusades" in locations not far from cities where Graham was coming or had just been. In the latter case, Graham often preached at the last service or two to give those unable to attend the larger crusade a chance to hear him in person. For Graham's major crusades, the associate evangelists typically join the larger team, filling in for Billy at various speaking engagements and simply enjoying the chance to visit with other members of the association. During the Chicago crusade, Graham needed a nap one afternoon and asked T.W. to handle a handful of small tasks—returning a few telephone calls, conveying a message to an aide, answering a question for the public relations staff, and the like. A well-organized man, Wilson finished the entire list before Graham awoke. When Billy expressed amazement, T.W. said, "You wanted them done, didn't you? Well, I did them."

About two o'clock the next morning, Graham went to Wilson's room and woke him. "I want you to come with me and help me," he said. The sleepy Wilson groaned. "Billy," he said, "we've been over this before and the answer is the same. I appreciate you more than I can tell you, but I know what I am supposed to do, and that is preach."

Graham quickly trotted out the reasoning he had used so effectively so many times before: "I want to ask you a question. Are you more concerned about the number of times you can speak or the most good you can do for Almighty God?"

"Man, that's beside the point," Wilson objected.

"Is it? Think about it. First of all, I need somebody who knows me, knows my family, knows my friends, and who is an evangelist himself."

"Billy, I just can't do this. I know what I'm supposed to do."

"Will you pray about it?"

"I don't need to pray about it."

"Oh? There's something in your life you don't need to pray about?"

"You know what I mean."

"No, I don't know what you mean."

"Anyway," Wilson recalled with a chuckle, "he was a super salesman. I tried to go back to sleep and couldn't. I tossed and turned all night. I called my wife back in Dothan, Alabama, but she didn't help me at all with a decision. She said, 'Just promise me one thing. Make sure you are in God's will, because if you are not, you will be miserable, and if you are miserable, we will all be miserable. Just make sure you are in God's will.' Well, I didn't sleep any that night, and I couldn't sleep the next night either. Finally, I said, 'Lord, I've got to get some sleep. Please help me.' Then it just seemed like he was impressing on me that this was what I ought to do. And I've been doing it ever since."

After that afternoon in 1962, T. W. Wilson spent most days of the rest of his life at the side or within easy reach of Billy Graham, serving as his gatekeeper, travel agent, valet, nurse, adviser, buffer, booster, defender, listener, jollier, minesweeper, and constant chaperon. Some team members occasionally referred to mild feelings of resentment toward T.W. because of his unique relationship with their leader—inevitably, they perceived such feelings in others rather than in themselves—but colleagues and knowledgeable observers of the Graham organization alike almost invariably described him as "an amazing man," "one of the strong backbones of the entire association," "a man who is able to subordinate himself without ever worrying about it a minute," and "a man who knows how to take care of Billy without making everyone mad."

T.W.'s chaperonage efforts did not always work out perfectly. Not long after he assumed his new post, Graham fell ill with pneumonia on his way to a meeting in the Philippines and had to be hospitalized in Honolulu. Checking himself out of the hospital against his doctors' advice, he and Wilson headed back to Montreat. The doctors had been right. By the time the two men reached Los Angeles, Graham's fever had soared, and he was miserable with a severe bronchial infection, but he insisted on returning home, where Nelson Bell could look after him. When their plane landed in Atlanta, tornadoes and pouring rain made it impossible for airplanes to leave for Asheville, so Graham insisted that T.W. rent a car and head out for home. When they got to Jefferson, Georgia, well after dark, Wilson stopped at a service station to ask for directions. Graham, who had gone to sleep in the back seat, groggily appraised the situation and staggered through the heavy rain to the restroom at the side of the building. When Wilson returned to the car, he never thought to check the back seat but simply jumped in and drove off—leaving Graham in the restroom. The interstate highway had not yet been built, and winding through the hills in a driving rain fully occupied his attention until he finally stopped for gas about midnight in Oteen, North Carolina, less than twenty miles from Montreat. When he turned around to wake Billy up and tell him they were almost home, he was astonished to find an empty back seat. He called Ruth to see if she had heard from her husband. "No," she said, "I thought he was with you." Wilson had recalled that, as he pushed along those last few miles wondering what on earth had happened, he could not help considering the possibility that the rapture had occurred and that he and Ruth had not been invited to make the trip.

Graham, of course, knew exactly what had happened, but that did not provide a simple solution. He had heard Wilson preparing to drive off but had not been in a position to pursue him. Sick, rumpled, and unshaven, he went into a cafe attached to the station and tried to call home. Unfortunately, he had just gotten a new unlisted number and could not remember it. With his famous voice rendered unrecognizable by laryngitis, neither could he convince the operator that he was in fact the registered owner of that number. Eventually, he persuaded the driver of the town's lone taxicab to take him to nearby Greenville, South Carolina, where he knew he could get a ride on to Montreat. The old man insisted Graham put down twenty dollars in advance and refused to believe his claim to be Billy Graham ("I think you are on the lam," he said) until they reached Greenville's Holiday Inn, where the manager recognized the evangelist and helped him arrange to rent a car to drive the rest of the way to Montreat.

Back at home, Ruth continued to care for her maturing brood of children and their ever-changing menagerie of dogs, goats, rabbits, ponies, and assorted wildlife. Anne continued to be a kind and tenderhearted girl who gave little trouble to anyone, and youngest daughter Bunny displayed much the same pleasant and pliable spirit. Franklin was cut from different cloth. An independent spirit from the start, he had started experimenting with cigarettes at age three, picking up butts from carpenters working on his mother's dream home. A few years later, Ruth decided to end the allure of smoking by offering him a pack and inviting him to smoke right in front of her. To her uncomfortable surprise, he quickly drew it down to a stub, then immediately lit up another. Other efforts to break his spirit were no more successful. Once, on the way to a drive-in restaurant in Asheville, his pestering the other children became so aggravating that Ruth stopped the car, pulled him out, and after checking to make sure he could get enough air, locked him in the trunk. When she let him out at the restaurant, he popped out and chirruped to the carhop, "I'll have a cheeseburger without the meat."

Ned, six years younger, was an easy target for Franklin's aggression. Ruth told of an overheard conversation in which Franklin, polishing his shoes by the fireplace, asked his younger brother, "Ned, do you love me?"

Ned, always described as having a gentle spirit, answered, "Yes, my love you."

Then Franklin sprang the trap: "Well, I don't love you."

Reflecting his father's ability to handle rebuff, Ned leaned back against the hearth and said after a few moments' thought, "Well, my love you."

Franklin shot back, "Well, I don't love you."

Ned knew where to go for help: "The Bible says ..."

Franklin cut him off. "The Bible doesn't say I have to love you, does it?"

"Well ...," Ned ventured, "the Bible says some nice things."

The soft answer apparently had its effect. Not long afterward, while Ruth was tucking Franklin into bed, she noticed Ned standing at the doorway of Franklin's bedroom—Franklin had trained him not to enter without permission. The tiny figure shyly asked his brother, "Can I come in and kiss you good night?" This time, Franklin accepted Ned's affection, and mission accomplished, little brother padded happily off to bed. "You know," Franklin admitted to his mother, "he's a pretty good little boy."

Seventeen-year-old GiGi had lost none of her spunk, but boarding school had removed her from Montreat for most of the year, and a new development was about to remove her forever. During the summer of 1960, while Graham was touring in Europe, his family stayed in Montreux, Switzerland, as the guest of Ara Tchividjian, a wealthy Swiss Armenian who became a Christian after reading *Peace with God*, flew to New York in 1957 to hear Graham preach, and had been an enthusiastic backer ever since. Over the course of the summer, GiGi, then fourteen, met Tchividjian's eldest son, Stephan, who was twenty-one. "I thought he was an old man," she recalled, but Stephan's grandmother told him, "That is the girl you are going to marry." Stephan, who was already engaged to a woman his age, thought it absurd, but his grandmother confidently informed him, "God has told me." The Grahams also admired Stephan. Late one afternoon, looking across a bejeweled mountain lake from the terrace of their home, Billy mused, "Wouldn't it be wonderful if GiGi and Stephan grew up and fell in love?" Ruth conceded his point, but noting the years and geography that separated them, added, "It's not going to happen. Let's pray that she finds someone like Stephan."

A year passed, and Stephan's fiancée decided she did not want to marry him. A devout Christian who fully accepted Billy Graham's exhortation to make everything of consequence a matter for prayer, Stephan began to ask God for help in finding a wife. As he told it, the image that kept coming to his mind and heart was that of GiGi Graham. Because he thought it might be unseemly to approach a girl so young, Tchividjian hesitated making direct contact. "He would start to write," GiGi recounted, "but he'd always tear up the letters. I never received anything from him—card, flowers, nothing." Unaware of what was going on in Stephan's mind, GiGi was dating T. W. Wilson's son, Jim. Shortly after her seventeenth birthday, she and Jim went off to Wheaton, both assuming they would eventually marry. Early in the fall, Billy and Ruth received a letter from Stephan Tchividjian asking permission to seek their daughter's hand in marriage. If they consented, he asked them to forward his enclosed letter of proposal to GiGi. If they disapproved, they were to destroy the letter and never tell their daughter he had written.

Ruth and Billy, who had been praying for someone like Stephan, could not help feeling God had given them an even better answer than they had hoped for. They agreed to let GiGi know of the proposal, but not immediately, lest the certain emotional turmoil disrupt her schoolwork. Better to wait until the Christmas holidays. Still, hints must have been dropped, because GiGi said she somehow knew something was going on and, feeling she was going to have to face some momentous decision, began to pray for guidance. As soon as she got back to Little Piney Cove, she asked, "Mother, what's going on?" Ruth conceded that they had something to discuss but thought it better to wait until the next morning, after a good night's rest.

GiGi pressed: "Mother, someone wants to marry me, doesn't he?"

Ruth was taken aback. "How did you know?"

GiGi admitted she had nothing concrete to go on but spilled out her hunches. "I don't know, but he's not American, is he?" Then, "Stephan Tchividjian has asked for my hand in marriage, hasn't he?"

"When Mother said yes," GiGi recalled, "I knew it was serious. I told her, 'I need to do some real praying, and I need to see him.' But Mother said, 'No. You are in love with Jim. If Stephan arrived, you are not emotionally involved with him, and you will make the wrong decision.'"

Ruth's response, if correctly remembered, seemed to reveal that she felt confident about what the right decision would be and was concerned only with strategy. Billy apparently felt no qualms on either score. When GiGi got him alone in the kitchen and told him she needed to see Stephan, he said, "No problem," and dialed the Tchividjian home, forgetting it was the middle of the night in Switzerland. After a few moments on the telephone, he informed Ruth that Stephan would be joining them for Christmas.

"I spent the next few days either on my knees or sitting in my window seat," GiGi recounted, "seeking God's direction. I wanted to give Stephan an answer when he got there and not go through the regular courtship routine. I prayed that the Lord would tell me what answer to give, but no answer came. The night before he was to come in, I asked Daddy if I could drive to the airport to pick him up. I hadn't driven much, and Daddy didn't think it would be safe, since there was snow on the ground. I asked, 'If the snow has melted and it's a pretty day, will you let me do it?' And he said, 'Okay.' Well, it was a clear, beautiful day. All the way to the airport, I prayed and prayed, but of course I got no answer. Then when the plane landed and he stepped out, the answer came: 'Yes.' That's all. I didn't feel any love or any other emotion. Just 'yes.' When we got in the car, I told him, 'Stephan, the Lord has told me to say yes.' He expected that I would want to finish my education, but we talked about it with Mother and Daddy, and because of Daddy's schedule, they thought it would be better if we got married in Europe in May. That took Stephan by surprise."

Meanwhile, Jim Wilson had been in the dark. GiGi remembered going down the mountain to the Wilsons' modest home and breaking the news to the unsuspecting young man. "It was the hardest thing I ever did. I wanted to throw my arms around him and tell him how sorry I was, but I asked the Lord to control my emotions. I was acting in obedience. Jim also wanted God's will for our lives, and he handled it with absolute grace and maturity. He and Stephan had a long talk, and he was so impressed by Stephan." For all his maturity, however, GiGi admitted that "it took Jim awhile to trust a girl again."

Would GiGi recommend a similar course of action for her own seven children? "I think it's crazy," she said with a laugh. "It had to be an exception. Stephan was older. I can't see a seventeen-year-old getting married to another seventeen-year-old. My children think the whole story is crazy, and they have no desire to follow in my footsteps."

Graham spent the first half of 1963 in a series of crusades and rallies in France and West Germany, with the now-standard set of European reactions: denunciation from leftist politicians, condescending opposition from clerics of the state churches and liberal theologians, secular skepticism from journalists and intellectuals, and sufficient enthusiasm from Evangelicals and the general populace to guarantee larger-than-expected crowds and expressions of grudging admiration from former critics. The major event of the second half of the year was a return engagement in Los Angeles, the scene of his first great crusade. This time, instead of a tent set up on a vacant lot, Graham held forth in the Coliseum, the nation's largest stadium. For most of the three-and-a-half weeks, crowds of between 30,000 and 60,000 people, most representing or invited by members of the 3,500 participating churches, heard Graham preach. Then, at the last service, 134,254 souls jammed into the sprawling stadium, while an estimated 20,000 others milled around disappointedly outside. It not only eclipsed the 1962 Soldier Field assembly as Graham's largest American crowd but set a record for the Coliseum that according to television commentators at the 1984 Olympics, still stands, commemorated by a bronze plaque bearing a bas-relief sculpture of the evangelist's head.

In Fundamentalist eyes, the Los Angeles campaign set another, less glorious record, when Graham acquiesced in the choice of Methodist bishop Gerald Kennedy as the chairman of the crusade's general committee. Though the position was largely honorary—most of the real oversight of the crusade was done by Graham's team and the local executive committee, which was usually dominated by Evangelicals—Kennedy was, in truth, a surprising choice. His theology was frankly liberal—he had once ventured that he doubted the deity of Christ and admitted he had never believed in the Virgin Birth. Fundamentalist critics also charged him with leftist political views "of the rankest sort," noting that he belonged to such "Communist front" organizations as the National Council of Churches and the Methodist Federation for Social Action. Allowing such a man to have a prominent public role in an evangelistic crusade, critics charged, marked "the farthest reach yet into the apostasy for Crusade leadership." Graham chose not to trouble himself with Fundamentalist carpings, but Robert Ferm, his chief apologist, pointed out that Kennedy had been appointed by local churchmen, that the actual conduct of the crusade would be controlled "by Mr. Graham and our Team only," and that he found it difficult to believe Kennedy would have accepted the post "if he did not believe in the basic Christian truths." Further, in the spirit of pragmatism that had long typified professional revivalism, Ferm observed that "it is so easy to find someone who believes all the fundamentals but who won't work." Kennedy was working, the crusade was succeeding, souls were being saved, and that, dear brothers, was that.

But pragmatism was not the only factor at work. Graham's fundamental beliefs and theological method had changed little, but as he put it in an article for *Christian Century*, "[A]fter a decade of intimate contact with Christians the world over I am now aware that the family of God contains people of various ethnological, cultural, class, and denominational differences. I have learned that there can even be minor disagreements of theology, methods, and motives, but that within the true church there is a mysterious unity that overrides all divisive factors. In groups which in my ignorant piousness I formerly 'frowned upon' I have found men so dedicated to Christ and so in love with the truth that I have felt unworthy to be in their presence. I have learned that although Christians do not always agree, they can disagree agreeably, and that what is most needed in the church today is for us to show an unbelieving world that we love one another."

Graham's ever-widening acceptance of others who professed to be Christians manifested itself not only in his continued association with the World Council of Churches—he attended its general assembly in New Delhi in 1961 at the council's invitation—but also in an improved relationship with Catholics, especially after John XXIII assumed the papal chair. Following John Kennedy's election, he scrupulously avoided any statements that could be construed as anti-Catholic, a relaxation of wariness that bothered some of Graham's colleagues. Robert Ferm, a man of catholic spirit but emphatically Protestant theology, exemplified the ambivalence some team members felt about consorting with Catholics. Whenever Graham's supporters or critics inquired about the evangelist's apparently weakening resistance to papist wiles, Ferm was quick to draw a firm baseline. "Certainly Catholic priests do not attend [crusade services]," he told a Kansas minister who had heard rumors of apostate fraternizing at the Chicago crusade. "[They] have not been invited to participate in any way. Nor would they do so if they were invited. They know altogether too well the gospel that Mr. Graham preaches." That knowledge, Ferm felt certain, explained why priests sometimes discouraged parishioners from attending Graham's meetings. "As you know," he wrote, "Roman Catholicism flourishes on ignorance. As long as people are not informed, Catholicism can prosper. It is only when people are informed that the hierarchy of the Roman Church gets into trouble. That is why it is so important for each one of us to be constantly active in informing people of the teaching and the political aspirations of the Roman Communion." Ferm admitted that Graham seemed to admire Pope John and what he was trying to accomplish in the Roman Church but felt it should be remembered that this particular pope was "a rare exception ... and one of the few concerning whom a particularly complimentary statement might be made."

Observers who applauded Graham's softening attitude toward liberal Protestants and Catholics found his stand on racial issues less satisfying. To be sure, he maintained his commitment to "non-segregated" crusades—he shied away from the term *integration* lest he be associated with civil rights radicalism—and even in the South, he insisted that black leaders be seated on the platform and have a visible role on the program. Though he expressly told Martin Luther King he did not intend to join him in the streets (and has claimed King felt that to be a wise and prudent course of action), he called for the prosecution of whites who attacked blacks who were peacefully demonstrating to obtain the rights that should unquestionably be theirs. Still, he stopped short of articulating any practical course of action that churches or communities might take to ease racial discrimination, and he cautioned that although confrontational marches and freedom rides were effective, they might create resistance that could never be broken down. "Jim Crow must go," he told a press conference just prior to his 1962 Chicago crusade, "but I am convinced that some extreme Negro leaders are going too far and too fast." Even while Dr. King languished in the Birmingham jail in the spring of 1963, Graham told a *New York Times* interviewer that his "good personal friend" would be well-advised to "put on the brakes a little bit," that his timing was "questionable," and that blacks and whites alike would benefit from "a period of quietness in which moderation prevails."

In the summer of 1963, Graham not only refused to take part in the March on Washington, the most memorable civil rights demonstration in

American history, but challenged King's most arresting image: "I have a dream that my four little children one day will live in a nation where they will not be judged by the color of their skin, but by the content of their character." Graham had no quibble with the dream, but his theology and philosophy of change left no room for such a vision of harmony. "Only when Christ comes again," he said, "will the little white children of Alabama walk hand in hand with little black children." In the meantime even proximate harmony could be achieved only by "Christians working in love from both sides." Graham's apparent discounting of human efforts to achieve social justice and his criticism of clergymen who make "the race issue their gospel" dismayed black churchmen. A Presbyterian pastor who actively supported the Coliseum crusade in Los Angeles nevertheless lamented that Graham chose neither to condemn racism nor to advocate equal rights during the campaign, despite the national preoccupation with these issues. The president of the National Association of Negro Evangelicals lamented that "Dr. Graham consistently fails to appreciate the intensity of this great social dilemma which cries out to be met head-on." As for Graham's contention that forced integration would not work, the black clergyman said simply and accurately, "It has worked time and time again."

When a racist cabal set a bomb that exploded in a Sunday-school room of Birmingham's Sixteenth Street Baptist Church, killing four little black girls, Graham not only shared in the revulsion felt throughout the nation but joined Drew Pearson in spearheading a fund drive to rebuild the damaged church. On the strength of this effort, and because of his long-standing policy on integrated crusades, BGEA associate evangelist Howard Jones and another pro-Graham minister, Ralph Bell, were able to persuade the National Association of Negro Evangelicals to pass a resolution commending Graham for his efforts on behalf of racial justice and harmony, but the sentiment was far from unanimous, and it is doubtful the resolution would have passed without active lobbying by Jones and Bell. Two years later, Bell would join BGEA as a full-time associate evangelist.

Apart from his unavoidable entanglement in the race issue, Graham was far less involved in social and political matters during the Kennedy administration than in the previous decade. He decried the Supreme Court's decisions to ban devotional Bible reading and prayer from public schools but commended Kennedy for opposing federal aid to parochial schools. He continued to describe Communist advances as an apocalyptic threat that was "almost surely a sign of the Second Coming" and regarded "a virile, dynamic, orthodox Christianity" as the only philosophical weapon with "any possibility of combatting the Communist conspiracy," but he repudiated John Birch Society founder Robert Welch's charge that America's pulpits were filled with legions of covert Communists, noting that he had never met a single minister in the United States whom he suspected of being a Communist. As a further sign of his retreat from the hard-line anticommunism he espoused in the 1950s, he recommended that the United States send massive quantities of surplus food to Communist China during a 1961 food shortage. "We are not at war with the people of China," he said. "I feel we have a moral and spiritual responsibility to share our surpluses with them. We cannot compromise with their ideology, but we should feed them when they are hungry."

In part, Graham's diminishing dogmatism reflected a growing awareness, nurtured by travel and association with a wide range of religious and political leaders on six continents, that the Manichaean dichotomies of Fundamentalism were a bit too neat, that people and positions and motives were often more complicated than he had once believed. But at least part of his lower political profile stemmed from the fact that his man, Richard Nixon, had lost the election, and the winner, John Kennedy, still regarded him with some reserve. The two men exchanged Christmas greetings and sat next to each other at the Presidential Prayer Breakfast, and Graham recalled that Kennedy told him he was the only Protestant minister he felt comfortable with, but he admitted he was never in the First Family's private quarters, and visited the Oval Office no more than three or four times. It was said that the President could mimic the evangelist's distinctive manner of speaking, that he "gritted his teeth sometimes" when they were together, and that Jackie Kennedy saw no reason whatever to cultivate closer ties with the Graham family. The coolness was mutual. In January 1963, Graham implied that four years of Kennedy leadership would be quite enough by gratuitously remarking that "John Connally has the necessary abilities to be President of the United States, but I'm not making an endorsement. I'm just giving advice to the Democratic Party."

Despite their limited contact, Graham respected Kennedy and doubtless hoped for a closer relationship in the future. In that spirit he had grave misgivings about Kennedy's trip to Texas in 1963. Not long before the trip, he tried to contact the President through Senator Smathers. When he told Smathers of his fear, based on conversations with his many friends in Texas, that the situation in Dallas would be tense, perhaps even dangerous, Smathers assured him that "the President probably already knows that," but indicated he would convey the message to Kennedy. Graham never heard from the White House and decided he was being unnecessarily apprehensive. "I had such a strong feeling about it," he recalled, "but then it occurred to me what a ridiculous thing it was, and I didn't pursue the matter any further." A few days later, while playing golf with T. W. Wilson at a club near Montreat, Graham received word that the President and Governor Connally had been shot. They sped to a nearby BGEA-owned radio station, where Graham went on the air while Wilson called Parkland Hospital in Dallas. By a fluke of timing, they learned Kennedy was dead before the national media released the news. Graham recalls that he withheld confirmation of the death until the major networks announced it; Wilson remembers holding a scribbled note to the glass on the booth where Graham was speaking and believes the evangelist may in fact have been the first to tell a public audience, however small, that the nation had lost its leader. In the days that followed, Graham was, of course, repeatedly asked for comments on the tragedy. The death of the young President, whom he described as "intensely interested in spiritual things," was, he conceded, "a terrible thing," but he hoped some good might yet come of it. Noting the marked increase in the number of people who attended church on the Sunday following the assassination, he observed that "we must have a terrible shock sometimes to rouse us out of our spiritual neglect and apathy."

The decade following John Kennedy's death hardly delivered the revival Billy Graham dared hope for in the aftermath of the assassination, but it did produce a notable resuscitation of his own involvement in affairs of state. His well-known friendship with Richard Nixon, coupled with his awkward involvement in the 1960 campaign, made it seem likely that his return to favor at the White House would probably have to await the return to power of the GOP. Insofar as Graham imagined that to be the case, he underestimated Lyndon Johnson.

19

Billy and Lyndon

Billy Graham and Lyndon Johnson met through Sid Richardson shortly after Johnson was elected to the Senate. They had not been close friends but liked one another and had maintained cordial contact, largely at Johnson's initiative. Immediately after Kennedy's assassination, Graham contacted the new President to let him know he would be praying for him and stood ready to help in any way he could during the difficult days that lay ahead. Whether for spiritual or political reasons, Johnson eagerly accepted the offer. "Your message met the need," he wrote. "The knowledge that one of God's greatest messengers was seeking Divine Counsel in my behalf provided me with the strong source of strength, courage, and comfort during the extremely trying days immediately after the tragic event in Dallas." Within a week after he moved into the White House, Johnson summoned Graham to Washington. A visit scheduled for fifteen minutes stretched to five hours as two farm boys who had ridden their talent, ambition, and energy to the pinnacle of their respective professions found they had more to offer each other than either had ever imagined.

That first visit was not all solace and solicitude. Graham had brought Grady Wilson with him, and Johnson insisted they all take a swim in the White House pool. "I was somewhat startled," Graham recalled, "because they didn't have any bathing suits. You just went as you were." Afterward, Grady regaled the group with stories so outrageously funny that Johnson called for an aide to make notes so that he could remember them and as an accomplished storyteller himself, perhaps put them to good use in another setting. Graham enjoyed Johnson's affability but felt obliged to remind the new President of his need to rely on God's guidance and power. Johnson's great-grandfather had been an Evangelical preacher, and Graham had no qualms about stating just what the Reverend Mr. Baines would have said or done in this or that situation, since he assumed that the good cleric's views would approximate his own. Graham conceded that Johnson probably recognized the value of associating himself with a major religious symbol at a time of national mourning and crisis but felt certain his interest in matters spiritual was genuine. A few days later, he told the press that Lyndon Johnson was "the best qualified man we've had in the White House," a man who would doubtless "provide moral leadership for the country." And he told the President that, as God had been with George Washington at Valley Forge and with Abraham Lincoln during the Civil War, he would now stand close to Lyndon Johnson, ready to strengthen him when the awesome burdens of his office threatened to overwhelm him.

Not long after reestablishing ties to the White House, Graham found himself at the center of a rumor that could have strained his friendship with Johnson. For several years, Dallas oil billionaire H. L. Hunt had admired Graham and his team, particularly Grady Wilson, whom he wanted to support in a series of wildcat revivals along the entire Gulf coast. Grady turned him down, at least in part because Hunt thought BGEA's policy of cooperating with local clergymen and organizing laypeople was foolishness: "You don't need the preachers, Grady. They'll just get in your way. Forget all that other stuff. Just go from town to town." Hunt let Grady off the hook, but he apparently tried out an even bolder notion on Billy Graham: an offer of 6 million dollars if Graham would run for president against Lyndon Johnson. According to Grady Wilson and other close friends, the old tycoon reached Graham in the Shamrock Hotel in Houston, informing him that the money would be deposited in his personal bank account if he allowed his name to be put in nomination at the Republican convention that summer. Witnesses insist that Billy took no more than fifteen seconds to tell his would-be benefactor that he was flattered but had no interest in relinquishing a post he regarded as more important than the presidency. Given his notorious penchant for wasting huge sums of money on conservative pipe dreams, particularly those in which unfettered capitalist individualism and uncritical patriotism were served up in a stew of Scripture, Hunt either could not imagine that Graham would actually refuse such an offer or sought to force his hand. In any case, he leaked his plan to the media, which, along with the entire Scripps Howard newspaper chain, ran the story immediately. That evening, Walter Cronkite told viewers of CBS News that evangelist Billy Graham was considering a bid for the presidency.

Prior to the 1952 election, Graham speculated that he might be elected president if he were to run on a platform calling the nation "back to God, back to Christ, and back to the Bible," but that seemed clearly to be a rhetorical ploy aimed at influencing the bona fide candidates to take a similar line. In the interim he had waved off several opportunities to run for public office in North Carolina, and his instant refusal of Hunt's offer seemed genuine. Still, the *Houston Press* reported that a source close to Graham indicated that "he is deeply interested in the opportunity for service, and ... is giving earnest and prayerful consideration to the idea," adding that if he did accept a draft, "it would be as a Republican." If Graham had such second thoughts, his friends and family quickly dispelled them. Ruth called from Montreat to tell him that she did not think the American people would vote for a divorced president, and if he left the ministry to enter politics, he would certainly have a divorce on his hands. Hunt's call came on a Friday. Graham proposed to call a press conference for the following Monday to deny the rumors. Calvin Thielman, pastor of the Presbyterian church in Montreat and an old friend of Lyndon Johnson's as well, told him that would be like waiting three days to deny that he was running around on his wife. "You deny that immediately," Thielman insisted. "You are not going to run for President. No use to fool with that one." Graham summoned the press, and by Sunday morning his short career as a putative candidate for national office had ended. H. L. Hunt was not the only party who felt the press conference was a mistake; the *Christian Century*, showing little sympathy for Graham's unsought plight, hooted at the entire affair. "This denial of an intention nobody except perhaps a few of his entourage suspected he entertained was remarkable," the *Century* observed. "That he should feel it necessary ... to take himself out of a race few even dreamed he might enter indicates just how far out of touch with political reality a man who stands in front of crowds can get."

If Lyndon Johnson considered Billy Graham a potential rival, he did not show it. Contact between the two men appears to have been limited during 1964. Graham invited the President to attend a crusade, and though he did not accept, Johnson reciprocated with an invitation for the Grahams to spend a night in the White House, which they did accept. That visit, Graham's first overnight stay in the private quarters—in recalling it, he noted that Richard Nixon had never been invited to Eisenhower's private quarters during his entire eight years as vice-president—sealed the friendship and led Graham to urge the President to "call on us any time we could ever be of the slightest service to you." Graham also forged ties with such key members of the Johnson administration as Bill Moyers and Marvin Watson.

Not long after her father's overnight visit to the White House, Anne Graham, then a freshman in college, attended a rally for Barry Goldwater and declared herself in favor of the Republican candidate. Johnson may have figured Anne was voicing sentiments uttered at the family dinner table, but he overlooked that possibility when he called Graham to say, "Billy, I know about those things. I have two daughters of my own, and I have trouble sometimes controlling what they say. When the election is over, you bring Anne up to the White House. I'd like to get acquainted with her." Conservative political operatives, however, seized on what Johnson chose to ignore. In a well-organized last-ditch effort to stem the tide that seemed certain to carry the President to a crashing victory, Republican campaign offices around the country received telegrams indicating that Billy Graham would endorse Goldwater if enough people asked him to. In the few remaining days before the November election, Graham received over a million telegrams, some bearing lists of names stretching three feet in length. The Western

Union office in Charlotte called in extra operators, used emergency circuits, and operated at full tilt around the clock. Circuits in Asheville were similarly jammed, and tens of thousands of additional messages poured into Montreat by airplane and motor courier. The manager of the telegraph office in Asheville declared that in thirty-five years of working for Western Union, he had never heard of such a campaign directed at one individual. On hearing of the avalanche in Asheville, Lyndon Johnson placed another call, delivering the simple, ostensibly avuncular message, "Now Billy, you stay out of politics." He also took the precaution of inviting Graham to spend the weekend before the election at the White House, where he would not be tempted to read his mail. Whether from preference or prudence, Graham disappointed Goldwater backers by refraining from endorsing either candidate, but when the election turned out as all the polls predicted, he congratulated the victorious President on his "tremendous victory" and declared expansively that he was "convinced that you were not only the choice of the American people—but of God. You are as truly a servant of God as was your great-grandfather Baines when he preached the gospel." As for being impressed with the telegram campaign, he observed dryly that the money "might have been better spent for evangelism."

The election behind them, Graham and Johnson unleashed their enthusiasm on each other. Billy led the Protestant prayer at the inauguration and preached at a special dedication service Johnson arranged at the National City Christian Church. Using as his text the words from a letter that legendary Texas hero Sam Houston had written to Johnson's grandfather, Graham exhorted the President, his cabinet, the justices of the Supreme Court, and a delegation from Congress not to forget the spiritual dimensions of leadership. Over the next four years, White House files reveal a continuous exchange of letters, cards, and small gifts between the two men, as well as repeated reports of intercessory prayer aimed at everything from hastening Johnson's recovery from the flu to supplying him with deep draughts of supernatural wisdom.

Johnson and Graham, of course, had much to give each other. For Billy, just to be welcome once again at the White House meant that he and his people—good, decent, God-fearing, Bible-believing, patriotic, middle-class, middle-American folk—were back in charge, or at least back in favor, as many felt they had not been during the Kennedy years. More specifically, the legitimation Evangelicals worked for and won in the years after World War II had not been lost. Now, their plans to rekindle a spirit the nation had not known since the days of the Benevolent Empire could proceed apace. Beyond that reclamation of stature and staging ground for himself and his constituency, Graham clearly savored the renewed opportunity to share in the experience and secrets of presidential power. Bill Moyers has recalled how the evangelist's eyes lit up as he sat riveted with fascination while the man who wanted to be "President of All the People" talked of his hopes for the Utopian enterprise he called the War on Poverty, while the Commander in Chief explained how he personally selected bombing targets in a much darker war in Southeast Asia, and while the Great Manipulator shared stories of the peccadilloes and peculiarities of powerful men he intended to turn to his will.

Graham always seemed surprised that famous and important people sought him out as assiduously as he sought them, and for reasons not remarkably dissimilar. Neither did he seem to realize fully, though he was certainly not innocent of all understanding on this score, that he gave as good as he got in such associations. Without question, and apart from the genuine affection he appears to have felt for Graham and the intrinsic satisfactions he found in their friendship, Lyndon Johnson understood the advantages of being Billy's buddy. If Billy Graham was the President's friend, then millions of Americans would conclude that the President must be a good man, a decent man, a noble man, perhaps even a Christian man. And if he possessed those qualities, then his causes—his War on Poverty, his civil rights act, his effort to preserve freedom and democracy in Southeast Asia—must also be good, decent, noble, perhaps even Christian, and therefore precisely the causes Christian folk ought to support. "Johnson always had a high appreciation of men as symbols," Moyers observed. "[If] a man comes clothed in symbols like Billy did, you never have to ask that man to do anything for you; he's done everything just by being there.... So Billy didn't have to do anything to help him, and Billy, in turn, never asked him for a thing. He was helped by being there as much as Johnson was helped by having him there." Public-opinion polls regularly placed both men at or quite near the top of the list of the world's most-admired men. Each clearly shared in that high view of the other, and each cherished the other's appreciation. Johnson once acknowledged that he often contacted Graham to "get a new injection" of confidence and optimism, recalling that during one particularly difficult period "when I was being called a crook and a thug and all," he invited Graham to spend a weekend with him, and "we bragged on each other. I told him he was the greatest religious leader in the world and he said I was the greatest political leader."

Perhaps because his own political career and opinions owed little to his meager academic training at the tiny teacher's college he attended in San Marcos, Texas, Johnson appeared to feel that Graham, another man whose success and appeal to millions of people owed more to intuition and personal qualities than to formal education, might be a resource fully as valuable as the Harvard brain trust inherited from John Kennedy. According to Graham and several associates, Johnson frequently sought his counsel on a variety of issues, ranging from general guidance about the War on Poverty to an offer to let him try to figure some way to cut 10 million dollars from a proposed budget. After Sargent Shriver flew to Montreat in a helicopter to enlist his aid, Graham did participate in a film supporting the poverty program but claims he generally limited his involvement to spiritual matters. Johnson did not always accept this reticence at face value. Shortly before the 1964 Democratic National Convention, the two families were having dinner at the White House, and the President asked Graham who he thought would be a good vice-president. Ruth immediately gave her husband a sharp kick under the table and interjected that "Bill really shouldn't get into political matters." Graham quickly agreed and Johnson let it drop for the moment, but when Lady Bird and Ruth walked into an adjoining room after the meal, the President grabbed Graham's arm and said with the insistent intensity few men found easy to resist, "Now Billy, tell me what you really think about that." Without taking credit for the eventual outcome, Graham has acknowledged that he recommended Hubert Humphrey.

In keeping with his long-standing tendency to interpret friendly behavior or polite attention as evidence of deep spiritual interest, Graham perceived Lyndon Johnson to be a somewhat more pious man than did many of his colleagues or various secular observers. It is of course possible to fake religiosity, and politicians in both ancient and recent memory have demonstrated notable talent for that particular artifice. Perhaps less well appreciated is the fact that it is also possible to hold deeply felt (if not always precisely articulated) religious beliefs, including belief in the worth of religion, right alongside and perhaps in conscious tension with patently secular and instrumental beliefs, values, and habits of mind and body. Billy Graham acknowledged this duality within Johnson. He understood that he served to legitimate Johnson to an Evangelical constituency, particularly in the South and Southwest. "I think he was attracted to me at least partially because I was well-known in Texas.... I think he was more afraid of what the editor of the *Baptist Standard* [a weekly Southern Baptist newspaper] was going to say about him than of the *Washington Post* or the *New York Times*." But the memory of a mother who hoped he would be a preacher, to follow in the steps of her own grandfather, also burdened the President's *complex soul, and his friendship with Graham forced him to struggle under that weight.* "He *wanted to live up to his mother's goals*," observed Graham, who knew something of what that could mean. "I think he had a conflict within himself about religion. He wanted to go all the way in his commitment to Christ. He knew what it meant to be 'saved' or 'lost,' using our terminology, and he knew what it was to be 'born again.' And yet he somehow felt that he never quite had that experience. I think he tried to make up for it by having many of the outward forms of religion, in the sense of going to church almost fanatically, even while he was President. Sometimes he'd go to church three times on a Sunday."

In addition to his penchant for attending public worship, which might easily be dismissed as a political gambit, Johnson manifested a less-visible piety that, even if it reminded one more of a St. Bernard than a St. Francis, was probably genuine. Graham recalled that "a number of times I had prayer with him in his bedroom at the White House, usually early in the morning. He would get out of bed and get on his knees while I prayed. I never had very many people do that." The President also liked to have people read the Bible to him—"He liked the plain-language versions"—and felt that others could benefit equally. On occasion, he would summon members of his staff a day or two after these devotional sessions, read the same passages to them that Graham or some other preacher had read to him, and admonish his minions to apply the truths they contained both to affairs of state and to their personal behavior. Johnson also believed that those who worked with him could benefit from some old-fashioned gospel preaching and sometimes invited Graham to conduct services and preach at Camp David or at his ranch on the Pedernales River in the Texas Hill Country. And if it seemed too much of an imposition to ask Graham to preach, Johnson always had a worthy backup he could call on: his own great-grandfather Baines. Trying hard but unsuccessfully to conceal his amusement at the memory of the scene, Graham recalled an impromptu service Johnson arranged at Camp David: "Ruth and I got up a little bit later than the others did. We walked over to the President's cabin, and there out on the porch several people were standing around, including [Attorney General Nicholas] Katzenbach and several other Jewish people, and there was Jack Valenti, an Italian Catholic, reading a sermon that Johnson's great grandfather had preached, on 'How to Be Saved.' The President thought they ought to hear it, and everybody had to listen."

The White House was not the only venue where Graham drew lavish attention during this period. For two six-month periods spanning the summers of 1964 and 1965, the Billy Graham Pavilion at the World's Fair in Flushing Meadow Park, New York, gave five million visitors a slick high-tech overview of his worldwide ministry and an opportunity to hear a well-polished, wide-screen, soul-winning sermon. Most Protestant denominations and parachurch organizations presented their case to fairgoers in the sprawling Protestant Pavilion. Graham could easily have obtained a section of that exhibit hall, but he dreamed of something grander and more distinctive. Soon after plans for the fair were announced, Robert Ferm and George Wilson met with the fair's director, Robert Moses, to discuss a separate BGEA-sponsored pavilion. Moses not only agreed to allow Graham to have his own building but promised to assign him a prime spot not far from the main gate. Typically, Billy embraced the idea with great enthusiasm at first, then suffered severe second thoughts. While recuperating from pneumonia, he decided the pavilion was too grandiose and was about to back out when one of his board members counseled him never to make a major decision when he was ill. When asked for his opinion on the matter, Wheaton president V. Raymond Edman reminded him of the huge response D. L. Moody had stirred at the

Chicago World's Fair in 1893. The opportunity to repeat and perhaps surpass an accomplishment of one of his heroes appealed to Graham. After George Wilson, who did not customarily spend money with much relish, declared that BGEA could afford to build the pavilion, Graham's enthusiasm returned. When the fair opened in the spring of 1964, one of its most prominent and recognizable landmarks was the Billy Graham Pavilion, designed by famed architect Edward Durrell Stone and crowned by a 117-foot tower covered with 4,000 gold-anodized disks.

Inside the pavilion, visitors found exhibits tracing Graham's ministry from the first great crusade in the Canvas Cathedral to the triumphant tours of six continents and dozens of countries. The central focus of the structure was a 350-seat theater in which curious visitors—more than one million in all, from more than 125 countries—saw Billy Graham, twelve times a day for twelve months, larger than life on the sweeping Todd-AO screen, and using a translation system that enabled them to hear "each man in his own language," as on the Day of Pentecost, listened to him deliver a comprehensive jeremiad that ended with the inevitable call to accept Jesus Christ as savior. Critics blasted the fair's religious exhibits for sharing in the general atmosphere of "chaos and greed" they saw pervading the exposition. Graham offered a more upbeat assessment. The New York World's Fair, at which nations from all over the world were sharing the brightest and most beautiful aspects of their respective cultures, was, he declared, "an indication that man is on the threshold of paradise." As for the Billy Graham Pavilion in particular, an editorial in *Decision* magazine pronounced that "there is definitely a taste of heaven about the place."

The World's Fair film, entitled *Man in the Fifth Dimension*, reflected the evolution Graham's film ministry had undergone since the days of *Mr. Texas* and *Oiltown, U.S.A.* Amateurish as they were, those first films proved so popular with church audiences that Graham used them to launch a reasonably successful series of films. The real breakthrough, however, came with the production of *The Restless Ones* in 1963. The full-length black-and-white picture told the story of the Wintons, an upper-middle-class family that had begun to lose its moorings in a sea of Southern California secularity but had found new meaning and the ability to withstand the temptations of sex and alcohol after attending Billy Graham's great crusade in the Los Angeles Coliseum. The film is far from subtle, and its attempts to capture the flavor of youthful wildness and early-sixties argot are often amusing. Still, to the young people most likely to see it, it apparently served as a strong warning against giving in to raging hormones. During the first four years after its release, it was seen by 4.5 million people and stimulated 346,000 known decisions. It also paid for itself. "On this one," film-ministry evangelist Dave Barr explained, "we decided to charge admission for the first time. This was a whole new concept, and we tried it in several cities to see if it would work.

If the churches were too critical or if it looked like we were going to get crucified, then we would back away from it." The films would be shown in public auditoriums or commercial theaters on a "four-walled" basis in which the sponsoring committee rented the facility and were then free to offer the invitation, counsel inquirers, or do anything else they felt was appropriate. The first big showing was at the 5,000-seat Aerie Crown Theater in Chicago. Barr recalled that "the Aerie Crown had a ninety-foot screen, and when you stood alongside the screen, you could see everybody's face in the light reflected off the screen, even though they didn't know you were looking at them. We'd have hundreds of young people in the audience, and as soon as the lights went out, you could see them start hugging and kissing and playing around with each other. But when Billy came on, his finger must have looked forty-five feet long. And when he started to preach, those kids would just sit there spellbound. The story is good, but not super. But his message was just so powerful; I think it's one of the best ever put on film. By the time he gave the invitation, the Holy Spirit had taken over. It was every bit as effective as when Billy is there in person."

Encouraged by the success of the Chicago showing, the Graham team decided to experiment further and met similar enthusiasm in other cities. At no cost to BGEA, dairies placed ads on the side of milk cartons and bottling companies run by Christians inserted fliers in six-packs of their soft drinks, so that by the time the film opened, a sellout had been guaranteed. In Albuquerque, a scheduled one-week run in a conventional movie theater stretched to three weeks. In San Antonio, the engagement lasted twelve weeks, and approximately one fourth of the audience responded to the invitation, a far higher percentage than Graham ever reaped in person.

Despite the adolescent awkwardness that accompanied rapid growth, the new approach was a walloping success. Dave Barr credited the intrinsic impact of the medium itself. "Films are so real," he observed. "Several years after *The Restless Ones* came out, a lady who had seen it in New Mexico wrote Billy to tell him she had seen Kim Darby [who played an unmarried pregnant girl in *The Restless Ones*] in another show on television. She said, 'I've often wondered what happened to April and her baby. Thank God, she's happily married and the baby is OK.' Later, we had another film about two guys that ran a gas station in Denver. A man wrote in to say that if he could find the station, he would give them his business for the rest of his life. Then he added a P.S.: 'Do you know if they give S & H Green Stamps?' That's precious, but it's also frightening to realize what a powerful tool film can be. I wouldn't have stayed with [the film ministry] for more than two years after *Mr. Texas*, no matter how much they paid me, if it hadn't been for the soul-winning aspects, but a tool that can make that kind of impact on people's minds can be used to win people to Christ. That's why God has given us this medium."

While Graham's celluloid self addressed millions of pilgrims from around the world, he gave his personal attention to a more modest aggregation situated at the Hub of the Universe. He had not been back to Boston for an extended campaign since his stunning victories in 1950, and many of the ministers and leading laymen who remembered that visit longed for his return and were primed to make the most of it. The 1964 crusade was typical in most respects. Instead of winding up in Boston Garden, Graham started there, filling it for each of ten nights, then addressing a throng of 75,000 at a closing rally on Boston Common. On the political and public relations front, the evangelist visited Ted Kennedy, hospitalized by severe injuries suffered in a plane crash, and drew praise from Governor Endicott Peabody, both for the contribution he was making to Boston's spiritual and moral life and for the quality of his sound system, which Peabody wished the Garden would purchase for its own use. Graham also professed to see signs of a growing interest in matters spiritual, signs he had not seen fourteen years earlier, signs that made him suspect Boston might be on the verge of a great religious awakening.

Billy's rosy vision was understandable. After a Saturday-evening service, he made an unscheduled but well-photographed visit to the Combat Zone, Boston's raunchy red-light district, where he brought traffic to a standstill as squealing young girls flocked around him while patrons of the tattered melange of bars, cafes, and strip joints poured into the street to catch a glimpse of the man who condemned their way of life each night. One club owner approached him to say, "I'd be proud if you stepped inside." When he entered the dark, smoky den of iniquity, the band stopped and the emcee, accustomed to welcoming "the very lovely and talented Miss Velva La-Voom," invited him to say a few words to the assemblage. Perhaps remembering that awkward gathering at the air force base in Newfoundland, when he and Chuck Templeton found themselves facing a crowd of servicemen more interested in girls than the gospel, Graham observed that "this is a very unusual congregation." But as on that occasion years before, he remembered his personal dictum, "This one thing I do," and he did it. He told the boozy auditors that they needed to fill their souls with a spirit that did not come in bottles, and he urged them to attend church the next morning. Guilt is magic, and darkened rooms are full of it. Instead of tossing him out, as a Tampa barman had done twenty-five years earlier, they applauded heartily and banged their glasses on the bar, and as he picked his way past the crowded tables, shaking every hand he could reach and radiating compassionate goodwill for people whose pleasure he could scarcely comprehend, several hundred new sinful seekers greeted his reappearance on the street with a rousing cheer. Despite that gratifying response, not many of the Combat Zone's denizens made it to the Garden. The crusade crowds, as usual, were heavily populated with sinners of a less spectacular sort. Reporters could not help noticing that on the whole, the legion of believers who packed the Garden each night were rather different from those who gathered to sip champagne while Arthur Fiedler conducted the Boston Pops or to bellow their outrage when Bruin tough guy Teddy Green went to the penalty box for high-sticking some fancy-skating Canadian. On the contrary, Graham's crowds were sober, almost homespun, in appearance and demeanor. "You would think you were in Kansas or Indiana or some place else," one journalist wrote. "It doesn't seem quite like Boston." But it was Boston, and those earnest people whose presence the journalist had previously failed to notice came in such numbers that in an echo of the 1950 campaign, Graham elected to go back to the Garden for an additional week after a few days off. The high point of the second stage, one that would have a lasting impact on Graham's ministry, was a meeting with Boston's fabled Roman Catholic prelate, Richard Cardinal Cushing.

Cardinal Cushing had long looked on Graham with favor. During the 1950 campaign, he had written an editorial entitled "Bravo, Billy!" for the diocesan newspaper. Just before the 1964 crusade got under way, he sounded another approving note by announcing that the crusade would "surely be of great importance for many Christians in the Greater Boston area," and assuring Graham that he and other Catholics would be praying for God's blessing on him in the expectation that he would "lead many to the knowledge of Our Lord." Because Cushing flew off to attend the Second Vatican Council in Rome immediately after making that statement, the two men did not meet during the crusade's first phase, but Graham made a point of stressing his own "tremendous admiration" for the cardinal. As soon as Graham announced he was staying on, America's favorite cardinal and the man some called "the Protestant Pope" began an amusing game of Muhammad and the Mountain. A diocesan spokesman later claimed that Graham initiated the request for a meeting, but Robert Ferm insisted he was present in the crusade office when the cardinal's secretary called to ask if Billy would come to the chancery. Sensitive to issues of relative prestige and still not convinced Catholicism was a benign force, Ferm vetoed that suggestion but indicated the cardinal would be welcome to drop by Graham's hotel. After a few minutes of consultation, the secretary called back to say that the cardinal would be happy to meet Billy on neutral ground and was offering to have their meeting presented live on local television. Ferm was skeptical. "How can you just have the television people schedule something like that?" he asked. The answer was simple: "The cardinal owns the TV station."

The forty-five-minute televised conversation surely rivaled any of Graham's mutual-admiration sessions with Lyndon Johnson. The cardinal, dressed in street clothes rather than in the ornate robes of his office, generously declared that "I have never known of a religious crusade that was more effective" than Graham's and assured the evangelist and his supporters that "although we Catholics do not join with them in body, yet in spirit and heart we unite with them in praying God's blessing upon this Christian and Christlike experience in our community." He urged Catholic young people to attend the crusade services with no fear of disloyalty to their church, assuring them that Graham's message "is one of Christ crucified, and no Catholic can do anything but become a better Catholic from hearing him.... I'm one hundred percent for Dr. Graham. He is extraordinarily gifted. The hand of God must be upon him." Then, in a mild rebuke to priests who might contrast Graham's populist appeal with the majesty of the Roman liturgy, Cushing added that if the Catholic Church had half a dozen men of Graham's caliber, he would stop worrying about its future in America. Never one to be outcomplimented, Graham professed to regard his new friend as "the leading ecumenist in America," lavished further praise on Pope John XXIII and his successor, Paul VI, and heralded Vatican II as a major step in dissipating the clouds of resentment and mistrust that had separated Catholics and Protestants. As for himself, he announced that he felt "much closer to Roman Catholic traditions than to some of the more liberal Protestants."

While most observers either praised or paid little attention to the conversation, some in both camps showed discomfort at its amicable spirit. On reading newspaper accounts of Cushing's endorsement of Graham, a leading Catholic official in New Hampshire insisted that the cardinal had been misquoted. In the Graham camp, Robert Ferm assured a troubled supporter that the evangelist had not really meant to imply that Catholics might be closer to the truth than some Protestants. But both men had meant what they said, leading Graham to observe that in contrast to the rancor and suspicion that attended the 1960 election, "this is sort of a new day." The encounter thus stands as a significant marker on the course that Graham steadfastly chose to follow, a course that led him from the narrow confines of the strictest sort of sectarianism to the open ground upon which one is reluctant to deny anyone the right to be called, if not brother, at least neighbor.

Graham opened 1965 with a quite modest crusade in Hawaii, where the average crowd was less than 6,600. He followed that with two weeks of preaching in Alabama, including a rally at the all-black Tuskegee Institute, an eight-day effort in Copenhagen, and ten-day campaigns in Denver and Houston. After more than fifteen years of independent ministry, Graham and his team could organize and execute a major crusade in their sleep, but a back-region episode at the Houston crusade revealed that Billy did not feel himself capable of flying on automatic pilot. That crusade, scheduled to be one of the first nonsporting events to be held in the brand-new Astrodome, had to be postponed several weeks when Graham underwent prostate surgery in late summer. During his recuperation period, he called several members of his board to Montreat and confided to them that he was considering backing out of the Houston meeting because he was not certain he would be able to preach. They assumed he was still feeling weak from the effects of his surgery and urged him to stick to the plan, to which he agreed. At a subsequent board meeting, however, he told Carloss Morris, a prominent Houston lawyer who had played a key role in organizing the crusade, that he was still not sure he could preach. Morris did not take him too seriously, assuming that the problem was physical and would clear up with a few more days of rest. But a night or two before the opening service, Graham addressed a precrusade gathering on the University of Houston campus. The next day, during a golf game at the River Oaks Country Club, he told Morris that he could preach after all. "I'd been speaking about five minutes last night," he reported, "and I felt the Holy Spirit take over, and it's back. I can preach. We are going to have a great meeting in Houston." Shaking his head at the memory, Morris finally understood what Graham had been trying to tell him: "Billy just didn't know whether or not the Lord was going to have his hand on him again so he'd be able to preach. I was astonished, but he had really been in doubt up to that point."

The Houston crusade was notable not only for the late arrival of the Holy Spirit but also because it marked the first time that Graham was able to persuade a sitting President to attend one of his services. The President and First Lady flew over from their Texas Hill Country ranch to be present at the climactic Sunday-afternoon service, at which 61,000 packed the spectacular domed arena. Reporters noted that Mrs. Johnson paid attention, but the President, for all his putative piety, spent most of the afternoon chatting with the Astrodome's visionary builder, Judge Roy Hofheinz, whose private box they shared. Johnson did, however, register his appreciation when Graham lambasted Vietnam protesters, comparing them unfavorably to the more religiously minded young people who had come to the dome that afternoon to show their loyalty to their Lord and their President.

Graham's position on Vietnam, like that of most of his countrymen, was never as definite as his stand on World War II and the Korean conflict. On the other hand, as a loyal friend and staunch patriot accustomed to giving those in authority the benefit of the doubt, he tended to take the President's side. And even though he had toned down his anti-Communist tirades of a decade earlier, he still warned against the encroachment of "Communist tyranny," urged his fellow Americans not to listen "to the siren song which would have us believe that the tide has turned or that communism has changed its goal for world revolution," and insisted that it was incumbent upon the United States to maintain "the strongest military establishment on earth." Early in 1965, during the Hawaii crusade, he asked a crowd to pray that President Johnson might obtain wisdom to help him lead the United States out of the "mess in Southeast Asia." The President, he reminded them, had inherited, not started, the war in Vietnam, but it was his painful responsibility to do something about it, and quickly. If the United States dallied, Graham speculated, "We either face an all-out war with Red China, or a retreat that will cause us to lose face throughout Asia. Make no mistake about it. We are in a mess." In an address to the Denver Press Club in late summer, he said, "I have no sympathy for those clergymen who [urge] the U.S. to get out of Vietnam. Communism has to be stopped somewhere, whether it is in Hawaii or on the West Coast. The President believes it should be stopped in Vietnam." Later in the year, he pointed out that "95 percent of the Congress is back of the President," adding that "these people know the facts." Such statements, infrequent as they were, led many war critics to conclude that Graham was a hawk. Even he recognized the charge was not entirely unfounded. In a letter to Bill Moyers in October of that year, he complained that he was "constantly taking a beating from some of these extremists because of my support of the President's Vietnam policy."

Graham had less problem with Johnson's Great Society programs, since their aims generally coincided with his own generous impulses toward those in need. He continued to believe in the worth of industry and self-discipline, but he also felt that those more favored by ability and circumstance had an obligation to share with those of meaner estate. In a departure from the pietistic individualism that characterized much of Evangelicalism, he acknowledged that "there is a social aspect of the Gospel that many people ignore. Jesus was interested in the hungry, the diseased, and the illiterate. A great deal of his time and preaching was taken up with this aspect of the ministry. The church should be deeply concerned about the poor, the illiterate, the diseased, and those oppressed by tyranny or prejudice." Graham understood that the problem extended beyond American shores and, moreover, that America could not pretend that the poverty of Third World countries was unrelated to its own affluence. "Three-fifths of the world live in squalor, misery, and hunger," he thundered. "Too long have the privileged few exploited and ignored the underprivileged millions of our world. Our selfishness is at long last catching up with us. Unless we begin to act, to share and to do something about this great army of starving humanity, God will judge us."

Graham's clearest stand on social issues continued to be in the realm of race relations. A few months after the bombing of Birmingham's Sixteenth Street Baptist Church, and in the face of acute misgivings on the part of city officials and dissension within both black and white ministerial associations, he held a fully integrated United Evangelistic Rally in that city's 60,000-seat municipal stadium on the afternoon of Easter Sunday. Threats of violence from both black and white racists limited the crowd to no more than 35,000 people, but that number was divided almost evenly between blacks and whites, who appeared to go out of their way to be friendly to each other. In his sermon, "The Great Reconciliation," Graham decried the hatred and prejudice that was tearing communities apart but offered no concrete recommendations for solving the problems of segregation. A week later, however, speaking before the annual meeting of the National Association of Evangelicals, he said, "We should have been leading the way to racial justice but we failed. Let's confess it, let's admit it, and let's do something about it." In recognition of these statements, moderate as they were, the George Washington Carver Memorial Institute gave Graham its Supreme Award of Merit, citing him "for outstanding contribution to the betterment of race relations and human understanding."

Not all black clergy agreed with the Carver Institute's assessment. Most accepted Graham's desire for racial harmony and understanding at face value, but many felt that his tepid support of Martin Luther King, his disavowal of protest tactics, and his skepticism about legislative solutions to racial problems, including the monumental Johnson-engineered Civil Rights Act of 1964, marked him as something less than a champion of their cause. It did not help his or white Evangelicalism's ratings in black circles that *Christianity Today* had not given its endorsement to the civil rights act. One of the magazine's editors, Frank Gaebelein, wanted to offer strong editorial support for the bill when it was under discussion, but Nelson Bell demurred, sticking to his hard-line insistence that true social change could come only with genuine spiritual conversion. Graham declined to take a definite stand on the civil rights act when he addressed the NAE meeting, excusing himself by claiming he had not had time to study the bill's provisions adequately. But he had said that "Evangelicals are going to have to give an account to God for our stand on the racial crisis," and the normally cautious organization adopted a resolution favoring the legislation then before Congress.

Such perceived half measures did not persuade Graham's black critics. A columnist for a black newspaper in Chicago called him "the most magnificent phony in America" and mocked his prescription of " 'kneeling at the cross,' waiting for a miracle to transform our souls." Graham would not walk with protesters or call for open housing or desegregated churches, the journalist jabbed, because "he's too busy praying." These charges stung, and Graham tapped his top troubleshooter, Robert Ferm, to investigate the possibility of organizing a crusade especially for blacks and other minorities on Chicago's South Side. After a week of visiting church leaders in that troubled quarter, Ferm reported that it was "one of the most explosive situations I ever got into" and seemed ripe for an outbreak of serious violence. Many black churchmen, including some who participated in the 1962 crusade, now found Graham guilty of tokenism and other half measures, evincing little more commitment to racial justice than other representatives of the exploitative "white power structure"—a label, Ferm noted, that "they have borrowed from Communist ideology." Graham's deputy told of the tension he felt in one meeting as blacks shouted angrily at him and at each other and admitted that he had never appreciated just "how serious a situation we have confronting us in interracial relations" in large cities. Any crusade, he concluded, would have to originate from the black community itself, and that seemed an unlikely prospect. Apparently sobered by Ferm's evaluation, Graham scuttled plans for a South Side crusade.

Blacks may have found Billy Graham ineffectual, but Lyndon Johnson did not. When violence broke out in Selma, Alabama, and elsewhere in the South in the spring of 1965, Johnson dispatched 4,000 troops to protect freedom marchers, then encouraged Graham to visit the troubled state and use his influence to restore a measure of calm. Graham canceled meetings planned for Great Britain to comply with the President's request, and for a brief moment it appeared he was coming to appreciate Martin Luther King's advocacy of civil disobedience. "It's true I haven't been to jail yet," he conceded to students in Honolulu, but added, "I underscore the word *yet*. Maybe I haven't done all I could or should do." Then, when he returned to the mainland, he told the *New York Times* that "I never felt that we should attain our rights by illegal means, yet I confess that the demonstrations have served to arouse the conscience of the world." When he addressed the situation in Alabama, however, his observations were of the nonconfrontational, blame-diffusing sort that black and white civil rights activists so resented. Alabama had its problems, he conceded, but so did other parts of the country, and using Alabama as a whipping boy diverted attention "from other areas where the problem is just as acute." Further, as he had been saying all along, only "a spiritual and moral awakening" could solve such problems. In the meantime, all parties should obey all laws, "no matter how much we may dislike them. If the law says that I cannot march or I cannot demonstrate, I ought not to march and I ought not to demonstrate. And if the law tells me that I should send my children to a school where there are both races, I should obey that law also. Only by maintaining law and order are we going to keep our democracy and our nation great."

Unable to countenance any kind of unseemly behavior, and equally unable to denounce his fellow southerners as peculiarly wicked people, Graham nevertheless took a firm position on the side of civil rights and racial integration. Behind the scenes, he met with hundreds of pastors, laypeople, civic leaders, and even with Governor George Wallace, repeatedly calling for tolerance and understanding and confidently reporting signs of "great progress" on every hand. If blacks found this too tame, segregationists found it too radical, but Graham received an enthusiastic rating from the man who sent him to the troubled region. In a warm and effusive letter, President Johnson assured him that "you are doing a brave and fine thing for your country in your courageous effort to contribute to the understanding and brotherhood of the Americans in the South." He stressed how much the evangelist's support and prayers meant to him and urged him to visit in person whenever he

Shortly before his inauguration in January 1961,
President-elect John F. Kennedy poses with Graham,
a fervent Nixon supporter, in Palm Beach.

Lyndon Johnson once admitted that he and Billy Graham often stroked each other's egos: "I told him he was the greatest religious leader in the world and he said I was the greatest political leader," 1971.

Graham and Richard Nixon bow in prayer on the platform at the Knoxville crusade, 1970.

AP/Wide World Photos

The Nixons and the Grahams at the White House, after a 1973 Christmas service.

AP/Wide World Photos

Billy Graham, sometimes called the High Priest of American Civil Religion, addresses an audience aboard a U.S. Navy destroyer, U.S.S. *Cushing*, 1990.

Graham with President Gerald Ford, one of the evangelist's many famous golfing partners, 1974.

Photograph by Russ Busby

A throng of 250,000 people packs Brazil's Maracana Stadium to hear Graham speak.

Graham addresses a crowd estimated at more than one million people, Yoido Plaza, Seoul, South Korea, 1973.

Photograph by Russ Busby

Religious News Service Photo

Graham chats with Queen Elizabeth, 1984.

AP/Wide World Photos

Graham with President Jimmy Carter and Vice-President-elect George H. W. Bush outside the Georgetown Baptist Church where Graham had preached, 1980.

could: "Please know that this door is always open—and your room is always waiting. I hope you will come often."

With the coming of summer, Graham continued to assert that if the Klan would quiet down and civil rights extremists would give southerners a chance to get used to the new laws and court orders, and if politicians would quit trying to exploit the situation for their own selfish ends, Alabama and other southern states would not only make peace but would provide a model for the rest of the country to follow. In the meantime, those who pointed accusing fingers at the South should take care, because his own observations indicated that racial violence could easily break out in dozens of cities far from the Deep South. Before that long hot summer was over, Graham's dire prophecy came true in a manner more terrifying than he had dreamt possible. When a routine police encounter in a black district of Los Angeles one stifling August evening erupted into a days-long conflagration that made it forever impossible to think of Watts without thinking of riot, Graham flew to Los Angeles. After donning a bulletproof vest and taking a reconnaissance helicopter flight over the swirling, smoking turmoil, the appalled evangelist declared what seemed to him obvious, even in the absence of concrete evidence. The rioters, he announced, were "being exploited by a small, hard core of leftists." He felt sure that 97 percent of the rioters were not Communists, "but it cannot be overlooked that this kind of disturbance is being used by those whose ultimate end is to overthrow the American government." It was, he believed, "a dress rehearsal for a revolution," stimulated by the "hate literature of the right and the left." Then, apparently feeling black rioters were not as susceptible to the reformation by evangelism he recommended for white racists, Graham called on Congress to devise "new tough laws ... to curb this kind of thing." He also urged Martin Luther King, Jr., who had been walking the streets of Watts in an effort to restore a semblance of peace, "to call for a moratorium on demonstrations for the time being." The *Christian Century* blasted his "fervent generalities" as "a vague emotional outburst [by] a man who knows something is dreadfully wrong but who hadn't the slightest idea what caused it," but Graham's hometown Charlotte *News* observed that "in the entire country, only one national figure of substance seems concerned enough to suggest corrective steps and to travel to the scene to offer his help."

Graham appealed to President Johnson to identify publicly those "who are teaching and advocating violence, training in guerilla tactics and defying authority" in the apparent hope that once these troublemakers had been exposed and branded, black folk would settle down and wait patiently for converted white people to open the doors they had deliberately held shut so long. His views on campus antiwar protests and widespread relaxation of conventional norms regarding sex and drugs took similar form. In commenting on disruptions in American universities, he revealed an unmistakably conformist and anti-intellectual strain. “You see some guy on every campus,” he said disdainfully, “and he usually has a beard. I’d like to shave a few of them. And he has a cigarette dangling out of one side and he’s got a book by Jean-Paul Sartre under the other arm. And he’s called an intellectual.... Now, who are the intellectuals? Usually the intellectuals are somebody who is sort of an extreme left-winger and he’s considered an intellectual especially if he smokes a pipe and has horn-rimmed glasses and sits in an ivory tower in a university.” Graham’s suspicion of the nontraditional extended beyond the university campus to high art and popular culture. “We can judge our times by the paintings produced by some modern artists,” he asserted. “We see indiscriminate splashes of color with no recognizable pattern or design. The incomprehensible mixture of pigment merely denotes the confused minds and values of our day. Many of the playwrights, novelists, and scriptwriters for television and movies give us unadulterated doses of violence, sex, and murder. Ours indeed is a sick generation in need of salvation.” Young people, he warned, were particularly vulnerable to the loss of structure and authority. “Drinking fathers and drug-dancing mothers are breeding a generation of unstable youngsters,” with the result that “one out of twelve college students is under some kind of psychiatric care.”

The only dependable guideline for restoring order and sanity to a troubled nation was, of course, to be found in Scripture. “I have a deeper conviction than when I began,” Graham insisted, “that the Bible has the answer to every moral situation known to man.” He conceded that Scripture might not provide a foolproof formula for settling every dispute, and that honest Christians might disagree over some issues, but he insisted that race is a different matter: “When it comes to specific moral issues that we can really pinpoint, like the race question, let’s say, I think our duty is clear.” Even so, he sometimes despaired that human effort, even when informed by Holy Scripture, would be able to wrest order from the chaos of the midsixties, and speculated that the only conceivable denouement to the tragic drama being played out on the national stage was a deus ex machina. “On the dark horizon of the present moment,” he confessed, “I see no other hope. There is really no other possibility I see ... for solving the problems of the world than the coming again of Jesus Christ.”

20

Second Comings

In the midst of distracting turmoil, Graham scheduled only three major events in 1966, but each was significant in its own way. The first, a crusade in Greenville, South Carolina, now the home of Bob Jones University, underlined the permanence of his separation from Fundamentalists. The second, a monthlong return to London, revealed that the kind of overwhelming spirit of revival that prevailed during the Harringay meetings could not be summoned at will, even by an organization whose technical skills were far more developed than they had been twelve years earlier. The third, a gathering in Berlin of Evangelical leaders from over a hundred countries around the world, set in motion a spirit and enthusiasm that played a significant role in the worldwide resurgence of Evangelical Christianity over the next two decades.

Had it not divided people who should have been friends and erected barriers where encompassing circles would have been more appropriate, the Southern Piedmont Crusade in Greenville could have been enjoyed as an amusing example of the ability of intransigent Fundamentalists to pollute almost any stream, all in the name of purity. In typical egocentric fashion, Bob Jones fulminated that the only conceivable reason Graham would come to Greenville was to attack and embarrass him. But the charges did not stop there. By consorting with Catholics, having fellowship with "rank, unbelieving agnostics," and attending conclaves of the World Council of Churches (which Jones identified as the forerunner to "the kingdom of Antichrist"), Graham had, according to Dr. Bob, "led thousands into compromise and alliance with infidelity and Romanism" and was "doing more harm to the cause of Jesus Christ than any living man." Jones warned his faculty and students that any who dared attend even one of Graham's services would be fired or expelled. He acknowledged that he could not control what people did when they knelt by their beds in the privacy of their rooms, but if they wanted to speak to God on behalf of Billy Graham, he recommended they recite the following prayer: "Dear Lord, bless the man who leads Christian people into disobeying the word of God, who prepares the way for Antichrist by building the apostate church and turning his so-called converts over to infidels and unbelieving preachers. Bless the man who flatters the Pope and defers to the purple and scarlet-clothed Antichrist who heads the church that the word of God describes as the old whore of Babylon." Dr. Bob's warning fell mostly on deaf ears. Billy, Cliff Barrows, and the Wilson brothers, all of whom Jones attacked as BJU products gone dreadfully wrong, professed to feel disappointment at their erstwhile mentor's attitude, but they had long since given up on winning his favor and rested content with the response that had always served them so well. Over a ten-day meeting, the Greenville crusade chalked up an aggregate attendance of 278,700, of whom 7,311 answered the invitation.

After more than a decade of holding revivals throughout the world, the 1954 Harringay crusade still stood out as the highest peak in a career that was coming more and more to resemble a mountain range. Understandably, the lure of a return visit was strong, but in London interest in another Billy Graham crusade was decidedly tepid. In 1963, when Maurice Rowlandson, who headed BGEA's London operation, approached the leaders of the Evangelical Alliance to see if they wanted to invite Billy back for another go, they surprised him with a unanimous and categorical rejection. By rounding up a group of Evangelical laymen, however, Rowlandson cobbled together an invitation that Graham agreed to accept, at which point Evangelical Alliance leaders changed their minds and agreed to become the official sponsors.

By early 1964 most of the major committees were in place, often headed and manned by the same people who staffed them in 1954. But this was not 1954. A decade earlier, Britain had still been crawling out of the ruins of war and seemed more willing to listen to a message of solace in a world still short on earthly satisfactions. Now, prosperity and self-confidence had returned, and spiritual hunger seemed to have abated. Major denominations were suffering severe losses in membership and attendance, all denominations were short of ministers, and secularism was ascendant. John A. T. Robinson, bishop of Woolwich, had just written a book called *Honest to God*, in which he confessed that like many of his fellow clergymen, he no longer found much meaning in the old formulations of the faith. As the renowned Evangelical scholar and rector of All Souls, Langham Place, John R. W. Stott, put it, "The church is simply not cutting any ice in our country." In an attempt to pierce this shield of indifference, Graham directed his team to organize the most thorough preparation ever undertaken for one of his crusades. Charlie Riggs oversaw the training of 30,000 would-be counselors. Thousands of additional volunteers attempted to distribute advertising leaflets to every household in the city. And for two solid years, Lane Adams and Robert Ferm visited with more than 4,000 British clergymen, mostly Anglicans, listening to their questions and complaints, patiently explaining the approach and rationale of the Graham crusades, and trying to enlist their support. Both men recalled that it was a hard two years. Adams felt frequent frustration at having to convince ministers that Billy Graham had any real concern for the British people. Adams himself had no doubts on that score. The night before they had left for England, he and Ferm had met with Graham, who led them in prayer. "We all three knelt down," he recalled, "and I have often thought that if I could have had a copy or a recording of that ad-lib prayer, it would have broken the heart of Great Britain to realize that an American citizen had Britain so much in his heart, cared so much, longed so much for the best of God to come to those people."

Robert Ferm also believed in Billy Graham; had he not, he would probably never have agreed to transfer his family to London just five days after they moved into a new home in Atlanta. Still, his correspondence from this period and his recollections years later make it clear that collaring diffident clergymen and wrestling with them like Jacob with the angel, determined not to give up until he wrested a blessing from them, had often left him weary and limping. Resistance began as soon as he hit the ground at Heathrow Airport. When he explained to the customs official who he was and why he had come to England, the man snapped, "We don't need you in Britain. We don't want you." As the officer launched into a virtual harangue, threatening to prohibit the Ferms from entering the country, Maurice Rowlandson appeared to meet them and on hearing the story, drew Ferm aside and began to pray for guidance. When they finished, Rowlandson told Ferm, "The London crusade just started." Ferm went back to the customs desk and began telling the officer of his own Christian experience and recommending that he let Jesus come into his heart. The man softened a bit and agreed to let the Ferms enter, but on one condition. "I'll let you stay if you'll find me one thug who was converted [during the Harringay crusade]. I want to meet him. If you can't find one, you can stay only six months." Rowlandson, who had done evangelistic work in prisons, was able to find a young man who almost fit the officer's requirements. The man had not attended Harringay but had been moved by hearing Bev Shea sing "Softly and Tenderly" in a film Rowlandson had shown in Dartmoor Prison, and by the time Billy Graham finished preaching in the film, he had decided to become a Christian. He subsequently organized Bible classes among his fellow inmates. When Lois Ferm produced the young ex-thug to the customs officer, the officer initially accused him of lying, then spilled out the reason behind his own sense of spiritual alienation. During World War II, he had killed eighty-seven men and could not believe God would ever forgive such a transgression. The former convict told the story of his own crimes, suggesting that since the man had been serving His Majesty's government at the time, God would surely not regard him as a murderer but in any case would forgive whatever sins he might have committed. Not long afterward, Bob Ferm took the man to dinner, and "right there in the airport, he accepted Christ as his savior."

Men whose souls are stained with guilt and remorse often make better subjects for conversion than do clergymen, who are likely to be afflicted with more amiable agonies. In their thousands of conversations with ministers, Ferm and Adams had to deal less with defiant hostility than with lukewarm languor. Liberal and High Church Anglicans, including the arch bishop of Canterbury, generally remained aloof from crusade preparations. On the right, strict Fundamentalists followed their American brethren in refusing fellowship with those of impure doctrine, and doctrinaire Calvinists regarded evangelism as a kind of heresy, since it implied that free will and human effort could play some role in salvation. In the great middle, those who resisted the crusade did so out of disillusion, doubt, and disinterest. Many felt that Billy Graham was old hat. People had already caught his act and would not go see it again. In 1954, one journalist observed, Billy had been an attractive, winsome young man with "a simple [message] for simple people in simple times. His message has not changed, but the times have." Some Britishers frankly admitted that the problem was cultural. "We don't specially like an evangelistic organization which presents to us a face clouded with executives, experts, and mailing lists," a Baptist paper noted. "There is a genuine difficulty of communication across an Atlantic full of differing temperament and mental habits." To be sure, Graham was not without his defenders. *The Christian*, the only conservative journalistic voice in the Church of England, noted that much of the criticism of the evangelist's organization stemmed "from that odd British notion that only the second best does for religion" and ventured that "Billy Graham's real offense is that he has disproved one of modern churchmen's most firmly held beliefs: that it is still possible to get crowds of people to come hear the preaching of the gospel.... This cannot fail to antagonize those who no longer have any gospel to preach." The impact of that defense, however, was blunted by the fact that since 1962 *The Christian* had been owned and operated by the Billy Graham Evangelistic Association.

Graham, of course, was aware of the tepid response he was receiving but handled it in his usual trusting manner. Before leaving for England, he mused that the London crusade "may be the biggest disaster of my entire life. In my heart I'm ready to be laughed at. But I do feel that in Britain there are hearts whom God has prepared. I've prayed about going to England; I felt 'this is of God,' and I haven't any doubts that we've made the right decision. I can do no more than just put myself in God's hands." Laughter, however, was not as much a problem as indifference. In sharp contrast to 1954, the secular press gave Graham and his crusade little more than obligatory coverage, and what little hostility reporters and other critics manifested was easily defused with a bit of wit or openhanded ingenuousess. When a professor asked Grady Wilson why, when Jesus had ridden into Jerusalem on an ass, Billy Graham found it necessary to book a first-class cabin on the *Queen Mary*, Grady replied, "Well, brother, if you'll find us an ass that can swim the Atlantic, he'll be glad to try it." When another man wondered if the humble Savior would go on television, Graham earnestly responded that "since He went as far as He could by foot and spoke to as many as He could by every means available because He wanted everyone to hear the message of salvation, I believe that if there had been any other way to reach more people, He would have used it." When he was asked, as he always was, why he found it necessary to advertise himself and his campaigns so extensively, he said, as if the matter were out of his hands, "I've wondered about that many times. I don't have the answer." And when David Frost asked him during a television interview, "How do you know you're not wrong [about the essentials of your message]?" he gave an answer that defied the usual canons of criticism: "Because I've had a personal experience with Christ. Because my faith is grounded in a relationship with God that has been proved in the laboratory of personal experience through these years."

On the lone occasion when the opposition mounted a sharper attack, Graham still managed to escape with only minor wounds. Under the impression that he would be discussing and promoting John Pollock's newly released and unfailingly flattering authorized biography, the evangelist agreed to appear on a BBC television program, *Twenty-four Hours*. When he arrived at the studio, he found himself facing two of his most virulent public critics, a psychiatrist who had described him as "psychologically sick ... a man on the run from an ever-threatening sense of depression," and George W. Target, a clever novelist who subsequently wrote an acerbic broadside in which he sought to portray every aspect of Graham's operation as a calculated and self-serving assault on human emotions and gullibility. Though he arrived in plenty of time, Graham was offered no makeup and, in contrast to his antagonists, was described by Pollock as looking "rather unhealthy and a trifle wild." The program's host never mentioned Pollock's biography but, after introductory remarks about "the great Billy Graham and his Evangelical roadshow," turned his other two guests loose on the unsuspecting evangelist. Target criticized Graham's heavy reliance on publicity and accused him and his team of telling "sanctified lies" to enlist volunteers and draw crowds. The psychiatrist revealed that he had gone forward at Harringay for the wrong reason—"It was you I wanted, it wasn't the Christ behind you"—and had been emotionally damaged when he was unable to have any personal contact with Graham in the counseling room. Graham remained courteous and even-tempered in the face of the assault, and his associates ventured gamely that he had gained more than he had lost, since the public would doubtless be offended by the unfair treatment he had received, but old hands on the team still remember the program as a low point in five decades of media exposure.

Its aftershocks probably had some role in stimulating Ruth Graham to dream a night or two before the crusade opened that no more than thirty people would be present for the inaugural service.

Ruth's dream proved unprophetic. From the beginning, the crowds were quite good. Princeton Rhodes scholar Bill Bradley, later a professional basketball player and U.S. senator from New Jersey, inspired crowds by telling of his personal faith in Jesus Christ, and British pop-music and movie star Cliff Richard's testimony was the widely covered highlight of a Youth Night that packed 30,000 people into the arena, despite the opinion of some young people that it was not really a youth night but "middle-aged people's idea of a youth night." On another evening, during the invitation, a sizable group of antiwar demonstrators began chanting "Pray for the souls in Vietnam," while a contingent of their fellows dropped leaflets through ventilation holes in the ceiling, but an ensuing scuffle between the protesters and ushers was quickly brought under control by bobbies from the Christian Police Association, several dozen of whom worked as volunteer security guards each evening.

Graham made a strong effort to overcome what had been perceived as weaknesses in the Harringay campaign. Even before the crusade began, the team underlined its commitment to racial justice. When a landlady asked Howard Jones to vacate the flat BGEA had booked for him, two other team members also left in protest. Graham personally ordered that all the leases in the block be canceled and that all team members relocate to an area that would accept Jones and other black members of the team. He also paid a long visit to the mostly black Brixton neighborhood, where he visited with residents in their homes and on the street before preaching to them from the back of a coal truck. Threats of hostile disruptions by neighborhood toughs proved groundless, and while Billy sped away to tea at Lambeth Palace with the archbishop of Canterbury, counselors worked with 136 people who had made decisions at the conclusion of his sermon.

Graham had been criticized during the Harringay crusade for his ostensible lack of concern for the workingman. To offset that image, team members visited dozens of factories, where they spoke with the joint approval of management and trade-union shop stewards. Graham appeared at few of these, but when he did, he reminded workers of the contributions revivalists had made to the welfare of working people. He also addressed a crowd of approximately 12,000 East Enders at a rally in Victoria Park, where hecklers gave him a hard time for a while but eventually quieted during the heart of his sermon. Other efforts to crack London's shell yielded little result. Graham's Indian associate Akbar Abdul-Haqq and John Wesley White, an Oxford-educated evangelist who had joined the team to help Graham with sermon preparation, found little success when they attempted to stem the tide of ridicule and abuse that greets most presentations of the gospel at Hyde Park's famed Speakers' Corner. Team evangelists suffered less abuse but won few more souls during repeated forays into Trafalgar Square. In one of the most widely reported sorties against Satan, Billy Graham himself made an abortive run into the garish Soho district, where what reporters described as a "200-second sermon" came to an abrupt end when he leapt down from a car hood to avoid being photographed with a local stripper who had flounced up beside him.

However their success or failure might be judged, factory meetings and street preaching were time-honored revivalist tactics. The 1966 London crusade, however, began a new chapter in Billy Graham's ministry in that it marked his first use of closed-circuit television to carry crusade services to audiences far from the central arena. He had, of course, pioneered the use of landline audio relays during the Harringay crusade, and his sermons had been broadcast regularly on television since the 1957 Madison Square Garden campaign, but this was his first use of television technology to beam his message into auditoriums and stadiums in cities where the ground had been prepared as if he were going to be present for a full-scale live crusade. By using all of the Eidophor projection equipment available in Britain, the team's electronic engineers were able to supply a television feed to ten cities at a time, usually for three days running. Crowds were surprisingly good in virtually every city, often filling whatever arenas or meeting halls were available, with the largest averaging well over 5,000 souls a night. In Manchester demand for tickets was so heavy that local organizers decided to charge admission—a unique occurrence in the annals of Graham's ministry—and still drew SRO crowds. Inevitably, technical glitches marred some of the transmissions, but the closed-circuit services displayed some singular strengths. Most notable was the heightened impact of Billy Graham's preaching. In the absence of distracting echoes and inevitable visual diversions and in the presence of a fourteen-foot image of Graham's head and shoulders, viewers were able to see and hear the evangelist—and thus to concentrate on his message and absorb the full impact of his rhetorical skills—far better than his live audience in London could. It was, one team member observed, as if they were "locked in with the gospel." As a consequence, the proportion of inquirers in the satellite services consistently ran higher than at Earls Court. Other factors, of course, may have figured into this welcome result, but it was immediately and abundantly clear that apart from the understandable desire to see the famous evangelist in the flesh, closed-circuit television could provide the basis for an effective out reach in cities too small to justify an in-person crusade. From that time onward, television relays became yet another standard weapon in Billy Graham's evangelistic arsenal.

By all the usual measures, London '66 was a success. Total attendance (1,055,368) was only half that of the 1954 meeting, but the crusade itself was only one third as long, so that average attendance was higher. More important, 42,000 people made decisions for Christ at Earls Court, 4,000 more than at Harringay. And whereas 90 percent of the inquirers at Harringay had reported at least some connection to a church, only 76 percent of the Earls Court inquirers did so, indicating that this crusade had a greater impact among the unchurched, always a closely watched barometer of evangelistic effectiveness. As for recognition of Graham's eminence, he was entertained by the American ambassador, honored at a luncheon hosted by the lord mayor of London, treated as a guest of honor by Princess Margaret at a charity affair attended by a thousand lords and ladies of the realm, and invited for a quiet lunch with the queen at Buckingham Palace. Against the possibility that a steady diet of royal food might cause him to forget his roots, a planeload of Nashville supporters entertained him at the Hilton Hotel with a traditional southern breakfast of Tennessee ham, gravy, sorghum molasses, and biscuits brought from home.

For all these marks of achievement, however, a slight air of defensiveness pervades team descriptions of the 1966 crusade. Graham declared it to have been "much more successful than Harringay" but acknowledged that the 1954 effort excited British Christians to a unique and unexpected degree. Admitting the resistance he met from clergy, Bob Ferm noted that "things went well when the crusade actually came off; Earls Court was not really unsuccessful, pound for pound." Others observed that given the hedonistic character of London's culture in the midsixties, "Billy was brave even to have it." In his brief chronicle, *Crusade '66*, John Pollock complained that with few exceptions, the British media "seemed oblivious of the Crusade's importance to the nation's future, and anxious to restrict news of Earls Court." It seems doubtful the media were engaged in a conspiracy to hide Graham's light under a bushel. More likely, it was simply that Billy Graham was a victim of his own success. There was little new the papers could say. It might be significant that Billy and his team could fill a large arena and several outlying auditoriums for a month, but it was no longer surprising. Because the novelty had worn off, media interest had waned and most of the papers seemed to agree with the *Daily Mail*, which ho-hummed, "We've grown accustomed to his faith."

Of those who managed to keep their enthusiasm in check, none were more conspicuous than the leaders of the Evangelical Alliance (EA). As their American counterparts had done periodically since the days of Charles Finney, EA leaders had become convinced that mass evangelism was more flash and sparkle than substance, and that individual and small-group efforts were ultimately more effective at winning souls and keeping them won than were giant public rallies, which they regarded as booster sessions for believers. The heart of EA's criticism, published in a 1968 report, *On the Other Side*, rested on a survey of British churches. The recurring theme of the responses from eighty-five churches in the sample was that the 1966 crusade and a

1967 follow-up effort that concentrated more on television than on the live service in London made no lasting impact on people who were outside the churches. Most of the unchurched had simply ignored the meetings; of the few who bothered to attend, only a small number had any lasting positive response. If they went forward at Graham's invitation, they often remained confused about what they had done or why they had done it. If they found their way into church, they usually found their way out again rather quickly. As for television relays, faithful church members enjoyed them and believed they must be effective, but the impact on outsiders appeared to be minimal. Overall, clergymen who returned the questionnaires expressed a clear belief that locally based evangelism, particularly when working with young people, was more effective than crusade evangelism. Graham's approach, they suggested, was something of a clumsy dinosaur, still throwing its weight around but unable to adapt to changing times and destined for extinction.

Because it was produced by Evangelicals, some of whom had worked diligently in Graham's crusades, and because its approach was thoughtful and measured rather than captiously critical, the report's conclusions were all the more devastating. In 1986 Maurice Rowlandson ventured that *On the Other Side* had "put crusade evangelism back at least ten years in Britain. It meant Mr. Graham couldn't even consider coming back in that time. In fact, it was 1984 before he came again. It had an amazing influence, that book. It was a very unhappy event, and we have only just emerged from it."

Though not everyone approved of his methods or held him in high esteem, even Graham's sharpest critics usually conceded that he was a man of sincere commitment and unquestioned integrity, and none denied he had played a major role in revivifying and reshaping Evangelicalism, helping it to become an increasingly dynamic and self-confident movement. But to Graham, these achievements were not enough. As he came to sense the breadth of his influence, he grew ever more determined to use it not just to build his own ministry but to change the fundamental direction of contemporary Christianity. That determination showed itself in a new and momentous way in late 1966 with the convening of the World Congress on Evangelism in Berlin. Since his earliest days at Florida Bible Institute, Graham had longed to stand in the line of men he considered to be great servants of God. The Berlin Congress was a conscious effort both to repair and forge a link in the chain that ran back to D. L. Moody, whose spirit and career Graham admired more than any other of his predecessors.

The nineteenth century had been a great era for missions, and no one had been more supportive than Moody, who helped finance major mission conferences and whose campaigns and summer meetings at Northfield had provided inspiration and impetus for the intensely mission-minded Student

Volunteer Movement in America and England and the World Student Christian Federation in Europe. One summer at Moody's Northfield Conference, more than 2,100 college students volunteered for missionary service. One of those inspired by Moody's example and encouragement was John R. Mott, who devoted the remainder of his ninety years in efforts to fulfill the student movement's ambitious slogan, The evangelization of the world in this generation. When Mott saw classical soul-winning evangelism continually lose ground to a growing concern to minister to the body and to alter social structures—both of which he regarded as legitimate Christian endeavors—he spearheaded the World Missionary Conference in Edinburgh, Scotland, at which he hoped to reconcile differences between his Evangelical and Modernist colleagues and then to rekindle their zeal for the winning of souls. To Mott's disappointment, his plan did not work. On the surface, the conference had an Evangelical flavor, but a majority of the 1,206 participants felt uncomfortable with making the kinds of claims to exclusive truth that had given birth and purpose to the missionary movement. In two significant manifestations of this reluctance, they declined to espouse belief in an infallible Scripture, preferring instead to ground their endeavors in a more ambiguous "authority of Christ," and they declared that Roman Catholic and Greek Orthodox countries should no longer be considered as mission fields. In a further show of ecumenical spirit, they agreed not to issue any resolutions that involved "questions of doctrine or church polity with regard to which the Churches or Societies taking part in the Conference differ among themselves." No doctrine, no principle would be more important than unity.

Upset by what they considered unacceptable compromise, the more Fundamentalist churches and agencies began to drop out of the ecumenical mission movement. By 1921, when the ever-hopeful Mott convened the inaugural meeting of the International Missionary Council (IMC), which had grown out of the Edinburgh conference, the Modernists were firmly in control and soul-winning evangelism had all but disappeared from the ecumenical agenda. Subsequent development was not in a straight line. An IMC conference in Madras in 1938, once again directed by Mott, called for a return to an emphasis on the Bible, though it explicitly rejected the orthodox Fundamentalist view of Scripture. Mott and some of the tiny remnant band of Evangelicals in the IMC tried to forge a synthesis between historical evangelism and the Social Gospel, but no one any longer talked seriously of evangelizing the world in this or any other generation. Not only was the task too big, but the ecumenists had largely abandoned the conviction that their message was intrinsically superior to that of the other great world religions. Instead, mainline missionaries, whose number was rapidly diminishing, were urged to discover and encourage the common and compatible elements between Christianity and the religions practiced by the people among whom they worked. In 1946, at the age of eighty-one, John R. Mott received the

Nobel Peace Prize for his efforts to bridge gaps of misunderstanding and to bring all human beings into loving fellowship. When asked how he wished to be identified, he gave a one-word reply: "Evangelist!" He had never surrendered his conviction that all people everywhere needed the salvation that could come only through Jesus Christ, but the institutions he led had never been further from believing it was their solemn duty to "go therefore and make disciples of all nations, baptizing them in the name of the Father, the Son, and the Holy Spirit" (Matt. 28:19).

The ecumenical movement reached a new milestone in 1948 with the founding of the World Council of Churches in Amsterdam, a meeting Billy Graham attended as an observer representing Youth for Christ. At this initial meeting, evangelism received a polite nod, but verbal proclamation of the *kerygma* was seen as clearly subordinate to the ostensibly more powerful nonverbal testimony of a united Christendom. Subsequent international conferences of the World Council, particularly those at Evanston in 1954 and New Delhi in 1961, acknowledged the surge of evangelistic efforts in conservative churches but explicitly marked off the differences between the council's view of mission and the ministry of Billy Graham, which the Evanston meeting characterized as "verbalism," claiming that it represented "an old form of evangelism," now seen to be in decline. By the time of the New Delhi meeting, which Graham also attended, the Evangelical view that individuals and churches should "send the light and preach the word" had been rendered inoperative by "universalism," the belief that, however one might conceive of salvation, all human beings will ultimately receive it. The mission of the church, therefore, consists of transforming sinful structures and has nothing to do with rescuing lost souls from eternal punishment in hell.

All this, of course, was anathema to Evangelicals, Billy Graham included. He attended the World Council's meetings, rejoiced in the fellowship of renowned ecclesiastics, even when they singled him out for criticism, and "thrilled at the whole process of seeing world churchmen sitting down together, praying together, discussing together." Even so, he felt their attitude toward evangelism was a grievous error. By the late 1950s as he reflected on his own success with the old evangelism and saw that *Christianity Today* had struck a responsive chord with tens of thousands of ministers in mainline denominations, he began to ponder ways of gathering Evangelicals together to recapture the vision D. L. Moody and John R. Mott had cherished. A three-day meeting of approximately two dozen Evangelical leaders at Montreux, Switzerland, in 1960 set others to thinking and exchanging ideas. Nothing happened right away, but early in 1964, during a taxi ride to the airport after a visit to the White House, Graham told Carl Henry that he wanted to convene a global conference on evangelism. To do so under the aegis of BGEA would seem too self-promoting, and he suspected "the Billy Graham Association didn't have the intellectual respectability to gather the type of person we wanted to come—professors and presidents of seminaries and people like that." He thought the best solution would be for *Christianity Today* to undertake it as a tenth-anniversary project, to be held in 1966. He also felt Henry should head the conference but agreed to give it his stamp of approval by serving as honorary chairman.

No one sitting in on the program-planning sessions would have mistaken the Berlin Congress for a meeting of the World Council of Churches, but the agenda would have delighted John R. Mott. The congress, announced BGEA executive Stan Mooneyham, would define biblical evangelism, expound its relevance to the modern world, identify and mark its opponents, stress the urgency of proclaiming the orthodox gospel through out the world, discover new methods and share little-known techniques of proclaiming it more effectively, and summon the church to recognize the priority of the evangelistic task. *Christianity Today* described the congress as "a Council of War," and Carl Henry called it a "once-for-all shot" at turning back the enemies of evangelism and reasserting the validity of a mission strategy "built on the clear exclusivity of Jesus Christ."

The 1,200 leaders invited to the congress included evangelists, theologians, scholars concerned with evangelism, and denominational and parachurch leaders from 104 nations. Inevitably, decisions as to who would attend created friction. Theologians thought it a waste of money to invite evangelists to a serious theological conference ("They are doctrinally anemic"), and evangelists doubted that a gathering of theologians would have much to say that would be useful ("They don't know how to lead souls to Christ"). Delegates from the Third World felt the invitation list was weighted too heavily in favor of the West, and Americans anxious to participate in what promised to be a historic meeting grumbled that congress leaders had set a limit of one hundred invitees from the United States. Some evangelists and parachurch leaders who received invitations quickly exploited them in fund-raising appeals, implying that their ministers had received endorsement from the highest levels of world Evangelicalism. Eventually, an impressive and eclectic group of Evangelicals assembled in Berlin. The scope of the gathering was underlined by the presence of Kimo Yaeti and Komi Gikita, Auca Indians who had participated in the 1956 killing of five missionaries in the jungles of Ecuador but had subsequently been converted to Christ. In addition to these erstwhile heathen, the roster also included representatives from both the National and World Council of Churches, as well as from Roman Catholic and Jewish observers. It was, however, notably free of separatist Fundamentalists, an omission that would not go unnoticed. To some, the experience of sitting at a common table with this ecumenical, international, and multicultural melange was enough to transform a simple meal into a foretaste of the messianic banquet. One observer reported there was not "the slightest hint of any racial divergence as those of many colours mingled together in full and free Christian fellowship. One could almost imagine that the Rapture had taken place, and we were all at the other end of the line!"

For ten days beginning on October 28, the ultramodern Kongresshalle, on the banks of the river Spree near the Berlin Wall, rang with clarion calls for a return to old-fashioned evangelistic preaching, carried out with the latest and most efficient techniques and technology. To underscore the sense of urgency, a large digital clock in the lobby emitted a loud pulse that signaled the birth of a new baby—Another Soul to Win—somewhere in the world, remorselessly hammering home the reminder that at 150 births per minute, the population of the planet was growing ten times faster than was Christianity. "No delegate," one journalist wrote, "can escape the significance of that clicking counter which constantly gate-crashes conversation and stabs the conscience as it emphasizes the enormity and desperate urgency of the one task we have—to communicate one gospel to the one race of all mankind."

In his opening address to the congress, Billy Graham tried to live up to a prominent Lutheran bishop's characterization of him as "the personification of the moving spirit of Evangelism." Explicitly linking himself and the congress to the tradition of D. L. Moody and John R. Mott, he announced at the outset that the primary purpose of the gathering would be to dispel confusion about the meaning, the motive, the message, and the methods of evangelism, as well as about the devious strategies of "the enemy," a category that included both natural and supernatural foes. Graham usually rested content simply to state what he believed without attacking positions that differed from his, particularly when his opponents were churchmen. On this occasion, however, he lashed out at the ecumenical advocates of universalism. The widespread but softheaded belief that God would not really let people go to hell, he said, had "done more to blunt evangelism and take the heart out of the missionary movement than anything else." Then, lest any think he believed that men born into other religious traditions might somehow find God by following those ill-lit paths, he declared flatly, "I believe the Scriptures teach that men outside of Jesus Christ are lost! To me, the doctrine of future judgment, where men will be held accountable to God, is clearly taught in the Scriptures." If the church could recover its conviction on these matters, he said, "it would become a burning incentive to evangelize with a zeal and a passion that we are in danger of losing." Graham acknowledged that modern biblical criticism had sown much doubt about the veracity of Scripture and the claims it made about Jesus and salvation, but he remained unshakable in his confidence that when an evangelist proclaimed the *kerygma*, he wielded a sword no biblical critic could blunt. "I have found," he assured his rapt listeners, who desperately wanted to learn whatever secrets he possessed, "that there is a supernatural power in this message that cannot be rationally explained. It may appear ridiculous and foolish to the intellectuals of our day, but it is the power of God unto salvation."

Just prior to the opening of the congress, the World Council of Churches had sponsored a conference in Geneva on social action at which it recognized a "need for revolutionary change in social and political structures" and sanctioned the use of violence, as long as it was kept to the minimum necessary to accomplish the desired goals. Specifically aligning themselves against Billy Graham, whom they characterized as a pawn Lyndon Johnson was using to rally support for American policy in Vietnam, some participants compared "the evangelistic type" to "Nazi Christians who by insisting that the Church concentrate on 'traditional' concerns betrayed the cause of justice" and depicted Graham's type of evangelist as "traitors to Christ's cause." Graham realized that religion reporters covering the congress would remark on these attacks and the juxtaposition of the two meetings, but he did not shrink from articulating his oft-stated conviction that "if the Church went back to its main task of proclaiming the Gospel and getting people converted to Christ, it would have a far greater impact on the social, moral, and psychological needs of men than it could achieve through any other thing it could possibly do." To face the overwhelming magnitude of the task before them, Graham urged a spirit of openness toward every possible avenue of evangelism, including the mass media and computers, "on a scale the church has never known before." To stick with old-fashioned methods would be to invite the wrath of God upon their heads. Finally, he emphasized the need for cooperative action, a unity based not on a desire not to hurt anyone's feelings, but a unity that grows out of working together in a common task. "Do we want unity among true believers throughout the world?" he asked. "Then evangelize!" Was there a model for the kind of unity he envisioned? Yes, there was. "I believe," he said, "that some of the greatest demonstrations of ecumenicity in the world today are these evangelistic crusades where people have been meeting by the thousands from various denominations with the purpose of evangelizing." So saying, Billy Graham made it clear that he was not only pointing the troops in the right direction; he was ready to lead the way.

The handpicked nature of the assembly precluded any serious disagreement over the essentials of Graham's address, and subsequent speakers reinforced and elaborated most of his major points in more than 180 meetings over the remaining ten days of the conference. The one gnat of contention that could not be strained out was his prescription regarding social action. The sponsoring organization itself was divided on this matter. Carl Henry and some other key people at *Christianity Today* (*CT*) had wanted the congress to devote more attention to social responsibility, and some speakers did address such issues as the relationship between Evangelism and race. But Howard Pew, who still provided major support to the magazine, firmly believed involvement in social action would spell "the end of Protestantism as a spiritual and ecclesiastical institution" and wanted the congress to stand firm against efforts by church bodies to influence economic and political institutions in any kind of direct manner. Graham took a middle position, wanting to emphasize evangelism without denigrating social action, which he thought would inevitably follow individual conversion.

Black participants generally criticized the tendency of Evangelicalism to manifest "not only passivity in social matters, but also, by default, a tacit support of the status quo." And BGEA evangelist Howard Jones charged that racism "is the question on which the whole cause of evangelism will stand or fall in the non-white countries of the world, and we are ignoring it." When BGEA and *CT* board member Maxey Jarman warned against being "tempted by the seeming strength [of] political power to force reforms and improvements among people" and recommended depending instead on "the faith and hope and love that comes from God" to effect social change, a black minister from Detroit responded, "Law did for me and my people in America what empty and high-powered Evangelical preaching never did for 100 years." Overall, social issues received short shrift on the agenda, but the congress did issue a 950-word statement condemning "racialism whenever it appears," asking forgiveness for "the failure of many of us in the recent past to speak with sufficient clarity and force upon the biblical unity of the human race" and asserting flatly that "we reject the notion that men are unequal because of distinctions of race or color."

Given the tightly controlled nature of both membership and message, the Berlin Congress held few real surprises, but the unlikely appearance of three remarkably disparate men, all religious leaders in their own distinctive way, provided a dash of panache that participants recalled with wonder, and some amusement, twenty years later. To appeal to Third World participants and to lend a measure of prestige to the congress, Stan Mooneyham used Billy Graham's name and his own ingenuity to arrange for Haile Selassie, emperor of Ethiopia and protector of the Ethiopian Orthodox (Coptic) Church, to attend and address the opening session of the congress. Since visits by heads of state are ordinarily handled by government officials, German leaders were stunned, and a bit miffed, to learn that the emperor was coming to Berlin at the behest of a staff member of an ad hoc Evangelical conference. Berlin mayor Willy Brandt's office moved quickly to take control of the visit, even going so far as to leave Billy Graham and other congress officials off the dais at a reception for Selassie, but the emperor gave Graham what he wanted when he told the gathering of the "great struggle to preserve Ethiopia as an island of Christianity" and urged the delegates to do all in their power to carry the message of salvation "to those of our fellows for whom Christ our Savior was sacrificed but who have not had the benefit of hearing the Good News."

A second congress attendee stirred far more lasting interest, in large measure because his participation in the conference was not just a product of an enterprising public relations machine but had real and patently obvious long-term implications for Evangelical Christianity. When Carl Henry wrote Oral Roberts in 1965 to tell him he would soon receive an invitation to the Berlin Congress, he noted his reservations about such Pentecostal phenomena as glossolalia (speaking in tongues) and healing, particularly "if these are made to be central and indispensable facets of normative Christian experience." Roberts understood all too well that Henry and Harold Ockenga, and even Billy Graham, who had always treated him with courtesy and respect, regarded his ministry and, indeed, Pentecostalism as a whole, as a peripheral and somewhat embarrassing relative. As a consequence, he accepted the invitation with considerable misgiving, later confessing that "since the healing ministry had not been understood to be an integral part of the mainstream of the Gospel, we were not sure how our ministry would be accepted or what our contribution could be to the Congress."

Oral's apprehensions were not unwarranted. Mainstream Evangelicals at the congress tended to give him wide berth, and Roberts responded by spending as much time as possible holed up in his room at the Berlin Hilton. Calvin Thielman, Ruth Graham's friendly and unpretentious pastor, made it a personal project to melt the wall of wariness that Oral and the Evangelicals had erected to protect themselves from each other. At their first encounter, which both men enjoyed, Roberts warned Thielman that being seen with him carried some risk, but Calvin pressed on. He arranged a luncheon, which he persuaded Roberts to pay for, and invited a pride of ecclesiastical lions, including the bishop of London, to sit down with the Oklahoma preacher and ask him hard questions. When Oral fielded their queries with both grace and skill, Calvin undertook to introduce his new friend to anyone who would hold still long enough to meet him.

Inevitably, word of Thielman's activities got back to Billy Graham, who sent a note asking Calvin to come to his room. As Thielman recounted the incident, Graham was sitting up in bed when he entered the room. Looking over his glasses, he said "T.W. tells me that you're getting together everywhere to eat with Oral Roberts." Feeling he was about to be cautioned, perhaps even reprimanded, Calvin protested, "Well, Billy, we invited him here and he is being avoided by people.... They treat him like an honorary leper." At that, Graham interrupted, his eyes filling with tears. "God bless you for that," he said. "You tell Oral that I want him to eat with me." Billy followed through by inviting Oral to dinner with a small gathering of conference leaders. At the end of the evening, as he spoke briefly with each of the departing guests, he asked Roberts, "Oral, when are you going to invite me to speak to your campus?" Wary he might be, but Oral Roberts recognized a public relations bonanza when he saw one, and he shot back, "How would you like to come to the campus not only to speak but to dedicate the university?" Graham declared, "I'd be honored to do it," and Oral Roberts suddenly found himself knee-deep in the mainstream of conservative Christianity.

Roberts acquitted himself well as chair of a panel discussion on healing, but his most significant triumph came in an unplanned address to a plenary session. In a characteristically warm introduction, Graham said, "Our prayer is going to be led by a man that I have come to love and appreciate in the ministry of evangelism. He is in the process of building a great university. He is known throughout the world through his radio and television work, and millions of people listen to him. They read what he writes and they thank God for his ministry. I am speaking of Dr. Oral Roberts, and I'm going to ask him to say a word of greeting to us before he leads the prayer." When the applause subsided, Roberts mesmerized the congregation with his humble confession that his doubts and fears had been "conquered by love." "I shall always be glad that I came," he said. "I needed to sit down and listen to someone else for a change." As one accustomed to being the leading light in Pentecostal circles, he noted his amazement at realizing that he had been "out-preached, out-prayed, and out-organized" by the men in whose presence he stood. "I thank you, Billy, and Dr. Henry," he said, "for helping to open my eyes to the mainstream of Christianity, and to bring me a little closer to my Lord. I have come to see the Holy Spirit in men who are here today. Yesterday I even had lunch with a Bishop. Can you imagine a Pentecostal evangelist eating with a Bishop of London?" Then he added, "We have talked of the glories of Pentecost in our denomination, but I wonder if we have thought enough of the unity of Pentecost. I think we Pentecostals owe a debt to the historic churches, and you might owe a small debt to us, for we have held on to Pentecost. We have learned new dimensions about it, and I thank God, Billy, and all of you for that." After thunderous and prolonged applause, Roberts led the assembly in a moving prayer in which, among other blessings sought, he adjured Satan to keep his hands off "this man, God's servant," Billy Graham, and implored God to anoint Billy with the Spirit as he had never before been anointed, "that he shall speak with a new force, a new power, a new vision, to this whole generation."

Perhaps only God knows whether Billy Graham got a new vision, but it was soon palpably obvious that Oral Roberts did, and he set out immediately to "capitalize upon our acceptance in Berlin." For several months, he filled his *Abundant Life* magazine with pictures and stories of the Berlin Congress, even quoting verbatim his remarks and prayer at the triumphant plenary session. He pumped Calvin Thielman for ideas as to how he could widen the circle of friends he had made in Berlin. "You don't realize what happened out there," he told Calvin. "Those kind of people never spoke to me before. They have avoided me and there was no way I could ever break through it until now. This is bigger than you understand. Because you've lived in these circles all your life and I haven't. I've been on the outside looking in." He invited Leighton Ford and Harold Ockenga to speak at his fledgling school. And of course he held Billy Graham to his offer to give the dedication address at his university the following April. Oral knew that most of Billy's colleagues felt he could only be harmed by the association, and the mail that came into the Minneapolis offices of BGEA confirmed that suspicion, but Graham had given his word and he kept it. Nearly 20,000 people attended the ceremony, and the media carried the word to any with eyes to see and ears to hear that Billy Graham had placed his stamp of approval on Oral Roberts and by implication on Pentecostal and charismatic Christianity. Roberts exploited the relationship and the endorsement for every advantage it would yield, but he had been deeply and sincerely touched by the risk Billy Graham had taken. "I knew that Billy loved me," he told a group of his supporters, "but I don't think the public knew it."

A third notable swirl eddied around a man who, unlike Haile Selassie and Oral Roberts, had not been invited to the Congress. Of the Fundamentalist triumvirate of Bob Jones, John R. Rice, and Carl McIntire, only McIntire had never been personally associated with Billy Graham. He had written and published numerous critical articles about the evangelist in his newspaper, the *Christian Beacon*, and had sent Graham a stream of multipage letters detailing his shortcomings and calling for public renunciation of his damnable ways and apostate friends. If Graham took notice at all, he did so simply by penning a short cheek-turning note informing his attacker that "I have received your letter and have taken note of its contents. God bless you." As one who had built a long and noisy career on rancorous confrontation, McIntire found his inability to get a rise out of Graham too much to bear and decided to smoke him out and expose him before the world Evangelical community as an appeaser of evil and error.

McIntire neither received nor expected an invitation to attend the congress as a delegate, but he was understandably stunned when Carl Henry told him he had applied too late to receive press credentials. Henry did, however, offer him observer or visitor status with the understanding that he would not be permitted to attend press conferences or interview delegates. McIntire hooted at what he took to be a legalistic ploy to exclude him and his critical perspective. He had come to report, he snorted, not to *observe* or *visit.* Denying him access to delegates meant he would not be able to document the degree to which Communist agents, posing as faithful Christians from Eastern European countries, had wormed their way onto the delegate list and planned to use the congress to spread their poisonous ideology throughout the Christian world. As a vehement anti-Communist, McIntire was incensed that speakers had been instructed to avoid attacking communism, lest they mar the "ecumenical policy and atmosphere" of the gathering. He professed shock and chagrin that Carl Henry and his henchmen would seek to thwart the free press, especially to appease the very communism Billy Graham had once courageously opposed, and he determined not to let such high-handed tactics and disreputable motives go unnoticed. He proved true to his resolution.

In an effort to put himself in the hallowed Reformed tradition of nailing theses to the door, McIntire issued a statement of protest against Billy Graham's brand of ecumenical evangelism and taped it to the glass partitions at the entrance to the Kongresshalle. Then, for the duration of the congress, from morning till late evening, in bright sun and biting cold, the Fundamentalist fulminator stood outside the entrance, distributing mimeographed tirades against Graham and the apostate ecumenical evangelism he represented to any who would receive them, and declaring that the meetings inside were the most tightly controlled "of any non-Roman religious gathering I have ever seen." McIntire recorded his putative ordeal and replayed the familiar Fundamentalist objections to Graham's ministry in a self-published and self-absorbed harangue, aptly titled *Outside the Gate.* A lesser man might have been tempted to go along with the crowd and accept the status of observer or visitor, but Carl McIntire was not such a man. "Thank God I retained my liberty," he wrote. "My separatist convictions begot such freedom." His antagonists, he reckoned, would not enjoy the same purity of conscience. He felt certain their shameful treatment of him "will be a major issue hanging over this Congress and over Henry and Graham the rest of their lives."

Though McIntire was capable of venting full fury on any deviation from his own rigid canons of orthodoxy, he saw Graham's ecumenical tendencies as more serious than everyday apostasy simply because the evangelist's eminent stature made it possible for him to influence so many people. In premillennial teaching, one sign of the impending arrival of the Antichrist will be the formation of a single, worldwide religion. To many Fundamentalists, the near-global reach of Roman Catholicism had long made that body seem a likely candidate to smooth the path for the coming of "the beast." Since its founding in 1948, the World Council of Churches, which sought to bring all Protestant bodies under its umbrella, had furnished another ready suspect. In *Outside the Gate*, McIntire attempted to fix the yoke of guilt around Billy Graham's neck as well. By collaborating with liberals and by downplaying differences between conservatives as if the tiniest jots and tittles of doctrine were not matters of eternal consequence, Graham and his colleagues in the New Evangelical camp were in danger of participating in what "could very easily be the church of the Antichrist, Babylon the Great, the Scarlet Woman, the Harlot Church, described in Revelation 17 and 18." By summoning Evangelical leaders from all over the world to Berlin, and by arranging and controlling the program so that virtually all dissent over matters of doctrine was squelched, Graham was conditioning Evangelicals for eventual membership in the World Council, after which the rapture and the tribulation could not be far behind.

Carl McIntire may have accorded Billy Graham and the Berlin Congress a more pivotal role in cosmic history than they deserved, but it was not an insignificant gathering. The *New York Times* published daily stories about it, and scores of major daily newspapers gave it front-page treatment. The Religious News Service reported that its coverage matched that given the Second Vatican Council, and Vatican Radio itself took sympathetic notice. A Religious News Service reporter, in fact, went so far as to compare Graham to Pope John XXIII. "The spirit of Pope John," he said, "hovered over the council. Billy Graham was physically, palpably, and inescapably present at the Congress, speaking admirably and holding together forces that would unquestionably have exploded in all directions save for his presence." That assessment may have overstated the assembly's potential fissiparousness, but it was certainly the case that hundreds of people who ordinarily had little or nothing to do with each other found barriers crumbling and suspicions melting as they came to feel that their shared enthusiasm for evangelism more than offset their differences over doctrine and polity. Perhaps the most important discovery came with the recognition by representatives of traditionally Evangelical denominations that even members of traditionally non-Evangelical bodies might share many of their same concerns. Religion journalist Jim Newton recalled that the Berlin Congress was "the first really big conference for Evangelicals. It was a mind-blowing experience [for Evangelicals] to meet with Methodists, Presbyterians, Coptics, and Orthodox who were concerned about evangelism. They all had this image that any church affiliated with the World Council was bound to be a liberal church and, therefore, not concerned about evangelism. Berlin shattered that stereotype. Just exploded it, as nothing had ever done before." Carl Henry agreed that the congress "shaped a mood in which Evangelicals sensed their larger need of each other and of mutual encouragement and enrichment." Western delegates, long accustomed to furnishing the impetus for mission efforts in non-Western countries, seemed particularly surprised and affected by what one observer called "the dynamic surge of evangelistic emphasis coming from the newer churches of Latin America, Africa, and Asia."

Evangelicals were not the only ones stirred by the Berlin Congress. At the triennial meeting of the General Assembly of the National Council of Churches, which convened in Miami in December of the same year, Dr. Willis E. Elliott of the NCC's Christian Life and Mission Division released a scathing denunciation of the congress, which he attended as an official observer. It had been, he said, "a promotional meeting for a party within Protestantism," a group that under the leadership of Billy Graham and Carl F. H. Henry was seeking to have itself recognized as the Evangelical party within the ecumenical movement. He professed to admire Graham and to stand in awe of "his godlike transcendence over the masses, the Sistine-ceiling frowning-God eyebrows, the Olympian masculinity, you name it, he's got it; both clarity and power of image." But he did not admire what he saw as Graham's obsession "with the promotion and protection of a particular angle on the Bible," an angle he characterized as "scribal evangelism," with an outlook that was "Biblicistic rather than Biblical" and had little room for an overtly social dimension. Recalling the reference by many congress speakers to the ever-ticking population clock, he noted that not one had suggested that Christians might assume some responsibility for damping the population explosion, and that this failure stemmed from an individualistic ideology that kept Evangelicalism from contemplating collective solutions to social problems.

Elliott called on the NCC "to establish a polar position for dialogue with the old evangelism as represented by Billy Graham," but he hardly succeeded in turning the evangelist into an enemy. In fact, while Elliott was merely releasing a report, Billy Graham was one of the assembly's two featured speakers, along with Vice-President Hubert Humphrey. Graham described the Berlin Congress as "a step" toward greater unity among Christians. In return, an official of the World Council announced that his organization would thenceforth seek opportunities to cooperate with Graham and his colleagues in evangelistic endeavors. Carl McIntire took this to mean that the National Association of Evangelicals (NAE) would soon be absorbed into a one-world church, where wheat and tares were equally valued, where Pentecostals would lie down with popes and men of scant conviction would sacrifice their souls on altars of compromise. In truth, ecclesiastical unity was not on the immediate horizon. The NAE neither disappeared nor linked arms with either the National or World Council, and the councils never quite got around to reviving the spirit of John R. Mott. Still, the Berlin Congress did prove to be a pivotal event for Evangelical Christianity, helping to create a kind of third worldwide ecumenical force alongside Vatican II and the WCC and establishing Evangelicalism as an international movement capable of accomplishing more than its constituents had dreamed possible.

21

Dreams and Wars

By the mid-1960s, Graham seemed to be following through on his oft-announced intention to cut back on full-scale crusades. In 1967 he held weeklong crusades in Puerto Rico, Winnipeg, Kansas City, and Tokyo, in addition to the television campaign from Earls Court. The following year, partly because of illness, he restricted himself to domestic crusades in Portland and Pittsburgh, a four-day stint at the Hemisfair in San Antonio, and a two-week visit to Australia. By this time, North American and British crusades could run on automatic pilot. No one could surpass Billy Graham at conquering critics and silencing skeptics by trotting out well-tested responses to troublesome questions, and no one seemed better able to convince himself that the effort then in progress was somehow distinct and more remarkable than those that had gone before. Still, though he could answer the same questions, preach the same sermons, and draw in impressive numbers of inquirers, world without end, Graham could never quite be content simply doing what he had done before. Always, he needed a new challenge for himself, a new way to stretch the boundaries and influence of Evangelicalism, a new opportunity "to do some great thing for God."

Still heady with the ecumenical excitement and international enthusiasm generated by the Berlin Congress, Graham made a brief visit during the summer of 1967 to Turin, Italy, where he preached at services hosted by the Waldensians, a famed sect that espoused Protestant principles centuries before Martin Luther and that many Evangelicals regard as the lone outpost of true Christianity during the dark ages of Catholic domination of the Western world. Reflecting the more expansive atmosphere of post–Vatican II Catholicism and acknowledging Graham's own ecumenical gestures toward them in the Berlin Congress, representatives of both the Roman Catholic and Greek Orthodox churches attended and were warmly received at one of these services.

From Italy, Graham foreshadowed what would become one of the most significant aspects of his later ministry when he preached for the first time in a Communist country. Early in 1966 he announced that he had been invited by Protestant churches in Poland, with approval from the Communist government's Ministry of Religious Affairs, to participate in the celebration of a thousand years of Christianity in that country, and that he intended to accept. That prospect of access to iron curtain countries doubtless influenced the directive to participants in the Berlin Congress to refrain from open criticism of Communist theory or practice. Shortly afterward, however, under pressure to grant a similar privilege to Pope Paul VI, the Polish government rescinded its permission, and the visit was canceled. Graham might easily have used this widely publicized rebuff as a pretext for retooling his old harangues against the godless Communists, but he limited himself to a scrupulously diplomatic "I hope we may be permitted to go at a later time." The Polish door would not crack open again for nearly two decades, but the evangelist received a consolation prize in 1967 in the form of an opportunity to visit and preach in Yugoslavia, heretical as far as Moscow was concerned, but still Communist and thus still a minor milestone for his ministry.

Graham spent only two days in Yugoslavia, both in Zagreb, but they were rich and emotion-laden. After discreet intervention by Billy's old friend, Liberian vice-president William Tolbert, the Yugoslav government permitted his entry, but the small community of Baptists who invited him were uncertain as to what officials would permit or what opposition Roman Catholics would mount. Their apprehensions proved groundless. Government policy banned religious advertising, but when a Baptist church erected a large sign announcing the meetings, officials looked the other way. Similarly, Catholics not only approved of Graham's visit, but when it became clear no Protestant church would hold the expected crowds and the government rejected a request for use of a municipal stadium, the prelate offered Graham the use of a soccer field adjoining a Catholic seminary and military hospital.

No Yugoslavian media mentioned Graham's appearance, but missionary radio broadcasts from Monte Carlo and word-of-mouth communication among Yugoslavian Christians brought at least two thousand worshipers to a Sunday morning service on the soccer field. When black clouds began to spill a driving rain on the crowd, Graham announced he would cut his sermon short, but a chorus of protests begged him not to, and after one lone voice pleaded "We've waited too long for this," he preached for an hour in a downpour relieved only by occasional drizzle. Aware that his status as a visiting cleric was a fragile one, but also in keeping with his theological convictions and personal predilections, Graham delivered a straight evangelistic sermon, referring only obliquely to the "difficult" situation of Yugoslavian Christians and exhorting them to demonstrate their benign intentions by following the scriptural injunction to "obey those in authority." Whatever they had expected, his message evidently more than satisfied the modest gathering. When the service ended, they rushed to greet and touch and kiss him, their eyes filled with joy and gratitude that such a famous preacher not only knew of their existence but had come to visit them.

In the fall of 1967, after years of importunate urging by Don Hoke, a veteran missionary he had known at Wheaton and in Youth for Christ, Graham registered a new first by holding a crusade in Tokyo. Not only was the Christian church in Japan at the time pitifully small—no more than 16,000 of Tokyo's 11 million citizens attended church on a given Sunday—-but it was divided into multiplied dozens of tiny sects and coalitions, most run by dictatorial old men jealous of their modest store of power and prestige and disinclined to cooperate with anyone else, including those of their own denomination. Predictably, many of these men resisted falling into line behind Graham's team, and some of those most in favor of his coming feared a major crusade might be scuttled by the unwillingness or inability of Japanese Christians to join hands with each other. But in a signal demonstration of one of the most important effects of Graham's ministry, the variegated cells of Tokyo's Christian life came together to form a reasonably united body. The unity, however, was not complete. In a striking demonstration of Western influence, the Fundamentalist Bible Council of Japan attacked Graham because he tolerated Roman Catholics and cozied up to the World Council of Churches. On the Left, the Japanese Christians' Peace Organization criticized what they took to be his support of American action in Vietnam. But these were minor cavils, and most Japanese church members seemed delighted that Graham was bringing some public recognition to their tiny movement.

Tokyo was not turned upside down, but the crusade greatly encouraged what was becoming a Christian community. The fully packed 15,000-seat Budokan indoor arena rang with the sounds of a Nipponized version of "What a Friend We Have in Jesus." Cliff Richard and baseball star Bobby Richardson gave their testimonies as if they were in Lansing or London. And when the time came for the sermon, diminutive interpreter Akira Hatori, standing on a platform to bring him nearly to Graham's height, translated stories of Belshazzar and the Rich Young Ruler and conveyed Graham's invitation to sinners. By the end of ten days, nearly 16,000 inquirers came forward. Compared to Tokyo's masses, such numbers were infinitesimal, and some doubtless returned to traditional religion, or joined one of the country's vigorous new religions, or simply slipped back into that city's sea of secularity, but mission veterans insist that the hundreds who endured provided an encouraging and permanent surge forward for Tokyo's churches. Though he did so with some misgiving, feeling he might be spreading his organization too thin by expanding to a country where Christianity was so weak, Graham authorized publication of a Japanese version of *Decision* and established a branch office of BGEA in Tokyo to provide expertise and encouragement to Japanese churches, as well as to serve as a staging base for other Graham forays into the Far East.

As Graham moved in ever-widening circles, he became increasingly aware of the need for Evangelicals to develop the intellectual skills needed for effective engagement with liberal Christianity and the secular world. Perhaps inspired by Oral Roberts's example, he revived his decade-old dream of establishing a high-quality Christian educational institution. In what amounted to a public solicitation, he told a reporter in 1966, "If someone came along with $10 million to invest in such a school, I'd consider it. I think a great university with high academics is needed." The following year, he announced he had formed a nonprofit group to look into the matter more seriously. If the group decided such a school was feasible, Graham would not serve as president, he said, but he would be associated with it in a formal and significant way. To emphasize that point, he added, "I consider this a major decision in my life."

The bait Graham tossed out was tempting. More than twenty cities offered him property and the promise of financing for the proposed school. By far the best offer, however, came from insurance magnate John D. MacArthur. The son of a Christian and Missionary Alliance evangelist whom Graham had admired, MacArthur offered to donate a thousand acres of prime property adjacent to the PGA golf center in Palm Beach Gardens, Florida, and to provide major financing for a university. The only condition on the offer was that the school would include a vocational component to teach young people a trade or other skills directly related to subsequent employment. Since his early benefactor, R. G. LeTourneau, had built a vocational school in Texas, Graham saw no problem with that, and the pace of planning for Graham University quickened smartly. Within a few months, the exploration group produced a working document that described the physical plant, the philosophy, and the financial feasibility of the proposed institution. In addition to MacArthur's promises, several gifts in excess of $200,000 had been pledged, including one of sufficient size to provide 100,000 volumes for the library. BGEA expected to contribute 10 million dollars during the first year and 3 million dollars for five consecutive years thereafter. Faculty salaries would be competitive with many secular institutions and higher than those paid in most Christian colleges and Bible schools. A statement of the school's philosophy of education explicitly affirmed that students would "fearlessly" pursue "truths about the physical universe" and world cultures, using the empirical and rational procedures common to the natural and social sciences. To discover "Truths concerning God," however, they would be expected to consult "the Hebrew and Christian Scriptures" and their account of the revelation of God "in the Person of His Son, Jesus Christ." To further circumscribe the search for religious truth, all board members, administrators, and faculty would subscribe each year to a statement of Evangelical faith whose first tenet asserted that the Scriptures "as originally communicated by God to men were fully and verbally inspired without error of any kind" and are "the supreme and final authority in all matters of faith and life; the infallible Word of God." Students at Graham University would receive computer-aided instruction and would obtain hands-on experience that would enable them "to easily function in a surround of television, computers, data processors, and in formation retrieval." The university would also boast a double handful of firsts—first to use the computer "for all conceivable services" (including a computerized "apologetic resource center"), first to offer Christian-led courses on applied computer programming, first to establish a Christian school of business, first to pioneer in undersea farming, and grandest of all, "first to offer courses of study on space platforms orbiting the earth (projected for 1975)."

Given Graham's proven ability to attract as much money as he needed for any project he backed, it seemed likely the university would become a reality. But the evangelist's public optimism about his crusades and other ventures frequently masked substantial private doubts, a fact that inspired Ruth and the children to nickname him Puddleglum, after a figure in a C. S. Lewis children's story who, Ruth explained, "has the boundless capacity for seeing the grim side of every situation." To illustrate her own Puddleglum's talent along this line, she recalled an occasion when she was scheduled to fly from Miami to Asheville via Atlanta. After checking the weather in Atlanta, Billy told her, "You probably won't be able to land. If not, I don't know where you will go—probably on to New York City. But if they try to land, I hope you make it; Atlanta is one of the busiest airports in the United States. And if you do, I'd advise you to spend the night in a motel—if you can get a room, which I doubt—as a lot of planes will be grounded and the motels will be full. In that case, rent a car, if you can get one, and drive home. But drive carefully because you could have a wreck." Graham's overly cautious nature normally would have made him hesitate before moving forward with so daunting a project as a full-scale university, but when co-workers and members of his board voiced concerns that the university might be too great a burden on the organization, he suddenly backed out, a decision that offended and permanently alienated John MacArthur and the directors of the foundation that ultimately administered his great wealth.

By pulling out of the university project, Graham was able to step back from what would surely have become an enormous drain on his time and his association's resources. He was less successful at extricating himself from other conflicts of interest and expression. In a send-up of his tendency to waffle or withhold comment on controversial subjects, the *Christian Century* published excerpts from an interview in which Graham seemed especially reluctant to say anything that might generate disagreement. Asked his views on capital punishment, he said, "I take no position." On therapeutic abortion: "That's a complicated question. I'm not going to get involved." On whether he approved of a bill to restrict the teaching of evolution in California schools: "I'd have to see the bill." On Vietnam: "We ought to leave that to our leaders—they know the facts."

On some issues, however, Graham was taking a more definite stand. At the Miami meeting of the NCC shortly after the Berlin Congress, he had criticized church leaders who "call for social service without also providing a solid spiritual basis for it." Less than a year later, however, he sent the central committee of the World Council a surprising paper in which he said, "There is no doubt that the Social Gospel has directed its energies toward the relief of many of the problems of suffering humanity. I am for it! I believe it is Biblical." This reference to biblical warrant for Christian social action was not a mere rhetorical flourish. In fact, Graham had carefully searched the Scriptures, using such reference tools as the Nave's Topical Bible, in which all the passages on a given subject are grouped together, and had been deeply impressed at the tremendous amount of attention paid to the poor in Holy Writ. Confronted with this evidence, he felt he had little choice but to take a more active and public stand against poverty. To Lyndon Johnson's great and understandable delight, Graham openly and unmistakably placed his blessing on the poverty program. During one stretch, he spent several days calling congressmen to drum up support for the War on Poverty, and he told a gathering made up of national business leaders and congressmen from both parties that if the American people did not support the programs of the Office of Economic Opportunity (OEO), the nation would "pay for it spiritually, morally, and in every phase of society." When Congress funded the poverty program, Graham clambered into a helicopter with Sargent Shriver and barnstormed around Appalachia, trying to persuade local officials to lend their cooperation to OEO efforts. Finally, he taped a pro-OEO interview for distribution to southern radio stations and even participated in *Beyond These Hills*, an antipoverty film shown throughout the South. In response to these efforts, the *Christian Century* grudgingly tendered its "problematic congratulations," the *Baptist Standard* marveled that GRAHAM NOW FAVORS WAR ON POVERTY, and Sargent Shriver acknowledged, in a memo to a White House colleague, that "we are extremely pleased."

If Graham's stand on racial issues was not all his critics wished, it was at least tolerably consistent: Integrate crusades, treat people of all races in a fair and loving manner, and avoid disruptive protests. His stance on the other great issue cleaving the country—the war in Vietnam—was less clear, even to him. As a matter of policy, he doubted the corporate body of the church should take explicit political stands, and he questioned especially whether pastors and leaders of denominations and such bodies as the National and World councils had the right to make political statements as if they were speaking for their entire constituencies. He also doubted that most ministers had the requisite expertise to offer an opinion on many nontheological issues. "I fear," he observed, "that if the church, as the church, begins to try to dictate in politics, we're way off the main track." In part this stemmed from theological conviction, commendable modesty, and deeply ingrained deference to authority. It probably also reflected his recognition that clerical spoutings irritated his friend, Lyndon Johnson. "A President of the United States told me," he volunteered, "that he was sick and tired of hearing preachers give advice on international affairs when they did not have the facts straight." As American involvement in Vietnam grew deeper and more tortuous, Graham found himself pulled in contradictory directions. On one side, his still-staunch anticommunism, his loyalty to the President and official national policy, and his long-standing admiration for the military made it difficult to question his government's actions. On the other side, his compassion for the enormous suffering being visited on Vietnam and the young soldiers who had been sent to defend it, the moral murkiness of his country's presence and role in that faraway conflict, and his frustration at American unwillingness or inability to bring the war to a satisfactory conclusion undermined the assurance he liked to feel about U.S. policy. He was convinced the President anguished over the war: "He carried a tremendous burden for the boys in Vietnam. He felt he was personally responsible for boys being killed." Aware that Graham would be addressing church leaders from around the world at the Berlin Congress, Johnson had told him before that meeting, "Billy, if anyone asks you about Vietnam, you say the President of the United States wants peace and will go anywhere in the world to talk peace." Graham remembered that "he pounded the table so hard as he spoke that I said, 'Mr. President, I am the only other person here and you don't have to convince me.'"

Armed with the confidence that his President wanted to do the right thing, Graham let it be known that he wanted to visit the troops at Christmastime 1966. White House staffers thought this could be a big plus for the administration. An official invitation from General William Westmoreland followed shortly afterward, and the President asked Graham for a full report when he returned. Despite his willingness to go, Billy recognized that his visit could be interpreted as approval of government policy and kept his plans quiet until shortly before he left. In London a BGEA committee planning for the 1967 television campaign registered its own hope that he would hold off mentioning the trip as long as possible, since it "might cause controversy in some sections." On his arrival in Vietnam, Graham studiously disavowed any political predisposition. His only purpose in being there, he insisted, was "to minister to our troops by my prayers and spiritual help wherever I can." He added, however, that "millions of people view [the war] with frustrated impatience" and indicated his and his association's willingness to support pacification programs to help Vietnamese people whose lives had been disrupted by the conflict. Billy remembered the trip as a harrowing one: "Much of the time we were there, it was cloudy and rainy, and we had to fly into these little places where they didn't even have an airport—just a grass strip. Once, conditions were so bad that we couldn't get anybody to fly us. They said, 'You shouldn't fly in this weather,' but I was scheduled, and I said we should go, no matter what the risk. We finally found this colonel who had guts enough to fly us. Several times, it looked like a bad mistake. Once, we came straight toward a mountain in dense clouds. We were in one of those two-motor planes with the big hole in the back, and this colonel pulled it up as hard as he could and the back end scraped the trees. I looked over at Bev Shea and he was just sitting there. He's never afraid of anything. Nothing ever bothers him—no nervousness at all."

The trip did not quiet all Graham's misgivings. In his first encounter with reporters, he confessed that he continued to view the war as "complicated, confusing, and frustrating," adding that "I leave with more pessimism about an early end to the war than when I arrived. How can we have peace? I don't know. I don't have any answers. I had hoped there would be some formula, but I don't see it. I don't know how it could end." Perhaps because he or someone else had found this assessment too downbeat, Graham gave the Associated Press a more positive statement the following day. "The stakes are much higher in Vietnam than anybody realizes," he said, especially for the Western world. "Every American can be proud of the men in uniform who are representing our nation on that far-flung battle front. They are paying a great price for the victory they are almost certainly winning there." And the following day, as part of a greeting relayed from servicemen to their families, he reported that he had found the troops to be "extremely religious," manifesting both high morale and high morals.

In late January Graham and Cardinal Spellman, who had also made a Christmas visit to Vietnam, came to the White House to report to the President and Secretary of State Dean Rusk. According to Joseph Califano, who apparently sat in on the meeting, both clerics stressed "the incredibly high morale of the troops." Graham recalled, however, that this news did not completely mollify the President, who pressed them for some insight: "Now, what do you think? We can't go on with this thing. The American people are not going to take it. We've got to get out of it. How do we do it?" Spellman was decidedly hawkish and favored an all-out military push. Graham claims he begged off from giving any political or military advice but did agree that "the American people are getting restless over this thing." In his conversations with the press after this meeting, he again reminded reporters that Johnson had not started the war but had inherited it from Kennedy and that while he would make no judgments as to whether it had been proper for America to make a commitment to South Vietnam, he felt there was an obligation to "see it through to a satisfactory conclusion."

Because he was out of the country during most of 1967, Graham found it relatively easy to steer clear of the explosive controversies surrounding Vietnam, though he was interrupted by protesters in London the night he preached on "The Cause of War" (which he identified as lust), and reporters usually tried to elicit some statement from him whenever he held a press conference. In the few public statements he did make, he typically maintained a slight proadministration bias. And after Martin Luther King began to speak out against the war, interpreting it as another injustice wrought by a sinful system, Graham scolded him for what he regarded as "an affront to the thousands of loyal Negro troops who are in Vietnam." However Graham perceived his own stance, the White House considered him a valuable ally. When a Gallup poll revealed widespread public opposition to the draft lottery, on the grounds that lotteries are associated with gambling and that many felt "it isn't right to gamble with lives," Johnson aides recommended substituting equal service for lottery and suggested that the President ask friendly religious leaders "to speak out on the misconception—especially Billy Graham." Later in the year, after most Western media outlets charged South Vietnam officials with wholesale rigging of what had been touted as free elections, Graham preached a radio sermon in which he used his familiar tactic of down-playing the seriousness of an offense and deflecting blame by pointing to a wider range of offenders. It would have been naive, he asserted, to expect the elections to be entirely fair and aboveboard. But wasn't it remarkable that these courageous people were even trying to have elections—after all, Britain held no elections during World War II! It was also likely, he thought, that some journalists were being unfair: "Many of the reporters are hostile, and will report the slightest rumor—and build headline-catching stories out of nothing." Besides, he reminded his listeners, "There are many areas in America where shenanigans go on on election day. Whatever you think of the merit of the war, I believe we should give the Vietnamese the same benefit of the doubt that we give ourselves." Some doubtless found even in such oblique remarks a sign that Graham's ties to the White House had short-circuited his critical acumen, but he insisted he had not been compromised. After George Romney's notorious reference to having been "brainwashed" by American military leaders during a visit to Vietnam, Graham observed, "I underwent the same briefings as Mr. Romney, and I wasn't brainwashed. I even lived with General Westmoreland for a time. All the men were trying to do was give us the facts. I didn't feel like they were trying to sell me a bill of goods."

Illness kept Graham from returning to Vietnam for Christmas 1967, and he made even fewer public statements on the war during 1968 than in previous years. He recommended, however, that the President and his administration must decide, and quickly, whether to take whatever steps might be necessary to follow through on their commitment, or admit that America had failed in that commitment and pull out—the first time, apparently, that he considered a conclusion other than military victory or negotiated peace. Despite this growing ambivalence over the war, in a patriotic burst that must have given young Franklin Graham something to think about, he declared, "I hope my son, who is nearing draft age, will gladly go and be willing to give his life."

As troubling as the war was, Graham seemed fully as disturbed by the protests and riots at home, predicting that terrorism and guerilla warfare would soon engulf the nation. Indeed, he did not see how the American dream could survive without a drastic shift in direction and thought it likely that "in less than ten years there will be internal chaos and a political tyranny in the form of some sort of left-wing or right-wing dictatorship, even if there is no war." Other observations were less Armageddon-like in tone but carried echoes of some off-the-mark statements he made during the early years of his ministry. In a warm endorsement of the muscular Christianity espoused by the Fellowship of Christian Athletes, he implied that the disruptive war-protest movement could have been avoided if America's youth gave more attention to sports. "I think athletics turn the great energy of young people in the right direction," he said. "People who are carrying Viet Cong flags around the country are not athletes. If our people would spend more time in gymnasiums and on playing fields, we'd be a better nation!" He also minimized the dangers and horrors of the war by making the statistically spurious and astonishingly blithe comment that "we say that the slaughter in Vietnam has been terrible but we lose more people in one month on the highways of America than the total Vietnam war has cost us. So it's far safer to be fighting in Vietnam than driving on the highways!"

Graham returned to Vietnam at Christmas, this time at the importunate invitation of General Creighton Abrams, Jr., who replaced Westmoreland. Perhaps hoping to gain some leverage with a Congress that consistently refused to provide the manpower and weaponry they felt they needed, the military accorded Graham full VIP treatment. He preached nearly twenty-five times, occasionally teaming up with Bob Hope, who flew in each day from Bangkok to entertain the troops. On Christmas Day he hopped by helicopter to several fire posts along the Cambodian border. Whenever possible he also visited military hospitals, taking time to talk with every patient in each unit and praying with those in intensive care. Once again he found morale "unbelievably high" and assured the home folk that American soldiers "know why they are fighting in Vietnam, and they believe what they are doing is right." He also perceived an improved political situation and reported to the President that "the change in the Vietnam situation since I was there two years ago is like night and day. I came back enthusiastically optimistic about the prospects of Vietnam becoming a strong free nation in Southeast Asia. I am certain that history is going to vindicate the American commitment if we don't lose the peace in Paris." He found the military situation equally encouraging and told reporters. "There is no question: the war is won militarily." When the *Charlotte Observer* received this bit of intelligence on wire-service dispatch, someone in the newsroom wrote in the margins of the printout, "This statement has been made before by lesser evangelists but greater generals."

Graham's optimism regarding the end of the war was of a piece with his evergreen prediction that revival loomed just on the edge of the horizon, but it also stemmed from an aching hope that his tormented friend in the White House might find some relief from his burdens. He estimates that he spent perhaps twenty nights at the White House, at Camp David, and on the LBJ Ranch in the Texas Hill Country, including several visits after Johnson left Washington, and his recollections indicate that Johnson was more candid with him than Nixon ever was. He marveled at Johnson's enormous capacity for work, recalling that sometimes, after they talked far into the night, Johnson would have a massage, usually asking Billy to read the Bible to him while the masseur kneaded and pounded his ponderous frame. Then, instead of sleeping, he would go back to his bedroom and spend hours working through a great stack of papers he needed to process before morning. Graham readily acknowledged the President's rough, blustery, calculating, bullying side, but he also saw a warm and tender Lyndon Johnson who like himself was concerned to do some great thing, if not for God, then for his country. He conceded that the programs of the Great Society were motivated in part by political aims and by a desire to leave a tangible personal legacy but insisted that "on a scale from one to ten, I'd say about eight that it was a ... very deep conviction that he had, that he wanted to do something for the underprivileged and the people that were oppressed in our society, especially black people." Even after he left the White House, when no photographers were around to record and publicize his actions, Johnson showed a personal concern. "I used to think it was sort of a political thing," Graham confessed, but "I visited the ranch a number of times after he left office and he still had that compassion. He would fill his car up with little black children and take them for rides and stop at the store and buy them candy and pick them up in his arms. He just had this built-in compassion for them. This had no political motivation whatsoever. He also had a great feeling for the Hispanic people. His compassion for the poor and the blacks was a very real thing."

When Lyndon Johnson announced on March 31, 1968, that in the interest of national unity, he would not seek reelection, Billy Graham was one of the few Americans not surprised. Nearly a year earlier, before public confidence in his handling of the war dipped to abysmal levels, before Bobby Kennedy revealed his intention to seek the Democratic nomination, Johnson confided to Graham that he did not expect to run for a second term. That decision, Graham has contended, stemmed less from weariness with the struggle than from fears about his health. "My people don't live too long," Johnson had said. "My father died when he was about my age. I don't think I could live out another term, and I don't want the country to have to deal with that." Such fears were not rare for Johnson, according to Graham. "He thought a great deal about death, and he talked to me about it several times." As part of these conversations, Graham quite naturally took the opportunity to speak to the President about the state of his soul. "I had a number of quiet, private talks with him about his relationship with the Lord," the always-on-duty evangelist recalled. "One of them was not long before he died. We were sitting in his convertible Lincoln, where he'd been chasing some of the deer right across the fields. We were stopped, looking out, and the sun was sinking. We had a very emotional time, because I just told him straight out that if he had any doubts about his relationship with God, that he'd better get it settled. I said, 'Mr. President'—I still called him 'Mr. President' then; before he became President, I called him Lyndon—'According to what you say, you don't think you have much longer to live. You'd better be sure you're right with God and have made your peace with him.' He bowed his head over the steering wheel and said, 'Billy, would you pray for me?' I said, 'Yessir,' and I did. He was very reflective after that. We must have sat there for another hour, hardly talking at all, just looking at the sunset."

Later during that same visit, Johnson told Graham that he wanted him to preach at his funeral and gave him the choice of presiding over a memorial service in Washington or the burial at the ranch. Graham said he felt more comfortable at the ranch, which seemed to please the President. He led the preacher over to a small grave plot and said, "I want to be buried right here. My father's grave is right there, my mother's right there." Then he stopped and looked Graham in the eye: "Billy, will I ever see my mother and father again?" Graham provided him with the promise that gives Evangelical faith its greatest power: "Well, Mr. President, if you're a Christian and they were Christians, then someday you'll have a great home-going." Johnson pulled out a handkerchief and began brushing tears from his eyes. Then he decided that others needed to hear what he had just heard. Returning to discussion of the funeral, he said, "Obviously, there'll be members of the press here. I don't know how many, but maybe they'll come from around the world. Billy, I want you to look in those cameras and just tell 'em what Christianity is all about. Tell 'em how they can be sure they can go to heaven. I want you to preach the gospel." He paused. "But somewhere in there, you tell 'em a few things I did for this country." As he recalled this memory, Graham smiled with obvious affection for a flawed but titanic figure who had also been his friend. His voice trailing off as he looked into the distance, perhaps catching an afterimage of a Hill Country sunset, he summed up Lyndon Johnson with head-shaking understatement: "He was quite a combination."

22

Nixon Revived

As fond as he was of Lyndon Johnson, eight years of Democratic occupancy of the White House did little to shake Billy Graham's conviction that America still needed his old friend Richard Nixon. Pneumonia prevented Graham from going to Vietnam during the Christmas holidays in 1967, but when Nixon invited him to spend a few days in Florida to help him reach a decision about making another try for the presidency, Graham rose from his sickbed and took a private plane to Key Biscayne, declaring bravely that "there are times when some things are more important than health." The two men spent several days together, talking, watching football games, going for long walks on the beach, studying the Bible and praying, and of course, speculating about whether Nixon would have a chance at the Republican nomination, and if he got it, whether he could defeat Lyndon Johnson, who he assumed would seek reelection.

Because of his loyalty to Johnson, and perhaps because he did not want Nixon to risk another crushing disappointment, Graham withheld his counsel. Finally, near the end of their visit, Nixon said, "You still haven't told me what I ought to do." Billy told him all he needed to hear: "Well, if you don't, you'll worry for the rest of your life whether you should have, won't you?" That was enough for both of them. Nixon would report on several later occasions that Graham had been more responsible than anyone else for his decision to run, and Billy began immediately to resume knitting the fabric of fellowship that would very nearly become a pall on his ministry. When the press learned of his visit and asked if he would like to see Richard Nixon on the Republican ticket in 1968, he conceded that "I would go that far." Mindful of his ties to the incumbent, he added that "I would not say who I would vote for as President, but I would say he is the most experienced Republican for the type of conflict we have today." He stressed that he was a registered Democrat but reserved the right to be flexible. "I vote independently," he said, "and I usually split. I vote for the man and not the party."

The following spring was routine for Graham but wrenching for America, with the Tet offensive in Vietnam, Johnson's decision not to run again, an increase in campus disturbances, and the assassinations of Martin Luther

King and Robert Kennedy. At the time of King's death, Graham was in an Australian crusade, part of which had to be rescheduled for 1969 because of yet another bout of illness, this time a serious lung problem. Graham interpreted the assassination as further evidence that America was unraveling, calling it "dramatic indication that we have tens of thousands of mentally deranged people in America. In some respects it has become an anarchy." Unable to return home for the funeral, he sent telegrams and flowers and gave the press a muted tribute to King: "Many people who have not agreed with Dr. King can admire him for his non-violent policies and in the eyes of the world he has become one of the greatest Americans." King's death did not lead Graham to believe he needed to take more daring action. A few weeks after the assassination, Howard Jones and Ralph Bell sent him a long letter in which they recalled that riots had erupted in 125 cities after King's death and that other trouble could be expected during the coming summer. They suggested that he and BGEA had an unparalleled opportunity to step into the gap and provide responsible leadership on the racial issues. Specifically, they urged him to commission a film aimed at both blacks and whites that would enable him to use his enormous influence to address burning questions in a bold and forthright way. Perhaps to avoid a confrontation that might have resulted in long-term strain, Graham chose not to respond directly. Instead, he directed an aide to assure Jones and Bell that he felt his long-standing practice of integrated crusades and his increased use of black musicians, black clergy, and black celebrities were having a more beneficial effect than anything else he could do. A few weeks after that, at Bobby Kennedy's funeral, he stood beside Ralph Abernathy, who was aggressively defining himself as King's legitimate successor, and thought to himself, Wouldn't it be wonderful if we could see Dr. King's dream come true? But he moved no closer to using, or even fully approving, King's tactics of prophetic confrontation and challenge of the establishment.

By late spring it seemed increasingly likely that Nixon would capture the Republican nomination. Before President Johnson withdrew from the campaign, Graham insisted he was "studiously trying to avoid political involvement this year." With Johnson out, however, and with the country "going through its greatest crisis since the Civil War," he acknowledged that "many people who just don't know how to cast their vote might accept what I have to say." Did that mean he might endorse a specific candidate? "I might find I will," he allowed; "I do believe I could influence a great number of people." At a Portland crusade in May, he introduced Julie and Tricia Nixon to the assembly, noting that "there is no American I admire more than Richard Nixon." And from that point until the election in November, he dropped so many favorable statements about Nixon that none but a dunce could have mistaken his intentions. Certainly, Democrats understood. A Johnson aide reported to the President that several senators and other leading Democrats were "disturbed at Billy Graham's intention to support Richard Nixon." Recalling that the evangelist had been talked out of an open endorsement in 1960, the aide added, "I know and understand (and approve) the rules you are operating under, but there must be some way or suggestion you can make on how to prevent Billy Graham from doing this." A handwritten note on the memo indicates the "President has no influence." Another note, from Johnson himself and partly illegible, reads, "Call him. [I'm just] his friend. I can't control him."

National Council of Churches executive Dan Potter, a staunch Graham admirer since the 1957 New York crusade, observed that even without explicitly endorsing Nixon, Graham could play a significant role in an election. "Billy has tremendous power," he noted; "almost frightening power. I think he uses this with a degree of discretion. But such power in a single individual ... I say it's frightening. Because I think that Billy's presence, in terms of Nixon's election, has a real influence. And when he sits by a prospective [candidate], even though he tries to be in every way a friend of all Presidents and Kings, he has to guard this very carefully. Because he does have the power of a person who is a symbol to millions of persons who watch his every move, and even a casual gesture becomes a significant signal. I think he is partially aware of the truth of this and therefore his influence is quite tremendous."

At the Republican convention in Miami in August, Graham (at Nixon's request) led the closing prayer after the nominee made his acceptance speech. As the evangelist offered congratulations and said his good-byes, Nixon caught him by the arm and offered him a delicious perk: a chance to sit in on the selection of his running mate. "You'll be interested in this," he said. "It's part of history." Back in a hotel suite, Graham stood at the edge of a circle of twenty or so Nixon insiders and prominent Republican leaders, listening with fascination as they discussed possibilities. Deep into the night and without warning, Nixon turned to him and said, "Billy, what do you think?" Graham was taken aback, "afraid I was putting myself in a political thing I didn't want to get into," but unable to pass up a chance to offer his opinion. "I would prefer [Oregon] Senator Mark Hatfield," he said. "First of all, he's a great Christian leader. He's almost a clergyman. He's been an educator and has taken a more liberal stand on most issues than you, and I think the ticket needs that kind of a balance." Whatever Nixon thought of Graham's advice, Hatfield's well-known opposition to American policy in Southeast Asia and his support of Arab interests in the Middle East made him unacceptable to others in the room. Perhaps sensing he had already said too much, Graham decided it was time to head back to his hotel in Key Biscayne. The next morning Nixon called Graham to tell him he had decided on Maryland governor Spiro Agnew. Graham was utterly surprised: "I'm sure Nixon didn't know him very well. I said, 'Why did you choose him?' He gave me his answers, which I don't want to reveal, and I said, 'Well, I hope he loves the Lord and will be a Christian Vice-President.' And he said, 'Well, you listen at about twelve o'clock and you'll hear the announcement.' Then about ten or eleven his communications director called me and said, 'Billy, Dick wanted me to call you and tell you it's still up in the air. It's between Agnew and Hatfield.' So I listened at twelve o'clock and, of course, it was Agnew. That night I went to the convention as the guest of Senator Frank Carlson, a very close friend of mine. We sat there and you could just feel a pall over the convention. I said, 'If my assessment's right, this is not a popular choice.' And he said, 'You're right. We don't know him.' I was called to platform to lead a prayer that night and I met Agnew for the first time. I never saw him after the campaign, I think, except at the inauguration and maybe once at the White House at a religious service. I never knew him at all. The night he resigned, I called him on the phone and told him I'd be praying for him, whatever the future held, because that's the time I think a minister has some input spiritually. That's the only contact I ever had with Mr. Agnew."

The Democrats' selection of Hubert Humphrey, another old friend, kept some check on Graham's expressions of enthusiasm for Nixon, but his preference was transparent. At a September crusade in Pittsburgh, he read a telegram of greeting from Humphrey, but he invited Nixon to take a prominent seat in the VIP section, where the television cameras could easily find him, and he lauded him from the platform, citing his generosity, his "tremendous constraint of temper," and his "integrity in counting his golf score," and calling their friendship "one of the most cherished I have had with anyone." Nixon described the occasion as "one of the most moving religious experiences of my life." The telecast of that particular service, broadcast just before the election, was added to Graham's TV schedule at the last minute because of "the urgency of the hour."

A few days after his crusade appearance, Nixon made a well-announced and thoroughly photographed call on Morrow Graham in Charlotte, displaying his ease and charm by observing three times that he felt obligated to visit Billy's mother, since Billy had preached at his own mother's funeral a few months earlier. Three weeks later, Julie Nixon turned up in Montreat for a visit at the Graham home, furnishing Billy with another opportunity to note that he was contemplating an endorsement but was not quite ready to give one at that point—without explaining what constituted the difference between an official endorsement and a clear and frequent statement of preference. Sometimes Graham's support came disguised as his own assessment of the political climate, as when he professed to discern a rightward trend among "a big segment of the population," a segment whose members did not carry placards or demonstrate or take what they wanted by violence, but who were nevertheless out there and ready to act, "a great unheard-from group" who were likely "to be heard from loudly at the polls." No one sensitive to campaign rhetoric would likely have missed the similarity between this group—presumably people Billy Graham had seen in his own audiences—-and the "Silent Majority" the Republicans were courting so assiduously. At other times Graham presented his nonendorsement as if he were no more than a neutral friend of the court. When Democrats trotted out their old reliable slurs on Nixon's basic character, Graham declared that his friend "has a great sense of moral integrity. I have never seen any indication of, or agreed with, the label that his enemies have given him of 'Tricky Dick.' In the years I've known him, he's never given any indication of being tricky." He acknowledged that Nixon was "reticent about speaking of his religious life" but declared he knew him to be "a devout person and a man of high principles, with a profound philosophy of government," and characterized him as having "the qualities to make an American Churchill in time of national crisis." After offering yet another such defense, he added, "While I do not intend to publicly endorse any political candidate, as some clergymen are doing, I maintain the right to help put the record straight when a friend is smeared."

Two decades later, Graham insisted that while Nixon's aides may have wanted to exploit their friendship, Nixon tried to protect him from possible backlash. "It seems to me, as I look back," he said, "that he wanted to guard me. I was in Atlanta when he was giving a speech and he said, 'Don't come. It'll be too political.' But Ruth and I wanted to go, so we went and sat in the back so nobody would see us. His aides did see us and we rode back to the hotel with him. I remember that somebody had asked him what he intended to do about the fire-ant problem if he were elected president. He said, 'I'll tell you this: When we get to the White House, we're going to deal with them. We're going to handle that.' We teased him about that in the car. That was the only time I ever went to one of his campaign meetings." Graham apparently overlooked his much-publicized presence in the studio audience of one of the carefully managed question-and-answer shows Nixon used during the campaign. On a later show the moderator asked the candidate if it was true that evangelist Billy Graham was supporting him; Nixon replied that he felt safe in reporting that it was true. A few days later, Graham himself provided confirmation. In an interview published four days before the election, he revealed that he had already cast his absentee vote for Richard Nixon. Nixon campaign operative Harry Dent freely admitted he had exploited that bit of good news in television ads that ran right down to the wire on the following Tuesday. Less readily acknowledged was that according to some sources, the new ads had been in production for at least three weeks before Graham made his well-timed announcement.

Nixon invited Graham to watch the election returns with him in New York, but Billy demurred. He did, however, agree to stay at a nearby hotel to be available to pray with him if he lost the election. About nine the next morning, when it appeared certain that Nixon had edged Humphrey by approximately half a million votes, Bebe Rebozo called to say that "Dick wants you to come over and have prayer with the family." It was hardly the consolation in defeat he had been prepared to offer, but it was close enough, and he and T. W. Wilson hustled over to the president-elect's hotel suite, where Rebozo ushered him in to see the Nixons and their two daughters. After a few minutes of congratulations and election talk, Nixon said, "Billy, I want you to lead us in prayer. We want to rededicate our lives." Graham recalled that "we all held hands and I led prayer. And then he went straight off to meet the press. He always had that spiritual side to him. It was always coming out."

Graham remained impressed by the irrepressible outcroppings of Nixon's spirituality, though he did feel it needed some channeling and pointing-up on occasion. As he recalled, Nixon wanted him to be the only clergyman to pray at the inauguration, but "I told him, 'You cannot leave the Jewish people out. You cannot leave out the Catholics and the Orthodox.' But he said, 'No, I want you, and I want you to take ten minutes.' I told him, "No, Sir, I can't do that.' Finally, someone did persuade him that he had to have all the major religious groups, but I think I did take three or four minutes, which *Time* called 'Billy Graham's mini-inaugural address.'" In the process of that extended prayer, which *Christian Century* characterized as a "raucous harangue" that made Nixon's inaugural speech seem "simple and winsome" by comparison, Graham thanked God that "thou hast permitted Richard Nixon to lead us at this momentous hour of history" and expressed confidence that America was headed toward "the dawning of a new day."

One may doubt that God arranged Nixon's victory over Hubert Humphrey, especially since the margin of his triumph (less than 1 percent) was not as impressive as, for example, that of the Israelites over the Amalekites, but Richard Nixon's term in office unquestionably initiated a new era for "civil religion," that blend of religious and political culture that has potential to both call a nation to acknowledge and honor its transcendent ideals and to delude it into thinking it has already done so. Every president in American history had invoked the name and blessings of God during his inauguration address, and many, including Billy Graham's friends Dwight Eisenhower and Lyndon Johnson, had made some notable public display of their putative piety, but none ever made such a conscious, calculating use of religion as a political instrument as did Richard Nixon.

Like other presidents before him, Nixon appeared at prayer breakfasts and made the standard salutes in heaven's direction, but the keystone of his effort to present himself as a man deeply concerned with religion and religious values was the White House church service, which he initiated on the first Sunday after his inauguration, with Billy Graham as the preacher. Other presidents had held religious services in the White House; indeed, Lyndon Johnson had invited the cabinet, leading staff members, and some of his personal friends to a service in the White House on the Sunday immediately following John Kennedy's funeral, and Billy Graham was the speaker on that occasion as well. But none before Nixon had ever sponsored a regular schedule of Sunday services. Throughout Nixon's presidency, an uncommon amount of his staff's time and attention went into the White House Sunday services. Surely some genuine spiritual benefit was obtained—by the participants, by the guests, perhaps even by the President himself—and Billy Graham still maintained, fifteen years after the last "Amen," that they were basically beneficial, though he recognized that the negative publicity they drew in some quarters had "backfired" on the President. "I thought it was a good idea at the time," he said, "and in hindsight, I still think it was a good idea. It was better than not going to church at all, and the President was worried about security and the commotion it would cause if he went to a regular church. Some people thought it was practicing civil religion—Mark Hatfield had that view—but I never thought of it in those terms. I just thought it was a great idea that the President of the United States would have services in the White House. I don't think there was any political connotation. There might have been, but I think Nixon was being very sincere. He wanted to set an example for the whole country."

Time magazine asserted that after the first three months of the Nixon presidency, "Billy Graham's spirituality pervades" the White House, but documents from the Nixon archives make it clear that his was not the only spirit roaming the halls of the national mansion. Early memos regarding the Sunday services dealt with format, frequency, possible speakers and musical groups, and denominational representation. The staff sought Graham's advice on these matters, and he submitted a long list of possible speakers, stuffing it with such Evangelical colleagues as Stephen Olford, Harold Lindsell, Leighton Ford, and Nelson Bell, but also taking care to include old friends like Gerald Kennedy, several prominent black ministers, Roman Catholic archbishop H. E. Cardinale, and spokesmen from both the National Council and World Council of Churches. Within a short time, however, the staff was clearly less interested in setting the tone for the republic than in forging a tool for Republicans. An early "action memo" to Charles Colson instructed him to get moving on the "President's request that you develop a list of rich people with strong religious interest to be invited to the White House church services." Colson and his colleagues apparently performed quite admirably; the guest list for a subsequent service included the presidents or board chairmen of AT&T, General Electric, General Motors, Chrysler, Goodyear Tire & Rubber, Westinghouse, Pepsico, Bechtel, Boise Cascade, Republic Steel, Federated Department Stores, and Continental Can Corporation.

Not every boatload of pilgrims to the White House packed such corporate weight, but none was composed of seekers plucked randomly from the shore. One memo, allocating a quota of invitees to various personnel—-

Cabinet members, Charles Colson, and Nixon's secretary Rosemary Woods got approximately fifty slots each; Pat Nixon and Harry Dent received ten apiece; POW wives were allotted six seats—specifically recommended that "non-VIPs" be limited to no more than 25 percent of the congregation. In another memo, Nixon's chief of staff, H. R. Haldeman, noted that "we are now covering the members of the regulatory agencies," pointing out that while that was not objectionable in itself, "all of our Assistant Secretaries and other Presidential appointees should be covered first. It isn't going to do us one bit of good to have a member of a regulatory agency at the Church Service or any other function. If they are to be invited, please limit the invitations to the Chairman or to an appointee we [are] working on for a specific purpose."

As might be expected for such an explicitly instrumental device, every effort was made to make sure that no preacher breached protocol by pretending to be a prophet and that all reports of the services be as favorable as possible. When Billy Graham was not in the pulpit (contrary to the popular impression that he was a regular performer, he preached at only four White House services in the six years they were held, though he did sometimes show up on other occasions to lead prayer and confer a blessing simply by being present), the staff tried to be sure their pastor-for-the-day was a conservative, a Nixon backer, and in touch with a major constituency. When Cincinnati archbishop Joseph Bernardin was invited to participate in a service shortly before St. Patrick's Day, a memo explained that "Bernardin was selected because he is the most prominent Catholic of Irish extraction and *a strong supporter of the President. We have verified this.*" At times, safe men were hard to find; when Harry Dent submitted a list of "some good conservative Protestant Southern Baptists," he felt moved to add, "They are the only good conservative Protestant ministers." Sometimes even conservatives were hard to trust. Elton Trueblood, theologically conservative but dovish in sentiment and independent in character, was given two handwritten notes prior to entering the pulpit, both stressing that he was not to raise any political issues in his sermon. The staff recognized, of course, that an invitation to speak at the White House could enhance a preacher's reputation and was willing to confer that blessing in return for expected political favors. In June 1970, after Nixon raised Baptist hackles by appointing Henry Cabot Lodge as his unofficial emissary to the Vatican, Graham suggested that inviting Carl Bates, president of the Southern Baptist Convention, might offset some of the criticism Nixon was receiving. Then, a few months before the annual meeting of the Southern Baptist Convention in 1971, he recommended that lay preacher Fred Rhodes, who expected to seek the presidency of that twelve-million-member denomination, be invited to preach. A staffer noted that Rhodes was a "staunch Nixon loyalist" and that "a White House invitation to speak would aid greatly in his campaign for this office." The quid pro quo was no mystery: "[I]f elected, Colson feels that Rhodes would be quite helpful to the President in 1972."

Perhaps feeling Nixon's decision to create a religious sanctuary in the White House meant he was finally going to go public with the deep religious convictions Graham had been attributing to him for fifteen years, Billy tried to edge him a bit closer to the altar, to get the President to own up to the piety the preacher felt certain was present. Before Nixon's first appearance at the Presidential Prayer Breakfast (sponsored not by the President but by the International Christian Leadership organization), Graham recommended that "the President's remarks probably should be very low-key and appear to be impromptu." It would also be good, he thought, if the President would "talk about his religious childhood and the impact of religious people on his life, mainly Sunday School teachers, the pastor of the Whittier church where he attended as a child, and other people such as this." Graham figured, no doubt, that such a reminiscence would both appeal to the assemblage and reopen the springs of Nixon's religious sentiments. The evangelist told any who would listen that no one who saw Nixon perform on such occasions could fail to be impressed, but he privately pressed for more, urging Nixon, in the fall of 1969, to make "a statement similar to the one Lincoln gave" before the end of the Civil War, issuing "an anguished call to prayer." At about the same time, he sent along a plan suggested to him by Jane Pickens Langley, the wife of William C. Langley, former president of the New York Stock Exchange, in which she suggested that "at noon each day, everything, including television and radio, could be stopped for two minutes of silent prayer with a definite subject suggested." With a siren serving as a call to prayer, Ms. Langley felt virtually certain that "very few people in this country would fail to comply—even if only out of superstition.... It should be an act of patriotism in which everyone wants voluntarily to participate, and if it is presented correctly, it can become that." To this singularly blatant suggestion that the nation adopt a new ritual for its burgeoning civil religion, Graham appended a simple note: "I personally think she has a point."

Nixon chose not to push for a daily prayer break, but he clearly valued most of Graham's efforts on behalf of his administration's religious program. He was dependably effusive over his White House sermons and treated his appearances as more special than those of other preachers; on one occasion, he not only invited eighty-year-old Morrow Graham and Nelson Bell to attend a service at which Billy was preaching but gave Graham the right to invite as many as thirty additional guests—a singular allocation of scarce political resources. Nixon also appreciated the fact that when Billy Graham was preaching he never had to worry about surprises. Graham would not say anything to embarrass him and would smooth over any rough spots that might arise. At one interfaith service at which Graham appeared on the program with Rabbi Edgar Magnin and John Cardinal Krol, the elderly rabbi got up to speak before his time had come, thus inadvertently cutting out a second number the Mormon Tabernacle Choir was prepared to sing. He also used more than the ten minutes or so the staff had allotted for his remarks. When his own time came to speak, Graham graciously observed that he thought it might be best to have a few moments to reflect on Rabbi Magnin's wisdom before his own sermon, and wondered if the choir might be able to grace the congregation with another offering. The choir happily complied, Graham cut his own prepared remarks short, and the service ended on time, just as if it had been a television program. Members of the congregation may never have noticed, but Richard Nixon did, and wrote a note of gratitude for his friend's skillful handling of an awkward situation.

Charles Colson, whose reputation as the most cynical of Nixon's aides has been badly tarnished by what appears to be a thoroughly genuine religious conversion and by subsequent years of leadership of the Prison Fellowship ministry, believed that Nixon's interest in religion had an authentic aspect. "Sure," he admitted, "we used the prayer breakfasts and church services and all that for political ends. I was part of doing that. But Nixon was an interesting guy. There was an ambivalence about him. There were times when I thought he was genuinely spiritually seeking. The things he'd believed as a young man, he said he no longer believed. He didn't believe in the Resurrection, or in Jonah being swallowed by the whale. He believed those were symbols. But then he'd talk about Catholics and how they had a set of firm beliefs. He'd say he wished he could be a Catholic because they had a set of beliefs and were comfortable with them. You could tell he was struggling inside. That was probably his mother's influence working on him. At the same time, he was a very shrewd politician. He knew how to use religious people to maximum advantage. He used to write orders on giving aid to religious schools or he'd take Cardinal Krol out on the *Sequoia* [the presidential yacht]. That was aimed at winning the Catholic vote. But that's what politicians do."

Billy Graham saw less of the calculating Nixon and recognized that many observers saw little or nothing of the pious Nixon, but he too insisted that his friend never quite shed the religious impulses that had sent him and his brother striding down the aisle at evangelist Paul Rader's tent meeting in Los Angeles years before. "There is a very deep religious side to Richard Nixon that never came out," he insisted. "He is a Quaker and Quakers don't believe in expressing their religion much, but he would [talk about it] to me privately. I made a deal with him. I said, 'I will not keep any notes or diary on my relationship with you, because you deserve privacy. You deserve to have some people around you whom you know are not going to divulge conversations, and especially a clergyman. I want you to have somebody that you can talk to in confidence.' I think he felt that with me, and with Ruth. He told us some things that I am sure he would never want anyone to know. He would take off his shoes and talk by the hour."

The closeness between the two men extended well beyond the confessional, and each felt at ease trading favors with the other. Sometimes the favors were minor, as when someone on the White House staff persuaded Duke Ellington to include vocalist Jimmie McDonald, who had recently left Graham's crusade team, in a concert of sacred music the famed bandleader was presenting on the West Coast. On another occasion, after spending a weekend at Lyndon Johnson's ranch in Texas, Graham tactfully conveyed word that the former president would greatly appreciate an invitation to come to Cape Kennedy to watch the launching of the rocket that would send Neil Armstrong, Buzz Aldrin, and Michael Collins to the moon; the request was promptly granted, with Nixon himself making the call to his predecessor. Other exchanges were more substantial. When it appeared that perhaps as many as four thousand unordained but "full-time Christian workers," including a sizable contingent from Bill Bright's Campus Crusade for Christ movement, were about to be drafted in 1969, Graham placed an urgent call to the White House, contending that they should receive the same exemption granted to ordained ministers. Previously, most local draft boards had routinely granted the exemption; when they had not, the National Selective Service System Appeal Board had upheld the right of such workers for the ministerial exemption. As the war wore on, however, many local draft boards tightened up and the appeal board began to turn down requests to exempt Campus Crusade workers on the grounds that they were not actually ministers. In a memo to Haldeman and John Ehrlichman, Dwight Chapin reported that "Dr. Graham states that ... on the President's Review Board there are one or two gentlemen who are antagonistic toward the work done by these Christian leaders. Needless to say, Graham is very anxious to have someone look into this matter and to see that the policy of exempting these 'full-time Christian leaders' is carried through." The White House obviously considered this as more than a minor annoyance to be finessed as gracefully as possible. Several staffers got involved in seeking a resolution, and one memo noted that "since the board serves at the pleasure of the President, the most quiet and expeditious method of obtaining a review of this matter would be to replace at least some of its members." Graham professed not to recall this episode, but the matter of deferring "Billy Graham's people" was on the White House agenda for at least two months and a "talking paper" for a telephone conversation with the evangelist directed that he be told there was "little danger of a wholesale draft of these ministers."

Predictably, Graham's friendship with Nixon drew heavy fire from several quarters. Liberal clergymen and others opposed to the war in Vietnam regularly condemned the evangelist for his failure to behave as a prophet, a stance that in their opinion required him to use whatever influence he possessed to persuade Nixon to refrain from bombing and to bring the war to a swift end, even at the price of conceding a defeat in American policy, if not in actual combat. Will Campbell, an iconoclastic southern preacher whose efforts to minister to both the victims and perpetrators of racial hatred and whose calls for peace in Vietnam had won him status as a true prophet, branded Graham "a false court prophet who tells Nixon and the Pentagon what they want to hear." Nicholas von Hoffman unleashed such a stinging assault on Graham that Herb Klein felt moved to register a complaint with the editor of the *Washington Post*. Gary Wills called the friendship between the two men "an alliance of moral dwarfs," and I. F. Stone called the clergyman "[Nixon's] smoother Rasputin." And so it went. In part, the criticism stemmed from the perception that Graham had an undiscriminating sense of sin, that because he regarded all sins as manifestations of the same fallen nature and all humans as equally sinful (though perhaps redeemed), he found it difficult to distinguish between, for example, pornography and saturation bombing of civilians. His critics also resented his decided preference for obedience to authority—virtually any authority that did not expressly forbid worship of God or compel worship of some other being—and his underlying assumption that those in power, particularly in the United States, were more likely to be right than wrong. Finally, they charged him with abdicating responsibility for improving the world by preaching that such problems as racial injustice, poverty, and war would never be solved until Jesus returned to inaugurate the millennium.

None of the charges was groundless. Since the end of the Benevolent Empire created by Charles Finney and his contemporaries before the Civil War, Evangelicals had concentrated on problems of individual behavior and character rather than on the shortcomings of corporate bodies. In *Moral Man and Immoral Society*, Reinhold Niebuhr brilliantly described how men of good character and impeccable personal morals could and did participate in business, government, and other large-scale institutions that were engaged in unjust, sinful, exceedingly destructive behavior, without any clear sense of incongruity or paradox. Evangelicals, with Billy Graham as a classic example, seemed never to have grasped Niebuhr's point. To Graham, structures were immoral because they were made up of immoral individuals. If these individuals could be redeemed, then the structures would automatically right themselves and begin to behave in a Christian manner. For that reason, calling for repentance on the part of small-time sinners—"the bartender who sells beer to minors, the income-tax chiseler, the college grad whose diploma is won by cribbing rather than cramming"—seemed to Graham to be as important a part of "The Answer to Corruption" as passing laws to curb wholesale abuses by corporations and the politicians.

It was also easy, at a time when millions of Americans were challenging all forms of authority, to find support for the view that despite an irenic spirit and ostensible commitment to individualism, Billy Graham was an authoritarian personality. He had said, "I once asked an army officer which he would rather have on the field of battle—courage or obedience. He flashed right back, 'Obedience.' God would rather have your obedience than anything else." He repeatedly asserted that young people had rallied to Hitler and Mussolini and various Communist leaders because they wanted a master to be the center of their lives. And he believed that nothing—not racism, not a divisive war in Southeast Asia—was likely to be so dangerous to the security of the nation and so odious in the eyes of God as angry protests in the street and rebellious assault on "the system" by student radicals. As for clergymen who led protests against the war, in an address before the Southern Baptist Convention he said, "Where many of these men get the 'Reverend' in front of their names, I do not know. Certainly they don't get it from God." A man who openly challenged the standing order, he seemed to be saying, could not be a man of God. "It is interesting to me," he observed, "that God does not tolerate disorder. He laid down precise laws in the physical, chemical and electrical world." Since God did not tolerate disorder, Graham saw little reason for his appointed representatives to do so either. He told a gathering of Protestant policemen in New York City that they were agents of God with "a tremendous responsibility at this hour of revolution and anarchy and rebellion against all authority that is sweeping across our nation," and he lamented that "the Supreme Court, in trying to protect freedom, is giving the nation dangerous license." He huddled with J. Edgar Hoover to receive a report on radical students and declared a few days later that "there is a small, highly organized group of radicals" who were "determined to destroy what they call 'the system'" and were "very dangerous to the security of our nation." In an interview on NBC television, he revealed that he had information that approximately one hundred terrorist groups would soon begin a campaign to destroy established order in the nation.

With regard to the third objection his critics raised, Graham always acknowledged that he saw no lasting solution to most of the world's problems short of the Second Coming. Without question, this conviction seriously weakened his and other Evangelicals' commitment to movements dedicated to major social change. But he did not invoke this belief as a means of escaping responsibility; he invoked it because he believed it was true, because he believed the Bible taught it. Even so, his views on the two great social issues of the decade—race and Vietnam—were neither as individualistic nor as patently acquiescent to governmental authority as his critics charged.

On the question of race, Graham stuck to his long-standing policy of insisting on integrated crusades, urging brotherhood and understanding, and warning that demonstrations and protests were likely to prove futile and counterproductive. In the summer of 1969, when Graham returned to Madison Square Garden for a ten-day crusade, civil rights activist James Forman was presenting his Black Manifesto to white churches and synagogues, demanding they pay $500 million in reparations to black Americans. When asked at a precrusade news conference if he expected Forman to present his demands at the Garden, Graham replied drily that "I don't think we're going to have any outside speakers. I'm going to do the preaching. If he were to come, we would welcome him with a big smile and hope he enjoyed the service." Perhaps sensing he would never get past the Garden's security force, or if he did, that he would not be able to work the guilt of Graham's congregation as successfully as that of, say, New York's liberal Riverside Church, Forman made no attempt to interrupt the crusade's services, and Graham never mentioned the Black Manifesto in his sermons. He did, however, attract more blacks to the Garden than he had in 1957. *Time* magazine estimated that at least a quarter of his audience on most nights was nonwhite.

For all his distance from the main arenas of conflict, Graham's frequent references to racial injustice and his principled adherence to what he did believe made it easier for other Evangelicals to take stronger stands. An important manifestation of that phenomenon came in September 1969, at the U.S. Congress on Evangelism. Though BGEA had no official role in this gathering, its leaders consciously saw themselves as extending the work of the 1966 Berlin Congress; Graham served as honorary chairman and gave a major address, the meeting was held in Minneapolis, and a book containing the speeches delivered at the gathering was edited by George Wilson and produced by BGEA's World Wide Publications. This congress, which attracted 5,000 delegates from 93 denominations and most states, served as a kind of springboard, enabling Evangelicals to identify more boldly with social action. Many of the old familiar notes were struck by the old familiar people, but the meeting also offered bolder fare. Leighton Ford, who had begun to appear on the *Hour of Decision* broadcasts almost as often as Graham and was unofficially being groomed to succeed him, declared it a shame the church had been "so slow to face the demands of the Gospel in the racial revolution of our time," and Stephen Olford warned of what could happen when church people clung to segregation. When he arrived at New York's Calvary Baptist Church, he reported, he found it staunchly segregationist. After he preached and taught a series of lessons on the evils of such an arrangement, all but eleven members voted to integrate the church. Of those eleven, four soon confessed their sin and repented; of the stonyhearted remainder, all seven died shortly thereafter. In the dramatic, riveting manner that had arrested a young Billy Graham's attention more than twenty years earlier, Olford thundered the explanation of their deaths: "God's judgment fell!"

Black delegates to the congress moved well beyond their white brethren. Tom Skinner, a former Harlem gang leader who admitted stabbing at least twenty-two people before being converted by a gospel radio broadcast, acknowledged that "Mr. Graham has been an outstanding spokesman in terms of the Gospel of Jesus Christ in healing the relationship between Black and White in this country," but he noted that religion had not always improved the lot of the oppressed and suffering. He reminded the delegates that religion had also undergirded slavery and that the church had been guilty of gross negligence of minorities and the poor. And then he got specific. "When I move to your community and buy a home and I'm being given a rough time," he asked, "will you take a stand? If my daughter falls in love with your son and they decide to get married, will you allow them to marry in peace? Will you reciprocate by accepting me as a brother? This is what black Christian brethren are crying out for, a genuine relationship." Skinner challenged his white brethren to open the doors to their institutions, to provide black faculty and recruit black students for their colleges, to grant black writers and ministers access to their magazines and radio stations, and to let them talk about race, not just about communism and sex and movies and nightclubs. To do less than this, to mouth platitudes about equality and then to censure blacks who participated in protests and riots, or to relocate their congregations when blacks moved into the neighborhood was to cry "Give us Barabbas" and to crucify Christ anew. In another uncomfortable historical allusion, Ralph Abernathy, the black Baptist minister who succeeded Martin Luther King as the head of the Southern Christian Leadership Conference, compared the law-and-order campaigns mounted by many politicians in 1968 to the campaign that elevated Hitler to chancellor of Germany in 1933. Finally, a group of nearly fifty black ministers presented the congress with a list of complaints, calling on white Christians to "confess in word and action to the sins committed against black people," urging representatives of church agencies to foster equal-employment practices and asking church leaders to help blacks obtain improved urban housing.

The Minneapolis congress neither took nor recommended any specific direct action on racial issues, but Evangelicals concerned for social action regard it as an important moment, and Graham himself took seriously the need to move beyond rhetoric and personal example. Though skeptical about the efficacy of forced busing, he made a series of five spot announcements urging southern parents to "obey the law" on school integration. Then, during a crusade in Anaheim, California, a few days later, he met E. V. Hill, a successful and influential Baptist pastor and close friend of Martin Luther King's. A conversation scheduled for forty minutes stretched into six hours as Hill detailed with considerable emotion the impatience many black churchmen felt toward their white brethren. Shortly afterward, Graham arranged a meeting between a group of key black ministers and the President of the United States. He acknowledged that "they would never have gotten to him in a hundred years if I had not opened the door," but Nixon treated it as more than a courtesy visit. Though internal memos reveal that the President thought the meeting had run on much too long (over three and a half hours),

Graham recalled that "they let him have it with both barrels and he sat there and took it." And at least on the short run and not without an eye for political advantage, Nixon responded to their complaints. The clergymen were quite specific, discussing such matters as their difficulty in getting funds from the Office of Economic Opportunity and the Department of Housing and Urban Development for housing projects for senior citizens and bonding restrictions that seemed to favor contractors. These appeals touched Nixon's compassionate as well as his calculating side. A Haldeman memo prior to the meeting indicated that "the President is extremely interested in following up with Billy Graham in the work he is doing with Negro ministers across the country. He feels, as does Graham, that this may be our best chance to make inroads into the Negro community." But more than unvarnished political tactic was at work. Immediately after the April 1970 meeting, Haldeman informed Ehrlichman that Nixon wanted "one of the projects cleared and done tomorrow. He points out that you can always find a way to do the things for the people on the other side and that just for once he'd like to see us find a way to do something right for the people on our side.... [He] wants to see at least one of their projects approved and under way if it means the staff at OEO have to take up a collection from their own pockets to raise the money to do it." Another staff memo indicated that "we are exploring additional ways in which we can involve these men and assist in their efforts to solve the problems of their communities." Whatever the controlling motive, help fulaction did occur, and at least some black ministers moved closer to the Republican camp. In May 1970, E. V. Hill wrote to Nixon to say that "upon your instructions, your staff intervened and within a few days caused the program to commence and also enabled the program to have as its contractors two very able Negroes.... I have not been quiet in proclaiming what you have personally done in this matter. I shall continue to tell my community ... of the interest of the President in a 'local matter.'"

When Graham looked at Vietnam, his stance continued to be less clear than his views on civil rights. Just weeks after Nixon took office, the evangelist told reporters that "we must have peace in Vietnam. I'm not only going to say I'm for peace, but I'm going to try to do something. In my particular area it must be done in rather a quiet way." What he did immediately was to gather a group of missionary leaders from various parts of Southeast Asia for a three-day meeting in Bangkok, where they shared their perceptions on the war and offered specific recommendations for ending it. The men were not tyros who had spent a few months in the area and were now calling for a worldwide day of prayer. Most had been in Vietnam from five to twenty years, and some enjoyed regular access to President Thieu and other members of the South Vietnamese government. Prior to the meeting, they interviewed hundreds of Vietnamese officials and other key people. In a thirteen-page confidential report to Nixon, Graham characterized them as a "hawkish" group, making their criticisms of the war all the more telling.

According to the missionaries, the South Vietnamese people were overwhelmingly pro-American and pro-Nixon, but the Paris peace talks had generated a fear that "a coalition government will be imposed on them that in the long run may lead to a Communist takeover." The group also manifested a growing sense of disillusionment with Americans in Vietnam, citing reports that "more than 40 percent of American troops are now on some form of dope or narcotics." They also charged that South Vietnamese officials and other citizens were enmeshed in a massive web of corruption largely traceable to the actions of Americans, particularly contractors and other businessmen, whom one missionary described as "the 'crud' of American society." As a result, at least a third of all the goods shipped to Vietnam from America eventually found their way onto the black market, and multiplied millions were being spent on programs that were colossal failures, creating disillusionment at the "glaring corruption, incompetence and waste of American civilians working for companies doing business in Vietnam." The missionaries believed that American policy was hopelessly misguided. Americanizing the war by providing extensive manpower and taking over the decision making not only robbed the South Vietnamese of their dignity but enabled the Vietcong and the North Vietnamese to appear like a "little boy" being beaten by an American giant, which gave them a tremendous propaganda weapon, even though their own giant—the Communist world—stood directly behind them. To make matters worse, the American giant often appeared clumsy and ineffective, "using methods of warfare learned at West Point and more appropriate in the battle theaters of World War II than in the jungles of Vietnam." Equally damaging, the missionaries felt, was "the overwhelming cultural intrusion," particularly the flood of American consumer goods readily available through post exchanges and on the black market. If this kept up, they warned, "we will have destroyed what we came to save, and that is the Vietnamese, their culture, and their freedom."

The missionaries felt it was still possible to win the war if the Paris peace talks produced no honorable settlement. The first step would be to return the war to the Vietnamese, letting them fight it in "the Oriental way." Guerilla warfare, encouraged by Eisenhower and Kennedy but deemphasized by Johnson, should be resumed, "using Oriental methods which seem brutal and cruel in sophisticated Western eyes, but which are being used every day by the Viet Cong to spread terror and fear to the people." The North Vietnamese, they believed, feared a well-equipped and well-trained South Vietnamese army using guerilla tactics far more than they feared American soldiers. Especially valuable in a renewed emphasis on guerilla warfare would be the mountain people, whom the missionaries felt they could control for another year or two, despite intense efforts by the Chinese to win their allegiance. America should also encourage and equip North Vietnamese defectors to return to the north to engage in guerilla warfare and ultimately to attempt a coup. "Why," Graham asked, "should all the fighting be in the south?" By missionary estimates, perhaps no more than 10,000 of the 27 million North Vietnamese were hard-core Communists. The rest, they suspected, would welcome liberation by anti-Communist forces.

Because ineffective and insensitive American policy provided the Vietcong with important psychological advantages, Graham and his colleagues recommended major attention to propaganda. "Instead of showing 10 hours of American movies a day," he said, "use our vast television investment for propaganda purposes," with concentrated attention to boosting Vietnamese morale, helping them feel a kinship with free nations throughout the world, and exposing Communist tyranny by such methods as interviewing Vietcong defectors and showing "the terrorism by the Communists right on television." This last tactic alone, he felt, "would do more than anything we can think of." Used properly, Graham believed, the multimillion-dollar radio and television system devoted almost entirely to entertainment purposes would produce 5,000 or more defectors from the Vietcong every month. Finally, he recommended that the Southeast Asian Treaty Organization be reorganized—"It is totally out of date"—and that Nixon convene an Asian summit conference.

When Graham's report, which varied somewhat from his repeated public insistence that he limited his counsel with political leaders to spiritual matters, became available for public inspection in February 1989, he noted characteristically that the views contained in it were largely those of the missionaries and that he had merely conveyed those views to the President. It is clear, however, that he agreed with them, not only from his own statements in the report but also from the fact that six months after he had sent it to Nixon, he sent a copy to Henry Kissinger, assistant to the President for national security affairs, noting that Defense Secretary Melvin Laird had been impressed with it and expressing his hope that Kissinger would also pay heed to it. Kissinger, too, had "found it quite useful" and was "looking into the points which they raised." Less concretely, Graham also began to voice an ambivalence about the war, reflecting the missionaries' influence. In an interview with Dotson Rader (grandson of evangelist Paul Rader, under whose preaching Nixon made his boyhood commitment to Christ) Graham revealed that he understood the feelings of "the people of Southeast Asia who are frightened that we might pull out" but added that America "can't be the world's policeman. We have far too many problems at home, growing too dangerous. And, also, I am not at all sure that the war is supportable, morally supportable. I am simply not sure at all."

Despite his misgivings, Graham could not bring himself to disagree openly with government policy, and he was at pains to show himself in sympathy with the views of Richard Nixon. When the *Christian Herald*, one of his early boosters, published an editorial opposing U.S. policy in Vietnam on both moral and legal grounds, Nixon asked Graham to find out who, specifically, had been responsible. Graham reported that the culprit was David Poling, who "openly professes his liberal thinking on practically all matters" and had led the magazine "increasingly to the left" during his tenure as president of the Christian Herald Association. Graham suggested, however, that Nixon need not be too concerned about the editorial. The circulation and influence of the magazine had been declining steadily in recent years and he believed it "definitely could not have any kind of impact on American Protestant thinking at the present time." Besides, he added, "*Christianity Today* ... is well-known as the most influential Protestant news journal, and it consistently takes stands opposite to those of the *Christian Herald*."

In addition to his efforts to help find some solution to the war in Vietnam, Graham stood ready to serve his President at any other promising juncture where he might be needed. Before a meeting with Israeli primeminister Golda Meir, he told Nixon, "If you have any suggestions as to how I may contribute in this delicate Middle East situation, please let me know." The White House evidently did not feel the evangelist was overreaching. One staffer suggested to Kissinger that Graham should convey to Mrs. Meir a sense of American unease over Israeli military strategy—specifically, a series of aggressive air strikes against its neighbors during the summer of 1969. Nixon also relayed Graham's offer to Kissinger and asked for a report on the meeting between Graham and Meir. There seems to be no record of the meeting itself, but Graham was clearly perceived during this period as one of Israel's valued friends. The World Wide Pictures film *His Land*, released in 1969, outlined Graham's theological understanding of the role of Israel in God's grand historical plan and was well received by Jewish leaders both in Israel and America. The film moved prominent Rabbi Marc Tanenbaum to declare that "for acts of friendship toward the Jewish people at a time of turmoil which has not been altogether congenial to Jewish security, Billy Graham deserves better than a stereotyped skeptical response from thoughtful Jews and many others, while not ignoring basic differences."

Graham offered to provide similar diplomatic services, as well as to gain entree to yet another world leader, when he asked Dwight Chapin to see about having the American ambassador to France arrange a meeting with that nation's new president, Georges Pompidou. A few months later, when Graham's schedule placed him in Paris at the time of Charles de Gaulle's death, he wired the White House to let Nixon know that he "would be available for anything he might want me to do in connection with De Gaulle's death." In each of these cases, Graham probably had more to gain than the

President, but on two other occasions in 1970 he exposed himself to sharp criticism and enthusiastically lent himself and his prestige to efforts that Nixon's staff hoped would shore up the President's policies and popularity and rally support for the administration.

In May 1970 Graham held a crusade in the stadium at the University of Tennessee at Knoxville and invited the President not only to attend but to address the crowd, another crusade first—Lyndon Johnson had attended a crusade while President but had not spoken. Graham, of course, insisted his invitation was free from political intent and professed bafflement that anyone should think otherwise. "If Mr. Nixon had been running for election," he acknowledged, "I could understand the charge of politics. But he is the President. I wouldn't think that you'd call the President political." Years later, he still maintained that his only concern had been spiritual: "I was going to preach the straight gospel. I thought he needed to hear it. I had him sit on the platform, of course; he was President of the United States." Not everyone agreed with Graham's assessment. In a CBS News editorial, Dan Rather asserted that whatever the evangelist's intent, Nixon had leapt at the chance to make a safe, popular appearance in the South. By identifying with Graham, who was enormously popular in his native region, the President hoped to give a boost to Republican candidates in that year's elections. He was particularly interested in the race for governor of Alabama, where a defeat to George Wallace would derail his troublesome presidential ambitions, and in the Republican attempt to unseat Democratic senator Albert Gore, Sr., in Tennessee. He did not think it seemly to campaign directly against the two men, but his advisers were said to feel that standing with Billy Graham would provide "just the right touch." Secondarily, at a time when colleges were erupting in protest against the Vietnam War—the killings at Kent State had occurred just ten days earlier—Nixon sought to prove he could appear on a major campus without creating an uproar, and it seemed unlikely that a stadium full of Billy Graham supporters gathered from conservative East Tennessee would explode into anti-establishment chaos, especially since a state law made it a crime to disrupt a religious service.

The evening proved to be less than the total triumph Nixon and his advisers hoped for. As he and Graham strode across the stadium turf on their way to the platform, a sweeping ovation washed over them, and a contingent of volunteers from the Fellowship of Christian Athletes and the unsmiling and vigilant corps of Secret Service agents provided an impenetrable defense against a small band of protesters holding placards recalling the biblical injunctions against killing or kneeling at the edge of the field in memory of those who had died in Vietnam. After Graham introduced Nixon, noting that "I'm for change—but the Bible teaches us to obey authority," the President urged the youth night crowd to depend upon "those great spiritual sources that have made America the great country that it is." When several hundred hecklers scattered about the stadium responded to that bit of piety with chants of "Bullshit! Bullshit!" and "Stop the crap and end the war!" the huge crowd swamped them with new waves of applause and cheers of approval that continued for several minutes. At one point, Nixon asked for attention, but he knew that most of the crowd was with him. He acknowledged the existence of different points of view and asserted his own belief in dissent, but added, with a triumphant smile, "I'm just glad that there seems to be a rather solid majority on one side rather than on the other side tonight," a verdict that touched off still another torrential ovation. Overall, it was a satisfying evening for the President—*Time* called it "one of the most effective speeches he has yet delivered," and when the service was telecast a few weeks later, most of the protest had been edited out, making it appear even better. Later that evening, after *Air Force One* arrived in California, Henry Kissinger called from San Clemente to tell Graham how much Nixon had appreciated the opportunity to have a part in the service.

Graham's other key effort to quiet the turmoil bedeviling the President occurred when he and Bob Hope teamed with Disney personnel, *Reader's Digest* publisher Hobart Lewis, and hotel magnate J. Willard Marriot, Sr., to produce a July 4 religiopatriotic extravaganza known as Honor America Day. The exact genesis of the Super Salute to God and Country is is difficult to pin down, but Graham was obviously involved at the earliest stages, and despite insistence that it was strictly a nongovernmental affair, the White House played a central role in its planning and execution. The official rationale for the event was that in those troubled times, a divided nation needed an opportunity to renew and express its commitment to its deepest and most precious ideals and values and to celebrate the glorious joys of being an American—a combination revival meeting and national birthday party. In keeping with that aim, the organizers attempted to sound all the major chords in America's heart song, with little sense that excess might detract from effectiveness. When told that a team of marathoners would relay an American flag from Philadelphia to Washington, and that the flag's arrival at the Lincoln Memorial would touch off a worship service presided over by Billy Graham, H. R. Haldeman did not wince in fear that many Americans might find the blending of civil and sacred symbols too blatant. Instead, he wrote on the memo, "Great idea! Start from Liberty Bell. Maybe others from Williamsburg, Jamestown, Mt. Vernon, etc." Later, he suggested that "most of all we need a solid cornball program developer."

Billy Graham's participation went far beyond letting his name appear at the top of the stationery and showing up to preach. BGEA seconded Walter Smyth to work on the project full time, and Cliff Barrows oversaw the planning of the music for the religious service. Graham mentioned Honor America Day on his *Hour of Decision* broadcast, sent a special letter urging his East Coast supporters to attend the celebration, and dispatched several staffers to stir up interest among churches within reasonable driving distance of Washington. He personally encouraged black ministers to support the event, since an all-white gathering would appear too flagrantly Republican. He also tried to make sure that others did their part. In a memo to Charles Colson, Dwight Chapin noted that Graham "is pushing everyone very hard and when we run up against problems, Billy immediately reacts to the call and gets people tracking right. A call of thanks [to] keep him charged up would be a good touch."

The festivities themselves went smoothly. Rabbi Tanenbaum, Bishop Sheen, and E. V. Hill led prayers, and astronaut Frank Borman, "the first man to pray publicly in outer space," was on hand to remind the assembly of the glories of prayers past. The U.S. Army Band and the Southern Baptist Male Chorus lent collective gravity to the occasion; Pat Boone, Kate Smith, and Johnny Cash sang patriotic favorites; and country singer Jeannie C. Riley warned that "when you're running down my country, Hoss, you're walking on the fighting side of me." On the ideological edges of the crowd, leftist and other antiwar groups protested the American presence in Southeast Asia, and right-wingers damned the administration for not really trying to win in Vietnam. In the center, where he felt most comfortable, Billy Graham ticked off the reasons why America was worthy of honor. A generous America, he said, had repeatedly opened its doors to the distressed. Instead of hiding and denying its problems, it recognized and tried to solve them, giving all the right to voice their opinions freely, even when they ran counter to the policies of the government and will of the majority. And, most important of all, America should be honored because of its pervasive faith in God Almighty. It was vintage Fourth of July fare and vintage Graham, a shining example of his ability to articulate the beliefs and sentiments of the great and decent center segment of American culture. The crowds on hand were disappointingly small—CBS estimated the total turnout at approximately 15,000—but millions watching network news heard Graham proclaim that "we honor America because she defends the right of her citizens to dissent"; call dissent "the hallmark of our freedom in America"; and thunder in conclusion, "Honor the nation!... And as you move to do it, never give in. Never give in! Never! Never! Never! Never!" Despite failure to attract the hoped-for "vast crowd," the White House was pleased. Patrick Buchanan urged Chapin to distribute pictures of Graham preaching in front of the Lincoln Memorial to "all publications," to mail a copy of his sermon to every minister in America, and to see to it that the sermon was reprinted in the *Reader's Digest*. No one appeared more appreciative than Nixon, who both called and wrote Graham to commend him on his speech, assuring him that he had touched the hearts of millions and noting that "the Honor America Day ceremonies reinforced my own conviction that it is time to strike back—not in anger, and not in a mean spirit, but in affirmation of those enduring values that have proved themselves in crisis and trouble, generation after generation, and given our nation its greatness." Graham never imagined for a moment that Nixon's values varied from his own or doubted that Richard Nixon was God's man for that critical hour in American history. In a handwritten note near the end of the President's second year in office, Graham wrote, "My expectations were high when you took office nearly two years ago but you have exceeded [them] in every way! You have given moral and spiritual leadership to the nation at a time when we desperately needed it—in addition to courageous political leadership! Thank you!" He signed the letter "With Affection."

23

The Power and the Glory

Despite his enthusiasm for the task, Graham's dabbling in the political arena occupied only a small portion of his time. His primary commitment and energy still went into preaching the gospel as effectively and widely as possible and encouraging movements and institutions that would enhance the growth and respectability of middle-of-the-road Evangelicalism. A lung problem that caused him to cut back on his crusade schedule in 1968 left him time not only to offer counsel to candidate Nixon but also to pursue his continuing interest in a school that would serve the East Coast as Fuller and Wheaton served the West and Midwest.

Graham apparently entertained few regrets about declining John MacArthur's offer to underwrite a full-scale university, but when the opportunity came to create an eastern counterpart to Fuller Seminary—a smaller and more manageable project that would not require him to neglect evangelism—he could not resist. That possibility arose as a result of an unusual set of circumstances involving the usual cast of characters. When Temple University in Philadelphia began to accept government funds in the midsixties, it was forced by law to divest itself of its seminary, the Conwell School of Theology, named for Temple's founder, nineteenth-century Evangelical philanthropist Russell Conwell. The seminary was small, with only five faculty members, a couple of buildings, and fewer than fifty students. The easiest course would have been simply to close down, but institutions resist death. Daniel Poling, a prominent clergyman and friend of Graham who was a member of Temple's board, had another plan. At a quickly arranged meeting in Penn Station, while Graham awaited a train to Montreat, Poling put the kind of pressure on Billy that Billy often put on others. "We've got to do something," he told Graham, "and I've got it on my heart that you should have it," adding that J. Howard Pew had it on his heart as well. Smarting from the United Presbyterian Church's recent refusal of his offer to build an Evangelical seminary that would stand for the integrity of Scripture, Pew pledged to throw generous support behind Conwell if Billy Graham would take charge. Graham resisted, but Poling pressed and, apparently thinking he saw a glimmer of interest, kept on pressing. Finally, echoing William Bell Riley's words twenty years earlier, he told Graham, "I'll just have to meet you at the Judgment of God with this, because I know you're the one to take it." The threat that he might be out of God's will if he spurned Poling's offer pushed Billy's balky camel on through the eye of the needle. "To make a long story short," he recalled, "I took it, but with this understanding: all the board and all the faculty would resign, and I would name a new board and a new faculty. Of course, that created some problems." Perhaps only Billy Graham would have dared set such conditions, but Poling accepted, and the Temple board agreed in essence to give Conwell to Graham, to let him do with it whatever he wanted.

What he wanted was a board and faculty whose judgment and theology he trusted, and that is what he got. He packed the eighteen-member board with old friends and associates: Leighton Ford, Stephen Olford, Allan Emery, Carloss Morris, Robert Van Kampen, Roger Hull, and other dependables, mostly from the Northeast; only four of the resigning trustees were asked to stay on. An all-new Evangelical faculty was formed, led by Stuart Babbage, a professor of theology at the Columbia Presbyterian Seminary in Atlanta. In an innovative attempt to recruit and train black clergymen, Graham arranged to have regular seminary classes taught in a black section of the city to make it easier on students who might find it difficult to come to the Temple campus for all their classes. After about a year, Graham began working on Harold Ockenga to take over the day-to-day leadership of the school. Ockenga was favorably inclined but was also considering an offer to become president of Gordon College and Divinity School, an Evangelical school in Wenham, Massachusetts, north of Boston. "One day we were talking on the phone," Graham recalled, "and I honestly don't remember which one of us said it, but one of us said, 'Why should we try to build two schools on the East Coast? We have one great school—Fuller—on the West Coast. Why not have one great school on the East Coast?'" The prospect of merger, with the attendant advantage of avoiding competition for faculty, students, and money, appealed to both men.

Because the Temple campus was crowded, and because Graham felt a location in the Boston area would provide the most desirable intellectual cachet, it made sense for Conwell to move to New England. Since Graham had that school's board in his pocket, his suggestion of a merger met little resistance. The Gordon board took more persuading, but Ockenga handled those negotiations, a task doubtless made easier by the prospect that access to Howard Pew's millions might finally end the little school's chronic financial problems. Pew was entirely willing to make good on his offer to back Graham's project, but not without qualification. Because he was convinced that association with an undergraduate college would divert attention from the seminary's primary task, and ultimately, that a liberal arts curriculum would undermine the authority of Scripture, he insisted that the new seminary divorce itself from Gordon College. Faced with the need to find a new home for a school that did not yet even exist, Graham approached another of his New England friends: Richard Cardinal Cushing. Billy pointed out to the cardinal that a Carmelite seminary in South Hamilton, near Wenham, had only two dozen or so students. "We want to put a major institution out there," he told Cushing. "We need that seminary." The prelate got on the telephone immediately ("He didn't always use Evangelical Protestant language when he talked to his assistants," Graham remembered) and found out that the seminary was indeed quite underutilized. Not long afterward, J. Howard Pew put up 2 million dollars to buy the land and several million more to refurbish existing facilities and to build and stock a library. With a new and attractive setting, a Graham-appointed board and faculty, and the combined 310-member student body from the two constituent schools, the Gordon-Conwell Theological Seminary got off to a brisk start in 1970. Enrollment quickly boomed, and two decades later, more than 550 students were preparing for the ministry in one of the largest and most vigorous seminaries in the country. And Billy Graham was still chairman of the board.

In the midst of establishing a new educational institution, Graham rebounded sufficiently from his health problems to return to Australia and New Zealand early in 1969 to finish a series of meetings cut short the year before. In 1970 he used an ambitious and innovative television relay system to transmit a crusade in Dortmund, Germany, to theaters, arenas, and stadiums throughout Western Europe and into Yugoslavia—"unscrambling Babel," as one aide put it, to reach speakers of eight different languages. Then, after more than three years of attending mainly to foreign fields, he returned to America for two full years of domestic crusades, in Anaheim, New York City, Knoxville, Baton Rouge, Lexington, Chicago, Oakland, Dallas-Fort Worth, Charlotte, Birmingham, and Cleveland. For the most part, these were standard crusades with standard results, including the standard announcements of record-breaking closing-day crowds and higher-than-average rates of response to the invitation. They were not, however, performed in a vacuum, and Graham found that wherever he went, he was obliged to adapt not only to current events and improved technology but also to his status as a symbol friends and foes alike could use in service of their own agendas.

The two-part visit to Australia and New Zealand was a mixture of joyous reunion and rude rebuff. Perhaps no event in that region's history had affected religious life more than Graham's triumphant tour in 1959. Now, a decade later, crusade committees and counseling classes and the pulpits of cooperating churches contained hundreds of people who proudly identified themselves as Fifty-Niners, men and women who had first come to faith in Graham's original crusade and were happily "going on in the Lord." The response in Sydney, where Evangelicals uncharacteristically had the strongest voice in Anglican circles, was generally warm and enthusiastic. Crowds were good—over 500,000 in eight days—and first-timers made up an unusually high 70 percent of the inquirers, a statistic that delighted both team and sponsors, since first-timers are more likely to represent a net addition to church rolls than are "rededicators." Graham's postponing of scheduled crusades in Melbourne and New Zealand may have made it harder to regenerate excitement when he returned in 1969; whatever the explanation, neither proved as receptive as they had been in 1959.

The evangelist managed to sidestep discussion of Vietnam during his 1968 visit to Sydney, but his perceived closeness to Nixon and the increased unpopularity of American policy made him the target of sharper questioning from newspaper and TV reporters during the 1969 tour. Unidentified antagonists threatened to bomb his meeting in Auckland, and a group of antiwar protesters interrupted a service at the Myer Music Bowl in Melbourne. When Leighton Ford, normally well received by college groups, spoke at the University of Adelaide, he was heckled by students who launched dozens of paper airplanes at him as he spoke. Perturbed that the ever-polite Graham and his associates could be treated so rudely, *Christianity Today* speculated that the day might soon return when Christians would be stoned for their faith. Despite these problems, the 1969 tour was far from a failure. An estimated 85,000 came to the cricket grounds for the closing service in Melbourne, and an unusually large number of youthful inquirers gave promise of long-term benefit to the churches.

Graham's continuing ability to draw large numbers of young people to his crusade encouraged and intrigued him, and moved him to make an honest, if limited, attempt to understand the sixties youth culture. He purchased a stack of rock albums, and after he and Ruth listened to them at least once, declared that he had been "frankly surprised to find that a lot of rock music is deeply religious" in the sense that the lyrics asked, "What is the purpose of my life?" "Where did I come from?" and "Where am I going?" He tried to mingle inconspicuously with hippies and protesters at several festivals and demonstrations, at least once donning fake whiskers to disguise his appearance. While he continued to deplore discourtesy and disorder and still regarded student radicals as a menace to society, he came away with a mostly positive view of what he had seen and heard. "With their talk of Jesus boots and almost biblical language," he said, probably not intending to assign all the language of the counterculture to this near-canonical category, "they show an unconscious longing for Christ." To be sure, he disapproved of some tactics favored by young protesters; still, he felt that "they're asking the right questions" and insisted that "they have a right to want to change the system."

In an effort to reach young people, Graham changed his own system somewhat. At his 1969 New York crusade, the team rented a ballroom near Madison Square Garden and operated what they billed as "America's Largest Coffeehouse," complete with strobe lights and screens that flashed "Jesus" and "Love" while the *apres-crusade* set gathered to talk with each other and a covey of youth counselors "in an atmosphere of psychedelic lighting and amplified folk-rock music" played by young Christian musicians, some of whom testified to their recent rescue from drugs and "digging the sex scene." Later that year, Graham accepted an invitation to speak at a rock festival in Miami. His audience on that occasion seemed more interested in leaflets urging the legalization of marijuana than in his hearty approbation of the "terrific music" he had heard and his promises of a way "to get high without hang-ups and hangovers," but he told reporters he had received a "tremendous response" and declared that he planned to attend more such gatherings, because "this is where the young people are [that] I want to reach. I love these kids. I really do."

Not all young people returned such expressions of goodwill. During a Chicago crusade, a group of approximately three hundred protesters identified by the *Chicago Daily News* as hippies, but branded as Satanists by Graham and *Christianity Today*, tried to disrupt a youth service at McCormick Place. Notified in advance of their plans, Graham prayed for forgiveness of and kindness toward the disrupters, but made it plain they would not be allowed to take over the service. "There's a small group of people here highly organized and ready to demonstrate," he informed the crowd of 27,000. "You came here to hear the Gospel and we paid for this hall. I'm sure you will know what to do when the time comes—and there are enough of you here to do it." When a contingent of troublemakers came forward during the second hymn of the service, Graham interrupted the choir and asked the thousands of young Christians in the arena to surround them and to "Love them. Pray for them. Sing to them. And gradually ease them back toward the entrances through which they have come." A small band of about thirty "Jesus People" joined hands to form a circle around the primary disrupters, chanting "Jesus is the Way," "Join the Jesus Revolution," and simply "Jesus! Jesus! Jesus! Jesus! Jesus!" Some singled out individual "Satanists" and began to share their faith with them or, in more dramatic fashion, threw their arms around them and began to pray for their salvation. Thousands remained in their seats, imploring God's Spirit "to confound the work of Satan in our midst," while hundreds of other young people formed an irresistible human wave that swept the interlopers toward the exits. A scuffle broke out briefly when one of the protesters tossed a firecracker, but swift police intervention forestalled any serious conflict, and the service resumed with an exhilarating sense of triumph over the Enemy. A similar incident in Oakland the following month was handled in the same manner.

Billy's concern for understanding young people no doubt stemmed in part from watching his own brood move into adulthood. Second daughter Anne, described by siblings and nonfamily members alike as a near-model child, had limited her flirtation with the world to bleaching her hair and paying considerable attention to makeup, but the results had been appealing enough to win her part-time work as a model for several of Asheville's better clothing stores. Some dour Fundamentalists may have clucked at such behavior, but the Grahams saw no harm in it. Anne recalled quite simply that "Mother totally trusted me and encouraged me and loved me. Therefore I was always the person she thought I was." Like sister GiGi, Anne was married at eighteen—in her case to former University of North Carolina basketball star Danny Lotz, who subsequently became a dentist and an active worker in the Fellowship of Christian Athletes. Bunny, who attended the Stony Brook School for girls on Long Island, followed her older sisters' example, also marrying at eighteen; the groom was Fred and Millie Dienert's son Ted, whom she met for the first time at the 1966 London crusade. Ted subsequently entered his father's advertising business and eventually became producer of Graham's syndicated television programs.

Ruth and Billy were mildly disappointed that none of their daughters got more than a smattering of college but were pleased with the men they chose for husbands, all of them older and competent, all of them active Christians. Franklin gave them more cause for concern. More than any of the siblings, Franklin chafed at the role of son and namesake of the world's most famous preacher, and he determined not to wear his father's mantle gracefully. At age ten he supposedly "asked Christ to come into his heart," but if the invitation was accepted, Christ found but a small and disorderly back room in which to dwell. As a teenager, Franklin flaunted the very behaviors Evangelicals shunned. He smoked and drank, wore long hair, drove fast cars, rode a Harley-Davidson motorcycle, and stayed out past midnight with girls who did not seem well suited for life in a parsonage. He fired his shotgun through his bedroom window and set his stereo in front of the intercom system just to irritate his family, and he warted poor Ned unconscionably. After a brief stay at Stony Brook School for boys, where his parents hoped he might straighten up, he came home to finish at the local public high school. But he was never a good student, as one old friend delicately observed. "Franklin's schooling was a matter of prayer for some time within the family." Friends despaired over Franklin, fearing he might fit the mold of the preacher's child gone bad. "There was a period in there," one observed, "when I thought Ruth and Billy had a moral casualty on their hands." Ruth and Billy were apparently never quite as worried as their friends. "I never pretended to be the stereotype of a fellow with a Bible under my arm," Franklin recalled, "but my parents pretty much let me be.... They knew the Lord would deal with me on these things." Not that his behavior was ignored or winked at; after telling him she preferred he smoke and drink at home rather than sneak away to indulge his vices, Ruth grew so disgusted with his smoking that she once emptied his ashtray on his head while he slept. Their relationship, however, was less truly adversarial than like a sparring match, with each protagonist respecting the other's point of view and neither regarding the other as an enemy. Always jealous of his privacy, Franklin habitually locked his bedroom door to keep his mother out. One morning, after he had come in later than she deemed appropriate, Ruth crawled out on the roof, a tin cup full of water in her mouth, intending to creep over to his open window and splash him into wakefulness. Franklin heard her coming and slammed the window down just in time to stop the deluge. A sporting loser, Ruth sat on the shingles and joined her son in a good laugh.

Ruth was able to show a special forbearance toward Franklin, it seems, because she understood his rambunctious spirit. She too sometimes became aggressive with machines, so much so that novice drivers in Montreat were warned to "watch out for Mrs. Graham," who seemed to regard speed limits and lane dividers as optional suggestions rather than legal boundaries. As she sped along, quite aware she was breaking the law, she frequently offered a brief exculpatory prayer: "Father, I'm sorry, but you understand." Whatever God thought, a state trooper who caught her doing eighty on old U.S. 70 between Waynesville and Montreat thought she needed reproof and correction. Anxious to get home to serve tea to Billy and a favored guest, Ruth accepted the ticket without arguing or trading on her name, but she stopped short of repentance. "Could you please hurry with that," she asked. "And when you finish, please don't follow me, because I'm going to have to do it again." For a time, it appeared Ruth might add motorcycles to her arsenal of offensive weapons. Instead of scolding Franklin for roaring through the sleepy campus of Montreat-Anderson College on his Harley hog, she asked him to teach her how to ride it. She was not a natural, but neither was she a quitter. The first time she climbed aboard by herself, she drove it over an embankment on the highway. When a worried truck driver got out to offer help, she assured him she was fine. "If you could just get it on the pavement headed in the other direction," she said, "I've a friend at the end of the road who'll help me stop." That experience didn't stop her; her second try ended when she plunged into a lake. Not until her third effort, when she mistook the accelerator for the brake, ending in yet another scary heap and severing a vein in her leg, did this middle-aged preacher's wife abandon this particular form of fun on the open road.

Graham's 1969 New York crusade drew capacity crowds to the Garden, but it differed from previous American crusades in that the primary focus was on the television audience. The successful use of television relays in the 1966

and 1967 British crusades convinced the evangelist to experiment further with that medium. This time, in addition to relaying the service to various auditoriums in outlying areas, he arranged to have local television stations broadcast all ten of the Garden services three times each in the New York area and once each in a dozen other cities. Response was good, and the team regarded the experiment as a success, but the saturation live coverage in specific cities proved no more effective than the customary three-night nationwide broadcast several weeks after the crusade, and this particular strategy was not repeated. Graham and his team, however, remained convinced that nothing could multiply the impact of a crusade so effectively and economically as television, and that although an arena or stadium crusade might draw more people overall, the proportion of inquirers tended to be a bit higher in the relay halls. In 1970 they launched an elaborate and ambitious effort to reach Western Europe and Yugoslavia with simultaneous transmission (and translation) of crusade services from Dortmund, Germany. To offset initial skepticism, BGEA paid to bring a sizable number of clergymen from all over Europe to Frankfurt for a demonstration of the Eidophor big-screen projection system to show them how effective it could be. Most were sufficiently convinced to return home and attempt to enlist other clergy in their regions to support the project, soon to be known as Euro '70.

Cooperation did not follow automatically; in some cases, it never came at all. Evangelical churches in France, where Graham's old friend Bob Evans was still active, signed on immediately and enthusiastically, as did Denmark and Norway; Sweden and Finland chose to remain uninvolved. Holland and Belgium agreed, but not until the last minute, in Belgium's case because of resistance from Roman Catholic influence within the state-run television authority. Small Evangelical populations and noncooperation from Catholics left Spain and Italy out of the network. In Yugoslavia, however, the only Eastern European country to participate, the Roman Catholic Church, still warm with the memory of Graham's 1967 visit, not only publicized the crusade but offered St. Marko Krizevcanin's Church in Zagreb as the meeting site. Great Britain was represented among the venues, but London and other major cities chose not to participate. According to a journalist covering the event for both *Christianity Today* (*CT*) and World Wide Publications, British Evangelicals were not keen on broadcasting a crusade originating in Germany with a German translator standing alongside Graham.

Ironically, perhaps the strongest opposition among participating countries came from within Germany itself, where, according to *CT*, "the theological centers of influence and the churches ... [lay] under the devastating spell of humanism and theological liberalism." In addition to the same theological objections they had raised against Graham's meetings since his days with Youth for Christ, they now objected to spending great sums of money on a television extravaganza when the money could be used to feed the hungry.

Probably more significant, a number of socially liberal German clergymen objected vehemently to Graham's political views and activities. At a meeting in Dortmund of nearly five hundred ministers whose divided opinions led to outbreaks of boos, hisses, and table banging, Graham was asked why he had not participated in the demonstrations in America against racism and the war. On the question of race, he replied, "I'm already holding demonstrations in the biggest stadiums and halls in the world, but because they are nonviolent, people think that's not a demonstration. It is a demonstration." When pressed to make some clear statement on Vietnam, his artful use of Martin Luther's image of "two kingdoms" elided much of his effort on behalf of the Nixon administration and probably would have caused his friend in the White House to wince, but it turned away the wrath of most of the challenging clergymen. "You greatly misunderstand my ministry," he said. "I do not represent the U.S. government. I represent the Kingdom of God.... My flag is the flag of Christ. Why did Jesus Christ not lead a demonstration against the tyranny of Rome? Why did Paul not lead a demonstration? Because they represented a different Kingdom. I cannot defend the United States, any more than you can defend what went on in the '30s and '40s in Germany." Then, to turn away wrath on the issue of Vietnam, he said, "Now concerning Vietnam, I promise you this. If Germany is invaded by a foreign power, and the U.S. comes to your aid, I will not lead a demonstration down Pennsylvania Avenue against giving you that aid." According to one witness, that statement brought "prolonged and unanimous applause." Still, out of fear that antiwar activists would use the crusade to mount some kind of dramatic protest, the speaker's platform was constructed at a height and in such a manner that allowed the television cameras to remain focused on Graham and ignore any disturbance that might be going on below. As a further hedge against disruption, a secure backup studio was installed underneath the platform, where Graham and his interpreter could carry on alone in the event of a truly serious outbreak. The logistics of Euro '70 were far more complicated than those for its British predecessors. Though the All-Britain Crusade had been fed to twenty-five cities whose inhabitants all spoke the same language, the technicians in each city followed a common set of technical specifications to effect the transmission. Euro '70 used the international television links of the Euro-vision system, but engineers still had to cope with different sets of "specs" and the problems inherent in the simultaneous translation of one sermon into the language of each participating nation.

When the crusade finally got under way in April 1970, nearly a thousand men at thirty-nine venues in ten nations (Austria and Switzerland had joined those already named) were involved in the largest closed-circuit television network ever organized in Europe. In addition to the television transmission, the crusade was also carried by Trans-World Radio, a powerful missionary station in Monte Carlo, to Africa and the Middle East, as well as to all of

Eastern and Western Europe. To adhere to the strict time demands of radio, technicians would begin to edit tapes a few minutes after the services began, start the landline transmission from Dortmund to Monte Carlo, then hope they could edit the remainder of the service and sermon to fit their allotted one-hour time slot. On several of the eight evenings of the crusade, their transmission exceeded fifty-eight minutes—on one evening, it ran a scant two seconds short of the sixty-minute cutoff point—but no broadcast ran over. Not everything worked so well; one evening at the Westfalenhalle in Dortmund, a British lighting engineer's attempt to make a cup of coffee in an electric kettle blew out a fuse that temporarily killed the sound transmission to all thirty-nine cities in the network.

Response to the crusade reflected the religious situation in participating countries. In Norway, where Evangelicals were cooperating on a nationwide scale for the first time in their history, interest and enthusiasm ran so high that church leaders predicted Graham could hold successful crusades in any city in the country. In neighboring Denmark, however, one of Copenhagen's finest auditoriums was no more than a quarter full on opening night and never reached capacity. Austria showed similar diversity, with near indifference in Vienna, better reception in Graz, and excellent crowds and response at Salzburg, where the services were piped into the Mozarteum. In strongly secular France, attendance was rather poor, but those who came responded warmly to Graham and his message. In Zagreb large crowds overflowed from the cathedral into an auxiliary hall. Once again Graham proved to be exceedingly popular with German audiences, leading the Reverend Johannes Heider, pastor of Dortmund's largest state (Lutheran) church, to observe that "the simple proclamation of the Bible by Billy Graham has brought more results than we ever expected and it, too, has brought many problems to modern German theologians. The hearts of Protestant pastors in Germany, through the preaching of evangelist Graham, have been opened to the unchanged, authoritative Gospel message."

Not all of the unusual occurrences at crusades involved opposition to Graham and his message. The 1969 Anaheim crusade stands out in the memory of several team members because of a small personal drama. By marrying Leighton Ford, Jean Graham traveled in her brother's circles and shared at least to some extent in his triumphs. Their sister Catherine married Samuel McElroy, who had also taken a position with BGEA, working in the organization's small Charlotte office. But Melvin, six years Billy's junior and so different in appearance as to appear almost unrelated, remained at home, where he continued to farm and run a dairy. For years he repeatedly declined the inevitable invitations to speak, since he realized they stemmed from his being Billy Graham's brother and not from any prowess as a pulpiteer. "This made me withdraw into a shell," he told a reporter in 1968. "I felt far beneath [Billy Frank]. Maybe in a sense I still do. But in recent years, I've come to think that God has placed us all in strategic jobs. Billy has the gospel to preach. And I have my farming. Since I took that outlook, the world has changed for me."

A man of good humor, Melvin learned to laugh at some of the ironies of being brother to the world's most renowned preacher. "A lady called me several years ago in the wintertime," he remembered. "She wanted some manure for her rose garden, in one of the great big homes here in Charlotte, over in the exclusive part of the city. Of course, I had a lot of it from the dairy, so I took her a load. Her regular yardman had the flu and she asked me if I would mind spreading it, so I did, even though I didn't usually do that. She came out there and sat on the back steps to watch me. I was throwing that stuff all over that big old formal rose bed, with a rock wall around it—must have been about two hundred beautiful rosebushes in it. And she started kind of laughing to herself, and I said, 'What are you laughing at?' I thought maybe I was doing something wrong. She said, 'Are you Dr. Billy Graham's brother?' I told her I was, and she said, 'Well, it seems you brothers have sort of drifted apart.' I said, 'What do you mean?' and she said, 'Doesn't he spread the gospel?' I said, 'Yes, Ma'am,' and I told her where he was in a crusade right then—it was in Chicago. And she said, 'And you're out here spreading manure. That seems pretty far apart.' I told her, 'No, Ma'am, it's not. He's up there working on poor souls, and I'm down here working on poor soil.'"

As he grew older and more comfortable with himself, Melvin began to speak a bit at his home church, but he never spoke at one of Billy's meetings until the Anaheim crusade; indeed, he had never even been to California, since, as he explained, "A dairy farmer stays home." But as he stood before the giant crowd in the stadium where the California Angels played baseball—-drawing only twice as many fans over a whole season as his brother would draw in ten days—his weather-beaten face, thin hair, and country accent heightening the contrast with his smooth, urbane sibling, he told a moving story. Fighting understandable nervousness, he related how he had sometimes felt "squashed and pressed down" by comparison to a brother who spoke to millions in public and to some of the world's most powerful and famous individuals in private. Then he told of reading in the Bible "about Moses, who complained to the Lord that he had a slow mind and a slow tongue." He also read what God said to Moses, and as it had with Moses, "the fire began to burn," and he recognized his own responsibility to tell others about Jesus. According to one eyewitness, countless people in the stands found it impossible to hold back tears of empathy and appreciation, and many of those who came forward at Billy Graham's invitation told their counselors that they had made their decision during Melvin's testimony. Twenty years later, Melvin would be preaching at least twice a month at churches throughout and beyond the Piedmont region and could easily fill the other Sundays if he did not prefer to be at home. Reflecting on his abilities as a speaker, he offered a modest, but not falsely self-deprecating, assessment: "I'm not an ordained preacher, but I think I've studied the Bible to the point that I can get up a message." He recognized that he would not have received many of the invitations had he not been Billy Graham's brother, but he had come to regard that as an advantage rather than a burden. "For years," he admitted, "I never would speak. I just wouldn't do it. I'd get the idea that they were comparing me to Billy, you know, and I knew that wouldn't work." Now, however, "After all these years, it doesn't bother me as it once did. Besides, I'm proud of him. What I'm saying is that I think a lot of him."

Millions shared Melvin Graham's admiration for his brother. In the 1970 list of men most admired by Americans, Billy Graham placed second, right behind Richard Nixon and just ahead of Spiro Agnew. He also made the list of best-dressed men, an accolade that seemed to puzzle as much as please him. He reported that he always wore Jarman shoes, out of loyalty to BGEA board member Maxey Jarman, but indicated he took a more passive role in selecting his wardrobe than did other members of the best-dressed club, which included Liberace. "Nearly all the clothes I wear are given to me," he revealed, "so I guess they must be the latest style." (In fact, off camera, Graham dresses almost entirely for comfort rather than style, sometimes with comical results. Ruth recalled an afternoon on a European beach when she saw "the strangest-looking apparition coming toward me. It was a tall, lean male in bright-red trunks [wearing] laced-up hushpuppies, yellow socks, and a baby-blue windbreaker, topped by a funny yellow hat that was slightly too small for him but rammed down to his ears. And as if that weren't enough, he had on the largest pair of sunglasses I'd ever seen. I was both amused and fascinated, when all of a sudden it dawned on me: 'Oh, no, he's mine!' ") Sartorial splendor, of course, was not the real point. Americans placed him in the same rank with the President and admired the way he dressed because they saw in him an apotheosis of their own best selves—an upright, honest, attractive man dedicated to the fundamental verities they, too, espoused. To admire him was to admire not just themselves, but the best and most attractive in themselves. He had his critics, to be sure, but just as the folk who chose him to be the grand marshal of the 1971 Parade of the Roses explained, he was to most Americans "a symbol of hope, peace, and renewed faith in God and a world-recognized leader as well as a friend of mankind."

Graham understood that his role in the Parade of the Roses would draw wide attention and was willing to share the sunlight with a friend; on the morning of the parade, he tried to reach Nixon and told an aide that if the President could return his call within an hour, he would make a point of mentioning their conversation publicly "as opportunities presented themselves throughout the day." But the tribute that pleased him most came when the people of Charlotte, North Carolina, declared him a prophet with abundant honor in his own country and proclaimed October 15, 1971, as Billy Graham

Day. Once again Graham thought it would be a fine thing if he and Richard Nixon could give each other a boost on this occasion. As soon as the Charlotte Chamber of Commerce announced its plans to praise its native son, the Nixon staff began to assess the event's potential to aid the President. Television executive and Chamber of Commerce president Charles Crutchfield, an old friend of Graham's and a strong pro-Nixon man, informed White House aides that Graham was "not sure it's something the President should do," that after Knoxville, "this one would be reaching." Still, Crutchfield felt if the President could see his way clear to take part in the ceremonies, "it would be a tremendous thing for Graham and his family." Even before details of the day were roughed out, H. R. Haldeman readily agreed that Nixon should try to attend, and he and other staffers began to calculate how Billy Graham Day could work to Richard Nixon's benefit. As soon as Nixon agreed to participate, White House staffers seized control, noting in one memo that the suggestions of the local organizing committee were "totally impractical in terms of benefit to us" and that one of Nixon's advance men would "have to make all of the decisions" about logistics, in part because the local leaders were "socially prominent appointments" who were "not prepared to work."

Graham's concern about the President's participation seems to have stemmed from his fear that opponents of the administration's Vietnam policy might use the occasion to mount an embarrassing protest, a prospect he naturally wished to avoid. The President's men also foresaw that possibility—and leapt at the chance to have Nixon stand beside Billy Graham in the face of unholy persecution. A few days before the celebration, a Secret Service reconnaissance team informed the White House that "very serious intelligence reports" indicated a high probability that a Nixon visit would set off disruptions, with "extremely obscene signs" and, quite likely, attempts at violence against both Nixon and Graham. Instead of arranging a last-minute, face-saving emergency pullout, Haldeman wrote "Great" and "Good" in the margins of the report. He approved of plans to keep demonstrators out of the coliseum where the President would speak, but only "as long as it is local police and volunteers doing it—*not* our people."

On the eve of the grand celebration, at a country-club reception arranged by Holiday Inns (whose key executives were avid supporters of his ministry), Graham could not resist reflecting on how far he and his profession had come since the days of Mordecai Ham. "When I started preaching twenty-five years ago," he remarked as he scanned the elegant assembly gathered to honor him, "people associated evangelism with emotionalism and nonintellectualism. Religion itself was back-page copy. But now, just look at all this!" That sense of satisfied accomplishment could scarcely have diminished as October 15 broke cool and clear over his native city. School children got the day off, municipal courts and many of the city's largest stores closed (at Charles Crutchfield's suggestion), and Western Union delivered stacks of congratulatory telegrams from such respectable souls as Arnold Palmer, Bob Hope, Pat Boone, Jimmy Stewart, Robert Stack, Randolph Scott, Ronald Reagan, Roy Rogers and Dale Evans, Lawrence Welk, General William Westmoreland, and from across the waters, Haile Selassie and Prince Rainier. On hand to pay tribute in person were South Carolina senator Strom Thurmond, a delegation of North Carolina lawmakers led by Senator Sam Ervin and Governor Bob Scott, *Reader's Digest* publisher Hobart Lewis, and Treasury Secretary John Connally.

Obviously, the brightest star in Graham's earthly crown that day was the appearance of the President of the United States, the most powerful man in the free world, who descended into Charlotte to pay homage to a native son who had once ridden a bicycle out on Park Road and preached to passersby in front of Belk's department store. As he deplaned from the gleaming *Spirit of '76*, Nixon looked properly presidential in a conservatively tailored dark gray suit and silverfish tie. Waiting to meet him on the tarmac, Graham looked embarrassingly evangelistic in a blue-checked, bell-bottomed outfit that he admitted was "a little louder than I thought it was. I bought it at Finchley's in New York especially for the occasion but I didn't know the blue checks would light up in the sun." Any discomfort he felt, however, quickly turned to exhilaration as the two friends rode into the city in the presidential limousine. As their motorcade pushed its way along streets jammed with well-wishers thrilled at the chance to see such a concentration of celebrities, Nixon showed Billy how to wave and how to allow the adoring throngs to touch him without risking injury—"With the palm turned backwards—-this way you can't hurt them by getting your hand pushed back, and you won't hurt your hand, either." Meanwhile, at the downtown coliseum, Secret Service agents, local police, and a band of volunteer marshals worked to sanitize the crowd by purging it of people carrying anti- administration signs ("One-Two-Three-Four—We don't want your F_____g War"), sporting beards or wearing non-Republican clothes, looking as if they might be about to shout obscenities, or behaving in any manner deemed to be suspicious. The marshals, identified only by unmarked red armbands, hustled obvious nonconformers away, sometimes quite roughly, from areas where they could confront or even be seen by Graham and Nixon. They confiscated film from cameras, as well as critical signs and banners, and in the *Observer's* delicate phrase, "exchanged derogatory titles" with those who objected to their heavy-handed tactics. Scores of suspected troublemakers bearing valid passes to the coliseum ceremony were told their tickets were counterfeit and were barred or ejected from the building. A mother whose grade-school son had asked her to take him to the celebration "so Billy Graham could save him" made the mistake of picking up a small banner one of the protesters had dropped and was rudely shunted away from the entrance. Another woman was ejected simply because she laughed at the sight of Secret Service agents dragging a teenage girl from a ladies' restroom. Even Governor Scott complained that he had been jostled and rudely treated by the Secret Service, perhaps because of what the *Charlotte Observer* described as a "mod-bangs hair style."

The precise identity and affiliation of the marshals was something of a mystery at the time, but a later investigation identified them as members of a local VFW post, recruited through contacts in Washington with the knowledge and approval of the White House. Following the event, Nixon sent a letter of commendation to the group's leader, Ernie Lee Helms. Then, when fourteen people ejected or excluded from the coliseum brought an $840,000 case against Helms and his cohorts, Nixon lawyer John Dean flew to Charlotte to advise Helms to keep quiet and the lawyer representing Helms stayed in frequent touch with Dean by letter and telephone as the case progressed. Eventually, a jury decided that both the damage suit and federal indictments against the self-deputized marshals were invalid—"against the weight of the evidence," according to the judge in the case—but not before White House aides acknowledged collaboration in the vigilante effort. As one witness explained, the President's staff regarded such heavy-handed measures as justified, since the occasion was not just another visit by the chief executive, but was "in some respects a religious ceremony."

The heart of the ostensibly sacred occasion was an outpouring of mutual admiration between Graham and Nixon. After characterizing his fellow Carolinians as the finest people in America, Graham asserted that if the nation had more people like them, "we would have little of the problems we have today in the country." Becoming more specific, and perhaps aware that none of the people who knew better would contradict him, he said, "In our home, we also wrestled with poverty, if you go by today's standards, except we didn't know we were poor. We did not have sociologists, educators, and newscasters constantly reminding us of how poor we were. We also had the problem of rats. The only difference between then and now is we did not call upon the government to kill them. We killed our own!" When the applause for that bit of revisionist autobiography and Republican orthodoxy died down, Graham began to praise his honored guest. He recalled having made a suggestion to Nixon and having the President reply, "Billy, I don't think that would be morally right." When he thought about it more carefully, he said, "I realized he was right. At that moment I felt that he was the preacher and I was the sinner."

When the time came for Nixon to return the compliments, he did not disappoint. He commended the proud people of the Piedmont for having "contributed to America and the world one of the greatest leaders of our time—the top preacher in the world!" He praised Graham for decades of inspiring Americans to espouse and uphold a strong religious faith, without which, he ventured, no nation can be great. Finally, he allowed that it was not farfetched to think that "when the history of this time is written," it would not be a scientist or statesman or some other secular leader but their own beloved Billy Graham who would be credited with having performed "the most important works."

Despite the overzealous efforts of Ernie Helms and his VFW buddies, not all the opposition could be screened out. Some ordinary-appearing citizens managed to chant or wave signs damning Nixon, the war, and occasionally, Billy Graham's role in rendering unto Caesar what belonged to God. After the ceremony, as the two men and their wives walked through a sea of people on their way to a small and extremely exclusive reception a short distance from the coliseum, a young man pushed his way through to Nixon, grasped his hand, and loudly accused him of being "a murderer" who had "spoken platitudes for the proletariat." Even though clearly euphoric over the glory that had come to him that day from "the kingdoms of this world," and perhaps rendered amnesiac by the cross-shaped sandwiches and a thirty-pound biblicoform cake served at the reception, Graham could not have failed to notice these vigorous exceptions to the triumphant mood of the occasion. That, however, is precisely what he claimed. Asked a few days later about the sputterings of protest and the unnecessarily aggressive action against the protesters, he blithely replied, "I'm sorry, I haven't heard about it.... It's unfortunate if it did happen, but I'm sure [the overreaction] was not deliberate. Anyway, you can't blame it on the President."

Graham's remarkable ability to overlook or trivialize the unpleasant, particularly when it involved powerful friends whose favor he curried, continued to draw fire. On the evening of Billy Graham Day, NBC News correspondent Herbert Kaplow observed that "if indeed you can tell a man by his friends, politicians seem to feel that with enough friends like Billy Graham, a fellow can do pretty well in American politics." Expressing a similar sentiment, the *Charlotte Observer* noted that "the President and the Chamber of Commerce draw honor to themselves by honoring Mr. Graham. He, in turn, moves closer to the places of power, anointing those who are there." Not everyone felt comfortable with this cozy symbiosis of Church and State. A few days before the grand celebration, Union Seminary President John C. Bennett charged that Graham's frequent resort to the Second Coming as the only viable solution to serious social problems "enables him to chastise America without disturbing the particular respectable forms of power in our midst, especially those responsible for the use of power by our nation abroad. He has a personal message that may help many individuals to live free of private burdens of sin and guilt and aimlessness, but he lets down those who see themselves as the victims of institutionalized injustice and those who are outraged by many acts of their Government abroad. When people claim to be above politics, it is axiomatic that they in effect support the status quo. This is true when they do nothing, but it is far more true when they advertise their close relations with the powerful." Bennett, of course, was a social and theological liberal and could thus be dismissed by Graham's supporters, but not all the criticism came from the opposing camp. On the same day Billy and the President were praising each other in Charlotte, Diane Sawyer, assistant to press secretary Ron Ziegler, sent her boss a memo drawing attention to an editorial in the *Charlotte Observer* in which it was noted that some of Graham's fellow Southern Baptists felt the evangelist "is too close to the powerful and too fond of the things of the world, [and] have likened him to the prophets of old who told the kings of Israel what they wanted to hear."

Without question, Graham had a remarkable talent for tickling the ears of those he admired, and a strong tendency to admire the famous and powerful. He was never a liar who blatantly said things he did not believe, nor a demagogue who cynically manipulated audiences for personal or party ends, but his desire to please often combined with his innate conservative instincts—abhorrence of disorder, belief in self-reliance and self-control, trust in authority—to produce a soothing balm when an astringent was needed. When chastised for an unconsidered remark, he could be abjectly repentant. Religion writer George Plagenz called his hand on his crowd-pleasing comment about poor people and rats, noting, "It is one thing to be in favor of self-reliance. It is quite another to be insensitive to the plight and feelings of those who for various reasons are not self-reliant." Graham dashed off an apology, admitting he had been wrong and urging Plagenz to "kick me in the pants" whenever necessary. More telling, he quit using the line. Still, he never shed a tendency to make statements whose logic and sense of proportion sometimes bordered on the bizarre. Without a hint that the upheaval spawned during the sixties might have more complex causes, he observed, "It is interesting to note that as soon as prayer was taken out of the schools ... drugs, sex permissiveness, and even crime entered the schools." That assertion, however weak the chain of causation it posited, was common in conservative religious circles. It was vintage Graham, however, to reflect on Lieutenant William Calley's notorious massacre of a Vietnam village and declare that "we have all had our My Lais in one way or another ... with a thoughtless word, an arrogant act, or a selfish deed," as if that heinous atrocity were just a notch or two further up the scale from grumpiness.

Knowing he could count on Graham to cast whatever he did in as favorable a light as possible doubtless pleased and reassured the President, and he rewarded his loyal friend with numerous attractive perks: an invitation to an evening at the White House with Beverly Sills; dinner aboard the *Sequoia* with Nixon and his inner circle of Henry Kissinger, H. R. Haldeman, John Ehrlichman, John Mitchell, Donald Rumsfeld, and Harry Dent; an overnight stay in the First Family's private quarters, with instructions to Julie and Tricia to "pick an appropriate movie" for viewing after dinner. In every case, aides had orders to give Graham full VIP treatment; on one occasion, after an aide failed to place the evangelist in the first limousine to arrive for a group of guests at a presidential party, Haldeman dispatched a memo noting how awkward and embarrassing that had been and asked that such a breach of protocol not recur.

In return for such care and cultivation, Nixon sought and received Graham's sincere friendship and goodwill, which translated into the priceless political coin of obvious approval and palpable, if coyly unspoken, endorsement. But he got more than symbolic benefit from Graham. Because of his peerless reputation and international contacts, Graham was able to serve in an informal ambassadorial role in situations in which a member of the diplomatic corps might have been less effective. "We thought highly of his abilities in that regard," Haldeman acknowledged. "He had contact at a very personal level with people of enormous diplomatic importance. He was astute in those situations, in the sense of his being a keen observer and understander of people. People tend to confide in him more than they would to other people. He draws out their inner feelings. That can be enormously important diplomatically."

A key instance of this occurred after the United States began to assume a more positive stance toward the People's Republic of China in 1971. This action, eventually regarded as one of the crowning achievements of the Nixon presidency, caused considerable unease among many of his conservative supporters in America and galloping anxiety in Taiwan. Graham proved a valuable ally on both fronts. At Nixon's request, he assembled a group of over thirty conservative religious and business leaders, at least a third of whom had close ties to BGEA, for an extensive briefing on the China situation from Henry Kissinger in the hope and expectation that they would convey a favorable reading to their sizable constituencies.

A second opportunity to serve came at the initiative of Generalissimo and Madame Chiang Kai-shek. A November 1971 memo from Haldeman to Kissinger reveals that the Chiangs had asked Graham to come to Taipei to discuss the change in American policy portended for their small and vulnerable Republic of China (ROC). They were "deeply troubled," Haldeman said, and "Billy Graham is the one person from this country that they will listen to and would like to meet with." Nixon approved a visit and Graham agreed that he would "try to explain things to them in whatever way we want them explained, and also meet with the missionaries in Formosa, among whom there is now a problem of strong resentment and anger towards the U.S." At Haldeman's request, Kissinger prepared a briefing paper for Graham to study before meeting with the President, at which time he expected Nixon to cover "other, more sensitive points." If he had any questions about the briefing paper, he was told that "Al Haig will be able to help you." The more sensitive points Nixon was to provide in his pretrip briefing were removed from the Nixon archives, ostensibly for reasons of national security, but the key points of the "talker" Kissinger prepared for Graham were that the President sent his warmest personal greetings, regretted deeply that the United Nations had decided to strip Chiang's republic of its representation in that body, pledged to honor America's long-standing diplomatic ties and mutual-defense commitments to the ROC ("You should avoid being drawn out," Graham was instructed, "on the particulars of our military assistance, such as levels of assistance and projections into the future"), and would work to preserve the ROC's standing in such organizations as the International Monetary Fund and the World Bank. The President asked Graham to convey his recognition of the pains the Chiangs must be feeling over the dramatic shift in American policy, and to assure them that "no secret deals have been or will be struck" that permit "improvement in relations with Peking at the expense of the vital interests of our allies in Asia, especially the Republic of China." When asked about this incident in early 1989, Graham professed barely to remember it and felt it could not have been significant. "The President may have asked me to give them greetings," he conceded. "You know, I preached Chiang's funeral at the Washington Cathedral. Mrs. Chiang was a very devout Christian. Ruth goes out to see her on Long Island. She and her sister studied here in Montreat for a time."

Graham's memory for other events of this period tend to follow a similar pattern. Mention of amply and precisely documented meetings, letters, telephone calls, and public statements were met with verbal and facial expressions of vague puzzlement and turned away by denial, modest acknowledgment of a faulty memory, or a shifting of the subject to some extraneous personal recollection. Nowhere was this tendency more obvious than in discussion of Richard Nixon's second election in 1972, a sequence of events that marked what was probably the closest Graham ever came to succumbing to the classic temptations offered by "the kingdoms of the world and the glory of them" (Matt. 4:8).

24

"Billy, You Stay Out of Politics"

In late November 1970, Nixon told Haldeman, "On the political front, it is important to start an early liaison with BG and his people. He was enormously helpful to us in the Border South in '68 and will continue to be in '72." Early in 1971, following a conversation with the President, H. R. Haldeman wrote himself the following note: "Graham wants to be helpful next year.... Point him in areas where do most good. He thinks there are real stirrings in religious directions, especially re young people.... I call him and set up date. No other level—can't have leak." Two days later, he scribbled a follow-up reminder: "Must mobilize him and his crowd." If the archival records are to be trusted, what followed was a close collaboration between Billy Graham and the White House that not only helped reelect Richard Nixon, but contributed importantly to the emergence, eight years later and under different leadership, of the New Religious Right. On the same day he penned the "must mobilize" memo, Haldeman prepared a "talking paper" for a conversation he expected to have with Graham. In that conversation, according to Haldeman's notes, Graham mentioned the crucial importance of the 1972 election and discussed what he regarded as a significant move to the right among religious people. Haldeman apparently felt it was possible to "mobilize him and his troops," but not if the administration began making too many concessions to liberal critics. "He's willing to do it," Haldeman wrote, "if we take firm line. Feels we're not getting firm enough line to the right."

A busy crusade schedule limited what Graham could do during 1971, though he did apparently make some effort to persuade the administration's leading Republican critic, Mark Hatfield, not to challenge Nixon for their party's nomination in 1972, with the understanding that the White House would provide full support for his campaign for reelection to the Senate. The White House staff, however, clearly regarded the evangelist as a front line heavyweight; in an August 1971 memo, Haldeman recommended setting up a group of eight to ten loyal "Conservatives for the President," who would "support the President down the line from a conservative viewpoint," to counterbalance criticism Nixon was receiving from "some of the conservative publications." Such a group should include, he thought, "Hobie Lewis, [*National Review* editor] Jeff Hart, Clare Luce, Billy Graham, etc." The staff also saw to it that Graham continued to receive rewards commensurate with the value the President placed on his friendship and support. When his old friend and admirer, William R. Tolbert, was elected president of Liberia, Kissinger recommended that Billy attend the inauguration as the President's personal representative. The other dignitaries representing America were the U.S. ambassador to Liberia, New York Stock Exchange chairman Bernard Lasker, and Mrs. Nixon. In deference to Graham's stature and tight schedule, Alexander Haig assured him that an aircraft would be provided to return him to the United States immediately after the required appearances in Liberia and that "he would have complete service with respect to accommodations, appropriate briefings, and the complete satisfaction of all his personal and official requirements."

In February 1972 Graham and Nixon met for more than an hour to discuss how and where he could be of greatest use to the campaign. In his summary of this meeting, Haldeman recorded that "it was agreed that Pennsylvania, Ohio, Illinois, and New York were most important, since California and Texas are already covered." Graham assured the President he would try to be helpful "in every possible way" and was promised solid briefings on domestic and foreign political matters so that he would always know where the administration stood on crucial questions. This would include another meeting at which Kissinger would brief key Evangelical editors, broadcasters, and denominational leaders about ongoing developments in the new policy toward communist China, apparently to gain support for the shift in policy. Haldeman's report also shows that Graham used the meeting to ask at least two specific favors of the President. Despite meeting what seems to have been resistance, he wrested a promise from Nixon to include a religion writer in the press corps for his momentous trip to China. He informed the President that the religious community would be deeply offended if no religion writer made the trip and assured him that the consensus choice of the religious press was David E. Kucharsky of *Christianity Today*. On a second matter that affected both *CT* and *Decision*, Graham complained that a recent change in postal rates had raised the cost of mailing religious publications by 400 percent, while pornographic literature suffered a hike of only 25 percent. "Needless to say," Haldeman told John Ehrlichman, "the President was horrified to learn of this state of affairs and wants to know what we are doing about it."

Haldeman was assigned primary responsibility for maintaining regular contact with Graham. Nixon directed him to call Graham "about once every 2 weeks to discuss the political situation," explaining that "I would prefer not to get into these matters as directly with him but I do want a continuing contact kept with him so that he doesn't feel that we are not interested in the support of his group in those key states where they can be helpful." In yet another February memo, Nixon aide Lawrence Higby noted, "Two that we can't let drop—Bob [Haldeman] needs to call the Secretary of Treasury John Connally and Billy Graham about once a week and just fill them in on what's happening and maybe raise a point or two with them. Let's make sure we put some sort of reminder in here on a weekly basis." Gordon Strachan, and perhaps others, fed Haldeman a steady stream of talking papers at least biweekly from mid-February until the election in November. These recommended that Graham be given advance notice of such matters as John Mitchell's leaving the attorney general's office to head the President's reelection campaign, details of Nixon's forthcoming trip to Moscow and Poland, the administration's strategy for dealing with busing on a regional basis, and the appointment of Patrick Gray as FBI chief. In exchange for this kind of insider information, the White House sought his reaction to Kissinger's secret diplomatic forays, his sense of whether George McGovern could actually capture the Democratic nomination, his assessment of the effectiveness of the administration's "recent attacks on certain members of the media" (including "Pat Buchanan—type comments"), and any suggestions he might have for the role Pat Nixon should play during the President's trip to Russia.

It may not be possible to establish with certainty how many of these "talkers" were acted upon until all the tapes made by the Nixon's infamous recording system are finally released for public inspection, but telephone logs and other archival records referring to conversations with Graham on the same date or shortly following the date of the talking papers strongly suggest that a substantial proportion of the recommended calls were indeed made. Haldeman confirmed that "I definitely made a good number of calls. I'm not sure just how frequently; ordinarily, it was not weekly, but it was probably more than monthly. Some weeks, it was more than once a week. That was probably true of the President as well." Sometimes the calls came from Nixon himself. Charles Colson recalled that "Nixon would call different people whose judgment he respected to get their opinions and also to see how the public was reacting to different issues. He was probably looking for affirmation, but also, I think, he was sounding out people whose judgment and insights he respected. He and Billy had a close personal relationship. Nixon would call Billy because he felt like talking to him. He'd use Billy as a kind of sounding board to find out what was happening on campus or across the country." Haldeman and Ehrlichman agreed with this assessment. "Billy was definitely in [Nixon's] inner circle," Haldeman said. "The President had enormous admiration and affection for him and relied on his counsel. Billy's political acumen is very high, and he had a talent for seeing the best of everything that is happening—not choosing to see the bad." Ehrlichman saw part of Nixon's interest as purely pragmatic: "Nixon felt Dr. Graham represented and spoke for a substantial segment of religious America. He was interested in his views on various subjects. It would be very important for the President to know how Dr. Graham and the people he talked to felt about, for example, abortion. This is purely hypothetical, but Dr. Graham might say, 'I was at a rally in Charleston, West Virginia, and eight out of ten people I talked to raised the issue of abortion.' That kind of thing." Like Haldeman, however, Ehrlichman agreed that Nixon's respect for Graham was unfeigned. "I think the President saw Dr. Graham as an icon of sorts. He had unqualified admiration for him. If anything, he overestimated his influence on the American people." With a wry chuckle, he added, "He certainly didn't underestimate it."

The seductive personal attention Graham received from the President doubtless helped raise his esteem for Nixon, and he did not hesitate to voice it. In an interview with the *Saturday Evening Post*, he observed that the presidency was "just really beyond a man to deal with" but reckoned that "Mr. Nixon is coming as close to it as anybody. Contrary to what people think about him, he is a true intellectual. We haven't had an intellectual in the White House in a long time. Kennedy was no intellectual—I mean, he was written up by the Eastern press as an intellectual because he agreed with the Eastern Establishment. But Nixon is a true intellectual, and he is a student, particularly a student of history. In that respect, he's a De Gaulle type."

Nixon's staff and friends not only valued Billy Graham's affirmation of the President but felt the President would do well to emulate some of Graham's more impressive skills, particularly those related to public speaking. Charlotte television executive Charles Crutchfield recommended that Nixon make greater use of teleprompters in his public speeches, noting that Billy Graham used them in all his filmed presentations. Haldeman suggested to Nixon that he cultivate the ability "to tell a story like Billy Graham." And Graham himself, while lauding Nixon for his ability to speak extemporaneously, thought he might be more effective if he restricted himself to only one major point in each speech and threw in a few quotes from the Bible.

Graham's suggestion that Nixon quote the Bible more often was part of a larger effort to enhance the President's appeal to the conservative religious folk he believed were poised to make their voices heard in the political arena, and his willingness to help strengthen that appeal involved more than cosmetic touches. In mid-1971, he urged the White House to cultivate Bill Bright, whose widespread and aggressive Campus Crusade organization might prove helpful among Evangelical young people in particular. At his meeting with Nixon at the time of the prayer breakfast, he had expressed his desire to have the President address Explo '72, a mammoth youth festival he and Bright were planning for Dallas in June. Haldeman indicated that "the President definitely wants to try to attend that" but noted that Graham and Bright had had a "stormy session re whether to invite President," and that Bright felt it would not be appropriate, particularly if Nixon gave a "major address that was not religious in nature." Whether because Graham could not change Bright's mind or because the President could not arrange a visit, Nixon did not attend Explo '72, but while the weeklong event was in progress, Billy called the White House and urged him to send a telegram of greeting to the 85,000 young people gathered for what he called "a religious Woodstock."

When it became clear that McGovern was indeed going to capture the Democratic nomination, the President's religious posture became a more critical issue. Graham pointed out to Lawrence Hibgy that because McGovern was an ordained minister who would likely receive strong support from clergymen associated with both the National Council and World Council of Churches, he might be able to woo the religious vote, particularly that of moderate and conservative people who might not agree fully with his antiwar and other liberal views but would favor having a pastor as President. A few days later, Charles Colson discussed these same matters, apparently with the President. His handwritten notes on their conversation contain the instruction, "Use Graham's organization." In a subsequent note, Haldeman outlined the strategy to be used: Graham and Bright would "stay in the shadows" themselves but would put "top operatives" in the Nixon camp in touch with "top guys in religious wing." Graham had apparently indicated that he and Bright could provide entree to fifty major conservative religious youth organizations with massive mailing lists. He felt sure that some people in these organizations—"seasoned, trusted people"—would take leaves of absence to work full time in an effort to counteract McGovern's campaign to capture the religious vote. In late June Haldeman noted, "Wait till Billy Graham pulls it together. Will work on this more." In a talking paper for a conversation scheduled two weeks later, Haldeman planned to ask Graham, "What is our best approach to McGovern? Should he be hit now or after the Democratic Convention? Is it now appropriate for [campaign worker] Ron Walker to work with T. W. Wilson to bring some staff of the Committee for the Re-election of the President together with Bright of the Campus Crusade?"

Bill Bright was not the only conservative religious leader Graham felt Nixon should cultivate. When Nelson Bell was elected moderator of the Presbyterian Church in the United States, Graham drafted a congratulatory telegram he thought would be appropriate for the President to send—a gesture that would be appreciated not only by his father-in-law but by the sizable group of clergymen and influential laymen in the denomination he now led. Graham also recommended that Nixon establish a tie to Oral Roberts. After a conversation with Graham, Harry Dent told Nixon that "both from the national and Oklahoma perspectives, it has become quite important that we get some visibility with Roberts. Millions of conservative voters soak up his TV performances, and he is quite a substantial figure in his home state of Oklahoma." Dent further noted that, through his university, its basketball team, and the World Action Singers, Roberts "has close identification with clean-cut youth, as well as conservative folk in general Roberts prayed at the Democratic Convention, but has indicated to me he wants to help your re-election." Nixon proved to be more interested in these suggestions than did Haldeman. In a note to Dwight Chapin, the protective chief of staff reported that "the President wants to consider the possibility of his going to the dedication of a new building at Oral Roberts' college in Oklahoma. This would be for the purpose of the effect it would have on Oral Roberts' following, not for the chance to go to Oklahoma, but it would also be an appearance at a college where there are 2,000 kids. I think it's a terrible idea, but he wanted it considered."

Graham sought to avoid controversy by declining invitations either to speak or to pray at both the Democratic and Republican conventions, but he did try to have an impact on the latter. In a memo to the President just before the convention in late August, Haldeman told his boss that Graham had stressed that it would be "a serious mistake if you do not include a spiritual note in your [acceptance] speech. Many of our hard-core supporters have a strong belief in God and will be looking for a spiritual note." Graham also recommended some specific biblical passages Nixon might draw upon: Psalm 33:12 ("Blessed is the nation whose God is the Lord"); Proverbs 14:34 ("Righteousness exalteth a nation: but sin is a reproach to any people"); Psalm 20:7 ("Some trust in chariots, and some in horses: but we will remember the name of the Lord our God"); and Joshua 24:15 ("Choose you this day whom ye will serve ... but as for me and my house, we will serve the Lord"). He felt this last verse might be the most appropriate, since it would appeal to both Christians and Jews. In a final message, Graham had asked Haldeman to inform the President that "he played golf yesterday at San Clemente and had a wonderful time. He shot a 32 for nine holes."

After the campaign got under way in earnest following the conventions, Graham's communications with the White House seem mainly to deal with how to keep McGovern from capturing the mantle of "the religion candidate." Haldeman's talking papers posed such questions as "What do you think of the new 'Religious Leaders for McGovern' group?" "Should our surrogates lash out at McGovern now?" and a striking example of the struggle between pragmatism and principle, "Should the President attack McGovern or should he carry on the theme of 'Bring Us Together'?" Graham was particularly concerned about the Religious Leaders for McGovern group. Organized by Methodist bishop James Armstrong and consisting of over two hundred liberal religious leaders, the group had set about to correct what its members believed to be Republican misstatements about McGovern and was pushing McGovern's candidacy in advertisements, letters to newspapers, and according to Graham, even in church services. Graham both liked and admired Armstrong and feared the movement might have considerable impact. If it seemed necessary, he might be willing to help establish a counterorganization, but Armstrong's actions had caught him by surprise, and he needed time to think about what role he might play. In the meantime, the evangelist recommended that the President attend church regularly and arrange to address a ministerial group whose ministers were not critical of his policy in Vietnam. Finally, Graham noted that he had been making quite complimentary statements about the President and that the campaign should feel free to use them, "once they have been put into public print."

Interestingly, the Committee to Re-elect the President felt Graham should not mount a countermovement to Armstrong's group. Speaking for the committee, journalist (and Jesuit priest) John McLaughlin judged that it would not be "in the interest of the public good to organize clergy, by reason of their clerical profession, to participate in partisan political activity." The Republicans were delighted, however, by Graham's glowing quasi-endorsements of Nixon. Graham announced to the Associated Press that he expected Nixon to carry every state in the union, with the possible exception of South Dakota, McGovern's home state. He told the *Charlotte Observer* that Nixon would "go down in history as the greatest President because he studied, prepared himself, disciplined himself for the Presidency, and the effects now show." More important, in what amounted to an official endorsement, Graham once again voted absentee, enabling him to announce five days before the election that to no one's surprise, he had indeed cast his vote for Richard Nixon. He had known Nixon since 1950, he said, and knew him to be a man of "deep religious commitment" and great "personal honesty." He had voted for him "because I know what he is made of. He was just born to be President."

Graham's prediction about the outcome of the election was remarkably accurate, except that the one state McGovern carried was not South Dakota but Massachusetts. And when the magnitude of the triumph became apparent on election night, Graham was among the first people the President called to share a moment of rejoicing—other members of the inner circle included John Connally, Nelson Rockefeller, Ronald Reagan, John Mitchell, Maurice Stans, Clark McGregor, Robert Dole, and several key labor leaders who had cast their lot with the Republicans. Obviously, Richard Nixon regarded Billy Graham not just as a close friend but also as a political ally.

It appears that nothing Graham did during the 1972 election was contrary to his rights as a private citizen or even as the most public of ministers. Clergymen have a right to hold and voice partisan opinions and to use their personal influence to persuade others to espouse those opinions. Most Americans agree that the pulpit is not the proper forum for announcing those opinions, but Graham seldom violated that convention, and then not blatantly. Neither did he abuse the privileges of his tax-exempt organization; in fact, Charles Colson recalled that "the only thing he did that was political—and he didn't know it was political—was [helping us] pull together Evangelical leaders to tell them what was going on in military and foreign policy issues.

He would give us the names of people. He didn't see it as political, but we did. We were scheming to win their support. We were looking at the conservative Evangelical vote as the political [movement] that actually did emerge in the eighties." Graham would not cooperate in other ways, however. "We tried to get his mailing list," Colson noted, "but he refused. At the time, I was disappointed because I thought he ought to help his friend, but now I respect him for it." One may quibble, as many of his fellow clergymen did, with his judgment of and loyalty to Richard Nixon, but a landslide majority of Americans agreed with him, in effect if not in intensity. It is therefore puzzling that he has repeatedly insisted that his relationship to Nixon was almost entirely one of friendship and pastoral concern. In perhaps his most explicit statement of that position, he told David Frost in 1972 that Nixon had told him repeatedly, "Billy, at all costs, you stay out of politics," insisting that "your ministry is more important to me than my election." Though he naturally assumed that his friend appreciated the few random remarks he had made on his behalf, he was certain he did not require or expect them, and insisted that "he would never, never try to use me politically."

When faced with extensive evidence that he had been viewed in the White House as an ally with a good deal more to offer than pastoral counsel and had, in fact, taken an active and independent role in abetting Nixon's reelection, Graham seemed genuinely baffled. He admitted that "I wanted to be used in '68, I suppose, behind the scenes, with the public not knowing much about it, because I thought he was the best-prepared man to be President of any man I had ever known. But I didn't want to be used in '72. I was still his friend, but I was not as close to him during that period. He didn't have time to be close to anybody. He was too busy and I was going all over the world preaching and planning conferences. Besides, I thought it was a shoo-in and so I wasn't involved. I didn't think McGovern would be a strong candidate. I wouldn't have taken any position anyway." He revealed that he had been aware that Lyndon Johnson "was not a McGovern man" but did not exploit that information. "I think I told Larry Higby a little about it, but I never even told Bob Haldeman and I never told Nixon. I didn't think that was something I ought to say. Johnson was pretty strong in some of the things he said. I figured it was one of those private things and he was just blowing off steam to me. Why me, I didn't know. But I thought the world of Shriver. He and I were very good friends. I've been a guest in their home." As for having played any role in mobilizing an embryonic religious right in 1972, he recalled the three-hour meeting between Nixon and the black ministers and a briefing on foreign affairs when "Oral Roberts came and brought his photographer. That was probably the one on China." Other than that, he insisted, "I don't recall anything. I certainly didn't try to organize Evangelicals in any way, shape, or form. I couldn't have. I didn't have that kind of influence."

Graham admitted that some members of the White House staff may have tried to use him at times. "I could sense that. Sometimes they were successful, sometimes they were unsuccessful. Sometimes I knew it, and sometimes, in hindsight, I see that I didn't know it. I wasn't used most times, I think. I'm sure there were a few times when I was." He dismissed most of the talking papers as little more than White House busywork: "Everybody writes memos in the White House—just shuffling papers. Chuck Colson told me there were thousands of memos that never meant anything. Some fellow would write it, and that was the end of it."

Graham's insistence that most of the talking papers were never converted into actual telephone calls seems clearly contradicted both by Haldeman's acknowledgment that he made the calls and by the unlikelihood that aides would continue to produce the papers if they were not acted upon. Similarly, his assertion that he took little interest or role in overtly political aspects of the campaign does not square with the documentary evidence. He freely admitted to a faulty memory, and during the two-day conversation of which these matters were a part occasionally had difficulty recalling the name of close and longtime associates, a problem that vexed him noticeably. Just two weeks before this conversation, his physicians had increased the dosage of his blood-pressure medicine, which can affect recall, though he did not cite this as an excuse. More important, Graham seemed eager not to appear to dissemble. In response to an advance list of questions, sent not at his request but in an effort to enable him to gather specific materials, he noted with some surprise that he had no memory whatsoever of a particular action in question—in this case, his efforts to persuade Mark Hatfield not to seek the Presidency—but that his secretary had produced letters clearly indicating he had indeed taken such action. "If you have anything like that," he said, "that shows I'm wrong about something I say, please tell me. It's important to get this right, and my memory is not all that good." But when the evidence did not come from his own hand, no matter how compelling it might appear, he consistently met it with some statement such as "That's the first I ever heard of it," brushed it off as an example of bureaucratic busywork unrelated to related events, or explained in a manner he seemed to find convincing that it simply could not be accurate because it ran counter to his deeply felt views about restricting his role in the political arena to matters spiritual. He did not believe a minister should do such things, and therefore, he could not believe he had done them.*

*In February 1991, when furnished with a copy of the manuscript of this book to permit him to check for factual errors (but with his own explicit disavowal of editorial control), Graham acknowledged that he had been surprised by much that he had read. "I knew what I had said to the President," he remarked, "and I knew what he had said to me. But I was unaware of all those memos circulating in the background. When I read about that, I felt like a sheep led to the slaughter."

25

A Ministry of Reconciliation

Billy Graham enjoyed proximity to power. He liked being able to have a hand, or at least a finger, in shaping national and international policy, in helping a friend gain and remain in the White House, in abetting the defeat of those whose religious and political views he believed to be mistaken. Such pleasures, of course, could arise from purely secular motives, which may help explain his abiding reluctance to acknowledge either participation or interest in them. But seductive as the siren song of secular power could be, it never drowned out the fundamental theme of his life and ministry: reconciling men and women to God and to each other. Thus, even during the period when he was involved in partisan politics to a degree that he has found difficult to acknowledge even to himself, most of his time and energy were spent not in trying to hoist flags of victory over conquered enemies but in trying to tear down barriers separating people who might, if given a chance, be friends.

Graham's efforts to help Nixon explain his China policy fit this pattern. Though not too many years earlier he had called the People's Republic "the most dangerous enemy of freedom in the world," he welcomed the President's dramatic move to reestablish formal ties with the nation and people his wife still loved so much, and he used his great influence to stanch criticism from quarters accustomed to regarding China as a menace even more threatening than the Soviet Union. In this case, he was merely a facilitator, a supplier of names and endorser of invitations. In other cases—in Ireland, India, South Africa, and Korea—Graham acted, sometimes at the risk of his life, as a living symbol and active agent of reconciliation and brotherhood.

Graham visited Ireland in late May of 1972 in the hope that by meeting with both Protestant and Catholic religious and political leaders in Northern Ireland and the Republic of Ireland and by judicious appearances on television, he might lay the groundwork for an eventual crusade or some venture that would help ease the tension between Catholics and Protestants, as his American crusades had promoted better relationships between blacks and whites. One strategy he considered, exemplifying his own deep conviction that people who got to know each other personally would find it extremely difficult to remain enemies, was to encourage religious leaders to establish hundreds of "dialogue groups," consisting of five Catholics and five Protestants each, as a way of substituting webs of personal friendship for walls of blind prejudice. Significantly, his visit came a few days after he completed a large and successful integrated crusade in Birmingham, Alabama, where his Easter service eight years earlier had been an important first step toward reducing overt tensions in that city's explosive racial situation. An exploratory foray by members of the London office of BGEA had met with warm assurances that a visit by Graham to Northern Ireland might well have a healing effect on the divided region, but tense conditions at the time of his arrival made it clear that a misstep could easily have serious negative consequences, including his assassination.

Graham landed in Belfast, the troubled capital of Northern Ireland, on a Saturday, with an appointment to preach on Sunday evening. Also in Belfast at the time was Arthur Blessit, a colorful and controversial street preacher who gained notoriety for his work with the "Jesus People" on Sunset Strip and was satisfying his continuing need for publicity by traveling about the world dragging a large cross on his shoulder, in the presumed manner of Jesus on the Via Dolorosa. Some doubted that self-promotion should be added to the catalog of spiritual gifts listed in the twelfth chapter of I Corinthians, but few questioned Blessit's physical courage, which he had already demonstrated in Belfast by openly consorting with both Catholics and Protestants, a tactic hardly calculated to endear him to either group. Blessit, however, thrived on audacious behavior and delighted at the chance to invite Billy Graham to join him on a bipartisan Sunday-morning sortie. As they entered the most troubled district in the city, with no police or private security guards to protect them, Graham managed to contain whatever fear he may have felt for his personal safety, but he could not completely conquer his anxiety. In a touching display of both humility and self-knowledge, the most successful public soul winner in Christian history turned to his guide and said, "You're going to have to teach me and consider me as a student of personal evangelism. I don't consider myself to be a man that's gifted of God just to deal with an individual." Fortunately, Blessit felt quite comfortable taking the lead—and enjoying Graham's vulnerability. As they approached the Peace Line, a barricade that divided a single road into Roman Catholic and Protestant lanes, and prepared to walk along it, Blessit informed his charge that he would be watched every step of the way. If the IRA deemed his presence unacceptable, they would announce their objection in an unambiguous manner—with a bullet in his back. Bolstered by faith that if he were assassinated he would proceed directly through heaven's portals, but not overly anxious to surrender his earthly ministry just yet, Graham walked along the barricade with a feeling of anxious peace. At a point where they could see Protestant and Catholic worshipers going in and out of their respective houses of worship, where they professed to love God but learned to hate their neighbors, the two men knelt to pray, asking God to send a revival that might bring peace in its train.

Graham and Blessit spent two and a half hours walking in both the Catholic and Protestant sectors, passing out tracts and talking with individuals. At one point, in the Falls Road district, where anti-Protestant feelings ran highest, they dropped into a *skabena*, an unlicensed pub, situated in back of a hairdresser's salon and known to be an IRA hangout. Encouraged by some of the men who recognized Graham, the two clergymen told a few jokes and did a bit of preaching, all to a good-natured response, including a reciprocal offering by a tipsy Irishman who boozily rumbled through "The Devil and the Deep Blue Sea." Later, Graham spent several minutes standing in a bombed-out dwelling, consoling a bus conductor whose wife had been killed by a terrorist's bomb that had ripped through their home a few hours earlier.

While Graham preached at Ravenhill Presbyterian Church on Sunday evening, a pulpit he had filled in 1946 on a Youth for Christ tour, the most prominent Protestant preacher in Northern Ireland, Ian Paisley, preached a countersermon in his own church, spilling out vitriolic condemnation of the evangelist and his compromising attitude toward Roman Catholics, and announcing that "the church which has Billy Graham in its pulpit will have the curse of the Almighty upon it." The tirade, one of two Paisley delivered during Graham's visit, was no surprise. The surprise had come two years earlier when the dogmatic separatist had written a book entitled *Billy Graham and the Church of Rome: A Startling Exposure.* Since Graham had seldom commented on Ireland, the book was not a criticism of his political views, but of his increasingly cozy relationship with Catholicism. It consisted mainly of quotations documenting his friendship with Catholic leaders such as Cardinal Cushing and denunciations of his ecumenical policies by such unyielding Fundamentalists as Bob Jones, whose university had presented Paisley with an honorary degree and had published the American edition of his book. Graham offered to meet with his antagonist while he was in Belfast, but Paisley declined the opportunity, explaining that he did not "have fellowship with those who deny the faith."

A small, singular event momentarily stirred fears in Graham's camp that his visit to the troubled city might be misconstrued as a piece of American meddling. On this same weekend, Richard Nixon was visiting the Soviet Union. As was his practice, Graham had urged him to visit some church in Moscow to demonstrate the importance Americans place on spiritual matters and the right to worship freely. Nixon, whose record on heeding Graham's spiritual counsel was spotty, had followed his advice on this occasion and wanted to let him know it. Unaware of Billy's whereabouts, he called the White House, which tracked Graham down and patched the call through to his hotel in Belfast, where the switchboard operator strongly resisted ringing his room, since he knew the evangelist had already retired. Then, in a two-minute conversation that bounced from Moscow to Washington and back to Belfast, the President of the United States happily reported to his itinerant pastor that he had attended the Moscow Baptist Church that morning. Just this once, Graham might have preferred a postcard. He and his associates understandably fretted that if word of the call leaked out, sensitive Irishmen would never believe its true purpose but would assume he was acting as an agent of American foreign policy. Inevitably, news of the communication did spread, but Graham's account of the matter was accepted, and no problem ensued.

During the next two days, Graham met with hundreds of Northern Ireland's political, religious, and social leaders—at a dinner for two hundred, a breakfast for one thousand, and numerous gatherings of much smaller groups. He also spoke at the Queen's University in Belfast, on invitation from both Roman Catholic and Protestant chaplains, and appeared several times on Ulster TV and the BBC. In each case, theologians, journalists, and secular intellectuals criticized the shallowness of his understanding of the situation in Ireland and dismissed his assertion that most of the problems bedeviling the Emerald Isle could be swept into the sea by a good revival. On those same occasions, however, many others professed to be deeply impressed by his humility ("He put it over with so much love," one student commented), his sincere desire to help bring peace to their nation, and his straightforward presentation of the faith that gave meaning to his own life.

Ultimately, example proved more important than utterances. In every meeting, Graham insisted that both Catholics and Protestants be present in proportions as equal as feasible, a requirement that brought together people who had never met or, if they knew each other at all, had certainly never sat down to eat or talk or pray with one another. In an encouraging coincidence—"He'll get the credit for it," an Irish MP wryly noted—the official IRA announced it was suspending military action in a truce it hoped might lead to lasting peace. The more violent Provisional IRA did not immediately consent to the truce, but radical Catholics seeking independence from England were not the only disturbers of the peace. Whether followers of Ian Paisley or not, many Protestants rejected Graham's efforts to build bridges of friendship across an abyss of prejudice and hatred. Despite his uncommon ability to feel hope when others could not, the peace-seeking evangelist acknowledged a discouraging hardness of heart among his Protestant brethren that he recognized might be a formidable hindrance to lasting peace.

Paradoxically, Graham received a much warmer reception in the Catholic-dominated Republic of Ireland, where he was hosted by the Irish branch of International Christian Leadership. As in Ulster, he met publicly and privately with hundreds of Protestant and Catholic leaders; the *Irish Times* said of one large breakfast meeting that "the guest list was startling for the brains and wealth and influence it represented." In a clandestine encounter complete with police disapproval, back-alley connections, switched vehicles, and secret routes, the Dublin leader of the IRA received Graham for a long conversation in which he explained his organization's view of the conflict with England and the Protestant Unionists in Ireland. Afterward, Graham refused to divulge details of their conversation but observed that he had "the distinct feeling that the issues involved were not religious but political," apparently overlooking the fact that these powerful forces in human life could seldom be neatly separated. In another temporary triumph of hope over history, he predicted confidently that a complete cease-fire in Northern Ireland was in the offing. In fact, the Provisional IRA in Ulster did join the previously announced truce three weeks later, but soon resorted to the bombs and bullets they seemed unable to abandon; by midsummer, England dispatched new troops to quell fresh outbreaks of violence.

If it did not bring peace to Ireland, Graham's visit was nevertheless a sincere and salutary step toward increased understanding among separated people. In contrast to the coolness of spirit he felt in Belfast, particularly from Protestants, he reported that he had seldom experienced such kindness and genuine religious fervor as he had in Dublin. Repeatedly, priests and nuns offered fervent expressions of gratitude for his visit and his ministry and replayed tapes of his addresses in convents and rectories, establishing the fact that Billy Graham was no enemy of Roman Catholics. He did not follow up on his expressed desire to hold a crusade in Ireland—largely because of opposition from the Protestant clergy—but eighteen months after his visit, BGEA associate evangelist Akbar Abdul-Haqq held a full-scale campaign in Dublin with extensive cooperation from the Catholic community.

Later in 1972, just after the election, Graham made another visit to a strife-torn region, this time to Nagaland, a state in the northeast of India, along the border with Burma. In a situation similar in some respects to that in Ireland, the predominantly Christian Nagas had sought independence from the Hindu-dominated New Delhi government since 1947, when India obtained independence from Great Britain. Guerilla action against national troops was a constant feature of Naga life, creating a situation so explosive that Westerners were seldom permitted to enter Nagaland. Graham did not visit Nagaland during his 1956 tour, but the Nagas knew well of his ministry and longed to have him hold a crusade in their region. In 1967 Akbar Abdul-Haqq held a crusade in the city of Kohima and indicated that Graham might respond positively to an invitation. Five years later, the Naga dream seemed about to come true when the evangelist agreed, pending government approval, to come to Kohima in November 1972.

Seldom, if ever, did a proposed crusade face such obstacles. During Abdul-Haqq's preliminary visit to prepare the churches for Graham's visit, a guerilla band killed three people in an attempt to assassinate the chief minister of Nagaland, a development that led to a stiff increase in state security measures and appeared likely to destroy chances of getting a permit for Graham. With endorsement from the chief minister (a Christian himself) and gracious but lukewarm assistance from a well-known young liberal Indian clergyman named Robert Cunville, a delegation of Naga churchmen went to New Delhi to beseech the minister for home affairs not to prohibit Graham's visit. The minister had no objection to Graham's coming but feared the rebels might kidnap or kill him in an effort to draw attention to their cause, thus creating a severe embarrassment for the Indian government. Finally, in an almost laughable gesture of governmental hand washing, the home minister agreed to allow Graham to come if the Baptist Church in Naga would take responsibility for maintaining peace during the crusade. Readily conceding, at least to themselves, the essential absurdity of that request, the churchmen agreed and dispatched one of their number into the mountainous jungle, where he met with rebel leaders and won from them a written promise not to engage in disruptive action during the crusade. Even so, the home minister, on a visit to the United Nations in New York, met with Graham and explained to him that while the government viewed his coming in a positive light, it stood ready to withdraw the permits on a moment's notice if the situation in Nagaland became too volatile.

Meanwhile, the Nagas were getting ready. To raise money for crusade expenses—as always, BGEA picked up the costs incurred by Graham and his associates—the churches obtained a contract from the government to build a road connecting a major artery to an airstrip four miles away. In less than two days, 7,000 volunteers cleared a path through steep jungle terrain with hand tools brought from their homes. The same spirit of commitment flourished in Kohima. Because crusade organizers expected as many as 100,000 souls to descend on the relatively small town, nearly every family opened its doors to guests, the town government allowed pilgrims to sleep in schools and other public buildings, and the Indian Army provided hundreds of tents as additional shelter. Villagers also sold meat and produce at low prices and gave away firewood on which to cook it.

Early in November, Baptists in Nagaland had celebrated the centennial anniversary of their denomination's presence in the state. That event, which the central government watched closely to see if the promised cease-fire would hold, passed without incident. Then, less than a week before the crusade was to begin, and after 80,000 pilgrims had arrived in Kohima, some walking for five or six days, guerillas ambushed an army convoy, killing and wounding several soldiers. The Naga church leaders were aghast, but remarkably, the government did not cancel the permits for Graham and his team, who were already in the Far East. Several of Graham's own advisers, however, including Akbar Abdul-Haqq, urged the evangelist to cancel the crusade, fearing either that the guerillas might stage an uprising and kill or injure innocent parties or that the central government would use the event as an excuse to dispatch more troops to Nagaland. In either case, the embarrassment to Christianity might outweigh any good a crusade could do.

In Bangkok Graham reluctantly decided to cancel the crusade, something he had never before done, except for illness. On Saturday he prepared a press release and directed Walter Smyth to take it to New Delhi for publication the following Monday. Back in Calcutta, Robert Cunville, who had become enthusiastic about the crusade, was crushed at the news but refused to accept it as final. "God can still do a miracle," he insisted, and he placed a call to Kohima, urging the multitudes gathered there to begin assaulting heaven with requests for deliverance from this quite real dilemma. Recalling this incident fourteen years later, Cunville insisted that God an swered those prayers with nothing less than a miracle. During the night, Graham received several cables, including messages from the U.S. State Department, acknowledging the risk but suggesting it might be better not to cancel the crusade. Early the next morning, Graham answered an insistent knock at his door and found himself facing a Naga Christian and a young American who had once been a missionary to Nagaland. The missionary announced dramatically that "I have come here as the servant of the Lord. You've *got* to go to Nagaland." He and his Naga friend explained the harm that a cancellation would bring to the church and, because church leaders had a key role in trying to bring peace to the region, to the whole state. They also challenged his faith, assuring him that God would protect him from danger. Ever susceptible to intimations that his ministry was part of some grander divine plan, Graham seized upon their importuning as the very sign from God that he had been seeking through a prayer-filled night, and he set out immediately to join several team members waiting for him in Calcutta. Monday afternoon, following attendance at a cricket match and a visit with Mother Teresa in Calcutta on Sunday, Graham and the team descended on Kohima, where the assembly, now swollen to an estimated 100,000 and packed onto a soccer field tucked in front of dark green mountains, cheered ecstatically at his long-awaited arrival. Later, he wrote in his diary, "Tears came to my eyes. I felt rebuked that I had even doubted about coming to these mountain people to minister the gospel. I felt terribly unworthy."

Graham stayed in Kohima four days. When he spoke at the morning Bible study sessions and at the late-afternoon crusade services, twenty interpreters translated his words into regional languages and dialects, not from soundproof booths wired to individual headsets or closed-circuit TV screens, but standing throughout the crowd, using bullhorns and mega phones to carry their voices to clumps of people gathered in the various language groups. No tongues of fire appeared, but the comparison to Pentecost, when "each one heard them speaking in his own language," could not be avoided. Perhaps the inescapable association with that event stimulated the expectation that other Pentecostal flowers might blossom in that remote jungle. In any case, crusade leaders responded to numerous requests by allowing people who sought healing of physical or spiritual affliction for themselves or for others to put the names of the afflicted person in a large box, which was then presented to Graham. The evangelist carefully explained that he did not claim the gift of healing nor believe that his prayers were more valuable than those of any other faithful Christians. Still, he did believe that God answers prayer and, if he willed, could meet any need. With that qualification, Graham prayed that those whose names were in the box might be healed if it pleased God. No lame people cast crutches aside and no blind men professed to see, but within a few days, grateful believers began to report what they could only interpret as miracles—recovery from epilepsy, from tetanus, from undiagnosed but apparently life-threatening ailments, and from the grip of soul-deadening sin. Graham's colleagues recall these incidents with an amusing mixture of mild skepticism, humility in the face of evidence, and unmistakable satisfaction. They tend not to approve of Pentecostal healing ministries, but they stop short of denying that God can intervene supernaturally in human life today if he so chooses. Best of all, they seem to relish the conviction that even in a field in which he does not specialize, Billy Graham still got good results.

Unfortunately, not every service had such a happy outcome. During the Wednesday morning Bible class, attended by tens of thousands, gunfire rang out at a point where the edge of the crowd lay close to the jungle. Graham called for calm and no panic ensued, but a guerilla's bullet had found its mark, leaving one man dead. As the service ended, a skirmish between guerillas and government troops resulted in several more deaths, but crusade leaders decided to proceed according to schedule, and no further incidents marred the meetings.

Though Nagaland was one of the few Christian strongholds in India, Graham's audiences contained Hindus, Muslims, and syncretists who might profess some form of Christianity but had no clear sense of the exclusivity Western Christians believed it entailed. Aware that many of his hearers might affirm allegiance to Christ but regard him as only one of many beings worthy of honor, Billy took great care in his invitation to stress that the God he proclaimed was not "one of the gods" but "*the* God," and that pledging allegiance to him involved renunciation of all other gods. Seating arrangements at Kohima did not permit inquirers to come forward or make it possible for counselors to talk with them individually. Even so, observers believe that more than 4,000 people made decisions for Christ during the three days that Graham preached.

Whatever the true number of decisions made at Kohima, Indian Evangelicals insist that the effects of the crusade involved more than an immediate net gain in church membership. Christianity is still a minority religion in India, claiming only about 3 percent of the population. That minority, however, is heavily Evangelical, especially in the northeast region of India that includes Nagaland and neighboring states. As in numerous other locales, nearly all of the growth among Christians is posted among Evangelicals, as conservative seminaries consistently turn out far more clergymen than do those of more liberal bent. And occasionally, men trained at the liberal seminaries find themselves attracted to the vitality they see in Evangelical circles. One such man was Robert Cunville. Exposure to Billy Graham and his team at Kohima so impressed Cunville that he gave up his more socially oriented ministry and came to America to enroll at the School of World Mission at Fuller Theological Seminary, supported by a scholarship from BGEA. Three years later, he returned to India with a doctorate in missions, and he has served since that time as an associate evangelist with the Graham organization. The crusade also seems to have had an impact on the tense political situation. Cunville and others believe that the rebel cease-fire negotiated by crusade leaders created a lull that provided opportunity for reflection and led ultimately to the writing of a peace motion that resulted in a stable government for Nagaland. Some government officials doubted that Graham's appearance had much effect on the peace process one way or the other. Still, the Naga church leader most responsible for bringing Graham to his homeland and for persuading the guerillas to allow the crusade to proceed was also intimately involved in the deliberations that led to a 1975 agreement that ended the Naga rebellion, and he emphatically regarded the Graham crusade as a turning point in the quest for peace. And Robert Cunville, who was not prepared for what he saw, summed up his account by saying, "In Nagaland, we never call it the Billy Graham Crusade. To this day, we call it the Kohima Miracle."

Immediately after Kohima, Graham returned to New Delhi for a meeting with Indira Gandhi. At President Nixon's request ("He knew I was a friend of hers"), the evangelist asked the prime minister what kind of ambassador she wanted the President to appoint. "She told me, 'I want one who has the ear of the President, who knows economics, and who knows something about India.' So I went right over to the embassy and said that straight to the President, and he appointed [Daniel Patrick] Moynihan." Graham called the appointment "an absolute master stroke" and offered to share his insights about India, particularly information he had gotten from three Christians in Mrs. Gandhi's cabinet. Moynihan was more than receptive. "When I got back to Washington," Graham recalled, "Moynihan came over to my hotel and thanked me. He thought I had had him appointed. We got down on our knees and prayed together about his going to India."

In another notable brush with world leaders, Graham wound up his Eastern tour with a stop in Tehran, where he discussed biblical prophecies with the shah of Iran.

Shortly after Nixon was elected in 1968, Graham began to contemplate returning to Washington for a major crusade. Noting that he was "convinced that the type of crusade we now hold could have a great impact," he suggested to a friend that he contact several of the men who had spearheaded the recent New York City crusade to see how to organize an appropriate invitation. Nothing happened immediately, but early in 1972, a group of leaders that included Congressman (and former major-league ballplayer) Wilmer "Vinegar Bend" Mizell approached Nixon to see if he would sign an invitation to Graham, as he had done for the 1969 New York crusade. On John Dean's advice that it would not be in keeping "with our general policy or the dignity of the Presidency," Nixon chose not to sign but informed Graham in a warm letter that he wanted him to know "how pleased I would be to see you lead such a Crusade here." Graham indicated that the current exploratory effort was "news to me" and that he would be unwilling to hold a crusade in the capital during an election year lest it embarrass the President in some way, but he did say that "after the election, I will get some of my people to investigate the possibilities."

True to his word, Graham began to put out feelers shortly after the election. The response was clear—and sharply divided. White churches wanted him; blacks did not. The board of the Council of Churches, with heavy black representation, voted to dissociate itself from the proposed crusade. The Reverend Ernest Gibson, later executive director of the council and cochair of the 1986 crusade, explained what he and his colleagues had felt at the time: "Tension between blacks and whites was high in 1972. Black leaders who were part of the civil rights movement were trying to identify friends. One of the criteria was whether whites would stand with us, support us, use their influence and positions of power to help. Mr. Graham was a frequent visitor to the White House, and we hoped he would say something supportive about the rights of black people in this country. But he didn't. He said nothing at all." That indictment was not quite accurate, but it was certainly true that Graham avoided movement rhetoric. To complicate the situation, according to Gibson, white church leaders did not so much consult blacks as to whether the evangelist would be welcome as inform them he was coming. "We resented that," he recalled, obviously still feeling whites had miscalculated. "We decided we would not cooperate with the call for a crusade. We were a pretty consolidated group." That decision killed a Washington crusade, erecting a barrier that had to be surmounted before the 1986 crusade could occur.

Ironically, at the very time American blacks were finding fault with Billy Graham, blacks and mixed-race "coloreds" in South Africa were hailing him as a principled and effective enemy of apartheid. Consistent with his long-standing policy, Graham spurned all invitations to preach in South Africa until he could be assured that any service in which he participated would be fully and freely integrated. Then, in 1972, a breakthrough came when South African evangelist Michael Cassidy managed to wrest from his wary brethren an invitation that satisfied Graham's criteria. Cassidy was a spiritual grandchild and avid admirer of Graham's; won to Christ by a Harringay convert, he heard Graham preach at Cambridge in 1955 and again in New York in 1957. After studying at Fuller Seminary, he returned to his homeland and established a small multiracial team of evangelists who held revivals throughout Africa. At the Berlin Congress, he delivered a brief and quite moderate paper on "The Ethics of Political Nationalism," in which he took an essentially Graham-like position, acknowledging the complexity of the South African situation, observing that the excesses of black nationalists were no more acceptable than those of their Afrikaner oppressors, and calling for government informed by love and justice for all rather than group self-interest. Unexceptional as it was, the paper generated heated response from South African representatives of the Dutch Reformed Church, who asked that it not be included in the official proceedings. That bit of attempted censorship failed, but Cassidy agreed to allow the proceedings to carry an appendix noting that the South African government observed and protected "complete freedom of evangelism" and stating that the policy of "parallel development" had a long and complicated historical background and "has been generally accepted by all the various racial groups" in the country.

Inspired by the Berlin Congress and follow-up gatherings in other parts of the world, Cassidy organized a South African meeting, to be held in Durban in 1973. To his utter surprise, when he mentioned the meeting to Graham during a visit to the United States early in 1972, Graham volunteered to participate if he would be welcome. Elated at this unexpected offer, Cassidy was dumbfounded when the organizing committee decided by a narrow margin that it would be best if the famous evangelist were not invited, ostensibly out of fear he might dominate the meetings and divert attention from the primary agenda. Beneath the surface, the decision was more complex. Black members of the committee, appreciative of Graham's long-standing refusal to wink at apartheid, wanted him to come. The more socially liberal white members tended to be suspicious of evangelism and feared that Graham might emphasize soul winning to the detriment of anti-apartheid efforts. A third and smaller contingent of staunch white Evangelicals either favored or had made peace with apartheid and correctly anticipated that a Graham visit would involve public criticism of that policy. Few of the resisters, however, were adamant in their opposition, and with a bit of active lobbying, Cassidy was able to win a reversal and official confirmation of his own informal invitation.

When he volunteered to break his personal boycott of South Africa, Graham expected only to participate in the Congress of Mission and Evangelism in South Africa, which would be the largest fully interracial meeting that nation had ever seen, with whites, blacks, coloreds, and Indians all living and eating in the same hotel. At the urging of Cassidy and others, however, he agreed to hold a public rally at the King's Park rugby stadium on condition that it would be open to all races and colors, with no separate seating arrangements. Then, both to appease Evangelicals who looked askance at his consorting with some of the liberal churchmen who would be present at the Durban Congress and to offer an additional witness against apartheid, he agreed to hold another public service in Johannesburg, this time under the aegis of Youth for Christ. Lest his hosts in either city later complain that he had misled them, Graham explicitly warned them that while he did not intend to launch an attack on apartheid, he would, if asked, state flatly that he disapproved of it.

Because he was speaking only twice, with one of those occasions an addendum to the congress, Graham did not field a full team for his South African appearances, but one bit of preparatory work stood out for both its short- and long-term effects. Millie Dienert, who for several years had been in charge of the prayer campaign prior to Graham's crusades, worked with a prominent South African Anglican woman to organize more than five thousand women into small interracial groups that met regularly to pray for the rallies. The groups proved so rewarding to the participants that instead of disbanding when the rallies were over, they became the nucleus of an interracial women's prayer movement that claimed 350,000 members just five years later.

Saturday, March 17, 1973, was a historic day in Durban, as 45,000 people from every racial and ethnic group in South Africa pressed into King's Park stadium for the first major public interracial gathering in that nation's history. Overcome by the sight of white ushers courteously welcoming blacks and of blacks and whites sitting together with no display of animosity or discomfort, a Zulu Christian said, through tears of joy, "Even if Billy Graham doesn't stand up to preach, this has been enough of a testimony." Graham did, of course, stand up to preach. Without mentioning apartheid, he repeated the same theme he had sounded during his 1960 African tour. Jesus was neither a white nor a black man, he said. "He came from that part of the world that touches Africa, and Asia, and Europe, and he probably had a brown skin. Very much like some of the Indian people here today. Christianity is not a white man's religion, and don't let anybody ever tell you that it's white or black. Christ belongs to all people! He belongs to the whole world! His gospel is for everyone, whoever you are." It was hardly a harangue against apartheid, but after 4,000 people answered the invitation, many for repentance of sins unspecified but surely including prejudice and discrimination, the headline of Durban's Sunday newspaper proclaimed: APARTHEID DOOMED.

Socially progressive churchmen who appreciated the significance of Graham's King's Park rally were disappointed that the evangelist did not mention apartheid in his address to the congress, where the risk would have been small and the possible impact great. To make matters worse, he left the convention hall immediately following his speech and departed for Johannesburg, leaving what Cassidy described as "an acute sense of vacuum and frustration" among delegates who had sought to elicit some more satisfying and helpful statement from him. Leighton Ford eased the situation by a more critical assessment of apartheid in his address to the assembly, and Graham's representative insisted that the early departure had been planned all along and was in no way an effort to duck controversy, but many delegates who had hoped for more could sympathize with their American colleagues who felt that throughout his ministry Billy Graham repeatedly stepped back from the courageous statement or action that might have made a crucial difference in critical situations.

If Graham's aim was to avoid controversy, he should not have been in such a hurry to reach Johannesburg. On his first day in the city, he held a press conference at which he described racial separation as "un-Christian and unworkable." He also moved a step beyond his oft-voiced position that changing hearts, not laws, was the only solution to the racial problem. Admitting that while in many respects America was no model for other countries to follow in addressing their racial problems, he pointed out that the U.S. Congress had enacted "the finest civil rights legislation in the history of the human race," and asserted that "at least legally, we are on the right footing." Then came a shot that hit his foot but ricocheted around the world. Aware that the United States Supreme Court had recently handed down the *Roe v. Wade* decision, a reporter asked Graham if he regarded abortion as the taking of human life. He said that he did but conceded it might be justified in some situations, such as pregnancy caused by rape. In an egregious example of a notorious tendency to allow a key word or image to send him down what his colleagues refer to as "rabbit trails," he referred to a newspaper article he had read the day before about the gang raping of a twelve-year-old girl. He volunteered that he advocated stiff punishment for rape, adding, "I think when a person is found guilty of rape he should be castrated. That would stop him pretty quick." Graham recalls that he immediately realized he had gone too far. "It was an offhand, hasty, spontaneous remark that I regretted almost as soon as I said it," he said. "I meant to get back to it, but I got sidetracked." Fortunately, South African papers paid little attention to the comment, but when it reached America, it created such a flap that White House staff members quickly prepared a memo for the President, alerting him to be ready to discuss it with Graham should the occasion arise. The remark drew fire because of a perceived barbaric quality and also because it was allegedly racist, since a disproportionate number of convicted rapists in America are black. Without trying to justify the statement, Graham explained that he had a deep concern about sex-oriented crimes and had been profoundly affected by the story of the young victim, who doctors said would probably be a psychological invalid for the rest of her life. He also noted that he had made a point of saying that any such penalty "should be administered fairly, objectively, equally and swiftly to all, without regard to race or wealth," and observed that it was odd that his critics seemed more disturbed by his commendation of castration than by the crime of rape.

Cries of racism from critics in America must have seemed incongruous to blacks and other nonwhites in Johannesburg, for whom Graham's rally at the Wanderers Cricket Ground was the first interracial public meeting most had ever attended. The service not only drew a thoroughly integrated crowd of 60,000, smashing the week-old record for integrated meetings by 15,000, but was carried live to the nation by the state-run radio network (television did not come to South Africa until 1975). No foreigner had ever been granted that privilege before, and the broadcast drew the third-largest audience ever registered by the network. Ever the gracious guest, Graham complimented South Africans for giving him "one of the finest receptions of my entire ministry" and showed himself worthy of such treatment by public association with two of the country's most popular figures, cricket star Trevor Goddard and golfer Gary Player. Both men helped with press relations, and Player gave Graham and his entourage a well-publicized reception at his home. The evangelist also garnered favorable publicity for a generous gift of more than $70,000 to famine victims in West Africa, an effort that exemplified his growing determination to make a tangible response to physical as well as spiritual needs.

Graham's conviction that this could be a valid and important part of his ministry led to the formation of the World Emergency Fund, a BGEA outreach that channels several hundred thousand dollars to disaster victims annually. But it was the simple, profound fact that by force of reputation and principle he had been able to set aside South Africa's dominant and infamous social arrangement that made the greatest impression on that nation. Shortly after his visit, a popular magazine proclaimed, "Apartheid gets three knockout blows." One blow was an international, multiracial athletic festival; the other two were Billy Graham's rallies in Durban and Johannesburg. The nefarious system did not, of course, stay down for the count. But undeniably, two successive giant demonstrations at which blacks and coloreds and Indians and whites could meet and mingle, could stand and sit and sing and pray side by side without breach of peace or threat to order, could confess that they were all flawed and sinful creatures who alike needed forgiveness from a God who was "no respecter of persons," could not but leave their mark.

Unhappily for Graham, many American blacks continued to view his efforts on their behalf to be less than adequate. That summer in Atlanta, his crusade drew a noticeably small turnout from the city's large black population. A major bus strike played some role, but with the notable exception of the Reverend Martin Luther King, Sr., most of the city's key black leaders urged blacks to stay away. Ralph Abernathy, successor to Martin Luther King, Jr., as head of the Southern Christian Leadership Conference, complained that blacks had not been involved in preparation for the crusade. Hosea Williams, of the conference's Atlanta chapter, charged that Graham had a poor record on race and poverty issues. The president of a black seminary criticized Graham's role as "chaplain to the Establishment" and his tendency to take "an oblique stand" on issues that vitally affect blacks, and for supporting Richard Nixon, who cut programs to benefit the poor. Others dragged up his allegedly racist comment about castrating rapists and faulted the "culturally white" style of his services.

Graham faced a similar boycott in Minneapolis a month later. Perhaps because black poverty was a less serious problem in Minnesota than in Georgia, Minneapolis ministers focused most of their hostility on his prescription of castration for rapists. At a long and frank meeting with the critical clergymen, Graham noted that a black friend counseled him not to apologize to blacks for the statement, since that would imply that he associated rape with blacks. He had decided, however, not to follow that advice. The statement, he said, had been "wrong and inflammatory," and he was sorry he had made it. He also agreed that he had not done enough to aid the poor, adding that he would not simply assert his repentance but would demonstrate it. Then, after a tour of black neighborhoods in the Twin Cities, he made a little-noticed but significant change in theology when he told the men that he had come to believe that the gospel should aim at saving not just individuals but society itself. All but two of the critical clergymen declared themselves convinced of Graham's sincerity and with drew their opposition to the crusade, but winning the confidence and cooperation of black Christians would continue to be a hill that had to be climbed, sometimes a wall that had to be scaled, in crusade after crusade throughout the remainder of his career.

Two months after the South African meetings, Graham returned to the Far East for a stunningly triumphant campaign in Korea. Perhaps no nation in the world has experienced such an explosive growth of Christianity as South Korea. Rather small and insignificant at the end of World War II, the Christian church claimed 10 percent of the population in 1970 and was experiencing a growth rate four times faster than that of the population as a whole. (By 1990 the proportion had grown to 28 percent, and at least one congregation claimed more than 500,000 members.) Favorable political conditions helped. In contrast to the anti-Christian bias found in some oriental countries, the South Korean government accorded favored treatment to Christianity, regarding it as a useful bulwark against, and counterforce to, communism. "Anything that promotes anticommunism," one prominent Korean leader explained, "the Korean government favors." But more important, Korean Christians display a level of commitment that amazes even the most dedicated of American Evangelicals. In hundreds of churches all over the nation, thousands of earnest believers gather every morning at four-thirty or five o'clock for fervent prayer meetings and enthusiastic preaching. Though not especially charmed by the dawn's early light himself, Abdul-Haqq conceded that such habits inevitably create "a psychological ethos that is spiritual" and attributes much of the success of Korean Christianity to the fact that "fifty years ago, someone started to pray."

The invitation to Graham came from a blue-ribbon committee representing sixteen hundred churches and led by Dr. Han Kyung Chile, a Presbyterian pastor who had served as the evangelist's interpreter in 1951 when he addressed Korean audiences following his visit with American troops at Christmastime. Reflecting the influence of American missionaries, some extreme Fundamentalist churches with ties to Carl McIntire and Bob Jones refused to cooperate either with each other or with Graham, whom they had been taught to regard as an archcompromiser. Eventually, however, the overwhelming majority of Christians in Korea supported the crusade, initiating a new era of ecumenical cooperation. "It was really the first time," Dr. Han observed, "that all the Christian people, not only in Seoul but also in a good many provincial towns, gathered together. In that sense, it was unique. When we knelt together, we found we were all friends."

To oversee crusade preparation, Graham dispatched Henry Holley, a former Marine staff sergeant who had joined BGEA several years earlier after impressing team members with the administrative skills he showed while working as a volunteer during Graham's 1960 Washington crusade. A thoroughly cordial but nevertheless spit-and-polish man accustomed to acting decisively, Holley clashed at times with local committeemen, who tended also to have definite notions about how things should be done. Holley was accustomed to thinking in large-scale terms, but the Koreans' aspirations and plans seemed at times too grand to be realistic and generated considerable anxiety both for him and dubious team members back in Atlanta, where team operations were now headquartered.

Nothing illustrated the Korean vision better than the proposal to stage the crusade on the People's Plaza, a mile-long former airstrip on Yoido Island in the middle of the Ham River. Holley and some Korean committee members feared that the facility was simply too big, so that even a huge crowd — 100,000, for example — would be swallowed up in the vast expanse and appear insignificant in newspaper and television pictures. Still, the only other large facility, Seoul's 25,000-seat National Stadium, was almost certainly too small, so there was little real choice. Yoido was also a fitting symbolic site; nearly ninety years earlier, the first American missionary to arrive in Seoul had been stoned when he stepped off the boat onto that same island. Ordinarily, the plaza was restricted to military parades and state-sponsored events.

In keeping with its pro-Christian policy, however, the government not only gave approval, but dispatched the Army Corps of Engineers to build a platform large enough to hold a 10,000-voice choir and to install powerful arc lights.

The crusade was originally planned for 1972, but an effort to control Graham's chronic high blood pressure had forced a postponement until 1973. Even then, at his physicians' direction, the evangelist notified Holley that he would not be able to follow through on his original plan to appear for the final service of six crusades to be held by his associate evangelists in Korea's other major population centers. This news stunned local organizers, who believed not being able to deliver Billy Graham as promised would result in a severe loss of face for themselves and the church. They also suggested that Graham was suffering from what they saw as an occidental weakness. "Americans," one observed, "always follow medical doctor's way. But the Oriental, even though his health is a little bad, if we promise, then we should be there." Graham stuck by his decision, but perhaps in the hope that he might change his mind at the last minute, the local committees did not publicize his withdrawal.

A second, less serious crisis involved the choice of interpreter. Dr. Han feared he was too old to perform the rigorous and stressful task of translating the evangelist's words for a huge audience. The obvious second choice for the role was a thirty-nine-year-old Baptist pastor named Kim Jang Whan, now better known in Evangelical circles as Billy Kim. During the Korean War, Kim had been converted and adopted by an American soldier who took him back to America and financed his education — at Bob Jones University. Equipped with Fundamentalist fire and southern-revivalist technique, as well as with an American wife, Kim quickly rose to prominence in the Korean Church as a pastor, a powerful evangelist, and a director in several international Christian organizations, including the missionary-run Far East Broadcasting Company and Billy Graham's old fraternity, Youth for Christ. He had also proved himself an effective translator by serving in the role for Carl McIntire, whose virulent anticommunism had gained him a considerable following in Korea.

At Bob Jones University, Kim had never heard either of the Doctors Bob or any guest speaker describe Graham as anything other than an enemy of true Christianity. Carl McIntire, of course, held the same opinion. Back in South Korea, where the minority status of Christians made shunning other believers less feasible than in South Carolina, Kim had moved away from strict separatism. He had attended the Berlin Congress, which had heightened his appreciation for Graham, and he had come to recognize that missionaries trained at BJU sometimes "talked of issues that were not central." Still, he was not so great a fan of Graham's that he felt he could not pass up the honor of standing beside him, and even more important, he feared that identification with Graham might cause some of his more conservative supporters in America to cut off contributions to programs in which he was involved. On the other hand, he could not escape the force of what both he and others believed: He was the right man for the job. In particular, he believed no one else could communicate Graham's offer of the invitation as well as he could. Presbyterians, by far the dominant Protestant body in Korea, did not really believe in the invitation, and no other Korean Baptist had sat through hundreds of pleas for sinners to come to Jesus just as they were. If the maximum number of souls were to be snatched from the sea of sin, Billy Graham would need Billy Kim to help hold the net. Finally, after praying almost continually for three days and calling a key American backer who assured him that he would not withdraw his support, Kim notified Graham that he would be his translator. Ugly letters damning him for his apostasy came in as and whence expected, but Kim put them aside and immersed himself in preparation, listening to tapes, watching films, studying Graham's tempo, even imitating his voice and gestures.

Bob Jones, Sr., had often spoken of Billy Graham as a man filled with self-importance and pride. An incident on the day Graham arrived in Seoul erased that image from Billy Kim's mind. As they prepared to leave the hotel for a reception and dinner with the crusade committee, Graham was abashed to find a caravan of four black limousines, each with a uniformed chauffeur, waiting for him and his party, and a motorcycle escort ready to clear their way of traffic. Fearful that such ostentation would create a negative impression, Graham asked if it might be possible to use a smaller car. Kim was impressed that a world figure would respond with such modesty but gave him a quick lesson in protocol. "These cars are the courtesy of the Korean government," he explained. "If you don't accept this gesture, you will offend the government. Also, you will make the Korean people feel you are not important enough to rate a limousine. If you ride around in a taxi or a small car, your credibility will be shot with Korean people. Billy, for the sake of the Korean mentality, please get in the car. Just say thank you. If the press picks it up, that's their problem." Graham doubtless acted wisely when he decided not to risk offending President Park Chung Hee's oppressive government. Though neither he nor the crusade could plausibly represent a threat to order or ideology, team members feel certain their hotel rooms and automobiles were bugged, and reflecting apparent conviction that any large gathering needed to be closely monitored, the army assigned an estimated 7,000 soldiers to the crusade services, ostensibly to help direct traffic, which seldom amounted to more than a few hundred cars.

Hours before the first crusade service, it was already obvious that the crusade committee had not overreached by securing Yoido Plaza. To provide some estimate of attendance, as well as to facilitate crowd control and the handling of possible emergencies, the physical-arrangements committee laid down a grid of paper strips glued to the asphalt pavement. Each square held six to twelve people seated on mats or pieces of paper or cloth they brought with them, and each section of 250 squares, roped off to form aisles, held approximately 2,000 people when all units were filled. By the time Billy and Ruth (who had spent time at a boarding school in North Korea as a girl) arrived at the island in the late afternoon, the crowd-control chart indicated that the dreamed-of throng of 300,000 was already in place. By the time the service started, it appeared that half a million people were sitting quietly, waiting to worship God and to listen to Billy Graham. Ruth later wrote in her diary that it was "one of those things impossible to take in," and Billy could not hide the awe in his voice as he told the happy crowd that they were not only the largest audience he had ever preached to, but "the largest audience ever to hear a preacher in person anywhere in the world."

Almost always in top form when preaching with an interpreter, Graham seemed even more effective than usual in Seoul as Billy Kim performed what almost anyone discussing these meetings seems convinced was the most impressive display of translation they had ever witnessed. Kim was so good, in fact, that some Korean television viewers assumed he was the featured preacher, with Graham interpreting his message for American military personnel. As usual, some pastors and theologians criticized the sermons for their theological thinness. And also as usual, the multitudes filled themselves happily with the simple loaves and fishes he offered them. When the services ended in the evening, thousands stayed afterward to pray, then bedded down right on the tarmac, so they could attend a 5:00 A.M. prayer meeting before returning home or hurrying off to work or, if they were from out of town, simply because they had no place else to go.

The huge crowds continued to gather, and the secular press and television paid the crusade an unprecedented amount of positive attention. Even the North Korean media noted that a remarkable kind of witchcraft event was occurring in Seoul. Then, for the closing service on Sunday afternoon, an incredible, impossible thing happened. When Billy Graham stood up to speak, he faced a densely packed ribbon of people stretching 200 yards in front of him and half a mile to either side—according to the crowd-control grid, 1,120,000 people, almost certainly the largest public religious gathering in history. Amazingly, what could have been a teeming multitude became instead a quiet congregation, able, with the aid of a superb sound system, to hear every word even at the farthest distance from the platform. The thousands of military policemen had little to do: One man in a million created a momentary stir with a brief and apparently aimless outburst; a few dozen people experienced minor medical problems, not one of which was serious. Few cities of a million inhabitants could match that record on any given afternoon.

During his twelve weeks in London in 1954 and again during the sixteen weeks in New York in 1957, Billy Graham had spoken to aggregate audiences of more than two million people. Now, in five days in Korea, he had addressed, in person, crowds totaling more than three million. Another million and a half attended the six associate crusades in other major cities. Inquirer cards from all the meetings exceeded 100,000. Billy Kim's church increased almost immediately by 30 percent in a spurt of growth, and its pastor, turned into a national figure by the crusade, gained a permanent spot in the front rank of Asian church leaders. The effect on Korean churchpeople, as astonished as outsiders by what they had seen and wrought, was also immediate and dramatic. Kim speculates that Graham came to Korea in what Scripture calls "the fullness of time," a time when momentum had reached a takeoff stage. "If he had come in '63 or '83," he reflected, "I doubt we could have pulled off a '73-style crusade. No question, '73 was a critical time." Dr. Han agreed that "with the Billy Graham crusade, the Korean church came of age." Denominations and missionary agencies that had fought or ignored each other began to perceive each other as brethren who could accomplish more by working side by side. The already high growth rate nearly tripled over the next two years as Presbyterians established seven hundred new churches, while Baptists and charismatic churches totted up proportionately similar gains. In 1977 a group of Korean evangelists secured Yoido Plaza for a crusade of their own with no help from Americans; according to Kim, they matched Billy Graham's million every night of the crusade. Finally, the Korean Church began to see itself as a sender, not just a receiver, of missionaries, as men trained in churches and denominational seminaries and at such ecumenical institutions as the Asian Center for Theological Studies and Mission (whose library was endowed by a generous gift from BGEA) began themselves to take the gospel to foreign lands. By the mid-1980s, South Korea was producing more foreign missionaries than any nation in the world save America and possibly India.

No one could foresee the details of these extraordinary developments following in the wake of the 1973 crusade, but only the most obtuse could fail to recognize they were witnessing a wondrous thing. Secular observers would inevitably point to timing, to organization, to publicity, to the efforts of an eager minority to secure a place in a rapidly advancing society. But as a helicopter lifted him from Yoido Plaza and skimmed over the mile-long sea of handkerchiefs and white programs waving beneath in adoring gratitude, Billy Graham blinked with wonder and pronounced the only benediction he could fathom: "This is the work of God. There is no other explanation."

26

Vietnam and Watergate

Graham fervently wanted to believe that America and Richard Nixon were also involved in the work of God. He had long seen America as especially blessed in return for its allegiance to Judeo-Christian principles and, since the mid-1950s, had repeatedly urged Nixon to make his commitment to those principles more explicit, to say in public what Graham felt certain he believed deep in his heart. The goodness of America (if it would seek anew the vision of its founders), the greatness of Richard Nixon (if he would let it come to full flower), and his own ability to discern right from wrong—these were fundamental articles of Billy Graham's faith. Bedrock beliefs can withstand enormous challenge, but never in Graham's life had he been forced to deal with the cognitive dissonance posed for him by the two key issues of Richard Nixon's presidency: Vietnam and Watergate. And perhaps never in his life did he experience so much difficulty in facing the limits and inconsistencies and distortions of his own perceptions than in his efforts to try to come to terms with these egregious episodes in American history.

The Nixon presidency had been a heady experience for Graham. His closeness to the White House had brought increased criticism, but that was bearable. Nixon won reelection in a landslide, and both he and his policies were generally admired by Graham's own constituency. Besides, for the most part, the detractors were people who had never much cared for Graham or his ministry. Even more important, Nixon's establishment of the White House church services and his encouragement of Graham's evangelistic efforts seemed part of the return to spiritual concerns that Billy perpetually longed for and frequently professed to see appearing on the horizon. After the second inauguration, he wrote a gushing note commending Nixon on what he deemed "by far the finest Inaugural address I have ever heard any President give. I have received many comments concerning the spiritual emphasis at the end. The note you struck touched a deep chord in America.... You are one of the most thoughtful men I have ever known." Unhappily, he could not add that Nixon was one of the most generous people he had ever known. When the media reported that of $2 million he had earned during his presidency, Nixon contributed only $13,510 to charities and churches, including a paltry $1,250 to the Whittier Congregation of Friends and $4,500 to BGEA, Graham registered surprise at "the small amount he reported giving to charities in relation to his total income," but added that "there may be some other explanation, in that his finances and contributions were left to other people."

Graham's perception of increased spiritual concern on Nixon's part emboldened him to push for measures he hoped might nudge America closer to becoming the righteous republic he was certain God wanted it to be. He had been predictably upset in 1962 and 1963 by the Supreme Court decisions banning prayer and devotional reading of the Bible in public schools. He once opined that "the few atheists who object to Bible reading in schools should be overruled by the majority" and briefly considered leading a movement to restore school-mandated prayer. He bowed for a time to the court's commitment to pluralism, though its secularist tendencies so dismayed him that in 1970 he recommended that Protestants consider establishing a massive system of parochial schools, a vision whose incarnation (though largely independent of action on his part) became one of the key institutional segments of the Christian New Right within a decade. Now, however, he seemed ready to experiment with the civil religion he and Richard Nixon were constantly being accused of trying to impose on America.

At the first White House service following the 1973 inauguration, Graham recommended that the Ten Commandments be read in every public-school classroom in America. It would, he ventured, be less controversial than prayer, and surely, all Judeo-Christian people could agree on its precepts. He failed to acknowledge that a rapidly growing segment of Americans did not fit into the categories of Jew or Christian. Neither did he seem to appreciate that with their prohibitions of worshiping gods other than Yahweh, taking God's name in vain, making graven images, and violating the Sabbath, the Ten Commandments were not simply general moral principles but explicit theological tenets. When reporters asked Chief Justice Warren Burger, who was present at the service, if Graham's suggestion might raise constitutional questions, Burger replied, "At this time, it would," but that seemed not to discourage the evangelist. At one point, he volunteered that if the Ten Commandments would not pass the court's test of neutrality, he would settle for Mao's Eight Values: Speak politely, pay fairly for what you damage, repay debts fairly, do not hit or swear at people, do not damage crops, do not take liberties with women, and do not mistreat captives. But when that concession to pluralism drew fire from some who feared he might be growing soft on communism, he returned to recommending the Ten Commandments.

Graham's critics were quick to point out the problems and inconsistencies of such positions, but it was not these issues that disturbed them most. Of far greater concern were Vietnam and Watergate, issues on which they felt no man who had the President's ear should remain silent. Graham liked to say, "I am not a Nathan," referring to the prophet who had called King David to account for his adulterous relationship with Bathsheba. In his mind, the alternative was an evangelist like Paul, who preached wherever he was given opportunity, including the courts of kings and governors, but did not occupy himself with trying to rectify the injustices of the Roman Empire. His critics, however, continued to feel that his refusal to speak out early and boldly against American policy in Vietnam and, later, against the Nixon administration's role in the execution and attempted cover-up of the Watergate break-in smacked not of the Apostle Paul, whose preaching resulted in his own imprisonment and martyrdom, but of Zedekiah, the proud and colorful false prophet of Israel who won a favored spot in the court of Ahab by telling the king what he wanted to hear, confirming a course of action that ended his reign in death and disgrace, with the dogs of Samaria licking up his blood.

Graham dealt with his confusion over Vietnam by refusing to comment on it during 1972. He was flushed out of that bunker, however, when the United States resumed heavy bombing of North Vietnam in mid-December of that year, setting off fresh waves of angry protest across America. Prodded by the press and fellow clergymen, including the Reverend Ernest Campbell of New York's Riverside Church, who preached a sermon entitled "An Open Letter to Billy Graham," in which he implored the evangelist to use his influence with Nixon to try to stop the bombing, Graham broke his self-imposed silence early in January 1973. In a widely distributed press release, he set forth what he claimed was the posture he had assumed throughout the war. "In regard to the conflict in Southeast Asia," he said, "I have avoided expressions as to who was right and who was wrong. Naturally, I have come under criticism from both hawks and doves for my position. During all this time, though, I had repeatedly indicated my hope for a rapid and just peace in Southeast Asia. I have regretted that this war has gone on so long and has been such a divisive force in America. I hope and pray that there will be an early armistice." He pointed out that although the Bible "would indicate we will always have wars on the earth until the coming again of the Prince of Peace," he did not take that as justification for indifference or complacency. "I have never advocated war," he said. "I deplore it! I also deplore the violence everywhere throughout the world that evidences man's inhumanity to man. I am therefore praying for every responsible effort which seeks true peace in our time."

In response to the suggestion that he urge Nixon to stop the bombing (which had, in fact, been stopped a few days before he released his statement), Graham scoffed at the popular picture of him as some kind of "White House Chaplain," pointing out that his relationship to Nixon was little different from Cardinal Cushing's relationship to John Kennedy. He also insisted that his influence on Nixon had been overdrawn: "The President doesn't call me up and say, 'Billy, shall we do this or that?' That just doesn't happen. I'm not one of his confidants; I'm not one of his advisers. I'm just a personal friend. That's all. In no way would he ask me military strategy. He's never even discussed it with me. If I have something to say to President Nixon, I'll do it privately and I won't announce it from the housetops with a lot of publicity." Even if the President did seek his advice on secular matters, Graham claimed, he would be reluctant to give it, a statement that neatly finessed two decades of documented action to the contrary. "I am convinced," he asserted, "that God has called me to be a New Testament evangelist, not an Old Testament prophet! While some may interpret an evangelist to be primarily a social reformer or political activist, I do not! An evangelist is a proclaimer of the message of God's love and grace in Jesus Christ and the necessity of repentance and faith."

The *New York Times* published another interview with Graham on the weekend of the inauguration, just six days before the signing of the truce agreement in Paris on January 27, 1973. He claimed he had "doubted from the beginning" the wisdom of "sending American troops anywhere without the will to win." It seemed to him, he said, that "we entered the war almost deliberately to lose it. I don't think we should ever fight these long-drawn-out, half-hearted wars. It's like cutting a cat's tail off a half-inch at a time." Still, he conceded that the December resumption of the bombing of North Vietnam had dismayed him. "I'll be honest with you," he said. "I felt gloomy. Like all Americans, I thought a cease-fire was imminent." Rather than let those widely shared and quite comprehensible statements stand alone, however, Graham minimized the significance of the war by noting once again that it was just one example of violence in a world filled with tragedy. "There are hundreds of thousands of deaths attributed to smoking," he said. "A thousand people are killed every week on the American highways," he noted, "and half of those are attributed to alcohol. Where are the demonstrations against alcohol?"

By this time, Graham had settled on an official version of his role with regard to the war. He told the *New York Times*, *Christianity Today*, and anyone else who asked that in all the history of the Vietnam conflict, he had made only one public comment that could be construed as support for the war. That lone remark, made before the United States became deeply involved in the war, had been an offhand response to a question. Moreover, he wasn't even certain what he had said on that occasion, "but I know that as soon as I said it, I wished I hadn't." Graham's critics were not impressed. Union Seminary's John C. Bennett observed that "when people claim to be above politics it is axiomatic that they in effect support the status quo." Elaborating on this point, others charged that it was precisely Graham's silence that accounted for his popularity with the president. Since he was unwilling to criticize them on any matter of substance, he was perceived by them and by the public to be in favor of whatever policy they espoused. In specific response to that criticism, a BGEA spokesman explained that "if he took a position for or against certain policies, he would alienate people on one side or another—and this he is not what he set out to do."

It is true that Graham had felt deep disquiet over the war for several years. It is true that he made some effort, as in his Bangkok meeting with missionaries, to discern both the positives and negatives of American policy and conduct and to suggest ways in which the war might be brought to a swift and satisfactory conclusion. It is also true, however, that his consistent characterization of war protesters as misguided, extremist, or even disloyal and his refusal to criticize American policy in Southeast Asia could easily be interpreted as support for that policy. That is how much of the public and many of his fellow clergy viewed his position, and that is certainly how the White House viewed it. In April 1972 Haldeman had instructed Colson that "calls should be made before the President's Wednesday night speech to Billy Graham, Bob Hope, Cardinal Krol, and others of that sort—the hard-line type—who support us. They should be urged to watch the speech because the President will be making some very important points that they will find helpful." Apparently, Graham wanted the White House to consider him a supporter. As soon as the media began to pick up on his press release deploring all war and violence and urging a rapid and just peace in Southeast Asia, Dwight Chapin informed Haldeman that Graham wanted to be in touch with him and with the President. "He is very disturbed," Chapin reported, "by some press reports which quote him as saying the war is deplorable."

When the Paris accord ended the war less than a week into the second Nixon administration, Graham could not resist a bit of private crowing; in a note of congratulations, he told the President, "Some of the liberal commentators seem to be disappointed that you were able to do it!" Now, perhaps, with the war behind him, Nixon could unshackle his latent spirituality and help heal America's wounds by leading it back to God. First, of course, he would have to attend to his own salvation. "It is my prayer," the evangelist wrote, "that during these next four years you will put your total trust in the same Christ that your dear Mother so firmly believed in." Unfortunately for Nixon, for Graham, and for the nation, the dark form taking shape on the horizon was not a whirlwind of revival, but the specter of Watergate.

When operatives of the Committee to Re-elect the President (CREEP) broke into offices of the Democratic National Committee in the Watergate apartment complex in June 1972, few could have foreseen that the early trickles of indignation would eventually become a flood of outrage that would sweep Richard Nixon from office and deposit several of his key associates in prison. Clearly, Graham did not treat it as an act of great consequence.

When George McGovern depicted what some were calling a caper as instead an example of the ethical poverty of the Republican administration, Graham characterized his attack as a "desperate" move, a sign that he knew he could not defeat Nixon on the more important issues of the campaign. In a note to Haldeman, he observed that "it is amazing to me that people who made a hero of [Daniel] Ellsburg for stealing the Pentagon Papers are so deeply concerned about the alleged escapade at Watergate."

Five months later, after federal judge John Sirica ordered seven defendants in the case, including G. Gordon Liddy and James W. McCord, Jr., to appear before a grand jury to explore possible high-level involvement in the break-in, and after McCord told a closed Senate hearing that John Mitchell, former attorney general and head of CREEP, had known of plans for the break-in before it occurred, Graham's primary response was one of admiration for the aplomb Nixon demonstrated while his enemies snapped at his ankles. "I have marveled at your restraint as the rumors fly about Watergate," he wrote. "King David had the same experience. He said: 'They accuse me of things I have never even heard about. I do them good but they return me harm.' (Psalm 35:11–12)." Graham apparently believed Nixon was certain to emerge unscathed. Quoting a modern-language translation of Proverbs 19:20, he predicted, "If you profit from constructive criticism, you will be elected to the wise men's hall of fame."

As evidence mounted that, indeed, Watergate had not been simply a caper performed by an overzealous free-lance cadre of CREEP "plumbers" but a carefully planned expedition ordered and subsequently covered up by men quite close to and possibly including Richard Nixon himself, Graham took some steps to clear himself of any possible stain that might wash over him. "[*New York Times* publisher Arthur Ochs] Punch Sulzberger was a good friend," he explained. "During Watergate, he offered me the use of his op-ed page to write whatever I wanted, and I wrote two articles distancing myself to some extent." He also gave interviews to AP religion writer George Cornell and the *Today* show and made some of the same observations on an *Hour of Decision* broadcast in May. "Of course," he acknowledged, "I have been mystified and confused and sick about the whole thing, as I think every American is." He felt certain the President was not seriously involved, since "his moral and ethical principles wouldn't allow him to do anything illegal like that," and he decried the "trial by media and by rumor." At the same time, he called for the dismissal and punishment of "everybody connected with Watergate," labeled the scandal as "a symptom of the deeper moral crisis" brought on by "amoral permissiveness that would make Sodom blush," and called on Americans "to engage in some deep soul-searching about the underpinnings of our society and our goals as a nation," to "take the law of Moses and the Sermon on the Mount seriously," and to show concern for "an honest and efficient government at all levels."

As he called on the nation to learn the deeper lessons of Watergate, Graham was counseling the White House to make that task more difficult. After Haldeman, Ehrlichman, John Dean, and Attorney General Richard Kleindienst resigned in anticipation of the Senate hearings scheduled to begin in mid-May, Graham called Larry Higby to suggest that Nixon and his staff take immediate measures to divert the public's attention from the Watergate affair. He suggested, Higby told the President, that "wherever possible we create picture situations such as the one yesterday with you and Willy Brandt. This causes public focus on the fact that the President is not bogged down on one issue, but is working in other areas. He feels the more of this type of thing we can do, the better. The American people need to be diverted from Watergate...." Two days later, North Carolina senator Jesse Helms dropped a note to Nixon, reporting that "I chatted at some length yesterday afternoon with Billy Graham. I need not tell you that you have a real friend there. Do not allow the present circumstances to worry you. Your friends understand, and we are confident that right will prevail. God bless you." These letters and verbal messages delivered through aides and friends served a double purpose. Not only did they transmit information he wanted the President to have; they also enabled him to say with a straight face and, perhaps, a clear conscience that he and the President had never discussed Watergate.

By midsummer it was clear that Watergate might well become Waterloo. Senator Sam Ervin opened the Senate hearings by announcing the investigating committee's intention to uncover all the relevant facts "and spare no one, whatever his station in life might be." John Dean pointed his finger at several folk of quite high station, and Alex Butterfield astonished the committee and the public by revealing that nearly all of the conversations in the Oval Office since early 1971 had been taped on a secret recording system. Now, with the possibility of finding out exactly what had gone on in that office, no series of "picture situations," however well orchestrated, stood a chance of diverting attention from Watergate. This was *the* story, and it would be played out to the end.

Graham had not visited the White House since the inauguration and had talked with the President on the telephone only four times since February, so his views on Watergate were necessarily rather speculative. In one of his more memorable speculations, he ventured that Watergate was just "another sign of permissiveness," a diagnosis that seemed a bit off the mark when applied to Gordon Liddy and John Mitchell, who helped plan it, and the arrow-straight gentlemen in the White House who helped cover it up. He also volunteered that it was too early to make any moral judgments about what had happened, apparently overlooking the fact that if the conspirators in the case had not considered burglary and illegal wiretapping to be at least borderline behavior, they would probably not have made blackmail payments and suborned perjury to try to keep it from coming to light.

As the year ground on, Nixon's situation worsened. Spiro Agnew, a man seldom accused of permissiveness, resigned in disgrace after pleading no contest to government charges of income-tax evasion related to kickbacks received from government contractors when he was governor of Maryland. Nixon at first refused Judge Sirica's request that the secret tapes be turned over to Watergate special prosecutor Archibald Cox. Then he fired Cox and lost Attorney General Elliot Richardson and Deputy Attorney General William Ruckelshaus in the infamous Saturday Night Massacre. Faced with the growing threat of impeachment, he finally agreed to release the tapes. In the face of this monumental and truculent recalcitrance, Graham issued a Thanksgiving statement in which he said, "I applaud the President for his courageous revelation of detailed facts of Watergate. I think the people want the facts and I am confident he will continue to give them." Despite his ability to discern courage where few others spotted it, Graham could not avoid seeing that his friend was in deep trouble. Still, he expected him to survive. Those who suspected he was weakening physically and psychologically should be reassured, he said, adding that "it is quite evident that the President is not going to resign, and . . . I doubt that the Senate would vote to remove him from office. If that is the case, and I believe it is, we should rally around the three branches of our government with our prayers and our support." Then, in the first of what would become a series of subtle distancing maneuvers, Graham admitted that "I do not always agree with the judgment and policies of his Administration, but President Nixon has my support and prayers." Since "even the dissenters and the doubters should realize that, in all probability, Mr. Nixon will be the only President we have for the next three years," he thought it reasonable that "all Americans, Democrats and Republicans, liberals and conservatives," offer that same kind of support. He concluded the statement with the hopeful prediction that "the tragic events of Watergate will probably make him a strong man and a better President." It was less than unqualified approbation, and it lacked the usual promise of certain victory, but Richard Nixon could not afford to turn down any offer of support. On Thanksgiving afternoon the President called Graham at his home in Montreat to thank him for his kind words.

On Sunday, December 16, Graham officiated at the White House Christmas service and, either before or afterward, spoke briefly with the President by telephone. In a letter thanking Nixon for the invitation and the conversation, Graham reaffirmed "my personal affection for you as a man, my appreciation for our long friendship, and my complete confidence in your personal integrity." Later that week and again in a note at Christmas, he complimented Nixon for being so "chipper" and "full of fun" in the face of adversity. "Certainly the Lord has sustained you in a remarkable way. Lesser men would have folded long ago." Then, offering a prediction that showed the wisdom in his consistent rejection of the status of prophet, he said, "I am sure that this coming year will be far better than 1973."

The new year began on a low note for the President, as his old and dear friend put a bit more distance between himself and the mess of Watergate. In an interview published in the January 4, 1974, edition of *Christianity Today*, Graham decided he finally had sufficient evidence to justify handing down a moral decision. He characterized both the break-in and the cover-up as "not only unethical but criminal," and said, "I can make no excuses for Watergate. I condemn it and I deplore it. It has hurt America." While acknowledging that Nixon had shown poor judgment "especially in the selection of certain people," he noted that there was as yet no proof the President was directly involved in either the break-in or the cover-up, and he reasserted his continuing confidence in Nixon's integrity. He had made mistakes, to be sure, but if he admitted them and thereby regained his credibility with the public, he could be a stronger President than ever before. In a similar vein, Graham denied that his having spoken at the White House Christmas service was in any sense a benediction of what had been going on there.

Graham gave Nixon advance warning of the *CT* interview and wrote a note thanking him for understanding why he felt it necessary to say what he had said. Nixon's actual response has not been preserved, but some of his supporters regarded Graham's statements as little short of outright betrayal. A staunch Republican business executive, George Stringfellow, wrote to ask why he had found it necessary to note that Nixon had made mistakes—"Did you need publicity?" He noted further that in a television speech Graham had made a point of associating himself with the late President Johnson. "I suppose this was done to further disassociate yourself [from] President Nixon." Then, in a parting shot, Stringfellow reported that he had recently attended a dinner at which Graham's remarks had been brought up, prompting an observation by one of the men present that "Nixon's ship is listing. When the water reaches the upper level the rats leave the ship." In concluding his letter, Stringfellow noted the diners had agreed that "the ship will right itself by next June and, if it serves your vanity at that time, you will be headed up the gangplank again." Stringfellow was not alone in his judgment of Graham's behavior and motives. Norman Vincent Peale, who reaffirmed his own admiration and affection for Graham, wrote to say, "Billy, I have just got to tell you that I was saddened by your recent reported statements about President Nixon. It appeared that you were trying to get out from under and were not standing by the man for whom you have professed abiding friendship." Peale had seen a copy of Stringfellow's letter and, while admitting it was "direct," said, "I must confess that it represents the views of many, myself included. As for me, I am sticking with President Nixon one hundred percent, all the way. I believe in him absolutely and have been totally unaffected by the vicious attacks upon him." Peale subsequently sent a copy of his letter to Nixon, who responded with a gracious note of appreciation.

Graham, however, was not alone among Nixon's friends in seeing the need for the chief executive to admit his mistakes. Charles Colson, regarded as one of the toughest in Nixon's inner circle, the man said to have boasted he would run over his grandmother if she got in his way, responded to the pressures of Watergate by accepting an invitation to join a small group of Washington political figures who met regularly for prayer and discussion. Within a short time, Colson experienced what the intervening years have shown to be a genuine, life-changing conversion. When word of that conversion leaked out, cynics hooted at what they took to be a blatant effort to gain sympathy with the public and, more importantly, with any judge or jury that might try him for his role in the Watergate cover-up. Internal White House memos, however, suggest that Colson's transformation was not only genuine but posed a bit of an inconvenience for the staff. In late November, as he looked ahead to the National Prayer Breakfast in January, Colson complained to the President that the breakfast had become "simply another big Washington gathering that people 'must' attend." Asserting that "its religious significance as a day for government leaders to join together in sincere prayer has been lost," he urged Nixon to schedule a second, smaller breakfast with a bipartisan group that "unanimously wants to pray with and for you." Colson believed such attention to spiritual matters was essential: "I have thought long and hard about how the ordeal of Watergate will finally come to an end. I believe that the country has to be lifted out of the doldrums of Watergate. Our best hope is to bring about a rebirth of faith and a renewed commitment to God; it is that national commitment that has seen America through its darkest and most perilous times.... I know that there are millions of Americans who would pray with and for you if they were asked to do so. The experiment may well in fact renew the American Spirit.... I believe, too, that this would begin the reconciliation that would enable you to lead the country out of these troubled times." Colson continued to press for a second, "real" prayer breakfast, but Nixon brought the matter to an end by dispatching a succinct verdict on the matter: "Two breakfasts are too many."

As one of the prayer breakfast's pioneers, Graham saw no particular need to revamp its format, but he did think it would be a splendid opportunity for the President to come clean. On several previous occasions, he had offered suggestions as to what Nixon might say in addresses before religious groups. His recommendations for this occasion included the statement "I hope I shall not be judged as hiding behind religion when I say that I have, like many of my predecessors before me, been driven to my knees in prayer.... [W]e are all in need of God's forgiveness, not only for mistakes in judgment, but our sins as well." He also urged the President to sprinkle some verses of Scripture into his talks. One of the most appropriate, he thought, might be

God's instruction to King Solomon in II Chronicles 7:14: "If my people, who are called by my name, shall humble themselves, and pray, and seek my face, and turn from their wicked ways; then will I hear from heaven, and will forgive their sin, and will heal their land." For a closing line, Graham suggested that the President say, "I want to take this opportunity today to rededicate myself to the God that I first learned about at my mother's knee." The White House was not thrilled to receive Graham's suggestions. Alexander Haig passed them along to Nixon with the recommendation that he read them, "since [Graham] may ask about them," but he characterized them as "replete with Watergate mea culpa" and branded them "totally unacceptable from my point of view." Apparently, Nixon also found them unacceptable. He recalled a conversation with his Quaker grandmother about prayer but chose not to use the breakfast as an occasion either to confess fault or rededicate his life to Christ.

In the months that followed, the President was named a Watergate coconspirator, his top aides were sentenced to federal prison, and after resisting a House Judiciary Committee subpoena on grounds of executive privilege, Nixon finally released extensive edited transcripts of the White House tapes. In recalling that period of national anguish, Graham has often claimed that he had been informed that Nixon had told his staff, "Don't let Billy Graham near me. I don't want to drag him into this mess." Without claiming perfect recall, he has told various inquirers that he and the President talked once, twice, or perhaps not at all between January 31 (the date of the prayer breakfast) and August 23, when Nixon resigned, and that several attempts to reach Nixon met a stone wall. The White House contact file lists four conversations between the two men, one each in February, April, May, and June, but only one of these lasted more than six minutes. Charles Colson did not remember any such directive from Nixon. "I wasn't aware of it," he said, "and it would surprise me if that were true. I don't know how Watergate would have touched Billy. In those days, [Nixon] was looking for friends, and I would think Billy could get through just like that." Haldeman echoed Colson's skepticism. "Based on my knowledge of Nixon and the way he worked," he said, "I would need a lot more proof before I would believe it." The contact file, which records uncompleted calls or the name of the person who took the call in the President's stead, reflects no unsuccessful attempts. Whatever the precise details, it is clear Graham had only limited contact with Nixon during his last seven months in office, at least in part because he spent much of that period in South Africa, Korea, and Europe.

On the last day of April, Nixon went on television to announce that he was releasing edited transcripts of the Watergate tapes. The House Judiciary Committee insisted that edited transcripts were not an adequate substitute for the tapes themselves, but the transcripts were hardly a disappointment to those who had long viewed Richard Nixon as the dark beast of American politics. As excerpts began to appear in the national media, reporters pressed Graham for a reaction. In a striking manifestation of an all-too-common tendency of Fundamentalists and Evangelicals to focus on readily observed and easily categorized externals of behavior rather than on deeper and more fundamental pathologies, Graham fastened on the omnipresent profanity in the conversation between Nixon and his aides, a characteristic of the transcripts that made *expletive deleted* a household phrase for a time. Though he recognized that Nixon was not the first occupant of the White House to use profanity, he could not agree with Father John McLaughlin's blithe dismissal of the President's language as "a form of therapy . . . with no moral meaning." He noted that "I have known five Presidents, and I suspect if we had the transcripts of their conversations, they too would contain salty language." Still, he confessed, "I just didn't know that he used this type of language in talking to others. I rarely heard him say anything except 'hell' or 'damn,' and he would usually say, 'Excuse me, Billy.'" That the President of the United States, a man he considered to be one of his dearest friends, a man charged with conspiring to commit and cover up political espionage and facing almost certain impeachment, had been revealed to the world as a secret swearer seemed almost incomprehensible. "I don't approve of that kind of language," he said. "God will not hold him guiltless."

After the first of these reactions had been reported, Nixon reached Graham early one morning in his hotel room in Scottsdale, Arizona, the day before he would begin a crusade in Phoenix. They talked for only three minutes, and Graham reported that "he just wanted to say hello." Perhaps the President hoped for some expression of forgiveness, which Graham would surely have given if asked. More likely, since he knew what else the transcripts told and Billy did not, he wanted one last conversation, however brief, in which at least a remnant of the mutual assumptions that had sustained their friendship for nearly twenty-five years was still intact.

Graham finished the Phoenix crusade (attendance 240,195, with 9,718 inquirers) in mid-May and returned home to Montreat. At first he avoided the grim task he knew he must eventually face. But finally, after fretting and moping about for several days, he shut himself in his study and began working through the *New York Times* edition of excerpts from the transcripts. What he found there devastated him. He wept. He threw up. And he almost lost his innocence about Richard Nixon. "Those tapes revealed a man I never knew," he confessed. "I never saw that side of him." Recalling his profound disillusionment years later—Ruth called it "the hardest thing that Bill has ever gone through personally"—he confided to an inquirer that "I'd had a real love for him. He'd always been very attentive to his friends, he never forgot a birthday. He seemed to love his country, love his children, love Pat. His thoughtfulness—there's a reason why so many people were loyal to him for so many years. I'd thought he was a man of such great integrity. I really believed, I really looked upon him as the greatest possibility ever for leading this country on into its greatest and finest days. He had the character for it. I'd never, ever, heard him tell a lie. But then the way it sounded in those tapes—it was all something totally foreign to me in him. He was just suddenly somebody else." The pain of that perception grew even sharper as Graham confronted the possibility that Lyndon Johnson and John Kennedy and Dwight Eisenhower might also have shown him only one of several faces. And inevitably, he had to confront his own possible, if unwitting, collusion in helping to do unto others as had been done unto him.

Graham told one reporter that as he pored through the transcripts, there were moments when "I thought like Wesley when he said: 'When I look into my heart, it looks like hell.'" That may be, but a few days later, when he issued a press release containing his considered reaction to the transcripts, his angst had shrunk back to quite manageable dimensions. One might reasonably have hoped that he would comment on the manipulation of appearances, on the cynical use of power and people, on the willful obstruction of justice, on the threat Watergate posed to a government of laws. Instead, the transgression Graham once again singled out as most distressing to him was one whose guilt he did not share. "I must confess," he said, that "this has been a profoundly disturbing and disappointing experience. One cannot but deplore the moral tone implied in these papers, and though we know that other Presidents have used equally objectionable language, it does not make it right. 'Thou shalt not take the name of the Lord thy God in vain' is a commandment which has not been suspended, regardless of any need to release tensions." He then offered the surprising observation that "a nation confused for years by the teaching of situational ethics now finds itself dismayed by those in Government who apparently practiced it." This oblique admission that profanity did not exhaust the evil practiced in the White House was welcome, but the implication that burglary, bribery, extortion, and perjury were somehow the result of an ethical approach whose primary tenet was, "In all situations, seek to perform the truly loving act," underscored the truth in Graham's frequent insistence that he was no scholar. He did, however, claim to be a faithful friend, and he reiterated that claim in this statement. Nixon, he said, "is my friend, and I have no intention of forsaking him now. Nor will I judge him as a man in totality on the basis of these relatively few hours of conversation under such severe pressure."

Four days after Graham released this statement, Nixon called from Camp David for a fourteen-minute conversation, the longest the two men had had in ten months and apparently their last while Nixon was President. The content of that conversation is unknown, at least until the Watergate tapes themselves are eventually made public, but it did not restore the relationship to its former level of closeness. Graham spent most of July in Switzerland in connection with an international conference that would prove to be one of the most significant enterprises of his entire ministry. (In his major address to the assembly, he drew sustained applause when he warned that evangelists must be careful not "to identify the Gospel with any one political program or culture," adding that "this has been my own danger.") When he returned to the United States, Nixon was all but finished. "I tried to get to him," he remembered, "to go have prayer with him, but I couldn't. The night before he resigned, I went to Washington at the urging of Senator Robert Griffin of Michigan, who asked me to come. He said, 'Billy, you are the only one who can talk to Nixon, and he needs you. I just talked to Ed Cox, his son-in-law, and he said to tell you to come just as quick as you can.' And I went, but I couldn't even get the operator to answer. I couldn't get anything."

The day following Nixon's retreat to San Clemente, Graham observed that he felt sorry for the President and his family, adding that "I shall always consider him a personal friend. His personal suffering must be almost unbearable. He deserves the prayers even of those who feel betrayed and let down.... We should let President Nixon and his family have some privacy now." When the new President, Gerald Ford, pardoned Nixon on September 8, Graham gave his blessing, stating that prosecuting the fallen leaders "would have torn the country apart more than Watergate itself." By acting mercifully, Ford "saved the country from the emotional division and agony that could have further weakened America at home and abroad." Ten days later, while he was in Los Angeles celebrating the twenty-fifth anniversary of the great crusade in the Canvas Cathedral, he talked briefly with the former President on the telephone; he asked if he might drop in for a visit, but Nixon, who "seemed depressed," indicated it would not be a good time, both because he had a great deal of work to do and because phlebitis was causing terrible pain in his leg. Not long afterward, the phlebitis produced a blood clot that sent Nixon to the hospital, where Graham did manage to pay him a visit. "He came pretty close to dying," Graham recalled. "He was much sicker than people realized." After his return to San Clemente to recuperate, "Ruth hired an airplane and had a big sign following the plane, saying Nixon, God Loves You and So Do We. She did that because we couldn't get to him. The picture was in *Time* magazine, but nobody knew it was Ruth."

Graham and Nixon finally reconciled the following spring over a two-and-a-half-hour candlelight dinner at San Clemente. According to Graham, they never specifically mentioned Watergate—"I'd say there was a studious avoidance of the subject by both of us. I certainly didn't want to bring it up!"—but Nixon did express some regret that he had let his friends down. Most of their conversation, he said, had been about the Bible and a book about the life of Christ that Nixon was reading. After dinner, the two of them had repaired to the study for a session of prayer. The former President, Graham said, had obviously suffered a great deal, but he voiced no recrimination and harbored no rancor toward those responsible for his downfall. Most important, it seemed obvious to Billy that Nixon had become deeply religious since his resignation.

And that, it seemed, put the matter to rest. The Evangelical doctrine of human depravity provided a useful clue to understanding what had happened, and Graham was quick to remind those with stones in their hands that "there's a little bit of Watergate in all of us. Let's don't go around so self-righteous, talking about all those bad people." But that same theological system made it possible for him to shift the primary blame to external forces. As his official biography puts it, he eventually decided that "Satan was somehow involved in the downfall of Nixon." He speculated that the Enemy's weapons of choice had been sleeping pills and demons. As he explained to another chronicler, Nixon "took all those sleeping pills that would give him a low in the morning and a high in the evening, you know. And all through history, drugs and demons have gone together—demons have always worked through drugs. Even the Greek word for them both is the same. My conclusion is that it was just all those sleeping pills, they just let a demon-power come in and play over him...."

As time passed, Graham seemed to have decided that what Satan had wrought may not have been so dreadful after all. When allegations concerning John Kennedy's amorous adventures surfaced late in 1975, he noted that at least Nixon "didn't have nude women running around in the private quarters of the White House." And a decade later, he had come to regard Watergate as little more than standard operating procedure for presidents. "They've all done that sort of thing," he pointed out—correctly, it appears. "I could tell you about Johnson, about what he did, what he was doing to Goldwater, but I won't get into that—at this point. I also read where Kennedy had certain conferences taped. And even back in Roosevelt's day they had things on wire recordings. I don't guess they were private conversations, but they were things that he wanted to record. Nixon wasn't much different, but the difficulty is that he had it on tape. Sid Richardson told me years ago, 'Don't put anything in writing. If you use the telephone, they can never use it against you.' I follow that pretty well. I don't have much in writing. All my business is on telephones. You know, if Nixon hadn't kept those tapes, he never would have been in all that trouble. To keep a tape of his private conversations was his greatest mistake. But he made other mistakes."

Though he indicated he and Nixon remained in touch—"I see him very often, in fact, almost every time I go to New York"—he acknowledged that their friendship was probably asymmetrical. "For years, I considered him among my very closest friends. I never thought of him for who he was. I just thought a great deal of him as a friend. He is one of the great people I have ever known personally who was a real gentleman. He's always courteous, always thoughtful. He would always ask about our meetings and the television programs, and he would comment on it. He was always very receptive when I would talk to him about spiritual things and his own relationship to the Lord and his family's relationship. He was always very respectful and very quiet. He didn't respond that much, but I could sense that he was responding inside. I think he considered me a close friend, but not one of his closest. I guess everybody has different levels of friendship." Reflecting on the possibility that the friendship between Graham and Nixon may have been asymmetrical, Charles Colson said, "That's true about Nixon with everyone. Nixon had a penchant for knowing how to use and manipulate people. He was the consummate politician. He would demand great loyalty, but as Watergate proved, he never quite gave it back."

Although Graham acknowledged that "maybe I was naive at that time; maybe I was used," he continued to insist that if any politician ever exploited a relationship with him, Richard Nixon was "certainly not one of them." Still, the episode sobered him mightily and made him far more wary of patrolling the corridors of power. Early in 1989 he observed that "inside the Beltway is a different world. That's the reason I don't go there anymore if I can help it. I'm glad I live down here on these mountains. I don't go to Washington much and I don't go to the Hill much. I used to have lots of friends that I'd go back and see—congressmen and senators—but for years I haven't done that. I just don't want to go. I feel God has called me to a much higher calling."

Friends and close co-workers confirm that the revelations of Watergate had a profound and chastening impact on the evangelist. Colson reported that "Billy told me he would never make the mistake again of getting that close to someone in office. And I think he has been more careful with Reagan and Bush than he was with Nixon." Leighton Ford conceded that "it was a great mystery to him. I don't think he's ever gotten over it." All seem to agree, however, that Graham's insistence that Nixon's friendship was entirely nonpolitical is sincere. Without tipping his own hand on the matter, Ford volunteered, "I have never heard him say one thing that made me believe he thought he was being used." Another close associate framed his assessment a bit more directly. "For the life of me," he said, "I honestly believe that after all these years, Billy still has no idea of how badly Nixon snookered him."

Part 5

Keeping the Faith (1974–1990)

27
Lausanne

In the gospel accounts of Jesus' final meeting with his eleven faithful apostles a few moments before he ascended into heaven, he gave them what came to be known as the Great Commission: "Go forth to every part of the world, and proclaim the Good News to the whole creation. Those who believe it and receive baptism will find salvation; those who do not believe it will be condemned." In August 1974 *Time* magazine noted that "millions of Christians still take that commission of Christ literally, still believe that one of their foremost tasks is to preach the Gospel to the unbaptized." Taken alone, that was a commonplace observation, but *Time* saw something uncommon afoot in the Christian world. "Last week," it announced, "in the lakeshore resort of Lausanne, Switzerland, that belief found a formidable forum, possibly the widest-ranging meeting of Christians ever held. Brought together largely through the efforts of the Rev. Billy Graham, some 2,400 Protestant Evangelical leaders from 150 countries ended a ten-day International Congress on World Evangelization that served notice of the vigor of conservative, resolutely biblical, fervently mission-minded Christianity." That notice and the congress that had served it, *Time* suggested, "constituted a considerable challenge to the prevailing philosophy in the World Council of Churches, headquartered some 30 miles down Lake Leman in Geneva." The WCC, the magazine noted, had all but abandoned any attempt "to disturb the honest faith" of adherents to non-Christian religions and had redefined its mission as "more of a campaign to achieve a sort of secular salvation, a human liberation in the political and social sense." The Lausanne Congress had arisen, at least in part, as a direct response to that departure from the evangelistic motive that had impelled John Mott to convene the meetings and form the organizations that eventually led to the founding of the WCC in 1948. Now, *Time* ventured, "the Evangelicals at Lausanne [had] laid the groundwork for a post-congress 'fellowship' that could eventually develop into a rival international body." Seventeen years later, no Evangelical world council had been formed, but the spirit of Lausanne was still vibrantly alive and the WCC's good ship *Oikumene* has unquestionably felt the waves generated when Billy Graham's band of Evangelicals dropped the Rock of Ages in their ocean.

Evangelism had steadily lost ground throughout the century in WCC-affiliated churches, but the turmoil of the 1960s had accelerated that process. In the West, liberal theologians and seminaries had flirted with and, in some cases, openly embraced views so unorthodox that it became fashionable to contend that one was being most "honest to God" when proclaiming God's death, a stance that obviously undermined any plausible theological rationale for preaching a gospel of otherworldly salvation. In America this progressive diminution of confidence in the basic historic claims of Christianity combined with increased attention to civil rights, poverty, and Vietnam to detract even further from interest in evangelism and traditional missions. In the United Presbyterian Church, for example, the number of missionaries declined from 1,300 in 1958 to only 580 in 1973. In the Third World, anti-colonialist movements often encouraged or viewed with favor by the World Council also served to discourage the sending of missionaries, who were seen to represent not only the Christian religion but Western culture as well. In addition, a tendency in liberal circles toward cultural relativity made it seem impolite and presumptuous to try to impose the Christian religion on sincere practitioners of another faith. Reacting to these several forces, the WCC and its member denominations began to speak more and more of a "moratorium on missions," a shutting down of traditional attempts to win people to Christ through proclamation or other forms of explicit evangelism.

All this, of course, was anathema to Evangelicals, including those whose denominations belonged to the World Council. For thirty years, they had seen tremendous response to unabashed proclamation of the old-fashioned gospel, not least in Billy Graham's crusades on six continents. Conservative Christians, including Evangelicals, Fundamentalists, Pentecostals, and charismatics, had founded scores of new evangelistic and mission agencies, and their several versions of Christianity were booming, particularly in the Third World. In 1974, for example, Protestant churches (largely Pentecostal) in Brazil were growing at a rate three times faster than the population as a whole. In Korea the figure was four to one. In sub-Saharan Africa Christians constituted almost 30 percent of the population and were expected to be a majority by the year 2000. The number of Christians in Taiwan—650,000—was twenty times larger than in 1946. As one important consequence, Third World churches were coming to see themselves not only as receivers but as senders of missionaries. And in America, as National Council of Churches executive Dean Kelley documented in his 1972 book, *Why Conservative Churches Are Growing*, liberal churches were losing members, ministers, and money, while Evangelical bodies such as Southern Baptists and the Assemblies of God were experiencing vigorous growth. Furthermore, the prospect for at least the near term seemed equally rosy, as Fundamentalist and Evangelical seminaries overflowed with students at a time when liberal schools were suffering steady attrition in the number and quality of applicants.

Still missing, however, was a firm sense among Evangelicals that they were part of a coherent worldwide movement. The 1966 Berlin Congress had helped, but it had been predominantly Western in composition, and its participants had been chosen with an eye for the role they could play in hammering out a viable Evangelical theology to undergird their triple themes of "One Race, One Gospel, One Task." In succeeding years BGEA financed and helped organize regional conferences in Asia, Latin America, Africa, the United States, and Europe, taking care in Third World meetings to encourage men from those areas to assume as much of the leadership and direction as possible to facilitate the development of a sense of independent fellowship and vision. In some cases, Graham did not even attend the meetings. "I felt I should not go," he explained, "for fear that they would think I was in a dominant role." The success of the post-Berlin regional conferences led naturally to consideration of another world congress, this time to move beyond theology to specific strategies for reviving and implementing John R. Mott's dream of "the evangelization of the world in this generation." Billy Graham was interested but understandably cautious, since it was clear that only he had the prestige to summon such a gathering and raise the money to pay for it. After consulting and receiving strong encouragement from approximately 150 Evangelical leaders around the world, Graham convened several small gatherings of what Carl Henry described as "international champions of evangelism," all of whom had worked with him closely in the past. Finally, in December 1971, he had the team he wanted. Leighton Ford would chair the program committee. Japan missionary Donald Hoke would serve as executive director, assisted by Stan Mooneyham, who would oversee the actual management of the meeting. Victor Nelson, a wise and profoundly respected pillar of BGEA's Minneapolis office, would mediate between various factions and use his remarkable organizational skills to keep the project afloat while the more visible public figures drummed up interest and support. Jack Dain's wide international experience and superb diplomatic skills made him an ideal choice for chairman, though he accepted only on the explicit condition that Billy Graham accept the designation of honorary chairman and that all concerned clearly understand that he, Dain, was acting as Graham's surrogate and was carrying out the evangelist's personal instructions. As he explained to the reluctant evangelist, since "I cannot see anyone but yourself being raised up by God to take an initiative at this time in this direction," it made no sense to pretend that Graham was not ultimately in charge. With the approval of his board, Graham agreed that BGEA would assume financial responsibility for the congress, slated for the summer of 1974.

For obvious symbolic reasons, and also because it would be a popular choice with delegates, Graham leaned toward Rome as the site for the conference, but the possibility of rankling Catholic feelings or of raising Fundamentalist suspicions that he was planning to have all the delegates kiss the pope's toe dictated the choice of a more neutral site, the magnificent Palais de Beaulieu conference center in Lausanne. As soon as Don Hoke and Walter Smyth settled on Lausanne, Graham dispatched several key people from his association to help prepare for the congress. Though he insisted throughout that he and his team should not dominate the planning and execution of the gathering, both Dain and Leighton Ford acknowledged that "he was the recognized, unquestioned leader." As Ford observed, "It would not have been possible without Billy. He had traveled throughout the world and met Evangelical leaders worldwide. Evangelicals of every stripe had worked together in practical ecumenism on Billy's crusades, and they got to know him and trust him." Still, though Graham clearly "could have been an autocrat, settling all the policies, [he] chose not to be."

Graham did insist on at least two points. To the disappointment of some, he refused to style the congress as an anti-WCC gathering, explaining that he was pro-Evangelical but not anti-ecumenical. His second demand concerned the criteria for choosing participants, and he made it clear that no liberals need apply. "Radical theology has had its heyday," he declared. "In the next world congress, every participant must be totally and thoroughly Evangelical." Jack Dain readily agreed with Graham, contending that wrangling over basic questions of belief would undermine the effectiveness of such a meeting. He professed to believe there is a proper place for dialogue but added, "Lausanne . . . is not it."

In Graham's vision of the meeting, every country in the world that allowed people to attend would be represented. At least half the participants would be from the Third World. Fully one third would be laypeople; the rest would be involved in cross-cultural mission efforts, full-time evangelistic ministries such as crusades and radio, denominational or parachurch mission agencies, theological and mission education, and other activities concerned with evangelization, which was seen as involving not just proclamation (evangelism), but the entire process of incorporating converts into churches and training them to teach and serve others. To make sure that what was learned would not be lost on those too old to put it into practice, Graham urged that 60 percent of the participants be under forty-five, with only 10 percent of the invitations going to elder statesmen over sixty-five. In a significant departure from the common Evangelical practice of barring women from public roles, Graham suggested that 10 percent of the participants be women. Inevitably, regional leaders fudged a bit to make sure that some of their cronies got invitations, but the final list of 2,400 included an impressive mix of cultures, ages, abilities, experience, and points of view. (Originally, Graham had wanted to invite 3,000 participants, but the cost, increased by three successive boosts in airfare in one year, forced a cutback.) Not everyone who was invited was able or willing to attend. Citing objections to the size and expense of the conference, more than half of the UK invitees declined their invitations, even though the British Evangelical Alliance put together a package that included travel and ten days in a Lausanne hotel for a hundred pounds. The East German government, apparently still regarding Billy Graham as an enemy, refused visas to all forty GDR delegates. In surprising contrast, Cuba not only permitted four men to attend the conference but loaned two of them money for the trip.

As with any BGEA project, little was left to chance. Planning in every area was extensive and meticulous, but no aspect received more attention than the program itself. Rather than risk having veteran speakers rely on glibness rather than on thorough preparation, Leighton Ford's committee not only insisted that papers be submitted months in advance but distributed copies to all invitees, inviting them to submit any responses they might have, as a condition of attending the congress, and instructing each speaker to prepare a revised address that incorporated the feedback. The final published compendium contained both the original and revised versions of the papers, making clear that the exercise was not taken lightly. One controversial paper received more than twelve hundred responses; in Haiti two hundred clergymen worked on the papers, though only one had been invited to Lausanne. An official working with Ford's committee explained, "We are trying to pick the brains of the church around the world." Given such unprecedented participation by Evangelical Christians from almost every nation in the world, Don Hoke felt justified in daring to hope that the Lausanne Congress would become a sort of twentieth-century Pentecost, an explosion of imagination and energy that would generate "a great spiritual fission whose chain reaction worldwide will speed the completion of Christ's great commission in this century."

By the time the congress opened in mid-July, it seemed clear something remarkable was in the offing. In his keynote address, which some associates have characterized as the most carefully crafted presentation of his career, Graham observed that the decline of evangelism in liberal churches could be traced to three primary causes: the loss of confidence in the Bible and thus in the authority of the gospel message; preoccupation with social and political problems, particularly at the leadership levels of denominations and interchurch agencies; and greater concern with an artificial organizational unity than with unity that develops naturally around a common task—specifically, evangelism. To counteract those ever-present dangers, he called for reaffirmation of the authority of Scripture and the formulation of a biblical declaration on evangelism that would not only serve as a rallying point for Evangelicals but would challenge the World Council of Churches, which would hold its septennial meeting in Djakarta the following year. Next, he expressed his hope that the conference would help clarify the proper relationship between evangelism and social responsibility, so that Evangelicals neither denied their obligation to meet tangible human needs nor became so consumed with social concerns that they, like the WCC, abandoned evangelism. In this connection, he warned against identifying the Christian gospel with any particular political program or culture—again drawing warm applause, particularly from Third World participants—and noted that "when I go to preach the Gospel, I go as an ambassador for the Kingdom of God—not America." And finally, following his unextinguishable ecumenical instincts, Graham expressed a strong hope that the gathering would help Evangelicals of every stripe in every nation feel they were part of a worldwide movement, and that it would encourage them to examine ways to identify and pool their resources to accomplish the awesome task of world evangelization.

The Lausanne Congress resembled the 1966 Berlin meeting in many ways. Once again, the lobby of the main convention hall was dominated by a "population clock" that ticked off the number of unsaved folk being born every minute—nearly two million by the time the meeting adjourned. And once again, some participants evinced great surprise to learn that so many others believed as they did. In Berlin it had been the formerly murderous Auca Indians; at Lausanne it was the more civilized but similarly isolated Cuban delegation. Don Hoke remembered that on about the third day of the congress, the four Cuban ministers stopped him in the huge almost-empty lobby. "They were about this high," he recalled, placing his hand at his sternum. "They were dancing around me and just dancing with joy. I don't speak any Spanish, but one of them spoke English. What they felt was an exuberance to find out there were so many Christians in the world, that these people all believed what they believed, that people from all over the world sang the same songs they sang and heard the same Bible passages preached. They had never dreamed they were anything but a persecuted minority, and here they found people from many nations and churches, all united in biblical evangelism. It just blew their minds, as the young people say." More widely traveled but also aglow with delight at seeing the melange of believers from 150 nations, Ugandan bishop Festo Kivengere observed that "you didn't have to say, 'They are one.' You saw it. It was a demonstration of how Christians can be one in spite of their different backgrounds."

Despite such similarities, Lausanne moved beyond Berlin in important ways. At the earlier meeting, the population clock hammered home the fact that millions being born might never hear of Jesus Christ. At Lausanne an attempt was made to identify those people and locate where they lived. Most Evangelical observers credit the Lausanne Congress with giving high-profile visibility to the concept of "unreached peoples," which has dominated mission efforts since 1974. The concept itself was not new; for generations, missionaries raised money and traveled to far countries to take the Christian gospel to those never before exposed to it. It had, however, been brought into sharper focus and refined by Evangelicalism's unquestioned experts in missiology, Donald McGavran and Ralph Winter, both of whom taught at the Fuller Seminary School of World Mission, which came into being after delegates at the Berlin Congress strongly encouraged McGavran to found a school dedicated entirely to mission endeavors. Because some form of Christianity can be found in most *nations* of the world, some assumed that the need for foreign mission efforts had passed. McGavran and Winter's contribution was to demonstrate unmistakably that most *peoples*, defined as sizable sociological groupings of "people who perceive themselves to have a common affinity for one another"—groups united, for example, by ethnic, religious, political, or other cultural attributes—were *unreached*, defined as having "no indigenous community of believing Christians with adequate numbers and resources to evangelize [their] people group without outside (cross-cultural) assistance." These concepts served to destroy complacency about the success of Christian missions. Westerners reading that Billy Graham had preached to 100,000 in Nagaland might imagine that Christianity was about to drive the last remants of Hinduism into the Ganges. In fact, it was largely confined to distinct and anomalous subcultural pockets scattered here and there around the country, and Christian believers made up no more than approximately 2 percent of India's population. In southern India, for example, nearly all Christians were drawn from only five of the one hundred subcastes, or peoples, found in that state. Similar examples exist in virtually every country. Identifying such groups made it possible not only to determine who needed to be evangelized but also to tailor mission efforts to a particular people, much as a secular advertiser attempts to target a specific audience. Instead of deciding to be a missionary to Bolivia, one might now train to work primarily among that nation's Aymara Indians. Instead of taking a gospel shotgun to Nigeria, a properly equipped missionary might aim a redemption rifle at the Maguzawas, a people known to dislike Islam and therefore possibly open to Christianity.

To drive home the scope and specific dimensions of the mission challenge, the congress's steering committee commissioned World Vision, the respected Evangelical benevolent agency with extensive international contacts, to collaborate with the Fuller School of World Mission to produce a *Handbook of Unreached Peoples*, containing a detailed analysis of the state of Christianity in virtually every country in the world, with specific attention to the people groups deemed most in need and most amenable to evangelization. Realization that of the 2.7 billion non-Christians in the world, nearly 2 billion were in areas without a significant Christian witness of any kind, and that many people groups in countries where Christianity was reasonably strong had been overlooked, had a stunning and lasting effect on congress participants. In subsequent years World Vision has continued to produce an annual *Handbook*, regarded as a basic reference tool for world mission. Its 1982 publication, the 1,400-page *World Christian Encyclopedia*, also funded in part by the Lausanne Committee, a continuation organization spawned by the congress, is regarded by many as perhaps the most impressive demographic study of Christianity ever assembled. In addition, the concept of unreached peoples has become one of the fundamental principles of Evangelical Christian mission. To reach the unreached, Winter and McGavran explicitly rejected the liberal view that cross-cultural mission efforts are no longer appropriate. They readily admitted that evangelism is easiest and most effective when performed by people similar to those they are trying to convert. Upper-middle-class white Americans are more likely to be attracted to an upper-middle-class church in their own neighborhood than to a black Pentecostal church in a ghetto storefront. Conversely, Presbyterian converts from Islam will find it difficult to share their newfound faith with upper-caste Hindus. But since "near-neighbor evangelism" is impossible when none of the neighbors are Christians, cross-cultural evangelism is imperative if people in unreached areas are to be won to Christ. And since Evangelicals devoutly believe that those not won to Christ will spend eternity in hell, there is little choice for compassionate souls but to accept the challenge and do the job as well as they can, despite the inevitable difficulties.

At Lausanne, in what some Evangelicals regard as "one of the milestone events in missiology," Winter delineated three types of evangelism, which he code-named El (near-neighbor evangelism, in which the only barrier is the gospel), E2 (evangelism involving "significant but not monumental differences of language and culture," as when North American missionaries attempt to establish Evangelical churches in Scandinavia or in the major cities of South America), and E3 (evangelism involving radical differences in culture, as when educated Western Christians plunge into African jungles or when Korean charismatics employed in Saudi oil refineries try to share their enthusiastic faith with their Arab co-workers). Obviously, Winter conceded, E3 evangelism is the most difficult, the most expensive, the least likely to succeed. But if Christians are to take seriously Jesus' final instruction to his disciples, they have no choice but to attempt it. The master pattern for world evangelization, he and McGavran contended, is to use E3 and E2 evangelism to cross cultural barriers and establish strong indigenous churches, and then to step back and allow those churches to perform the easier and more fruitful El evangelism.

That clarion call to a renewed emphasis on cross-cultural evangelism, coming at a time when both the institutional church and formal mission efforts were under sharp criticism, not only in ecumenical circles but also among some Evangelicals, was not the most popular address at Lausanne, but it may have been the most influential. Don Hoke observed that "those concepts were an in-house thing at Fuller. It would have taken years to get them out to the church. But Lausanne gave them instant worldwide visibility." Not long afterward, tension on the Fuller faculty led Winter to leave the seminary to found the U.S. Center for World Mission, also headquartered in Pasadena and now regarded as perhaps even more important and influential than the program at Fuller. While acknowledging that Winter's own abilities and efforts were the primary force in these developments, Hoke pointed out that Lausanne played a crucial role: "By giving Ralph that platform, we gave him worldwide visibility in one night. The press picked it up, mission leaders picked it up, and the whole thing has gone forward since then."

The resistance to cross-cultural evangelism stemmed largely from resentment of attempts by Western missionaries to impose aspects of Western culture on target peoples as if those aspects were part of the gospel itself. Many participants noted the need for greater cultural sensitivity when presenting the gospel to other cultures, citing such offenses as the use of music deemed irreverent or secular, inappropriate dress, disregard of dietary customs, and particularly among young people, activities in which males and females were expected to mingle in ways that might be perfectly normal at an American church camp but appeared scandalous in less permissive cultures. Participants also urged greater understanding after conversion occurred. Winter observed that if African converts from Islam want to pray five times a day and hold services on Friday (the Muslim day of worship), there was no pressing need to dissuade them from such practices. On a matter of greater significance, a majority of those who prepared a report on evangelizing polygamous cultures concluded that converts should not leave their spouses after becoming Christians, though they should be instructed not to acquire any additional partners.

Lausanne also moved beyond Berlin by giving greater attention to Christian social responsibility. At the earlier meeting, concern for social action, particularly with respect to race, came primarily from the floor rather than from scheduled speakers and was regarded as something of a protest against a carefully controlled individualistic emphasis. At Lausanne plenary speakers provided the stimulus that led to a deserved identification of the congress with renewed concern in Evangelical circles for social action. The two most significant statements were those of Argentinian Rene Padilla and Canadian (with Latin roots) Samuel Escobar. Padilla sharply criticized the tendency of American Evangelicals to identify Christianity with a politically and economically conservative middle-class American way of life. Such a standpoint, he charged, created "innumerable prejudices" against Christianity in Third World countries and lent support to the Marxist critique of religion as the "opium of the people." Effective mission, he insisted, could not be exclusively otherworldly. Perhaps thinking of the dramatic population clock in the lobby, he observed that "there is no place for statistics on 'how many souls die without Christ every minute,' if they do not take into account how many of those who die, die victims of hunger." Escobar mounted a similar attack on the biased social views of American Evangelicals, noting their tendency to oppose the violence of revolution but not the violence of war, to condemn the totalitarianism of the Left, but not that of the Right; to speak openly in favor of Israel, but to say little about the plight of Palestinian refugees; to tell the poor to be content with their poverty, but not to call on the rich exploiter to surrender his possessions; to encourage the victims of racial discrimination to look forward to a color-blind heaven, but not to condemn segregation if that might cause their churches to lose members; and to condemn "all the sins that well-behaved middle-class people condemn, but say nothing about exploitation, intrigue, and dirty political maneuvering done by great multinational corporations around the world." As for Billy Graham's contention that concentration on the social implications of the gospel would lead to abandonment of evangelism, Escobar stated flatly, "I would like to affirm that *I do not believe in that statement*. I think the social gospel ... deterioriated because of poor theology. The sad thing is that those who have the right theology have not applied it to social issues." With a bit more balance than Padilla, Escobar acknowledged that many First World missionaries in Latin America gave their lives in selfless service to the poor and oppressed, and that many indigenous Evangelicals displayed little concern for their countrymen. Still, because the lion's share of resources were concentrated in Western nations, Western Christians must take seriously the "complex issues and ambiguities by which the missionary task is surrounded" and must not only proclaim that "the end is at hand" but also seek to make this world "a bit less unjust and cruel, as an evidence of our expectation of a new creation."

It would have been a simple matter to polarize the assembly on this issue. Billy Graham, as usual, paced back and forth across the middle line, insisting that "our witness must be by both word and deed" but wary lest undue attention to works sap the faith that produced them. The resolution, or something approaching it, came in the formulation of another of the congress's major achievements: the Lausanne Covenant. The covenant evolved from months of effort overseen by John Stott, president of the British Evangelical Alliance and, almost by common consent, the leading intellectual in the Evangelical world. After months of input from congress participants and feedback from those who read preliminary drafts, Stott and a committee that included Ford, Escobar, Art Johnston, Harold Lindsell, Wheaton president Hudson Armerding, and J. D. Douglas (an erstwhile *CT* staffer and editor of BGEA's British newspaper, *The Christian and Christianity Today*) set to work. With Billy Graham as an unofficial but vitally interested hovering figure who read and commented on every draft, the committee crafted a document that Ford, no lightweight himself, characterized as "one of this century's exemplary statements on Christian beliefs, concerns, and commitment."

In fifteen paragraphs and three thousand words the covenant covered the major bases of Evangelical belief and strongly affirmed the need for both a renewed commitment to world evangelization and unselfish cooperation between churches and parachurch agencies engaged in the task. Most of its statements demanded much but occasioned little disagreement among people whose very presence signified their dedication to evangelism. Several paragraphs, however, represented long hours of intense agonizing over precise words and meanings and continued to draw attention fifteen years later. One of the most controversial addressed the proper balance between evangelism and social responsibility. With both the drafting committee and the assembly divided on this issue, utmost care was essential if the sought-for unity was to last. The result was a set of statements that gave unmistakable primacy to evangelism, explicitly defined as "the proclamation of the historical, biblical Christ as Saviour and Lord, with a view to persuading people to come to him personally and so be reconciled to God," while making it clear that "the results of evangelism include ... responsible service in the world." More specifically, the covenant stated that Christians are obliged to share God's "concern for justice and reconciliation throughout human society and for the liberation of men from every kind of oppression," expressed penitence "for having sometimes regarded evangelism and social concern as mutually exclusive," and declared that "although reconciliation with man is not reconciliation with God, nor is social action evangelism, nor is political liberation salvation, nevertheless we affirm that evangelism and socio-political involvement are both part of our Christian duty.... Faith without works is dead." The following paragraph, however, worked out after long debate between the two factions on the committee, contained the crucial affirmation that "in the church's mission of sacrificial service, evangelism is primary." It was a cautious, even hedging sort of statement, and evangelism still held its position as the master motive, but the Lausanne Covenant furnished Evangelical Christianity with a rationale for social action that it had lacked since the days of Charles Finney.

The covenant was formally presented to the congress at a climactic communion service. At the conclusion of the service, Jack Dain and Billy Graham signed the document itself and approximately 2,000 of the 2,400 participants turned in Covenant Cards indicating their desire to be regarded as signers. One of those who chose not to sign was Ruth Graham, primarily because Stott insisted on inserting the following statement: "Those of us who live in affluent circumstances accept our duty to develop a simple lifestyle in order to contribute more generously to both relief and evangelism." Stott, a bachelor, lives quite simply in a cozy book-lined flat in London. Most of his substantial book royalties have been used to support Third World students engaged in advanced theological studies. Ruth admires Stott but found his espousal of a simple lifestyle too confining. "If it said 'simpler,'" she told him," I would sign it. But what is 'simple'? You live in two rooms; I have a bigger home. You have no children; I have five. You say your life is simple and mine isn't." Stott refused to delete the offending sentence, and Ruth decided, just as she had decided long ago that she did not need to be baptized by immersion, that she could be a quite acceptable Christian without signing something she regarded as a bit self-righteous and precious. Others chose not to sign on various grounds, but signing or not signing was never regarded as a major issue. "It was a covenant, not a creed," Leighton Ford explained. "It was never intended as a testimony of orthodoxy. It was a banner to rally people, not a knife to cut them down." Interestingly, the names of the signatories were sealed away and never made public. Ford claimed not even to know where they are located.

Graham brought the congress to a rousing close with a demonstration of his own masterful form of evangelism by packing Lausanne's largest stadium for an afternoon rally. Severe pain from an infected jaw that deviled him throughout the conference forced him to cut his sermon short, but he graciously stayed around for over an hour after the service, shaking hands, signing autographs, posing for pictures alongside admiring participants, and generally playing the role of World Christian Statesman, a man who had done what only he was in a position to do, bringing together Evangelical leaders from all over the world, mixing them together in bubbling ferment, impressing them with what they had already done, and sending them forth filled with visions of what yet might be.

Not everything had gone exactly as Graham had planned. Given his preference, the Lausanne Congress would have ended forever that summer afternoon on the steps of the Stade-Lausanne. He had insisted since the first discussion that no ongoing institutional structure be created because he did not want BGEA to be financially responsible for another organization, and also, according to friends, because he feared that what might start as a staunch Evangelical body could easily turn left after he died, leaving a monument that would cast a distorted shadow over his legacy. That preference went unheeded. Congress participants, particularly those from the Third World, became so intoxicated with the feeling of belonging to a worldwide fellowship of like-minded believers that they simply refused to let it sink back into Lake Leman. Responding to a groundswell of interest, congress leaders circulated a questionnaire asking whether some sort of continuing structure was desired; 86 percent of those who responded gave a definite yes. "You have to realize," Don Hoke explained, "that this was the greatest thing that had ever happened to many of these people. The World Council of Churches is an old-boys club. Basically, most of them are liberal or have liberal tendencies. The Evangelical churches started by American missionaries around the world are not represented in the council. The great independent churches of Africa, some with a million members apiece, have no voice in the council. Those Third World people knew they had a voice here, and they did not want to lose it."

Graham was adamant that any continuing structure not be construed as an anti-WCC body but finally agreed to go along with a continuation committee that would facilitate communication and information sharing among Evangelicals throughout the world. Before the congress ended, participants met in regional groups to select representatives to a forty-eight-person committee, stratified, like the congress itself, by geography, denomination, age, sex, and culture. In January 1975 that committee met at the Hotel del Prado in Mexico City, which was convenient for Graham, who was on his way to a vacation in Acapulco. In this meeting, the tension between evangelism and social action resurfaced and threatened to abort the newly conceived organization, as Graham and John Stott disagreed over what the Lausanne mandate to the continuation committee had actually been. Stott felt the committee should address the entire range of concerns found in the Lausanne Covenant. Graham contended, with equal fervor, that the focus should be on the narrower task of evangelization. Evangelicals should be involved in social action, he acknowledged, but the Lausanne Continuation Committee "should stick with reconciliation with God!" and not try to "get involved in all the things that God wants done in our generation." In the years to come, both men downplayed their differences and continued to hold each other in the highest regard, but their differences, though not enormous, remained real and significant. The friction between their two positions was such that when a majority of the committee pressed Billy to serve as honorary chairman of the continuation committee, believing that his imprimatur and leadership were essential to its success, he resisted, agreeing only to pray about it overnight. When he left the room to permit free discussion of his continuing role, Stott and—to the surprise of most—Jack Dain argued that it would be best if Graham were not the honarary chairman. The discussion was intense and not always friendly, with some feeling that Graham and the cause of evangelism were being betrayed. Had Graham wished, it would have been rather simple either to insist on control of the committee, since BGEA would probably have to fund it during the early stages of its existence, or to register public disapproval, which would effectively render it impotent. Instead, at the first meeting the following morning, he asked permission to speak first. He accepted the honorary chairmanship, but instead of requiring that his own point of view be accepted as a condition of his acceptance, he conceded the validity of Stott's interpretation.

The effect was extraordinary. One observer recalled that "as he began to open his heart, sharing with us his deep personal feelings, I never witnessed a more magnanimous expression of tenderness and understanding. His insight to the situation, his sensitivity to personalities, amplified by his own transparent humility, literally melted us together. What differences we had were largely resolved in an enveloping sense of trust and purpose." Another man, the youngest member of the committee, agreed with this assessment of

Graham's spirit. On seeing "his humility, the graciousness of his spirit, and his genuine desire to be open to the Lord and to the counsel of the Lord's people," he said, "I became convinced that Dr. Graham actually felt that he had much yet to learn and that he needed the counsel and help of other Christians. For a man in his position actually to reflect that kind of attitude is to me remarkable and a great challenge." In response, the Lausanne Continuation Committee accepted as a guideline that its purpose would be "to further the total Biblical mission of the church, recognizing that in this mission of sacrificial service, evangelism is primary, and that our particular concern must be the evangelization of the 2,700 million unreached people of our world."

At the Mexico City meeting, the Lausanne Continuation Committee for World Evangelization (*Continuation* was later dropped from the name, and the committee came to be known as LCWE) became a permanent entity, with Jack Dain as its first chairman, to be succeeded a year later by Leighton Ford. Gottfried Osei-Mensah, a Ghanaian-born, British-educated Baptist pastor with an electrifying pulpit presence, was chosen as executive secretary, a full-time post he held until 1986. Loose plans were made for future meetings of a two-hundred-member consultative committee, which Graham also agreed to serve as honorary chairman, but primary oversight was put in the hands of an eleven-member executive committee on which Graham did not serve. That committee agreed to operate on a modest budget and to serve as a "catalyst and stimulator" rather than attempt to give directions to the Evangelical world. Graham pledged $100,000 in BGEA funds to underwrite expenses for the first year.

The impact of Lausanne began to be felt almost immediately. American and European Christians had long been accustomed to regional, national, and international meetings at which they shared viewpoints and stimulated each other's enthusiasm and confidence. For most Third World churchmen, however, the fellowship and inspiration they had found at Lausanne was new, and they quickly set about to sustain and recreate it in their own circles. Congress participants began to report on follow-up meetings they led in their local areas. Soon, Lausanne veterans, with the help of the continuation committee, began to organize the first of dozens of what were inevitably labeled mini-Lausannes throughout the world, some covering a wide range of topics, some focusing on a specific issue, such as improvement of theological education, more effective use of media, and coordination of efforts between churches and parachurch agencies. A series of meetings in Singapore in 1977 and 1978, supported strongly by Billy Graham, gave rise to coalitions of Asian Evangelicals who had scarcely been aware of each other's existence before Lausanne but who joined together enthusiastically to create research centers, cooperative programs of conservative theological education in newly formed seminaries and extension programs, and at least two hundred agencies that began to train and send missionaries to neighboring nations. Chinese Christians in particular took fire from Lausanne and sent it leaping across continents. By the mid-1980s, the Chinese Coordinating Committee for World Evangelization, headquartered in Hong Kong with a permanent staff of seventy, was involved in the evangelistic efforts of 5,000 Chinese churches throughout the world, including the United States. In 1986 its leader, Thomas Wang, became executive director of the Lausanne Committee.

Other meetings produced thoughtful interchange on key theoretical and strategic issues and resulted in booklets, known as *Occasional Papers*, that have been widely distributed and seminal in their effect on world Evangelicalism. In these and myriad extensions of what has come to be called the Spirit of Lausanne, the Lausanne Covenant has played a major unifying role—again, particularly in the Third World, where it provided a formal basis on which Baptists, Mennonites, Methodists, Pentecostals, and others, including Evangelical members of WCC-affiliated denominations, could agree to work together. "It's a coalescence of the spirit of evangelism as exemplified by Billy Graham," Don Hoke explained. "It is not so well known in America or in some parts of Europe, but it's a household word in Third World churches. If we want to organize a meeting in Africa, we can say, 'This is what we believe,' and that is all we need. It is a very, very significant document." Hoke is by no means alone in this assessment; the *International Bulletin of Mission Research* has asserted that the covenant "may now be the broadest umbrella in the world under which professing Christians can be gathered to pray and strategize for the salvation of their cities."

Some of Lausanne's impact occurred closer to Billy Graham's home. After finishing high school, Franklin Graham, who was twenty-two at the time of the conference, had formed a loose tie with his father's ministry, accompanying Roy Gustafson on several of the Holy Land tours he led as part of his work for BGEA. Acting as a kind of surrogate father who knew when to press the case for reform and when to hold back, the wise and witty Gustafson assured Billy and Ruth that Franklin would come around eventually, but he seemed to be going more on hope than tangible evidence, and Ruth shuddered when she heard stories of her son's driving a Land Rover across Middle Eastern desert terrain with the steering wheel in one hand and a bottle of whiskey in the other, explaining that he drove better when he was relaxed. With his experience as a tour aide serving more as an excuse than a reason, Franklin attended the Lausanne Congress as a worker in the travel department. At long last the Grahams' patience paid off, and a lifetime of exposure to much of the best of Evangelical Christianity finally took effect. Mingling with Third World Christians and recognizing the physical hardships many of them suffered moved Franklin tremendously. A few weeks later, in a Jerusalem hotel room where he and Gustafson were staying, he threw a wadded-up pack of cigarettes in the trash, knelt by his bed, and told

God, "I want you to be lord of my life. I am willing to give up any area that is not pleasing to you. And I'm sick and tired of being sick and tired." Shortly afterward, with his life on a straighter and narrower path, Franklin married and went back to school at Appalachian State University, announcing that he planned to dedicate himself to a life of Christian service.

Ironically, what Third World Evangelical leaders regard as a prophetic force in contemporary Christianity is viewed with less honor in the founding prophet's own circle. American Evangelicals, for whom Youth for Christ, the NAE, and other interdenominational fellowships have long provided similar association and inspiration, tend to be less caught up in the spirit of Lausanne. This is particularly true within BGEA itself, where some key figures regard the Lausanne Committee as both a rival for Evangelical funds and, should it follow its more liberal instincts, a possible blotch on Billy Graham's record. George Wilson, never one to look kindly on unnecessary expenditure, hinted strongly that the original Lausanne Continuation Committee arose more from a desire to get "a free trip from the ends of the world at least once a year" than from a selfless dedication to soul winning. Other BGEA stalwarts registered their misgivings about Lausanne either by discounting its effectiveness or by falling uncomfortably silent when the topic arose. To a considerable extent, their reservations reflect dissatisfaction with the role Leighton Ford has played in the "Lausanne Movement." Almost from the establishment of the continuation committee, Ford spent at least half his time on its activities—raising money, traveling all over the world to speak at follow-up conferences, and bearing the lion's share of the administrative burden after Gottfried Osei-Mensah proved to be more adept at inspiration than administration. "Gottfried is a wonderful front man," Don Hoke observed. "He is black, articulate, biblical, evangelistic, from the Third World—but he is no administrator. He would give these wonderful addresses and pray with people and everybody would be happy and excited, but that would be the end of it. He didn't know how to bring groups together or help people organize or let them know what the committee could do to help them. So the burden quickly fell to Leighton."

That burden inevitably detracted from Ford's work with BGEA and raised fiscal concerns, both because of the expenses he incurred on behalf of the LCWE—"Leighton operates like Billy," Hoke observed. "He's not extravagant, but he doesn't count the cost if something needs to be done."—-and because he raised money from some of the same sources Graham liked to tap. Eventually, the LCWE set up its permanent headquarters in Charlotte, where Ford lives. Both men minimize any direct conflict between themselves. Ford noted that "I was asked by Billy himself to take over the chairmanship after Bishop Dain resigned. He said, 'I want you to do it. I'll stand behind you and we'll make the funds available. We need you in there to keep it going in the right way.' He's always been very supportive." He acknowledged, however, that "some of the people around Billy have not been supportive. They probably felt that if Billy wasn't running it, there was no point to being involved in it. You will certainly pick up some ambivalent feelings. I think Lausanne represents Billy. I don't think it represents his organization, which is centered on actually doing evangelism. Billy's broad view of evangelism and social issues and theology and churchmanship are not represented as much in the organization as in Billy himself."

Graham also insisted in 1989 that he felt no tension with either Ford or the LCWE and believed the Lausanne movement is "on the right track," though he noted, in his familiar way of raising points for which he preferred not to bear responsibility, that "some feel they spend far too much time on conferences and meetings. Some feel they spend too much money. And some have thought they were sort of turning left from the original positions." No one denies that real tensions existed, and insiders admit that Graham himself felt more reservations than he was willing to acknowledge for the record. In fact, at one point he grew sufficiently irritated with the expense involved in mounting a 1989 Lausanne II meeting in Manila that he threatened to withdraw from the position of honorary chairman. Further, though other factors were involved, few knowledgeable participants or observers deny that Ford's decision to leave BGEA in 1986 to found Leighton Ford Ministries was motivated at least in some degree by continuing friction within the Graham organization.

The evidence indicates that Lausanne's impact has been greater than its detractors admit. Without question, key leaders among Third World Evangelicals regard it as of historic importance, and its yeast continues to leaven the lump of world Christianity. Choosing another metaphor, John Stott aptly observed that "many a conference has resembled a [display] of fireworks. It has made a loud noise and illumined the night sky for a few brief brilliant seconds, only to fall to the ground with smoke, silence, and darkness. What is exciting about Lausanne, however, is that its fire continues to spark off other fires. [It] refuses to die down." Less poetically, but with no less conviction, the widely respected Brazilian Evangelical Nilson Fanini stated flatly his belief that Lausanne had, in fact, fulfilled Don Hoke's vision of a "twentieth-century Pentecost. God has used the Lausanne Committee to revive the spirit of evangelism and missions throughout the world. I have been in eighty-two countries. I have seen the impact of Lausanne all over the world. It is not just theoretical. I saw it!"

28

Higher Ground

Barely one month after Nixon's resignation left Graham filled with feelings of profound sorrow, confusion, and perhaps betrayal, he returned to Los Angeles for a three-night reprise of the 1949 crusade that had hurled him into the nation's consciousness twenty-five years earlier. This exercise in nostalgia, however, was no harbinger of a ministry in decline. Two weeks later, Graham headed for Rio de Janeiro to make another run on the continent that had largely resisted his incursions twelve years earlier. Of all the South American countries he visited in 1962, Brazil had been among the friendliest. In the intervening years, the country had experienced impressive growth in its Protestant ranks, particularly among Pentecostals, and the stage seemed set for a satisfying visit. After a shaky start marked by audio problems that contributed to plummeting attendance after the opening service, the crusade gained momentum and wound up with close to 250,000 people jammed into the huge Maracana soccer stadium. The president of Brazil, himself an Evangelical, authorized the largest television station in Rio to carry the service, making it available to over 100 million people; according to Crusade Director Henry Holley, station officials believed perhaps 50 million saw at least part of the unprecedented broadcast. Evangelicals were not the only ones impressed with the crowd. Graham asked the archbishop of Canterbury, Michael Ramsey, who was in Brazil at the time, to bring a brief greeting to the assembly. The British prelate rankled a few feelings when he arrived at the stadium in a chauffeured Rolls-Royce ("There was some insensitivity—-the people are awfully poor") and violated Graham's request that he limit his remarks by speaking for nearly twenty minutes. Bemused at the memory, Holley provided a simple explanation for the archbishop's failure to observe the protocol: Unlike Billy Graham, "the Archbishop had never seen that many people gathered in one place before."

The Brazilian campaign burned itself into Graham's memory not only for triumphs registered at a time when he needed triumph but also because it coincided with one of the most frightening and unsettling events of his life. While visiting daughter GiGi and her family in Milwaukee, where GiGi's husband, Stephan Tchividjian, was doing graduate work in clinical psychology, Ruth decided to rig up a pipe slide for her grandchildren. The simple device consisted of a strong wire strung at a sharp angle between two trees with a section of pipe threaded onto it. The plan was for the children to climb one tree, grab hold of the pipe, and sail across the yard to the ground. To make sure it was safe, Ruth (age fifty-four but giving that fact no more respect than she felt it deserved) acted as test pilot. She had no trouble scaling the taller tree, but when she grabbed the pipe and launched herself, the wire snapped as she picked up speed and she crashed into the ground from a height of fifteen feet—and did not move. For a split second, GiGi considered the possibility that her mother was faking injury, trying to salvage a laugh from an embarrassing situation, but when the family dog licked Ruth's face and she did not react, it was clear this was no joke. At the hospital, GiGi learned her mother had shattered her left heel, broken a rib, and crushed a vertebra. More frightening, she had suffered a concussion that left her unconscious for a week, causing her family and physicians to wonder if she would live, and if she lived, whether she had suffered irreparable brain damage.

Shortly after arriving in Brazil, Billy got a confused and incomplete message that Ruth had been in a serious accident. It was one o'clock in the morning, but he immediately began preparing to return home, directing Grady Wilson to preach in his stead. Grady told his friend, "Buddy, we never know why God allows these things to happen, but Ruth's unconscious. She'd rather you stay here and preach, and do what God called you to do." At that moment, Graham's call to be an evangelist gave way to his covenant to be a husband; he looked at Grady and, feeling utterly helpless, said, "I can't." After several abortive efforts with an eccentric telephone system, they made contact with GiGi, who unexpectedly subscribed to Grady's theology. Her mother was in good hands, she assured her father, and was doing just fine—a diagnosis for which she had no good evidence. He should by all means finish the crusade as scheduled and not worry for a moment.

Billy did as family and friends urged, but with a fearful aching in his heart. He had always demonstrated a remarkable ability to shut out all distractions when he stepped into the pulpit, but his offstage tendency to anticipate the worst now tormented him terribly, as he suspected—correctly—that his family was protecting him from the full truth. When he returned to America, he learned just how serious Ruth's injury had been. And then Ruth herself learned. On regaining consciousness, she discovered to her horror that her memory was seriously impaired; among the missing items were hundreds of Bible verses memorized throughout her life. As her faculties returned with vexing slowness, she prayed, "Lord, take anything from me, but *please* give me back my Bible verses." Gradually, the precious memories straggled back into her mind, sometimes alone, sometimes in small groups, sometimes bringing with them companions she did not remember ever having seen before, much less having committed to memory. Visible signs of the accident eventually passed, but it left its mark, including mild impairment to her short-term memory and physical problems that necessitated replacement of her hip, part of a wrist joint, and, possibly related, reconstruction of her esophagus. She also began to suffer from a nerve disorder whose effects she likened to being attacked by swarms of ants, and from a chronic wracking cough that disturbs her sleep and sometimes threatens to expel the life from her small body. She emphatically did not suffer from a delight in talking about her misfortunes. One morning in 1987, while her obviously worried husband talked about her problems, noting that she had been awake most of the night, she came into the room to stir the coals in the giant walk-in fireplace. "Did you ever hear the definition of a bore?" she asked, looking back over one shoulder. "A bore is someone who, when you ask them how they feel, will tell you the truth. Change the subject!" With that, she walked out brightly and began rounding up some lunch. That same afternoon, Graham went into another room to take a call from their daughter, Bunny Dienert. When he came back, he announced that Ted and Bunny would cancel their vacation and go with her to the Mayo Clinic the following Monday. She listened tensely and did not respond directly, but she was clearly irritated that he had taken this action without consulting her. The subject, one sensed, would be discussed in further detail when they were alone. When she left the room, Billy broke the tension by recalling an occasion when she had gone into a severe coughing fit in the midst of receiving an honorary degree. "The papers said she had been greatly moved," he said with a smile. "She didn't even want the degree."

In the mid-1970s, Graham adopted a conscious policy of holding more crusades in medium-sized cities such as Albuquerque, Lubbock, Jackson, Asheville, and South Bend. This saved money and focused on the television broadcasts as much as on immediate results in the crusade cities themselves. On foreign outings, however, the team still pulled out all the stops, trying always for the largest possible crowds and the greatest possible penetration of the gospel in lands where it was less familiar. Not every foray onto foreign soil met with great success—a ten-day crusade in Brussels produced only 2,557 inquirers—but stronger showings in Taiwan and Hong Kong indicated Graham was in no danger of losing his prowess. The Taiwan crusade had strong official and popular support. Earlier in the year, Graham had presided at a memorial service for Chiang Kai-shek at the National Cathedral in Washington, and Madame Chiang returned the favor by serving as honorary chair of the crusade, which drew more than 250,000 over five days, despite heavy rainfall during each service. Strong anti-American sentiment in Hong Kong made crusade organizers so anxious that they considered taking Graham's name off the publicity materials, but crowds were large—nearly twice as many as the pope had drawn, team members noted—and the inquirer rate was a whopping 9.4 percent, about twice the standard response.

In 1977 a five-day crusade in Manila marked another politician's effort to use Graham to polish a public image. Under heavy fire for what *CT* called "allegedly repressive politics," Ferdinand and Imelda Marcos went out of their way to associate themselves with Graham and his mission. They received him in private audience, had him spend the night in the presidential palace when the water system at his hotel broke down, and hosted a state dinner in his honor, the first time a head of state had ever so honored him, despite his many visits with presidents, queens, and chancellors. At a National Prayer Breakfast, which both Marcoses attended, the president declared he had come "to demonstrate to our people and to the whole world my personal belief in prayer.... The time has come again to pray." At the School of Evangelism, where she gave the opening address, Mrs. Marcos proclaimed that "it is only those who are Christ-informed and Christ-conscious who are strong." Apparently, she counted herself and her husband among those so empowered. "The president and I," she said, "are fully conscious that our temporal powers are bestowed by God, and we clearly realize that this gift of love can only be used in the purest of motives."

On the other side of the world, Graham held two crusades in Scandinavia during 1977 and 1978. The first installment, in Goteburg, Sweden, was modest in the numbers it generated but encouraging in spirit. The second tour, which included visits to Norway and Sweden, was marred by some of the most bitter and concentrated opposition the evangelist had ever faced. In Oslo, a coalition of scientists, psychologists, actors, writers, and miscellaneous humanists opposed the crusade. Voicing some of the same complaints, but with greater vituperation, a group calling itself the Heathen Society loudly vowed to disrupt the services and made good on their pledge. At a meeting for pastors, a young woman barely missed dousing Graham with a mixture of red paint and chemicals. As security men trundled her out of the room, Billy benignly declared, "I love that young woman because Christ loves her," a statement that contained the requisite cheek turning while making it clear he did not find her intrinsically winsome. At a stadium rally, the same woman slashed the ropes holding a huge crusade banner, then climbed a tall light tower where she unfurled a sign reading WHEN CHRISTIANS GET POWER, THEY WILL KILL. A female companion on another light tower loosed a long blast from a powerful air horn and showered the crowd with anti-Graham leaflets, while other heathens chanted, "Billy, go home!" Police hustled the demonstrators away, allowing Graham to finish the service, but as he left, still more hecklers hurled rotten fruit, cream-filled cakes, and small bags of garbage at him, none of which scored a direct hit. In Stockholm protesters pelted Billy with tomatoes, this time hitting their mark, and criticized him for terrorizing children with the fear of hell. Faculty and students at a Lutheran seminary in Uppsala so opposed his coming to Sweden that they released a paperback book subjecting his theology and approach to severe criticism, leveling charges of unreasonable expense and psychological manipulation of crowds (his use of the invitation, they said, was "spiritual rape") and criticizing the evangelist for his association with Nixon, his support of the war in Vietnam, and his strong opposition to communism. The attacks had their effect. The inquirer rate for all services was less than 1 percent, the lowest ever recorded in forty years of crusades.

Most of Graham's foreign crusades during this period met with far better results. Repeatedly—in Singapore 1978, Australia 1979, Japan 1980, and Mexico City 1981—participants and team members reported larger-than-expected crowds, high percentages of first-timer responses to the invitation, and occasional doubling and tripling of church membership. Repeatedly, they delighted in generous and even-handed treatment by the media and government officials and at ecumenical cooperation that crossed virtually all barriers, except those protecting McIntire-type Fundamentalists from contamination by compromise and those insulating liberals from people who believed more fervently than they deemed appropriate.

Back in America, Graham continued to demonstrate increasing openness to Roman Catholics, and they returned the favor. In a crusade in Asheville early in 1977, a Catholic church opened its doors to allow overflow crowds to view the crusade on closed-circuit television. And in May Graham held a five-day crusade on the campus of Notre Dame University. Though he altered his sermons mainly by adding references to Bishop Fulton Sheen and Mother Teresa, *Christianity Today* aptly observed that this remarkable event showed that Graham "is not afraid to go deep into Roman Catholic territory. It also showed that many elements in the once-hostile Catholic community are now receptive to Graham's type of ministry." *CT* reported that one priest had taken off his collar as he came forward, telling a counselor he was accepting Christ for the first time, but Graham required no such renunciation of past allegiance. On the contrary, he assured Catholics that he was not asking them either to break or to form a relationship with a particular denomination. And as one measure of the impact of his ecumenism on his own team, Robert Ferm, who had often assured anxious supporters that Mr. Graham would never compromise the gospel by consorting with Catholics, addressed the faculty and students at the Notre Dame seminary prior to the crusade. It was, Ferm admitted ten years later, in a bit of charming understatement, "significant."

Graham acknowledged continuing differences between Catholic and Evangelical theology. "From my point of view," he noted, "the Roman Catholic Church emphasizes Mary too much, but I think Protestants have gone the other direction in denying the greatness of Mary. The Scripture says she was the most blessed of women. Also, the infallibility of the pope is something Protestants can never accept, but I have a great deal of admiration for the pope, even though I don't accept all of his theology. I don't think the differences are important as far as personal salvation is concerned." In a similar vein, T. W. Wilson observed that television evangelist Jimmy Swaggart was "absolutely wrong" in his insistence that Catholics are not Christians in the eyes of God. "A number of doctrines they teach," Wilson said, "we don't subscribe to, nor would we ever. But to say that they are not Christians—-man alive! Anybody that receives Jesus Christ as their Lord and Savior is converted! They're born again! I believe the pope is a converted man. I believe a lot of these wonderful Catholics are Christians. I'd like to shake them and turn them around and tell them, 'You don't need all this. You don't need to go to the confession booth and confess all your sins to that priest. He's just a man.' So there are differences, but that doesn't mean they're not converted."

Immersion in his crusades provided Graham with a convenient reason to retreat from the national spotlight after the Watergate debacle, but the 1976 election campaign forced him to clarify his political stance. Though clearly scorched by his association with Nixon, he had not deemed it necessary to break all ties with the White House. He had played golf with Gerald Ford while Ford was still a congressman and, shortly after he became President, had called to offer congratulations and assurances of goodwill. He followed that with a long visit during which he and the new President prayed and read the Bible and a few weeks later allowed the *Ladies' Home Journal* to publish a prayer affirming that "we acknowledge thy sovereignty in the selection of our leaders." Still, early in 1976 he told a reporter he planned to "stay a million miles away from politics this year," and he came close to a public breach with Campus Crusade leader Bill Bright over the latter's efforts to launch a conservative Christian political bloc. Graham charged that Bright had contacted prayer and Bible-study groups spawned by his crusades in an effort to enlist them in his movement. He did not resign from Campus Crusade's board, but he refused to serve as chairman of the Christian Embassy, a Washington mansion Bright purchased for use as a staging ground for evangelizing legislators and other government officials; and when the embassy opened, he chose not to participate in the dedication ceremonies. "Bright has been using me and my name for twenty years," he complained. "But now I'm concerned about the political direction he seems to be taking." Graham and Bright subsequently patched up their differences, but Graham never became a supporter of the Christian Embassy.

Perhaps ignoring signs of Graham's increased skittishness at political partisanship, Gerald Ford made no effort to distance himself from his predecessor's favorite preacher. The new President declined an offer to attend a crusade in Norfolk, Virginia, but asked to be kept informed about future crusades, and he maintained occasional contact with the evangelist, assuring him that "Betty and I think of you and Ruth often, and we are deeply grateful for your wonderful friendship." As he began gearing up for reelection, he clearly hoped to count on Graham for more than prayer. When Ruth's health prevented Billy from attending the National Prayer Breakfast, an event at which an incumbent President typically displays all the piety he can muster, White House memos indicate that Ford's staff was disturbed at his absence, and the President invited him to be in touch as soon as he felt free to travel, "so that arrangements may be made for us to get together for a visit." Ford was known to share the Evangelical sentiments common to his Grand Rapids, Michigan, congressional district, but his interest in Billy Graham was not exclusively spiritual. As it began to look more likely that the Democratic candidate would be a southern Evangelical Christian, it seemed especially important for Ford to cultivate whatever ties he had within the Evangelical community. In late April a White House staffer directed colleagues to "keep your eye open for possible events that we could help hook Billy Graham into with the President." Two days later, Ford sent a note to the Highland Park Presbyterian Church in Dallas, congratulating it on its fiftieth anniversary and sending warm greetings to its pastor—Ruth Graham's brother, Clayton Bell. That summer, when Queen Elizabeth and Prince Philip visited the United States, Billy and Ruth Graham were one of only 150 couples invited to attend a state dinner in their honor. "All America wanted to come," he recalled, "but they couldn't invite but about 150 to 175 couples. Ruth and I were quite surprised to be invited. The invitation could have come from the Palace."

Graham thought well of Ford, but he thought better of maintaining a stance of political neutrality. At some point during late summer, after Carter's nomination, the President decided to exercise his option to attend a crusade service. Graham was preaching in Pontiac, Michigan, in Ford's home state, and it would have been easy to justify inviting the President to sit on the platform and offer a few words of greeting to the crowd. But in a letter that showed how far Billy Graham had come since the days when he fairly begged Harry Truman and Dwight Eisenhower to grace his ministry with a visit, he told the President, apparently in response to a telephone inquiry, that he felt it would be impossible to ask him to address a crusade audience. "I think the backlash would not only hurt our ministry," he wrote, "but would hurt you as people would think you were 'using' me." He did, however, offer a fair-sized crumb: "If you came and sat in whatever area the Secret Service would decide is best, and were recognized from the platform, I am sure you would get a rousing reception." Lest Ford envision that such an invitation might be interpreted as an endorsement, Graham added, "Of course, since I am maintaining a neutral position, as I always try to do in politics, I will also extend a similar invitation to Governor Carter. In the meantime, I am praying that God's will will be done on November 2, and that the man of God's choice will be elected."

Though Graham's general political stance was closer to Ford's than to Jimmy Carter's, he faced a stronger-than-usual dilemma. In 1966 Carter chaired a film crusade in Americus, Georgia. He had not been particularly impressed with *The Restless Ones*, the crusade's centerpiece film, but he was a devout, born-again Southern Baptist (truly converted, it was said, not long after hearing his pastor preach a sermon borrowed from Billy Graham) and he affirmed the main points of Evangelical belief. He was also one of the few church leaders willing to oversee an integrated public program, which Graham insisted upon. At the conclusion of the film each evening, Carter himself explained the gospel briefly and gave the invitation. Seven years later, while governor of Georgia, Carter chaired Graham's Atlanta crusade and hosted the evangelist for an overnight stay in the Governor's mansion. Still, the man who so fervently longed for piety in his presidents that he sometimes perceived it where others could not carefully avoided indicating a preference for his fellow Southern Baptist. To the contrary, he told a *Los Angeles Times* reporter that "I would rather have a man in office who is highly qualified to be President who didn't make much of a religious profession than to have a man who had no qualifications but who made a religious profession." In an ostensible and perhaps sincere show of the promised neutrality, he added that Ford and Carter held similar religious views, but some in the Carter camp, apparently including the candidate himself, felt Graham had been giving Evangelicals permission not to vote for the governor. Carter snapped, "I think what people should look out for is people like Billy Graham, who go around telling people how to live their lives." In a similar display of pique, Carter's son Jeff also criticized Graham's statement, gratuitously (and erroneously) adding that Graham's doctorate was a mail-order degree.

Graham sought to defuse the building tension by dropping a note to Rosalyn Carter, telling her "to give Jeff a big hug. I have two sons and I understand." Carter's resentment was eased by winning the election. Graham immediately told the press that although he was not one of Carter's advisers, they had been friends for years. The president-elect was, he asserted, "a leader we can trust and follow," and he would personally be praying and "rootin' and tootin' for him." Graham skipped the inauguration, the first he had missed since 1949, but he did attend a special presidential Prayer Breakfast a few days later, and he and Ruth spent yet another night in the White House. "Rosalyn asked if we wanted to sleep in the Lincoln Room," Graham recalled, "and I told her, 'No, I don't. That bed has a hump right in the middle.' I'd been there with both the Johnsons and the Nixons, so I knew how the beds slept. She said, 'Really?' She went back and felt it and said, 'You're right.' So we slept in the Queen's Room, across the hall. The same thing happened with the Reagans, but I think Mrs. Reagan got a new mattress for the Lincoln Room." The two men had occasional contact after that, and Graham later characterized Carter as "the hardest-working President we've ever had." He noted that "he doesn't inspire love or loyalty in the way that Reagan does," but added, "At the same time, you know he would struggle with you and do anything in the world you asked him to, if he felt like he could."

It was understandable that the relationship between Carter and Graham never became particularly close. Graham was wary of the political spotlight, and given the evangelist's ties to Nixon, Carter had little reason to believe Billy would ever become a major ally. Further, within months after Carter's inauguration, BGEA was plunged into a crisis that made association with Graham seem more a liability than an asset. To the chagrin of his admirers and the snide smiles of cynics, it appeared for a time that Billy Graham and his righteous band, like so many of their predecessors, had been caught trying to serve both God and mammon.

That Graham might be guilty of financial malfeasance came as a shock even to those who had excoriated him for his theology and his politics. After he made the decision in 1952 to stop taking love offerings and to place BGEA's finances under the direction of a board of respected business-people, the association enjoyed a mostly unblemished record for financial integrity. No one receiving mail from several of the leading independent ministries can fail to be struck by the contrast between Graham's fund-raising techniques and those of most of his colleagues. As frequently as every two weeks, others send letters bordered in red or black or Western Union yellow and labeled "Crisis-gram" or "Disaster-gram," and claiming their ostensible author had been in prayer in the middle of the night ("My doctor says I have to get more rest, but how can I sleep with a heart so burdened for lost souls?") when he realized the only hope for his financially strapped ministry lay in writing "you, Sister Chapman, one of the most faithful supporters I have had in twenty-seven years of serving God." Graham's letters, arriving once a month in a simple window envelope, report on what the ministry has recently accomplished and what lies just ahead, request continued prayer and, usually in no more than four or five sentences, apologetically asks supporters to send "as generous and sacrificial a gift as the Lord lays it on your heart to give." And that's it. No cries of desperation. No threats. No promises of a tenfold or hundredfold miraculous return on whatever they contribute. No requests for seventy dollars to celebrate his seventieth birthday, or forty dollars to commemorate forty years of crusade evangelism, or twelve dollars in honor of the twelve apostles or the twelve tribes of Israel or the twelve white Edsels he had seen on the way to his prayer tower. Just "Here's what we are doing. We think it's the Lord's will. If you'll pray for us and send us a little money, we surely would appreciate it." Ed Plowman, a veteran Graham associate, observed that the monthly letter "is one of the few things Billy does entirely himself.

George Wilson applies his editorial touches and there's very little besides that. It's no professional fund-raising agency. It's Billy. And it's refreshing."

The radio and TV pitches follow a similar pattern. Unlike colleagues whose programs are often little more than hour-long begging bouts, Graham's prime-time specials seldom devote more than two or three minutes to finances, and those appeals are carefully couched to avoid any hint of charlatanry. The refusal to employ half-truths, heart-tugging petitions, and misleading promises has saved Graham from a load of opprobrium. "Let's face it," Plowman said, "you don't identify the Graham organization as being one of the sob sisters out with a tin cup, or with its hat in its hand all the time. Whatever problems the organization has had, they aren't problems of exploiting the masses or shaking down little old ladies. Billy has so soft-pedaled the appeal for funds that this has contributed to the aura of integrity. People say, 'I believe this man. I can trust him. I believe he is telling the truth.'" As a result of that approach, Plowman estimated that BGEA "is probably realizing only one fourth or one fifth of its potential income." Plowman was not calling for a shift in tactics: "What I'm saying is that respectability and the impression of respectability comes at a high price to the Graham organization."

In addition to paying its own formidable bills, BGEA regularly makes substantial contributions to numerous other ministries and charities, a practice extremely unusual among parachurch ministries. Graham's conviction that BGEA should spend all the money it receives, except for a prudent short-term reserve, made it difficult for his board to convince him he needed to establish a pension fund for himself and other members of the association. "We don't worry about anything like that," he told Carloss Morris during the mid-1950s. "It's not the way we operate. We use whatever we get to put our radio program on new stations." Morris countered with an example he could not ignore. "Old Mordecai Ham would come into Houston after he was way up in years," Morris recalled, "and he would try to conduct a revival and not draw enough people to pay his expenses. I'd call some friends and we'd bail him out of the Rice Hotel and give him enough money to get to the next town. I told Billy, 'No one takes care of old evangelists. If you don't need anything for yourself, you need to make plans for Cliff and Bev and the others.' Well, we finally got Roger Hull on the board. He was chairman of Mutual of New York—that's a big one—and he pushed it and we finally got a pension plan put in." Once convinced of the need, Graham not only accepted it graciously but insisted it be retroactive. Willis Haymaker, for example, was too old to qualify for benefits, but Graham saw to it that his old crusade mentor received what amounted to a full pension until the day he died.

In a similar spirit of "taking no thought for the morrow," Graham also resisted setting up a program of trusts, annuities, and life-estate agreements by means of which supporters could donate money, stocks, real estate, and other types of property to the association, gaining an immediate tax deduction and drawing regular interest income from the annuity until their death or some other designated point, at which time the property would belong fully to BGEA, to do with as it wished. "Billy didn't want to become an institution," George Wilson recalled, "but every day we lived we became more and more an institution, and people kept writing in, wanting to set up annuities. He didn't understand it and I didn't push it." Finally, under continued prodding from the board and patient explanation by Wilson, Graham agreed to an annuity program, but only with the stipulation that donors would be completely protected against loss. Most ministries and other nonprofit organizations using this popular fund-raising strategy feel free to put a hefty portion of the gift—40 percent to 50 percent or, in some cases, substantially more—-directly into working funds in the actuarially reasonable expectation that the remainder will provide enough to cover the promised interest payments. In an unusually conservative policy, Graham and Wilson both insisted that none of the principal be touched as long as the donor was alive, so that if, for whatever reason, the ministry went bankrupt, no donor would be hurt financially. "We don't need it and we don't want to touch it," Wilson explained. "There's been too much religious skulduggery at that point."

To cultivate possible donors to this program, BGEA representatives call on people who make sizable donations to the ministry or who specifically express interest in some kind of annuity program. On a typical first visit, the field reps offer to take the prospect to dinner, always letting them pick the place, "so they won't think we're being too cheap or too expensive," and if asked, explain how the annuity program works. They are instructed not to ask for money and are forbidden to accept any gifts themselves. They are also admonished not to use their contacts to set up their own organizations. But as one admitted, "It happens—as Billy Graham started by using his YFC contacts."

In 1977 approximately $147,000 worth of annuities were sold to a handful of supporters in Minnesota, where the association had not yet met all the requirements of an amended registration procedure and were not properly licensed to offer such investment instruments. The sticking point was BGEA's reluctance to provide extensive financial information about its operations. When pressed by reporters, Graham claimed the Minnesota Securities Commission's letter asking for fuller data had been lost and that as soon as he had learned the association was not in compliance, he had directed George Wilson to furnish whatever information was needed. Wilson also described BGEA's failure to provide the information as an "oversight caused by a clerical error." That defense had flaws. The commission agreed that a letter had been lost, but the loss had occurred two years earlier. For the past nine months, a commission spokesman said, he had been negotiating with BGEA attorneys over whether the annuities were a security and needed to be registered, whether BGEA had to file a report at all, and if it did, how much information it must provide. "I would hardly call nine months of negotiations an 'oversight,'" the agent tersely observed. While covering the story, reporters learned that the Better Business Bureau (BBB) had been trying unsuccessfully for five years to get Wilson to provide a copy of BGEA's annual audit; because he had refused, the bureau would not put BGEA on its list of trustworthy charities. Such pressures quickly moved the association to meet the Securities Commission requests, and the annuity sales were approved as expected. The BBB would probably have been left hanging, however, had it not been for a nearly simultaneous revelation that threatened for a while to leave a sizable stain on Graham's reputation for fiscal rectitude.

During the spring of 1977, the *Charlotte Observer* published a four-part series on Graham and BGEA by investigative reporters Mary Bishop and Robert Hodierne. After a year of scrutinizing the ministry's operations and receiving what they believed had been a full disclosure of all its facets, Bishop and Hodierne gave Graham and his organization a clean bill of health. The ministry, they said, was financially upright and refreshingly free of scandal. In their report they quoted Graham as saying the association spent nearly everything it raised each year and was seldom more than a million or so long or short. He also volunteered that he thought it would be wrong for BGEA to own stock, since ownership could be construed as an endorsement of a corporation. Just a few weeks later, however, the *Observer* broke a story that delighted doubters and caused millions of true believers to wonder if even Billy Graham had succumbed to the lure of lucre. The paper revealed the existence of the World Evangelism and Christian Education Fund (WECEF), incorporated in Dallas and worth $22.9 million. Most of the holdings of the seven-year-old fund, which the paper said had been "carefully shielded from public view," were in blue-chip stocks and bonds, but assets also included $3.9 million worth of prime undeveloped land in the Blue Ridge Mountains of North Carolina, purchased by Dallas attorney Jerry John Crawford in 1973 and held in his name until 1975. Though he used WECEF money, the *Observer* reported, Crawford did not mention Graham or any of his organizations while making the purchase. Further, when owners of land next to the tract asked if Graham or any of his people owned the land, they had been told no as recently as the spring of 1977. That WECEF was a Graham organization was beyond question. Almost all of its funds had been funneled into it from BGEA. Nine of its eleven board members were also directors of BGEA; the other two were Ruth Graham and her brother, Clayton Bell.

The explicit and implied charges in the article stung Graham, and in contrast to his standard policy of turning the other cheek to his critics, he characterized the *Observer* article as "grossly misleading" and used an *Hour of Decision* broadcast to offer a detailed statement, which was then released to the press and sent to his supporters. WECEF, he explained, had been established for three purposes: to provide support for such student-oriented programs as Campus Crusade, the Fellowship of Christian Athletes, and Young Life; to establish an evangelism institute on the campus of Wheaton College; and to develop a layman's training center in Asheville. The fund's extraordinarily low profile, he said, had been seen as desirable to avoid giving the impression that the ministry was so rich that it did not need small contributions and also to avoid a flood of requests from needy projects. In a more scriptural but less persuasive defense, he quoted Matthew 6:3–4:

"But when thou doest alms, let not thy left hand know what thy right hand doeth: That thine alms may be in secret: and thy Father which seeth in secret himself shall reward thee openly." As for his previous statements about holding stock, well, this was different, since WECEF did not bear his name.

Neither the legality of the fund nor the way its monies were spent was ever questioned. It was fully registered as a nonprofit corporation in Texas, it filed yearly 990 forms with the IRS, it was overseen by unpaid board members and had virtually no overhead expenses, and the money was being disbursed exactly as Graham said. Between 1971 and 1975, for example, WECEF had donated more than $1 million to the Billy Graham Center at Wheaton, a center for the study of evangelism and the repository of Graham's extensive archives; $260,000 to Montreat-Anderson College; $120,000 to Gordon-Conwell Seminary; $72,000 to the Fellowship of Christian Athletes; and smaller amounts to more than a dozen other Evangelical groups. (It also channeled $240,000 into the coffers of *Christianity Today*, a detail that magazine omitted in a listing of major recipients of WECEF funds. When asked why he had not included *CT*, editor Harold Lindsell said he "saw no need to do so.") Despite the legitimacy of the fund and its beneficiaries, Bishop and Hodierne understandably felt they had been deceived. When Graham and his associates sketched the ministry's various financial components, the reporters asked if that covered everything and were assured that it did. Now, that seemed plainly not to be true. The claim that they had not even thought about WECEF, since it was a legally separate entity, persuaded no one. The claim that the fund was not a secret, since 990 forms are available to any wishing to see them, was equally unconvincing, since even the most diligent sleuths are unlikely to ask for information about an organization they do not know exists.

Feeling burned, Hodierne took a closer look at the real estate owned by the fund, and for awhile it appeared he had uncovered the real dirt. Not only had Jerry John Crawford purchased land without revealing his use of WECEF money, but it seemed possible that several of Graham's relatives and associates in the ministry might have benefited financially from the transactions. Hodierne's investigation centered on a payment of $2.75 million for Porter's Cove, a 1,050-acre piece of stunning mountain property on the edge of Asheville where Graham planned to build the proposed training center.

The owners of the property received $2.1 million; the remaining $650,000 went to the North Carolina firm of Pharr Yarns, which had purchased an option to buy the property for $2.1 million just three months earlier. The option had cost Pharr $25,000. Real estate experts told Hodierne that no one would assess the property as worth more than $2 million, that the highest offer prior to Pharr's had been $1.5 million, and that it was simply unheard of for a $25,000 option to produce a $625,000 profit in so short a time. The plot got even thicker when William Pharr revealed that he had shared the profit with McLain Hall, a Greenville, South Carolina, real estate broker. Hall and Melvin Graham, who speculates in land, were involved in several land deals at this time, some of which involved not only Pharr Yarns but Morrow Graham, Catherine Graham McElroy, and Leighton Ford as well. Further, Grady Wilson and Cliff Barrows had also made real estate investments with Hall. Because William Pharr indicated that he and Hall had shared $465,000 of the profit for the option but would not account for the remaining $160,000, it seemed possible that Melvin, and perhaps some of his relatives and close friends, might have pocketed some of that money. Since Melvin was a member of the WECEF board, such action would be not only unethical but illegal. Asked about that possibility, an IRS official replied, "If these are the facts, then they have a problem with us."

Neither Hodierne nor the IRS nor anyone else was able to establish that Pharr or Hall knew the foundation was looking for property when they bought the option. Melvin Graham emphatically denied that he or any relative or board member or ministry employee received any profit whatsoever on the transaction, and no evidence to the contrary ever surfaced. Billy Graham declined to say whether he was aware of prior ties between his relatives and the owners of the option, but T. W. Wilson said he felt sure Billy knew nothing about these dealings. When pressed as to why the foundation had paid such an inflated price for both the property and the option, without so much as getting an appraisal or haggling over the premium, WECEF and BGEA board member Bill Mead, CEO of Campbell-Taggart Industries, said, "We didn't consider it necessary. If [a piece of land] fits the purpose and you can make [the deal], you do it.... That's the one we felt we had to have to accomplish our purpose, so we bought it at the best price we could." Melvin Graham snorted, "You pay what a man's asking... or you don't get the property. If you've got any common sense, you know that." Those with more than rudimentary common sense, of course, felt that anyone who paid the initial asking price on such a piece of property had not had much experience with real estate, a description that did not fit Melvin Graham.

It was not a happy time for the Graham organization. Even the most charitable reading of the evidence made it appear that BGEA had not been completely straightforward with either the press or their supporters, and that key leaders in the association had exercised poor business judgment and displayed uncalled-for generosity in allowing some of their friends to make an unreasonable profit on the deal. Letters and calls to the *Observer* and to BGEA, even from people sympathetic to the ministry, urged Graham to come clean and clear the air, admitting mistakes if there were any, and then get on with his ministry. Others, of course, condemned the newspaper for attacking a trustworthy man of God. Ironically, some letters defended both Graham and another homegrown ministry to which the paper was beginning to give a hard time: Jim Bakker's PTL Ministries.

Though Graham acknowledged the fund had not been widely publicized, he denied it had been a complete secret. Its creation in 1970 had been announced at a news conference in Minneapolis, and the Religious News Service, whose subscribers include the *New York Times*, the *Washington Post*, *Time*, *Newsweek*, and CBS, had carried stories about it during the first year or two of its existence. More pointedly, Graham noted that he had talked about it freely in 1972 with Peter Geiger, a respected religion reporter with the *Akron Beacon Journal*, a newspaper in the Knight-Ridder chain, which also owned the *Observer*. The *Observer's* response to that particular bit of intelligence seems to have been less than exemplary. According to Geiger, whose memory of the incident remained fresh in 1989, he had gone to North Carolina in 1972 to gather information for an extended piece about Graham prior to an upcoming crusade in Cleveland. While visiting his boyhood home, by then surrounded by a new industrial park, Graham volunteered that when his family sold the land, he had put his share of the money into a foundation headquartered in Dallas and headed by one of his board members. Monies from this fund, which had grown to $2.5 million at the time, would be used to further world evangelism. Geiger mentioned the fund in his story but thought little more about it until he read the 1977 *Observer* series and listened to Graham's defense on the *Hour of Decision*.

As a kind of memento of the visit, Geiger had kept the tapes of the interview. On checking them, he confirmed his memory that Graham had indeed talked freely about the fund and that he had written about the fund in his story. He immediately sent a copy of his story and a transcript of the interview to David Lawrence, editor of the *Observer*. Lawrence did not respond, but Geiger's own editor advised him not to make a fuss about the matter. A few days later, Graham called to ask Geiger if he remembered their conversation. Not sure just what force his editor's cautionary statement carried, Geiger answered carefully: "Mr. Graham, if you had told me about the fund, I would have had it in a tape recording and would have written about it. If that were true, I would have sent it to the *Observer*. Do you hear me?" Graham exulted, "I hear you loud and clear. Thanks a lot!" Several weeks later, Charlotte television executive and longtime Graham friend Charles Crutchfield called to ask Geiger if he had indeed sent a transcript and a clipping to David Lawrence. Geiger gave Crutchfield the same answer. Shortly afterward, Geiger's editor asked him, "What have you done?" Geiger explained, "I tried to set the story straight." He then learned that Lawrence had said he was going to Montreat to check with Graham. Geiger asked how long that would take and was told it was none of his business. About six weeks later, Graham called Geiger to say, "I'm hurting. What can you do for me?" Lawrence had indeed visited with him, but had written nothing as yet. "Shall I call in [AP religion writer] George Cornell?" the evangelist asked. Geiger told him that was a brilliant idea. By contract, the Associated Press was free to use everything he published, and he would be happy to send Cornell the tape and his article. Shortly afterward, Cornell called, got the information he needed, and wrote a column explaining Graham's side of the story and chiding the *Observer* for its own failure to come clean. The story went out on the wire on Wednesday, for Saturday publication. On Friday Lawrence called the managing editor of the AP, demanding it be withdrawn. The editor refused. "The *Beacon Journal* never carried the column," Geiger said. "I don't think the *Observer* did."

The following week, Graham called again. "You're in trouble, aren't you?" he asked. Geiger admitted he was. He had been called into his editor's office and told, "We will hear no more of this. You have done your good deed. Now keep your mouth shut." Graham told him not to worry—"I'll hire you." Geiger pointed out that no matter what happened, he could never come to work for BGEA without destroying his own credibility. Graham conceded that point but assured him, "I know ten editors who would hire you tomorrow."

In a rare occurrence, BGEA and its affiliate organizations ran a deficit of $3.2 million in 1977, and *CT* speculated that the hubbub over the WECEF may have contributed to a drop in contributions, but most of the deficit was due to a $2.7 million rise in expenditures. The association was back in the black the following year, and the ministry seemed to suffer no lasting negative effects. More significant, BGEA began making an audited financial statement available to anyone who requested it, for whatever reason. The memory of that incident still rankled people within the Graham organization ten years later, but Billy himself has long since made peace with his antagonists. "David Lawrence and I became friends, eventually," he said. "When he got a big award in Detroit from the National Conference of Christians and Jews, they wanted me to be their speaker. He did, too. I went up there and gave the address, praising him. I didn't want to hold a grudge against him. There was no way we could quite explain it to their satisfaction, but it didn't cause us too much trouble. I spoke to the National Press Club around that time also, and Bob Hodierne was in the audience. They asked me some questions about the incident and I said, 'Bob Hodierne has taught us some good lessons. We have learned some things from him.'"

Ruth Graham, cleaning up after lunch while her husband recounted this episode, interjected sarcastically, "That was very gracious of you."

"No, it wasn't gracious," Billy gently responded. "It was the truth."

Ruth snapped back: "He came up here and we told him everything, right out there on the porch, and he went back and what he wrote didn't have one word of fact in it."

"Well, darling, I wouldn't say 'not one word.' There were a few misstatements, but it had a lot of truth in it."

"My husband is more gracious than I am," she said, banging pots as she spoke.

"We didn't mention the fund," Graham continued, "because it was a separate corporation. And they didn't ask about it. That was a little bit on the fence line, I think. We should have said, 'We've got another fund down in Texas that we are going to do thus and such with.' We told the government about it, but we didn't think the newspapers necessarily had a legitimate right to know about everything. I've changed my mind on that. I think they do. Because I think we should be publicly accountable for everything."

Having proved to himself anew the value of setting up external mechanisms to ensure one's virtue, Graham became a zealous advocate of full disclosure by parachurch organizations. In 1979 he played a key role in founding the Evangelical Council for Financial Accountability (ECFA), and George Wilson served as the first chairman of its board. The organization's stated purpose is "to enunciate, maintain and manifest a code of financial accountability and reporting which is consistent with enlightened and responsible Christian faith and practice." Membership in ECFA is voluntary, and almost none of the well-known television preachers opted to join, but Graham soon began to call on his colleagues to come aboard and to warn Christians against being too trusting. "It is common for most religious leaders to be very secretive about the finances of their organization," he wrote. "Unfortunately, when legitimate Christian organizations and churches refuse to be completely open about finances, they are conditioning people to accept unquestioningly the contention of the cult leader that he is not accountable to anyone for his financial dealings. If you give to any Christian charity (including the Billy Graham Evangelistic Association) and you don't insist on an understandable financial accounting of your gift, you are in danger of falling prey to [dishonesty]."

During the closing years of the 1970s, Graham was nudged out of his traditional spot as the nation's most newsworthy Christian leader by Jerry Falwell, who was soon joined by Pat Robertson, James Robison, and a gaggle of other religious broadcasters and parachurch leaders who were forming what came to be called the Christian New Right. Graham was not tempted to throw in with the new movement. Instead, he began to try on the role of elder statesman. In *Christianity Today's* first issue of 1980, he drew on personal experience to warn his newly politicized brethren to "be wary of exercising political influence" lest they lose their spiritual impact. A few days later, in a

AP/Wide World Photos

Graham addresses members of a Baptist youth camp assembled for the closing service, Hungary, 1977. Though not advertised publicly, the meeting was attended by more than five thousand Hungarians and other Eastern Europeans. At Graham's right is his interpreter, Dr. Alexander Haraszti.

Religious News Service Photo

Graham receives the prestigious Templeton Prize from Prince Philip, 1982.

The Reverend Robert Runcie, archbishop of Canterbury, serves coffee to Graham at Lambeth Palace, 1989.

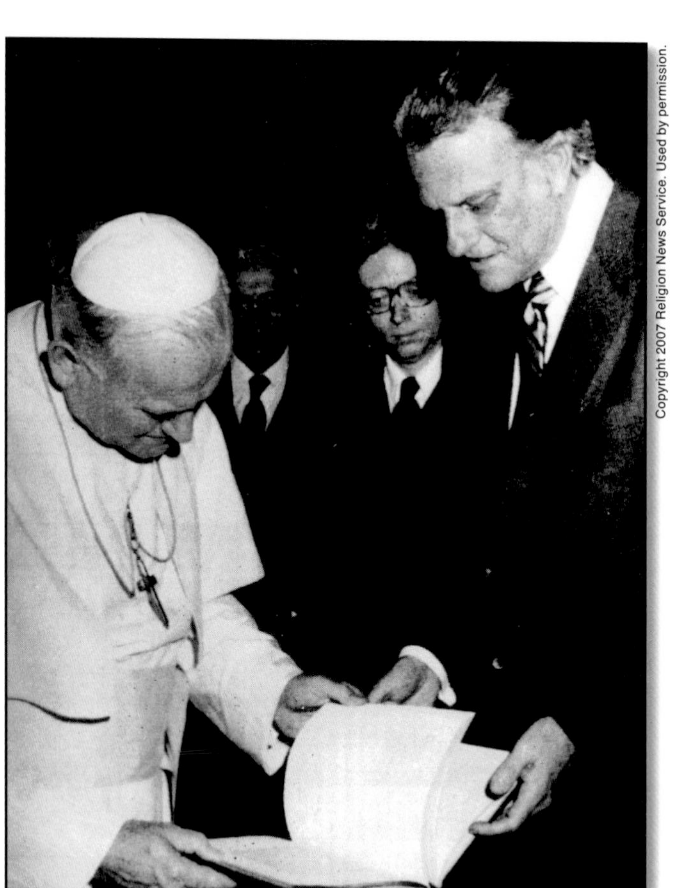

His Holiness John Paul II welcomes Graham, sometimes called the Protestant Pope, to the Vatican, 1981.

Graham shares a light moment with
President and Mrs. Reagan, 1981.

Religious News Service Photo

The original Billy Graham evangelistic team in a 1975 photo. *Front row:* Tedd Smith, Graham, Grady Wilson. *Back row:* Cliff Barrows, George Beverly Shea.

AP/Wide World Photos

Franklin and Billy Graham on the Great Wall of China during a seventeen-day tour, 1988.

Religious News Service Photo

Graham sings a song with a group of Chinese schoolchildren encountered during his visit to the Great Wall, 1988.

Billy Graham gives a Paris audience his familiar message: "La Bible dit ..."

© Bettmann/CORBIS

Forty years into his public ministry, Graham tells a closing-day crowd at his 1986 Greater Washington Crusade that "the Bible [still] says . . . !"

Religious News Service Photo

Billy gets his star on Hollywood Boulevard, making him the one thousandth celebrity to be so honored, 1990.

President Ronald Reagan presents Billy Graham with the Presidential Medal of Freedom, 1983.

The Graham family celebrates Ruth and Billy's 50th wedding anniversary, 1993.

Billy Graham, evangelist.

press conference prior to a preaching mission at Oxford University, he noted that, "in my earlier days and [crusades], I tended to identify the Kingdom of the God with the American way of life. I don't think like that now." Though he still favored free-enterprise capitalism, he believed Christians could live under various economic systems. A few days later, in a dialogue at Cambridge with the archbishop of Canterbury, he sounded a similar note, observing that he no longer associated a Christian understanding of society with American nationalism. These were not just throwaway lines designed to please a British audience. In various press conferences and interviews in the United States, he warned against "the mingling of spiritual and political goals," observing, in notable contrast to his earlier willingness to offer prescriptions for national policy, that "we as clergy know so very little to speak out with such authority on the Panama Canal or superiority of armaments. I do not intend to use what little influence I may have on [such] secular, non-moral, non-religious issues."

As he had in 1976, Graham kept a low profile during the 1980 election, but his sympathies lay with Ronald Reagan, whom he had known since 1953. "I met him through his mother-in-law," he recalled. "I was playing golf with Henry Luce at the Biltmore Country Club in Phoenix, and Mrs. Davis came out on the course. She said, 'I want you to meet my new son-in-law. You two have many things in common.'" And indeed they did. Both reached the pinnacle of their professions by dint of a gift for articulating, in terms easily grasped by masses of people, a large but essentially simple vision. Neither demonstrated any notable talent for critical analysis or practical detail. They understood intuitively how to inspire and how to lead, and how to assemble teams to implement their visions. They trusted fully in a small number of firmly held principles, and as long their friends and associates pledged allegiance to those principles, they assumed they had no reason to be wary of anything else those friends or associates might believe or do. And when that assumption proved faulty and expectations went awry, they possessed a remarkable ability to dismiss the troublesome evidence as a blip, a momentary aberration—certainly not a fundamental weakness in their own vision or judgment. The friendship flourished, and Billy and Ruth often visited the Reagans when they were in California. Graham recalled that on one occasion, while Reagan was governor, "I spoke to a group of Democratic leaders, and they had a big battle as to whether to invite him, because they knew I was a big friend of his." Reagan did not attend the speech but invited Graham to visit with him and his cabinet in his office, which was in the same building. As soon as they sat down, Reagan said, "Billy, tell us what the Bible teaches about things that are happening today, and where you think we stand in the prophetic scriptures." Graham observed, "I knew he had an interest in prophecy, but I don't know where it came from. I understand his mother was interested in all that."

Despite this background, Graham declined to jump on board Reagan's campaign train, but he did manage to give it a well-publicized friendly wave. Fortuitously for the candidate, Graham was holding a crusade in Indianapolis at the time of the Indiana primary, and he gave Reagan a nice boost by joining him for breakfast, during which he congratulated him warmly on his strong showing in the Texas primary the day before. Reagan was duly appreciative, and all three major television networks suggested that the meeting had given him a remarkably well-timed boost. Graham professed to see it as no more than a courtesy visit, noting that "I refused to endorse him. He never asked me, but one of his aides did. I never had Nixon or any of his aides ask [for an endorsement]. Nixon told me to stay out of politics. Always. Of course, everybody knew pretty well how I stood with Nixon."

After Reagan's election, Graham enjoyed many other breakfasts with him—at the White House. By his reckoning, he spent more nights in the presidential quarters during Reagan's time in office than during either Johnson's or Nixon's presidency, though little was made of most of the visits. After the first of these overnight stays, which included a five-hour conversation, he characterized Reagan as "laughing, kidding, a lot of fun, yet a brilliant man" who "thinks positively and is optimistic about the country." The country, Graham volunteered, was in capable hands: "Ronald Reagan runs it but, like Ike, he lets others handle the details, which gives him time to think of bigger things." The friendship was sufficiently close that when the President was shot on March 30, 1981, the White House sent out an emergency call for Graham, and the evangelist came immediately to the capital to comfort and pray with Mrs. Reagan. He also contacted the father of John Hinckley, the President's assailant, and prayed with him over the telephone.

Graham once noted that Reagan liked to talk about "the old days in Hollywood" more than about politics and indicated that he probably had less influence over him than over some past Presidents. Columnists Rowland Evans and Robert Novak reported that in the fall of 1981 Graham successfully lobbied several key senators on behalf of the President's plan to sell AWAC airplanes to Saudi Arabia, a measure actively opposed by Jerry Falwell and his avidly pro-Israel troops in the Moral Majority. Graham minimized his role, but did not deny that at the President's request he had indicated to several legislators that putting AWACs in Saudi hands posed no military threat to Israel. Still, it appears that his relationship with Reagan had far less political implications than those with Eisenhower, Johnson, and Nixon. This is not to say that Billy Graham had lost interest in affecting the secular order, particularly as it impinged on the sacred realm. Quite to the contrary, he was at that moment, and had been for several years, involved in a slow, quiet, occasionally awkward but nonetheless remarkable campaign aimed at nothing less than inducing the leadership of the Soviet Union and its Eastern bloc satellites to grant full religious freedom to the citizens of their respective nations.

29

A Crack in the Curtain

Few, if any, developments in Billy Graham's ministry were more surprising or controversial than his success in penetrating the iron curtain. It was not surprising that he would want to preach in Communist-dominated lands. He wanted to preach everywhere, and he had at least a modicum of confidence that, aided by the Holy Spirit, his preaching could achieve wondrous results in even the most unpromising of environments. It was, however, a notable turn of events when first one and then another and another Warsaw Pact country not only allowed him to visit, but progressively extended privileges to him that no other churchman, including the most prominent and politically docile native leaders, had ever received. Graham had, after all, been described in America as "Communism's Public Enemy Number One" and touted as an effective force for warning neutral and left-leaning nations against the perils of collaborating with the Russians. The Communist press had also depicted him as a threat, calling him a charlatan and a warmonger and claiming he was an active and not-so-covert agent of American foreign policy. But as early as the mid-1950s, Graham began to express interest in preaching behind the iron curtain, as long as no restrictions were placed on what he could say. During his tourist trip in 1959, he knelt in Red Square and prayed that he might one day preach the gospel on that very site and also at Moscow's great public stadium. The Polish government's cancellation of its 1966 invitation disappointed him, and his brief trip to Yugoslavia did not have the same cachet, since that country had cut its ties with Moscow and was regarded as a Communist renegade. Graham was stymied. He wanted to add Eastern Europe and the Soviet Union to his life list of preaching venues, but he could not just barge in and set up a tent or hire a hall. Lyndon Johnson had approved of the proposed visit to Poland but made no effort to push it, and neither the Nixon nor Ford administrations volunteered to intercede on his behalf with any Communist government. It seemed unlikely that the tiny Evangelical minorities in any of the Soviet bloc countries would have sufficient influence to persuade their governments to permit an American evangelist to propagate a message explicitly challenging the official atheism of the Communist system. In short, it appeared that a ministry behind the iron curtain, if it ever came at all, might have to wait for a political upheaval of the magnitude of what eventually occurred in 1989. And then came Alexander Haraszti.

In a milieu peopled mainly with good old southern boys, sobersided midwestern Evangelicals, a phalanx of brisk young sales-executive types, and a sprinkling of witty British clergymen, Alexander Haraszti, M.D., Ph.D., stands out. Rumpled and gruff-looking in a setting where neatness and smiling are the rule, cannily calculating in the midst of men whose stock-in-trade is disingenuousness, authentically well educated (a master's degree in Latin and Hungarian literature, a seminary degree, a doctorate in linguistics, and a medical degree with specialties in gynecology and general surgery) in an environment abounding in honorary doctorates conferred by friends, and equipped with apparently inexhaustible energy, monomaniacal tenacity, and virtually total recall, he has left an indelible mark on a ministry that would scarcely acknowledge he existed for the first five years he labored on its behalf.

Born and reared a Baptist in Hungary and married to the daughter of a Baptist minister, Haraszti supported himself as a pastor and theological professor from 1944 to 1956 while he and his wife completed medical degrees. In the mid-1950s, he began to learn of Billy Graham's ministry from typewritten pages passed from hand to hand in Hungarian Baptist circles. In 1955 he obtained an English copy of *Peace with God* and, with the help of a German edition, translated Graham's best-seller into Hungarian. Since he saw little chance of obtaining government permission to publish the book through regular channels, he distributed mimeographed copies to his students at the Baptist theological seminary in Budapest on the pretense that its chapters were examples of sermons and suitable for homiletic instruction. Soon afterward, this pirated edition of *Peace with God*, which he subtitled *Lessons in Homiletics for Students of Theology*, made its way into the Lutheran, Reformed, and Roman Catholic seminaries in Hungary.

Haraszti's talent for accomplishing his goals without running afoul of the authorities had already shown itself a few years earlier. The Communist government had long and correctly viewed the Catholic Church as a formidable opponent, but Catholics were not the only perceived enemy. Because the Ministry of the Interior, which oversaw all religious affairs, knew the United States was a stronghold of Baptist religion, it regarded the Baptist Church in Hungary as little more than a front for an American-inspired, antigovernment political association. By chance, during a preaching tour that took him through the little village of Korosszakall in eastern Hungary, Haraszti met an elderly Baptist couple who told him that their son, now the minister of the interior, had grown up in the Baptist church in the village. A few months later, at the request of his fellow churchmen, Haraszti met with the minister in an effort to persuade him that Baptists were politically harmless and should not be persecuted. When the bureaucrat raised the familiar charge that "Baptists are American agents," Haraszti was ready. First, with great politeness, he asked if the minister had grown up in Korosszakall and if his parents still lived there. When the minister acknowledged this to be the case, Haraszti told of having met them and of knowing he had attended the Baptist church before moving to the capital. "I cannot imagine," Haraszti said, "that you would ever go to a place that has any American contacts. You would not go to people who are American agents or who have in any way some secret contacts with American agencies." His apparent gruffness dissolving into gleeful delight at the memory, Haraszti recalled that "the man became red up to the top of his head. He was most embarrassed—most embarrassed—and the entire collection of data [about Baptists] was stopped immediately. If they continued presenting Baptists as American agents, what happens to His Excellency?"

From that point forward, the Ministry of the Interior began to give Baptists and other Evangelicals greater license to carry out normal church activities. Though it granted these rights rather grudgingly, Haraszti noted that "this was the price they had to pay for peaceful people who otherwise were not dangerous, who were reliable, and actually, who were very good workers. In the government's view, they were a little odd. They believed in their Jesus Christ. They liked to read the Bible and sing their hymns and so on—a little strange, but otherwise good people." Gradually, the government softened its resistance to all religion as part of a larger effort by János Kádár's Communist regime to polish its image and gain most-favored-nation trade status with the United States. Regular church meetings and some special events could be held, though not advertised, as long as the Ministry of the Interior was informed about them. Ministers could preach and teach Christian doctrines, but could not preach against the government. The churches, in turn, were expected to encourage workers to work hard and refrain from stealing from their factories, and to support the government's position on such key issues as peace. The established religious bodies—Catholic, Lutheran, Reformed, and Jewish—received financial support from the state in return for their acknowledgment of the state's authority in world matters and their pledge of political allegiance to it. Free churches neither sought nor received such assistance, but they did receive equal standing at the Ministry of the Interior, and they were protected from harassment at the hands of the numerically dominant Catholic Church so that in many ways their situation was better than it had been prior to the Communist takeover.

In 1956, shortly after the beginning of the Hungarian uprising, the Harasztis emigrated to America with the intention of becoming medical missionaries to Africa for the Southern Baptist Convention (it was this lifelong ambition, he insists, not political dissent, that led them to leave their homeland). However, by the time they completed their training and received citizenship status, both were over forty and too old to be accepted as new missionaries. Learning of the situation, Albert Schweitzer sent Haraszti a seven-page letter inviting the family to join him at his hospital at Lambarene. Haraszti was flattered, but wrote back to ask the famed humanitarian, "Do you do a soul-winning service?" When he received no answer, he resigned himself to working with Hungarian Baptists in America and to opening channels to facilitate Evangelical preaching in his homeland. After he and his wife established their medical practice in Atlanta, they met several members of Billy Graham's team who had begun to use that city as the central staging base for both domestic and foreign crusades, but he made no effort to contact Graham himself, not even to tell him of his use of *Peace with God*. (He had reason to lie low on that score. Shortly after coming to America, he had notified Doubleday of the warm reception his translation received in Hungary, naively believing Graham's publisher would be pleased. Doubleday was not amused and instructed him sternly in the ways of American publishing.) He did not meet Graham until sixteen years after he arrived in the United States.

In 1972, Haraszti, now an American citizen, used contacts with fellow Atlantans Walter Smyth and BGEA public relations director Don Bailey to arrange a meeting between Graham and two prominent Hungarian Evangelical leaders, Dr. János Laczkovszki, president of an organization of 20,000 Baptists in Hungary, and Seventh-day Adventist clergyman Sandor Palotay, president of Hungary's Council of Free Churches, an association representing eight Evangelical denominations. Both men were well known to Haraszti from earlier days. Both were shrewdly skilled at dealing with Hungarian authorities. And largely because of this skill, both were widely regarded as Communist agents by American Baptists who knew anything about them.

In the midst of a crusade in Cleveland, Graham received Haraszti and his two friends warmly, and Palotay invited the evangelist to come to Hungary under the auspices of the Council of Free Churches. Graham announced and accepted the invitation from the platform that same evening but found himself in a bind when Palotay later admitted he had no authority to issue the invitation without government approval and when critics, including some of the evangelist's most trusted confidants, warned against dealing with suspected Communist agents. When Smyth informed Haraszti that a news release confirming the meeting and the invitation might be canceled to avoid embarrassment and criticism, Haraszti leveled with him. Aware that Palotay's considerable ego had been bruised by his perception that Graham and Smyth doubted he could make good on his invitation, Haraszti said, "All right.

Since he is an agent, we do not accept an invitation from him. Therefore, we shall not go to Hungary. Period. Because we cannot get an invitation from anybody else." The only plausible strategy for a Graham visit, he insisted, was to go "above ground," with the full knowledge and approval of the Communist government. If they rejected the assistance of Laczkovszki and Palotay, the only possible source of an invitation would be "some not-respected, not-acknowledged, little bitty underground Baptist leader, who will be happy to give us an invitation," but whose lack of clout would result in Graham's having to dig an underground tunnel, emerge secretly in some forest, "and there [he] will preach to the birds." Even to get a visa, he pointed out, it would be necessary to contact the Hungarian ambassador to the United States. The ambassador would contact his government, the government would contact the churches, and the churches he contacted would be those cooperating with the government. If the leaders of those churches were not involved, Haraszti said, "we will continue where we have been so far: nowhere." The two Hungarians, he insisted, were not Communists, but pragmatists. When he had preached and taught in Hungary, he had done so with government approval. That did not make him a Communist agent. Laczkovszki and Palotay, he assured Smyth, were no more Communist than he.

Somewhat calmed by this discussion and by additional material Haraszti produced in Palotay's defense, Smyth authorized the physician to travel to Hungary to finalize the plans. Haraszti smiled at such naïveté. "They thought it was just like in India or Japan or Australia. If it is agreed upon between church leaders and Dr. Graham, then the rest is just a matter of letter writing. Little did they know." In Hungary he met not only with leaders of the Council of Free Churches but with the presiding bishops of both the Lutheran and Reformed churches—Graham had expressed a strong hope that all Protestant groups would support a visit—and, most importantly, with Imre Miklos, the secretary of the Ministry for Church Affairs and the government official who would give final approval to any visit by the evangelist.

Miklos made it clear the Hungarian state had deep misgivings about Graham's coming, alleging that he was "a burning anti-Communist"; that his evangelistic techniques were alien to Hungary; that he did not understand Eastern European political, religious, or social life; and that he was a war monger. Haraszti took exception only to the last of these charges. On a subsequent visit with the secretary, he produced photographs and other documentation of Graham's visits to the troops in Korea and Vietnam. He pointed out that while the evangelist had indeed been critical of communism, he urged American soldiers not to exploit or behave arrogantly toward native people in the lands where they were fighting, and he had prayed not only for America and the nations they were defending but for North Korea and North Vietnam as well. "Your excellency," he said to Miklos, "if this is warmongering, please teach me how to do *peace* mongering." Miklos made no promises, but he smiled broadly and told Haraszti, "I see Dr. Graham in a different light now than I did before. I am very grateful to you for bringing this information." Then he added, "We, as the State, could order the churches to accept [Dr. Graham], and smile at his coming, and be happy. We could order it, but we don't want to. We have to discuss this matter with the churches. And we must get their consent. If the leading churches agree, and if the Hungarian government agrees, and if the governments of other Socialist countries agree—there are no independent actions—then we can speak about Dr. Graham's coming."

For the next five years, Haraszti dedicated himself to gaining an official invitation for Graham to visit Hungary. Never in that time did he meet with the evangelist again, and BGEA paid for none of his numerous trips to Hungary or for telephone bills that ran into the thousands of dollars, though it did supply him with whatever publications and other documentary materials he needed. "If I came to Dr. Smyth and said, 'Would you agree that I go to Hungary and speak with Palotay?' he said, 'No objection.' But he would never mention [paying for the trip]." Haraszti attributes this stance not to stinginess on the part of BGEA but to the simple fact that no one in the Graham organization thought he could produce an invitation. "They knew what I was doing. If I succeed, OK. If not, it's just another attempt that backfired. Haraszti's an independent agent. If he has this obsession that he wants to take Billy Graham to Hungary, [let him try,] but who can believe that it is ever possible?" Haraszti insisted he does not resent having to spend his own money, but the memory of dealing with the unspoken skepticism was obviously still fresh and, viewed from a position of success, rather delicious.

Working closely with Palotay, whom he characterized as a "daredevil" with a superior talent for public relations and governmental relations, Haraszti fed Miklos with a stream of materials to use in his conversations with his counterparts in Moscow and in other Eastern bloc capitals. He stressed that Graham had long ago moderated his virulent anti-Communist rhetoric and convinced the minister that the 1967 trip to heretical Yugoslavia had been an innocent response to an unexpected opportunity, not a willful attempt to embarrass orthodox Communists. "This was very suspicious," Haraszti recalled. "It weighed heavily against Dr. Graham. He has not gone back to Yugoslavia since, and not because he has not been invited." More importantly, he was able to demonstrate, by chronicling the evangelist's past behavior in countries troubled by political tension, that a visit would create no public embarrassment or subsequent strain for the government.

Haraszti did not limit his lobbying efforts to Palotay and Miklos. In Hungary he continued to court the Lutheran and Reformed bishops, informing them of Graham's ecumenical approach and assuring them that a visit by the evangelist would, at worst, do their churches no harm. He also established contact with Hungarian Jews and managed to forge a friendship with Roman

Catholic bishop Joœef Czerháti. Aware that Haraszti was prominent in the American Hungarian community, Czerhati asked for his help in getting U.S. permission for Hungarian priests and nuns to serve in churches catering to people of Hungarian descent in the United States and Canada. Haraszti agreed, but on the condition that as bishop of Hungary's largest religious body, Czerháti drop the church's well-known opposition to Graham's proposed visit. "The bishop grabbed my hand," Haraszti recalled, "and said: 'I will welcome Dr. Graham in my chancery when he comes. I will also support his coming at the Ministry for Church Affairs.'" With obvious satisfaction, Haraszti said, "Bishop Czerháti kept his word." In addition, because of his work with the Hungarian-American community and his many trips to his homeland, Haraszti became well acquainted with the Hungarian ambassador and embassy personnel in Washington, where he pressed the case for Graham at every opportunity. And whenever his travels for the Southern Baptist Foreign Mission Board took him to countries with a Hungarian embassy, he made a point of visiting the ambassador and mentioning what a fine thing it would be for Billy Graham to visit Hungary.

In the course of these visits, Haraszti picked up two valuable pieces of information. Near the end of World War II, the Crown of St. Stephen, named for Hungary's patron saint and regarded as the nation's most precious symbolic treasure, was given to the U.S. Army to avoid confiscation by the Russians. After the Communist takeover, the United States declined to return it, on the grounds that the government was a Soviet puppet rather than a legitimate representative of the Hungarian people. Secondly, the Kádár regime still fervently sought most-favored-nation status for Hungary. In July 1977 Haraszti raised both of these issues with Walter Smyth, suggesting that a few words in the right places would be viewed favorably by the Hungarian government. Smyth bridled at the suggestion. "Alex," he said, "Billy is not going to get involved in politics!" Having monitored Graham's career for twenty years, Haraszti shot back, "Dr. Smyth, since when has he not been involved in politics?" Haraszti sensed an invitation was close at hand and pressed his case: "Billy wants to go. You want him to go. I want him to go. We cannot turn back. We must deliver something. We must look into this matter."

With approval from Smyth, Haraszti visited the Hungarian ambassador in Washington to learn exactly what Hungary wanted. Frenetic back-corridor negotiations then began in earnest. Late in July the physician arranged a brief meeting in Paris between Graham and Palotay, who gave the evangelist a written but still unofficial invitation, stipulating that he must not make it public until the official state-sanctioned invitation came through. The visit was tentatively scheduled for the first week of September, less than six weeks away, but Graham still had no tangible assurance the invitation was bona fide. A week later Smyth contacted Haraszti in Atlanta and implored him to go to Hungary immediately to obtain an official invitation. A trip Graham regarded as one of the most momentous of his entire ministry needed some planning and publicity. It simply would not do for him to show up in Budapest, preach to a handful of Baptists, and come home with no tales of triumph or pictures of victory over Satan. Scrubbing a full schedule of surgery, Haraszti made the trip, helped Palotay word an invitation that both Graham and the government could approve, got it signed, sped back to the United States, and delivered it in person to Montreat.

A man with a keen sense of deference and protocol, Haraszti was impressed that Graham had personally driven to the Ashveille airport to meet him but surprised to find the famous evangelist filled with trepidation about the whole Hungarian venture. He remembered that Graham "was shaky, trembling, worried." He desperately wanted to go, but just as desperately feared the adverse reaction that might descend upon him if he were seen to be a willing dupe of Communist manipulation. Content to let others talk with Haraszti for the previous five years, Graham now pressed the man who had become his unofficial spokesman to Eastern Europe. "Why would they invite me, Alex? What is behind it?"

Haraszti leveled with him. "I will say it straight, Dr. Graham. It is not for your big blue eyes. And they have not invited you because they want to hear the Gospel."

"Then why am I going?" Graham asked.

"To preach the gospel," Haraszti said.

"But you said they don't want to hear the gospel."

"They don't want to hear it, but they will. There is a purpose. You go to preach the gospel. They invite you because they would like to have the crown back and to get the 'most-favored-nation status.' "

"Then this is a swap? A quid pro quo?"

At that, the Hungarian physician-diplomat gave the southern evangelist a lesson in obliqueness. The Hungarians had demanded nothing, he said. "The invitation is in your hands. I have delivered it. They have already acted in faith in generously giving you something which no Communist government ever gave. This is an all-time first, and even if there is no continuation, you still have it." Then he held out a carrot Graham could not resist. It was true that other Western religious leaders had spoken at a church in Moscow or sung at a gathering in Poland, but no evangelist from East or West had ever toured a Communist country, speaking in crowded churches and addressing open-air meetings. He would be the first. Haraszti then produced a photocopy of his 1956 translation of *Peace with God*—the first time Graham had heard of that particular enterprise. "In this book," he told the amazed evangelist, "I described you as an evangelist to five continents. In my next preface, I will call you Billy Graham, 'Evangelist to the World.' In my opinion, this is the beginning of things to come: first, the approval of the Hungarian government; second, the approval of other Communist governments; third, the approval of the churches—the organized, established churches in Hungary, not just little bitty Baptist churches. They will spread what they have seen and heard and experienced. And so, after Hungary, there shall be another meeting."

"I would not accept if there were any conditions," Graham protested mildly.

"The Hungarian government would not invite you if you set any conditions," Haraszti countered. "This was in faith on both sides, because the Hungarian government knew that I was close enough to you that you would accept my advice, and you know that I am close enough to the Hungarian government that it accepts my advice. The government of Hungary did not ask me to do this, but I did tell them I would call these matters to your attention. And they were happy to hear it. They were very happy to hear it. Therefore, I take it upon myself to ask you to please use the services of your good office to see that Hungary gets the crown and the most-favored-nation status."

Graham sputtered, "But Alex . . ." But Alex could not be dissuaded. He knew from his contacts that President Carter already had both matters on his desk and could act on his own without legislation if he felt concessions to Hungary would not cause problems in America. He also knew that János Kádár was willing to take a softer line toward religion. For a year his government had been making public and well-received concessions to Catholics and had recently restored diplomatic contacts with the Vatican. Kádár was aware that Jimmy Carter was a Baptist and thought it plausible that a gesture of goodwill toward Graham might be looked upon with favor in the White House. He also knew that Carter was a zealous advocate of human rights and that Eastern bloc restriction of Jewish emigration was a key obstacle to improved relations between the two countries. Kádár faced a ticklish dilemma on this issue. If Hungary applied for most-favored-nation status, Washington would insist that it allow Jews to emigrate freely, a provision the Soviet Union did not observe. If Hungary openly agreed to this demand, it would offend the Soviet Union, something it did not wish to do. If, however, the United States were to offer the desired status without making an explicit demand, Hungary would voluntarily but without fanfare allow Jews to leave the country.

Now in too far to back out and at some level doubtless enjoying the reunion with power, Graham relayed this information to old friend John Sparkman, chair of the Senate Foreign Relations Committee, who wrote a letter to his counterpart in the Hungarian government, Deputy Premier Gyorgi Aczel. Graham also spoke with Jimmy Carter, who told him he was aware of his plans to visit Hungary and asked him to express his warm greetings to the government and all the people of Hungary, especially the Christians he would be visiting. When Haraszti informed the Hungarian government that

Graham had been fully briefed on all matters of concern, and that he had made some "high contacts" and would be coming "with certain things in his pocket," the government was pleased. As word spread that the Foreign Ministry, which far outranked the Ministry for Church Affairs, would welcome Graham warmly, the Lutheran and Reformed bishops, both of whom had been quite cool toward his coming, suddenly decided it would be marvelous if the evangelist would consent to preach in some of their churches as well as in the Evangelical churches that were his ostensible hosts. That, of course, pleased Billy Graham and Alexander Haraszti. It did not please Sandor Palotay and his colleagues in the Council of Free Churches.

Palotay had gotten state approval of the invitation by convincing Imre Miklos and other government officials that the meetings at which Graham would preach would be small and meaningless, heartening to Evangelical Christians but of no consequence to anyone else. Palotay's ego also entered into the picture. It might not be a glorious tour, but it would be *his* tour, and he was not anxious to have it taken from his hands. Billy Graham, on the other hand, had no intention of letting his first real foray behind the iron curtain fall flat. "He does not say, 'I don't go,'" Haraszti recalled; "but he asked me, 'Alex, if only two hundred people will be there, I just don't see how I can do it. What shall I tell people in America?'"

Working feverishly over an eight-day period in Montreat, Graham, Haraszti, and John Akers, former dean of Montreat-Anderson College, fashioned a several-ends-against-the-middle approach to the problem. Haraszti informed the Hungarian ambassador in Washington of the evangelist's concern over the modest agenda the Council of Free Churches had set for him. If at all possible, Graham wished to broaden the scope of the visit just a bit; specifically, to include preaching appointments at major Reformed and Catholic churches and a meeting with key leaders of the Jewish faith. Unless such additions could be made, Haraszti told the ambassador, "Dr. Graham will not come." Graham's concern, he said, was for Hungary. If Americans read or saw on television that he preached only to small crowds in tiny churches, they would believe that the government prohibited the people from attending. That would be bad propaganda, Haraszti pointed out—"just the opposite of what the government hopes to achieve." The ambassador, who had come to hope Graham's visit might produce solutions to some of the key problems he was charged with solving, immediately informed Palotay and Imre Miklos that it would be a serious mistake if Graham's visit were conducted at a low level. On the heels of this ploy, Graham cabled a message to Miklos. Cooing warm greetings with the innocence of a dove, but making his points with the wisdom of a serpent, Graham asked for more information about his itinerary. Would he be preaching in the Reformed church in Debrecen, the center of Calvinism in eastern Hungary? And were any plans being made for him to preach at the large Roman Catholic cathedral in Pecs, in southern Hungary?

And just one other thing: Had any provision been made for him to meet with Hungary's Jewish leaders?

Palotay was understandably livid when he learned of the cablegram. He had worked five years to arrange the invitation. Now, what he had regarded as a signal triumph the Foreign Ministry was calling a potential disaster, and Billy Graham was complaining about the itinerary. When Haraszti returned to Hungary in late August with Walter Smyth to make final preparations for Graham's visit, the Council of Free Churches summoned him to what amounted to a kangaroo court, demanding that he give a full report of his activities following his receipt of the official invitation from Palotay. Haraszti, who relishes a battle of wits, expressed surprise that he was facing an inquiry, when what seemed appropriate was some expression of appreciation. When Palotay pushed him further, Haraszti played his trump. "I am not sure it is proper," he said, "that I give a report to a lay gathering about the action of Hungary's official representative to the United States, and also a report about my discussions with the U.S. State Department. Also, I am not sure if it is proper that I divulge here letters of which I am privy through the confidence of Dr. Graham, from the highest-ranking official in the United States to the highest-ranking official of Hungary. But if I am forced, I will do it under protest, but then somebody must be responsible for forcing me to divulge state secrets of both Hungary and the United States." Haraszti smiled broadly at the memory of the occasion. "State secrets," he said with a chuckle. "They called off the meeting. This was the end." Frustrated by Haraszti's cleverness, Palotay badgered him in private for a few days, but the two men soon reconciled their differences and became a formidable team in presenting Graham's case in Eastern Europe. "Palotay was in an embarrassing situation," Haraszti admitted years later, but "[like] something comes up from underwater, he emerged fine and dandy. He was able to make the best out of it. He realized that he could not have done it without Haraszti. At the same time, Haraszti also realized that without Palotay I could not do it. So we had to make peace. Palotay [did] the groundwork for me in Communist countries. He [was] a man of energy and dynamism and contacts, contacts, contacts. He [was] a mediator for me in many, many cases. He did a tremendous pioneer work for me."

The tour, though modest when compared to Graham's standard crusades, was an unqualified success. When he and his team arrived at the Budapest airport, they were met by Palotay, the protocol chief from the Ministry for Church Affairs, and American ambassador Philip Kaiser, then whisked away to the lovely and secluded Grand Hotel on Margaret Island in the middle of the Danube in downtown Budapest. At his first public appearance, hundreds who had packed into the city's largest Baptist church heard him acknowledge that the anti-Communist message he had preached was out of date. He had come to Hungary with "an open heart and an open mind," he declared. "I want to learn about your nation, I want to learn about your churches, I want to learn about your Christian dedication and sense of responsibility within your own social structure. But most of all, I want both of us to learn together from the Word of God."

In keeping with his wishes, Graham spoke in Hungary's largest Reformed church in Debrecen and melted the resistance of both the Reformed and Lutheran bishops. At Pecs, Bishop Czerháti not only welcomed him to the chancery but expressed a hope that he would return someday to preach from the cathedral steps. As requested, he met with Hungary's key Jewish leaders, who also received him warmly and confirmed their government's claims that Jews enjoyed impressive religious liberty, marked by the presence in the capital of thirty synagogues, including the largest in the world, and the only Jewish seminary in an Eastern European country. Ambassador Kaiser, himself a Jew, confirmed the accuracy of their account.

Not all the stops on the tour were under the aegis of religion. At a government-arranged visit to a lightbulb and appliance factory, Graham accepted a souvenir lightbulb with the promise that it would shine in his home in North Carolina as a bright reminder of one of the most unforgettable experiences in his life. He then noted that "I have also brought a souvenir to you, my dear friends, something that shineth much brighter than this lightbulb. I have brought to you the light of the world, Jesus Christ." According to Haraszti, many of the workers began to weep openly and unashamedly, aware that "this was the very first time in Communist Hungary that any minister would preach about Jesus Christ in a state-owned factory."

The high point of the ten-day visit came when Graham addressed a large open-air meeting at a Baptist youth camp in Tahi, in the mountains along the Danube. The most conservative estimates of the size of the crowd placed it between 5,000 and 15,000. Haraszti noted that reliable informants, using automobiles parked along the river as an index, estimated the number to be closer to 30,000. Whether one accepts the low or high figure, it was apparently the largest religious meeting in Hungary's history. Like all the other meetings, there was no advance notice in either the secular or religious media, but word-of-mouth advertising, much by long-distance telephone, brought Evangelical Christians streaming into the camp from all over Hungary and from at least six other Eastern bloc countries as well. A decade after this notable event, Haraszti is careful to point out that Graham had not been invited to address a large public gathering. Hungarian Baptist youth meet at the camp every year. Graham was present "to watch how the Baptist youth camp hold their closing service.... I hope you hear clearly what I said. It was not an evangelization rally; it was a closing service. Now, of course, some people might say, 'If this is the closing service, how does an evangelization [rally] look?' I don't know the difference between the two." No one, of course, was fooled by this semantic ploy. Ambassador Kaiser and his wife sat in the front row alongside ranking officials from the French embassy, and the thousands of people who traveled hundreds of miles and sat on blankets throughout the night just to have a good view of the closing services were not surprised when Billy Graham was asked to make a few remarks. At the same time, the government was not forced either to grant or to deny permission for him to address the crowd.

Prior to the visit, Haraszti impressed upon Graham the critical importance of telling the truth about what he found in Hungary. It would be simple, sensational, and gratifying to his American supporters to make a whirlwind tour, then return to decry the lack of religious freedom behind the iron curtain. If he expected to be invited back, however, it would be wiser to acknowledge the degree of religious freedom that in fact existed in Hungary. Graham understood the point. In his public statements and in interviews with Western reporters, he steadfastly refused to criticize the Hungarian government or even to comment on East-West relations, except to urge greater effort to achieve world peace. Instead, aware that the government was permitting the Council of Free Churches to sell tapes and transcripts of his sermons, he noted that "things are far more open than I had supposed. There is religious liberty in Hungary.... The church is alive in Hungary." To reporters aware of his early anti-Communist tirades he explained, "I have not joined the Communist Party since coming to Hungary, nor have I been asked to. But I think the world is changing and on both sides we're beginning to understand each other more." He added that key leaders of the Communist party were calling for and practicing greater cooperation between Church and State.

This approach paid rapid dividends. In a conversation near the end of the tour, Imre Miklos warned Graham that he would be accused of having been brainwashed by the Communists but consoled him by saying, "I shall also be accused of having joined the Christian church." He indicated clearly, however, that he was prepared to take the heat and that Graham's gracious tact would be rewarded. This visit, he assured the evangelist, would be only the beginning of his ministry to the Socialist countries of Eastern Europe. He also made it clear that another visit to Hungary would be welcomed. "For friends," he said, "it is not enough to meet only once." The friendship was doubtless sealed more strongly when, not long after Graham returned home and stopped by the White House to give his report, the Crown of St. Stephen was returned to its homeland and the United States welcomed Hungary to most-favored-nation status. Graham makes no claim that his was the sole or even the pivotal role in the return of the crown, but does acknowledge that he discussed the matter with "the proper authorities." Politically, it was not a cost-free gesture; expatriate Hungarians in America, who tended to be staunchly anti-Communist, bitterly resented the return of the crown to a Communist government and subjected Haraszti to a torrent of criticism for collaborating with the enemy.

Haraszti stayed on in Budapest a few days to tie up loose ends. Curious to learn if the visit made any impact on "the everyday man," he asked a waiter at the Grand Hotel, "Do you know who is Billy Graham?" The man snapped to attention—"straight, strict, stiff"—and said, "Yes, sir. He is second only to the Pope." Haraszti neither smiled nor offered a correction. "Thank you for your answer," he said. "I know now you know who he is."

Imre Miklos was correct in predicting that Graham's visit to Hungary was only the beginning of a ministry in Eastern Europe. In 1978 the long-delayed visit to Poland finally became a reality. Once again, Alexander Haraszti played a decisive role. The Hungarian experience had convinced Graham and his colleagues both that Haraszti knew what he was doing and that a man from the United States who had contacts within a Communist country's government could often accomplish more than Evangelical brethren within that country. Perhaps still not certain Haraszti could be equally effective outside his native Hungary, Walter Smyth authorized him to submit his expenses for reimbursement but still held back from giving him the right to act as Billy Graham's official representative.

Haraszti's visit to Warsaw in January 1978 went smoothly. Graham's tactful behavior in Hungary had calmed any misgivings the free churches or state officials might have, and an official invitation for an October visit was arranged with minimal difficulty, but Roman Catholic authorities, far more powerful in Poland than in any other Eastern bloc country and far more antagonistic toward the government than the Hungarian Catholic Church, had strong reservations about the American evangelist. During the spring of 1978, an envoy of the Polish primate, Stefan Cardinal Wyszynski, traveled to Atlanta to inform Haraszti that the cardinal resented his having started negotiations with the government before coming to the head of the Church. With an arch show of surprise, Haraszti indicated that the cardinal had not invited him to be in contact and that, in any case, the cardinal's record on influencing his government was not superb. "He did invite the pope, but he never got him. But I did get Dr. Graham to Hungary, and the cardinal did not get anybody of importance to Poland."

Recognizing that Haraszti could not be bullied, the envoy warned that Graham's visit would be an embarrassment, since Catholics would not attend his meetings and the small number of Protestants in Poland would not make much of an audience. Haraszti called the bluff. Handing the man a copy of a new BGEA publication, *Billy Graham in Hungary*, he pointed out that wherever Billy Graham went, the *New York Times*, the *Chicago Tribune*, the *Washington Post*, the *Los Angeles Times*, the *Miami Herald*, *Time*, *Life*, AP, UPI, Reuters, U.S. television networks, the BBC, West German television, and Graham's own television crew followed. Hundreds of thousands would see pictures of the trip in a book like the one he was now holding. Millions would watch a television program like the one about the Hungary tour, which had just aired on 326 stations in prime time. If the envoy's prediction was accurate, Haraszti said, "then the world will see that under the wise leadership of Cardinal Wyszynski, Roman Catholicism has been wiped out in Poland, because not even a cathedral remained — not one. Because on our films, which we will present to the Canadian and American public, there will be only Jews — not many, unfortunately — a large number of communists, a few Baptists and other Protestants, but not a single Roman Catholic church or priest or professing Catholic. So the world will see that Roman Catholicism has disappeared from the face of Poland." The envoy, gaining appreciation for the surgical precision with which Haraszti had dissected his threat, said in German, *"Sie sind schlau"* ("You are shrewd"). The physician demurred: "I am not shrewd, and this is not even a threat. This is a promise. If the cardinal wants this, I cannot help. This is not my doing, not my making; this is his making. And if you are honestly the representative of the cardinal, you will report this to him."

As it happened, both parties were unsure of the other's motives. Graham wanted an invitation from the Catholic hierarchy but did not want the Church to control the visit. Haraszti and Walter Smyth made it clear that although the evangelist fully understood that generally speaking "to be a Pole is to be a Roman Catholic," he felt that Christ is also present in other churches, and he wanted to preach the gospel in those churches as well. Furthermore, the official sponsors of the visit would continue to be the Polish Baptist Union and the Polish Ecumenical Council, the inclusive Protestant body. For its part, the Church was willing to cooperate but did not want to be embarrassed by offering an invitation that might be refused. Cardinal Wyszynski also feared that as a Protestant on friendly terms with the Communist government, Graham might say things that would harm the Catholic Church's relationship with the state. After a further bit of stalking and fencing when Haraszti returned to Poland in July, Graham's and the cardinal's representatives decided they could trust one another and reached an agreement that the evangelist would speak at four cathedrals (he was invited to seven) and visit the shrine of the Black Madonna at Czgstochowa. At each meeting, Smyth explained, the service would consist of a solo, a prayer, a Bible reading, another solo, and a sermon by Billy Graham. The cardinal's men agreed, clearly aware that this format left no room for a Catholic mass. Haraszti assured the bishop (Dabrowski) serving as secretary of the Polish episcopate that Graham fully understood the status and problems of the Polish Church. From that point forward, Graham and his team enjoyed "the utmost cooperation of the Polish Church."

The Polish tour (October 6–16, 1978) went smoothly. The official state press accorded it little attention, but religious publications were permitted to provide extensive advance promotion and thorough coverage. In Warsaw

Graham spoke to an overflow crowd of nearly 1,000 and led an evangelism workshop for more than 450 clergy and other religious workers, including several Catholic seminary professors and teaching nuns. From that beginning visible signs of ecumenical warmings, in a climate Protestant leaders typically described as unfriendly, accompanied Graham's appearances. At Warsaw's Catholic seminary, the dean of theology introduced Graham by recalling how, during a sojourn in Chicago a few years earlier, a black woman on a bus had asked him if he was saved. He had responded, "Can't you see my collar?" The woman, a Baptist, had been unimpressed. "I don't care about that," she had said. "Have you been born again?" The dean related that, stunned by this challenge, he had gone back to his room, read the third chapter of John once again, and had a new experience of Christ that led him to rededicate his life. He was grateful to Baptists, he said, and he welcomed the most famous Baptist of all to Poland.

Graham's first sermon ever in a Catholic church occurred at Poznah in western Poland, where he prayed that the Holy Spirit would unite the hearts of the Roman Catholics and Protestants worshiping together on that occasion. In Krakow his host was to have been Karol Cardinal Wojtyla, but because the cardinal was, as a Graham staffer put it, "out of town getting elected pope," the forging of that particular crucial ecumenical bond would have to wait awhile. In the Communist-dominated city of Katowice, where nearly 6,500—a high percentage of them young people—jammed into the cathedral, a corps of approximately 300 priests and nuns sitting together in a high balcony watched skeptically. As Graham rose to speak, a priest said to a colleague, "Now the show is to begin." When the evangelist finished his sermon on Galatians 6:14 ("Far be it from me to glory except in the cross of our Lord Jesus Christ") and asked those who wished to recommit their lives to Christ to raise their hands, all three hundred priests and nuns did so.

As part of what he later described as the busiest ten days of his entire ministry, Graham paid a visit to Auschwitz, where the sight of crematorium chimneys and baby shoes and hair shorn from Jewish prisoners bound for the gas chambers profoundly affected his tender conscience and, according to aides, played a major role in stiffening his growing resolve to work for peace and reconciliation. Warning that the mentality that had produced Auschwitz could resurface, he repeatedly urged his audiences to work for "unity, peace, and the spread of God's love" and stressed his willingness to cooperate with church and government leaders in efforts to achieve world peace. By all the standard criteria, the tour was a smashing success. Protestant pastors soon began to report that Catholics continued to show warmth toward them after Graham left, and Graham's standing with Catholics was epitomized when Bishop Herbert Bednorz asked him to autograph a stack of copies of the Polish translation of *How to Be Born Again*, offering the simple explanation, "I want to give them to my friends."

30

The Preacher and the Bear

Billy Graham returned briefly to Hungary and Poland in 1981 to receive honorary doctorates from the Debrecen Theological Academy (the oldest Protestant theological seminary in the world) and the Christian Theological Academy in Warsaw. It was clear, however, that Protestants were not the only ones who approved of him. In Hungary János Kádár gave him the use of his private train, and after the visit to Poland, the cardinal who had been "out of town" in 1978, now His Holiness John Paul II, welcomed him to the Vatican for a half-hour visit, the first time any pope had received him. Noting that they had talked of "inter-church relations, the emergence of Evangelicalism, evangelization, and Christian responsibility towards modern moral issues" (an indication it had been a full half-hour), Graham told a press conference that "we had a spiritual time. He is so down-to-earth and human, I almost forgot he was the pope."

The next major visit to a Communist land, however, was the one Billy Graham had been seeking for at least twenty-five years. In 1982 he finally gained entrance to Russia as more than a tourist. Preliminary negotations for the visit began during the 1977 Hungarian visit, when Soviet Baptist leader Alexei Bychkov came to the closing service at Tahi and assured Graham he would work to arrange an invitation. Higher-level inquiry began in October 1978, when PepsiCo CEO Don Kendall, a personal friend of Soviet premier Leonid Brezhnev's, arranged a meeting in Washington between Graham and Soviet ambassador Anatoly Dobrynin. The appointment came through with only a few hours' notice, and at Graham's importunate urging, Haraszti began a scheduled hysterectomy a few minutes early, then left the finishing touches to assistants so he could grab a plane that would get him to Washington in time for a four o'clock meeting. During the ride between the hotel and the embassy, Graham introduced Haraszti to Kendall. "Alex is a very remarkable man," he said. "I think nobody else understands world politics on a global basis as much as he does. Henry Kissinger may be an exception, but as far as Eastern Europe is concerned, even Henry does not know that much."

Perhaps familiar with Graham's penchant for overstatement, Kendall asked, "And what does Henry say about this?" Graham did not back off: "I don't know what Henry says, but he is not my adviser. He never took me to any Communist country, and Alex did. And I think Alex knows things which Henry does not. And I think he has a much [better grasp] of Communist lands, and particularly State-Church relations, than Henry will ever have."

The compliment pleased Haraszti—"I felt Dr. Graham meant it." A few minutes later, he received an even greater show of confidence. After an exchange of polite greetings at the embassy, Dobrynin asked Graham point-blank, "Why do you want to come?" Without prior warning, Graham replied, "Mr. Ambassador, I'd like to ask Dr. Haraszti to make a statement on my behalf. He is my adviser in Eastern European matters, and he could put it in words better than I can. With your kind permission, he will express my feelings about a visit to an Eastern European country, and also my policies."

Haraszti, a man whose deserved self-confidence—"I admit the truth," he likes to say, "even when it favors me"—and humble deference to Billy Graham ricochet incongruously through every conversation, recalled the occasion with pleasure: "Of course, this is an honor. This means that he somehow remembers me." He also smiled at the memory of Graham's ploy. "He is wise. If my answer is good, I did it under his instructions. If it is bad, then I did not actually represent his thoughts." Haraszti was not tongue-tied by the responsibility. After pointing out that Graham's calling obliged him to preach the gospel of Christ to the entire world, Communist and non-Communist alike, Haraszti astonished the ambassador by stating that Graham wanted to go to Russia to express his gratitude to Vladimir Ilych Ulyanov Lenin for what he had accomplished in the great Socialist revolution of 1917. By breaking the back of the Orthodox Church, whose intimate ties with the state enabled it to suppress all competitors, the revolution had made possible the development of Evangelical movements throughout the Soviet Union, with the result that Evangelical Christianity had never been stronger, as the existence of perhaps three million Soviet Baptists and other Evangelicals proved. Haraszti admitted this had not been Lenin's aim, but suggested that if the revolutionary leader were alive today, he would change his opinion. He would see that the problem lay with the political nature of the Church, not with Christians themselves, and that even though the government discriminated against them in many ways, Christians were nevertheless the best workers and citizens, people who gave their testimony not only in words but also in deeds.

Dobrynin gave no response to this remarkable interpretation of history, but Haraszti continued. It was not only Evangelicals who had flourished under communism, he asserted. Throughout the Soviet Union he had found a revitalized Christianity in the Orthodox Church. When revolutionaries murdered priests and stripped the churches of their gold and silver, they had forced Christians to realize they were blind, naked, sick, and weak with nowhere to turn except to Jesus Christ. It was true the Church had shrunk in numbers, but it was also true that it had grown in fidelity to Christ. "Sir," he said, "you have forty to fifty million dedicated Orthodox Church members today. I have seen them, young and old, people and priests, and I saw Jesus Christ and the Holy Spirit beaming in their faces. They are an invincible Church. They are not subject to intimidation, because they are willing to sacrifice their lives. If you put them in concentration camps, you give them an audience. If you execute them, they lift up their hands and eyes to the Lord, who is to receive them into his happiness. In addition to these millions of Evangelicals and Orthodox Christians, you also have other millions of Catholics, Protestants, and Jews, and perhaps fifty million Muslims—over one hundred million believers in God, and only seventeen million Communist party members. You must make peace with them, or one day they will revolt. You know history. They will revolt when they feel strong enough. If you do not make peace with them, sir, you are going to face a very serious problem." As long as the Communist countries restricted religious freedom, Western countries, and America in particular, would continue to view them with suspicion and resentment. If the atheistic state were to become involved in intense conflict with religious believers, Western powers might well intervene on behalf of the believers. And if that were to happen, not even the unthinkable would be unthinkable. "Sir," he said, "we know what is the end of it if we do not check this situation. It does not matter then who shall be responsible for what, who is to blame, when both nations are blown up."

Haraszti moved in for the kill. "We are not begging the Soviet government to invite Dr. Graham," he told Dobrynin. "We believe it is in the interest of the Soviet government to invite him. Why? Because Billy Graham is not just an evangelist; he is also a newsmaker. You have been in this country long enough to know how public opinion works in America. Dr. Graham is a public-opinion maker. People listen to what he says and follow his leadership." If he found some modicum of religious freedom in the Soviet Union, and a sincere desire for peace on the part of the Soviet people, and if he honestly reported what he had seen to the American public and to the President and Congress and other leaders, he could serve as a tremendous positive force for peace between the two great nations. No other person in the world, Haraszti averred, could have such an effect on public opinion, with the possible exception of the pope. Then, without speaking ill of the pope, he drew a comparison between the two men. Graham was an accomplished statesman—Haraszti told Dobrynin that Nixon had appointed Henry Kissinger to be secretary of state only after Graham turned down the post, an assertion Graham later dismissed as fanciful—with thirty years of quasi-diplomatic experience in the West, extensive political contacts on all the continents, and now, with successful trips to Hungary and Poland in his dossier and negotiations under way for visits to other Eastern bloc nations. The pope, by contrast, had lived in only one Communist land and had no experience in the West. He might develop into a great statesman and world leader, but it was too early to tell. If the pope were to visit the Soviet Union, the result might be good—or it might not be. "We don't know what the pope will say; we do know what Dr. Graham will say. I think it is in the interest of the Soviet Union to invite Dr. Graham before somebody else is invited."

Dobrynin finally spoke. "Dr. Haraszti," he said, "I could not disgree with one word you said. I report this to my government. I am for Dr. Graham's coming to the Soviet Union. But I'm an ambassador only; I'm not the policy-making body."

"Mr. Ambassador," Haraszti reminded him, "you are also a member of the Central Committee."

"Yes," Dobrynin acknowledged, "I am."

Dobrynin stood by his word, and within a few weeks, it became clear that an invitation would eventually be forthcoming. Haraszti let it be known that Graham wanted to preach at as many places as possible, but would adjust to whatever schedule the government approved. Contrary to his 1959 prayer, he would not expect to preach in Red Square or in a stadium. He would want to preach in Orthodox as well as Protestant churches, and he felt it would be crucial to meet with Jewish leaders, as he had done in Hungary and Poland. He would accept appointments with political or religious dissidents but would not embarrass the government by publicizing their cases after his return to the United States. With these tacit understandings in place, preliminary plans were made for a visit during the fall of 1979, then postponed because of Soviet preoccupation with U.S.-Chinese relations, generated by Deputy Premier Deng Xiaoping's visit to the United States that year. The Moscow Olympics and the friction generated by America's boycott of the games made 1980 seem unpropitious as well.

The coveted invitation, which finally arrived in 1982, involved some of the most delicate, controversial, and peril-fraught negotiations of Graham's entire ministry. During the summer of 1981, the head of the Russian Orthodox Church, Patriarch Pimen, announced that key religious leaders from all over the world would convene in Moscow in May 1982 for a World Conference of Religious Workers for Saving the Sacred Gift of Life from Nuclear Catastrophe. Though ostensibly sponsored by the Orthodox Church, the conference was obviously endorsed by the Communist party and was widely viewed in the West as a transparent government-engineered propaganda enterprise. When he first learned of it, Alex Haraszti shared this view and informed Soviet Baptist leaders that Billy Graham would have no part in such a charade. Without denying that the party fully approved of the conference, Baptist leader Alexei Bychkov insisted that the Orthodox Church's sponsorship was entirely sincere and at least semi-independent. He also revealed that

Baptist churches, as well as virtually all other religious groups in the Soviet Union, had contributed generously toward financing the conference. At least partially convinced, Haraszti contacted the Orthodox leaders he and Walter Smyth had been cultivating to devise an invitation Billy Graham would feel able to accept.

Haraszti's primary contact, Father Vitaly Borovoy, the Orthodox patriarchate's representative to the World Council of Churches, let it be known that the Orthodox hierarchy was extremely interested in having Graham attend the conference but did not want to risk the embarrassment of offering an invitation that might be rejected. Before an explicit personal invitation could be issued, there would have to be some guarantee that Graham would accept it. Haraszti assured Borovoy that Graham wished to embarrass no one, that he was a strong advocate of peace, and that he was deeply interested in witnessing firsthand the way in which brave Russian Christians had been able to keep faith alive despite repressive government policies. At the same time, he would almost certainly not be interested in coming to Moscow simply to attend a conference that many Westerners would inevitably regard as a Communist-conceived, anti-American event but would also expect to preach in both Baptist and Orthodox churches, and to meet with Jewish leaders.

Borovoy saw no problems with the Baptist and Jewish appointments but observed that canon law forbade having an unconsecrated priest preaching in an Orthodox Church. Haraszti, surprising the priest with a brief recital of serious disputes over small points in canon law, suggested it should be possible to find a way around the law. Borovoy thought for a moment, then brightened. "You are right," he said. "The patriarch could introduce him to the faithful, and he could extend greetings." Haraszti was pleased. "And Father Borovoy," he said, "you know and I know that these 'greetings' will be centered around Jesus Christ. You will call it 'greetings' and we will call it 'preaching.' What is the difference?"

In a subsequent meeting with Metropolitan Filaret, the chair of the conference's International Preparatory Committee, Haraszti repeated Graham's "basic wishes," adding that any invitation to the evangelist should be accompanied by invitations to his key advisers, specifically, Smyth, Akers, and Haraszti. Filaret objected that other participants would be restricted to a single secretary and that bending those restrictions to accommodate Graham would offend participants from other countries, such as the various African nations. Haraszti was not in a yielding mood. Working a bit of diplomatic jujitsu, he informed Filaret that when he had visited the pope, Graham had been accompanied by three advisers. "I do not think," he said, "that His Holiness, Patriarch Pimen, is so much smaller in stature than the pope that he could not afford having Dr. Graham with three of his closest advisers." Certainly, if Patriarch Pimen were coming to America, Graham would not cavil over how many metropolitans he brought with him. As for offending

Africans, Haraszti countered, "Your Eminence, I see your problem. But I would never have dared to compare the Soviet Union with Chad, or even Sudan, for that matter. I also would not realize that America should be in the same category as Chad." Then, perhaps piqued by what he regarded as a specious excuse, Haraszti let his unbounded esteem for Graham soar to heights that would have stunned the evangelist. "I don't compare Dr. Graham with the patriarch or the pope," he told Filaret, "because Dr. Graham is not the head of a church. He is the head of all Christianity. He actually is the head of the Roman Catholics, the Orthodox, the Protestants—everybody—in a spiritual way, because the pope cannot preach to all the Protestants, but Billy Graham can preach to all the Roman Catholics. The patriarch cannot preach to all the Roman Catholics; they will not listen to him. But Billy Graham can preach to all the Orthodox, and they will listen to him, because he is above these religious strifes. He is a man of much higher stature than any of these people. I do not mean any offense to His Holiness, the patriarch, but Billy Graham deserves more than three metropolitans or three cardinals."

Remarkably, instead of taking umbrage at Haraszti's demotion of both pope and patriarch, Filaret stepped from the room. When he returned ten minutes later, his face was wreathed in a relaxed smile. "All right," he said. "He can have his three co-workers." With these feet in the door, Haraszti then gained permission to enlarge Graham's entourage to include T. W. Wilson, a secretary, an aide to handle press relations, and a photographer. He reminded Filaret to arrange Graham's preaching appointments and meetings with one or two high-ranking Soviet officials, and he made it clear Graham would expect to give a major address at the conference. In return, the evangelist would make no statements criticizing Soviet foreign policy or religious or social conditions in the Soviet Union. He would come not as a social critic but as an evangelist, "a man of God, and a gracious guest who would not abuse the friendship of his hosts" or embarrass them in any way.

With this impressive collection of concessions safely tucked into his diplomatic pouch ("He was the world figure whom they wanted to invite to their world conference," Haraszti explained, "and cost what it may, they were ready to pay the price") the good doctor raised one last point, almost as if it were an afterthought: If Billy Graham visited the Soviet Union, it would be imperative for him to visit the six Siberian Pentecostals who, claiming to be victims of religious persecution, had sought asylum in the U.S. Embassy in 1978 and had been living in its basement ever since.

Filaret's face fell. The Siberian Six ("Seven" before one of their number went on a hunger strike and had to be removed to a hospital) had become a vexing source of tension between the Soviet and U.S. governments, and a cause célèbre for champions of religious freedom around the world. Soviet authorities persistently claimed the Pentecostals were not sincere religionists persecuted for their faith but opportunists using religion as a means to force the government to allow them to leave the country, as they had been trying to do for over twenty years. Several Graham associates eventually came to share this view, as did many American reporters assigned to Moscow, but the publicity generated by the group's virtual imprisonment (they refused to leave and the U.S. government allowed them to remain in the embassy until the Soviet government guaranteed they would be allowed to emigrate unharmed) made them impossible for Graham to ignore. Fully aware of the metropolitan's chagrin that he had raised the issue, Haraszti explained that if Graham returned to America and said the Soviet government had not allowed him to see the Siberians, it would reflect badly on the government and on the peace conference. If he said he had freely chosen not to see them, he would suffer an enormous loss of respect in America, either because he lacked compassion or commitment to religious freedom or because he was lying. And if he said the Pentecostals had not wanted to receive him, Americans would scoff, charging him with swallowing obvious propaganda. Uncomfortable as it might be for all concerned, Graham had to see the Siberians. Once more, Filaret reluctantly agreed but expressed his fervent hope that by the time of Graham's visit, there would no longer be a "Pentecostal problem."

Filaret promised to put his accession to Graham's basic wishes in writing as part of the official invitation Haraszti would deliver by hand to the evangelist. He insisted, however, that the envoy obtain a verbal guarantee from Graham that if the invitation were tendered, it would be accepted. Haraszti called John Akers that night. Akers relayed the information to Graham, and Graham spoke with the White House and the State Department. When Akers called Haraszti back, he reported that the invitation was acceptable "on the highest level," and that Graham would accept it. Haraszti relayed that news to Filaret, not failing to mention that high levels had approved the evangelist's participation in the conference—"I wanted the Soviet government to know that Dr. Graham does not come as a simple American citizen. The message was not missed." When he returned to New York with a five-page invitation, he discovered, to his considerable agitation, that the assurances conveyed to Metropolitan Filaret were unraveling at the seams. In the brief period since he had signaled his acceptance, Graham had come under strong pressures from within his organization, from various Evangelical leaders, and from the State Department—with U.S. ambassador to the Soviet Union Arthur Hartman among the most vociferous—to decline the invitation and refuse to add respectability to the so-called Peace Conference. When Haraszti joined Graham and his inner circle of advisers in his suite at the Essex House in New York, he expected to bask in their appreciation. Instead, Graham anxiously asked, "Alex, do you realize I am risking my entire ministry if I accept this invitation?"

Haraszti responded with crystalline logic. "The thirty-five years already behind you," he said, "is history. You cannot jeopardize it. You cannot risk it. It is historical fact. Now, you must not jeopardize the ten years to come. This is the beginning. For years you have been praying that the Lord may bring the time when this becomes possible. Here is the time. This will be your first coming to the Soviet Union, but not your last one. If you accept this invitation, all the other satellite countries will fall in line. These things are interwoven. No Moscow, no satellite countries. Please, Dr. Graham, don't let me down. *Do not let me down*."

Graham invited Haraszti to play the devil's advocate. What arguments could be made against his going? Haraszti leapt at the opportunity. The main reason not to go, he said, would be unbelief. "If we don't believe in the Word of the Lord, and if we don't believe in our cause, then we must not accept." As a man of faith, however, he had no choice. "You have no way out if you want to be honest, and I am sure you want to be honest."

This struck home, but Graham raised again the question of governmental opposition. "If the President should come and tell me [not to go], I will not go." Haraszti observed that Western Christians sometimes criticize Christians in Communist lands for giving Caesar more than his due. Considering that Stalin murdered tens of thousands of believers, that Khrushchev closed thousands of churches, that Brezhnev demanded that Soviet people deny God, yet more than 100 million refused to do so, what moral right did an American have to charge them with compromise or weak faith, especially when the American was risking nothing more than a few hostile attacks by the press?

"Alex," Graham said, "do you know that I receive hate letters by the thousands?"

"I expect that you receive them," Haraszti responded, "but if I may compare my little case with your great case, you don't know how many hate letters I receive, and how much adverse publicity I receive in the American Hungarian papers, because I opened the way for Billy Graham to go to Communist countries—this poor, naive, good American, and Haraszti the evil spirit. I considered it a privilege not only to trust and believe in Jesus Christ, but also to suffer for him. I think that, spiritually, the same applies to you."

While they debated, a call came from Vice-President George Bush. Scribbling in one of the black notebooks to which he habitually commits precise details of anything he considers significant, Haraszti recorded the half of the conversation he could hear. "George, I am sorry," Graham said, "but I have accepted it. It is too late. I had the nod from the highest place. I took it seriously and I accepted it. I cannot do anything now." He went on to express confidence that his visit to the Soviet Union would not only promote the cause of Christ but would help improve relations between the two great countries. As a loyal American, he felt it was his duty to go.

Graham later reported that Bush had said he was neutral about the visit and was simply conveying the expressions of concern received from others.

"I'm reading to you without comment," the Vice-President had said. "You are preaching the gospel, and I don't dare tell you what to do." Graham also received private approval from Ronald Reagan. "The newspapers were saying that the President was opposed," he recalled, "but the Sunday before I went, George Bush invited me to lunch at his home, and I went with Punch Sulzberger, of the *New York Times*, and his family. When we got there, George said, 'I don't think the Reagans have any plans for lunch. I'll call them up. I'll bet they're lonesome.' He called them up, and in about half an hour, here they came, with several cars that go with them everywhere. Almost the first thing the President did when he came in was pull me aside and say, 'Now Billy, don't you worry about this trip. God works in mysterious ways.' In fact, he gave me a handwritten note saying, 'We'll be praying for you every mile of the way.'" Graham also reported that a White House official had told him, "If you don't go now, it would look as though we stopped you and it is going to hurt us. You have to go."

Whatever the President and Vice-President thought, the State Department adamantly opposed Graham's participation in the conference, fearing his appearance and comments would be used to stir public opinion against American plans for a significant increase in missile deployment, a measure designed to force the Soviets to begin serious disarmament negotiations. Both Arthur Hartman and William Wilson, U.S. ambassador to the Vatican, repeatedly importuned Haraszti to urge Graham to rescind his acceptance. "Whatever he says," they contended, "will be good for the Russians." During Haraszti's repeated visits to the Vatican ("Just about every time I went to Moscow," he blithely explained, "I also went to Rome") Wilson "warned me, begged me, cajoled me, in no uncertain terms," always claiming that the State Department and the President himself opposed Graham's going to Moscow, but always stopping short of stating, in so many words, that the President had specifically authorized him to tell Graham not to go. Haraszti dutifully reported what both ambassadors had told him, but Graham stood firm. "If the President is so [dead set] against it," he said, "he's welcome to tell me. But until and unless I hear it in person from him, I will not accept coded messages." Unquestionably, the simple desire to preach in the Soviet Union played a role in Graham's decision to press on. In retrospect, however, he insisted that his controlling motive was to draw attention to his increasing commitment to the avoidance of nuclear war. "I had started speaking out against nuclear weapons and calling for the elimination of all weapons of mass destruction, whether chemical or nuclear, but it was never in the press. So I decided the only way I could make my statement known was to accept the invitation to come to the peace conference in Moscow. 'Then they will listen to me,' I thought."

Whatever other motives may have been operating, Graham's assertion that he wanted to draw attention to his increased concern for peace was not an ex post facto rewriting of history. At least as early as 1963, he allowed that he would be in favor of universal nuclear disarmament, but that was an occasional and quite lightly sounded note. More typical were his reminders that Christ had described himself as one who brings fire and bears a sword, and that Christians and other freedom-loving people must also stand ready to bear a sword against any who would try to destroy their families or their country. No single event was responsible for what would be a notable shift in tone and emphasis, but several Graham associates observed that he seemed to regard issues of peace and disarmament in a new light after his early visits to Eastern Europe, particularly after his 1978 pilgrimage to Auschwitz, where the meaning of the Holocaust burned itself into his consciousness. In addition, said one man who had accompanied him on the tour of Poland, "He saw that the commitment of [Eastern European] religious leaders for peace and reconciliation was serious."

A few months after the Polish tour, when the World Council of Churches began to call for approval of the new SALT II accords, Graham added his voice to their chorus. "The people of the U.S. want peace," he observed, as do the people of China and the Soviet Union. "Why can't we have peace?" He conceded that defenses were necessary "to keep madmen from taking over the world and robbing the world of its liberties" but noted that he had begun to take a new view of nuclear weapons. Moreover, he observed, it seemed his fellow Evangelicals were beginning to share his concerns—the Southern Baptist Convention had passed resolutions calling for multilateral nuclear disarmament and support of SALT II. Perhaps they had reached the same conclusion he had: "I didn't really give it the thought that I should have given it in my earlier years, but I have come to the conviction that this is the teaching of the Bible." While denying he was a pacifist and insisting he did not favor unilateral disarmament, he flatly declared, "I'm in favor of disarmament. I'm in favor of trust. I'm in favor of having agreements, not only to reduce but to eliminate. Why should any nation have atomic bombs? As I look back—I'm sure many people will disagree with me on this—but as I look back, I think Truman made a mistake in dropping that first atomic bomb. I wish we had never developed it." In short, he seemed to be saying communism might be bad, but not so bad as to risk global annihilation to stop it. "I have seen," he said, "that we must seek the good of the whole human race, and not just the good of any one nation or race."

From these beginnings, Graham began to call for "SALT 10," a leapfrogging over the small incremental gains that might be won in a series of arms-limitation talks to "the bilateral, verifiable eradication of all nuclear, biochemical and laser weapons used for mass destruction." Noting that "we are spending a million dollars a minute on armaments all over the world" while "people are hungry and starving in Somalia and other places," he raised reasonable questions: "Have we gone mad? Are we seeking the genocide of the whole human race?... Suppose we were spending that much for food?" Such statements began to crop up not only in press interviews but also in crusade sermons, but that was different from voicing them in a setting organized and controlled by America's most formidable rival, and Graham was hesitant. "Ruth and I prayed about it, of course, and I vacillated quite a bit as to whether or not I should go. I called a number of friends, including Mr. Nixon, Henry Kissinger, people like that, and asked their opinions." Nixon, who had surprised the world by reestablishing ties with the People's Republic of China, pondered the matter for several days, then called to tell him, "Billy, you know I believe in taking big risks. This is a big risk, but I believe that in the long run it will be for the benefit of the gospel that you preach. You'll be criticized, but take the long view." Kissinger also approved and even helped with the speech he eventually delivered at the conference. "But the thing that finally turned it for me," Graham said, "was the Bible." Getting up to select a Phillips translation of Paul's epistles from a row of Bibles on a bookshelf, he turned to the ninth chapter of I Corinthians. "The Apostle Paul's experience has been a key to my decisions on this sort of thing," he explained. "When he had a doubt as to where he should go and how he should handle himself, he said, 'I have, in short, been all things to all sorts of men that by every possible means I might win some to God. I do all this for the sake of the Gospel; I want to play my part in it properly.'" He closed the book and said with utter conviction, "Those verses have been the key to a great deal of what I have done in my life. I decided I was going to do my very best to preach the gospel in Eastern Europe or China or wherever else, whatever government they have. I never had a doubt from the moment I made the decision that the Lord was with me in this."

The decision made, Graham and his colleagues carefully drafted a letter of acceptance, which Haraszti delivered to Filaret and the Soviet Baptist leaders with strict instructions that it not be announced until Graham had a chance to prepare his supporters and the public for the news, and to work out several tricky scheduling problems. One such problem was extricating himself from a series of addresses at college campuses in New England. He managed that by postponing part of the appearances until after the conference and by using the rest to draw wide public attention to his still-developing views, with the result that his trip to Moscow would not be a complete surprise to either his supporters or his critics. His announced topic for full-house appearances at Harvard, MIT, Boston College, Northeastern, the University of Massachusetts, Dartmouth, and Yale was "Peace in a Nuclear Age," and at some campuses his appearance coincided with an antinuclear effort known as Ground Zero Week. Students at some gatherings were disappointed that he seemed to use nuclear issues simply as a ploy for segueing into a standard crusade address. (At UMass, he received a standing ovation at the beginning but not at the end, and some students walked out when he shifted into evangelistic gear, and at MIT, students were stunned when he proclaimed that lasting peace could never be achieved until Christ returned to inaugurate the millennium.) Still, he made an impression. To be sure, his message was far from radical, but it was equally far from the hawkish sentiments with which he had long been associated. He plumped repeatedly for "SALT 10," and, at Yale, even endorsed Ground Zero. "You and I," he told the Elis, "have a responsibility to work for the poor, the needy, the starving of the world. And also for peace now." At Harvard he not only denounced the arms race but called for an end to South African apartheid, racial discrimination anywhere in the world, and "American exploitation of a disproportionate share of the world's resources." The response was gratifying. An unlikely ally, the *Christian Century*, observed that Graham "has used his prestige to announce his opposition to the arms race. He obviously does this out of conviction, not for ego enhancement, as some of his secular critics assume." Other socially liberal churchmen who remembered his reluctance to criticize the war policies of Lyndon Johnson and Richard Nixon praised his new stance. Harvard theologian Harvey Cox gave him credit for having the courage to take a position sure to be unpopular with many of his conservative supporters, and Will Campbell declared, "I once accused him of being the court prophet to Richard Nixon, but I have to say, he's God's prophet now."

A second scheduling problem gave Graham another opportunity to score important points before leaving for Moscow. He had been named recipient of the prestigious Templeton Award, given to persons who had made outstanding contributions to religion—other winners have included Sarvepalli Radhakrishnan, Aleksandr Solzhenitsyn, and Mother Teresa—and was slated to receive the award from Prince Philip in London on May 9, the same date he was scheduled to preach in the Orthodox and Baptist churches in Moscow. He was able to get the date of the award presentation shifted, a circumstance Haraszti used to good advantage in his conversation with the Russians. He told them Billy Graham was a man of his word who would stick by his commitment to come to Moscow, even if it meant giving up the $200,000 that came with the prize, a revelation that stunned the Russians, particularly after Haraszti informed them Graham would donate the money to charity and various evangelistic efforts. But also, he noted, the evangelist had been received at Buckingham Palace and had visited with the Queen of England many times, whereas he had not yet met President Brezhnev even once. Did Graham expect to see Brezhnev, the Russians asked? That, Haraszti replied, would be up to Soviet authorities; as a guest, Graham would not dream of making any demands. Still, Brezhnev had received Muhammad Ali, and it did seem that Billy Graham represented far more people than Ali, whether one used American citizens or world Christians as the relevant constituency.

In late March Filaret's office and BGEA released news of Graham's intention to participate in the peace conference. Against Haraszti's strong pleadings, the BGEA release, picked up and relayed to the Soviet Union by the Voice of America and Radio Free Europe, announced that Graham would preach in the patriarchal Cathedral of the Epiphany at eleven o'clock on May 9, the Sunday morning prior to the conference, and in the Baptist church at six o'clock that evening. The Soviets had strongly urged that the dates and times not be publicized lest the crowds be so large as to be either dangerous or simply embarrassing to the state, and thus ultimately troublesome for the churches. But Graham, revealing an apparent belief that believers can bombard heaven with pinpoint precision, insisted that "I just cannot tell the American public that I will preach in Moscow and not tell them when, because they won't know when to pray for me." Not surprisingly, the Russian announcement contained no mention of appearances outside the conference, and when a wire-service reporter in Moscow checked with both churches, he received the same response: "We know nothing about it." In both cases, Haraszti explained, church leaders had routed the calls to low-ranking members who could honestly profess ignorance of the entire matter. Embarrassed, Graham wanted to release the text of the invitation to the press, but Haraszti prevailed against that notion, convincing him that publicizing the confidential document would result in withdrawal of the invitation and would destroy his credibility with both church and government leaders in the Soviet orbit. Eventually, Graham agreed to a brief statement that simply reaffirmed the truth of the first release and indicated no further comment would be forthcoming.

The gaffe left its mark. When Graham's party arrived at the Moscow airport on Friday afternoon, a troubled Alexei Bychkov, the Baptist leader, explained to Haraszti that the plans had changed. Instead of preaching at the Baptist church on Sunday evening, as part of a scheduled five-hour visit, Graham would preach at the 8:00 A.M. service. He would then rush to the Orthodox church, whose service would already be in progress, and deliver a brief message. The evening period would be devoted to a visit to the publishing department of the Orthodox Church, to allow the American evangelist to see for himself that Bibles and other religious materials could be printed in the Soviet Union. Haraszti protested vigorously, but to no avail. The new schedule would stand.

Graham's insistence on announcing his preaching schedule had offended the government. On the day after his arrival, he gave equal offense to the Orthodox Church, though he did not realize it until after he left Russia. The evangelist was informed on Saturday morning that he was to go immediately to a meeting with Georgi Arbatov, director of the U.S. Canada Institute, a member of the Central Committee of the Communist party and a confidant of Yuri Andropov, who had succeeded Brezhnev as leader of the Soviet government. Graham and his colleagues thought it awkward that his first official visit would be with a secular leader, since he was a guest of the Orthodox

Church, but the Arbatov contact was a good one and they decided not to question the instruction. In fact, Orthodox leaders viewed Arbatov's first-strike offensive as a blatant attempt to upstage the Church, and they fumed quietly throughout the week at what they took to be a callously opportunistic slight on Graham's part.

After preliminary pleasantries, Arbatov gave a long presentation about the need and the prospects for world peace, and particularly about Soviet concern over America's continuing buildup and deployment of missiles. Graham countered with his own concern for peace and his now-standard SALT 10 proposal. Then, as he did in all his meetings with Eastern bloc leaders, the Christian diplomat shared his belief that the only true peace was peace with God and bore witness to his own belief in the transforming power of Jesus Christ. Arbatov, an intelligent and sophisticated internationalist, listened attentively, with no hint of how he felt about what he was hearing. When the three-hour visit ended, he told Graham he hoped they would visit again. Graham leapt at the bait: "Now that we know each other and have become friends, why don't you call me Billy?" Not overly eager to lose control of the situation, Arbatov responded, "Of course, my name would be George. But why don't we wait till next time?" Graham had no choice but to accede, which he did with grace; he also promised that when he returned to the United States, he would give a thorough report of their conversation to the President.

Throughout the rest of the visit, a deputy of Arbatov's stuck so close by Graham's side that he became a source of considerable irritation to Billy and his associates, as well as to a Baptist official who jockeyed with him constantly to see who could stand closer whenever a camera pointed in the evangelist's direction. At times Graham grew almost desperate to rid himself of his uninvited companions, but lack of certainty over exactly whom they represented and what authority they possessed left him with little alternative but to follow the example of the Apostle Paul and regard them as thorns in the flesh which he must bear for the gospel's sake. Despite this irritation, he felt confident the meeting with Arbatov had opened a wide door for his ministry. Unable to sleep that night, he called Haraszti to his room at 2:00 A.M. "Alex," he said, "I feel that I'm in the will of God. I feel that my present visit will have an effect upon the fate of our two nations, and also upon the fate of mankind." Haraszti readily agreed. This was the beginning, he felt, of Evangelicalism's penetration of the Soviet Union. "Other people write history," he said. "We are making history."

Despite such high expectations, the long-awaited day of triumph, when Billy Graham would finally preach Christ in the capital of communism, was, quite simply, a fizzle. Exhausted and still suffering from jet lag, he was pulled out of bed early Sunday morning and trundled over to the Baptist church. The unannounced change and the early hour, when public transportation was limited, short-circuited the development of an unwieldy crowd. As a further control, entrance to the service was by government-approved passes dispensed by Baptist leaders, with at least some direction from state officials. Of nearly 1,000 people present for the service, only about one third were from the church; another third were reporters and delegates from the peace conference, and the remainder were "outsiders," generally conceded to contain an undetermined but probably substantial contingent of KGB security personnel. (Questioned later about the presence of KGB agents at the service, Graham said he hoped that was true: "Those are the kinds of people I've been trying to reach for a long time.") Several hundred Soviet Evangelicals arrived late, but instead of being allowed to sit in normally open overflow rooms, they were kept behind barricades a block away, where they sang hymns to signal their presence, a bold gesture that could have led to their arrest under normal circumstances.

When Bychkov introduced Graham to the congregation, he asked how many had read his book, *Peace with God*. Though most could have had access only to hand-copied or other duplicated versions, nearly half the people in the audience raised their hands. Graham preached a rousing hour-long sermon on the healing of the paralytic man described in the fifth chapter of John, likening the man's change to religious conversion. Ticking off the marks of a convert's life, he mentioned that believers should be diligent workers and loyal citizens, "because in the thirteenth [chapter] of Romans, we're told to obey the authorities." A wire-service reporter erroneously converted that sentence into Graham's text, and newspaper accounts all over America subsequently indicated that Graham had preached a sermon on the thirteenth chapter of Romans urging Christians to be submissive to authorities.

Bychkov called Graham's visit "a great event in the history of our church," but not all Baptists agreed. At least three people brandished signs or banners protesting the persecution and imprisonment of religious workers in the Soviet Union. A plainclothesman ripped a sign away from one woman, and another was detained briefly by authorities after the service. When told of this, Graham once again showed his attachment to decency and order by responding blandly, "We detain people in the United States if we catch them doing something wrong. I have had people coming to my services in the United States and causing disturbances and they have been taken out by the police." He could not be prodded into a more provocative comment. "In a host country like this," he said, "it's been my practice through the years never to take political sides and get involved in local problems." In a subsequent discussion of the same incident, he explained that, if he were to follow any other policy, "then it means that my own ministry is limited." One disappointed Baptist commented, "I don't see any difference between Dr. Billy Graham and our own timid churchmen, who are scared to death to offend the authorities. We hoped for better things from him. He could be very helpful if he wanted to be." And a disillusioned woman said, "I'm sure our authorities are very reassured by what they heard today. If they could trust him to be so uncontroversial every time, they'd probably let him have his crusade and then use it to prove that there is freedom of religion in our country."

Graham's behavior was not a bold public stand for freedom, to be sure, but neither was it the sycophant self-aggrandizement some thought. The detained woman, for example, had held up a banner reading, "We have more than 150 prisoners for the work of the gospel," apparently referring to a well-known aggregation of imprisoned pastors. Because he felt a public statement would be less effective than private diplomacy, Graham did not reveal that he had the names, addresses, pictures, and other relevant information on 147 of these prisoners and that he was in serious conversation with Soviet authorities about them.

As soon as he ended his sermon at the Baptist church, Graham was whisked back into a car for a dash to the patriarchal cathedral. There Father Borovoy introduced him to a crowd of approximately 5,000 and allowed him to speak for a few minutes to worshipers who had stood throughout the three-hour liturgy. He attempted a condensed version of the same sermon he had just given, but whatever effect it might have had was diminished by the lack of a microphone and his interpreter's soft voice, a combination that led a sizable segment at the rear of the church to shout repeatedly, "We can't hear! Louder! Louder!" Graham was able to declare, however, that he had experienced three conversions in his lifetime: his first acknowledgment of Christ as his Lord and Savior, his determination to work for a racially just society, and more recently, his commitment to work for world peace for the rest of his life. After a quick lunch with the patriarch in a private room on the third floor, he was treated to a four-hour tour of the publishing facility. "Who wanted ever to see the publishing department of the Orthodox Church?" Haraszti later fumed, barely able to control his frustration at the still-fresh memory. "It was a made-up meeting. It had no real meaning or significance. All the good time was taken up, just to be sure there would be no opportunity for anything." Some blamed the Russians for the fiasco. Haraszti saw it otherwise. "We blew it! It is we who blew our chances. Moscow could have been a world affair—all splendor, Billy Graham with the patriarch in the cathedral, with the patriarch of Alexandria, the patriarch of Romania, the metropolitan of Poland, the metropolitan of Finland all present, and the great evangelist talking to the people." Failure to understand the Soviet situation and an unbridled penchant for publicity that led to announcement of the visit had tarnished a golden opportunity. "I will control my expressions," Haraszti said, but "this is the lack of wisdom of American Evangelical people to the capital of the atheistic world. You see? A lack of wisdom.... We misused, abused, and breached the verbal contract. I actually am unhappy."

The early sessions of the peace conference, held at the International Trade Center rather than at a religious site, immediately confirmed the suspicion of critics. Patriarch Pimen opened the proceedings with an assault on the West for "blackening the honest and openly peace-loving policy of our fatherland." That theme continued as speakers from Soviet-influenced nations praised President Brezhnev and Soviet policies and laid the blame for the arms race squarely at the feet of Western warmongers. Graham had said beforehand that he would walk out if the proceedings grew too one sided. That threshold was apparently not crossed, but when a Syrian delegate scheduled to give a three-minute greeting launched into a slashing half-hour diatribe against the United States, Graham, who was sitting on the platform and visible to all, removed his headphones to signal his unwillingness to listen further to attacks on his country. In response to these broadsides, Arie Brouwer, general secretary of the Reformed Church in America, and David Preus, presiding bishop of the American Lutheran Church, warned that if such unproductive harangues continued, the American contingent would walk out. Either by coincidence or, more likely, at explicit instructions from Soviet authorities—-shortly after Graham removed his headphones, Metropolitan Filaret and other Orthodox leaders began passing slips of paper back and forth—the attacks on the United States abruptly ceased.

When Graham's turn came to speak late Tuesday morning, he acquitted himself admirably. Other speakers had run over their allotted time so much that speakers were being urged to cut nonessential remarks in the interest of time. Always unusually conscious of time, Graham fretted and tried to decide on what he might omit until Filaret came to him privately and said, "Regardless of everything else, don't curtail your message. Say everything that is on your heart." Whether or not he said everything, he said a great deal. After making the expected statements of appreciation to Pimen and Filaret, he summoned an image Billy Sunday or Mordecai Ham would have appreciated. The United States and Russia, he said, reminded him of two boys, their hands filled with lighted matches, standing in a room knee-deep with gasoline. Though they might argue immaturely over who had the most matches and how they could arrive at an equal distribution, both knew full well that if either dropped just one match, mutual destruction was certain. While disclaiming technical expertise that would enable him to set forth a comprehensive plan for disarmament, and reasserting his conviction that no lasting peace could come until the advent of Christ, Graham insisted nonetheless that Christian leaders had a solemn obligation to call the nations to repentance—all nations. "No nation, large or small," he stressed, "is exempt from blame for the present state of international affairs." The "unchecked production of weapons of mass destruction," he charged, "is a mindless fever which threatens to consume much of our world and destroy the sacred gift of life," but even if nuclear war never comes, "the nuclear arms race has already indirectly caused a hidden holocaust of unimaginable proportions in our world. Every day, millions upon millions of people live on the knife-edge of survival because of starvation, poverty, and disease. At the same time, we are told the nations of the world are spending an estimated $600 billion per year on weapons. If even one-tenth of that amount were diverted to long-range development programs that would help the world's poor and starving, millions of lives could be saved each year. The standard of living in underdeveloped countries would be raised significantly. If we do not see our moral and spiritual responsibility concerning this life-and-death matter, I firmly believe the living God will judge us for our blindness and lack of compassion."

In his specific recommendations, Graham called on world leaders to turn down the volume on hostile rhetoric and listen carefully and emphatically to what those on the other side were saying. Reflecting his own convictions regarding the importance of personal relationships, he recommended an increase in every sort of cultural interchange between Eastern and Western nations. Then, in the only mention of the topic by any speaker, he called on all nations to respect "the rights of religious believers as outlined in the United Nations Universal Declaration of Human Rights" and agreed to by those who signed the Final Act at Helsinki, to "recognize and respect the freedom of the individual to profess and practice, alone or in community with others, religion or belief acting in accordance with the dictates of his own conscience." After renewing his call for a SALT 10 elimination of weapons, Graham closed by recalling that thirty-seven years earlier, almost to the day, the Nazi forces had surrendered in Berlin, bringing to an end a devastating war in which the United States and the Soviet Union had fought side by side against a common enemy. Today, he said, these two, and all other nations on earth, again faced a common enemy: the threat of impending nuclear destruction. "May all of us," he pleaded, "whether we are from large nations or small nations, do all we can to remove this deadly blight from our midst and save the sacred gift of life from nuclear catastrophe."

Graham's address met with three minutes of sustained applause and Cossack-style foot stamping, but he was not permitted to savor that moment long. Violating a trust, however unwittingly, by publicizing his schedule had caused him one set of problems. Keeping a trust created another set of at least equal magnitude. Metropolitan Filaret's hope that the Pentecostal problem would be resolved before Graham arrived in Moscow had not been realized. The dissidents were still in the embassy basement and the United States was still trying to embarrass the Soviet government into guaranteeing them the right to emigrate if they emerged. Ambassador Hartman, irked that Graham had agreed to participate in the peace conference, refused to meet him at the airport or to hear him preach at the patriarchal cathedral lest he seem to be approving his visit, but he did invite the evangelist to dinner at the ambassadorial residence and seemed determined to use him as a weapon in the struggle over the Pentecostals.

In deference to the strong anxieties of both the Soviet government and the Orthodox Church, Graham had given his assurance that any visit with the dissidents would be private and pastoral, not public and political, and that he would make every effort to keep the visit low-key and confidential, with no reporters, photographers, or television cameras present. That assurance, accepted by the Russians "with grinding teeth," proved hard to uphold. As Graham headed for his car after a brief press conference on his arrival at the airport, a reporter from a Charlotte television station, with cameras whirring behind him, pushed toward him with a thick packet, calling out, "Dr. Graham! Dr. Graham! These are letters from the Pentecostals." Graham was taken aback and instructed Haraszti to take the letters, in which the Pentecostals urged Graham either not to visit them at all, or if he did visit, to demand first that the Soviet government agree to their emigration. Neither option seemed viable, but Graham and his colleagues saw immediately that press determination to give full publicity to any contact with the Pentecostals put him in an extremely delicate position.

Alerted that the press planned to be present for Graham's scheduled visit to the embassy, Akers complained to Ambassador Hartman, then said that Graham would not visit the Pentecostals if the media were involved. Hartman reluctantly agreed to keep the press away from the evangelist during his visit and provided aides who helped Graham and his party push through a swarm of at least fifty reporters who met them when they arrived at the embassy on Tuesday evening. After keeping Graham's party waiting for a long period in a bare room outside his ninth-floor office—Haraszti felt it was a deliberate "royal waiting time" designed to establish rank—Hartman informed Graham that the Pentecostals insisted on television and photographic coverage of the visit. While Akers and Smyth went downstairs to talk with the Pentecostals, Hartman pressed Graham to accept their demand. In an adjoining room, the deputy chief of mission, Warren Zimmerman, urged Haraszti to convince Graham that he had a responsibility to take a bold stand for religious freedom. Hartman's pressure weighed heavily on Graham's shoulders. When the ambassador and his deputy left the two men alone, Graham said, "Alex, I don't know what to do. I feel like I'm letting the Pentecostals down."

Haraszti called on his experience as a physician to give an answer. Medical disaster plans, he explained, include a system known as triage. Of three categories of casualties, those who will survive without attention and those who will perish no matter how much attention they receive are ignored. The responsible physician makes his decision, then gives his attention to those who truly need his help to survive. "You are in a similar situation," he said. The Soviet Union and its satellite nations contained 400 million people; the U.S.

embassy contained six Pentecostals. Based on his extensive negotiations over this matter, Haraszti felt certain the Soviet government was willing to allow the dissidents to leave the country but had made it a matter of honor not to give in to U.S. pressure and would let them go only when it could be accomplished in a nonsensational way that would preserve Soviet dignity. Even if Graham were somehow to create a stir sufficient to embarrass the government into releasing the Pentecostals, he would immediately and forever end any chance of a further ministry in Eastern Europe. "Which is more important," Haraszti asked, "six or four hundred million? To do what the Pentecostals want or to come back to Russia on a greater scale?" Haraszti enjoyed telling the story. "I will never forget," he said. "He stuck out his chin—you know, he has a strong chin—and he said, 'I have made my decision. If they insist on cameras, I will not visit them.'"

At that point, Akers and Smyth returned to confirm that the Pentecostals were insisting on photographic coverage. Graham stood firm, and after two more visits by Akers and Smyth the dissidents agreed to an unrecorded visit. A consul took them downstairs, through an inner courtyard where photographers had been allowed to congregate, and into the basement rooms where the Pentecostals were living. Once inside, Haraszti and Akers both immediately noticed that a curtain over the basement window had been pulled open to permit photographers standing outside to take pictures of the gathering. While Akers waved his hands to spoil the cameramen's view, Haraszti pulled the curtain to close the gap. "I looked around," he recalled. "If they could have killed me by looks, they would have. I would not be here."

The Pentecostals seemed obviously dejected and resentful, but Graham greeted each one warmly, "with a hug and a kiss. All of them. Very nice." But as soon as he sat down at a table to talk with them, Lyubov Vaschenko, a girl of seventeen or eighteen, opened a spiral notebook and began to read questions from it. Haraszti could not believe it. "There was no Thank you for coming.... We have heard of you.... No appreciation. Nothing." The questions, which he felt certain had been prepared by American reporters, were sharp and accusing. Why had Graham refused to have their meeting photographed? Why had he come? What would we tell the American President? Why was he not interested in helping them gain release? Graham explained that his visit was pastoral and that he never televised a pastoral visit. He did not yet know what he would tell the President. He was working to help them, but privately, and felt that a public furor would not be in their interest.

After further sparring, the highlight of which was an unsuccessful attempt to get Graham to identify the red horse in the book of Revelation as communism, Graham interrupted Lyubov Vaschenko's questions by reading from Psalm 37: "Wait for the Lord and be patient, and He will bring up your sun." He counseled the Pentecostals to be patient, expressing his sympathy for their situation and his hope that it would soon be resolved. Then, using a classic Evangelical technique for escaping from a tense encounter, he suggested they pray together. When Graham finished his own prayer, in which he asked God to give the Pentecostals wisdom to understand and accept the present situation, he fell silent, expecting other members of the group to offer their own prayers. When a long period of utter silence made it clear no one else would speak, Graham and his colleagues, and then the Pentecostals, stood up. The visit was over.

"They were just full of rage," Haraszti recalled. "Two thirds of the questions had not been read. Billy would not say the red horse was the Communist government. They were just outraged." In a last attempt to snatch some victory, Vaschenko asked Graham "in a very nice way" if she might take a picture of him, "just for our family album. We would like to have a memory that we were with you." Graham, congenitally unable to say no easily, looked at his associates for help, murmuring that he had no objection as long as they promised not to use it to publicize his visit. Akers stepped in quickly and reminded him that they had agreed no photographs would be taken and that agreement must be kept. Relieved to let someone else don the black hat, Graham agreed, and after awkwardly stiff good-byes, he and his party adjourned to the ambassador's residence for dinner. The next morning, the American press reported that the Pentecostals had been not at all impressed with Billy Graham—"He was like all the other religious figures who have visited us, nothing special"—and had been disappointed with the visit and with his failure to offer any help other than prayer.

Though it was a public relations fiasco and seemed, on the surface, to lend credence to the charge that Graham was more concerned with chalking up new preaching victories than with standing up for oppressed people, the eventual resolution of the Pentecostal problem proved to be a singular example of the Graham team's diplomatic skill and the evangelist's unique influence in Soviet circles. During a return visit to Moscow in the summer of that year, Haraszti spoke about the Pentecostals with Metropolitan Filaret and with Georgi Arbatov; with ministers of the Soviet State Council for Religious Affairs; and with the first deputy to Boris Ponomarev, chief of the party's International Affairs Department and the highest-ranking Soviet official Graham had met during his visit. He also discussed the situation thoroughly with the State Department and with staff members at the Soviet embassy in Washington. His message was simple and straightforward: The Pentecostal situation is a problem for both the United States and the Soviet Union. Neither side invited it, neither side wants it, but both sides have it, and negotiation through regular diplomatic channels has failed to resolve the problem. Billy Graham realizes this is not a simple case of religious persecution, but the American public does not, and public opinion is such that it will be extremely difficult for the President to start arms-reduction negotiations with the Soviets until this matter is resolved. Graham also understands that neither party can appear to yield on this issue without losing face. Therefore, as a private citizen, he offers his personal guarantee, backed by his own person as a hostage to the Soviets, if necessary—in fact, Haraszti made this offer without Graham's knowledge or agreement—that if the Soviet Union will guarantee to allow the Pentecostals to leave the country, the United States will not use the issue for propaganda against the Soviet government.

When Haraszti carried this message to Arthur Hartman, the ambassador laughed in derision. Who does Billy Graham think he is, that the Pentecostals would believe he could persuade the Soviets to guarantee their freedom? And if Soviet authorities gave him such a promise, what reason was there to believe they would not lie to him? Haraszti went back to Ponomarev's deputy, who told him that Soviet dignity demanded that the Pentecostals not leave the country as a result of pressure from the U.S. government. Soviet law would not allow them to apply for a visa from the U.S. embassy, because the embassy is a foreign territory. If they wanted an exit visa, they had to leave the embassy, return to their homes in Siberia and apply for a permit there. If they did that, the Deputy promised, "They will leave the Soviet Union without any delay. They must trust the Soviet government that we keep our word." Haraszti stressed the risk to Billy Graham if he used his reputation and influence to assure both the Pentecostals and the U.S. government that the Soviet government could be trusted.

The deputy looked Haraszti squarely in the eye. "The Soviet Union," he said, "will not lie to Billy Graham."

"This is what we believe," Haraszti responded. "We are sure about this. Billy Graham trusts the Soviet government. So, we have an agreement."

"You do and we do," the deputy said, "because we have no interest in keeping the Pentecostals if they leave the U.S. embassy. Our interest is to get rid of this issue. Our interest is to forget it and never remember it."

This, unfortunately, did not convince Hartman, who dismissed Haraszti's report as wishful thinking and counseled the Pentecostals to remain in the embassy. Metropolitan Filaret tried to help by writing a letter to Graham, stating that it was the conviction of the Orthodox Church that if the Pentecostals left the embassy on their own and returned to Siberia, they would be allowed to leave the Soviet Union. Still, Hartman would not budge. Haraszti felt he knew the reason: "The ambassador obviously was jealous.... [He] did not want the Pentecostals to leave under Billy Graham's negotiations." Whatever Hartman's motives—and wariness toward Soviet promises could hardly be considered a diplomatic weakness—Graham and his associates continued to press their case. Finally, during the spring of 1983, Graham wrote a letter to the Pentecostals outlining the steps he felt they should take. A few days later, on the evening of April 13, a consul from the U.S. embassy called on Alexander Haraszti in his Moscow hotel room to inform him that the Pentecostals had left the embassy and were at that moment on a plane to Siberia. Not long afterward, the two families, together with several relatives who had not been with them in the embassy, were allowed to emigrate, one group to Israel and the other to St. Louis. Billy Graham and Alexander Haraszti never received any further word of explanation from the Soviets or appreciation from the Pentecostals. John Akers claimed that Soviet church leaders informed him that Graham's influence had been decisive but acknowledged that other groups had also claimed an influence and added, "We have to be very careful about what we claim. We're not trying to get onto that bandwagon." Asked in 1989 to assess his role in the incident, Graham smiled faintly and wrapped himself in the familiar and becoming old cloak of astute humility. "I think [the Soviets] eventually did what we asked them to," he said, as if he could barely remember. "I have no way of knowing whether [what we did] was a factor or not. But I think it was."

31

Tribulation and Triumph

Graham's visit to the Siberian Pentecostals and his address at the peace conference made modest news in America, and the Moscow trip might easily have slipped into the historical record with little notice had it not been for the evangelist's encounters with the press. Ed Plowman, a veteran journalist who handled Graham's press relations on the tour, could not remember a week in which Billy spent more time with the press, and it seemed to him, from the first confrontation at the airport to the last press conference, that the primary goal of some reporters was to goad their quarry into making a headline-grabbing anti-Soviet statement. For his part, Graham did his best to stay on a tightrope between violating his conscience and irritating his hosts. His performance was wobbly at times, but an intrinsically difficult trick was made even harder by reporters who were shaking the wire.

At a press conference just before Graham left Moscow, the Charlotte reporter who had handed him the letters from the Pentecostals on his arrival asked him for his conclusions about religious freedom in the Soviet Union. His answer, as captured on Plowman's tape recorder, involved hedging and omissions but cast a moderately favorable light. Noting that he had been in Russia only six days, nearly all of that in a small area of Moscow and all heavily scheduled, he said he could not possibly make any valid personal evaluation of the state of religious freedom throughout the vast Soviet Union. "There are differences," he acknowledged, "between religion as it's practiced here and, let's say, in the United States, but that doesn't mean there is no religious freedom." He observed that "not one single person has ever suggested what I put in the address I gave to the congress or the sermons I preached here," and no one had tried to stop him from presenting the gospel to everyone he had called upon during his visit. "So I have experienced total liberty in what I wanted to say." He also mentioned that most nations place some limits on the practice of religion: In the United States, for example, "a public school teacher cannot lead her pupils in Bible study and prayer."

Was he saying, the reporter pressed, that the purported lack of religious freedom in the Soviet Union is a myth? "Not necessarily," Graham replied. "I'm just telling you that I don't know all about it.... I haven't had a chance [to see everything]." Had he stopped there, he might have gotten off lightly, but he continued. "Saturday night, I went to three Orthodox churches. They were jammed to capacity on a Saturday night. You'd never get that in Charlotte, North Carolina [Laughter]. On Sunday morning the same was true of the churches I went to, and it seemed to me that the churches that are open, of which there are thousands, seem to have liberty of worship services." This indicated that at least "a measure of freedom" existed in the Soviet Union, "perhaps more than many Americans think." Also, life in Russia was not as grim as the popular impression had it. "The meals I've had are among the finest I've ever eaten. In the United States, you have to be a millionaire to have caviar, but I've had caviar with almost every meal I've eaten." Later, while walking with an AP reporter through a tunnel in the Moscow airport on the way to his plane, he repeated the assertion that "thousands of churches are open," and followed up with a factually accurate but easily distortable excursus on church polity. These churches, he said in stunning understatement, "may have different relationships [with the state] than, say, they have in Canada or Great Britain. And in Great Britain you have a state church and in other countries you have state churches. Here the church is not a state church. It is a 'free' church in the sense that it is not directly headed, as the church in England is headed, by the Queen."

These statements, which reached the United States before Graham reached London, created a furor in America. Problematic enough on their own, they were more often than not twisted just enough to make them sound incredibly naive. It was frequently reported Graham had said that there was no religious repression in the Soviet Union, that religion was more fervent in Moscow than in Charlotte, and freer from state control than in England. He was also roundly chastised for having preached on Romans, chapter 13, implying that Christians should not resist religious intolerance by the authorities. Did Billy Graham not realize that the "liberty" he "personally experienced" was no more generally available to Soviet citizens than were the caviar he ate or the Chaika limousine that shuttled him around the city while other delegates to the conference rode in buses? Did he not count the Siberian Pentecostals he had visited or the 147 imprisoned religious workers as tangible evidence of religious repression? Had no one pointed out that the churches were filled not only because there were so few of them but also because it was the anniversary of V-E Day, when Soviets celebrate what they regard as a virtually unaided Russian victory over Hitler's army? And was he truly so credulous as to believe that by complimenting his hosts in public he would be in a stronger position to press the case for religious freedom in private? *Christianity Today* quoted an unnamed but leading newsman who charged that "mouthing the gospel to Soviet leadership and privately urging them to act contrary to their basic convictions was an utter waste of time. Of course, he could preach his gospel and tell them in private to relax their restrictions against religion. But do you think Graham will convert those Communists or move them to lower their tyrannic grip? Of course not. Graham was a fool to think so. He was duped by them to fit into their propaganda and their Marxist program for nothing in return." Even the *New York Times*, which Ed Plowman admitted had been "a towering exception" to what he regarded as rampantly inaccurate and biased reporting, observed that "heaven only knows what Mr. Graham wanted to accomplish with his misguided denials of Soviet repression." And at Wheaton College, approximately fifty peaceful protesters milled and marched outside the Billy Graham Center, carrying signs that proclaimed BILLY GRAHAM HAS BEEN DUPED BY THE SOVIETS and GRAHAM EATS CAVIAR AS RUSSIAN CHRISTIANS SUFFER IN JAILS.

Graham was astonished at the reaction. Interviewed from London by satellite on *This Week with David Brinkley*, he complained with good reason that the press had distorted his statements in Moscow. He attended the peace conference, he said, "totally because I wanted to preach the gospel of Christ in atheistic Russia." Of course, he was aware that his visit and his statements might be used for propaganda purposes, but "I believe my propaganda of the gospel of Christ is far stronger than any other propaganda in the world." Confronting him in the interview were United Methodist minister Edmund Robb, who charged that whatever his intentions, Graham had been manipulated to lend credibility to a rigged conference, and Soviet dissident Mark Azbel, who stated point-blank that "people in Russia ... think that you've betrayed their hopes. They think that you are not knowledgeable enough to bring the message about the situation with religion in Russia." When Graham freely admitted he was not an expert on the situation, Azbel shot back, "Then keep out of the discussion."

Immediately upon his arrival in New York a few days later, Graham held a press conference and gave interviews in which he tried to explain himself once again, with scarcely better results. He expressed deep regret at his failure to cite the plight of the Siberian Pentecostals and the 147 imprisoned religious workers as evidence of formal religious repression. He pointed out that his sermon at the Baptist church had been on John chapter 5, and conceded that the reference to the thirteenth chapter of Romans had been a mistake, lamely contending that when he called on citizens to *obey authority*, he had meant "the authority of Christ," and that "it never occurred to me until after I preached the sermon that somebody might take it as applying to that situation there. (He had tried to make that same point on the Brinkley show, visibly befuddling both Sam Donaldson and George Will.) He patiently explained that he had used *free church* in the technical sense of "lacking state support," and would "never in a million years" have suggested that churches had greater freedom in the Soviet Union than in Britain. And he repeatedly denied that he had pulled his punches in the hope of gaining permission to hold a full-scale crusade in the Soviet Union but counted it significant that he had met more "top Soviet officials" than he had ever dreamed possible and had told each one how he had been saved and what the Bible says every man must do to be saved. It was in these meetings, he insisted, that he had said the things the press and his detractors wanted him to say in public: "There's a diplomatic language in public, but behind the scenes, you get tough." He also asserted that at least part of the reason for the outcry over his visit was "an irrational fear" many Americans felt toward the Soviet Union, a fear that made it impossible for them to believe that he could establish cordial and sincere relationships with Soviet leaders. "They are not all alike any more than we're all alike," he said, and such outmoded stereotypes constitute a barrier to peace.

Not all of Graham's problems, however, stemmed from misquotation or misconstruction by American reporters, and not every use of his words by the Soviets was innocent of deceit. A BGEA press release of May 19, 1982, quoted him as saying, "In the Soviet Union there are an estimated 20,000 places of worship of various religions open and each year hundreds of permits are granted for new churches." That statement, apparently based on information furnished Graham by his hosts, was inaccurate. A 1987 statement by the chairman of the Soviet State Council for Religious Affairs revealed that the actual number of religious organizations operating in the Soviet Union in 1981 was 15,687 and that the number of registrations had dropped by approximately 7,000 during the previous two decades and continued to drop until 1986. Moreover, long after Graham had tried to explain his statement to Western reporters, Soviet commentators were proclaiming them as gospel truth. On an August 1982 Radio Moscow broadcast, the program's host responded to an inquiry concerning religious freedom by noting that his own words, or those by any representative of Radio Moscow, might be distrusted. For that reason, he said, "I will instead quote the testimony of unimpeachable witnesses. The latest of these has been the American evangelist, Dr. Billy Graham, whom no one in his right mind would suspect of sympathizing with the Soviet system. At the conclusion of his visit to the Soviet Union earlier this summer, Billy Graham said he had found more religious freedom in the Soviet Union than in Britain, with its established Church of England."

Graham's explanations and apologias neither convinced nor silenced his critics. A gang of seventeen members of the radical Jewish Defense League ransacked the New York offices of the World Council of Churches, demanding that the WCC renounce Graham's visit. Dan Rather asserted that Soviet bloc immigrants and Graham's Evangelical friends alike believed that the evangelist, "to put it bluntly, was had—deceived and used." And the author of a letter to *Christianity Today* claimed that "one of the world's best informed commentators on Soviet religious life," following a visit to Russia shortly after Graham's remarks were publicized, "did not find a single believer who was not numbed and shocked by Graham's apparent lack of sensitivity to the persecuted." Clicking off a list of Soviet abuses during a CBS News commentary, former Baptist minister and old friend Bill Moyers said, "Religious freedom is tolerated, as long as you don't exercise it. Billy Graham did not miss this, so much as he ignored it, partly from Southern courtesy, partly for tactical reasons, partly as the price of celebrity. He's a popular and pleasant fellow who doesn't like offending his hosts, whether in Washington or Moscow. But it's never easy to sup with power and get up from the table spotless. That's why the prophets of old preferred the wilderness. When they came forth, it was not to speak softly with kings and governors, but to call them to judgment."

Once again, as he had done when challenged to be bolder on civil rights and Vietnam, Graham took refuge in his role as evangelist. He acknowledged he could understand how some could view him as a self-aggrandizing opportunist—"It looks that way to the outsider and probably looks a little bit that way to me"—but insisted that "wanting to preach in Russia is not my ego; it's my calling." He had been shocked and shaken by the reaction to his visit and comments, he said, but now he had "a feeling of serenity" about the whole episode. "I have the greatest sense of peace that I was in the will of the Lord.... There might have been one or two little things I would have changed, like that verse of Scripture ... but I believe the whole thing was of God."

Much as Graham and his colleagues hoped, his behavior at the Moscow conference convinced Soviet authorities that he was no apparent threat to public order or political stability. Before 1982 was out, the German Democratic Republic (GDR) and Czechoslovakia, two countries with which Haraszti had been negotiating for several years, allowed Graham to make carefully controlled but satisfying visits. The GDR was the tougher of the two to crack. During the five years Haraszti and Sandor Palotay had negotiated with Imre Miklos over the invitation to Hungary, the governments of East Germany and Romania were the only two Communist regimes to disapprove of the 1977 visit. The reasons behind East German reticence were political—and quite understandable. At least partly because many church and Communist party leaders had come to know and respect one another while imprisoned by Hitler as enemies of the Third Reich, believers in East Germany enjoyed a fair amount of freedom—Christian books and periodicals were available in religious bookstores, religious programs were aired regularly over state-run radio and television networks, the state-supported Lutheran Church operated six university-level seminaries, the government paid the operating expenses of the Church's numerous social agencies, and more than fifty full-time Lutheran evangelists were allowed to proclaim the gospel as long as they adhered to certain tolerable restrictions. That accommodation, however, had been strained as large numbers of young people began to show interest in religion. A monthly service in Karl Marxstadt, for example, regularly drew between 5,000 and 10,000 young people, some of whom admitted that attending church was a way of making a statement against the government when few other such expressions would be tolerated. To counteract this trend, the state had begun to bar young people from universities and good jobs for no apparent reason other than their status as active Christians. In addition, many East Germans longed for reunification with West Germany. If Billy Graham visited the GDR and rallied young people to the church or further stirred up already-restive dissidents, the results could be unfortunate.

To allay fears that he would push for reunification, Graham acceded to the urgings of East German officials and canceled plans for a preaching tour of West Germany. The Moscow visit finally toppled the last barriers to state approval for a trip to the GDR, but another premature leak of the news, this time by a staff member in BGEA's Berlin office, almost undid nearly four years of backstage negotations. When Graham finally visited six East German cities in October 1982, he met with enthusiastic response from young people but notable restraint on the part of church and state leaders. He recalled a meeting with Lutheran pastors of the Synod of Saxony as extremely uncomfortable. "When I walked in," he said, "I did not see a warm eye in the place. I shook hands with several people, and they gave me a very cold look. When I stood up, I told them that I'm a fellow believer. I believe in the Lord Jesus Christ with all my heart. So do you. We profess the same faith. But you all looked at me with such hostility when I came in. I could see it in your eyes. I didn't see the warmth a Christian should be having toward a fellow Christian.'" He acknowledged that this sort of challenge was unusual for him. "I had never done that in my whole life, to any group of people. But when I finished, they gave me a nice ovation, and when I went out, I shook hands with many of them and their eyes were just smiling."

Graham's appointments with state leaders were similarly cool. At a meeting with party leader Erich Honecker's first deputy and other top officials, he listened to a series of predictable statements about the peace-seeking ideals of the Soviet bloc nations. When his turn came, he got right to the point. "Your country doesn't trust my country," he said, "and my country doesn't trust your country. And that makes it pretty difficult to live with each other." He then spoke of the atomic bomb and subsequent nuclear weapons. Men had built them, dropped them, and now stood ready to use them again. The problem, it seemed, was something wrong with the hearts of men. With that as his "sermon starter," he proceeded to tell them how Jesus Christ could renew the heart of any man who seeks him. Ed Plowman recalled that "they were ill at ease, but fascinated. They couldn't say much. He hit them right where they lived. He felt good about it."

From East Germany, Graham went directly to Czechoslovakia for a rather tense four-day visit. Clergymen in all the Soviet bloc countries had to make some accommodation to the state in order to operate with any measure of freedom. In Czechoslovakia state control of the clergy was so strict, and sometimes capricious, that ministers operated in constant anxiety over the possibility that a misstep, or even an internal church squabble that displeased state authorities, would cost them their license and their ministry. As a result, Graham found churchmen more wary of his visit than were government officials. The government, however, had its own agenda and clearly hoped to use Graham's visit to bolster its image. Admission to Graham's several appearances was by ticket only, and tickets were given only to those who the government felt certain would not be whipped into some kind of antigovernment uprising. "They tried to keep this silent," Haraszti recalled. "They wanted the propaganda advantage of [making it appear they had a] free society, while keeping control of a closed society."

In one blatant effort, they arranged for him to visit a war memorial in Bratislava and suggested he deliver a speech praising the Russian soldiers who had died in the liberation of Czechoslovakia at the end of World War II. He had already learned that in official Soviet history America's role in defeating Germany had been virtually elided. He agreed to speak at the memorial but gave clear notice he would pay tribute not just to Soviet soldiers but to Russians and Americans alike. "Oh, they did not like it! They took strong exception," Haraszti recalled. "But we gave them two alternatives: Either Billy Graham does not visit the war memorial or he does visit and speaks according to history, not according to your history. He visited the memorial. I had to be there all the time, to check the history, to be sure that he would not be led astray."

Graham continued his practice of speaking to government officials about the need for greater religious freedom and the reduction of tension between Church and State. He also gained an unprecedented bit of national exposure for religion when a television interview by one of the country's best-known news commentators aired uncut in prime time over the state-run network. Once again Graham made a positive impression on government officials. Several years after the visit, Reinhold Kerstan, a Baptist World Alliance executive who had accompanied Graham on this tour, ran into visa problems while traveling through Czechoslovakia on his way to Austria. Unable to make headway through normal channels, he called the head of the Ministry of Religious Affairs, identified himself as a member of Graham's 1982 party, and asked for help. Within forty-five minutes, Kerstan was on his way, with the assurance that "it was a delight to do something for the friend of my friend, Dr. Billy Graham."

Graham's plane had barely soared out of the Moscow airport at the end of his 1982 visit when Alexander Haraszti began preparing the ground for a return visit. His first task was to make amends to Orthodox leaders who resented Graham's attention to government authorities. They had hoped his visit would strengthen the Church's hand in dealing with the State; by spending so much time with state officials, and particularly by visiting Arbatov before attending an official church function, Graham seemed to have indicated he held the state in higher regard. "We were ready," one clergyman told him, "not to ever see Billy Graham in the future." Haraszti carefully explained that the Graham team had been uncertain about just who was in charge. When Arbatov sent for him, he had assumed it was with the knowledge and approval of church leaders. When he spoke to other high officials, he had done so not to upstage the church but to represent its interests in a way that church leaders might not be free to do. That seemed to satisfy the Orthodox clergy, as did Haraszti's explanation that Graham's remark that he would like to conduct a "crusade" in the Soviet Union meant simply that he wished to have a chance to preach the gospel, not that he wanted to conquer either the Orthodox Church or the Soviet people. Over the next two years, a dozen more trips, most involving Haraszti, led at last to the extended preaching tour Graham had been seeking so long.

During twelve days in September 1984, Graham spoke more than fifty times in four cities: Moscow and Leningrad, the Estonian city of Tallinn, just across the bay from Finland, and Novosibirsk, deep in the heart of Siberia. The itinerary was tightly controlled, and all speaking engagements were in churches and other religious settings rather than open to the public, but Graham was able to speak to thousands of Christians face-to-face, something no Westerner had ever been allowed to do. In Leningrad he addressed nearly six hundred students and faculty at the Russian Orthodox Theological Academy, telling them how to communicate the gospel effectively. He had prepared a formal lecture, but seminary officials told him, "Oh, no. We'll get this printed and hand it out. We want you to tell us how to preach." So, he recalled, "I just got up and told them how I got started, what methods I use in study, what kind of sermons I prepare, how I deliver them, how I give an invitation to receive Christ, and all that. And then I answered questions. It's the same thing I try to do at every university I visit." He told the seminarians that wherever he went, he found four omnipresent problems: emptiness, loneliness, guilt, and fear of death. All four problems have the same solution—-the gospel of Jesus Christ, simply and authoritatively proclaimed. "In some societies," he admitted, "you cannot go outside and preach as in others," but in every society Christians could manifest such "fruits of the Spirit" as love, joy, peace, long-suffering, gentleness, kindness, and self-control. "People will see you," he assured them, "and after awhile they will say, 'What makes you different?'" And that question would provide the opportunity to bear witness to saving faith. Graham's address was videotaped for use in homiletics classes at the seminary, and one professor grandly declared that Graham's visit "could change the style of preaching in the Orthodox Church." Graham also spoke at Leningrad's patriarchal cathedral, where Metropolitan Antonii shattered precedent by interrupting the three-hour liturgy to introduce him to the congregation of 6,000 as "a great preacher and a great peacemaker" and to allow him to deliver a full-length sermon on "The Glory of the Cross." He followed this triumph with an emotional service at the city's 3,000-member Baptist church, packed to the rafters with eager worshipers, many of whom held microphones to capture every word on their tape recorders.

In Tallinn, Graham spoke at the Orthodox cathedral and two large Baptist churches. At one of the Baptist churches, the 4,500 people who managed to squeeze into the sanctuary were treated to a highlight in the evangelist's life, when he and son Franklin, newly ordained to the ministry, participated together in a service for the first time. The setting, though auspicious, could not have seemed entirely foreign; at the end of the service, two choirs, with full orchestral accompaniment, sang a song that had somehow made its way from the American South a full century earlier: "When the Roll Is Called Up Yonder, I'll Be There." In the academic city of Novosibirsk, five time zones to the east, Graham visited the Siberian Division of the Academy of Sciences of the USSR, where he surprised a group of scientists by asserting that his anthropology professor at Wheaton, a Russian, had taught him that a Siberian had traveled to the New World long before Columbus made the trip. At the city's flourishing Baptist church—one of fifty-four in western Siberia—several thousand people who could not get into the church listened to him over loudspeakers set up in a fenced-in area around the church. The evangelist's request that the congregation pray for the upcoming meeting between President Reagan and Foreign Minister Gromyko surprised the worshipers and caused his advisers to wince; the meeting, revealed to Graham by Reagan, had not yet been announced by either government.

In Moscow, Graham preached at the cathedrals overseen by Patriarch Pimen and Metropolitan Filaret. Remembering the frustrating problems of his first visit, he arranged this time for a special sound system that enabled the thousands of worshipers in both cathedrals to hear him clearly. He also returned to the Baptist church, once for a regular worship service and a second time to address more than 250 Baptist ministers who were gathered to celebrate the hundredth anniversary of the beginning of Baptist mission work in Russia.

In every city, Graham visited with key government leaders, sharing his Christian faith on every occasion—without exception—and stressing the need for all people to work together to achieve lasting peace. In Moscow he renewed his acquaintance with ministers Kuroyedov and Fitsev, who had cleared the way for his visit, and with academician Arbatov. But the most significant visit of this trip was a meeting of nearly two hours with Boris Ponomarev. Chief of the International Affairs Department for the Central Committee of the Communist party and a member of the Politburo, Ponomarev was the most influential Soviet leader to receive Graham on either of his visits and the man Graham felt could do most to improve the situation for Soviet believers. This was the moment he had been waiting for, the moment when all the careful preparation and the quiet bearing up under criticism of his motives would be rewarded. Ponomarev began the conversation with a forty-five-minute monologue on Soviet foreign policy. "I am sure he was trying to get to Reagan through me," Graham admitted. "When he finished, I asked him, 'Now that you have told me what you wanted to say, can I tell you about America? About religion in America? Because you can never understand America until you understand its religious life. Would you like to know what I preach about, and why so many come to hear me preach?' "

Drawing on a statement he had prepared and which he left with Ponomarev at the end of their conversation, Graham explained that a major reason for his tour of the Soviet Union was to "make some contribution to the search for peace in our world." He admitted, "I am not a politician, nor do I consider myself able to deal with the very complex details which are involved in arms control," but as a follower and representative of the Prince of Peace, he felt compelled to call upon the leaders of powerful nations to have the vision and courage to renew their efforts to eliminate such weapons. He acknowledged the ideological and social differences between the United States and the USSR but expressed his conviction that "we must learn to coexist, and even be friends." But before that could happen, he felt Soviet leaders would have to improve the situation with respect to religious believers, "a situation which has a direct and important bearing on relations between our two countries." Graham readily admitted that religious believers had more freedom in 1984 than in earlier periods, as when Nikita Khrushchev closed thousands of churches and subjected believers to severe oppression during the 1960s. He commended the government for relaxing some of its restrictions on believers (as a case in point, he found nine of his own books in print in Russia) but urged that more be done. Pointing to the more than 100 million believers, he observed that trying to control the religious beliefs and practices of so many people created a complicated and unnecessary problem for the government. It also cast the government in an unfavorable light internationally, particularly in the United States, where over 90 percent of the population professes to believe in God and cannot feel much kinship for a society that attempts to establish atheism as its official philosophical position. "We in America," he said, "have fought for decades against discrimination among our citizens because of race, religious creed, color, or national origin. It was a long time before these ideas germinated, but presently it is accepted and more and more practiced by the majority of our people. It also is fully backed by our laws." To people with such a tradition, however imperfectly realized, Soviet restriction of religious freedom constitutes "a deep gulf" between the two nations. "To put it clearly," he explained, "a major reason the American public does not support closer ties with the Soviet Union is because of what is perceived as religious discrimination and even oppression, especially of [Christians] and Jews. You will never reach a satisfactory understanding with the United States as long as you keep up this anti-Semitic and anti-Christian thing. Many Americans are concerned over the very low number of Jews who have been permitted to migrate from the Soviet Union in the last year or two, and other issues affecting people of Jewish background, such as rabbinical training and language teaching in Hebrew. It is difficult for detente to be successful as long as these problems remain."

Graham recalled the barrage of criticism he had received in 1982, when he observed that religious freedom in the Soviet Union was greater than many Americans realized. The media would be lying in wait for him when he returned home this time. People would pay attention to how he answered. "I would like to be able to say in good conscience that in the Soviet Union there is a trend toward granting more and more freedom of religion, and toward lifting regulations and administrative measures which discriminate against believers." He specifically recommended allowing young people to practice religion openly without fear of being barred from universities or desirable occupations, removing all restrictions from the publication of Bibles and other types of religious literature, allowing people to build new church buildings and alter old ones as needed, and permitting churches to operate more seminaries and other institutions for theological training. A man with a keen intuitive understanding of the value of symbols, Graham assured Ponomarev that these and other steps would do much to overcome the negative image Westerners have about Soviet life, "a negative image which again I stress is a major barrier in friendly U.S.-Soviet relations."

The old statesman told Graham, "We will discuss this among ourselves." Four years later, as Graham and former Ambassador Dobrynin entered the building housing the offices of the Central Committee, they ran into Ponomarev. "He was so warm and friendly," the evangelist recalled. "He said, 'I will never forget the things that you said. We have deeply appreciated it and have discussed it many times.'"

Both the Orthodox Church and the Soviet government should also have appreciated the account of Graham's trip that aired on prime-time television in the United States and Canada. The hour-long documentary gave a rather detailed and sympathetic description of Orthodox religion and painted a positive picture of life in the Soviet Union. It also paid tribute to the importance of Moscow as a world city, lauded the richness of its cultural life, and reflecting Graham's appreciation for cleanliness and order, praised the immaculateness of its subway system and made note of the fact that the trains run on time.

The next Communist country to allow Graham to preach was perhaps the most repressive of all: Romania. Alex Haraszti had been working to obtain an invitation since 1978. The Ceauşescu government, badly in need of gestures to mask its true character, agreed to permit a visit as early as 1983, but the Orthodox patriarch resisted for two more years, fearing a Graham tour would boost the fortunes of the large Hungarian Catholic minority and the smaller but vigorous Protestant sects, particularly Baptists and Pentecostals. Despite, or more likely, in direct response to, strict government controls on religion, Romania has been one of the world's revival hot spots during the 1970s and 1980s, and when Graham finally got permission to enter the country in 1985, he was met by the largest crowds he had faced anywhere in Eastern Europe, even though Romanian media gave no advance notice of his visit. In Timisoara, an estimated 150,000 who had gathered on a large square around an Orthodox cathedral grew so frustrated at the government's refusal to allow Graham to address them over loudspeakers that only a strong show of potential force by the state police averted a riot. At one point, as the Orthodox metropolitan led Graham and his party through a dense crowd, the sheer pressure of thousands of people struggling to get close to him caused the evangelist to list to his left at almost a forty-five-degree angle. "What a telling way to die," he gasped, "dying by the crowds which did not hear the gospel." Though he later admitted he had feared for his life, Dr. Haraszti did not count the appearance a failure. "These people," he said, "will speak about what they did not hear."

In Sibiu police averted a repeat of the scene in Timisoara by cordoning Graham off so that no crowds were allowed to form anywhere close to him, but throngs estimated as high as 40,000 heard him in Voronet, Arad, and Oradea. In Bucharest, where he preached at several sites, the government reneged on a promise to allow overflow crowds to hear him by loudspeakers, but at one location, a Baptist minister successfully bluffed a Securitate officer into leaving the loudspeakers in place, warning him that the crowd would kill him if he tried to take them down. Overall, according to Haraszti, approximately 150,000 people heard Graham in Romania; another 150,000 to 250,000 saw but did not hear him because of the lack of loudspeakers. Without question, these were the largest religious gatherings in Romanian history.

As in his first visit to the Soviet Union, Graham baffled and upset many Romanian Christians by expressing his "gratitude to the leadership of their country, which gives full and genuine freedom to all religious denominations," a description they found quite at variance with the true situation, even with respect to his visit.

Interestingly, government officials made little effort to mask their cynicism. Every sermon was introduced with long, self-serving paeans to the Ceauşescu regime, and host churches not only were required to provide expensive gifts to Securitate officials traveling with Graham but were charged exorbitant sums to cover travel and accommodations for the evangelist's party (expenses BGEA had already covered) and for accompanying Romanian officials, apparently including the hundreds of Securitate personnel whose major role was to frustrate efforts of church people to see and hear the evangelist preach. Still, even one Romanian Baptist who reported these disappointments, which he shared, acknowledged that Graham's visit had been "a blessing" and "the greatest public miracle I have experienced" under Communist rule.

Graham followed the Romanian trip with yet another visit, in 1985, to Hungary, whose government demonstrated its cordiality by extending privileges he had received in no other Communist country. In Pecs a crowd of more than 20,000 assembled in front of the Roman Catholic cathedral not only heard Graham speak from the cathedral steps but were able to see his face on a twelve-by-eight-meter Diamond Vision screen brought in from Great Britain. This was the first outdoor public religious meeting since World War II. In Budapest he chalked up another postwar first when he was permitted to speak in a state-owned sports arena that normally seated 12,500 people. When authorities saw that the crowd was a model of deportment, they allowed over 2,000 more to enter, to sit on steps and stand in walkways. At both services and in four other cities where John Akers and Franklin Graham preached, Bibles and copies of *Peace with God* and *The Holy Spirit* were given away or sold at reduced prices at open bookstalls.

After taking note of Graham's two appearances, Cardinal Lékai, Catholic primate of Hungary, told the evangelist in the presence of U.S. ambassador Nicholas Salgo, "There are three people who are great manipulators of crowds in the present world: President Reagan, a former actor; Pope John Paul II, a former actor; and Billy Graham." Haraszti noted with a wry smile that the cardinal "did not add any qualifications after Dr. Graham's name." These men, the cardinal noted, could influence crowds both large and small. They know how to hold attention, how to get people to do what they want them to do, even how to manipulate them. They know what people want to hear and do not want to hear, what causes negative sentiments and what causes positive sentiments. "To be perfectly honest, Dr. Graham," he said, "and please don't be offended, but I call you one of the greatest actors on the human scene. Without all the resources that the President has, or the built-in influential factors that the pope has, you have built yourself up and gone further than either one." Graham, recalled Haraszti, did not respond. "He was very friendly, like always, but he was not taken with it. He has thought of it many times, of course."

Graham felt he achieved a measure of success in the iron curtain countries. He understood that the Communist governments had their own agendas, and that preaching the Christian gospel was not one of them. "People ask us all the time," Walter Smyth observed," 'Don't you realize they are using you?' Of course, they are using us. But we are using them as well, to get the gospel out to their people. And we have an element on our side with which they are not familiar, and that's the Holy Spirit, who continues his work after we are gone. We feel it is worth whatever advantage it is to them to gain prestige out of Billy Graham's visit or to prove that there is greater religious freedom than many Westerners think." Often echoing this "our-propaganda-is-greater-than-theirs" line, Graham insisted only that he not be asked to criticize the American government or its foreign policy, and that no attempt be made to influence what he would say, either in the pulpit or at any other public gathering. If granted these freedoms, he felt he had little to fear from efforts of his hosts to turn his visits to their advantage. While he may have overestimated his own ability to resist manipulation, he was not so naive as to imagine manipulation would not be tried, and he accepted as a given that his every move was under careful surveillance. "I always go with the assumption that we are being recorded," he said, "in bedrooms, at tables, even in automobiles. But I have felt that in Korea and the Philippines, and in some Western countries, too." Rather than view this as oppressive, he chose to use it as an opportunity for evangelism. "In several countries," he recalled with a chuckle, "Ruth would read the Bible, and then I would read the Bible, and when she prayed, she would pray real loud for the people who were listening to our conversation. And we explained the gospel to each other over and over, so that whoever recorded that would have the gospel message. We have done that everywhere."

After more than a decade of experience, Graham and his associates are convinced they have accomplished real evangelism in Eastern Europe. In most places it was not feasible for inquirers to respond to the invitation as in a Western crusade, but Billy regularly asked those who wished to make a decision for Christ to stand or raise their hands, and uncounted thousands complied. As in American crusades, many were doubtless simply renewing their Christian commitment. Others, quite likely, were making firm a resolution toward which they had been moving for some time. Still others may have been taken by surprise by their own positive response to what the evangelist had to say. Ed Plowman told of a government official in Moscow who confided to him that "when Billy Graham asked people to raise their hands, it touched my heart. And in my heart, I raised my hand." Graham and his men also felt their visits have improved the situation for Eastern European believers. In the spring of 1989, John Akers observed, "We found that political leaders in that part of the world had very little sensitivity to the American religious scene or to the sensitivity American Christians felt about the persecution of their fellow Christians in other parts of the world. I think the Jewish people have done a much better job than Christians have of bringing pressure to bear, being noisy about the treatment of Jews in other parts of the world, specifically in Eastern Europe. We have tried to get the Eastern European governments to understand that people in this part of the world feel strongly about how churches are treated." A primary concern has been to elevate the standing of Evangelical churches and to improve their relations with Orthodox and Catholic bodies. Haraszti noted that Baptists were prominently involved in every Socialist country the evangelist visited. By appearing in Orthodox and Catholic cathedrals, flanked always by a Baptist minister who served as his interpreter, Graham gave "credibility, visibility, and respectability to Baptists, and also to Pentecostals and other small churches." But concern was not limited to Evangelicals. One quite self-conscious tactic the Graham team used was to win concessions for themselves that could then be passed on to native Christians. Repeatedly, Alex Haraszti urged local religious leaders to press the team's case for greater freedom by asking the minister of religious affairs, "If Billy Graham, an American, can appear on our television and preach in stadiums with loudspeakers and Diamond Vision screens, why can't our bishop or patriarch do the same? Why can't Protestants have a mass meeting? If he can sell religious books, why can't we?" "I gave them this argument," Haraszti said, "and they are using it." Graham undergirded this approach by his consistent exhortation to Christians to be good workers and loyal citizens, and thus to reduce their governments' perception of them as real or potential enemies. "We are bringing new images of believers and churches," Haraszti noted. "They are seeing us as an honest Church, a nonpowerful Church, a loyal Church." He was not implying, however, that the Church simply bend itself to the will of the State. Drawing on an image Jesus had used, he asserted that the churches would also wield a transforming influence. "We penetrate these societies and change them like leaven."

As part of this leavening process, Graham has been quick to take advantage of any opportunity. After the devastating earthquake in Soviet Armenia in 1988, BGEA donated $50,000 in relief money, channeling $30,000 through the Orthodox Church and $20,000 through the All-Union Evangelical Council. "One reason we did that," Akers acknowledged, "was because the churches are now being permitted in small ways to do some social work. And quite frankly, a gift like this is a way to help that process continue. We are concerned about the earthquake victims, of course. It's not just a gimmick, by any means, but it was an opportunity for us to hit the wedge and open that crack a bit more—a way to strengthen the position of the churches.

We are also exploring the possibility of assisting in the printing of some religious literature. We have informal permission to print perhaps 200,000 copies of Billy's books in the Soviet Union. There is virtually no religious literature of any kind in the churches, so that would be a real breakthrough. Here, our book would be just one of 15,000 or 16,000 titles. Over there, it may be one of only fifteen or sixteen, so it's enormously significant.

"No one can estimate," Akers continued, "how much [Graham's visits] have done to bring about the changes we have seen in the last year or two, particularly in the Soviet Union, but it is interesting that virtually every point Mr. Graham made [in his 1984 meeting with Ponomarev] has become a reality, point by point, little by little. That's not to say that everything is just rosy, but it is to say that a number of points [on which] there has been substantial progress are precisely the points that Mr. Graham did raise. I am not trying to claim we are the catalyst, and we will probably never know exactly what our role has been, but it is true that Billy is alone among Western churchmen at having had a unique kind of access to Eastern European leadership."

Again without claiming many specific victories, Graham's associates clearly feel that, criticisms of his early visits notwithstanding, he has served his country well as an unofficial ambassador. "There is a lot of artificial, government-nurtured anti-Americanism in these countries," Haraszti pointed out. "And here a great and famous American comes, and he behaves humbly and shakes hands and deals with people on all levels. People were able to get acquainted with a nonugly American who was equally at home in government limousines and simple family homes. He was a magnificent goodwill ambassador."

Graham enjoyed White House support throughout the Reagan years, and clearly expected similar encouragement from old friends George Bush and his secretary of state, James Baker. "I have known Jim Baker for several years," he explained, "and Susan [his wife] is a really committed Christian. She is all-out for Christ. I can't evaluate what his position would be about any particular visit I might make, but I know that if he found it within the scope of policies he approved, he would be very warm to me. He believes in what we are doing." When Gorbachev visited the United States in 1988, Graham was the lone Protestant clergyman invited to the White House for the full round of celebrations. At one gathering, the two men sat directly across from each other. "I have read that he has cold eyes," the evangelist recalled. "I never saw those cold eyes. His eyes were always warm or they were dancing. He has a tremendous sense of charisma about him." Graham clearly doubted that the Soviet leader was a committed atheist, pointing out that "when he got off the plane, if you remember, he said, 'May God help us.' And then in his talk to that group at the embassy, an hour and a half where I was sitting right in front of him, he used the word *spiritual* three times."

In July 1991 Billy Graham and his associates conducted a five-day School of Evangelism in Moscow. More than 4,900 Protestant pastors, evangelists, and other church workers from throughout the Soviet Union attended the school. The event was held in a state-owned sports arena, and participants were housed at Moscow State University at BGEA's expense. While he was in Moscow, Graham had long conversations with Boris Yeltsin, newly inaugurated president of the Russian Republic, and with Soviet president Mikhail Gorbachev. The visit with Gorbachev was given prominent coverage on a top-rated Soviet TV news show aired nationwide. Declaring that "it is harvest time" in the USSR, Graham revealed that he was considering an invitation to return to Moscow in 1992 to conduct a crusade in Lenin Stadium.

32

Amsterdam

Billy Graham knew why men and women needed to be saved, and he knew how to show them the way. As he saw his own life and ministry moving inexorably toward the end, what he wanted more than anything else was to share that quite simple, quite practical knowledge with others who like himself found their greatest joy in going about from place to place, preaching the word and winning souls. The upshot of that impulse was a pair of conferences in Amsterdam in 1983 and 1986, which, one participant noted, "[if they had happened] in the time of the Early Church, they . . . would have been written up in the Book of Acts."

According to Walter Smyth, the idea of a practical, instructional conference for itinerant evangelists was "something that had been burning in [Graham's] heart for years." He had been pleased with Lausanne as "a movement to reach leaders," but wanted something "to reach the little guys out in the bushes," the uneducated evangelists in Calcutta or the Congo whose primary need was not a treatise on how to establish dialogue with a Marxist or a Muslim but basic instruction in such mundane matters as sermon composition, fund-raising, and effective use of films and videotapes. He had thought of such a conference as early as 1954, but it was not until 1977 that he finally pushed the wheels into motion. And what he had in mind was such a mammoth undertaking that it did not come to pass for another six years. The kind of gathering Graham envisioned was far more difficult to organize than the Berlin and Lausanne congresses. The first challenge lay in identifying and then contacting "the little guys out in the bushes." Simply by virtue of being little guys, most of the men whom Graham sought to help were unknown to the people in charge of sending invitations. German Evangelical leader Werner Burklin, a YFC veteran who had worked for BGEA on other projects and who served as executive director for both conferences, acknowledged as they set about to construct an invitation list that he and his colleagues had no idea how many itinerant evangelists there were in the world or how to get in touch with them. By contacting church and parachurch leaders for names and references and putting out word that such an event was being planned, conference organizers eventually assembled a list of approximately 10,000 itinerant evangelists in 133 countries. After screening them as carefully as possible and allocating quotas to various countries, nearly 3,900 (70 percent from Third World countries) were invited to assemble in Amsterdam for an International Conference for Itinerant Evangelists (ICIE). Amsterdam was selected because, of the few locations in the world capable of providing food, lodging, and meeting places for a gathering of this size, the Netherlands had the additional advantages of being a major international airline center, with its own KLM Royal Dutch Airlines offering service from many parts of the world, and a tradition of allowing people from most other countries to obtain visas with little difficulty.

Burklin estimated that at least 90 percent of the invitees who descended on the cosmopolitan Dutch city in July 1983—most of them supported in part or whole by BGEA funds—had never previously attended any kind of conference; many, perhaps most, had never traveled outside their own countries. The inevitable clash of cultures produced both poignant and comic moments. A Third World participant who was taken by bus to the convention center for registration, then directed to board another bus for a ride to his hotel, refused to leave the center. Though he could not speak English or any other language represented at the registration desk, he finally managed, with tears filling his eyes, to make clear that after having come so far and gotten so close, he feared he was about to be deported. On the first day of the conference, several participants unfamiliar with the concept of a coffee break abashed Western colleagues by drinking directly from the cream pitchers. And in a similar misreading of cues, a group of Africans, told to "relax and dress casually" during a day off at the midpoint of the conference, startled unwary tourists by lounging barefoot in the lobby of the downtown Marriott hotel. Other contrasts between the affluent, sophisticated West and the world's poorer nations made the West seem incredibly prodigal. An Indian man who operated a mission school in Kashmir was appalled to see thousands of plastic water cups thrown into the trash after each coffee break and meal. His little school used similar cups but, instead of throwing them away, it managed to make them last as long as three years. With the aid of a food-service consultant, he took a large supply of the precious once-used vessels back to his village. With a similar eye for utility, several Africans sacked up large quantities of the rectangular food dishes used by KLM caterers to serve airline-type meals to the participants. The dishes, they explained, would make marvelous roof tiles for their homemade dwellings.

The ten-day conference, held during a scorching heat wave, featured dozens of plenary addresses by the redoubtable workhorses in Billy Graham's stable of associates—Stephen Olford, Luis Palau, Bill Bright, Gottfried Osei-Mensah, E. V. Hill, Akbar Abdul-Haqq, Charlie Riggs, Charles Colson—and more than a hundred workshops on such practical topics as "Finding and Securing New Sources of Financial Aid," "Effective Street Preaching," and "The Evangelist's Family Life." At the opening session, Graham himself repeated advice distilled from his own decades of preaching. At a special wives program—"for those who fill the important role of homemaker for itinerant evangelists"—Ruth Graham spoke of "growing beautiful, not bitter, in adapting to a husband's needs," and Bill Bright's wife, Vonette, contrasted the roles and attitudes of the "secular woman" concerned primarily with self-image, personal achievement, and professional success with those of the "spirit-filled woman" who looks to Jesus Christ for her identity.

When Graham and his colleagues first began to plan for Amsterdam '83, they expected it might attract as many as 2,000 evangelists. When actual attendance nearly doubled that, with thousands more having to be turned down and additional thousands writing to plead that another conference be held as soon as possible, the bureaucratic machine that had produced the first conference barely stopped to refuel before getting into gear to organize a 1986 sequel that would be even grander in scope and impact. This time around, organizers knew they would not have trouble drawing a crowd; they did not, however, anticipate the flood of applications generated by announcement of a second conference. By soliciting church leaders around the world for the names of active itinerant evangelists who might benefit from such a meeting, ICIE organizers soon had a list of nearly 62,000 potential invitees, from whom less than 10,000 would be chosen. Interestingly, thousands of those—-perhaps as many as a third of the total number—had been encouraged to become evangelists by alumni of the 1983 conference. According to Associate Conference Director Bob Williams, who served as the major hands-on organizer for the gathering, the winnowing-out process was a heartbreaking endeavor. "We sent applications to 48,000 people," he explained. "We wrote the other 14,000 and told them we had received so many applications from their part of the world that there was no point in raising their hopes falsely. To get the kind of spread we wanted, we had to set quotas and cut off some countries after the number of applications reached a certain point. We might send an application to someone in a country whose quota had been filled if he came highly recommended, but he'd nearly have to be able to walk on water. From those 48,000, we received 28,000 applications, and we could only take 9,000."

Applicants were rated according to a point system designed to favor those likely to benefit most from such a conference, rather than those who already had effective ministries. Those between the ages of twenty-five and forty-five received more points than either younger or older candidates. Those affiliated with "known, solid Evangelical" denominations scored higher than those from "known non-Evangelical" groups. Those with "some education" (up to completing high school) outpointed those who had attended college as well as those with little or no education. Those engaged in full-time itinerant evangelism ranked above those who spent only part of their time preaching. The selection committee also favored applicants with a commitment to effective follow-up of their preaching over those who thought it sufficient to preach a few sermons and move on to the next town. In addition, applicants could receive bonus points if they had been recommended by a person known and trusted by the committee, and "general response" points, "according to how the Holy Spirit leads."

Not all of the selection was done around a table in Amsterdam. Whenever possible, usually while following up the results of the 1983 conference or building support for the 1986 meeting, Williams and his associates made site visits, verifying that applicants were indeed legitimate evangelists engaged in ministries whose aims and ethos were in harmony with those of Billy Graham's. During a 1985 trip to Nairobi, Williams decided to check out a man reported to be an effective open-air preacher. When he came to a city square where he expected to find the man, he was dismayed to hear a preacher ranting and raving in front of a small band of hecklers ("It was not the kind of preaching we want to encourage"), then relieved to learn that the man he sought was holding forth on the other side of the square before a crowd of over a thousand people. "He gave an invitation," Williams recalled, "and at least fifty people came forward. Afterwards, we asked him how he accounted for his success. He said, 'In 1983 a friend of mine went to Amsterdam '83 and attended a workshop on how to do open-air campaigns. Three years ago I was doing what that guy on the other side of the square is doing, with no success. No one was paying any attention, except to laugh at me. From my friend I learned a few basic techniques about how to gather a crowd, how to keep their attention, how to preach a message in a few minutes—because a lot of people walk up for five minutes and leave—and how to get church members to work with me. Simple, practical things that people had been using for years, but that were new to me. I just applied them, and they worked.' "

On the same trip, Williams decided to visit an alumnus of the 1983 conference who reportedly had won 8,000 people to Christ since returning home from Amsterdam. "That sounded," Williams said, "as if he might be 'speaking evangelistically'—they stretch it sometimes. So we went down to see about it. We flew in a little Missionary Aviation Fellowship plane, and a missionary met us at a mission hospital about 200 miles from Nairobi. We said, 'Tell us about this man. We hear that he has had 8,000 decisions since 1983. Is that true?' The missionary said, 'No, it's not true. It's 8,000 each year since 1983.' We asked him if he could document it, and he said he could. They had followed up on every one of them. We learned that before Amsterdam '83, he had approximately 130 decisions over a 10-year period. When we found the man, we asked him what he was doing differently. He picked up a notebook he had gotten at the 1983 conference. 'I've been doing this and this before I start preaching,' he said, pointing to different sections in the notebook. 'And when I preach, I do this and this and this.' We asked him, 'What about follow-up?' and he said, 'This and this and this,' just pointing to sections in his notebook. Sometimes we get so technical, and it's all so basic."

When the final selections were made, more than three fourths of the nearly 8,200 invitees were from the Third World. Africa was most heavily represented, with 2,337 evangelists from 49 countries. In keeping with the principles of the unreached-peoples strategy articulated at Lausanne, effort was made to cover as many subgroups as possible within each country. In Nigeria, for example, at least one evangelist was selected from 136 of that nation's 137 major tribes. "We looked hard for an evangelist from the last tribe," a recruiter said, "but we just couldn't find one." Asia and Latin America each furnished approximately 1,500 envoys. The North American contingent numbered 1,361, and 32 countries of Eastern and Western Europe provided 1,009 delegates. The remainder of the contingent came mainly from the Middle East, Oceania, and the Caribbean. Graham was unable to obtain permission for twenty evangelists from the People's Republic of China to attend, but two PRC representatives, neither of whom were evangelists, were present. In the last accounting, evangelists streamed into Amsterdam from 173 countries—more, it appears, than had ever been represented at any gathering, religious or secular, in the history of the world.

The selection committee had made a few mistakes. One man identified as a witch doctor was sent home as soon as his true colors were discovered. Several others used the conference to run a minor-league scam—collecting names of Westerners, writing them later to request donations of Bibles and reference books for the libraries of their mission schools, then selling the books and pocketing the money for themselves. But some who showed up felt that they, not the selection committee, had been deceived. On registering, each delegate was tagged with a hospital-type wrist strap, to be worn throughout the ten-day conference. Printed on it was an emergency telephone number: 42-51-51. At least two delegates left for home after noticing that each pair of numbers added up to six, making it seem plausible that these straps were the dreaded mark of the beast and that the conference itself was a major step in setting up the one-world church that would be the tool of the Antichrist.

After due allowance for the inevitable tares among the wheat, it was an enthusiastic, dedicated, and extraordinarily variegated group of men and women who gathered for the conference. Some were crusade evangelists who moved from town to town holding revivals in the conventional and time-honored fashion. Others specialized in working with young people, prisoners, hospital patients, refugees, migrant-worker camps, military personnel, lepers, or even, as in the case of two Dutch women, the prostitutes who ply their trade in Amsterdam's notorious red-light district. Of 7,604 participants who responded to a survey, approximately one third had some college or seminary training, but 601 had no formal training whatever. "These are not high-powered TV evangelists," a conference staffer observed. "These are guys walking twenty or thirty miles to share the gospel, going to Borneo and South Africa and Papua New Guinea" The overwhelming majority were in the favored age range of twenty-five to forty-five, with thirty-one the average age. Most of the older evangelists came from the Orient, where respect for age made it difficult to persuade prospective delegates that the available slots should go to younger men. More participants came from Baptist backgrounds than from any other single denomination, but in striking testimony to Billy Graham's commitment to fellowship with those outside the old Evangelical pale, members of various Pentecostal groups outnumbered even the Baptists. In another adjustment to changing times, approximately five hundred participants were women.

Most evangelists from North America and Western Europe paid their own travel and lodging expenses. Third World preachers were encouraged to raise some portion of their expenses, as a token of commitment, but BGEA underwrote most of their costs, as well as the substantial expense involved in planning the conference and in renting the sprawling RAI exhibition complex where it was held. When all the bills were tallied, the association had demonstrated its commitment to world evangelism by contributing approximately 21 million dollars toward Amsterdam '86. Nearly all of it came from regulation-size donations. No foundations or wealthy donors were approached; when a friend of the ministry offered a donation of 2 million dollars a few days before the conference opened, Graham told him, "It's already paid for. Give your money to something else." In typical BGEA fashion, conference organizers paid great attention to doing things as economically as possible. Graham's hometown travel agency arranged bargain flights from all over the world. Staff members negotiated favorable rates with eighty-five Amsterdam hotels and saved great sums by housing 4,000 men in a makeshift dormitory set up in the Jaarbeurs exhibition center in Utrecht, twenty-five miles away. Special arrangements were made with Amsterdam's elaborate public-transportation system so that anyone wearing an ICIE armband was allowed to ride anywhere the system's carriers went, without buying a ticket. Equally typical, however, was a disregard for trouble or expense when a grand gesture was needed. A two-hundred-person delegation from Argentina and Uruguay found itself stranded in Buenos Aires by a pilots' strike. Because it was the height of the tourist season, staffers had to scour the world looking for a suitable aircraft to charter and send for the stranded evangelists. Eventually, they located a DC-8, described as "the only airplane free in the entire world," and dispatched it from New York to Buenos Aires. The plight of the Argentine contingent became a dramatic focus for the conference during its opening sessions. Graham's announcement that a plane had been found met with thunderous applause. When a heavy fog made it impossible to land in Buenos Aires, thousands of fog-dispersing prayers flew upward. And when the weary Latins finally walked into the great hall where the plenary sessions were held, they were greeted as if they had been the last load to make the rapture. It was marvelous drama, and the Argentines became the darlings of the conference. It also cost a half-million dollars, causing one of Billy Graham's staunchest admirers to volunteer that "one cannot help wondering if the money might not have been better spent."

Some participants overcame even greater obstacles than the Argentines. A Sri Lankan evangelist spent forty hours dodging gunfire and bombs and picking his way around land mines as he crossed sixty miles of civil-war zone on his way to the airport in Colombo. Others bore the scars of persecution inflicted by people hostile to them and the gospel they preached. Still others spoke matter-of-factly of the perils they faced in trying to carry out the Great Commission. "We cannot go easily into the Muslim areas to preach and spread the gospel," a Lebanese evangelist explained. Why not? "Because they will kill us." On several occasions Billy Graham personally greeted delegations as they arrived at the RAI center by bus. At one such encounter, a knot of diminutive Indian evangelists was obviously stunned to find the tall, tanned evangelist, who seemed to them more a legend than a flesh-and-blood person, suddenly plunging into their midst, pumping their hands, and thanking them for coming. They were not alone in being moved. A few days later, Graham told a press conference that when he met men who had gone to prison and been beaten and reviled for trying to do what he had been able to do with great reward and honor, "I felt like a worm."

Even in cosmopolitan, polyglot Amsterdam, the sheer variety of the visitors drew attention. Dutch television carried stories of African men who began digging latrines shortly after arriving at Jaarbeurs, and of blacks astonished to see white stewards bring breakfast to their bedsides, not realizing such a thing could occur anywhere in the world. The participants themselves were staggered at the experience of seeing so many Christians from so many other parts of the world. "They suddenly realized," Werner Burklin remarked, "that we are all one in Christ. We have the same Savior, the same gospel, the same call." One man, an African bishop accustomed to and expecting more plush accommodations, decided to stay on at Jaarbeurs a day or two before arranging for something a bit less Spartan. After imbibing the rich spirit of the multicultural fellowship for a short time, however, he chose not to leave, declaring grandly that "this place is like heaven!"

The conference began with Olympic-style pageantry as six runners, symbolizing the six continents, carried torches from the far reaches of the great Europehall and together lit a central flame that would burn throughout the conference, symbolizing the Light of the World that participants were preparing to reveal more brightly. Then, as Cliff Barrows read the names of the 173 countries represented in that assembly and a brace of trumpets filled the air with the stirring strains of "Onward, Christian Soldiers," stewards bearing the flags of those countries crisscrossed the vast auditorium, itself already festooned with maroon and gray banners bearing the legend DO THE WORK OF AN EVANGELIST in dozens of different languages. Iraqi and Iranian Christians, both representing tiny minority populations, stood alongside each other, their eyes glistening with tears, as did Jewish and Arab Christians from Palestine and evangelists from both South and North Korea. A white South African embraced his black countryman and brother in Christ. Though it is unlikely anyone missed the symbolism, a narrator reminded the diverse assembly that "we are not strangers or enemies but fellow citizens of a heavenly kingdom." As they joined together to sing "Crown Him with Many Crowns," some holding hands, many shedding tears of joy, almost all were caught up in a transcendent unity of spirit.

Though Graham has been remarkable in his ability to stimulate response around the world by preaching essentially the same sermon, ICIE organizers did not believe a one-size-fits-all approach would be effective for the average native evangelist. "We cannot adapt to the culture," Program Director John Corts said, "to the extent that we change the message, but we need to be sensitive to it, so that we will not seem to be demanding an American, Western, high-tech kind of approach. For example, only two African countries have a literacy rate as high as 65 percent. Distributing Bibles may not be the key factor in such a country. We can't tell people to 'write to Billy Graham, Minneapolis, Minnesota, that's all the address you need.' They live in an entirely different world, and we have to be sensitive to that. I've been part of Billy's big American crusades, with the highly polished formats. I've helped shape that. But that is not what we are doing here. I have never served out in the bush, but I've been there and I know what goes on in that setting. I've seen what they are doing, and I have tried to listen to what they are saying as we set up this program."

During the conference, Billy Graham and his stalwart band of associates from around the world sounded the great themes of the gospel message, each elaborating on one of the Amsterdam Affirmations, a set of fifteen brief principal statements agreed upon by participants at the 1983 conference. Graham himself gave four plenary addresses, though not at his own insistence. Prior to the conference, he repeatedly, and apparently quite sincerely, argued for a smaller role. "I raise the money rather than do the work," he said. "It has not taken much of my personal time. I have a great staff, and I was able to delegate responsibility and leave them alone almost from the beginning." Because he had not done the work, he seemed to feel he had not earned the right to take a major role. "We polled people who are coming to this conference," Walter Smyth said, "to see what they wanted to hear. Ninety percent of them want to hear from Billy Graham, to learn how he does it. And we have had the hardest time getting the poor man to speak. He keeps saying, 'Look, I don't want to dominate this. This is not a Billy Graham show.' But we have had to say to him, 'Billy, these evangelists look to you. They want to hear you. They will listen to others, but nobody is going to take your place in this conference.' It's like pulling teeth to get him to speak more than once." John Corts told a similar story: "You see the dynamic preacher out front," he observed. "I see the guy sitting in his hotel room in his baseball cap and dungarees, asking, 'What am I supposed to say to these people? How am I supposed to answer their questions?' "

As powerful a presence as he inevitably was, Graham was far from being the whole show. Argentine Baptist leader Samuel Libert held forthably with a discourse on "The Evangelist's Authority: The Word and the Spirit," and evangelist/professor Ravi Zacharias spoke eloquently of "The Lostness of Man." Billy Kim thrilled the assembly with an electrifying, if often quite funny, explication of the conditions required to bring about "The Revival We Need." Gottfried Osei-Mensah spoke on "The Great Commission," Moody Bible Institute president George Sweeting described "The Evangelist's Passion for the Lost," Nilson Fanini stressed the importance of "The Evangelist's Commitment to the Church," and Franklin Graham spoke movingly about "The Evangelist's Ministry Among Situations of Human Need." Layered in with these exhortations to action were sermon after sermon on the importance of the character of evangelists. Stephen Olford issued a thundering summons to "The Personal Life of Holiness," and in a stunning display of a genetic gift for capturing the attention of a great assembly, Graham's daughter Anne Lotz delivered a riveting address on "The Evangelist's Faithfulness," driving her points home with the same two-pistol hand gesture and hammering cadence her father had used so effectively for forty years.

Each plenary address was set in the context of a worship service. In addition to prayers and congregational singing, most sessions featured "Up with Jesus" music from the Continental Brass and Singers, a talented group of young people in *Miami Vice* clothes who served as the house band, or from one of more than twenty other multinational groups and soloists, including a fifteen-member choir from the Moscow Baptist Church. At least once each day, a dramatic troupe known as The Lamb's Players and headed by Walter Smyth's son Bob presented brief playlets closely geared to the theme of that session. One skit, on the pitfalls that lie on the path of charismatic leaders, drew knowing laughter and self-conscious winces as it presaged the scandals that would explode within the world of television evangelism a scant few months later.

The plenary sessions gave "the little guys" a chance to see "the big guys," and for the most part, the big guys showed why they were at the top of their profession. But much of the most important work of the conference, the detailed transmission of pragmatic instruction, went on in more than 160 seminars and workshops. Every participant was obliged to attend five seminars, one each on "Preparation for an Evangelistic Event," "Preparation and Delivery of an Evangelistic Message" "Giving the Evangelistic Invitation," "Counselor Training," and "Follow-up Methods." While the plenary sessions were delivered in English and translated simultaneously into fifteen languages, any one of which could be tuned in on the headphones attached to wireless receivers available to all participants, the seminars were broken into nineteen language and regional groups to enable materials developed by "master teachers" to be adapted to a wide range of situations.

The workshops were far more varied in content and more limited as to the number of languages in which a given topic was discussed, but few participants had difficulty finding topics of interest among the two dozen or so dealt with each day, ranging from "Working with Pre-literates" to "Getting on Secular Television and Radio Talk Shows," and including a host of sessions on such themes as open-air preaching, writing for publication, working with prisoners and the disabled, preaching to Muslims, management techniques for an evangelistic ministry, and training other evangelists. Women evangelists and wives of male participants were free to attend any session they wished, but a limited "Women's Program" was also available. The most memorable session on that agenda was led jointly by Cliff and Billie Barrows's daughter, Bonnie Barrows Thomas, and by Ruth Graham, who talked frankly and engagingly about the high and low points of the life of an evangelist's wife, drawing warm appreciation for such frank and commonsensical observations as "I find Christian parents without problem children can be stuffy. If you have a prodigal, you will love all prodigals."

John Corts and other program organizers often pointed out that they were following a "technical education model" in the seminars and work shops, dealing with concrete technique far more than abstract theory. To help participants implement their new knowledge more readily, 7,000 evangelists from Third World countries received canvas knapsacks filled with books, sermon outlines, and other preaching aids, cassette recordings of sermons by Graham and others, and to play them in villages and homes where electricity was nonexistent and batteries unobtainable, a hand-cranked tape player. As a logical extension of that pragmatic approach, the next-to-last afternoon of the conference was designated a "Day of Witness" on which participants tried to put into action what they had learned in face-to-face confrontation with the unsaved. "It's a little phony," Corts admitted, "because, let's face it, they don't speak Dutch, but it's an attempt to give them an experience of going out into the street and seeing what it means to use what they have learned in a real situation."

The Netherlands had surely never experienced such a concentrated display of concern for its lost condition. After a brief demonstration to let them know what kind of responses they might expect, evangelists clambered onto 120 chartered buses that dispatched them to 68 locations in 49 Dutch cities and villages. Predictably, many encounters misfired, as when an American evangelist who approached a group of women engaged in animated conversation soon found himself the target of the evangelistic efforts of the Lesbian Collective to Get the U.S. Out of Nicaragua. A small but imaginative band of Latin American messengers met with no greater success when they assayed to bring Christ to nude bathers on a beach at Scheveningen. Billy Graham himself, ostensibly camouflaged in dark glasses, windbreaker, and baseball cap, spent time in Amsterdam's sprawling Vondel Park. When he was able to avoid the efforts of unwary ICIE delegates to convert him, he spoke with several small groups, one of which asked him to leave them alone and another whose members seemed more interested in what they were smoking than in what he was saying. Some evangelists met negative, even abusive, reactions, but most seemed encouraged by the experience. When results were tallied at the end of the day, they were told that the gospel had been communicated to more than 40,000 people on that single afternoon, and that more than 300 firm commitments were known to have been made, the firstfruits of the great harvest expected from Amsterdam '86.

In many respects, Amsterdam '86 bore little resemblance to the first major Graham-sponsored conference at Berlin, but the two did share at least one notable feature: Carl McIntire came to both, uninvited and unwelcome. Well past eighty but still capable of red-eyed fury, McIntire set up a booth in the lobby of a large hotel adjacent to the RAI center and offered FREE BILLY GRAHAM BOOKS to the many evangelists quartered there and to any others who dropped in on their way to a nearby train station. The books were free, and they were about Billy Graham. They were also, of course, highly critical of the evangelist whom McIntire had long characterized as "the greatest disappointment in the Christian Church." With fellow Graham basher Edgar C. Bundy nodding agreement at his side, McIntire reported that in the week he had been at his post he had talked to "dozens and dozens" of evangelists who were "astonished at what I told them." He fumed that Graham had allowed a Russian chorus to sing and identified a Russian evangelist at the conference as "a hard-core KGB strong man who has broken necks and killed people." He pointed to the large numbers of Pentecostals and charismatics at the conference as evidence that Graham's lack of concern for pure doctrine was leading to a one-world church, just as predicted in the book of Revelation. And, though he grudgingly conceded that "Graham does know how to raise money and put on a conference," he made it clear he thought the $21 million BGEA had spent on the conference was a damnable bit of stewardship. "They spent $2 million just on food—food and hell!"

After a moving communion service that despite the use of a wine substitute tasting remarkably like strawberry Kool-Aid inevitably summoned images of a messianic banquet, the conference ended on Sunday evening, July 20. Billy Graham preached on the Second Coming, and 10,000 Evangelical Christians from the ends of the earth prepared to depart for their homelands, fully aware that most of them would never meet again unless and until that longed-for Advent actually came to pass. As a final galvanizing act, Graham read the fifteen Amsterdam Affirmations and the largest gathering of evangelists ever to assemble in one place fairly shouted "We affirm!" in response to each. Then six torchbearers lit their lamps from the flame that had burned throughout the conference and headed back toward the world's six continents. As the bearers of 173 flags followed in train, Graham solemnly intoned, "You are witnesses to that Light. Go preach the Good News to your nations. You are His messengers.... The glory of the Lord is upon you, for the Lord has turned our darkness into light, that we may proclaim the salvation of our God to all the nations. *Do the work of an evangelist!*"

Had Billy Graham and BGEA done nothing further than send 12,000 fully charged and freshly prepared evangelists back to their homelands, the results of the Amsterdam conferences would probably have a significant impact on hundreds of thousands of individual lives before the wheels set in motion there finally rolled to a stop. But three and a half years later, the model developed for these gatherings was being emulated in dozens of smaller gatherings throughout the world. In 1988 26 "Mini-Amsterdams" were held in Latin America alone, culminating in a Los Angeles gathering that drew 6,000 evangelists working with Latins in both North and South America. Other meetings drew between 2,000 and 3,000 participants, and at the beginning of 1990, John Corts reported that BGEA had supported and helped organize 88 such conferences, with an aggregate attendance of more than 46,000 evangelists from 97 countries. There were no plans to discontinue the program.

33

The Constituted Means

Dramatic and pathbreaking as they were, Graham's visits to the Soviet bloc nations and the Amsterdam conferences did not long divert him from the well-worn crusade trail. During the early 1980s, he held crusades in Canada, Japan, Mexico, Baltimore, Boston, Boise, San Jose, Houston, Spokane, Chapel Hill, Orlando, Fort Lauderdale, Tacoma, Sacramento, Anchorage, Oklahoma City, Hartford, and Anaheim. In 1984–85 he conducted a highly successful two-stage Mission England that included seven full-scale campaigns in major cities other than London and live-link satellite video meetings in fifty additional cities. In 1986 he followed up the Washington, D.C., crusade with a meeting in Tallahassee and with Mission France, an effective effort that originated in Paris in the midst of terrorist bomb scares and sent the gospel flying by satellite to thirty-one cities throughout that nation. In 1987 he opened the season in Columbia, South Carolina, in the same stadium where Henry Luce had first heard him thirty-seven years earlier, then checked off all the remaining parts of the country in which he had never held crusades in a five-state Peaks to Plains barnstorming tour that wound up in Denver's Mile High Stadium. He closed that year with an encouraging campaign in Helsinki. Then, as the decade ended, the premier evangelist of the second half of the twentieth century consciously sought to associate himself with his counterpart from the first half of the nineteenth by beginning a series of crusades that would take him to the same cities in upstate New York where Charles Grandison Finney had stamped his indelible mark on American revivalism.

With forty years of experience in the vault, Graham's crusade team unquestionably had its act together, so that when an invitation to hold a crusade was received, pondered, and accepted, it could roll into a city and roll out a crusade along well-established lines, pursuing what Charles Finney called "the right use of the constituted means." Most of the time its accomplishments were quite predictable, within a modest range of variance, although the results were often not exactly what the sponsoring churches expected or what the Graham team implied, and the process was not quite the automatic, self-contained, flawless operation it may have appeared to be from the outside.

Still, a Billy Graham Greater Anywhere Crusade, however much it may have depended on the Spirit of God for its success, was a remarkable exercise in rational organization and action.

Team members did not want to appear as manipulators of ostensibly spiritual phenomena and were invariably careful not to relegate Deity to the sidelines, but Sterling Huston, director of North American crusades, freely acknowledged that "yes, we have a plan. We know one way, and it will work for local congregations if they will follow it. We try to be flexible and adapt the plan to a local situation, but when they invite Mr. Graham to come, this is the only plan we know that really works. We want it contextualized, but the skeleton, the principles, the goals don't change." The degree to which the plan was followed varied somewhat with the personality of the particular crusade director assigned to a given campaign, but David Bruce, a Denver pastor who worked with the follow-up program on numerous crusades, noted that "there is a sense in which, because you have a short time line, you almost have to come in and say, 'Look, we've done this for forty years. This is the game plan. Get on board with us.'" This approach often worked better at home than abroad. In the 1986 Mission France, resistance to what French churchmen dubbed an *entreprise parachutée*—a complete system dropped from an American gospel transport plane—made it necessary to give more control to local leaders. The resulting blend of local custom and imported practice was both successful and amusing. In Strasbourg, the lovely old Alsatian city near France's northeastern border with Germany, satellite-service organizers saw nothing incongruous in having concessionaires sell beer and sausage or in allowing worshipers to smoke during the services, and the Graham people apparently felt no need to complain about these breaches of American pietistic practice, as long as the soccer-stadium scoreboard proclaimed that *"Jésus dit, 'Je suis Le Chemin, La Vérité, et La Vie,'"* and the book tables had plenty of copies of *La Paix avec Dieu* and *Un Monde en Flamme*. But some American Evangelicals felt the Graham method was too inflexible. One pastor who had worked in several Graham crusades over the years charged the team with putting on "a dog-and-pony show with little evidence of struggle or growth or ambiguity. The concern for people is great, no question about that. But there is some going through the motions. It would seem that there is such a dramatic difference between Spokane, Boise, Houston, and Boston that there's got to be some reflection of that, and that a great organization like BGEA ought not to be just transplanting the same thing in every community." Instead he felt the team and "the plan" had "developed a kind of rigidity that does not listen. Most of the crusade directors have done this so often that they are weary of [it]." John Bisagno, pastor of Houston's 21,000-member First Baptist Church, agreed that greater flexibility was needed but conceded that "when you have a thirty-year track record of the most successful evangelism in the world, why should they [let] local committees come in and get them to change their plans?"

Graham's remarkable record did indeed enable him to overcome obstacles that would surely thwart a lesser figure. Seldom was this more clearly in evidence than in Mission France. To help the evangelist gain permission to use the sparkling new 15,000-seat Palais Omnisport de Paris-Bercy, U.S. ambassador Joe M. Rodgers, a former Tennessee contractor who had attended Graham's crusades in both Knoxville and Nashville, successfully interceded with Paris mayor Jacques Chirac. Rodgers, it happens, was not acting entirely on his own. With some bemusement, he observed that two years into his term as his country's ambassador to France, President Reagan had given him only two assignments, one of which was to help Billy Graham get the use of Bercy. The other was to arrange a meeting between Graham and President François Mitterrand. Similar cooperation obtained at other levels. When terrorists initiated a frightening series of bombings in public places a few days before the crusade opened, the city responded by providing Graham and his team with bullet-proof automobiles and deploying 2,500 heavily armed policemen and soldiers to stand guard at the arena and search everyone who entered each night of the crusade.

Security was seldom the obvious problem that it was during the Paris campaign, but great care was always taken both to protect Graham and his team from injury or harassment and to preclude or short-circuit any attempts to disrupt the services. In most cities the team worked closely with local police or, in some places, national police, military, and intelligence forces for months before a crusade to map out detailed security and crowd-control plans. When circumstances seemed to justify it, the association hired former Secret Servicemen to oversee security operations. "People try to get to him," Tex Reardon said simply. "You don't always know for what purpose. We try to protect him from strangers walking off the street." The team's own security personnel downplayed physical threats to avoid setting up challenges for addled publicity seekers and also to protect Graham from anxiety. For the most part, their efforts were limited to greater attentiveness to possible problems. "If someone comes in with a package," Reardon explained, "we don't deliberately search it or anything, but we note it. We log where it is." In addition, they altered a long-standing practice of storing programs and counseling materials under the speaker's platform: "If you were going to do anything, what better place than a cardboard box under a platform? So we eliminate boxes. We also have guards watching the facilities all night." Graham knew of such measures, but if they bothered him, he managed not to show it. He told Ruth and his colleagues not to pay ransom if he were ever kidnapped and he appeared to believe, in good Presbyterian fashion, that nothing would happen to him unless God willed it. Ruth shared his view, contending that "nothing can touch a child of God without his permission."

Still, Graham and his staff took precautions against the twisted fantasies and misplaced hatreds demented souls sometimes direct toward public figures. According to T. W. Wilson, the evangelist received more threats of violence during the mid-1980s than during the thirty years prior to that. Pulling out a four-inch folder filled with vile imprecations that documented his point, he said, "We turn all threats over to the FBI, and they look into it. Some of the language is so filthy, and the hatred so bitter, you wouldn't believe it." One warned, "I'm going to get you. I'm going to cut up your wife's body in small pieces, feed her innards to wild animals, and bury the rest in a shallow grave. I have never been arrested and have no police record." It was signed with a swastika. Because the letter bore a California postmark and had been addressed to a BGEA post-office box, it seemed likely the writer was on the ministry's mailing list. The FBI narrowed the field to 4,000 neo-Nazis in the San Diego area, cut that number to a dozen most-likely candidates, and assigned agents to stake out each one of them. When the would-be assailant, a young woman, sent the fifth such letter, agents arrested her, went to her home and found the typewriter on which she had punched out her malevolent missives, and confronted her shocked parents with what their daughter had been doing. Apparently feeling little real danger existed, Graham decided not to press charges. "If they really want you," Wilson conceded, "they can usually get you, but we take all the threats seriously. We have more trouble with religious nuts than anything else."

One part of the crusade plan that seldom worked perfectly, even after forty years, was the effort to increase black participation in crusade preparations and black attendance at services. Team members admit that despite their efforts to integrate the crusades, blacks still regarded them as predominantly a white enterprise and did not usually participate as fully as had been hoped. Charges that BGEA was not sensitive to black issues and sensibilities stung Graham, and he directed his associates to make every conceivable effort to involve blacks in the 1986 Greater Washington Crusade. John Akers acknowledged that "we made our best shot with regard to blacks in Washington. We have tended to do what whites tend to do: make plans and invite blacks to join in. This time we made a deliberate effort to involve black churches and black leadership from the beginning. Every committee had a black cochair. But we did not do this in Tallahassee a few months later." Ralph Bell agreed that "the association really went out of its way in Washington. If that same effort were made in other crusades, I think it would be much better. But we have not made as much effort since then. We forget really quickly. I think it is in Billy's mind, but I don't think it is in the minds of the guys who carry it out to really involve themselves in the black community. At times in a team meeting, we have talked about developing a strategy to reach black America.

We've said we were going to talk about it, and cry over it, and pray about it, and get ideas, and call in resource people, and explore opportunities, and so forth. It's a good idea, but it never happens. It's a matter of commitment. If it were a matter of technology, they would explore the avenues, figure out how to do it, and go ahead and do it. But I don't think that, apart from Billy himself, that we have been committed to that goal with respect to the black community."

Some blacks have noted that the decorous style of Graham's crusades lacked the spirit and demonstrative character of the worship services to which they are accustomed. Some white supporters felt the same way. John Bisagno, whose church in Houston is a model of Baptist respectability, ventured that "Cliff and the team have overreacted a little bit too much over the years to criticism. They're trying a little too hard not to be specifically emotional in the services. I'm hearing people say they are surprised that the services seem kind of structured and flat. They're not experiencing the kind of life and excitement that they anticipate. We shouldn't program the joy of the Lord and natural excitement out of the services." Barrows's intention was not simply to be innocuous but to try to create a service that would be familiar and reassuring to people who do not go to church regularly. While it is true that the music in many Evangelical churches is far livelier than that in Graham's crusades, he felt that the limits are set not by what Christians would enjoy but by what non-Christians will find comfortable and reassuring. For that reason, crusade hymns were usually those likely to be recognized by nonregular attenders—"Bless the Lord, O My Soul," "Amazing Grace," and "When We All Get to Heaven." This ruled out most newer songs and choruses. Barrows also avoided choosing hymns that contain such words or phrases as "I worship," "I adore," or "I praise your name," which might embarrass outsiders or make them feel they don't belong. These sentiments were left to the choir or soloists, who presumably could sing them with a clearer conscience. Barrows was not adamant in resisting change and adjusted to some more recent developments in Christian music, but organist John Innes acknowledged that "Cliff keeps a pretty tight rein. He talks to the special artists carefully, but his more nervous moments are likely to come with the people who give testimony than with the singers, because you don't know how long they are going to take or, really, what they are going to say when they get up there."

Crusade guests did generate a bit of anxiety for the platform team, particularly when they were appearing for the first time. Some, like Grammy-winning vocalists Sandi Patti and Larnell Harris, country-music performer George Hamilton IV, and British singer Cliff Richard were known and dependable entities. Johnny Cash, another regular, caused little worry about his performance, but his occasional relapse into drug use caused some problems for Graham, who doggedly stuck by his longtime friend and put him back on the platform, penitent and presumably forgiven, as soon as he was physically and emotionally able to get there. In addition to musicians, crusades typically featured several Christians from the sports world, such as former Dallas Cowboy coach Tom Landry, former baseball standout Pat Kelly (who was director of Christian Fan Outreach and husband of Howard Jones's daughter, Phyllis), and various local sports figures who affirmed that their greatest accomplishment in life came when they became a member of the Greatest Team, under Coach Jesus, who will never cut them from the squad. Former NBA basketball star Pete Maravich had just begun to give testimony at Graham's crusades a few months before he died of a heart attack in 1987, and professional wrestler Hulk Hogan may have been auditioning for a spot in Evangelicalism's main event when he made a point of visiting Graham during the Denver crusade, talking with the evangelist about his own roots in the Baptist church, his personal faith in God, and "the privilege of leading his father to Christ shortly before his death."

Guest artists, celebrity testifiers, announcement makers, and prayer givers were all urged to keep their remarks short and succinct to make sure they "leave plenty of time for Mr. Graham." Though he was pleased to use celebrities to draw crowds and to demonstrate that Christianity need not be a drab and lifeless affair, Graham unquestionably felt that the main event of his meetings was the sermon itself, and he expected Cliff Barrows to see to it that people didn't have to wait too long to hear him and that he had plenty of time to say what he wanted to say. When a singer threw in a gratuitous testimony, or a testimony giver took an extra two minutes to reveal an unexpected defeat or triumph in the struggle with Satan, Graham began to cast impatient glances at Cliff and to nibble anxiously at his fingernails.

The team's largely successful efforts to knock off rough edges, polish away the bumps, and remove any burrs that might make a visitor uncomfortable produced a service that for whatever it may have lacked in the thrills produced at revivals featuring dramatic healings, outbursts of tongue speaking, and rows of ecstatic believers strewn around the pulpit after having been "slain in the Spirit," nevertheless provided an important and impressive kind of ritual reassurance and reaffirmation. In America, at least, most people who attended the crusades either belonged to or grew up in churches where such middle-of-the-road styles and sentiments were the norm. For them, a Billy Graham crusade was like a gigantic homecoming reunion, an upbeat, friendly, nonthreatening festival that assured them that the old verities are still to be believed, the old songs and prayers still sung and prayed, the old threats and dangers still out there huffing and puffing, but still equally easy to keep at bay if one will "only believe."

Crucial to the success of this ritual and to Billy Graham's remarkable longevity as a crusader was his ability to enlist representatives of the mass media as key soldiers in his campaigns. On occasion, of course, the press was anything but friendly toward him, but anyone who spends several days in the

BGEA headquarters browsing through the oversize scrapbooks that fill an entire room cannot help but be impressed with the overwhelmingly positive treatment the media lavished upon him for four decades. That response was neither unsought nor uncultivated. Larry Ross, a Walter Bennett Communications employee assigned almost exclusively to the Graham organization (which was the agency's only major continuing account), speculated that the favorable treatment Graham typically received from reporters is an example of the benefits of following the Golden Rule. The press generally treated him well "because of how well he treats the press. He is so gracious even when he is dealing with reporters who have written stories that are not in his best interest. He gives them more time than they request or expect. Many times, I have seen him bless those who curse him. I think the Lord has honored that. Even those who don't agree with his message respect the man and his transparent goodness." Veteran AP religion writer George Cornell agreed that Graham seemed able to parry even the most pointed thrusts from hostile reporters: "He has the plain, ingenuous directness of a genuinely free human being." A further reason Graham was able to maintain good relations with the press was his habit of paying them public praise during his crusade services. In 1950 he asked his Boston audiences to write to the editors or publishers of the local newspapers to thank them for the marvelous coverage the crusade had received. Forty years later, he was still making the same request, some times even singling out one or two reporters—typically, the key religion writers from the crusade city's major papers—for special praise.

The Bennett agency counted on the local press to provide an abundance of free publicity for Graham's crusades and sometimes kept careful score of the results. After the 1984 phase of Mission England, for example, Gavin Reid reported that "the national press had published 157 items and eleven editorials covering nearly 3,000 column inches. The regional press (and we were deliberately working to capitalize on regional awareness) published 1,262 items plus eighteen editorials taking up no less than 37,116 column inches! Radio time amounted to nearly eight and a half hours and television time amounted to five hours seven minutes." Reid and his assistants had made these tallies at the specific request of the Graham organization. Predictably, however, the agency did not rely solely on cooperative journalists. Every crusade involved a saturation advertising campaign, and though Graham sometimes professed to wish he never had to see his name on another billboard or banner, even his closest friends and staunchest backers admit that he handled whatever embarrassment he felt with considerable equanimity. Bob Evans recalled that shortly before the 1986 crusade, "when he came to Paris, he said, 'Get some more pictures up. I don't see my picture up enough.' He got special permission to put posters in the Metro stations. He felt like he needed more publicity." And Fred Dienert, who was personally responsible for puffing Graham for forty years, said, in unambiguous admiration,

"Bill understands the value of publicity. At night, when he can't sleep, God evidently gives him thoughts—about the ministry, about promotion, about what to do here and there. It's uncanny, and they work out well. And it's because the Lord's got his hand on him. It's not us. We do the newspapers. We do the billboards, we buy the spots, and everything else. I believe all that helps, but I think the real answer is God."

Of course, the bottom-line goal of every crusade was the number of people who responded to Graham's call. Though from his early days he had an uncanny gift for the invitation, his colleagues acknowledged that especially since he achieved world renown, several quite unmiraculous factors entered into Graham's unprecedented success at "drawing in the net." Gavin Reid admitted that "Billy gets good results because more uncommitted people come to his meetings than is true with other evangelists. He is a 'name.'" And all gave much credit to the planting and cultivation that went on before the harvester hit town with his evangelistic combine. In giving the invitation, Graham often described the decision to come forward as a difficult one. That can be the case, of course, particularly in foreign countries where Christianity is a minority religion and becoming a Christian may involve painful breaks with one's family and friends. But for most inquirers, the decision to walk down the aisle is relatively easy; indeed, in some cases, it is easier than staying put. Everyone who has been to a crusade service or watched one on television, which almost certainly includes most of those in attendance, knows that hundreds of others would be streaming to the front and that no embarrassing emotional demonstrations would be expected (or even tolerated). Further, those who came with a friend as part of the Operation Andrew program surely understood that failure to respond would be a bit of a disappointment to the friendly folk who got them a ticket and saved them a place on the bus, and would make the trip home less enjoyable than if they had behaved as hoped—as some of the other invitees were almost certainly likely to have done. Such pressures were not enormous, but they were real, and they helped swell inquirer ranks.

The inevitable success of the invitation could not help but have an exhilarating effect on the counselors who assisted inquirers in clarifying and confirming their decision. Evangelical Christians feel they should be leading others to Christ, but many find it difficult to talk to their friends and relatives about salvation out of fear they will be thought intrusive or odd. But at the crusade, they talked with people who, by their complete willingness to buy what is being sold, furnished them with the opportunity to do precisely what they thought they should be doing, with an almost perfect guarantee of success. This happy experience almost surely bolstered their confidence and willingness to approach others once the crusade ended.

In a diffuse and invisible way, this process was repeated a few weeks later, when the crusade was aired on television and viewers were given opportunity to respond to his preaching by calling a number on their screens. More than a fourth of the 12,000 or so people who called one of BGEA's eight regional telephone centers during the week of Graham's quarterly television specials made some kind of decision for Christ. And, as at the live crusades, some of the greatest benefits accrued to the counselors themselves. Terry Wilken, a team member who worked with the telephone ministry from its inception, observed that "nothing increases faith like trying to give it away. Every night counselors go out of here several feet off the ground talking about the blessings they have received from participating. When you look at it from their perspective, its probably the easiest kind of witnessing you could do."

As one who long compared himself to the harvester who reaps what others have sown and cultivated, Billy Graham recognized that the harvest, to be of significant use to any but scavengers, must be gathered into barns and protected against hostile elements. By his own criterion, then, it is disciple making rather than decision counting that must serve as the ultimate measure of an evangelist's accomplishments. Neither he nor his associates pretended that every person who comes forward or calls a counseling center is making a meaningful response. When one watches a father shrug his shoulders and shuffle down the aisle after his grown daughter tells him she is disgusted with him for holding back—"That was the whole point in coming, for God's sake!"—or sees two prepubescent boys poke one another and toss their caps in the air as they skip across the stadium infield toward the counseling area, or listen to a teenage girl tell her friend, "Well, if I can, you can. There's nothing to it," one comes to understand that not every decision flows from the deepest wellsprings of heart or mind. Graham long admitted that people come for different reasons and that some of the reasons are quite superficial. "We never call them 'converts,'" he said early in his career. "We much prefer to call them 'inquirers.' Only God knows when or if a man is truly converted. Many come forward in our meetings who are seekers but not finders."

As Graham and his team always graciously admitted, the trip down the aisle is just one segment of a journey on a path that many others have helped prepare and on which the seeker had already started to walk. "I am not sure I have ever led a soul to Christ," he has said. "There are so many factors—a mother, a Sunday school teacher, a preacher who has been slugging it out for years. I simply come along as a way-shower. I say, 'Do you see that door? That's the way in.'" Of those who made first-time decisions in Graham's crusades, a small minority—but still a substantial number—were doubtless truly won to Christ from a stance of antagonism, indifference, or apathy, as a sampling of the mail received in Minneapolis clearly reveals. For the majority, however, particularly in America, the decision they made is one they would have made at some point in their lives even if Billy Graham had not come to town—when they reached a certain age, when peers in their Sunday-school class responded, when pressure from their spouses reached a sufficient level, or at a revival held by a lesser evangelist. Similarly, some "rededicators" were genuine reprobates, dragooned into the stadium against their will or perhaps come to scoff and moved instead by terror or love to repent and turn from their evil ways. Far more were people of tender conscience who feared they had not done all they might to win souls, or who were more concerned with their own affairs than about their Father's business, or who felt guilty because they sometimes daydreamed during the pastor's sermon. But, like the decision to attend college or to marry, a decision to say "I am now ready to assume the responsibility of living as a Christian" was not less momentous simply because it was an expected part of one's life agenda. Similarly, if a substantial number of church folk whose light had begun to dim were plugged back into their systems on a high-voltage line, the crusade performed an important function for both the individual and the systems in question.

While the great stadium crusades remained the hallmark of his ministry, and while he drew crowds to them for a far longer period than any other evangelist has ever managed to do, it is indisputably the case that Billy Graham magnified his voice and multiplied his words tremendously by his ability and willingness to use modern mass media. To the end, he made use of the two media that served him longest: print and radio. In 1990 his "My Answer" column ran in over a hundred newspapers, but that was far below its peak during the 1950s and 1960s. Aides insist he tried to check them to approve of their content, but conceded, as the column itself noted once each year, that staff members did the actual writing. No one seemed to think the column was living up to its potential. Even Fred Dienert, who was usually relentless in his determination to put a positive spin on anything connected with the ministry, admitted that "something should be done. There's an opportunity to handle it in a way that meets the needs of people today. For example, if you talk about divorce, you're talking about the whole country. It's in every church in America. Families breaking up, loneliness, singles, people who are hurting and crying. You can't just give them a verse about casting all of your cares on Jesus because he'll take care of you. It would probably take a full-time crew to do a better column, but it could grow again, because nobody has the audience Billy has."

Rather than wait for a newspaper squib to hit upon their particular problem, those who wanted a fuller and more satisfying answer to a specific question could write directly to Graham at his Minneapolis headquarters. Correct spelling and a precise address were unnecessary. The letter collection contains missives sent to "Belly Grayem, Menihapuls, Menisoldiem"; "Rev. Billy Graham, Many Applause, Many Sorrow, Los Angeles"; "Mr. Belly Graham, Baptist Church's Preacher, will you find him out, please, NY"; "Billy Graham (World Citizen), care of American Government"; and "The

Rev. Billy Graham—Dear Mr. Postman, I don't know the address of Rev. Graham, but please try and get this letter to him. It really is important. Love, Linda." In marked contrast to other well-known media ministers who not only claim to read every letter they receive but authorize responses in which a computer has slugged in the correspondent's name in a display of ersatz intimacy, Graham freely admitted he did not and could not read more than a tiny fraction of his mail. Moreover, the responses were signed by the people who actually prepared them.

Prepare is often more accurate than *write.* Ralph Williams, director of BGEA's Christian Guidance Department, explained how his staff of approximately twenty-five men and women handled most of the more than 200,000 inquiries people addressed to Billy Graham each year. Large notebooks contained standardized responses on a host of subjects; each sentence and verse of Scripture were numbered, so that a mail counselor could construct an appropriate response simply by typing the proper codes on a computer. Most of the topics were routine, of the sort a secular therapist might face: Anxiety, Bereavement, Birth Control, Drugs, Jealousy, Marriage, Smoking, and War. Others made it clear that this was a religious enterprise: Age of Accountability, Bible Translations, Daughter Wants to Marry Non-Christian, Frequent Writers ("We keep a file of people who just write to us again and again, so we can refer back to previous letters"), Heaven (Description of), Jehovah's Witnesses, Ministry (Call to), Non-Christian Friends for Children, Parents (How to Deal with Child's Waywardness), Perilous Times, Poem Acknowledgment ("We get a lot of poems"), Purgatory, Sabbath, and Witnessing. The responses were not quotations from Billy Graham, but Williams felt they were "pretty much abreast of how Billy feels. We've built them up over the years and feel we're in tune with him and his thoughts and position on these topics, whether it's in the area of theology or social action or whatever." When a topic loomed large in the public consciousness—for example, abortion, AIDS, cults, herpes, or as in 1987, television evangelism—the counseling department typically prepared a few paragraphs, a special letter, or even a complete pamphlet on the subject. Sometimes such letters called for a delicate balancing act. "We are inclined to be a bit ambiguous on AIDS," Williams noted. "We feel it's important to give a sense of hope. While some are saying AIDS is a judgment from God, we just say that our sin as a nation brings its own harvest."

When an inquiry was too complex or sensitive for a prepackaged response, it was forwarded to an "advanced counseling reader," typically a minister or counselor with more experience than the first tier of readers. Advanced counselors also had notebooks to draw on but could adapt the responses to fit a particular situation; regular counselors were not permitted to deviate from the printed responses. When it appeared that correspondents needed something more than a one- or two-page letter, the counselors could refer them to specialists near their homes. "We have a list of 'helping people' around the country," Williams explained. "We know something about their background, their specialty, and their staff, so that we are sure they have a Christian perspective. It may be a church or a pastoral counselor or a Christian who specializes in crisis intervention. There are so many people who are without purpose, who don't know why they should live and think they don't want to live, who are just awash in life, and can't find help from pastors who believe the answer is simply to tell them to have more faith." In August 1987 BGEA's operations chief John Corts noted that 27 women in the mail division had answered 17,000 letters during the previous 60 days. "The people who wrote don't know those ladies," he admitted. "The only name they know is Billy Graham. They write because they want him to tell them whether they should buy a house or move into a rest home down the street, or whatever. We can't answer all those questions, but at least we can go back to them with some kind of love, care, and concern."

Decision still rolls along as the world's most widely distributed religious magazine, with two million copies mailed to subscribers in 163 countries, and Graham continues to reach millions through his many books. In 1972 the *Saturday Evening Post* quoted him as saying, "I do all of my own writing." The quote may have been accurate, but the reality was not, and Graham was said to be quite sensitive about his extensive reliance on researchers and ghostwriters. That sensitivity ebbed noticeably, so that he became quite open about the help he received from others, maintaining only that he participated actively in his writing projects and, at the least, carefully examined anything that went out under his name to make certain it accurately represented his beliefs and opinions. John Akers, who helped with several books, explained that Graham provided the essence of his books and others helped fill in the outlines, "including Ruth, who has a great gift for illustration."

The Hour of Decision was still being aired weekly over 690 stations in 1990 (including 151 international stations broadcasting six foreign-language versions of the program), but the Graham team had come to view it less as a prime evangelistic tool than as a vehicle for keeping the ministry's "prayer partners" informed as to what the evangelist is doing. In addition to its radio program, BGEA also owns and operates two radio stations, one near Montreat and one in Honolulu. "We didn't want to be in that business," Graham said, "but we are in it. It's never really been an interest of mine, and I don't give it top priority." T. W. Wilson, who monitored the stations, agreed with that assessment. "When a station's going real good," he said with a chuckle, "it's *our station*. When there are problems, it's *T's station*." Graham apparently had a similar lack of passion for making films. According to John Akers, "The film ministry has always driven him crazy. Basically, it's an exercise in deficit financing." World Wide Pictures became the largest producer and distributor of Christian films in the world: An estimated 150 million people have seen at least one of the films and at least 1.5 million have made decisions for Christ at film showings. (Expense and concern over diminished effectiveness led to a 1988 decision to close the Burbank studios and relocate production facilities in Minneapolis.) *Caught*, a 1986 film about drugs and a boy's search for his natural father, did not draw well in the United States, but worldwide more than 600,000 people saw it during the first two months after it was released—far less than had been expected, but not an insignificant number—and Dave Barr, World Wide's international representative, ventured that "this one may do for the international program what *The Restless Ones* did for the United States. We think it is going to be a great blessing."

Radio gave Billy Graham his first truly national exposure, and films legitimated the use of that medium by people who regarded cinema as the devil's tool, but it was television that kept him in the public eye. Other preachers appear on television more often, but none used the medium more efficiently and effectively than Graham. One key to his success was the decision not to attempt a weekly Sunday-morning program. As years of Nielsen and Arbitron ratings have demonstrated, the audiences for his programs, usually aired in groups of three on a quarterly basis, were far larger than those for the syndicated Sunday programs of other religious broadcasters. This larger audience also appeared to contain far more unchurched people than did the Sunday shows. The 1978 Gallup study, *The Unchurched American*, for example, discovered that 11 percent of the 61 million unchurched in this country said they had watched Billy Graham on television. The only other preacher to attract more than 4 percent was Oral Roberts, then also using prime-time specials in addition to his Sunday-morning program. The audience of the Sunday programs produced by Roberts, Jimmy Swaggart, Jerry Falwell, and their colleagues appeared to be composed primarily of faithful church members, which is why most of the programs aired before ten o'clock; if they came on later, their audience would be in church. If a program was geared to teach, nurture, and encourage believers, early Sunday morning would be the best time for it. If it aimed to reach the lost and the lukewarm, it would be hard to think of a less promising time slot. Since Graham's compelling mission was to present his message to people who are not already hearing it several times a week, he chose to run his programs during prime-time early evening hours.

Despite the success Graham's quarterly specials enjoyed and the near-automatic ease with which they could be produced, there had been in creasing pressure to modernize the format in the later years. TV director Roger Flessing put the matter bluntly: "We have a Good News show with an hour on the anchor man. I'd like to see more graphics, file footage, other things that would illustrate points Mr. Graham is making. Jesus was a visual teacher—-

'Look at the lilies,' 'Look at the fisherman,' 'Look at the farmer,' 'Look at the . . . Look at the. . . .' With television, we have the capacity to *look* but we're not doing it. We're right here just looking at the preacher. And we can't even be as visual as we'd like with what we've got." Pointing to a shot of the choir on one of the monitors arrayed before him on the control panel in the television truck, he said, "Most church choirs look better than this. We don't really try to shoot 'tights,' because when you zoom in, these people don't know what they're singing, or they're three beats off, or one person is just gung ho and the person next to her doesn't even know what's going on. A church choir is more disciplined."

Ted Dienert—Fred's son, Graham's son-in-law, and TV producer beginning in 1982—agreed with Flessing. Sitting in a hotel restaurant one morning during the 1987 Columbia crusade, he said, "There's a constant effort to try to figure out what will hook the secular audience. The crusades haven't changed for twenty years, and the TV format has been virtually the same. We are integrating new elements into that format because the viewer's taste and sophistication has changed, and we need to keep up with that. At times maybe I get a little avant-garde for the ministry, but my job is to see if we can get the job done more effectively. I don't care whether I like it, or Cliff likes it, or even whether Billy Graham likes it. We want to be sensitive, of course, but my goal is that audience out there."

To create a more appealing product, Dienert and Flessing altered the old practice of filming only three crusade services and hoping for the best, with editing limited to cutting a few dead spots here and there to squeeze the program into a one-hour time frame. They began to film all the services and used only those segments they felt would make the most effective package. A few weeks after the Denver crusade, for example, the two men and other members of their crew, armed with stacks of film and thick notebooks, met at Third Coast Studios in Austin, Texas, to piece together the master videotape they would send to a duplicator, who would make 350 copies to be distributed to television stations in the United States and Canada.

With seven or eight nights of entertainers and testifiers, it was relatively simple to come up with a good mix that fit the time constraints for a particular program and to edit out anything that might be jarring to the viewing audience. On this occasion someone noted that the sky was dark while Bev Shea sang but light when Graham got up to preach afterward. "We try to keep the songs with the night of the sermon," Dienert explained, "but Bev blew the words that night," and his segment was taken from another service.

When it came time to plug in Graham's sermon, Dienert and his technicians referred to notebooks that contained transcripts of every word spoken on the videotape, with a precise indication of the time each sentence took. The evangelist's "misspeaks" were always excised. "Either we or someone else points out mistakes, and we clip them," an assistant producer explained. "If he misquotes *Time* magazine or says the King of Spain died last week, that comes out. Or anything controversial—that comes out." Jokes and stories Graham had repeated for years also came out, as did meandering trips down what the TV crew called "rabbit trails." The editors might also cover up such minor irregularities as reference to "my fourth point" when no third point was ever made. After the sermon's obvious errors and weak spots were eliminated and its length set, it was strengthened even further by skillful use of reaction shots of the crowd that could be matched with various parts of the sermon. By the time the program aired a few weeks later, Billy Graham had become a better preacher than he actually was on the night he delivered the sermon in person, and those who watched the program could see that he held the crowd in the palm of his hand.

Graham's policy of appearing quarterly instead of weekly may have won him a larger audience, but it also saddled the Dienerts with a tougher task than that faced by the media representatives for other television ministers. Instead of negotiating long-term contracts for a regular weekly time slot, the Dienerts and other Bennett company agents had to wrangle anew with station representatives every time they wanted to put Graham on the air. Partly as a measure to save money, the Bennett company moved Graham's programs onto UHF stations in many cities and in some markets dropped local stations entirely, relying on the Turner cable network to provide a sufficient audience. Economic pressures also led to a dropping of the foreign-language programs that were once a standard component of Graham's television outreach. Despite these cutbacks, there was no sign that Graham or his colleagues had serious misgivings about television's efficacy as an evangelistic tool.

A major advantage of television, of course, is that it enabled Billy Graham to do what he could not possibly do in person. Larry Ross elaborated on that obvious but important fact. "Television," he said, "enables Mr. Graham to reach more people with less demands on his time and energy as he gets older. We try to maximize a limited resource that has been blessed by God over the years and try to maximize his effectiveness in his remaining years." Ross was not implying that Billy Graham had gone into semiretirement and planned to sit at home in Montreat, talking to television cameras and playing out the string. At that time, early in 1988, the team was actively engaged in setting up Mission World, a project that would carry crusades originating in London, Hong Kong, and Buenos Aires to satellite centers in hundreds of cities throughout the world. In underdeveloped nations or away from major cities, the satellite signal would be picked up by low-cost portable receiving dishes that could be transported in a case the size of a golf bag, then unfolded like a fan and made operational in eighteen minutes. In more remote spots, the program would be videotaped and shown in small villages a day or two later on portable VCR equipment. "Mr. Graham is not afraid of the technology at all," Ted Dienert insisted. "He welcomes it. He wants God to use him until it is all over, and he is willing to take the necessary risks. It would be easy for him to stay in the same pattern, but he is a visionary man, and I feel that God has really honored that."

Dienert had good reason to appreciate his father-in-law. BGEA was unusual among large independent ministries in having continued to use an outside agency rather than creating an in-house agency that would perform the same roles without receiving the 15 percent to 17 percent commissions typically paid to agencies for their work. The savings were substantial; for example, if an agency receiving a 15 percent commission bought $20 million in television air time, its share was $3 million. Fred Dienert, who prospered handsomely from the arrangement, saw it as a mark of Graham's character that he remained with Bennett. "Bill remembers his friends," he said. "He's very faithful to his friends, and he's been faithful to us. He could have gone in-house a long time ago, but he doesn't want to. He doesn't want to be bothered with it. He has enough problems as it is, and he's happy with what we've been doing, and he appreciates it."

Not everyone within BGEA was completely at ease with the arrangement. Overt criticism was muted or ventured on a not-for-attribution basis, in part because Fred Dienert had been connected with the ministry for longer than all but the inner circle; in part because Millie Dienert, who received no pay for her extensive work in building the prayer program, was held in unfailingly high regard; in part because Bennett company personnel unquestionably did a first-rate job and appeared genuinely committed to the ministry's primary goals; and in part because Ted Dienert was married to the Graham's youngest daughter, Bunny. Still, an undercurrent of uneasiness occasionally bubbled to the surface. Asked where Fred Dienert could be found, a plainly dressed Graham lieutenant might name a location, then add, "You'll be able to spot him," a mild dig at Dienert's preference for somewhat flashier clothes than were common in BGEA. Another would commend Franklin Graham for living in "just an ordinary house with a tin roof" and driving "a car just like yours or mine—not a Porsche, like some people drive." Again, the reference was clear: BGEA salaries would not support a lifestyle that includes Porsches, airplanes, and Arabian horses; Ted and Bunny Dienert somehow managed to have them all.

When the only issue was standard payment for work well done, few people seem to have objected, though when Walter Bennett died in 1982, some board members reportedly suggested it might be time to form an inhouse agency, under the direction of Cliff Barrows. Those vague feelings of discontent were reinforced when Ted Dienert, who had worked on the Graham account since 1967, took charge of producing the TV programs that same year, giving rise to inevitable murmurs of nepotism. In 1987, however, the Dienerts found themselves at the center of a small stir that illustrated both the constant need to monitor the ministry's financial affairs and a willingness to take swift and decisive action when the situation demanded it. For several years, postproduction work (final editing and preparation for duplication) on the television programs had been done at CVS, a video facility in Dallas, where the Bennett company's main headquarters are located. In 1986, however, the contract was shifted to Third Coast Studios, a small operation in Austin. Some board members questioned the shift and wondered why Third Coast had been selected without competitive bidding. When the answer came to light, it was not inspiring.

Early in October 1987, when asked about ties between Third Coast and the Bennett company, Fred Dienert acknowledged that "we are related. We have a small portion." CVS, he explained, had not always been able to get the postproduction work done as rapidly as was needed. Owning a small portion of Third Coast provided enough leverage to make certain the turnaround time for production was minimal. What Dienert characterized as a small portion turned out to be 45 percent, with an additional 5 percent belonging to a Bennett employee. When Cliff Barrows learned the extent of Bennett's ownership, he is said, in suitably Evangelical language, to have "hit the ceiling." In a year when the biggest story in American religion was the fall of Jim Bakker's PTL empire, the one major ministry that had managed to emerge as a model of probity did not need a revelation that Billy Graham's son-in-law and one of his oldest friends not only benefited handsomely from handling his media account but had also hired their own company to help produce his programs. It was neither illegal nor more expensive than the arrangement with CVS, and it may have been efficient, but it could easily cast Graham and his ministry in an unfavorable light if zealous reporters got hold of the information. Almost immediately, while Ted Dienert was in Austin supervising work on programs drawn from Graham's Denver crusade, Barrows flew in for a brief but intense set of discussions. No one would speak freely about the details of their conversations, and it is not clear Barrows knew precisely what he was looking for when he arrived, but the upshot was unambiguous. Within days the postproduction contract was shifted back to CVS. Not long afterward, Graham's board appointed one of its members to serve as a special liaison between BGEA and the Bennett agency to make certain their financial relationships remained well within ethically defensible limits.

34

Decently and in Order

The swift end to which Cliff Barrows brought the ambiguous operation in Austin was not simply the product of one man's determination to follow the scriptural injunction to "abstain from all appearance of evil" (I Thessalonians 5:22). Rather, it reflected the conscious and remarkably well-observed philosophy that permeated another key foundation stone in Billy Graham's enduring success, the Billy Graham Evangelistic Association itself. Graham was quick to admit that his ability to travel the world, to stand before great throngs, to send his words to the farthest reaches of the planet, to visit and befriend the famous and powerful, to influence the policies of great nations, and to raise up legions to take his place were enormously enhanced by the tireless and dedicated efforts of several hundred men and women who labored in quiet anonymity in downtown Minneapolis.

For nearly forty years, from 1950 until he reluctantly went into semiretirement in 1987, George Wilson ran BGEA's headquarters with an iron hand. A stout, squarish man with a bulldog face and a taste for iridescent suits and sport coats that clash with the kindly-pastor image of most BGEA staffmembers, Wilson enjoyed the respect, if not always the affection, of those who labored in his vineyard. One team member characterized Wilson as having "a unique gift for giving directions." From a position of greater occupational security, Billy Graham put it more pointedly: "George is a dictator. Maybe I shouldn't use that word, but he's a strong man. He doesn't mind telling somebody off if they need telling off. He's not the most popular man in the world, but he does use Sunday-school language, and he's a real Christian. He's part preacher, part lawyer, part financial wizard." A former staffer cited frustration with Wilson as a major reason he had left the organization. "He's hard to deal with," he explained. "He deals carefully, particularly when he doesn't know how close someone is to Billy, because he doesn't want direct competition. He deals by instinct, and little more, and he can throw cold water on any idea." But even he acknowledged Wilson's effectiveness: "George knows how everything is wired. He's like an indispensable engineer."

To a considerable extent what aggravated Wilson's detractors was his zealous concern for the bottom line. That near obsession with saving money, however, helped shield Graham from the kind of criticism heaped on evangelists who live in opulent mansions, drive fleets of luxury automobiles, and air-condition their doghouses. BGEA's Minneapolis complex, comprising an old and unremarkable three-story office building purchased from Standard Oil and a newer structure that was once a parking garage for the Willys Overland automobile company, had a Spartan quality that made it easy to believe the association obtained it for only $2.25 per square foot. In contrast to the elaborate and sometimes garish personal monuments erected by other media ministers, it could easily pass for the regional headquarters of a medium-size insurance company, and were it not associated with Billy Graham, it would surely not have been a stop on the Chamber of Commerce tour of the city. But as he walked through it, George Wilson's pride in what he had built and in the money he had saved in building it was unmistakable.

The lifeline of every major independent ministry is its direct-mail operation. Howard Pew, Maxey Jarman, and other members of BGEA's board provided major funding for several large projects, but the bulk of the ministry's support comes in small bills and modest checks tucked into the millions of letters that pour into the headquarters—140,000 to 150,000 during a normal week, twice that *per day* during the quarterly television broadcasts. With multiplied millions of letters involved, minuscule savings per unit quickly become substantial amounts. No one understood that better than George Wilson, and he loved to show off procedural shortcuts or mechanical gimmicks he had devised to save money for the association. Pausing to give some whirring apparatus an affectionate pat, like a coach commending a running back, he observed, "This saves about half a penny a letter. When you're talking about millions of checks a year, it's worthwhile," then cocked his head as if to say, "What do you think of that?"

Officially, Wilson stepped down from his post as BGEA's chief of operations in 1987, but he continued to work full-time as a consultant on various projects. Fortunately for the organization, any reluctance he felt about moving out of the top spot was eased by his having a major role in picking his successor, John Corts. Like Graham, Corts attended Florida Bible Institute, and he worked with YFC for years before signing on to help with the 1964 Boston crusade. Intending to stay with the association only six months, he wound up staying sixteen years, until he resigned to take a pastorate in 1980. Following a successful run in a local church, he moved into the presidency of his alma mater, now known as Trinity College and located in Dunedin, Florida, but Graham was reluctant to let him go. After obtaining leaves of absence to take key roles in both Amsterdam conferences, where he showed unusual administrative competence, Corts finally agreed to take over the reins at BGEA. It appears to have been a happy choice. He was sufficiently tough but less prickly and protective than Wilson, and he clearly had the boss's confidence. "George picked him," Graham reported, "and that helps. Whoever sits in that office is sort of the main center of the thing. The executive committee and the board call the ultimate shots, but it's that day-by-day running of it that sets the tone. John's a man of the Scriptures. He loves the Lord, and he will keep the organization on a firm biblical keel, and that's what I want."

It is difficult to imagine that any visitor to BGEA headquarters in Minneapolis would have failed to notice a distinctive atmosphere. It was simple enough to dismiss almost universal participation in ten-minute daily devotionals and twice-weekly chapel services as prudent conformity, but casual conversation and consistent behavior quickly dispelled suspicions that this was just another job for these folk. At lunch the cafeteria resembled a fellowship dinner at a middle-size midwestern church, with little attention to distinctions of rank. Corts sat and talked easily with a minor official's secretary and a man from the art department, and nearby, a printer and the head of the estate-planning division speculated about why even the most vigorous churches seemed to be having trouble drawing a good crowd for Wednesday-night prayer meetings. It was no surprise to hear several people observe that "we're really more like a family than a business," but the easy analogy was not far off the mark.

Watching Billy Graham interact with BGEA personnel made it clear that though he depended heavily on men like George Wilson and John Corts, he was no figurehead who simply showed up at press conferences or popped into the pulpit to do whatever his "handlers" told him to do. No one doubted he was the undisputed leader of his team and that both the strengths and short comings of his leadership style left indelible marks on the association. Those who worked with him for years uniformly praised his vision, his intuition, his sense of strategy, and his ability to choose people he could trust and to motivate them to put his dreams into operation. "He is much brighter than most people, including himself, give him credit for being," John Akers insisted. "He may not quote Aquinas in Latin, but he sees the essence of a problem quicker than most people. He has an ability to intuit the heart of a problem that is sometimes little short of brilliant." George Wilson, who prefered performance to pedigree, made a similar assessment: "He has innate common sense. That's something you don't get with a Ph.D. When he gets the facts, he can usually come up with the right decision." Sometimes, the decision-making process was more calculating than it might appear on the surface. "He plays it down," T. W. Wilson said, "but he's a real administrator. Many times he has shared with me in private what he thinks ought to be done. Then, in a meeting with the board, he will ask someone, 'What do you think?' Then he'll look at another one and ask, 'What do you think?' When he gathers all their comments, he will say, 'Well, I think most of us would agree that this is what we ought to do,' and it will be exactly what he had been planning to do all along. His timing is almost as good as his strategy."

One of Graham's greatest gifts was his ability to gather and hold on to a collection of men and women who proved to be far more able than any objective analysis of their portfolio would have predicted. As Sterling Huston diplomatically phrased it, "Mr. Graham has a remarkable ability to respond to intuitive promptings." Further, once he had chosen someone, Graham accorded a remarkable amount of trust. "Billy is a great delegator," T. W. Wilson observed. "He gives you a job and he trusts you to get it done. He doesn't stand over your shoulder and monitor what you are doing, but he expects you to do the job and do it right. He doesn't want you to tell him, 'I can't.' He'll say, 'You keep working at it. If you want to, you can tell me how you accomplished it when you get it done.' At the same time, he's a good forgiver. He forgives all of us our mistakes." Graham was also extraordinarily generous with praise toward those who worked with him. Allan Emery, who took early retirement in 1978 to devote full time to serving as BGEA's unpaid president, observed that "[he has] one of those rare qualities that the greatest of leaders have—being able to share the glory. He always shares the reward publicly. He never stints in the praise he gives anyone. It has to be earned, to a degree, but he's very generous with it. Sometimes I think he goes a little overboard."

The obverse side of Graham's willingness to let his underlings work without specific direction was his own resistance to being pinned down on the details of whatever it was he wanted to do. One former associate described BGEA operations, particularly those directly involving Graham, as "more process than structure. Plans are made and unmade all the time. The inside circle tries to anticipate his movements, and there is some manipulation—they know what he responds to. But he tries to keep all his options open. It is hard to tie him down on anything. You can never get him to say yes or no. If you ask him to do something, he is apt to say yes, but that doesn't mean he will do it. He doesn't want to commit, because something else might come up—an important meeting or a TV show or something like that. He is the inspiration and the mover, but he is also the bottleneck."

T. W. Wilson, who laughingly admitted to having to buy several sets of plane tickets for any trip Graham made, put a more positive face on Graham's resistance to being pinned down. "How can you be in God's will and pray for His leadership if you've already got a fixed idea about what you are going to do? The very fact that he's willing to change, that he's flexible—that's because he always seeks God's guidance. And he does that with his schedule. If there's a part of the world where he feels God is impressing him to go, he'll postpone something and go." Wilson's theological gloss on Graham's notorious flexibility would not have displeased the boss. Recalling that "a lot of times I would go into a city [to help prepare for a crusade] and he wouldn't even know where I was for a year," Robert Ferm once faced Graham with the frustrations his open-ended way of operating generated in his staff. "It would help all of us," Ferm told him, "if you would be more specific as to what you want us to do." Graham hesitated not a moment. "When God called me to the work of evangelism," he shot back, "I had to realize that it's only the Holy Spirit that can give the answer to questions. And if that same Holy Spirit can't guide you, you'll know it yourself and you'll probably drop off the team. But don't expect me to tell you what to do." Ferm smiled at the memory. "That was a definite point of view of his," he said. "I only brought it up that one time."

Graham relied heavily on his board of directors. An all-too-familiar pattern in independent evangelistic ministries has been for the ministry's board (which is required for the ministry to qualify as a nonprofit, tax-free organization) to consist of the evangelist, his wife, son, son-in-law, brother-in-law, closest assistant, lawyer, and one or two ciphers. In such an arrangement, the chances for financial and ethical laxity are enormous. Perhaps no single organizational measure Billy Graham took did more to keep him out of hot water and to undergird his reputation for fiscal integrity than his recruitment of and submission to an impressively strong board. Graham, Cliff Barrows, T. W. Wilson, George Wilson, and Franklin Graham were all on the board, as were E. V. Hill and another minister or two, but they were surrounded by such successful Christian business and professional men as CEOs Robert Van Kampen, William Walton (Holiday Inns), Bill Mead (Campbell-Taggart Industries), Bill Pollard (ServiceMaster); Carloss Morris (Stewart Title Company), Frank Coy (Day Company department stores in Cleveland); Montgomery *Advertiser* editor and publisher Harold Martin; former Minnesota governor Harold LeVander; financial manager and former Harvard University Corporation treasurer George Bennett; Dallas banking executives Bill Seay and Dewey Presley; and former postmaster general Marvin Watson. The larger board, which stood at twenty-seven in 1990, had final jurisdiction, but much of the real work of oversight was performed by a nine-member executive committee, chaired by Allan Emery. This committee met approximately ten times a year in person and convened on the telephone as needed. Neither Graham nor any other person paid by the association or in a position to benefit financially from any of its operations served on the executive committee. "That board has people on it," Ed Plowman observed, "who are not accustomed to having someone walk in [as some well-known evangelists do] and say, 'Here is the way we are going to go.' They took what Billy said seriously, but not as a blank check they would sign without examination. And they took a much stronger stand in later years than they used to. The board would definitely call his hand on certain things—'Who gave you authority to do that? We have a budget here and we have to stick with it.' That happens." George Bennett, the former Harvard treasurer, agreed. "I have served on many boards," he noted, "but I have never been associated with an organization that has such high standards of business procedure and financial controls as BGEA."

Graham's handling of his personal finances long reflected this same concern for propriety. Since he made the decision in 1952 to accept a specified salary instead of the much higher love offerings he could have reaped from his crusades, he and his board agreed that the benchmark for his wage would be the salary earned by a prominent minister in a large urban church. At the time, the figure was approximately $15,000. And when money was tight, as during both the marathon 1954 London crusade and the Madison Square Garden campaign in 1957, both Graham and his team took half-salary to keep expenses down. By the late 1980s, BGEA's income was running over $70 million a year and the evangelist's salary had risen to nearly $80,000, a figure he readily acknowledged to be an imprecise gauge of his true financial status, both because many of his expenses when he was away from Montreat were either paid for by the association or picked up by friends and supporters and because of the huge royalties his books earned. Still, repeated efforts of reporters and other Graham watchers failed to turn up any of the usual signs of great personal wealth or evidence that he was squirreling away stockpiles of money to squander during some long-postponed rainy season. His mountain home is worth perhaps $500,000 today, but more for the 150 acres it sits on than for the log-and-asbestos-siding structure itself. It is unquestionably a marvelous dwelling, but that is due more to Ruth Graham's taste and ingenuity than to any obvious outlay of money.

Graham stopped accepting free clothes during the 1960s but did not follow a rigid policy of refusing all gifts. When he played golf regularly, he paid for membership in the Black Mountain and Biltmore country clubs, both near Asheville, but his membership at Grandfather Mountain, another North Carolina club, was paid for by the developer, and Jack Nicklaus gave him a membership at John's Island Country Club in Vero Beach, Florida. He long accepted free rooms at Marriott Hotels and Holiday Inns and was often the guest of admiring hoteliers in crusade cities. He defended this practice by pointing out that "there's nothing in the Bible that says I can't accept freebies," but he routinely turned down ultraluxurious accommodations to avoid creating an impression that might harm his ministry. Fending off generous well-wishers could be difficult. June Carter Cash, after watching Ruth shiver on a crusade platform one evening, presented her with a full-length hooded mink coat. Ruth told June she could not even appear in public wearing such an obviously expensive coat, much less on a crusade platform. June told her to "wear it to the barn. Wear it in the car. Wear it out walking with Billy in the snow on the mountain. But stay warm!" She followed that directive for a while, using the coat as an everyday wrap—once showing up at a friend's house with asbestos gloves as accessories—but eventually got June's permission to donate it to a charity auction. Friends who knew what she had done, however, bought it for twice its true value and gave it back to her, with strict instructions that she not try to get rid of it again. In similar fashion, Billy turned down the offer of several board members to provide him with a corporate jet with all expenses paid for five years. "Ruth and I couldn't sleep for thinking about it," he recalled. "We just felt BGEA couldn't have an airplane."

If he so chose, Graham could have easily amassed considerable wealth from honoraria for speeches and royalties from his books, virtually all of which have been best-sellers. He received thousands of invitations to speak each year, many with the promise of large fees, but he turned down most and took no honoraria for those he accepted. Since 1960 all his royalties went into a general trust administered by the First Union National Bank in Charlotte, which disbursed it to facets of his ministry or to other charities. Much of more than a million dollars earned by *Angels*, for example, went to the Billy Graham Center at Wheaton. The royalties from *Approaching Hoofbeats*, which sold over 500,000 copies, helped pay for the follow-up after Amsterdam '83. He explained that he had the right to make an exception and hold out a portion of the money each year but said in 1989, "I've only done it once and that was this last year because Ruth and I felt we just had to have some extra money coming in. We had to help some of our children and grandchildren a little bit. Especially with the education of grandchildren." Then, quite accurately, he added, "Of course, I could have kept it all."

The Grahams' tastes were far from exotic or expensive. At home they had a housekeeper, but Ruth did most of the cooking herself and the fare was delicious but absolutely unpretentious: homemade soup, pounded steak or leftover ham, turnip greens and creamed corn, and marvelous made-from-scratch biscuits. But Billy didn't require even that level of preparation. "If I'm not here," she said, "his favorite meal is baked beans, Vienna sausages, and canned tomatoes. Can you think of anything worse? They're all the same color, for one thing." He chuckled at his own plebeian preferences, adding, "I share the beans with the dogs." None of it seemed to be an act. In an early conversation over club sandwiches in a New York hotel room, he explained that he seldom went out to restaurants because constant interruptions from well-meaning admirers made it difficult to finish a meal. He had made a rare exception the night before. "Fred Dienert loves to go out to real nice restaurants, so he just insisted we go to Trader Vic's."

Graham's personal offices in both Minneapolis and Montreat served as an index of his attitude toward vulgar display. The Minneapolis office, which he seldom used, was extremely modest, smaller than several in the same area, and it opened directly onto a large warren of modular "action offices" filled with secretaries and middle-level managers. Its simple furnishings and few pictures conveyed no sense that it belonged to the central figure in the organization, and staff members felt little hesitation at saying, "Why don't you just work in Mr. Graham's office? Nobody's using it today." His office at the Montreat headquarters was larger, but scarcely more opulent. Were it not for several family photographs and a copper plaque bearing a likeness of L. Nelson Bell, few would suspect its occupant's identity.

Team members generally followed Graham's example of frugality. Their modest middle-class homes gave no hint they were occupied by world travelers. Cliff and Billie Barrows, for example, live in a thoroughly pleasant wooden home on a hilltop on the edge of Greenville, South Carolina. The view from the kitchen window is lovely, and the house is large enough to have reared five children comfortably, but it lacks any sign of ostentation. A few feet away stands a small cabin that houses offices for Barrows, his associate Johnny Lenning, and their secretary. It also contains a tiny studio where Cliff and Lenning produced the *Hour of Decision* broadcasts. The two men built the cabin themselves, and BGEA paid no rental for its use. Barrows paid a yardman out of his own pocket, but he and his two co-workers handled the janitorial duties themselves. He did not seem to count it remarkable that the most popular religious radio program in history was put together in a little wooden building in his backyard. "That's just one of the phases of our job," he said with a shrug. "A very small part."

Graham and his associates clearly felt that reliance on a strong board invested with real authority was a major factor in protecting him from the scandals that rocked the world of television evangelism in the late 1980s. "I don't think Jim Bakker intended to do those things," George Wilson observed. "He just slid into it. He didn't have anybody around to tell him it was wrong. I don't think he started out to be dishonest. Billy knows that any man has feet of clay and had better mind his steps." Precisely because neither Graham nor his lieutenants felt immune to temptation, they consistently stressed the need for help in keeping a check on their baser inclinations. Millie Dienert volunteered that "I have always appreciated, from a moral point of view, how clean the men have been in their attitude toward the [secretaries]. The doors are always left open. There is a high regard for the lack of any kind of privacy where a boss and his secretary are involved. At times, I thought they were going a little too far, that it wasn't necessary, but I'm glad they did it, especially today. They have kept everything above reproach. When you are working on a long-term basis with the same person, constantly, in hotels, where the wife is not there and the secretary is, that is a highly explosive situation. You have to take precautions. I have always respected the way they have handled that. It has been beautifully done."

Graham himself lamented the tribulations Bakker, Jimmy Swaggart, and Oral Roberts had brought on themselves by illegal, immoral, and outrageous behavior. "I've prayed for them a lot," he said, and he seemed to mean it. He maintained positive feelings about his old friend, Oral Roberts, but acknowledged substantial misgivings about some of the directions Roberts had taken in later years. "Oral invited me to give the dedication speech at the City of Faith. He also invited Gene Mayberry from the Mayo Clinic. I called Gene to ask him what he was going to do, and he said he was waiting to see what I was going to do, because his colleagues didn't think he should lend the prestige of the Mayo Clinic to Oral's university. I told Gene I just didn't feel led to go. It was very inconvenient for me—I was supposed to be in Dallas that day for a Billy Graham Day at the First Baptist Church—but there was also something in my heart that said, 'Don't go.' I love Oral. I believe at times he is a real man of God. At times, though—that tall Jesus and all those other things he has said—he talks about things that are just foreign to me. Among all those people, I like Oral best, but when he does things like that, people outside of Christ get very skeptical and cynical."

Graham barely knew Bakker and Swaggart, and when the scandals broke, he resolutely tried to refrain from making any public comments about their plight. As reporters besieged him with requests for interviews and editors offered him space in their magazines and newspapers, he anguished over what he might say. "Forty years ago," he noted, in a pained voice, "we took steps to avoid this, but if I say that, I'll come off sounding self-righteous, and I don't want to do that. I may still make some bad mistakes." As much as the debacle saddened him, he was able to see a bright side to the series of seamy episodes. "A couple of big names have crashed," he observed, "but it's like the thousands of flights at O'Hare in Chicago. The overwhelming majority don't crash. We have so many television evangelists doing marvelous work for God.... Jesus had just twelve people. One betrayed him, one denied him, one doubted him,... [so] we've had it all through the history of the church.... I don't think the church-at-large has been hurt in any way. 'The gates of hell will not prevail against it,' Jesus said. Things like this have happened down through church history—Protestant and Catholic—but the work goes on.... The work of the Lord continues. In its own backhanded way, I think it may help the church.... It's making everybody look to their financial integrity and responsibility. And to their personal lifestyles. Public evangelists must watch themselves very carefully."

Most observers credit Allan Emery with bringing some needed bureaucratic rationality to the association when he agreed in 1978 to serve as president of the association and chair of the executive committee. Emery handled a number of uncomfortable situations for which Graham was unsuited either by temperament or by image. "Billy always wears the white hat," he explained, "and he has to. He does it very beautifully." If someone has to make a mistake or rankle sensitive feelings, it works better if Graham is not the culprit. "I'm expendable and he isn't," Emery said. "I'm perfectly happy in this system." As Emery's comments imply, even in an organization with an unusual record for harmony, unpopular decisions must sometimes be made and unsuitable people must sometimes be fired. Graham seldom participated directly in those proceedings. "Confrontation is not a thing Bill likes to do," Cliff Barrows acknowledged. Some people are able to confront and say no and move right ahead. We've got people in our organization who can do that, but I don't think that's my forte, nor Bill's. We don't relish it. That has characterized his whole life—and mine, to a certain extent. We don't want to disappoint anybody. We say yes to everybody as much as we can. That's been one of the most difficult things we have had to deal with over the years." Asked about this, Graham conceded both that he avoided confrontation and that this trait sometimes caused frustration for those around him. "Whether it's a fault or an asset," he said, "I don't know. But my father was that way. I never saw him lose his temper more than once or twice in my whole life. I think I inherited some of his characteristics along that line. Ruth thinks I am far too easygoing. She says, 'You ought to talk stronger. You ought to stand up to some of these people and say what you feel.'" He paused, chuckled, and added, "So far, I have resisted, quite largely, her advice."

Not surprisingly, most of the people who held key positions in the organization—with George Wilson a notable exception—manifested a similarly conciliatory style, a circumstance that created awkwardness when a team member was not performing adequately or when colleagues found it difficult to work together. "We have been so blessed," T.W. said. "So many in our organization have been with us for decades. But we've had to get rid of a few. We talk to them and try to get them to shape up. On occasion, we ask them, 'Are you sure you are where God wants you?' If they can't change, they will usually resign. That makes it easy on us." A staffer guilty of legal or moral trespass would likely be confronted swiftly and either dismissed immediately or given explicit instructions as to what steps needed to be taken. Inadequate performance or an irritating personal style were apt to elicit a far more uncertain set of signals. In discussing former colleagues, association veterans sometimes observed, with a wry smile, that "it was felt the gifts God had given him could work most effectively outside the organization," or "he came to sense that his presence was no longer required at every meeting." Addressing the issue more explicitly, Lane Adams explained that if Graham felt someone no longer fit the ministry's needs, "probably, that man would begin to be bypassed. Things that he was invited to participate in before, he would be left out of. Slowly but surely, it would dawn on him that he was getting a very gentle message that perhaps the time had come for him to put his feelers out and find something else to do." According to Robert and Lois Ferm, what may seem to be a rather cowardly way of dealing with conflicts stemmed at least in part from Graham's own generous nature. "Billy won't believe anything bad about a person. He is so lenient and fair. Not long ago, he had to let one man go, but he gave him a year's wages, so that he could maintain his family until he found another job. He would never leave anyone hanging."

No characteristic of Billy Graham's organization stood out more clearly, or was accorded more importance by those who have viewed the ministry at close range, than the fact that nearly all of the men who started out with him in the 1940s were still by his side in 1990, and that most of the "newcomers" had been with him for at least a quarter of a century. While in some Evangelical circles vaunting ambition, fragile egos, and naked pride have created chronic tension and high turnover, BGEA is famous for its organizational stability and internal harmony. It is not without spot or wrinkle, and almost any member of the association can point to minor flaws, but it is nevertheless an impressive monument to Billy Graham's leadership and a remarkable example of effective nontraditional bureaucratic organization.

At the heart stood the inner circle of Graham, Barrows, George Wilson, T. W. Wilson, and Walter Smyth. Nelson Bell held a spot there until his death, as did Grady Wilson until heart disease moved him to the sidelines in the late 1970s. Bev Shea and Tedd Smith, who were at Graham's side as long as the others, are beloved and respected figures but have not wielded the same kind of influence and power. "You cannot break into that circle," Lane Adams observed. "There is no way to catch up. It isn't that they don't care about what you think. It's simply that you haven't been around for forty years." Johnny Lenning, who worked at Cliff Barrows's side since 1959, agreed. "Quite a few of us have been around for twenty or twenty-five years," he noted, "but that's not forty years."

These men, in essence, spent almost all of their adult lives together, united in spirit and by telephone even when separated geographically. "When you have been together and worked together for so many years," Barrows pointed out, "you just know one another. You know what the others are thinking, how they are going to react." None, perhaps, was more important to the unity of the organization than Barrows himself. In a brief but singular tribute in 1986, Graham told the nearly 10,000 evangelists gathered at Amsterdam that "God has given me mighty men, but the mightiest of all has been Cliff Barrows." Graham knew Barrows was ill, suffering from what proved to be a tumor that sidelined him for almost a year, but it was not compensatory praise. No man in the association, save Graham himself, comes in for higher praise, and several ministry veterans admitted that "Cliff is the guy to go to if there is a real problem." One key function Barrows served was to discourage power plays on the part of other members of the association. "If anybody could have built a following for himself," Lenning observed, "it would have been Cliff, because he is such a warm person. But he has not done that. He has been a model for other people in the organization. If the number two man isn't grabbing for power, it's harder for anyone else to do it."

T. W. Wilson, almost invisible publicly, continued to be almost indispensable privately. As Graham's servitor, shadow, and shield, he arranged travel and lodging, provided confidential companionship, protected the evangelist from the endless stream of petitioners who want "just fifteen minutes" of his time, and performed any other task, large or small, that needed performing. With Graham since the night they answered Mordecai Ham's challenging call together, Grady Wilson played a vital role in the organization until serious heart attacks in 1977 and 1978 forced him to curtail his activities. After illness made it impossible for him to keep a full schedule, Grady still made it to several of Graham's crusade services each year and continued to preach on occasion, even when congestive heart disease made it necessary for him to spend a fair portion of each day in bed. He remained a beloved figure until his death early in the fall of 1987. At the Columbia crusade during the spring of that same year, he drew affectionate greetings and smiles as he strolled through the hotel lobby, wearing a raffish plantation hat and sporting a cane over which a rattlesnake skin had been stretched, so that its ferocious fanged head appeared to emerge out of his gnarled fist. The cane seldom failed to attract a comment, and Grady never failed to point out that he was "the only snake handler on the Billy Graham team." The offspring of other team members, young adults themselves, pumped his hand and hugged him and instructed their children to "love Uncle Grady's neck." When old friends asked him how he felt, he assured them he didn't fear meeting his Maker but was enjoying what time he had left in this earthly realm. "I'm ready to go," he said more than once, "but I'm not getting up a load right now." And when an old friend asked when might be a good time to get together for a visit, he told him, "I'm free between now and the rapture."

When it finally came time for Grady to go, his spirits seldom sagged. Doctors and nurses told family members he had changed their lives as they watched him face death with such equanimity. When a young nurse asked him, "Aren't you just a little bit afraid?" he replied, "Honey, why should I be afraid? I'm going to see Jesus." His daughter Nancy, a nurse and missionary herself, sat with him as death came near. The last words he heard as he drew his final breaths were the soft reassurance that "we love you. It won't be long till we see you in glory." At the funeral Billy Graham told the story of Grady's first sermon, when he borrowed and twisted the stem off Billy's watch, and he used the four points Grady had made in that first sermon to structure his own remarks. The last point called for listeners to make a decision for Christ. Bev Shea sang, and friends and family spent at least as much time laughing as crying. They missed Grady, to be sure, but none doubted where he had gone, and all of them expected to see him again.

Walter Smyth did not spend as much time in Graham's physical presence as some other members of the inner circle, but contact between the two men was constant, particularly since the early 1960s, when Smyth moved into position as head of team operations and, later, as vice president of the association with special responsibility for international operations. When Smyth left Youth for Christ to go to work for Graham in 1950, Evangelical publisher

William B. Eerdmans raised a caution. "Why put all your eggs in one basket?" he asked. "What if something happens to Billy Graham?" Smyth told Eerdmans that if something happened, God would have some other work for him to do. Reflecting on that memory in his small office in Amsterdam, waiting for the 9,600 evangelists who would soon start pouring in from all over the world, he said, "And here we sit, thirty-six years later. When I started out, I had no idea all this could happen. We were fumbling. We were stumbling. We didn't know what was going on. Nobody in the longest stretch of the imagination ever expected it to run this long. And here we are today with more invitations and larger crowds and bigger responses than ever." How did he account for that? "You can't explain it, except for God."

Knowledgeable observers often acknowledged a low-key but discernible rivalry between Smyth and George Wilson, perhaps inevitable in a situation in which one man's job is to control the purse strings and the other's is to see to it that his projects get the resources they need, and several suggested that a major reason the team's offices were in Atlanta from 1965 to 1977 was because Smyth and other team members wanted to get out from under Wilson's close supervision. However real and deep that rivalry—and Billy Graham's men do not speak freely of friction in their ranks—Smyth enjoyed an enviable reputation for spotless character, great personal warmth and wisdom, indefatigable commitment to the ministry's goals, and astonishing patience with his underlings. Bob Williams, who adopted Smyth as a mentor, recalled an occasion when a staff member was causing notable tension among his colleagues. "I found Dr. Smyth sitting in his office, praying and weeping about this man—the man we all wanted to choke." Then, with a smile that acknowledged the tensions his own ego and brisk style had sometimes created, Williams added, "I have heard several times that he has wept over me." Billy Graham paid a similar tribute to Smyth's forgiving spirit. "I don't know that I ever had an argument with Walter," he mused, "and it's his fault."

Pressed up against this inner circle, vital to the organization and held in high esteem, were second and third tiers comprised of such men as John Corts, Sterling Huston, Howard Jones, Ralph Bell, John Wesley White, Alexander Haraszti, John Akers, and the various crusade directors and special-purpose men and women who attended to whatever task needed doing. Leighton Ford was a kind of first among equals in this company before leaving BGEA in 1986. One insightful observer with close ties to the association described Ford as theologically "so conservative he squeaks" but credited him with being "just about the only one who was not absolutely sure of everything" and with having a special sensitivity to the social implications of the gospel and the concerns of non-Western people. Now, under the aegis of the Leighton Ford Ministries, he holds crusades and devotes special attention to training younger evangelists in what he characterizes as an effort to repay the encouragement Billy Graham gave to him. For his part, Graham seemed happy with the arrangement. "I told Leighton twenty years ago, 'You cannot establish yourself as long as you are staying in my shadow.' And I've talked to him several times since, and finally, he began to see it. So he worked out a plan and we agreed to help him financially, which we have done. I think this last year we gave him about $400,000. We'll continue to do that if we have enough ourselves." (In fact, BGEA's IRS returns indicate that contributions to Ford's ministry during the year in question amounted to $226,494. No contributions were listed for 1987 or 1988.)

The problem of living in Billy Graham's shadow was not peculiar to Leighton Ford. "We only need one preacher and one song leader," Johnny Lenning pointed out, "so there's not room for a lot of competition. We have lost some good men who did not want to be subjugated to Billy and who left to form their own ministries." Tedd Smith agreed. "People come to hear Billy Graham," he observed. "You know that and you work with that. You are either very happy with that, or you don't work out." Fortunately, most team members found satisfaction in being part of the first rank of big-league evangelism. To be sure, pride found its outlets. Veterans sure of their own place will smile and suggest that one watch the little shuffles that occurred when Graham left his hotel for a crusade service or a press conference as certain members of the organization jockeyed to see who got to ride with Billy and who rode in the second car or the van. And in a circle where honorary doctorates from Christian colleges are as ubiquitous as pocket testaments, those who never managed to garner one or who chose not to flaunt either earned or honorary distinctions poked gentle fun at those who introduced themselves as "Doctor." Despite such occasional outcroppings of vainglory, members of the Graham team appeared remarkable in their ability to divert attention from themselves to their leader and to the cause they served. "There's not much upward mobility," Lois Ferm observed, "but you just have to come to grips with that. My own personal attitude is that I feel very honored and thrilled to be a part of this great movement in history. An important factor, of course, is that Billy himself thinks you are the greatest thing that ever came down the pike. He's convinced of it. You know that anybody else with your credentials could do the job just as well as you, but he doesn't believe that. As long as he doesn't believe it, who am I to disagree with him?"

No one pretends that working for Billy Graham was an unbroken idyll. Crusade directors write and speak of the loneliness they sometimes felt when moving to a new city, even though they typically took a small core of associates with them. Men who spent more than half their time away from home acknowledged that this put a strain on even the most long-suffering of wives and understanding of children. Faithful workers down in the ranks devoted their lives to Billy Graham's ministry, then sometimes wondered if he knew they exist. And those who have experienced dark nights of the soul occasionally admit that the genuine closeness and family spirit that pervaded the organization when things were going well, or when illness or death or other kinds of externally caused problems to arise, were not always manifest in less straightforward circumstances. "There is a need for more pastoral care within the team," one former team member alleged. "There could have been more closeness in times of trouble, more help when there were pressures and problems. People in the association have an enormously hard time facing conflicts and personal problems. It's almost considered a sign of weakness if you confess a problem. They tend to give you a straight spiritual answer—if they ever discover the problem—without looking at the sociological or psychological aspects. They can win an argument without helping the person. There can be a sort of condemnation for failures, faults, and sins, instead of a spirit of helping people seek and find forgiveness, and work out their problems."

Whatever the truth of that assessment—and a sufficient number of present and former team members sounded similar notes to make it seem plausible—it is also quite apparent that the level of personal harmony and mutual commitment among at least a fairly wide circle of key personnel was truly remarkable. John Stott, who lauded Graham for surrounding himself with able men, observed that competence was not their only distinguishing mark. "They truly love each other. And they are extremely loyal to each other. They're like overgrown schoolboys. It's endearing." Stott's country man, the Reverend Gilbert Kirby, agreed: "It's the most effective small team I have ever seen. You can liken it to the apostolic party with Paul, traveling around Asia Minor, going to strategic places. I don't know when there has been another small team like it. Certainly not in this century."

35

The Bible [Still] Says

More than forty years into his public ministry, Billy Graham had few, if any, peers as a Christian leader. Still, he regularly insisted that he lacked depth and profundity as a theologian and that his sermons and books were rather ordinary in both form and content. Few of his closest colleagues seemed inclined to dispute him. Robert Ferm, who spent a career putting the best possible face on Graham's actions and words, described him as "a theologian of the highest realm" but made the mark of his greatness his ability to simplify. "I have read the major theologians," Ferm said, "and he is in an entirely different category. He is a man who knows God. Knowing God, he has a concept of the inspiration of Scripture that he can put into fifteen or twenty words, while other men would write a whole book about it." Other associates and friends acknowledge the simplicity of Graham's theology but do not assign it the same depth. John Akers tactfully observed, "I have found from time to time that he had more understanding about certain theological issues than is perhaps the popular perception." Carl Henry admitted that "I keep my fingers crossed about the books Billy writes" and characterized Graham's theology as a conservative "people's theology" that gained its authority from the evangelist's total reliance on Scripture. Still another veteran colleague was more blunt: "Billy has never worked through his theology."

The theology Graham espoused in his later years differed a bit from that of his early ministry, but warnings by his Fundamentalist detractors that association with liberal churchmen would undermine his allegiance to the pillars of Evangelical orthodoxy proved unwarranted. He made room for more liberal views than his own but remained loyal to traditional formulations. He refused, for example, to damn those who espouse some form of theistic evolution—"I seriously doubt if differences at this point really make too much sense"—but made it clear he believed Adam and Eve were real people who lived in a real Garden of Eden "that many scholars think was in the area now occupied by Iraq and Iran." Similarly, he acknowledged he could find nothing in the New Testament that made belief in the Virgin Birth essential to salvation but unequivocally stated that "I most certainly believe Jesus Christ was born of a virgin." As for the nature of Scripture itself, he shied away from the shibboleth term *inerrancy*, by which conservatives mean the Bible contains no scientific or historical error, but he regularly asserted his belief in the "plenary verbal inspiration" of the Bible, noting that "it has always been clear to me that we cannot have inspired ideas without inspired words." And he never wandered far from his conviction that when he used the phrase *"The Bible says . . . ,"* it was tantamount to saying, "The Bible means. . . ." Even so, he did not insist that all Christians hold a conservative view of Scripture. "We are not saved because of our view of the Bible," he said. "We are saved by our view of Jesus Christ and our acceptance or rejection of him and the life we live after we come to Christ."

Graham's reflections about other key aspects of systematic theology were equally innocent of struggle or conflict. "I cannot prove the existence of God," he said, "but deep inside, everyone knows there must be some sort of supernatural being." Though he confessed that "I can't explain the Trinity satisfactorily," he noted that "it's not what I don't understand about God that troubles me. It's what I do understand and don't do. That's not original with me, by the way. I've heard a lot of people say that." His view of humanity and its deepest need also remained essentially unchanged from the portrait he drew in the 1950s. The complexities of human nature plumbed by Shakespeare and Sartre, by Camus and Chekhov, by Bergman and, indeed, by the Bible itself need not occupy us unduly, he seemed to say, since virtually all human problems can be explained by reference to "something that happened in the Garden of Eden long ago." In the early years of his ministry, Graham had proclaimed that "Christ is the answer" to virtually any problem his hearers might face. Wider experience and honest reflection eventually taught him to admit to inquirers that "coming to Christ is not going to solve all your problems. It may create some new problems. Because when you've been going one way and suddenly turn around and go the other way, against the tide of evil in the world, that's going to create some friction and difficulty." Still, those fearing they were doomed to days of persecution and long nights of existential wrestling were surely relieved to hear in his next sentence that they could successfully meet and master these challenges if they had "certain things, and we're going to give them to you in just a moment." The promised buckler and shield consisted of a copy of the Gospel of John, a few memory verses, the first lesson of a Bible correspondence course, and assurance that God would not allow Satan to subject them to doubt or temptation too compelling to resist.

One of the thorniest problems for Evangelical Christians is the fate of the heathen who never hear Billy Graham or any other Christian evangelist proclaim the gospel. A 1978 article in *McCall's* magazine quoted Graham as having said "I used to believe that pagans in far countries were lost if they did not have the gospel of Christ preached to them. I no longer believe that." Predictably, that apparent widening of the circle of the saved scandalized some of

Graham's supporters and led to a hasty assurance by *Christianity Today* that the evangelist's beliefs had been misrepresented. Graham was careful not to make any subsequent statements that appeared to exempt anyone from the need to make an explicit commitment to Christ, but he did not automatically consign to hell all who never hear the Christian gospel preached. "They are in the hands of a God of love and mercy and grace," he said. "I don't think I can play God." He was willing to venture, however, that he doubted a righteous God would consign an Albert Schweitzer, who denied the deity of Christ but gave his life to good works, to the same fate reserved for such consummately evil men as Hitler and Eichmann. "Hitler and Schweitzer should not be in the same place." Beyond that, he would not speculate: "I'm going to have to wait until I get to heaven, and ask the theologians up there and get the answer."

That he might not get the opportunity to press his query seemed never to occur to him. "I know beyond the shadow of a doubt," he said, "that if I died at this moment, I would go straight to the presence of God." Moreover, "I look forward to dying, because I know that I'll be relieved from all the bondage of this body. And all the temptations and all the pressures of this life will be gone. What a glorious future we have in Christ." Throughout his career, Graham has talked of his readiness to die with a kind of wistful serenity that has led some to suggest that he nursed a fairly transparent death wish. His associates chuckle at that hypothesis, noting that his supposed romance with death does not deter him from rushing off to the Mayo Clinic at the slightest sign of illness, and Graham himself acknowledges that when death actually stares him in the face he experiences quite normal reactions. In 1987, while returning home from Europe, a small bomb went off in the baggage compartment of the plane, causing a momentary fear of crashing. "I wouldn't say I was afraid," he recalled, "because I'm ready to go at any time. I'd say I was nervous. I thought to myself, 'Am I afraid to die?' and then I thought again that it's instinctive to want to live. I mean, that's something God gave us and if we don't have that sense of self-preservation we would all die. We might go out and commit suicide. But I am not afraid of death." Still, he admitted, "I'm not looking forward to the dying process We're all afraid of the unknown. We're not quite certain of how it's going to be. I'm not afraid of being dead. I'm afraid of the period of dying, catching fire or suffering before death. I hope I don't have to go through that. But I may. I'm ready."

Graham's readiness to die stemmed in large measure from his firm conviction that good as this life has been to him, it cannot compare with an eternity in heaven, which he believed to be an actual physical place, though not necessarily in our particular solar system. "Some people have speculated that it's the North Star," he once volunteered, "but this is all speculative." Next to basking in the presence of Father, Son, and Holy Spirit throughout eternity, the greatest joy of all will come from being united with the great saints of all ages and reunited with one's own family and friends. Among those Graham looked forward to visiting is Elvis Presley. "I never met him," he said, "but I believe I will see him in heaven, because Elvis was very deeply religious, especially in the last two or three years [of his life]."

As a younger man, Graham was prone to blaming a roaring lion's share of the world's suffering on the active agency of Satan and his cohort of demons. With the passage of time and the accumulation of experience, he resorted to such dualistic explanations less often. "Suffering is simply a fact," he wrote in 1983. Christians should remember that they are not exempted from suffering, and should keep in mind as well that "when one bears suffering faithfully, God is glorified and honored." He admitted he had no answer to why some evangelists carry scars from being beaten and burned for Christ's sake, while his life had been free from physical persecution, or why "some people appear to glide effortlessly through life while others seem constantly to be in the throes of pain and sorrow." In 1962 he speculated that God may have used a French air disaster that killed 130 people, including a large delegation from Atlanta, Georgia, as a tool to move many others to be converted. In 1988 when a Pan Am crash in Scotland took the lives of dozens of students from Syracuse University, where he was holding a crusade, he avoided any suggestion that God was killing young people to boost conversion rates. Asked how he would minister to the parents of the dead young people, he said, in a voice filled with compassion, "I would put my arms around them and weep with them, and quote Scripture. I would try to tell them there is hope for those who put their trust in God." As for trying to discern the will of God in human suffering, he resorted humbly to citing a charming image favored by Evangelical saint Corrie Ten Boom: "Picture a piece of embroidery placed between you and God, with the right side up toward God. Man sees the loose, frayed ends; but God sees the pattern."

Just as Graham believed that some, though not all, evil could be laid at Satan's hooves, so he maintained that Christians often enjoy the beneficent ministration of angels, whom he dubbed "God's Secret Agents." In *Angels*, a 1975 book that sold over two million copies, he asserted that while everything in the book was supported in Scripture, he also believed in angels "because I have sensed their presence in my life on special occasions." Asserting that "some biblical scholars believe that angels can be numbered potentially in the millions," he described them as ageless and immortal, free of sickness, and able "to move instantaneously and with unlimited speed from place to place," though only some of them have wings. Nothing indicates they have to eat to stay alive, and the Bible gives no hint that they are concerned with sex, an attribute that "may indicate that angels enjoy relationships that are far more thrilling and exciting than sex." The possibility that being sexless may be one of the drawbacks of angelhood—perhaps the short end of a trade for immortality or ubiquity—seems not to have occurred to him. He did, however, acknowledge that humans had some advantages over angels. No angel, for example, can pastor a church, serve as an evangelist, or counsel inquirers at a crusade. Still, because they possess detailed knowledge of earthly affairs, they can participate in many mundane activities. Graham thought it at least plausible, for example, that angels had piloted fighter planes for dead men during the battle for Britain in World War II, though he acknowledged that this was a hypothesis that "we cannot finally prove."

As a young man, Graham had been deeply impressed with dispensationalist premillennialism and its detailed scenarios of the course human history was taking. With exposure to alternative theological views, and the repeated experience of seeing the precise predictions of dispensationalist teachers go unfulfilled, he modified his personal eschatological beliefs and toned down his public statements about the Second Coming even further. "I used to be able to preach to an audience and sort of outline exactly what the events would be that would precede the Second Coming of Christ," he mused. "I don't do that anymore. I still hold some views on it, but I don't make them public. I think there is something to dispensationalist teaching, but I just can't accept the way some dispensationalists apply biblical prophecy to current newspaper headlines. I don't believe, for example, that the Common Market is the organization of the beast, as some of them say." Though no longer willing to predict the timing of the rapture—"I don't think anyone knows when Christ is coming back, and Jesus warned us not to speculate about dates. It could be tonight. It could be a million years from now. I don't know"—he had lost none of his confidence that Jesus is indeed coming again, probably sooner rather than later, and that the broad outlines of premillennial teaching are reasonably trustworthy. He clearly believes that a time will come when "a counterfeit world system or ruler will establish a false Utopia for an extremely short time. The economic and political problems of the world will seem to be solved. But after a brief rule the whole thing will come apart.... This massive upheaval will be the world's last war—the battle of Armageddon." This climactic battle will be followed by Christ's millennial reign, during which "political confusion will be turned to order and harmony, social injustices will be abolished, and moral corruption will be replaced by integrity. For the first time in history the whole world will know what it is like to live in a society governed by God's principles. And Satan's influence will not be present to hinder world progress toward peace, unity, equality, and justice. Man's dream for global harmony will be realized!"

Like other premillennialists, Graham saw such phenomena as the AIDS plague, continuing and apparently irresolvable conflict in the Middle East, the decline in private and public morality, the increase in lawlessness, the proliferation of wars, and the rise of religious cults as other signs that the end is near. He did not follow the lead of some who insisted the rapture would come in less than forty years after the establishment of the nation of Israel in

1948 but expressed his belief that "there is a special place for Israel in God's plan. I think it is significant that they are a nation and are in the land that God promised them. I think it is one of the signs that we are told to look for in connection with the coming again of the Lord." On several occasions he has even ventured that his own worldwide ministry, in person and on radio and television, may be part of the universal evangelization process premillennialists believe will occur just prior to the Second Coming. "With all the media we have," he told an international gathering of evangelists in 1986, "we can reach the world quickly and bring back the King. I believe we could be living in the last period of history. I hear the Four Horsemen. They are on the way!"

One notable change in Graham's theology, pressed on him by external developments, was his greater acceptance of charismatic phenomena. "I believe God has used the charismatic movement throughout the world to wake up a lot of communities," he observed. "It fits in with the temperaments of many cultures. I think it has been raised up by the Lord. But I have never spoken in tongues. I know many godly people who have, but who never talk about it except privately, and it has brought great change in their lives." Did he yearn for such gifts himself? "I have asked God to give me all he wants me to have, but I have never been given tongues. Oral Roberts once told me that if I ever spoke in tongues, not to tell anybody. I believe it is one of the gifts of the Spirit, but our Lord never mentioned it. Paul dealt with it in only one book, and that was with a troublesome church [at Corinth]. It was a carnal church, and the gift of tongues was giving a lot of trouble. At certain periods of history, I think it has been a gift of the Holy Spirit, but it is easily counterfeited and we have a tremendous amount of false speaking in tongues today. I have never asked for that gift. Paul said it was the least of all the gifts. The greatest of all the gifts is love."

Graham's assessment of divine healing follows a similar pattern. He professed not to doubt that miraculous healing can occur but warned that one must exercise "spiritual discernment" to avoid being duped by the "many frauds and charlatans" involved in faith healing. He also conceded the possibility that some Christians might have a genuine gift of prophecy but warned that it should be heeded only when "it does not involve new revelation" that contradicts "the written Word of God" He was even less tolerant of the popular charismatic teaching that God wants Christians to be wealthy, particularly those Christians who are willing to make generous contributions to the television preachers who espouse this teaching. Though the doctrine is taught by some of the most popular television ministers—Oral Roberts, Pat Robertson, Kenneth Copeland, and, before his fall, Jim Bakker—Graham abandoned his usual conciliatory attitude when discussing this teaching. "I don't like it at all," he snapped. "I think it is contrary to Scripture. God promised wealth to certain people, like Abraham and other great men of the

Old Testament. But in the New Testament, we are told to deny ourselves." He then rolled into a monologue that revealed something of his own struggle with the ease and prosperity of his own life. "In our culture," he said, "it is hard to deny yourself. When we came up here, we thought we were denying ourselves, with this twelve-dollar-an-acre property and two log cabins. But we added on as the children came, and today it's a big, fine house. Ruth and I talk quite often about what standard we should live by. When I go to places like India and Bangladesh and Africa, it bothers me no end that I have three good meals a day. We have never been tempted along the lines of money so much, but we do have money. We have too much. What do you do? I guess it's individual conscience in our culture. But I think that teaching is heresy. I just don't agree with it at all."

Those who acknowledge that Billy Graham was no theological sophisticate recognize that his fame did not rest on his ability to spin theological webs or split fine hairs of doctrine, and even members of his own team, who heard him preach hundreds, even thousands, of times, do not regard him as a remarkably gifted pulpiteer. Without being prodded, his closest associates and most ardent admirers volunteer rather readily that "Billy's sermons are quite ordinary, even sub-ordinary," or that "he'd be the first one to tell you there are lots better preachers." Over the years Graham's preaching changed somewhat in both content and delivery. Though he still preached regularly on John 3:16 and Belshazzar and the Second Coming, his later sermons were much shorter and less densely packed than in earlier years. He also used a much calmer and quieter style, a change fostered not only by age but by the demands of television. He could still summon the old fire on occasion, but as early as the 1970s, his preaching became much more avuncular, befitting his passage from young firebrand to senior statesman. The later preaching still followed the pattern of attacking the complacency of his audience by confronting them with their fears and discontents, but the focus had shifted noticeably. The flames of hell and nuclear holocaust that caused audiences to sweat in terror from the 1940s well into the 1960s gradually gave way to the chillier discomforts of loneliness, emptiness, guilt, and the fear of death, and to such high-profile threats to society as drugs and AIDS. Graham freely acknowledged his use of fear as a motivator for conversion, but the anger that critics had professed to see in his early preaching seemed mostly absent. Certainly, Graham hoped it was gone. "We need to preach with compassion," he told a group of aspiring evangelists. "People should sense that you love them, that you are interested in them. Even when you preach about hell, you need to convey that both the author [God] and the messenger speak from a broken heart."

It would be gratifying to report that Graham's use of jokes and humor had taken on a finer and subtler tone as well, but such was not the case. Most of the jokes in his relatively small stockpile were the very same ones he had been using for thirty years, and age had not sharpened their effect. Aides said they had often advised him to refresh his store of anecdotes or, perhaps even better, to quit trying to be a humorist, but their pleas were outweighed by the unfailing willingness of his audiences to laugh at even the hoariest of his pocketful of chestnuts. They also failed in efforts to get him to purge his sermons of worn-out illustrations and resigned themselves to finding them a source of some amusement. In the spring of 1986, he quoted the popular song, "Show Me the Way to Go Home," and said, "There's a movie out, *And God Created Woman*, starring Brigitte Bardot," as if they were parts of current popular culture rather than artifacts of earlier decades. In the same crusade, in a less anachronistic but even more glaring example of obliviousness, he told a long story that he claimed had happened just a few weeks earlier. With no apparent sense that the account might have a familiar ring to it, he told, in full detail, the story of a newly released prisoner who eagerly returned home, to be welcomed by a plethora of yellow ribbons tied around an old oak tree. A few people applauded as if hearing the story for the first time, but others indicated by quizzical expressions that at least the broad outlines of the story seemed vaguely familiar. When a team member was asked the next morning if he thought that story might serve well as a theme for a movie, or perhaps a popular song, he broke into laughter and said, "Oh, you caught a mild version. Sometimes he has rags and dish towels and sheets hanging from telephone poles and skyscrapers."

One might easily assume that such oddities reflect a habit of reusing old sermons without feeling any impulse to update them, but that is apparently not the case. Weeks before every crusade, Graham began to fret about what he would preach and to hound staff members to help him come up with new material, and one of his secretary's primary tasks in the final days before the opening service was to type new sermon manuscripts on a large-print typewriter. Wisely, Graham made no attempt to deny that he reused much old material. Waving his hand at a row of black notebooks in the small office in his home, he said, "Those are sermons I have preached in the last fifteen years. The old ones are down at the office. Some of those are better than the ones I've preached more recently. What I'll do is take and rework those." Reworking tried-and-true sermons—a perfectly honorable practice among preachers—consists largely in sparking them up with new factual data, new references to current events, and new illustrations. And well before a crusade began, aides prepared briefing documents that he could draw on to illustrate his sermons as well as answer questions from the press. Associate Evangelist John Wesley White for a long time was Graham's primary sermon illustrator. White, who held a doctorate from Oxford, viewed his work modestly.

"I'm often cast as an intellectual," he said, "which I'm not. I'm not reading heavy philosophical literature. I'm reading *Time*, *Newsweek*, *USA Today*, the Toronto *Star*, and that kind of thing. I contribute substantiating quotes, convincing statistics, colorful little—I hesitate to say this—*National Inquirer* ham-and-eggsy things. I'd like to think they're true." Ed Plowman observed that "like a lot of public speakers, Billy tends to pull usable quotes from various sources, and sometimes these are taken out of context. More and more these days, he speaks from a text, and John Akers and others go over it with him to make sure of the wording and the accuracy, particularly on historical and political matters. When he departs from the text, he sometimes gets into trouble."

Graham's reliance on the work of others, and the concomitant superficial acquaintance with the material he cited, betrayed itself in mispronunciations, as when he spoke of "the great Jewish scholar, Maiodes," or "the famous writer, Eli Weasel," and in such superfluities as identifying Dostoevski as "the greatest novelist in the Soviet Union," then adding, "He was. He's dead now." Some of Graham's illustrative imports were jarringly imprecise, as when he said, "A famous man committed suicide the other day," or "A psychologist in Chicago said the other day ..." or "A sociologist at Oxford said last year ..." or "That's like the girl at Harvard who was searching for something and didn't know what it was—and it was written up in *Time* magazine." At other times the ostensible precision was itself rather astonishing. Without citing supporting documentation, he might announce that "over four hundred people in Los Angeles claim to be Jesus Christ" or reveal that "84 percent of the modern novel is illicit, illegal, or immoral." At a service in Columbia, he repeated his familiar claim that sexual chastity is virtually impossible without supernatural assistance, then noted that this is especially the case for a man, whose sex drive "is six times greater than in a woman." At that revelation, a young woman handling press relations for the crusade dropped her head on the table and mumbled in despair, "Where did he get that? How could anybody measure that? *Ohhhhhh*." Other team members apparently suffered a similar reaction. At breakfast the next morning, when John Wesley White was asked if he would comment on something Graham had said the evening before, he did not require further elaboration. "That did not come from me," he quickly interjected. "Kathleen [his wife] and I were sitting right behind a row of girls and in front of them was a bunch of Army recruits. I don't think they had had a dosage of saltpeter that day. There was a fascinating reaction on their faces when Billy said that. I had gone through that sermon and given him a lot of material, and Kathleen turned to me and said, 'Did you give him that?' I said, 'No, I did not!' I believe if you asked T.W., he would say right quickly, 'Didn't get it from me.' You would have some trouble getting anyone to own up to that one."

Fortunately, Graham recognized this tendency in himself. The next evening, he said, "The United States owes a trillion dollars. Do you know how much that is? If you stacked dollar bills all the way to the moon and back, you wouldn't have a trillion dollars." Then, perhaps having been chided by friends for his previous remark, or simply finding his own illustration implausible, he paused, then said, "I heard that. I think that's an exaggeration. I believe you would have a trillion." Generous chuckles rippled through the audience. Caught up in the amusement, he added, "But I read that in some paper, and I always believe everything I read in the paper. Especially the *Inquirer*." Laughter rolled out of the stands, and no one appeared to enjoy the self-deprecating humor more than Graham's own colleagues. Perhaps the evangelist's ability to poke fun at his own foibles was aided by the insightful aphorism he quoted a few moments later: "Today is the first day of the rest of your life."

Analysts from within Graham's camp believe it was precisely his trusting simplicity that made him so effective as a preacher. Whatever his audiences thought about his intellectual acumen, they viewed him as utterly sincere about what he said in the pulpit. "There is no magic, no manipulation," observed Gavin Reid. "The man just obviously believes what he says, and he comes over as a very human person." In the end, however, they insist that any attempt to explain Billy Graham in secular terms was bound to fail. "There is something quite miraculous about his power," John Innes said. "I think people believe they are going to hear something from God when Mr. Graham gets up there, and I believe they do. They hear another voice through him—the voice of God." Graham agreed with these observations but thought they apply to all true evangelists, not just himself. "An evangelist," he said, "is a person with a special gift and a special calling from the Holy Spirit to announce the good news of the gospel. You're an announcer, a proclaimer, an ambassador. And it's a gift from God. You can't manufacture it, you can't organize it, you can't manipulate it.... I study and read and prepare all the time, but my gift seems to be from the Lord in giving an appeal to get people to make a decision for Christ. That seems to be the gift. Something happens that I cannot explain. I have never given an invitation in my whole life when no one came." According to Graham, exercising his gift took a tangible physical toll on his energy: "In the five or ten minutes that this appeal lasts, when I'm standing there, not saying a word, it's when most of my strength leaves me. I don't usually get tired quickly, but I get tired in the invitation. This is when I become exhausted. I don't know what it is, but something is going out at the moment."

Perhaps the most notable development in Graham's preaching over the years was a shift in his stance on various moral and social issues of high interest to Evangelicals. His code for personal behavior remained quite conservative, but he displayed a more tolerant attitude toward human frailty than he once did, he recognized differences between cultures, and he stressed forgiveness more than judgment. He also developed an increased appreciation for the need to change social structures and conditions as well as individual hearts.

While many Evangelicals and Fundamentalists continue to regard the use of alcohol as one of the surest signs of a corrupt lifestyle, Graham frequently noted that "I do not believe the Bible teaches teetotalism. I can't believe that. Jesus drank wine. Jesus turned water into wine at a wedding feast. That wasn't grape juice as some of them try to claim. The Greek word is the same as the Bible uses everywhere else for wine." When he first went public with that assertion in 1976, in defense of Jimmy Carter's admission that he enjoyed an occasional highball, Graham drew a fusillade of criticism from stunned supporters, but he refused to back down. Drunkenness is clearly a sin, he said, and distilled liquors make the use of alcohol far more risky than it was in biblical times. He even agreed that it was better for Christians to abstain completely from alcohol than to risk falling into the problems it could cause. But in contrast to his occasional tactic of claiming he had been misquoted and misunderstood, he not only continued to defend and repeat his earlier statement but acknowledged that he used alcohol himself from time to time, and that he knew something of its effects. "Once in a while I will have a sip of wine before I go to bed," he told a reporter. "I only have to drink a little wine and my mind becomes foggy and I don't like it. After all, a clear mind is what I have been striving for all my life."

The years did not diminish Graham's conviction that sex offers perhaps the most formidable temptation human beings can face, and that abstinence from fleshly lusts is the proper course to follow, but he displayed considerable compassion for young people growing up in a sex-saturated culture. "It's very, very difficult," he acknowledged. "If I had grown up in the present society, I'm not sure I could have coped at all. I think the only way a person can live clean today is if he has had a very real experience with God. I think they are given a supernatural power to live a clean life." Perhaps recalling evenings of delicious temptation in his father's shiny Plymouth automobile, he recommended that dating couples put a Bible on the car seat between them as a reminder that "Christ is the cure of even the most torrid of earthly temptations," and assured them that if they would make the decision to resist temptation, "God provides a way of escape. The Holy Spirit is there to help." Graham professed to have direct knowledge of the Spirit's power to manage sexual tension. "I've been away from my wife as long as six months," he volunteered, "but I never engaged in any sort of sexual practice. This means that a person can control his sex desires with the help of God." Though he clearly believed tha. sex is wonderful in its place—at home, between loving marriage partners—he frequently reminded his audiences that "you don't have to have sex to live. It is not like water or bread. Many have lived without sex. They have taken a chastity vow, and they have a strength and a power and an alertness that other people don't have.... God can give you power to control that part of your body."

And yet he refrained from making people feel guilty about every sexual thought they may have. When speaking of lust, he noted that "I'm not talking about looking at a beautiful girl and admiring her. That's natural, and God gave us these sex instincts, and I don't think we should deny them. But he drew some circles around it and said, 'Thus far, and no further.' And if you do [go further], you hurt yourself." He recognized, of course, that many devout Christians do go further, but his response to such slips was hardly a bluenosed harshness. If he had children who he knew engaged in premarital sex, he said, "I would tell [them] that I totally disapprove, but I would love them even if they did."

Graham showed similar flexibility in his attitude toward homosexuality and abortion, two other issues on which Evangelicals have taken a generally rigid stance. He continued to regard homosexuality as a sin but refused to put it in the category of special heinousness. "The Bible teaches these practices are wrong," he said, "but no more so than adultery." More boldly, he asserted, "I love them and don't treat them any differently than my other friends. There are worse sins." Clearly, he felt that treating homosexuals as pariahs was an un-Christian response. Just as clearly, however, he believed that conversion would lead to a change in sexual orientation, or at least to an ability to control homosexual behavior. "You have to take a vow to God," he recommended, "and ask God to help you, and he will." He recognized that not everyone in his audience would share his views, but rather than write them off as hopeless and hell-bound, he offered them the best advice he could find. In a 1988 telecast focusing on AIDS, he included an extended appearance by Surgeon General C. Everett Koop, who made it clear he believed abstinence is the proper course for unmarried people but urged those who were not being abstinent to use condoms, a notable departure from the standard Evangelical television program.

On the volatile question of abortion, Graham took a conservative but not absolutist line. "The Bible does not support the indiscriminate practice of abortion," he said, but added that "an exception might be made in the case of incest, rape, or when the mother's life is in danger," noting that "this is about the same position as Pope John Paul II takes. I know some people feel that is not the right position, but that's my position." He disagreed with the pope's position on birth control. "I am a strong advocate of birth control," he said, acknowledging that this runs counter to official Catholic doctrine, but added, "I suspect that many Catholics practice it." Protestants have typically favored birth control, but Graham's position explicitly reflected his expanded social consciousness. "When you travel through India, Pakistan, etc., you have to believe in some form of control of the population. I don't think it should ever be state control, . . . but the population explosion is a very serious thing."

Demographic realities also pressed Graham, along with other Evangelical leaders, to relax long-standing strictures regarding divorce and remarriage. Traditionally, strict Evangelical teaching has frowned strongly on divorce and sanctioned remarriage only for those whose spouses were guilty of adultery. In practice, many people who divorce for reasons other than adultery remarry and continue to attend church, but they are often the cause of some awkwardness for all parties, and many divorced Evangelicals either remain single out of explicit fear of eternal punishment, or if they choose to remarry, move to new churches to give themselves a fresh start. As the high divorce rates prevalent in the larger society began to appear in Evangelical circles, the churches have not only shown a greater tolerance for what they once regarded as a notable aberration but have made the "singles ministry," which typically includes a substantial divorced contingent, a major feature of many successful congregations. Graham felt more comfortable with the traditional teaching; in describing a case in which a divorced woman had remarried, he discreetly noted without giving details that "she was free to remarry," meaning that her husband had committed adultery. And what of those who are the sinners instead of the sinned against? "If they are not the innocent party," he replied, "there is a question in my mind. Not a definite yes or no. I am not a legalist. Some of these things have to be taken case by case, point by point. God can forgive adultery." His frequent use of the phrase "You can't unscramble eggs" when referring to such cases indicated a pragmatic belief that trusting God to forgive all sorts of past mistakes is a more viable course of action than trying to rewrite history.

Graham also moderated other views regarding the family. In earlier years he spoke of the husband as "the master of the house" who "organizes it, holds it together, and controls it," and had counseled wives "to remain in subjection" to their husbands. By the mid-1970s, he had absorbed enough feminist rhetoric to cause him to rethink his position. Volunteering that he had based his earlier views on a misinterpretation of the Bible, he said, "I believe the Biblical position on women's rights is that the husband and wife are equal." He still believed that "in the governing organization of the home, the husband is the head," but was willing to concede that "the woman is also the head in certain areas and there is an equal responsibility in the home." Like vice-presidents in a corporation, they have equal status but manage different divisions. In this kind of arrangement, subjection would not be an issue. Husbands and wives would "submit to each other." Predictably, he decried a feminist tendency to devalue the role of wife and mother as "a Satanic deception of modern times" but conceded that "there are things in today's feminist movement that I like because I think women have been discriminated against."

Such views, of course, were hardly radical, even in Evangelical circles, but Graham took a somewhat bolder step by lending support, or at least not offering opposition, to the ordination of women. In 1975 he admitted that he was simply not sure about what position to take on this touchy subject. Two years later he said, "I don't object to it like some do because so many of the leaders of the early church were women. They prophesied. They taught. You go on the mission fields today and many of our missionaries are women who are preachers and teachers." As for women as pastors, "I think it's coming probably, and I think it will be accepted more and more. I know a lot of women who are far superior to men when it comes to ministering to others." Men might resist giving them full rights in the church, but such women "are ordained of God whether they had men to lay hands on them and give them a piece of paper or not. I think God called them." A decade later, following the pattern he had set in dealing with blacks during the 1950s, Graham had quietly placed his stamp of approval on women ministers by including them (albeit in small numbers) in BGEA-sponsored conferences and by inviting them to lead prayer and take other public roles in his crusades.

Just as association with world church leaders had given Graham a more flexible attitude toward theological positions different from the Fundamentalist revivalism in which he had been raised, so his exposure to the full range of the world's political and economic systems had made him less confident that Western-style free-enterprise capitalism would be the system of choice in the millennium. While still voicing a clear preference for the free-enterprise system, he said, "I don't think it's the only one that Christians can support. We are a socialist society compared to, let's say, the days of Franklin Roosevelt. There has to be a certain amount of socialism." The inequity between rich and poor, including disparities between wealthy and developing nations, he observed, "is going to have to change somehow, whether voluntarily or by law. You can't have some people driving Cadillacs and other people driving oxcarts and expect peace in the community. There is a crying need for more social justice. It's a problem whose solution is beyond me, but I've found about 250 verses in the Bible on our responsibility to the poor."

Even though he had supported Lyndon Johnson's War on Poverty, Graham had retained a slight cynicism toward such government programs. In 1969 he spoke with approval at having seen a poster that read, I FIGHT POVERTY. I WORK. And he criticized the motives of those who backed anti-poverty legislation by observing that "many people carry a heavy load for poverty because they want votes, and others want to get involved in the problems so they can get their hand in the till." He conceded that the existence of opportunists and grifters "should never do away with our responsibility for the legitimate poor," but his portrait surely gave comfort to those inclined to blame the poor for their own plight. He also continued to maintain a somewhat fatalistic attitude toward poverty, citing Jesus' observation, "The poor you have with you always," and reiterating his belief that only the Second Coming and the millennium would bring true relief from the world's enduring problems. Repeated firsthand exposure to human suffering eventually had its effect on Graham's native compassion, and he gradually began both to enlist his organization in the struggle against poverty and to acknowledge that poverty had other than individual roots and that something more sweeping than philanthropy would be required to ease the world's suffering. "From the very beginning," he said, "I felt that if I came upon a person who had been beaten and robbed and left for dead, that I'd do my best to help him. I also felt that this applied to my relatives and friends and immediate neighbors. But I never thought of it in terms of corporate responsibility. I had no real idea that millions of people throughout the world lived on the knife edge of starvation and that the teachings of [the Bible] demanded that I have a response toward them.... As I've traveled around through India and Africa and Latin America and all those places for all these years, it can't help but be a heavy pressure.... For a person who hasn't been there and touched those people and seen those people, it is really difficult to explain ... [but] as I traveled and studied the Bible more, I changed."

In 1973 BGEA inaugurated its World Emergency Fund to provide a more routinized way of responding to similar needs. Aware of the criticism some relief agencies receive for the proportion of their incomes they spend in overhead, Graham took deserved pleasure in noting that "not one penny" of the monies contributed specifically to this fund was siphoned off for administrative purposes. More as an example than as a serious attempt to alleviate hunger, Graham's later crusades included a program called Love-in-Action in which people were asked to contribute nonperishable food to the service for distribution through reputable social agencies. Typically, this effort brought in several tons of canned and boxed goods, but Graham freely admitted its limitations and symbolic purpose: "Of course, we can't feed all the hungry people. It's only a gesture, to demonstrate what we ought to do all the time. If the churches and synagogues did what they could do, we would not have to have such a confused welfare system."

By the early 1980s, Graham was beginning to echo Roman Catholic statements about God's presumed "preferential option for the poor." During an address at the Kennedy School of Government at Harvard, he astonished the school's dean, a former resident of Charlotte, and many of the students gathered to hear him, when he said, "As a Christian, I believe that God has a special concern for the poor of the world, and public policy should in some way reflect this concern. I believe God has a special concern for things like peace, racism, the responsible use of Earth's resources, economic and social justice, the use of power, and the sacredness of human life." He admitted that "how these matters are to be implemented is a very complex matter" and confessed that "I have not always seen many of the complexities.... I am still learning.... But I have come to see in deeper ways some of the implications of my faith and the message that I have been proclaiming." In *Approaching Hoofbeats*, which appeared the following year, he offered details on the worldwide scope of such problems as hunger and infant mortality, asserted that the disparity between the rich and the poor is "one of the basic causes of social unrest in Central America and other parts of the world," and condemned "the indifference of certain governments to the plight of their own people." And by the end of the 1980s, he was insisting that the United States do its part for underprivileged nations by helping them gain relief from international debt. Though he recognized that Americans would bridle at the austerity such a policy would entail, since it would inevitably increase the tax burden on Americans, he saw no other alternative. "I think we've got to help them with this debt," he said. "It's threatening Latin countries and countries throughout the world, and we've got to do something about it."

The evangelist was also willing to identify, or at least to sympathize publicly, with groups that had once drawn his barely disguised scorn. During a two-installment tour of British cities in 1984 and 1985, he repeatedly expressed concern for the unemployed, making it clear that he no longer regarded people who were out of work as willfully lazy. "The most important thing, apart from finding jobs," he said, "is that unemployed people should not be made to feel that they are second-class citizens. Christians should be deeply concerned for the problems of society and should be supportive of those who are socially deprived." While preaching in the industrial city of Sheffield, he met with miners who had been involved in a brutal union dispute to suggest how Christian teaching might apply to their situation. Details of their conversations were not revealed, but they apparently went beyond the pious palliatives that have led many British working people to give up on the church. The president of the National Union of Mineworkers called the meeting "extremely useful," and Graham, while insisting he did not know enough about the situation to take sides, did the miners' cause no harm by saying, "My heart goes out to people who hurt." British churchmen, who have often faulted Graham for excessive individualism, professed to be gratified "by the way in which the social awareness of his maturity finally tempers the fundamentalist fires of his youth."

Graham's views on crime and punishment also took on a more liberal cast. He grew more aware that not all crime is street crime or committed by poor people—"Many of our crimes are committed in upper-middle-class or affluent environments"—and believed that some form of gun control would be appropriate. He also developed reservations about capital punishment. "One of the hesitations I've had," he told a reporter, "is that so many blacks are executed. The system has always been too one sided, and many of the people on death row are poor people who couldn't afford good lawyers. There is no perfect system of justice on this earth. God will have it at judgment. But this is a very imperfect system. And execution makes the imperfection final." At hearing her husband backtrack on some of his earlier law-and-order sentiments, Ruth frowned and bluntly interjected, "I'm for capital punishment. I think it is a deterrent. I know in countries where they have it, I feel safer walking down the streets." Unwilling to start an argument but also unwilling to abandon his position, Graham gently responded, "Darling, there are countries where they have executions in which I don't feel safe at all."

No shift in Graham's social thought drew more attention than his increased concern for peace and nuclear disarmament. Given the flak his 1982 visit to Moscow drew, he might easily have backed off his more dovish sentiments or claimed he had been misunderstood or misquoted. Instead, he stood by his ploughshares and included an extended statement of his views on disarmament in his 1983 book, *Approaching Hoofbeats.* He began with a confession and a statement of repentance. "To limit the growing threat of nuclear warfare seems perfectly in line with Christ's call to be peacemakers on the earth," he said, but admitted that "in those first years of the nuclear age I did very little in this particular area. I preached the gospel throughout the world, which was my primary calling, and I warned people against war in my sermons from the very beginning.... But perhaps I should have done more ... I wish now that I had taken a much stronger stand against the nuclear arms race at its beginning when there was a chance of stopping it." He repeated his by now standard statement that he was neither a pacifist nor an advocate of unilateral disarmament and acknowledged that, given the sinful nature of humankind, police and military forces would always be necessary in this temporal realm. Still, he regarded a worldwide concern for peace as a heartening sign, and he called on all Christians "to rise above narrow national interests and to give all of humanity a spiritual vision of the way to peace." He then repeated the recommendations he had made at the 1982 Moscow conference: Urge all governments to respect the rights of religious believers, get to know one another personally, and encourage world leaders to work toward eliminating all nuclear and biochemical weapons of mass destruction.

Graham's fear that either the Soviet Union or the United States would set off a major conflagration ebbed in the 1980s, but it was offset by concern over nuclear proliferation and the problems inherent in a situation in which "the smaller nations, many nations not quite as stable," had or would soon have nuclear capability. Showing his willingness to draft such possibilities into the service of his invitation, he told a South Carolina audience, "Fifteen to twenty-five nations have a nuclear capacity. Terrorists are also working on it, and may have it. That's the reason you ought to come to Christ." He also continued to insist that "no Secretary of State or government official shuttling back and forth between countries can lessen these international tensions. It may patch things up for a while, but only the coming of Christ will solve the problems." Still, his shift from a fatalistic view of nuclear war as the likely means God would use to launch Armageddon to a vision of world peace as "a realistic, present hope" for which Christians ought to strive, and his seconding Dwight Eisenhower's 1953 observation that "every gun that is made, every warship launched, every rocket fired signifies—in a final sense—a theft from those who are hungry and are not fed, those who are cold and are not clothed" was real and significant. *Christianity Today* correctly characterized his interest in nuclear issues as something other than "the scare tactics of a preacher who wants responses to his sermons." It reflected instead the agony of "an evangelist and international diplomat" who had "discussed these problems with seven U.S. Presidents and other heads of state and world leaders, and has dealt with more people searching for God than perhaps any man in history."

Did Graham honestly think his vision of SALT 10 could ever be realized? "Not likely," he admitted. "But does that mean I should cease praying, speaking, and working for that day when the people of the earth will unite to remove the ever-present threat of nuclear holocaust? Again, no! . . . I do not plan to be a leader in a peace movement or organization. I am an evangelist. But I am a man who is still in process."

36

What Manner of Man?

Billy Graham genuinely believed what he preached, and his organization provided him with the means to accomplish what lesser lights can only dream about. But the crucial factor in explaining Billy Graham's unprecedented accomplishments as an evangelist and world Christian leader is Billy Graham himself. In good Evangelical fashion, his associates and admirers insist that any attempt to account for him on the human level is destined to seem trite, even foolish. Allan Emery uses the image of a turtle on a fence post. Any sensible person encountering that unlikely sight would immediately realize that the turtle had not crawled up there by himself but had been placed there by some larger and more powerful force. The Reverend Maurice Wood, bishop of Norwich and member of Britain's House of Lords, offered a similar assessment: "I believe that in each generation God raises up certain people he can trust with success. I would put Billy in line with the Wesleys and St. Augustine. Toss Francis in, if you like. He's in that league, anyway. And what's extraordinary is that he doesn't seem to know it. He doesn't want a Graham church. He is more interested in sharing the load than in grabbing the limelight. He wants to be a servant of the Church, to challenge and spark the churches to be what they must become: the evangelizing agents of God and his Word. But there's no doubt about it; he is the most spiritually productive servant of God in our time."

Some think it a waste of effort to speculate as to when or where the next such figure might arise. "I honestly believe with all my heart that Billy Graham is the most important single thing God has done since the Apostle Paul," Lane Adams volunteered. "He is the only man who has ever had the ear of the world this long. Could it be that he is like John the Baptist, making straight the way of the Lord? Perhaps he is giving one last clarion cry for the Second Coming of the Savior. When you consider the advent of satellite communications, which makes it possible to have such a broad outreach, you can't help but stop and wonder."

It is true that no person in modern history has done more than Billy Graham to bring to the world's attention the message and testimony of Evangelical Christianity. Through his crusades, his conferences, his radio and television programs, his newspaper columns and magazine articles and books, his friendship with kings and queens and presidents and prime ministers, and his enduring omnipresence as a public figure, he forced millions of people to pay attention to a kind of religion that ordinarily astute observers predicted would vanish from all but the remotest and most backward of locations by the end of the twentieth century. He stood for and personified the Evangelical conviction that what the Bible says is what the Bible means, but he did so without encouraging the blatantly anti-intellectual tendencies that have often characterized Fundamentalist and, to a lesser degree, Evangelical Christianity. Moreover, his warm ecumenical heart melted barriers that traditionally separated Evangelicals from more liberal Christians and repeatedly opened itself to non-Christians as well. Prominent rabbi Marc Tanenbaum said of him, "The American Jewish Committee can tell in moving chapter and verse how Dr. Graham came time and again to the aid of the embattled people of Israel, when his voice and influence in high places made a crucial and, at times, a decisive difference Dr. Billy Graham has been and continues to be one of the greatest friends of the Jewish people and of Israel in the entire Christian world in the twentieth century." And in recent years, when Muslims could easily have provided him with a convenient target for demagogic attacks, he repeatedly called attention to the commonality between Islam and the Judeo-Christian tradition, recommending that Christians "go out of our way to love them," and pointing out that his son Franklin has visited Lebanon nearly thirty times to help rebuild Muslim homes destroyed by bombs. "[Franklin] felt he needed to do something to show Islamic people that Christians could love them, in spite of the wars and the troubles."

Just as he helped Evangelicals make their presence felt in the mainstream of American religion, Graham also encouraged them to take a more active political role. Though he disliked being labeled the High Priest of the American Civil Religion during the Johnson and Nixon years and admitted he sometimes acted imprudently on behalf of his friends in the White House, he continued to encourage Evangelicals to be involved in the political process and showed them that their involvement need not be as fanatical and narrow-gauged as some of the efforts of the Christian New Right. In the process, his own political outlook had broadened and deepened. "Eisenhower once said publicly that I was the greatest ambassador that America had," he recalled. "Of course, at the moment he said it in the 1950s, I was pleased. Now I would not be pleased because I feel that my ministry today is a world ministry. Now when I say something, I think, 'How is this going to sound in India? How is it going to sound to my friends in Hungary or Poland?' I don't ever want to dodge the truth, and I don't ever want to back down on my convictions. But I'm beginning to see that there are more sides to some of these questions than I once thought. I am not as dogmatic."

Graham's ability to speak to American culture so successfully for sixty years stemmed in some measure from the fact that he was in many ways an apotheosis of the core values of that culture. If results are the metric, he was the best who ever was at what he did, but he attained that height through hard and honest work, not through inheritance or blind chance. Always ready to use the latest technology to accomplish his goals and maintain his prominence, he nevertheless insisted that his most valuable asset was a circle of loyal friends. He walked with royalty and received unprecedented media attention for over four decades but was still something of a small-town boy, astonished that anyone would think him special. In a profession stained by scandal, he stands out as the clearly identified exemplar of clean-living integrity. In a society riven by divorce, he and the wife of his youth reared five attractive and capable children, all of whom are faithful Christians with their own intact families. He is, in short, an authentic American hero.

Billy Graham was, for most of his life, a genuinely charismatic figure. Using such a term as *charisma* may seem a resort to a supernatural, and therefore nonverifiable, explanation, but social observers as uncongenial to the supernatural as Max Weber and Eric Hoffer have regarded charisma as palpably real and historically important. The term owes its presence in sociological literature to Weber, one of that discipline's patriarchs, who described the charismatic leader as a man able to inspire people to follow him and accept his authority, not out of fear or hope of material gain but out of love, devotion, and enthusiasm. He typically possesses a strong sense of mission, a conviction that his mission is admirable and obtainable, and a confidence that he is particularly well equipped to accomplish that mission—either because he has been chosen by God or some impersonal destiny, or simply because his peculiar set of talents seem so well matched to the historical circumstance. Hoffer added to these elements "a cunning estimate of human nature; a delight in symbols (spectacles and ceremonials); ... a recognition that the innermost craving of a following is for communion and that there can never be too much of it; a capacity for winning and holding the utmost loyalty of a group of able lieutenants." Graham's associates and enthusiasts would doubtless object to having their hero lumped in with some of the figures to whom students of politics and religion have applied the concept—Lenin, Hitler, Mussolini, Sun Myung Moon, Jim Jones, and L. Ron Hubbard—and would probably quibble over the cynical tone of Hoffer's characterization, but whenever they move beyond the sovereignty of God as an explanatory variable, they speak in terms that fit easily into these accounts of charisma.

British Evangelical John Stott agreed that "what is most captivating about Billy is his sincerity. There isn't an iota of hypocrisy in the man. He is real. I sat in Harringay night after night asking over and over, 'What is the reason [for his success]?' I finally decided that this was the first time most of these people had heard a transparently honest evangelist who was speaking from his heart and who meant and believed what he was saying. There is something captivating about that." Another old friend echoed Hoffer's "cunning estimate of human nature." Graham, he said, "is not an intellectual in the academic sense of the word, but he is a genius. He preaches to presidents and kings and queens in a way that no other man has ever been able to do. He is so 'people sensitive.' He knows just what to say without either compromising the gospel or turning anyone off. I've watched him with a telescope and I've watched him with a microscope but I haven't changed my views of him. He has his faults. Everyone does. But he is just an amazing, amazing man."

Without doubt, it was Graham's prowess as a soul winner that commended him most powerfully to Evangelical Christians, since no activity has higher standing in their minds than bringing the lost to Christ. But he was also an exemplar in other aspects of his personal life, leading the kind of life they feel they should lead but seldom actually manage on a sustained basis. He arose around seven o'clock each morning and performed a round of devotions that included prayer and the reading of five psalms and one chapter of proverbs—"Psalms for how to get along with God, Proverbs for how to get along with man." After breakfast he spent an hour in Bible study, tried to get some exercise—in later years, usually a brisk walk—and rounded out the workday with writing, reading, meetings, and telephone calls. During crusades he rested most of the afternoon—"We don't bother him, except for emergencies." He socialized little apart from obligatory planned events and, when he was in Montreat, rarely left his mountain retreat. He was strongly conscious of time and expected others to share his concern. "I become impatient if I feel I'm being used," he admitted. "I value my time. I only have a certain amount left, and I want it to be put to the best use. Also, I hate to be late for an appointment. I don't mind waiting for someone for an hour if he's late"—an assertion no visitor should take seriously—"but I hate to be late."

T. W. Wilson called him "the most completely disciplined person I have ever known." What Wilson calls discipline, others label compulsion, even venturing to suggest that Graham was a classic workaholic. Bob Terrell, a perceptive Asheville newspaperman who worked for BGEA for several years, observed that Graham "feels the urge to accomplish, and he doesn't think he is accomplishing anything when he is sitting by a fire on top of the mountain. He uses *compelled* quite frequently—'I feel compelled to preach the gospel to as many people as I can, for as long as I can'—and he is not satisfied if he is not busy. It's hard for him to relax and rest. He has the busiest schedule of any person I have ever known, but I think he likes it that way. Whenever he is on the road, he is constantly busy, sometimes for months at a time. If he goes to the Caribbean, he is always working on a book. He will say he would like nothing better than to stay home and rock and relax, but he really can't stand to be idle."

Graham recognized that he took on more than he could handle with ease, but felt he sometimes had little choice. "One of the things we are blessed with," he explained, "is that I get opportunities that no other Evangelical will ever get. For example, the realtors convention in Honolulu, or the bankers convention, or the National Chamber of Commerce. I've spoken to all of them. Or the American Bar Association; I've spoken to them two or three times. It takes so long to prepare those addresses, and I have to get help on them, because they're specialized things. I don't mind speaking. If they'd ask me to come and give an evangelistic address, that's down my line. But these other kinds of speeches are so time-consuming." Ruth obviously felt her husband could exercise a bit more discipline without harming the Evangelical cause. "It's not necessary to speak at all," she interjected; "I don't think the Lord called you to give all those strange addresses." Billy did not argue with her, but his response perhaps offered a clue as to why he kept accepting invitations. "At the last ABA meeting, I stood around and shook hands and shook hands until they finally told me that I had to go, that my plane was going to leave. So I just said, 'I have to go,' and left. I didn't realize until about two days later that the next person in line was Justice [Lewis F.] Powell of the Supreme Court. But not long after that, he wrote me the most tremendous letter I have ever received about my ministry."

Students of charismatic leaders have often noted that such men tend to stir a variety of emotions in the bosoms of their followers, a robust portion of which feelings are distinctly sexual. Leading a movement requires enormous energy, and the lines between political, spiritual, and sexual energy are not finely drawn on the map of the human psyche. That dynamic leaders, including religious leaders, experience and arouse strong sexual feeling should come as no particular surprise to anyone who pays attention. Thus, in light of his own quite obvious awareness of the imperious heights to which sexual temptation can mount, Billy Graham's spotless record as a faithful husband is an accomplishment his followers regarded with due appreciation. Marshall Frady, in an overwrought but often insightful biography, likened Graham to Billy Budd, a man with "exactly that quality of raw childlike unblinking goodness," possessing "a staggering passion for the pure, the sanitary, the wholesome, the upright." The allusion to Melville's classic American innocent is a natural one, and by no means completely off the mark, but it falls short at a crucial point, and that point is a theological one. Billy Budd was naturally good and unable to believe that others did not share his elemental guilelessness. Billy Graham suffered from no such fantasies. He did indeed seem to have "a passion for the pure," but never for a minute did he imagine that he, or anyone else, was beyond corruption. And that is the secret of his ability to avoid public scandal. No one listening to Graham warn against succumbing to the pleasures of the flesh would imagine that he derived his information solely from survey research data. Just as he had the wisdom to put others in charge of the purse, he had long clearly understood that his best strategy for avoiding sexual temptation was to keep himself out of its path. "I'm sure I've been tempted," he said, "especially in my younger years. But there has never been anything close to an incident." How had he managed that record? "I took precautions. From the earliest days I've never had a meal alone with a woman other than Ruth, not even in a restaurant. I've never ridden in an automobile alone with a woman." Even past seventy, on the rare occasions when only he and his secretary were in a room together, he kept the door opened wide so that none would suspect him of unseemly behavior. Before Graham entered a hotel room, T. W. Wilson checked it out to make sure no woman was hiding in the closet or the bathroom or lurking behind the drapes. Once he was in the room alone, he would not answer the door unless he knew for certain who had knocked. These are not measures taken by a man whose goodness is entirely childlike. At the same time, they are not hedges planted by a bloodless prude. He never suggested that he longed for the life of a monk, nor did he seem overly concerned simply with appearances. In 1983, shortly after actress Joan Collins appeared in a widely publicized nude spread in *Playboy*, Graham and Collins were booked onto *The Merv Griffin Show* on the same day. His staff was worried. Larry Ross pointed out that "everything she stood for was a complete about-face from what Mr. Graham stands for. For example, she talked about how to raise a thirteen-year-old daughter with a live-in boyfriend. Several times the audience booed some of her statements, just because of the values they represented. I didn't know what to do. I thought, 'This is good television, but it's going to be a real shifting of gears.' I thought Mr. Graham may not know everything she stands for. So I told him. He said, 'Yes, I know.' Well, when he went on, the first thing Merv said was, 'Billy, were you aware that Joan Collins has appeared in *Playboy*?' Mr. Graham said, "Yes, I've seen it. Someone showed it to me in the barbershop.' Right on national television, he said that! And then he went right into sharing the gospel. I'm sure he was concerned about his position on that program, but he was so confident in his message and what he stood for that he wasn't concerned about showing a side of Billy Graham people hadn't seen."

In 1989, with the fallout from the Jim Bakker and Jimmy Swaggart scandals far from settled, he noted in a casual (but openly recorded) exchange about current movies that he had recently seen *Dangerous Liaisons*. "I was staying near Times Square," he explained, "so I went to see it. It was based in the eighteenth century in France. It was very interesting. There were a couple of scenes that were pretty steamy. The people were about half nude. But you could see that anywhere." That a universally recognizable evangelist would attend such a movie in Times Square would scandalize many Evangelicals. That he would talk about it freely to a writer with a tape recorder and give no indication that he preferred it not be mentioned would cause anxiety among some of his colleagues. But just as he had freely acknowledged that he sometimes looked at the pictures in *Playboy*, he seemed unworried that someone might discover he had seen a "pretty steamy" movie without launching a boycott of the Satanic film industry. In short, he seemed to know when he needed external controls, and when he did not.

Graham's passion for sexual fidelity doubtless stemmed primarily from his unshakable conviction that fidelity is God's will and infidelity a mortal sin. But he also enjoyed an uncommon bond with Ruth, an uncommon woman. "There would have been no Billy Graham as we know him today had it not been for Ruth," T. W. Wilson contended. "They have been a great team. A model couple." Cliff Barrows described her as "a tower. She has great insight, great sensitivity. She is a woman of the Bible, a scholar with the great capacities and gifts of her father, who was probably Bill's greatest teacher." Graham readily seconded these assessments. "She knows the Bible a lot better than I do," he admitted. "A lot of my sermons, I read to her and she gives me little pointers and illustrations and Scriptures to go with them. My son Ned said to me on the phone just last night, 'Dad, she's the most remarkable woman in the world. She has stayed in the background, but I just don't know any other person like her.' Of course, that's a boy talking about his mother, but as I look at her as objectively as I can, I think he's right. She really is remarkable."

Ruth's contributions to her husband's success were not limited to Scripture verses and sermon illustrations. She also provided him with a measure of grit lacking in his own palliative style and a willingness to question and challenge him when his colleagues would not. "Ruth is a power," one former associate noted. "She has a little tougher mind than Billy's. She is not as afraid of offending. Billy is always auditioning." Ruth had sometimes been critical of the women's liberation movement—"I think we're being taken for a ride. It's men's lib because it's relieving them of the responsibility of supporting and caring for their families"—but she seemed never to have felt that the biblical injunction to wives to be in subjection to their husbands required her to hide her opinions or feelings under a bushel, nor did she seem the least bit awed to be married to one of the world's most famous men. Honorary degrees, red-carpet treatment, and lavish compliments did not impress her. When Billy spoke glowingly of a reception given him by the president of Mexico—"He even embraced me"—she quickly brought him down to earth: "Oh, Bill, don't be flattered. He did that to Castro, too." And unlike the wives of most of the prominent television evangelists, she never tried to insert herself into the limelight: "That's not my wad of gum." She did, however, quietly pursue her own forms of ministry. When she inherited a nice sum of money at her father's death, she gave it all away, bestowing much of it on an orphanage in Mexico. She also maintained an interest in female prisoners. In a case that received minor public attention, she befriended Velma Barfield, a North Carolina woman convicted and eventually executed for murder. After making her commitment to Christ while in prison, Barfield would call out from her cell, "I'm guilty. I did what I shouldn't have done. But please listen to me. Read your Bibles and pray; turn to Jesus." From all appearances, her conversion did not appear to be a case of trying to impress the governor or the board of pardons and paroles in the hope of winning a stay of execution. T. W. Wilson told of going with Billy Graham to visit the prison a week or two after Barfield had been executed. "One person after another told Billy, 'Velma Barfield was the finest person I ever met.' The warden said, 'She made an impact on our prison.' Billy spoke, and when he gave the invitation, he said, 'How many would like to adopt Velma's Jesus.' Without exaggeration, fully half of them stood up. Even the warden's father stood. I'm telling you, it was impressive."

However extensive or effective her work with felons and orphans, Ruth's primary ministry, by all accounts, was with her children. "PKs" (preachers' kids) who rebel against a strict and public upbringing are standard figures in the lore of religious communities, but the children of itinerant evangelists, who spend substantial portions of their lives away from home, may be at special risk. Billy Graham and his team knew that their own fame and personal dedication would not guarantee that their children would stay on the straight and narrow path. Grady Wilson recalled an evening early in Graham's ministry when the inner circle went out for a snack in Atlanta and invited Ma Sunday to go with them. "Boys," she said, "whatever you do, don't neglect your family. I did. I traveled with Pa all over the country, and I sacrificed my children. I saw all four of them go straight to hell." Grady remembered that "she sat there with tears running down her cheeks. I know one of her sons jumped out of a hotel window somewhere in California. He was on drugs or something. Another one came to me in Phoenix, Arizona, just a panhandler. I gave him twenty-five dollars. Ma said, 'I wish you hadn't done it. He'll just take it out and buy more whiskey.' We remembered that. I know Billy has prayed night and day by the hour, all around the world, for his children. All of them have been filled with plenty of adrenaline, from the oldest to the youngest, but Ruth stayed up on that mountain and took care of them and all of them have turned out to be just exceptional Christians."

For a time, as had been true of Franklin, it appeared that Ned, the youngest son, might spoil the family record. After graduating from the Stony Brook School, Ned dabbled briefly with college, spent two years as a mountaineering instructor while living at home, then sampled the curriculum at three more schools before he finally graduated from Pacific Lutheran University in Tacoma. He admits to a rebellious impulse but insists it was aimed not at his parents: "I never had any reason to rebel against them." Rather, he asserted, he was resisting "God's call on my life to go into the ministry. It wasn't that I had had bad examples. It was that I knew what entering the ministry would mean: turning everything over to God." Ned manifested his rebellion by turning to more than a casual use of drugs, including cocaine. Once again, the Graham philosophy of child rearing prevailed. "While I was embroiled in all that," he recalled, "my parents were just very patient. They expressed concern and displeasure over the behavior, but never once did they make me feel they rejected me as a person. Their love for me was always unconditional. Their home was always open, no matter what condition I was in. They gave themselves to me, and I never felt their love was conditioned on meeting some requirement. Eventually, their grace and love were just irresistible." Also once again, the formula worked. In mid-1991, at age thirty-three, Ned lacked only one course before finishing a degree at Fuller Seminary and was serving as pastor of adult ministries in a Tacoma Baptist church. He also serves as president of East Gates Ministry, an American-based operation dedicated to assisting a wide range of mission and indigenous Christian efforts in the People's Republic of China.

Though it obviously cannot explain the success that brought him fame, the very fact that he was extraordinarily famous unquestionably added to Billy Graham's appeal, and the way he handled that fame further warmed those who were drawn to the glow of his celebrity. No person in the twentieth century received as much sustained popular attention and was as widely admired as Billy Graham. He placed high on public-opinion poll listings of the nation's and the world's most admired men virtually every year since 1951. In a survey conducted by *Christian Century* to discover which of eleven "living giants of the Christian faith" could be identified by American churchpeople, 67 percent of respondents correctly identified Billy Graham; the next most familiar "giant" was known to only five percent. Contestants in the 1976 Miss U.S.A. beauty pageant in Niagara Falls named him "Greatest Person in the World Today," and in a 1978 *Ladies' Home Journal* survey, only God outpointed him in the category "achievements in religion." He was once named *Time's* "Man of the Year," and in 1990 *Life* listed him among "The 100 Most Important Americans of the 20th Century." The only other figure from the world of religion to make the list was his old adversary, Reinhold Niebuhr. In 1990 Graham was honored with a star on Hollywood Boulevard.

Graham's celebrity gave him entrée to others of similar repute. When Mikhail Gorbachev visited the United States for a summit meeting with Ronald Reagan in 1988, for example, Graham was the only clergyman invited to be present at his arrival and attend the state dinner in his honor. The evangelist long defended his association with celebrities and the publicity machinery that kept his star well polished and ascendant by contending that though he personally abhorred the attention he received, he went along with it as essential to attracting an audience for his message. He admitted that might have paid more attention to public-opinion polls than he ought to—"I wonder sometimes if

I'm pleasing God or man"—but his awareness of and concern over his need for approval served to keep what could easily be a colossal ego in admirable check. His standard opening offer—"Please call me 'Billy'"—seemed utterly genuine and reflected his uneasiness with honorific treatment he felt he had not earned. "I don't really like these honorary degrees at all," he said. "They've given me so many that they've become meaningless, and I don't ever list them. I couldn't even name all the places I've received degrees from. Many times, if they invite you to speak at commencement, it's just automatic that they give you a degree. In the beginning—I think the first degree I got was from Houghton College—I was quite pleased. And the first degree I got from a Catholic institution, Belmont Abbey, I was honored. I should be honored about the others, I suppose, but I don't have the feeling of appreciation that maybe I ought to. It's just something I sort of endure. Unless, of course, some major school like Harvard or Yale or Princeton were to give me one...."

His oft-expressed desire to move about the world incognito was understandable. Johnny Lenning observed that "sometimes he must feel like a piece of meat, just being pushed into a room, told that the person in the gray coat is the most important man in the room, and the one he ought to pay most attention to, then twenty minutes later pushed into another room and told that the lady in the green dress is the prime minister, and then trying to talk to those people through an interpreter, knowing that everything he says is loaded with political implications—it must be so draining on him." Even when no one expected anything in particular from him, the simple fact that every eye in the room was on him took an inevitable toll. Robert Ferm recalled a dinner he had shared with Graham in a nondescript restaurant in San Francisco. "All through the meal, people would walk by and just reach out and touch him lightly on the shoulder, or brush his sleeve. There must have been twenty people who did that. A few stopped and said, 'Hello, Billy Graham.' One or two teen-aged girls came over and got his autograph. Here in Asheville, he is pretty free to go out in restaurants. People recognize him and leave him alone. But no where else." The wish for privacy, however, was mixed with a measure of gratification at being recognized. Graham's sister, Jean Ford, noted that "he very much wants to be able to be in a restaurant or walk through a hotel lobby in privacy, and yet he would almost feel hurt if people didn't recognize him. We were on an elevator with him a couple of weeks ago in the Washington Hilton, and people didn't recognize him, and he initiated the 'Good morning, how are you?' He wouldn't say, 'I'm Billy Graham,' but as soon as they looked at him they knew who he was immediately. I think there's a paradox there in his personality. But also, I think he never wants to pass anybody up and have them think he is aloof or unapproachable, because he's not. I think he very much wants to be warm. People around him sometimes try to make him out to be unapproachable, but that's not the way he is. He is still very much a southern gentleman."

Those who knew Graham best insisted convincingly that his fame had not gone to his head. BGEA photographer Russ Busby, who probably spent more time in the evangelist's presence than any member of the association except Cliff Barrows and the Wilson brothers, and who is noted for his wry humor and independent spirit, proposed that "the biggest asset Billy has is his honest humility. He has an ego, like the rest of us. Sometimes it takes off, but he brings it back under control. To my knowledge, he seldom thinks more highly of himself than he ought to. When he does, it only lasts briefly—I don't mean weeks; I mean a day or two, and that's it. Billy Graham is human, but he works on it. It takes a big ego to be a big preacher, but the difference between Billy and the others is that when God wants to speak to him, at least he can get his attention."

Like his twin desires for privacy and recognition, Graham's humility stood in paradoxical tension with his understandable delight, also real, in his fame and accomplishments. He would muse about "our little ministry," suggest that its heyday was long past, and express doubt that future historians will have any real interest in it, then note almost offhandedly that a recent crusade crowd was "the largest gathering of any kind in that whole region," or he would make some reference to Wheaton's Billy Graham Center, whose voluminous and carefully tended archives virtually guarantee that he will not be forgotten. He also could not completely free his spirit of all traces of competition. At Columbia, South Carolina, in 1987, a few months before Pope John Paul II was scheduled to appear in the same stadium, he urged his supporters to do whatever they could to fill the stadium for the closing service on Sunday afternoon. "We don't have to wait for the pope to come to fill it," he said. Then, as his overwhelmingly Protestant audience broke into enthusiastic applause, he seemed to sense that he had said more than he intended, and he tried to regain the high ground. "I hope he does fill it," he said. "I think he will. He's a wonderful pope. But it would be good preparation for him. It would show people what it looks like filled."

Though he worked hard to be humble about himself, Graham allowed his natural ebullience to run free when talking of others. His penchant for hyperbole is legendary and good-naturedly discounted by his friends and associates. Crusade organist John Innes recalled a service at which the evangelist had introduced his old friend Stuart Hamblen as "the greatest hymn writer in America today." Innes said, "We were all thinking, 'He's got to be kidding.' Stuart had written 'It Is No Secret What God Can Do' and a couple like that, but he was hardly the greatest hymn writer in America. Another time, Billy described a [crusade] city as one of the most beautiful he had ever visited. We were all wondering what part of the city he had been in. It was one of the ugliest places you could imagine." Innes, however, did not regard such statements as either conscious untruths or insincere flattery. "I don't think Billy has ever been a liar. I think at the moment he says those things he truly means them. He builds people up. He's a natural builder-upper." Asked about this tendency, T. W. Wilson chuckled wryly and told of seeing a note Graham had addressed to a mutual friend with the inscription, "To my best buddy." "Well," Wilson said, "I had one addressed the same way. But he really means it. He might say the same thing to a number of people, and he means it with everybody he says it to."

Graham's siblings deny that their brother inherited the tendency to exaggerate from their parents, but insist that whatever its source, it was a trait of long standing. "It's always been there, as far as I know," said Jean Ford, and Melvin Graham acknowledged that "Billy Frank has very seldom had anything negative to say about folks. He's never been anywhere that he doesn't come home and say, 'I just love that place. I love those people. Never seen anybody like them.' With the team, he's always bragging on this one and that one, talking about what a tremendous influence they have had on him, telling them, 'Without you, I don't know how we'd have made it.' That's something he's done for years and years. If he's with you, he's going to make you feel like you're just about the most important person he's ever met. And you know"—he leaned forward and a big, knowing smile flashed across his open farmer's face—"that don't make anybody mad. And, of course, it works both ways. That's one reason people like him so."

Graham professed no great insight about himself. "I am not a self-analyzer," he said. "I know some people who just sit and analyze themselves all the time. I just don't do that. I don't ask myself why I do this or that. I rarely think introspectively like that." He may not have spent much time thinking about what kind of person he was, but he thought a great deal about what kind of person he wanted to be. When asked what one word he would like people of future generations to use when they characterized his life and his ministry, he hesitated not a moment. Snapping his head slightly, as if to lock it into position to fire precisely at a key target, he thrust out his jaw and said, "Integrity! That's what I've worked for all my life: integrity!" Depending on how one chooses to interpret his occasional reconstructions of his past actions and motives—his relationship with Richard Nixon offers a key example—Graham's record may not turn out absolutely free of spot or wrinkle, but it is nonetheless remarkable. Bob Evans, who is quite aware of his friend's private insecurities and imperfections, said of him, "There is no dark side to Billy Graham. I don't feel there is any secret insincerity or hidden agenda. He is as transparent a person as I have ever known. He makes mistakes. He is human. He has made some false moves and has tried to correct them. But it is not like the movie stars' biographies where you find that Rock Hudson was a secret homosexual or anything like that. There is nothing of that sort with Billy Graham."

Happily, such laudations are not limited to professional colleagues or others with a stake in putting the best face on the ministry. George Bergin, a rough-hewn handyman who acts as caretaker for the Grahams' home in

Montreat and whose wife helped Ruth with the cooking and housework, volunteered as he maneuvered a Jeep down the steep and narrow road that connects Little Piney Cove to the village below, "You've been visiting some mighty good people today. My wife and I have been knowing Mister and Miz Graham for fifteen years, and I'm telling you, they're the same inside the house as out." But perhaps the most succinct assessment of the evangelist's character came from his old friend, Chuck Templeton. Though still convinced that Graham had committed "intellectual suicide" back in 1949, that his theology was untenable, and that his vulnerability to being used by the famous and powerful was a notable shortcoming, Templeton observed with considerable feeling, "Whatever you may think about him, you've simply got to recognize that Billy Graham is a *good guy.*"

Early in his ministry, Graham occasionally suggested that he felt he would not live to be an old man. In part, that may have been a symptom of an overall preoccupation with doom that he seemed to manifest. But it was also a reasonable conclusion to draw from a life that for all its vigor had been marked with illness and affliction. In addition to the publicized ailments that forced him to cancel or postpone crusades, Graham suffered from an astonishing assortment of ailments, including hernias, ulcers, tumors, cysts, polyps, infections, pneumonia, chronic high blood pressure, throbbing headaches, spider bites, and a series of falls that broke eighteen of his ribs. Most of his associates shy away from labeling him an indisputable hypochondriac, but they admit that he sometimes got high mileage from his disabilities. Jean Ford smiled as she compared her brother to his wife: "Ruth will go to her grave saying, 'I'm fine. Never felt better.' And Billy will say, 'You see, I told you I was sick.' The things that are wrong with him are real things, and some of them are very odd and peculiar, but he is very open with his hurts. I don't know whether there's any hypochondria there or not, but he doesn't mind letting you know if he's not feeling well. I'm sure anyone in his position would be tempted to use that. This is one area where he can really be human." Leighton Ford agreed. "I don't think it's escapist," he said, "but it is a way of being like other people. He can't sit in a restaurant and have a quiet dinner like anyone else, but he can have a sore knee like anyone else."

As he entered into the eighth decade of his life, Graham freely admitted, "I have declined some. I'm not anything like I was ten years ago. I've slowed down some. I notice when I go down steps, I always use the railing if there's one there." His colleagues, however, marveled at his vigor, and Melvin Graham thought his brother was being too hard on himself. "Billy Frank thinks his age is hurting him," Melvin said. "He thinks people are going to say he's over the hill. Now he may not have the stamina he once had. Used to, he could preach all night long, wide open. He doesn't do that anymore. And maybe it's true that he can't keep going full steam much longer. I don't know. But I'll be honest with you, I don't think he's over the hill too far."

37

"To the Ends of the Earth"*

Billy Graham and his men found well-deserved satisfaction at having managed to stand in the public eye for more than four decades while suffering only occasional seasons of doubts about their integrity or judgment. They were pleased with their past. They were less settled about their future, though they realized that the end of Graham's ministry could not be far off. Graham acknowledged that "we have a committee that looks into that once in a while" but hinted that his own preference might simply be to let his ministry end when he died or retired. "It would take a lot of courage from the Lord just to close it," he said. "Nobody's ever done that—just said, 'God had this ministry for a period of time, and now it's finished.' We have certain things that could be continued, like our little magazine and World Wide Pictures. Some of the television ministry could go on in other parts of the world for ten or fifteen years if I suddenly died today." He conceded it was not likely anyone could simply pick up his crusade ministry and carry it forward at the same level. His voice conveying realistic assessment rather than obvious pride, he said, "There are a lot of wonderful young men around, but I don't think anyone has arisen, probably, to be the kind of evangelist I have been."

When Franklin Graham was ordained to the ministry in 1982, his father understandably began to think of him as a possible successor. Kenneth Chafin, former dean of the School of Evangelism, recalled when Graham first began to play with that idea. "We were in a crusade, and Billy called to say he wanted to see me right away. I told him I needed to introduce Robert Schuller at the School of Evangelism, but he insisted. He wanted to sit in the sun, so we went out to the stadium and sat on towels with our shirts off. T.W. sat off about fifty yards away. Billy asked me point-blank, 'Do you think Franklin can succeed me?' I told him, 'I don't think so. God chose you. He'll choose your successor.' He said, 'But the staff says he's good.' I told him, 'He is good, but he's a novice. He can't preach the way you do.' Billy didn't want to hear that."

It must have been difficult for Graham to believe that God might not want his son to take over his ministry, since it seemed almost miraculous that he was even a Christian. Franklin was an able preacher and occasionally held

* "That you may bring salvation to the ends of the earth" (Acts 13:47 NIV).

crusades but saw his primary role as that of facilitating evangelism by demonstrating Christian love and compassion through two admirable Christian relief organizations he heads, Samaritan's Purse and World Medical Missions. "I'm not an evangelist," he said back then, "though I'm concerned about evangelism. Where my father has used the large stadiums of the world—the crusades—to reach people, I believe I can use the gutters. So we're going down the same road. But he's going high, and I'm looking low."

With a staff of nearly forty people and combined budgets, in 1990, of approximately $7 million, less than 20 percent of which was spent for administration and fund-raising, the two organizations concentrate more on long-term benefits than on flashy one-time contributions. World Medical Missions coordinates the efforts of American physicians who visit Third World nations for four to six weeks at a time, performing surgery and assisting in establishing basic health care programs. The work of Samaritan's Purse is more varied. In dozens of trips to Lebanon, some of which have put him at considerable personal peril, Franklin has overseen the building (and subsequent rebuilding) of much-needed hospitals in that war-torn land. In Ethiopia, rather than add to shipments of food that lay unused or rotting on loading docks, the organization provided local Christian leaders with money to buy diesel fuel, which enabled them to distribute the goods, then initiated an extensive program of drilling water wells and installing drip-irrigation systems that allowed farmers to grow food with less than half the water previously needed. In India, where women often trudge for miles to get a day's supply of water, Franklin and his colleagues hit on the idea of drilling wells on the grounds of Evangelical churches and providing water freely to people in their villages. As villagers flock to the church grounds, pastors and lay leaders engage them in conversation about Christ. By the end of 1990, Samaritan's Purse had fully funded 130 wells, providing approximately 350,000 people with access to fresh, clear water. In a similar gesture, the organization gives away coconut trees, which provide poor families with food and other materials that can cause a marked rise in their meager standard of living. By using these gifts to create bridges to Hindu families, one native evangelist was able to establish nearly 150 new churches in a single year. Additional programs tailored to local needs and possibilities have been launched in Pakistan, Malaysia, Thailand, Haiti, and several African countries.

Because of his firm insistence that winning souls is more important than ministering to bodies, coupled with impressive evidence that the latter facilitates the former, Franklin Graham largely managed to avoid the suspicion that he was trying to lead Evangelical Christianity into a rebirth of the old Social Gospel. On the contrary, his quiet, self-effacing dedication to his ministries greatly enhanced his stature in Evangelical circles and made his taking over the reins at BGEA seem less farfetched.

Despite his growing prominence and respect, Franklin was obviously skittish about trying to follow too closely in his father's footsteps. "I really feel sorry," he said, "when I see people like Richard Roberts [son of Oral Roberts], who is trying so hard to assume his father's identity—by the way he combs his hair, his facial expressions when he looks into the camera. He'll never be his father.... And I'm not my father. For me to try to comb my hair and act and look like him, I would always be a disappointment in people's minds." Few believed Franklin would attempt a major crusade ministry modeled on his father's, but he was clearly a possibility to lead whatever would be left of BGEA when the elder Graham passed from the scene. "Franklin says he doesn't want to do it right now," Billy observed, "but it would be advantageous in some ways, because he has my name, he's had experience in management, and he's preaching. It would be easier for people who have given to us financially to give to him." Board member Carloss Morris felt something might be worked out. "I think the Lord decides these things, but from the human side I can envision it. I think we could have a great ministry under Franklin. That boy's got a big heart for the Lord and a big heart for helping people all around the world." T. W. Wilson agreed. "Franklin is totally committed to the cause of Christ," he said. "He has a world vision. And who better than a son would preserve Billy's good name and that of his ministry? I've told Billy, 'If a man has to lean one way or the other, I'd rather see him lean too far in the direction of conservatism than have one drop of liberalism in his blood. And Franklin believes something, thank God. He'll keep this thing going for God's glory, and honor you as well.' Now, I haven't always felt that way. He was a rounder, I'm telling you. But then he really got turned on for the Lord. I think he is one of the most highly improved young men that I know."

Franklin's theological conservatism was definitely in his favor. T. W. Wilson was not alone in fearing that a successor might depart from the course Billy Graham had followed, and some suspect that is one reason the evangelist had been reluctant to settle on a definite plan for succession. Johnny Lenning wondered aloud "if Billy would not just as soon have the whole thing closed down when he finishes, so there would be nothing left to go apostate. Then you would have had a ministry that for four decades has been clean and aboveboard, so that you could look back and praise God for what was done, instead of looking back and seeing what its roots were before it degenerated." Despite such sentiments, however, few people seemed seriously to believe that BGEA would simply close its doors when Graham retired or died, but true to their professed belief that their own work had been divinely ordained and guided, most key figures in the association seemed willing to leave the future in the sure hands of God. Asked what he thought would happen when Graham passed from the scene, Maurice Rowlandson said, "My answer to that, in the true meaning of the words is, 'God only knows.' It isn't man's job to provide the successor. When men did that in the days of the apostles, they chose Matthias, and you never heard of him again. God's choice was Paul. Our choice could be quite wrong. But if God lays his hand on the right man at the right time, he'll provide him with the right organization." Cliff Barrows sounded a similar note. "I don't have the foggiest idea what will happen," he said. "I don't know whether there will ever be anyone to take Bill's place or not. Somehow, I feel this has been an era that God has allowed to happen, and that now he is going to do it another way rather than continue to gather huge crowds together. But then, God may surprise us all."

John Corts agreed that no single individual seemed ready to receive Graham's mantle but thought it possible BGEA could continue to serve as an important enabler of world evangelistic efforts. "We've been struggling with this," he said, "without a real design. We don't have a formalized plan for the future, but a lot of us are thinking about it. Long term, the challenge is to take the resources that have been developed to support Billy Graham and use them in a way that will make them a resource for the Church of Jesus Christ for many years to come. Perhaps we could support a consortium of evangelists who need the kind of help we can give: promotion, accounting, spiritual counseling, literature, follow-up, mobilization of prayer and church support. We could become a support base, perhaps, for a number of ministries. We're not quite sure that's possible. If it's not, then someday we may just have a funeral service. The honest answer is, nobody knows."

As 1990 ended, there had been no funeral service, nor any indication one was being planned, but Graham had quietly set about to dismantle a substantial part of the ministry's far-flung operations. Between 1986 and 1990, BGEA offices in London, Sydney, Buenos Aires, Hong Kong, Tokyo, Taiwan, Paris, and Munich had shut down, usually after turning over their tasks to other organizations. Russ Busby still operated a small photographic studio in Burbank, but virtually all other BGEA operations now proceeded from Minneapolis and Montreat. Whatever course BGEA took at Graham's demise would be simpler to navigate with fewer ships in the armada.

As he moved inexorably toward the end of his life, Graham seemed to agree with those who felt that the most promising way to preserve and extend his ministry lay not so much in finding a single successor to carry on his work as in multiplying the resources for equipping and encouraging tens of thousands of evangelists. At the 1986 Amsterdam conference, Nilson Fanini observed that it would be impossible to imagine another evangelist of Graham's stature. "There will be just one Billy Graham in church history," he said. "You would need a thousand evangelists to do his job. And I believe that is what the Holy Spirit is going to have: a thousand Billy Grahams in Africa, a thousand Billy Grahams in Asia, a thousand Billy Grahams in South America." The dozens of mini-Amsterdams organized around the world since 1986, most with assistance from BGEA, made Fanini's prediction seem plausible.

The best bet for transmitting the inspiration and experience of the Graham team, however, was believed to be a new institution, the Billy Graham Training Center, just outside Asheville on Porter's Cove, the parcel of land whose purchase by the WECEF raised so many eyebrows in 1978. Long before authorizing purchase of the Cove, Graham had toyed with the idea of establishing a center where Bible conferences of the sort D. L. Moody once sponsored could be held and where ministers and laymen could come to study the Bible in a retreat-type setting and to receive intensive instruction in the theory and practice of evangelism. In 1968 he went so far as to send George Wilson to talk to representatives of the Cunard Line about the possibility of buying the *Queen Elizabeth* ocean liner for that purpose. A stunning piece of land near the southern end of the Blue Ridge Parkway, the Cove seemed ideally suited for such a center. Graham insistsed it would be neither a monument to him nor an embarrassment to fellow Christians. "It won't be like PTL. It will be unpublicized, quiet, a place where people can come and study the Bible. It won't be a showplace. It probably won't even have a sign." True to that promise, the buildings erected during the first phase of construction were modest structures, clearly fashioned for function rather than fame. Ruth Graham helped architects design a chapel, arguing for and getting a higher steeple than originally planned, and she decided where her and her husband's graves would be. "We've already got the graveyard built," Billy said brightly; "I've gone down and lain there."

Some saw the Cove, rather than the Minneapolis office, as the place where the memory of Billy Graham's ministry would be most faithfully preserved and his vision most imaginatively embodied. It could easily become the central location for continuing the work of the School of Evangelism that accompanied the crusades—a pilot effort in 1990 drew eight hundred pastors from forty states and fifty-six denominations. Since Graham never played any significant role in the school, younger men could conduct sessions throughout the year, both at the Cove and at other locations around the country. But some of the old warhorses were not quite ready to retire. "I see the latter part of our ministry as one of doing some basic teaching in the areas of evangelism," Cliff Barrows said, his eyes gleaming at the possibilities. "I think we could have a communications center where Bill, when he is no longer able to travel, could still, by satellite, speak and minister about evangelism and discipleship and training and counseling and follow-up and Christian life and character—the whole business. Basically the same things Amsterdam '86 was committed to. We could talk to Christian leadership around the world. With portable satellite dishes and technology just leaping ahead, you can conceivably get a little dish into every hamlet in the world. Technologically, it's already available, and the price is coming down all the time. Through communications technology, the association can still have a great encouraging ministry. Bill can still make a tremendous impact on the world."

Graham acknowledged that he could not maintain the pace he once did—"I'm slowing down. I can feel it. My mind tells me I ought to get out there and go, but I just can't do it"—but insisted that "I'll preach until there is no breath left in my body. I was called by God, and until God tells me to retire, *I cannot. I may preach to smaller groups. I may go back to the streets where I began.* But whatever strength I have, whatever time God lets me have, is going to be dedicated to doing the work of an evangelist, as long as I live."

Street preaching in front of saloons, however, was not a likely finale to Billy Graham's career. For more than fifty years as an evangelist, he fought the good fight and kept the faith. Now, surely on either God's or nature's gun lap, he was ready to finish the course and seemed determined to let the world know he planned to cross the line with an impressively strong kick. In 1988 he embarked on a missionary journey that not only added a new and important country to his own life list but also fulfilled a long-simmering dream of Ruth's: to return to China, where she had been born and where her family had spent a quarter century, to encourage the spread of the gospel among a people who had never been far out of her mind. In 1980 she and her three siblings returned to the site of the mission compound where they had been reared, and people she met on that trip helped arrange the invitation that made it possible for her husband to accompany her on a return visit. Reminiscent of the circumstances of Graham's visits to Eastern Europe, the invitation was a cooperative effort between the China Christian Council, a government-approved (and unofficially controlled) body that includes most of the nation's regular Protestant churches (as distinguished from thousands of "house churches" not affiliated with Western denominations), and a state agency known as the Chinese People's Association for Friendship with Foreign Countries. Like the Soviet bloc visits, the China trip was anything but a haphazard, spur-of-the-moment venture. A few months before leaving, Graham explained offhandedly that "Ruth has formed a committee of China experts," then tossed off the names of a few of her committee members: "Richard Nixon has been helping; George Bush—people of that sort. We had a study group of luminaries pulled from the State Department here all day yesterday to give us suggestions. A China expert from Johns Hopkins is helping a great deal, and a man from *Time* magazine. We've gotten tremendous help from Zhang Wenjin, the former Chinese ambassador to the United States; he's a member of the Politburo now, and head of the Friendship Association that's invited us. He's the one that Chou Enlai sent to negotiate with Kissinger to get Nixon to come to China." Another who played a key role was an American-born resident of China, Sidney Rittenberg. Fresh out of the University of North Carolina and filled with idealistic notions of communism, Rittenberg had gone to China in 1946 to help build the Utopian society he expected the

Communist revolutionaries to create. His idealism suffered a sharp comeuppance when, suspected first of being a spy and then of being an enemy of the Cultural Revolution, he spent sixteen years in prison, mostly in solitary confinement. In more recent years Rittenberg had been deeply involved in the modernization process in China, particularly with regard to greater use of computers, and had served as an interpreter and consultant to American media and commercial enterprises seeking to do business with China. "He charges [American businesses] seven thousand dollars a day for consultations," Graham reported, "but he didn't charge us a cent. He thought it would be a tremendous thing for relations between the U.S. and China for us to visit. He was the one who really started the ball rolling for us in China. He and his wife were visiting in [California] in 1979, and he saw one of our programs on television and said, 'Let's get that man to China.' And he started doing what Dr. Haraszti was doing in Eastern Europe."

The message the Grahams took to China was much the same as what Billy and Alexander Haraszti had delivered in Eastern Europe. "First," Ruth said, "we want to explain what Christians believe and help [government leaders] understand that Christians make their best citizens—the most reliable, the hardest working, the most honest. They don't get drunk and they don't run around or gamble away everything they make. They are good family people." A second aim would be to assure Chinese Christians that their efforts and successes were known and prayed about throughout the world and to help make them feel they are a vital part of international Christianity. And thirdly, "Bill will emphasize peace," Ruth said. "Peace with God. They will be celebrating an International Year of Peace while we are there. It is interesting to read articles from the Beijing government. They all talk about peace. They want peace. But they don't realize that they cut themselves off from the real source of peace."

This ambitious three-pronged mission—originally scheduled for the fall of 1987 but aborted when Graham tripped over his briefcase in a Tokyo hotel room and broke several ribs—finally got under way in April 1988. The five-city, seventeen-day trip got off to a rousing start in Beijing, where Graham was feted at a welcoming banquet hosted by Ambassador Zhang in the Great Hall of the People. The ambassador welcomed Ruth as a "daughter of China" and introduced her husband as "a man of peace." Subsequently, U.S. ambassador Winston Lord and his wife, Betty Bao Lord, hosted a luncheon for Graham and a collection of religious and political leaders. The diplomatic coup of the trip came when the Grahams were received by Premier Li Peng, who spent nearly an hour in conversation with the evangelist, discussing such topics as the role of religion in China's future. Graham, as always, bore witness to his own faith, and Li, while stressing that he was and expected to remain an atheist, acknowledged that the constitutional guarantees of freedom of religion had not always been faith fully observed, and conceded that

China needed "moral power" and "spiritual forces" to undergird its efforts at modernization. The previously unannounced visit was featured on Chinese television and made the front pages of newspapers throughout the country—-the only other foreign dignitary the premier had received was Philippine president Corazon Aquino—and generated widespread public interest in the rest of Graham's visit.

Other notable sessions included lectures at the Chinese Academy of Social Sciences and at Beijing University (both of which have sprung from institutions founded by American missionaries), a preaching appearance before an overflow crowd of approximately 1,500 at the Beijing Christian Church, and an address to a large gathering of foreign diplomats and business people at Beijing's International Club. Having been advised by Ambassador Zhang that if he did not ask to visit major historical sites, "People will notice," Graham visited a section of the Great Wall. When someone explained to a lively group of third graders that their fellow tourist was a famous American, they entertained him with several patriotic songs, and he did his best to respond in kind. When one of his guides taught the children to sing "Jesus Loves Me" in both Chinese and English, the evangelist gamely joined in, making it clear both that his tone deafness is cross-cultural and his memory for lyrics less than flawless. If any of the children could understand his words, they heard the smiling tall man sitting cross-legged in their midst proclaim the un-Evangelical news that "He is weak, but we are strong." Still, an Australian couple who were taken aback when they recognized him correctly guessed his intentions. "What do you think he's doing here," the husband asked. His wife gave the only answer that made sense: "Probably what he does everywhere."

Other cities on the agenda included Huayin (where Ruth had spent her childhood), Nanjing, Shanghai, and Guangzhou. In each, he spoke to large gatherings of Christians and met with key political and civic leaders to discuss the necessity and social advantages of removing all restrictions on religious belief and practice. He found the clearest example of a growing tolerance toward religion in Nanjing, where he visited a thriving new religious press. During the Cultural Revolution, most copies of the Bible had been destroyed; if believers had access to a copy at all, it was likely to be one that some dedicated saint had laboriously copied by hand. Now, in the first year of its operation, Amity Press was in the process of printing 600,000 copies of the Bible, with plans to print and distribute a million copies a year after that. Graham also spoke to students at Nanjing Seminary, where he gave the ministers-in-training his familiar exhortation to preach the gospel with authority; to preach it simply, boldly, and urgently; and to preach it again and again. After an extended question-and-answer session, a representative of the student body gave Graham a banner to remind the evangelist to pray for him and his fellow seminarians. Then, with touching timidity, he said, "All of our students hope someday to be like you."

China had never received so prestigious a religious leader before, and Chinese media gave the visit impressive attention. Various events on Graham's itinerary, particularly his visit with the premier, drew wide radio, television, and newspaper coverage, both at the national and local levels. The influential *World Economic Herald*, published in Shanghai, carried an interview with the evangelist on its front pages, and Ruth Graham was interviewed by writers for the Beijing *Review* and *Chinese Women* magazines. While no one would dare suggest that any substantial proportion of China's billion-plus population was about to convert to Christianity, Sidney Rittenberg did venture that Graham had represented Christianity to Chinese leaders as "a powerful moral force to support the Chinese people in their mighty, backbreaking efforts to escape from poverty, both moral and material," and that he had impressed them with his suggestions on "how they might better shape and administer their policy on religious freedom. In this manner, Mr. Graham is opening the big door for the advance of Christianity in China. In doing so, he will promote the opening of all the little doors."

Shortly after the China visit, Graham returned to Russia to celebrate one thousand years of Christianity's presence in that country. As a guest of the Russian Orthodox Church, he was treated as a major dignitary. "The millennium celebration was fantastic," he reported. "Television and newspapers were filled with it all day long. That's the first time the present generation of Soviet people realized their roots were in Christianity. This made a real impact on them. I suppose I was the main foreign speaker. They put me right up there behind Mrs. Gorbachev, and I had an opportunity to talk with her twice during breaks. They received me everywhere—the Central Committee, the Politburo, everywhere. They gave a luncheon for me the last day I was there, and Georgi Arbatov came and gave a speech. He talked about what I had contributed to better relations between the United States and the Soviet Union. I was amazed he was even there, and even more amazed he was a speaker. I thought the way they treated us was a little bit historic."

When he returned to the United States after that visit, Graham found himself faced with another political campaign and the quadrennial challenge to be a neutral observer. "I almost got into it this time," he said, "because I went to Atlanta to the Democratic convention and led a prayer there. I had a good talk with Governor Dukakis out at the [Georgia] governor's home. All the [Democratic] governors were there, and I was the only outsider. I was there to lead in prayer, and they put me right beside Governor Dukakis. The chairman of the Democratic party was there, but the conversation was almost totally between Governor Dukakis and me." At the convention itself, Graham led another prayer, in which he invoked both Scripture and the memory of John F. Kennedy. He noted that in contrast to some conventions he had attended, the mood seemed "quiet and reverent. It was sort of a religious spirit. While I was praying and when I finished, you could hear a pin drop. Usually, they're just walking and talking, but they were just as quiet as could be. And when I finished, there were 'amens' from all over the place. I think it had something to do with the fact that there were so many blacks there. And I noticed that the whites began to dress up, because the blacks were dressed up just like they were going to church, and this had a great impact on some of those white delegates. I felt that, from a religious point of view, the black people made a very positive impact. It was very interesting. My talk—my prayer—came at the prime time of the evening, but no one carried it except CNN and C-SPAN. And one other network, maybe for a minute, I heard later."

Some political observers surmised that Graham's prominent presence at the convention might be a signal that the Democratic party was once again acceptable to the white Evangelicals who had so largely deserted it in the two previous presidential elections, but that interpretation did not last long. The Republicans were not about to concede Billy Graham to the Democrats. "I was invited to the Republican convention," Graham recalled, "and I went. And they wanted me to lead the prayer after Reagan spoke, and I did. Then they asked me if I would stay over for the Bush speech, and I was glad to do it. I didn't know I was going to be sitting with Mrs. Bush the whole time." But there he was, smiling and applauding the nominee, and looking every inch as if he felt quite comfortable in the Republican box, even though he told the Associated Press, "I always stay politically neutral." Five months later, he would once again look quite comfortable as he mounted the platform at the inauguration and thanked God that "in Thy sovereignty Thou has permitted George Bush to lead us at this momentous hour of our history for the next four years."

Graham took no public—and, as far as is known, no private—role in the campaign, but he never claimed he had no favorite in the race. Graham and Bush had, in fact, been friends for many years—"the best friend I have in the whole world, outside my immediate staff," according to one account. The evangelist met George's father, Prescott Bush, through friends converted during the 1957 New York crusade, and the Grahams had spent several short vacations at the family's summer home in Hobe Sound, Florida. "George's mother [was] one of the most remarkable Christian women I had ever known," Graham observed. "Whenever we went down there, she would ask me to teach a Bible class. I don't remember exactly when I met George, but we were thrown together at several things, and we became good friends. Then they began to invite us up to Kennebunkport. We've been up there five of the last seven years, I think. In fact, he just invited us to come to Camp David. I was there with Johnson twice and with Nixon once. Interestingly, George and I have never talked politics. Not one time. Never mentioned them. He's never asked me to do anything for him." Perhaps not, but on the evening of January 16, 1991, when American and allied forces launched the devastating air attack on Iraq, Billy Graham's well-publicized presence in the White House and his oversight of a worship service for key political and military leaders the next morning lent powerful symbolic legitimation to the president's claim to be conducting a just war.

Graham also continued to stay in touch with another old Republican friend, Richard Nixon. "I visited him in New Jersey just recently," he reported. "He was explaining his vision of America and the world in foreign policy. But he talked more about spiritual things and the Lord about as much as I had ever heard him talk before. I had a feeling that he was willing to talk now about things that he used to be reluctant to talk about. I think part of that was his Quaker background. He was a very staunch Quaker, and it was hard to express things having to do with spiritual matters. But I never had a doubt from the time I got to know him that he was a very religious man."

In 1982, Alexander Haraszti, who had accomplished what many believed impossible, conceded that "it is, humanly speaking, just impossible, even unimaginable, that a Christian minister of the gospel would actually be allowed in any communist country to preach from an open place like in a stadium, a large square, or on any secular premises." Just seven short years later, in the summer of 1989, Haraszti stood at Billy Graham's side on a platform erected in the center of Hungary's largest stadium, and there, before an estimated 110,000 people—inevitably, a stadium record—and the largest known religious gathering in Hungary's history, he translated into his native tongue a sermon the evangelist had based on Galatians 6:14: "But God forbid that I should glory, save in the cross of our Lord Jesus Christ...." At the conclusion of the sermon, which Haraszti reproduced right down to the classic Graham gestures and the story of the ex-convict who came home to find a yard filled with yellow ribbons, more than 35,000 people came forward—nearly one third of the crowd and the largest response the evangelist had seen in more than a half-century of inviting people to accept Jesus Christ. When the service was carried on the state television network a week later, many others contacted the sponsoring religious bodies, pushing the decision total even higher. One newspaper headlined its front-page story on the event with "An angel came upon the stadium." Matyos Szuros, the president of the Hungarian parliament, filmed an interview for Graham to use on the television program that would air a few months later in America. Hungary was changing, he said. There was now greater freedom of religion, freedom for Christians to speak out about what they believed, freedom even, he noted with some sense of historical awareness, to preach in public to 100,000 people. The churches of Hungary, he said, were in the process of renewal, and that was good, because the nation needed to have them involved in the moral education of its people. Szuros's statement amounted to an official admission that the ideological reasons for the suppression of religion had been proven wrong. These were not empty words. A month after this interview, the State Office for Religious Affairs was abolished as the government announced it was removing all barriers to the free development of church life in Hungary.

The following spring, Graham registered another triumph over long odds. In 1960, shortly before the Berlin wall went up, he preached to a huge throng gathered in front of the historic Reichstag building near the Brandenburg Gate. The East German government and press denounced him as a warmonger, and Communist military troops tried to drown out his sermon by staging artillery practice a few hundred yards away. Thirty years later, the wall was in ruins, the Communist government in a state of collapse, and Billy Graham, the Great Survivor, was again preaching on the steps of the Reichstag, this time as the guest of both West and East German churches, which had jointly invited him to bring a spiritual dimension to the momentous upheavals destined to produce a reunified Germany, a reconfigured Europe, and an end to the cold war. As 15,000 people, most from East Germany, huddled in near-freezing rain under umbrellas and plastic sheeting, Graham told of the tears of joy he shed while watching the grim symbol of enmity come tumbling down and declared that "God has answered our prayers for peace." He warned, however, that abandoning moral and spiritual values at this critical point in human history "could be just as devastating to society in the long run as weapons of mass destruction." Announcing that "God is giving this country another chance," he proclaimed the same message he had preached for over fifty years in more than sixty countries: "There is no hope for the future of Europe, America, or any other part of the world outside of the gospel of Christ." His text was John 3:16.

Dan Rather, who had scored Graham for naïveté at the time of his 1982 visit to the Soviet Union, acknowledged that "before anybody else I knew of, and more consistently than anyone else I have known, of any nationality, race, or religion, Reverend Graham was saying, 'Spirituality is alive in the Marxist-Leninist-Stalinist states.... Frankly, there were those years when I thought he was wrong, or that he didn't know what he was talking about. It turns out he was right. And give him credit—he also took the time to go and see for himself." And Richard Nixon volunteered, "There is no question that he helped bring about the liberation, the peaceful liberation of Eastern Europe, and some of the present opposition to Communism in the Soviet Union."

These dramatic ventures underlined Graham's stature as a Christian world figure, but they did not displace his dedication to his primary and continuing call: preaching the gospel to as many people as humanly possible in whatever time is left to him. Fittingly, the undertaking he and his colleagues devised to provide a climax, though not a finale, to his career as a globe-circling evangelist, is known as Mission World. The original plan was to have him address crusade audiences in virtually every country on the planet simultaneously—or nearly so, with brief delays to accommodate differences in time zones. As the project took shape, Graham and his colleagues, including a skeptical BGEA board, decided that the logistic complexity and enormous financial requirements of a one-shot, worldwide mission were too great to justify, and that a more modest, stage-by-stage approach would be more effective and efficient in achieving the desired goals. Had it not been for the scope of the original vision, however, no one would have dreamed that what actually occurred was a scaled-down version of something even grander. "Mission World arose as a response to cries for help from men and women who attended Amsterdam '83 and '86," Bob Williams explained. "We can't keep pushing Mr. Graham physically, but wherever he goes, we try to let his shadow fall as far as possible, through available technology, without having to extend him personally."

In Mission World's 1989 incarnation, Graham's shadow stretched across the British Isles and over 33 countries of Africa. In London itself he addressed nearly 400,000 people at services in four venues and more than 800,000 in 247 "live-link" centers throughout the United Kingdom and the Republic of Ireland. In Africa the satellite signal from London was aired live on the national television network in 13 countries. Another 20 nations received the program by videotape a week or two later, usually after translation into one of nine different languages. The initial African effort included 16,000 fully prepared crusades, with an aggregate attendance of 8.5 million. An additional 4,000 film and videotape missions in areas without TV reception were still going on six months later. As Williams pointed out, "We are not talking million-dollar high tech. We have been working with manufacturers. For five hundred dollars, and the cost is dropping all the time, we can buy a whole set of video equipment that a little guy in the jungle can learn to use right away. We put that into the hands of evangelists from Amsterdam '83 and '86 and let them tramp all across the country with it. They don't have the stature to organize a crusade in Lagos, but they copy tapes just by jacking between recorders and then courier them out by bicycle or train or bus to locations all over Nigeria. We figure we were able to reach Africans at a cost of about 3.5 cents per viewer." No attempt was made to get an accurate accounting of decisions from all meetings, but crusade leaders distributed 2.5 million pieces of follow-up literature. "We are not claiming there were 2.5 million inquirers," Williams said, not mentioning that such a response would be larger than the number of inquirers who responded to the invitation in all of Graham's crusades over the previous forty years. Still, he observed, "We can think and hope and dream and pray and wonder about how many there were and about what will happen now." Furthermore, developments in technology have been so astonishing that achievements undreamt of when Mission World was first conceived now seem almost quaintly modest. "Five or six years ago," Williams noted, "there were 140,000 television sets in all of India. Today, there are 30 million. In Thailand, one of every four homes has a VCR; five years ago, they were unknown. Now we have avenues and vehicles that would work only in more developed countries just a few years back. This approach could be a key to the ministry's future after his death. People know exactly what you mean when you talk about Billy Graham evangelism or a Billy Graham School of Evangelism or an Amsterdam-type conference. They know what BGEA is and what it stands for. We can still have a tremendous ministry in being a catalyst and providing resources for genuine biblical evangelism. I don't know what the Lord wants to do. We are getting a lot done now in Africa, Asia, and Latin America because of what we have done in the past. That doesn't mean we have a future. But the Lord has gone before us, and He'll have his hand on what happens next." For now, however, Williams did not think it necessary to worry about what happened when Billy Graham departed the scene, for the evangelist was still on hand and going strong. "I've seen a greater passion, a greater urgency in Mr. Graham during the last five or six years," he said. "I think he has a renewed strength and vision and courage. He won't stop. I don't know if he feels the days are coming when the world will be less receptive to the gospel, or if it's something about the Second Coming, or what. Maybe it's just that the helplessness and hopelessness of the world is becoming more evident. But there is a definite sense of urgency. It's always been there, but it's greater today than ever."

And so it seemed. Late in 1990, as crusade organizers in 70,000 locations in twenty-six countries of Asia eagerly awaited the falling of his shadow on their lands, Billy Graham launched the oriental expression of Mission World. On November 7, exactly seventy-two years to the day after Frank and Morrow Graham first proudly beheld their firstborn son and wondered what lay in store for him, he stood on the deck of a traditional Chinese junk as it crossed Victoria Harbor on its way to Hong Kong, whence, yet again, he would address the largest aggregate audience—an estimated 100 million souls—ever to hear the good news concerning Jesus Christ.

Part 6

Finishing the Course
(The Final Years)

38

The Work of an Evangelist

When the original edition of this book appeared, the story closed on Billy Graham's seventy-second birthday. No other major evangelist in Christian history had enjoyed a significant ministry of comparable length, and no one would have faulted Graham had he decided to enter into quiet retirement, especially after his growing problems with trembling and weakness were diagnosed as Parkinson's disease. But Bob Williams had been correct when he predicted, "He won't stop." Indeed, some of the most impressive achievements of Billy Graham's entire ministry would come during his last decades.

The most ambitious and logistically complex accomplishment was undoubtedly the completion of Mission World. The first phase, in 1989, had gone from London to more than 30 countries in Africa. The second phase, Mission World Asia, dispatched the Christian gospel, translated into 45 languages, from Hong Kong to more than 70,000 satellite and video crusades in 30 countries in Asia and the Pacific. Each Crusade was prepared as if Graham were coming personally; more than 400,000 counselors were trained and 10 million pieces of follow-up literature were printed in 30 languages. As in all subsequent Mission World efforts, the programs were culturally adapted, with pre-produced musical segments and testimonies designed to appeal to audiences in given regions. Although a precise count was impossible to obtain, available reports indicated that the goal of reaching 100 million people with each program had been met. It was clearly the largest single outreach in over 40 years of Billy Graham's international ministry.

Two years later, in November 1991, Crusade services originating in Buenos Aires reached an estimated 65 million people in 20 countries of South America, Central America, and Spanish-speaking countries in the Caribbean. The European edition of Mission World, dubbed ProChrist 93, called for greater technological sophistication than the three previous efforts. For some time, German Christians had wanted to sponsor a Billy Graham mission, but, perhaps still anxious to avoid association with the Nazi rallies of the 1930s and 1940s, wanted the evangelist to tour 20 cities over a 30-day period instead of holding a standard crusade in a large stadium. Graham's health and stamina precluded such an exhaustive undertaking, but the Mission World format provided a satisfactory alternative. From a 7000-seat hall in Essen that served as a studio, Graham's sermons, delivered alongside a German interpreter but translated simultaneously into 44 other languages, were transmitted by satellite to 386 remote sites in Germany, Austria, and Switzerland. In addition, eight uplink trucks beamed up to 14 daily transmissions of the program via various satellites to more than a thousand venues in 56 countries and territories in 16 time zones. An estimated 2 million people attended the services nightly and countless others viewed them later in thousands of video crusades, including many throughout the former Soviet Union. This venture brought the total of countries reached through Mission World since 1989 to 141, involving at least 95 different languages.

By 1995, what had seemed unfeasible, perhaps even impossible, when Billy Graham first began to dream about preaching to the entire world at once, now seemed achievable. Bob Williams, still serving as director of the project, spoke of "a double-hung window of opportunity," referring to a relaxation of government restrictions in many areas and the dramatic reduction in the cost of satellite technology. Some things, of course, had not changed; one of those was time zones. Apart from being able to boast that the gospel had been preached to all nations at the same moment, actually trying to do so made no sense. As Mike Southworth, BGEA manager of satellite services, observed, "For Christians to get up in the middle of the night to go to a program is difficult enough. To ask non-Christians to do that is next to impossible, [and they] are really the ones we want to reach."

Instead, culturally adapted programs, molded around sermons Billy Graham preached in Hiram Bithom Stadium in San Juan, Puerto Rico, on March 16–18, 1995, were—after translation into 116 different languages—bounced off 30 separate satellites to 3000 downlink sites in 185 countries in all 29 time zones, to be viewed at appropriate hours. In addition to stadiums, theaters, churches, and village gatherings at which the programs were projected onto bed sheets tacked to walls, the three programs were aired over national television networks in 117 countries and seen in the U.S. over several cable television systems and in national syndication. BGEA, not given to exaggerated claims regarding its audiences, estimated that more than a billion people heard at least one of the programs. With the possible exception of the Olympics, this project, dubbed Global Mission, may well have been the most technologically complex example of worldwide communication ever attempted.

As with all of Billy Graham's evangelistic endeavors, precise assessment of Global Mission's effectiveness is impossible. That said, one can share the wonder expressed by David Barrett, co-author of the *World Christian Ency-*

clopedia and widely regarded as a top authority on world missions. "How," Barrett asked, "can you envisage one man speaking to a billion people? I think there are only two people in the world who could have attained this: Billy Graham and John Paul II." Future students of world religion, Barrett thought, would view Mission World "as one of the most significant events in the worldwide spread of Christianity."

Heartened by the success of Global Mission and unwilling to abandon the hundreds of thousands of contacts involved in that immense effort, BGEA followed it in 1996 with two additional globe-girdling initiatives known as the World Television Series. Both efforts made use of satellite transmission and national television networks, but instead of trying to attract people to stadiums and other large-scale gatherings, they enlisted approximately one million churches worldwide to help set up video house parties to which church members could invite their friends and neighbors. Reminiscent of Operation Andrew, in which Christians bring their friends to stadiums to hear Graham preach, this was called Operation Matthew, after the tax collector (and, subsequently, apostle and gospel writer) who invited his friends to his home to meet Jesus.

In a second innovation, instead of the traditional format of music and testimony followed by a sermon, the entire program was based upon a sermon during which Graham's message was illustrated and amplified by music and drama, often quick-cut in MTV style, and by statements from such internationally famous figures as Nelson Mandela, Archbishop Desmond Tutu, and President Jimmy Carter. Prior to these home meetings, hosts were provided with discussion guides, follow-up materials, and literature to distribute to guests. In all, approximately 450 million pieces, culturally adapted and in dozens of languages, were sent to more than 150 countries for each of the two programs. BGEA estimated that between 30 and 40 million house parties were held and that more than 2 billion people watched at least one of the programs.

On a more modest scale, Graham continued to press his attempts to preach the gospel in lands still dominated by or barely emerging from the shadow of communism. In 1986 Alexander Haraszti had said, "We don't expect that Billy Graham will ever be able to preach in public in Moscow." The next five years, of course, confounded most expectations about what would happen there. While other developments understandably attracted greater worldwide attention, the relaxation of restrictions on religious organizations, particularly those other than the Russian Orthodox Church, was certainly a significant indicator of sweeping change. In July 1991 Billy Graham engineered a breakthrough for Russian Evangelicals by gaining permission to hold a full-fledged school of evangelism in Stadium Druzba, an annex of Lenin Stadium. Almost 5000 pastors and lay leaders not only were permitted to attend the school, but also were housed and fed in dormitories at Moscow

State University. As a further indication that Graham's careful cultivation of Russian secular and religious authorities in earlier years had convinced them of his integrity, he was urged and agreed to warn participants to watch out for false teachers and exploiters from the West who would split indigenous churches and exaggerate accounts of their visits in order to raise money for their own use back home. During his time in Moscow the evangelist met with Mikhail Gorbachev and Boris Yeltsin. He reported that he had found both men to be interested in spiritual matters and said that his long conversation with Yeltsin had been primarily about moral and religious subjects.

A fuller answer to Graham's 1959 prayer for revival in Red Square (p. 264) came the following year, with Vozrozhdeniye (Renewal) 92, hailed by *Decision* magazine as "Something beyond all expectations." With the support of 150 churches in the Moscow area and 3000 more from elsewhere in Russia, Graham proclaimed the gospel of Christ in the huge indoor Olympic Stadium. The stadium's previous attendance record of 38,000, set at the 1988 Goodwill Games, was surpassed at each of the three services. At the final meeting on Sunday, 50,000 people jammed into the stadium and an additional 20,000 watched the proceedings on a large screen outside. More than a quarter of the audience responded to the invitation at each service. The cooperation of Russian authorities and institutions echoed that of Graham's 1989 Hungary mission. The Moscow postal system distributed 3.2 million promotional leaflets, enough for every home in Moscow; *Isvestia* ran an in-depth interview; and Graham appeared on several national television programs. At one service the famed Russian Army Chorus sang "The Battle Hymn of the Republic," bringing the audience to its feet for the refrain, "Glory, glory hallelujah/His truth is marching on."

A few months before the Moscow mission, Graham had finally cracked through the shell surrounding the most closed of communist societies, North Korea. Once a country that contained so many Christian churches that it was sometimes called "The Jerusalem of the East," Korea had ruthlessly repressed virtually all religious expression for more than half a century. Now only a tiny percentage of the population still identified itself as Christian; indeed, the capital city of Pyongyang had only two church buildings, one Protestant and one Catholic. Still, perhaps aware of Graham's efforts on behalf of religious freedom in the former Soviet Union and its satellite states, the Korean (Protestant) Christians Federation and the Korean Catholics Association, with governmental approval, invited Graham to visit, with the understanding that his appearances would be quite limited. After gaining approval from President George Bush and Secretary of State James A. Baker III, Graham accepted the invitation.

In Pyongyang, Graham preached at both of the city's churches and spoke to about 400 students at Kim Il Sung University, laying out the basics of Christian faith and telling them something of the role religion had played in

American history. He also met with the Minister of Foreign Affairs and, more importantly, with the aged and iron-fisted President Kim Il Sung. North Korean television, which featured their meeting as its lead story, described the conversation as "warm and cordial" and noted that President Kim had expressed hope that "a new spring will come in the relations between our two countries."

Two years later, Graham received a second invitation, once again coming from the two Christian associations. Graham announced that his primary reason for going was to preach the gospel of Christ, but acknowledged a willingness to explore more fully President Kim's hope for "a new spring." Graham spoke at the same venues as during his first visit and also to a public meeting that included some of the nation's top leaders. But the centerpiece of this trip was a three-hour meeting with President Kim. This time Graham brought a message from the new American president, Bill Clinton, holding out hope of a warmer relationship once North Korea formally agreed to allow international teams to inspect its nuclear weapons facilities.

According to Stephen Linton, an expert on Korea who accompanied Graham on the trip and was present at this meeting, Kim responded in an agitated fashion, shaking his fist and declaring that "President Clinton had the logic reversed: first the two presidents should establish a relationship. Then they could talk about the problems." Linton described the conversation as "two old men bantering," with Kim Il Sung loud and emotional, and Graham trying to assure him that Clinton, who "represents a new generation of Americans," was "doing the best he can, under the circumstances." Linton reported that even though Kim Il Sung did not agree with Clinton's approach, he was open to the possibility that the young American president was sincere. Graham's phrasing, Linton discerned, was "a polite way for one old man to tell another old man that they were dealing with young men, and that young men can sometimes be brash." This "provided an explanation for the U.S. position in a way that made sense to an old village elder like Kim Il Sung" and also served as "a character reference for the young United States administration."

Once again, Billy Graham's informal diplomacy may have had a significant impact. President Kim made no commitment at the time, but a few weeks later he formally agreed to allow international inspectors to visit North Korea's nuclear sites. In Linton's view, Graham's explanation "provided a motive for allowing the inspections that didn't hurt Kim Il Sung's pride. It made it more a favor that he was bestowing than a concession that had been wrung out of him."

Graham's efforts in China did not progress far beyond his earlier visits, but he did visit again briefly in early 1994, just prior to his second trip to North Korea. When Chinese President Jiang Zemin visited the U.S. in 1997, he requested a meeting with the evangelist in Los Angeles, where they reportedly discussed religious life in both the United States and China, including issues of human rights and religious freedom.

As indicated by his government-approved visits to Pyongyang, Billy Graham retained his position as Chaplain to the Nation and occasional ambassador without portfolio. The media still sought his opinion on matters of state, and he still managed to provide transparent support for his political friends, as when he commended Ronald Reagan in 1991 by observing that "one of his greatest achievements was having the wisdom and courage [to choose] George Bush as his running mate." When the nation proved unwilling to choose his old friend George Bush to fill a second term in the White House, Graham found much to admire in Bill Clinton and was pleased to lead prayers at both of his inaugurations, giving him the distinction of participating in eight inaugurations for six presidents — more than any other figure in American history except John Marshall, who was Chief Justice of the Supreme Court from 1801 to 1835.

Graham maintained his friendship with Ronald Reagan, visiting him on occasion and noting with regret the toll Alzheimer's disease was taking on another Great Communicator. When Richard Nixon died in 1994, Graham presided over the internationally televised services and also at the more private graveside committal of his complex and controversial old friend's body, a fitting end to a relationship that had drawn him further into the political vortex than any other of his flirtations with power and, in the process, had shown him the dangers of trying to swim in a whirlpool. In another manifestation of his role as the People's Pastor, Graham joined President Clinton in a moving prayer service in the aftermath of the bombing of the Oklahoma City federal office building in April 1995.

In May 1996 the U.S. Congress honored Billy and Ruth Graham by presenting them with the Congressional Gold Medal, the highest honor Congress can bestow on a citizen. The first citizen to receive the award was George Washington; only 112 others had been so honored in more than two centuries. This was only the second time the award had gone to a clergyman, and the third time it had been given to a couple. Speaker of the House Newt Gingrich, who hosted the event attended by more than 700 congressional, diplomatic, and religious leaders, called Graham "one of the great civic leaders of the 20th century" and lauded him and Ruth for having "given up their lives as a model for serving humanity, and [standing] as role models for generations to come." Gingrich added, "By receiving this medal, you join about as exalted a group of citizens as we have in this country, and you frankly honor us by being here to receive it." Physically frail and obviously moved by such tribute, Graham responded by saying, "As Ruth and I receive this award, we know that some day we will lay it at the feet of the One we seek to serve."

In addition to the several phases of Mission World and despite progressive physical decline brought on by what was thought to be Parkinson's, Graham maintained a relatively full schedule of crusades during the last decade of the century, though most of these lasted only three to five nights instead of the eight days that had been customary in the 1980s. On what amounted to a decade-long farewell tour, he brought his team and his message to New Jersey, New York, three cities in Scotland, Philadelphia, Portland, Pittsburgh, Tokyo, Cleveland, Toronto, Minneapolis, Charlotte, San Antonio, Ottawa, Indianapolis, St. Louis, Nashville, and Jacksonville, breaking stadium records in almost every city.

None of these gatherings drew more national attention than "An Afternoon in the Park with Billy" on September 22, 1991. As the conclusion to a three-year Mission New York that began in Buffalo and included major events in Albany and on Long Island, Graham climaxed a successful crusade at the Meadowlands in neighboring New Jersey—topping popular singer Bruce Springsteen's former record turnout for that venue by more than 10,000 people—with a three-hour music and message extravaganza on the 15-acre Great Lawn of Manhattan's Central Park.

At least one New York City official scoffed at hearing that Graham and his team were hoping for as many as 50,000 people to show up for the event. "Surely their draw in the Northeast is not what it's going to be in the South," he said, "but this is New York City." Evidently unaware of Graham's earlier success at bringing the gospel to Gotham—and Boston, Chicago, Los Angeles, and other locations far from the Bible Belt—this gentleman also failed to recognize that, if BGEA representatives were publicly setting a goal of 50,000, they probably had already confirmed bus reservations for at least 75,000. It was never their practice to set themselves up for public disappointment, and they certainly did not intend to do so in full view of the nation's major media. Preparation had been extensive. Beyond the standard measures, 2.5 million brochures had been distributed house-to-house in all five boroughs of the city. In contrast to 1957, when Catholics were urged to stay away from Billy Graham's Madison Square Garden Crusade and priests were provided materials to help them counter Evangelical teaching, on this occasion in 1991 John Cardinal O'Connor, Archbishop of the Catholic Archdiocese of New York, and Bishop Thomas V. Daily of the Diocese of Brooklyn wrote to their priests in 630 Catholic churches, urging them to invite their parishioners to go hear Billy Graham, and encouraged the distribution of brochures to hundreds of daily visitors to St. Patrick's Cathedral. In addition to greater participation by African-American churches than in earlier years, at least a hundred Chinese churches actively promoted the event to their members.

Once again, thorough planning, extravagant publicity, and the prospect of hearing the world's most famous evangelist preach from the front porch of America's cultural capital produced an astonishing result. By police estimates, 250,000 people turned out for what the *New York Daily News* called "the largest religious assembly in New York City history." It was also more than twice as large as any audience ever to hear Graham in the United States. Mayor David Dinkins called it "perhaps the most multi-cultural revival meeting the world has ever seen." More than 200 reporters crowded into the press area. The *New York Times* gave it glowing front-page coverage, and the *Wall Street Journal* exclaimed that "we live in a time when . . . such a large gathering turning out for a religious message is a phenomenon."

No other domestic event matched the Central Park rally in terms of a live audience, but the crusades of the 1990s were not simply formulaic reprises of what had gone before. Increasingly, crusade budgets included $50,000 to $100,000 in funds for distribution through social service agencies; collections of food and other items for the hungry and homeless became standard. At the Philadelphia crusade in 1992, 100,000 pounds of food was donated for distribution through local agencies, and 35,000 personal-care kits containing a variety of hygiene products were assembled and distributed to homeless people in Philadelphia and in Chester, Pennsylvania, and Camden, New Jersey. That crusade also continued a growing emphasis on developing a multicultural appeal, as the 7,400-voice choir sang hymns in English and Spanish and Korean.

While these changes were significant, they were mild compared to what, starting in Cleveland in 1994, would become a hallmark of Billy Graham crusades during the last years of his public ministry. Recall that Graham first gained national and international attention with Youth for Christ, which featured vital young men dressed in loud clothes and accompanied by contemporary music and such novelties as a horse that could tap out the number of Jesus' apostles or the number of persons in the Trinity. As Graham and Neo-Evangelical Christianity matured and entered the mainstream, this youthful exuberance disappeared. The Graham team made a conscious effort to fashion services that would be thoroughly familiar to their middle-class constituency and would reassure backsliders and those who had never made a Christian commitment that coming forward at a Billy Graham crusade would plug them back into a community and cultural experience quite similar to what most of them had known in their youth. By the 1990s, however, high proportions of those attending the crusades—and, more importantly, of the younger generations Graham particularly wanted to reach—had never been to a "Little Brown Church in the Wildwood" and would not likely regard an invitation "just to trust and obey" as a particularly appealing offer.

As Graham spoke of what Evangelicals call a "burden" for young people in his grandchildren's generation, he found a receptive spirit in Rick Marshall, a crusade director with several teenage youngsters. Marshall had felt for some time that crusade services were not meeting the needs of young people and that a crucial step would be to introduce more music of the sort they enjoyed. Predictably, Billy Graham had no feel for the contemporary music scene, but he observed that when he went into different countries and cultures, he often needed an interpreter to put his message into a language people could understand. If popular music, however jarring to his own ears, could serve as a medium of translation, he was willing to give it a try.

The experiment was launched in June 1994, in Cleveland's venerable Municipal Stadium. Marshall enlisted popular Christian musicians Michael W. Smith and rock group dcTalk and publicized the event on MTV and the two most popular rock stations in the Cleveland market. Instead of having these artists simply sing a number or two and give a brief testimony, the idea was to have them present a full concert of high-energy music, then follow that with a message from Billy Graham, a caring adult who would attempt to let them know that he understood their world and wanted to help them find purpose and meaning in their lives. Tedd Smith, who by this time had assumed the lead role in producing the actual crusade program, admitted that "we didn't know what was going to happen in Cleveland. I think there was some hesitation. Is this going to work? People who had been around so many years and had not been in a concert atmosphere wondered, 'Are they going to behave?'"

The answer to the first concern—"Will they show up?"—came early. Five hours before the concert was to start, an estimated 50,000 kids were waiting to get into the stadium. That sight hardly eased the concerns about behavior. Larry Ross, who now had primary responsibility for Graham's public relations, recalled that Roger Flessing, by then in charge of BGEA media but still something of a free spirit, had provided his crew with T-shirts that read, "The Billy Graham It-Seemed-Like-a-Good-Idea-at-the-Time Tour." In a similar spirit of giddy anxiety, Ross and several others sported clip-on earrings backstage. As the time for Graham to go on approached, Ross peeked out from backstage to see a mass of young humanity "pogo-ing" in front of the stage and a "wave" whipping around the upper deck of the stadium. Later he remembered thinking, "'There is no way we are going to get control of this crowd. What are we going to do?' But then, when Mr. Graham got up to speak, they settled down and you could hear a pin drop. Whether it is the grandfatherly image or the respect for his generation, I don't know, but it was amazing. And it's like that everywhere we go."

Tedd Smith gave a similar account. "We've never had anything like drugs," he observed. "When the music is on, the kids are listening, doing what they do at a concert. Then here comes granddaddy on stage. The musicians give Billy Graham a hug. The kids say, 'Oh, gee, these guys are hugging him. He's a good person.' And all of a sudden, they become very, very quiet. We have found that in every single city. What he says is very much what they want to hear."

Clearly, the experiment was a success, and Youth Night became a standard feature of Graham crusades, as did a Saturday morning Kidz Gig, aimed at younger children and often drawing upwards of 20,000 kids and their parents for a Christian music review featuring Psalty the Singing Songbook, a cartoon character popular in Evangelical circles. In a remarkably short time, Michael W. Smith, Kirk Franklin, dc Talk, Jars of Clay, Third Day, Steven Curtis Chapman, Crystal Lewis, Ricky Skaggs, the Gaither Vocal Band, the Tommy Coomes Band, Dennis Agajanian and the Praise Band, and other young Christian musicians were just as likely to be part of a Billy Graham crusade as were Sandi Patti or Johnny Cash and June Carter Cash.

Ross acknowledged that not all of the old guard were easily won over. "It has been tough. Let's put it this way—it has been an education process. Though they were very progressive in the early days, this was a whole genre of music they were not used to," an observation underscored by watching team members remove ear plugs and grimace as they tried to communicate through the noise coming from the stage. The team was not alone. Franklin noted that "Daddy is not too comfortable with the music," or, more pointedly, "Daddy doesn't like it. He won't even listen to it. But he's willing to give it a try. They're stocking the pond so he can go fishing."

The old evangelist was also willing to adjust his preaching to a new audience. Instead of hauling out a classic sermon about King Manassas, "The Wickedest Man Who Ever Lived," he preached about Solomon, "the richest, most powerful, and sexiest man of his time," moving somewhat beyond strict exegesis of Scripture to assert that Solomon had several Ph.D.s from the universities of his day and used drugs, not to mention all those wives and concubines, but still could not find happiness in pleasure and power. Instead of quoting *Reader's Digest* or a world leader he had personally known, he cited MTV and shared nuggets of disillusionment from the lead singer of Nine-Inch Nails and the rapping Notorious B.I.G., or referred to Kurt Cobain's widely publicized suicide.

In city after city, Youth Night not only consistently drew the largest crowd for the crusade, but set stadium records in almost every venue—78,000 in Atlanta, 73,500 in Toronto, 82,000 in Minneapolis, 88,000 in Charlotte, 75,000 in San Antonio, 70,000 in Jacksonville. And so it went. In 1996 a special Youth Night television special was translated in 48 languages and sent to 160 countries. While asserting that "these programs have become not only a hallmark for his ministry, but a model for pastors who are trying to reach this generation," Larry Ross admitted that the phenomenon continued to amaze him. "Sometimes," he said, chuckling and shaking his head, "they will chant, 'BILL-Y, BILL-Y, BILL-Y' for a minute or two before they settle down. And then they hang on every word. To have an 82-year-old evangelist setting stadium attendance records on Youth Night—go figure. I think it just confirms the search for meaning."

Bev Shea and Billy at the 2004 Los Angeles Crusade. This marked the 55th anniversary of the conclusion of the historic, eight-week "Canvas Cathedral" tent revival in Los Angeles.

Billy and Ruth in their home in Montreat, North Carolina, Christmas 2005.

Billy Graham's original home (moved and reassembled from its previous site) and Billy Graham Library and Visitor Center, located on the grounds of the Billy Graham Evangelistic Association in Charlotte, North Carolina.

The dedication ceremony for the Billy Graham Library and Visitor Center on May 31, 2007, featured (from left) former presidents George H. W. Bush and William J. Clinton, Billy and Franklin Graham, and former president James Earl Carter.

President Barack Obama meets with Billy Graham, 91,
at his home in North Carolina on April 25, 2010.

Billy speaks at his final crusade in New York, 2005.

Charles Ommanney/Getty Images

Billy Graham at his home, July 25, 2006.

The Youth Night programs had another quite visible effect on Billy Graham crusades. To accommodate the bands and such high-tech items as the JumboTron screens, the stage settings underwent radical transformation. Before Youth Nights began, the standard setting was a simple draped platform with several rows of chairs for key committee personnel, local clergy, and various dignitaries. Sometimes, in outdoor venues, a small canopy might be erected over the pulpit to protect the evangelist from sun or rain. In the new arrangement, the stage resembled those erected for major rock concerts, with a huge boxlike superstructure that stretched, with the screens and protective fencing, almost completely across the end zone of a football stadium and extended eighty feet upward. This provided protection from the elements and lent a much more theatrical air to the event. The rows of chairs for dignitaries were gone; only the few people with key roles appeared on the stage. Musicians entered through a curtain at the rear and performed before large screens that could be illuminated in dramatic ways, then lifted out of the way by cables when the performance ended. Billy Graham still spoke from a simple pulpit—a tiny, even lonely figure on a huge sound stage. Yet, as he summoned his strength and began to preach, it was easy to forget the new trappings and to remember the old days when he dominated the platform, even though that memory would have been far dimmer had his audience not been able to view him on the huge screens on each side of the stage works. As had been the case for more than a half-century of public ministry, the old evangelist was still anchored to the rock, geared to the times.

Apparently Graham's appeal to youth was not limited to Evangelical circles. In 1999 two addresses at Harvard drew capacity crowds. At the John F. Kennedy School of Government, where he spoke on "The Relevance of God in the Twenty-first Century," he received a long standing ovation from students and faculty after his address and forty-minute question-and-answer session. The demand to hear him was so great that a lottery system was used to select those allowed to attend the event. The only other person to require such a measure that year was Governor Jesse Ventura of Minnesota. During the same visit Graham spoke at Memorial Church in Harvard Yard. No lottery was used, but many students spent the night on the front steps of the church to make sure they could get seats the next morning. The Rev. Peter Gomes, a university minister and himself an unusually able and eloquent preacher, said Graham's sermon on the meaning of the cross was one of the highlights of his twenty-five-year career at Harvard. The visit received extensive positive coverage in the college newspaper, the *Harvard Crimson*, not usually regarded as an Evangelical organ.

Of all Billy Graham's efforts to encourage the spread of the Christian gospel throughout the world, it is possible that none meant more to him, or ultimately will prove to have greater impact, than the mammoth Amsterdam conferences for itinerant evangelists. The 1983 and 1986 conferences described earlier in this book, together with numerous smaller regional conferences organized along the same lines, have trained tens of thousands of evangelists from all over the world in the arts, crafts, and commitment required to fulfill their calling in an effective manner. Glowing reports from participants in these programs regarding the efficacy of this training continue to support the view that the answer to the oft-asked question, "Who will be the next Billy Graham?" is not a single towering figure, but the thousands of men and women trained by BGEA to carry on his kind of ministry, not in great stadiums or via synchronous-orbit satellite, but in the highways and byways of the world, largely unknown outside their modest spheres. It was fitting, then, that the capstone to Billy Graham's ministry was Amsterdam 2000, an expanded version of the earlier conferences.

This nine-day gathering, held in July and August 2000, involved 10,732 participants from 209 countries and territories. It was undoubtedly the most international conference in the history of the world. Three-fourths of these men and women—while women constituted only eight percent of the total, they were still present by the hundreds—were from developing nations and most of these, approximately 7000 in all, lived in the same mass dormitory in Utrecht that had been used in the earlier conferences. Once again, preference was given to evangelists in the presumed prime of their careers, between ages twenty-five and forty-five, and to those whose formal educational opportunities had been limited. The twenty-two plenary sessions featured many of the familiar luminaries—Ravi Zacharias, Billy Kim, Luis Palau, Stephen Olford, J. I. Packer, John Stott, Bill and Vonette Bright, Charles Colson, Franklin Graham, Anne Graham Lotz, and George Carey, Archbishop of Canterbury, among others. Hundreds of other Evangelical stalwarts led 130 seminars and more than 200 workshops. To his great disappointment, and certainly to that of the participants, Billy Graham himself was unable to attend, due to a setback in the treatment of his disease, now re-diagnosed as hydrocephalus, which produces Parkinson's-like symptoms. He did, however, watch the plenary sessions over the Internet, and Franklin delivered the message his father had prepared for the opening session of the conference.

In addition to the larger enrollment, Amsterdam 2000 went beyond its two predecessors by widening the scope of its concern to include elements addressed by the other BGEA-supported international conferences, Berlin and Lausanne. (See pp. 325ff. and 439ff.) Echoing the concerns of the 1966 Berlin Conference, a Church Leaders Task Group focused on ways churches might become more evangelistic and cooperate more effectively with independent evangelists. Recalling the 1974 Lausanne Conference's call for a greater sensitivity to cultural differences, a Theologians Task Group concentrated on problems encountered by evangelists trying to proclaim a uniform gospel message in a pluralistic world. A third contingent, the Strategists Task Group, focused on ways of implementing more fully Jesus' Great Commission, developing specific strategies to plant churches by the end of 2002 in each of 253 population groups designated as "unreached peoples." At the end of the conference these task groups produced what they called the "Amsterdam Declaration: A Charter for Evangelism in the 21st Century," comprising a list of fourteen pledges they urged upon those called to evangelistic ministry. Like the previous conferences, the final session of Amsterdam 2000 included a massive communion service. Richard Bewes, Rector of All Souls Church, Langham Place, London, who officiated at that service, did not exaggerate when he called it "the most internationally representative Christian service of all time."

The thousands of participants for whom Billy Graham was a legendary hero were understandably disappointed at not having a chance to see him in person. The BGEA family itself, however, suffered a greater sadness. Bob Williams, who had played a major role in all three of the Amsterdam conferences, had contracted pulmonary fibrosis, a serious lung disease, during the course of his travels for the association as director of international ministries. Although seriously restricted by this condition, Williams remained heavily involved in the planning and oversight of this last great effort, all the while wearing a special pager that would notify him the moment a lung became available for transplant. The call never came. Bob Williams, age fifty-one, died on August 7, one day after the close of Amsterdam 2000.

39

"Guard What Has Been Entrusted to You"

*Bob Williams's death was untimely, but the Graham organization had been confronted with the realities of aging and death for several years. No one had believed Billy Graham would live forever, but questions of who, if anyone, would succeed him at his passing and of what would happen to BGEA at that point had been difficult to face. Graham and some of his closest associates clearly hoped Franklin would assume the mantle as leader of the organization and perhaps even as primary evangelist, even though Franklin had expressed considerable ambivalence about taking either role. Others were less sanguine at the prospect of transferring their loyalty and devotion to a man whose style differed significantly from his father's and who, some thought, had not yet fully proved he was ready to assume such a position. And understandably, many people who had grown comfortable with a system and organization that had shown remarkable stability over more than four decades were anxious at the prospect of any significant change. As an obscure but wise philosopher once remarked, "When you start changing things, something different might happen." But when Billy Graham was diagnosed with serious progressive illness in 1992, the pressure to attend to BGEA's future began to mount, as it became increasingly clear that "someday" was, unavoidably, now at hand. Inevitably, Franklin Graham edged closer to center stage and the spotlight he had never seemed to crave.

Franklin had been ordained in 1982, but he doubted the pulpit would be a major focus of his ministry, and he clearly did not aspire to follow in his father's footsteps as a crusade evangelist. In 1983, while he was assisting at a crusade in Saskatoon, Saskatchewan, led by BGEA associate evangelist John Wesley White, White persuaded him to preach one evening. When not a single person in the crowd of approximately 1,000 responded to the invitation, Franklin was devastated. "Don't you ever ask me to do that again," he told White. "I'm not Billy Graham." He was serious. Not until 1989 did he

*"Guard what has been entrusted to you" (I Timothy 6:20 NRSV).

preach in another crusade and then only after strong urging from his friend, hunting companion, motorcycle buddy, and born-again country guitar picker Dennis Agajanian, who gave him a rifle as an added inducement to join White in a crusade in Juneau, Alaska. The first effort in Juneau was hardly more successful than the Saskatoon outing. As Franklin told the story, only nine people came forward, and four of them were Dennis Agajanian's friends. "He wanted to make sure that somebody went up," Franklin recalled. "I didn't find out about that until several years later. I asked him, 'Dennis, why in the world would you do that? If God is in this and we try to manipulate the invitation, God will curse us. He won't bless us.' "

A night or two later, Franklin used one of his father's favorite sermons, and the unmanipulated response to that one was much better. Franklin took this as a sign. "I realized that I had nothing to do with that. That was the Holy Spirit of God touching the lives of these people. They were responding to God's invitation. I went back to my room that night and said, 'God, if this is something you want me to do, I'll be glad to do it. I will make it the number one priority in my life and I will do it as long as you will allow me to do it, but I will need your help.' " While he had no intention of shortchanging his work at Samaritan's Purse, Franklin pledged to devote one-tenth of his time to evangelistic preaching and was soon holding eight to ten crusades around the world each year, at first alternating with John Wesley White and later as sole preacher, to progressively larger crowds.

The success of these crusades surprised no one more than Franklin Graham himself. In 1994 he told Ken Garfield of the *Charlotte Observer* that he had avoided evangelistic preaching, because "I didn't want to be compared to Daddy. There is enough pressure in life. I didn't need that one." And even with five years of preaching under his belt, he said, "It's not that I want Daddy's mantle. The Lord in heaven called me to do it."

Although convinced of his own call, Franklin understood that many people had come to hear him, at least during the early years of his evangelistic ministry, to see how he stacked up against his famous father. "I don't know if I can avoid comparisons," he admitted. "Billy Graham is my father. I'm his son." But, he added, "I love my father. How can you be tired of being compared to someone you love and admire so much?" He frequently told his audiences that "because I am the son of Billy Graham, that did not impress God one bit," but he realized it might impress others, so when he conducted a campaign in Australia in 1996, billboards proclaimed that "Over 40 years with Billy Graham makes him worth hearing." The family resemblance is clearly there, with the strong, classic features and piercing, direct gaze. His preaching style is nothing like his father's early, spellbinding, Gatling-gun delivery, but it had been decades since Billy's own preaching, tamed by television, had borne much resemblance to the impassioned oratory that took him to fame in the 1950s.

Franklin calls his campaigns "festivals" instead of "crusades," explaining that "a crusade is not something unchurched people understand. What does that mean? A crusade for what? People understand festivals. You have beer festivals, art festivals, and music festivals. Albuquerque has a balloon festival. I would rather have a name that, if we're going to publicize something in the community, people will say, 'Well, sure, if there's going to be a festival, I will be there.' I majored in marketing. This is a way to attract people. You don't want to turn people off. You want them to taste your product." His festivals certainly have music and perhaps a few balloons, and JumboTron screens flash with video clips aimed at holding his audience's attention, but the product they are invited to taste is hardly all milk and honey.

While his services often resemble the Youth Nights in his father's crusades, he is quick to note the differences. Shortly before Billy Graham's Greater Louisville Crusade in June 2001, Franklin observed that "Daddy's Youth Nights are a little more edgy than mine. We have had some discussions about that. It is not so much Daddy as it is the people around him that are pushing him in that direction. I think they have pushed Daddy a little too far. I know he has felt uncomfortable, and his board has felt uncomfortable. *I* have felt uncomfortable. For me, Billy Graham is a standard, and when Billy Graham does something, we're saying to the churches of America, 'This is okay,' and churches will say, 'Billy Graham is doing it, so we can do it too.' Some of these groups, you can't understand them, and I'm thinking, 'Why do I want them?' They make a noise. A crusade or festival should not be there solely to entertain. We should have good music, which is part of the magnet that helps attract people, but it has to be music that's focusing on what we want. If we lose that, if we bring groups that are just doing a gig, I don't want them. The key is having everything point to the cross—your music, your musicians, everything—so that when I stand up to preach, the platform has been set. Everything has to focus toward the Lord Jesus Christ and preparing people for that invitation."

When he preaches, Franklin speaks directly and with authority. He has a good sense of humor, but relies little on jokes or other devices many preachers use to seduce and hold an audience. Instead, he moves quickly into the heart of his rather short sermons, identifying sins by name and warning that death and hell are their consequence, declaring what God has done through his Son to repair the breach between himself and fallen humanity, and calling on his audiences to repent at the foot of the cross, ask for the needed and promised forgiveness, and accept Christ as Lord of their lives. Whereas his father told of other people who rebelled against God, Franklin draws on his own biography. "For years I didn't want Jesus Christ in my life," he confesses. "I ran from him. I was afraid if I gave my life to him I'd have a spiritual straitjacket all my life. I wanted to be free. I wanted to make myself happy. There was a lot of fun, no question, but there was an emptiness. There was a big hole in the middle of Franklin Graham."

Accounts of wickedness overcome have long been a staple of evangelistic preaching, but Franklin's message of rebellion fired by emptiness obviously strikes a chord with his audiences, heavily populated with "baby boomers" and their offspring. Their awareness that Franklin was indeed a bit of a rebel—even if smoking, drinking, and driving fast do not hold the top positions in everyone's list of sins—provides an authentic touch. This image is undergirded by his having Dennis Agajanian, Ricky Skaggs, and other tough-looking contemporary musicians open his programs and his own habit of preaching in jeans, boots, a black leather jacket, and a Harley-Davidson baseball cap. ("I dress this way not because it's an image. I just enjoy it. When I was at the White House ... I wore a suit. I know when to put a tie on.") Most of his listeners also know that Franklin actually rides a Harley, flies his own plane into dangerous regions and dodges artillery fire and snipers' bullets in his work with Samaritan's Purse, and once famously cut down a tree with more than 700 rounds from an assault rifle. The combination of being both William Franklin Graham III and Franklin Graham, Rebel with a Cause and Christian Soldier of Fortune, has powerful appeal, and Franklin has used his legacy, his license, and his liberty to good effect, drawing ever larger crowds to his services.

As Billy Graham's medical problems continued their slow but inexorable course, the need to think seriously and concretely about the future of BGEA became more pressing. Franklin's expanding ministry, both in the pulpit and with Samaritan's Purse, had improved his stature among organization stalwarts and generated increasing speculation that he would eventually take the reins. According to *Time*, Ruth Graham "became increasingly vocal in her belief that Franklin should eventually be his father's successor." Franklin apparently also thought it possible and reportedly broached the subject with his father early in 1995. Apparently the elder Graham was not ready to make a decision. Some accounts say he "rebuffed" his son's inquiry. Franklin said only that, while it was plausible that he might one day head BGEA, "[my father] didn't say it to *me*." Neither did he say it to anyone else, at least publicly. However, the option to remain noncommittal would soon be taken from him by circumstances beyond his control.

In conversations among BGEA insiders, some words serve as shorthand for signal moments in Billy Graham's ministry: The Canvas Cathedral, Harringay, Madison Square Garden, Berlin, Lausanne, Amsterdam. For less glorious reasons, Toronto joined that list in June 1995. At a standard appearance before a large civic club on the day before a crusade was scheduled to begin at Toronto's Sky Dome, Graham collapsed, felled by a bleeding colon. From his hospital bed he asked T. W. Wilson to contact Franklin and ask him to take his place in the pulpit at the opening service. What followed is variously described, depending on one's place in the audience, backstage, or among the dramatis personae, as a series of innocent misunderstandings, an unattractive struggle for power, or, less darkly, a mirthless comedy of errors.

Wilson called Ruth Graham, who called Franklin and told him his father was ill and wanted him to preach in his stead. Franklin had returned from Rwanda the day before, and his plane was being serviced. But he quickly arranged for a substitute and, with his wife and a daughter, flew to Montreat the next morning to pick up Ruth, then headed for Toronto. Before leaving, Franklin had called his sister Anne Lotz and asked her to pray for him. Concerned about their father and also recognizing the symbolic significance of having her brother step into the famed evangelist's shoes in a major international setting with the spotlight at full wattage, Anne booked a flight and arrived in Toronto in mid-afternoon. Not long after she checked into her hotel, she received a call from a distraught Franklin, who told her he had just been informed that he would not be preaching that evening. Instead, associate evangelist Ralph Bell, an Ontario native, would fill in for their father. The decision had been made that morning, but no one had told Franklin when he was met at the airport. "My mother went straight to the hospital to see Daddy," Franklin recalled, "and I went to the hotel room to work on my notes. About 5:00 o'clock—two hours after BGEA issued a press release naming Bell as the speaker for that evening—one of Daddy's aides dropped by my room and said, 'Franklin, I've got to talk to you.'"

Anne was furious and demanded to know who was responsible for this turn of events. Franklin wasn't sure, but gave her the names of the people he presumed were involved. The basic outlines of what happened next are not in much dispute. Anne and Franklin had emotional meetings with their father, with members of the crusade committee, and with key BGEA personnel, including Rick Marshall, who was directing the Toronto crusade. Anne and Franklin thought it important that their father's wishes be honored; Marshall and the committee contended that Billy Graham crusades had always been characterized as local events and therefore the local committee should have the final say in such matters. The committee refused to change its decision but would allow Franklin to "bring a greeting" from his father and give a brief report on his mission to Rwanda. They would get back to him the next day about whether he could preach at subsequent services. That evening Franklin used his allotted time to give a quite brief evangelistic message rather than a report on Rwanda, and Ralph Bell preached as planned. The next morning, when representatives of the crusade committee tried to reach Franklin to tell him they wanted Bell to preach at the remaining services as well, they learned that he had already flown back to North Carolina.

Beneath that consensus view of the known facts lie several conflicting explanations and attributions of motive. It appears that the Canadian committee did make the decision to ask Ralph Bell to fill in for Billy Graham and, when pressed by the younger Grahams, stood by their decision. Why they did so is less clear. Although Bell is a Canadian and had filled in for Graham on other occasions, some insiders doubt the local committee was even aware of that and assert that BGEA representatives must have suggested him to the local committee. They also note that John Wesley White is a Canadian but was apparently not mentioned as a candidate for the task, perhaps because he was known as one of Franklin's staunchest advocates. That the push for Bell as Billy's replacement came from inside BGEA also fits with a report that the chairman of the local committee claimed not to have known of Billy Graham's wish until he met with Anne and Franklin.

Those who feel the decision to go with Bell was at least defensible point to BGEA's tradition of local control of the crusades, but they also speculate that both Rick Marshall and the local committee probably felt it unwise, after long months of extensive and expensive preparation, to turn Billy Graham's pulpit over to a relatively unseasoned evangelist, even if he did have his father's name, genes, and blessing. Franklin and those who take his side have a less sanguine view. Franklin questioned both the behavior and motive of those who had countered his father's request. He and Anne certainly understood the potential symbolic power involved in picking up his fallen father's mantle at an event already making international news because of Billy's collapse. "That's what some people were afraid of," he said. "I was honored that my father wanted me to preach, that he thought I was ready to fill in for him. I don't think my father's crusade directors were loyal to him. That is what he asked for, and they didn't support him."

In an interview not long after that event, Franklin showed his awareness that religious organizations, even those with the finest reputations, are not immune to the forces that characterize "worldly" organizations. Noting that control of BGEA's $90-million annual budget could provide significant incentive to those wanting to shape the organization's—and their own—future, he said, "Listen, people will shoot you for $20. For $90 million, who knows?"

It is worth noting that no one believed Ralph Bell had a hand in stirring the pot, and Anne has said that Bell encouraged her to try to persuade the committee to let Franklin preach. By all accounts, Bell acquitted himself admirably, in and out of the pulpit, throughout this trying time, preaching to huge crowds each of the first three nights. Billy Graham recovered sufficiently to preach at the last two services.

Franklin's family and friends worried about the impact this would have on him. Years later, both Anne and Franklin acknowledged that she had displayed more open outrage than he, and she speculated that perhaps both her presence and anger had been providential. "Franklin handled it so well," she said, "but I feel like maybe God had me there to go with him, and that for me to be outraged helped him. He was concerned with calming me down, so maybe I was able to vent some of the anger he felt and also stand by him." Less angry than concerned, BGEA photographer Russ Busby sat down with Franklin a few days later and told him, "I don't know what happened, but there is one thing you need to consider. What really matters is what happens inside us. Don't let this turn you bitter against God or anyone else. Make sure in your own heart that you've got it worked out. Because that's where the problem could lie."

For a time, Franklin insisted that he did not know the details of the Toronto affair, that he never wanted to learn them, and further, that it really didn't matter. But years later, in a softer mood, he acknowledged, "There have been politics for a number of years in BGEA. And at some point there were people who worked very hard—I won't say against me, but they certainly didn't work for me." He recalled a widely publicized dispute between Samaritan's Purse and the Evangelical Council for Financial Accountability in 1992. Questioned by the watchdog group for some of his organization's accounting practices and for his personal use of the company plane, Franklin withdrew Samaritan's Purse from the ECFA in April 1992, dismissing the investigation as the work of "crummy little Evangelical busybodies" who were jealous of his success. He insisted that "[ECFA] cannot hold up one piece of paper, not one document, and say, 'This is where we got him.' They can't do it." Whatever problems existed were cleared up quickly, and Samaritan's Purse membership in ECFA was reinstated in January 1993. Two years later, the organization's president dismissed it as "a bump in the road. And now it's gone." Looking back, Franklin saw it as part of an effort to sidetrack his ascension to leadership of BGEA. "That whole thing with ECFA," he said, was all political. It was an effort by some people to tarnish Franklin. " 'We don't want to destroy him, but let's taint him so that he's not in the running, so that his credibility is blackened a little bit.' "

The awkwardness and tension generated by the turmoil in Toronto forced Billy Graham to recognize that, by leaving questions of succession and leadership unresolved, he ran the risk of having members of his team, long noted for its harmony and relative lack of infighting, split into factions that could undercut its effectiveness after he passed from the scene. This would hurt not only the organization he had led for nearly half a century but the entire Evangelical world. A few months later, Graham took action. First, he joined Franklin in a father-and-son crusade in Saskatoon, which coincided with the publication of Franklin's autobiography, *Rebel with a Cause: Finally Comfortable with Being Graham*. That symbolic joint lifting of the torch was followed shortly afterward, on November 7, by the BGEA board's electing Franklin to the newly created position of first vice-chairman, "with direct succession to become chairman and CEO should his father ever become incapacitated." Billy Graham retained his position as chairman of the association, but Franklin gradually took increased responsibility and in November 2000 was officially named CEO. John Corts remained as president and continued to oversee the Minneapolis operation on a day-to-day basis, but Franklin began to spend more time at the headquarters and to take a real leadership role. In January 2002, Corts retired, and Franklin assumed the additional role of BGEA president.

Not long after it became clear that Franklin would eventually head the ministry, a BGEA veteran advised him to "keep one thing in mind. Most of the people in the Minneapolis office honestly believe, and I believe with them, that they have given their lives to your father's ministry and, through that, to God. Don't lose sight of that. Whatever differences you may have with them, keep in mind that they really have dedicated their lives to your father's ministry and to God's work." Franklin appeared to have heard that counsel, volunteering that "with BGEA we have a leadership that is older and retiring. I'm coming in and trying not to step on toes and slowly trying to fit in."

Those who knew Franklin best recognized the potential for friction, because of both his new authority and his old personality. Soon after he was named Vice-Chairman and Successor, a cousin, Mel Graham, observed that "the handful that would resist Franklin clearly see him as a threat. Uncle Billy has got a lot more timid, a lot more easygoing here in his later years. And Franklin is a man of action. If somebody's chain needs to be jerked, he'll jerk it." No one doubts that Franklin is more direct and less averse to conflict than was his father, but most observers gave him high marks—improving significantly over time—for his sensitivity both to his father's continuing position as the dominant figure in the association and to the predictable anxiety felt by people about possible changes in the roles they had occupied for decades, and perhaps even about how secure their positions would be in a new regime.

One BGEA staffer attributed what difficulty existed not only to normal resistance to change on the part of entrenched team veterans, but also to Billy Graham's reluctance to cede control even in the face of clearly diminished abilities. "We have a relay race, and the guy who created the baton and has been carrying it for fifty years has come to the point where he ought to hand it off, but he wants to take another lap. That has been a problem. Some of the people who are extremely loyal to him and to the ways we have always done things want to point out everything that Franklin is going to do or trying to do or thought about doing or mentioned in an elevator, and when they bring it up to Billy, he says he is not sure about that. But when you pin him down, he says, 'Sure, that's what I want to do.' I think eventually it is going to work out fine, but has it been a model transition? No. I think everybody would say that."

Russ Busby also acknowledged Billy Graham's difficulty in passing the baton, but felt he had loosened his grip sufficiently by mid-2001 to effect a relatively smooth transfer. "It took a little bit of time, but I think God has given Mr. Graham peace about this. I think he has peace about Franklin's motives for preaching. They are not, from my viewpoint, self-serving. I don't think he's ever wanted to run the Billy Graham Association. He's got his own organization. But in the present situation, someone needs to take over. I think Billy also had some concern as to whether Franklin was ready for it. And when it is your own son, you want to make sure this is right, that you are not pushing your son into a place God has not prepared for him. In my mind, that would have been Billy's biggest concern. I think he has peace about that now. I also think God has worked in Franklin's life and accomplished what needed to be done there for him to take over. In my mind, God has put his stamp of approval on Franklin."

Without a doubt, the spectacular growth and success of Samaritan's Purse greatly enhanced Franklin's standing in the Evangelical world and helped convince skeptics that he had the ability to run BGEA. In fiscal year 2001, Samaritan's Purse income topped $179 million, including nearly $24 million from its Canadian affiliate. This outstripped BGEA revenues by approximately $62 million, a bracing response to those who feared that Franklin would never be able to attract the financial support that had come to his father. Audited statements revealed that 91 percent of Samaritan's Purse income was expended on ministry, an admirably high proportion for any nonprofit organization. The organization's facilities are extensive, modern, and comfortable, but neither lavish nor designed to draw attention to or pay homage to their leader. Located several miles from Boone, North Carolina, the complex is not only rather difficult to find, but has no signage to indicate one has arrived.

A visit to the ministry's website (*www.samaritanspurse.org*) reveals the impressive range and scope of its efforts to bring relief and support for people in need around the world. In the wake of hurricanes, earthquakes, and tsunamis in Central America, Turkey, India, Indonesia, and the U.S. Gulf Coast, Samaritan's Purse has airlifted emergency supplies such as food, blankets, and temporary shelters, then followed up by building thousands of durable one-room homes — a project so impressive that the U.S. government AID program funneled money through the organization to build additional houses. In other initiatives, the ministry has built an orphanage in Moldova; set up a big water-filtering project in Ethiopia; helped establish a silk-production industry in Laos by distributing 600,000 mulberry saplings (to provide food for silkworms) to help families increase their income; delivered planeloads of food, medicine, and supplies to homeless people in Rwanda and to refugees in Afghanistan; and dispatched hundreds of medical professionals to different parts of the world as volunteers under its medical arm, World Medical Mission. In 2012, the organization sent disaster relief units and hundreds of volunteers to help survivors of Hurricane Sandy.

Greg Laurie, a noted California evangelist and pastor and a member of the Samaritan's Purse board, observed that Franklin "will go into virtually impossible situations and get something done. He won't take no for an answer."

For several years Samaritan's Purse has been heavily involved in Sudan in response to pleas from southern Sudanese Christians who had suffered atrocities at the hands of their own countrymen, mostly northern Muslims who have killed nearly two million of them and have tortured and displaced millions more, even selling them into slavery. Flying into areas officially off-limits to international agencies, Samaritan's Purse pilots delivered emergency supplies that included bags of maize and sorghum seed (staples of the Sudanese diet), basic medical supplies, mosquito-nets dipped in natural insecticide to help ward off malaria, and tools to help refugees reestablish their lives. In 2014 the organization distributed more than 1,500 metric tons of food each month to nearly 90,000 people in refugee camps in the region. Opened in September 1997, the eighty-bed Samaritan's Purse hospital, staffed primarily by international volunteer medical professionals working for a few weeks at a time, has treated more than 100,000 patients in an area that had been without adequate medical care for more than two decades. The hospital has been bombed repeatedly, killing some personnel. Because of his organization's work in Sudan, Franklin Graham was asked to testify before the U.S. Senate Foreign Relations Committee, where he called on the United States to join with other world powers to bring down what he regarded as "an illegitimate government."

In February 2002 Franklin took on a significant—and to some, surprising—challenge when to date when Samaritan's Purse, in cooperation with BGEA and at a cost of $2.3 million, organized "Prescription for Hope," an international Christian conference on HIV/AIDS that drew more than 900 frontline AIDS workers, church and government leaders, and medical providers from 87 countries to Washington D.C. During the five days of the conference—which featured such speakers as Senators Jesse Helms (R-N.C.) and Bill Frist (R-Tenn.) and the First Lady of Uganda, Janet Museveni—Franklin called on Christians to show "Christ-like care and compassion for the infected and affected." This was not simply an attention-grabbing venture. Since 2002, Samaritan's Purse has worked with AIDS patients and their families in more than forty-two countries. In another bold effort to fight a deadly epidemic, Samaritan's Purse attracted international acclaim in 2014 when its extensive efforts to combat the Ebola outbreak in Liberia led to its being named, along with a small number of other organizations, as *Time* magazine's Person of the Year.

Interestingly, and in contrast to these dramatic, often life-saving efforts, a program that began in 1993 as a heart-warming little venture to brighten a few children's lives at Christmas time has become Samaritan's Purse's largest program, at least from a budgetary standpoint. The program, known as Operation Christmas Child, is simple in its essence. Donors, mostly children from affluent Western countries, pack a shoebox with candy, small toys, school supplies, and perhaps a pair of socks or mittens and send it to Boone along with nine dollars to cover shipping costs. After being checked at large processing centers in Boone and Charlotte to make sure they contain no inappropriate items such as food that might spoil or dangerous or inappropriate toys, the boxes are securely wrapped, then packed with others for eventual distribution to children in countries ravaged by war, poverty, or natural disasters. Imagining the delight in the eyes of a child in Albania or Zimbabwe as she opens her little box has proved irresistible, as has the opportunity to have one's own children and grandchildren feel some connection with and responsibility for those less fortunate. In the weeks before Christmas 2016, Samaritan's Purse planes and trucks delivered more than 11.5 million shoeboxes to distribution points in 104 countries. The total cost of Operation Christmas Child for that year topped $281 million, over 54 percent of total expenses for the combined U.S. and Canadian organizations. One might argue that this substantial amount of money could be used to meet more vital needs, but most of it is generated by the program itself and would probably not otherwise be available. Perhaps more importantly, hundreds of thousands of families who might not think of giving money to buy wood stoves or water filters or mulberry saplings will form a bond with an organization that *has* thought about such things.

Throughout the growth of this ministry Franklin has insisted that his efforts at social amelioration are subordinate to evangelism. "Our goal and our purpose," he asserted, "is to take an ugly situation and turn it around so we can preach the Lord Jesus Christ—not in a crusade environment or a mass rally, but one on one, in small groups. People will listen out of respect—'I am interested that you would come all the way from America to my corner of the world. You are here and you helped me. I am interested in who you are and what you believe.' Our being there in those circumstances generates a sincere interest. We planted over a hundred churches in Kosovo alone." His obvious success at both kinds of ministry has drawn real admiration from within BGEA, including the admission that "when you think about it, his ministry is really more complete than his father's ... and that's good." There is also a recognition by some that many contemporary young people are attracted more strongly by a demonstrated commitment to relieve human suffering than by a passionate proclamation of original sin or substitutionary atonement.

One of the fears expressed by and for the generation of Evangelical leaders reaching the end of their careers at the close of the twentieth century was that their successors, having grown up in times of affluence and relative ease and having experienced Evangelicalism as a significant part of the cultural mainstream rather than a marginal movement fighting for respectability, would be too soft, too willing to compromise with "the world," too willing to water down their message to gain popularity. Ironically, despite his early wildness, Franklin Graham seems not only firmly committed to a quite conservative view of Scripture and Evangelical theology, but also more willing than his father to condemn both sin and sinners in blunt, unyielding terms. In this respect, as one observer noted, he is more like the young Billy Graham than the older one and may even be more like that earlier notable exponent of "muscular Christianity," Billy Sunday. "I want to confront you in love," Franklin has said, "But I'm warning you that there's a hell and there's a heaven, and your soul lives for eternity. [God] has a standard, and that standard doesn't change.... [I]f you continue this behavior, you may die, and your soul will be separated from God for eternity."

Franklin certainly says things his father probably would not have said after becoming a national and international figure. He exhorted a 1999 Wheaton College graduation class not to "lower the flag" by being "tolerant of people who live in sin," and was clearly willing to follow his own admonition. His father surprised many during the Monica Lewinsky scandal by saying, on NBC's *Today* show, "I forgive [President Clinton] ... because I know the frailty of human nature and I know how hard it is—especially a strong, vigorous young man like he is.... He has such a tremendous personality that I think the ladies just go wild over him." In contrast, Franklin said flatly, "A lie is a sin, and sex outside marriage is a sin. It doesn't matter if you're the president of the United States or Franklin Graham or a busboy in a hotel." He didn't deny the reality of temptation, but felt it could be avoided by following the same rules that had helped his father avoid scandal for so many years: "I will never be alone with another woman or travel with my secretary alone," he told a radio interviewer. "I'll always make sure there are other people with me." As for Bill Clinton, Franklin said, "For the sake of the country, the best thing he can do is quietly resign. Let Al Gore pardon him and get it off the front pages and into history."

In the same spirit, Franklin differed with Evangelicals who had given positive reviews to Robert Duvall's movie *The Apostle.* Franklin told his Wheaton audience, "When Hollywood portrays the Church of Jesus Christ as immoral, no, don't you tell me this is a great film. No way. Hollywood portrays a minister of God's Word as a murderer, a womanizer, a drinker, bringing the level of the pastor of the Church of Jesus Christ down to the level of trash." On the other hand, Franklin brought Jim Bakker to his father's home for Sunday dinner the weekend after the disgraced evangelist got out of jail, and he continued to act in a supportive fashion, in keeping with his belief that God not only condemns sin but also forgives it. Bakker, incidentally, had a more favorable view of Duvall's movie, seeing it as "the story of a man who did a terrible thing, but his heart, like David's, was toward God.... Either we believe in grace or we don't. So I have to accept the grace in that story."

Franklin also sounded harder than his father on other "sins of the flesh." To the consternation of many conservative and abstemious Christians, Billy Graham freely acknowledged that Jesus and his companions drank wine, that the Bible does not command total abstinence, and that he occasionally lifted a glass himself. Franklin, a former drinker, draws a sharper line: "The world says, 'You want to drink? That's great. Just be responsible [and] have a designated driver.' No, it's not OK. It's wrong. It's a sin." When asked his opinion of American drug policy, he said, "I think that people who sell drugs—I'm not talking about people who use it, but about those who traffic in it—I think they ought to be executed. They are killing and destroying lives. They are no different than Timothy McVeigh. You want to stop drugs? Then [make it clear,] 'You deal in it, you get caught, you pay with your life, because you are taking lives. You are a murderer, a killer, a destroyer of families.' I tell you, if you get that tough, you are going to clean up the streets pretty quick." He readily acknowledged that the American drug war in South America is "crazy" and riddled with corruption, he urged enlargement of treatment programs to help people get free of drugs, and he conceded that execution might be too harsh for lower-level dealers. But, he said, "If we are serious about it, we need to be tough. We have to be a little bit meaner. We are so timid about the death penalty. For people who deal and traffic in drugs, there need to be severe, severe penalties." To discourage users, he also favored a policy that relies heavily on punishment as a deterrent: "You can cut off demand pretty quickly with laws that make it such a risk that you never, ever want to get caught with drugs. Singapore doesn't have too much of a drug problem. It's a great place to live. It's a wonderful society. It's clean, it's beautiful. A beautiful place."

Franklin's decisive, sometimes authoritarian opinions and statements may help account for his appeal to a generation grown skeptical of moral relativism. Even those not inclined to share his views may have little quarrel with his call for a more stringent sexual morality and abstention from alcohol and drugs; his approval of harsh penal sanctions obviously resonates widely throughout society, at least among white Americans. But some of his comments on international political issues have been bolder and more controversial than those of his father, who typically tried either to sidestep controversy or to express any criticism he might have of a current administration in circumspect language and muted tone.

In a 1999 interview with *Christianity Today* writer Wendy Murray Zoba, Franklin said, on the record, that the United States should not have gotten involved when Saddam Hussein invaded Kuwait in 1990. "He was just taking back what originally belonged to Iraq.... Kuwait is part of Iraq. It is." Samaritan's Purse not only provided aid to Iraq after the Gulf War, but also sent young single men into the area, hoping they would marry Christian Iraqi women and remain in the country as missionaries. (In another attempt to use the Gulf War as an opportunity for evangelism, Franklin helped U.S. troops smuggle Arabic-language New Testaments into Saudi Arabia.) Years later, after watching a video of Serbian soldiers brutalizing Bosnians in Sarajevo, Franklin said he would have had them executed. Commenting on atrocities in Sudan, he threw a combination punch, noting that "black brothers in Africa are being annihilated by the Muslims, who are Arabs.... But Jesse Jackson is silent. What is that?"

During a festival in Lexington, Kentucky, in October 2000, Franklin stirred the ire of Arab Americans when he reacted to violence in the Middle East by saying, "The Arabs will not be happy until every Jew is dead. They hate the state of Israel. They all hate the Jews. God gave that land to the Jews. The Arabs will never accept that. Why can't they live in peace?" The American-Arab Anti-Discrimination Committee immediately called on BGEA "to repudiate these shockingly racist comments which condemn each and every Arab as a genocidal bigot and suggest that Palestinians have no rights in their own country because 'God gave that land to the Jews.'" None of these provocative statements or actions is of a kind one associated with Billy Graham. In fact, in the days immediately following Franklin's statements about Arabs, the elder Graham issued a statement saying he was "praying for and supporting the efforts among leaders of both sides in the search for peace."

In a similar vein, Franklin has been more pointed than his father in claiming unique superiority for Christianity over other religions. While Billy never wavered in his effort to proclaim the acceptance of Christ as the only reliable road to salvation, he was clearly troubled by the prospect that people who had never heard the gospel message would be condemned to eternal damnation (see p. 576), and he was often at pains to avoid appearing to be an opponent or critic of other faiths, particularly the major world religions. Franklin seems untroubled by the prospect that his comments might offend some who do not share his convictions. To the familiar, if naive, question as to whether Muslims, Hindus, and Buddhists were not all serving the same God that Christians worship, he said, "It's not the same God. There's one God and he has a son, Jesus Christ. Friends, there's no other way." On another occasion, he said, "It wasn't Mohammed of Islam who died for the sins of the world. It wasn't Buddha who died for the sins of this world.... It was the Lord Jesus Christ." And after a trip to India, he marveled at "hundreds of millions of people locked in the darkness of Hinduism. It was an unbelievable eye-opener for me to see how pagan religion blinds and enslaves people. These people were bound by Satan's power."

Further, Franklin's response to the terrorist attacks of September 11, 2001, and the U.S. military campaign in Afghanistan differed sharply from his father's irenic observations. Twice, including on the *NBC Nightly News*, he called Islam "a very evil and wicked religion." Predictably, these words brought a strong response, from the Council on American-Islamic Relations (which failed to get a meeting with Franklin), but also from the president of Stop Hunger, a relief organization. Franklin backtracked slightly, noting the millions of dollars Samaritan's Purse had poured into Muslim countries and claiming he had been "greatly misunderstood." Yet in the *Wall Street Journal*, he observed that "The persecution or elimination of non-Moslems has been a cornerstone of Islamic conquest and rule for centuries," adding that the Qur'an "provides ample evidence that Islam encourages violence in order to win converts and to reach the ultimate goal of an Islamic world."

This is not to say that Franklin sees no virtue in religions other than Christianity. In discussing President George W. Bush's controversial "Faith-Based Initiative," Franklin parted company with Pat Robertson and Jerry Falwell, both of whom had said that Muslim groups should not be eligible for assistance under the proposed program. "Let's say that Muslims have a way to get kids off the street after school," he volunteered. "I may not like the fact that they're Muslims, but why should they be discriminated against? If they are doing a good job, I say thank God somebody cares enough to [help those kids]."

Franklin has also followed his father's lead in welcoming virtually all denominations, including Roman Catholics, to participate in his festivals as full partners. Still, he feels bound by conscience and calling always to make it clear that he is a minister of Jesus Christ, not a spokesman for some kind of civil religion guaranteed to offend no one. At a memorial service for the victims of the massacre at Columbine High School in Littleton, Colorado, in 1999, he asked the 70,000 mourners gathered before him and the millions more watching the live CNN broadcast, "Do you believe in the Lord Jesus Christ? Have you trusted him as your Savior?" Extolling the example of seventeen-year-old Cassie Bernall, whose confession, "Yes, I believe in God," apparently prompted Eric Harris and Dylan Klebold to kill her, making her a born-again martyr and heroine, Graham told his hearers that the only way they could be prepared to meet God should their own lives end suddenly was "to confess our sins, repent of our sins, and ask God for his forgiveness and to receive his son, Jesus Christ, by faith into our hearts and into our lives."

Not surprisingly, Franklin's use of this occasion to preach what amounted to an Evangelical sermon drew fire from several quarters. Rabbi Fred Greenspahn, chairman of the religious studies department at the University of Denver and the only non-Christian on the program, said it showed a "pretty ignorant narrow-minded streak of Christianity." He told Graham afterward that he had found his remarks "hurtful because they weren't inclusive of other religions." According to Greenspahn, "He looked at me and ignored me.... It seemed to me at that service if you weren't 'saved,' you weren't acceptable." Another rabbi said that he had felt "disenfranchised" because the service was "clearly Evangelical," adding that a service of that sort should be religiously inclusive. This one, he said, "didn't pass the smell test. It shut out a lot of people." Not all the criticism came from non-Christians. The Rev. Michael Carrier, a Presbyterian pastor and president of the Interfaith Alliance of Colorado, said, "I felt like he was trying to terrorize us into heaven instead loving us into heaven.... [This service] was supposed to be for all the people of Colorado and the nation to find solace, not an Evangelical Christian service." Franklin himself apparently had no second thoughts. Interviewed about the event a few days later, he said he had felt an "awesome responsibility" at the Columbine service "to give people a rope to hold on to. I had about five or six minutes. The families of the 13 were there looking and the whole world was watching on TV. I just wanted to tell people that there is a God, that he loves us, and that he gave his only son 2,000 years ago."

Franklin stirred a similar response in January 2001, when he led the invocation at the presidential inauguration of George W. Bush and delivered the sermon at a service the next morning in the National Cathedral. He concluded his inaugural prayer by saying, "May this be the beginning of a new dawn for America as we humble ourselves before you and acknowledge you alone as our Lord, our Savior, and our Redeemer. We pray this in the name of the Father, and of the Son, the Lord Jesus Christ, and of the Holy Spirit. Amen." At the worship service the following morning, he spoke of "Christ, whom the Bible speaks of as the source of all wisdom," and proclaimed that "it's not enough just to be moral; it's not enough just to believe in God. The Bible says in John 3 that you must be born again." He asserted his belief that God is calling America to repentance and faith and that "to repent is to acknowledge our need of the Great Physician in our lives ... and to accept his prescription for healing of our souls found in his son, Jesus Christ, and by faith receiving him into our heart and trusting him as our savior and follow him as our Lord.... Jesus said in John 14:6, "I am the way, the truth and the life. No man comes to the father but by me.... May we as a nation again place our hope and trust in the almighty God and his Son, the Lord Jesus Christ, our Savior, our Redeemer, and our Friend. May God bless you, and may God bless America."

These statements drew critical comments from Jews, Muslims, and other non-Christians, and also from Christians who felt that the inauguration—the preeminent ritual of American civil religion—should be an occasion to bring the nation together, not symbolically exclude people of different faiths or of no faith at all. When asked about what he had said and the reactions to it, Graham made it clear that his distinctly Christian statements were not the product of thoughtlessness or habit. At a rehearsal the day before the inauguration, he recalled, the Rev. Kirbyjon Caldwell, an African-American pastor from Houston who was scheduled to give the benediction, had asked him if he planned to pray in the name of Jesus. "I said, 'Absolutely. Yes sir. This isn't a platform I have sought. I think God has put me here, and I think it would be wrong not to pray in the name of the Lord Jesus.' And he said, 'Good. I'll do it too.'" And he did. Caldwell drew even more fire than Graham when he closed his benediction with the words, "We respectfully submit this humble prayer in the name that's above all other names, Jesus the Christ. Let all who agree say 'Amen.'"

Picking up a Bible during this interview, Graham continued, "The President put his hand on the Bible. Is he excluding Muslims because he doesn't have the Qur'an? Or how about the Hindu Book of the Dead? How long does the list have to be? Did he exclude all of these and other Americans because he had his hand on the Holy Bible? The President is a Methodist—a born-again Methodist—a Christian who wants to have a Christian prayer to open the inauguration and a Christian benediction to close it. It is his inauguration. He is a Christian. Because the United States voted for a Methodist, did we exclude the Jews because [vice presidential candidate U.S. Sen. Joseph] Lieberman didn't get elected? Come on! Why fault me because, as a Christian, I invoke the name of the Lord Jesus Christ, the Son of the living God?" My Father in heaven prepared me for that moment, and I wasn't about to sell out his Son Jesus Christ because of what people might say. I'm a minister of the gospel. If you don't want me mentioning the name of the Lord Jesus Christ, don't invite me. That's just the way I feel."

Billy Graham made pointedly Christian statements and led Trinitarian prayers in public for decades without stirring much notice, but Billy Graham was an icon, and he achieved iconic status when America was a far less diverse nation than at the beginning of the twenty-first century. Franklin's form of insistent Evangelicalism has kept him from assuming his father's mantle as Chaplain to the Nation. Though seen as a major spokesman for Evangelical Christianity, Franklin recognizes that at such occasions as the Columbine memorial service and the inauguration, he served as a stand-in for his incapacitated father, and he professed not to care about assuming the role of the People's Pastor. "That is not something I want to do," he said. "If the President asked, I would go to something, but I don't see myself being the kind of figure my father was. This is not a role I want. I have enough roles right now. Managing Samaritan's Purse and BGEA is enough." Franklin did, however, make a quick round trip to Philadelphia during Amsterdam 2000 just to give the closing prayer on opening night of the Republican National Convention. (The official convention website, incidentally, posted the text of his prayer but did not include the closing line, "We ask this tonight in the precious name of thy Son, the Lord Jesus Christ.")

Russ Busby expressed what seemed to be the emerging assessment of Franklin's fitness for the challenging position he inherited. "God prepares new people for new times," he said, "and I think he has prepared Franklin. After being around him for many years and traveling with him and being in all of his meetings in the last three or four years, I have seen God working in his life. No one can replace Mr. Graham. Franklin is different from his father, so a few things will be different. That's what causes all of us to get a little apprehensive. But Franklin has a heart for God, and it shows. And the more you are around him and hear his message and talk to people and see him out with Samaritan's Purse—really down with the people, wanting to help, so that ultimately he can present God's love to them through Jesus Christ—you can see that he is real."

Franklin's standing with long-term BGEA supporters has doubtless been enhanced by his increasing success as an evangelist, in the United States and internationally. Although his festivals in the U.S. have not matched those of his father's crusades, they have typically attracted tens of thousands in cities such as Mobile, New Orleans, Baltimore, and Norfolk. Far larger crowds have flocked to his meetings in other countries, with aggregate attendance of 71,000 in Montevideo, Uruguay; 76,000 in Timisoara, Romania; 93,000 in Moldova in 2005; 112,000 in Villahermosa, Mexico; 186,000 in Ecuador in 2006; 183,000 in Taipei; and 317,600 in Manila. And in 2008, Franklin obtained permission to visit Pyongyang, North Korea, where he met with both religious and political leaders and preached in one of the city's two Protestant churches.Such results reassure those who may have feared that Franklin's commitment to Samaritan's Purse might cause him to neglect the public evangelism that was the heart of his father's ministry. And those taking an even longer view are surely heartened by the knowledge that Franklin's oldest son, Will—a pastor in Raleigh, North Carolina, and a graduate of Jerry Falwell's Liberty University—has laid claim to the family mantle. In 2006, Will held his first large "Celebration" in the U.S. in Gastonia, N.C. (He had previously held a similar mission in Barrie, Ontario, in 2004.) He preached to overflow crowds and saw more than 300 people respond to the invitation. Fittingly, as a sign of patriarchal blessing, his choir leader for the event was Cliff Barrows. Will seasoned quickly, leading successful evangelistic outreaches in several states and in South America, Australia, and India. By 2013, he was a full-fledged BGEA Associate Evangelist and Executive Director of the Billy Graham Training Center at the Cove.

40

"Having Faithful Children"

*Franklin Graham's emergence as a respected evangelist and Christian leader surprised many who had watched him grow up. Middle sister Anne Morrow also seemed an unlikely candidate for public ministry, not because she ever displayed a wild streak, but because she professed to be terrified of speaking to any sort of audience and, more importantly, because she had been groomed to be a Southern Christian Woman in the Southern Baptist Church.

After marrying Danny Lotz when she was eighteen, with the expectation of following her mother's example as a full-time wife and mother, Anne went through years of infertility and miscarriages before finally giving birth to three children, a son and two daughters. Instead of feeling fulfilled, she felt "immersed in small talk and small toys and small clothes and small, sticky fingerprints.... I felt trapped.... My whole life was small." She struggled through bouts of depression and guilt over feelings of inadequacy. Trying to fathom how her own mother had maintained such a relentlessly positive disposition while spending much of her life as essentially a single mother of five, Anne recalled the many times she had gone into Ruth's room and found her with an open Bible on her lap or kneeling in prayer by the side of her bed. "My mother raised five of us, and I never saw her lose her temper. And I knew she drew that kind of strength from her time in Scripture and her time in prayer, and I wasn't doing that."

Finally, in 1976, to meet her need for intellectual stimulation and spiritual nourishment, Anne organized a Bible class for women, using guidelines furnished by an international organization called Bible Study Fellowship. She didn't realize when she filled out an application for the program that she was expected to become the teacher. Hundreds of women signed up, probably assuming that Billy Graham's daughter was bound to be an experienced instructor. "They didn't know I couldn't teach," she said. "I'd never taught Sunday school or anything in my life. It was totally contrary to my personality. Surely God wouldn't call me outside of my personality—yet he did! He called me to do something I didn't have a clue that I had a gift for."

*"Having faithful children" (Titus 1:6 KJV).

Anne admits that her parents had mixed feelings about her undertaking such a demanding role. "It wasn't so much my daddy," she said, "as my mother. Her call in life was to stay at home and raise us, to free up Daddy to do what he has done, and I think in her mind she transferred that to a Christian woman's role—a Christian wife stays at home and raises the children and serves the husband, so he can be free to serve the Lord in whatever capacity. That was her mind-set, even though she had a mother who was very strong, who ran the nurses clinic in China and did a lot outside the home. I think Mother felt I had to devote all my time to raising my children, cleaning and cooking and that kind of thing, because that's what she had done." That changed within the first year, after Billy and Ruth showed up at the class unannounced as a birthday surprise for Anne. "I didn't know they were coming until I stood up in class that day and looked out and there they were. I don't like surprises like that, but as a result, Mother was able to see me in a normal week, to see that my children were happy and well behaved, my house was clean, and I had a wonderful meal on the table. She and Daddy were thrilled at the class itself as they saw 500 women with their Bibles opened, taking notes, and they saw the seriousness of the commitment. They just sensed God's presence in that place. And just like that, their attitude totally changed and they knew this was of God. I can't tell you how supportive they were after that."

The classes were nondenominational and included women from approximately 120 churches, but they met at the Hayes Barton Baptist Church, Anne's home church. After nine years of sustained success, church leaders asked her to take her classes elsewhere. While acknowledging that "there were other things going on, swirling around underneath, as is usually the case," she felt the primary reason for the church's action was her strong view of biblical inerrancy. Since the late 1970s, the Southern Baptist Convention has been embroiled in controversy between a hard-line conservative faction that insists that the Bible is divinely inspired, even to the precise words in the original manuscripts (which no longer exist), and entirely free of error, and a more moderate faction that allows for somewhat greater latitude in interpretation. "I do believe with all my heart that the Scriptures are true," Anne explained. The Hayes Barton church, she said, was "aligned with that side of the convention that takes a more liberal view. I think because they knew how I felt, they believed I would be aligned with the more conservative side of the convention, and they didn't want that identification."

Scarcely missing a beat, Anne moved her class—and her church membership—to Providence Baptist Church in Raleigh and continued to teach the class there until 1988. At that point, her reputation as a speaker had generated so many invitations that she felt she could no longer continue the task of teaching the class and "discipling" the sixty-five assistant teachers who led the discussion groups. "It was like pastoring a church," she said. She also knew the class could continue without her. The Providence class continues at full strength—Bible Study Fellowship insists on a limit of 500 women—and has spawned several more classes of similar size in Raleigh.

Freed from the class, Anne founded AnGeL ministries, using her initials as pillars and filling in with her view of angels. "Angels in the Bible," she explained, "were messengers of God, and they went where God sent them and gave the message He put on their heart. I felt that describes what I do." The prime message on Anne Lotz's heart is the need for revival in the churches, even in the South, even in a city where thousands of women engage in regular Bible study.

"Many people still go to church in the South," Anne acknowledged, "unlike Seattle and some of these other places, but I feel like a lot of it is cultural. On Sunday, you go to church. That's where you meet your friends, dress up, and maybe have a special lunch afterwards. A lot of your social life is rooted in the church. It is just part of the way we live in the South. Yet many people sitting in church, going through all the ceremonies and traditions and rituals, don't have a personal relationship with God. I get frustrated even with professing Christians. They add Jesus to their lives, but when it comes to a choice and they would have to give up something—whether it is vacation time, time with their families, a social event, or a club membership, or even a friendship—they don't choose to put Christ first. He's not that important to them. And that's why we're not passing our faith on to the next generation, because if you treat Jesus as if He's not important enough to make a sacrifice for, your kids—I don't care what you teach them—pick up on that and it's not only as if He's not important; it's as if He doesn't even exist.

"I think our culture across the board is deteriorating morally and spiritually. We can point our finger at the politicians and the media, but I would point my finger at church. If we had kept our focus and were transmitting real faith in Christ, if He were preeminent in every person's life who professes to be a Christian, so that we live only for Him and He dictates what we think, what we see, where we go, what we do, I don't think our country would be in the shape it is in. In [II Chronicles 7:14], God promised Solomon that when things are not going right in your country, 'If my people which are called by my name will humble themselves and pray and seek my face and turn from their wicked ways, then I will hear from heaven and I will forgive their sins and will heal their land.' So the believer's faith and relationship with God directly impacts the land. But even if it makes no impact on America, I feel like the church needs to be what God has called us to be. I believe God has called me to do whatever I can to help professing Christians refocus on the person of Jesus Christ and His preeminence in their lives."

As her reputation grew, Anne had many opportunities to speak at churches, retreats, and conferences, but grew frustrated that her call for revival was often lost amid the clutter of announcements and business sessions. "There were times when I thought revival could have broken out," she recalled, "but it wasn't on the program." AnGeL Ministries gave her a greater opportunity to control both the content and the context of her presentations. To reduce distractions, she developed a format of two-day revival meetings, primarily but not exclusively for women, usually scheduled for a Friday evening and an all-day session on Saturday. (Still influenced by her mother's example, she makes a point of being at home on Sunday, to attend church and cook Sunday dinner.) She is often joined by other noted Evangelical women teachers such as Kay Arthur and Jill Briscoe, but the centerpiece of her programs are three hour-long messages on the theme "Just Give Me Jesus." Reminiscent of her father's crusades, the revivals are followed by an eight-week Bible study taught in local churches. Also reminiscent of her father, she said she expects to see real revival as a product of her meetings. "It will be characterized by repentance of sin growing out of a deep conviction of sin . . . , by a recommitment to Jesus as Lord and Savior . . . , by a recommitment to the word of God, [and] to obeying God's word. When revival comes, it's not just for a weekend. It's a lifetime commitment."

Anne explained that the title of her revivals, "Just Give Me Jesus," arose from "a desperate cry of my own heart." Interviewed for television by Larry King in May 2000, she ticked off the tribulations she had experienced in recent years—hurricanes, floods, snowstorms that had devastated their property in eastern Carolina; the destruction of her husband's dental offices by fire; the diagnosis and successful treatment of her son's cancer; the marriage of all three of her children within an eight-month period; and her parents' deteriorating health. "I don't want to be entertained," she said. "I don't want visuals or musicals. I don't want a vacation. I don't want to quit. I don't want sympathy. The cry of my heart is, 'Just give me Jesus.'" She has also written a book with that title, structuring it around the Gospel of John. Several other books, some with companion CDs and videos, have sold widely and garnered awards from the Evangelical Christian Publishers Association. In most of these she moves through the text systematically, expounding on its meaning and applying it to the lives of her audience. In 1998 the International Bible Society honored her, along with her father, with the Golden Word Award for "her special ability to encourage people to search the Scriptures for themselves."

Interestingly, Anne prefers to call herself a "Biblical Expositor" rather than a preacher, but adds that when she speaks to Southern Baptist pastors, she describes herself as a waitress simply trying to serve the Bread of Life. Yet, when she enters a pulpit or stands on a simple stage, bare except for a thick, rather short wooden cross, precise labels don't really matter. Anne Lotz can preach.

Like many preachers, especially from the South, Billy Graham usually began his sermons by telling a joke or two, recycling the same jokes for half a century. Anne occasionally allows herself a small ironic chuckle after describing some foolish human behavior, but she is not in the entertainment business, even as a warm-up technique. In a typical session, after a few introductory remarks she consciously focuses attention by saying, "Listen to me!" and launches into a brief set-piece in praise of Jesus. An example:

His office is manifold and His promise is sure.
His life is matchless and His goodness is limitless.
His mercy is enough and His grace is sufficient.
His reign is righteous, His yoke is easy, and His burden is light.
He is indestructible, He is incomprehensible, He is inescapable;
He is invincible, He is irresistible, He is irrefutable, He is indescribable.
I can't get Him out of my mind and I can't get Him out of my heart.
I can't outlive Him and I can't live without Him.
The Pharisees couldn't stand Him but they found they couldn't stop Him.
Satan tried to tempt Him, but found he couldn't trip Him.
Pilate cross-examined Him but found no fault in Him.
The Romans crucified Him but couldn't take His life.
Death couldn't handle Him and the grave couldn't hold Him.
Just give me Jesus!
(Applause)

Then, during the presentations that last nearly an hour each, she might tell a single story of the non-humorous sermon-illustration genre or refer to some difficult period or episode in her own life, but mostly she draws again and again from biblical texts to note the fallen nature of all humans, the failures of Christians, the inevitability of suffering, and the need for repentance and recommitment. Despite a strong emphasis on the complete sufficiency of God's grace, made available through Christ's sacrifice, she does not portray the redeemed life as an easy one. In a pointed reference to the optimistic and materialistic "Name-it-and-claim-it-God-wants-you-to-be-rich" message so popular in some conservative Christian quarters, particularly among Pentecostals, she told a Kansas City audience, "Don't listen to that health and wealth and prosperity gospel, because it's a lie. Let me tell you something: Jesus didn't promise us health and wealth and prosperity. He promised us a cross. And after the cross comes the resurrection and the glory. But you've got to deny yourself and take up the cross and follow him."

Anne speaks in a direct, intense, driving style that, though lacking much variety in tone or pace and practically free of self-conscious dramatic technique, is nonetheless quite arresting. She is a serious woman with a serious message, and she imparts that seriousness to her listeners. Renowned preaching expert Stephen Olford, who directed a school for evangelists in Memphis and had also been something of a mentor to Anne before his death in 2004, said of her rhetorical style, "In a day of superficiality, in a day when so much preaching is tickling people's ears—she eschews all that. She has something to say. It's solid. It's biblical. It's a no-nonsense presentation. That's what makes her attractive.... She has a tremendous gift of communication, and a dignity and presence which is most impressive." Other notable observers have agreed. Billy Graham was often quoted as calling her "the best preacher in the family," and *Time* magazine agreed that she had "inherited the greatest share of Billy's gift." With no trace of sibling rivalry, brother Franklin has described her as "an anointed, powerful speaker" who is "the best in the country, or anywhere in the world for that matter, at what she does."

Addressing the inevitable comparisons to her father and brother, Anne observed that "we're on the same team, but our gifts are different.... Franklin and Daddy are like the obstetrician; they bring the baby into the world. We at AnGeL Ministries are like the pediatrician; we help the baby grow up." Although she offers an invitation at her revivals, Anne aims her message mainly at people who already profess to be Christians, for she sees her mission as a continuation of the work of evangelists, who seek to bring people to Christ for the first time. She sees her role as supporting people after they are converted and and restoring them to active faith and commitment when they have drifted away. On occasion, however, she is quite willing to assume the role of evangelist. Invited to speak at the Millennium World Summit for Religious and Spiritual Leaders at the General Assembly of the United Nations, she made no effort to note the commonalities among world religions, but preached a brief sermon on John 3:16, observing afterward that "I did my best in seven and a half minutes to present the gospel as clearly as I knew how."

Many conservative Christians are far less concerned with the distinctions between an evangelist, an expositor, and a preacher than between that most basic of human distinctions: male and female. Even among those who have wholeheartedly supported her father's ministry and agree completely with the aim and content of Anne's revival message, opposition to a woman in the pulpit is widespread. Anne encountered a striking manifestation of this attitude in the late 1980s when she addressed a pastors' conference. Although she has referred to this frequently, she declines to identify the organization, except to say that it was not a Southern Baptist event, but regional and nondenominational. "I was the only woman on the program for the convention. I was always afraid to stand in the pulpit before a large group, but it never crossed my mind to be afraid because there were men in the audience. I guess that's how naive I was. I was astounded when I stood up and looked out and saw that some of them had just turned their chairs around and put their backs to me. I don't know how many did that, but there were enough that it caught my attention. Today, I can still see them in my mind's eye. I finished the message, but it terrified me. I had an experience right after that in a much smaller group, in a totally different region of the country, with another group of pastors. They didn't say anything or do anything, but when I stood up, it was like a glass wall, and my voice got softer and softer until they turned up the microphone full force, and they still had trouble hearing. I was just shutting down. I could just feel the hostility. But I'm glad I had those experiences, because I needed to get on my face before God and find out what He was saying to me. My concern was that—because these were pastors and men of God, men who knew the Scriptures—in my zeal to serve the Lord I was serving Him outside of what He had expressly commanded in His word. I didn't want to be in ministry that contradicted what God had said. And as I knelt before God and prayed that through—it wasn't quick; it was a process—I feel like He clarified it for me in such a way that my confidence is unshaken."

The key, Anne said, was the story of Mary Magdalene. "After the resurrection of Christ, He appeared first to the women, and Mary Magdalene was among them. He told her and these other women, 'I want you to go back to Jerusalem and tell My disciples—eleven men—what you have experienced today, that you have seen Me and have had an experience with the risen Christ. And I want you to tell them to meet Me up in Galilee.' So He was telling those women to do two things: (1) to share their personal testimony as to who Jesus was in their lives, and (2) to give out His words to the disciples. I felt like God was letting me know that He has commissioned women and that commission has never changed, that we are commissioned just like anybody else to be ready 'in season and out of season' to share a word of personal testimony as to who Jesus is and what He means to us—our experience of the risen Christ. When people have a problem with women in ministry, they need to take it up with Jesus, because He is the one who put it there." That sharing, she continued, can be with one's children or neighbors, but it can also include "a more formal presentation from the pulpit."

As for the pivotal verse in the dispute over women preachers, I Timothy 2:12—"I permit not a woman to teach or have authority over a man"—Anne is convinced that the emphasis is on "authority," not teaching. Unlike some women, including Southern Baptist women, she feels it would be improper for her to be a senior pastor, with authority over men in a church. "That has nothing to do with just presenting the word from the pulpit when I am invited," she insists. "The authority that I speak with has nothing to do with my position. I'm not a scholar. I don't know Greek and Hebrew. It is the authority of God's Word. It is the authority of the Holy Spirit Himself as He speaks through us to our hearts. It has nothing to do with my having authority over my audience. I know He has called me, and I know He has told me that the audience is not my concern, that He will put into that audience whom He wants to put there, whether they are men or women or young or old or Americans or Africans or Russians. The audience is His responsibility. My responsibility is to be faithful to the message He has put on my heart."

Anne expressed rueful amusement at the ways some church leaders have tried to deal with the issue. "I've spoken in church sanctuaries where I'm not allowed in the pulpit. They will put a podium down on the platform or on the floor. That doesn't bother me—in fact, I've gotten to where I prefer nothing at all, but just stand in front of the audience without any barrier—but I don't see any scriptural basis for that." Referring to the television program *60 Minutes*, which had aired a segment about her a few weeks earlier that had mentioned the chair-turning incident, she said, "When the world looks at something like that, . . . they immediately spot the hypocrisy and inconsistency, and then they just throw out the baby with the bath water. And they miss the message of the church that is true, the gospel that should be preeminent in our teaching and our presentation and the way we live. They miss that because they see this prejudice and hypocrisy and they just don't get it. And I don't get it either. I don't want to be in anybody's pulpit or podium. I just want lives changed. They have no problem if I am sitting on a plane and sharing the gospel with a man next to me. Why do they have a problem with my sharing the gospel in an arena when men are in the audience? Where does the Bible say I can do it with one, but I can't do with 10,000? They have no answer for me on that."

Resistance has clearly diminished. In the summer of 2000 Anne became the first woman ever to address a plenary session at the 125-year-old Keswick Bible Conference in England, where she not only spoke but also shared the program for an entire week with John Stott, one of England's most prominent clerics and theologians. The male leaders at Keswick, she said, "couldn't have been more supportive or affirming. It was almost as if they were my big brothers and wanted to encourage me and support me and promote me. It was precious. I've felt that at Amsterdam and a lot of places I have been. And it has been the sweetest thing to have my mother and daddy and both of my brothers and both of my sisters totally supportive, without blinking. That has been really special."

The Keswick appearance led to an invitation to do a leadership retreat for Operation Mobilization, an Evangelical mission organization based in the Netherlands. "I think [resistance] has softened," Anne said. "Eastern Europe might still have a problem with this, and any Arab country, but I have been all through South America and Central America, where men are so macho, and have been so warmly received. I don't want women to assert themselves and lord it over others in the church out of a prideful attitude. But I wouldn't want a man to do that, either. Some denominations out there are struggling with this, and I just pray that it will balance out and the leadership would look at it in the light of what God's Word actually says and not just in the way they were raised to believe or [from] some kind of cultural prejudice."

Anne acknowledged that position statements by her own denomination, the Southern Baptist Convention, had exacerbated tensions over this issue. In 1998 the SBC had drawn widespread attention by its instruction to women "to submit herself graciously to the servant leadership of her husband even as the church willingly submits to the headship of Christ." Then, at its annual convention in Orlando, Florida, in June 2000, another clause was added to the "Baptist Faith and Message," stipulating that "while both men and women are gifted for service in the church, the office of pastor is limited to men as qualified by Scripture." Of this, Anne said, "I think a lot of pastors took that statement—even though that's not what it says—as a reason to deny women any position in ministry, unless it's in the nursery or with a woman's group. I think that stirred up some hostility that wasn't there before, or maybe it was just sort of dormant. The line was much fuzzier, but now it's drawn, and the way many people are drawing it, I don't think it's biblical." She attributes such actions as a reaction to the feminist movement. "I think there are women in ministry," she observed, "who, like the feminists, are trying to assert themselves and take a role in the church that is not really Spirit-led but [stems from] pride. That, coupled with the atmosphere in our country about women—women's rights, women's positions, that sort of thing—[the pastors] feel the world may be creeping into the church. But when there is an issue like that, we can't react on the basis of how we feel. We have to take it back to Scripture, and some of their positions have no basis in Scripture at all. I think it is just coming out of their own prejudice."

At its 2001 convention, the SBC took an additional step, declaring women ineligible for future ordination, though it did not insist that Southern Baptist women who had already been ordained renounce their status. Anne has expressed some uncertainty over whether women should be eligible for ordination, but considers it irrelevant in her own case. "To me, to be ordained means that you can marry, bury, and baptize. That is not something that I aspire to at all. I have no desire to be pastor of a church. I feel like that would almost limit what God has called me to do. I believe God has forbidden me to be ordained. But," she has conceded, "if another godly woman searches the Scriptures and believes God wants her to be ordained and to be a pastor, that is between her and God. I respect her view."

As her parents neared the end of their remarkable lives, Anne reflected on the influence they had exerted on her. "I was raised primarily by my mother," she told one interviewer, but added, "Although [my father] was gone for months at a time, he was adored. I believe he's been a biblical father in that by living his life he has passed on the reality of his faith and taught us about God. It wasn't just the things that he said that impacted us, but the way he lived and stayed faithful to his call. To me, that's the best a father can do. I love, honor, and respect him." She speculated that her father's prolonged absences might even have had a positive spiritual effect on her. "Because he wasn't there," she explained, "I developed a relationship with God that I may not have had with a more normal relationship with my father. I may have looked to my earthly father to meet my needs, or depended on him to fill the voids in my life. I didn't have that, so I looked to God for those things. And God has been my father in the most precious ways, which I wouldn't trade for anything. I thank God for the family that He gave me."

Ned (Nelson Edman), the youngest of the five Graham siblings, still runs East Gates Ministries International, which has been deeply involved in the publication and distribution of Bibles in China as well as supporting the construction of churches, training of ministers, and equipping churches to provide Christian education for children in that country's restrictive atmosphere. Following his father's example, Ned has sought to work within the confines of Chinese law rather than engage in Bible smuggling or other activities that might antagonize authorities and cause problems for Chinese Christians. Also like his father, he has been criticized by Christian groups that feel he is not being sufficiently critical of a regime that closely regulates religious behavior and uses forced abortions and compulsory sterilization to restrict population growth.

More severe criticism has stemmed from difficulties in Ned's personal life. During the mid–1990s the stresses inherent in his ministry, tension with a key member of his board, and an increasingly troubled marriage led him first to take refuge in alcohol and then to enter a holistic recovery program that he says not only helped him gain control over alcohol abuse but greatly improved his general health and vitality. After returning to his post at East Gates, he and Carol, his wife of nineteen years, agreed to seek individual and joint counseling to heal their marriage. But in October 1998, as he arrived at the Seattle airport from a trip to China, she had him served with divorce papers accusing him of a variety of misbehaviors. He categorically denies most of them, characterizing them as inventions of an aggressive lawyer who was counting on him and his family to provide a generous settlement to avoid public embarrassment. He did, however, acknowledge that the marriage had long been a hollow shell. The divorce was handled through mediation, and records of the proceedings were sealed. Ned and Carol were awarded joint custody of their two sons.

Troubled by these developments, several members of the ministry's staff and board members resigned. In addition, the Grace Community Church (in the Seattle suburb of Auburn), whose senior pastor was Ned's chief antagonist on the East Gates board, revoked his ministerial credentials and enjoined him to stop using the title "Reverend" in East Gates materials and correspondence. Instead of resigning from the organization, which his mother had helped found and which BGEA had supported generously, Ned appointed new board members, including his sister Ruth (Bunny) and his then-brother-in-law Stephan Tchividjian, and persuaded sister GiGi Tchividjian to work in the office until the crisis passed. In an even more important familial contribution to the rehabilitation of his son's image, Billy Graham provided a statement for the East Gates website and other publicity materials assuring the ministry's supporters that "Ruth and I are proud of and grateful to God for our son Ned." Noting that East Gates has distributed two million Bibles to Christians in China, the elder Graham added, "Our family stands solidly behind East Gates and all it stands for and would encourage Christians interested in China to back this unique and effective ministry." In February 2001 Ned and Christina Rae Kuo, a Chinese-American woman who is now actively involved in the East Gates ministry, were married in Ruth Graham's bedroom at Little Piney Cove. Billy Graham performed the ceremony. During the last years of Ruth's life, Ned spent most of his time in Montreat, caring for his mother.

The oldest of the Graham offspring, GiGi (Virginia), though not heading a formal Evangelical institution, has nonetheless engaged in an extensive ministry of speaking and writing. She has written several well-regarded books for various Evangelical publishers and helped her mother produce *Footprints of a Pilgrim*, an effective recounting of Ruth's life that uses her prose and poetry together with new anecdotes and comments from some of the many famous people the Grahams have known. As age and illness kept her parents confined more and more to their home, GiGi spent long stretches with them, living in a small residence in Montreat, where one of their sons also lived.

GiGi has long been in demand as an inspirational speaker at women's conferences in the United States, Canada, and Europe, and while living in Montreat took a strong interest in the children's health center of the Mission Hospitals in Asheville. After settling in Montreat when World War II forced him to leave his beloved medical mission in China, Ruth's father, Dr. L. Nelson Bell, joined the staff of Mission Hospital in Asheville. There he played a key role in merging four smaller medical facilities to form Memorial Mission Hospital, seeking to bring a higher level of medical care to the families of Appalachia, and to children in particular. Thus it seemed fitting that when the hospital system opened a major new health center for children in 1994 and named it for two of Asheville's most famous citizens, Ruth's name came first, in recognition of her father's concern for and contributions to the health needs of people in that region. Renamed the Ruth and Billy Graham Children's Hospital in 2001, the center can deal with virtually the entire range of children's health problems except for open-heart surgery and burn treatment. It also sends "Toothbuses," fully equipped mobile dental clinics, into rural areas to provide free care to children without regular access to professional dental services. "Most people simply don't realize that many people in Southern Appalachia live in Third World conditions," GiGi observed. "Many counties, for example, don't have a single physician to provide obstetrical services." Seeking to keep alive her grandfather's and her mother's commitment, GiGi has devoted considerable time to raising money for the institution. In 2005, to avoid confusion over funding and organizational ties, the Graham name was dropped from the center, but the Missions Hospitals website identifies them as great friends of the program, and pictures of Ruth and Billy are prominently displayed in the facility.

In 2004, GiGi and Stephan Tchividjian surprised family and friends by ending their marriage of more than thirty years. The following year she married Chad Foreman, an ex-Marine and Florida-based private investigator. A squabble in a parking lot in June 2005 drew the attention of passersby and the police and resulted in a charge of misdemeanor domestic violence against GiGi and a night in jail, a charge and penalty she and her husband both characterized as distinctly inappropriate. After a brief flurry of public attention, the incident drew little further notice. Stephan Tchividjian, whose work included counseling, business consulting, and hosting a radio talk shown, also remarried.

Franklin's early rebellion, its memory kept alive in story and sermon, and Ned's divorce and problems with alcohol and drugs, not widely publicized but well known to Evangelical insiders, made it clear that Billy and Ruth Graham had not escaped the problems and heartaches that trouble millions of American families. Yet many continued to hold up their family as an ideal toward which all Christian households should strive. Armchair and professional psychiatrists alike might reasonably point to the nonconforming behavior of both sons and the teenage marriage of all three daughters as evidence of a less-than-perfect home environment. But publicly, and to a large extent privately, the five Graham siblings have seldom said anything more detracting than "we weren't perfect," followed by a nearly complete lack of supporting evidence or a willingness to shoulder all the blame themselves. In recent years, youngest daughter Ruth — formerly but emphatically no longer known as "Bunny" — has been more outspoken about what she regards as the disadvantages of growing up in a famous family.

In a conversation in mid–2001, Ruth referred to an insightful *Atlantic Monthly* article by Sue Erikson Bloland, daughter of the famed psychiatrist Erik Erikson, about the costs fame extracts from famous people and their families. Ruth obviously saw many parallels in her own life. She said, "My father's relation with the family has been awkward, because he has two families: BGEA and us. I always resented that. We were footnotes in books — literally. Well, we're not footnotes. We are real, living, breathing people. There is no question Daddy loves us, but his ministry has been all-consuming. And we have understood, by and large. We've done a good job. We have coped. We have not rejected them or Christ. We're all involved in some form of ministry. That's remarkable. We have done well at living up to people's expectations, but it is a burden. We were not a perfect family and I'm tired of people saying it. I don't want to be indiscreet, but God inhabits honesty, and I'm not good at image-management."

As a child, Ruth said, "I felt adopted. A TV crew came to our house when I was about nine or ten to do a program about *The World of Billy Graham.* I remember that the director called me 'Sad Eyes.'" As for the Grahams' practice of sending their children to boarding school, Ruth acknowledged that part of their motivation might have been to obtain a better education than was available locally and added, only half in jest, that her mother felt that "if the royal family sent their children away to school, it was probably a good idea. And, of course, she had been sent away as a girl." But these, she thought, were minor factors. "Daddy was burdened, Mother was overwhelmed. It was easier to send us away. When GiGi wanted to come home, they wouldn't let her. And then they sent her off to Europe and [helped arrange for her to marry Stephan Tchividjian] as a teenager. That was really weird."

Like Anne, Ruth remembers being groomed for the life of wife, homemaker, and mother. "There was never an idea of a career for us," she said. "I wanted to go to nursing school — Wheaton had a five-year program — but Daddy said no. No reason, no explanation, just 'No.' It wasn't confrontational and he wasn't angry, but when he decided, that was the end of it." She added, "He has forgotten that. Mother has not." With a career ruled out, Ruth followed the path laid out for her: She married Ted Dienert, son of Fred, who handled Billy Graham's media ministry, and Millie, who organized the prayer campaign for the crusades. "I married Ted," she said, "because I wanted to feel special to someone. I didn't feel that way in my family. I was too immature. I chose not to see a lot. Ted was not interested in me. He was interested in Ted, in the image. It was all part of a picture. And Fred wanted it."

Ruth fell easily into the expected routine, rearing three children, maintaining an active personal spiritual life, and organizing women's retreats. Later she worked part-time as an acquisitions editor for HarperCollins. Then, in the mid–1980s, after nearly twenty years of marriage, she learned that Ted had been having an affair for more than five years. Writing about this traumatic discovery, she said, "At first I resorted to my familiar pattern of denial — covering over my hurt with spiritual platitudes. I prayed. I fasted. I forgave. I claimed Bible promises. I did all I'd been taught to do. I also hid my problems from everyone, humiliated that others — especially my family — would find out."

Her family did find out, of course, and her father strongly urged Ruth not to divorce Ted, telling her it would hurt millions of Evangelical Christians who looked to his ministry and their family for inspiration. After one crucial conversation, Ruth recalled that "Daddy put his arms around Ted and said, 'Nothing will change.' I saw how important the ministry was to him — and how little the family was. Things had to look right, and divorce didn't fit." By that time, however, she had already determined that "there was nothing to go back to" in her marriage, and she went through with the divorce. Although she spent little time counseling with her parents during the breakup, she acknowledged that both her parents were "always very loving" toward her once they realized the marriage was over. "Inside," she said, "there was that core of love and grace and gentleness. I'm not sure Daddy could understand the hurt I felt, but he could understand broken trust. That's where we could communicate. He has been betrayed, hurt, and gone ahead."

Ruth sought professional counseling to help her through her marital trials, overcoming an old bias among some Christians that resorting to a psychologist or psychiatrist was a sign of "spiritual problems." She also acknowledged, at least to herself, that her simple faith that "if you serve God, he will take care of you" was too simple. Immersing herself in the Old Testament, she came to realize that God was not depending on her to protect his reputation. Israel disappointed God repeatedly, yet "his plans kept moving right along.... I've learned that he isn't threatened by my anger or doubts.... Many Christian leaders are weighed down by this idea of 'be perfect—or else!' So when I finally laid this burden down, I was free.... In fact, when I ask questions and express doubt, it's a sign of faith because I'm assuming God is listening and that he's the source of the answers. As long as I'm in dialogue with God, I'm expressing faith and nurturing hope."

Ruth also soon learned that countless Christian families have been torn apart or severely injured by similar stresses and that, contrary to her and her father's fears, her divorce was "barely a blip on the radar screen." Indeed, she has used her own experiences as a way of communicating the truth that even the most famous Christians are not exempt from the problems that trouble most members of the human race. "We all," she said, "still have to work through the mess and muck of life."

At age forty Ruth determined to "reinvent myself." A significant symbolic step was to insist that she no longer be referred to as "Bunny," a name she felt kept her from being taken seriously. Franklin has pointedly ignored her wishes in this matter, and other members of the family have acknowledged difficulty in making the switch, often electing to call her "Bunny Ruth." None, however, fails to note how serious she is about making the change. She also went back to college and, in the spring of 2001, graduated with honors from Mary Baldwin College—the only one of the Graham daughters to finish college. Though she has left Bunny behind, she has never considered renouncing her status as a Graham. At Mary Baldwin, she wrote her senior thesis on the topic "Cross-cultural Communication of the Concept of Sin," analyzing the spiritual depth, cultural sensitivity, and rhetorical artfulness Billy Graham manifested in addressing audiences in such disparate locales as China, the USSR, South Africa, and Alabama. He was, she offered, "a very special man. It was wonderful, as a daughter, to step outside and see the balance he had to maintain, with the whole world watching." Commenting further on her father's qualities, she said, "He was always a learner, never a know-it-all. He has never been dogmatic. He was able to sit down with theologians with a genuine curiosity and have real dialogue. He had an ego, but he was not egotistical. He was always amazed at what he had achieved—'How did I get here?' "

Ruth has participated in both of her brothers' ministries and has established her own Ruth Graham Ministries, aimed particularly at addressing the woundedness of women whom she feels have too often been neglected by the church or met with unsatisfactory pat answers. "You can't just slap a Bible verse over a wound and expect it to heal," she has poignantly noted. She continues to write for Christian publications, speak at Evangelical gatherings, and hold "Ruth Graham & Friends" conferences, where she is joined by other articulate women who share their stories of coping with the pains of such troubles as infidelity, spousal abuse, divorce, illness, and addiction. Her 2004 book, *In Every Pew Sits a Broken Heart—Hope for the Hurting*, laid bare the stories of her divorce from Ted Deinert, an unhappy and brief second marriage, a third marriage that ended in divorce, and the pain of dealing with a daughter's eating disorder and two out-of-wedlock pregnancies. She shared the spiritual resources that enabled her to emerge from these crises and offered a series of wise and sensitive "Tips for Those Who Care" for people in pain. As in that book, her speeches also use illustrations from her own life to say that "God doesn't love Billy Graham or his family any more than he loves you." In two subsequent books, *A Legacy of Faith: Things I Learned from My Father* and *A Legacy of Love: Things I Learned from My Mother,* Ruth wrote of both the difficulties and blessings of being part of an often idealized but still quite human family. Yet even while insisting that her parents and family were not perfect, she spoke of them with great tenderness, "I know what their core is. That has never wavered. I respect that. I admire it. I aspire to it."

41
The Last Days

All the Graham offspring acknowledge that their father had a difficult time growing old. During the summer of 2001 GiGi observed that "it has been very difficult for Daddy. He has the impression that he is sort of a has-been, that he is no longer in control of anything—especially his work. In many ways, he has retired, but it's real, real hard for him to turn loose. He's used to having people talking to him, asking his advice, seeking his counsel, and it's just not the same anymore."

Daughter Ruth noted some of the same things. "The other day I was at the house," she recalled, "and Daddy had been watching [an old video] of himself preaching on TBN [a Christian television network]. He said, 'I watched myself. I wonder what it felt like to have that power. I don't have that power and strength now.' I think he underestimates himself. He underestimates the power of gentleness. There is a power in gentleness that is not in fire and brimstone." Ruth also noted the greater vulnerability her parents had shown as age and illness overtook them, but thought they had been true to their natures. "Mother was always sweet," she said. "There's never a problem. It's all sunshine. She won't talk about herself. And that gets worse as she gets older. She'll never tell you how she feels. It's always been that way, but it has intensified. She's not supposed to lift anything, but she'll get up from her chair and walk slowly across the room to put a log on the fire when I'm right there by the fire. One of the nurses told me that she checked on her late one night and found her kneeling by her bed in prayer. She had every excuse not to kneel—her broken body, hurting and aching—but nothing would stop her from worshiping her Lord, and that's how she has done it. That's Mom."

Her father, Ruth noted (as others did through the years), had played the sick role in a different manner. "Daddy complains all the time. When he had shingles, he was in so much pain and he would say, 'I'm dying,' and we'd all rush to his bedside. And then he'd get better. Finally, Mother said, 'Would you please just hush up and die like a Christian?' But it's so sweet to see him toddle in to kiss her goodnight and she raises her face to him, her eyes just sparkling to receive his kiss. Daddy is a clay pot that has allowed God to fill him with his grace."

Anne Lotz also showed appreciation for her father's increased vulnerability and for the opportunity to be of service to him as his earthly life drew to a close. She spoke with obvious gratitude at his request that she be with him at the Mayo Clinic when, in June 2000, a shunt was placed in his brain to reduce the pressure from hydrocephalus. Within a day of returning to North Carolina, she learned that the procedure had not worked as hoped and that additional surgery was required. She quickly booked another flight to Minnesota. "It happened to be on Father's Day," she recalled. "I got there and was sitting in the chair. Daddy was asleep, and I just started to cry, because his head was now totally shaved and he had this little green cap on, and he looked so frail. I asked God to help me get hold of myself, and he did. When Daddy woke up, I was fine. I was under control. He looked at me, and his eyes focused, and he said, 'Anne, what are you doing here?' and I told him, 'Happy Father's Day.' I couldn't remember a Father's Day when I knew where he was, much less be able to be with him. I told him I was on my way to New York [to be on the *Today* show] and wanted to spend Father's Day with him. He just grinned and said, 'Anne, this isn't on the way to New York.' We both got really emotional. I stayed with him once again until I knew he was out of the woods. It is one of the most precious blessings I feel God has ever given to me.

"When I'm with Daddy, I feel like we communicate on a level that is not verbal. The Lord is just present when we're together, and he seems strengthened and encouraged and blessed by it. For years and years, I felt like Daddy gave more attention even to the local reporter at the newspaper than to us, because that was where his focus was, and Mother had encouraged him in that. Then, at the end of his life, to see him come back and have the time with us is really wonderful. So precious! And my mother also. I have been with her in the hospital when she has had surgeries. She is always afraid she is going to be a burden to us. I told her it isn't a burden; it is a blessing. For all these years, they have been so self-sufficient, so selfless, and if they had a need, they had a whole staff to answer it. We have not been able to do things for our parents. And then to find that I can actually do something for them that would be a blessing and help to them is just the highest privilege and the greatest blessing of my life. Daddy just hates growing old, but in the midst of all his physical infirmities and limits, to see the sweetness of his character and the gentleness and the same concern for others, it's incredible. It's such a testimony to a life that has been lived for Christ and focused on Christ, so that in the end you actually take on his characteristics. I look at my daddy and mother and I can see Christ in their faces. Sometimes when they are feeling the worst, are hurting the most, or things are not going right for whatever reason, you can see the countenance of Christ in them. And it gives me hope."

Concerned at both a personal and professional level, Franklin Graham made the eighty-mile trip from Boone to Montreat as often as his schedule permitted and often astride his Harley, but he also took extra pains to see that his father was well cared for when he was away from home. To take the place of T. W. Wilson, forced by a stroke in 1999 to relinquish his role as Billy's faithful traveling companion, Franklin assigned two longtime staffers, David Bruce and Maury Scobee, to the task so that his father was never without one of them close at hand. In addition to handling details of travel, appointments, and meals, the men were also enjoined to make sure Billy's hearing aid always had fresh batteries and to watch for such things as a crooked tie or a minor food stain on a lapel—details an older man might overlook before an interview or a television appearance. But Franklin's overwhelming commitment was to help his father "finish well" and to provide him with ample assurance that the Billy Graham Evangelistic Association would remain faithful to its mission. At least in part to facilitate his own ability to keep close watch on the operation, Franklin surprised many by announcing in mid-November 2001 that BGEA would move its headquarters from Minneapolis to a new and larger facility to be erected on the Billy Graham parkway in Charlotte, thus bringing the ministry back at last to the soul from which it sprung.

Franklin faced the future with little obvious trepidation. Samaritan's Purse is solidly positioned to continue its work indefinitely. As for BGEA without BG, he felt it could long continue what it was born to do and had done best for decades: evangelism. He and other associate evangelists will continue to hold crusades, using the time-tested model that seems always to bring out the crowds and gather in the harvest. And for a time, his father will also continue to proclaim the gospel—by means of the technology whose use he and his team pioneered.

While still thinking big, Franklin thought that available technologies could be used in a more efficient and effective manner than in such undertakings as Mission World and Global Mission. "I never was totally comfortable with those," he said, "especially when we came out of San Juan. I think what we were trying to do was good, but the world is a pretty big place and you just can't do something all the way around the world at the same time. There are too many time zones. When it's day here, it's night there. What we ended up having to do was video it and delay it so that we could go around the world within a twenty-four-hour period of time. And I was thinking, 'So what?' What was so wonderful about that, other than that we could say we had done it? What I want to do is focus. We can take one of my father's old telecasts and lip-sync it so that Daddy is speaking Chinese if we show it in China, Spanish if we show it in Central or South America, Swahili in Africa, and Hindi in India. Let's just go in with the money and buy the time on state television and show it in prime time. That's what we do in this country. And let's go around the world. Let's say we start with Central America. We put a local address and local telephone number on the screen and work with a local mission group or local church to be our representative for that telecast, so that all the requests will come in to them, and we provide the materials and pay them to mail them out for us and we keep that little office open for a month or two. We do that in every nation, so that people can respond to a local address. When we finish Central America, we move to South America, and when we finish South America, we move to Europe, and then to Africa and the Middle East and on into India. It might take us three years to go around the world and do it right in every country. And once we go around the world and complete it, we do it again with a different program, and the next time around we will be a little smarter, because we have been there before."

In addition to the immediate results, Franklin added, "By having a crusade on television, we would be giving a model to the church. People would say, 'So that's what a Billy Graham crusade is. That's what the message is about. That's how you give an invitation.' That would spark an interest so that people will say, 'We want to have a crusade like that in our city. Who has the gift of evangelism in our country? Let's get together and help them. Let's do this in our town, with one of our own.'" It would be far better, Franklin thought, to let people see a crusade on their state-run television at prime time than at four in the morning on some UHF Christian station that was coming in all scratchy."

Franklin also determined to extend his father's ministry by using BGEA's enormous collection of videotapes. "We have sat on my father's videos," he explained. "I am making them available to Jan and Paul Crouch [of Trinity Broadcasting Network]. Some people wonder why we want to give it to them, because they are 'different.' I'll tell you why: They have a network. [Skeptics of the plan] say, 'Yeah, but they are Pentecostals.' So? At least they love the Lord Jesus Christ. We pay to be on NBC and ABC and CBS, and Daddy [would] be on and the program right after [would] be some godless program, with immorality and killing and violence and everything. I'd much rather be on Trinity Broadcasting, and I don't have to pay for that. They are going to take my father's telecasts and play them for free, and they are thrilled to have that opportunity. I think you can take some of these old telecasts and show them on Trinity Broadcasting. We're going to put a little subtitle down on the bottom — Billy Graham Classic — so people will realize this is not live — and fifty years from now people can still come to know Jesus Christ. But sitting on those tapes isn't leading one person to Christ." TBN began airing "Billy Graham Classics" twice weekly in mid-2001.

Franklin's creative rethinking of ways to combine BGEA's extensive archival resources, various forms of media, and time-tested organizational methods has proved astonishingly successful in an initiative known as "My Hope World TV Project." Begun in 2002 and continuing to evolve, the program centers on regional telecasts of programs featuring Billy Graham "classics," current presentations by Franklin, and films from Worldwide Pictures. Local churches cooperate to stir interest and support, as in traditional Graham revivals, but instead of gathering people into churches or public venues, church members trained in sharing their faith and leading people to Christ invite small groups into their homes to view the programs, as the World Television Series had pioneered with Operation Matthew in the 1990s. The results far exceeded expectations. In the first five years of the program, more than 2.2 million "Matthews" posted such gatherings, with 6.4 million people making decisions for Christ. Local churches reported explosive growth overnight, with 40 to 70 percent of those making decisions following through and becoming integrated with the congregation. Several Latin American countries reported remarkable harvests — Venezuela, 234,000; Argentina, 321,000; Colombia, 705,000 — and three Russian installments have garnered more than 320,000 decisions. But the clear standout has been India, with a total in excess of four million.

Although he thought it plausible that within a few years BGEA and Samaritan's Purse would share common boards, Franklin thought it unlikely the two organizations would ever merge formally. "I think we will keep them separate," he said, explaining that "Samaritan's Purse complements BGEA. The criticism that my father and his generation got, that people are more concerned with the soul and not the body — they can't make that charge against me. Even the most liberal of liberal groups receive me because I had twenty years with Samaritan's Purse before I started my evangelism. In their minds, that gives me credibility. I didn't design it this way. This is just the way it happened. I never dreamed the media and others would treat me differently because of the humanitarian work, and I am going to use that to the advantage of evangelism."

Despite his intention to keep the two organizations separate, Franklin did see an advantage in having BGEA headquarters closer at hand. In November 2001 he announced that the central operation would move from Minneapolis, "all the address you need" for more than fifty years, to Charlotte. Dedicated in April 2005, the spacious new facilities (200,000 square feet) sit on sixty-three acres alongside the Billy Graham Parkway. The new location, not far from the Charlotte airport, is much closer to Samaritan's Purse in Boone and the Cove in Asheville.

The Billy Graham Training Center at the Cove has become and will doubtless continue to be a major component of BGEA ministries. Prominent Evangelical teachers lead seminars, most lasting three to five days apiece and focusing on such topics as "A Hunger for the Holy," "Following Jesus in Tough Times," "Shepherding the Heart of a Woman," "Five Lies That Ruin Relationships," "Christ's Take on Investing the Rest of Your Life," "Successful Aging," and "Who Wants to Have a Million-Dollar Marriage?" The main conference auditorium seats 500 and features state-of-the-art electronic equipment. Two reasonably priced inns are tastefully furnished, but offer guests no radio or television sets, and recreation is limited to walks through the woods of the beautifully maintained 1,500-acre property. In the future the Cove will likely serve as the site for "mini-Amsterdam" conferences (now called "Beyond Amsterdam") to provide intensive training in evangelism.

In all these ways and others that may present themselves, Franklin Graham intends to use the resources of BGEA to further evangelism (to use the words of the association's original charter), "by any and all means." The great desire of his heart, he said convincingly and with a sense of urgency, is "to help other evangelists. I want BGEA to be in the forefront of the battle. We are not going to sit on the sidelines and say, 'The glory days are behind us.' We are going to be pro-active, out there, in the face of the devil and every demon in hell. We are going to fight for every soul we can, to give them a chance to hear the gospel, give them a chance to confess and repent before God, give them a chance to receive God's provision through his Son, Jesus Christ. I like to build. For twenty years I've been building a ministry for my Father in heaven, and I don't have any intention of quitting that. I want to build BGEA, and I want to build Samaritan's Purse, and we want to take it for another generation. I'm forty-eight now; fifty-eight ... sixty-eight ... seventy-eight.... Maybe I've got thirty more years. You can say, 'That's a long time.' But I've been here twenty years and it feels like it's gone just like that. We don't have a lot of time. So if we are going to do something, we had better do it now."

When he spoke these words in the spring of 2001, Franklin's awareness of the swiftness of the stream of life had doubtless been quickened by the passing of those who had so long held up his father's arms. Fred and Ted Dienert, Billie Barrows, Robert Ferm, Victor Nelson, Alexander Haraszti, and George Wilson had all died during the 1990s. Just two weeks after that conversation and a few days after finally making his retirement official, T. W. Wilson suffered a fatal heart attack in a restaurant near his home in Montreat. Walter Smyth had retired and was in poor health. John Wesley White was still recovering slowly from a devastating stroke suffered in 1996. Another of Franklin's mentors, Roy Gustafson, died in April 2002. Cliff Barrows and George Beverly Shea appeared to be in good health, but Cliff was seventy-eight and Bev was ninety-two. And, of course, his own father's precarious health was seldom far out of Franklin's mind. Obviously and inexorably, the little team that had done so much to lead Evangelical Christianity out of the wilderness and into the central arenas of the religious world over the past six decades was about to pass into history.

Awareness that an era was ending was not limited to Evangelical Christians. On September 14, 2001, three days after the terrorist attacks on the World Trade Center and the Pentagon, Billy Graham was once again called upon to fill the role of People's Pastor at the observance of National Day of Prayer and Remembrance in Washington. Representatives of Judaism, Islam, and various segments of Christianity spoke, and spoke well, but the task of delivering the central message fell to the man who had borne its weight so many times before. Although he was obviously frail and accepted the assistance of two escorts to help him to his place on the dais at the National Cathedral, Graham's voice was strong and his manner sure. He acknowledged that, when asked how God could allow such tragedy and suffering, "I have to confess that I really do not know the answer totally, even to my own satisfaction. I have to accept, by faith, that God is sovereign, and He's a God of love and mercy and compassion in the midst of suffering."

Graham noted how the events of the week had underscored the brevity and uncertainty of life, cited the heroism and courage so many had shown in the aftermath of the attacks, called for spiritual renewal, and pointed to the cross as the symbol of hope for Christians—making it clear that "I'm speaking for the Christian now," a tacit acknowledgment that not all present or watching on television shared the same convictions. Toward the end, he said, "I've become an old man now," confirming that he understood what many in this global audience were seeing for themselves for the first time, "and I've preached all over the world, and the older I get the more I cling to that hope that I started with many years ago and proclaimed in many languages to many parts of the world." The wounded nation and its people would recover, he felt confident, and he called upon them to rebuild on the solid rock of faith in God, quoting the words of the familiar hymn, "How Firm a Foundation":

Fear not, I am with thee; O be not dismayed,
For I am thy God, and will still give thee aid;
I'll strengthen thee, help thee, and cause thee to stand,
Upheld by my righteous, omnipotent hand.

As Billy Graham returned slowly to his seat, the huge audience, silent throughout most of the service, signaled its respect and gratitude for the venerable evangelist with a sustained wave of warm applause for one whose like would not pass their way again.

Sadly, troubling shadows soon clouded the aura of expansive goodwill Billy Graham and his ministry had come to symbolize. A few weeks after the National Day of Prayer and Remembrance, many Christian leaders were working to ease and forestall expressions of enmity against Arabs and

Muslims. On a day when President Bush was wishing Muslims "health, prosperity, and happiness during [the Islamic holy month of] Ramadan," Franklin Graham publicly observed that he did not regard Islam as "this wonderful, peaceful religion." On the contrary, he said, it is "wicked, violent, and not of the same God.... It wasn't Methodists flying into those buildings, it wasn't Lutherans. It was an attack on this country by people of the Islamic faith." Irate Muslim leaders decried these comments, but when representatives of the Council on American-Islamic Relations asked to meet with him to foster better understanding, Franklin declined, claiming he could not fit them into his schedule.

He did, however, offer a clarifying statement, in which he claimed he had been "greatly misunderstood" and said he did not believe Muslims "are evil people because of their faith." He acknowledged that much evil has been done in the name of religion, including Christianity. Still, he did not temper his criticism of Islam, expressing concern about the treatment of women in Muslim lands and observing that the Qur'an "provides ample evidence that Islam encourages violence in order to win converts and to reach the ultimate goal of an Islamic world." Muslims, of course, were hardly satisfied by such putative clarifications, but other observers also expressed bafflement. The White House distanced itself from Graham's remarks, saying that President Bush "views Islam as a religion that preaches peace." The president of an international relief organization lamented, "It doesn't help the cause of Christianity. It doesn't bring the faiths together. My question is, 'What's he trying to accomplish?' I hope he was caught off guard." More pointedly, veteran *Newsweek* religion editor Ken Woodward, a longtime Graham observer, volunteered that "obviously, Mr. Graham is tone deaf in this respect. He's certainly not his father's son in terms of discretion."

Unfortunately, in late February 2002 evidence surfaced that caused many to wonder if at least part of the father's "discretion" had not been, in fact, "deception." A newly released batch of tapes from the Nixon White House included a 90-minute conversation Graham had had with the President and Chief of Staff H. R. Haldeman on February 1, 1972, during which all three men made anti–Semitic statements. Although they both expressed admiration for Israelis, Nixon and Graham agreed that liberal American Jews played a prominent role in what they regarded as the largely unpatriotic news media and in the production and dissemination of an increasingly corrosive popular culture. Graham noted that he was not talking about all Jews and that he had many Jewish friends, but he admitted that, when in the company of liberal Jews such as those at the *New York Times*, he did not let them know "how I really feel about what they're doing to this country. And I have no power, no way to handle them, but I would stand up if under proper circumstances."

Predictably, Jewish leaders, many of whom had professed great admiration for Graham, expressed disappointment, dismay, and disgust at these remarks. According to staff members close to him, Graham immediately saw the implications of these revelations and quickly issued a statement saying that, although he did not remember the conversation, he deeply regretted what he had obviously said and insisted it did not reflect his feelings toward Jews. He noted that he had long sought to build bridges between Jews and Christians and would "continue to strongly support all future efforts to advance understanding and mutual respect between our communities." In a more extended statement, issued a day or two later, he said,

> I cannot imagine what caused me to make those comments, which I totally repudiate. Whatever the reason, I was wrong for not disagreeing with the President, and I sincerely apologize to anyone I have offended.
>
> I don't ever recall having those feelings about any group, especially the Jews, and I certainly do not have them now. My remarks did not reflect my love for the Jewish people. I humbly ask the Jewish community to reflect on my actions on behalf of Jews over the years that contradict my words in the Oval Office that day.
>
> Much of my life has been a pilgrimage—constantly learning, changing, growing, and maturing. I have come to see in deeper ways some of the implications of my faith and message, not the least of which is in the area of human rights and racial and ethnic understanding.

Some Jewish leaders as well as others who had been taken aback by the tapes accepted his apology, recalling that he had been a strong supporter of Israel, had urged Soviet leaders to allow Jews to emigrate to Israel, had assured Jewish leaders in New York that he would not be targeting Jews for conversion during his 1991 crusade there, and, more recently, had criticized his fellow Southern Baptists for announcing a special campaign of evangelism aimed at Jews. They also noted that his remarks on this occasion stood out as virtually unique in his known oral or written statements.

Although not all were convinced by such arguments, it seems plausible that, just as Billy Graham moved from acceptance of segregation and male dominance to a firm insistence on racial integration and equal opportunity for women, and from denunciation of all forms of socialism to a more flexible political stance, he had also grown beyond whatever validity he had once assigned to anti–Semitic stereotypes that were more widely held and voiced in the general culture in 1972 than was the case three decades later.

Graham's later life had become quiet, as disease, accidents, and age kept both Ruth and him confined mostly to Little Piney Cove or hospitals, except for brief periods when he emerged to hold crusades—in Dallas/Fort Worth, San Diego, Oklahoma City, Kansas City, and Los Angeles. Despite delays because of health and fears that he might not be able to handle the rigors of such outings, he rallied repeatedly and, in virtually every case, drew record crowds as multiplied thousands turned out for what they reasonably expected would be their last chance to hear the fabled evangelist.

It was fitting that the final crusade of Graham's career, in June 2005, was in New York City, the scene of his most memorable American crusade, the 1957 marathon in Madison Square Garden. He had hoped to return to the Garden, for nostalgia's sake, but realization that it could not possibly hold the expected multitude forced a shift to Corona Park in Flushing Meadow, the site of the 1964–65 World's Fair. Death had continued to winnow the ranks of Billy's family, friends, and associates — Montreat pastor and friend Calvin Thielman died in 2002; Walter Smyth followed in 2003, as did old friends Johnny and June Cash and beloved brother Melvin Graham; and Stephen Olford died in 2004 — but the core platform team was there. Cliff Barrows, age eighty and nearly blind from macular degeneration, looked robust and was in fine voice and spirit, though direction of the 1,500-voice choir had been surrendered to Tom Bledsoe. George Beverly Shea, age ninety-six, was still able to sing "How Great Thou Art," the song he had introduced to America at the 1957 Crusade, with remarkable volume and vibrancy. (Three years earlier, in Dallas, he had said, "I think I sounded better at ninety.")

In the weeks prior to the event, reporters who interviewed the aging evangelist commented on the toll taken by disease, failing sight and hearing, and two serious falls that had hospitalized him for long periods in 2004. He seemed feeble, they said, his voice sometimes barely above a whisper, a weak echo of the clarion instrument that had been his trademark, and he seemed at times to grope for words. At a press conference two days before the crusade, however, Graham seemed visibly and audibly revived. His voice had grown noticeably stronger, and his answers came without hesitation or imprecision. Newspapers continued to report that he would be able to sit on a high stool behind a specially built pulpit and that Franklin would stand ready to take over if his father were unable to finish a sermon. They need not have worried. Though he remained offstage in an air-conditioned tent until minutes before he was to preach, and proceeded to the platform slowly, using a walker and with Franklin supporting him at his side, Billy Graham was ready.

When his time came on opening night, his snowy mane flowing down to his collar, the venerable old evangelist accepted the tremendous standing ovation for a few moments, then signaled the audience to settle down. Never one to shed tears, in part because of a tear-duct limitation, he said, "I have stars in my eyes. I can't see you very well just yet." That he should be moved is understandable. Arrayed before him like sheep on a thousand hills, the huge crowd — attendance for the three nights topped 230,000 — may well have been the most ethnically and culturally diverse crowd ever to attend a Billy Graham Crusade and perhaps as diverse a large audience as ever assembled anywhere.

As Graham spoke, his voice was clear and strong, little different from other crusades in the previous decade. He stood throughout all three sermons, using the stool only during the invitation. The sermons were short—about fifteen minutes, with the exception of the last afternoon, when he spoke at greater length on the Second Coming—but the response was, one last time, impressive, as nearly 10,000 people streamed forward in response to the familiar call, "I'm going to ask you to come.... Come now," and the encouraging strains of "Just as I Am."

After the New York Crusade, Graham spent most of his time either at Little Piney Cove with Ruth or traveling to the Mayo Clinic for treatment of his various ailments, newly including an aggressive form of macular degeneration. Although he was unable to withstand the rigors of even a shortened crusade, he did make one-night guest appearances at Franklin's festivals in New Orleans and Baltimore in 2006. In April of that year, he battled illness to appear at the George H. W. Bush Presidential Library and Museum at Texas A&M University to receive the George Bush Award for Excellence in Public Service. Despite being mostly offstage, however, the venerable evangelist was not forgotten. *Newsweek* profiled him in a thoughtful cover story and *Time* reporters Michael Duffy and Nancy Gibbs interviewed him extensively for a book, *The Preacher and the Presidents: Billy Graham in the White House.* Graham also achieved distinction as apparently the oldest person to hit the best-seller lists, with the publication of *The Journey: How to Live By Faith in an Uncertain World.* And on May 31, 2007, his status as an eminent figure was confirmed yet again as the nation's major media converged on Charlotte for the formal dedication of the Billy Graham Library and Visitor Center, where the Mayor of Charlotte, the Governor of North Carolina, and former Presidents Jimmy Carter, George H. W. Bush, and Bill Clinton lauded Graham for his contributions to the world and for the personal spiritual guidance and moral example he had provided them over decades.

The complex, sharing space with BGEA headquarters, was expected to attract 250,000 tourists a year. The grounds have a rustic quality that echoes the rural setting of Graham's original home. The handsome two-story brick structure itself, which had been moved from its original Park Road location just four miles away to Jim Bakker's PTL Christian amusement park in Fort Mill, South Carolina, was repurchased and reassembled on the new site. The main attraction, however, is the library, a designation that is something of a misnomer. Unlike presidential or other special-purpose libraries, it is not designed to be a research facility; although it contains some of Graham's personal papers, most of his archives remain at Wheaton. The library's major functions are to serve as a memorial to the evangelist's life and ministry; as an evangelistic tool, since guests are repeatedly exposed to presentations of the Gospel; and, not insignificantly, as a way to keep people informed about and loyal to the Billy Graham Evangelistic Association.

Visitors enter the library through a forty-foot-high cross-shaped portal in a huge barn that recalls Billy's early days on the dairy farm. They are met there by a mechanical talking cow named Bessie, designed to engage the attention of children. Inside, visitors watch a video of people asking the great life questions Graham sought to address during his long ministry, together with highlights from that ministry. They then move through display rooms that—using realistic sets, photos and artifacts gathered over a lifetime, and a variety of media—recreate key episodes and facets of the evangelist's life: the 1949 Los Angeles Crusade; his use of radio, television, and movies; his response to such issues as Communism and racial strife; his relationships with eleven U.S. presidents; the great international conferences for evangelists at Lausanne and Amsterdam; and regularly updated information about current BGEA ministries. One room is devoted to Ruth's life, both as a young girl in China and Korea and as devoted wife and mother in one of the world's most famous families.

Early reaction to the venture was mixed. Numerous observers regarded the talking cow as inappropriately hokey; others found it a fitting reminder of Graham's dairy-farm origins and a charming way to introduce the evangelist and his message to children. Some viewed the enterprise as glorifying the evangelist instead of the Christ he preached. Graham himself was said to have resisted the project at first, claiming he did not want a monument to himself. Franklin and members of the BGEA board assured him that the library tour would have a strong evangelistic dimension, which it emphatically does—virtually every exhibit involves pointed exposure to the gospel Graham preached, and the tour ends with a montage, taken from crusades over the decades, of his offering the invitation to repeat the Sinner's Prayer and meet with counselors awaiting outside the cross-shaped exit. With that understanding, Graham relented. "When it was presented as an ongoing ministry and people would have the opportunity to be won to Christ," he said, "I changed my mind."

The sharpest and most public controversy arose over whether the complex would also contain the graves of Billy and Ruth Graham. It had long been assumed that the Grahams would be buried at the Cove, but Franklin and at least some members of the BGEA board thought the library would be more appropriate. Indeed, plans had been made for the tour to end in a garden that would serve as their final earthly resting place. When Ruth learned of the plan, however, she would have none of it. Supported by Ned, at least one of his sisters—an exact count was difficult to obtain—and crime novelist and lifetime family friend Patricia Cornwell, Ruth adamantly insisted that she intended to be buried in the mountains where she had raised her children and that "she hopes her husband will join her there." She underscored her determination by signing a notarized statement, witnessed by six people, stating that she expected Billy to stand by their agreement. "My final wish," it said, "is to be buried at the Cove. Under no circumstances am I to be buried in Charlotte, North Carolina."

The dust-up drew wide, if brief, attention after the *Washington Post* published a detailed account of the family dispute, quoting Ruth as having dismissed the library complex as a "circus" and "a tourist attraction." Franklin defended the library as an appropriate burial place and said that his father had approved of the plan. He lamented the opposition from his siblings, conceded that his parents should have the last word, and observed that he was preparing both sites. A few days later, he would say only that a decision had been reached, but that the family had agreed not to discuss it any further.

The indomitable feistiness that Ruth displayed as she talked about her burial could not mask the fact that she was indeed dying. Finally, aware that she had reached the end of her earthly road and in consultation with her family, she asked to be taken off artificial life support. On June 14, 2007, surrounded by her five children and her husband of nearly 64 years, she died, at age 87. Two days later, a great cloud of witnesses turned out to express their love and respect as the cortege bearing her body traveled from the funeral home in Asheville, along U.S. Highway 70 past her beloved Cove, through the streets of Black Mountain and the narrow roads of Montreat, to Anderson Auditorium on the campus of Montreat College.

At the service, attended by more than 2,000 people and carried live on local and cable television as well as the Internet, the congregation sang, "Great Is Thy Faithfulness"; George Beverly Shea sang one of Ruth's favorite hymns, "In Tenderness He Sought Me"; and Ruth's older sister, Rosa, charmed the audience with amusing stories of their childhood in China. Each of the Graham children spoke briefly, blending reminiscence with evidence of the faith she had instilled in them. Daughter Ruth noted that early in her life their mother had chosen Christ as "as her center, her home, her purpose, her partner, her confidante, her example, and her vision, and we can all make that choice today." Ned read a Puritan prayer that Ruth had often requested as part of their daily devotions in recent years. GiGi, who said she was losing her best friend, told of standing at her mother's bedside in the last days as "she looked past us into what I believe was eternity," then read a poem, "Time to Adore," that Ruth had written about hoping she would ascend to heaven slowly rather than "in the twinkling of an eye," so that she might have "time to adore" both what she was leaving and the "joy unspeakable" that lay in store. Franklin drew laughter with stories of Ruth's trying to catch a rattlesnake with a marshmallow fork and of rousting him out of bed by pouring a can of cigarette butts and ashes on his head, but stressed that her belief in the Bible and in Jesus as the Son of God was her most important gift to her children. "I thank you, Mama," he said, "for your example, for your love, for your wit, for your humor, for your craziness. I love you for all of it, and I'm going to miss you terribly." More serious by temperament than her siblings, Anne noted their mother's love for their father, but said even that paled in comparison to her love for Jesus and for God's Word. She then read from Romans 8, the same passage she had read to Ruth on "the morning she went to heaven, to our Father's house."

Throughout the service, Billy, his white hair still long and full, had listened pensively from the front row. He had not been scheduled to speak, but decided he did have something to say. Helped to his feet by two aides and clutching his walker, he thanked people for coming and noted the presence of a large contingent of grandchildren and great-grandchildren. "As you have already heard," he said, "she was an incredible woman." Nodding toward the simple wooden casket, aware that an inmate at Louisiana's Angola prison had made a matching one for him, he added, "I wish you could look in that casket, because she's so beautiful. I sat there a long time last night just looking at her and praying, because I know that she'll have a great reception in heaven." In a statement released earlier, he had said, "Although I will miss her more than I can possibly say, I rejoice that some day soon we will be reunited in the presence of the Lord she loved and served so faithfully."

At the close of the service, the Graham children stationed themselves at the major exits from the auditorium, to greet and visit with all those who had come to honor their mother. Their father had said that he wished he could greet them all as well, but apart from his diminished strength, he would soon be accompanying Ruth's body to Charlotte, where she would be buried the following day in the memorial garden at the Billy Graham library.

Even in death, Ruth's personality shone through. Her headstone reads, "End of Construction—Thank You for Your Patience."

Some closest to him predicted that Billy's grief at Ruth's death would hasten his own, but it did not. Age continued to take its inexorable toll, further degrading his eyesight and hearing and largely restricting him to his home except for visits to his doctors in Asheville, outings he sometimes used to have lunch at TGI Friday's or to get a corn dog at the Sonic drive-in. As he was able, he wrote the book *Nearing Home: Life, Faith, and Finishing Well,* a thoughtful book about aging (published in 2011). He followed the 2008 presidential campaign on television and welcomed Republican candidate John McCain to his home. A temporary health episode forced cancellation of a similar visit with Barack Obama.

Graham himself gave no public indication of his preference between the candidates and said, "I'm not making any endorsements, and I'm staying out of partisan politics." Franklin also professed not to be offering an endorsement, but noted that the differences between the two candidates were substantial and "the choice Americans make in November will affect our nation for years to come." The mass mailing that contained that observation included a picture of Senator McCain seated between Billy and Franklin and a picture of Franklin with Fox News journalist Greta Van Susteren, who had accompanied him on his trip to North Korea. As had often been the case in previous elections, the implication was not difficult to divine.

Billy Graham turned ninety on November 7, 2008. A small gathering of family, caregivers, close friends, and staff members from the Montreat area celebrated with him at Little Piney Cove on the day of record, followed by a larger celebration a few days later at the Greenbrier resort in White Sulphur Springs, West Virginia. That event opened with a short video, narrated by veteran radio broadcaster and old friend Paul Harvey, who sat at Graham's table, had recently turned ninety himself, and would die in early 2009. Dignitaries including former President George H. W. Bush and his wife, Barbara, sent warm greetings, as did then-President George W. Bush in a separate video greeting. Stephan Nelson Tchividjian, the oldest of Graham's nineteen grandchildren, thanked "Daddy Bill" for the many valuable lessons he had taught them in both word and deed. Daughter Ruth recounted the enveloping grace her father had shown when she drove home after a failed marriage they had tried to discourage. Billy's younger sister, Jean Ford, recalled incidents from their childhood, noting that "All of us knew from Day One that he was Mother's favorite." And a notable musical trio of Michael W. Smith, Cliff Barrows, and Bev Shea, who would soon turn 100, led the assembly in "Happy Birthday."

Throughout the program, Graham sat staring emptily and impassively, reminding one of elderly nursing-home patients whose minds have long departed. When she spoke, Ruth even said, "Daddy, it's Bunny." But then, when he was handed a microphone for a response to the tributes and gifts, he spoke for nearly five minutes, his voice weak but his mind still clearly intact. He expressed gratitude to his family, his staff, and his many friends and gratitude for the opportunity to preach the gospel of Christ for so many years. Then he said he hoped to see everyone again at his ninety-fifth birthday party.

In preparation for that evening, Franklin had sent out a message asking anyone who had come to Christ under his father's ministry to send a letter or e-mail telling their story and sending birthday greetings. Like the multitudes that had streamed down the aisles at Graham's crusades, the response was visibly impressive, as waiters rolled in the first of several large carts containing more than 120,000 messages. Franklin noted that one had come from a woman converted in 1938, surely one of the first in Billy's crown, and it summarized thousands of others with the words, "We love you and we thank you." Graham managed a weak "Love you" that set off a prolonged and, for many, tearful outpouring of applause.

Franklin announced that his father was tired and needed to go to bed, wheeling him out while dessert was being served. Ruth, looking back on the occasion later, was not so sure. "Daddy thought Franklin took him out too soon. He wanted to stay longer. He talked about that night for weeks. He absolutely loved it."

Billy Graham may seriously have intended to stay free of partisan politics, but Franklin made that difficult for him. In November 2009, he invited John McCain's 2008 running mate and former Alaska governor Sarah Palin and her family to meet with his father for dinner at Little Piney Cove. After the gathering, Graham issued a statement calling it an honor to have Governor Palin in his home and noting, "I, like many people, have been impressed with her strong commitment to her faith, to family and love of country." Afterward, Franklin told the *Charlotte Observer*, "Daddy feels God was using her to wake America up." He later took Palin with him on a Samaritan's Purse relief effort to Haiti and featured her in a Samaritan's Purse video wearing one of the organization's sweatshirts as she and husband, Todd, helped clean up after the May 2011 tornadoes in Alabama.

In April 2010, at a request from the White House, the elder Graham received President Obama, marking the first time an incumbent president had ever visited him at his Montreat home. With Franklin present, they met for half an hour and prayed together, president for preacher as well as preacher for president. After the meeting, Graham issued a statement expressing pleasure at the visit and adding, "As we approach the National Day of Prayer on May 6, I want to encourage Christians everywhere to pray for our President, and for all those in positions of authority, and especially for the men and women serving in our military."

The reference to the Day of Prayer and the military was surely a conscious allusion to the fact that a week earlier, the Pentagon had rescinded an invitation to Franklin to lead a prayer service on that day, responding to public criticism of his repeated negative statements about Islam.

Franklin later described Obama as "a very nice man" and "very gracious," but indicated he was not sure if Obama was a true Christian, criticized him for appearing to be more concerned about Muslims than about Christians persecuted by Muslims, and told Fox News host Sean Hannity that he wished "the president could come under some good, sound biblical teaching."

When Mitt Romney became the Republican candidate in the 2012 presidential election, Franklin noted that "He's a Mormon" and "Most Christians would not recognize Mormons as part of the Christian faith," but added, "He would be a good president if he won the nomination, because I think he's got the strength, business-wise, politics-wise. He's a sharp guy. And he's proven himself."

Perhaps as a caution to his less circumspect son, Billy had told *Christianity Today* in early 2011 that if he had a chance to "go back and do anything differently, I would have steered clear of politics." Though grateful for the opportunities to minister to powerful people, he admitted that, "looking back, I know I sometimes crossed the line, and I wouldn't do that now." But in 2012, he appeared once again to cross that self-drawn line. In October, with the election only weeks away, Franklin brought Governor Romney to Montreat to visit his father.

That visit led immediately to a report that the elder Graham had said he would do all he could to help Governor Romney in the campaign "and you can quote me on that," and that Franklin had pledged to help turn out Evangelical Christians to vote for the governor. Soon after, BGEA produced full-page ads bearing Billy Graham's iconic visage and signature alongside copy urging voters to support "those who protect the sanctity of life and support the biblical definition of marriage between a man and a woman." The ads appeared in *USA Today*, the *Wall Street Journal*, and newspapers in battleground states, with smaller versions sent to churches to insert in their Sunday bulletins. Graham representatives note that the ads do not mention a specific candidate or party, an observation surely intended more for the IRS than for the target audience. Given that Governor Romney opposed same-sex marriage and that President Obama supported it and by doing so had, to use Franklin's words, "shaken his fist" at God, the ads left no doubt about their intent. To clarify matters further, Franklin wrote a piece in the October issue of *Decision* explaining "Why Evangelicals can vote for a Mormon," and the BGEA website deleted a long-running item identifying Mormonism as a cult. The explanation offered for the latter action was that BGEA did not want "to participate in a theological debate about something that has become politicized during this campaign."

Because of Graham's reentering the political arena "out of due season" by offering an endorsement of Romney and focusing on a topic that had never been central to his ministry when he was active, some observers charged that Franklin had steered his father in that direction, perhaps against his will or at least without full enthusiasm. Skeptics, including former and then-current BGEA employees, wondered if Graham actually made the pro-Romney statements attributed to him or had much to do with the advertising campaign. Franklin turned away reporters seeking direct confirmation or clarification from Mr. Graham himself, on the grounds that his father's infirmities made that impossible. A disappointed insider familiar with the ministry for decades suggested that, in the absence of a definitive statement by Billy Graham himself, or even if one should be forthcoming, perhaps the best course would be "to remember him as he was for most of his ministry."

When President Obama was reelected by nearly five million votes, Franklin saw a dark future. "If we are allowed to go down this road in the path that this president wants us to go down," he lamented, "I think it will be to our peril and to the destruction of this nation." Fewer than half of evangelical voters showed up to vote, and Graham considered that an insufficient turnout. "If Christians are upset," he said, "they need to be upset at themselves. We need to do a better job of getting our people—the Church—to vote.... If Christians would just vote, then elections in this country would be much different."

Franklin determined to do what he could to achieve a better result in the 2016 election. While many people were surprised by the popularity of Donald Trump, Franklin turned out to be remarkably prescient about Trump's appeal. In fact, in his 2011 interview with Christiane Amanpour, Franklin had said of Donald Trump, who had floated the idea of a 2012 run, "When I first saw that he was getting in, I thought, well, this has got to be a joke. But the more you listen to him, the more you say to yourself, you know, maybe this guy's right."

"So, he might be your candidate of choice?" Amanpour asked.

"Sure, yes," he responded.

In the same interview, Franklin had echoed Trump's "birther" views by saying that if Obama had a legitimate birth certificate, he should produce it. Not surprisingly, Trump liked the sound of those views and called Franklin a few days later to tell him so. Graham chose not to reveal the content of their conversation beyond saying, "I never told him he should run. I don't feel that's my role." But their exchange obviously went well. In 2012, BGEA received a $100,000 donation from Trump's Foundation; Samaritan's Purse received $25,000. On November 7, 2013, Donald and Melania Trump sat alongside News Corp. chairman and CEO Rupert Murdoch at a table next to Billy Graham as more than eight hundred people gathered in a hotel ballroom in Asheville to celebrate the evangelist's ninety-fifth birthday. A photo of the two tables, with then Fox News Host Greta Van Susteren leading the crowd in singing "Happy Birthday" to Graham, appeared in the January 2014 issue of *Decision*.

In keeping with his determination to light a fire under lukewarm Christians during the 2016 election campaign, Franklin led a "Decision America Tour" that featured rallies at the capitols of all fifty states. He professed to be nonpartisan—"My hope is not in either party. Both have failed miserably over the past few decades, compromising with evil all too often, and refusing to take a bold stand for righteous behavior." The aim of his campaign, he said, was "to put God back in the political process." He left little doubt, however, as to how he thought God wanted people to vote "according to His will and purpose." He repeatedly decried the policies and actions of "our government today" and opined that, despite the widely publicized blots in his copybook, "I think Donald Trump has changed. I think God is working on his heart and in his life."

When Trump surprised the world by defeating the heavily favored Democratic candidate Hillary Clinton, with the help of 81 percent of the evangelical vote, Franklin professed not to be surprised by what he called "the biggest political upset of our lifetime." After large crowds showed up for his rallies at the capitols during his fifty-state tour, he told the *Washington Post*, "I could sense God was going to do something this year. Prayer groups were started. Families prayed. Churches prayed. Then Christians went to the polls, and God showed up." As for the political pundits and secular media, "None of them understood the God-factor."

Though Graham never explicitly endorsed Trump during the campaign, the president-elect invited Franklin to join him at a "thank you" event in Alabama a few weeks after the election and acknowledged the boost Graham had provided: "Having Franklin Graham, who was so instrumental, we won so big, with evangelical Christians." At Trump's inauguration on January 20, Franklin continued the long tradition of Graham participation in signal rituals of American civil religion by reading from I Timothy 2:1–2, which urges "that supplications, prayers, intercessions, and thanksgivings be made for all men, for kings and all who are in high positions, that we may lead a quiet and peaceable life, godly and respectful in every way."

At his ninety-fifth birthday celebration in Asheville, Billy Graham was quite frail and said little, but his few words were directed to Cliff Barrows, who had turned ninety himself a few months earlier. "Cliff," he said, "I want to thank you. This celebration is partly for you as well. I want to thank you for all you have meant to me all these years. Thank you, and God bless you." Barrows responded, "Happy Birthday, dear Bill. I thank God for every remembrance of you." Notably missing was the third member of the seventy-year inner circle, George Beverly Shea, who had died in April of that year at age 104.

The evening also served as the occasion to draw attention to a new nationwide effort called "My Hope America," in which Christians across the country are encouraged to invite friends and neighbors into their homes to watch BGEA-produced videos that include messages from Billy Graham. The first of these, "The Cross," which aired on nationwide television a few days later, featured dramatic testimonies of people whose lives had been transformed by accepting Christ, punctuated by scenes of individuals struggling up a mountain to reach a large cross covered with ugly, misshapen pieces of wood that represented the sins of the world. Also interspersed were film clips of Graham's proclaiming the old, old story at various points in his long life and contemporary scenes of the venerable evangelist sitting in a chair at his home in Little Piney

Cove. Although his eyes had dimmed and his natural force had abated, his conviction remained as strong and powerful as ever as he told the familiar story at the heart of the gospel he had preached since boyhood. Near the end of the video, as a young woman stood at the foot of the cross and sang of Jesus' resurrection, the ugly branches and tangles fell away, leaving an unblemished symbol of redemption and salvation. A younger Graham, recorded at the height of his powers, proclaimed, "God says, 'Receive Him. Believe Him. Put your trust and your confidence in Him, and I will forgive your sins, and I will guarantee you eternity in heaven. It's all yours, and it's all free. All you have to do is receive it.'" Then, for the last time in his legendary ministry, Billy Graham exercised his remarkable gift of the invitation: "Today, I'm asking you to put your trust in Christ and pray this prayer, sentence by sentence after me. 'Dear Heavenly Father, I know that I'm a sinner. And I ask for your forgiveness. I believe you've died for my sins and rose from the dead. I turn from my sins. I repent of my sins. I invite you to come into my heart and my life. I want to trust and follow you as my Lord and Savior. In Jesus' name, Amen.'"

As the program ended, Graham was shown sitting in a rocker on his porch, rubbing his large black dog's neck and looking past the old rail fence at the border of the yard to the Blue Ridge mountains in the distance as the voice of his younger self said, with blessed assurance, "He's given me a reason for existence. I know where I've come from. I know why I'm here. I know where I'm going. Do you?"

Earlier in the year, Graham had published *The Reason for My Hope: Salvation*, which proclaimed a similar positive message and seemed to be an appropriate valedictory volume. Indeed, that was said to be the expectation within the Graham family and BGEA, but in September 2015 another book appeared, this one officially identified as the thirty-third and last in the string of (mostly) bestsellers. The title, *Where I Am: Heaven, Eternity, and Our Life Beyond*, would have attracted little attention in itself, but early reviewers were surprised by a greater emphasis on hell, described as "a place of wailing and a furnace of fire; a place of torment, a place of outer darkness, a place where people scream for mercy; a place of everlasting punishment" and the stark warning, "If you accept any part of the Bible, you are forced to accept the reality of hell, the place for punishment for those who reject Christ."

In the early years of his preaching, Graham used familiar fire-and-brimstone imagery and language when speaking of the ultimate fate of the unredeemed, but for most of his long career, he spoke of hell more as a state of separation from God, without much allusion to or description of the agonies of eternal physical fire. In 2005 he had told CNN's Larry King, "That's not my calling. My call is to preach the love of God and the forgiveness of God and the fact that he does forgive us. That's what the cross is all about, what the Resurrection is about. That's the Gospel." He acknowledged that he had once preached a harder line: "In my earlier ministry, I did the same. But as I got older, I guess I became more mellow and more forgiving and more loving."

Inevitably, some observers reckoned that the harsher tone of the new book reflected Franklin's views and temperament more closely than those of his father. Franklin rejected such speculation. "This isn't a cut-and-paste of his old sermons or anything like that," he insisted. He acknowledged that his former secretary, Donna Lee Toney, had helped with the actual writing of the book, but insisted that the idea, the organization, and the actual content were entirely his father's. "It's a new book. Where we needed to fill in some gaps, we went back and checked his sermons to make sure it was accurate.... It's all him. Nothing in the book was written that's not in his words." As for a perceived difference in tone and emphasis, Franklin said, "Maybe this was a burden, that he felt he didn't preach (about hell) strong enough in his latter years. I don't know."

As the years rolled past, Billy Graham continued to outlive those who had stood by his side through the decades. Howard Jones, BGEA's first black associate evangelist, died in 2010. Maurice Rowlandson, longtime head of the BGEA offices in the UK, followed in 2015, as did Graham's son-in-law Danny Lotz, Anne's husband. The following year saw the passing of researcher and sermon writer John Wesley White and Billy's faithful companion and closest friend, Cliff Barrows. Photographer Russ Busby died in 2017.

For many years Graham had said repeatedly and convincingly that death held no terror for him. That fearlessness was rooted, of course, in his absolute confidence that death was but a passage to the glorious eternal life that he had invited millions of his fellow humans to share with him. On at least one occasion he had spoken of heaven in terms harking back to his earliest preaching. In 1992 he said, "I don't think I'll miss anything about earth, because I think everything that is for my happiness and well-being will be in heaven. If there's a golf course there and golf makes me happy, there'll be a golf course."

More typically, Graham spoke of the ineffable but surely matchless glories of being in the presence of God the Father, Son, and Holy Spirit and reunion with the redeemed of the ages. He talked of questions he wanted to ask God when they had a few minutes together, such as why there is suffering in the world and whether those who have never heard the Christian gospel will truly be damned forever and ever. He wondered, no doubt, about what people would say of him in the days and decades after his death, but only one accolade seemed truly important: "I want to hear one person say something nice about me and that's the Lord, when I face him. I want him to say to me, 'Well done, thou good and faithful servant.' I'm not sure I am going to, but that's what I'd like to hear."

Surely, few Evangelical Christians doubted Billy Graham would receive that Ultimate Compliment. But many, both within and without those circles, had a more immediate question. In the famed evangelist's waning years, it became common for observers of the religious scene to speculate as to who would be "The Next Billy Graham." The answer is quite likely, "No one." Billy Graham is not, like the Pope or the Archbishop of Canterbury, an office in the Christian church that must be filled by the likeliest candidate. Graham rose to prominence at a rather low point in the history of Evangelical Christianity, when candidates for leadership were relatively few and it was easier for one person to stand out above others. Half a century later, Evangelicals had become a movement at least equal in size and strength to Catholics and "Mainline" Protestants in the United States, and most of the Christian missionary work conducted throughout the world was done under the aegis of some Evangelical/Fundamentalist/Pentecostal denomination or parachurch agency. Many faithful and talented men and women contributed mightily to that remarkable transformation. Still, from his crusades to the great international conferences, to the fostering of religious freedom in godless regimes, to the training of tens of thousands of individual itinerant evangelists, to the pioneering use of media, it was Billy Graham who, more than any other, shaped and inspired that movement. And, to the world's good fortune, he consistently manifested an expansive spirit that reached out to enlist an ever-widening circle of individuals and groups to join him in that effort. From revivals supported by small knots of Fundamentalists and Evangelicals to crusades and conferences and global missions in which Christians of every stripe and color and culture work together in common cause, Graham was a powerful, even unique force for Christian ecumenism. Individual lives and nations, the world, and the Church of Jesus Christ are richer for that fact.

The remarkable success, scope, and complexity of the movement to which Billy Graham contributed so much make it unlikely that any single figure could ever match or exceed his influence over it. It is possible, of course, that ten, fifty, or a hundred years from now, some young man or woman with just the right combination—a combination easy to describe but apparently harder to embody—will manifest comparable achievement and leadership. It may be that developments in transportation and communication will enable this New Light to shine more brightly than Billy Graham's ever could, just as jet power and radio and television and satellite and computer technology enabled him to reach more people than any of his predecessors could have dreamed possible. But unless and until that happens, William Franklin Graham, Jr., can safely be regarded as the best who ever lived at what he did—"a workman," as Scripture says, "who needeth not to be ashamed."

Notes

In the source notes that follow, page designations refer to the page on which the reference appears. In addition, the following abbreviations will appear frequently:

Throughout

BG: Billy Graham
BGCA: Billy Graham Center Archives
BGEA: Billy Graham Evangelistic Association
CN: Collection
MF: Microfilm

Part IV

LBJLA: Lyndon Baines Johnson Library Archives
JFKLA: John Fitzgerald Kennedy Library Archives
NARS: National Archives and Record Service
NPM: Nixon Presidential Materials
(National Archives and Record Service)
HRH: H. R. Haldeman
WHCF: White House Central Files
WHSF: White House Special Files

Part V

AH: Alexander S. Haraszati

Chapter 1: Mr. Graham Goes to Washington

Page

26. The description of the crusade service is necessarily a composite, since it was not possible to be simultaneously present at all facets described. The service around which the account is primarily based occurred on April 27, 1986. Some aspects of the description, however, are drawn from interviews and observations of other services during the crusade, whose dates were April 27–May 4, 1986. The story of the traffic-directing police officer was published in the July/August 1986 issue of *Decision*, the official magazine of the Billy Graham Evangelistic Association (BGEA). All other material in this chapter is drawn from personal observation.

27. "Redeemer Nation" and "soul of a church." The phrases are borrowed from Ernest Lee Tuveson, *Redeemer Nation: The Idea of America's Millenial Role* (Chicago: University of Chicago Press, 1968), and Sidney E. Mead, *The Nation with the Soul of a Church* (New York: Harper & Row, 1975).
27. "like Queen Esther." Esther 4:14.
28. "his wonders to perform." I am well aware of the strong feelings and complex theological issues involved in the use of *inclusive language*, which does not assign a masculine gender to God. Because Billy Graham, his evangelistic predecessors, and most of his contemporary Evangelical followers emphatically do not use such gender-neutral language, I have elected, for good or ill, to abide by the conventional practice of using masculine pronouns to refer to deity.
29. "Just As I Am." Lyrics by Charlotte Elliot, music by William B. Bradbury.

Chapter 2: A Great Cloud of Witnesses

32. "Seek good and not evil." Amos 5:14.
32. "as soon as God's Ordinances cease." John Cotton, "God's Promise to His Plantation," quoted in Harry S. Stout, *The New England Soul* (New York: Oxford University Press, 1986), p. 16.
33. Puritans envision "the New Heaven and the New Earth." Ibid., p. 62.
34. "one of the greatest company-keepers." Jonathan Edwards, "A Faithful Narrative of the Surprising Work of God in the Conversion of Many Hundred Souls, in Northampton, and the neighboring towns and villages of New Hampshire, in New England, in a Letter to the Reverend Dr. Colman, of Boston," in *The Works of President Edwards*, vol. III (New York: S. Converse, 1830), p. 16.
34. The revival "very much at a stop." ... "a new people." Stout, *New England Soul*, p. 72.
34. Advance publicity for Whitefield. Ibid., p. 26.
34. People leaping from the balcony. Edwin Scott Gaustad, *The Great Awakening in New England* (New York: Harper & Brothers, 1957), p. 27.
35. "the old Spirit of Preaching." George Whitefield, *Journals*, cited in Gaustad, *Great Awakening*, p. 30.
35. Whitefield criticizes local pastors. Whitefield, *Journals*, quoted by Stout, *New England Soul*, pp. 192, 194.
35. "the Word ran like lightning." Whitefield, *Letters*, quoted in Gaustad, *Great Awakening*, p. 27.
35. "not since the earthquake of 1727." Thomas Prince, "An Account of the Revival of Religion in Boston," p. 9, cited by Gaustad, *Great Awakening*, pp. 27–28.
35. Revival greatest where roots ranshallow. Stout, *New England Soul*, p. 196.
36. Edwards on the millennium. Jonathan Edwards, *Some Thoughts Concerning the Present Revival* (Boston, 1742), quoted in Stout, *New England Soul*, p. 204.
36. Marshall, Voltaire, and Paine on religion in America. J. Edwin Orr, *The Role of Prayer in Spiritual Awakening* (Los Angeles: Oxford Association for Research in Revival, n.d.), p. 1, quoted in Lewis Drummond, *A Fresh Look at the Life and Ministry of Charles G. Finney* (Minneapolis: Bethany House, 1983), p. 18.
37. James McGready's revival techniques. Charles A. Johnson, *The Frontier Camp Meeting: Religion's Harvest Time* (Dallas: Southern Methodist University Press, 1955), pp. 32–37. Much of the description of the camp meetings is based on Johnson, pp. 41–68, which quotes frequently from eyewitness accounts.
37. "liquid boiling waves" and "flaming abyss." James McGready, "A Short Narrative of the Revival of Religion," in *New York Missionary Magazine and Repository of Religious Intelligence* IV (1803), p. 228, quoted in Johnson, *Frontier Meeting*, p. 55.

38. "slain ... laid in neat rows." John Lyle, "Diary of John Lyle (1801–1803)," typed manuscript, Durrett Collection, University of Chicago, pp. 21–35. Cited by Johnson, *Frontier Meeting*, p. 58.
38. "ground was crowded with bleeding bodies." B. W. McDonnald, *History of the Cumberland Presbyterian Church* (Nashville, 1888), p. 47, cited by Johnson, *Frontier Meeting*, p. 59.
38. "like the roar of Niagara." James B. Finley, *Autobiography of Rev. James B. Finley; or, Pioneer Life in the West*, ed. William P. Strickland (Cincinnati, 1856), pp. 166–67, cited in Johnson, *Frontier Meeting*, p. 64.
41. "like cannonballs through ... eggs." Drummond, *Fresh Look*, p. 62.
41. Finney "attracted widespread criticism." Keith J. Hardman, *Charles Grandison Finney, 1792–1875* (Syracuse: Syracuse University Press, 1987), pp. 84–85.
41. "weepers seldom receive any lasting good." Finney, quoted in George W. Gale, *Auto biography of Rev. George W. Gale* (New York, 1864), p. 272.
41. The Benevolent Empire. For further information, see Donald W. Dayton, *Discovering an Evangelical Heritage* (New York: Harper & Row, 1976); Clifford Griffin, *Their Brother's Keepers: Moral Stewardship in the United States, 1800–1865* (New Brunswick: Rutgers University Press, 1960); Winthrop Hudson, *The Great Tradition of the American Churches* (New York: Harper & Row, 1963); Timothy L. Smith, *Revivalism and Social Reform* (Nashville: Abingdon Press, 1957).
42. *"the right use of the constituted means."* Charles Grandison Finney, *Lectures on Revivals of Religion* (Cambridge, Mass.: Belknap Press of Harvard University, 1960), p. 13. Italics added.
42. "a SOLEMN FACT ... Seldom." Ibid., pp. 186–88.
42. "the only way to preach." Ibid., pp. 208–9.
42. "A good preacher would also pay attention to the faces." Ibid., pp. 210–11.
42. "not hesitate to use theatrics." Ibid., p. 220.
42. "When the blessing evidently follows" ... "converting sinners." Ibid., p. 189.
42. "the great business of the church ... every kind of sin." Charles Grandison Finney, "The Pernicious Attitude of the Church on the Reforms of the Age," Letters on Revivals, no. 23, *The Oberlin Evangelist*, January 21, 1846, p. 11. This letter is reprinted in full in Dayton, *Evangelical Heritage*, pp. 20–22.
43. "useful in the highest degree possible." Finney, *Lectures*, p. 404.
43. "the millennium may come ... in three years." Ibid., p. 306.
43. "church cannot turn away ... slavery a sin." Ibid., p. 288.
43. "Finney's converts became active participants." See, for example, William Warren Sweet, *Revivalism in America* (New York: Scribners, 1945), p. 160.
46. "the public will think ... it must succeed." Letter from Moody to McCormick, April 5, 1866. Cyrus H. McCormick Papers, quoted in James F. Findlay, *Dwight L. Moody: American Evangelist 1837–1899* (Chicago: University of Chicago Press, 1969), p. 117.
46. "Moody, save all you can." D. L. Moody, *New Sermons, Addresses, and Prayers*, p. 535, quoted in Findlay, *Dwight L. Moody*, p. 253.
47. "a fair, square, practical thing." Quoted in William G. McLoughlin, Jr., *Modern Revivalism: Charles Grandison Finney to Billy Graham* (New York: Ronald Press, 1959), p. 248.
47. Eton meeting canceled. Findlay, *Dwight L. Moody*, pp. 176–77.
47. "Moody made it a big business." McLoughlin, *Modern Revivalism*, p. 166.
48. "the Calliope of Zion." This phrase originated with H. L. Mencken, *The Truth Seeker*, April 15, 1916, p. 246, quoted in William G. McLoughlin, *Billy Sunday Was His Real Name* (Chicago: University of Chicago Press, 1955), p. 155.
49. Sunday's baseball career. Joseph L. Reichler, ed., *The Baseball Encyclopedia* (New York: Macmillan, 1982), p. 1389. McLoughlin, *Billy Sunday*, pp. 3–8; "Evangelist Types Vary Over Years," Detroit *Free Press*, February 2, 1952. McLoughlin states that Sunday claimed to have stolen 95 bases. The Detroit *Free Press* credited him with 96 thefts in 116 games.

The story is better with 95 stolen bases; unfortunately, *The Baseball Encyclopedia* is probably correct. According to McLoughlin, Sunday also claimed to have batted .359 one year, but *The Baseball Encyclopedia* records no such figure. Statistics for Cobb and Wills are from *The Baseball Encyclopedia*, pp. 751 and 1474, respectively.

49. Sunday's tabernacles. To help disperse and amplify the sound, Sunday often used an Augaphone, a cone-and-umbrella-shaped device designed to disperse the voice of speaker, who stood directly under it, to all parts of the building.
49. "the devil's been hunting his hole." Sunday, quoted in Homer Rodeheaver, *Twenty Years with Billy Sunday* (Nashville: Cokesbury, 1936), p. 98.
50. "As he became flashier ... sort of woman." McLoughlin, *Billy Sunday*, pp. 174, 159, 175.
50. Sunday's preaching style. Ibid., pp. 154–56.
50. "he used his athleticism." Ibid.
50. "With Christ you are saved ... decide now." Boston *Herald*, December 9, 1916, p. 3, quoted in McLoughlin, *Modern Revivalism*, p. 409.
50. "converted without any fuss." Quoted by Mencken in *The Truth Seeker*, April 15, 1916, p. 246, quoted in McLoughlin, *Billy Sunday*, p. 128.
50. "They will not have much to change." *Life and Labors of Rev. William A. (Billy) Sunday, with Selected Sermons* (Decatur, Ill.: Herman, Poole, 1908), p. 324, quoted in McLoughlin, *Billy Sunday*, p. 129.
50. "So it sums up.... Gee whizz!" *Boston Herald*, December 15, 1916, p. 14, quoted in McLoughlin, *Billy Sunday*, p. 130.
51. Sunday's patriotism. McLoughlin, *Billy Sunday*, pp. xxvi, 258–59.
51. "godless social service nonsense." Ibid., p. 140.
51. "be a horticulturist." Ibid., p. 136.
51. "he cooperated with Prohibitionist forces." Ibid., pp. 231–35.
52. "a giant for God." W. T. Ellis, *Billy Sunday: The Man and His Message* (Philadelphia: John T. Winston, 1936), p. 277, quoted in Douglas W. Frank, *Less Than Conquerors* (Grand Rapids: Eerdmans, 1986), p. 238.
52. "easier for people to do right." McLoughlin, *Billy Sunday*, p. 293.
52. "If I had my way with these ornery wild-eyed socialists." Sydney E. Ahlstrom, *A Religious History of the American People* (New Haven: Yale University Press, 1972), p. 900.
52. "aggregate number exceeded 100 million." McLoughlin, *Billy Sunday*, p. 29. Professor McLoughlin took this figure from an obituary notice. Though he readily acknowledged it may have been exaggerated, he calculated that Sunday held, on average, 6 campaigns a year for 40 years, preaching approximately 50 sermons per campaign, with an average audience of 10,000 per sermon (in his heyday, he regularly packed tabernacles designed to hold more than 20,000 people), producing a total of 120 million. McLoughlin thought it reasonable to discount this figure by at least 20 million but did not regard the estimate of 100 million as totally implausible. Conversation, July 2, 1991.
53. "a gangly teenager." The Reverend Fred Brown, an evangelist who was holding a revival in Charlotte on November 6, 1935, the date of Sunday's death, recalled that, on learning the evangelist had died, he and two associates went into a bedroom to pray that someone would rise up to stand in the gap left by his passing. A friend of the Graham family's, he professed to remember that Billy Graham came forward that evening and made his decision to enter the ministry. Young Evangelicals often make several commitments to "full-time Christian service" during their teenage years. Billy Graham has no specific memory of such an incident, but did not deny its possibility. Fred and Donella Brown, oral history, 1976, CN 141, Box 2, Folder 39, BGCA.

Chapter 3: Billy Frank

57. "her first child." Technically, Billy was the second child. The first, a daughter, had died shortly after birth. Patricia Daniels Cornwell, *A Time for Remembering: The Ruth Bell Graham Story* (San Francisco: Harper & Row, 1983), p. 60.

57. "no aged Simeon." See Luke 2:22–35.
58. "Frank, be a good boy." Marshall Frady, *Billy Graham: Parable of American Righteousness* (Boston: Little, Brown, 1979), p. 24.
58. Frank Graham "on the sidelines of worldly pleasure." Billy Graham, "Billy Graham's Own Story: 'God Is My Witness,'" Part I, *McCall's*, April 1964, p. 124; Melvin Graham, interview, November 17, 1987.
58. Graham family's beach visits. Frady, *Parable*, p. 37.
58. "Frank purchased a house across the road." Morrow Graham, oral history, June 3, 1977, CN 141, Box 7, Folder 40, BGCA.
59. "running and zooming." Morrow Graham, interview with Michael Hooser of World Wide Pictures (a subsidiary of BGEA), April 30, 1971. A tape of this interview was furnished by BGEA.
59. "never any quietness about Billy." Morrow Graham, interview (Hooser).
59. "relieved when he started school." Morrow Coffey Graham, *They Call Me Mother Graham* (Old Tappan, N.J.: Fleming H. Revell, 1977), p. 21.
59. "he never wears down." Ibid., p. 35.
59. "sugar baby." Morrow Graham, interview (Hooser).
59. She'll "just love you for it." Ibid.
60. Whippings. Graham, "God Is My Witness," Part I, April 1964, p. 124.
60. Morrow Graham on corporal punishment. Morrow Graham, *Mother Graham*, p. 28; Morrow Graham, interview (Hooser). "The children didn't die" is a reference to Prov. 23:13: "Do not withhold discipline from a child; if you beat him with a rod, he will not die."
60. Frank Graham's conversion. Vernon W. Patterson, oral history, 1971, CN 141, Box 5, Folder 29, BGCA.
61. "I knew I was born again." Morrow Graham, oral history.
61. "family altar." Morrow Graham, interview (Hooser).
61. Graham children learn Scripture verses. Ibid.; Melvin Graham interview, November 17, 1987.
61. "Are there more gods than one?... enjoy him forever." Questions 5 and 1, *The West minster Shorter Catechism* (Richmond: Presbyterian Committee of Publications, n.d.), ratified by the General Assembly of the Presbyterian Church in the United States, December 4, 1961.
61. Sabbath rules and ice-cream cones. Melvin Graham, interview.
62. "Be quiet, or he'll call your name." BG, sermon, Washington, D.C., May 3, 1986.
62. "you couldn't get mad." Noel Houston, "Billy Graham," *Holiday*, February 1958, p. 136.
62. "You couldn't resist him." Frady, *Parable*, p. 61. A shorter version of this quote appears in Houston, "Billy Graham," p. 136.
62. "Read!" Melvin Graham, interview.
62. "obedient simians." Melvin Graham, oral history, June 2, 1977, CN 141, Box 4, Folder 6, BGCA; Catherine Graham McElroy, oral history, July 7, 1976, CN 141, Box 5, Folder 13, BGCA.
62. Billy Frank's early reading habits. BG, interview, March 1, 1988. Morrow Graham, interview (Hooser).
62. "He didn't pick up his lessons too quick." Melvin Graham, interview.
62. "ability to listen intently." Morrow Graham, interview (Hooser).
63. "my father eked out a bare existence." Graham, "'God Is My Witness,'" Part I, April 1964, p. 124.
63. Graham family's affluence. Most interviewees who knew the Grahams during this period mentioned their affluence; for example: classmate Winston W. "Wint" Covington, Jr., interview, August 9, 1988; Albert McMakin (chief tenant), telephone conversation, August 12, 1988; Sam Paxton, interview, April 27, 1988.
63. "My daddy was my idol." Melvin Graham, oral history.

63. "That was just his life, to play ball." Morrow Graham, interview (Hooser).
63. "He really did like the girls." Catherine Graham McElroy, interview, March 31, 1988. Billy's friend Wint Covington observed that "Billy always was a ladies man. He was quite a thinker, too. That's all he thought about." Covington, quoted in *Charlotte Observer*, September 21, 1968, on story of BG Appreciation Day, 1968.
63. "I never went any further." TV profile of BG, *Legends*, CNN, 1986.
63. Parents expected them "to be clean." Graham, "'God Is My Witness,'" Part I, April 1964, p. 124.
63. "get down deep into the Word." Morrow Graham, *Mother Graham*, p. 256.
64. All-day prayer meetings. *Charlotte Observer*, August 10, 1958; Morrow Graham, *Mother Graham*, p. 34, and Morrow Graham, oral history; Patterson, oral history; Patterson, "The Prayer Heard Round the World," *Decision*, October 1975, pp. 3, 12. This particular meeting was the fourth marathon prayer session the men's group had held. In some accounts, the men's group was identified as the Charlotte Layman's Evangelical Association. It appears likely that the group went by both names at different times in its existence. T. W. Wilson, whose father was a participant, felt certain it was called the Christian Men's Club at the time of this incident. Conversation, February 14, 1991.
64. "shake up the whole state." Albert McMakin, interview, March 21, 1988.
64. "out of Charlotte." John Pollock, *Billy Graham: The Authorized Biography* (New York: McGraw-Hill, 1966), p. 5; Frady, *Parable*, pp. 77–79; Morrow Graham, *Mother Graham*, p. 35.
64. "just some fanatics." Patterson, "The Prayer Heard Round the World," p. 12.
65. Ham's anti-Semitism. Houston, "Billy Graham," p. 135. Ham's tactics included quoting extensively from the notorious anti-Semitic tract, *Protocols of the Elders of Zion*, and accusing Julius Rosenwald, a philanthropist who contributed millions to develop schools for southern blacks, of planning to use these schools as vice quarters where black men and white women could cohabit.
65. "It made you think your mother had been talking to him." Graham, sermon, Washington, D.C., May 3, 1986.
65. "Almost—but lost!" "Almost Persuaded," lyrics and music by P. P. Bliss. Grady had responded to the invitation two years earlier during a meeting held by evangelist George Stephens, but he counted this response as the more important of the two.
66. "I made my decision for Christ." BG, sermons, Washington, D.C., May 3, 1986, and Columbia, S.C., April 29,1987. See also, Pollock, *Authorized Biography*, pp. 6–7; Frady, *Parable*, pp. 82–83; David Lockard, *The Unheard Billy Graham* (Waco, Tex.: Word Books, 1971), p. 14.
66. "I'm a changed boy." Morrow Graham, interview (Hooser).
66. "Oh God, I don't understand." BG, sermon, Columbia, S.C., April 29, 1987.
66. "much nicer to me." Catherine Graham McElroy, interview.
66. "it didn't change all at once." Melvin Graham, interview.
66. "right up on the sidewalk." T. W. Wilson, interview February 26, 1987.
66. "just too worldly." *Charlotte Observer*, September 24, 1956.
66. BG "had to retake a final exam." Sam Paxton, interview.
66. "wasn't any dumb bunny." Wint Covington, interview.
66. "roll up our sleeves to show our watches." Wint Covington, interview.
66. "deep down inside me." BG, sermon, Columbia, S.C., April 29, 1987. Graham has often repeated this account in quite similar form.
66. "like Sonny, Buddy, or Junior." *Boston Globe*, March 27, 1950.
67. "Grady borrowed my watch." Graham told this story on numerous occasions, usually when introducing or talking about Grady. He even repeated it in his eulogy at Wilson's funeral, November 3, 1987. Like other key stories in the oral tradition, variations exist. In some ver-

sions, perhaps the most accurate, Graham only feared the watch would be ruined. Grady sometimes responded by insisting that his nervousness stemmed not from preaching but from the fact that Billy Frank was sitting right on the front row, holding his (Grady's) girlfriend's hand. Grady Wilson, BGEA team meeting, Disney World, 1976. Tape provided by BGEA.

Chapter 4: The Boy Preacher

68. T. W. Wilson "got saved." Vernon W. Patterson, oral history, 1971, CN 141, Box 5, Folder 29, BGCA.
69. "if he could just preach like Jimmie Johnson." Melvin Graham, interview, November 17, 1987. 67 "I'll give him two weeks." Albert McMakin, interview, March 21, 1988.
69. "Sincerity" ... "a matter of principle." Stanley High, *Billy Graham: The Personal Story of the Man, His Message, and His Mission* (New York: McGraw-Hill, 1956), p. 108. 67 "Myrtle Beach." *Charlotte Observer*, September 18, 1958.
69. "man is weak." Grady Wilson, *Billy Graham as a Teenager* (Wheaton, Ill.: Miracle Books, 1957), p. 23.
70. "I'm glad to see so many of you out." Grady Wilson, *Count It All Joy* (Nashville: Broadman Press, 1984; Minneapolis: Grason, 1984), p. 59.
70. BG's first sermon. Noel Houston, "Billy Graham," *Holiday*, February 1958, p. 138.
70. To "take over the freshman class!" Grady Wilson, *Graham as Teenager*, p. 25.
71. "Griping Not Tolerated." John Pollock, *Billy Graham: The Authorized Biography* (New York: McGraw-Hill, 1966), p. 11.
71. "his classwork was a shambles." Grady Wilson, *Graham as Teenager*, p. 25, citing an article about Graham in a 1956 issue of the *American Weekly* Sunday Supplement; no other reference given.
71. Missionary visits Graham home, reconnaissance visit to Florida. BG, interview, March 1, 1988.
72. "Billy, if you leave." Pollock, *Authorized Biography*, p. 12.
72. "a voice that pulls." Wendell Phillips, interview, July 1, 1988. Phillips is the primary source of the description of the encounter with Jones. The frequently reported assertion that Graham was expelled from Bob Jones College is untrue, though he has conceded that absence from class and poor performance might well have led to dismissal on academic grounds had he remained in school. Florida Bible Institute founder and president W. T. Watson later reported that "a well-known Christian educator wrote me after being advised that Billy would be coming to our school—'Billy belongs to a good family in North Carolina. His father is an orthodox, substantial Christian man. Billy has possibilities. He will do good work if you hold his feet to the fire and insist on his taking a regular course.'" W. T. Watson, *The Bible Schooldays of Billy Graham* (Dunedin, Fla.: Trinity College, n.d.), p. 23. (Florida Bible Institute changed its name to Trinity College.) In a later oral history, Watson confirms that the educator was indeed Bob Jones, whose calmer judgment, at least on this occasion, overcame his sense of personal affront. W. T. Watson, oral history, February 14, 1977, CN 141, Box 5, Folder 42, BGCA; also, AP, March 9, 1973.
72. Letters from Phillips, oranges outside dorm windows. T. W. Wilson, oral history, January 30, 1971, CN 141, Box 4, Folder 46, BGCA.
72. BG leaves Bob Jones. The chronologies found in various accounts of these events cannot be harmonized. Some versions are clearly mistaken. After careful consideration of the evidence, I believe this version to be accurate. Fortunately, nothing of real consequence is at stake. Sources consulted include T. W. Wilson, oral history; John Minder, oral history, September 28, 1977, CN 141, Box 5, Folder 25, BGCA; Morrow Graham, oral history, June 3, 1977, CN 141, Box 7, Folder 40, BGCA; BG, interview, March 31, 1988; Wendell Phillips, interview.

72. "a picture of a roulette wheel." Vera Resue, oral history, April 18, 1980, CN 141, Box 5, Folder 30, BGCA.
72. "I spent the afternoon." Pollock, *Authorized Biography*, pp. 12–13.
73. "a lanky Ichabod." Roy Gustafson, interview, June 27, 1988.
73. "glorified tourist." BG, interview, March 31, 1988.
73. "not a digger." Vera Resue, oral history.
73. "Billy always wanted to do something big." Marshall Frady, *Billy Graham: Parable of American Righteousness* (Boston: Little, Brown, 1979), p. 130.
73. "a combination man." Watson, oral history.
73. BG admires visitors, feels call to ministry. Various accounts; e.g., Morrow Graham, oral history and *They Call Me Mother Graham* (Old Tappan, N.J.: Fleming H. Revell, 1977), p. 40; Lois Ferm, "Billy Graham in Florida," *The Florida Historical Review* (October 1981): 173–85.
73. "there is more where this came from." Watson, *Bible Schooldays*, p. 21.
74. BG pledged never to refuse autographs. Watson, oral history.
74. The ten-thousand-dollar answer to prayer. Watson, oral history; also, BillyGraham, "Billy Graham's Own Story: 'God Is My Witness,'" Part II, *McCall's*, May 1964, p. 200.
74. "couldn't preach for sour apples." Roy Gustafson provided this phrase in interview, June 27, 1988; others provided the same assessment.
74. "an all-round wonderful man." BG, interview, March 1, 1988.
74. "the gift of helps." I Cor. 12:28.
74. "I polish the apple." John Minder, oral history, February 24, 1977, CN 141, Box 5, Folder 42, BGCA.
75. BG's first formal sermon. John Minder, oral history; Graham, "'God Is My Witness,'" Part II, May 1964, pp. 200–201. Graham has told this story on numerous occasions. Roy Gustafson offers a variation, claiming that the first formal effort, complete with multiple sermons, occurred at a tent meeting in Tampa at which the other student ministers were Norman Vernon and Steve Cloud. Roy Gustafson, interview.
75. BG becomes youth director. Unidentified Tampa newspaper clipping, CN 15, Box 1, Folder 1, Scrapbook, BGCA.
75. "FBI did not lack for rules." Emily Cavanaugh Massey, oral history, March 15, 1977, CN 141, Box 5, Folder 18, BGCA.
75. Sexual scandal at FBI. Pollock, *Authorized Biography*, pp. 15–16; Frady, *Parable*, pp. 117–18; Roy Gustafson, interview.
76. "Emily thinks a great deal of me." Pollock, *Authorized Biography*, p. 16; Morrow Graham, *Mother Graham*, p. 43.
76. Emily breaks engagement. Emily Cavanaugh Massey, oral history.
76. "All the stars have fallen." High, *Personal Story*, p. 76.
76. "There is nothing to live for." Charlotte *News*, September 8, 1958; Wendell Phillips, interview. Phillips no longer has this letter but confirms the essential accuracy of the quotation.
76. Emily's rebuff affects decision to enter ministry. Allen Thomason, *Boston Post*, January 12, 1950. Frady, *Parable*, pp. 108–17, provides the most detailed account of the relationship between Billy and Emily, but both protagonists and several eyewitnesses challenge both its accuracy and the importance he assigned to it. The oral tradition on the matter is hopelessly muddled. The romance seems to have obtained an overblown and apparently permanent position in the Graham legend as a consequence of newspaper stories written shortly after he burst on the national scene. That it was significant, however, seems beyond doubt. In addition to Graham's siblings, Grady Wilson, who was not on the scene, also insisted that Billy's personality took on a more serious dimension as a direct consequence of the breakup.

    When Emily and Charles Massey married, Billy attended the wedding, sitting with the family of the bride. He recalled that everyone in the church was aware of his presence and his second-place finish. Roy Gustafson remembered that as he came down the aisle, Charles Massey looked over at Billy and winked, as if to say, "I got her." Gustafson, interview. Over the years, Billy has stayed in touch with the Masseys, once calling them from the White House. According to Marshall Frady, Charles Massey did not imagine that Graham made the call simply because he was near a convenient telephone (Frady, *Parable*, p. 117). At a 1976 testimonial dinner at their alma mater, where her husband had become a professor after turns in the army chaplaincy and several pastorates, Emily Cavanaugh Massey acknowledged her pleasure at having been loved by two good men, and early in 1987 Graham described a recent visit with "my former fiancée and her husband" as "very nostalgic and pleasant." BG, interview, February 26,1987. In general, the Masseys appear to believe the Graham-Cavanaugh romance has been sufficiently documented for historical purposes.

77. "I used to have the strangest glimpses." Pollock, *Authorized Biography*, p. 17.
77. "All right, Lord." BG, interview, March 1, 1988.
77. "bartender knocked him down." Pollock, *Authorized Biography*, p. 19; Frady, *Parable*, p. 128.
77. "Folks, pray for me." Watson, *Bible Schooldays*, p. 21.
77. "his gospel gun was always loaded." Ibid., p. 19. Graham has recalled that although the station, WFOY, had only 250 watts of power, "we thought we were reaching the whole world through that little station." Jerry B. Jenkins, "A Conversation with Billy Graham," *IRTV Guide*, vol. 2, no. 4, 1974, pp. 7–8.
78. "a young man who is going to be known." Pollock, *Authorized Biography*, p. 22.
78. "quarter pound of butter." The Reverend Cecil Underwood, oral history, March 14, 1977, CN 141, Box 5, Folder 38, BGCA.
78. "young Graham does not mince words." Unidentified newspaper clipping, scrapbook, CN 15, Box 1, Folder 1, BGCA. Some accounts place this meeting at the Peniel Baptist Church in East Palatka, but this clipping, obviously from a local newspaper, identifies the church as the East Palatka Baptist Church, noting that the revival was sponsored by the young people of the Peniel Baptist Church, where Underwood had become pastor.
78. "the first little inkling." "The New Evangelist," *Time*, October 25, 1954, p. 55.
78. Baptism in Silver Lake. Underwood, oral history. Some accounts identify the lake as Crystal Lake. Interestingly, Dean Minder had personally immersed Billy just a few weeks earlier, raising the possibility that his submission to Underwood's suggestion stemmed more from a desire to please his hosts than from any burning conviction that something was missing in his life. This third baptism (the first having been his baptism as an infant) is also mentioned in a clipping from the Park Ridge, Illinois, *Herald*, January 16, 1942, and was confirmed by Graham in conversation, February 15, 1991. Graham also indicated that he believed his baptism as an infant had been in the Methodist church to which his father had originally belonged, rather than the Presbyterian church to which the family belonged during most of his boyhood.
79. "called on stumps to repent or perish." Watson, *Bible Schooldays*, p. 7; Melvin Graham, interview; TV profile of BG, *Legends*, CNN, 1986.
79. "Poor little Bobby." Watson, oral history.
79. "as if he were God casting the planets." Watson, *Bible Schooldays*, pp. 12–13.
79. "Billy's fervor." Morrow Graham, *Mother Graham*, p. 54.
79. Sermon titles. Fliers and newspaper advertisements, CN 15, Box 1, Folder 1, Scrapbook, BGCA.
80. "crime has increased" ... "fearful damage." Billy Graham, "Signs of the Times," sermon manuscript, CN 15, Box 1, Folder 11, BGCA.
80. "Hear Billy Graham." Watson, *Bible Schooldays*, p. 21.
80. Handmade fliers. CN 15, Box 1, Folder 1, Scrapbook, BGCA.

80. "Dynamic Youthful Evangelist." Grady Wilson, BGEA team meeting, 1976. Recording provided by BGEA.
80. "A Great Gospel Preacher at 21." Flier for York, Pennsylvania, campaign, 1940, CN 15, Box 1, Folder 1, Scrapbook, BGCA.
80. "One of America's Outstanding Young Evangelists." Promotional flyer, CN 15, Box 1, Folder 6, BGCA.
80. "Good Songs Each Night." Handbill for meeting at W. T. Watson's Gospel Tabernacle, CN 15, Box 1, Folder 1, Scrapbook, BGCA.
80. "The Melody Three." Handbill, ibid.
80. "Your Friends Will Be There" appeared as the tag line on most of Graham's fliers from this period.
81. Capitola revival. Wilson, BGEA team meeting, 1976.
81. "Saul among the Benjaminites." I Sam. 10:20–24.
81. Vera Resue's valedictory. Watson, *Bible Schooldays*, p. 17. This prophetic address, now part of the Graham legend, was quoted extensively by Paul Harvey on his radio program of June 13, 1964. Vera Resue, oral history.

Chapter 5: Ruth

83. Billy meets Ruth. Patricia Daniels Cornwell, *A Time for Remembering: The Ruth Bell Graham Story* (San Francisco: Harper & Row, 1983), p. 59. I freely acknowledge a considerable debt to this excellent biography by Ms. Cornwell, who has since turned her hand to a well-regarded series of mystery novels.
84. Lutherans held "very strange beliefs." Billy Graham, "Billy Graham's Own Story: 'God Is My Witness,'" Part I, *McCall's*, April 1964, p. 125.
84. Ruth's childhood. Cornwell, *A Time for Remembering*, pp. 12–30.
84. Ruth's clothes and piety. Ibid., p. 60.
85. "I had never heard anyone pray like [that] before." John Pollock, *Billy Graham: The Authorized Biography* (New York: McGraw-Hill, 1966), p. 24.
85. "we didn't pay much attention." Jean Graham Ford, oral history, CN 141, Box 3, Folder 44, BGCA.
85. "if you let me serve you with that man." Cornwell, *A Time for Remembering*, pp. 60–61. See also Pollock, *Authorized Biography*, pp. 24–25, and Marshall Frady, *Billy Graham: Parable of American Righteousness* (Boston: Little, Brown, 1979), p. 140.
85. The courtship. Cornwell, *A Time for Remembering*, pp. 60–68.
86. "I'll do the leading." Cornwell, *A Time for Remembering*, p. 73; Pollock, *Authorized Biography*, p. 26. Despite this assertion of authority, Billy may have been prepared to compromise. A story in the college newspaper a few weeks later revealed that he "wants to head for a Far Eastern missionary field immediately after his graduation, but will go into evangelistic work if the war interferes with his plans." Wheaton *Record*, March 24, 1942.
87. Speaking across the upper Midwest. Curtis Mitchell, *Billy Graham: The Making of an Evangelist* (Philadelphia: Chilton Books, 1966), p. 175. Newspaper clipping from Whea-ton *Daily Journal*, September 13, 1941, CN 74, Box 1, Folder 4, Scrapbook, BGCA; V. Raymond Edman, "Random Recollections on Billy Graham as an Undergraduate," n.d., CN 74 (Ephemera of William Franklin Graham), Folder 11, Box 2, Supplement 1, BGCA, "A Young Southern Evangelist," handbill for meeting in Moline, Minnesota, CN 15, Box 1, Folder 6, BGCA.
87. BG replaces Dr. Edman at "the Tab." Clipping from Wheaton *Daily Journal*, September 13, 1941, Graham scrapbook, CN 15, Box 1, Folder 4, BGCA; Edman, "Random Recollections"; Pollock, *Authorized Biography*, p. 27.
87. LeTourneau "Number One Christian Layman." Undated newspaper advertisement, CN 15, Box 1, Folder 1, Scrapbook, BGCA.

87. Identical sermons. Robert Van Kampen, oral history, May 17, 1976, CN 141, Box 5, Folder 39, BGCA.
88. Army rejected application for the chaplaincy. Cornwell, *A Time for Remembering*, p. 75.
88. BG absent while Ruth is ill. Ibid., p. 78. At almost the same time, Jean Graham, who had shadowed Ruth throughout the wedding process, fell ill with bulbar polio, and Ruth may have had a light, nonparalyzing case of the same disease. Jean recovered, but suffered some lasting paralysis in one arm and in her throat. Jean Graham Ford, oral history, CN 141, Box 3, Folder 44, BGCA.
88. "businessmen's dinner series." Van Kampen, oral history. See also William G. Mc-Loughlin, *Billy Graham, Revivalist in a Secular Age* (New York: Ronald Press, 1960), p. 35; Pollock, *Authorized Biography*, p. 30; Frady, *Parable*, p. 145, etc.
88. Other accomplishments at the Village Church. Van Kampen, oral history.
88. "Billy's not a pastor." Torrey Johnson, oral history (interview conducted by Robert Shuster, BGC archivist), December 13, 1984, CN 285, BGCA.
88. "Get in there and preach." Stanley High, *Billy Graham: The Personal Story of the Man, His Message, and His Mission* (New York: McGraw-Hill, 1956), pp. 138–39.
89. WCFL. Some accounts identify the station as WENR, but Johnson claims it was WCFL. Torrey Johnson, oral history.
89. BG persuades congregation to sponsor *Songs in the Night*. Van Kampen, oral history. This task was not particularly difficult; Bob Van Kampen had provided key financial support for the program when Johnson ran it and believed in its potential.
89. "Imagine! That's our Billy Frank." Morrow Coffey Graham, *They Call Me Mother Graham* (Old Tappan, N.J.: Fleming H. Revell, 1977), p. 47; Catherine Graham McElroy, interview, March 31, 1988. Also, Cornwell, *A Time for Remembering*, p. 80.
89. Van Kampen Press. Van Kampen, oral history.
89. Effectiveness of *Songs in the Night*. George Beverly Shea, interview, March 5, 1989; Torrey Johnson, oral history; Cornwell, *A Time for Remembering*, p. 80; etc.
89. "another Billy Sunday or Moody" ... "It was obvious." Van Kampen, oral history.
90. Growth in Bible institutes. Sydney E. Ahlstrom, *A Religious History of the American People* (New Haven: Yale University Press, 1972), p. 913.

Chapter 6: "Geared to the Times, Anchored to the Rock"

92. Beginnings of youth rallies. James C. Hefley, *God Goes to High School* (Waco, Tex.: Words Books, 1970), p. 21. The "Youth" section of *United Evangelical Action*, the journal published by the National Association of Evangelicals, regularly carried stories of Wyrtzen's rallies, some of which drew more than twenty thousand young people. See, for example, the April 1944, May 1944, and October 1944 issues. These publications were made available to me by the staff at the National Association of Evangelicals, Carol Stream, Illinois.
92. Bev Shea encourages Johnson to start youth program. Torrey Johnson, oral history (interview with Robert Shuster, BGC archivist), December 13, 1984, CN 285, BGCA. Also, Torrey Johnson, oral history (interview with Lois Ferm), February 8, 1977, CN 141, Box 24, Folder 23, BGCA. There is substantial overlap between these two oral histories, and no noticeable contradictions, but the interview in CN 285 is more extensive and thorough than that in CN 141. Both are extremely rich interviews.
93. "the worst fit of stage fright of my life." John Pollock, *Billy Graham: The Authorized Biography* (New York: McGraw-Hill, 1966), p. 32.
93. "He electrified the gathering." Merrill Dunlop (musical director for the service), interview with Robert Shuster, CN 50, Tape T2A, BGCA. Though I have consulted this and other sources for myself, I acknowledge a debt for having been guided to them by Ron Frank, a graduate student in Church history at the Graham Center in Wheaton during the period of my research there. My appreciation for the importance of the YFC years was greatly

enhanced by conversation with Mr. Frank and by his unpublished seminar paper, "Graham's Youth for Christ Years: What Was Their Significance?" May 15, 1986.

93. "forty-two people responded" at May 27, 1944, Chicago rally. Hefley, *High School*, p. 22; Pollock, *Authorized Biography*, p. 32; etc.

93. "the Bobby-Sox Evangelist." *United Evangelical Action*, November 1, 1944.

93. "spent much of his time on the telephone." James T. "Jimmie" Johnson, oral history, January 10, 1979, CN 141, Box 17, Folder 14, BGCA.

94. Torrey Johnson persuades Graham to join YFC. In some accounts of this meeting, Johnson and the Grahams found themselves booked into the same hotel, or into propinquitous hotels, quite by accident (Patricia Daniels Cornwell, *A Time for Remembering: The Ruth Bell Graham Story* [San Francisco: Harper & Row, 1983], p. 81), though Graham has been quoted as saying it was "not by chance. The Lord was in it." Stanley High, *Billy Graham: The Personal Story of the Man, His Message, and His Mission* (New York: McGraw-Hill, 1956), p. 140. In an oral history interview (CN 285, BGCA), Johnson states the two couples made the trip together. In yet another version, Johnson was in Miami and requested hotel reservations for both parties. Don Mott, oral history, April 18, 1983, CN 141, Box 14, Folder 1, BGCA. Given Johnson's single-minded pursuit of his goals, it is doubtful their meeting was a coincidence.

94. "will you come join us?" BG, interview, March 1, 1988.

94. Leaving Western Springs, gaining release from chaplaincy commitment. BG, interview, March 1, 1988.

94. "not one bit of paper work." Hefley, *High School*, p. 24.

94. Winona Lake conference of Youth for Christ. Also present at this and subsequent meetings were businessmen who backed the movement and college presidents such as Bob Jones and V. Raymond Edman, who hoped the organization would send their schools a fresh supply of students. Other college presidents who supported the movement included John Brown of John Brown University in Arkansas, Louis Talbot of the Bible Institute of Los Angeles, and Will Houghton of the Moody Bible Institute. No school seems to have benefited from the movement more than Bob Jones College. Several of the YFC evangelists were enamored of the school, and several directed as many as forty or fifty students to it each year. Torrey Johnson, oral history, CN 285, BGCA.

94. "We never inquired." Ibid.

95. BG is "top civilian passenger." Hefley, *High School*, p. 32. Some estimates run as high as 200,000 miles.

95. T. W. Wilson joins YFC. T. W. Wilson, interview, February 26, 1987.

95. "We were just these dynamic, handsome young guys." Marshall Frady, *Billy Graham: Parable of American Righteousness* (Boston: Little, Brown, 1979), p. 161.

96. "consecrated saxophone." "YFC Girds for Action," *United Evangelical Action*, August 15, 1945.

96. MacArthur, "the Gospel Horse." Hefley, *High School*, p. 17. Torrey Johnson claims the Gospel Horse was not a YFC attraction, but the story is well attested, and the BGCA contain material on such a horse. It may be that Johnson was never directly associated with such an act. Johnson, oral history, CN 285, BGCA.

96. "We punched them right between the eyes." William G. McLoughlin, *Billy Graham, Revivalist in a Secular Age* (New York: Ronald Press, 1960), p. 38.

96. 1945 Memorial Day Rally. "70,000 Attend Memorial Day Rally," *United Evangelical Action*, June 15, 1945; "Billy Graham Tours Country for YFC," *United Evangelical Action*, April 4, 1945); Torrey Johnson, oral history (interview with Lois Ferm), February 8, 1977, CN 141, Box 24, Folder 23, BGCA.

97. "I believe God wants you to go to . . ." Hefley, *High School*, p. 31.

97. First meeting between Graham and Barrows. Cliff Barrows, interview, February 24, 1987.

97. "Graham might turn out to be a top newsmaker." Wesley Hartzell and Jim Huffman, "Billy Graham's Twenty Years as a World Crusader," Chicago *Sunday American Magazine*, March 13, 1966, p. 4, in CN 224 (Shufelt Papers), Box 1, Folder 18, BGCA.
98. "Puff YFC." Torrey Johnson, oral history, CN 285, BGCA; "Youth for Christ," *Time*, February 4, 1946, pp. 46–47. According to Johnson, the telegram, whose wording was notably similar to Hearst's later and more famous directive, "Puff Graham," fell into the hands of Wesley Hartzell, who relayed its contents to Johnson.
98. Hartzell's reports give BG wide exposure. Hefley, *High School*, p. 25; cf. also Pollock, *Authorized Biography*, p. 21.
98. Preparation for trip to England. Torrey Johnson, oral history, CN 285, BGCA; *United Evangelical Action*, March 1, 1946; Charles Templeton, interview, December 2, 1987; Frady, *Parable*, p. 164; Pollock, *Authorized Biography*, pp. 34–35.
99. Fiasco at Gander AFB. Charles Templeton, interview.
99. "like a breath from heaven." Torrey Johnson, oral history, CN 141, BGCA.
99. "We want you just like you were." Ibid.
99. "He spoke for fifty-seven minutes." . . . "It was terrific." Canon Thomas Livermore, oral history, 1971, CN 141, Box 10, Folder 9, BGCA. The memory of the bow tie and the clerical robe was provided by BG in a talk before the Youth for Christ Council Convocation, July 26–August 4, 1974, CN 141, Box 11, Folder 55, Tape 15A, BGCA.
100. Paul Maddox assists Graham. Torrey Johnson, oral history, CN 141, BGCA.
100. "God really knit our hearts together." Cliff Barrows, interview, February 24, 1987.
100. Fog in churches. Don E. Hoke, article in *Christian Life*, reprinted in *The Fundamentalist*, January 6, 1950, in CN 360, MF Reel 1, BGCA.
100. Manchester campaign. "Billy Graham on Evangelism," *Christian Life*, January 1951, p. 11, cited by Frank, "Graham's YFC Years," fn. 22.
100. "not to argue, only to explain." Stanley High, *Billy Graham: The Personal Story of the Man, His Message, and His Mission* (New York: McGraw-Hill, 1956), p. 143.
100. "Billy called on me." An unidentified clergyman quoted in High, *Personal Story*, p. 144.
101. "the greatest spiritual revival." *United Evangelical Action*, January 1, 1947, p. 17.
101. Olford's meeting with Graham. Stephen Olford, interview, April 21, 1988; Stephen Olford, oral history, CN 141, Box 5, Folder 27, BGCA; BG, interview, March 1, 1988. The three sources of this account differ in minor details, mostly with respect to chronology. Based primarily on the personnel making the two YFC trips, the version presented here seems accurate. With the passage of time, the significance of the event seems to have diminished somewhat in Graham's assessment, but since he assigned it a prominent role in earlier accounts, it seems fair to assume that it was a pivotal occasion.
102. "It became fascinating." Templeton, quoted in Frady, *Parable*, pp. 172–73.
102. "a similar Southern Baptist youth revival movement." During the summer of 1946, Reiji Hoshizaki, a Nisei student at Baylor University in Waco, Texas, participated in activities of the Chicagoland Youth for Christ. That fall, his enthusiasm generated interest at Baylor for a similar program. The following year, after Hoshizaki and a fellow student, M. D. Oates, observed additional YFC activities in San Diego, they returned to Baylor committed to a youth-led revival effort, which they called Waco Youth for Christ. Months of preparation and hours-long prayer meetings culminated in dramatically successful citywide revivals in Waco, Dallas, and Houston. Then, under the aegis of the Baptist General Convention of Texas, the movement organized similarly fruitful efforts throughout the South and in Hawaii. Numerous participants in what came to be known as the Youth Revival movement—since they were not affiliated with YFCI, they were asked to drop the original designation—have become key leaders in the Southern Baptist Convention, and historians of the movement credit it with giving rise to organized youth programs in Baptist and other churches. For a concise sketch of this movement, see Katy Jennings Stokes, "Those Halcyon Days," *The*

Baylor Line, April 1981, pp. 23–27. The Texas Collection at Baylor contains scrapbooks, correspondence, and oral histories pertaining to the movement. I am also indebted to conversations with former participant William Cody for helpful background information and insights regarding the movement.

102. Hearst: YFC a "good and growing thing." Quoted in Hefley, *High School*, p. 13. No source given.

103. "Modernism was on the ropes." From a Graham sermon quoted by Charles Cook, *The Billy Graham Story: "One Thing I Do"* (London: Marshall, Morgan and Scott, 1955), pp. 90–91, cited by McLoughlin, *Revivalist*, pp. 39–40.

103. "America's foremost youth leader." Song sheet from YFC rally, Grand Rapids, Michigan, September 1947, CN 224 (Shufelt Papers), Box 1, Folder 18, BGCA. Cited in Ron Frank, "Billy Graham and Los Angeles 1949: A Date with Destiny," (unpublished paper, Wheaton College, 1986), pp. 4–5.

103. "A Young Athlete." Crusade brochure, Grand Rapids, September 1947, ibid.

103. Advertising for Charlotte campaign. "Crusade Report—Billy Graham Revival in Charlotte, North Carolina," CN 5 (Patterson Papers), Box 1, Folder 8, BGCA.

103. "a gaggle of gospel variety acts." *Charlotte Observer*, November 23, 1947, and August 10, 1958; "Crusade Report," Patterson Papers; Mel Larson, *Youth for Christ: Twentieth-Century Wonder* (Grand Rapids: Zondervan, 1947); quotes from Grady Wilson are from Frady, *Parable*, p. 174.

104. "We didn't really ask Grady." BG, interview, March 5, 1989.

104. Raising Shea's pay. Vernon W. Patterson, oral history, 1971, CN 141, Box 5, Folder 29, BGCA.

104. "Communism ... South America" and "Unless ... isolated in the world." *Charlotte Observer*, November 23, 1947.

104. "You should see Europe." Tom Fesperman, Charlotte *News*, November 10, 1947.

104. "Jesus Christ is the Hero of my soul." *Charlotte Observer*, November 23, 1947.

104. Advertisement for Northwestern College. "Northwestern College Opens September, 1944," *United Evangelical Action*, August 15, 1944, p. 3.

104. Riley talks to both Johnson and Graham. On March 12, 1946, the Northwestern board officially invited Johnson to become president of the schools, with Graham to serve as his assistant and "field representative." Torrey Johnson, oral history, CN 141, BGCA. Some people familiar with the story believe Graham was Riley's first choice and that the decision to invite Johnson was at Graham's urging (see, for example, Pollock, *Authorized Biography*, p. 42), but the early date of this invitation makes this somewhat improbable. W. T. Watson stated that Riley had first developed an interest in Graham during his visits to FBI. Watson, oral history, January 30, 1971, CN 141, Box 4, Folder 46, BGCA.

105. W. B. Riley's search for a successor. George Wilson, interview, August 3, 1987; Torrey Johnson, oral history, CN 141, BGCA; High, *Personal Story*, p. 145.

105. Riley: "I'll meet you at the judgment seat." High, *Personal Story*, p. 145. Several versions of this story exist, none of which can be certified as accurate, since no recording of the occasion exists, and Graham's own memory for such details is imprecise. Pollock, for example, has Riley using the biblical image of Elijah's conferring his mantle upon Elisha, *Authorized Biography*, p. 42. Frady's account appears to be a conflation of the High and Pollock versions. Frady, *Parable*, p. 175. Since Graham has been the ostensible source of all the accounts, I have chosen to accept High's version because it was obtained closer to the event itself. There seems no doubt that Riley called Graham to his bedside and invoked some biblical story of succession.

105. BG agrees only to interim presidency. Graham's reluctance to assume the position is made clear in a letter written to the school's board of directors eleven days after Riley's death. In it he stated that he would become the interim president "with the clear understanding that

my present responsibilities and commitments to Youth for Christ International before September 1, 1948, are to be fulfilled.... I have never sought this position. It has been thrust upon me. I wrote Dr. Riley several letters in which I turned down the position flatly, even requesting that he neither negotiate nor write to me anymore; but you know Dr. Riley. When he thought he was right, he held on as ferociously as a bulldog until he made me give him this promise and commitment. I intend to fulfill my obligation and commitment to Dr. Riley...." Letter from BG to Northwestern Schools Board of Directors, December 17, 1947, in Minutes of Youth for Christ Board of Directors, CN 48 (Youth for Christ International), Box 9, Folder 4, BGCA. Cited by R. Frank, "Graham's YFC Years," n. 44.

105. Ruth "never" moving to Minneapolis. Cornwell, *A Time for Remembering*, p. 85.

106. T. W. Wilson a successful YFC evangelist. See, for example, an account of his British campaign in *United Evangelical Action*, December 1, 1948, p. 20.

106. "I would be a miserable flop." T. W. Wilson, interview, February 28, 1987.

106. T. W. comes to Northwestern; Beavan helps with publicity. Wilson never shared Graham's confidence that God wanted him at the schools. "I told him one day," he recalled, "Billy, I'm here, but I think you called me instead of God." T. W. Wilson, oral history, January 30, 1971, CN 141, Box 6, Folder 1, BGCA.

106. "Dear Gang." Pollock, *Authorized Biography*, p. 44.

106. "He hired him because he liked him." T. W. Wilson, interview, February 26, 1987.

106. Growth at Northwestern Schools. Exact figures are hard to pin down. Authoritatively offered accounts have ranged from a low of 400 students at the beginning of Graham's presidency to a high of 1,259 when he resigned in 1951. In an annual report of the enrollment of Evangelical colleges and Bible schools, *United Evangelical Action* tended to round off enrollment to the nearest hundred. For example, one article pegged the enrollment at Northwestern at 1,000 and that at Bob Jones at 3,000. *United Evangelical Action*, July 1, 1948, pp. 11–12.

106. Honorary degrees. *Charlotte Observer*, September 15, 1948.

106. Bob Jones gives commencement address. *United Evangelical Action*, July 1, 1948, p. 27.

107. Graham attends WCC meeting in Amsterdam. Pollock, *Authorized Biography*, p. 47.

107. "I think Bill knows that." Cliff Barrows, interview, March 25, 1987.

Chapter 7: The Canvas Cathedral

109. The postwar revival. Most data cited here are from George Cornell, AP, February 5, 1951. The best accounts of the postwar healing revival are David E. Harrell's two books, *All Things Are Possible* (Bloomington: Indiana University Press, 1975) and *Oral Roberts: An American Life* (Bloomington: Indiana University Press, 1985).

110. The Modesto Manifesto. This account, including all quotes, is based primarily on material from Cliff Barrows, interview, March 25, 1987, Greenville, South Carolina. Graham, Shea, and Wilson have all spoken frequently of this occasion, and various writers have mentioned it. Other problems they pledged to avoid included sensationalism, overemotionalism, excessive emphasis on biblical prophecy or other controversial topics, anti-intellectualism, and the lack of proper follow-up on inquirers.

110. Bev Shea sends laundry money. Ira Eshelman (member of sponsoring committee), oral history, February 10, 1977, CN 141, Box 3, Folder 43, BGCA.

111. "the sorriest crusade." Grady Wilson, interview, March 1, 1987.

111. Altoona "not one of the most blessed of events." Cliff Barrows, interview, February 24, 1987.

111. Deranged woman. Barrows, interview, February 24, 1987; Grady Wilson, interview, March 1, 1987.

111. "We didn't do much in Altoona." Barrows, interview, February 24, 1987.

112. Graham's prayer at Maranatha Bible Conference. Roy Gustafson, interview, June 27, 1988. Several biographical works contain accounts of the prayer in the field.

112. Templeton "not an expositor." Torrey Johnson, oral history (interview with Robert Shuster, BGC archivist), December 13, 1984, CN 285, BGCA.
113. BG "got more results." Charles B. Templeton, interview, December 2, 1987. 110 Templeton "best used of God." *United Evangelical Action*, April 15, 1946, pp. 6–7.
113. "That was before he went to seminary." Lawrence Young, oral history, July 1971, CN 141, Box 5, Folder 49, BGCA.
113. "Chuck, go to Oxford." Templeton, interview.
114. "Bill, you cannot refuse to think." Templeton, interview. For the full text of the great commandment, see Mark 12:29–30.
115. "of all men most miserable." I Cor. 15:17–19.
115. Graham's Forest Home "surrender." John Pollock, *Billy Graham: The Authorized Biography* (New York: McGraw-Hill, 1966), p. 53. Frady's account of this incident has Graham saying, "Lord, help me. I don't have the knowledge. I'm placing myself completely, heart and mind, without intellectual reservations, in your hands.... Oh, Lord, I do! accept this as your word! Come what may, without question or falter, I believe in this as your holy word!" Marshall Frady, *Billy Graham: Parable of American Righteousness* (Boston: Little, Brown, 1979) pp. 183–84. Since Graham was alone, he is obviously the only possible source for any reliable reconstruction of what he actually said, aloud or to himself, and here, as elsewhere, Frady's recollections were apparently unaided by a tape recorder. The possibilities for variant accounts of the exact wording of this prayer are thus quite substantial, and Graham's more recent accounts of the incident have become quite succinct—e.g., "Oh God, from this moment on, I am going to accept this book as Thy word." I have used Pollock's version because it lay closer to the original event and received Graham's approval as an authentic account. Given the familiarity with which Graham's longtime associates speak of "the Forest Home experience" and the subsequent erection of a monument on the spot where he accepted the authority of the Scriptures, there seems little reason to doubt the essential substance of such accounts.
115. "I could not live without facing my doubts." Charles Templeton, interview.
115. Templeton "the most gifted." *National Council Outlook*, June 1951, p. 14. Cited in Lawrence Leland LaCour, *A Study of the Revival Method in America, 1920–1955, with Special Reference to Billy Sunday, Aimee Semple McPherson, and Billy Graham* (Ph.D. diss., Northwestern University, 1956), p. 276.
115. "gave [me] power and authority." Maynard Good Stoddard, "Billy Graham: The World Is His Pulpit," *Saturday Evening Post*, March 1986, p. 44.
115. "I felt as though I had a rapier." Billy Graham, "The Authority of Scriptures in Evangelistic Preaching," *Christianity Today*, October 15, 1956, p. 6. This was Graham's first article in the inaugural issue of the magazine.
115. "a bronze tablet." The tablet reads: "To the praise of God for the life and ministry of Dr. Billy Graham, who had a life-changing encounter with God here at Forest Home when, as a young preacher, he knelt with the Bible in his hands and promised God he would 'take the Bible by faith and preach it without reservation.' From that time his preaching was marked by a new and God-given authority. Preaching the scriptures in the power of the Holy Spirit, he has seen multiplied thousands turn to the Lord Jesus Christ in repentance and faith (Heb. 4:12). This tablet was placed here on April 9, 1967, when Dr. Graham preached by this lakeside." Forest Home officials commissioned the tablet in appreciation for Graham's role in a major fund-raising drive on behalf of the center.
116. Groups supporting "Christ for Greater Los Angeles" efforts. Report on Billy Graham Crusade, CN 141, Box 5, Folder 14, BGCA. An estimated 250 churches, most affiliated with the National Association of Evangelicals, supported the campaign. Most of the "mainline" denominations belonging to the Los Angeles Council of Churches took no role in the early stages.

116. Edwin Orr and Armin Gesswein conduct preparatory meetings. "Ripples of the Revival," *Youth for Christ Magazine*, January 1950, p. 23. I. A. "Daddy" Moon also helped, especially in working with counselors.
116. "around-the-clock prayer chains." Stanley High, *Billy Graham: The Personal Story of the Man, His Message, and His Mission* (New York: McGraw-Hill, 1956), p. 148.
116. "a garish midway-style picture." The museum at the Billy Graham Center at Wheaton College contains an exhibit focused on the Los Angeles campaign. In an interesting bit of revisionist pictorial history, the picture of Graham on the marquee has been retouched to give it a less carnival-style appearance.
116. Hollywood Christian Group. Several accounts of the Los Angeles revival identify this organization as the Stars Christian Fellowship Group, but participants in the group confirm that the name used here was correct.
116. Endorsement from the mayor. "Ripples of the Revival," *Youth for Christ Magazine*, January 1950, p. 23.
117. "Dr. Graham." *The Canvas Cathedral*, a motion picture documentary account of the crusade that serves not only as a valuable record of the event itself but as an index of Graham's confidence, or at least hope, that future generations might want a record of this event. CN 113, BGCA.
117. "We don't believe it is a concert." "Sickle for the Harvest," *Time*, November 14, 1949, p. 64. At the end of the crusade, *Life* magazine noted that "Graham frowned on flashy, crowd-drawing showmanship." "A New Evangelist Arises," *Life*, November 21, 1949, pp. 97–98. See also Mel Larson, "Tasting Revival," *Revival in Our Time* (Wheaton: Van Kampen Press, 1950), pp. 18–19.
117. An "authority that impressed even his colleagues." Shortly after the crusade, Bev Shea wrote that following the Forest Home experience, "God spoke through Billy in a way I had not seen before." George Beverly Shea, "God Was There," *Youth for Christ Magazine*, January 1950, p. 16.
117. Graham's preaching. This account of Graham's preaching is based on sermons published shortly after the Los Angeles crusade in *Revival in Our Time*, and on the film, *The Canvas Cathedral*.
117. "a mile per sermon." I do not find this estimate incredible. Maturity and television have reigned in Graham's pulpit peregrinations, but I have made similar calculations about other peripatetic preachers.
117. "wire recording." AP, February 19, 1950.
117. "I've learned ... delivery that holds them." Tom Fesperman, Charlotte *News*, November 10, 1947.
118. Soviet Union "had successfully tested the bomb." *Charlotte Observer*, October 2, 1948.
118. Sermon on communism. Billy Graham, "Prepare to Meet Thy God," *Revival in Our Time*, p. 124.
119. "I pray that He would." Ibid.
119. "little ... distinguished the revival." Larson, "Tasting Revival," *Revival in Our Time*, p. 13.
119. Wide spacing of seats. Lawrence Young, oral history. Young admitted that "the crusade was pretty well bogged down as far as numbers were concerned."
119. "put out a fleece." This figure of speech, indicating a practical experiment by means of which an individual seeks to discern God's will, is drawn from the biblical story of Gideon, who set out a fleece one evening, asking God to indicate his will by causing the fleece to become wet with dew while the surrounding ground remained dry. When this occurred, he set out the fleece a second time, with the more difficult request that the fleece remain dry while the dew moistened the ground around it. When this condition was also met, Gideon concluded that the Lord was indeed with him and led three hundred Israelites in a rout of the much larger Midianite army. See Judg. 6:33–7:25. The story of the weather fleece was

related by the motion maker, Lionel Mayell, oral history, October 28, 1977, CN 141, Box 5, Folder 20, BGCA.

119. Hamblen "a key man in the area." Larson, "Tasting Revival," *Revival in Our Time*, p. 14.

119. "Someone ... who is a phoney." Pollock, *Authorized Biography*, p. 57.

120. "I heard the heavenly switchboard click." Stuart Hamblen, "Lord, You're Hearing a New Voice," *Youth for Christ Magazine*, January 1950, p. 72. The account of Hamblen's conversion is based primarily on oral histories by Lionel Mayell and Don Mott. Similar versions occur in various accounts of this crusade. Most state, incorrectly I believe, that Hamblen was drunk from a night of rebellious barhopping.

120. "I will keep El Lobo." Toronto *Daily Star*, November 2, 1949.

120. "Puff Graham." BG, interview, February 27, 1987.

120. "Puff Graham" background. Roy McKeown, interview, August 10, 1988; Roy McKeown, oral history, October 28, 1977, CN 141, Box 5, Folder 14, BGCA. Several other stories have arisen to account for Hearst's decision to step in at this particular point. In one, a maid at Hearst's San Simeon castle commended the meetings to her employer. In another, Hearst and Marion Davies attended the revival in disguise. In yet another, a Mrs. Edwards, an older woman who belonged to a prayer group that prayed regularly for Charles Fuller and his *Old-Fashioned Revival Hour* and had devoted temporary attention to BG, had somehow managed to get through to Hearst on the telephone and had shared her conviction that BG was "God's man for this nation." According to her testimony, Hearst made no commitment but treated her politely. Mrs. Edwards's confidence in Graham persisted. She spent several years traveling to cities where Graham was preaching to pray for his crusades. For her story, see Pat Robertson, *Shout It from the Housetops* (Plainfield, N.J.: Logos International, 1972), pp. 48–53. All three stories could, of course, be true. I have personally pressed Roy McKeown for details and believe the sequence of events described here to be the most significant. Cornwell, based on her conversation with Don Goodenow, the *Examiner's* picture editor, asserts that Hearst's teletype message to his managing editors was a more prosaic "give attention to Billy Graham's meetings." Patricia Daniels Cornwell, *A Time for Remembering: The Ruth Bell Graham Story* (San Francisco: Harper & Row, 1983), pp. 86–88.

121. "The press will work for nothing." J. Edwin Orr, interview, July 14, 1986.

121. "I never thought [Hearst] would see a person like me." BG, interview, February 27, 1987.

121. Hearst interested in "whatever attracted the greatest number." Cornwell, *A Time for Remembering*, p. 86.

121. "missionary just back from Korea." Mayell, oral history. 118 Graham uses Edwards's sermon. Cornwell, *A Time for Remembering*, p. 87.

122. Zamperini. For the story of Zamperini's conversion and subsequent ministry to troubled youth, see Louis Zamperini, *Trouble at My Heels: The Story of Louis Zamperini* (London: Peter Davies, 1956). See also, Louis Zamperini, "I Had Turned My Back on God," *Youth for Christ Magazine*, January 1950, p. 31.

122. Jim Vaus. Most of the material on Vaus is from an interview conducted on August 4, 1988. Some details are from Jim Vaus, oral history, May 26, 1976, CN 141, Box 5, Folder 40, BGCA; McKeown, oral history; Jim Vaus, *The Devil Loves a Shining Mark: The Story of My Life* (Waco, Tex.: Word Books, 1974); *Los Angeles Herald*, November 8, 1945; and Lewis W. Gillenson, *Billy Graham and Seven Who Were Saved* (New York: Trident Press, 1967), pp. 87–114.

122. Graham meets Mickey Cohen. Vaus interview; also, BG, "Billy Graham's Own Story: 'God Is My Witness,'" Part II, *McCall's*, May 1964, p. 180. Like Hamblen's, the Zamperini and Vaus conversions stood the test of time. Zamperini established a camp for troubled boys. Vaus worked with street gangs in East Harlem for twelve years, then returned to California, where he founded an elaborate program to locate and assist runaway youth.

123. "Louella Parsons interviewed him." McKeown, oral history.

119. AP assessment. Quoted in Stanley High, *Billy Graham: The Personal Story of the Man, His Message, and His Mission* (New York: McGraw-Hill, 1956), p. 133. Precise reference not given.
123. "biggest revival ... since the death of Aimee Semple McPherson. "A New Evangelist Arises," *Life*, November 21, 1949, p. 97.
123. "the revival sickle." "Sickle for the Harvest," p. 63.
123. "I wouldn't go without him." Morrow Coffey Graham, *They Call Me Mother Graham* (Old Tappan, N.J.: Fleming H. Revell, 1977), p. 51.
123. "Prostitutes and skid-row derelicts showed up." Benjamin Weiss, oral history, July 1971, CN 141, Box 5, Folder 43, BGCA.
123. Campaign statistics. The estimate of inquirers is from BGEA statistical sheets, updated after each crusade. Other published accounts set the number within a range between 4,100 and 6,000.
123. "hot-rodders in wide ties." McKeown, oral history. The information about Fuller's support is from Armin Gesswein, oral history, July 13, 1971, CN 141, Box 3, Folder 55, BGCA. Shuler's support is noted in Lawrence Young, oral history. According to Young, Shuler claimed the cancellation of services to allow members to attend the revival cost his Trinity Methodist Church at least twenty thousand dollars.
123. "something ... way beyond me." Gesswein, oral history.

Chapter 8: Evangelism Incorporated

127. Ockenga's attitude toward BG. Allan Emery, oral history, April 9, 1979, CN 141, Box 10, Folder 4, BGCA; Harold John Ockenga, oral history, March 19, 1972, CN 141, Box 11, Folder 38, BGCA.
128. "my lips will turn to clay." Allan Emery, oral history. Emery reported that Billy Sunday's crusade had resulted in fifty-four new churches in Boston. See also "Evangelist Graham Depicts U.S. at Crossroads in Boston Debut," *Boston Herald*, December 31, 1949; "Gospel Rally Attracts 6,000," *Boston Sunday Post*, January 1, 1950; "7,500 Hear Dr. Graham in Crusade," *Boston Post*, January 2, 1950; "Evangelist Calls City to Week of Penitence," *Boston Herald*, January 2, 1950. All clippings from CN 17, Mid-Century Campaign Scrapbook, 1949, BGCA.
128. "A spirit ... I've never seen since." Mrs. Allan Emery, in Allan Emery, oral history.
128. Boston Press Conference. Lawrence Dame, *Boston Herald*, December 30, 1949; Allan Emery, interview, July 19, 1986. See also Allan Emery, oral history. In another press conference two weeks later, BG once again explained the details of the financing of the campaign. *Boston Herald*, January 10, 1950; *Boston Post* and *Record*, January 12, 1950. Emery reported BG's salary as "something like $7,500." Joseph F. Dineen, in a complimentary series carried in the *Boston Globe*, pegged BG's salary at $12,500, April 3, 1950; *Look* placed it at $8,500 but noted he had taken in approximately $13,000 the previous year from love offerings and had returned his salary to Northwestern. Lewis Gillenson, "Billy Graham: God's Ball of Fire," *Look*, July 18, 1950, p. 27.
129. "swashbuckling southerner." Grace Davidson, *Boston Post*, December 30, 1949.
129. "imminent deification of Joseph Stalin." Gene Casey, "Evangelist Sees Return of Christ in 10–15 Years," *Boston Globe*, December 30, 1949.
129. "Wait till those gravestones start popping." Boston *American*, January 13, 1950.
129. Description of heaven. *Boston Post*, January 16, 1950. BG offered a virtually identical description of heaven a few weeks later in Columbia, South Carolina. Columbia *State*, March 6, 1950. I have not found any evidence that he made such statements after these two occasions.
130. Prayer meetings in hell. "500 Become Converted After Sermon on Hell," *Boston Herald*, January 14, 1950, CN17, Mid-Century Campaign, Scrapbook 1, 1949, BGCA; "Immortality," *Hour of Decision*, 1957.

130. Belshazzar sermon. *Boston Globe,* January 6, 1950. Also in Boston *Traveler,* January 6, 1950, and Gillenson, "God's Ball of Fire," *Look,* p. 27.
130. Prodigal Son sermon. *Boston Globe,* January 10, 1950. The "uppity pig" impression was described by a reporter for the Pittsburgh *Press,* September 18, 1952, p. 2, reporting on the Prodigal Son sermon as rendered in that city. Quoted in William G. McLoughlin, *Billy Graham, Revivalist in a Secular Age* (New York: Ronald Press, 1960), p. 125.
131. Ruth's reaction to Billy's acting. Stanley High, *Billy Graham: The Personal Story of the Man, His Message, and His Mission* (New York: McGraw-Hill, 1956), p. 88.
131. Ruth discusses marriage. *Boston Globe,* January 17, 1950; Dorothy Cremin, *Atlanta Journal,* February 9, 1950; Betty Cody, Columbia *State,* March 12, 1950.
131. "They hate the gospel." *Boston Globe,* January 15, 1950.
132. BG not mercenary. Joseph F. Dineen, *Boston Globe,* April 3, 1950; Gordon W. Sanders (assistant city editor of *Boston Herald*), testimonial letter, March 1, 1950, CN 360, MF Reel 3, BGCA.
132. "aiming for diamond greatness." *Boston Post* souvenir edition, n.d., CN 360, Scrapbook 16, MF Reel 3, BGCA.
132. Death penalty. "Billy Graham, Others, Discuss Sander Case from Boston Pulpits," *Boston Globe,* January 9, 1950, pp. 1, 16. CN 17, Mid-Century Campaign Scrapbook.
132. "Don't anybody tell Mr. Truman." "Revival Better than Europe Aid—Graham," Boston *Record,* January 11, 1950; "We May Spend Selves into Depression, Graham Says," *Boston Globe,* January 10, 1950.
132. O'Neill "introduced him to the assembly." BG, interview, March 5, 1989.
132. "Peter on the Mount of Transfiguration." Matt. 17:4.
132. "possibly disobeyed the voice of God." Allan Emery, oral history. See also John Pollock, *Billy Graham: The Authorized Biography* (New York: McGraw-Hill, 1966), p. 68.
132. Haymaker's contributions. Grady Wilson, interview, March 1, 1987; McLoughlin, *Revivalist,* pp. 54–55.
133. "crusade." Willis Haymaker, oral history, January 29, 1971, CN 141, Box 4, Folder 22, BGCA; Pollock, *Authorized Biography,* p. 69.
133. Strom Thurmond's help. Grady Wilson, interview, March 1, 1987; Cliff Barrows, interview, March 25, 1987; Columbia *State,* March 5, 1950.
133. Appearance at Bob Jones University. *Little Moby's Post,* March/April 1950, p. 1. *Little Moby's Post* is a BJU Alumni publication.
133. *Time* story on Columbia crusade. "Heaven, Hell, and Judgment Day," *Time,* March 20, 1950, pp. 72–73. On the night Luce attended the crusade, BG preached on the Judgment and Hell. See also Pollock, *Authorized Biography,* pp. 70–71 f.
134. *Peace with God.* Gerald Beavan, interview, July 27, 1988. Wyrtzen fills in, *Boston Post,* April 11, 1950.
135. BG requests visit with Truman. Letter from BG to White House, February 9, 1949; Letter from Charles G. Ross, secretary to President Truman, February 9, 1949; Letter from BG to Mr. Ross, February 17, 1949. CN 74, MF Reel (Harry S. Truman Presidential Library, Letters and Telegrams), BGCA. Unless otherwise noted, subsequent correspondence pertaining to Truman is from this same collection.
135. "his whole ambition was 'to get President Truman's ear.'" AP, February 19, 1950.
135. "national day of repentance." "Gospel Rally Attracts 6,000," *Boston Sunday Post,* January 1, 1950.
135. Appointment with Truman granted. Letters, Congressman Joseph R. Bryson to John McCormack, May 25, 1950; Matthew J. Connelly (secretary to the President) to BG, June 1, 1950; Connelly to BG, June 20, 1950.
135. BG visits Truman. BG, Grady Wilson, Gerald Beavan, interviews; Cliff Barrows, "We Met the President," *Youth for Christ Magazine,* n.d. (shortly after July 1950 visit), CN 360, MF

Reel 3, BGCA; "persona non grata," Billy Graham, "Billy Graham's Own Story: 'God Is My Witness,'" Part II, *McCall's*, May 1964, pp. 180–81; photo of group, AP wirephoto, *Oregon Journal*, July 22, 1950; Charles Cook, *The Billy Graham Story: "One Thing I Do"* (London: Marshall, Morgan and Scott, 1955), p. 40. Participants reported that they wore white suits, and the AP wirephoto seems to confirm this. *Time*, however, described BG's suit as "pistachio-colored." Graham did indeed have a green suit, which he sometimes wore with matching green shoes. *Time* may have been correct; I have chosen to accept the report of the participants.

136. "I talk to more people." Letter, BG to Truman, July 18, 1950.

136. Truman refuses to send telegram. Letter, presidential secretary Matthew Connelly to William M. Boyle, Jr., chairman of Democratic National Committee, August 23, 1950, declining request made by Evangelical leader Carl F. H. Henry. Connelly noted that "the president ... has not in a single instance commended any one particular religious meeting."

136. "publicity-grabbing God-huckster." See Truman's assessment of Graham in Merle Miller, *Plain Speaking* (New York: Berkeley, 1973), p. 363.

137. Meeting with Truman. BG, Mayor's Prayer Breakfast, Washington, D.C., April 30, 1986. Grady Wilson, interview, March 1, 1987; see also, Grady Wilson, *Count It All Joy* (Nashville: Broadman Press, 1984), pp. 206–208; Gerald Beavan interview; Graham, "'God Is My Witness,'" Part II, p. 180.

137. Portland Tabernacle. Brochure, CN 360, MF Reel 3, BGCA. The structure had modern restrooms, a first-aid room and nursery, and fifty thousand watts of lighting.

137. Boisterous women. Portland *Oregonian*, August 22, 1950; Louis Hofferbert, "The Billy Graham Story," *Houston Press*, n.d., ch. 11. This syndicated newspaper biography, by Hofferbert, was first published during the 1952 Houston crusade.

137. Portland crusade attendance. Newspaper accounts of the revival generally peg the attendance at close to 650,000. BGEA claims a more modest 520,000.

137. Eisner meets with BG. I was told this story by Fred Dienert, Eisner's son-in-law, who claims Eisner had no idea BG was within a thousand miles. In the version related by John Pollock (*Authorized Biography*, pp. 80–82), Eisner had narrowed the field in which Providence was called upon to act. Both accounts credit Eisner with a strong propensity to follow "impressions," which he regarded as God's way of directing his life.

139. BG considers a radio program. Raising money for radio. This account is based primarily on an interview with Fred Dienert, October 5, 1987. Dienert acknowledges a certain fuzziness on precise details. For slightly differing versions, see High, *Personal Story*, pp. 153–64; McLoughlin, *Revivalist*, pp. 63–64; Pollock, *Authorized Biography*, pp. 80–83; and BG and T. W. Wilson, oral history, March 3, 1976, CN 141, Box 32, Folder 28, BGCA. In his 1964 autobiographical series for *McCall's*, in which he appears to have made several minor factual errors, BG placed the figure contributed at the service at $24,000. Graham, "'God Is My Witness,'" Part II, p. 181. Gerald Beavan, whose claim to a good memory for details is supported by cross-checking with other sources, insists, along with several others, that $23,500 is the correct amount. Bill Mead and Howard Butt, Jr., both eventually became members of BGEA's board of directors. Butt's practice of spending six months a year in evangelistic work, which won him the sobriquet, God's Grocery man, is mentioned in *United Evangelical Action*, 1954, p. 148.

140. Formation of BGEA. George Wilson, interview, August 3, 1987; BG and T. W. Wilson, oral history. Though usually regarded as the first business manager of BGEA, Wilson was technically the second. Because Wilson was still fully employed by Northwestern Schools, BG sent Frank Phillips, the YFC director who headed the Portland crusade committee, to head up the operation during its first few weeks of operation, and he traveled to Minneapolis approximately every other week during the first six to ten months of the organization's existence. Graham and Wilson, oral history.

140. *Hour of Decision* premier broadcast. *Hour of Decision*, radio script, program 1, November 5, 1950, in folder with Paul S. James, oral history, March 17, 1977, CN 141, Box 4, Folder 40, BGCA; Paul Mickelson, oral history, May 19, 1976, CN 141, Box 21, Folder 14, BGCA. Mickelson was BG's organist during this period and played on this first program. See also McLoughlin, *Revivalist*, p. 65; *Authorized Biography*, p. 85.
141. "About ten years before he was born." Vernon W. Patterson, oral history, 1971, CN 141, Box 5, Folder 29, Addendum, BGCA.
141. Nielsen rating. Billy Graham, *America's Hour of Decision* (Wheaton, Ill.: Van Kampen Press, 1951), pp. 64–66, quoted in McLoughlin, *Revivalist*, p. 65.
141. Expansion of radio program. McLoughlin, *Revivalist*, p. 65.
141. "an estimated twenty million people." In light of the erroneously outsize claims made in recent years about the size of the audiences for television evangelists, this estimate may be overblown. See, for example, William Martin, "The Birth of a Media Myth," *The Atlantic*, June 1981, pp. 7–16.
142. *Hour of Decision* television program. According to BG, the impetus to produce a television program came from Leonard Goldenson, president of United Paramount Theaters, Paramount studio's distribution division. Goldenson had met BG during a visit to Paramount, whose president, Frank Freeman, was an ardent supporter of his crusades, and he had heard the evangelist turn down a lucrative offer to star in a Paramount movie. When ABC, owned by Paramount, decided to produce a weekly religious television program, Goldenson contacted BG and persuaded him to star in it. At first, ABC donated the time; then BGEA began to pay for it to insure freedom to produce the kind of program BG wanted. When ABC, under pressure from NBC and CBS, decided in 1954 to stop selling time for religious programming, BGEA discontinued the program. BG, interview, March 5, 1989.
142. "no one remembers." Jerry B. Jenkins, "A Conversation with Billy Graham," *IRTV Guide*, 1974, p. 8.
142. The mail operation. BG and T. W. Wilson, oral history.
142. BG begins "My Answer." Pollock, *Authorized Biography*, p. 87.
143. Photos in Atlanta *Constitution*, December 11, 1950, p. 2; Paul James, oral history, various interviews.
143. Atlanta love offering of $9,268.60. AP, January 6, 1951. Total contributions during the Atlanta crusade came to $127,241. BG received 55 percent of a love offering amounting to $16,852, with the remainder going to Barrows. BG told reporters that the money would be "reinvested in the service of the Lord."
143. BG goes on salary. BG, interview; Graham, "'God Is My Witness,'" Part II, pp. 181–82; McLoughlin, *Revivalist*, p. 67; Pollock, *Authorized Biography*, p. 88. The November 1951 Greensboro crusade was apparently the last in which a love offering was taken.
143. Russell Maguire's background. "Trouble for the Mercury," *Time*, December 8, 1952, p. 42. The occasion of this article was Maguire's purchase of the conservative journal of opinion, *The American Mercury*. At the news of the purchase, a substantial portion of the magazine's staff resigned.
144. Maguire offers money. W. T. Watson, oral history, February 14, 1977, CN 141, Box 5, Folder 42, BGCA.
144. *Oiltown U.S.A.* promotion. McLoughlin, *Revivalist*, pp. 98–99. *Mr. Texas* appeared in 1951; *Oiltown* appeared in 1952. At least part of the funding for *Mr. Texas* was provided by the Tarrant County Baptist Association. Fort Worth is in Tarrant County, and the sermons that led to Redd Harper's conversion were filmed during the Fort Worth crusade.
144. TV program funded by Texans. Pollock, *Authorized Biography*, pp. 100–101.
144. Western hat, green suit, "Gabriel in Gabardine." According to Barrows, the hat was a gift from the team. Though he liked it, BG eventually stopped wearing the hat because he felt it drew too much attention. Barrows, interview, February 24, 1987. Grady Wilson remem-

bered the green suit: "I was with Billy at Boston-Hoffman in Fort Lauderdale, Florida, when he bought that green suit. I thought it was so pretty. It was what they call Charmaine gabardine. Had a real sheen to it. Some reporter called him a 'Gabriel in Gabardine.' [After that article], Billy got self-conscious and put [it] aside. Gave it to his brother or somebody in his family, I think." Grady Wilson, interview, May 1, 1987. Green suede shoes were mentioned by J. Mabel Clark in an article that apparently appeared in the Austin *American-Statesman*, April 27, 1952. The citation is unclear in BGCA scrapbooks. In other stories from this period, reporters called BG a "Barrymore of the Bible," a "Hollywood John the Baptist," and a "Matinee Idol Revivalist." In one story, published in the Midland *News*, January 23, 1952, a reporter indicated that BG insisted that photographers always take his "good" profile.

144. Graham holds "an airborne service." AP, June 9, 1951; Paul Mickelson, oral history.
144. Governor Langlie chairs crusade. Hilding Halvarson, oral history, May 12, 1976, CN 141, Box 4, Folder 15, BGCA.
144. Premier of *Mr. Texas*. AP, October 2, 1951. The crowd for the premier and other services during the Hollywood Bowl meeting was built with the aid of Henrietta Mears's Sunday-school students, who divided up the metropolitan telephone book and tried to call everyone in it. BG packed the Hollywood Bowl night after night. Ethel May Baldwin and David V. Benson, *Henrietta Mears and How She Did It!* (Ventura, Calif.: Regal, 1966), pp. 151–52.
145. "a wonderful ride." *Mr. Texas*, Billy Graham Evangelistic Films, 1951. Print furnished by BGEA.
145. "God's seal of approval." Pollock, *Authorized Biography*, p. 100.
145. Dave Barr recalls early days of film ministry. Interview, November 14, 1987.
145. BG expects short ministry. "Billy Graham Predicts He Hasn't Long to Live," Pittsburgh *Press*, September 8, 1952.
145. "on Communist purge lists." Unidentified clipping, apparently from Portland *Oregonian*, August 22, 1950.

Chapter 9: Principalities and Powers

147. "your Waterloo." Minneapolis *Star*, January 19, 1952.
147. Washington crusade statistics. "Rockin' the Capitol," *Time*, March 3, 1952, p. 76.
147. "high point of the crusade." "40,000 Heard Billy Graham in Drizzle on Capitol Steps," Washington *Times-Herald*, February 4, 1952. Most newspapers used a similar figure, although a Red Wing, Minnesota, paper carried a small article noting that an experienced crowd estimator claimed no more than five thousand people were at the service. Inexperienced observers often exaggerate crowd size, but an eightfold error seems unlikely.
147. "you didn't need anything but Sam Rayburn's word." BG, press conference, National Press Club, Washington, D.C., April 24, 1986.
147. Involvement of congressmen in crusade. UP, January 23, 1952.
147. "Harry is doing the best he can." Warren Ashby, "The Message of Billy Graham," unpublished article, n.d., quoted by William G. McLoughlin, *Billy Graham, Revivalist in a Secular Age* (New York: Ronald Press, 1960), pp. 243–44, fn. 47.
148. Truman: "he was never a friend of mine." Harry S Truman, in Merle Miller, *Plain Speaking* (New York: Berkeley, 1973), p. 363.
148. "Truman eventually softened his assessment." During his 1967 crusade in Kansas City, BG made a point of visiting Truman in Independence, Missouri. Obviously still embarrassed at the memory, when he apologized for his awkward visit to the White House in 1950, Truman countered with his own apology that his assistants had not made the rules of protocol clearer and assured the evangelist he bore him no ill will. Graham has told this story on several occasions, and members of his team have confirmed it.
148. "when, as, and if a request comes." Memo, Matthew Connelly to "WDH." CN 74, MF Reel (Harry S Truman Presidential Library, Letters and Telegrams), BGCA. Unless otherwise noted, subsequent correspondence pertaining to Truman is from this same collection.

148. BG invites Truman to address a crusade service. BG to Truman, December 23, 1951.
148. "at Key West" ... "not want it repeated." Memo, WDH to Matthew Connelly, December 28, 1951.
148. "disappointing reply," Connelly to BG, December 31, 1951.
149. "advantageous for the President." BG to Connelly, January 9, 1952.
149. "225 ministers who urged him to be present." Gerald Beavan to Truman, January 28, 1952.
149. "would rejoice to know that their chief executive was in attendance." BG to Truman, January 29, 1952.
149. BG calls the White House. Memo, ACM to Connelly, January 31, 1952.
149. The President sends best wishes. Connelly to BG, February 1, 1952.
149. "I guess he was just too busy." "Rockin' the Capitol," p. 76. As a gesture of good will, BG sent the president a copy of *Communism and Christ*, a book he apparently thought might prove useful in confrontations with the Red Menace. An aide noted that the volume "was respectfully referred to the Department of State for appropriate acknowledgment." White House memo, March 3, 1952.
149. Congressmen support the crusade. Prebendary Colin C. Kerr, "Is America in Revival?" *The Life of Faith* (British Evangelical publication), February 20, 1952.
149. Attendance at Capitol rally. "Graham Converts Congressmen," Minneapolis *Star*, February 4, 1952.
149. Pentagon prayer meetings. "Rockin' the Capitol," p. 76.
150. Senator Robertson's resolution. AP, February 15, 1952.
150. "we can hold the balance of power." INS, October 17, 1951, in CN 74, Box 1, Folder 12, BGCA.
150. MacArthur is "deeply religious." "Rockin' the Capitol," p. 76; see also AP, February 20, 1952.
150. Religious leaders "will use my views as a guide." Ruth Gmeiner, "Billy Graham Making Check of Candidates' Spirituality," UP, February 2, 1952.
150. "I'd be elected." AP, February 4, 1952. A slightly different account, setting this statement in the context of a conversation with a presidential candidate, presumably Estes Kefauver, was reported in the Aberdeen, Maryland, *World*, February 9, 1952.
150. BG is encouraged to run for Senate. AP, February 19, 1950.
150. "estimated he could swing at least sixteen million votes." UPI, July 9, 1952.
151. Eisenhower thanks BG for interest. Letter, Dwight D. Eisenhower to BG, November 8, 1951, CN 74, Box 1, Folder 12, BGCA. Unless otherwise noted, further correspondence between Graham and Eisenhower or other members of the Eisenhower administration with the exception of Richard Nixon is from this source. On February 14, 1952, Graham requested an interview with General Eisenhower, noting that Sid Richardson had suggested he write. In a letter written to Graham on February 21, Eisenhower tentatively granted the interview. Graham's enthusiasm for Eisenhower may have been generated by the general's penchant for making such statements as "the churches of America are citadels of our faith in individual freedom and human dignity. This faith is the living source of all our spiritual strength. And this strength is our matchless armor in our worldwide struggle against the forces of Godless tyranny and oppression." Quoted in the *New York Times*, September 8, 1947, cited in Mark Silk, *Spiritual Politics* (New York: Simon & Schuster, 1988), p. 91.
151. Richardson prompts Graham to write Ike. Billy Graham, "Billy Graham's Own Story: 'God Is My Witness,'" Part III, *McCall's*, June 1964, p. 64.
151. BG urges Ike to run for office. Gerald Beavan, interview, July 27, 1988. Beavan claims, and there seems to be no reason to dispute the claim, that largely on the strength of their Fontainebleau meeting, Eisenhower invited him to join his campaign staff to become his primary public relations man. Though he declined a full-time position, he did some work for the campaign.

151. "one man sitting in Washington." *Hour of Decision*, July 26, 1953, quoted in McLoughlin, *Revivalist*, p. 114.
151. Truman and Adam compared. Quoted in ibid., p. 114.
151. "the nation's leaders blundered." *Houston Post*, May 4, 1952, Section II, p. 1, quoted in ibid., p. 112.
151. Truman faulted for failing to follow MacArthur's advice. "Grace Versus Wrath," sermon, *Hour of Decision*, 1951, quoted in ibid., p. 115. McLoughlin reported that in a personal letter to him, Graham insisted he had studiously attempted to remain neutral in his statements about Korea, ibid., pp. 244–45, n. 64.
152. "a new foreign policy." *Hour of Decision*, November 2, 1952, quoted in ibid., p. 115.
152. "we all seem to agree." Pittsburgh *Press*, September 7, 1952, II, p. 25, quoted in ibid., p. 243.
152. "nation desperately needs a strong spiritual leader." BG, sermon *Hour of Decision*, June 29, 1952.
152. "fortitude and courage." *Houston Post*, May 4, 1952.
152. "a Moses or a Daniel." Charles Cook, *The Billy Graham Story: "One Thing I Do"* (London: Marshall, Morgan and Scott, 1955), p. 100. All quoted in McLoughlin, *Revivalist*, pp. 117, 120.
152. Ike's religiosity. Graham, "'God Is My Witness,'" Part III, June 1964, p. 64.
152. Eisenhower to Langliere BG's possible involvement in campaign. Letter, August 11, 1952, CN 74, Box 1, Folder 12, BGCA.
152. Eisenhower staff ambivalence toward BG. Internal memos from the campaign staff reveal that James Hagerty felt Eisenhower should not bother with BG, but Gabe Hogue favored communication. A memo approving a visit bears the handwritten note, "Five minutes only." Note to General Paul Carroll from Alice S., October 2, 1952, CN 74, Box 1, Folder 12, BGCA.
152. Graham's "personal survey." "Billy Graham: Churchmen Favor Ike," Minneapolis *Morning Tribune*, October 27, 1952.
153. Graham's efforts to visit Korea. "Army Refuses to Sponsor Graham Revival in Korea," *Boston Globe*, November 28, 1952.
153. Ockenga criticism of government policy. *Boston Post*, November 29, 1952.
153. Beavan and congressional friends help. Billy Graham, *I Saw Your Sons at War: The Korean Diary of Billy Graham* (Minneapolis: Billy Graham Evangelistic Association, 1953), p. 12. The congressmen were L. Mendel Rivers (Democrat-South Carolina) and Senator Clinton Anderson (Democrat-South Dakota).
153. Graham visits Korea. "Two Visits to Korea," *Time*, January 5, 1953, p. 34.
153. "duck from bunker to bunker." Minnesota *Star*, December 13, 1952, CN 360, MF Reel 23, BGCA.
153. "750 missionaries." Graham, *I Saw Your Sons*, p. 16. All profits from the sale of this book were directed to war relief and mission efforts in Korea.
153. "We all became VIPs!" ... "assigned by protocol to [generals]." Ibid., pp. 19, 35, 49, 52, 54.
153. BG visits orphanages, hospitals. Ibid., pp. 29–31, 46, 55.
154. "wept more ... come out a man." Ibid., pp. 34, 55. The United Press also reported that BG was truly shaken by scenes of battle and the wounds of soldiers, December 27, 1952.
154. Reports of preaching services, commitment of Korean Christians. Ibid., pp. 24, 38, 44, 54; AP, December 15, 1952.
155. "rugged he-man" ... "no pinup picture." Graham, *I Saw Your Sons*, p. 50.
155. "If President Truman had taken time to visit Korea." Widely quoted in news accounts of Korean trip. Ernie Hill, "I've Got Plan to End Korean War—Graham," *Chicago Daily News*, December 13, 1952.
155. BG's plan to end war. UP, December 27, 1952.
155. "It has been my privilege ... born-again Christians." From a sermon, "Peace in Our Time," preached early in 1953, quoted in McLoughlin, *Revivalist*, p. 96. Graham would later

observe that "I am convinced [Eisenhower] made his personal commitment to Christ as a boy; but he made it publicly after he had become President of the United States." John Pollock, *Crusades: 20 Years with Billy Graham* (Minneapolis: World Wide Publications, 1969), pp. 283–84. BG claimed on other occasions that both Eisenhower and Secretary of State John Foster Dulles had told him America's only hope lay in religious revival. Also, Asheville *Citizen*, November 9, 1953.

156. BG requests "a short chat" with the President. Letter, BG to Eisenhower, June 29, 1953.
156. Why BG belongs to First Baptist, Dallas. Noel Houston, "Billy Graham," *Holiday*, March 1958, p. 113.
156. Review of *Peace with God* and Templeton's *Life Looks Up*. Theodore A. Gill, "Evangelists Three," *Christian Century*, March 23, 1955, pp. 369–70. Templeton's book was published by Harper & Row. The third evangelist of the title was Dale Evans Rogers, whose inspirational book, *My Spiritual Diary*, Gill also reviewed.
156. "for the man in the streets." Billy Graham, *Peace with God* (Garden City, N.Y.: Doubleday, 1953). Introduction, p. vii.
156. BG sends *Peace with God* to Eisenhower. Thank-you note, Eisenhower to BG, November 3, 1953, CN 74, Box 1, Folder 12, BGCA.
156. "I have seen it happen." Greensboro *Daily News*, October 15, 1951.
156. "appealing to a higher type of social strata." Quoted by Richard H. Rovere, "Letter from Washington," *The New Yorker*, February 23, 1952, pp. 78–85.
157. BG rejects Billy Sunday role and NBC offer. Minnesota *Sunday Tribune*, October 1, 1950; "Billy Graham Spurns Millions," *Christian Century*, March 17, 1954, p. 351; Billy Graham, *America's Hour of Decision* (Wheaton, Ill.: Van Kampen, 1951), p. 33.
157. Bunny and Franklin are born. Patricia Daniels Cornwell, *A Time for Remembering: The Ruth Bell Graham Story* (San Francisco: Harper & Row, 1983), pp. 88–89.
157. Billy fails to recognize his daughter. Ibid., p. 87.
157. Baptist tourists. Ruth Graham, oral history, August 26, 1978, CN 141, Box 4, Folder 8, BGCA. According to Graham, some tourists actually forced themselves into their home. "'God Is My Witness,'" Part II, May 1964, p. 176.
157. Bunny's fund-raising gambit. Ruth Graham, oral history.
158. GiGi remembered father's absences. Virginia "GiGi" Tchividjian, interview, October 25, 1990.
158. "Bye, Daddy!" Ruth Graham, *It's My Turn* (Old Tappan, N.J.: Fleming H. Revell, 1982), p. 106.
158. Satisfying the need for a father. Graham, "'God Is My Witness,'" Part II, May 1964, p. 176.

Chapter 10: Trust and Obey

159. "I can feel the tug." "What Is God Like," sermon, *Hour of Decision*, 1951; Billy Graham, *Peace with God* (Garden City, N.Y.: Doubleday, 1953; New York: Pocket Books, 1965), p. 31. Unless otherwise noted, all page references are to 1965 edition. NB: quotations from *Hour of Decision* sermons are taken primarily from printed copies of the sermons. The dates cited are taken from these reprints but may not be completely accurate in every case, since some revisions obviously occurred in later versions. For example, a sermon entitled "The Invitation of Christ" and dated 1959 includes a reference to "the late president John F. Kennedy," who did not die until 1963.
160. "we prayed once out in Portland, Oregon, and it poured down." *Hour of Decision* television program, 1952, CN 113, Film 188, BGCA.
160. God as Great Bookkeeper. Charlotte *News*, May 22, 1957, quoted in Marshall Frady, *Billy Graham: Parable of American Righteousness* (Boston: Little, Brown, 1979) p. 303.
160. Satan described. Graham, *Peace with God*, p. 48.
160. Adam "created full grown." Ibid., p. 33.

161. "Christ was the substitute!" Ibid., pp. 82–83.
161. "Only the Christian knows how to live." Billy Graham, *My Answer* (Garden City, N.Y.: Doubleday, 1960), p. 139.
161. "The Christian should stand out ..." Ibid., p. 160.
161. BG, "The Life That Wins," sermon, *Hour of Decision*, 1952.
162. Profanity and lying. BG, "Sins of the Tongue," sermon, *Hour of Decision*, 1952.
162. Georgia considers prohibition. "The Whiskey Rebellion," *Time*, February 20, 1950, p. 18.
162. Graham hopes Mississippi will remain dry. Jackson *Clarion-Ledger*, July 10, 1952, CN 360, MF Reel 5, BGCA.
162. Sexual content of *My Answer*. G. W. Target counts and categorizes these statements in *Evangelism, Inc.* (London: Penguin Books, 1968), p. 156.
162. "never lick it without Christ." Sherwood Eliot Wirt, "New Life Surges in 'Graveyard of Evangelists,'" *United Evangelical Action*, August 1, 1958, p. 16.
162. Death penalty for adultery. BG, "The Responsibilities of the Home," sermon, *Hour of Decision*, 1954.
162. Perils of "innocent friendship." Graham, *My Answer*, p. 42.
162. "adultery can be forgiven." Ibid., p. 149.
163. "make certain that my suspicions were justified." Ibid., p. 34.
163. "an either/or deal." Ibid., pp. 39–40.
163. Advises against confession of adultery. Ibid., pp. 27, 36.
163. "on the question of abortion." Ibid., p. 111.
163. The role of women. Billy Graham, "The Home God Honors," sermon in *Revival in Our Time* (Wheaton, Ill.: Van Kampen Press, 1950), p. 95, and BG, "Responsibilities sermon."
163. "Wife should adapt continually." BG, "My Answer," newspaper column, February 15, 1953.
163. Women "entitled to choose" to become pregnant. Graham, *My Answer*, p. 29.
164. The Bible sanctions corporal punishment. "Responsibilities."
164. "calluses on my backbone." BG, "Home God Honors," p. 99.
164. "Do not be afraid to use it." Ibid., p. 100.
164. disintegration of Roman Empire due to broken home. BG, "The Answer to Broken Homes," sermon, *Hour of Decision*, 1953.
164. Divorce survey. BG, "Broken Homes."
164. "the secret of America" ... "homes of our fair land." BG, "The Home," sermon, *Hour of Decision*, 1956. Quoted in William G. McLoughlin, *Billy Graham, Revivalist in a Secular Age* (New York: Ronald Press, 1960) p. 129. This passage does not appear in later reprints of this sermon. It is not uncommon, however, for the printed sermons to undergo revision, sometimes to remove distracting references to events no longer familiar to contemporary readers or, apparently, to delete passages that have drawn unfavorable notice from journalists or scholars.
164. Moody-style pathos: open front door and fatally ill girl. BG, "Mother's Day Message," sermon, *Hour of Decision*, 1953.
165. "stepping in Daddy's tracks." BG, "Father," sermon, *Hour of Decision*, 1956.
165. Graham on emotional preaching. Frank Colquhoun, *The Harringay Story: The Official Story of the Billy Graham Greater London Crusade*, 1954 (London: Hodder & Stoughton, 1955), p. 19.
165. Revival more likely in difficult times. *U.S. News & World Report*, August 27, 1954, p. 87.
165. Social problems listed by Graham. The reference to high-speed objects is from "Immortality," sermon, *Hour of Decision*, 1957. The other references are generic and appear in many sermons.
167. Graham silent at invitation. Graham's silence at the invitation was not invariable. In the film *Mr. Texas*, he urges the audience in typical revivalist fashion: "That's it. Quickly. Come on." Newspaper accounts of the notable absence of this technique, however, make it appear the silent approach was his standard method of giving the invitation.

167. "almost all ministers ... agree." BG, "Christianity Versus Communism," sermon, *Hour of Decision*, 1951.
167. "victory over the tongue." BG, "The Sins of the Tongue," sermon, *Hour of Decision*, 1952.
167. Reasons for youthful immorality. "Young Evangelist Graham Flays Girls' Loose Morals," Boston *Traveler*, January 4, 1950.
167. Jefferson's theology. "Billy Graham Tours National Shrines, Asks Moral Awakening," the *Washington Post*, January 13, 1952.
167. "behavioristic philosophies." BG, "The Bible and Dr. Kinsey," sermon *Hour of Decision*, 1953.
167. Ministers should hide doubts. "Billy's Conquest," *Newsweek*, July 12, 1954, p. 68.
167. "People want to be told." Wayne S. Bond, "The Rhetoric of Billy Graham," Ph.D. diss., Southern Illinois University, August 1973, p. 28.
168. Ockenga on the social conscience of the New Evangelicalism. Quoted in Lowell D. Streiker and Gerald S. Strober, *Religion and the New Majority: Billy Graham, Middle America, and the Politics of the 70's* (New York: Association Press, 1972), p. 112.
168. Favorable observations on labor. BG, "Labor, Christ and the Cross," sermon, *Hour of Decision*, 1953; Billy Graham, *Peace with God* (Garden City, N.Y.: Doubleday, 1953), p. 181; Graham, interview, March 26, 1987.
169. Admonitions to employers. Graham, *Peace with God*, pp. 180–81.
169. Prayer groups in cities. Stanley High, *Billy Graham: The Personal Story of the Man, His Message, and His Mission* (New York: McGraw-Hill, 1956), p. 63.
169. "an industrial Utopia." BG, "Organized Labor and the Church," sermon, *Hour of Decision*, 1952.
169. "no union dues" in the Garden of Eden. Quoted in James L. McAllister, "Evangelical Faith and Billy Graham," *Social Action* XIX (March 1953): 23, cited in McLoughlin, *Revivalist*, p. 99.
169. "The only one I mention is communism." "Rabbi Criticizes Evangelist Billy Graham; Southern Baptist Ministers Offer Defense," Portland *Oregonian*, February 17, 1950 CN 360, MF Reel 2, BGCA. Quoted again in July 25, 1950 edition.
169. "a battle to the death." BG, "Satan's Religion," sermon *Hour of Decision*, 1953. In another sermon, "Christianity Versus Communism," *Hour of Decision*, 1951, he called communism "a fanatical religion that has declared war upon the Christian God."
169. Communism's "power from the devil." Asheville *Citizen*, November 20, 1953.
169. "The Devil is their god." BG, "Satan's Religion."
169. "Then let's do it." *Hour of Decision*, June 10, 1951, quoted in McLoughlin, *Revivalist*, p. 112.
170. "While nobody likes a watch dog." BG, "Labor, Christ and the Cross," sermon, *Hour of Decision*, 1953. Later reprints of this sermon delete "the lavenders," probably in an effort not to offend homosexuals unnecessarily.
170. BG did not know of Marxists in churches. AP, March 30, 1953.
170. "put under suspicion." Asheville *Citizen*, November 20, 1953.
170. "I am not answering that." London *Daily Herald*, February 26, 1954, p. 7, quoted in McLoughlin, *Revivalist*, p. 112.
170. "most people laughing off McCarthy." Letter, BG to Eisenhower, May 10, 1954, CN 74, Box 1, Folder 12, BGCA. 166 "Senate was fiddling over trifles." *Hour of Decision*, December 5, 1954; also BG, "Christ Is Coming," sermon, *Hour of Decision*, 1955, quoted in McLoughlin, *Revivalist*, p. 112.
170. Warnings against appeasement. BG, "America's Decision," sermon *Hour of Decision*, 1953.
171. "We shed the blood and pay the bills." Ibid., quoted in McLoughlin, *Revivalist*, p. 116.
171. UN weakness. BG, "Teach Us to Pray," sermon, *Hour of Decision*, March 1953, quoted in McLoughlin, *Revivalist*, pp. 116–17.

171. "Communism's Public Enemy Number One." *Chicago Daily News*, June 11, 1955, p. 1.
171. East German papers call Graham "a hypocritical demagogue." "Billy Graham's Messages Arouse the Red Devil," AP, in *Chicago Daily News*, February 27, 1952.
171. Racism "an unspoken assumption." Graham, interview, March 28, 1987.
172. God "no respecter of persons." Acts 10:34.
172. Reporters question Columbia segregation. *Boston Post*, March 27, 28, 31, 1950; Portland, Maine, *Evening Express*, March 27, 1950. In CN 1 (Haymaker Papers), Box 1, Folders 1–2, BGCA. Cited in Jerry Berl Hopkins, *Billy Graham and the Race Problem, 1949–1969* (Ph. D. diss., University of Kentucky, 1986), p. 33. I am grateful to Dr. Hopkins for having ferreted out some materials of which I was previously unaware, as well as for his generally evenhanded treatment of Graham's developing position on race.
172. "All men are created equal." "Rabbi Criticizes Billy Graham," quoting a statement Graham had made on August 15, 1950. CN 360, MF Reel 3, BGCA.
173. Offer to hold service for blacks only. Atlanta *Daily World* (November–December 1950); Atlanta *Constitution*, November 27, 1950; *Christian Science Monitor*, January 1, 1951.
173. Communists behind reform efforts. *Los Angeles Times*, September 15, 1951.
173. "You can't clean up a city." BG, quoted in Hopkins, *Race Problem*, p. 37. 169 "race with race." Ibid., p. 38.
173. No discrimination in Washington crusade. "Graham Begins Plans for Big Four-Week Washington Revival," *Charlotte Observer*, January 12, 1952, CN 360, Reel 5, BGCA.
173. "love, love, love." The *Washington Post*, January 21, 25, 1952; February 18, 1952, quoted in Hopkins, *Race Problem*, p. 39.
173. Segregation at the Houston crusade. John Pollock, *Billy Graham: The Authorized Biography* (New York: McGraw-Hill, 1966), p. 97.
173. Service for black leaders. "Negroes Ask Graham to Stay Over" *Houston Chronicle*, June 6, 1952.
173. Baptist colleges should admit blacks. "Billy Graham Urges Negroes in Colleges," Memphis *Commercial Appeal*, May 18, 1952, CN 360, Reel 5, BGCA.
174. Race problem "something you're going to have to face." Billy Graham, "Why Don't Our Churches Practice the Brotherhood They Preach?" *Reader's Digest*, August 1960, p. 116; also Pollock, *Authorized Biography*, p. 97.
174. No segregation at the cross. UP, July 9, 1952.
174. *Christian Century* applauds BG. *Christian Century*, August 13, 1952, p. 934.
174. "I feel I have been misinterpreted." Jackson *Clarion-Ledger*, July 10, 1951.
174. "I cannot be hypocritical on this matter." G. Merrill Lenox to BG, July 8, 1952; BG to Lenox, July 12, 1952, CN 1 (Haymaker Papers), Box 1, Folder 18, BGCA; quoted in Hopkins, *Race Problem*, pp. 43–44.
175. "personally removed ropes." BG, sermon, Washington, D.C., May 3, 1986. Also, personal conversation.
175. Detroit pastor complains; Haymaker responds. Charles A. Hill to Haymaker, June 11, 1953; Haymaker to Hill, June 15, 1953, CN 1 (Haymaker Papers), Box 1, Folder 18, BGCA, quoted in Hopkins, *Race Problem*, pp. 47–48.
175. "The church must practice Christianity." *Michigan Chronicle* (Detroit), October 3, 1953, quoted in Hopkins, *Race Problem*, p. 49.
175. "A great spiritual revival is needed." Ibid.
175. *Christian Century* commends BG. Frank Fitt, "In the Wake of Billy Graham," *Christian Century*, December 1, 1953, pp. 1438–39.
176. BG rejects "curse of Canaan" argument. Detroit *Sunday Times*, September 27, 1953, quoted in Hopkins, *Race Problem*, p. 51.
176. "There is no 'Master Race.'" "My Answer," in Asheville *Citizen-Times*, November 15, 1953, quoted in Hopkins, *Race Problem*, pp. 52–53.

176. "The church should have been the pace-setter." Graham, *Peace with God*, p. 181.
176. "When true Christians look at other people." Ibid., p. 182.
176. BG's lukewarmness toward integration during Nashville crusade. Hopkins, *Race Problem*, pp. 60–61. BG to James M. Gregg, July 24, 1954, CN 1 (Haymaker Papers), Box 1, Folder 24, BGCA.

Chapter 11: Harringay

177. "From vict'ry unto vict'ry." From George Duffield and George J. Webb, "Stand Up, Stand Up for Jesus," popular Evangelical hymn.
177. Limited support, even among Evangelicals. Robert O. Ferm, oral history, 1978, CN 141, Box 3, Folder 37, BGCA. In an interview with *U.S. News & World Report*, BG asserted that approximately one thousand churches had been involved in the invitation and that he imagined approximately two thirds of them were Anglican churches. This appears to be a gross overestimate. Billy Graham (interview) "Billy Graham's Story: New Crusade in Europe," *U.S. News & World Report*, August 27, 1954, p. 82.
177. Resistance to a crusade. The Reverend A. Jack Dain, interview, July 14, 1986, Amsterdam. See also Frank Colquhoun, *The Harringay Story: The Official Story of the Billy Graham Greater London Crusade*, 1954. (London: Hodder &C Stoughton, 1955), p. 18.
177. "His theology is fifty years behind contemporary scholarship." Reynolds' *News*, May 22, 1955, quoting Dr. Brian Wellbeck, a psychologist who contended after the crusade that BG had harmed British churches.
177. Forms of opposition to the crusade. Various interviewees made similar observations. One of the most articulate and analytical was Brian Kingsmore, a Scottish Presbyterian minister interviewed in Amsterdam, July 10, 1986.
178. hope "to start a spark." *Hour of Decision* television program, April 1954, CN 54, Film 99, BGCA.
178. Earl Warren attends prayer service. *United Evangelical Action*, 1954, p. 15.
178. "Spiritual vacuum." BG's use of this term with respect to England is cited in Louis Hofferbert, "The Billy Graham Story," *Houston Press*, May 1952, Chapter 16, CN 360, Reel 5, BGCA.
178. Award-winning public relations campaign. Gerald Beavan, interview, March 1988. BGEA shared one of the awards with Craven-A Cigarettes. Colquhoun, *Harringay Story*, p. 44.
178. "Hear Billy Graham," *World Press News*, October 15, 1954.
178. Eisenhower endorses crusade, Dulles to help. Letter, BG to Willis Haymaker, n.d., CN 3 1 (Haymaker Papers), Box 1, Folder 21 (London 1954, 10/53–6/54); "Billy Graham: Young Thunderer of Revival," *Newsweek*, February 1, 1954, p. 42; John Pollock, *Billy Graham: The Authorized Biography* (New York: McGraw-Hill, 1966), p. 113.
178. "like a Biblical Baedeker." "100,000 Pounds Worth of Hot Gospel," London *Evening News*, February 23, 1954, CN 360, Reel 6, BGCA. Unless otherwise noted, all newspaper clippings relating to the Harringay crusade can be found in CN 360, Reel 6.
179. Text of "Socialism" brochure. The *New York Times*, February 21, 1954. The basic account of this snafu was provided by Gerald Beavan, interview. Pollock and Graham have written that the offending word was to have been changed to *secularism*. Beavan, who wrote the copy, insists that the only change suggested or made was from an upper case to a lowercase s.
180. "Apologize—or stay away!" Hannen Swaffer, in London *Daily Herald*, February 20, 1954.
180. "interfering in British politics." Radio news sheet, February 20, 1954, quoted in Pollock, *Authorized Biography*, p. 115.
180. "an attack on the British Labor government." London *Daily Mirror*, February 22, 1954.
180. Reporters board the liner. Billy Graham, "'God Is My Witness,'" Part II, *McCall's*, May 1964, p. 183.

180. "never attacked Socialism." London *Daily Herald*, February 22, 1954, p. 1.
180. George Wilson takes blame. Montreal *Daily Star*, February 22, 1954.
180. Beavan claims to have ordered change in calendar, Glasgow *Sunday Mail*, n.d. (1954). Beavan insisted he was responsible for using the word *socialism* but observes that it would never have surfaced had not Wilson used the text in the calendar without his (Beavan's) knowledge. Beavan, interview.
180. Socialism an equivalent to theatergoing. Montreal *Daily Star*, February 22, 1954.
180. BG response "fatuous." London *Daily Herald*, February 24, 1954.
180. "less than fully convincing." A spokesman for the crusade committee told reporters, "You caught him on the High Seas without his documents or his adviser." London *Daily Herald*, February 22, 1954.
180. Marx "a subtle, clever, degenerate materialist." BG, "Satan's Religion," sermon, *Hour of Decision*, December 1953.
181. BG calls for revolt against socialism. BG, "Revival or the Spirit of the Age," sermon, *Hour of Decision*, 1952, quoted by William G. McLoughlin, *Billy Graham, Revivalist in a Secular Age* (New York: Ronald Press, 1960), p. 102. 177 "England would turn to Marxist socialism." BG, "World Reds Hit by Billy Graham," sermon, Miami *Daily News*, May 18, 1952.
181. BG might go to England to help halt Socialist trend. BG, "Our Spiritual Debt to England," sermon, *Hour of Decision*, June 8, 1952.
181. Aneurin Bevan "a dangerous man." "British Call Billy Graham Back, but Must Wait for Two Years," *Chicago Daily News*, March 21, 1952.
181. Bevan agent of "Communist advance." BG, "The Urgency of Revival," sermon, *Hour of Decision*, 1954.
181. "Labor [party] is killing all initiative." Quoted by Cassandra (nom de plume of columnist William Conner), "What Is Billy Graham Up To?" London *Daily Mirror*, February 28, 1954.
181. De Courcey's approval. Quoted without citation in McLoughlin, *Revivalist*, p. 106.
181. BG "not partial to Socialism." Quoted without citation, ibid.
181. Awakening would detach people from socialism. *Intelligence Digest*, June 1954, p. 5, quoted in McLoughlin, *Revivalist*, p. 107.
181. London *Free Press* advertisement in London *Times*, quoted in McLoughlin, *Revivalist*, p. 105.
181. De Freitas impressed by BG's Christianity. Glasgow *Daily Record*, February 27, 1954.
181. BG greeted like a celebrity. "4,000 Women Mob Hot Gospeler," London *Daily Mail*, February 25, 1954.
181. "It's time we let out the lions." Pollock, *Authorized Biography*, p. 117.
182. "I thought I heard [Bill] praying." Ruth Graham's diary, quoted in Pollock, *Authorized Biography*, p. 119.
182. Beavan's message garbled. Ibid.; Beavan, interview.
182. "The building is packed." Noel Houston, "Billy Graham," *Holiday*, February 1958, p. 143; Graham, "'God Is My Witness,'" Part II, May 1964, p. 183.
182. Symington and Bridges. Glasgow *Daily Record*, March 2, 1954; Beavan, interview; Houston, "Billy Graham," February 1958, p. 143; Graham, "'God Is My Witness,'" Part II, May 1964, p. 183; Patricia Daniels Cornwell, *A Time for Remembering: The Ruth Bell Graham Story* (San Francisco: Harper & Row, 1983), pp. 95–97; Pollock, *Authorized Biography*, pp. 119–21.
182. 178 souls. Graham, "'God Is My Witness,'" Part II, May 1964, p. 184.
182. Attendance at Harringay. Grady Wilson, "Three-Month Miracle," *Moody Monthly*, October 1954; Pollock, *Authorized Biography*, p. 121.
183. Operation Andrew beginnings. Stephen Olford, interview, April 21, 1988; Robert O. Ferm, manuscript for article on the history of Operation Andrew, CN 19 (Ferm Papers), Box 11, Folder 3 (February-March, 1965), BGCA.

183. "landline relays." Herbert Lockyer, Jr., "The Relay Meetings," *Moody Monthly*, October 1954; "Graham London Crusade Is Breaking All Records," *United Evangelical Action*, 1954, p. 148; Colquhoun, *Harringay Story*, pp. 130–32.
184. Banquet at Claridge's. Pollock, *Authorized Biography*, p. 117.
184. "reminds me of my ancestors." Ibid., p. 122; Graham, interview, March 28, 1987.
184. Roy Rogers and Dale Evans. Cornwell, *A Time for Remembering*, p. 99.
184. Giant rallies. "34,586 Decisions," *Time*, May 31, 1954, pp. 58–59; Cornwell, *A Time for Remembering*, p. 108; Pollock, *Authorized Biography*, pp. 129–30; Charles T. Cook, "Memorable Climax to London Crusade," *The Christian*, May 28, 1954.
185. "It could have been better." Bishop A. W. Goodwin-Hudson, oral history, January 7, 1976, CN 141, Box 4, Folder 5, BGCA.
185. "Brother Archbishop." This oft-repeated story is perhaps the best known of the many anecdotes regarding Grady Wilson. BG repeated it at Grady's funeral in September 1987. Grady told me the same story, noting that "he outranks the prime minister. He is second in line only to the queen, and here I was calling him 'Brother Archbishop.' " Wilson added that the day before, BG had driven him past Lambeth Palace, the arch bishop's residence in London, and had told him that the palace contained thirty-two bathrooms. "I couldn't see the reason for that," Grady said, still marveling more than thirty years later. "To a country boy from North Carolina, that was just sort of overwhelming." Interview, March 1, 1987.
185. Frank Martin's change of heart. Quoted in Colquhoun, *Harringay Story*, p. 175.
185. Donald Soper's reaction. J. Erskine Tuck, "Winning the Press," *Moody Monthly*, October 1954.
185. Weatherhead: "what does fundamentalist theology matter?" Ibid.
185. BG hears sharp criticism. Colleen Evans, remarks at National Press Club, April 24, 1986.
185. BG "teachable and humble." "Why Not Export Billy Graham?" *Christian Century*, March 24, 1954, p. 357.
186. "my eyes were scalding with tears." "William Hickey Meets Billy Graham," London *Daily Express*, March 1, 1954.
186. The bloke means everything he says." Cassandra, "What Is Billy Graham Up To," *Daily Mirror*, February 28, 1954.
187. "Mr. History." Pollock, *Authorized Biography*, p. 132.
187. BG disowns descriptions of heaven. British press conference response, quoted in Colquhoun, *Harringay Story*, p. 79; BG, "The Ten Commandments," *Hour of Decision*, 1958.
187. "As for hell, . . ." British press conference, Colquhoun, *Harringay Story*, p. 79.
187. Invitation hymn dropped. "The Crusade for Britain," *Time*, March 8, 1954, pp. 72–74. Other changes noted by crusade organist Paul Mickelson, oral history, May 19, 1976, CN 141, Box 21, Folder 14, BGCA.
187. BG changes views on socialism. Ralph Lord Roy, "Billy Graham's Crusade," *The New Leader*, August 1, 1955, p. 8, quoted in McLoughlin, *Revivalist*, p. 222.
187. Positive view toward organized labor. AP, in *Charlotte Observer*, September 6, 1954.
188. BG permits cessation of collections. Bishop A. W. Goodwin-Hudson, a key member of the crusade's executive committee, wanted to continue the collections, but the crusade chairman, General D. J. Wilson-Haffenden, felt it was important to stop the collections as early as possible to offset any criticism of financial arrangements. Goodwin-Hudson, oral history.
188. Harringay statistics. "Assess Permanent Results of the Graham London Campaign," *Christian Century*, March 2, 1955, p. 262; "Billy's Britain," *Time*, March 22, 1954, p. 67; also, Colquhoun, *Harringay Story*, passim.
188. Results comparable to Wesley. "Old-Time Religion," *U.S. News & World Report*, July 9, 1954, pp. 42–43.
188. Indifference a veneer. London *Sunday Times*, May 30, 1954.

188. *Evening Standard* poll. "Where Are the Billy Graham Converts?" London *Evening Standard*, December 6, 1954.
188. "The effect ... very little." Denis Duncan, in *British Weekly*, May 29, 1958, p. 1, quoted in McLoughlin, *Revivalist*, pp. 192–93.
189. Archbishop of Canterbury assesses BG. Dr. Geoffrey Fisher, *Canterbury Diocesan Notes*, June 1954.
189. "very little to show." *Viewpoint*, a Protestant Episcopal Church television program, Mutual Broadcasting System, quoted in *Charlotte Observer*, June 15, 1958.
189. A contrast between two churches. I have heard several such stories, of London and other cities. The one alluded to here was told to me by Maurice Rowlandson, a longtime BGEA representative in London. He compared Edgeware Parish Church, St. Martin's, with St. Lawrence Whit Church. St. Lawrence was the little engine that couldn't. Interview, July 10, 1986.
189. Few new members. One pastor told of receiving ninety referrals, of which only two were still active in his church a few months later. Errol Hulse, *Billy Graham: The Pastor's Dilemma* (Houslow, Middlesex: Maurice Allan, 1966), pp. 11–12.
189. Ordained Evangelicals in 1956. *Charlotte Observer*, November 13, 1956, citing British religious journals; John Pollock, "England Four Years After Graham," *Christianity Today*, April 28, 1958, pp. 10–12.
189. Growth of Evangelicalism among Anglicans. Various supporting statistics and anecdotal material were furnished to me by the Reverend Dr. John R. W. Stott, interview, September 29, 1986; The Reverend A. Jack Dain, oral history, December 1, 1971, CN 141, Box 3, Folder 12, BGCA; Bishop Maurice A. Wood, interview, October 2, 1986; The Reverend Richard Bewes, Rector, All Souls, London, interview, October 1, 1986; The Reverend Gilbert W. Kirby, interview, September 29, 1986.
189. "I am deeply grateful." Letter, BG to Dwight D. Eisenhower, May 10, 1954, CN 74, Box 1, Folder 12, BGCA. Also, Graham (interview), "New Crusade," p. 88.

Chapter 12: Fields White Unto Harvest

190. European Tour. Billy Graham (interview) "Billy Graham's Story: New Crusade in Europe," *U.S. News & World Report*, August 27, 1954, p. 86; *United Evangelical Action*, August 1, 1954.
190. "a salesman in God's company." Unidentified newspaper with Berlin dateline, July 3, 1954; *Abendpost*, June 12, 1955.
190. "God has a TV camera focused on you." BG criticized in letter to editor of unidentified German newspaper (translation), CN 360, MF Reel 8, BGCA.
191. East German newspaper criticism. Graham (interview), "New Crusade in Europe," p. 83; *Abendpost*, June 12, 1955; *Zeitung*, June 27, 1954; other German newspapers in CN 360, MF Reel 8, BGCA.
191. BG on German rearmament, reactions. London *Daily Express*, June 24, 1954, ibid; unidentified German newspaper, June 24, 1954, ibid.
191. BG denies political mission. Unidentified Düsseldorf newspaper, June 25, 1954, ibid.
191. BG's kidney stone. Jerry Beavan believed the stone had a more mundane origin. "I saw the stone [after it was removed.] It looked like a chip out of a coke bottle. They did an analysis at North Carolina or Duke or someplace, and they found the stone had a heavy phosphorus content. A homeopathic physician named Brown Henry had dosed Billy up with lots of white pills. We provided the lab with those pills, and they were loaded with phosphorus." Gerald Beavan, interview, July 7, 1988.
192. Bolten with BG in Berlin. John Pollock, *Billy Graham: The Authorized Biography* (New York: McGraw-Hill, 1966), pp. 136–37; Beavan, interview; "New Crusade in Europe," p. 83. Estimates of the numbers of East Germans were possible because most had come across the border in buses.

192. BG's alleged nightclub visits. Unidentified newspaper clipping, March 3, 1955, citing reports in East Berlin newspapers, CN 360, MF Reel 8, BGCA.
193. Wembley crusade and meeting the royal family. Pollock, *Authorized Biography*, pp. 151–54; George Burnham, *Mission Accomplished* (Westwood, N.J.: Fleming H. Revell, 1955) pp. 101–103.
193. "The French just sin and sin." "Billy Graham Preaches to Americans in Paris," *Chicago Daily News* Service, in Minneapolis *Star*, March 24, 1952.
193. BG's Cambridge mission. Pollock, *Authorized Biography*, pp. 154–58; Stephen Olford, interview, April 21, 1988.
194. Divinity professor's introduction ... students applaud. "Billy in the Lion's Den," *Time*, November 25, 1955, p. 54.
194. Dain had doubts. The Reverend A. Jack Dain, interview, July 14, 1986.
195. "As I was with Moses ..." (Josh. 1:5) George Burnham, *To the Far Corners: With Billy Graham in Asia* (Westwood, N.J.: Fleming H. Revell, 1956) p. 14.
195. Dulles calls for "dynamic faith." John Foster Dulles, *War or Peace* (New York: Macmillan, 1951), pp. 251–56, cited in Mark Silk, *Spiritual Politics* (New York: Simon & Schuster, 1988), pp. 91–92.
195. Telegram from Eisenhower, Dulles's advice. From a letter from Billy to Ruth Graham, quoted in "The Sweep of God in India—Billy Graham's Diary," *Christian Life*, July 1956, pp. 14–19. In CN 74, MF Reel 1, from Box 299, (Pre-Presidential Papers of Richard Nixon, National Archives and Record Service).
195. Dulles: India needs message of authority. Burnham, *To the Far Corners*, p. 14.
196. "Beggars were all around in Bombay." Quoted in ibid., p. 21. Throughout this book, Burnham quotes from what is ostensibly "Billy's diary." Graham claimed the quotations were not from a diary but from letters he wrote to Ruth, which Burnham obtained and used, presumably with permission. BG later wrote, "I am sorry Mr. Burnham was able to get hold of [this material]." Graham, Letter to Editor, Madras *Daily Journal*, February 24, 1957.
196. Riots laid to Communists. Burnham, *To the Far Corners*, pp. 18–19.
196. "I smiled and they smiled back." Noel Houston, "Billy Graham," *Holiday*, March 1958, p. 81.
197. Bombay press conference. Pollock, *Authorized Biography*, p. 162; Chuck Ashman, *The Gospel According to Billy* (Secaucus, N.J.: Lyle Stuart, 1977), p. 107; Marshall Frady, *Billy Graham: Parable of American Righteousness* (Boston: Little, Brown, 1979), p. 339. Accounts of journalists' reception to BG vary wildly. Pollock, the authorized biographer, asserts that BG was responding to a spiritual hunger the reporters manifested. Ashman asserts that reporters complained the press conference had been like a sermon. Frady speaks of "venomous" accounts. Articles in English in the scrapbooks in the BGC Archives differ little from those written about BG in other foreign countries during this period.
197. "the tramp, tramp, tramp of bare feet." Pollock, *Authorized Biography*, pp. 162–63.
197. "Dr. Graham can be dreadfully effective." P. Lai, "Billy Graham in India," *The Nation*, April 7, 1957, pp. 276–77, quoted in Frady, *Parable*, p. 336.
198. Bishop Jacob's cobras. The Reverend A. Jack Dain, oral history, December 1, 1971.
198. Kottayam services. Dain, oral history and interview. Dain recalled that no food or drink was available other than what people had themselves brought. Pollock, *Authorized Biography*, p. 163, speaks of food vendors falling silent during the service.
198. BG follows Bishop from platform. Graham's "diary," in Burnham, *To the Far Corners*, p. 49.
198. Hindus more open than Muslims. "Billy in India," *Time*, February 13, 1956, p. 72.
199. BG quiets crowd at Palamcottah. Burnham, *To the Far Corners*, pp. 53–54.
199. BG confronts worshiping crowds. Ibid., pp. 54–55; Houston, "Billy Graham," March 1958, p. 81.

200. Reserved seats in New Delhi. *Hindustan Times*, February 5, 1956.
200. BG in Benares temple. Burnham, *To the Far Corners*, pp. 43, 79–80.
200. Nehru's lack of enthusiasm about BG. Noel Houston, "Billy Graham," *Holiday*, February 1958, p. 138.
200. Nixon's role in arranging the appointment. Letter, BG to Nixon, January 7, 1956; Cable, Nixon to Cooper, January 20, 1956. A cable from New Delhi, January 24, 1956, confirmed that the appointment had been made.
200. Encounter with Hammarskjold. Burnham, *To the Far Corners*, pp. 60–61.
200. BG's meeting with Nehru. Ibid., pp. 61–63; Houston, "Billy Graham," February 1958, p. 138.
201. Nehru seen as pro-Christian. Burnham, *To the Far Corners*, p. 58.
201. Men are the same the world over. BG often made this observation. This particular formulation is quoted in Houston, "Billy Graham," March 1958, p. 81.
201. "average Communist in India doesn't know what it's all about." Burnham, *To the Far Corners*, pp. 68–69.
202. Indians thrilled at personal visits. Ibid., p. 60.
202. A Cadillac for Nehru. Ibid., pp. 71–72. This suggestion drew a withering blast from the *Christian Century*, which charged that BG "hasn't a glimmer of a notion about what is really going on in the world. . . . If there were any sense at all of the real nature of the world's revolution, a man couldn't even think of such irrelevances as a train or a car, much less utter them. . . . [I]t is wretched politics and impossible Christianity." "Whose Ambassador?" *Christian Century*, February 29, 1956, pp. 261–63. Filipino newspapers also scored the evangelist heavily, damning him for "insulting the Indian sense of values" and charging that he was a "publicity-mad preacher," a Liberace of the religious world who was trying "to sell American friendship to India in the same manner that she sells, say, toothpaste or brassieres." Manila *Chronicle*, *Herald*, and *Daily Mirror*, all quoted in *Christian Century* article.
202. BG chooses Abdul-Haqq. Pollock, *Authorized Biography*, p. 164.
203. "like the prophet Elijah." See I Kings 19.
203. Indian resentment of Burnham's book. "Billy Graham Answers His Critics," Letter to the Editor, Madras *Sunday Standard*, February 24, 1957. Also, Pollock, *Authorized Biography*, p. 165.
203. "Everything has been perfect." Burnham, *To the Far Corners*, pp. 154–55. The commentator was Marshall Frady, *Parable*, p. 342.
203. Never had better platforms. Billy Graham (interview), "Asia Can Be Won," *U.S. News & World Report*, April 6, 1956.
204. Ruth builds a house. Ruth Graham, oral history, CN 141, Box 4, Folder 8, BGCA; Patricia Daniels Cornwall, *A Time for Remembering: The Ruth Bell Graham Story* (San Francisco: Harper & Row, 1983), pp. 111–21; personal observation.
205. "quiet it down and go easy." Letter, Frank W. Boykin to Eisenhower, March 19, 1956, CN 74, Box 1, Folder 1, BGCA.
205. Eisenhower's letter to BG. Letter, March 22, 1956, CN 74, Box 1, Folder 12, BGCA.
206. BG agrees to help. Letter, BG to Eisenhower, March 27, 1956, ibid.
206. BG's progress report to Eisenhower. Letter, June 4, 1956, ibid.
206. Gradual repentance of racism. One of BG's 1956 *Hour of Decision* sermons was entitled "The Sin of Tolerance."
206. Niebuhr chides BG. See particularly Reinhold Niebuhr, "Literalism, Individualism, and Billy Graham," *Christian Century*, May 23, 1956, pp. 640–42; "Proposal to Billy Graham," *Christian Century*, August 8, 1956, pp. 921–22.
207. *Life* article about racial problems. Billy Graham, "Billy Graham Makes Plea for End to Intolerance," *Life*, October 1, 1956, pp. 138–40.

Chapter 13: New Evangelicals, Old Fundamentalists

208. "go ahead and buy it." John Pollock, *Billy Graham: The Authorized Biography* (New York: McGraw-Hill, 1966), p. 170.
209. T. W. Wilson joins BGEA ... "more like a gentleman." T. W. Wilson, oral history, January 30, 1971, CN 141, Box 4, Folder 46, BGCA.
209. Leighton Ford. Jean Graham Ford, oral history, July 7, 1976, CN 141, Box 3, Folder 44, BGCA; Leighton Ford, oral history, July 7, 1976, CN 141, Box 3, Folder 43, BGCA.
211. "It is wrong to abdicate responsibility." H. J. Ockenga, quoted in David Moberg, *The Great Reversal: Evangelism Versus Social Concern* (Philadelphia: Lippincott, 1972), p. 228–29.
211. "an urgent matter." BG to Eisenhower, June 29, 1953, and September 28, 1953, CN 74, Box 1, Folder 12, BGCA. Unless otherwise noted, further correspondence between Graham and Eisenhower or members of the Eisenhower administration other than Richard Nixon are from this source.
211. "extremely vital information." White House memo, quoting a message from Betty Lowery, a BGEA secretary, who sought to set up a meeting with the President after BG returned from the Middle East in 1956.
212. "an unforgettable experience ... GOP-controlled this fall." BG to Eisenhower, February 8, 1954.
212. "Still thinking you are the greatest." Letter, BG to Eisenhower, January 7, 1956.
212. "my unqualified support." Letter, BG to Eisenhower, August 15, 1955.
212. Nixon's "all-important sense of humor ... better still, in Hawaii." Letter, BG to Nixon, September 13, 1955, in CN 74, MF Reel 1, from Box 299, (Pre-Presidential Papers of Richard Nixon, National Archives and Record Service), BGCA. Unless otherwise noted, all subsequent pre-presidential correspondence between BG and Nixon is also from this source.
212. "Governor Dewey said ... integrity and Christian principles." Letter, BG to Nixon, October 8, 1955.
213. "Your political advice was on the beam." Letter, Nixon to BG, November 7, 1955.
213. "How thoughtful of you." Thank-you note, BG to Nixon, June 4, 1956.
213. Nixon viewed as "man of the people." Billy Graham (interview), "Asia Can Be Won," *U.S. News & World Report*, April 5,1956, pp. 62–71. The Vice-President's staff clearly understood the advantages of having Graham on their side. Shortly after the *U.S. News & World Report* article appeared, an aide wrote to Nixon, "I hope that you also noted the tribute paid to your visit to India by Billy Graham in the *U.S. News & World Report*. It seems to me that Graham's statements in this regard could be disseminated more widely." Memo, Pat Hillings to Nixon, April 10, 1956. A few days later, Nixon dropped Graham a note thanking him for the kind words; Nixon to BG, April 18, 1956.
213. Nixon "a splendid churchman." Graham, quoted in Newark *Sunday News*, September 4, 1955, quoted in William G. McLoughlin, *Revivalist in a Secular Age* (New York: Ronald Press, 1960), p. 118.
213. BG sends speech. Letter, BG to Nixon, July 14, 1956.
213. "three air-conditioned rooms." BG to Nixon, June 4, 1956.
213. "a cause that cannot lose." Letter, BG to Eisenhower, August 24, 1956.
214. "Democrats are going to use every trick." Letter, BG to Nixon, August 24, 1956.
214. Lament over divorced presidential candidates. "The Home," *Hour of Decision*, 1956.
214. "possibilities in the making." Letter, BG to Nixon, November 10, 1956.
214. "talk concerning Bible prophecy." Ibid. Sometime in 1956, apparently, BG and Nixon had discussed biblical prophecy during a visit in the home of Evangelical senator A. Willis Robertson, father of religious broadcaster and presidential candidate M. G. "Pat" Robertson.
214. "in case added responsibilities are yours." Letter, BG to Nixon, December 2, 1957.
214. First Presidential Prayer Breakfast. Donald Scott McAlpine, "Mr. Christian of Washington," *United Evangelical Action*, July 1, 1954, pp. 266–67.

215. The founding of Fuller Theological Seminary. George Marsden, *Reforming Fundamentalism: Fuller Seminary and the New Evangelicalism* (Grand Rapids: Eerdmans, 1987), pp. 13–30, 53–54, passim. This meticulous and thoughtful account of Fuller Theological Seminary's short history provides an excellent window into Evangelical Christianity since the 1940s.
215. Wilbur Smith's vision of a journal. Letter, Smith to BG, February 22,1951, Smith Papers, Fuller Theological Seminary, quoted in ibid., p. 158.
215. BG begins to plan for *Christianity Today* (*CT*). Graham (interview), "In the Beginning," *Christianity Today*, July 17, 1981, p. 26.
216. BG's vision of *CT*'s stance. Letter, BG to Lindsell, January 25, 1955, CN 192 (Lindsell Papers), Box 6, Folder 2, BGCA.
216. The "big love" approach. Ibid.
217. *CT* in D.C. Graham (interview), "In the Beginning," p. 27.
217. *CT* offices in Washington. L. Nelson Bell, oral history, November 8, 1970, CN 141, Box 2, Folder 23, BGCA.
217. "a silent group of non-published men." Letter, BG to J. Howard Pew, April 13, 1955, quoted in Carl F. H. Henry, *Confessions of a Theologian: An Autobiography* (Waco, Tex.: Word Books, 1986), p. 146.
217. Pew's views. See, for example, "The Resourceful Mr. Pew," *Christianity and Crisis*, June 11, 1956, p. 75; Also, Pew, draft of speech, included in letter to L. Nelson Bell, May 15, 1959, CN 8 (*Christianity Today* [*CT*] collection), Box 1, Folder 57, BGCA.
217. Pew: U.S. should drive Communists from UN. Letter, Pew to Bell, October 5, 1961, CN 8 (*CT* Collection), Box 1, Folder 57, BGCA.
218. Pew's contributions to *CT*. Financial reports in annual meetings of the *CT* board, for 1955–59, in CN 8 (*CT* Collection), BGCA. See also Henry, *Confessions*, p. 145.
218. "Would Carl be ready?" Letter, BG to Lindsell, January 25, 1955, CN 192 (Lindsell Papers), Box 6, Folder 2, BGCA.
218. Henry "too well known as a Fundamentalist." BG to Bell, June 5,1955, quoted in Henry, *Confessions*, p. 141.
219. "Liberalism and Evangelicalism do not have equal rights." Henry to BG, June 20, 1955, CN 192 (Lindsell Papers), Box 6, Folder 2, BGCA.
219. Henry's questions about capitalism. Ibid.; Carl F. H. Henry, "Christianity and Economic Crisis," *United Evangelical Action*, May 1, 1955, pp. 7–11, quoted in Marsden, *Reforming Fundamentalism*, p. 160.
219. "truth without love will be ignored." Henry to BG and Bell, August 18, 1955, quoted in Marsden, *Reforming Fundamentalism*, p. 161.
219. "we will seek it elsewhere." Bell to Board, quoted in Henry, *Confessions*, p. 162.
219. A board should trust an editor. Ibid., p. 163.
220. Public notice of *CT*'s appearance. Ibid., p. 162; Paul Harvey's endorsement is also mentioned in a letter, Bell to Ockenga, October 1, 1956, CN 8 (*CT* Collection), Box 1, Folder 56, BGCA.
220. BG critiques first issue of *CT*. Letter, BG to Henry, October 28, 1956, CN 192 (Lindsell Papers), BGCA.
220. Vita Safe and Supra Vite. Ads and letters contained in report to *CT* board, May 28, 1957, CN 8 (*CT* Collection), BGCA.
220. Poor response to circulation efforts. Report of circulation manager Linda Jane Kik to *CT* board, January 6, 1958. Minutes of board meetings, CN 8 (*CT* Collection), BGCA. George Wilson had apparently estimated that BG's appeal might garner fifty thousand subscriptions. Bell to Wilson, March 14, 1958, CN 8 (*CT* Collection), Box 1, BGCA.
220. *CT* adopts more effective circulation techniques. Linda Jane Kik report to *CT* board, June 5, 1958. David Lawrence's help noted in minutes of board meeting, September 13, 1956. CN 8 (*CT* Collection), BGCA.

221. *Look's* assessment, quoted by Henry, report to *CT* board, May 28, 1957. NAE assessment cited in Henry's report, June 18, 1959, CN 8 (*CT* Collection), Box 1, Folder 56, BGCA.
223. McIntire: NAE little better than NCC. Marsden, *Reforming Fundamentalism*, p. 49.
223. Jones's criticism of BG. Quoted in R. K. Johnson, *Builder of Bridges: The Biography of Dr. Bob Jones, Sr.* (Murfreesboro, Tenn.: Sword of the Lord, 1969), pp. 287, 278, 286. Carl McIntire agreed that liberals were exploiting the unwary BG. In the November 22, 1956, issue of the *Christian Beacon*, he quoted an unnamed official of the World Council who allegedly said, "We do not agree with Billy Graham's theology, but we are using him to build our churches."
223. "the more Dr. Bob turned against him." Several interviewees confirmed this account and interpretation of Jones's animus against BG.
223. *Sword of the Lord*, any edition. This is a shortened version of the paper's official statement of faith. For the longer version, see "The Statement of Faith and Agreement Signed Annually by Directors of The Sword of the Lord Foundation," *Sword of the Lord*, September 10, 1954, p. 2.
224. BG endorses RSV. *Sword of the Lord*, June 17, 1955, p. 9. A year earlier, BG had backed off a bit from a strict Fundamentalist view of Scripture when he told the *Methodist Recorder*, "What do you mean by a 'fundamentalist'? Do you mean by that someone who believes God dictated the Bible to certain men as if they were dictaphones and had no part in the matter except insofar as they recorded the words of God? If so, then I am certainly not a fundamentalist. If on the other hand you mean by a fundamentalist one who believes the great fundamental truths of the Bible and man's need of a savior, then I certainly am!" *Methodist Recorder*, May 20, 1954, p. 251. Most professors at Fuller Seminary held positive views toward the new book, a fact that reportedly cost Charles Fuller thousands of supporters. Marsden, *Reforming Fundamentalism*, pp. 136–37.
224. "no one in his right mind." Robert Leslie Sumner, *Man Sent from God: A Biography of Dr. John R. Rice* (Grand Rapids: Eerdmans, 1959), p. 211. Sumner's account of BG's remarks is based on a report in the Colgate-Rochester Divinity School *Bulletin*, referred to without citation.
224. BG at Union. Carl F. H. McIntire, "Billy Graham at Union Seminary," *Christian Beacon*, March 16, 1955, pp. 1–2 (Note: this article appeared a full year after BG's address); John R. Rice, "Billy Graham at Union Seminary," *Sword of the Lord*, April 22, 1955, p. 3.
224. "I am neither a Fundamentalist nor a Modernist." John R. Rice, "Questions Answered About Billy Graham," *Sword of the Lord*, June 17, 1955, p. 10.
224. "God has people in all the churches." Edward B. Fiske, the *New York Times*, July 17, 1956. The article identifies the statement as having been made after the London crusade.
225. Rice: "No one could possibly say that Billy Graham is a modernist." Rice, "Graham at Union," p. 3.
225. "every Christian … ought to rejoice." Rice, "Questions Answered," pp. 9, 11; Rice, "Graham at Union," p. 3.
225. Modernist opposition proves BG preaching the truth. "Modernist Critics Beset Fundamentalist Billy Graham," *Sword of the Lord*, April 6, 1956, p. 7.
225. Negative mention by nonregular contributors. Chester E. Tulga, "More Than Evangelicals," *Sword of the Lord*, July 27, 1956; Tom Malone, "What Do You Think of Billy Graham?" *Sword of the Lord*, September 14, 1956.
226. "What difference does it make who sponsors …?" "What's the Next Step?" interview with Billy Graham, *Christian Life*, June 1956, pp. 20–23, as quoted and paraphrased in Marsden, *Reforming Fundamentalism*, p. 163.
226. Paul did not give convert names to pagans. Joseph T. Bayly (editor of the Intervarsity magazine, *His*), letter to *Christian Life*, August 1956, p. 4, quoted in Marsden, *Reforming Fundamentalism*, p. 163.

226. "The *Sword of the Lord* does not speak for you." John R. Rice, "Which Way, Billy Graham?" *Sword of the Lord*, November 23, 1956, p. 2.
226. "breaking down of convictions." John R. Rice, "Billy Graham's New York Crusade," *Sword of the Lord*, April 19, 1957, p. 8.
226. Rice attacks BG's motives. John R. Rice, "Dr. Rees Defends Billy's Unequal Yoke," *Sword of the Lord*, April 26, 1957. Dr. Rees is Paul Rees, an evangelist and, at the time, president of the NAE, who often worked closely with BG and who had offered a defense of BG's policy of cooperative evangelism. See Paul Rees, "What About the Criticism?" *Christian Life*, April 1957, pp. 14–16.
227. "I intend to continue." John R. Rice, quoted in *Christian Beacon*, April 4, 1957. The address was given on April 3.
227. "principal sparkplug." Rice, "Dr. Rees," p. 7.
227. New York committees short on Fundamentalists. James Bennet, *Christian Beacon*, April 25, 1957, p. 3. Bennet, an attorney and prominent Fundamentalist layman, had spoken at BG's businessmen's dinners during his pastorate at Western Springs, Illinois. Graham, interview, March 26, 1987. John R. Rice made a similar charge: "Of the one hundred fifty-five men and women from the general crusade committee, only a small minority claim to be out-and-out Bible believers and converted people and most are openly liberal." Rice, "Billy Graham's New York Crusade," p. 8. The discrepancy in numbers may be due to Rice's lumping the general and executive committees together.
227. "They are *not* godly men." McIntire, quoted in Robert Dunzweiler, *Billy Graham: A Critique*, (Elkins Park, Pa.: Faith Theological Seminary, 1961), p. 17. The committee list was published in the November 22, 1956, issue of *Christian Beacon*. John R. Rice published the same list in *Sword of the Lord*, July 5, 1974, p. 4.
227. "not orthodoxy, but love." BG's NAE statement, quoted in "The Lost Chord of Evangelism," *Christianity Today*, April 1, 1957, p. 26.
227. "only question is: Are you committed to Christ?" Andrew Tully, "Billy Graham Doesn't Anticipate Overnight Miracles from Crusade," New York *World-Telegraph and Sun*, May 29, 1957, p. 6.
227. "we'll send them to their own churches." New York *Evening Journal*, September 18, 1956. In the September 29, 1956, issue of the Protestant Council's publication, *Protestant Church Life*, Graham was quoted as saying, "We're coming to New York ... to get people to dedicate themselves to God and to send them on to their own churches—Catholic, Protestant or Jewish." Quoted in Edgar Bundy, *Billy Graham: Performer, Politician, Preacher, Prophet?* (Miami Shores, Fla.: Edgar Bundy Ministries, 1982), p. 10. According to Bundy (p. 9), BG told Wyrtzen and Bennet in a private conversation in 1955 that "he would always tell his converts that they should go to the church of their choice, whether it is Catholic, Jewish, or Protestant." A virtually identical statement was reported in the San Francisco *News*, November 11, 1957, p. 3. In contrast, Nelson Bell told Bob Jones, Sr., in 1957, just prior to the New York crusade, that BG "never has sent one card to a Catholic church." Letter, Bell to Jones, May 7, 1957, in CN 8 (*CT* Collection), Box 1, Folder 32, BGCA.
227. Billy's "amiable personality" leads him to countenance error. William Ward Ayer, "Aftermath of the Billy Graham Crusade in New York," apparently unpublished article, quoted in Dunzweiler, *Graham: A Critique*, p. 30.
228. BG's "policy never to answer critics." BG, "The Life That Wins," sermon, *Hour of Decision*, 1952.
228. "petty little fights over non-essentials." BG, "Peace vs. Chaos," sermon, *Hour of Decision*, 1951.
228. "little love notes." Stephen Olford, interview, April 21, 1988.
228. Others speak on BG's behalf. Letter, Bell to Jones, May 7, 1957, CN 8 (*CT* Collection), Box 1, Folder 32, BGCA; "Dare We Renew the Controversy," *Christianity Today*, June 24, 1957, p. 26. Other articles followed in July.

228. "no major evangelist," Robert O. Ferm, *Cooperative Evangelism* (Grand Rapids: Zondervan, 1958), p. 31.

Chapter 14: God in the Garden

230. "fear and trembling." AP, March 15, 1957.
230. "I'm prepared to be crucified." "A Great Revival Coming: Billy." New York *Mirror*, May 11, 1947.
230. Crusade committee members. "Billy Graham Crusade Aims at Awakening City." *New York World-Telegram and Sun*, March 4, 1957, p. 1; "A Talk with Billy Graham," *New York Post*, May 12, 1957. Roger Hull had become interested in BG after his wife and son heard the evangelist in Memphis in 1951, an event that sparked a significant change in the son's life and eventually led to his entering the ministry and becoming pastor of New York's Broadway Presbyterian Church. Roger Hull, oral history, December 10, 1970, CN 141, Box 4, Folder 37, BGCA. During the crusade, Jane Pickens Langley, whose husband was president of the New York Stock Exchange, entertained BG at a private luncheon to which she had invited several friends associated with New York's oldest money, and during the middle of the crusade, the entire team enjoyed a daylong outing with 150 guests at the Long Island estate of Mr. and Mrs. Cornelius Vanderbilt Whitney. Curtis Mitchell, *God in the Garden* (Garden City, N.Y.: Doubleday, 1957), p. 101.
231. Wealthy backers. William G. McLoughlin, *Billy Graham, Revivalist in a Secular Age* (New York: Ronald Press, 1960), p. 159; also, p. 102.
231. African tribesmen pray for BG. Herbert Weiner, "Billy Graham: Respectable Evangelism," *Commentary*, September 1957, p. 258.
231. Far East prayer groups. Mitchell, *God in the Garden*, pp. 80–81; "One Hundred Cities in Prayers for Graham Crusade," *New York Herald Tribune*, May 26, 1957, p. 23.
231. New York prayer groups. David Bazar, "Billy Graham Relies on Power of Prayer at Crusade Next Month," *New York Journal-American*, April 20, 1957.
231. "Every time I see my name up in lights ..." Quoted in Mitchell, *God in the Garden*, p. 63. BG has made this same observation countless times throughout his ministry.
231. BG spends fifty times more than Billy Sunday on publicity. Unidentified clipping from publication that appeared during the crusade. CN 360, MF Reel 9, BGCA.
232. "The campaign will spin along." "In the Garden," *Christian Century*, May 15, 1957, pp. 614–15.
232. BG at Yale. *Yale Daily News*, February 12, 13, 15, 1957. I am indebted to Jim Ford, Yale 1988, for his assistance in seeking out the pertinent issues of the *Daily News.*
232. "Billy ... master artist." Lane Adams, interview, February 9, 1987.
233. Niebuhr's criticisms. "Salvation," *Newsweek*, April 23, 1956; Reinhold Niebuhr, "Proposal to Billy Graham," *Christian Century*, August 8, 1956, p. 921–22; "After Comment, the Deluge," *Christian Century*, September 4, 1957, pp. 1034–35; quoted in McLoughlin, *Revivalist*, p. 503.
233. "merely by signing a card." Reinhold Niebuhr, "Differing Views on Billy Graham," *Life*, July 1, 1957.
233. "It simply would not do." Reinhold Niebuhr, "Literalism, Individualism, and Billy Graham," *Christian Century*, May 23, 1956, p. 641.
233. "even less complicated answers." Reinhold Niebuhr, *Life*, July 1, 1957; "Graham Ballyhoo Cheapens Ministry, Niebuhr Says," *New York Post*, June 2, 1957, quoting Niebuhr's comments in *Advance*, the official magazine of Congregational Christian Churches, June 14, 1957.
233. "Theologians don't seem to understand." *Saturday Evening Post*, April 13, 1957, quoted in David Poling, *Why Billy Graham?* (Grand Rapids: Zondervan, 1977), p. 99. In fact, Graham did touch on such matters as housing, poverty, race relations, employment, and public

education in his sermons during the New York crusade, and he did so not just offhandedly but after substantial research by his assistants and himself. Social concerns by no means dominated his preaching, but neither were they completely absent. Dan Potter, oral history, CN 141, Box 10, Folder 17, BGCA.

234. "If I tried to preach as he writes." Quoted in Noel Houston, "Billy Graham," *Holiday*, February 1958, pp. 140–41. Some liberal churchmen agreed with BG. Henry P. Van Dusen admitted that "there are multitudes whom Mr. Graham may reach who are not now and never will be touched by a more sophisticated interpretation of the gospel." "A Talk with Billy Graham," *New York Post*, May 12, 1957.

234. "I knew he wouldn't see me." BG, quoted in George Champion, oral history, CN 141, Box 23, Folder 14, BGCA.

234. "Catholics seemed to appreciate" BG. During his 1952 Washington crusade, an editorial in the diocesan *Catholic Standard* had commended him for exhorting people to return to the law of Christ and noted with approval the contrast between his services and those Fundamentalist gatherings at which Catholics had been attacked. This irenic spirit, the paper said, was "a great assurance to our Catholic people who have long known not to confuse the majority of Protestants with a vocal few." Editorial, *Catholic Standard*, February 1, 1952, quoted in "Catholic Standard Supports Graham," Arlington, Virginia, unidentified newspaper, February 8, 1952; *The Tablet* (Brooklyn, N.Y.), February 9, 1952. In a similar spirit, the national Roman Catholic weekly, *America*, reported on his five-day crusade in France in 1955, noting that "he is evidently intelligent, sincere, and genuinely zealous. Undoubtedly he is doing a lot of good among devout Protestants here and abroad." *America*, quoted in *Chicago Daily News*, June 11, 1955, p. 1.

234. Weigel on BG. Gustave Weigel, quoted in *America*, May 4, 1957, pp. 161–64.

234. "nine sermons on Catholic doctrine." "Catholic Sermons on Doctrine Set," *New York Journal-American*, May 5, 1957, p. 10; "St. Patrick's Sermon," the *New York Times*, May 6, 1957. In a letter to his friend, Richard Nixon, BG optimistically interpreted this directive as an attempt by the archbishop to assist the crusade by contributing to "genuine spiritual awakening." Letter, BG to Nixon, in CN 74, MF 1, from Box 299, (Pre-Presidential Papers of Richard Nixon, National Archives and Record Service), BGCA. Unless otherwise noted, correspondence between BG and Nixon (and members of their staffs) prior to Nixon's becoming President is from this source.

234. Catholics forbidden to hear BG. Rev. John E. Kelly, in *Homiletic and Pastoral Review*, April 1957, quoted in "Don't Be Half Saved?" *Time*, May 6, 1957, p. 86; "Gentle but Firm," *Newsweek*, May 6, 1957, p. 80; "Catholics Warned on Graham Talks," *New York World-Telegram and Sun*, April 24, 1957.

234. "a danger to the faith." The *New York Times*, April 25, 1957. It is interesting to note that this story of conflict was the first story about the crusade to make the first page of the *Times*.

234. BG's heart grew cold. "This Can Happen in New York," unidentified clipping in BGC scrapbook. Appears to be from *Chritianity Today*.

235. "like our Lord weeping over Jerusalem." Stephen Olford, interview, April 21, 1988.

235. "We do not expect to see a city transformed." "Graham's Viewpoint," *New York Herald Tribune*, May 12, 1957, pp. 1, 25.

235. "largest-ever opening-night attendance." Stanley Rowland, Jr., the *New York Times*, May 16, 1957, p. 22.

235. *Times* coverage of the crusade. Ibid., May 16, 1957.

235. "garish red headlines." *New York Journal-American*, April 13, 1957.

235. "part Dick Nixon." "Graham's Great Appeal," *New York World-Telegram and Sun*, July 18, 1957.

235. "He is like an excellent salesman." Mitchell, *God in the Garden*, pp. 57–58.

236. BG on *Life's* cover. *Life*, July 1, 1957.

236. Telephone counseling. "Scores of Students at Crusade," *New York Herald Tribune*, May 19, 1957, p. 30.
236. Inaugural TV program. Trendex ratings, "TV, Radio Today," June 4, 1957, p. 7; also, "Great Medium for Messages," *Time*, June 17, 1957, p. 61. For J. Howard Pew's role, Stephen Olford interview and John Pollock, *Billy Graham: The Authorized Biography* (New York: McGraw-Hill, 1966), p. 180. Some estimates of Pew's contribution run as high as $400,000. The *New York Times* set the figure at $200,000, but this seems based on an estimated cost of $50,000 apiece for the first four programs. The $100,000 figure is approximately correct, but it appears Pew's contribution was geared to cover the first two weeks of programming, even though the original contract negotiated by Bennett and Dienert was for four weeks. BG furnished the information about Goldenson and the fact that Pew was not required to make good on his guarantee pledge. Graham, interview, March 5, 1989.
237. "Gallup poll revealed." Gallup poll, June 1, 1957.
237. "This will affect Graham's ministry." "Amazing TV," *Christian Life*, September 1957.
238. TV show reviewed. Quotations from reviews are from Mitchell, *God in the Garden*, p. 119, and *Variety*, June 5, 1957, p. 1957, p. 31. Quotation explaining appeal of live services is from Tedd Seelye, cited by Pollock, *Authorized Biography*, p. 180.
238. Wall Street meeting. *New York Daily News*, July 11, 1957, p. 1; *New York World-Telegram and Sun*, July 10, 1957, p. 21.
238. Yankee Stadium rally. "Held Over," *Time*, July 29, 1957, p. 48; "Billy Graham Draws Biggest Stadium Crowd," *New York Herald Tribune*, July 21, 1957; "100,000 Fill Yankee Stadium to Hear Graham," the *New York Times*, July 21, 1957, p. 1.
238. BG commends Martin Luther King, Jr. Stanley Rowland, Jr., "As Billy Graham Sees His Role," the *New York Times Magazine*, April 21, 1957, pp. 17, 25.
239. Racial hatred breaks several commandments. "Cohen, Bodyguards Hear Graham," *New York World-Telegram and Sun*, May 22, 1957, p. 14.
239. Black ministers invite BG to North Carolina. "North Carolina Negroes Ask Graham to Lead Anti-bias Campaign," *New York Post*, May 21, 1957, p. 16.
239. Antidiscrimination legislation needed. "Speak Up Against Racial Bias: Graham," New York *Mirror*, July 15, 1957.
239. Black attendance improves. "Does a Religious Crusade Do Any Good," *U.S. News & World Report*, September 27, 1957.
239. Angry letters and calls. Interview, Howard Jones, May 3, 1988.
239. Kasper's comments. *New York Herald Tribune*, July 2, 1957.
239. Segregationists to be disillusioned with heaven. "No Color Line in Heaven," *Ebony*, September 1957, pp. 99–100.
240. BG and King hold sensitizing meetings. Graham interview, February 27, 1987.
240. Prayer and the Holy Spirit. Jones, interview.
240. BG's introduction and King's prayer. Tape recording of service, in Billy Graham Collection at James E. Boyer Centennial Library, Southern Baptist Seminary, Louisville, quoted in Edward Lee Moore, *Billy Graham and Martin Luther King, Jr.: An Inquiry into White and Black Revivalistic Traditions*, (Ph.D. diss., Vanderbilt University, 1979), p. 455.
240. King approves BG's strategy. Jones and BG, interviews. This particular quote is from Jones.
240. Angry response to BG's endorsement of King. Jones, interview; "Billy Lost South When He Jumped to Politics," *Life*, October 19, 1957.
240. Bob Jones on BG's stand. "BJU Founder Feels Billy Graham Won't Hold Local Crusade," Greenville, South Carolina, *Piedmont*, September 10, 1957.
241. BG fails to recognize Ruth. George Burnham and Lee Fisher, *Billy Graham and the New York Crusade* (Grand Rapids: Zondervan, 1957), p. 143.
241. Beavan's ideas for a wind-up rally. Letter, Beavan to Graham, July 24, 1957, CN 17 (BGEA Vice-President, 1954–1977), Box 1, Folder 4 (New York crusade miscellany), BGCA.

241. Crowd estimates for Times Square rally. Police estimated the crowd at 75,000. United Press reporters pegged it at perhaps as high as 200,000. Uncharacteristically, BG at first accepted the UP figures, then later acknowledged they were probably too high. Beavan felt 160,000 was a fair figure; other BG team members were willing to settle for 125,000. The *New York Times*, September 2, 1957; Mitchell, *God in the Garden*, p. 179.

241. BG's Times Square sermon. Quoted in Mitchell, *God in the Garden*, p. 180.

242. Christian Arts Fellowship. Lane Adams, interview; oral history, May 9, 1978, CN 141, Box 2, Folder 4, BGCA.

242. Celebrities at the crusade. "Crusade Windup," *Time*, September 9, 1957; *Charlotte Observer*, June 4, 1957; Mitchell, *God in the Garden*, p. 64.

242. Perle Mesta. *Charlotte Observer*, June 4, 1957.

242. Gloria Swanson. Mitchell, *God in the Garden*, p. 43.

242. Mickey Cohen. In a book filled with hip shots and dubious allegations, Chuck Ashman alleges that Cohen boasted of his ability to get loans and cash payoffs from members of the Graham organization and claims that he believed Graham himself was behind these efforts as part of a plan to lure him into becoming a headline-making convert. Ashman claimed to have documentary evidence to support Cohen's claims, but when challenged to produce them, failed to do so. Jim Vaus, who stayed in touch with Cohen until his death, acknowledges that Cohen took advantage of him financially but describes this as simply part of a "conning" pattern Cohen was quite willing to use on anyone. In particular, he is known to have pretended to have had financial problems as part of an effort to convince the Internal Revenue Service that he was not cheating on his income tax. The IRS did not believe him and successfully brought charges that resulted in his imprisonment in federal prison. BG visited him at least twice during his first stay in jail, which began not long after the Los Angeles crusade, and maintained some contact with him in later years, mostly through associates and Dr. and Mrs. Nelson Bell, but Cohen soured on the relationship in later years. "If anybody should win this year's Academy Award," he wrote to Charlie Riggs, "It should be him." Michael Mickey Cohen, *Mickey Cohen, in My Own Words: The Underworld Autobiography of Michael Mickey Cohen, as told to John Peer Nugent* (Englewood Cliffs, N.J.: Prentice-Hall, 1975), p. 227. BG may well have believed and hoped Cohen might convert to Christianity, and may or may not have known that friends were helping him financially, but Cohen's word on any subject was quite unreliable. For further information, see Chuck Ashman, *The Gospel According to Billy*, (Secaucus, N.J.: Lyle Stuart, 1977), pp. 17–20; "Mickey Cohen and Billy Graham Pray and Read Bible Together," *New York Herald Tribune*, April 2, 1957; Mitchell, *God in the Garden*, p. 27; "Cohen, Bodyguards Hear Graham," *New York World-Telegram and Sun*, May 22, 1957, p. 14; "New Graham Book: It's Cheeky but Is It True?" *Charlotte Observer*, September 11, 1977; Louis Hofferbert, "The Billy Graham Story," Chapter 8, *Houston Press*, May 15,1952; Pollock, *A Foreign Devil in China: The Story of Dr. L. Nelson Bell, an American Surgeon in China* (Grand Rapids: Zondervan, 1971; Minneapolis: World Wide Publications, 1988), p. 311; Jim Vaus, interview.

242. Ethel Waters. Ethel Waters, oral history, October 1970, CN 141, Box 5, Folder 141, BGCA; Grady Wilson, interview, March 31, 1987; Mitchell, *God in the Garden*, p. 137.

242. "Analysis of decisions." Robert Ferm interviewed 231 ministers (most had cooperated with the crusade, but some had actively opposed it) and over 2,000 inquirers were selected in a somewhat random fashion. Ferm chose his sample by taking 100 names from each alphabetical grouping of inquirers. This obviously gave inquirers whose names began with such letters as *Q* or *Z* a much larger chance of being included than those whose name began with, for example, *B* or *M* or *S* or *W*. Ferm apparently took this into some account, and it seems clear he was in no way trying to select a sample that would skew findings in a direction that would guarantee an outcome favorable to BG. Ferm, interview, March 28, 1987. Crusade results. "The New York Billy Graham Crusade Report," typed report, n.d., but apparently

1958. CN 19 (Ferm Papers), Box 5, Folder 36 (New York 1957 Crusade Reports), BGCA; "One Year Later," *Christian Life*, September 1958, pp. 11–15. Reports from individual congregations are found on p. 13 of this article.

243. Post crusade follow-up effort. "Billy Graham Is Back to Follow Up Crusade," *New York Herald Tribune*, September 25, 1957.

243. "There is a difference!" BG, quoted in Mitchell, *God in the Garden*, p. 12.

Chapter 15: Reaping the Whirlwind

245. Fundamentalists sign pledge. *Sword of the Lord*, January 24, 1958, pp. 4–8. Cited in Farley Porter Butler, *Billy Graham and the End of Evangelical Unity* (Ph.D. diss., University of Florida, 1976), p. 232.

245. Liberal and Fundamentalist opposition in San Francisco. Butler, *End of Unity*, p. 243; Sherwood E. Wirt, "New Life Surges in 'Graveyard of Evangelism,'" *United Evangelical Action*, August 1, 1958, p. 3.

245. "What makes San Francisco significant ... which divide them" *Christianity Today*, quoted in Butler, *End of Unity*, pp. 243–44.

245. BG's open letter. CN 192 (Lindsell Papers), Box 6, Folder 2, BGCA.

246. "no way I could answer them." BG, interview, March 26, 1987.

246. BG and Bob Jones in Birmingham. The basic story was told to me by Roy Gustafson, June 27, 1988. BG was able to recall fewer details but confirmed that such a meeting occurred in Birmingham and that he recalled nothing contradicting Gustafson's story. BG, interview, May 5, 1989.

246. T. W. Wilson not welcome at funeral. The *New York Times*, reprinted in *Charlotte Observer*, June 15, 1969; confirmed by Wilson, February 15, 1991.

246. "a little like Saul and David." BG, interview, March 26, 1987. Barrows recalled an incident in which famed Fundamentalist evangelist John R. Rice displayed a similar spirit. Several evangelists, including Rice and Jones, were involved in a long joint revival in Chicago. The campaign had not gone particularly well except on Saturday nights, when the young preachers from Youth For Christ handled the services. "I remember vividly," Barrows recalled, "standing in a corner while the executive committee discussed Saturday nights. John R. Rice felt that he and some of the older men should have Saturday nights. The rationale was that 'these young fellows can't carry it.' But in my perception there was also a feeling that 'if the big crowd came for the young fellows on Saturday night, it sort of shows up the rest of us who don't get the crowds the other nights.' There was that little element of tension. It was hard for the older men to move to one side and make room for the younger fellows coming along. I think there was a little jealousy. God forbid if I am wrong, but I don't think the issue was fundamental, if you press it right down. I don't want to be unkind. The Scripture says, 'Let God judge.'" Interview, March 28, 1987.

247. Ockenga calls BG the spokesman of New Evangelicalism. Press release, December 1957, quoted in *Christian Beacon*, January 9, 1958.

247. Bob Jones removes Fuller program from BJU station. George Marsden, *Reforming Fundamentalism: Fuller Seminary and the Hew Evangelicalism* (Grand Rapids: Eerdmans, 1987), p. 167.

247. BG's graciousness on airplane. Lane Adams, interview, February 9, 1987; oral history, May 9, 1978, CN 141, Box 2, Folder 4, BGCA.

248. Costs of celebrity. Patricia Daniels Cornwell, *A Time for Remembering: The Ruth Bell Graham Story* (San Francisco: Harper & Row, 1983), pp. 131–49.

248. GiGi recalls Ruth's child-rearing techniques. GiGi Tchividjian, interview, October 25, 1990.

248. "The children misbehave.... I must be careful." Cornwell, *A Time for Remembering*, p. 144.

249. Discipline when Billy was home. GiGi Tchividjian, interview.

249. "Some dad you are!" GiGi Tchividjian, interview. Cf. also Cornwell, *A Time for Remembering*, p. 145.
249. Ruth uses dog-training manual. Ruth Graham, *It's My Turn* (Old Tappan, N.J.: Fleming H. Revell, 1982), p. 100.
249. GiGi's difficulty at being good. Cornwell, *A Time for Remembering*, pp. 112, 141–42.
249. GiGi's "practical theology." Graham, *It's My Turn*, pp. 110, 92.
250. GiGi at boarding school. GiGi Tchividjian, interview.
250. "I never take sides." "A Talk with Billy Graham," *New York Post*, May 12, 1957. At about this same time, BG told reporter Noel Houston that a group of conservative Democratic senators had come to his home to urge him to enter the primaries against North Carolina's senator Kerr Scott. He had declined their offer by saying, "Why should I demote myself to be a senator?" The implication was not that he was more famous than any senator but that his work as an evangelist was more important. Over the following decades, he would often give similar answers when asked about possible political ambitions. Noel Houston, "Billy Graham," *Holiday*, March 1958, p. 114.
250. "religious issue would be very strong." Letter, BG to Nixon, December 2, 1957 in CN 74, Box 299 (Pre-Presidential Papers of Richard Nixon, National Archives and Record Service), MF 1, BGCA. Subsequent correspondence between BG and Nixon prior to Nixon's presidency is from this source.
250. "a split deep within democratic ranks on the race issue." Letter, BG to Nixon, August 27, 1958.
250. BG offers Nixon "moral and spiritual" opportunity. Letter, BG to Nixon, March 28, 1957.
251. "one of the most historic events of your administration." Letter, BG to Eisenhower, August 2, 1957. The President declined. Letter, Eisenhower to BG, August 9, 1957. BG was not alone in assuming a growing parity in his relationship with political leaders. During the New York crusade, a Long Island woman who had been unsuccessful in her efforts to arrange a personal visit with the evangelist wrote to Richard Nixon to see if he would intercede on her behalf. Letter, Mrs. L. Diess, Richmond Hill, Long Island, to Nixon, July 25, 1957.
251. "Dear Miss Counts ... Graham, D.D." quoted in "The Political Education of Billy Graham," the *Washington Post*, April 14, 1986. See also the *New York Times*, September 16, 1957.
251. Faubus attended New York crusade. *New York World-Telegram and Sun*, May 24, 1957, p. 6.
252. "duty of every Christian to obey the law." "Graham Hits Race, Hate in Talk to 10,000 on Long Island," *Newsday*, September 25, 1957.
252. Turmoil linked to outsiders. "Graham Links 'Outsiders' to School Rioting." *New York Journal-American*, September 27, 1957.
252. Communist newspapers report Little Rock trauma. Reported in the *New York Times*, September 19, 1957.
252. Oveta Culp Hobby and Richard Nixon communicate with BG. Long Island *Daily Press*, September 26, 1957, pp. 1, 22.
253. Ike consults BG about sending troops. BG, interview, February 27, 1987. Also, Billy Graham (interview), *USA Today*, August 15, 1988. Other details of the Little Rock conflict from the *New York Times*, September 4–9, 14–16, 21–26, 1957.
253. BG willing to visit Little Rock, but not without an invitation. *New York Times*, September 25, 1957; "Graham Hits Race," *Newsday*, September 25, 1957. Fundamentalists do not want him. Ernest Q. Campbell and Thomas F. Pettigrew, *Christians in Racial Crisis: A Study of Little Rock's Ministry* (Washington, D.C.: Public Affairs Press, 1959), p. 55. This provocative book shows that many clergymen favored school integration but chose not to speak out, primarily because they feared the effects their actions would have on their careers. For a replication of their study in a northern (Rochester, New York) setting, see William C. Martin, *Christians in Conflict* (Chicago: Center for the Scientific Study of Religion, 1972).

253. "the most remarkable man in history." Letter, BG to Eisenhower, December 2, 1957.
254. "largest religious gathering ever held in the southeast." "Graham Sets the South an Example," *Christian Century*, November 19, 1958, p. 1326.
254. BG in Columbia. *Charlotte Observer*, October 12, 14, 23, 27, 1958; Charlotte *News*, October 23, 1958. John Pollock, *Billy Graham: The Authorized Biography* (New York: McGraw-Hill, 1966), pp. 225–26; also, Columbia *State*, October 24, 1958, cited in Hopkins, *Race Problem*, pp. 89–91. Bonnell's letter is quoted in Pollock, *Authorized Biography*, p. 225. The *Christian Century* had commended BG's actions in an article, "Billy Graham Sets the South an Example," November 19, 1958, p. 1326.
255. BG calls bombings Hitler-like. AP, in *Charlotte Observer*, October 16, 1958.
255. BG in Clinton. UPI, December 15, 1958; Pollock, *Authorized Biography* p. 226; Drew Pearson, *Diaries, 1949–1959*, (New York, 1974), pp. 487–88, cited by Hopkins, *Race Problem*, p. 95.
255. BG visits Little Rock. AP, September 11,1959; UPI, September 14, 1959; Also, *Arkansas Democrat*, September 11–15, 17, 1959, cited in Hopkins, *Race Problem*, p. 98. Vaught's assessment of BG's influence, quoted in Pollock, *Authorized Biography*, p. 226.
256. "a breezy, easy-to-read style." BG's conception of the new magazine, quoted by Pollock, *Authorized Biography*, p. 240.
256. *Decision's* beginnings. Pollock, *Authorized Biography*, p. 240–41; Sherwood E. Wirt, oral history, January 6, 1976, CN 141, Box 5, Folder 47, BGCA.
256. Crusade University. Minutes, "Billy Graham Project," November 5, 1959, December 29, 1959, Washington, D.C., CN 313, Box 2, Folder 14, BGCA.
256. Brochure. The name *Crusade University* was a working designation only. At the November board meeting, BG apologized for the appearance of his name and picture on the brochure's cover and told the gathering that "I don't want this to be a Billy Graham College or a Billy Graham University." CN 313, Box 2, Folder 14, BGCA; Carl F. H. Henry, interview, February 10, 1987.

Chapter 16: Unto the Uttermost Parts of the Earth

258. "Less than a third . . ." Gallup poll. Stewart Barton Babbage and Ian Siggens, *Light Beneath the Cross* (New York: Doubleday, 1960), p. 18.
258. Australian opposition to previous evangelists. "An Evangelist Far Away," *Newsweek*, March 9, 1959, p. 104; "Real Cool, Billy," *Time*, March 23, 1959, p. 63; Babbage and Siggens, *Light Beneath the Cross*, passim. Brian Willersdorf (Australian evangelist), interview, July 15, 1986.
258. The invitation to hold a crusade in Australia. Babbage and Siggens, *Light Beneath the Cross*, pp. 20–22.
259. Feature films used to generate interest. Ibid., p. 26.
259. Edwin Orr's preparatory meetings. J. Edwin Orr, interview, July 14, 1986; Willersdorf, interview.
259. BG suffers eye problem, recuperates in Hawaii. Grady Wilson, interview, March 1, 1987. Also. "Billy Graham's Journey," *Newsweek*, February 16, 1959; "Conquest Down Under," *Newsweek*, May 25,1959; *Charlotte Observer*, January 15, 1959; UPI, January 13,1959; John Pollock, *Billy Graham: The Authorized Biography* (New York: McGraw-Hill, 1966), p. 205. BG's Canadian benefactor was Charles A. Pitts.
260. Melbourne venues and attendance figures. Babbage and Siggens, *Light Beneath the Cross*, p. 32; Pollock, *Authorized Biography*, pp. 190–96. The attendance figure of ten thousand for the original indoor stadium includes crowds watching on closed-circuit television in an auxiliary building.
260. Trains slow down by Cricket Grounds. Pollock, *Authorized Biography*, p. 196.
260. Letter from Eisenhower. *Charlotte Observer*, March 12, 1959.

260. Governor reads Ps. 23. Pollock, *Authorized Biography*, p. 196. Long before the campaign began, U.S. ambassador William J. Siebald, acting on a recommendation from Richard Nixon, had sponsored a reception for BG and a representative group of government and church leaders at the embassy in Canberra, thus making it clear that BG came to Australia with blessings of his own government. Noted in letter from BG to Nixon, October 14, 1958 in CN 74, MF Reel 1, from Box 299 (Pre-Presidential Papers of Richard Nixon, National Archives and Record Service).
260. New Zealand statistics. Babbage and Siggens, *Light Beneath the Cross*, pp. 35–36.
260. Sydney statistics. Ibid., p. 36.
260. BG's press coverage. "Inquiries re Crusade Results," notes in CN 19 (Ferm Papers), BGCA; Willersdorf, interview.
261. Telephone counseling. Babbage and Siggens, *Light Beneath the Cross*, p. 48. Pollock, *Authorized Biography*, p. 192.
261. Press and TV coverage. Babbage and Siggens, *Light Beneath the Cross*, pp. 49, 52; Willersdorf, interview.
261. "national adulation." Willersdorf, interview.
261. "biggest thing in ... church history of Australia." Bishop R. C. Kerle, quoted by AP, in Charlotte *News*, May 7, 1959.
261. Prestigious converts. Students and medical personnel converted. The Reverend Gordon Powell, pastor, St. Stephen's Presbyterian Church, "Six Months After Billy Graham," address at University of Sydney, "Folder Inquiries re Crusade Results," CN 19 (Ferm Papers), BGCA; Babbage and Siggens, *Light Beneath the Cross*, p. 110.
261. Governor's wife, business leaders, and lawyers converted. Babbage and Siggens, *Light Beneath the Cross*, pp. 56, 105, 113. At Sydney, a section of reserved seats was set aside for professional people, and doctors had access to a restricted parking lot.
261. Growth at St. Stephen's. Powell, "Six Months (address)"; Babbage and Siggens, *Light Beneath the Cross*, p. 138; Pollock, *Authorized Biography*, p. 212.
262. Results proportionate to effort. Various letters from pastors, in "Inquiries re Crusade Results," CN 19 (Ferm Papers), BGCA; John Mallison, interview, July 13, 1986.
262. Growth in volunteer ranks, cuts in crime. Babbage and Siggens, *Light Beneath the Cross*, pp. 27, 55.
262. Bible sales. Roy Gustafson, oral history, 1976, CN 141, Box 4, Folder 12, BGCA.
262. Stabbing. UPI, May 11, 1959.
262. Sydney clergymen encouraged by Graham crusade. The Reverend A. Jack Dain, inter view, July 14, 1986. Also, Walter Smyth, interview, June 11, 1986. The Most Reverend Archbishop Marcus L. Loane also reported that through the middle of the 1960s, a majority of applicants to the Church of England's Moore Theological College traced their conversion or sense of call to the ministry to the 1959 crusade, as did a substantial number of candidates seeking to become missionaries under the auspices of the Church Missionary Society. Loane, oral history, March 29, 1982, CN 141, Box 13, Folder 28, BGCA.
262. "Australia far from revived." Orr, interview.
263. Tea with the queen, sex in the parks, and Jayne Mansfield. *Charlotte Observer*, June 9, 1959; UPI, June 9, 19, 22, 1959; Charlotte *News*, July 3, 4, 1959.
263. "If the female bosom were covered." AP, May 22, 1958.
263. BG visit to Russia. UPI, July 7, 14, 19, 1959; Charlotte *News*, July 3, 1959
264. "it will put Khrushchev on the spot." AP, September 27, 1959.
264. Graham-sanctioned book about African tour. Tom McMahan, *Safari for Souls* (Columbia, S.C.: State-Record, 1960). Most of the citations in this chapter are to press releases prepared by McMahan and syndicated in American newspapers. The book was in large measure compiled from these releases. CN 19 (Ferm Papers), Box 5, Folder 50, Africa 1960, BGCA.

264. "documentary." The film *Africa on the Bridge* won the Golden Reel Award as documentary of the year, 1960.
264. Why BG has seldom returned to Africa. Graham, interview, February 26, 1987.
265. Documentary positive toward Nkrumah. *Africa on the Bridge*. McMahan reported that shortly before their visit, a group of women visiting Nkrumah's mother had chanted, "Blessed art thou among women." McMahan, *Safari*, pp. 26–27. Interestingly, in the 1966 coup in Ghana, Nkrumah's statue was one of the first symbols of his regime to be toppled.
265. Islamic opposition. "Moslems vs. Billy," *Time*, February 15, 1960, p. 86; "Graham Wins Friends but Alienates Moslems," *Christian Century*, February 17, 1960, pp. 180–81; "New Attitude," *Christian Century*, February 24, 1960, p. 214; UPI, February 4, 1960.
266. BG urges Eisenhower to visit Nigeria. McMahan, "Safari," press release; *Charlotte Observer*, April 1, 1960.
266. Islamic healing challenge. AP, March 5, 1960; McMahan, *Safari*, p. 101. The story of Elijah's challenge to the priests of Baal is found in I Kings 18.
266. "Country devil." McMahan, *Safari*, p. 14–16.
266. "Witchdoctors." Ibid., p. 68; "Have Graham's Crusades Helped Africa?" *Our Africa*, May 1960 (*Our Africa* is a magazine published in Durban, South Africa). Clipping in CN 19 (Ferm Papers), Box 5, Folder 50, Africa 1960, BGCA.
267. BG at leprosarium. Grady Wilson, *Count It All Joy* (Nashville: Broadman Press, 1984), pp. 296–97.
267. BG "put the cookies on a lower shelf." George F. Hall, "Billy Graham in Moshi," *Christian Century*, March 23, 1960, p. 366.
267. Fear of being misunderstood. McMahan, "Safari," press releases from Jos, Nigeria, and Nairobi, Kenya.
268. "Just this little visit." Unidentified clipping, March 4, 1960, in CN 19 (Ferm Papers), Box 5, Folder 50, Africa 1960, BGCA.
268. Drunken dance scene. *Chicago Daily Tribune*, February 29, 1960.
268. "All over Africa ... Christ belongs to all races." UPI, March 30, 1960; "Safari for Souls," *Time*, February 1, 1960; p. 37; Christianity associated with colonialism, McMahan, "Safari," press release, Jos, Nigeria.
268. First integrated meetings in Rhodesia. "Billy Graham's World," *Newsweek*, March 28, 1960, p. 86; McMahan, *Safari*, pp. 54, 57.
268. "God doesn't ... see color of skin." BG, sermon, in *Africa on the Bridge*.
268. White women shoulder to shoulder with blacks. South African Press Association/AP clipping, February 28, 1960. Numerous papers carried this statement. In CN 360, MF Reel 14, BGCA.
269. "While African laborers ... a dream of equal opportunity." *Africa on the Bridge*.
269. African nationalists oppose BG's visit. McMahan, *Safari*, p. 58; "Sixty Africans Demonstrate As Graham Talks," Cleveland *Press*, February 26, 1960; unidentified clipping from CN 360, MF Reel 14, BGCA.
269. "tempted to reconsider his boycott of South Africa." "Graham May Still Visit South Africa," Durban *P.E. Evening Post*, February 22, 1960.
269. "I don't see how the South African approach can possibly work." Unidentified clipping from press conference at Victoria Falls, in CN 360, MF Reel 14, BGCA.
269. Only Christ could bring change of heart. "Graham May Still Visit South Africa," February 22, 1960.
269. Racial separation won't work. AP, in Charlotte *News*, April 4, 1960; also, stories in *Charlotte Observer*, March 30, 1960, and April 1, 1960. McMahan, "Safari," press release.
269. "They doubt US will be a true friend." UPI story, *Observer*, March 20, 1960.
270. "70 percent ... all differences can be settled." "No Solution to Race Problem 'At the Point of Bayonets,'" *U.S. News & World Report*, April 25, 1960, pp. 94–95; UPI, March 30, 1960.

270. Received by patriarch and emperor in Ethiopia. McMahan, "Safari," press release.
270. Ethiopian and Egyptian visits aided by Nixon. Letter, Ambassador Raymond A. Hare to Richard Nixon, May 11, 1959, with copy to BG, reattempt to set up meeting between BG and Egyptian president Nasser; Letter, BG to Nixon, November 19, 1959, requesting letter of entree to Haile Selassie, CN 74, MF Reel 1, from Box 299 (National Archives Pre-Presidential Papers of Richard Nixon, National Archives and Record Service), BGCA. In fact, I could find no record that such a letter was furnished, but it seems likely. Selassie's independent approval of BG, however, was indicated by his attendance, in 1966, at a major BGEA-funded conference in Berlin. See Chapter 20, "Second Comings."
270. Why BG reluctant to hold a crusade in Cairo. BG, quoted in David Poling, *Why Billy Graham?* (Grand Rapids: Zondervan, 1977), p. 86.
270. BG and Barrows whoop at animal herds. Charlotte *News*, February, 1960 (exact date obscured). Also, McMahan, *Safari*, p. 48, quoting from BG's diary, and p. 52.
271. BG banned from, then visits Jordan. Charlotte *News*, December 8, 1959; *Charlotte Observer*, December 7, 1959; January 1, 1960; February 6, 1960; March 19, 1960; McMahan, *Safari*, p. 88.
271. Hussein welcomes, Muslim radio station plays sermon. Roy Gustafson, oral history, 1976, CN 141, Box 4, Folder 12, BGCA.
271. BG in Israel. McMahan, *Safari*, pp. 88–92; "Mission's End," *Time*, March 28, 1960, pp. 63–64; Graham, interview, February 26, 1987; Gustafson, oral history. BG did not meet with Ben-Gurion, who was in New York at the time.
272. BG with Rabbi Toledano. McMahan, *Safari*, p. 92.
272. Luce clipping service report. Atchison, Kansas, *Globe*, August 15, 1959, in CN 19 (Ferm Papers), BGCA.
272. BG stimulates newspaper and magazine coverage of religion. Letter, AP religion writer George Cornell to Robert Ferm, August 20, 1959, CN 19, BGCA. Calvin Thielman quoted a similar observation by *Time* religion writer Richard Ostling; interview, February 25, 1987. In another letter to Ferm, Henry Luce had said of BG, "In his personality and in his manner, [Graham] has shown a rare combination of strength and forcefulness, with kindness and pervasive friendliness. [His] ability to attract and to deliver a message to great numbers of people has been, it seems to me, providential at this time in America." August 22, 1959, CN 19 (Ferm papers), BGCA.
272. "all the kingdoms." Matt. 4:8, from the story of the Temptation of Jesus.

Chapter 17: Election and Free Will

275. BG urges Eisenhower to visit Africa. Tom McMahan, "Safari for Souls," press release, CN 19 (Ferm Papers), Box 5, Folder 50, Africa 1960, BGCA.
275. BG intercedes with Eisenhower on Nixon's behalf. Graham, interview, March 5, 1989.
276. BG urges Nixon to attend church. Letter, BG to Nixon, November 19, 1959, CN 74, MF Reel 1, from Box 299 (Pre-Presidential Papers of Richard Nixon, National Archives and Record Service), BGCA. Unless otherwise indicated, all correspondence between BG and Nixon and White House staffers referred to in this chapter is found in this collection.
276. "This is a time" ... "roared with laughter." The quote from Graham is a reconstruction of two reports, one in a story by Bill Lamkin, *Charlotte Observer*, May 21, 1960, and the other in an unidentified newspaper clipping, May 21, 1960, included in file of correspondence between Graham and Nixon.
276. BG willing to endorse Nixon on *Meet the Press*. Memo, Leonard W. Hall to RN, May 23, 1960.
276. BG on the U-2 and Communist attempts to affect election. Letter, BG to RN, May 27, 1960.
277. BG recommends Judd as Nixon's running mate. Letter, BG to RN, June 21, 1960.

277. Grady claims Catholics prayed for BG's death. UP1, *Charlotte Observer* and Chattanooga *Free Press*, August 8,1960; AP, in Gastonia, North Carolina, *Gazette*, August 10, 1960; and Columbia, South Carolina, *State*, August 13, 1960. If this allegation was not an invention of Wilson's, and it seems unlikely that it was, it was probably based on a report relayed to the Graham organization by missionaries in South America. Given the animosity that often existed between Protestant missionaries and local Catholic authorities, it is difficult to rule out either some sort of misguided effort by a local priest or a paranoid reaction by a missionary to some unfounded rumor. In fact, I don't know, and could not discover the source of this allegation. By the time I became aware of it, Grady Wilson had died. Kennedy's request for pledge noted in letter, R. Ferm to E. Loren Pugsley, July 31, 1962, CN 19 (Ferm Papers), Box 4, Folder 21 (general correspondence), BGCA.

277. Salinger's denial, Columbia *State*, August 13, 1960.

277. LBJ: JFK "obviously impressed by your attitude." BG to LBJ, August 8, 1960; LBJ to BG, August 16, 1960. Box 227a ("Billy Graham"), White House Central Files (WHCF), Lyndon Baines Johnson Library Archives (LBJLA). Unless otherwise noted, all correspondence between BG and LBJ is from this file.

278. "This conference" ... "minds of millions." Letter, BG to RN, August 23, 1960.

278. King: JFK lacks "depthed understanding." Taylor Branch, *Parting the Waters: America in the King Years*, 1954–63 (New York: Simon & Schuster, 1988), p. 314.

278. "I think I at least neutralized him." Letter, BG to RN, August 23, 1960.

278. Kennedy aids King's release from prison. For an extended description of the efforts of both parties to win the black vote without alienating whites, see Branch, *Parting the Waters*, pp. 347–76.

278. "a question as to your religious convictions." Letter, BG to RN, August 23, 1960.

279. "states in your column." Letter, BG to RN, August 23, 1960.

278. "keep Kennedy and Johnson off-balance." Letter, BG to Eisenhower, August 4, 1960, CN 74, Box 1, Folder 12, BGCA.

278. BG "delighted to cooperate." Letter, BG to RN, August 23, 1960.

280. BG in West Berlin. UPI stories, September 27, 28, 1960, and AP stories, September 25, 29, 1960, all in *Charlotte Observer.*

280. Ockenga's sermon on religion and politics. *Religion, Politics, and the Presidency* (Sea Cliff, N.Y. Christ's Mission, 1960), a sermon preached at Park Street Church, Boston, June 5, 1960.

281. Bell's warnings against Catholic domination. Speech, "Protestant Distinctives and the American Crisis," reprint, in CN 19 (Ferm Papers), Box 9, Folder 8 (Materials regarding Catholicism), BGCA. The speech was apparently given at least twice, on August 21, 1960, in Montreat and on September 7, 1960, in Washington.

281. NAE concerns over a Catholic president. Ford pamphlet filed in CN 19 (Ferm Papers), Box 9, Folder 9, BGCA. NAE plan of action located in 1960 Campaign Files, Religious Issues files of James Wine, John F. Kennedy Pre-Presidential Papers, Box 1018, John F. Kennedy Library Archives (JFKLA).

281. *Christianity Today* warns of Catholic opppresion. See, for example, *Christianity Today*, February 1, 1960, p. 20; June 20; 1960, p. 31; October 24, 1960, p. 25.

281. BGEA flyer. Contained in Wine Files, Box 1018, JFKLA.

281. Anti-Kennedy sentiment at Wheaton College. Lowell D. Streiker and Gerald S. Strober, *Religion and the New Majority: Billy Graham, Middle America, and the Politics of the 70's* (New York: Association Press, 1972), pp. 60–61.

281. JFK could not withstand Roman hierarchy. Theodore Sorenson, *Kennedy* (New York: Harper & Row, 1965), p. 188.

282. Oxnam and Blake "uneasy" about Kennedy. Mark Silk, *Spiritual Politics* (New York: Simon & Schuster, 1988), pp. 121–22.

282. "The Roman Catholic Church will take advantage of this." Letter, BG to Eisenhower, August 4, 1960, CN 71, Box 1, Folder 12, BGCA. Dr. Bell had made this same point in his speech, "Protestant Distinctives."
282. BG's statement to *Time* and *Newsweek*. Statement was dated August 28, 1960. A reprint was attached to a letter from BG to RN on the same date.
282. BG "detaching myself" ... "at this time." Letter, BG to RN, September 1, 1960.
283. "Kennedy's tactic" ... "wait for the developments." Letter, BG to RN, September 24, 1960. BG barely missed the barrage of criticism aimed at Peale. He had been scheduled to appear at the meeting, labeled the Study Conference on the Relationship of Religion and Freedom, but, for whatever reason, did not.
283. "shut the mouth of your opponent." Letter, BG to RN, October 17, 1960.
284. "I think this makes a hell of a lot of sense." Memo, RN to Len Hall and Bob Finch, October 5, 1960. This memo refers not to the October 17 letter from BG but to similar recommendations contained in his letter of September 24.
284. "Graham continued to be vexed" ... "praying needs to be done." Letter, BG to RN, October 17, 1960.
284. BG felt obliged to Luce. Graham, interview, March 6, 1989.
284. BG's article for *Life*. Unpublished manuscript, submitted to *Life*, CN 74, MF Reel 1, BGCA.
284. BG consults politically astute friends. Letter, BG to RN, June 21, 1961, explaining the episode to RN, who wanted full details for use in writing his book, *My Six Crises*.
286. "I had peace." Letter, BG to RN, June 21, 1961. Other letters pertinent to the *Life* article include Luce to BG, September 19 and December 9, 1960; BG to Luce, October 16 and 24, 1960; BG to RN, July 17, 1960; RN to BG, August 18, 1960, BG private files, Montreat. The second article ran as "We Are Electing a President of the World," *Life*, November 7, 1960, pp. 109–10.
286. "I shouldn't become involved in partisan politics." AP, October 30, 1960.
286. "There is a great deal of evidence" ... "you cannot win this election." Letter, BG to RN, November 2, 1960.
286. "Dixie no longer in the bag." Lowell D. Streiker and Gerald S. Strober, *Religion and the New Majority: Billy Graham, Middle America, and the Politics of the 70's* (New York: Association Press, 1972), p. 61.
286. "believe your great campaign ... in the future" Telegram, BG to RN, November 9, 1960.
286. "I understand there is to be a recount " Charlotte *News*, November 19, 1960.
287. BG explains luncheon with Kennedy. Memo, JDH (unidentified) to RN, November 23, 1960, CN 74, MF Reel 1 from Box 299 (Pre-Presidential Papers of Richard Nixon, National Archives and Record Services), BGCA.
287. Kennedy's curiosity about the Second Coming. Sermon, Washington, D.C., May 4, 1986; also, Billy Graham, "Billy Graham's Own Story: 'God Is My Witness,'" Part III, *McCall's*, June 1964, p. 145.
287. BG "tried to walk the middle line." Graham, interview, March 26, 1987.
287. "Dr. Graham hails Kennedy victory." The *New York Times*, January 17, 1961. In the copy of this article contained in Nixon's Pre-Presidential Papers, a Nixon staff member had circled the headline before routing it to his boss.
288. Photographs for personal use only. Letter, Pierre Salinger to Jack Ledden (photographer, *Palm Beach Post-Times*), February 24, 1961. Letters, White House Names File, Billy Graham, JFKLA.
288. "probably the best and most effective statement ..." "Ck for sure that his wife's name is Ruth." Draft of letter, RN to BG, January 15, 1961.
288. RN requests explanation of BG's decision on *Life* article. Letter, RN to BG, May 31, 1961.
288. "The more I listened ... I had hoped you would say." Letter, BG to RN, June 12, 1961.

289. BG fears he has offended Nixon. Letter, BG to RN, June 21, 1961.
289. "The *Life* article should have been published." Letter, RN to BG, August 17, 1961.
289. BG recommends a goodwill press conference. Letter, BG to RN, November 11, 1962.
289. "There are few men I have loved as I love you." Ibid.

Chapter 18: The Kennedy Years

290. "A decade of marathon campaigns … students." As early as the mid-1950s, BG began to predict that his life and ministry would be short.
290. JFK "will be your John the Baptist." BG, interview, March 26, 1987. The incident is recounted in several newspaper articles, including a story by Eustaquio Ramientos, Jr., "Billy Graham a Great American," Quezon City, Philippines, *Examiner-News Weekly*, March 1963, CN 360, MF Reel 50, BGCA.
291. "Stick around and try to get some pictures." Russ Busby, interview, April 30, 1986.
291. BG in Venezuela. AP stories, in *Charlotte Observer*, January 23,24, and 25, and February 2, 1962; Sandra Hill, story in Charlotte *News*, January 30, 1962; Norman Mydske (a BGEA operative who has specialized in Latin American ministry), interview, November 25, 1987; Russ Busby (BGEA photographer), interview, April 30, 1986.
291. Storm in Paraguay. Charles Ward, interview, October 21, 1986.
292. BG's impact on South American Evangelicalism. Dr. Kenneth Strachan, as quoted by Mydske, interview, November 25, 1987.
292. BG invited by a rising vote. The chair of the meeting was Herbert J. Taylor, who had sponsored Bev Shea and supported Youth for Christ years earlier. Letter, H. J. Taylor to BG, May 18, 1960, in CN 17 (BGEA Vice-President, 1954–1977), Box 2, Folder 23, Chicago 1962, BGCA.
292. BG returns to Soldier Field for dramatic TV finale. Chuck Ashman, *The Gospel According to Billy* (Secaucus, N.J.: Lyle Stuart, 1977), pp. 131–34; Pollock, *Authorized Biography*, pp. 237–39.
294. Beginnings of the Billy Graham School of Evangelism. John Pollock, *Billy Graham: The Authorized Biography* (New York: McGraw-Hill, 1966), pp. 234–36; George Wilson, interview, August 3, 1987; Victor Nelson, interview, August 5, 1987; John Dillon (dean of the Billy Graham School of Evangelism), interview, April 30, 1987.
294. T. W. Wilson becomes BG's personal assistant. Wilson, interview, February 27, 1987. Wilson told essentially the same story in his oral history, CN 141, Box 8, Folder 12, BGCA.
296. BG is stranded in a truck stop. Grady Wilson, *Count It All Joy* (Nashville: Broadman Press, 1984), pp. 244–47; Mary Bishop, *Billy Graham: The Man and His Ministry* (New York: Grosser & Dunlap, 1978), pp. 76–77; UPI, in *Charlotte Observer*, March 20, 1965.
296. Franklin learns to smoke. Patricia Daniels Cornwell, *A Time for Remembering: The Ruth Bell Graham Story* (San Francisco: Harper and Row, 1983), pp. 163–64.
297. "I'll have a cheeseburger." Ibid., p. 143.
297. Franklin and Ned on love. Ruth Graham, *It's My Turn* (Old Tappan, N.J.: Fleming H. Revell, 1982), p. 119.
297. "He's a pretty good little boy." Ibid., p. 20.
298. GiGi's courtship. GiGi Tchividjian, interview, October 25, 1990.
299. BG sets Los Angeles Coliseum record. Pollock, *Authorized Biography*, p. 253.
300. Fundamentalists object to Bishop Kennedy doubts about deity of Jesus. Gerald Kennedy, *God's Good News* (New York: Harper Bros., 1955), p. 125, quoted in Charles Emert, *Billy Graham's 23 Years of Theological Change*, ed. D. A. Waite (Collingswood, N.J.: Bible for Today, 1971), p. 13.
300. Kennedy on Virgin Birth. Letter from Kennedy to R. T. Ketcham, quoted in Emert, *23 Years of Change*, p. 37.

300. "farthest reach yet." Anonymous mimeographed document, "Bishop Gerald Kennedy to Head Billy Graham Los Angeles Campaign in 1963," in CN 19 (Ferm Papers), Box 6, Folder 18 (Southern California), BGCA.
300. Ferm answers critics. Letters, Ferm to C. H. Lewis, July 12, 1963, and the Reverend Gunnar Hoglund, October 30, 1963, in CN 19 (Ferm Papers), Box 4, Folder 29, BGCA.
300. Changes in BG's concept of the church. Billy Graham, "What Ten Years Have Taught Me," *Christian Century*, February 17, 1960, pp. 186, 188.
301. Ferm defends BG's relationship with Catholics: "Catholic priests do not attend" ... "the Roman communion." Letter, Ferm to E. Loren Pugsley, Newton, Kansas, July 31, 1962, CN 19 (Ferm Papers), Box 4, Folder 21 (General Correspondence), BGCA.
301. Pope John "a rare exception." Letter, Ferm to Murray W. Downey, CN 19 (Ferm Papers), Box 4, Folder 34 (Correspondence, May 1964), BGCA.
301. BG's attitudes on race, insistence on integrated crusades. Letters, Douglas M. Branch, general secretary of North Carolina Baptist Convention, to Haymaker, November 28, 1961; Haymaker to Branch, November 22, 1961; James J. Steward, Jr., to Branch, November 29, 1961, all in CN 1 (Haymaker Papers), Box 5, Folder 13, BGCA; Haymaker to Harold G. Sanders, pastor of First Baptist Church, Tallahassee, November 11, 1960, CN 1 (Haymaker Papers), Box 4, Folder 18, BGCA; *Florida Times-Union* Qacksonville), January 15, 1961; Keesing's Research Report, *Race Relations in the U.S.A., 1954–1968* (New York, 1970), pp. 146–50; the *New York Times*, May 18, 1961; Letter, Gordon Clark to Carl F. H. Henry, July 21, 1961, CN 8 (*CT* Collection), Box 15, Folder 13, BGCA, all cited in Jerry Berl Hopkins, "Billy Graham and the Race Problem" (Ph.D. diss., University of Kentucky, 1986), pp. 108–12. During this period, the AP and UP1 carried other similar expressions of the need for churchmen to take a leading role in desegregating churches and defusing racial tensions.
301. "Jim Crow must go ... too far and too fast." Chicago *Sun-Times*, May 31, 1962, quoted in Hopkins, "Race Problem," p. 112; also, AP, in *Charlotte Observer*, July 9, 1961.
301. BG feels King should "put on the brakes." The *New York Times*, April 18, 1963, p. 21.
302. BG discounts human efforts at racial harmony. *Los Angeles Times*, August 3 and 10, 1963; *Christianity Today*, September 13 and 30, 1963, pp. 1134, 1187–88, 1194–95.
302. Black churchmen criticize BG. Presbyterian pastor, L. David Cowie, "Apostolic Preaching in Los Angeles," *Christianity Today*, October 25, 1963, p. 69. It is noteworthy that Cowie's criticism appeared in *CT* in the context of an article generally complimentary of BG. The NANE president was Marvin Prentis, quoted in "The Crowded Coliseum," *Christianity Today*, September 27, 1963, p. 1245, and by AP, August 29, 1963.
302. Negro Evangelicals commend BG. Cowie, "Apostolic Preaching," p. 69.
302. BG's limited political statements. Criticizes Supreme Court decision on prayer and Bible reading, CN 19, Box 4, Folder 22 (General Correspondence), BGCA; quoted in "Prayer Still Legal in Public Schools," *Christian Century*, July 4, 1962, 79; quoted in Cort R. Flint, with the staff of *Quote* magazine, *Billy Graham Speaks!: The Quotable Billy Graham* (New York: Grosset & Dunlap, 1968), p. 126.
302. BG commends JFK stand on parochial-school aid. AP, in *Charlotte Observer*, August 19, 1961. On communism. Billy Graham, "Facing the Anti-God Colossus," *Christianity Today*, December 21, 1961, pp. 6–8.
302. BG, "The Ultimate Weapon," sermon, *Hour of Decision*, 1961; "My Answer" column, November 8, 1961.
302. BG repudiates Welch charges. AP, July 9, 1961.
303. BG recommends sending food to China. AP, February 13, 1961.
303. BG and Kennedy regard each other with reserve. Correspondence, BG to JFK, August 26, 1963; JFK to BG, January 6, 1962; August 26, 1963. Letters, White House Names File, Billy Graham, JFKLA.

303. Infrequent visits. BG, interview, February 27, 1987.
303. JFK "gritted his teeth." Edward Fiske, "The Closest Thing to a White House Chaplain," the *New York Times Magazine*, June 8, 1969, p. 114.
303. JFK and Jackie condescend to BG. Chuck Ashman, *The Gospel According to Billy* (Secaucus, N.J.: Lyle Stuart, 1977), p. 178.
303. BG puffs Connally. AP, January 16, 1963.
303. News of JFK's assassination. BG, interview, March 26, 1987; T. W. Wilson, interview, February 27, 1987.
304. "we must have a terrible shock sometimes." UPI, December 8, 1963.

Chapter 19: Billy and Lyndon

309. "Your message met the need." Letter, Lyndon B. Johnson (LBJ) to BG, December 9, 1963. Box 227a, "Billy Graham," White House Central Files (WHCF), Lyndon B. Johnson Library Archives (LBJLA). Unless otherwise noted, all correspondence between BG and the Johnson White House was found in this 266-page collection.
309. BG's first visit to the Johnson White House. BG, oral history (interview by Monroe Billington), AC 84–76, LBJLA.
305. BG concedes Johnson may have had political interest in him. Ibid.
306. LBJ "best qualified." Charlotte *News*, December 17, 1963. "as God had been with Washington ... Lincoln." Letter, BG to LBJ, December 29, 1963.
306. H. L. Hunt offers to back Grady Wilson and BG. Grady Wilson, interview, May 1, 1987; BG, press conference, Washington, D.C., April 24, 1986; Calvin Thielman, interviews, February 25, 1987, and May 29, 1991; Lane Adams, interviews, February 9, 1987, and May 29,1991; "Evangelist Graham Considers Draft for President—by GOP," *Houston Press*, January 31, 1964; Chuck Ashman, *The Gospel According to Billy*, (Secaucus, N.J.: Lyle Stuart, 1977), p. 163; "Billy Won't Run for President," *Christian Century*, February 12, 1964, p. 197. Several people were familiar with the Hunt offer. The amount of money Hunt offered was reported to be as large as $10 million in some versions of the story, but $6 million seems to be the preferred figure. Though confirming that he once flirted briefly with the possibility of running for the presidency and acknowledging that substantial financial support would have been forthcoming, Graham declined to say that H. L. Hunt had offered him the sum in question. T. W. Wilson asserted that Hunt made no such call but acknowledged that other factors had led Graham to consider a draft by the GOP. Another source asserted that such an offer had definitely been made but remembered the would-be supporter as Sid Richardson rather than H. L. Hunt. Since Richardson died in 1959—BG preached his funeral—this cannot have been true and probably reflects a slightly faulty memory. The *Houston Press* did not name Hunt, but confirmed that Graham "has been offered eye-popping support, running into the millions." In view of the existing evidence, I have chosen to accept the account reported here but acknowledge that the evidence is a bit ambiguous.
307. Invitation to LBJ to attend crusade. Reflected in LBJ's polite decline, July 22, 1964.
307. Grahams visit White House. Invitation, LBJ to BG, July 22, 1964; Thank-you letter, BG to LBJ, August 27, 1964.
307. BG forged ties with Moyers and Watson. Moyers letter to BG, January 8, 1964.
307. Marvin Watson ties. Numerous memos and letters.
307. Anne endorses Goldwater, LBJ's call. BG, oral history, pp. 10–11; *Charlotte Observer*, May 20, 1965 (a Johnson reminiscence).
308. Telegram campaign. Charlotte *News*, November 3, 1964; AP, December 23, 1964.
308. Weekend prior to election spent in White House. Marshall Frady, *Billy Graham: Parable of American Righteousness* (Boston: Little, Brown, 1979), p. 266.

308. "as truly a servant of God as was your great-grandfather." Letter, BG to LBJ, November 10, 1964.
308. Telegram money "might have been better spent." BG and Goldwater campaign.
308. BG speaks at inaugural church service. Calvin Thielman interview, February 25, 1987; Grady Wilson, interview, March 1, 1987.
308. BG and LBJ exchange greetings and gifts. Correspondence, LBJ or White House staff to or concerning BG: August 21, September 11, and December 4, 1965; May 3 and September 1, 1966; November 8 and 11, 1966; January 3 and June 21, 1968 (leisure shoes). BG or staff to LBJ or staff: August 27, November 20, and December 6, 1965; March 28, December 2, 1966, etc. Intercessory prayer for flu: BG to LBJ, January 30, 1965; for supernatural wisdom: BG to LBJ, February 12, 1965; BG to LBJ, June 21, 1968.
309. Moyers on Johnson's use of men as symbols. Frady, *Parable*, pp. 264–65. Moyers confirmed the accuracy of Frady's account in a letter received February 26, 1991.
309. Gallup polls of "most-admired" men. Reported in Detroit *Free Press*, January 2, 1966.
309. "We bragged on each other." *Charlotte Observer*, May 20, 1965.
309. LBJ seeks BG's advice. War on Poverty: Calvin Thielman, interview, February 25, 1987. 304 "cut ten million dollars." Frady, *Parable*, p. 263.
310. "Now Billy, tell me what you really think." Carloss Morris, oral history, January 10, 1978, CN 141, Box 10, Folder 14, BGCA.
310. BG recommended Humphrey. Frady, *Parable*, pp. 263–64.
310. "I was well-known in Texas." BG, oral history.
310. LBJ afraid of the *Baptist Standard*. BG, *Legends*, CNN, 1986; also, in slightly different form, in BG, oral history.
310. LBJ's religiosity. BG, oral history; interview, March 26, 1987; Calvin Thielman, interview, February 25, 1987.
311. BG Pavilion at New York World's Fair. Carloss Morris, oral history; John Pollock, *Billy Graham: The Authorized Biography* (New York: McGraw-Hill, 1966), p. 261; Cort R. Flint, with the staff of *Quote* magazine, *Billy Graham Speaks!: The Quotable Billy Graham* (New York: Grosset & Dunlap, 1968), pp. 168–69; Martin E. Marty, "Religious Cafeteria," *Christian Century*, June 10, 1964, pp. 758–59; "Some Clouds on a Summer's Day," *Christian Century*, July 1, 1964, p. 854; personal observation.
312. Four and a half million see *The Restless Ones*. Edward Fiske, "White House Chaplain," the *New York Times Magazine*, June 8, 1969, p. 113.
313. Effectiveness of film ministry. Dave Barr, interview, November 14, 1987.
313. "That's why God has given us this medium." Barr, interview.
314. 1964 Boston crusade. Allan Emery, oral history, April 9, 1979, CN 141, Box 10, Folder 4, BGCA.
314. BG visits Ted Kennedy. "Graham Chats with Kennedy in Hospital," *Boston Globe*, September 23, 1964; "Graham Blames Courts for Violence," *Boston Herald*, September 18, 964.
314. BG visits Combat Zone. "Graham Wins 'Combat Zone,'" Boston *Sunday Advertiser*, September 20, 1964; "The Aftermath of a Crusade," *Boston Herald*, September 27, 1964.
315. Visit with Cardinal Cushing arranged. George M. Collins, "Graham to Meet Cardinal Tomorrow," *Boston Globe*, October 6, 1964. In a statement Jews also found appealing, Graham declared that "it is high time that the church spoke authoritatively to Israel and assured all Jews that we do not hold them as a nation responsible for the crucifixion," a position Cushing had also espoused. "Graham Visits Bars in South End," *Boston Globe*, September 20, 1964.
316. BG meets Cardinal Cushing. "Secret of Billy Graham's Voice? It's the Tepid Water in That Pitcher," *Boston Globe*, October 5, 1964; "Cardinal Has Praise for Graham Crusade," *Boston Herald*, September 16, 1964; "Cardinal Lauds Graham, Then Flies to Rome," *Boston Globe*, September 16, 1964; "Graham Visits Bars in South End," *Boston Globe*, September 20,

1964 (re Cushing's efforts on behalf of Jews); Pollock, *Authorized Biography*, pp. 263–64, in which BG's official biographer indicates that the evangelist requested the meeting with Cushing; Robert Ferm (who disagrees with that interpretation), interview, March 28, 1987; Allan Emery, oral history; interview, July 19, 1986. "From a Cardinal: Praise for a Protestant Crusader," *U.S. News & World Report*, October 19, 1964, p. 24; "Go Hear Graham: Cardinal Cushing," *Boston Globe*, October 7, 1964; Kenneth L. Woodward, "Crusader and Cardinal," *Newsweek*, October 19, 1964, p. 71; "New England Revisited," *Christianity Today*, November 6, 1964, pp. 53–54; L. David Otte, "Graham Predicts Second Coming," *Boston Globe*, October 12, 1964; Leonard Marks, USIA, interview with Billy Graham, September 20, 1965, Folder EX ND 19/CO 312, September 1965, Box 217, LBJLA.

317. BG doubts he can preach in Houston. Carloss Morris, interview, May 5, 1987. Morris tells essentially the same story in his oral history.

317. LBJ attends Astrodome crusade. UPI, November 19, 1965, CN 17, Box 8, Folder 18 (Clippings, Houston 1965), BGCA.

317. BG warns against communism. Speech to North Carolina Press Association, reported by AP, in *Charlotte Observer*, July 31, 1965.

317. The "mess in Southeast Asia." "Billy Graham Asks Prayers for Johnson in Viet Crisis," San Juan, Puerto Rico, *Star*, February 15, 1965. CN 360, MF Reel 50 (Clippings, Misc. Foreign Countries, 1/1960–12/1965), BGCA.

318. "I have no sympathy ... stopped in Vietnam." *Rocky Mountain News*, August 25, 1965.

318. BG: "95 percent of the Congress ... know the facts." "Billy Graham on War, Religion (interview with Max Goldberg)," *Boston Globe*, December 12, 1965.

318. "my support of the President's Vietnam policy." Letter, BG to Moyers, October 19, 1965, Box 56, HU 2, LBJLA.

318. "God will judge us." Quoted without citation in Flint, *Billy Graham Speaks!* p. 129.

318. Birmingham Easter Rally. Birmingham *News*, March 5, 30, 1964; Birmingham *World*, March 28, 1964; the *New York Times*, March 30, 1964; Chicago *Sun-Times*, March 30, 1964. These newspapers are cited in Jerry Berl Hopkins, "Billy Graham and the Race Problem," 1949–1969, (Ph.D. diss., University of Kentucky, 1986), pp. 117–21. For correspondence confirming prior apprehensions, see CN 1 (Haymaker Papers), Box 6, Folder 8, BGCA, cited in Hopkins, *Race Problem.*

319. "The Great Reconciliation" sermon. "The Issue in Alabama," *Decision*, June 1964, pp. 1–3.

319. Speech to NAE, April 7, 1964, Religious News Service.

319. G. W. Carver Award. Letter, Howard Jones to Robert Ferm, July 14, 1968, CN 19 (Ferm Papers), Box 10, Folder 2 (1/68–3/71), BGCA.

319. *CT* does not endorse civil rights act. Carl F. H. Henry, *Confessions of a Theologian: An Autobiography* (Waco, Tex.: Word Books, 1986), p. 227.

319. NAE adoption of pro-civil-rights resolution. *Chicago Daily News*, April 7, 1964; *Chicago's American*, April 8, 1964; quoted in Hopkins, *Race Problem*, pp. 121–22.

319. Black columnist attacks BG. Chuck Stone, *Chicago Defender*, April 18–24, 1964, quoted in Hopkins, *Race Problem*, pp. 123–24.

319. Ferm reports on Chicago situation. Ferm, letter and "Preliminary Report," August 25, 1964, CN 1 (Haymaker Papers), Box 8, Folder 18, BGCA. Cited in Hopkins, *Race Problem*, pp. 124–27.

320. "I haven't been to jail yet." Religious News Service, March 3, 1965, quoted in Lowell D. Streiker and Gerald S. Strober, *Religion and the New Majority: Billy Graham, Middle America, and the Politics of the 70's* (New York: Association Press, 1972), p. 53.

320. "I never felt ... conscience of the world." The *New York Times*, April 17, 1965, p. 8.

320. BG's observations re Alabama. Montgomery *Advertiser*, April 19, 23, 24, 1965, and unidentified clippings, 1965 Clippings Box, April Folder, BGCA, cited and quoted in Hopkins, *Race Problem*, pp. 128–30.

320. "BG in Montgomery: A Stride Toward Reconciliation," *Christianity Today*, July 2, 1965, pp. 31–32.
320. Johnson commends BG. Letter, LBJ to BG, April 13, 1965.
321. "if the Klan would quiet down." See, for example, AP, June 21, 1965; "Graham Crusade Draws 100,000 in Montgomery," Crusade Information Service, quoted in Charlotte *News*, June 23, 1965.
321. BG responds to Watts riot: rioters being exploited. The *New York Times*, August 18, 1965; AP, in *Charlotte Observer*, August 15, 18, 1965.
321. BG urges Martin Luther King, Jr., to call for a moratorium. Charlotte *News*, August 17, 1965; Also, the *New York Times*, August 10, 1965, p. 18; "Does Anyone Really Care?" *Christian Century*, September 22, 1965, pp. 1148–49; Leonard Marks, US1A, interview with Graham.
321. Assessments of BG's comments on Watts riot. "Be Specific, Mr. Graham," *Christian Century*, September 1, 1965, p. 1053; editorial, Charlotte *News*, August 17, 1965.
321. Identify rioters, get rid of ghettos. *Charlotte Observer*, June 25, 1966; "Graham Asks LBJ to Act on Race Riots," *Boston Herald*, July 19, 1966. Also, "Billy Graham's Plea to President Johnson," *U.S. News & World Report*, August 7, 1967, p. 92.
322. "You see some guy on every campus." Houston crusade, 1965, quoted in Bill Adler, *The Wit and Wisdom of Billy Graham* (New York: Random House, 1967).
322. "Ours indeed is a sick generation." Sermon, *Hour of Decision*, 1966.
322. "frug-dancing mothers." Quoted in Lewis F. Brabham, *A New Song in the South: The Story of the Billy Graham Greenville, S.C., Crusade* (Grand Rapids: Zondervan, 1966), p. 62.
322. "one out of twelve college students." Letter, Robert Ferm to William G. Kelley, November 1, 1962, CN 19 (Ferm Papers), Box 4, Folder 25 (General Correspondence), BGCA. Kelley had asked for the source of BG's assertion that "one out of seven college students" was in psychiatric care. Ferm replied that BG had claimed only one in twelve and conceded that the charge was "undocumented" but "believed correct."
322. "When it comes to specific moral issues... our duty is clear." CN 74, VT-NBC, BGCA.
322. "I see no other hope." Quoted in Adler, *Wit and Wisdom*. A similar statement was reported by L. David Otte, "Graham Predicts Second Coming," *Boston Globe*, October 12, 1964.

Chapter 20: Second Comings

323. Bob Jones criticizes BG. AP, in Atlanta *Journal*, March 4, 1966; *Charlotte Observer*, March 4, 1966; "Graham in Greenville," *Christianity Today*, April 1, 1966; "Boycotting Billy," *Time*, March 18, 1966, p. 103; Lexington, North Carolina, *Dispatch*, March 14, 1966; Letter, Bob Jones, Jr., to editor of London *Christian*, May 6, 1966, CN 83–108, MF Reel 10 (Clippings, England 1/66–6/66), BGCA. Note: There is some inconsistency in the newspaper clippings. It is possible that Bob Jones, Jr., was responsible for some of these statements, particularly the charge regarding "alliance with infidelity and Romanism."
324. Greenville statistics. BGEA records.
324. Rowlandson finds a sponsor for crusade. Maurice Rowlandson, interview, July 10, 1986; UPI, June 5, 1956. BGEA-authorized stories of the crusade tell of the Evangelical Alliance sponsorship, but not of their reservations. Curtis Mitchell, *The Billy Graham London Crusade* (Minneapolis: World Wide Publications, 1966), p. 5; John Pollock, *Crusade '66* (Grand Rapids: Zondervan, 1966), p. 8. Church of England declines to sponsor. "London and Conversion," *America*, June 18, 1966, p. 114.
324. Stott: "the church is not cutting any ice." Quoted in Mitchell, *London Crusade*, p. 11.
325. Ferm and Adams visit with clergy. Robert Ferm, interview, March 28,1987; Lane Adams, interview, February 9, 1987; Memo, The Reverend A. W. Goodwin-Hudson to the Reverend Harold G. Owen, secretary of Berks Spiritual Preparation Committee, August 25, 1965, CN 19 (Ferm Papers), Box 11, Folder 2 (1/65–1/66), BGCA.

325. BG's prayer for Great Britain. Lane Adams, oral history, May 9, 1978, CN 141, Box 2, Folder 4, BGCA. In the first conversation I had with Adams, prior to a formal interview, he repeated this story in much the same form. More than twenty years after the incident, he remained impressed.
325. Ferm's encounter with customs officer. Ferm, interview.
326. "a simple message for simple people." Cecil Northcott, "The Graham Crusade: Abdication of Evangelism," *Christian Century*, May 25, 1966, pp. 673–75.
326. "We don't specially like ... mental habits." "Choose ye ... Sham!" *Baptist Times*, January 10, 1966.
326. "only the second best does for religion." David Lazell, "Objections to Evangelism," *The Christian*, July 15, 1966, p. 11.
326. "Billy Graham's real offense ..." David Orrock, "The Memorable Crusade," *The Christian*, March 25, 1966; CN 83–108, MF Reel 10 (Clippings, England, 1/66–6/66), BGCA.
326. "may be the biggest disaster." BG, quoted in Pollock, *Crusade '66*, p. 13.
327. BG and team answer questions. Mitchell, *London Crusade*, pp. 15, 33, 21, 43.
327. BG on Vietnam at church assembly. Pollock, *Crusade '66*, p. 80.
327. *Twenty-four Hours*. Pollock, *Crusade '66*, pp. 18–19; Mitchell, *London Crusade*, p. 14. Target's book was *Evangelism, Inc.* (London: Penguin Press, 1968). A transcript of the *Twenty-four Hours* with Kenneth Harris was printed in *The Christian and Christianity Today*, May 27, 1966. (*The Christian*, a long-established religious newspaper, was purchased by BGEA and for a time had a collaborative arrangement with *CT*. In 1966 the publication was bearing the double title and printed some of the same material that appeared in the American version of *CT*. I used these materials in BGEA's London office. They are now housed in the BGCA.)
328. Ruth Graham's dream. Mitchell, *London Crusade*, p. 34.
328. Bill Bradley and Cliff Richard. Ibid., pp. 38, 75.
328. "not a youth night." Pollock, *Crusade '66*, p. 52.
328. Antiwar demonstration. Ibid., p. 80.
328. Police volunteers. Mitchell, *London Crusade*, p. 36.
328. BG orders team relocation. Howard Jones, interview, May 1, 1987; also, Pollock, *Crusade '66*, p. 282.
328. BG visits Brixton. *The Christian and Christianity Today*, May 27, 1966. Also, Mitchell, *London Crusade*, p. 74; Pollock, *Crusade '66*, pp. 40–41.
328. Ministry to working people. Pollock, *Crusade '66*, pp. 60–62. Other references to Wesley, Hardie, Shaftesbury, William Wilberforce, and YMCA founder George Williams can be found in newspaper clippings from the period of the crusade, CN 360, MF Reels 17–18, BGCA.
329. Unsuccessful preaching efforts in Hyde Park and Trafalgar Square. Mitchell, *London Crusade*, p. 71.
329. Graham gives "200-second sermon" in Soho. Mitchell, *London Crusade*, pp. 79–80; and Pollock, *Crusade '66*, p. 43.
329. Closed-circuit TV transmissions. "London-Leeds TV Link-up," *Yorkshire Evening Post*, January 18, 1966; Robert Ferm, interview; Pollock, *Crusade '66*, pp. 53–59; Mitchell, *London Crusade*, pp. 100–102.
330. Earls Court statistics. BGEA crusade statistics.
330. BG honored by royalty and others. Mitchell, *London Crusade*, p. 73; Pollock, *Crusade '66*, pp. 81–82.
330. "a slight air of defensiveness pervades team descriptions." Interviews, BG, February 26, 1987; Robert Ferm, Lane Adams, others; Pollock, *Crusade '66*, p. 82.
330. "We've grown accustomed to his faith." Vincent Mulchrone, London *Daily Mail*, quoted in Mitchell, *London Crusade*, p. 13.

331. On the Other Side: The Report of the Evangelical Alliance's Commission on Evangelism (England: Scripture Union, 1968), pp. 135–45, 168–69; Rowlandson, interview.
332. John Mott. Mott's story is well-known. For one carefully researched and well-documented account, see Arthur E. Johnston, *World Evangelism and the Word of God* (Minneapolis: Bethany Fellowship, 1974).
332. No resolutions on issues on which participants differed. Minute 16 of the International Committee, meeting July 14–20, 1908, p. 8, Archives, World Council of Churches, Geneva. Quoted in Johnston, *World Evangelism*, p. 95.
332. IMC conference in Madras, 1938. See Johnston, *World Evangelism*, pp. 171–95.
333. Mott: "Evangelist!" Billy Graham, "Why the Berlin Congress?" *Christianity Today*, November 11, 1966, p. 3.
333. "an old form of evangelism." Quoted in Arthur E. Johnston, *The Battle for World Evangelism* (Wheaton, Ill.: Tyndale House, 1978), p. 105.
333. Universalism triumphs at New Delhi. Johnston, *Battle*, p. 147.
333. BG thrilled with World Council meetings. BG, interview, February 27, 1987.
333. Montreaux meeting. BG, interview, February 27, 1987.
333. BG asks Henry to lead Berlin Congress. Carl F. H. Henry, *Confessions of a Theologian: An Autobiography* (Waco, Tex.: Word Books, 1986), p. 252.
334. Purposes of the congress. Stanley Mooneyham, "Do It Again, Lord," unidentified clipping, March 4, 1966, CN 83–108, MF Reel 10 (Clippings, England 1/66–6/66), BGCA.
334. Berlin Congress a "Council of War". "The World Congress: Springboard for Evangelical Renewal," *Christianity Today*, November 25, 1966, p. 34.
334. a "once-for-all shot." Carl F. H. Henry, interview, February 10, 1987.
334. Friction over selection of delegates. Henry, *Confessions*, p. 253.
334. Delegates from 104 nations. "The World Congress," *Christianity Today*, November 25, 1966, p. 34; Dave Foster, "Flags of 100 Nations Fly in Berlin," *The Christian and Christianity Today*, November 4, 1966, p. 1; John Pollock, *Crusades: 20 Years with Billy Graham* (Minneapolis: World Wide Publications, 1969), p. 234.
334. Kimo and Komi. "Two Ex-Savages in a Big World," Miami *News*, November 26, 1966. In some reports, both Aucas are implicated in the missionary deaths; in others, only Kimo is mentioned, suggesting that Komi may not have been directly involved.
335. "One could almost imagine ... the Rapture." Foster, "Flags of 100 Nations," p. 1.
335. The "birth clock." Pollock, *Crusades*, p. 236; Foster, "Flags of 100 Nations," p. 1.
335. BG's definition of evangelism. Graham, "Why Berlin?" p. 5. The Luthern bishop who had praised BG was Otto Dibelius.
336. WCC sees "need for revolutionary change." WCC statement quoted in Johnston, *Battle*, pp. 153–54.
336. "evangelistic type" compared to "Nazi Christians." Henry, *Confessions*, p. 254.
336. BG's opening address. Graham, "Why Berlin?" *Christianity Today*, November 11, 1966, pp. 5–6; "The Heart of a Revolution," *The Christian and Christianity Today*, pp. 1, 12, 20, 22.
336. Pew resists social action. Henry, *Confessions*, pp. 264–66.
337. "not only passivity ..." William Pannell, "Spiritual Needs of the Negro," in *One Race, One Gospel, One Task*, vol. II of official reference volumes of the World Congress on Evangelism (Minneapolis World Wide Publications, 1957), pp. 376–80, and *Christianity Today*, November 11, 1966, p. 12.
337. Jones objects to omission of race from address. Harold Schachern, "Race Issue Sparks Row at Evangelical Congress," Detroit *News*, October 31, 1966.
337. Maxey Jarman warns against political power. "The World Congress," *Christianity Today*, November 25, 1966, p. 35.
337. Black minister (the Reverend Louis Johnson) responds: "Law did for me." Ibid.

337. "racialism ... distinctions of race or color." David E. Kucharsky, "Racialism Condemned at Berlin Congress," *Christianity Today*, November 4, 1966; UPI, November 4, 1966, CN 19, Box 10, Folder 2 (1/68–3/71), BGCA.
337. Haile Selassie appears at congress. Foster, "Flags of 100 Nations," p. 1; Henry, *Confessions*, pp. 257–58; Pollock, *Crusades*, p. 235.
338. Henry's reservations about Pentecostal phenomena. Letter, Henry to Roberts, May 17, 1965, in Oral Roberts University archives, quoted in David Edwin Harrell, Jr., *Oral Roberts: An American Life* (Bloomington: Indiana University Press, 1985), p. 199.
338. "we were not sure how our ministry would be accepted." Oral Roberts, "My Personal Impressions of the World Congress on Evangelism," *Abundant Life*, January 1967, p. 28, quoted in Harrell, *Oral Roberts*, p. 200.
338. BG discusses Roberts with Calvin Thielman. Harrell, *Oral Roberts*, p. 201, based on interview with Thielman.
338. BG agrees to speak at ORU. Ibid., p. 201.
339. Roberts chairs panel discussion on healing. Ibid., pp. 202–203.
339. BG introduces Oral Roberts. From Oral Roberts, "We Have Been Conquered by Love," *Abundant Life*, February 1967, p. 23, quoted in Harrell, *Oral Roberts*, p. 203.
339. Roberts addresses the congress. Roberts, "Conquered by Love," quoted in Harrell, *Oral Roberts*, p. 204.
339. Oral's prayer. Ibid.
339. "I've been on the outside looking in." Ibid., p. 206, quoting from Thielman interview.
340. "I knew that Billy loved me." Quoted in ibid., p. 206.
340. McIntire not invited to Berlin. Carl McIntire, *Outside the Gate* (Collingswood, N.J.: Christian Beacon Press, 1967), pp. 106, 117, 121–24, 134–35, 175; *Christianity Today*, November 25, 1966, p. 35; J. D. Douglas, interview, July 17, 1986.
340. Speakers told not to attack communism. McIntire, *Outside the Gate*, pp. 56, 141, 151.
341. McIntire tapes ACCC protest to Kongresshalle walls. Ibid., p. 108.
341. McIntire rejoices in his purity. Ibid., pp. 176, 138–39.
341. BG helping to build church of the Antichrist. Ibid., pp. 7, 12, 48, 95.
342. Media coverage of Congress. "The World Congress: Springboard for Evangelical Renewal," *Christianity Today*, November 25, 1966, p. 34; Henry, *Confessions*, p. 260; Religious News Service, quoted in McIntire, *Outside the Gate*, pp. 13–14.
342. "Berlin shattered that stereotype." Jim Newton, July 17, 1986.
342. "Congress shaped a mood." Henry, *Confessions*, p. 261.
342. Westerners surprised by non-Western evangelism. J. D. Douglas, *Japan Harvest*, Fall 1966.... From typed copy furnished by Douglas.
343. BG at NCC meeting. Reported in McIntire, *Outside the Gate*, pp. 233, 204.

Chapter 21: Dreams and Wars

344. BG at Turin. John Pollock, *Crusades: 20 Years with Billy Graham* (Minneapolis: World Wide Publications, 1969), p. 247.
345. Poland visit planned and canceled. UPI, *Charlotte Observer*, September 9, 1966. "I hope ... later time." Atlanta *Journal*, quoted in Carl McIntire, *Outside the Gate* (Collings wood, N.J.: Christian Beacon Press, 1967), p. 142. McIntire felt BG was foolish for wanting to visit Communist countries, whose leaders were certain to use him for propaganda purposes, *Outside the Gate*, pp. 142–58. He would still be making the same contention about BG's visits to the USSR and other Eastern bloc countries during the 1980s.
345. Pope Paul VI kept out of Poland. Alexander Haraszti, oral history, May 21, 1979, CN 141, Box 45, Folder 1, BGCA. For detailed information about Haraszti, see Part V, Chapters 29–31.

345. Yugoslavian visit. Pollock, *Crusades*, pp. 247–48, and *Billy Graham, Evangelist to the World* (New York: Harper & Row, 1979; Crusade Edition published by World Wide Publications), pp. 81–83; "Billy's Communist Rally," *Newsweek*, July 24, 1967, pp. 70–71; "In Motion," *Time*, July 21, 1967, pp. 60–61; J. D. Douglas, "Graham's Rousing Red Welcome," *Christianity Today*, August 18, 1967, p. 45; *Christian Century*, September 20, 1967, p. 1200.
346. The Tokyo crusade. Don Hoke, interview, March 6, 1989; Ken McVety, interview, July 18, 1986; Pollock, *Crusades*, pp. 255–61; "The Graham Crusade," *Christian Century*, February 21, 1968, pp. 240–42.
347. Graham University. Jim Huffman, "Questions Answered, This Time about Himself," Chicago *American* feature, in Oregon *Journal* (Portland), March 17, 1966; AP, in *Charlotte Observer*, October 3, 1967; untitled feasibility study for the proposed university, CN 313, Box 2, Folder 14, BGCA; BG, interview, February 27, 1987. In a notable irony, the MacArthur Foundation has underwritten the Fundamentalism Project, a major study of Fundamentalist ideology and culture conducted in the latter years of the 1980s.
348. Puddleglum. Ruth Graham, *It's My Turn* (Old Tappan, N.J.: Fleming H. Revell, 1982), pp. 62–63.
349. BG waffles on social issues. "Evangelical Springtime," *Christian Century*, April 26, 1967, p. 575, quoting an interview printed in the University of Minnesota's *Minnesota Daily*, February 14, 1967.
349. BG criticizes NCC leaders. The *New York Times*, December 6, 1966; "I am for it!" BG paper, quoted in Religious News Service dispatch, August 24, 1967.
349. BG backs poverty program: Scriptural warrant a crucial factor. BG, interview, March 6, 1989, and Leighton Ford, interview, March 4, 1989; "Now I'm a Convert," AP, June 15, 1967; calls congressmen and barnstorms Appalachia, Marshall Frady, *Billy Graham: Parable of American Righteousness* (Boston: Little, Brown, 1979) p. 397; addresses congressmen and business leaders, June 29, 1967, *Congressional Record*, 90th Cong., p. 16541, quoted in Edward Lee Moore, "Billy Graham and Martin Luther King, Jr.: An Inquiry into White and Black Revivalistic Traditions" (Ph.D. diss., Vanderbilt University, 1979), p. 198; radio program and film, letter, Robert Kintner to LBJ, June 19, 1967, Box 227a ("Billy Graham"), WHCF, LBJLA; "Problematic Congratulations," *Christian Century*, September 27, 1967, p. 1213, and October 4, 1967, p. 1271; *Baptist Standard*, June 21, 1967, quoted in Wayne S. Bond, "The Rhetoric of Billy Graham" (Ph.D. diss., Southern Illinois University, August 1973); "We are pleased," note, Shriver to George Christian, May 9, 1967, Box 227a ("Billy Graham"), WHCF, LBJLA.
349. BG's reticence re clerical pronouncements on social issues. Quoted in Cort R. Flint, with the staff of *Quote* magazine, *Billy Graham Speaks!: The Quotable Billy Graham* (New York: Grosset & Dunlap, 1968), pp. 105–106.
349. LBJ carried "tremendous burden for the boys in Vietnam." BG, interview, March 26, 1987.
349. "Billy, if anyone asks" ... "don't have to convince me." UPI, in *Charlotte Observer*, October 13, 1966.
350. BG wants to visit Vietnam, seen by LBJ as "a big plus": Memo, R. W. Komer to LBJ, August 1, 1966; Westmoreland invitation and LBJ request for report, November 28, 1966, Box 227a ("Billy Graham"), WHCF, LBJLA.
344. Vietnam visit "might cause controversy." Minutes, 1964–67, BGEA/London Office.
350. BG willing to support pacification programs. AP, December 20, 1966.
350. Only desire is to minister. Pollock, *Crusades*, p. 278.
351. Near airplane accident in Vietnam. BG, interview, March 5, 1989.
351. BG reports on the war. AP dispatches in Orlando *Star*, December 27, 1966; *Charlotte Observer*, December 28, 29, 30, 1966; and Charlotte *News*, December 30, 1966.

351. BG reports to LBJ. BG, oral history by Monroe Billington, October 12, 1983, AC 84–76, LBJLA; Memo, Joseph Califano to Marie Fehmer, January 20, 1967, Box 227a ("Billy Graham"), WHCF, LBJLA; AP, in *Charlotte Observer*, February 1, 1967; Dale Herendeen, "Graham Preaches Peace in Vietnam," *Christianity Today*, January 20, 1967, pp. 36–37; "Danger on the Home Front," *Christian Century*, January 25, 1967, pp. 99–100.
352. Slight pro-administration stance in public statements. "Not What He Meant," *Christian Century*, March 29, 1967, p. 411; radio program summarized in memo, Loyd Hackler to George Christian, April 28, 1967, Box 227a ("Billy Graham"), WHCF, LBJLA; half-hour color film, *Billy Graham on Vietnam*, produced by Lester Harmon (Wyncote, Pa.: Battle Advertising, 1967), briefly described in document located in Box 227a ("Billy Graham"), WHCF, LBJLA. The *Christian Century's* assertion that BG "endorses the war in Vietnam as a holy enterprise" appeared in an editorial, "Danger on the Home Front," January 25, 1967, p. 99.
352. BG scolds Martin Luther King, Jr. *Christian Century*, May 17, 1967, p. 645, quoting an address by the evangelist in Philadelphia.
352. White House wants BG to "speak out" on draft lottery. Memo, Fred Panzer to LBJ, March 10, 1967, Box 227a ("Billy Graham"), WHCF LBJLA.
352. BG defends Vietnam elections. *Hour of Decision*, September 3, 1967, reprint in Folder EX CO 312, Box 81 (1967), LBJLA.
352. BG not brainwashed. UPI, *Charlotte Observer*, September 10, 1967.
353. "I hope my son ... give his life." BG felt patriotism demanded that a young man accept the call to war but did not insist that actual combat be required. "I think when our nation makes a commitment," he said, "right or wrong, I have a responsibility to my nation." Still, noting that "we have these gigantic bases at Can Ranh Bay and Da Nang and Bien Hoa and all these places," he pointed out that there were many places a person could serve if his conscience did not allow him to fight. Press conference, WFGW Radio, Black Mountain, North Carolina, March 12, 1968, in CN 313 (Van Kampen Collection), Box 2, Folder 20, BGCA.
353. "I think athletics.... spiritual renaissance." Bob Myers, Charlotte *News*, September 20, 1968.
353. Vietnam safer than highways. Flint, *Billy Graham Speaks!* p. 15.
353. BG's 1968 Christmas visit to Vietnam. Letters, BG to LBJ, November 18, 1968 and January 3, 1969, Folder EX F05, Box 45, LBJLA; *Charlotte Observer*, November 28, and December 30, 1968, January 6, 1969; Pollock, *Crusades*, p. 277; "Questions Regarding Vietnam, Social Involvement, Race Relations," Memo to Executive Committee Members and Pastors, BG European Crusade, Berlin (for 1970 crusade), December 2, 1969, CN 19 (Ferm Papers), Box 6, Folder 44 (Misc., December 1969–March 1970), BGCA.
354. LBJ's work habits. BG, oral history, LBJLA.
354. LBJ's compassion. BG, interview, March 25, 1987; oral history (interview by Monroe Billington), October 12, 1983, AC 84–76, LBJLA.
355. LBJ's expectation of death affects decision not to run. BG, interview, March 25, 1987; oral history, LBJLA. George Christian, Johnson's secretary, gave a similar account of Johnson's decision in George Christian, "The Night Lyndon Quit," *Texas Monthly*, April 1988, pp. 109, 168–69.
355. BG talks to LBJ about the state of his soul. BG, interview, March 26, 1987.
355. LBJ's funeral plans. BG, interview, March 26, 1987; some details furnished by Grady Wilson, interview, March 1, 1987. Johnson perhaps hoped that BG would convey a more positive image of him to the press than he himself had been able to project. "I think President Johnson had a great difficulty in communicating on television," Graham observed. "He once told me when we were sitting alone watching a sunset down in Texas that television is what had killed him politically." BG, oral history.

Chapter 22: Nixon Revived

356. BG encourages Nixon to run. John Pollock, *Crusades: 20 Years with Billy Graham* (Minneapolis: World Wide Publications, 1969), p. 286; Flora Rheta Schreiber, *Good Housekeeping*, July 1968, quoted in Pollock, *Crusades*, p. 286; Marshall Frady, *Billy Graham: Parable of American Righteousness* (Boston: Little, Brown, 1979), pp. 446–47; *Christianity Today*, July 17, 1968; "Notes from the News," *Christian Century*, July 24, 1968; and Milton Karr, "Unbecoming Silence" (letter), *Christian Century*, January 8, 1969, p. 51.
356. "I would go that far ... not the party." AP, December 30, 1967.
357. BG responds to King's assassination. CN 24 (BG's Press Conferences), Tape 8, BGCA; editorial, *Decision*, August 1968, p. 2; *Southland Times*, June 4, 1968, quoted in Jerry Bed Hopkins, "Billy Graham and the Race Problem, 1949–1969" (Ph.D. diss., University of Kentucky, 1986), p. 150; BG, interview, February 27, 1987.
357. Jones and Bell urge BG to make film. Letter to BG, May 1, 1968; response, Forrest Layman to Jones, May 6, 1968, CN 12, Box 6, Folder 12, BGCA. Layman was manager of the BGEA office in Atlanta, which oversaw BG and associate evangelist crusades.
357. BG muses about King at Kennedy funeral. *Decision*, October 1969, pp. 8–9, quoted in Hopkins, *Race Problem*, p. 152.
357. "studiously trying ... this year." UPI, in *Charlotte Observer*, March 13, 1968.
357. "greatest crisis since the Civil War." "Billy's Political Pitch," *Newsweek*, June 10, 1968, p. 62.
357. "I do believe I could influence ... people." *Charlotte Observer*, May 14, 1968.
357. "no American I admire more." *Charlotte Observer*, May 27, 1968.
358. Democrats' reaction. Memo, James Rowe to LBJ, July 31, 1968, Box 227a ("Billy Graham"), WHCF, LBJLA.
358. Potter on BG's influence. Dan Potter, oral history, 1970, CN 141, Box 10, Folder 49, BGCA.
358. Nixon chooses a running mate. BG's advice is quoted in Edward B. Fiske, "The Closest Thing to a White House Chaplain," the *New York Times Magazine*, June 8, 1969, p. 108; the remainder is from Graham, interview, March 5, 1989. See also interview, *Christianity Today*, December 1973, and "Evangelists: The Politician's Preacher," *Time*, October 4, 1968, p. 58. Persistent rumor had it that Agnew had been recommended by Strom Thurmond, but BG disputes this account. According to him, Thurmond "was holding out for Reagan until the dying end." Fiske, "White House Chaplain," p. 108. Thurmond may, of course, have raised Agnew's name after BG left the gathering.
359. Nixon attends Pittsburgh crusade. "The Politician's Preacher," *Time*, October 4, 1968, p. 58; David E. Kucharsky, "Soul Search in the Steel City," *Christianity Today*, September 27, 1968, pp. 31–32.
359. Nixon visits Morrow Graham. *Charlotte Observer* and Charlotte *News*, September 12, 1968. Frady gives an extended and amusing account of this visit, *Parable*, pp. 447–49.
359. Julie Nixon visits Montreat. *Charlotte Observer*, October 18, 1968.
359. "a big segment" ... "at the polls." *Charlotte News*, September 19, 1968.
360. Nixon not "tricky." *Charlotte Observer*, September 30, 1968, and Dallas *Morning News*, September 30, 1968, p. 5A.
360. Nixon an "American Churchill." Billy Graham, "Billy Graham's Own Story: 'God Is My Witness,'" Part HI, *McCall's*, June 1964, p. 64.
360. "While I do not intend ... when a friend is smeared." Chuck Ashman, *The Gospel According to Billy* (Secaucus, N.J.: Lyle Stuart, 1977), p. 199; no source cited.
360. BG and Ruth attend campaign meeting. BG, interview, March 5, 1989.
360. Nixon confirms Graham's support, BG announces vote for Nixon. *Charlotte Observer*, November 1, 1968.
360. Dent exploits BG vote. "Preaching and the Power," *Newsweek*, July 20, 1970, p. 54.
361. BG prays with Nixons after victory. BG, interview, March 5, 1989.

361. BG and the inauguration. BG, interview, March 5, 1989; "The Inauguration," *Time*, January 31, 1969, p. 13; "The Inaugural Prayers," *Christianity Today*, February 14, 1969, p. 27. BG sat in the family box on the inaugural reviewing stand, and he and Ruth sat next to the Nixons at the inaugural concert. BG had been concerned that his backing of Nixon would strain his relationship with Johnson. Shortly after the election, he had written to the President, "I hope you will always remember that there is one country Baptist preacher from North Carolina who loves you, appreciates you, and hopes to see you often in the future." He went on to assure LBJ that Nixon was a good man and would certainly call on the former president for help, just as LBJ had called upon Eisenhower. Letter, BG to LBJ, November 18, 1968, Folder EX F05, Box 45, LBJLA. Early in January he wrote to Johnson again, noting that he would offer a prayer at the inauguration and observing that "it will be a unique experience for me to stand on that inaugural platform with you and Mr. Nixon. I love, admire and respect you both." If Johnson had been angry with him, he had apparently gotten over it. LBJ penned a note on the letter, "Ask him to call me and come in when he gets here on the 18th. And call Mayflower (hotel) on 18th and ask him over." BG to LBJ, January 3, 1969, Folder EX F05, Box 45, LBJLA.

362. BG preaches at White House on Sunday after Kennedy's funeral. BG, interview, March 5, 1989.

362. BG defends WH services. BG interview, March 5, 1989. UPI reported a similar statement on August 14, 1976. On a CBS News program, August 6, 1976 (CN 74, VT 2-CBS, BGCA) BG ventured that the services had perhaps been a mistake, but he seems to have changed his mind in the interim.

362. BG suggests preachers for WH services. Memo, Charles B. "Bud" Wilkinson to BG, January 24, 1969, requesting recommendations, Folder RM (Religious Matters) 2-1 "Religious Services in WH, Begin 3/31/69–," SF RM Box 6, WHCF, Nixon Presidential Materials Staff, National Archives and Record Service. Hereinafter, this archival source will be identified as NPM.

362. BG recommendations. Folder RM 2-1 "Religious Services in WH (1969–70)," CF (Confidential Files) 1969–74, Box 55, WHCF, NPM.

362. Recommendation of Cardinale. Letter, BG to RN, January 25, 1969, ibid.

362. Action Memo to Colson. Memo, February 23, 1970, Log no. 275, Folder RM 2-1 "Religious Services in WH, March 1–April 30, 1970," SF RM Box 12, WHCF, NPM.

362. Guest list of corporate leaders. Memo, Marge McFadden to Debbie Murray, October 12, 1970, Folder RM 2-1 "Religious Services in WH," SF RM Box 12, WHCF, NPM.

363. Allocation of invitations: Memo, Alex Butterfield to RN, March 15, 1971, Folder "Alex Butterfield," March 1971, Box 74, HRH Files, WHSF, NPM; HRH to Butterfield, Folder "February," Box 196 (HRH Chronological 1971–, A-H), WHSF, NPM.

363. BG preaches at four services. The dates were January 26, 1969, following the inauguration; March 15, 1970; September 12, 1971; and January 21, 1973, after the second inauguration.

363. BG prayed or was present at additional services. He gave benediction when Chattanooga minister Ben Haden preached, September 19, 1971, Folder RM 2-1 "Religious Services in WH, 9/1/71–9/30/71," SF RM, Box 15, WHCF, NPM. Present when Bill Bright spoke, W. R. Howard to Dave Parker, August 4, 1971, Folder RM 2-1 "Religious Services in WH, 6/1/71–8/31/71," SF RM Box 15, WHCF, NPM.

363. Selection of Bernardin to preach. Memo, Folder RM 2-1 "Religious Services in WH, 1/1/73–2/28/73," SF RM Box 17, WHCF, NPM.

363. "the only good conservative Protestant ministers." Harry Dent to Lucy Winchester, re Mother's Day service, 1970. Folder RM 2-1, "Religious Services in WH, 5/1/70–7/31/70," EX Box 12, WHCF, NPM.

363. Trueblood warned. Dwight Chapin to Stuart, August 31, 1971, Folder RM 2-1 "Religious Services in WH, 5/1/70–7/31/70," SF RM Box 12, WHCF, NPM.

363. Baptist opposition to Vatican appointment, "Baptists see Vatican 'Emissary' as 'Tragically Unwise Decision,'" RNS press release, June 11, 1970.

363. BG recommends Carl Bates. Letters, BG to Chapin, June 11 and 18, 1970, Folder RM 2-1 "Religious Services in WH, 6/1/70–6/30/70," SF RM Box 14, WHCF, NPM; Constance Stuart to George Bell, July 23, 1970, Folder RM 2-1 "Religious Services in WH, 5/1/70–7/31/70," SF RM Box 12, WHCF, NPM.

363. Invitation to Fred Rhodes. Deborah Sloan to Herbert Butterfield, August 3, 1971, Folder RM 2-1 "Religious Services in WH, 6/1/71–8/31/71," SF RM Box 15, WHCF, NPM.

364. BG's suggestions for Nixon's prayer breakfast remarks. Reported in memo, Chapin to Jim Keogh, January 23, 1969, re January 30 prayer breakfast. Chapin had asked BG to forward his suggestions to the President, but that letter, if written, apparently did not arrive. On the day of the breakfast, Haldeman (HRH), wrote a note to three aides (Chapin, Keogh, Cole) stating that the president was in a quandary as to what to say. Folder RM 2 "Prayers, 1/69–12/70," RM Box 3, WHSF, NPM.

364. BG recommends "anguished call to prayer." Letter, BG to Haldeman, 10/18/69, Box 40, HRH Files, WHSF; BG sends Langley letter, October 30, 1969, Folder RM 2, EX Box 3, WHCF, NPM.

365. BG, Rabbi Magnin, and the Mormon Tabernacle Choir. RN to BG, January 22, 1973, Folder RM 2-1 "Religious Services in WH, 1/1/73–2/28/73," RM Box 17, WHCF, NPM.

365. Colson on Nixon's religiosity. Colson, interview, April 18, 1989.

365. Nixon comes to Christ in Rader meeting. Nixon's story, told in November 1962 issue of *Decision*, was cited by Fiske, "White House Chaplain," p. 108.

365. BG pledges to hold Nixon's conversations in confidence. BG, interview, February 27, 1987. BG made essentially the same statement in other interviews.

366. WH persuades Ellington to use McDonald. Len Garment to HRH, July 8, 1969, Folder "Presidential handwriting, July 1969," Box 2, POF, WHSF, NPM.

366. BG suggests invitation to LBJ. Discussed in memo, John R. Brown to HRH, July 10, 1969, Folder EX "Outer Space 3, 7/1/69–7/21/69," Box 4, WHCF, NPM.

366. BG seeks deferments for Campus Crusade workers. Chapin to HRH and Ehrlichman. February 15, 1969, Folder RM 1/69–12/70, Box 1, WHCF, NPM; Jay Wilkinson to Robert Ellsworth, February 22, 1969; talking paper; memo, Jonathan Rose to Harry Dent, February 26, 1969; note dated April 23, 1969, labeled, "Two problems: Billy Graham's people want to be deferred," all in Box *63*, Egil Krogh (372-OA #2982), SMOF, WHSF, NPM.

367. Campbell and Wills criticisms of BG, quoted in Ashman, *Gospel According to Billy*, p. 202; I. F. Stone, quoted in "Preaching and Power," *Newsweek*, July 20, 1970, p. 50; Nicholas von Hoffman, "Don't Rock the Ark," the *Washington Post*, June 23, 1969, referred to in Butterfield to Klein, July 15, 1969 and Klein to RN, July 18, 1969, Folder RM 1/69–12/70, Box 1, WHCF, NPM.

367. "the bartender ... cramming." Billy Graham, "The Answer to Corruption," *Nation's Business*, September 1969, p. 47.

368. "I once asked an army officer ..." Quoted in Donald Meyer, "Billy Graham—and Success," *New Republic*, August 23, 1955.

368. "Where many of these men get the 'Reverend' ..." "Preaching and the Power," p. 55.

368. "It is interesting to me ... electrical world." *Hour of Decision*, quoted in AP, *Charlotte Observer*, July 17, 1969.

368. Police are "agents of God." Quoted in Fiske, "White House Chaplain," p. 111.

368. "The Supreme Court ... license." Quoted in Cort R. Flint, with the staff of *Quote* magazine, *Billy Graham Speaks!: The Quotable Billy Graham* (New York: Grosset & Dunlap, 1968), p. 82.

368. Student radicals. Meeting with Hoover, HRH note, April 25, 1969, and letter, HRH to BG, April 25, 1969, in Folder HU 3-1 "Civil Disturbances—Riots (1969–70)," Box 36, HRH Notes, Jan.–June 1969, WHSF, NPM; also in Folder EX HU 3-1 "Civil Disturbances-Riots," HU Box 23, WHCF, NPM. This letter has been withdrawn from public access.

368. "a small, highly organized group … our nation," AP, May 19, 1969.

368. One hundred terrorist groups. UPI, in *Charlotte Observer*, August 25, 1969.

369. "I don't think … hope he enjoyed the service." "Billy Graham, Here for Crusade, Says City Needs 'Awakening,'" the *New York Times*, June 10, 1969; "Mellowing Magic," *Time*, June 27, 1969, p. 48.

369. Forman and BG ignore each other. Tracy Early, "Graham in New York: Less of the Same," *Christian Century*, August 6, 1969, p. 86.

369. Book about U.S. Congress on Evangelism. George Wilson, ed., *Evangelism Now: The U.S. Congress on Evangelism* (Minneapolis: World Wide Publications, 1969).

369. Leighton Ford, "a shame the church …" Leighton Ford, "The Church and Evangelism," in ibid., p. 52.

369. "God's judgment fell!" Ibid., p. 193.

370. Skinner criticizes white Christians. Tom Skinner, "Evangelism in Our Modern Community," George Wilson, ed., *Evangelism Now: The U.S. Congress on Evangelism* (Minneapolis: World Wide Publications, 1969), pp. 137, 145, 147, 150.

370. Abernathy: "campaign that elevated Hitler." Ralph Abernathy, "What This Congress Can Mean to Society," ibid., pp. 176–78.

370. Black ministers list complaints. Chicago *Sun-Times*, September 14, 1969; Carey Moore, "Moving!" *Decision*, December 1969, pp. 6, 11; both cited in Hopkins, *Race Problem*, p. 154.

370. BG spot announcements on school integration. "Billy Graham Urges Compliance with School Integration Laws," *Christian Century*, September 23, 1970, p. 1115. In the spots, BG ventured that most southern parents were not opposed to school integration but only to long bus trips for their children.

371. Nixon meets with and responds to black ministers. "They would never have gotten to him … he sat there and took it," BG, quoted in William R. Eineke, "Graham Sides with Mrs. Ford on Issue of Pre-marital sex." Madison, Wisconsin, *State Journal*, March 13, 1976.

371. "the president is extremely interested …" HRH to Len Garment, January 16, 1970, Folder EX "HS 4/2/70–9/30/70," HS Box 1, WHCF, NPM.

371. Nixon "wants one of these projects done." HRH to Ehrlichman, April 30, 1970, Folder FA 5 "Housing 1969–70," Box 11, CF, WHSF, NPM.

371. "exploring additional ways." Memo, Tod Hullin to Don Murdoch, May 8, 1970, Folder EX HS 4/2/70–9/30/70, HS Box 1, WHCF, NPM.

371. E. V. Hill writes RN. E. V. Hill to RN, May 27, 1970, Folder EX HS 4/2/70–9/30/70, HS Box 1, WHCF, NPM.

371. "We must have peace …" AP, March 24, 1969.

373. "Confidential Missionary Plan for Ending the Vietnam War." BG to RN, April 15, 1969, CF ND 18/CO 165 RM Graham, WHCF, NPM; also, Folder ND 18/CO 165 "Vietnam, Jan–April 1969," Box 42 CF 1969–74, WHSF, NPM. Declassified February 22, 1989.

373. BG sends missionary report to Kissinger. BG to Kissinger, December 28, 1970, CO Box 84; Kissinger to BG, January 20, 1971, Folder EX CO 165 Vietnam, Box 84, WHCF, NPM. Kissinger and Graham had been acquainted for some time. "He'd come to our [New York] crusade in 1957," Graham recalled. "In fact, he was at the opening night. He was brought by the first person to come forward that night. Henry was a professor at Harvard and was down visiting for some reason. I think he came back one or two more nights. One night he came back to see me in my little office." Interview, March 5, 1989.

373. BG knows feelings of Asians, is "not sure at all." Dotson Rader, "Billy Graham and Friend," *Evergreen Review*, October 1969, p. 70.
374. Concern over *Christian Herald* editorial. BG is quoted in memo, Butterfield to RN, Folder RM 3-3, Prot. 69/70, RM Box 20, WHCF, NPM.
374. BG to talk with Golda Meir. BG to RN, September 20, 1969, EX CO 71 9/25/69–11/20/69, WHCF; Harold Saunders to Kissinger, September 24, 1969, CO 39, WHCF, NPM.
374. Marc Tanenbaum commends BG. From "Billy Graham and the Jewish Community," New York City radio program on WINS, May 31, 1970, quoted in Lowell D. Streiker and Gerald S. Strober, *Religion and the New Majority: Billy Graham, Middle America, and the Politics of the 70's* (New York: Association Press, 1972), p. 37.
374. BG wants to meet Pompidou. *BG to Chapin*, August 7, 1970, Folder EX FE 3, AR Box 2, WHCF; Chapin to Kissinger, July 21, 1970, Folder 8 "7/1/70–7/31/70," EX Box 27, WHCF, NPM.
374. BG offers services at de Gaulle's death. BG to Chapin, November 10, 1970, Folder EX FE 3-1/A-Z (1969–70), FE Box 2, WHCF, NPM.
375. "I wouldn't think that you'd call the President political." "The Preaching and the Power," *Newsweek*, July 20, 1970, p. 55. BG also defended against the charge of politics in David E. Kucharsky, "Graham in Gotham," *Christianity Today*, July 17, 1970.
375. "I was going to preach the straight gospel." BG, interview, March 5, 1989.
375. CBS News editorial, May 28, 1970, CN 74, VT 1-CBS, BGCA. Tennessee statute (TCA 39–1204) noted by Ashman, *Gospel According to Billy*, p. 205.
375. Knoxville service. CN 74, VT 1-CBS, and VT 4-NBC, BGCA; "The Presidency: In Praise of Youth," *Time*, June 8, 1970, p. 13; "Preaching and the Power," *Newsweek*, July 20, 1970, pp. 50, 54; BG, interview, March 5, 1989; Frady, *Parable*, pp. 452–54; Ashman, *Gospel According to Billy*, pp. 206–208.
376. Haldeman responses to program plans. "Great idea!" handwritten notes on memo, Gregg Petersmeyer to HRH, June 11, 1970, OA 3404; "cornball," HRH handwritten response on memo, Chapin to HRH, June 9, 1970, Folder EX HO/h 1969–70, SF HO Box 6, WHCF, NPM. Haldeman thought Ross Perot may have made the first suggestion for Honor America Day. Haldeman, interview, August 14, 1989.
376. BG takes active role in Honor America Day. Chapin to Colson, May 19, 1970, talking paper (n.d.), June 12, 1970, Folder OA #3404, Box HO 23, WHCF, NPM; undirected Chapin memo, Folder EX HO/h 1969–70, SF HO Box 6, WHCF, NPM.
377. Small crowd. CBS News, July 4, 1970, CN 74, VT 1-CBS, BGCA.
377. "Never!" "Preaching and the Power," *Newsweek*, July 20, 1970, p. 50.
377. The White House is pleased. Buchanan to Chapin, July 6, 1970, OA #3404, Box HO HO 23, WHCF; RN to BG, July 13, 1970, and Chapin to HRH, July 12, 1970 (mention of phone call), Folder EX HO/h 1969–70, SF HO Box 6, WHCF, NPM.
378. "My expectations were high." BG to RN, December 10, 1970, Folder EX HO 12–1, *II* 1/70, SF HO Box 24, WHCF, NPM.

Chapter 23: The Power and the Glory

379. BG helps establish Gordon-Conwell. Allan Emery, interview, July 19, 1986, and oral history, April 9, 1979, CN 141, Box 10, Folder 4, BGCA; BG, interview, March 5, 1989; Transcript of press conference, WGFW Radio, Black Mountain, North Carolina, March 12, 1968, in CN 313 (Van Kampen Collection), Box 2, Folder 20, BGCA; "Gordon and Conwell Announce Betrothal," *Christianity Today*, June 20, 1969, p. 32; "Gordon-Conwell Merger," *Christianity Today*, January 3, 1969, p. 35.
381. "unscrambling Babel." David C. Rennie, oral history, 1984, CN 141, Box 29, Folder 6, p. 5, BGCA.

382. Sydney crusade. The Reverend A. Jack Dain, interview; "Austrailia Crusade Begins," *Christianity Today*, April 12, 1968, pp. 42–43; "The Cross over Sydney," *Christianity Today*, May 24, 1968, pp. 43–44.
382. New Zealand and Melbourne. *Christian Century*, May 29, 1968, April 2, 1969; *Christianity Today*, March 28, 1969, p. 41; April 11, 1969, p. 45; John Pollock, *Crusades; 20 Years with Billy Graham* (Minneapolis: World Wide Publications, 1969), pp. 290–97.
382. "a lot of rock music is religious." Quoted by Louis Cassels, UPI, in *Charlotte Observer*, September 19, 1970.
382. "With their talk" ... "to change the system." Quoted in *Charlotte Observer*, January 24, 1969.
383. "America's Largest Coffeehouse." Described in Philip Tracy, "Billy Graham Plays the Garden," *Commonweal*, July 25, 1969, pp. 457–59; Pollock, *Crusades*, p. 302.
383. "terrific music" ... "I really do." *Charlotte Observer*, December 29, 1969.
383. Hippie Satanists disrupt service. *Chicago Daily News*, June 9, 1971; *Christianity Today*, July 2, 1971; Billy Graham, *Approaching Hoofbeats* (Waco, Tex.: Word Books, 1983), pp. 85–86. One observer recalled that "I saw these fellows not dressed in shabby clothes, but dressed in felt or satin robes, velvet robes, purple robes. I think they were devil worshipers smoking pot right there in the meeting." The Reverend Hubert Mitchell, oral history, 1976, CN 141, Box 13, Folder 16, BGCA.
384. Anne's modeling. Patricia Daniels Cornwell, *A Time for Remembering: The Ruth Bell Graham Story* (San Francisco: Harper & Row, 1983), p. 144.
384. Franklin's rebellion. Ibid., pp. 161–67. *Houston Chronicle*, March 5, 1988.
385. Ruth's vehicular adventures. Ibid., pp. 207–209.
386. 1969 New York television crusade. Pollock, *Crusades*, pp. 297–301.
386. Euro '70. Dave Foster, "Euro '70," *Christianity Today*, May 8, 1970, pp. 24–25; *Billy Graham: Euro '70*, (Minneapolis, World Wide Publications, 1971), passim. Information regarding special platform, synchronization of translation, and German Evangelical Alliance, John Pollock, *Billy Graham, Evangelist to the World* (New York: Harper & Row, 1979; Crusade Edition, Minneapolis: World Wide Publications,) pp. 76, 77, 80.
388. Melvin: "This made me withdraw into a shell." Quoted in Charlotte *News*, September 20, 1968.
389. Melvin spreads manure. Melvin Graham, interview, November 17, 1987. A brief version of this story appeared in the *Charlotte Observer*, September 21, 1968.
389. Melvin speaks at Anaheim crusade. Account based on John Wesley White segment on *Hour of Decision*, quoted in Pollock, *Crusades*, p. 310. "I'm not an ordained preacher." Melvin Graham, interview.
390. "I never would speak ... wouldn't work." Melvin Graham, interview.
390. "After all these years ... I think a lot of him." Charlotte *News*, September 20, 1968.
390. BG makes "most-admired" and "best-dressed" lists. *Charlotte Observer*, March 4, 1970; Charlotte *News*, January 28, 1970.
390. Billy on the beach. Ruth Graham, *It's My Turn* (Old Tappan, N.J.: Fleming H. Revell, 1982), p. 79.
390. BG "a symbol of hope ... a friend of mankind." Religious News Service, July 30, 1970, quoted in Lowell D. Streiker and Gerald S. Strober, *Religion and the New Majority: Billy Graham, Middle America, and the Politics of the 70's* (New York: Association Press, 1972), p. 30.
390. BG offers to mention conversation with RN. Memo, Butterfield to RN, January 1, 1971, Folder EX RE 10 "Football, 1/1/71," SF RE Box 5, WHCF, NPM.
391. "would be reaching." HRH note, February 14, 1971, Folder 2/15–3/31, Box 43, Haldeman Notes, HRH Files, WHSF, NPM.

391. HRH feels RN should attend Billy Graham Day. HRH Note, June 18, 1970, in Folder 5/20/71–6/30/71, Box 43, Haldeman Notes, HRH Files, WHSF, NPM.
391. White House takes control of Nixon appearance at Billy Graham Day. William Henkel, Jr., White House memo, reported by Michael Schwartz, *Charlotte Observer*, June 8, 1974.
391. HRH: "Great" ... "*not* our people." Memo reported on CBS *News*, August 1, 1973, CN 74, VT 1-CBS, BGCA; also *New York Times*, Charlotte *News*, etc. August 2, 1973, *Charlotte Observer*, June 8, 1974. Nixon's men were understandably frustrated by the demonstrations that dogged their leader but recognized the need to handle encounters in a planned way. In a sardonically playful note, Colson wrote the following memo to John Dean on May 23, 1972: "I have just received the Haldeman memo attached dated May 19 re contact with demonstrators. According to H's memo, I am to clear all contacts well in advance with you. This to advise you that I am planning tomorrow night to drive my Pontiac Station wagon upon the curb of Pennsylvania Avenue in front of the White House and run over all of the hippies who are lying there. My plan is to do this while they are asleep sometime between 2 and 3 a.m. Would you please let me know what coordination you would like to arrange?" Folder "May 1972," Box 5, John Dean Files, WHSF, NPM.
391. "When I started" ... "look at all this!" *Charlotte Observer*, October 15, 1971.
392. Telegrams and attendees on Billy Graham Day. *Charlotte Observer*, October 16, 1971.
392. BG's suit. *Charlotte Observer*, October 16, 1971. Descriptions of Billy Graham Day, *Charlotte Observer*, October 13, 14, and 16, 1971.
392. Nixon teaches BG how to wave. "Billy Graham: The Man at Home," *Saturday Evening Post*, September 1972, p. 45.
392. Secret Service, police, "marshals"; crowd screened for troublemakers, marshals sued. *Charlotte Observer*, October 16, 1971; Richard Mashcal, *Charlotte Observer*, November 5, 1971.
393. White House involved with marshals. *New York Post*, *Washington Post*, August 6, 1973; AP, April 24, 1974; *Charlotte Observer*, June 8, 1974; the *New York Times*, April 22, 26, 29, 30, and May 6, 1975.
393. Charges dismissed. The *New York Times*, May 6, 1975; *Charlotte Observer*, July 12, 1975.
393. "Against the weight of evidence," The *New York Times*, July 13, 1975.
393. "a religious ceremony." *Charlotte Observer*, May 2, 1975.
393. Carolinians kill their own rats. "Nation's Finest People Live Here, Billy Says," *Charlotte Observer*, October 16, 1971.
393. BG commends RN's morality. Ibid.
393. RN commends BG. *Charlotte Observer* and *News*, October 16, 1971; CN 74, VT 1-CBS, BGCA; David E. Kucharsky, "Billy Graham's Day," *Christianity Today*, November 5, 1971.
394. "murderer ... platitudes." Charlotte *News*, April 24, 1975. The young man, a student at Davidson College, had been ejected from the Coliseum after placing a black armband on his suit after finding a seat. He insisted he was conducting "a silent vigil" and had had no intention of disrupting the proceedings.
394. "cross-shaped sandwiches ... biblicoform cake." *Charlotte Observer*, October 16, 1971; "The Political Education of Billy Graham," the *Washington Post*, April 14, 1986, p. 8.
394. "You can't blame it on the President." *Charlotte Observer*, November 5, 1971.
394. Kaplow: "if indeed ... in American politics." NBC News, October 15, 1971, CN 74, VT 4-NBC, BGCA.
394. "the President and the Chamber of Commerce draw honor." Editorial, *Charlotte Observer*, October 15, 1971.
394. John C. Bennett's criticisms, "Billy Graham in Oakland," *Christianity and Crisis*, October 4, 1971, pp. 195–97.
395. Sawyer memo to Ziegler. Alpha names files, Box 155, WHSF, NPM.

395. Plagenz chastises Graham. UPI, December 31, 1971.
395. "It is interesting ... entered the schools." *Charlotte Observer*, November 5, 1971.
395. "We have all had our My Lais ..." Quoted in letter to *Charlotte Observer*, October 18, 1971. Shortly after the My Lai incident, the White House had called BG to solicit his views on Calley. HRH note, February 14, 1971, Folder 4/1/71–5/19/71, Box 43, Haldeman Notes, WHSF, HRH Files, NPM (Apparently misfiled).
395. Presidential perks to BG. White House dinners, Folder EX FG 12 1/1/72–1/31/71, Box 2, FG 12, WHCF, NPM.
395. *Sequoia* dinner, Folder CF WH 11–3 "Yacht," Box 70, WHCF, NPM.
395. Julie and Tricia pick film. Folder 5/20/71–6/30/71, Box 43, Haldeman notes, HRH Files, WHSF, NPM.
396. Haldeman embarrassed, HRH to Vern Coffey, August 11, 1971, Folder "HRH Chronological," Box 197, HRH Files, WHSF, NPM.
396. White House valued BG's diplomatic skills. H. R. Haldeman, interview, August 14, 1989.
396. Kissinger briefs BG's conservative friends. HRH to BG, July 17, 1971, Folder "China 1/1/71," Box 17, EX CO 34; Folder "HRH Chronological," Box 197, HRH Files WHSF, NPM; HRH to Kissinger, August 3, 1971, Folder "HRH Chronological," Box 197, HRH Files, WHSF, NPM. The briefing occurred on August 10, 1971.
396. Graham to visit Chiangs on Nixon's behalf. HRH to HAK, November 11, 1971, Folder "Kissinger, November 1971," Box 86 (Alpha names files, A-X Oct–Dec 1971, Kehrli 10/71–Klein 11/71), HRH Files, WHSF, NPM
396. Talking Points for BG's conversation with Chiangs. HRH to BG, November 22, 1971, Folder "HRH Chronological Nov. 1971, A–L," Box 197, HRH Files, WHSF, NPM.
397. BG barely remembers Chiang visit. Interview, March 5, 1989.

Chapter 24: "Billy, You Stay Out of Politics"

398. "On the political front ... in '72." Memo, RN to HRH, November 30, 1970, Folder "Memos from the President typed by Haldeman's office, 1970," Box 164, HRH Files, WHSF, NPM.
398. "Graham wants to be helpful ... can't have leak." HRH, handwritten notes, February 6 and 8, 1971, Folder 1/1/71–2/15/71, Box 43, Haldeman notes, HRH Files, WHSF, NPM. Haldeman notes, Part I, Jan–March '71, White House logs indicate that BG had seen the President on February 1, the date of the annual National Prayer Breakfast. WH Master List, Contacts File by Name, Graham p. 1413, WHCF, NPM.
398. BG wants "line to the right." Talking paper, February 8, 1971, Talking Papers, 1971–7/72, Box 153, HRH Files, WHSF, NPM; HRH note, May 10, 1971, Folder 4/1/71–5/ 19/71, Box 43, Haldeman notes, HRH Files, WHSF, NPM.
398. BG apparently dissuades Hatfield from seeking Republican nomination. Harry Dent gave BG authorization to tell Hatfield he would have full White House backing in Senate race if he did not seek the presidency. HRH note re call from Dent, HRH Notes, Box 179. Dent later noted that BG was "checking this out." Dent to Charles Colson, April 8, 1971, Colson Files Folder "Political Misc.," Box 99, WHSF, NPM. When I asked Graham about this, he insisted he had no memory of such an episode but, in a remarkable show of candor, said that his secretary had found correspondence confirming that he had indeed talked to both Nixon and Hatfield about this matter on several occasions. BG, interview, March 6, 1989.
398. BG a frontline heavyweight. Action Paper, August 2, 1971, Folder "HRH Chronological," Box 197, HRH Files, WHSF, NPM.
399. BG attends Tolbert inauguration. Talking Paper, Secretary Rogers, Folder "HRH Chronological," Box 197, HRH Files, WHSF, NPM; Kissinger to RN, September 11, 1971, Folder "EX CO 84, Liberia 1/1/71," WHSF, NPM; Haig to Higby, Folder "General Haig, Novem-

ber 1971," Box 86 (Alpha names files A–X Oct–Dec 1971, Kehrli 10/71–Klein 11/71), HRH Files, WHSF, NPM.

399. BG's February 1972 meetings with WH staff and RN. HRH note, January 31, 1972, "Haldeman notes, Folder 1/1/72–2/18/72," Box 45, HRH Files, WHSF, NPM; HRH meeting summary, March 9, 1972, Folder "HRH Subject," Box 163, HRH Files, WHSF, NPM; David E. Kucharsky, "Billy Graham's Day," *Christianity Today*, November 5, 1971; memo, Ziegler to HRH and DC, March 29, 1972, Folder "R. Ziegler," Box 94 (Alpha names files, Feb–April 1972), HRH Files, WHSF, NPM. 392 Second China Briefing. HRH to Colson, March 17, 1972, Folder "March 1972" Box 199 (HRH Chronological), HRH Files, WHSF, NPM; Higby to HRH, March 17, 1972, and HRH to Higby, March 29, 1972, Folder "Higby," Box 93 (Alpha names files, Feb–April 1972), HRH Files, WHSF, NPM.

399. Postal rates. HRH to John D. Ehrlichman, February 1, 1972, Folder "February 1972," Box 199 (HRH Chronological), HRH Files, WHSF, NPM.

399. Nixon wants HRH to keep "continuing contact" with BG. Memo, RN to HRH, March 14, 1972, Folder "HRH 1972, Memos from the President," Box 162, HRH Files, WHSF, NPM.

400. Higby memo to Strachan and Kehrli. Memo, February 1, 1972, Box 125 (Graham, marked "Administratively Confidential"), NPM, HRH Files, WHSF, Haldeman also told aides that he wanted to be kept informed of all calls between BG and the President. Memo, Butterfield to Higby, August 7, 1972, Folder "Butterfield, August 1972," Box 101 (HRH Alpha names files, July–August 1972) HRH Files, WHSF, NPM.

400. Talking paper topics, insider information. Talking papers, February 10, March 22, April 3, 11, and 26, May 8 and 16, 1972, HRH Box 125 (Graham), HRH Files, WHSF, NPM.

400. Talking papers and telephone calls. Most, but not all, telephone calls between BG and RN (or a specifically designated aide) are logged on a master list that begins with December 1971 and continues through June 1974. Some additional calls are mentioned in White House memos. Haldeman's calls are not logged in a systematic fashion; rather, various archival folders contain, often without an obvious rationale, little collections of telephone log slips. Haldeman's records alone log or mention at least seventeen different calls between February 1, 1972, the date of the National Prayer Breakfast, and November 9, the day following the election. It seems a safe assumption that points on the talking papers were discussed during a number of these calls.

400. Haldeman confirms calls. H. R. Haldeman, interview, August 14, 1989. John Connally also confirmed that Haldeman called him and that he was aware that Haldeman was making regular calls to BG. John B. Connally, interview, January 30, 1991.

400. Colson on RN conversations with BG. Charles Colson, interview, April 18, 1989.

400. "Billy was definitely in [Nixon's] inner circle . . . see the bad." H. R. Haldeman, interview, August 14, 1989.

401. Ehrlichman comments. Interview, August 15, 1989. John Connally made a similar observation: "[Presidents who sought Graham's counsel] felt he was in contact with more individuals than any other person in the United States and that he had a sense of America's feelings unlike anything they could otherwise obtain. None of them were in a position to probe the feelings and the reactions of the people that Billy Graham touched. He gave them a completely different perspective of what people saw, what they thought, how they felt, what moved them. That's why he was important to them. That's why they liked to have him around. He provided access to the minds of people that they otherwise had no entry into. They had no way of determining the feelings and the depths of emotions of the people that Billy Graham touched." Connally, interview, January 30, 1991.

401. "Mr. Nixon . . . a e Gaulle type." "Billy Graham: The Man at Home," *Saturday Evening Post*, September 1972, p. 105

401. Suggestions to Nixon on public speaking. February 8, 1971, Folder "Jan 1–Feb 15, 1971," Box 45, Haldeman Notes, HRH Files, WHSF, NPM.
401. BG wants WH to cultivate Bill Bright. Dave Parker to Colson, July 29, 1971, Folder RM 2-1 "Religious Services in White House 9/1/71–9/30/71," SF RM Box 15, WHCF, NPM. Explo '72. HRH to Parker, February 1, 1972, Folder "HRH Chronological," Box 199, 700 HRH Files, WHSF, NPM; HRH note, February 2, 1971, Folder "HRH Notes," Box 45, HRH Files, WHSF, NPM.
401. Explo '72. HRH to Parker, February 1, 1972, Folder "HRH Chronoligcal," Box 199, HRH Files, WHSF, NPM; HRH note, February 2, 1971, Folder "HRH Notes," Box 45, HRH Files, WHSF, NPM.
402. BG asks RN to send telegram to Explo '72. L. Higby to HRH, June 14, 1972, Folder "Higby, June 1972" Box 98 Alpha names files, June–July 1972, HRH Files, WHSF, NPM.
402. "religious Woodstock." in AP, *Charlotte Observer*, June 11, 1972.
402. Colson's notes: "Use Graham's organization." Colson's notes, made on June 27, 1972, do not mention Nixon specifically, but bear the letters *EOB*, a designation staff members used for a hideaway office Nixon maintained in the Executive Office Building, and are filed in a folder titled "Presidential Meeting Notes." Folder "Presidential Meeting Notes [1972–1973]," Box 16 (Meeting Files), Staff Member and Office Files—Charles W. Colson, WHSF, NMPS.
402. WH fears McGovern will win religious vote, mobilizes BG. Memo, Higby to HRH, June 14, 1972, Folder "Higby, June 1972," Box 98 (Alpha names files, June–July 1972); HRH note, Box 45 (Haldeman notes, May 9–June 30, 1972, Part II), HRH Files, WHSF, NPM. Harry Williams, a BGEA man whom Graham described as one of the best he had for organizing residential for crusades, apparently took such a leave of absence to organize precincts for Nixon. HRH to Ken Rietz, July 26, 1972, Box 200 (HRH Chronological, July, 1972), HRH Files, WHSF, NPM.
402. "What is our best approach ... Campus Crusade?" Talking Paper, June 27, 1972, HRH Box 125 (Graham), HRH Files, WHSF, NPM.
402. BG asks RN to send telegram to LNB. Higby to HRH, June 14, 1972, Folder "Higby June 1972, Box 98 (HRH Alpha names files, June–July 1972), HRH files, WHSF, NPM.
402. BG urges RN tie with OR. Dent to Parker, June 20, 1972, and Dent to RN, August 11, Folder "RM 1/1/71–12/72, Religious Services," SF RM Box 2, WHCF, NPM.
403. Haldeman dislikes the idea. HRH to DC, August 17, 1972, Box 200 (HRH Chronological, August 1972), HRH Files, WHSF, NPM.
403. BG declines invitations to conventions. David E. Kucharsky, "Graham on Demons," *Christianity Today*, June 7, 1974, pp. 49–50.
403. BG's advice to RN re acceptance speech, reported in memo, HRH to RN, August 19, 1972, Folder "August 1972," Box 200 (HRH Chronological), HRH Files, WHSF, NPM. The White House staff had arranged for Graham to be able to play at the San Clemente golf course as the President's guest. Folder "July 1972," Box 200 (HRH Chronological), HRH Files, WHSF, NPM.
403. Talking papers re McGovern. HRH talking papers, September 20, and October 25, 1972, Box 125 (Graham), HRH Files, WHSF NPM.
403. BG concerned about Religious Leaders group. LH to HRH, September 21, 1972, regarding BG call, September 20, Talking Papers 7/72–9/72, Box 153 (HRH Subject Files) WHSF, NPM.
404. McLaughlin recommends against organizing clergy. McLaughlin to Dave Parker, October 5, 1972, Folder RM 1/1/72–12/72, SF RM Box 2, WHCF, NPM.
404. BG reckons RN will carry all states but South Dakota. AP, in *Charlotte Observer*, August 13, 1972.
404. Nixon to "go down in history." *Charlotte Observer*, September 21, 1972.
404. RN "just born to be President." AP, November 3, 1972.

404. BG is called on election night. HRH Action Paper, October 30,1972, Box 125 (Graham), HRH Files, WHSF, NPM.
405. "We tried to get his mailing list." Colson, interview.
405. "Billy, ... you stay out of politics" ... "never try to use me." BG, quoted in David Frost, *Billy Graham Talks with David Frost* (London: Hodder and Stoughton, 1972), p. 66.
405. BG knew LBJ "not a McGovern man." BG, interview, March 5, 1989.
406. BG denies active involvement in 1972 election. BG, interviews, March 5 and 6, 1989.

Chapter 25: A Ministry of Reconciliation

407. China an "enemy of freedom," AP, July 31, 1965.
407. BG goes to Ireland. "Billy Graham: From Birmingham to Belfast," *Christianity Today*, June 9, 1972; John Pollock, *Billy Graham: Evangelist to the World* (Harper & Row, 1979), pp. 91–92.
408. BG and Blessit tour Belfast. Graham Lacey, oral history, 1974, CN 141, Box 11, Folder 27, BGCA. John Pollock, drawing on Lacey's account, tells much the same story in *Evangelist to the World*, pp. 93–95.
409. Paisley attacks BG. *Charlotte Observer*, June 8, 1972; J. D. Douglas, "He Put It over with Love," *Christianity Today*, July 7, 1972, p. 4. Douglas reported that in his pastoral prayer at one of the services, Paisley "thanked God that a bomb being handled by IRA officers a few hours earlier had accidentally exploded, killing several of them."
410. RN calls BG in Belfast. Pollock, *Evangelist to the World*, p. 95. WH Master List, Contact File by Name, Graham, WHCH, NPM. The call occurred on May 29, 1972, 4:29 P.M., EDT. That Nixon would call was not a complete surprise. He had also called Graham for a brief communication on February 26, during his visit to China.
410. BG meets with Roman Catholic and Protestant leaders, expects peace but recognizes problems. Pollock, *Evangelist to the World*, pp. 95–96; *Charlotte Observer*, June 8, 1972; Douglas, "He Put It over with Love," *Christianity Today*, July 7, 1972, p. 5.
411. BG in Dublin. Pollock, *Evangelist to the World*, pp. 98–102; *Charlotte Observer*, June 8, 1972; Brian Kingsmore, interview, July 7, 1986.
412. Nagas build road. Robert Cunville, oral history, CN 141, Box 3, Folder 9, BGCA; Pollock, *Evangelist to the World*, p. 9.
412. Kohima provides beds, food, wood. Pollock, *Evangelist to the World*, p. 9.
414. The Kohima crusade. Ibid., pp. 3–26; Cunville, oral history and interview, July 17, 1986; The Reverend A. Jack Dain, interview.
415. BG and Moynihan's ambassadorship. BG, interview, March 5, 1989. Graham's account is supported by internal memos between WH aides David Parker and Bruce Kehrli. Parker to Kehrli, December 20, 1972, and Kehrli to Parker, December 22, 1972, Folder "CF FO 2/CO-66–FO 2/CO-99," CF Box 30, WHSF, NPM.
416. BG meets with the Shah. Interview, March 5, 1989; "Graham and the Shah," *Christian Century*, January 10, 1973, p. 3. Graham recalled that "I was sort of overwhelmed at the magnificence of the palace. I talked my head off to him. I talked to him about Daniel the prophet, the beginning of Persia, what God would do, and Christ, and so forth. I vowed a long time ago that I'd never be in the presence of anybody like that without preaching the gospel. He was very gracious. I spent several hours. He pulled a screen and we watched Walter Cronkite give the news from the night before." Interview, March 5, 1989.
416. BG considers Washington crusade. Letters, BG to Robert Hancock, n.d.; John Dean to Rose Mary Woods, January 31, 1972; RN to BG, February 1,1972; BG to RN, February 4, 1972; all in Folder RM 3 1/1/71–12/31/72, RM Box 18, WHCH, NPM.
416. "We decided we would not cooperate." The Reverend Ernest Gibson, interview, May 2, 1986.

417. Cassidy's efforts to combat apartheid. Michael Cassidy, "The Ethics of Political Nationalism," in *One Race, One Gospel, One Task*, ed. Carl F. H. Henry and Stanley Mooneyham, vol. I of official reference volumes of the World Congress on Evangelism, Berlin, 1966 (Minneapolis: World Wide Publications, 1967), pp. 312–17.
417. BG accepts invitation to preach in South Africa. Pollock, *Evangelist to the World*, pp. 28–31.
418. Women's prayer movement in South Africa. Ibid., pp. 32–33.
418. Integrated stadium at Durban: "Even if Billy Graham ... enough of a testimony." Ibid., p. 33.
418. "Christ belongs to all people!" Film, *South Africa*, World Wide Pictures, 1973.
419. "Apartheid Doomed." Pollock, *Evangelist to the World*, p. 36.
419. Disappointment at BG's address and departure. Ibid., pp. 36–37.
419. BG recommends castration for rapists. UPI, March 20, 1973; AP, March 30, 1973; BG, interview, February 26, 1987; Talking paper, March 3, 1973, Folder "EX FO 8, 3/1/73–4/30/73," Box 73, WHCF, NPM. Also, "A Graham Follow-up," *Christian Century*, April 11, 1973, pp. 414–15; Pollock, *Evangelist to the World*, pp. 38–39.
420. Gary Player. Player and BG were already longtime friends. It was Player, in fact, whom BG credited with having broken him from his awkward cross-handed golf grip. Edwin Fiske, "The Closest Thing to a White House Chaplain," The *New York Times Magazine*, June 8, 1969, p. 106.
421. Black attendance low at Atlanta crusade. "Blacks Close Their Ears to Graham," St. Petersburg *Times*, July 7, 1973; Dr. Russell Dilday, oral history, March 5, 1980, CN 141, Box 11, Folder 10, BGCA; Edward E. Plowman, "Billy and the Blacks: Atlanta and Graham Revisited," *Christianity Today*, July 20, 1973, pp. 40–41.
421. BG responds to charges of black clergy in Minneapolis. "Graham to Tour Black Areas in Support Bid," Minneapolis *Star*, July 10, 1973; *Chicago Defender*, July 10, 1973; "Two City Ministers Stand Firm on Denouncement of Graham," St. Paul *Dispatch*, July 12, 1973.
422. Growth of Korean Christianity. Billy Kim, interview, July 17, 1986; Akbar Abdul-Haqq, interview, May 2, 1986.
422. Korean separatism and ecumenism. Kim, interview; Pollock, *Evangelist to the World*, pp. 46–47.
423. "Americans... follow doctor's way." Ibid., p. 46.
424. Billy Kim agrees to interpret. Kim, interview; Henry Holley, oral history, January 9, 1976, CN 141, Box 4, Folder 29, BGCA.
424. Limousines embarrass BG. Kim, interview.
425. Park regime monitors BG and crusade. David Poling, *Why Billy Graham?* (Grand Rapids: Zondervan, 1977), p. 85
426. Korean Crusade description. Pollock, *Evangelist to the World*, pp. 54–57; Kim, Abdul-Haqq, Holley, interviews; Holley, oral history.

Chapter 26: Vietnam and Watergate

428. BG commends RN's inaugural address. BG to RN, February 6,1973, Folder "Presidential and Pre-Presidential, 1/1/73," SF RM Box 2, WHCF, NPM.
429. BG surprised at Nixon's contributions. *Boston Globe*, December 29, 1973; *Charlotte Observer*, December 28, 1972. In 1972 Nixon contributed a total of $295 to charitable causes. The *New York Times*, December 23, 1973, p. 24.
429. BG upset at Supreme Court decisions on prayer and Bible reading: "atheists should be overruled." George Burnham and Lee Fisher, *Billy Graham: Man of God* (Westchester, Ill.: Good News Publishing, n.d.), p. 54, quoted by Marshall Frady, *Billy Graham: Parable of American Righteousness* (Boston: Little, Brown, 1979), p. 438.

429. BG recommends Protestant schools. David E. Kucharsky, "Billy Graham and 'Civil Religion,'" *Christianity Today*, November 6, 1970, pp. 56–58.

429. BG recommends reading Ten Commandments in schools. The *New York Times*, January 22, 1973, p. 38; NBC News, January 21, 1973, CN 74, VT 4-NBC, BGCA; Commends Mao's Eight Values, interview with Maureen D'Honau, Mainichi (Japan) *Daily News*, May 28, 1973. In responding to criticisms of his positive words for Mao's precepts, BGEA spokesmen said that the interviewer had not spoken good English and had misunderstood what BG was trying to say. Ms. D'Honau, who was American-born and spoke no language other than English, insisted she was quoting BG accurately. Reported in *Review of the News*, March 1974, quoted in Edgar Bundy, *Billy Graham: Performer, Politician, Preacher, Prophet?* (Miami Shores, Fla.: Edgar Bundy Ministries, 1982), p. 83. BG continues to recommend reading of Commandments in schools. "Graham on Demons: Milestone in Arizona," *Christianity Today*, June 7, 1974, p. 49.

430. Zedekiah and Ahab. I Kings 22. The comparison was made by, among others, Will Campbell, in "An Open Letter to Dr. Billy Graham," *Katallagete-Be Reconciled*, Winter 1971, p. 2. It was also alluded to in the *Charlotte Observer's* editorial on October 14, 1971, with the comment that "the unsucessful Micaiah," the courageous prophet who told King Ahab the truth, "is remembered and the others are forgotten."

430. "I have never advocated war." BGEA press release, attached to letter, Chapin to HRH, January 8, 1973, Box 125 (Graham), HRH Files, WHSF, NPM. Quoted in Joan Rattner Heilman, "Billy Graham's Daughter Answers His Critics," *Good Housekeeping*, June 1973, p. 154.

430. BG denies he is "White House Chaplain." BGEA press release, attached to letter, Chapin to HRH, January 8, 1973, Box 125 (Graham), HRH Files, WHSF, NPM.

431. "The President doesn't call me up ... that's all." AP, in *Charlotte Observer* and *News*, January 4, 1973; "Graham: 'Not White House Chaplain,'" Abilene *Reporter-News*, January 5, 1973; "Graham Calls Ministry Evangelistic, Not Political," *The Dallas Morning News*, January 4, 1973.

431. "I felt gloomy ... demonstrations against alcohol?" Edward Fiske, the *New York Times*, January 21, 1973. In response to a question from *Newsweek* reporter Jane Whitemore, Graham named smoking as a villain of similar scope; though not published in *Newsweek*, his comment was reported in "Quote of the Week," *New Republic*, January 6 and 13, p. 11; Referred to in Garry Wills, "A Prophet Gagged," Chicago *Sun-Times*, January 30, 1973; "Graham Discusses Viet War," Winston-Salem, North Carolina, *Twin City Sentinel*, January 30, 1973.

431. BG recalls only one remark in favor of war. January 1973 press release; "A Clarification," *Christianity Today*, January 19, 1973, p. 36; Graham has since identified his "lone remark" as one he made at the Denver Press Club in 1965, criticizing protesting ministers. BG, interview, March 6, 1989.

432. Bennett, "others," and BGEA spokesman, quoted in Joan Rattner Heilman, "Billy Graham's Daughter Answers His Critics," *Good Housekeeping*, June 1973, p. 154.

432. BG the "hard-line type." HRH to Colson, April 25, 1972, Folder "HRH Chronological," Box 199, HRH Files, WHSF, NPM.

432. BG "disturbed by some press reports." DC to HRH, January 8,1973, Box 125 (Graham), HRH Files, WHSF, NPM.

432. Liberal commentators disappointed. BG to RN, February 6, 1973, SF RM Box 2, WHCF, NPM.

433. McGovern "desperate." AP, in *Charlotte Observer*, November 3, 1972

433. BG amazed at furor over "alleged escapade." BG to HRH, October 20, 1972, Box 21 (Correspondence, personal, October 1972), HRH Files, WHSF, NPM.

433. "I have marveled . . . hall of fame." BG to RN, April 6, 1973, Folder EX F08 4/1/73–4/30/73, Box 73, WHCF, NPM.
433. BG "distancing myself." Interview, February 26, 1987.
433. BG speaks out on Watergate. The statements are from the *Today* interview, April 27, 1973, quoted in John Pollock, *Billy Graham: Evangelist to the World* (New York: Harper & Row, 1979), p. 176; *Billy Graham*, "Watergate and Its Lessons of Morality," op-ed page, the *New York Times*, May 6, 1973; *Hour of Decision*, May 13, 1973.
434. BG recommends "picture situations." Recounted in Higby to RN, May 2, 1973, Folder "Presidential Handwriting, May 1973," POF Box 22, WHSF, NPM.
434 "Your friends understand." Letter, Jesse Helms to RN, May 4, 1973, JL Box 12, WHCF, NMP.
434. BG and RN "had never discussed Watergate." Quoted in *Charlotte Observer*, June 15, 1973.
434. "another sign of permissiveness." The *New York Times*, May 1, 1973; cited in editorial, *Arkansas Gazette*, July 7, 1973.
435. Thanksgiving press release, November 22, 1973, sent to Rosemary Woods by Charles Crutchfield. PPF Box 8, WHCF, NPM.
435. RN calls BG. WH Master List, Contact File by Name, Graham, p. 1414, WHCF, NPM.
435. BG at White House Christmas Service. WH Master List, Contact File by Name, Graham, p. 1415, WHCF, NPM; telephone call and reaffirmations, letter, BG to RN, December 1973, Folder RM 2-1 "Religious Services in WH, 10/16/73–12/31/73," SF RM Box WHCF, NPM.
435. BG sees RN as "chipper." Charlotte *News*, December 17, 1973; 1973 to be better, BG to RN, December 26, 1973, Folder RM 2-1, "Religious Services in WH, 10/16/73–12/31/73," SF RM Box 17, WHCF, NPM.
436. Speaking at White House not "a benediction of what had been going on there." BG interview, "Watergate," *Christianity Today*, January 4, 1974, pp. 8–10. In an interview with *The Christian Science Monitor*, December 31, 1973, Graham repeated his opinion that Nixon would become a great president if he could get Watergate out of his system.
436. "if it serves your vanity." George E. Stringfellow to BG, January 9, 1974, Folder EX JL 3 80 of 89, 2/25/74–3/4/74, SF JL Box 21, WHCF, NPM.
436. "I was saddened by your statements." Peale to BG, February 4, 1974, and RN to Peak, March 4, 1974, Folder EX JL 3 80, 2/25/74–3/4/74, SF JL Box 21, WHCF, NPM.
437. Colson's conversion. CC to RN, November 21, 1973, CF SP 2-4/1969 (State of Union), and Folder "CF SP 3-162 Prayer Breakfast Remarks," Box 60, CF 1971–74, WHCF, NPM.
437. Colson presses for two breakfasts. Unsigned, undated memo, Folder CF SP 3-162, "Prayer Breakfast Remarks," Box 60, CF 1971–74, WHCF, NPM.
437. "Two Breakfasts are too many." Talking paper, Congressman Al Quie (Republican-Minnesota, president of National Prayer Breakfast Committee), ibid. The Prayer Breakfast Committee, which sponsored the larger breakfast, agreed with Colson on the need for a smaller event.
437. BG's suggestions for Prayer Breakfast remarks. Included, with Haig's assessment, in Haig to RN, January 30, 1974, Folder CF SP 3-162 "Prayer Breakfast Remarks," Box 60, CF 1969–74, WHCF, NPM.
438. Haldeman doubts RN shunned BG. Haldeman, interview, August 14, 1989.
438. BG and Nixon have limited contact. BG made the claim of limited access as least as early as August 1974 in an interview with John Dart, of the *Los Angeles Times*, reported in *Charlotte Observer*, August 17, 1974. He made the same claim in Donald H. Harrison, "Billy Graham Voices Doubts on 'Final Days,'" San Diego *Union*, April 1, 1976. He repeated it at least twice in interviews with me, on February 26, 1987 and March 5, 1989. Colson expressed his doubts in an interview, April 18, 1989. WH Master List, Contact File by Name, Billy

Graham, p. 1415, WHCF, NPM. The list records calls for February 25 (four minutes), April 15 (six minutes), May 4 (three minutes), and June 2 (14 minutes).

439. McLaughlin: Swearing "a form of therapy." "White House Priest Defends Profanity," *Charlotte Observer*, May 9, 1974. McLaughlin characterized swearing as a "form of emotional drainage" that is "good, valid, and sound" for men under high pressure. Observing that the "essence of morality is charity," he asserted that Nixon had done more to create a climate of charity "than any leader of this century." In response to those who were chastising Nixon for his language, he noted that Christ had reserved his "most scorching condemnation" for those guilty of "moral arrogance." He also insisted that Nixon had "not only a lawful privilege but a moral obligation" to resist Judge John Sirica's subpoena of the White House tapes.

439. "I have known ... salty language." Charlotte *News*, May 1, 1974. "I just didn't know ... 'Excuse me, Billy.'" *Observer*, May 9, 1974.

439. "I don't approve" ... "not hold him guiltless." *Charlotte Observer*, May 9, 1974.

439. Nixon called "to say hello." In George Cornell, AP, in Sumter, South Carolina, *Daily Item*, quoted in Frady, *Parable*, p. 477. Frady places the call on the day the tapes were released, but the tapes became available to the press on May 1, and the call came on May 4 (Contact File, Master List by Name, Billy Graham, p. 1415, WHCF, NPM). Frady also indicates that a response by BG on May 2 came after the call, which is incorrect. Frady's account makes a better story, perhaps, but it does not fit the evidence.

439. "I never saw that side of him." Quoted in John Dart, *Los Angeles Times News* Service, *Charlotte Observer*, August 17, 1974.

439. Ruth: "the hardest thing." Quoted in Pollock, *Evangelist to the World*, p. 181.

440. "I'd had a real love ... somebody else." Frady, *Parable*, p. 478.

440. "had to confront his own ... collusion." In an "Open Letter to Billy Graham," delivered on his syndicated TV show, Paul Harvey observed that people must be writing to the evangelist, saying, "So this is the man to whom you were spiritual adviser." Harvey's comment: "It hurts, Billy, but you asked for it ... For God's sake—and I use the expression as you would—in the future stay out of politics!" Harvey, who claimed he had warned Graham against getting involved in politics, called Graham after the program, and indicated he had accepted the advice "cordially." Noting that "no mortal means more to me than Billy," the commentator allowed that he was not sure he had done the right thing and would ask forgiveness if he came to believe he had made a mistake by airing his criticism publicly. *Charlotte Observer*, May 26, 1974.

440. "I thought like Wesley ... hell." Quoted by Frady, *Parable*, p. 479.

440. BG's press release, May 29, 1974. Printed in the *New York Times*, May 29, 1974; NBC News, CN 74, VT 4-NBC, BGCA, etc.

440. RN calls BG on June 2, 1974. WH Master List, Contact File by Name, Graham, p. 1415, WHCF, NPM.

441. "This has been my own danger." Billy Graham, "Why Lausanne?" in *Let the Earth Hear His Voice*, ed. J. D. Douglas, official reference volume of the International Congress on World Evangelism (Minneapolis: World Wide Publications, 1975), p. 30. The applause was reported in interviews with both Leighton Ford, March 4, 1989, and Don Hoke, March 6, 1989.

441. "I tried to get to him" ... "I couldn't get anything." BG, interview, March 26, 1987. Also, *Charlotte Observer*, August 17, 1974.

441. "I shall always consider ... some privacy now." BG statement quoted in the *New York Times*, August 9, 1974.

441. BG approves pardon of Nixon. AP, in Palo Alto *Times*, September 9, 1974.

441. Nixon declines to visit with BG. *Charlotte Observer*, September 17 and 18, 1974. From the Washington Post/Los Angeles Times News Service.

441. Ruth hires plane. BG, interview, March 26, 1987.
441. BG and RN dine at San Clemente. David E. Kucharsky, "Graham's Powwow: Springtime in the Rockies," *Christianity Today*, April 11, 1975, pp. 38–39; NBC News, March 18, 1975, CN 74, VT 4-NBC, BGCA; Saginaw, Michigan, *Catholic Weekly*, April 4, 1975.
442. "a bit of Watergate in all of us." NBC News, June 14, 1974, CN 74, VT 4-NBC, BGCA.
442. "Satan was ... Nixon." Pollock, *Evangelist to the World*, p. 181.
442. Sleeping pills and demons. Frady, *Parable*, p. 487.
442. Nixon "didn't have nude women ..." AP, January 2, 1976.
442. "They've all" ... "made other mistakes." BG, interview, March 5, 1989.
442. "I see him very often ... different levels of friendship." Ibid.
443. "That's true with Nixon with everyone." Charles Colson, interview, April 18, 1989.
443. "Maybe I was naive" ... "Nixon not one of them." *Charlotte Observer*, January 2, 1975; AP, in *Charlotte Observer*, May 18, 1975. One clergyman who disagreed was Pat Robertson, who asserted that "the Watergate tapes showed Christians were the victims of a cruel hoax. We were led to believe that the man who appeared as a confidant of Billy Graham ... was in truth a man of personal piety. We can surmise that Dr. Billy Graham has been used for political image building." *Charlotte Observer*, August 17, 1974.
443. "Inside the Beltway ... higher calling." BG, interview, March 5, 1989.
443. Associates assess BG's post-Watergate view of Nixon. Interviews with Colson; interviews with Ford; interviews with Graham associate.

Chapter 27: Lausanne

447. The Great Commission. Mark 16:15–16. Some ancient manuscripts of the Gospel according to Mark do not include verses 9–20. A similar wording of the Great Commission is found in Matt. 28:19–20. The account of the Ascension in Luke 24:44–53 does not include the Commission.
447. "A Challenge from Evangelicals," *Time*, August 5, 1974, p. 48. Interestingly, the chief religion writer for *Time* was (and is) Richard Ostling, a former *CT* staffer. I am indebted to Leighton Ford for the idea of using this article as the lead for this chapter. Ford followed a similar strategy in his 1986 Fuller Lectures, *A Vision Pursued: The Lausanne Movement 1974–1986* (photocopy for private distribution). Ford's lectures and conversation have been quite valuable in providing an overview and perspective on the Lausanne movement, which he has served as a principal leader.
448. "honest to God." The key document in this movement was John A. T. Robinson's *Honest to God* (Philadelphia: Westminster Press, 1963).
448. Decline in United Presbyterian Church in the U.S.A., missionaries. J. D. Douglas, press release, CN 53, Box 1, Folder 7 (Lausanne Press Releases), BGCA.
448. Evangelical growth in Third World countries. "Challenge," *Time*, p. 50.
449. "I felt I should not go," Billy Graham, quoted in John Pollock, *Billy Graham: Evangelist to the World* (New York: Harper & Row, 1979), p. 189.
449. Preparations for Lausanne. Carl F. H. Henry, *Confessions of a Theologian: An Autobiography* (Waco, Tex.: Word Books, 1986), p. 349; Donald E. Hoke, interview, March 6, 1989; Leighton Ford, interview, March 4, 1989; Dain: "I cannot see anyone ..." quoted by Pollock, *Evangelist to the World*, p. 189.
450. Ford: "It would not have been possible without Billy." Interview.
450. "could have been ... chose not to be." Ford, *Vision*, p. 9.
450. BG's demands. Ibid.
450. "Lausanne ... is not it." Dain, quoted in press release, May 2,1974, CN 53 (International Congress on World Evangelization), Box 1, Folder 7 (Lausanne Press Releases), BGCA.
450. Quotas for invitees. Information Bulletin No. 1, January 1974, CN 53, Box 1, Folder 7, BGCA.

450. Fudging on invitation list. Pollock, *Evangelist to the World*, p. 195.
450. Expenses force cutback in participants. Pollock, *Evangelist to the World*, p. 198.
451. British invitees decline. Hoke, interview.
451. GDR delegates refused, Cuba delegates permitted. Pollock, *Evangelist to the World*, p. 204.
451. Preparation of papers. Two weeks to respond, Pollock, *Evangelist to the World*, p. 197; "paper received more than twelve hundred responses," Ford, *Vision*, p. 10 (All participants were required to respond to papers, but not to each paper); two hundred Haiti clergymen and "pick the brains," ICOWE News Release, CN 53, Box 1, Folder 7, BGCA. The official was Paul Little, who served as program director (Ford was chair of the Program Committee). Little, a most promising young Evangelical leader, died in a car accident in 1975.
451. "a great spiritual fission." Donald E. Hoke, "Lausanne May Be a Bomb," *Christianity Today*, March 15, 1974, pp. 12–14.
452. Hoke surrounded by Cubans. Hoke, interview.
452. Kivengere: "They are one." Quoted in Pollock, *Evangelist to the World*, p. 205.
453. Definitions of "peoples" and "unreached peoples." Ford, *Vision*, p. 55.
453. Handbooks. Published regularly by the Missions Advisory Research Committee (MARC), a division of World Vision. Also, David Barrett, ed., *World Christian Encyclopedia* (New York: Oxford University Press, 1982).
454. El, E2, E3. Ralph D. Winter, "The Highest Priority: Cross-Cultural Evangelism," in *Let the Earth Hear His Voice*, official reference volume of the International Congress on World Evangelism, ed. J. D. Douglas (Minneapolis: World Wide Publications, 1975), pp. 213–41.
454. Ford and Hoke assessments of El, E2, E3. Ford, *Vision*, p. 13; Hoke interview. Winter agreed that the Lausanne meeting gave great visibility to his and McGavran's ideas. Interview, February 6, 1991.
455. Cultural sensitivity. ICOWE News Release, CN 53, Box 1, Folder 7, BGCA; Winter, "Highest Priority," p. 224.
455. Rene Padilla's address, "Evangelism and the World," in *Let the Earth Hear His Voice*, ed. J. D. Douglas, world official reference volume of the International Congress on Evangelism (Minneapolis: World Wide Publications, 1975), pp. 125, 129, 131.
456. Samuel Escobar's address, "Evangelism and Man's Search for Freedom, Justice and Fulfillment," in Douglas, *Let the Earth*, pp. 304, 324, 326.
456. "Our witness must be" Billy Graham, quoted in Ford, *Vision*, p. 14.
456. Stott drafts covenant, Ford assesses. John R. W. Stott, interview, September 29, 1986; Ford, *Vision*, pp. 22–24.
457. The covenant on social responsibility. Paragraphs 4 and 5, "The Lausanne Covenant," in Douglas, *Let the Earth*, pp. 3–9. Copies of the covenant appear in the text or appendix of numerous Evangelical publications.
457. Ruth chose not to sign. The recollection is from Hoke, but Ruth Graham volunteered a confirming account in a personal conversation during which I was not taking notes. Fourteen years after the incident, it was clear the memory still rankled her.
458. "a covenant, not a creed." Ford, interview.
458. BG at the Stade-Lausanne. Pollock, *Evangelist to the World*, pp. 213–14.
458. Questionnaire reveals 86 percent of delegates want continuation. *World Evangelization Handbook* (Charlotte: Lausanne Committee for World Evangelization, 1985), p. 14.
458. "Third World people knew they had a voice." Hoke, interview.
459. "stick with reconciliation." Billy Graham, "Our Mandate from Lausanne '74" (from address to the Mexico City meeting), *Christianity Today*, July 4, 1975, pp. 3–6.
459. "As he began ... trust and purpose." Robert E. Coleman of Asbury Seminary, quoted in Pollock, *Evangelist to the World*, p. 250.
460. Another, younger committee member. Rames Atallah, quoted in ibid., p. 251.

460. Compromise guideline. Quoted in Ford, *Vision*, p. 33.
460. Mexico City meeting. Hoke, interview; Pollock, *Evangelist to the World*, pp. 294–53; ICOWE Press Release; "Longevity for Lausanne," *Christianity Today*, February 14, 1975, pp. 58–59; "Continuing Lausanne: Regional Outreach," *Christianity Today*, February 13, 1976, p. 67.
460. Follow-up meetings. Hoke, interview; "Lausanne: Continuing the Action," *Christianity Today*, September 29, 1976, pp. 47–48; "Future in Focus," *Christianity Today*, November 5, 1976, pp. 62–63; Leighton Ford, "Update Lausanne," *Christianity Today*, December 9, 1977, pp. 344–81; Ford, *Vision*, pp. 30–31.
461. Asian meetings. Hoke, interview; Thomas Wang, interview, July 18, 1986; The Reverend A. Jack Dain, interview and oral history, CN 141, Box 3, Folder 12, BGCA. Leighton Ford continued as chairman of the committee.
461. Lausanne Covenant "the broadest umbrella." Hoke, interview; *International Bulletin of Mission Research*, October 1984.
462. Franklin's conversion. "Young Graham's Path Is All His Own," *Houston Chronicle*, March 5, 1988; Patricia Daniels Cornwell, *A Time for Remembering: The Ruth Bell Graham Story* (San Francisco: Harper & Row, 1983), p. 215; "Franklin Graham Enters Ministry," Mesa, Arizona, *Tribune*, January 11, 1982; UPI, January 11, 1982. "Graham's son to enter ministry," *The Dallas Morning News*, January 2, 1982.
462. "a free trip from the ends of the world." Recalled by Carl F. H. Henry, interview, February 19, 1987. Billy Melvin, executive director of the National Association of Evangelicals, also discounted the lasting significance of the Lausanne movement. Inter view, December 7, 1989.
462. "Gottfried was a wonderful front man." Hoke, interview. Osei-Mensah stepped down from his position in 1984. He was replaced by Carl J. Johansson, a pastor and missionary of the Lutheran Church of America. *Christianity Today*, October 19, 1984, p. 57.
462. "Leighton operates like Billy." Hoke, interview.
462. "I was asked ... Billy himself." Ford, interview.
463. BG acknowledges criticisms of Lausanne. Billy Graham, interview.
463. BG threatens to withdraw as honorary chairman of Lausanne II. Reported and confirmed by witnesses to a heated meeting at the International Congress of Itinerant Evangelists, a BGEA-sponsored gathering held in Amsterdam in 1986. Other information from Jim Newton, interview, July 17, 1986.
463. "Many a conference ... refuses to die down." John R. W. Stott, quoted in Ford, *Vision*, p. 25.
463. Nilson Fanini: "I saw it!" Interview, July 18, 1986.

Chapter 28: Higher Ground

464. Archbishop of Canterbury talks too long. Henry Holley, interview, November 25, 1987. The Evangelical president of Brazil was Ernesto Geisel.
465. Ruth's accident. Grady Wilson, interview, May 1, 1987; Patricia Daniels Cornwell, *A Time for Remembering: The Ruth Bell Graham Story* (San Francisco: Harper & Row, 1983), pp. 216–18; AP, in Charlotte *News*, October 3, 1974; Billy Graham, interviews and conversation.
466. "She didn't even want the degree." Billy Graham, interview, February 27, 1987.
467. Taipei and Hong Kong crusades. "Harvest Time on Taiwan," *Christianity Today*, November 21,1975, pp. 51–52; "Happiness in Hong Kong," *Christianity Today*, December 5, 1975, p. 51; Charlotte *News*, April 11, 1975; Henry Holley, oral history, January 9, 1976, CN 141, Box 4, Folder 29, BGCA.
467. Ferdinand Marcos statement. Quoted in John Pollock, *Billy Graham: Evangelist to the World* (New York: Harper & Row, 1979), p. 293.

467. Imelda Marcos statement. Quoted in Lindsell, "BG's Mission to Manila," *Christianity Today*, December 30, 1977, pp. 36–37.
467. Opposition in Oslo. Edward Plowman, "The Scandinavians: No Neutrality on Graham," *Christianity Today*, October 20, 1978, pp. 52–53; UPI, September 25, 1978.
468. Opposition to BG in Sweden. Plowman, "No Neutrality"; *Charlotte Observer*, October 5, 1978; Billy Graham, interview, March 26, 1987.
468. Singapore crusade. Lawson Lau, "Crusade Boosts Gospel Ground Swell," *Christianity Today*, January 19, 1979, pp. 43–44; The Reverend Alfred C. H. Yeo, Singapore clergyman, interview, July 18, 1986.
468. Australia crusade. Alan Nichols, "Graham Crusade Lifts Down-under Church," *Christianity Today*, June 29, 1979, p. 48; *Charlotte Observer*, June 10, 1979.
468. Japan crusade. Interviews with Robert Williams, June 6 and 10, 1986; Kenneth McVety, July 18, 1986; Holley, November 25, 1987; Mark Komake, "The Billy Graham Japan Crusades: Large Crowds in Spiritual Void," *Christianity Today*, November 21, 1980, pp. 44–46.
468. Mexico City crusade. Bill Conrad, "Graham in Mexico: A Protestant Impact in Spite of Obstructionism," *Christianity Today*, April 10, 1981, pp. 52–53.
468. Asheville crusade. Arthur H. Matthews, "Honoring a Homegrown Prophet," *Christianity Today*, April 15, 1977, pp. 55–56.
468. Crusade at University of Notre Dame "significant." Arthur H. Matthews, "Graham Scores at Notre Dame," *Christianity Today*, June 3, 1977, pp. 30–31; Robert Ferm, interview, March 28, 1987.
469. BG on differences between Evangelicals and Catholics. Billy Graham, interview, February 26, 1987; Graham's statements at Mayor's Prayer Breakfast, Washington, D.C., April 30, 1986; *Legends*, CNN. Graham would meet with the pope personally at the Vatican in 1981. Edward Plowman "The Evangelist and the Pope Confer Privately in Rome," *Christianity Today*, February 6, 1981, p. 88.
469. "Catholics are Christians." T. W. Wilson, interview, February 27, 1987.
469. BG's prayer for Ford. "Prayer for a President," *Ladies' Home Journal*, December 1974, p. 68.
469. "a million miles away from politics." "Graham Sides with Mrs. Ford on Issue of Premarital Sex," *Wisconsin State Journal* (Madison), March 13, 1976.
469. BG rift with Bill Bright. "Politics from the Pulpit," *Newsweek*, September 6, 1976, pp. 49–50; "Evangelist Billy Graham," *Houston Chronicle*, September 18, 1976; Edgar R. Cooper, "Graham Bows Back," *The Baptist Message* (Alexandria, Louisiana), October 14, 1976.
470. "so that arrangements ... visit." Letter, Gerald Ford to BG, January 29, 1976, WH Master List, Contact File by Name, Billy Graham, Gerald Ford Library.
470. "keep your eyes open." Memo, Jerry H. Jones to Bill Nicholson, April 20, 1976, CN 74, Box 1, Folder 12, BGCA.
470. Ford congratulates Highland Park Presbyterian Church, April 22, 1976. CN 74, Box 1, Folder 12, BGCA.
470. BG and Ruth invited to state dinner for Queen Elizabeth. Billy Graham, interview, May 5, 1989.
470. BG declines Ford request to speak at crusade. BG to Gerald Ford, September 10, 1976, CN 74 (Ephemera of William Franklin Graham), Box 1, Folder 12, BGCA.
471. Carter chairs Graham crusades. "Billy Graham Prophesy on Carter True," Rochester, Minnesota, *Post Bulletin*, July 15, 1976; "Carter Will Restore Confidence, Graham Says," *Miami Herald*, December 26, 1976; Billy Graham, interview, March 6, 1989.
471. "I would rather ... religious profession." Russ Chandler, "Graham: Undecided," *Christianity Today*, September 10, 1976. Chandler is a *Los Angeles Times* religion writer.
471. Jimmy Carter responds to BG statement. UPI, September 29, 1976.

471. Jeff Carter criticizes BG. AP, October 7, 1976.
471. Carter "a leader we can follow" ... "rootin' and tootin' for him." UPI, November 3, 1976.
471. BG missed 1977 inauguration. AP, January 6, 1977.
471. Lincoln's bed has hump, Carter "doesn't inspire love." Billy Graham, interview, February 27, 1987.
472. Carter "hardest-working." *Legends*, CNN, 1986.
473. "That letter.... is telling the truth." Edward Plowman, interview February 10, 1987.
473. "respectability comes high." Ibid.
473. BGEA begins pension fund. Carloss Morris, interview, May 5, 1987; T. W. Wilson, interview, February 26, 1987.
474. BGEA "field reps." Billy Graham, interview, February 26, 1987; Ken Taylor, interview, July 19, 1986.
474. Problems with BGEA annuities. UPI, September 28, 1977; Jim Fuller and Lori Sturdevant, "State Rejects Graham's Application," Minneapolis *Tribune*, October 9, 1977; Youngstown, Ohio, *Vindicator*, October 9, 1977; AP, October 10, 1977; "Billy's Bucks," *Time*, July 10, 1978, p. 70.
475. WECEF controversy. *Charlotte Observer*, June 16 and 26, 1977; July 7, 23, and 24, 1977; August 12, 1977; and September 25, 1977; Charlotte *News*, June 12, 1977; Mary Bishop, *Billy Graham, the Man and His Ministry* (New York: Grosset & Dunlap, 1978), pp. 49–51; "Honoring a Homegrown Prophet," *Christianity Today*, April 15, 1977, pp. 55–56; "Graham and the Press: New Look at Ledgers," *Christianity Today*, July 29, 1977, pp. 36–37; "Graham: The News Can Be Misleading," *Christianity Today*, August 18, 1978, p. 35; "Billy Graham on Financing Evangelism," *Christianity Today*, August 26, 1977, pp. 18–20; "On Billy Graham and the WECEF," and "Billy Graham: Issues and Answers," *Christianity Today*, October 21, 1977; Press release, quoted in Bishop, *Man and His Ministry*, p. 51; Art Toalston, "Kindling Fires Along the Ohio," *Christianity Today*, November 18, 1977, pp. 47–49; "Graham's Beliefs: Still Intact," *Christianity Today*, January 13, 1978, pp. 49–50; "Graham: A Deficit," *Christianity Today*, July 21, 1978, p. 44. Lester Kinsolving, "Billy Graham Conceals Assets," Ann Arbor *News*, July 9, 1977; Youngstown *Vindicator*, October 9, 1977; Charlotte *Weekly West*, September 21, 1977; Frank Coley, "Graham's Fund. He Isn't the One Covering Up," Charlotte *Weekly Star*, September 14, 1977. Wes Michaelson, "Financing the Billy Graham Organization," *Sojourners*, September 1977, pp. 7–8; "Graham Funding [of *CT*] Not Reported," ibid., p. 9; Interviews: Billy Graham, March 26, 1987; George Wilson; Peter Geiger, telephone conversation, fall 1989.
480. BG: "It is common ... [dishonesty]." Billy Graham, *Approaching Hoofbeats: The Four Horsemen of the Apocalypse* (Waco, Tex.: Word Books, 1983), p. 110.
480. BG: "be wary." Billy Graham, "An Agenda," *Christianity Today*, January 4, 1980, p. 25.
481. "In my early days ... like that now." Religious News Service, January 31, 1980. Quoted in Edgar Bundy, *Billy Graham: Performer, Politician, Preacher, Prophet?* (Miami Shores, Fla.: Edgar Bundy Ministries, 1982), p. 138.
481. "no longer associated ... American Nationalism." J. D. Douglas, "Ramsey-Graham Cambridge Bout Is Gloves-on Affair," *Christianity Today*, February 6, 1981, pp. 88–89.
481. "We as clergy" ... "non-religious issues." San Francisco *Examiner & Chronicle*, February 15, 1981; Chicago *Sun-Times*, January 29, 1981, quoting an article about to be published in *Parade* magazine, apparently on Sunday, January 31, 1981.
481. BG meets Reagan. Billy Graham, interview, March 26, 1987.
481. Reagan's interest in prophecy. Billy Graham interview, March 6, 1987.
482. "TV networks suggested ..." ABC, CBS, NBC, network news. May 4 and 6, 1980. CN 74, VT 13, BGCA. The Texas primary was held on May 3.
482. "I refused ... everybody knew how I stood." Billy Graham, interview, February 26, 1987.

482. Reagan "laughing ... brilliant man" and "like Ike." AP, July 18, 1981. "old days in Hollywood." Billy Graham, interview, February 21, 1986.
482. BG prays with Nancy Reagan and John Hinckley's father. San Antonio *Star* (Sunday magazine), April 26, 1981.
482. BG lobbied senators re AWAC sale. Rowland Evans and Robert Novak column, November 2, 1981; see also "Graham Calls for Nixon's Return in Foreign Affairs," *Dallas Morning News*, November 10, 1981.

Chapter 29: A Crack in the Curtain

483. BG as "Communism's Public Enemy Number One." See, for example, William H. Stonement, Daily News Foreign Service, in *Chicago Daily News*, June 11, 1955, in CN 74, Box 1, File 12, BGCA.
483. "He knelt in Red Square." Billy Graham, "Impressions of Moscow," *Christianity Today*, July 20, 1959, pp. 14–16.
484. Haraszti's near-total recall. Haraszti is a meticulous record keeper, taking extensive notes of events, conversations, and observations in dozens of small black notebooks. Before my first interview with him, I was informed of his prodigious memory. I was astonished by his ability to recall precise dates, the spelling of difficult names, and long sections of conversations, some of which had occurred fifteen years in the past. I was even more astonished to read oral histories taped from two to seven years in the past, and to find that his accounts of the conversations on those occasions were virtually identical with the accounts he had given to me.
484. Haraszti (AH) translates *Peace With God*. Alexander S. Haraszti (AH), interview, July 16, 1986, and oral history, May 21, 1979, CN 141, Box 45, Folder 1, BGCA.
485. "established religious bodies received financial support." The established churches had received this support since signing a concordat in 1948. AH, oral history, May 21, 1979, CN 141, Box 45, Folder 1, BGCA.
486. Unless otherwise noted, information on BG's first steps toward a visit to Hungary was furnished in interviews with Haraszti.
486. Palotay. AH, oral history, May 21, 1979. Sandor Palotay died in August 1979.
493. The Grand Hotel. The Graham team suspected that the Grand was chosen less for its ambience than for its isolation and consequent ease of observation; anyone going from or coming to it would be conspicuous. Of an apparent piece with this rationale was the insistence by the Hungarian hosts that members of the team room in pairs, an arrangement that would foster conversation that could be monitored. When members of the TV crew resisted this arrangement and announced their intention to find their own accommodations, Palotay assured them that if they did so, they would be put on a plane bound for home the next day. Conversation, John Akers, February 14, 1991.
494. BG "open heart ... Word of God." AP, September 5, 1977; CBS News, September 4, 1977, CN 74, VT 2-CBS, BGCA.
494. BG at Pecs. Denton Lotz, interview, April 30, 1986; AH, oral history, May 21, 1979.
494. BG receives lightbulb. AH, introduction to oral history, ibid.
494. Closing service at Tahi youth camp. AH, oral history, December 26, 1979, CN 141, Box 45, Folder 2, BGCA.
495. "things are more open ... in Hungary." UPI, September 6, 1977, quoted in Malachi Martin, "The Truth and Billy Graham," *National Review*, January 9, 1978, p. 722.
495. "I have not joined Communist party." AP, September 10, 1977; Bob Terrell, "Reflections on Hungary, Asheville *Citizen*, September 22, 1977.
495. "For friends ... once." AH, interview; also, oral history introduction.
495. Hungary regains crown and most-favored-nation status. AH, oral history, December 26, 1979. BG, interview, March 6, 1989.

496. "second only to the Pope." AH, oral history, December 26, 1979.
497. "Sie *sind schlau.*" Ibid.
498. Priest: "Can't you see my collar?" Denton Lotz and AH, interviews.
498. BG in Poznań. AP, Chicago *Sun-Times*, October 10, 1978.
498. three hundred priests and nuns raise hands. Lotz, interview.
498. BG at Auschwitz. Edward Plowman, "Billy Graham in Poland," pp. 54, 57; Lotz, interview.
498. Bednorz asks for autograph. Ibid., p. 57.

Chapter 30: The Preacher and the Bear

499. BG receives degrees, visits pope. AP, January 5, 6, 9, 23, 1981; Edward Plowman, "The Evangelist and the Pope Confer Privately in Rome," *Christianity Today*, February 6, 1981, p. 88.
500. "Alex knows things which Henry [Kissinger] does not." AH, interview, July 16, 1986, and oral history, December 26, 1979, CN 141, Box 45, Folder 2, BGCA.
500. BG meets with Dobrynin. AH, oral history, December 26, 1979.
502. Orthodox Church invites BG to conference. AH, oral history, June 16, 1982, and June 3, 1983, CN 141, Box 45, Folders 3–5, BGCA.
503. Haraszti meets with Filaret. AH, oral history, March 15, 1984, CN 141, Box 45, Folder 6, BGCA.
504. Negotiations about the Siberian Six. AH, interview; oral history, June 16, 1982, CN 141, Box 45, Folders 3–4, BGCA; Edward Plowman, "How the Press Got It Wrong in Moscow," *Christian Century*, June 23–30, 1982, p. 718.
505. Haraszti delivers invitation. AH, oral history, June 30, 1982, CN 141, Box 45, Folders 3–4, BGCA.
506. Haraszti persuades BG to accept invitation. AH, oral history, June 30, 1982.
506. Bush tells BG he is neutral. BG, interview, March 6, 1989.
507. Reagan privately approves of BG visit. Ibid.
507. White House official: "You have to go." Stephen L. Nordlinger, *Baltimore Sun*, May 17, 1982.
507. State Department opposition to visit. AH, oral history, March 14, 1984, CN 141, Box 45, Folder 6, BGCA.
508. "as early as 1963." Robert Ferm to Ruby Escue, October 28, 1963, explaining Graham's position. Ferm also indicated that Graham believed the UN was "the best possible hope that man has, but that, too, is an endorsement but with many qualifications." CN 19 (Ferm Papers), Box 4, Folder 28 (12/62–6/63), BGCA.
508. "he saw commitment ... was serious." Denton Lotz, interview, May 1, 1986. Lotz, a Baptist World Alliance executive who accompanied Graham on several forays behind the iron curtain, is the brother of Danny Lotz, husband of Graham's daughter, Anne.
508. BG shifts views on nuclear arms. CBS Evening News, March 29, 1979, CN 74, VT 2-CBS; Colman McCarthy, Charlotte *News*, June 29, 1979.
508. "I have seen ... race." Billy Graham (interview), "A Change of Heart," *Sojourners*, August 1979, reprinted in advertisement, *Yale Daily News*, April 16, 1982.
508. SALT 10. Billy Graham, *Approaching Hoofbeats: The Four Horsemen of the Apocalypse* (Waco, Tex.: Word Books, 1983), p. 146.
508. "Have we gone mad?" *Charlotte Observer*, June 10, 1979, and August 30, 1981.
509. Nixon: "take the long view." Harold L. Myra et al., "William Franklin Graham: Seventy Exceptional Years," *Christianity Today*, November 18, 1988, p. 18.
509. "These verses have been the key." Interview, March 6, 1989. In a 1988 interview with *Christianity Today*, he downplayed the importance of his views on nuclear disarmament. "We went with the understanding that we'd be invited back," he said. "The Russians kept their word, and we were invited back. Our purpose in going had nothing to do with political or

even peace problems—it was just the chance to preach the gospel." Myra et al., "Seventy Exceptional Years," *Christianity Today*, p. 19. Motives are some times complex.

510. "He has used his prestige . . ." "A few Kind Words for Billy Graham," *Christian Century*, May 26, 1982, p. 619.

510. BG preaches peace. *Charlotte Observer*, April 21, and May 9, 1982; *Yale Daily News*, April 16, 20, 21, 1982; Robert M. Randolph, associate dean of students, MIT, conversation, December 5, 1988; CBS Evening News, April 12 and 15, 1982, CN 74, VT 13, BGCA; Tom Minnery, "Stirring the Coals in New England," *Christianity Today*, May 21, 1982, pp. 28–29; Harry Genet, "Graham Will Preach in Moscow," *Christianity Today*, April 9, 1982, p. 44.

510. Templeton Prize. UPI, March 19, 1982; AP, May 15, 1982.

512. BG and Arbatov. AH, interview; oral history, March 15, 1984.

513. Admission by ticket. AH, oral history, March 15,1984; Reinhold Kerstan (Baptist World Alliance official), interview, May 2, 1986; ABC, NBC, CBS News, CN 74, VT 13, May 9, 1982; AP, *Charlotte Observer*, May 11, 1982.

513. Size of crowd. AH, oral history, March 15, 1984; *Christianity Today*, June 18, 1982, p. 42.

513. "I've been trying to reach [KGB] for a long time." Tom Minnery, "Graham in the Soviet Union," *Christianity Today*, May 21, 1982, p. 52; AH oral history, March 15, 1984.

513. Graham's sermon at Moscow church. "Billy Renders unto Caesar," *Newsweek*, May 24, 1982, pp. 89–90; Plowman, "Press Got It Wrong," p. 718.

513. "A great event," *Christianity Today*, June 18, 1982, p. 42.

513. "We detain people." John F. Burns, "Graham Offers Positive View of Religion in Soviet," the *New York Times*, May 13, 1982; "Billy Renders unto Caesar," *Newsweek*, p. 89; also, Mobile *Press Register*, May 16, 1982.

514. Soviet Christians criticize BG. Jim Gallagher, "Graham in Moscow, Preaches Obedience," *Chicago Tribune*, May 10, 1982; "Billy Renders unto Caesar," *Newsweek*, p. 89.

514. BG speaks to authorities about 147 prisoners. Minnery, "Graham in the Soviet Union," p. 56; audio tape, New York Press Conference, May 19, 1982, furnished by BGEA.

514. BG at Orthodox cathedral. "Billy Renders Unto Caesar," pp. 89–90; "Billy Renders unto Caesar," p. 53; J. Martin Bailey, "The Media Missed the Story," *Christianity and Crisis*, June 7, 1982, pp. 155, 172; AH, oral history, March 15, 1984. Some sources reported that Pimen introduced Graham, but Haraszti says it was Borovoy. Given Haraszti's acquaintance with both men, and Pimen's concern for status, it is likely that Haraszti's account is correct.

514. "A made-up meeting." AH, oral history, March 15, 1984; other quotes are from AH, oral history, June 30, 1982, CN 141, Box 45, Folders 3–5. Interestingly, AH reported that Graham preached for only twenty minutes. Oral history, March 15, 1984. All others' accounts, including those by eyewitnesses, placed the time at closer to an hour. "Billy Renders unto Caesar," pp. 89–90; Edward Plowman, interview, February 10, 1987.

515. Pimen's introductory statement, "Billy Renders unto Caesar," *Newsweek*, p. 90; "Inside Washington," *Human Events*, May 22, 1982, p. 5.

515. Graham's address. *Charlotte Observer*, May 12, 1982. This material is not found in the text of Graham's speech, "Graham's Mission to Moscow," *Christianity Today*, June 18, 1982, pp. 20–23.

516. Graham urges religious freedom and SALT 10. Graham, "Graham's Mission to Moscow," p. 23. The citation from the universal declaration is from Section VII of the Final Act of Helsinki.

516. Enthusiastic response to speech. AH, oral history, June 3, 1983, CN 141, Box 45, Folders 3–5, BGCA.

517. Reporters press BG re Pentecostals. AH, oral history, ibid. For reasons not entirely clear, Haraszti emphasized that publicity about the visit was kept down at the request of the Orthodox leaders. The government's only request was that Graham not visit the Pentecostals

at all. The letter from the Pentecostals had been sent to Graham in the United States but had arrived after Graham left Montreat. Jack Anderson, "Graham Asked to Cancel Moscow Trip," syndicated column, June 6, 1982.

517. AH advises BG re Pentecostals. AH, interview, July 16, 1986, and oral history, March 15, 1984. In the oral history, Haraszti sets the figure at 600 million people. This appears to be due to his having made a simple error. After giving the population of the USSR as 264 million (approximately correct), he used 464 as the base figure to which he added the population of the satellite countries. In his interview with me, he spoke of 400 million, which is the closer approximation.
518. BG visits Pentecostals. AH, ibid.
518. Ps. 37. The quotation from Ps. 37 is from Haraszti's memory and apparently not an exact rendering of any standard English version of the Bible.
519. Pentecostals disappointed. ABC, CBS, NBC, TV News, May 11, 1982, CN 74 VT 13, BGCA.
519. BG "nothing special." *Charlotte Observer*, May 12, 1982; "Billy Renders unto Caesar," *Newsweek*, p. 90.
520. BG role in release of Pentecostals. AH interview, and oral history, March 15, 1984; Graham, interview; John Akers, interview, March 6, 1989. For accounts of the emigration of the Pentecostals, see the *New York Times*, June 28, 29, and July 19, 1983.

Chapter 31: Tribulation and Triumph

522. BG statements on religious freedom in USSR. Edward Plowman, "Billy Graham: The Gospel Truth in Moscow," *Saturday Evening Post*, September 1982, p. 112; Plowman, interview, February 10, 1987; also, "Graham Says U.S. Wavered on Moscow Trip," *Baltimore Sun*, May 17, 1982; "Graham Offers Positive View of Life in Soviet, the *New York Times*, May 13, 1982, and "For Moscow's Guests, Life in a Luxurious Cocoon," the *New York Times*, May 15, 1982; *Charlotte Observer*, May 16, 1982; "Questionable Mission to Moscow," *Time*, May 24, 1982, p. 60; Tom Minnery, "Graham in the Soviet Union" *Christianity Today*, June 18, 1982, pp. 52, 56; ABC, CBS, NBC News, CN 74, VT 13, May 12, 1982, BGCA. Of the caviar, Graham later told reporters, "There is a lot of caviar in the Soviet Union and very little in the United States. It was available in Moscow and I wasn't going to let it sit there." AP, May 18, 1982.
523. Reaction to BG statements. Editorial, *Christianity Today*, June 18, 1982; see also George F. Will, "Listening to America's Most Embarrassing Export," column, May 13, 1982, *Charlotte Observer.*
524. "heaven only knows." The *New York Times*, May 16, 1982.
524. Wheaton students: "Billy Graham has been duped." AP, May 17, 1982.
524. "Then keep out of the discussion." *This Week with David Brinkley*, ABC TV, May 16, 1982, CN 74, VT 12, BGCA.
524. BG met "top Soviet officials." Minnery, "Graham in the Soviet Union," p. 56.
525. BG defends self. "Graham in Moscow: What Did He Really Say?" *Christianity Today*, June 18, 1982, p. 12; UPI, *Charlotte Observer*, May 17, 1982; Minnery, "Graham in the Soviet Union," June 18, 1982, pp. 52, 56; *Charlotte Observer*, May 23, 1982; CBS News, May 19, 1982, CN 74, VT 12, BGCA; AP, May 20, 1982; "Billy, Are You Blind?" *Los Angeles Times*, June 5, 1982.
525. BGEA press release. Crusade Information Service, May 19, 1982, quoted in Kent Hill, *The Puzzle of the Soviet Church* (Portland, Ore.: Multnomah Press, 1989), p. 196.
525. Soviets admit decline in churches. Hill, *Puzzle*, p. 196, quoting an interview with Council for Religious Affairs chairman Konstantin Kharchev, *Science and Religion* (November 1987): 23.

525. Radio Moscow broadcast quotes BG. "Vantage Point," Radio Moscow, August 4, 1982. Quoted in Hill, *Puzzle*, pp. 196–97.
525. JDL gang ransacks WCC offices, Dan Rather asserts BG was "deceived and used." CBS News, May 19, 1982, CN 74, VT 12, BGCA.
526. "best informed commentator ... persecuted." Letter, Michael Bordeaux to *Christianity Today*, September 3, 1982, p. 8, quoted in Hill, *Puzzle*, p. 197.
526. Moyer's assessment. CBS News, May 17, 1982. CN 74, VT 13, BGCA.
526. "It's my calling." "Graham Backs Moscow Visit as 'My Calling.'" Chicago *Sun Times*, May 17, 1982; Graham also mentioned the appearance of opportunism in an AP story, May 17, 1982.
526. BG has "feeling of serenity." Minnery, "Graham in the Soviet Union," p. 57.
526. GDR and Romania did not approve Hungary visit. AH, oral history, December 26, 1979, CN 141, Box 45, Folder 2, BGCA.
527. "When I walked in ... just smiling." BG, interview, February 26, 1987.
527. BG meets with GDR officials. "Hopeful Signs for the Church in East Germany," *Christianity Today*, December 17, 1982, pp. 40–43; BG, interview, February 26, 1987; Edward Plowman, interview, February 10, 1987.
528. Czechoslovakia visit. AH, interview, July 16, 1986.
528. Czechs warm to BG. "Billy Graham Gets a Friendly Reception in Czechoslovakia," *Christianity Today*, December 17, 1982, pp. 38–40; Reinhold Kerstan, interview, May 2, 1986.
528. Soviet church leaders angry with Graham. AH, oral history, March 15, 1984, CN 141, Box 45, Folder 6, BGCA.
529. BG in USSR, 1984. Bob Terrell, *Billy Graham in the Soviet Union* (Minneapolis: Billy Graham Evangelistic Association, 1985), pp. 21–30. "Billy Graham's Mission Improbable," *Time*, September 24, 1984, p. 48.
530. BG at Tallinn. Terrell, *Graham in the Soviet Union*, pp. 35–36.
530. BG at Novosibirsk. Ibid., pp. 47–48, 52; Beth Spring, "Billy Graham Sees Vitality and Dedication Among Russian Christians," *Christianity Today*, October 19, 1984, pp. 38–39; AH, oral history, June 16, 1982, CN 141, Box 45, Folders 3–4.
531. Ponomarev visit. BG, interview, March 6, 1989; unpublished document, statement of Billy Graham to His Excellency Boris N. Ponomarev, September 20, 1984. I am grateful to Mr. Graham for sharing this document with me. Graham said that with the exception of Ronald Reagan and Rabbi Marc Tanenbaum, he had shown the document to no one else outside his immediate circle of advisers.
531. Nine BG books in print in USSR. AP, September 28, 1984.
533. Romania tour. Edward Plowman, "Fanning the Flames of Revival in Romania," *Christianity Today*, November 8, 1985, pp. 59–61; Plowman, interview; AH, interview, July 16, 1986; AH report at Columbia crusade, May 1, 1987; Russ Busby, interview, April 30, 1987; BG, press conference, National Press Club, April 26, 1986.
533. BG lauds corrupt Romanian government. Janice Broun and Grazykna Sikorska, *Conscience and Captivity: Religion in Eastern Europe* (Washington: Ethics and Public Policy Center, 1988), p. 231.
534. Government gouges host churches. Ibid., pp. 347–349, quoting a *samizdat* document produced by a Romanian Baptist and furnished by the Keston News Service, no. 245, June 1986.
534. 1985 Hungary visit. Edward Plowman, "Relations Improve Between Church and State in Hungary," *Christianity Today*, November 22, 1985, pp. 64–66; Plowman, interview; AH, interview; Russ Busby, interview.
534. Cardinal calls BG an actor. AH, interview.
535. "People ask us ... many Westerners think." Walter Smyth interview, June 11, 1986.
535. BG assumes surveillance. BG, interview, March 6, 1989.

535. Soviet official: "I raised my hand." Plowman, interview.
536. BG gives credibility to small churches. AH, interview.
536. "We bring new images." Ibid.
537. Permission to print BG books. John Akers, interview, March 6, 1989.
537. "a magnificent goodwill ambassador." AH, interview.
537. BG expects Baker's support. BG, interview, March 6, 1989.
537. BG on Gorbachev's spirituality. Interview, CBS *Morning News*, December 25, 1987. Transcript.

Chapter 32: Amsterdam

539. "would have been in Book of Acts." Quoted in Dave Foster, *Billy Graham: A Vision Imparted. A Pictorial Report on the International Conference for Itinerant Evangelists* (Minneapolis: World Wide Publications, 1984), p. 23.
539. "According to Walter Smyth...." Foster, *A Vision Imparted*, p. 6 "to reach the little guy." BG, interview, February 27, 1987.
540. Burklin: "no idea as to how many ..." Werner Burlkin, interview, June 6, 1986.
540. Why Amsterdam was selected. Foster, *A Vision Imparted*, p. 17.
540. "poignant and comic moments." From Tom Minnery, "How to Be an Evangelist," *Christianity Today*, September 2, 1983, p. 44; Foster, *A Vision Imparted*, pp. 21–22.
541. Wives meeting. Foster, *A Vision Imparted*, pp. 62–63; Foster, "Billy Graham on What He Does Best," *Christianity Today*, September 2, 1983, pp. 28–31.
541. Processing applications for Amsterdam '86. Bob Williams, interview, June 9, 1986; application evaluation guidelines, ICIE 1986, furnished by Williams.
541. Distribution of invitees. "Summons to the 'Unknowns,'" *Time*, July 28, 1986, p. 69.
543. PRC representatives. Burklin, interview.
543. Evangelists operate book scams. T. W. Wilson confirmed that this had happened. Interview, February 26, 1987. I received several such requests from individuals whom I had noted hanging around the conference bookstore and telling Westerners of their needs.
544. Five hundred women participants. "Summons to the 'Unknowns,'" p. 69.
544. "It's already paid for." Bob Evans, interview, July 9, 1986. Graham acknowledged that this had happened. Several other team members told the same story, not always with a sense that their leader had acted prudently.
545. "might have been better spent." A. Jack Dain, interview, July 14, 1986.
545. Sri Lankan evangelist crosses war zone. Dave Foster, *Amsterdam 86* (Minneapolis: Billy Graham Evangelistic Association, 1987), p. 25.
545. "They will kill us." Foster, *Amsterdam 86*, p. 21.
545. "I felt like a worm." BG, ICIE press conference, July 18, 1986.
545. "we are all one in Christ." Burklin, interview.
545. "This place is like heaven!" Foster, *Amsterdam 86*, p. 83.
546. Cultural adaptation of program. John Corts, interview, June 9, 1986.
547. BG resists speaking. Ibid.; Walter Smyth, interview, June 11, 1986.
548. Ruth on problem children. Foster, *Amsterdam 86*, p. 61.
548. John Corts on Day of Witness. Interview.
548. Day of Witness. Personal observation; statistics from Foster, *Amsterdam 86*, pp. 83–66. McIntire. Luncheon conversation with McIntire and Bundy, July 18, 1986.
550. Corts's 1990 report on mini-Amsterdams. Letter, Corts to author, February 6, 1990.

Chapter 33: The Constituted Means

551. BG checked off remaining states. Graham has not actually held a crusade in Delaware, but his campaigns in Philadelphia and New York, and a New Jersey crusade scheduled for September 1991—his first in that state—have involved churches in Delaware.

552. "Yes, we have a plan ... don't change." Sterling Huston, interview, May 2, 1987.
552. "This is the game plan." David Bruce, interview, July 24, 1987.
552. "dog-and-pony show." Kenneth Chafin, oral history, 1981, CN 141, Box 11, Folder 8. Chafin was dean of the Billy Graham School of Evangelism from 1968 to 1983.
553. "When you have a thirty-year track record." John Bisagno, oral history, November 13, 1981, CN 141, Box 13, Folder 2, BGCA.
553. Ambassador Rodgers's only assignments pertained to BG. The Honorable Joe M. Rodgers, U.S. ambassador to France, interview, September 21, 1986.
553. Crusade security. Tex Reardon, interview, April 29, 1986.
553. Ruth Graham: "Nothing can touch a child of God." Mary Bishop, *Billy Graham, the Man and His Ministry* (New York: Grosset & Dunlap, 1978), p. 16.
554. "If they really want you." T. W. Wilson, Interview, February 27, 1987.
554. Akers on inclusion of blacks. John Akers, interview, February 25, 1987.
555. Jones and Bell observations on efforts to include blacks. Howard Jones and Ralph Bell, interviews, May 1, 1987.
555. Bisagno on crusade services. John Bisagno, oral history, 1981, CN 141, Box 13, Folder 2, BGCA.
555. Crusade music. Gavin Reid, interview, April 30, 1987, and *To Reach a Nation* (London: Hodder and Stoughton, 1987), pp. 78–80; John Innes, interview, May 1, 1987.
556. Hulk Hogan meets BG. Denver crusade, press release 87-8, BGEA Crusade Information Service.
557. BG blesses reporters who curse him. Larry Ross, interview, March 28, 1988.
557. George Cornell assesses BG. Letter, Cornell to Robert Ferm, August 20, 1959, CN 19 (Ferm Collection), BGCA.
557. Mission England press coverage. Reid, *To Reach a Nation*, p. 56, and interview.
557. "Get some more pictures up." Bob Evans, conversation, November 12, 1987.
558. Dienert on BG's gift for publicity. Interview, October 5, 1987.
558. Reid: "He is a 'name.'" Reid, *To Reach a Nation*, p. 76.
559. Telephone ministry. Terry Wilken, interview, June 11, 1986.
559. "We never call them 'converts.'" BG, quoted in Lewis F. Brabham, *A New Song in the South: The Story of the Billy Graham Greenville, S.C., Crusade* (Grand Rapids: Zondervan, 1966), p. 52.
559. BG: "not sure I have ever led a soul to Christ." Related by Roy Gustafson, interview, July 13, 1986.
559. Over the years, various journalists, sociologists, seminary professors, church-agency researchers, and members of Graham's own staff have studied individual crusades in attempts to determine how many inquirers were already members of, or in reasonably close touch with, a church before they went forward at a crusade service; how many were members or at least attending church at some specified point after the crusade; and how big a net gain in previously unaffiliated members the churches in a crusade city experienced. The studies vary in both design and result, but several findings appear again and again. In America, depending somewhat on the location of the crusade, between half and three quarters of the inquirers were already faithful in church attendance. Even larger percentages (as high as 96 percent in one study) had some kind of tie with a specific congregation or denomination. The net gain in new church members amounted to between only 5 percent and 16 percent of all inquirers, and a substantial portion of those were young people, who typically make up at least half of the total number of inquirers. When social class was considered, members of the respectable middle class, who compose the bulk of white Evangelical Protestant churches in America, clearly predominated. In short, what most inquirers in Graham's American crusades hear may be "Good," but it can hardly be counted as "News." For them, Graham is not so much an evangelist, bringing fresh tidings of a hitherto unknown truth, as he is a revivalist,

calling them to renew allegiance to that which they already believe, or to take a few more steps in the direction in which they were already leaning. See, for example, Kurt Lang and Gladys Engel Lang, "Decisions for Christ: Billy Graham in New York City," in *Identity and Anxiety, Survival of the Person in Mass Society*, ed. M. R. Stein (Glencoe, Ill.: Free Press, 1960); George Palmer Bowers, *An Evaluation of the Billy Graham Greater Louisville Evangelistic Crusade, 1958*, Th.M. Thesis, Southern Baptist Theological Seminary, Louisville, Kentucky, December 1958; Glenn Firebaugh, "How Effective are City-Wide Crusades?" *Christianity Today*, March 27, 1981, pp. 24–27; Lewis Drummond, *The Impact of Billy Graham Crusades: Are They Effective?* (Minneapolis: World Wide Publications, 1982); Win Arn, "Mass Evangelism: The Bottom Line," in Arn, ed., *The Pastor's Church Growth Handbook* (Pasadena: Church Growth Press, 1980), pp. 95–101; Frederick L. Whitham, "Revivalism as Institution alized Behavior: An Analysis of the Social Bases of a Billy Graham Crusade," *Social Science Quarterly*, 49, no. 1 (June 1968): 115–27; Various surveys of British crusades summarized in G. W. Target, *Evangelism Inc.* (London: Penguin, 1968), passim.

560. "My Answer" column written by others. William A. Doyle, "God, Mammon and the Men of BGEA, *Corporate Report*, June 1977, p. 30; Fred Dienert, interview, October 5, 1987.

561. Unusual addresses. From a collection of letters on display at the Billy Graham Museum, Billy Graham Center, Wheaton, Illinois.

561. BGEA Christian Guidance Department. Ralph Williams, interview, August 5, 1987.

561. Twenty-seven secretaries answer seventeen thousand letters. John Corts, interview, August 5, 1987.

562. "I do all of my own writing." "Billy Graham: The Man at Home," *Saturday Evening Post*, Spring 1972, p. 46; Ferms interview, March 28, 1987. Graham does receive extensive help on at least some books. In a March 18, 1976, memo to Harold Lindsell, apparently regarding Graham's book on the Holy Spirit, published in 1978, Graham's secretary, Stephanie Wills, informed Lindsell that she had asked Mr. Graham "if he'd like the book chapter by chapter or all at once. He said he doesn't have time to work on it right now, so he'd prefer it all at once. However, he then said that he might have time in early April.... If possible, I would like a copy of that first chapter as soon as possible. Since I need to retype it I would prefer to do it while he's gone than try to do it when he gets back." The reference to retyping seems to indicate that Graham had sent Lindsell a draft for editorial and other assistance. CN 192 (Lindsell Papers), Box 6, Folder 3, BGCA. *The Holy Spirit* is usually regarded as Graham's most substantial theological work. In its preface Graham thanks several people for reading and commenting on the manuscript. Lindsell's name is the first. Billy Graham, *The Holy Spirit* (Waco, Tex.: Word Books, 1978), p. 11.

562. Radio Stations. BGEA annual report, 1988; BG, interview, February 26, 1987; T. W. Wilson, Team and Staff Conference, The Homestead, Virginia, November 13, 1987.

562. "The film ministry ... deficit financing." John Akers, interview, February 26, 1987.

563. Dave Barr's view of film ministry. Barr, interview, November 14, 1987.

563. BG's TV audience. *The Unchurched American* (Princeton Religious Research Center and the Gallup Organization, Inc., 1978), p. 58.

564. "a Good News Show ... more disciplined." Roger Flessing, conversation, May 1, 1986.

564. Efforts to hook secular audience. Ted Dienert, interview, May 1, 1987.

565. Television maximizes BG's effectiveness. Ross, interview. 556 BG not afraid of technology. Ted Dienert, May 1, 1987.

566. BG sticks with Bennett agency. Fred Dienert, interview, February 1976. Several media agents have commended Graham for his policy.

567. Third Coast. The details of this story seeped out more or less by accident. Puzzled as to why Bennett had chosen Third Coast Studios, I asked Fred Dienert and received his "small portion" answer. It seemed slightly irregular, and when I raised the matter with several usually candid members of the Graham organization, they admitted to the existence of

some questions about the arrangement. At the Denver crusade, Ted Dienert had invited me to come to Austin to watch the editing process. When I called Bennett offices in Dallas to find out precisely when he would be in Austin, I was given the date but I sensed a certain uneasiness. That particular impression may have been erroneous; the tension in the air when I arrived at Third Coast Studios was palpable. It was clear I had come into the midst of a fairly serious family squabble. Dienert was cordial but visibly uncomfortable. Cliff Barrows, who arrived at about the same time I did, was cordial but seemed weary, a condition that could easily have resulted from Grady Wilson's death and funeral a few days earlier. Several others seemed almost pleased I was present. Cliff's questions about Third Coast's facilities, unexplained retreats by principal players into side rooms, and knowing glances exchanged between technicians and Bennett staff members made it obvious that something was up. Discreet inquiry made it just as obvious that I would probably not get the full story just by asking. In the course of the day, someone mentioned that Stellacom, a company somehow affiliated with the Walter Bennett Company, was doing work for NASA. Since NASA is a government agency, I knew that if that were the case, Stellacom's records, as well as those of all related companies, would be a matter of public record. A check of the pertinent records showed ties to Walter F. Bennett Company, Walter Bennett Company, Walter F. Bennett Advertising, Third Coast Studios, Third Coast Sound, and Third Coast Videos, Incorporated. Bennett ownership of Third Coast is given on various documents as 45 percent, 50 percent, and, in one case, 100 percent—a possible mistake. Subsequent conversations pegged the actual figure at 45 percent; an additional 5 percent was owned by a Bennett employee. With this information in hand, I asked several key participants and was able to piece together the story as related here. In fact, it appears that with the Walter Bennett Communications/BGEA work as its main account, Third Coast itself was losing money. Stellacom, a Third Coast subsidiary with a cost-plus contract guar anteed by the government, was a quite profitable operation, and likely to remain so. Not long after the Graham video work went back to CVS, leaving Third Coast even more unprofitable, Walter Bennett Communications and a business associate bought out the co-owner, thus gaining control of Stellacom, the most profitable part of the operation.

Chapter 34: Decently and in Order

568. "George is a … wizard." BG, interview, February 27, 1987.
568. "He's hard … like an indispensable engineer." Former BGEA employee, interview, July 15, 1986.
569. Wilson tour of BGEA. August 3, 1987.
570. BG on John Corts. BG, interview, February 26, 1987.
570. "He is much brighter … brilliant." John Akers, interview, February 26, 1987.
570. BG "has innate common sense." George Wilson, interview, August 3, 1987.
570. "He plays it down … his strategy." T. W. Wilson, interview, February 27, 1987.
571. "Mr. Graham … intuitive promptings." Sterling Huston, interview, May 2, 1987.
571. BG "a great delegator." T. W. Wilson, interview, February 26, 1987.
571. BG generous with praise. Emery, oral history April 9, 1979, CN 141, Box 10, Folder 4, BGCA.
571. "he is also the bottleneck." Former BG associate, interview.
571. T. W. on BG's "fickleness." Wilson, interview.
571. R. Ferm on BG's flexibility. Robert Ferm, interview, March 28, 1987.
572. Marvin Watson's appointment to the board raised some eyebrows, since he had pled Watson guilty to covering up an illegal fifty-four-thousand-dollar contribution to Richard Nixon's 1972 campaign. Graham defended the appointment by saying, "It hasn't been brought up and I don't think anybody would bring it up because I think the entire board has total and complete confidence in the integrity of Marvin Watson and also in his deep Christian com-

mitment.... I know the whole story. He explained it to me very carefully, point by point.... It was best for his sake and for his family's sake and for his Christian testimony's sake for him to do what he did. I personally don't think he was guilty." *Charlotte Observer*, February 7, 1977.

572. Plowman: "That board ... That happens." Edward Plowman, interview, February 10, 1987.

573. Bennett on BGEA fiscal standards. Quoted in "Billy Graham on Financing Evangelism," *Christianity Today*, August 26, 1977, p. 18.

573. BG and staff take reduced salaries during major crusades. Harold L. Myra et al., "William Franklin Graham: Seventy Exceptional Years," *Christianity Today*, November 18,1988, p. 22.

573. BG stopped taking free clothes. "A Contagious Faith in God," *Charlotte Observer*, February 9, 1977.

573. Country club memberships. Mary Bishop, *Billy Graham, the Man and His Ministry* (New York: Grosser & Dunlap, 1978), pp. 20, 22.

573. "freebies." *Publishers Weekly*, late summer 1977 (precise date unclear in BGCA scrap-book copy).

573. Ruth's coat. Patricia Daniels Cornwell, *A Time for Remembering: The Ruth Bell Graham Story* (San Francisco: Harper &c Row, 1983), p. 113

574. BG rejects plane. BG, interview, February 27, 1987.

574. "I could have kept it all." Ibid.

574. "Fred Dienert ... Trader Vic's." BG, conversation, February 22, 1986.

575. Barrows on home and office. Cliff Barrows, interviews, March 25, and February 24, 1987.

575. BG knows to "mind his steps." George Wilson, interview.

575. Mildred Dienert on BGEA morality. Interview, April 30, 1987.

576. BG on Oral Roberts. Interview, March 5, 1989.

576. "I may still make some bad mistakes." BG, interview, March 28, 1987.

576. BG on effects of TV scandals. "A couple of big names ... work for God," Myra et al., "Seventy Years," p. 20.

576. "Jesus had just twelve ... history of the church." *CBS Morning News*, December 25, 1987, transcript.

576. "I don't think ... it may help the church," George W. Cornell, AP, in the *Washington Post*, January 2, 1988.

576. "It's making everybody ... very carefully." Myra et al., "Seventy Years," p. 23.

576. Emery brings rationality, wears black hat. Emery oral history, April 9, 1979, CN 141 Box 10, Folder 4, BGCA.

577. "Confrontation difficult for BG and Barrows. Cliff Barrows, interview, March 25, 1987.

577. BG: "So far, I have resisted... her advice." BG, interview, March 26, 1987.

577. "We have been blessed ... easy on us." T. W. Wilson, interview.

577. How staffers are eased out. Interviews, Kenneth Taylor, July 19,1986; Plowman; Adams, February 9, 1987; Robert and Lois Ferm.

578. "You cannot break in.... " Lane Adams, interview, February 9, 1987.

578. "that's not forty years." John Lenning, interview, February 27, 1987.

578. "When you have been together ... react." Barrows, interview, February 27, 1987.

578. Lenning on Barrows. John Lenning, interview.

579. Grady in Columbia. Personal observation, May 1, 1987.

580. "Why put all our eggs ... except for God?" Walter Smyth, interview, June 11, 1986.

580. Comments on Walter Smyth. All were made as part of a special recognition for Smyth during the 1987 Team and Staff Conference at the Homestead, November 13, 1987.

581. "I think we gave him about $400,000." BG, interview, February 27, 1987.

581. Living in BG's shadow. John Lenning, interview; Tedd Smith, interview, April 30, 1987.

581. "You don't feel very important.... Who am I to disagree?" Lois Ferm, Interview March 28, 1987.

582. "There is a need ... work out their problems. Harvey Thomas, interview, June 16, 1987.

582. "They're like overgrown schoolboys." John Stott, interview, September 29, 1986.

582. "The most effective small team." The Reverend Gilbert Kirby, interview, September 29, 1986.

Chapter 35: The Bible [Still] Says

583. "I have read ... a whole book about it." Robert Ferm, oral history, June 21, 1978, and January 19, 1979, CN 141, Box 3, Folder 37, BGCA.

583. Colleagues comment on BG's theology. Interviews, Carl Henry, February 10, 1987; John Akers, February 26, 1987.

583. Garden of Eden location. BG, sermons, Washington, D.C., April 27, 1986, and Paris, September 27, 1986.

583. "Jesus born of virgin." BG, interview, United Church of Christ *Observer*, quoted in Carl McIntire, *Outside the Gate* (Collingswood, N.J.: Christian Beacon Press, 1967), p. 87.

584. "plenary verbal inspiration." Cf., e.g., Billy Graham, *The Holy Spirit* (Waco: Word Books, 1978, paperback edition), p. 60.

584. "not saved because of views of Bible." *Legends*, CNN, 1986.

584. "everyone knows ... supernatural being." BG, sermon, Paris, September 20, 1986.

584. "it's not what I don't understand." BG, interview, March 26, 1987.

584. "Garden of Eden long ago." BG, Mayor's Prayer Breakfast, Washington, D.C., April 30, 1986.

584. "coming to Christ ... in just a moment." Sermon, Washington, April 27, 1986.

584. "pagans ... no longer believe that." BG, quoted in James Michael Beam, "I Can't Play God Anymore," *McCall's*, January 1978.

585. Response in "Graham's Beliefs: Still Intact," *Christianity Today*, January 13, 1978, pp. 49–50.

585. "Hitler and Schweitzer," quoted in Ian R. K. Paisley, *Billy Graham and the Church of Rome* (Greenville, S.C.: Bob Jones University Press, 1970), p. 55, citing *Sunday Magazine*, June 1966.

585. "I don't think I can play God".... "ask the theologians up there in heaven." BG, interview, March 26, 1987.

585. BG sure of heaven. Sermons, Washington, April 28,1986, and Columbia, South Carolina, May 1, 1986.

585. BG not afraid to die. Billy Graham, on *Larry King Live*, CNN, January 18, 1988, and January 17, 1989. On the second of these programs, King, who had suffered a heart attack and was obviously fascinated by Graham's equanimity in the face of death, recalled the bomb incident and asked Graham to give his response again.

585. Heaven may be North Star. Edward Fiske, "The Closest Thing to a White House Chaplain," the *New York Times Magazine*, June 8, 1969, p. 109.

586. Heaven and Elvis. Heaven described in Billy Graham, *Till Armageddon* (Waco, Tex.: Word Books, 1981), pp. 214–15; BG expects to see Elvis, David Lawrence, "Conversations with Billy Graham," September 25, 1977.

586. "Suffering is simply ... pain and sorrow." Billy Graham, *Approaching Hoofbeats: The Four Horsemen of the Apocalypse* (Waco, Tex.: Word Books, 1983), pp. 61, 94.

586. Interpretations of suffering. 1962: Bulawayo *Chronicle*, June 16, 1962, CN 360, MF Reel 14, BGCA; 1988: TV show of Syracuse crusade.

586. Embroidery image, Graham, *Till Armageddon*, p. 53.

586. BG on angels. Billy Graham, *Angels* (New York: Doubleday, 1975; New York: Pocket Books, 1975), pp. 28, 34, 46, 124–25, 175–76.

587. BG alters dispensationalist beliefs. Interview, March 26, 1987.
587. BG will not speculate about dates. BG, interview, February 26, 1987.
587. "battle of Armageddon." Graham, *Approaching Hoofbeats*, p. 224.
587. "global harmony will be realized." Graham, *Till Armageddon*, pp. 22–23.
588. Middle East and the End. BG, interview, February 26, 1987; BG, sermon, Paris, September 27, 1986; Knotts, England, *Worksop Guardian*, May 17, 1985.
588. BG ministry may be preparation for Second Coming. Sermon, Washington, May 4, 1986.
588. Four Horsemen "on the way." BG, Sermon, Amsterdam, July 20, 1986.
588. BG on tongue speaking. Interview, March 26, 1987.
588. Healing and prophecy. Billy Graham, *The Holy Spirit* (Waco, Tex.: Word Books, 1978), pp. 241, 244, 207.
588. BG criticizes prosperity theology. Interview, March 26, 1987.
589. Colleagues comment on BG's preaching. John Corts, interview, August 5, 1987; T. W. Wilson, interviews; Robert Ferm, oral history, 1978, CN 141, Box 3, Folder 37, BGCA.
589. "preach with compassion." BG, sermon, Amsterdam, July 14, 1986.
590. BG's anachronisms. Sermon, Washington, D.C. April 27, 1986.
590. "Tie a Yellow Ribbon." BG, sermon, Washington, D.C. May 3, 1986, conversations following.
590. "I'll rework those." BG, interview, February 26, 1987.
590. John Wesley White aids BG. Akers, interview; John Wesley White, interview, May 2, 1987.
591. "Like a lot … trouble." Edward Plowman, interview, February 10, 1987.
591. "Maiodes." Sermon, Amsterdam, July 20, 1986.
591. "Eli Weasel." BG, sermon, Washington, April 25, 1986.
591. Dostoyevski "dead now." BG, sermon, Columbia, South Carolina, May 3, 1986.
591. BG's imprecisions: "psychologist." Sermon, Washington, April 28, 1986.
591. "sociologist." Washington, May 3, 1986. "Harvard … *Time*," BG, sermon, Paris, September 20, 1986.
591. "over four hundred …" BG, sermon, Paris, September 24, 1986.
591. "modern novel." Ibid.
591. "Male sex drive six times greater." BG, sermon, Columbia, South Carolina, May 1, 1987.
591. "Didn't get it from me." John Wesley White, interview. Graham's secretary, who types Graham's sermons and is thus aware of the sources of his quotes, believed Graham has based his comment on a comment by his brother-in-law, Clayton Bell, to the effect that "a recent study says that the average man thinks about sex six times an hour while he is awake." Letter, Stephanie Wills to William Martin, February 26, 1991.
592. BG jokes about his credulity. Columbia, South Carolina, April 30, 1987.
592. "There is no magic … human person." Reid: "You and Me as Well as BG," London *Church Times*, February 3, 1984.
592. "They hear another voice." John Innes, interview, May 1, 1987.
592. BG's assessment of his gift. Sermon, "The Evangelist's Gift and Calling," Amsterdam, July 13, 1986; Address, YFC Convention, 26 July–4 August 1974, YFC Archives, BGCA.
592. "I become exhausted." *Charlotte Observer*, June 15, 1969.
593. BG develops appreciation for structures. In a 1974 *Christianity Today* interview, Graham said, "I think we have to identify with the changing of structures in society and try to do our part." January 4, 1974, p. 17.
593. "I do not believe the Bible teaches teetotalism." "Carter Will Restore Confidence, Graham Says," *Miami Herald*, December 26, 1976. I have heard Graham make similar statements in recent crusades.
593. "Once in a while … a sip." BG, quoted in Angela Levin, London *Sunday Mail*, April 8, 1984. Graham has confirmed this to the author.

593. "It's very difficult ... to live a clean life." *Legends*, CNN, 1986.
593. Resisting temptation. *Charlotte Observer*, July 2, 1979; "Just Say NO," TV show of Peaks to Plains Crusade, September 9, 1987.
593. "you don't have to have sex ... part of your body." BG, sermon, Columbia, South Carolina, April 29, 1987, and interview, March 26, 1987.
594. "Thus far, and no further." *Legends*, CNN.
594. If BG children had pre-marital sex. BG, quoted in Madison, Wisconsin, *State Journal*, March 13, 1976.
594. Homosexuality no worse than adultery. Billy Graham, *Approaching Hoofbeats*, p. 97. In another context he listed jealousy, pride, greed, and lust as sins of equal magnitude. Page 4 of a transcript of a press conference (n.d.).
594. Homosexuals should "ask God to help you." *Legends*, CNN. 585 AIDS and condoms. BG syndicated telecast, March 1988.
594. Abortion: "individual cases." Graham, *Approaching Hoofbeats*, p. 157; view similar to pope's, National Press Club, April 24, 1986. Elsewhere as well.
594. Birth control. "Billy Graham: The Man at Home," *Saturday Evening Post*, Spring 1972, p. 105.
595. "God can forgive adultery." Interview, March 26, 1987.
595. Husband and wife should share power. "Of Religion and Politics," *Boston Globe*, August 16, 1976.
595. "Satanic deception." "'Lib Endangers Family, Graham Warns," San Diego *Tribune*, August 17, 1976.
595. "discriminated against." San Diego *Evening Tribune*, April 1, 1976; "A Chat with Billy: Religion and Politics," San Jose *Mercury*, September 27, 1981.
596. BG "not sure" about women as pastors. UPI, July 24, 1975.
596. "don't object ... God called them." "What Makes Graham Special," *Charlotte Observer*, February 7, 1977.
596. "a certain amount of socialism." Ibid.
596. 250 verses on the poor. "Why Broadcast Trends Worry Billy Graham," Belfast *Newsletter*, January 11, 1985.
596. "slight cynicism" toward government programs. "Don't Rock the Ark," the *Washington Post*, June 23, 1969.
597. Only the Second Coming can cure poverty. See, for example, Mary Bishop, *Billy Graham, the Man and His Ministry* (New York: Grosset & Dunlap, 1978), p. 68.
597. Travel and study changed BG. *Charlotte Observer*, April 15 and 25, 1982; "The Political Education of Billy Graham," *Washington Post*, April 14, 1986.
597. World Emergency Fund. Graham, *Approaching Hoofbeats*, p. 159.
597. Love-in-Action "a gesture, to demonstrate ..." BG, sermon, Denver, July 26, 1987.
597. BG on poverty. At Harvard, *Charlotte Observer*, April 25, 1982; "Political Education of Billy Graham;" Graham, *Approaching Hoofbeats*, p. 152, passim; interview, March 6, 1989.
598. Unemployed not second-class. "Billy is Worth Listening To," Newcastle *Sunday Sun*, May 27, 1984; also, Tom Minnery, "A Royal Reception for Billy Graham in England," *Christianity Today*, March 2, 1984, pp. 34–36.
598. "My heart goes out." "The President of Presence," Sheffield *Star*, June 20, 1985.
598. British churchmen gratified. Douglas Brown, "Billy's Back at Start of Heritage Year," London *Church Times*, May 4, 1984. Similar statements were made by Gilbert Kirby, John Stott, and Gavin Reid during interviews with the author.
598. "Many of our crimes." Graham, *Approaching Hoofbeats*, p. 166.
598. BG's views on gun control. "I am for some sort of restraint and registration. [We] should know where the 40 million handguns are." San Antonio *Express-News*, April 26, 1981.

599. BG and Ruth on capital punishment. *Charlotte Observer*, June 10, 1979. In 1973 the UPI quoted Graham as saying, "[W]hen capital punishment is administered equally, it's proved to be a deterrent," *Charlotte Observer*, March 23, 1973.
599. "extended statement" on disarmament. Graham, *Approaching Hoofbeats*, pp. 131, 133, 137, 141–43.
599. "Terrorists ... come to Christ." BG, sermon, Columbia, South Carolina, April 29, 1987.
599. "no Secretary of State." Press release, 1986 Greater Washington Crusade, BGEA.
600. Peace "a realistic present hope." BG, quoted in James E. Nash, "The Bomb, Rev. Billy, and the Second Coming," *Christianity and Crisis*, May 30, 1983, p. 215.
600. "Every gun ..." Graham, *Approaching Hoofbeats*, p. 170.
600. BG's approach "the scare tactics of a preacher." *Christianity Today*, April 6, 1984, p. 30.
600. "still in process." Graham, *Approaching Hoofbeats*, pp. 146, 144.

Chapter 36: What Manner of Man?

601. BG "the most spiritually productive servant of God in our time." Bishop Maurice Wood, interview, September 30, 1986.
601. "I honestly believe ... you have to wonder." Lane Adams, interview, February 9, 1987.
602. "Rabbi Tanenbaum Praises Work of Billy Graham," *Jewish Week-American Examiner* (New York, N.Y.), March 19, 1982.
602. BG on Muslims. Press conference, National Press Club, April 24, 1986; Dedication Service, Greater Washington Crusade, April 25, 1986; Mayor's Prayer Breakfast, April 30, 1986.
602. "Eisenhower once said ... not as dogmatic." *Charlotte Observer*, August 30, 1981.
603. Description of charisma. See Max Weber, *From Max Weber: Essays in Sociology*, trans., ed. H. H. Gerth and C. Wright Mills (New York: Oxford University Press, 1946), pp. 245–52; Robert C. Tucker, "The Theory of Charismatic Leadership," *Daedalus*, Summer 1968, pp. 731–56; Eric Hoffer, *The True Believer: Thoughts on the Nature of Mass Movements* (New York: Harper & Row), p. 112.
604. Stott on BG. Interview, September 29, 1986.
604. BG not an intellectual, but a genius. I cannot cite the source of this quotation. Somehow, in the process of lifting it from the data base in which it was originally placed, it was separated from its author. I do know it is an authentic quote from a person well acquainted with Graham, and it seemed better to admit I have lost the source than to omit the observation.
604. "Psalms for how to get along." T. W. Wilson, interviews.
604. "I hate to be late." "A Conversation with Billy Graham," *IRTV Guide*, 1974, p. 10.
604. BG "can't stand to be idle." Bob Terrell, interview, March 27, 1987.
605. BG's speeches to prestigious meetings. Conversation with Grahams, March 26, 1987.
605. Frady compares BG to Billy Budd. Marshall Frady, *Billy Graham: Parable of American Righteousness* (Boston: Little, Brown, 1979), pp. 11, 13, 437–40.
606. BG never alone with a woman. Harold L. Myra et al., "William Franklin Graham: Seventy Exceptional Years," *Christianity Today*, November 18, 1988, pp. 22–23.
606. BG and Joan Collins. Larry Ross, interview, March 28, 1988.
606. BG sees *Dangerous Liaisons*. Interview, March 5, 1989.
607. Plaudits for Ruth. Interviews, T. W. Wilson, February 27, 1987; Cliff Barrows, February 24, 1987; BG, February 26, 1987.
607. Ruth "a little tougher." Kenneth Chafin, interview, December 18, 1986.
607. Ruth on women's liberation. AP, April 15, 1976.
607. "He did that to Castro, too." *Charlotte Observer*, June 10, 1979.
607. Ruth and Velma Barfield. T. W. Wilson, February 27, 1987.
608. Grady on Ma Sunday and Ruth. Interview, March 1, 1987. Others told similar stories. In an oral history, Mrs. Donella Cochran Brown recalled that the Sundays had visited in her home often when she was a little girl and that "Ma Sunday always said, 'Take care of your

little boys; take care of your little boys.'" The Reverend Fred Brown and Donella Cochran Brown, oral history, December 29, 1976, CN 141, Box 2, Folder 39, BGCA.

608. Ned Graham. Interview, May 8, 1991.
609. BG "most admired." In 1990, The Gallup Organization reported that Graham had been named to its "most-admired" list 32 times in the 40 years it had conducted the poll, placing him "at the head of the list of the men the American public has admired the most over the past four decades." *Decision*, November 1990, p. 21.
609. BG best known of "living giants." Martin E. Marty, "Name Games," *Christian Century*, October 16, 1974, p. 975.
609. *Ladies' Home Journal* survey. *Charlotte Observer*, June 22, 1978, citing the July 1978 edition of *Ladies' Home Journal*. For the record, Abraham Lincoln and Eleanor Roosevelt edged both God and Graham in the competition to determine who had done the most good for the world.
609. BG only clergyman invited to meet Gorbachev. Larry Ross, interview.
609. "pleasing God or man?" BG, *Legends*, CNN, 1986.
610. "Unless, of course, some major school ..." BG, interview, February 27, 1987.
610. BG's problems with privacy. John Lenning, interview, February 24, 1987; Robert and Lois Ferm, interview, March 28, 1987.
610. "a paradox in his personality." Jean Graham Ford, interview, March 4, 1989.
611. God can get BG's attention. This quotation is a combination of two similar comments made by Busby, April 25, 1986, and April 30, 1987.
611. "We don't have to wait for the pope." BG, sermon, Columbia, South Carolina, April 30, 1987.
612. "To my best buddy." T. W. Wilson, interview, February 26, 1987.
612. BG's hyperbole "don't make anybody mad." Melvin Graham, interview, November 17, 1987.
612. "no dark side to Billy Graham." Robert Evans, interview, July 9, 1986.
613. BG "a *good guy*." Charles Templeton, interview, December 1, 1987.
613. Leighton and Jean Ford on Graham's ailments. Interview, March 4, 1989.
613. BG not "over the hill too far." Melvin Graham, interview.

Chapter 37: "To the Ends of the Earth"

614. BG ruminates about the future. Interview, March 5, 1989.
614. Chafin and BG discuss Franklin. Chafin, interview, spring 1986. After stepping down from his role with the School of Evangelism, a role he performed while serving as pastor of Houston's South Main Baptist Church, Chafin was the Billy Graham Professor of Evangelism at Southern [Baptist] Seminary in Louisville before taking a pastorate in that city.
615. Franklin: "I'm not an evangelist ... I'm looking low." Quoted in "Young Graham's Path Is All His Own," *Houston Chronicle*, March 5, 1988.
615. Franklin seen as plausible successor. Willmar Thorkelson, "Billy Graham to Ordain Son and Possible Protege," Minneapolis *Star*, December 25, 1981. Widely reprinted.
616. "I am not my father ..." Franklin Graham, quoted in White.
616. "Franklin says ... right now." BG, interview, March 5, 1989.
616. Carloss Morris on Franklin. Interview, May 5, 1987.
616. T. W. Wilson on Franklin. Interview, February 27, 1987.
616. John Lenning on problems of succession. Interview, February 24, 1987.
616. Rowlandson on the future of BGEA. Interview, July 10, 1986.
617. Barrows: "I don't have the foggiest idea." Interview, February 24, 1987.
617. Corts on the future. Interview, August 5, 1987.
617. Nilson Fanini: "You would need a thousand Billy Grahams." Interview, July 18, 1986.

618. Graham considers purchase of the *Queen Elizabeth*. Press conference, WFGW Radio, Black Mountain, North Carolina, March 12, 1968, CN 313, Box 2 Folder 20, BGCA. Apparently, Graham was only mildly serious about purchasing the liner, but he did note that, with its two thousand air-conditioned rooms, recreational facilities, and abundant meeting rooms, it would make "a tremendous conference center."
618. "It's the only piece ... won't even have a sign." BG, 1987 Team and Staff Conference, and interview, March 26, 1987; also, "Bible College Receives Gift of 1,440 Acres," Columbia, South Carolina, *State*, April 21, 1981. Eight hundred pastors attend School of Evangelism. BG monthly letter, September 1990. The school in question was held in August 1990. The total number of pastors who had attended a Billy Graham School of Evangelism stood at more than sixty-one thousand at the end of 1990.
618. Barrows: "I see the latter part ... impact on the world." February 24, 1987.
619. BG slowing down. BG, quoted by Bob Williams. Similar statement at Washington press conference, April 24, 1986. Others have made similar statements.
619. Grahams discuss China trip. Interviews, February 26, 27, 1987, and March 5, 1989.
620. BG received by Li Peng. Richard N. Ostling, "And Then There Was Billy," *Time*, November 14, 1988, p. 41; Edward Plowman, *Billy Graham in China* (Minneapolis: Billy Graham Evangelistic Association, 1988), pp. 10, 26.
621. BG as tourist. BGEA TV program, "Billy Graham in China;" Plowman, *Billy Graham in China*, pp. 14–15; Ruth and Billy Graham, interview, March 5, 1989.
621. BG at Nanjing Seminary. Plowman, *Billy Graham in China*, p. 46.
622. Rittenburg assesses BG visit. Ibid., p. 47.
622. Return to Russia. BG, interview, March 5, 1989.
622. Political conventions and campaign. Ibid.; Jim Castelli, Springfield, Missouri, *News and Leader*, July 23, 1988; BGEA reprint of prayer, January 20, 1989.
623. George Bush is BG's best friend. The *Washington Post*, January 25, 1991, citing Doug Wead, *George Bush, Man of Integrity* (Eugene, Ore.: Harvest House Publishers, 1988).
623. BG's relationship with Bush. BG, interview, March 5, 1989.
624. BG on Nixon. Ibid. The visit mentioned occurred in December 1988.
624. "It is, humanly speaking, impossible" AH, oral history, June 16, 1982, CN 141, Box 45, Folder 3-4, BGCA.
624. Hungary stadium service. Ed Plowman and John Akers, *Billy Graham in Budapest* (World Wide Publications, 1989), p. 18, quoting "Angyal Szallat a Stadionra," *Mai Map*, July 30, 1989; *Billy Graham in Hungary*, BG syndicated television program, January 1990.
625. Berlin rally. Quotations from BGEA press release 90-4.
625. Dan Rather and Richard Nixon on BG's Eastern Europe visits. *The Bible and the Wall*, BG syndicated television program, fall 1990.
626. Mission World. Bob Williams, interviews, February 28, 1990, June 12, 1987, June 9, 1986; "Soft Sell and Satellites Deliver Biggest Audience," *Christianity Today*, August 18, 1989, pp. 48–49.

Chapter 38: The Work of an Evangelist

631. Mission World Asia. BGEA press release 90-16. Richard S. Greene, "Gospel Message Goes to Millions in Asia," *Decision*, February 1991, p. 11; Richard S. Greene, "Mission World Asia Continues—Thirty Countries, Bringing the Gospel," *Decision*, April 1991, pp. 28–29.
631. Mission World, Latin America. Richard S. Greene, "In Buenos Aires: A Cause for Celebration," *Decision*, February 1992, pp. 7–10.
631. ProChrist 93. BGEA press releases 93-2, 93-6, and 93-7; David Neff, "Personal Evangelism on a Mass Scale," *Christianity Today*, March 8, 1993, pp. 64, 66.
633. World Television Series. BGEA publicity materials.
633. Russian school of evangelism. BGEA press release 91-15.

634. "beyond all expectations." "Something Beyond All Expectation," *Decision* (January 1993), pp. 7–13.
634. Korean visit. BGEA press release, March 27, 1992.
635. BG and Kim Il Sung. "Kim Il Sung, Up Close and Personal," *New Yorker*, March 1994, p. 33.
636. Graham and Jiang Zemin meet in Los Angeles. BGEA press release 97-17.
636. Grahams receive Congressional medal. BGEA press release 96-3, May 3, 1996.
637. "Surely their draw in the Northeast." David Briggs, Associated Press, "Graham seeks record crowds for New York City crusades," *Houston Chronicle*, May 18, 1991, Section Religion, page 3, 2 Star Edition.
637. Central Park rally. Roger C. Palms, "Central Park Rally: An Afternoon of Good News," *Decision*, December 1991, pp. 7–10. Also, Ari L. Goldman, "Billy Graham is Back to Save New York," *New York Times*, September 16, 1991, pp. B1, B7; Robert D. McFadden, "New York Hears Words of Hope From Billy Graham," *New York Times*, September 23, 1991, pp. B1, B6; Peter Steinfels, "Blunt Style of Preaching and a Message as Direct," *New York Times*, September 23, 1991, p. B6.
638. Charitable contributions at crusades. BGEA press release 92-9.
639. FG and Larry Ross on Youth Night. Interviews.
640. Youth Night. Larry Ross, interview, December 15, 2000; Rick Marshall, interview, June 24, 2001, Louisville, Kentucky; Franklin Graham quotes from comments in BGEA team devotional service, June 24, 2001, Louisville; Tedd Smith quotes from personal conversation, Louisville, Kentucky, June 23, 2001, and from Loydean Thomas, "Rock of Ages," *San Antonio Express-News*, March 30, 1997, p. 12G. Also, personal observation of Youth Night at the San Antonio Alamodome, March 29, 1997, and Louisville, Kentucky, June 23, 2001 (including Kidz Gig on the morning of the same day), and uncut video footage from Jacksonville, Florida, Youth Night, November 4, 2000, provided by BGEA.
641. Billy Graham at Harvard. BGEA press release 99-08.
642. Amsterdam 2000. Larry Ross, interview; conversation, Cathy Wood, BGEA, June 24, 2001; BGEA press release materials; *Decision*, October 2000; http://www.amsterdam2000.org. The description of the Task Groups is from "So That All May Hear . . . ," *Decision*, October 2000, pp. 20–21.

Chapter 39: "Guard What Has Been Entrusted to You"

644. "Obscure but wise philosopher." I first heard this from my brother-in-law, Philip Summerlin.
645. Franklin's first crusade experiences. Interview, Franklin Graham, May 8, 2001; Wendy Murray Zoba, "Not Your Father's Evangelist," *Christianity Today*, April 5, 1999, pp. 53–54. Agajanian gives gun and "The Lord . . . called me." Ken Garfield, "Father's Gift to Son: Evangelism," *Charlotte Observer*, September 28, 1994, p. 6A.
645. FG comparisons to BG. "I don't know if I can avoid comparisons." FG, quoted in Mark Pinsky (*Orlando Sentinel*), "Not Quite in Father's Footsteps," *Washington Post*, January 6, 1996, p. B8; "I love my father." FG, quoted in Andrew Barron, "Billy Graham's Son Has Own Style," *Greensboro News & Record*, September 29, 1994; "Because I am the son. . . ." FG, quoted in Gustav Niebuhr, "On a Wing and a Prayer," *New York Times*, October 12, 1994, pp. C1, C10; "Over 40 Years with Billy Graham," *Christianity Today*, April 29, 1996, p. 55.
646. "Festivals" instead of "Crusades." FG, interview, May 8, 2001.
646. FG criticisms of BG Youth Nights. Interview.
647. "For years a big hole." FG, in Zoba, "Not Your Father's Evangelist," p. 56.
647. "I dress this way." FG, in Pinsky, "Not Quite in Father's Footsteps."
647. FG's rugged image. The title of Franklin's first autobiographical work is *Rebel with A Cause: Finally Comfortable with Being Graham* (Nashville: Thomas Nelson, 1995).

647. Ruth "became increasingly vocal." "In the Name of the Father," *Time*, May 13, 1996; "My father didn't say it to me." Zoba, "Not Your Father's Evangelist," p. 54.
648. Toronto conflict. Interviews with FG, Anne Graham Lotz, Russ Busby, Tex Reardon, and others who preferred not to be identified. Also, Anne Saker, "Crusade Staff Turns Away Graham's Son," *Raleigh News & Observer*, June 9, 1995, p. A1; and Terrence Noland, "About My Father's Business," *Business/North Carolina*, November 1995, pp. 22–35. "People will shoot you" is from Noland, p. 24.
650. ECFA questions FG and Samaritan's Purse. "ECFA cannot hold up" and "bump in the road" are from Noland, "Father's Business," p. 32. "Crummy little evangelical busybodies" appears in Jeffery L. Sheler, "After the Legend," *U. S. News & World Report*, May 3, 1993, p. 73. Other quotations are from FG interview, May 8, 2001.
650. Franklin appointed vice-chair and successor. BGEA press release 95-32.
651. "Keep one thing in mind." Russ Busby, interview, June 22, 2001.
651. "Slowly trying to fit in." FG, interview.
651. Mel Graham quote. Noland, "About My Father's Business," p. 25.
651. "We have a relay race." Interview.
652. Russ Busby on Franklin's performance as successor. Interview.
653. Greg Laurie quote. Noland, "About My Father's Business," p. 28.
653. "Prescription for Hope" HIV/AIDS conference. "AIDS Victims Need Churches' Help," *USA Today*, Tuesday, February 26, 2002; "Franklin Graham Issues Challenge to Christians Worldwide: Join the Fight against HIV/AIDS," Samaritan's Purse Press Release, February 22, 2002; Tom Layton, "Christians Challenged to Confront AIDS," *Decision*, April 2002, pp. 26–27; Caryle Murphy, "'Army' of Christians Needed in AIDS Fight, Evangelist Says," *Washington Post*, Tuesday, February 19, 2002, p. B1.
653. The 2016 figures come from the organization's 2016 annual report. http://bit.ly/2vG72Q5.
653. More than 42 countries. http://www.samirtanspurse.org/donation-items/hivaids-ministries/.
654. Samaritan's Purse activities and finances. The 2012 figures come from http://s3.amazonams.com/static.samaritanspurse.org/pdfs/2012-SP-Form-990-Public-Disclosure.pdf. Unless otherwise noted, other information about Samaritan's Purse ministries is taken from the organization's website, http://www.samaritanspurse.org. Income figures are from the organization's annual report, available in print and on the website. Figures for BGEA are from that organization's annual report, available at http://www.graham-assn.org. Quotes from FG are from interviews.
655. FG similar to Billy Sunday. Zoba, "Not Your Father's Evangelist," p. 55.
655. "Billy Graham Forgives Clinton," *Maranatha Christian Journal*, March 15, 1998. Quoting *Today* Show. http://www.mcjonline.com/news/98/news2404.htm.
655. FG on Bill Clinton. "A lie is a sin." Zoba, "Not Your Father's Evangelist," p. 52; "I will never be alone. . . ." Bill Leslie interview with FG, November 1, 1996, WRAL-TV, Raleigh-Durham-Fayettville, NC, http://www.wral.com/features/specialreports/archive.html; "For the sake of the country. . . ." Quoted by Ken Garfield, "Franklin Graham: Step Down Quietly," *Charlotte Observer*, September 10, 1998, http://www.charlotte.com/special/clinton/pub/0911religion.htm.
656. FG, *The Apostle*, and Jim Bakker. Zoba, "Not Your Father's Evangelist," p. 55; FG invites Bakker to lunch. Ken Garfield, "Father's Gift to Son: Evangelism," *Charlotte Observer*, September 28, 1994, pp. 1A, 6A.
656. FG on drinking as a sin. Zoba, "Not Your Father's Evangelist," p. 55.
656. FG favors tough drug policies. Interview. As noted on p. 589, Billy Graham shared his son's preference for an ordered society, but later in life expressed reservations about the efficacy and fairness of capital punishment. FG's reference to Singapore pertains to the city's strin-

gent antidrug enforcement policies, which resulted in a Dutch businessman being executed on drug-trafficking charges in 1994 and also a narrow escape from the death penalty for a Canadian man in 1996.

657. FG on Gulf War. Quotes from Zoba, "Not Your Father's Evangelist," pp. 53, 55. Samaritan's Purse sends single men to Iraq: Noland, "About My Father's Business," p. 28. Smuggles Bibles into Saudi Arabia: Pinsky, "Not Quite in Father's Footsteps."

657. FG would have had Serbian soldiers executed. Pinsky, "Not Quite in Father's Footsteps."

657. "Jesse Jackson is silent." Zoba, "Not Your Father's Evangelist," p. 55.

657. "The Arabs will not be happy." This statement, apparently made during a television broadcast of a Franklin Graham festival, was originally reported by the Associated Press on October 14, 2000. It was then circulated by the American-Arab Anti-Discrimination Committee (ADC) in a press release, "Pattern of Hateful Anti-Arab Remarks Must be Condemned," October 16, 2000, and later included in the *1998–2000 Report on Hate Crimes and Discrimination Against Arab Americans* (Washington: ADC Research Institute, 2001), p. 71, edited by Hussein Ibish. According to ADC's Laila Al-Qatami, repeated attempts to contact Graham regarding his comments were unsuccessful. A *Religions and Ethics Newsweekly* program aired on WNET-NY on October 20, 2000, reported Franklin Graham subsequently amended his remarks by saying he had not meant to imply that all Arabs hated Jews. The same program reported Billy Graham's more moderate statement. http://www.thirteen.org/religionandethics/transcripts/408.html.

657. FG on world religions. "It's not the same God." Quoted by Ken Walker, "Franklin Graham Following in Famous Father's Footsteps," press release, Associated Baptist Press, October 18, 2000, vol. 00–94. "It wasn't Mohammed": Quoted in Anne Saker, "Graham Crusade Begins," *Raleigh News & Observer*, September 26, 1994. "Darkness of Hinduism": Pinsky, "Not Quite in Father's Footsteps."

658. Response to the terrorist attacks: "Christian leader condemns Islam," Jim Avila, *NBC News*, November 16, 2001. http://www.msnbc.com/news/659057/asp?cp1=1#body; "Muslim group wants Graham meeting," Associated Press, November 20, 2001; Richard N. Ostling, "Billy Graham hasn't retired, but son's era begins," Associated Press, November 24, 2001; "Rev. Franklin Graham says he doesn't believe Muslims to be 'evil people,'" Associated Press, December 4, 2001.

658. FG: Muslims should be included in aid to faith-based organizations. Interview.

658. FG remarks at Columbine Memorial Service. Full text at http://www.propheticroundtable.org/franklin-graham_Columbine_memorialservice.htm.

659. Criticism of FG's Columbine remarks. All quotes are from Virginia Culver, "Sunday Event Offended Some," *Denver Post*, April 29, 1999. http://sobek.colorado.edu/~glenn/media/dp/shot0429h.htm.

659. FG felt "awesome responsibility." Virginia Culver, "Voices of Columbine: Franklin Graham," *Denver Post*, April 16, 2000. http://63.147.65.175/news/chs0416p.htm.

659. FG's inaugural prayer and sermon. The texts of both of these were posted on the Samaritan's Purse website. Prayer: http://www.samaritanspurse.org/index.asp?section=News+Room&page=2001/jan/012001.txt; sermon: http://www.samaritanspurse.org/index.asp?section=News+Room&page=2001/jan/012101FGSpeech.txt.

660. FG defends inaugural prayer and sermon. Interview.

660. FG not seeking to be Chaplain to the Nation. Interview.

660. FG prayer at 2000 Republican National Convention. The complete text of the prayer, with the closing line and mention of its omission on the RNC site, was posted at http://www.myrightstart.com/Graham-prayer.php3.

661. Busby assessment of FG. Interview.

661. Will's Celebration. Jerri Menges, "Alive in Gastonia," *Decision* (December 2006), pp. 25–28.

Chapter 40: "Having Faithful Children"

662. "I was immersed ... fingerprints." Anne Graham Lotz, *Just Give Me Jesus* (Nashville: W Publishing, 2000); "I felt trapped.... My whole life was small." Wendy Murray Zoba, "Angel in the Pulpit," *Christianity Today*, April 5, 1999, p. 57.
662. AGL: "My mother raised five of us." "The Preacher's Daughter," *60 Minutes*, June 3, 2001. Interviewed by Morley Safer.
662. AGL: "They didn't know I couldn't teach." In Laurie Beyer, "Taking the Word Around the World," *Just Between Us—The Magazine of Encouragement for Women*, February 2000. http://www.justbetweenus.org/2_00/facetoface.html.
663. Anne's parents attend her class. Interview, July 11, 2001.
663. Anne is asked to move her class. Interview.
664. "Angels in the Bible." AGL on *Larry King Live*, May 18, 2000.
664. AGL on the need for revival. Interview.
665. Revival "wasn't on the program." Ken Camp, *Baptist Standard*, April 24, 2000. http://www.baptiststandard.com/2000/4_24/pages/lotz.html .
665. AGL expects revival. Camp, *Baptist Standard*, April 24, 2000.
665. Significance of "Just Give Me Jesus." AGL on *Larry King Live*, May 18, 2000.
665. AGL books and honors. *http://www.annegrahamlotz.com/*. Also, Zoba, "Angel in the Pulpit," p. 58.
666. AGL criticizes "prosperity gospel." *Just Give Me Jesus*, audiotape, Bridgeport, Ill.: Christian Audio Tapes, 2000, tape 2.
667. "In a day of superficiality." Randy Bishop, "Just Give Me Jesus," *Christian Reader*, September/October 2000; "She has a tremendous gift." "Billy Graham Ministries: A Family Affair," Capitol Broadcasting Company, Raleigh, N.C., November 2, 1996. www.wral.com/features/specialreports/archive.html.
667. AGL "inherited the greatest share." Zoba, "Angel," p. 57; "Best in the country," FG, interview.
667. AGL compared with BG and FG. "We're on the same team." "'Just Give Me Jesus' Revival to Feature Anne Graham Lotz," *Christian Times*, retrieved from Internet and no longer available. FG and BG "like the obstetrician." Quoted in Bishop, "Just Give Me Jesus."
667. AGL at UN. Lotz, *Just Give Me Jesus* audiotape 2.
667. AGL on women in ministry. Interview. Lotz has given the example of Mary Magdalene on several occasions. A similar version can be found on *Just Give Me Jesus* audiotape 2.
669. AGL on diminishing resistance to women in ministry. Interview.
670. Wife to submit to servant leadership. "Southern Baptist Faith and Message." http://sbc.net/default.asp?url=bfam_2000.html.
670. "Office of pastor limited to men." "Southern Baptist Faith and Message."
670. AGL: SBC reacting to feminism. Interview.
670. AGL on ordination. Interview. "If another godly woman ..." is from a press conference after Amsterdam 2000. http://challengeweekly.co.nz/lss31.htm.
670. BG as absent father. AGL: Laurie Beyer interview. Ms. Lotz made similar comments on Larry King Live.
671. Ned Graham's ministry. Terry Mattingly, "Christian Groups Don't Agree About China," syndicated column. http://www.gospelcom.net/tmattingly.
671. Ned Graham. The first major account of Ned's problems was Karen L. Willoughby's "Ministerial Oversight?" World Magazine, November 6, 1999. http://www.worldmag.com/world/issue/11-06-99/national_1.asp. This article asserted or strongly implied that in addition to abusing alcohol, Ned had been unfaithful to his wife, had physically abused her and the children, and had used pornography. Graham repudiated Willoughby's article, charging that she had "flat-out lied" to him about the auspices under which she was working and had proceeded dishonestly and bizarrely throughout preparation of her article. He

claims, for example, that she presented him with nine hundred single-spaced lines of questions, asking such things as whether it was true that he had arranged abortions for several women he had impregnated and was growing hallucinogenic mushrooms on the grounds of East Gates Ministries. Using this article and materials taken from Carol's divorce papers before they were sealed (and circulated by the senior pastor of their church), as well as further interviews, freelance writer Tony Carnes wrote, with Art Moore, "Woes Shake East Gates Ministries: Resignations Follow Allegations, Divorce," in the December 6, 1999, issue of *Christianity Today*. This experience, Ned said, "opened my eyes to where Evangelical Christianity has sunk. We are the one section of the population that shoots our own wounded. I haven't done an interview with a Christian [publication] since then. I have just focused on ministry." Interview, August 15, 2001. Billy Graham's approving statement appeared prominently on the home page of the East Gates website, http://www.egmi.org.

672. Ruth and Billy Graham Children's Health Center/Hospital. http://www.grahamhealthykids.org.
673. "Insightful Atlantic Monthly article." Sue Erikson Bloland, "Fame: The Power and Cost of a Fantasy," Atlantic Monthly, November 1999. http://www.theatlantic.com/issues/99nov/9911fame.htm.
674. Ruth Graham McIntyre on her family. The quotes "my familiar pattern ... find out" and "his plans kept moving ... nurturing hope" are from Ruth Graham McIntyre, "Growing Up Graham," Youthworker: The Contemporary Journal for Youth Ministry, May/June 2000. http://www.youthspecialties.com/ywj/articles/columns/mymindm-j00.html. All other quotes are from interview, July 24, 2001.

Chapter 41: The Last Days

677. AGL on her parents' aging. Interview.
680. *Billy Graham Classics* on TBN. By midsummer 2001, this plan had been implemented.
681. "My Hope World TV Project." *Decision*, October 2006, pp. 22–25.
681. BGEA to move to Charlotte. Richard N. Ostling, "Billy Graham Hasn't Retired, But Son's Era Begins," AP, November 21, 2001.
682. FG's plans for BGEA. Interview.
683. The observance of the National Day of Prayer and Remembrance, September 14, 2001, was aired on all major broadcasting networks. The text of Graham's remarks, as well as an audio recording, were reprinted in many newspapers and preserved on the BGEA website. http://www.billygraham.org/newsevents/ndprbgmessage.asp.
684. FG's comments on Islam. "This wonderful, peaceful religion," Jim Avila, NBC News, November 16, 2001. http://msnbc.com/local/wbal.g978991.asp; "a very evil and wicked religion" and "It wasn't Methodists ...," *NBC News*, November 16, 2001; Associated Press, November 20, 2001, and Richard N. Ostling, AP, November 24, 2001. Bush statement at Ramadan, Avila, *NBC News*, November 16, 2002.
684. FG declines offer to meet with Muslims, AP, November 21, 2001.
684. FG's clarifying statements. BGEA press release, November 18, 2001, and Graham op-ed piece in *Wall Street Journal*, November 19, 2001.
684. Bush: Islam "preaches peace." *NBC News*, November 16, 2001.
684. "It doesn't help ... off guard." Ray Buchanan, president of Stop Hunger, based in Raleigh, N.C., AP, November 21, 2001.
684. Ken Woodward, FG is "tone deaf." *NBC News*, November 16, 2001.
684. Response of Jewish leaders. David Firestone, "Billy Graham Responds to Lingering Anger Over 1972 Remarks on Jews," *New York Times*, March 17, 2002, p. A24.
684. BG sees implications. Private conversation.
685. BG apologizes. Press release, March 1, 2002, and "Excerpts from Billy Graham's Statement About Nixon Tape," *New York Times*, March 17, 2002, A24.

685. BG had grown. In the closing paragraph of my beliefnet article, referenced above, I wrote the following: "Billy Graham was 53 years old when his conversation with Nixon and Haldeman took place. Should he have known better than to say the things he said? Of course. Should he have played the role of prophet rather than court chaplain and boldly spoken truth to power? Absolutely. Should we, in light of all we know about him, which is a great deal indeed, condemn him as a duplicitous hater? That privilege would seem to be reserved only for those completely confident the stone they are poised to throw will leave no stain in their own hand."

687. Billy Graham Library and Visitor Center. Personal observation. See also Jim Dailey, "The Billy Graham Library—The Life of an Evangelist," *Decision* (February 2007), p. 19; Amanda Knoke, "The Billy Graham Library: Proclaiming Christ," *Decision* (April 2007), pp. 28f; Franklin Graham, "An Evangelistic Experience," *Decision* (May 2007), p. 40. For the controversy regarding the Library and its possible function as a burial site, see Laura Sessions Stepp, "A Family at Cross-Purposes," *Washington Post* (December 13, 2006), p. A01. For the record, I had no problems with the talking cow.

689. A golf course in heaven. BG on *Prime Time Live.* A 1992 program included in "Billy Graham: A Personal Crusade," A&E *Biography* (Pam Ridder, producer). First aired on May 22, 2000.

689. BG: "I want to hear." Ibid.

690. 2008 campaign. http://www.christianitytoday.com/ct/2008/novemberweb-only/145–52 .0.html.

692. Palin visit. http://www.christiantoday.com/article/sarah.palin.meets.billy.graham/24705.htm

692. Graham meets Obama. http://billygraham.org/story/president-obama-meets-with-billy-graham–2/ and http://www.thedailybeast.com/articles/2013/11/07/when-obama-visited-billy-graham-each-man-prayed-for-the-other.html.

692. Day of Prayer. http://thecaucus.blogs.nytimes.com/2010/04/25/obama-visits-the-rev-billy -graham/.

692. Franklin comments on Obama. "very nice man" http://www.christianpost.com/news/franklin-graham-troubled-by-obama-softening-to-donald-trump–49970/. Obama a true Christian? http://thecaucus.blogs.nytimes.com/2012/02/21/billy-grahams-son-questions-obamas-faith/. President needs sound biblical teaching. http://www.foxnews.com/on-air/hannity/transcript/franklin-graham-clarifies-controversial-comments-about-trump-obama.

692. Franklin assesses Mitt Romney. http://www.newsmax.com/Newsfront/franklin-graham -Romney-Mormon/2012/02/21/id/430049.

693. "I wouldn't do that now." http://www.christianitytoday.com/ct/2011/januaryweb-only/qabillygraham.html?start=2.

693. "you can quote me on that." http://articles.latimes.com/2012/oct/12/news/la-pn-billy -graham-romney-endorsement–20121011.

693. *Ads against same-sex marriage.* http://religion.blogs.cnn.com/2012/05/03/billy-graham-backs-north-carolinas-gay-marriage-ban and /http://danielsilliman.blogspot.com/2013/10/billy-grahams-big-ads.html.

693. Evangelicals can vote for a Mormon. http://billygraham.org/decision-magazine/october –2012/can-an-evangelical-christian-vote-for-a-mormon/.

693. Mormonism cult item deleted from BGEA website. http://newsfeed.time.com/2012/10/19/billy-graham-no-longer-thinks-mormonism-is-a-cult/.

694. Romney endorsement Billy or Franklin? http://www.ctlibrary.com/ct/2012/october-web-only/billy-graham-political-statements-history.html and http://www.dailykos.com/story/2012/10/18/1146371/-The-Hypocrisy-of-Billy-Franklin-Graham.

694. Graham's 95th birthday. http://www.foxnews.com/us/2013/11/07/billy-graham–5th -birthday-to-be-marked-by-party-in-nc/.

694. "My Hope" video. http://myhopewithbillygraham.org/programs/.

694. Franklin Graham, "If we are allowed. . . ." Stoyan Zaimov, "Billy [sic] Graham Responds to Obama Victory, Continues Evangelism Campaign," *The Christian Post*, November 9, 2012. http://bit.ly/2rLwUa9

Vote totals: http://bit.ly/2sKUbud

694. "If Christians are upset." Billy Hallowell, "Are Christians at Fault for Obama's Re-Election Win? Rev. Franklin Graham Says Yes," *TheBlaze*, November 19, 2012. http://bit.ly/2szVIEZ

694. Franklin Graham approves of Trump. Sarah Pulliam Bailey, "How Donald Trump is bringing Billy Graham's complicated family back into White House," *Washington Post*, January 12, 2017, http://wapo.st/2t3v6h6. Also, Jane C. Timm, "Trump's Foundation Wrote Many Checks on Path to Nomination, *NBC News*, October 5, 2016, https://www.nbcnews.com/politics/2016-election/trump-s-foundation-wrote-many-checks-path-nomination-n659811.

Billy Graham's 95th birthday party photo. Jim Dailey, "My Hope America With Billy Graham," *Decision*, January 2, 2014. http://bit.ly/2t4MNgl

694. "My hope is not in either party." Franklin Graham, "The Race for America's Future," *Decision*, October 2016, p. 5. http://bit.ly/2s073zN

694. "Put God back . . ." Jean Hopfensperger, "Evangelist Franklin Graham holds 'no hope' for either parties' candidates." *St. Paul Star Tribune*, June 16, 2016. http://strib.mn/2t3Rzua

695. "I think Donald Trump has changed . . ." Michael F. Haverluck, OneNewsNow.com, November 11, 2016. http://bit.ly/2t4cNb8

695. "biggest political upset." Michael F. Haverluck, OneNewsNow.com, November 11, 2016. http://bit.ly/2t4cNb8

695. "God showed up." Lindsey Bever, "Franklin Graham: The media didn't understand the 'God-factor' in Trump's win." *Washington Post*, November 10, 2016. http://wapo.st/2rLxJ2W;

Franklin Graham, "Evangelical Vote Fuels Historic Election Result," *Decision*, November 30, 2016. http://bit.ly/2sZRsiL

695. Trump: Franklin Graham "so instrumental." http://wapo.st/2t3v6h6

696. Billy Graham, *The Reason for My Hope: Salvation* (Nashville: Thomas Nelson, 2013).

696. "a place of wailing." Billy Graham, *Where I Am: Heaven, Eternity, and Our Life Beyond* (Nashville: Thomas Nelson, 2015), pp. 202f.

697. BG to Larry King. http://www.cnn.com/TRANSCRIPTS/0506/16/lkl.01.html. I thank *Charlotte Observer* writer Tim Funk for recalling and documenting this conversation.

697. "I don't know." Tim Funk, "New Billy Graham book echoes hardline preacher of '50s, not grandfatherly evangelist of love," *Charlotte Observer*, October 6, 2015. http://www.charlotteobserver.com/living/religion/article38008473.html. See also Adelle M. Banks, "Billy Graham warns of fire and brimstone in 'final' book," Religion News Service, October 2, 2015. http://religionnews.com/2015/10/02/billy-graham-warns-of-fire-and-brimstone-in-final-book/

Index